BUTLER'S
LIVES OF THE SAINTS

COMPLETE EDITION

HERBERT J. THURSTON, S.J.
AND DONALD ATTWATER

VOLUME I

RUARY · MARCH

< *in Volume IV*

NIHIL OBSTAT: PATRICIVS MORRIS, S.T.D., L.S.S.
CENSOR DEPVTATVS
IMPRIMATVR: E. MORROGH BERNARD
VICARIVS GENERALIS
WESTMONASTERII: DIE XXIII FEBRVARII MCMLIII

PREFACE TO THE SECOND EDITION

IT is now over a quarter of a century since Father Herbert Thurston, S.J., was asked to undertake a drastic revision and bringing up-to-date of Alban Butler's *Lives of the Saints*. The first, January, volume was published in 1926. Beginning with the second, February, volume (1930), Father Thurston invoked the help of Miss Norah Leeson in the revision or rewriting of many of the lives that appear in Butler and the compilation of others ; and Miss Leeson continued to contribute in this way down to the end of the June volume, as is testified by Father Thurston's repeated grateful acknowledgements to her in the pertinent prefaces (notably June, page viii). Beginning with the July volume (1932), the present editor was entrusted with the preparation of practically the whole of the text and the writing of additions thereto, down to the end of the series in 1938. Throughout the whole work Father Thurston himself always wrote the bibliographical and other notes at the end of each " life ". The general principles upon which the work was done are set out in Father Thurston's own words in the introduction which follows.

The issuing of this second edition of the "revised Butler" in four volumes has involved a certain abbreviation of the 1926–38 text (one tenth was the proportion aimed at). For example, while shortened forms of Butler's daily exhortations had generally been retained, it has now been found necessary to discard them entirely. While recognizing and welcoming the solid, unfanciful, scriptural character of Butler's homilies—so characteristic of eighteenth-century English Catholicism—it must also be recognized that they were often excessively repetitious and monotonous. Father Thurston points out that " Butler's main purpose in writing was undoubtedly the spiritual profit of his readers ". And it can hardly be denied that in our day and generation that purpose can be better served by letting the lives of the saints speak for themselves than by direct exhortation and " moralizing " about them. Moreover, some idea of the true life of a saint, such as we, and Butler, tried to give, must be more conducive to true devotion than a false or doubtful idea : as Abbot Fernand Cabrol once wrote, " The exact knowledge of facts is of the greatest assistance to true piety ". For a *Lives of the Saints* in English as wholly appropriate to our time as Butler's was to his, the work must be done again from the beginning : and for that we have to await the coming of another Alban Butler, another Herbert Thurston. It has also been necessary to omit, especially in certain months, some of the brief notices of the very obscure or uncertainly-venerated saints : Father Thurston himself expressed the desirability of this in his preface to the December volume. On the other hand, room has been made for the very considerable amount of fresh material provided by the beatifications and canonizations of the past fifteen years, and also for some earlier holy ones who were not included in the first edition. Butler's original work contained some 1,486 separate entries ; the present version contains about 2,565.

The excisions from the 1926–38 text vary in length from one word to a page or more. But need for compression, or the addition of fresh or different matter, has also sometimes involved the rewriting of passages, or even of a whole "life".* I have especially welcomed the opportunity to revise a great deal in July-December which I knew to be unsatisfactory, and to bring it at any rate more into line with Father Thurston's commentaries and with the text of January-June, written either by Father Thurston himself or more directly under his eye than were my contributions. Apart from verbal modifications, abbreviations and the like, the bibliographical and critical notes have been left as Father Thurston wrote them ; but some attempt has been made to bring the bibliographies up-to-date (May 1954). It was not possible to go through all the learned periodicals in various languages that have appeared since 1925, but due attention has been paid to the *Analecta Bollandiana ;* and I have added what is, I hope, a representative selection of new biographies and similar works. Among these last is included a number of "popular lives" for the general reader. Some of Father Thurston's critical notes have been incorporated at the end of the pertinent text for the convenience of the more casual reader.

In this edition a uniform order of presentation has been adopted. With a few special exceptions (*e.g.* March 1, June 9, July 9, September 26) the first saint (or feast) dealt with each day is that which is commemorated in the general calendar of the Western church, when there is one. The order of the rest is chronological. The choice of day of the month on which a saint should be entered is a far less simple matter. In general I have followed Father Thurston's arrangement (which has involved not a few alterations of date): *viz.* to adopt in the case of canonized saints the indications of the 1930 (*secunda post typicam*) edition of the *Martyrologium Romanum*, and in the case of saints and *beati* not included in the martyrology, to deal with them, so far as was ascertainable, on the days appointed locally for their liturgical observance. This last rule, however, does not always provide any satisfactory guidance, for the same saint may be commemorated in half a dozen different dioceses on half a dozen different days. But for those who belong to religious orders a feast-day is usually assigned in the order itself, and this I have done my best to adhere to. When for one reason or another (*e.g.* a very recently beatified subject) I have been unable to ascertain the feast-day, that person is entered under the day of his death. While this work was in progress, the Friars Minor adopted a new calendar, too late for me to make more than some of the consequent changes of date. In the title of each entry the saint is generally described according to the categories of Western liturgical usage, except that the description "confessor" is omitted throughout : any male saint not a martyr is a confessor. Occasionally the description does not agree with the office at present in use : *e.g.* on July 29, Felix "II" is referred to as "pope and martyr" by the Roman Martyrology and as "martyr" in the collects of the Missal and Breviary ; but he was neither a true pope nor a martyr.

As it has now been my privilege to have a considerable part in the revision of Alban Butler's *Lives of the Saints* it is not out of place perhaps for me here to express my complete submission to Father Thurston's judgement as to how and in what spirit that work should be done, and our full agreement in admiration of

---

* In doing which I have ever had in mind Alban Butler's own warning in his Introductory Discourse : "Authors who polish the style, or abridge the histories of others, are seldom to be trusted ".

Butler and his work. As I wrote in a foreword to the July volume, I first came to the work with a good deal of prejudice against Butler. But the prejudice was due to ignorance, and was soon dispelled. In common, I think, with most people who have never had occasion to read his *Lives* attentively, I had supposed him to be a tiresome, credulous and uncritical writer, an epitome of those hagiographers whose object is apparently at all costs to be "edifying", sometimes in a rather cheap and shallow way. Certainly his manner of writing is tiresome, but it does not obscure his sound sense and the solid traditional teaching of his exhortations. Credulous and uncritical he is not. He is as critical a hagiographer as the state of knowledge and available materials of his age would allow, and if he from time to time records as facts miracles and other events which we now, for one reason or another, have to question or definitely reject, he neither attaches undue importance to them nor seeks to multiply them : holiness meant to Butler humility and charity, not marvels. In only one respect does his critical faculty seriously fail him : he will hear nothing against a saint and nothing in favour of a saint's opponent, whether heretic, sinner or simply opposed. That is an attitude we can no longer tolerate : without wanting to remove St Jerome's name from the calendar or to canonize Photius, we now recognize that truth is better served by admitting that St Jerome gave rein to a censorious and hasty tongue and that Photius was a man of virtuous life and great learning : that people on the right side of a controversy do not always behave well or wisely and those on the wrong side not always badly or foolishly. It was a saint, and one no less than Francis de Sales, who wrote :

> There is no harm done to the saints if their faults are shown as well as their virtues. But great harm is done to everybody by those hagiographers who slur over the faults, be it for the purpose of honouring the saints . or through fear of diminishing our reverence for their holiness. It is not as they think. These writers commit a wrong against the saints and against the whole of posterity (*Œuvres*, Annecy ed., vol. x, p. 345).

In the *Analecta Bollandiana*, vol. lvii (1939), there appeared a general review of the revised edition of Butler's *Lives* from the pen of Father Hippolyte Delehaye, s.j., president of the Bollandists. Therein he enumerates some of the writers who, since the days of the *Golden Legend* of Bd James of Voragine, applied themselves to the task of adapting the lives of the saints to the ever-changing needs of time and place : " Among the more recent and the better known, who proceed above all from Ribadeneyra, may be named Rosweyde, Giry, Morin, Baillet, Butler, Godescard, down to the deplorable compilation of Mgr Guérin, to whom we owe the *Petits Bollandistes*." And he adds : " The palm goes to Alban Butler .." But it is only fitting that there should also be quoted here Father Delehaye's more lengthy appreciation of Father Herbert Thurston.

> Father Thurston is today unquestionably the *savant* who is best up in hagiographical literature, in all related matters and in the surest critical methods. His numerous writings in this field keep him always in touch with the understanding public that takes interest in this branch of knowledge ; and there was no one better qualified than he to find the answer to the delicate problem of recasting the old collection [*scil.*, Butler's *Lives*] in such a way as to satisfy piety without incurring the scorn of a category of readers generally difficult to please. The summary commentary as he uses it gives the new

"Butler" a scientific value which makes this work of edification a tool for students as well.

Referring to Father Thurston's writings in general Father Delehaye says :

The considerable body of work wherein this learned man exercised his unusual abilities of research and criticism nearly always bears a relation, direct or indirect, to our [scil., the Bollandists'] studies : such are his articles on the origin of Catholic feasts and devotions ; and on those wonderful phenomena that, rightly or wrongly, are looked on as supernatural, of which the lives of the saints are full : apparitions, stigmata, levitations—a world wherein one is continually brushing against illusion and fraud, into which one may venture only with a reliable and experienced guide.*

Those words had not long been in print when Herbert Thurston was called to his reward, on November 3, 1939, to be followed eighteen months later by their writer, Father Delehaye. There may suitably be applied to them certain words of Alban Butler : "Great men, the wisest, the most prudent and judicious, the most learned and most sincere, the most free from bias of interest or passion, the most disengaged from the world, whose very goodness was a visible miracle of divine grace, are in themselves vouchers of the truth of the divine revelation of the Christian religion. Their testimony is the more unexceptionable as they maintained it in a spirit of humility and charity, and in opposition to pride and all human interest."

I cannot leave this preface without expressing my warmest thanks to Father Paul Grosjean, Bollandist, for his great kindness in reading the proofs of this second edition. That he should have undertaken this task is one more example of the wide-spiritedness of the Society of Bollandists, whose learning is always at the service of the humblest student, and whose interest extends to the most modest work in the field of hagiography and associated subjects. Whatever errors, omissions and faults of judgement this edition contains are all mine : it is thanks to Father Grosjean that they are not more : and I owe to him a number of valuable corrections and references. It was thanks to the work of the Bollandists that in the first instance Father Thurston was able to accept the formidable undertaking of revising Butler. It is thanks to Father Grosjean that I can let this further revision go before the public with considerably less trepidation than I should have felt had the proofs not come under his eye : the eye, moreover, of a scholar whose learning is particularly exercised upon the hagiological history of Great Britain and Ireland.

DONALD ATTWATER.

FEAST OF ST BEDE THE VENERABLE,
    May 27, 1954.

---

* In 1952 Father Joseph Crehan, s.j., published a memoir of Father Thurston, which includes an invaluable bibliography of his writings, from his first article published in *The Month* in 1878 down to his death. Father Crehan has also edited in a single volume those of his articles that deal with stigmatization, levitation, second-sight and the like, as manifested in the lives of certain saints and others : *The Physical Phenomena of Mysticism* (1952).

INTRODUCTION

[The following introduction has been compiled from the relevant parts of Father Herbert Thurston's prefaces to the volumes of the 12-volume edition of the revised Butler's *Lives*, especially from the January preface. Words in square brackets are explanatory or connecting additions by the present editor. These prefaces were written between 1925 and 1938; and this must be borne in mind when reading, *e.g.* the second paragraph below, written in October 1925. The number of canonizations, etc., since then reinforces Father Thurston's words : it includes the beatification of groups of 191 French martyrs in 1926 and 136 English martyrs in 1929.]

THIS is not a book intended for scholars, though it is hoped that even scholars may sometimes find it useful. Its main object is to provide a short, but readable and trustworthy, account of the principal saints who are either venerated liturgically in the Western church, or whose names for one reason or another are generally familiar to Catholics of English speech. The work has developed out of a projected new edition of the well-known *Lives of the Saints* by the Rev. Alban Butler, which was originally published in London between 1756 and 1759.* Upon a more careful examination of the text—many times reprinted since the eighteenth century, but always without adequate revision—it soon became apparent that to render this venerable classic acceptable to modern readers very considerable changes were required, affecting both its form and its substance. Of these modifications it is necessary to give some brief account.

To begin with, Alban Butler died in 1773, rather more than 150 years ago. During the interval the Church's roll of honour has been enlarged by the addition of many new names. Even if we consider only the period which has elapsed since the death of Pope Pius IX in 1878—*i.e.* not quite half a century—there have been in that time twenty-five canonizations and fifty-one formal and independent† beatifications, some of them involving large groups of martyrs. But over and above this, we have a constant succession of equivalent beatifications, for the most part attracting little public notice, which take the form of what is called a *confirmatio cultus*. This is a decree sanctioning authoritatively and after due inquiry the

---

* The full title of the first edition, which appeared without the author's name, was " The Lives of the Fathers, Martyrs and Other Principal Saints ; compiled from original monuments and other authentick records ; illustrated with the remarks of judicious modern criticks and historians". Bishop Ward states that it was issued " nominally in four, really in seven octavo volumes " ; Mr Joseph Gillow, on the other hand, declares that there were five. The fact seems to be that there were only four paginations, but that the more bulky volumes, some of more than 1,000 pages, were divided into two parts by the binders and new title-pages supplied. On Bishop Challoner's advice some part of the notes, notably a long dissertation on the writings of St John Chrysostom, was omitted when the work was first published. These, however, with other supplementary matter, were printed from the author's manuscript in the second edition, which appeared in twelve volumes at Dublin in 1779–1780, after Butler's death.

† Each saint canonized is previously beatified. Only those beatifications are here numbered which have not so far been followed by canonization.

veneration alleged to have been paid from time immemorial to this or that servant of God who lived before 1634, when the enactments of Urban VIII regarding the canonization procedure came into force. Thus what is often called " the Beatification of the English Martyrs " [in 1886] was not, strictly speaking, a beatification at all. There was no solemn ceremony in St Peter's, no papal document taking the form of bull or brief, but simply a *confirmatio cultus*, published in 1886 with the pope's approval, but emanating from the Sacred Congregation of Rites. Nevertheless, the effect of the decree was equivalent to that of a formal beatification. It justifies, subject to certain restrictions, the public veneration of any of the fifty-four martyrs therein named ; it allows Mass to be celebrated in their honour ; and it permits the faithful to invoke them individually and collectively as " Blessed ". When it is remembered that in this group are included such champions of the faith as Cardinal Fisher, Sir Thomas More, several monks of the London Charterhouse, the Countess of Salisbury (mother of Cardinal Pole), and Father Edmund Campion, s.j., not to speak of many others, secular priests, religious and laymen, it becomes clear that in virtue of this one decree Butler's lists need to be supplemented by half a dozen new entries, or possibly more.

[But many others have been added to this edition, over and above those canonized or beatified since Butler's day. In the month of June, for example, over half the separate entries] are concerned with saints or groups of saints of whom there is no record in Alban Butler's original work. Of course such a computation of numbers warrants no inference as to the adequacy or inadequacy of the selection made. It would always be easy to add a multitude of other names borrowed from the martyrologies, from local service-books and calendars, or from the oriental synaxaries. But no good purpose would be served by attempting completeness . . . completeness of any sort is a simple impossibility. No authority save that of the Holy See can pronounce upon the claims of the thousands and thousands of alleged martyrs or ascetics whose names are heaped together in local martyrologies, synaxaries, episcopal or relic lists, and similar documents, and the Holy See very wisely has taken the course of remaining silent, unless on certain occasions when it has been specially appealed to. The oriental and Celtic "saints", so called, would alone create a most formidable problem. In the " Martyrology of Gorman ", a twelfth-century compilation, 72 presumably different Colmans are mentioned, and there are also 24 Aeds, 23 Aedans and 21 Fintans. Similarly anyone who will consult the index of the most recent edition of the *Martyrologium Romanum* will find that 67 saints named Felix are therein commemorated. Even in the sixty-six folio volumes of the Bollandist *Acta Sanctorum, quotquot toto orbe coluntar vel a catholicis scriptoribus celebrantur*, there is no assumption of exhaustiveness. Under each day a long list is printed of *praetermissi aut in alios dies rejecti*, and the reason why these names are passed over amounts in most cases either to a doubt whether a title to inclusion on the ground of *cultus* has been made out, or else to the lack of information concerning the facts of their individual history. At a period when the public recognition of holiness amounted to no more than a local veneration, sanctioned at least tacitly by the bishop, it is exceedingly hard to decide which of the devout servants of God who have had the epithet " sanctus " or " beatus " at one time or other attached to their names, are to be regarded as invested with the religious halo of an aequipollent canonization.

The principal aim of such a revision as the present must be to provide a brief account of the lives of those holy people whose claims to sanctity have either been attested by a formal pronouncement of the Holy See, or have met with definite liturgical recognition at an earlier period in response to popular acclaim. Unfortunately we must admit that in not a few cases veneration has been widely paid to personages of whose real history nothing certain is known, though the pious imagination of hagiographers has often run riot in supplying the deficiency. Further, there are names included in the Roman Martryology which stand only for phantom saints, some of them due to the strange blunders of medieval copyists, others representing nothing more than prehistoric sagas which have been embellished and transformed by a Christian colouring. Where such stories have become familiar and dear to the devout believers of earlier generations, it did not seem right to pass them by entirely unnoticed, even though the extravagance of the fiction is patent to all who read.*

It has been suggested above that in the case of holy people held in honour during the first thousand years of the Church's history either for their virtues or for their violent death in the cause of Christ, it is by no means easy to determine which among them should be recognized as saints and as entitled to the prefix often attached to their names in historical records. In none of these cases can we point to a papal bull of canonization or to any formal acceptance by the Holy See other than inclusion in the Missal or a notice in the official martyrology read at Prime. So far as such servants of God have a claim to the honour of saintship, they owe the privilege to what is called an "aequipollent" (i.e. virtual) canonization. It is a sort of courtesy title in fact. In view of the confused ideas entertained by many people upon this subject, I have ventured, in Appendix II of the [last] volume, to reproduce with some additions a brief statement on the matter which I had occasion to write in another connection and which appeared in *The Tablet* of January 15, 1938. Appendix I consists of some few biographical notes concerning Alban Butler himself. The memoir published in 1799 by his nephew, Mr Charles Butler, seemed to me too verbose and characteristic of the tone of the eighteenth century to bear reprinting entire, but I have borrowed from it a few passages and excerpts from letters which preserved matter of biographical interest.

More serious, however, than the comparatively simple task of supplying the lacunae of a book compiled nearly two centuries ago is the difficulty caused by the peculiarities of Butler's style. Charles Butler, in a memoir prefixed to an edition of the *Lives* brought out in 1798, seems to have formed an estimate of his uncle's literary gifts which most modern readers will find it difficult to endorse. He says, for example :

> Our Author's style is peculiar to himself ; it partakes more of the style of the writers of the last century than of the style of the present age. It possesses great merits, but sometimes is negligent and loose. Mr Gibbon mentioned it to the editor [i.e. Charles Butler] in warm terms of commendation ; and was astonished when he heard how much of Our Author's life had been spent abroad. Speaking of Our Author's *Lives of the Saints*, he calls it a "work of merit—the sense and learning belong to the author, his prejudices are those

---

* [Even exploded legends have their spiritual, and other, significance : one reader has pointed out what an excellent lesson in recollection and freedom from curiosity is provided by St Marina's sojourn undetected in the monastery (February 12). But didactic fiction has gone rather out of fashion, and it is not everyone who can say of his amusement at hagiographical excesses that "it is a sympathetic and tolerant smile and in no way disturbs the religious emotion excited by the picture of the virtues and heroic actions of the saints" (H. Delehaye).—D. A.]

of his profession ".[*]   As it is known what prejudice means in Mr Gibbon's vocabulary, Our Author's relatives accept the character.

It will be noticed that Gibbon's judgement upon the *style* of the *Lives of the Saints* is not recorded in his *Decline and Fall*.   We only know it by Charles Butler's report, and it is possible that the nephew was mistaken in attaching serious import- ance to phrases which may have been spoken merely out of politeness and not without a suspicion of irony.   Even when full allowance is made for the peculiarities of eighteenth-century diction, Butler's English impresses the reader nowadays as being almost intolerably verbose, slipshod in construction, and wanting in any sense of rhythm.   He is hardly ever content to use one verb or one adjective where he can possibly employ two, and it seems difficult to believe that when he had once written a passage, it ever occurred to him to revise it with a view to making his meaning clear.   As compared with the language of such contemporaries as David Hume, Smollett, Goldsmith, and even Samuel Johnson, I seem to detect a curiously foreign and latinized note in all that Butler published.   One gets the impression that while he wrote in English, he often thought in French, and that a good many of the oddities of phraseology which continually jar upon the modern ear are due less to the fact that his diction is archaic than to a certain lack of familiarity with the English idioms of his own time.

It may not perhaps be out of place to quote here a single example—and it is typical—of how Butler has often filled out his space with mere verbiage.   In his account of St Ethelbert, King of Kent, the *bretwalda* who received St Augustine and was converted by him to Christianity, Butler writes as follows.   I quote from the library edition of 1812 :

> Divine providence by these means [*i.e.* the marriage with Bertha, etc.] mercifully prepared the heart of a great king to entertain a favourable opinion of our holy religion, when St Augustine landed in his dominions : to whose life the reader is referred for an account of this monarch's happy conversion to the faith.   From that time he appeared quite changed into another man, it being for the remaining twenty years of his life his only ambition and endeavour to establish the perfect reign of Christ, both in his own soul and in the hearts of all his subjects.   His ardour in the exercises of penance and devotion never suffered any abatement, this being a property of true virtue, which is not to be acquired without much labour and pains, self-denial and watchfulness, resolution and constancy.   Great were, doubtless, the difficulties and dangers which he had to encounter in subduing his passions, and in vanquishing many obstacles which the world and devil failed not to raise ; but these trials were infinitely subservient to his spiritual advancement, by rousing him continually to greater vigilance and fervour, and by the many victories and the exercise of all heroic virtues of which they furnished the occasions.

Now this wordy panegyric is justified in precisely the measure in which such statements would probably be true of any other holy person.   We know absolutely nothing about St Ethelbert beyond what Bede tells us, and there is no hint in Bede of any of the things here dwelt upon.   He says not one syllable about a sudden change of conduct, or about unremitting " exercises of penance and devotion ", or

[*] See Gibbon's *Decline and Fall of the Roman Empire* (Bury's edition), vol. v (1911), p. 36, note 76.

about his struggles with temptation and the obstacles which the world and the Devil failed not to raise. The whole description has been evolved by Butler out of his inner sense of the probabilities of the case. This atmosphere of superlatives, without foundation in known facts, is surely regrettable. It can hardly fail to undermine all confidence in the author's statements, and when heroic deeds are recounted which really are based on trustworthy evidence, the reader is naturally led to ask himself whether these things also are mere padding introduced to give substance to a narrative which was too conspicuously jejune.

I must confess, then, that in the almost hopeless effort to secure some sort of harmony between Butler's *Lives* and the large number of biographies now added to bring the work up to date, I have constantly treated his original text with scant respect. It was impossible to leave unaltered such a description as the following —I quote one example out of hundreds—" melting away with the tenderest emotions of love, he [St Odilo] fell to the ground ; the ecstatic agitations of his body bearing evidence to that heavenly fire which glowed in his soul " ; or, again, a few lines lower down, " he excelled in an eminent spirit of compunction and contemplation. Whilst he was at prayer, trickling tears often watered his cheeks."* Moreover, some considerable economy of space was necessary in order to make room for the additional material and so I have more or less systematically eliminated the footnotes and the small-type excursuses which are found in the second and subsequent editions. Butler made excellent use of his authorities, and he undoubtedly went to the best sources then available, but in almost every department of knowledge new and momentous discoveries have been made since the beginning of the nineteenth century, so that almost all the English hagiographer's erudition is now out of date. The only practical course seemed to be to omit the notes, replacing them at the end of each biography by a few references to standard authorities, and adding, where the matter seemed to call for it, a brief discussion of the historical problems involved. In not a few instances it has, for one reason or another, seemed best to set aside not only the notes, but the biography itself, and to rewrite the whole.†

Butler's main purpose in writing was undoubtedly the spiritual profit of his readers, and from the beginning of January to the end of December it is his practice to conclude the first biography of the group belonging to each day with a short exhortation.‡ In this connection an extract or two from Butler's preface to the *Lives* will serve to illustrate the ideal which he had before him in compiling his *magnum opus*, and will at the same time furnish a more favourable specimen of his thought and of his style than is commonly met with in the body of the work. He says, for example, very truly :

> The method of forming men to virtue by example is, of all others, the shortest, the most easy, and the best adapted to all circumstances and dispositions. Pride recoils at precepts, but example instructs without usurping the authoritative air of a master ; for, by example, a man seems to advise and teach himself. . . In the lives of the saints we see the most perfect maxims

* In the life of St Odilo on January 1, vol. i, p. 43, of the edition of 1812.

† [On pages vi–viii of the March volume (1931), readers interested in the matter will find a note by Father Thurston about the relation between certain passages in the text of Butler's " Lives " and passages in *The Lives of the Saints* (1872–77) by the Reverend Sabine Baring-Gould.—D.A.]

‡ *Cf.* page v above.

of the gospel reduced to practice, and the most heroic virtue made the object of our senses, clothed as it were with a body, and exhibited to view in its most attractive dress.   Whilst we see many sanctifying themselves in all states, and making the very circumstances of their condition, whether on the throne, in the army, in the state of marriage, or in the deserts, the means of their virtue and penance, we are persuaded that the practice of perfection is possible also to us, in every lawful profession, and that we need only sanctify our employments by a perfect spirit, and the fervent exercises of religion, to become saints ourselves, without quitting our state in the world. .   Though we cannot imitate all the actions of the saints, we can learn from them to practise humility, patience, and other virtues in a manner suiting our circumstances and state of life ; and can pray that we may receive a share in the benedictions and glory of the saints. As they who have seen a beautiful flower-garden, gather a nosegay to smell at the whole day, so ought we, in reading, to cut out some flowers by selecting certain pious reflections and sentiments with which we are most affected ; and these we should often renew during the day ; lest we resemble a man who, having looked at himself in the glass, goeth away, and forgetteth what he had seen of himself.

CONTENTS OF VOLUME I

JANUARY

PAGE

FEBRUARY

MARCH

BIBLIOGRAPHICAL ABBREVIATIONS

Acta Sanctorum—This without qualification refers to the *Acta Sanctorum* of the Bollandists.

BHG.—The *Bibliotheca hagiographica graeca* of the Bollandists.

BHL.—The *Bibliotheca hagiographica latina* of the Bollandists.

BHO.—The *Bibliotheca hagiographica orientalis* of the Bollandists.

Burton and Pollen, LEM.—*Lives of the English Martyrs*, second series, ed. E. H. Burton and J. H. Pollen.

Camm, LEM.—*Lives of the English Martyrs*, first series, ed. Bede Camm.

CMH.—H. Delehaye's Commentary on the Hieronymian Martyrology, in the *Acta Sanctorum*, November, volume ii, part 2.

DAC.—*Dictionnaire d'Archéologie chrétienne et de Liturgie*, ed. F. Cabrol and H. Leclercq.

DCB.—*A Dictionary of Christian Biography*, ed. William Smith and Henry Wace.

DHG.—*Dictionnaire d'Histoire et de Géographie ecclésiastiques*, ed. A. Baudrillart *et al.*

DNB.—The *Dictionary of National Biography*, ed. Leslie Stephen *et al.*

DTC.—*Dictionnaire de Théologie catholique*, ed. A. Vacant *et al.*

KSS.—*Kalendars of Scottish Saints*, ed. A. P. Forbes.

LBS.—*Lives of the British Saints*, by S. Baring-Gould and John Fisher.

LIS.—*Lives of the Irish Saints*, by John O'Hanlon.

Mabillon—*Acta Sanctorum Ordinis Sancti Benedicti*, ed. J. Mabillon.

MGH.—*Monumenta Germaniae Historica*, ed. G. H. Pertz *et al.*

MMP.—*Memoirs of Missionary Priests*, by Richard Challoner, referred to in the edition of 1924, ed. J. H. Pollen.

PG.—*Patrologia graeca*, ed. J. P. Migne.

PL.—*Patrologia latina*, ed. J. P. Migne.

REPSJ.—*Records of the English Province of the Society of Jesus*, ed. Henry Foley.

Ruinart—*Acta primorum martyrum sincera et selecta*, ed. T. Ruinart.

Stanton's *Menology*—*A Menology of England and Wales*, by Richard Stanton.

VSH.—*Vitae Sanctorum Hiberniae*, ed. Charles Plummer.

Father H. Delehaye's *Les origines du culte des martyrs* is referred to in the " deuxième édition revue " of 1933.

There is an English translation by Mrs V. M. Crawford of Father Delehaye's *Les légendes hagiographiques* (" The Legends of the Saints "), made from the first edition. The third French edition (1927) is revised and is therefore sometimes referred to.

The English title of the work herein referred to as " Léon, *L'Auréole séraphique* (Eng. trans.) " is *Lives of the Saints and Blessed of the Three Orders of St Francis* (1885–87), by Father Léon (Vieu) de Clary. A corrected and enlarged edition of this work in Italian, by Father G. C. Guzzo, began publication in 1951 : *Aureola serafica*. By 1954 four volumes had appeared, covering January-August.

It has not been deemed necessary to give every reference to such standard works as the *Dictionary of Christian Biography*, the *Dictionnaires* published by Letouzey, and A. Fliche and V. Martin's *Histoire de l'Église*, though these are often referred to in the bibliographical notes. The first two volumes of Fliche and Martin, by J. Lebreton and J. Zeiller, have been translated into English by Dr E. C. Messenger (*The History of the Primitive Church*, 4 vols.), and the first two English volumes of the continuation, *The Church in the Christian Roman Empire*, are also published.

The reader may here be reminded once for all that for all modern saints and *beati* the surest source of information on the more strictly spiritual side is the *summarium de virtutibus* with the criticisms of the *Promotor fidei* which are printed in the process of beatification. Copies of these are occasionally to be met with in national or private libraries, though they are not published or offered for sale to the general public. And for all saints named in the Roman Martyrology the standard short reference is in the *Acta Sanctorum, Decembris Propylaeum : Martyrologium Romanum ad formam editionis typicae scholiis historicis instructum* (1940). This great work provides a running commentary on the entries in the Roman Martyrology, correcting where necessary conclusions expressed in the sixty-odd volumes of the *Acta Sanctorum*, and anticipating much that will be said at greater length in those volumes that have yet to appear ; and there are summary bibliographies throughout. It is indispensable for all serious study and reference.

Attention may be drawn to the following recently published general works :

R.-F. AGRAIN, *L'Hagiographie : ses sources, ses méthodes, son histoire* (Paris, 1953).

Les RR. PP. Bénédictins de Paris, *Vies des saints et des bienheureux.* January-December, 12 volumes. Especially the last six volumes.

E. G. BOWEN, *The Settlements of the Celtic Saints in Wales* (University of Wales Press, Cardiff, 1954).

E. DEKKERS, *Clavis Patrum Latinorum* (Bruges, 1951). The best guide to the editions of the Fathers from Tertullian to Bede.

J. DELORME, *Chronologie des civilisations* (Presses universitaires de France, 1949).

A. EHRHARD (continued by Fr Heseler), *Ueberlieferung und Bestand der hagio-graphischen und homiletischen Literatur der griechischen Kirche.* Three volumes in *Texte und Untersuchungen* (Leipzig, 1937–1943).

E. GRIFFE, *La Gaule chrétienne à l'époque romaine*, volume i (Paris, 1947). From the beginning to the end of the fourth century.

A. HAMANN, *La Geste du sang* (Paris, 1953). Translations of authentic texts of passions of the martyrs.

R. JANIN, *Les églises et les monastères* (de Constantinople), volume iii in *La Géographie ecclésiastique de l'empire byzantin*, Part I (Paris, 1954). Important for *cultus* and relics of saints.

Menologium cisterciense a monachis ordinis cisterciensis strictioris observantiae compositum (Westmalle, 1952).

And also, in relation to particular places in France, the work of J. Hubert and F. Benoit (Arles), M. de Laugardière (Bourges), J. de La Martinière (Orléans), J. Perrin (Sens) and, especially, René Louis (Auxerre). In the *Revue d'histoire ecclésiastique* (Louvain) the pertinent reviews of books and also the bibliographies (in a separate supplement) are particularly valuable.

BUTLER'S
LIVES OF THE SAINTS

JANUARY

1: OCTAVE OF BIRTH OF OUR LORD JESUS CHRIST

CIRCUMCISION was a sacrament of the Old Law, and the first legal observance required by Almighty God of that people which He had chosen preferably to all the nations of the earth to be the depositary of His revealed truths. These were the descendants of Abraham, upon whom He had enjoined it several hundred years before the giving of the law to Moses on Mount Sinai. And this on two accounts : First, as a distinguishing mark between them and the rest of mankind. Secondly, as a seal to a covenant between God and that patriarch : whereby it was stipulated on God's part to bless Abraham and his posterity ; whilst on their part it implied a holy engagement to be *His* people, by a strict conformity to His laws. It was therefore a sacrament of initiation in the service of God, and a promise and engagement to believe and act as He had revealed and directed.

This law of circumcision continued in force till the death of Christ : hence, our Saviour being born under the law, it became Him, who came to teach mankind obedience to the laws of God, to fulfil all justice and to submit to it. Therefore, He was " made under the law "—that is, was circumcised—that He might redeem them that were under the law, by freeing them from the servitude of it : and that those who were in the condition of servants before might be set at liberty, and receive the adoption of sons in baptism, which by Christ's institution succeeded to circumcision. On the day He was circumcised He received the name of JESUS, the same which had been appointed Him by the angel before He was conceived. The reason of His being called Jesus is mentioned in the gospel " For He shall save His people from their sins." This He effected by the greatest sufferings and humiliations, humbling Himself, as St Paul says, not only unto death, but even to the death of the cross ; for which cause God hath exalted Him, and hath given Him a name which is above all names, that at the name of JESUS every knee shall bow ; agreeably to what Christ says of Himself, " All power is given unto Me in heaven and in earth ".

Considered liturgically, three, if not four, distinct elements may be recognized in the festival which the Church keeps on the first day of each year. It is, to begin with, the octave of Christmas, and—possibly as a consequence of this—a special commemoration is made of the Virgin Mother whose pre-eminent share in the mystery could not adequately be recognized on the feast itself. Secondly, our ancient mass-books and other documents preserve many traces of the observance of the day in a spirit of penance, seemingly to protest against and atone for the debaucheries and other excesses customary among pagans at the outset of the new year. Thirdly, the eighth day after birth was the day when our Infant Saviour was circumcised, an incident pregnant with significance which called for suitable celebration on its own account.

So far as our liturgical evidence goes the earliest recognition of the feast is to be found in the Lectionary of Victor of Capua. This, which bears witness to the usage of southern Italy in the year 546, has an entry *De circumcisione Domini*, and indicates as a reading for that day the passage from St Paul to the Romans (xv. 4–14) in which our Lord is spoken of as " Minister of the circumcision for the truth of God to confirm the promises made to the fathers ". Only a very little later we find in the 17th canon of the second Council of Tours (A.D. 567) a statement that from Christmas to the Epiphany each day was treated as a feast except that triduum (apparently from January 1 to January 3) "during which our fathers, to stamp out the custom of the pagans, imposed a private celebration of litanies on the first of January, in order that psalmody might be carried on in the churches, and that on the day itself Mass of the Circumcision might be offered to God at the eighth hour ". Here, besides the reference to the Mass of the Circumcision, all the associations of the word *litaniae* were distinctly connected by the usage of the times with penitential practices. Further, in the archetype of the martyrology known as the *Hieronymianum*, which dates from about the year 600, the Circumcision is again mentioned, and this is also the case with the majority of the calendars, martyrologies, lectionaries and other service-books of the seventh and following centuries. Although in the present Roman liturgy no trace remains of the early efforts made to wean Christian converts from taking part in the pagan idolatries and debaucheries which ushered in the new year, still the so-called " Gelasian " sacramentaries, more or less modified by the uses which prevailed in Gaul, Germany and Spain, constantly provide a second Mass for this day which is headed " *ad prohibendum ab idolis* "—*i.e.* against idolatrous practices. In this Mass all the prayers echoed the petition that those who had been brought to the pure worship of the Christian faith might have the courage utterly to turn their backs upon the old, profane and evil ways of paganism. It is to be noted that even before any special church celebration can be connected with new year's day, we find St Augustine, in a sermon preached on that morning, exhorting his hearers to behave as Christians amid the excesses of their gentile neighbours at that season.

It is certain, then, that a wish to rescue the weaker members of the Christian community from the contamination of the new-year celebrations played a great part in the institution of a church festival on that day. St Augustine's words suggest that he realized how hopeless it was to impose a general fast upon an occasion which was a holiday for the rest of the world. Ordinary human nature would have rebelled if too much had been exacted of it. All that could be done in practice was to carry out the principles enunciated by such wise pastors as St Gregory Thaumaturgus and St Gregory the Great, that when pagan observances were ineradicably fixed in the customs of a people, the evil must be neutralized by establishing a Christian celebration in place of the heathen one. On the whole it would seem that outside Rome—in Gaul, Germany, Spain, and even at Milan and in the south of Italy—an effort was made to exalt the mystery of the Circumcision in the hope that it might fill the popular mind and win the revellers from their pagan superstitions. In Rome itself, however, there is no trace of any reference to the Circumcision until a relatively late period. What our actual missal preserves for us, even down to the present day, is a liturgy which, while echoing, as the octave naturally would, the sentiments proper to Christmas, refers in a very marked way to the Mother of God, *e.g.* in the collect for the feast. How comes it that our Lady is thus appealed to on the first day of the year ? This may, as mentioned above, be simply the result of her intimate connection with the mystery of the Incarnation, but there is some evidence that the liturgy for to-day represents the service for the octave of Christmas as solemnized in the ancient Roman basilica of our Lady, Old St Mary's (*cf.* D. Bünner in the bibliography). But whether or not a feast of special solemnity was observed on January 1 in this ancient church to serve as an antidote to pagan licence, it is unfortunately certain that the expedient was only partially successful, and that the riotous excesses of the season still survived in the " Feast of Fools " and other abuses, against which the better sort of ecclesiastics protested throughout the middle ages, but often protested in vain.

See Abbot Cabrol, *Les origines liturgiques* (1906), pp. 203-210 ; also in the *Revue du clergé français*, January, 1906, pp. 262 *seq.*, and in DAC., s.v. " Circoncision " ; F. Bünger, *Geschichte der Neujahrsfeier in der Kirche* (1909) ; D. Bünner, " La fête ancienne de la Circoncision ", in *La Vie et les Arts Liturgiques*, January, 1924 ; G. Morin in *Anecdota Maredsoluna*, vol. i, pp. 426-428. See also Mansi, *Concilia*, vol. ix, p. 796 ; Maasen, *Concilia Merov.*, p. 126 ; St Augustine, sermon 198 in Migne, PL., vol. xxxviii, c. 1025 ; and W. de Grüneisen, *Ste Marie Antique*, pp. 94, 493. There occurs above a reference to the *Hieronymianum*, which will be frequently mentioned in these notes. The " Martyrology of Jerome ", so called because it was erroneously attributed to St Jerome, was the foundation of all similar Western calendars of martyrs and other saints. It was compiled in Italy during the second half of the fifth century the archetype on which all existing manuscripts of it are based is a recension made in Gaul about the year 600. Father Delehaye's Commentary on the *Hieronymianum* (CMH) is printed in the *Acta Sanctorum*, November, vol. ii, part 2.

ST CONCORDIUS, Martyr   (*c.* A.D. 178)

A SUBDEACON who, in the reign of Marcus Aurelius, was apprehended in the desert, and brought before Torquatus, governor of Umbria, then residing at Spoleto. The martyr, paying no regard to promises or threats, in the first interrogatory was beaten with clubs, and in the second was stretched on the rack, but in the height of his torments he cheerfully sang, " Glory be to thee, Lord Jesus ! " Three days after, two soldiers were sent by Torquatus to behead him in the dungeon, unless he would offer sacrifice to an idol, which a priest who accompanied them carried with him for this purpose. The saint showed his indignation by spitting upon the idol, upon which one of the soldiers struck off his head.

See his acts in the *Acta Sanctorum*, January 1 ; and Tillemont, *Mémoires*   ., vol. ii, p. 439.

ST ALMACHIUS, or TELEMACHUS, Martyr   (*c.* A.D. 400)

ALL that we know of this interesting martyr is derived from two brief notices, the one contained in the *Ecclesiastical History* of Theodoret (bk v, c. 26), the other in the ancient " Martyrology of Jerome " referred to in the note above. In the first we read that the Emperor Honorius abolished the gladiatorial combats of the arena in consequence of the following incident : " An ascetic named Telemachus had come from the East to Rome animated with a holy purpose. Whilst the abominable games were in progress he entered the stadium and, going down into the arena, attempted to separate the combatants. The spectators of this cruel pastime were infuriated, and at the instigation of Satan, who delights in blood, they stoned to death the messenger of peace. On hearing what had happened the

3

excellent emperor had him enrolled in the glorious company of martyrs, and put an end to these criminal sports."

In the *Hieronymianum* the notice, preserved to the present day in the Roman Martyrology, reads : " January 1st　　　the feast of Almachius, who, when he said ' To-day is the octave day of the Lord, cease from the superstitions of idols and from polluted sacrifices ', was slain by gladiators at the command of Alipius, prefect of the city."　As against Dom Germain Morin, who is inclined to regard this alleged martyrdom as only an echo of the fantastic legend of the dragon of the Roman Forum, Father H. Delehaye, the Bollandist, believes the incident to be historical, and, in spite of certain difficulties, considers that the martyr's name was really Almachius, and that he perished about A.D. 400.

See *Analecta Bollandiana*, vol. xxxiii (1914), pp. 421-428.　*Cf.* Morin, in *Revue Bénédictine*, vol. xxxi (1914), pp. 321-326, and CMH., p. 21.

ST EUPHROSYNE, Virgin　　(Fifth Century ?)

THE Greeks call St Euphrosyne " Our Mother ", and pay her great honour, but we have no authentic accounts of her life.　Her so-called history is nothing but a replica of the story of St Pelagia, as narrated for Western readers in the *Vitae Patrum* or in the *Golden Legend*, a tale which struck the popular fancy and which, with slight variations, was adapted as an embellishment to the lives of St Marina, St Apollinaris, St Theodora, etc.

According to this fiction, St Euphrosyne was the daughter of Paphnutius, a pious and wealthy citizen of Alexandria.　He and his wife had long been childless, but Euphrosyne was born to them in answer to the prayers of a holy monk whose intercession they had sought.　The little girl was fascinating and marvellously beautiful, and because of the joy she caused to her parents they named her Euphrosyne.　When she was eleven, her mother died.　Her father set about finding her a husband and affianced her to a young man of great wealth.　At first she does not seem to have objected, but after an interview with the old monk who had prayed for her before her birth, she began to feel the call to a higher life and ceased to care for the things of this world.　She tore off her jewellery and gave it away to the poor, she avoided young people of her own age, consorting only with pious, elderly women, and, in order to make herself less attractive, we are told that she ceased washing her face " even with cold water ".　All this seems to have made no impression on her father, who went off to a three days' retreat in honour of the holy founder of a monastery of which he was a benefactor.　As soon as he was gone, Euphrosyne sent a servant she could trust to ask for an interview with the old monk. She told him how she felt, and he replied that our Lord had said that if anyone would not leave father, mother, brothers and everything for the kingdom of Heaven's sake, he could not be His disciple.　She then confessed that she feared to anger her father, as she was the only heir to his property.　The monk answered that her father could find as many heirs as he wanted among the poor and the sick. Finally she asked him to give her the veil—which he did then and there.

When the interview was over, and Euphrosyne began to think matters out, she came to the conclusion that she could not count upon being safe from her father in any nunnery in that country, for he would be sure to find her and carry her off by force.　She therefore secretly changed into man's attire and slipped out of the house by night—her father being still away.　She found her way to the very monastery her father frequented, and asked for the superior, who was surprised to see this exceptionally beautiful youth. Euphrosyne told him that her name was Smaragdus, that she had been attached to the court but had fled from the distractions of the city and the intrigues of the courtiers, and that she now desired to spend her life in peace and prayer. The abbot was greatly edified and offered to receive her if she would submit to the direction of an elder to teach her the discipline of the religious life—she being evidently quite inexperienced. She replied that, far from objecting to one, she would welcome many masters to teach her the way of perfection. No one ever suspected her sex, and she soon gave proof of extraordinary progress in virtue. She had many trials and temptations, but she overcame them all. Because her beauty and charm were a cause of distraction to the other monks, she retired to a solitary cell where she saw only those who desired her advice. Her fame for holiness and wisdom spread far and wide, and after a time her father, in his despair at losing her, asked leave to consult this venerated ascetic, Smaragdus. She recognized him, but he did not know her, since her face was almost hidden and she was much changed by her austerities. She gave him spiritual consolation, but did not make herself known to him till she was on her death-bed many years later. After her death, her father Paphnutius retired from the world and inhabited her cell for ten years.

See Delehaye, *Les légendes hagiographiques* (1927), pp. 189-192, and Quentin, *Les martyrologes historiques*, pp. 165-166. Although a commemoration of St Euphrosyne appears in the Roman Martyrology under January 1, and the Carmelites claim her as belonging to their order and keep her feast on January 2, there is the gravest reason to doubt whether such a person ever existed. No local *cultus* exists in this case to which we can trace the origin of the legend. In the Greek synaxaries she is commemorated on September 25, and in the majority of the Latin martyrologies her elogium occurs on January 1 ; but in the *Acta Sanctorum* her story is given on February 11. A Greek life is printed in the *Analecta Bollandiana*, vol. ii, pp. 196-205, and the Latin versions are catalogued in BHL., nn. 2722-2726. The atmosphere of all these is decidedly one of pure romance. At the same time there do seem to be authentic cases of women hiding themselves in male attire in monasteries and remaining for a while undetected. There is more or less contemporary evidence that this was done by the girl " Hildegund ", who died in the Cistercian abbey of Schönau on April 20, 1188 ; but the question of her sanctity is another matter.

ST EUGENDUS, or OYEND, Abbot   (*c.* A.D. 510)

After the death of the brothers St Romanus and St Lupicinus, founders of the abbey of Condat, under whose discipline he had been educated from the age of seven, Eugendus became coadjutor to Minausius, their immediate successor, and soon after, upon his demise, abbot of that famous monastery. His life was most austere, and he was so dead to himself as to seem incapable of betraying the least emotion of anger. His countenance was always cheerful ; yet he never laughed. He was well skilled in Greek and Latin and in the Holy Scriptures, and a great promoter of studies in his monastery, but no importunities could prevail upon him to consent to be ordained priest. In the lives of the first abbots of Condat it is mentioned that the monastery, which was built by St Romanus of timber, being consumed by fire, St Eugendus rebuilt it of stone ; and also that he built a handsome church in honour of SS. Peter, Paul and Andrew. His prayer was almost continual, and his devotion most ardent during his last illness. Having called the priest among his brethren to whom he had committed the office of anointing the sick, Eugendus caused him to anoint his breast according to the custom then prevalent, and he breathed forth his soul five days after, about the year 510, and of his age sixty-one.* The great abbey of Condat, seven leagues from Geneva, received from this saint the name of Saint-Oyend, till in the thirteenth century it exchanged it for that of Saint-Claude, after the bishop of Besançon who is honoured on June 6.

See the life of St Eugendus by a contemporary and disciple of his, which has been critically edited in modern times by Bruno Krusch in the MGH., *Scriptores Merov.*, vol. iii, pp. 154–166. Krusch, in his introduction and in a paper on " La falsification des vies des saints burgondes " in *Mélanges Julien Havet*, pp. 39–56, pronounces this life to be a forgery of much later date ; but Mgr L. Duchesne, in *Mélanges d'archéologie et d'histoire* (1898), vol. xviii, pp. 3–16, has successfully vindicated its authenticity and trustworthiness.

ST FULGENTIUS, BISHOP OF RUSPE   (A.D. 533)

FABIUS CLAUDIUS GORDIANUS FULGENTIUS was the descendant of a noble senatorial family of Carthage, born in 468, about thirty years after the Vandals had dismembered Africa from the Roman empire. He was educated with his younger brother under the care of his mother Mariana, who was left a young widow. Being by her particular direction taught Greek very young, he spoke it with as proper and exact an accent as if it had been his native language. He also applied himself to Latin ; yet he knew how to mingle business with study, for he took upon himself the administration of the family concerns in order to ease his mother of the burden. His prudence, his virtuous conduct, his mild carriage to all, and more especially his deference for his mother caused him to be respected wherever his name was known. He was chosen procurator—that is, lieutenant-governor and general receiver of the taxes of Byzacena. But it was not long before he grew disgusted with the world ; and being justly alarmed at its dangers, he armed himself against them by reading, prayer and severe fasts. His visits to monasteries were frequent ; and happening to read a sermon of St Augustine on the thirty-sixth psalm, in which that saint treats of the world and the short duration of human life, he felt within him strong desires of embracing the monastic state.

Huneric, the Arian king, had driven most of the orthodox bishops from their sees. One of these, named Faustus, had founded a monastery in Byzacena. It was to him that the young nobleman addressed himself; but Faustus, taking exception to the weakness of his constitution, discouraged his desires with words of some harshness : " Go ", said he, " and first learn to live in the world abstracted from its pleasures. Who can suppose that you, on a sudden relinquishing a life of ease, can put up with our coarse diet and clothing, and can inure yourself to our watchings and fastings ? " Fulgentius modestly replied that, " He who hath inspired me with the will to serve Him can also furnish me with courage and strength." This humble yet resolute answer induced Faustus to admit him on trial. The saint was then in the twenty-second year of his age. The news of so unthought of an event both surprised and edified the whole country ; but Mariana, his mother, ran to the monastery, crying out at the gates, " Faustus ! restore to me my son, and to the people their governor. The Church protects widows ; why, then, rob you me, a desolate widow, of my son ? " Nothing that Faustus could

* The rich abbey of Saint-Claude gave rise to a considerable town built about it, which was made an episcopal see by Pope Benedict XIV in 1748, who, secularizing the monastery, converted it into a cathedral. The canons to gain admittance were required to give proof of their nobility for sixteen degrees, eight paternal and as many maternal.

urge was sufficient to calm her.   This was certainly as great a trial of Fulgentius's resolution as it could well be put to ; but Faustus approved his vocation, and accordingly recommended him to the brethren.   But soon, persecution breaking out anew, Faustus was obliged to withdraw ; and our saint repaired to a neighbouring monastery, of which Felix, the abbot, would fain resign to him the government.   Fulgentius was much startled at the proposal, but at length was prevailed upon to consent that they should jointly execute the functions of superior.   It was admirable to observe with what harmony these two holy abbots for six years governed the house.   No contradiction ever took place between them : each always contended to comply with the will of his colleague.   Felix undertook the management of the temporal concerns ; Fulgentius's province was to preach and instruct.

In the year 499, the country being ravaged by an irruption of the Numidians, the two abbots were compelled to fly to Sicca Veneria, a city of the proconsular province of Africa.   Here it was that an Arian priest ordered them to be arrested and scourged on account of their preaching the consubstantiality of the Son of God. Felix, seeing the executioners seize first on Fulgentius, cried out, " Spare that poor brother of mine, who is too delicate for your brutalities : let them rather be my portion, who am strong of body."   They accordingly fell on Felix first, and the old man endured their stripes with unflinching resolution.   When it was Fulgentius's turn he bore the lashes patiently enough ; but feeling the pain excessive, that he might gain a little respite he requested his judge to give ear to something he had to impart to him.   The executioners being commanded to desist, he began to discourse pleasantly of his travels.   The cruel fanatic had expected an offer to surrender on terms, but finding himself disappointed he ordered the torments to be redoubled. At length the confessors were dismissed, their clothes rent, their bodies inhumanly torn, their beards and hair plucked out.   The very Arians were ashamed of such cruelty, and their bishop offered to punish the priest if Fulgentius would undertake his prosecution.   His answer was that a Christian is never allowed to seek revenge, and that a blessing is promised for the forgiveness of injuries.   Fulgentius went aboard a ship bound for Alexandria, wishing to visit the deserts of Egypt, renowned for the sanctity of the solitaries who dwelt there.   But the vessel touching at Sicily, Eulalius, abbot at Syracuse, diverted him from his intended voyage by assuring him that " a perfidious dissension had severed that country from the communion of Peter ", meaning that Egypt was full of heretics, with whom those who dwelt there were obliged either to join in communion, or be deprived of the sacraments.

Fulgentius, having laid aside the thought of visiting Alexandria, embarked for Rome, to offer up his prayers at the tombs of the apostles.   One day he saw Theodoric, the king of Italy, enthroned in state, surrounded by the senate and his court.   " Ah ! " said Fulgentius, " how beautiful must the heavenly Jerusalem be, if earthly Rome is so glorious !   What glory will God bestow on the saints in Heaven, since here He clothes with such splendour the lovers of vanity ! "   This happened towards the latter part of the year 500, when that king made his first entry into Rome.   Fulgentius returned home shortly after, and built a spacious monastery in Byzacena, but retired himself to a cell beside the seashore.   Faustus, his bishop, obliged him to resume the government of his monastery ; and many places at the same time sought him for their bishop, for King Thrasimund having prohibited by edict the ordination of orthodox bishops, several sees had long been vacant.   Among these was Ruspe, now a little place called Kudiat Rosfa in Tunisia.

7

For this see St Fulgentius was drawn out of his retreat and consecrated bishop in 508.

His new dignity made no alteration in his manners. He never wore the *orarium*, a kind of stole then used by bishops, nor other clothes than his usual coarse garb, which was the same in winter and summer. He went sometimes barefoot; he never undressed to take rest, and always rose for prayer before the midnight office. It was only when ill that he suffered a little wine to be mingled with the water which he drank; and he never could be prevailed upon to eat flesh-meat. His modesty, meekness and humility gained him the affections of all, even of an ambitious deacon Felix, who had opposed his election and whom the saint treated with cordial charity. His love of retirement induced him to build a monastery near his house at Ruspe; but before the building could be completed, orders were issued from King Thrasimund for his banishment to Sardinia, with others, to the number of sixty orthodox bishops. Fulgentius, though the youngest of the band, was their oracle when in doubt and their tongue and pen upon all occasions. Pope St Symmachus, out of his fatherly charity, sent every year provisions in money and clothes to these champions of Christ. A letter of this pope to them is still extant, in which he encourages and comforts them; and it was at the same time that he sent them certain relics of SS. Nazarius and Romanus, " that the example and patronage (*patrocinia*)," as he expresses it, " of those generous soldiers of Christ might animate the confessors to fight valiantly the battles of the Lord ".

St Fulgentius with some companions converted a house at Cagliari into a monastery, which immediately became the resort of all in affliction and of all who sought counsel. In this retirement the saint composed many learned treatises for the instruction of the faithful in Africa. King Thrasimund, hearing that he was their principal support and advocate, sent for him. The Arian king then drew up a set of objections, to which he required his answer; the saint complied with the demand: and this is supposed to be his book entitled *An Answer to Ten Objections*. The king admired his humility and learning, and the orthodox triumphed in the advantage their cause gained by this rejoinder. To prevent the same effect a second time, the king, when he sent him new objections, ordered them to be only read to him. Fulgentius refused to give answers in writing unless he was allowed to take a copy of them. He addressed, however, to the king an ample and modest confutation of Arianism, which we have under the title of his *Three Books to King Thrasimund*. The prince was pleased with the work, and granted him permission to reside at Carthage till, upon repeated complaints from the Arian bishops of the success of his preaching, he was sent back to Sardinia in 520. Being ready to go aboard the ship, he said to a Catholic whom he saw weeping, " Grieve not; I shall shortly return, and we shall see the true faith of Christ flourish again in this kingdom with full liberty; but divulge not this secret to any." The event confirmed the truth of the prediction. His humility concealed the multiplicity of miracles which he wrought; and he was wont to say, " A person may be endowed with the gift of miracles, and yet may lose his soul. Miracles insure not salvation; they may indeed procure esteem and applause; but what will it avail a man to be esteemed on earth and afterwards be delivered up to torments?" Having returned to Cagliari, he erected a new monastery near that city, and was careful to supply his monks with all necessaries, especially in sickness; but would not suffer them to ask for anything, alleging that " We ought to receive all things as from the hand of God, with resignation and gratitude ".

King Thrasimund died in 523, having nominated Hilderic his successor, and in Africa the professors of the true faith called home their pastors. The ship which brought them back was received at Carthage with great demonstrations of joy, more particularly when Fulgentius appeared on the upper-deck of the vessel. The confessors went straight to the church of St Agileus to return thanks to God ; on their way, being surprised by a sudden storm, the people, to show their singular regard for Fulgentius, made a kind of umbrella over his head with their cloaks to defend him from the downpour. The saint hastened to Ruspe and immediately set about reforming the abuses that had crept in during the seventy years of persecution ; but this reformation was carried on with a sweetness that won sooner or later the hearts of the most obdurate. St Fulgentius had a wonderful gift of oratory ; and Boniface, Archbishop of Carthage, never heard him without tears, thanking God for having given so great a pastor to His Church.

About a year before his death, Fulgentius retired into a monastery on the little island called Circinia to prepare himself for his passage to eternity. The importunities of his flock, however, recalled him to Ruspe a little before the end. He bore the pain of his last illness with admirable patience, having this prayer almost always upon his lips "Lord, grant me patience now, and hereafter mercy and pardon." The physicians advised him to take baths, to whom he answered, "Can baths make a mortal man escape death, when his life has reached its term ?" Summoning his clergy and monks, who were all in tears, he begged their forgiveness if he had ever offended any one of them ; he comforted them, gave them some moving instructions, and calmly breathed forth his soul in the year 533, of his age the sixty-fifth, on January 1, on which day his name occurs in many calendars. In some few churches his feast is kept on May 16, perhaps the day on which his relics were translated, about 714, to Bourges, in France, where they were destroyed in the Revolution. The veneration for his virtues was such that he was interred within the church, contrary to the law and custom of that age, as is remarked by the author of his life. St Fulgentius had chosen the great St Augustine for his model ; and as a true disciple, imitated him in his conduct, faithfully imbibing his spirit and expounding his doctrine.

There is a trustworthy biography of this saint, written by a contemporary, whom many believe to have been his disciple, Fulgentius Ferrandus. It has been printed in the *Acta Sanctorum*, January 1, and elsewhere. See the important work of G. G. Lapeyre, *St Fulgence de Ruspe* (1929), which includes the *vita* in a separate volume. For an account of the theological and controversial writings of St Fulgentius reference may be made to Bardenhewer's *Patrology*, pp. 616–618 in the English translation (1908) or to DTC., vol. vi, cc. 968 *seq.* See also Abbot Chapman in the *Catholic Encyclopedia*, vol. vi, pp. 316–317 ; and Dr H. R. Reynolds in DCB., vol. ii, pp. 576–583.

ST FELIX, BISHOP OF BOURGES (c. A.D. 580)

NOT very much is known of this saint, but there can be no doubt regarding his historical existence or the veneration in which he was held by his contemporaries. St Germanus of Paris officiated at his consecration ; we cannot be sure of the exact date. St Felix took part in the Council of Paris (A.D. 573), and Venantius Fortunatus addressed a little poem to him commending a golden pyx (*turris*) which he had had made for the reservation of the Eucharist. St Felix is commemorated in the diocese of Bourges on January 1, but the year of his death cannot be accurately determined. His tomb was in the church of St Austregisilus *de Castro*, outside the city walls.   Twelve years after his death, as we learn from Gregory of Tours, the slab covering his remains was replaced by another of more precious material.   The body was then found to be perfectly free from corruption, and numerous cures are said to have been obtained by those who drank water in which some of the dust of the old crumbling slab had been mingled.

See Duchesne, *Fastes épiscopaux de l'ancienne Gaule*, vol. ii (1900), p. 28.   Venantius Fortunatus, *Carmina*, bk iii, no. 25 (Migne, PL., vol. lxxxviii, c. 473 ; in the text edited for MGH. by F. Leo this poem is printed as bk iii, no. 20) ; and Gregory of Tours, *In gloria confessorum*, c. 102, in MGH., *Scriptores Merov.*, vol. i.

ST CLARUS, Abbot   (*c*. A.D. 660)

St Clarus, whose name was given him in his youth from his " brightness ", not so much in human learning as in his perception of the things of God, is believed to have been made abbot of the monastery of St Marcellus at Vienne in Dauphiné, early in the seventh century.   A Latin life, which must be more than a hundred years later in date, relates many marvellous stories of the miracles he worked,* but it is probably trustworthy when it tells us that Clarus was first a monk in the abbey of St Ferréol, that he was highly esteemed by Cadeoldus, Archbishop of Vienne, that he was made spiritual director of the convent of St Blandina, where his own mother and other widows took the veil, and that he ended his days (January 1, *c*. 660) as abbot of St Marcellus.   His *cultus* was confirmed in 1903.

See *Acta Sanctorum*, January 1, and M. Blanc, *Vie et culte de S. Clair* (2 vols., 1898).

ST PETER OF ATROA, Abbot   (A.D. 837)

A life of St Peter of Atroa, who was born in 773 near Ephesus, was written by one of his own disciples and is still extant.   It goes into some detail, but is principally made up of edifying anecdotes of no great interest, particulars of the saint's numerous journeys and, above all, accounts of his even more numerous miracles.

He was the eldest of three children, and was christened Theophylact, and nobody was surprised when, at the age of eighteen, he decided to be a monk.   Directed, it is said, by the All-holy Mother of God, he joined St Paul the Hesychast (Recluse) at his hermitage at Crypta in Phrygia, who clothed Theophylact with the holy habit and gave him the name of Peter.   Immediately after his ordination to the priest-hood at Zygos some years later, at the very door of the church, there happened the first wonder recorded of him, when he cured a man possessed by an unclean spirit.

Shortly afterwards St Peter accompanied his spiritual father on his first pil-grimage, when they directed their steps towards Jerusalem ; but God in a vision turned them aside, telling them to go to the Bithynian Olympus, where St Paul was to establish a monastery at the chapel of St Zachary on the edge of the Atroa.   This accordingly was done, the monastery flourished, and before his death in 805 Paul named Peter as his successor.   He was then thirty-two years old, and the access of responsibility made him redouble his fervour and his extreme austerities.

The monastery continued to flourish for another ten years, when St Peter decided to disperse his community in the face of the persecution by the Emperor

---

* It is perhaps desirable to remind the reader once for all that only Almighty God can do miracles.   The use of the above and similar expressions is permissible by custom, but in fact the miracle is done by God through the agency or at the intercession of the saint concerned.

Leo the Armenian of those who upheld the orthodox doctrine concerning the veneration of images. Peter himself went first to Ephesus and then to Cyprus; on his return, at a conference of some of his refugee brethren, he escaped arrest by imperial troops only by making himself invisible. Then, with one companion, Brother John, he continued his wanderings and visited his home, where his brother Christopher and his widowed mother received the monastic habit at his hands. He tried to settle down as a recluse in several places, one of which was Kalonoros, The Beautiful Mountain, at the end of the Hellespont; but so great was his reputation as a wonder-worker and reader of consciences that he was never left in peace for long. But at Kalonoros he remained for some years, making journeys about western Asia Minor from time to time, each of which was starred with miracles.

The death of Leo the Armenian in 820 made for a little more tranquillity in the Church, and with the stimulus of persecution taken away for a time the pettiness of small minds reasserted itself. Certain bishops and abbots, jealous of his popularity and his miracles, accused St Peter of practising magic and of casting out devils by the power of Beelzebub. When they refused to listen to his modest expostulations, Peter decided to seek the advice of St Theodore Studites, who was living in exile with some of his monks at Kreskentios, on the gulf of Nicomedia. When he had made careful enquiry and questioned Peter closely, St Theodore wrote a letter (it can be found in his works) to all the monks around Mount Olympus, declaring that the conduct and doctrine of Peter of Atroa were irreproachable and that he was as good a monk as could be found. The detractors were thus rebuked, and the vindicated Peter returned to Kalonoros.

He then undertook the restoration of St Zachary's and the reorganization of two other monasteries that he had established, taking up his own residence in a hermitage at Atroa. But a few years later the Iconoclast troubles began again and, the local bishop being an opponent of images, Peter judged it wise once more to disperse his monks to more remote houses. He was only just in time, for soon after the bishop came to St Zachary's with the intention of driving them out and arresting those who resisted. St Peter, meanwhile, having seen his community safely housed elsewhere, stayed for a period with a famous recluse called James, near the Monastery of the Eunuchs on Mount Olympus. It was while staying here that he miraculously cured of a fever St Paul, Bishop of Prusias, who had been driven from his see by the image-breakers: the instrument of the bishop's cure was a good square meal.

Persecution becoming more envenomed in Lydia, Peter and James retired to the monastery of St Porphyrios on the Hellespont, but soon after St Peter decided to go back to Olympus to visit his friend St Joannicius at Balea, from whence he returned to his hermitage at St Zachary's. A few weeks later St Joannicius had a vision: he seemed to be talking with Peter of Atroa, at the foot of a mountain whose crest reached to the heavenly courts; and as they talked, two shining figures appeared who, taking Peter one by each arm, bore him away upwards in a halo of glory. At the same moment, in the church of St Zachary's, while the monks were singing the night office with their abbot on a bed of sickness in the choir, death came to St Peter of Atroa, after he had lovingly addressed his brethren for the last time. It was January 1, 837.

There seems to have been no liturgical *cultus* of St Peter of Atroa, but it is nevertheless curious that his contemporary biography should have been ignored or overlooked by hagiologists for so long. As is said above, it is largely taken up with the saint's miracles, but it is interesting as a good specimen of ninth-century Byzantine hagiography and for what it tells of monastic life during the Iconoclast troubles.   Rescuing the manuscript " from wherever the caprice of the learned had hidden it ", as Fr V. Laurent puts it, Fr B. Menthon published a translation in *L'Unité de l'Église*, nos. 60 and 71 (1934–35), as one chapter from his work on *Les moines de l'Olympe*.   Father Menthon was pastor of the Latin Catholics at Brusa, and had an intimate knowledge of the topography and archaeology of the neighbouring mountain, where scanty ruins of St Peter's monastery of St Zachary, and of numerous others, can still be seen.

ST WILLIAM OF SAINT BENIGNUS, ABBOT   (A.D. 1031)

ST WILLIAM, who must be regarded as one of the remarkable men of his age, was born in the castle of the island of San Giuglio, near Novara, in 962, at the very time when this stronghold was being defended by his father, Count Robert of Volpiano, against the besieging forces of the Emperor Otto.   The garrison was eventually forced to capitulate upon honourable terms, and the emperor and his consort, laying aside all resentment, acted as sponsors to the newly-born infant. He was educated in a monastery, and later became a monk at Locadio, near Vercelli. In 987 he met St Majolus, and followed him to join the already famous abbey over which the latter ruled at Cluny.   The Cluniac reform was then rapidly extending its sphere of influence, and William, after being sent for a while to reorganize the monastery of Saint-Sernin on the Rhone, was finally chosen to go with twelve other monks to revive the ancient foundation of Saint Benignus at Dijon.   William now received the priesthood and was blessed as abbot.   In a short time the whole abbey underwent a transformation both materially and spiritually.   The edifice was enlarged, a great minster was built, schools were opened, the arts encouraged, hospitality developed, and works of charity in every form set on foot.   Ultimately the community of Saint Benignus became the centre of a great network of associated monasteries, either reformed or newly founded, in Burgundy, Lorraine and Italy.

St William's own character was one in which great zeal and firmness were joined with tender affection for his subjects.   He did not hesitate on occasion to oppose, both by action and by his writings, the most powerful rulers of his time, men like the Emperor St Henry, Robert, King of France, and Pope John XIX, when he felt the cause of justice was at stake.   In the interests of the Cluniac reform he was constantly active, making many journeys and travelling as far as Rome.   His biographer claims that he inspired St Odilo, who is also commemorated on this day, with the love of high perfection, and amongst his other works he refounded Fécamp in Normandy, a monastic institution which afterwards had an important influence on the religious life in England.   It was at Fécamp that St William breathed his last, as day was dawning, on Sunday, January 1, 1031.

The life of William, written by his disciple Ralph Glaber shortly after his death, has been printed by the Bollandists, by Mabillon, and others.   See also E. Sackur, *Die Cluniacenser;* Hauck, *Kirchengeschichte Deutschlands*, vol. iii ; G. Chevallier, *Le Vénérable Guillaume* (1875); and B.H.L., n. 1284.

ST ODILO, ABBOT   (A.D. 1049)

ODILO was very young when he received the monastic habit at Cluny from the hands of St Mayeul or Majolus, by whose appointment he was made his coadjutor in 991, though only twenty-nine years of age ; and from the death of St Mayeul in 994 he was charged with the entire government of that great abbey.   Notwithstanding the austerities practised on himself, his dealings with others were always gentle and kindly. It was usual with him to say that of the two extremes, he chose rather to offend by tenderness than by a too rigid severity. In a great famine in 1006 his liberality to the poor was by many censured as extravagant ; for to relieve their necessities he melted down the sacred vessels and ornaments, and sold the gold crown which St Henry had presented to the abbey. Odilo journeyed to Rome four times, and when out of devotion to St Benedict he paid a visit to Monte Cassino, he earnestly begged leave to kiss the feet of all the monks, obtaining his request with difficulty.

Under the rule of St Odilo the number of abbeys which accepted Cluniac customs and supervision increased, and a greater degree of organization and dependence of the subordinate monasteries on Cluny developed. The particulars varied somewhat according to the status of the monastery concerned and its distance from the mother-house : but many priories were dependent on Cluny in the strictest sense, and were controlled by her even to the extent of their superiors being nominated by Cluny. In this and in other developments there was a modification of principles laid down in the Rule of St Benedict, and historically a distinction is made between Cluniac monks and Benedictines pure and simple.

Massacres and pillage were so common in that age, owing to the right claimed by every petty lord to avenge his own injuries by private wars, that the agreement called " the truce of God " was set on foot. By this, among other articles, it was agreed that churches should be sanctuaries to all sorts of persons, except those that violated this truce, and that from the Wednesday till the Monday morning no one should offer violence to another. This pact met with much opposition among the Neustrians, but was at length received and observed in most provinces of France, through the exhortations and endeavours of St Odilo, and Richard, Abbot of Saint-Vanne, who were charged with this commission. Prince Casimir, son of Miceslaw, King of Poland, retired to Cluny, where he became a monk, and was ordained deacon. He was afterwards, by a deputation of the nobility, called to the crown. St Odilo referred the matter to Pope Benedict IX, by whose dispensation Casimir mounted the throne in 1041, married, had several children, and reigned till his death in 1058.

It was St Odilo who instituted the annual commemoration of all the faithful departed on November 2, to be observed by the members of his community with alms, prayers and sacrifices for the relief of the suffering souls in Purgatory ; and this charitable devotion he often much recommended. He was very devout to the Blessed Virgin ; and above all sacred mysteries to that of the divine Incarnation. As the monks were singing that verse in the church, " Thou, about to take upon thee to deliver man, didst not abhor the womb of a virgin ", he was rapt in ecstasy and swooned away. Most of his sermons and poems treat of the mysteries of our redemption or of the Blessed Virgin. Having patiently suffered during five years many painful diseases, St Odilo died at Souvigny, a priory in the Bourbonnais, whilst employed in the visitation of his monasteries, on January 1, 1049, being then eighty-seven years old, and having been fifty-six years abbot. He insisted on being carried to the church to assist at the Divine Office, and he died, having received the viaticum and extreme unction the day before, lying upon the ground on sack-cloth strewn with ashes.

See his life by his disciple Jotsald, edited by the Bollandists and Mabillon. A portion of the text lacking in these copies has been printed in the *Neues Archiv* (1890), vol. xv, pp.

117 *seq.* *Cf.* also E. Sackur, *Die Cluniacenser* ; P. Jardet, *Saint Odilon* (1898) ; BHL., n. 908 ; and Mabillon, *Annales*, vol. i, p. 57.   Ceillier demonstrates against Basnage that the Life of St Alice the Empress is the work of St Odilo, no less than the Life of St Mayeul. We have four letters, some poems, and several sermons of this saint, which may be found in Migne, PL., cxlii.   See also *Neues Archiv* (1899), vol. xxiv, pp. 628-735.

BD ZDISLAVA, Matron   (A.D. 1252)

This holy associate of the Dominican Order was born early in the thirteenth century in that part of Bohemia which now forms the diocese of Litomerice.   Her piety as a child was remarkable, and it is said that at the age of seven she ran off into the forest with the intention of leading a solitary life given up entirely to prayer and penance.   She was, of course, brought back, and some years later, in spite of her reluctance, she was constrained by her family to marry.   Her husband, a wealthy nobleman, to whom she bore four children, seems to have treated her somewhat brutally, though by her patience and gentleness she secured in the end considerable freedom of action in her practices of devotion, her austerities and her many works of charity.   She made herself at all times the mother of the poor, and especially of the fugitives who, in those troublous days of the Tartar invasion, poured down upon the castle of Gabel, where she and her husband resided.   On one occasion her husband, coming indignantly to eject a repulsive fever-stricken mendicant to whom she had given a bed in their house, found in his place, not a living man, but a figure of Christ crucified.   Deeply impressed by this (*cf.* what is said about a similar incident in the life of St Elizabeth of Hungary, November 19), he seems to have left his wife free to found a Dominican priory and to join their third order.

Zdislava had visions and ecstasies, and even in those days of infrequent communion she is said to have received the Blessed Sacrament almost daily.   When she fell grievously ill she consoled her husband and children by saying that she hoped to help them more from the next world than she had ever been able to do in this.   She died on January 1, 1252, was buried in the priory of St Laurence which she had founded, and is stated to have appeared to her husband in glory shortly after her death.   This greatly strengthened him in his conversion from a life of worldliness.   The cult paid to her in her native country was approved by Pope Pius X in 1907.   The alleged connection of Bd Zdislava Berka with the third order of St Dominic remains somewhat of a problem, for the first formal rule for Dominican tertiaries of which we have knowledge belongs to a later date.

See *Analecta Ecclesiastica* (1907), p. 393 ; and M. C. Ganay, *Les Bienheureuses Dominicaines* (Paris, 1913), pp. 49-67.

BD HUGOLINO OF GUALDO   (A.D. 1260)

Hardly anything appears to be recorded concerning the life of this religious beyond the fact that he entered the Order of the Hermits of St Augustine, and that somewhere about the year 1258 he took over a monastery in his native place, Gualdo in Umbria, which monastery had formerly belonged to the Benedictines.   There he died in the odour of sanctity only a short time afterwards on January 1, 1260. It would seem that a local cult gradually grew up in the diocese of Spoleto, and that his body, which for many months had remained incorrupt, was translated by

Bartholomew Accorambone, Bishop of Spoleto, to the parish church of SS. Antony and Antoninus. This cult was confirmed in 1919.

For the decree *confirmationis cultus* from which the above is taken, see the *Acta Apostolicae Sedis* for 1919, p. 181.

BD JOSEPH TOMMASI, CARDINAL OF THE HOLY ROMAN CHURCH (A.D. 1713)

BY the beatification of Cardinal Joseph Mary Tommasi, the Church may be said to have set her seal upon the principle that neither profound learning nor the critical spirit of accurate scholarship nor independence of judgement, so long as it is kept in check by regard for dogmatic truth, are inconsistent with the highest sanctity. Bd Joseph Tommasi has been described by a high modern authority, Edmund Bishop, as " the prince of liturgists ", and he has been honoured by Anglicans on that ground almost as much as by Catholics ; yet amid all his literary labours he practised heroic virtue, and was faithful to the minutest observances of a strict religious rule.

He was born on September 12, 1649, at Alicata in Sicily. His father was duke of Palermo and prince of Lampedusa, with other honourable titles ; his mother's name was Rosalia Traino. They had already four daughters, who became nuns in the Benedictine monastery at Palma founded by their father. One of them, Isabella, the cardinal's great confidant (in religion Maria Crocifissa), is also a candidate for beatification and may be styled " Venerable ". No pains were spared in Joseph's education, and even as a boy he was a good Greek scholar. The music of the Church also had ever a great attraction for him, and before he was fifteen the superior general of the Theatines was struck with his unusual ability. His distinct call to the religious life came about this time—manifested in his increasing love of prayer and solitude, and his growing distaste for the things of earth. Many obstacles were in the way, besides his father's wish that he should take up a position at court. One was most unexpected. His mother had already entered a convent as an oblate or tertiary, and now his father determined to do the same and to leave the world, making over everything to Joseph. However, after a time he gave his consent to his son's fulfilling his vocation. He was drawn to the Theatine clerks regular, as his uncle, Don Carlo, was a distinguished and most saintly member of that order, and his vocation was finally determined by a sermon which he heard. He entered the noviciate at Palermo in 1664, and after his profession, being very delicate, he was sent to Palma for change and rest, giving great edification to all he met. He next went to Messina to study Greek, thence to Rome and to the Universities of Ferrara and Modena. In the process of beatification is a letter from Mgr Cavalcante, Bishop of Pozzuoli, speaking of the great virtue, humility and love of silence of the young religious.

A few years later we hear of a prophecy of Maria Crocifissa that her brother would one day be a cardinal, accompanied by a sisterly reminder that, however fine a horse's trappings may be, he still remains a horse. In 1673 Joseph was called to Rome, being twenty-four years old. His superior offered to ordain him before the full time, but he refused the offer. Maria Crocifissa wrote him a letter of encouragement, telling him not to shrink from the priesthood, but to see that his soul was like wax, ready to receive its indelible seal. " I give you ", she wrote, " the great book of Christ crucified. Pass your time reading it, for I find your name inscribed there." He prepared most earnestly for his ordination, and sang his three Christmas Masses at San Silvestro, where for forty years, with the exception of a journey to Loreto, he lived the ordinary life of his order. He was already looked upon as a saint in Rome. At the very sight of him quarrels and disputes, unkind or loose talk ceased. But Don Joseph, like all the chosen of God, passed through a time of bitter spiritual trial and desolation. In 1675 he writes to Maria Crocifissa imploring her prayers. She answered exhorting him to patience and humility in accepting his cross from the hand of God, telling him that she, too, was not without her spiritual trials. He answered that the days of actual physical martyrdom are over, and that we are now in the days of hidden martyrdom, seen only by God ; the lesson of it all being trust in God. He was at this time so scrupulous that he could not be allowed to hear confessions or preach.

Don Joseph's life was almost that of a hermit, devoted to prayer and study. He made a special study of Greek philosophy, Holy Scripture and the Breviary. A knowledge of eastern languages was a necessity, and his Hebrew teacher, Rabbi Moses da Cave, owed his conversion from Judaism in 1698, at the age of seventy and after long years of resistance, to the prayers of Don Giuseppe and his sisters. His first book was an edition of the *Speculum* of St Augustine. In 1680 appeared the *Codices Sacramentorum*, being four texts of the most ancient liturgies he could meet with. These precious documents had been stolen from the library of Fleury Abbey, and dispersed by the Calvinists in the sixteenth century. They had been gradually collected together again in Rome, partly by Queen Christina of Sweden. Tommasi's work became celebrated and Mabillon transcribed a great part of it in his *Liturgia Gallicana*. Out of modesty his next book, the *Psalterium*, was published under the name of Giuseppe Caro. It was a work of very great learning, giving an account of the two most important translations of the psalms, the Roman and the Gallican, and it opened up for liturgists a whole new field of research. There were many other treatises of the same class, particularly on the *Antiphonarium*, all displaying great erudition and fervent piety. His work on the psalms attracted the notice of Pope Innocent XII, and in 1697 Tommasi entered the Vatican, under obedience, for the first time. The year 1704 saw him appointed theologian to the Congregation of Discipline of Regulars. In this latter capacity he laboured for the reform of the orders, and all who came in contact with him were impressed with his zeal and holiness.

Don Tommasi, having been chosen as confessor by Cardinal Albani, had required his penitent in 1700 to accept the papacy under pain of mortal sin. Soon after, Clement XI insisted on raising the Theatine scholar to the cardinalate, saying, *Tommasi l'ha fatto a Noi, e Noi lo faremo a lui.* (" What Tommasi did to us, we will do to him.") It was promptly refused, and the whole day was spent in discussion between Don Tommasi and the high ecclesiastics. Eventually he wrote the pope a grateful letter of thanks, " representing to your Holiness the obstacles and impediments, my grave sins, my passions ill-controlled, my ignorance and want of ability, and my conscience bound by vows never to accept any dignity, which make it imperative to implore from your Holiness the permission to refuse the honour ". This letter was read to the Congregation of the Holy Office, and Cardinal Ferrari was deputed by Clement to tell Tommasi that the same reasons applied to him as to the pope, whom he had urged to accept the still more onerous burden of the papacy. Being finally persuaded that it was the will of God, he submitted, saying, *Oh via ! sarà per pochi mese* (" Well ! it will only be for a few months "), and went to receive the hat from his Holiness. He wrote to Maria Crocifissa to implore her prayers, saying that Saul among the prophets fell terribly, and that Judas was an apostle and perished.

Joseph Tommasi continued his simple life, going to choir with his brethren, and as much as possible avoiding all ceremony. The members of his household were dressed as poor people ; amongst them was an old beggar, a converted Jew. His food was of the plainest, and even of that he ate so little that his doctor remonstrated. The new cardinal took the title of San Martino ai Monti, remembering that he had left home to begin his religious life on St Martin's day, and also because it had been the title of St Charles Borromeo, who was his great pattern in his life as cardinal. He found it necessary to leave his monastery in order to live near his church, which belonged to the Carmelites, with whom he frequently joined in their offices as one of themselves. People flocked from all over Rome to be present at his Mass, whereat he allowed nothing but plainsong, accompanied by the organ only. At the classes of Christian doctrine on Sunday he himself instructed the smallest children, explaining the catechism and singing hymns with them. Owing to the extreme moral laxity of the day, he, with the pope's approval and following the example of Borromeo, insisted on the separation of the sexes in the church and in approaching the altar. This raised a storm of opposition and abuse, but he persevered quietly in what he thought to be right.*

Bd Joseph was absorbed in the love of God, and often walked about hardly knowing what he was doing. Those who served his Mass bore witness to the extraordinary graces vouchsafed to him, and he was several times found in ecstasy before the Blessed Sacrament or his crucifix. He showed his love for God's creatures by his almsgiving and care for all who came to him in need—not even allowing the birds to go hungry. The poor and suffering besieged his house and pressed round him when he went out, just as long ago they pressed round his Master. His humility had even, at times, been exaggerated, and his uncle Don Carlo once reproved him for calling himself a ne'er-do-well, telling him not to be abject but humble. To Maria Crocifissa he once called himself a *tristo*, which may mean scoundrel, to which she replied that she must decline to correspond with such a character. We read also of his patience in bearing constant bad health ; of his very severe bodily mortifications, and of the wise moderation of the advice he gave to all who sought his help. He more than once foretold his own death, and when in December 1712 Pope Clement fell ill, the cardinal observed, " The pope will recover ; I shall die." He chose the spot where he should be buried in the crypt of his church, to which he went for the last time on St Thomas's day and joined the friars at Compline. After the office, he made arrangements with the prior about the alms to be given to the poor, advising him to keep back the coal as the cold would increase after Christmas.

On Christmas eve he was very ill, but insisted on attending the services at St Peter's, and offered his three Masses in his own chapel. He suffered greatly from cold, and, refusing all food, could only sit crouching over the fire. After two days he took to his bed. Hearing the lamentations of his *famiglia* and of the poor people who were crowding into the lower part of the house, he sent them word that he had asked the pope to provide for them. At times he was delirious, but his confessor

* Separation of men from women at public worship is normal in most parts of the East, and is considered theoretically desirable in the West too : *cf.* the Code of Canon Law, canon 1262, § 1.

repeating the name of Jesus he recovered consciousness at once.   He would not
have the prayers for the dying said until he asked for them.   Very shortly before
his death he received viaticum, and thus strengthened by the Lord he had so dearly
loved, he passed quietly through the *janua caeli* of death on January 1, 1713.   Even
before his death the sick were healed through touching his clothing, and when the
end had come cures multiplied round his bier.   Bd Joseph Tommasi was beatified
in 1803.

See D. Bernino, *Vita del V. Card. G. M. Tomasi* (1722) ; and the anonymous Theatine
biography compiled from the process of beatification, *Vita del B. Giuseppe M. Tommasi*
(1803).   Vezzosi published a collected edition of his works in eleven volumes in Rome,
1747–1769 ; but some few tractates have only been printed in recent times by Cardinal G.
Mercati (*Studi e Testi*, vol. xv, 1905), who points out that the *beatus* in signing his own name
spelt it with one " m " ; but the commonly received form is Tommasi.

2 : THE HOLY NAME OF JESUS

"THOU shalt call his name JESUS, for he shall save his people from their
sins " (Matt. i 21).   A feast of the Holy Name of Jesus is observed in the
Western church on the Sunday that falls between the Circumcision and
the Epiphany ; and when there is no such Sunday, on this date, January 2.   As
we honour Christ's passion summed up in the material cross, so the name Jesus
brings to the mind all that name stands for (*cf.* Phil. ii 9–10).   " To speak of it
gives light ; to think of it is the food of the soul ; to call on it calms and soothes
the heart " : so said St Bernard of Clairvaux, than whom no one has spoken of the
Holy Name more movingly or more profoundly.

The Council of Lyons in 1274 prescribed a special devotion towards the name
of Jesus, and it was to the Order of Preachers that Bd Gregory X specially turned
to spread it.   But its great diffusion—in the face of a good deal of opposition—was
due to the two Friars Minor, St Bernardino of Siena and St John of Capistrano.
It was they who popularized the use of the monogram IHS, which is simply an
abbreviation of the name Jesus (Ihesus).   The subsequent adoption of this monogram as part of the emblem of the Society of Jesus gave it a yet wider diffusion.   A
feast of the Holy Name was granted by the Holy See to the Franciscans in 1530
and was subsequently allowed elsewhere.   Not till 1721 was it extended to the
whole Western church, and it was not many years later that Pope Benedict XIV's
commission for the reform of the Breviary recommended that it should be withdrawn from the general calendar.   The feast is in a sense only a double of the
Circumcision, and the lessons of the third nocturn at Matins are taken from St
Bernard's sermons on that mystery.

It is interesting to note that the Name of Jesus figures in the calendar of the
Book of Common Prayer, on August 7, the date selected by some late medieval
bishops in England and Scotland when they adopted the feast on their own
initiative.   And Father Edward Caswall's translation of the lovely Vespers hymn,
Jesu dulcis memoria (anonymous, but often wrongly attributed to St Bernard), has
made it known perhaps better among Protestants than Catholics.   St Bernardino
and St John of Capistrano may have been the originators of the Litany of the Holy
Name, which in fact is concerned rather with the attributes of our Lord than with
His name : Bishop Challoner in the original *Garden of the Soul* calls it simply the

Litany of Our Lord Jesus Christ.   The great English contribution to the devotion was *Jesu's Psalter*, by the Bridgettine Richard Whytford, with its triple invocations of Jesu.   Nowadays it too often is printed in a debased form.

See the *Acta Sanctorum*, October, vol. x, pp. 319–320 ; C. Stengel, *Sacrosancti nominis Jesu cultus et miracula* (1613) : lives of St Bernardino of Siena ; F. G. Holweck, *Calendarium liturgicum festorum Dei et Dei Matris* (1925) ; and the issue of *La Vie Spirituelle* for January 1952.   For the Eastern tradition of the Holy Name, see *La prière de Jésus* (Chevetogne, 1951).   An account of the work and projects of Pope Benedict XIV's commission, referred to above and elsewhere herein, may be most easily found in S. Bäumer, *Histoire du bréviaire*, vol. ii (1905), cap. 12 (trans. from the German and supplemented by R. Biron).

ST MACARIUS OF ALEXANDRIA   (*c.* A D. 394)

ST MACARIUS the Younger, a citizen of Alexandria, followed the business of a confectioner.   Desirous to serve God with his whole heart, he forsook the world in the flower of his age and spent upwards of sixty years in the desert in penance and contemplation.   He first retired into the Thebaid about the year 335.   Having acquired some proficiency in virtue under masters renowned for their sanctity, he quitted Upper Egypt and came to the Lower before the year 373.   In this part were three deserts almost adjoining each other : that of Skete, on the borders of Libya, that of the Cells, contiguous to the former, this name being given to it on account of the hermit-cells with which it abounded ; and a third, which reached to the western branch of the Nile, called Nitria.   St Macarius had a cell in each of these deserts, but his chief residence was in that of the Cells.   Each anchoret had here a separate cell in which he spent his time, except on Saturday and Sunday when all assembled in one church to celebrate and receive the divine mysteries. When a stranger came to live among them, everyone offered him his cell, and was ready to build another for himself.   Their cells were not within sight of each other. Their manual labour, which was that of making baskets or mats, did not interrupt the prayer of the heart, and a profound silence reigned throughout the district. Our saint here received the priesthood, and shone as a bright sun influencing this holy company, whilst St Macarius the Elder lived no less eminent in the wilderness of Skete.   Palladius has recorded a memorable instance of the self-denial observed by these hermits.   A present was made to St Macarius of a newly-gathered bunch of grapes ; the holy man carried it to a neighbouring monk who was ill, and he sent it to another.   In this manner it passed to all the cells and was brought back to Macarius, who was exceedingly rejoiced to perceive the abstinence of his brethren, but would not eat the grapes himself.

The austerities of all the inhabitants of that desert were extraordinary, but St Macarius went far beyond the rest.   For seven years together he lived only on raw vegetables and beans, and for the three following years contented himself with four or five ounces of bread a day, and consumed only one little vessel of oil in a year, as Palladius assures us.   His watchings were not less surprising.   God had given him a body capable of bearing the greatest rigours ; and his fervour was so intense that whatever spiritual exercise he heard of or saw practised by others he resolved to adopt for himself.   The reputation of the monastery of Tabennisi, under St Pachomius, drew him to this place in disguise, some time before the year 349.   St Pachomius told him that he seemed too far advanced in years to accustom himself to their fastings and watchings ; but at length admitted him on condition he would observe all the rules.   Lent approaching soon after, the monks prepared to pass that holy time each according to his strength and fervour : some by fasting one, others two, three or four days, without any nourishment ; some standing all day, others only sitting at their work.　Macarius took palm-tree leaves steeped in water as materials with which to occupy himself, and standing in a retired place passed the whole time without eating, except for a few green cabbage leaves on Sundays. His hands were employed in almost continual labour, and his heart conversed with God.　Such a prodigy astonished the monks, who even remonstrated with the abbot at Easter deprecating a singularity which, if tolerated, might on several accounts be prejudicial to their community.　St Pachomius prayed to know who this stranger was ;　and learning by revelation that he was the great Macarius, embraced him, thanked him for the edification he had given, and desired him, when he returned to his desert, to offer up his prayers for them.

The virtue of this great saint was often exercised by temptations.　One was a suggestion to quit his desert and go to Rome to serve the sick in the hospitals ; which, on due reflection, he discovered to be a secret artifice of vainglory inciting him to attract the eyes and esteem of the world.　True humility alone could discover the snare which lurked under the specious disguise of charity.　Finding this enemy extremely importunate, he threw himself on the ground in his cell, and cried out to the fiends, " Drag me hence, if you can, by force, for I will not stir ".　Thus he lay till night, but as soon as he arose they renewed the assault ; and he, to stand firm against them, filled two baskets with sand, and laying them on his shoulders, set out to tramp the wilderness.　A friend, meeting him, asked him what he was doing, and made an offer to relieve him of his burden ; but the saint only replied, " I am tormenting my tormentor ".　He returned home in the evening, freed from the temptation.　Palladius informs us that St Macarius, desiring to enjoy heavenly contemplation at least for five days without interruption, immured himself within his cell, and said to his soul, " Having taken up thy abode in Heaven where thou hast God and His angels to converse with, see that thou descend not thence : regard not earthly things."　The first two days his heart overflowed with rapture ; but on the third he met with so violent a disturbance from the Devil, that he was obliged to return to his usual manner of life.　God oftentimes withdraws Himself, as the saint observed on this occasion, to make religious people sensible of their own weakness and to convince them that this life is a state of trial.　St Jerome and others relate that a certain anchoret in Nitria having left one hundred crowns at his death, which he had acquired by weaving cloth, the monks met to deliberate what should be done with the money.　Some were for having it given to the poor, others to the Church : but Macarius, Pambo, Isidore and others, who were called The Fathers, ordained that the one hundred crowns should be thrown into the grave, and that at the same time should be pronounced the words, " May thy money be with thee to perdition ".　This example struck terror into the monks and put an end to the hoarding of money.

Palladius, who from 391 lived for a time under our saint, was eye-witness of several miracles wrought by him.　He relates that a certain priest whose head was consumed by a cancerous sore came to his cell, but was refused admittance ; Macarius at first would not even speak to him.　Palladius strove to prevail upon him to give at least some answer to the unfortunate man.　Macarius on the contrary urged that God, to punish him for a sin of the flesh, had afflicted him with this disorder : however, that upon his sincere repentance and promise never more to celebrate the divine mysteries he would intercede for his cure.　The priest confessed his sin, with the promise required. The saint thereupon absolved him by the imposition of hands ; and a few days after the priest came back perfectly healed, glorifying God and giving thanks to his servant.

The two saints of the name of Macarius happened one day to cross the Nile together in a boat, when certain officers could not help observing to each other that these men, from the cheerfulness of their aspect, must be happy in their poverty. Macarius of Alexandria, alluding to their name, which in Greek signifies *happy*, made this answer, " You have reason to call us happy, for this is our name. But if we are happy in despising the world, are not you miserable who live slaves to it ? " These words, uttered with a tone of voice expressive of an interior conviction of their truth, had such an effect on the tribune who first spoke that, hastening home, he distributed his fortune among the poor, and embraced an eremitical life.

In the desert of Nitria a monastery bearing the name of St Macarius survived for many centuries. St Jerome, in his letter to Rusticus, seems to have copied many things from a set of constitutions attributed to this saint. The *Concordia Regularum*, or " collection of rules ", gives another code under the names of the two SS. Macarius, Serapion (of Arsinöe, or the other of Nitria), Paphnutius (of Bekbale, priest of Skete), and thirty-four other abbots. According to this latter, the monks fasted the whole year, except on Sundays and the time from Easter to Whitsuntide ; they observed the strictest poverty, and divided the day between manual labour and prayer. Hospitality was much recommended, but for the sake of recollection it was strictly forbidden for any monk, except one who was deputed to entertain guests, ever to speak to any stranger without leave. The definition of a monk or anchoret given by Abbot de Rancé, of La Trappe, seems to trace the portrait of the great Macarius in the desert. When, says he, a soul relishes God in solitude, she thinks no more of anything but Heaven. This Macarius is named in the canon of the Coptic Mass.

See Palladius, *Lausiac History*, ch. 18, and *Acta Sanctorum*, January 2. *Cf.* Schiwietz, *Morgenlandische Mönchtum* (1904), vol. i, pp. 104 *seq.* ; Amélineau in *Annales du Musée Guimet*, xxv, 235 *seq. ;* BHL., n. 757 ; *Codex Regularum* in Migne, PL., vol. ciii ; and *Concordia Regularum*, ed. H. Menard (1638). Although there may be some confusion in the stories told regarding the different ascetics who bore the name Macarius, it is impossible to identify this Macarius " the Younger " (of Alexandria) with Macarius the Elder (the Egyptian), for Palladius distinctly tells us that he knew them both.

ST MUNCHIN, Bishop   (Seventh Century)

The martyrologies of Oengus, Tallaght and Gorman all mention on this day a Munchin, who is also described as " the Wise ", but that he was ever bishop of Limerick, or bishop at all, seems most doubtful. There is no extant life of the saint and the only data about his ancestry and career are to be found in the pedigree of the Dal Cais, the ruling sept in north Munster during early Christian times. Among the sept is numbered " Sedna from whom Maincin of Luimneach " in the Book of Ui Maine. The rare references to Sedna's folk show that the territory of his people lay by the coast of the present County Clare. The connection of Maincin (the name means " Little Monk ") with the island at Limerick is explained in another entry in the genealogy : " Dioma had three sons, Dubduin, Aindlid and Feardomnach who gave Sibtand to Maincin of Luimneach ". The donor's brethren figure in well-vouched history and we are enabled to date the lifetime of Munchin to the late seventh century. Inis Sibtand was the island at the head of the Shannon tideway where in the early tenth century the Norsemen founded Limerick.

St Munchin is the principal patron of the diocese of Limerick, and his feast is kept throughout Ireland.

The substance of the above notice is due to Mgr Canon Michael Moloney, of Limerick. Canon J. Begley's surmise in his history of the diocese of Limerick (1906), pp. 71–72, is no more than an arbitrary guess. See also LIS., vol. i, pp. 27–34.

ST VINCENTIAN   (A.D. 672 ?)

THE only information which we possess concerning this saint is quite untrustworthy. It come to us in a biography which professes to have been written by a certain deacon Hermenbert, who was his tutor when a boy but survived him long enough to write this account. The life states that Vincentian lost his parents as a child and was brought up by one Berald, Duke of Aquitaine, who eventually agreed to the request of St Didier, Bishop of Cahors, that so promising a child should be trained for the priesthood. But Berald died soon after, and his son and successor compelled the bishop to send the youth back to the ducal household, where he was placed in charge of the stables. In the interval Vincentian had acquired the habits of the most fervent piety. He gave away to the poor his clothes and his food, he refused a bride who was pressed upon him, and, in the end, he was so cruelly beaten, persecuted and threatened that he ran away and hid himself in the forest, leading a solitary life as a hermit. It is useless to detail the extravagant miracles which mark the different stages of the story. Eventually death came to release Vincentian at the time which had been revealed to him in a vision, viz., January 2, 672. The dead body was placed on a car to be drawn by two oxen to the spot which his relics were destined to render famous. On the way a bear killed one of the oxen, but a disciple of the saint commanded the bear to drag the car in the place of the beast it had killed, and it at once obeyed.

The life has been printed by W. Levison in MGH., *Scriptores Merov.*, vol. v, pp. 112–128, with an introduction in which he proves that the story cannot he the work of a contemporary as pretended but that it is a pure fabrication, two or three hundred years later in date. See also Bruno Krusch in *Neues Archiv*, vol. xviii, p. 561. There is nothing even to show that such a person as St Vincentian ever existed.

ST ADALHARD, OR ADELARD, ABBOT   (A.D. 827)

THE family of this holy monk was most illustrious, his father Bernard being son of Charles Martel and brother of King Pepin, so that Adalhard was first cousin to Charlemagne. He was only twenty years old when, in 773, he took the monastic habit at Corbie in Picardy, a monastery that had been founded by Queen St Bathildis. The first employment assigned him was that of gardener, in which, whilst his hands were employed in digging or weeding, his thoughts were on God and heavenly things. The great example of his virtue defeated the projects of his humility and did not suffer him to live long unknown, and some years after he was chosen abbot. Being obliged by Charlemagne often to attend at court, he soon, in fact, became the first among the king's counsellors, as he is styled by Hincmar, who had seen him there in 796. He was even compelled by Charlemagne to quit his monastery altogether, and act as chief minister to that prince's eldest son Pepin, who, at his death at Milan in 810, appointed the saint tutor to his son Bernard.

After the death of Charlemagne, Adalhard was accused of supporting the revolt of Bernard against Louis the Debonair, who banished him to a monastery in the little island of Héri, called afterwards Noirmoutier, on the coast of Aquitaine. The saint's brother Wala (one of the great men of that age, as appears from his curious life, published by Mabillon) he obliged to become a monk at Lérins. This exile St Adalhard regarded as a great gain, and in it his tranquillity of soul met with no interruptions. The emperor at length was made sensible of his innocence, and after five years' banishment recalled him to court towards the close of the year 821 ; but he soon had again to retire to his abbey at Corbie, where he delighted to take upon himself the most humbling employments of the house. By his solicitude and powerful example his spiritual children grew daily in fervour ; and such was his zeal for their advancement, that he passed no week without speaking to every one of them in particular, and no day without exhorting them all in general by his discourses. The inhabitants of the country round had also a share in his labours, and he expended upon the poor the revenues of his monastery with a profusion which many condemned as excessive, but which Heaven sometimes approved by sensible miracles. The good old man would receive advice from the least of his monks. When entreated to moderate his austerities, he answered, " I will take care of your servant ", meaning himself, " that he may serve you the longer."

During his banishment another Adalhard, who governed the monastery by his appointment, began at our saint's suggestion to prepare the foundation of the monastery of New Corbie, commonly called Corvey, in the diocese of Paderborn, that it might be a nursery of evangelical labourers for the conversion of the northern nations. St Adalhard, after his return to Corbie, completed this undertaking, and to perpetuate the strict observance which he established in his two monasteries he compiled a book of statutes for their use, of which considerable fragments are extant. Other works of St Adalhard are lost, but by those which we have, and also by his disciples St Paschasius Radbertus, St Anskar and others, it is clear that he was a zealous promoter of literature in his monasteries. Paschasius assures us that he instructed the people not only in the Latin, but also in the Teutonic and vulgar French languages. Alcuin, in a letter addressed to him under the name of Antony, calls him his son, whence many infer that he had been scholar to that great man. St Adalhard had just returned from Germany to Corbie, when he fell ill three days before Christmas and died on January 2, 827, in his seventy-third year. Upon proof of several miracles the body of the saint was translated with solemnity in 1040 ; of which ceremony we have a full account, by an author, not St Gerard, who also composed an office in his honour, in gratitude for having been cured of intense pains in the head through his intercession.

See his life, compiled with accuracy but in a tone of panegyric, by his disciple, Paschasius Radbertus, printed in the *Acta Sanctorum*, and more correctly in Mabillon (vol. v, p. 306). *Cf.* also U. Berlière in DHG., vol. i, cc. 457–458 ; and BHL., n. 11.

BD AYRALD, Bishop of Maurienne   (A.D. 1146 ?)

THE identity of this holy bishop is involved in much confusion and obscurity. His *cultus* was confirmed in 1863, and in the decree published on that occasion a summary of his life is given.

If we may credit this account, he was a son of William II, Count of Burgundy. Of his three brothers, one was elected pope under the name of Callistus II ; another,

Raymond, became king of Castile; and the third, Henry, count of Portugal. Ayrald himself, however, according to the same summary, entered the Carthusian Order at Portes, and was made prior. From this life of seclusion he was called away to rule the see of Maurienne, but we are told that he still paid long visits to his old monastery to renew his spirit of fervour, and that he died at a comparatively early age. While one Carthusian chronicler, Dom Le Vasseur, is in substantial agreement with this account, assigning January 2, 1146, as the date of Ayrald's death, another, Dom Le Couteulx, contradicts it at almost every point. The fact seems to be that in the twelfth century there were three different bishops of Maurienne named Ayrald or Ayrard. One of these, either the first or the third, but not the second, had been a Carthusian monk at Portes.

In honour of the bishop who was beatified and with whom we are here concerned, the following epitaph was engraved of old upon his tomb in the cathedral of Maurienne:

> Hic jacet Airaldus, claro de sanguine natus,
>   Portarum monachus, Pontificumque decus;
> Ecclesiae lumen, miserorum atque columen,
>   Virtute et signis splendidus innumeris.

> "Here lies Ayrald, a man of noble blood, monk of Portes, glory of pontiffs, a light of the Church, stay of the unfortunate, shining with goodness and unnumbered miracles."

A lively controversy, of which a full bibliography may be found in U. Chevalier's *Répertoire—Bio-bibliographie*, has been carried on regarding the identity of Bd Ayrald. See especially C. F. Bellet, *Un problème d'hagiographie* (1901), and Truchet, *Le B. Ayrald* (1891); also Le Vasseur, *Ephemerides*, vol. i, pp. 3–6; Le Couteulx, *Annales Ord. Carth.*, vols. i, 382 *seq.*, and ii, 43 *seq. Cf. Historisches Jahrbuch*, 1903, p. 142, and 1904, p. 279.

BD STEPHANA QUINZANI, Virgin   (A.D. 1530)

STEPHANA QUINZANI was born in 1457 near Brescia, of a middle-class family. Strange things are related of her childhood, and she is said to have consecrated herself to God at a very early age. Her precise vocation, however, was not decided until her father and mother moved to Soncino, and she came under the influence of the Dominicans. There she had a vision of St Andrew the Apostle holding a cross. Receiving the habit of the third order of St Dominic, she spent her time in nursing the sick and relieving the poor until she was able herself to found a convent at Soncino. The most interesting document which has been preserved concerning her is a contemporary account, drawn up in 1497 and signed by twenty-one witnesses, describing one of the ecstasies in which she represented in her own person the different stages of the Passion, including the scourging, the crowning with thorns and the nailing to the cross. In these ecstasies the wound marks, or stigmata, seem to have shown themselves in her hands and feet, and her frame became so rigid that the onlookers could not change her position or bend her limbs. She is said to have performed many miracles of healing and to have multiplied food and money.

The *Legenda Volgare*, from which all accounts of Bd Stephana ultimately derive, is called by its editor, Mgr Guerrini, "a mystical romance in full flower, written as ascetical edification rather than history, full of elevations and mystical ramblings for women readers". Another source, the fragments of the *beata's* own letters, has not yet been properly explored and studied ; she corresponded with many people in northern Italy.   Bd Stephana died on January 2, 1530, and her *cultus* was confirmed in 1740.

See P. de Micheli, *La b. Stefana Quinzani   memorie e documenti*, and P. Guerrini, *La prima Legenda Volgare de la b. Stefana Quinzani* (1930).   See also M. C. Ganay, *Les Bses. Dominicaines* (1913), pp. 413–434, and pp. 545–548 where is printed part of the *relazione* referred to above.

ST CASPAR DEL BUFALO, FOUNDER OF THE MISSIONERS OF THE PRECIOUS BLOOD   (A.D. 1837)

CASPAR, who was born in Rome, the son of a chef, in 1786, received his education at the Collegio Romano and was ordained priest in 1808.   Shortly after this Rome was taken by Napoleon's army, and he, with most of the clergy, was exiled for refusing to abjure his allegiance to the Holy See.   He returned after the fall of Napoleon to find a wide scope for work, as Rome had for nearly five years been almost entirely without priests and sacraments.

In 1814 he conducted a mission at Giano, in the diocese of Spoleto, and there the idea of the Congregation of the Most Precious Blood first came to him.   He found a house at Giano suitable for his purpose, and with the help of Cardinal Cristaldi, ever his kind friend, and the hearty approval of Pope Pius VII, the new congregation was formally approved in 1815.   The house and adjoining church of San Felice in Giano were given him by the pope.   The second foundation was made in 1819 and the third shortly afterwards at Albano.   His wish was to have a house in every diocese, the most neglected and wicked town or district being chosen. The kingdom of Naples was in those days a nest of crime of every kind ; no one's life or property was safe, and in 1821 the pope wrote with his own hand to del Bufalo asking him to found six houses there.   He joyfully responded, but met with endless difficulties before subjects and funds were collected.   His biographer tells us that Providence had *scherzato* (played practical jokes) with him, as over and over again one difficulty was overcome only to be replaced by a greater ; but by degrees men gathered round him, and at last he could say he had more than all the money he wanted.

Grave difficulties arose under Pope Leo XII ; but these were cleared up, and in 1824, the houses of the congregation were opened to young clergy who wished to be trained specially as missioners.   The ideal was high, the work arduous.   A missioner, the founder said, like a soldier or sailor, must never give in, must be ready for anything.   He required from his sons not only devotion, but also hard study.   To evangelize the whole world, which was their aim, they must learn foreign languages besides theology and Holy Scripture.   In his life-time their work covered the whole of Italy.   Journeying from town to town, enduring endless hardships, threatened often even with death, their founder always taking the most arduous work himself, they preached their message.

Del Bufalo's biographer gives us a graphic account of a mission, describing its successive stages.   Some of his methods were distinctly dramatic, *e.g.* the missioners took the discipline in the public piazza, which always resulted in many conversions.   On the last day forbidden firearms, obscene books, and anything else that might offend Almighty God were publicly burnt.   A cross was erected *in memoriam*, a solemn *Te Deum* sung, and the missioners went away quietly.   Caspar would often say at the end of a mission, exhausted but thankful, " If it is so sweet to tire ourselves for God, what will it be to enjoy Him ! "   One of his principles was that everybody should be made to work.   He therefore founded works of charity in Rome for young and old, rich and poor of both sexes.   He opened the night oratory, where our Lord is worshipped all night by men, many coming to Him, like Nicodemus, by night who would not have the courage to go to confession by day.

His last mission was preached in Rome at the Chiesa Nuova during the cholera outbreak of 1836.   Feeling his strength failing, he returned at once to Albano, and made every preparation for death.   He suffered terribly from cold, and at night from parching thirst, but he would not take anything to drink, so that he might be able to celebrate Mass.   He asked to be left alone as much as possible, that his prayer might be less interrupted.   After the feast of St Francis Xavier he went to Rome to die.   On December 19 the doctor forbade him to say Mass ; he received the last sacraments on December 28, and he died the same day.

Various miracles had been worked by Don Caspar during his lifetime, and after his death many graces were obtained by his intercession.   We have, in fact, a long list of cures and other miraculous occurrences.   He was canonized in 1954.

See the *summarium* presented to the Congregation of Rites in the process of beatification, and Sardi, *Notizie intorno alla vita del beato Gaspare del Bufalo* (1904).   The English form of the name Caspar or Gaspar is properly Jasper.

3 : ST ANTHERUS, Pope and Martyr   (A.D. 236)

THE name of St Antherus occurs in the list of popes after that of St Pontian. He is believed to have been elected November 21, 235, and to have died January 3, 236, thus reigning only forty-three days.   Nothing certain is known regarding his martyrdom, though the *Liber Pontificalis* states that he was put to death for obtaining copies of the official proceedings against the martyrs with the view of preserving them in the episcopal archives.   He was buried in the " papal crypt " in the catacombs (Cemetery of St Callistus), and the site was discovered by de Rossi in 1854, together with the fragments of a Greek inscription.

See Allard, *Hist. des Persécutions*, vol. ii, p. 212 ; G. B. de Rossi, *Roma Sotteranea*, vol. ii, pp. 55 *seq.* and 180 *seq.* ; and the *Liber Pontificalis*, ed. L. Duchesne (1886–1892), vol. i, p. 147.

ST PETER BALSAM, Martyr   (A.D. 311)

PETER BALSAM, to follow the narrative of his published " acts ", was a native of the territory of Eleutheropolis in Palestine, who was apprehended at Aulana in the persecution of Maximinus.   Being brought before Severus, governor of the province, the interrogatory began by asking him his name.   Peter answered, " Balsam is the name of my family ; but I received that of Peter in baptism."

SEVERUS : " Of what family and of what country are you ? "

PETER : " I am a Christian."

SEVERUS : " What is your employment ? "

PETER : " What employment can I have more honourable, or what better thing can I do in the world, than to live as a Christian ? "

SEVERUS : " Do you know the imperial edicts ? "

PETER : " I know the laws of God, the sovereign of the universe."

SEVERUS : " You shall quickly know that there is an edict of the most clement emperors, commanding all to sacrifice to the gods, or be put to death."

PETER : " You will also know one day that there is a law of the eternal King, proclaiming that everyone shall perish who offers sacrifice to devils. Which do you counsel me to obey, and which, think you, ought I to choose—to die by your sword, or to be condemned to everlasting misery by the sentence of the great King, the true God ? "

SEVERUS : " Since you ask my advice, it is that you obey the edict, and sacrifice to the gods."

PETER : " I can never be prevailed upon to sacrifice to gods of wood and stone, as those are which you worship."

SEVERUS : " I would have you know that it is in my power to avenge these affronts by putting you to death."

PETER : " I had no intention of affronting you. I only expressed what is written in the divine law."

SEVERUS : " Have compassion on yourself, and sacrifice."

PETER : " If I am truly compassionate to myself, I ought not to sacrifice."

SEVERUS : " I want to be lenient ; I therefore still allow you time to reflect, that you may save your life."

PETER : " This delay will be to no purpose for I shall not alter my mind ; do now what you will be obliged to do soon, and complete the work which the devil, your father, has begun ; for I will never do what Jesus Christ forbids me."

Severus, on hearing these words, ordered him to be stretched upon the rack, and whilst he was suspended said to him scoffingly, " What say you now, Peter ; do you begin to know what the rack is ? Are you yet willing to sacrifice ? " Peter answered, " Tear me with hooks, and talk not of my sacrificing to your devils : I have already told you, that I will sacrifice only to that God for whom I suffer." Hereupon the governor commanded his tortures to be redoubled. The martyr, far from any complaint, sung with alacrity those verses of the royal prophet, " One thing I have asked of the Lord : this will I seek after : that I may dwell in the house of the Lord all the days of my life. I will take the chalice of salvation, and will call upon the name of the Lord." The spectators, seeing the martyr's blood run down in streams, cried out to him, " Obey the emperors ! Sacrifice, and rescue yourself from these torments ! " Peter replied, " Do you call these torments ? I feel no pain : but this I know, that if I be not faithful to my God I must expect real pain, such as cannot be conceived." The judge also said, " Sacrifice, Peter Balsam, or you will repent it."

PETER : " Neither will I sacrifice, nor shall I repent it."

SEVERUS : " I am on the point of pronouncing sentence."

PETER : " It is what I most earnestly desire." Severus then dictated the sentence in this manner : " It is our order that Peter Balsam, for having refused to obey the edict of the invincible emperors, and obstinately defending the law of a crucified man, be himself nailed to a cross." Thus it was that this glorious martyr finished his triumph, at Aulana, on January 11 ; but he is honoured in the Roman Martyrology on January 3.

There can be little doubt that Peter Balsam is to be identified with the martyr Peter Abselamus, whom Eusebius (*De Martyribus Palest.*, x, 2–3) describes as having been burnt to death at Caesarea.   For this and other reasons very different opinions have been held as to the trustworthiness of the narrative given above.   Ruinart, and even Bardenhewer (*Geschichte der althirchl. Literatur*, vol. ii, p. 640), treat the acts as authentic.   P. Allard (*Hist. des persécutions*, vol. v, p. 126) and H. Leclercq (*Les Martyrs*, vol. ii, p. 323) believe them to have been compiled inaccurately ; Father Delehaye more logically (*Légendes Hagiographiques*, p. 114) considers that the narrative must be regarded as a historical romance founded on a basis of genuine fact.   See also Harnack *Chronol. Altchrist. Lit.*, vol. ii, p. 474.

ST GENEVIEVE, or GENOVEFA, Virgin   (*c.* A.D. 500)

GENEVIEVE's father's name was Severus, and her mother's Gerontia ; she was born about the year 422 at Nanterre, a small village four miles from Paris, near Mont Valérien.   When St Germanus, Bishop of Auxerre, went with St Lupus into Britain to oppose the Pelagian heresy, he spent a night at Nanterre on his way.   The inhabitants flocked about them to receive their blessing, and St Germanus gave an address, during which he took particular notice of Genevieve, though she was only seven years of age.   After his sermon he inquired for her parents, and foretold their daughter's future sanctity.   He then asked Genevieve whether it was not her desire to serve God only and to be naught else but a spouse of Jesus Christ.   She answered that this was what she desired, and begged that by his blessing she might be from that moment consecrated to God.   The holy prelate went to the church, followed by the people, and during the long singing of psalms and prayers, says Constantius —that is, during the recital of None and Vespers, as one text of the Life of St Genevieve expresses it—he laid his hand upon the maiden's head.   After he had supped he dismissed her, telling her parents to bring her again to him the next morning.   The father obeyed, and St Germanus asked the child whether she remembered the promise she had made to God.   She said she did, and declared that she hoped to keep her word.   The bishop gave her a medal or coin, on which a cross was engraved, to wear about her neck, in memory of the consecration she had received the day before ; and he charged her never to wear bracelets or jewels or other trinkets.   The author of her life tells us that the child, begging one day that she might go to church, her mother struck her on the face, but in punishment lost her sight ; she only recovered it two months after, by washing her eyes with water which her daughter fetched from the well and over which she had made the sign of the cross.   Hence the people look upon the well at Nanterre as having been blessed by the saint.

When she was about fifteen years of age, Genevieve was presented to the bishop of Paris to receive the religious veil, together with two other girls.   Though she was the youngest of the three, the bishop gave her the first place, saying that Heaven had already sanctified her, by which he seems to have alluded to her promise of consecrating herself to God.   From that time she frequently ate only twice in the week, on Sundays and Thursdays, and her food was barley bread with a few beans.   After the death of her parents she left Nanterre, and settled with her godmother in Paris, but sometimes undertook journeys for motives of charity.   The cities of Meaux, Laon, Tours, Orleans and all other places she visited bore witness to her miracles and remarkable predictions.   God permitted her to meet with some

severe trials ; for at a certain time everybody seemed to be against her, and persecuted her under the opprobrious names of visionary, hypocrite and the like. The
arrival of St Germanus at Paris, probably on his second journey to Britain, for some
time silenced her calumniators ; but it was not long before the storm broke out
anew. Her enemies were fully determined to discredit and even to drown her,
when the archdeacon of Auxerre arrived with *eulogiae*, blessed bread, sent her by
St Germanus as a testimony of his particular esteem and a token of communion.
This seems to have happened whilst Germanus was absent in Italy in 448. The
tribute thus paid her converted the prejudices of her calumniators into veneration
for the remainder of her life.

The Franks had at this time gained possession of the better part of Gaul, and
Childeric, their king, took Paris. During the long blockade of that city, the citizens
being reduced to extremities by famine, St Genevieve, as the author of her life
relates, went out at the head of a company who were sent to procure provisions,
and brought back from Arcis-sur-Aube and Troyes several boats laden with corn.
Childeric, when he had made himself master of Paris, though always a pagan,
respected St Genevieve, and upon her intercession spared the lives of many
prisoners and did other generous acts. She also awakened the zeal of many persons
to build a church in honour of St Dionysius of Paris, which King Dagobert I
afterwards rebuilt with a monastery in 629. St Genevieve likewise undertook many
pilgrimages, in company with other maidens, to the shrine of St Martin at Tours,
and the reputation of her holiness is said to have been so great that her fame even
reached St Simeon Stylites in Syria. King Clovis, who embraced the faith in 496,
often listened with deference to St Genevieve, and more than once granted liberty
to captives at her request. Upon the report of the march of Attila with his army
of Huns the Parisians were preparing to abandon their city, but St Genevieve, like
a Christian Judith or Esther, encouraged them to avert the scourge by fasting and
prayer. Many of her own sex passed whole days with her in prayer in the baptistery ; from whence the particular devotion to St Genevieve, formerly practised
at S.-Jean-le-Rond, the ancient public baptistery of the church of Paris, seems to
have taken rise. She assured the people of the protection of Heaven, and though
she was treated by many as an impostor, the event verified the prediction, for the
barbarous invader suddenly changed the course of his march. Our author attributes to St Genevieve the first suggestion of the church which Clovis began to build
in honour of SS. Peter and Paul, in deference to the wishes of his wife, St Clotilda,
in which church the body of St Genevieve herself was enshrined after her death
about the year 500.

The miracles which were performed there from the time of her burial rendered
this church famous over all France, so that at length it began to be known by her
name. The fabric, however, fell into decay, and a new church was begun in 1764.
This has long been secularized and, under the name of the Pantheon, is now used
as a national mausoleum. The city of Paris has frequently received sensible proofs
of the divine protection, through St Genevieve's intercession. The most famous
instance is that called the miracle *des Ardents*, or of the burning fever. In 1129 a
disease, apparently poisoning by ergot, swept off in a short time many thousand
persons, nor could the art of physicians afford any relief. Stephen, Bishop of
Paris, with the clergy and people, implored the divine mercy by fasting and supplications. Yet the epidemic did not abate till the shrine of St Genevieve was
carried in a solemn procession to the cathedral. Many sick persons were cured by

touching the shrine, and of all who then were suffering from the disease in the whole town only three died, and no others fell ill.   Pope Innocent II, coming to Paris the year following, after due investigation ordered an annual festival in commemoration of the miracle on November 26, which is still kept in Paris.   It was formerly the custom, in extraordinary public calamities, to carry the shrine of St Genevieve in procession to the cathedral.   The greater part of the relics of the saint were destroyed or pillaged at the French Revolution.

The ancient life of S t Genevieve from which most of the above account is derived, and which purports to h ave been written by a contemporary eighteen years after the saint's death, has been the subjec t of keen controversy.   There are three principal recensions of it, known respectively as the A, B and C texts.   Text A has been edited by B. Krusch in MGII., *Scriptores Merov.*, vol. iii (1896).   Text B is printed in the very valuable essay of C. Kohler, *Étude critique sur le texte de la vie latine de Sainte Geneviève* (1881), and Text C may be found in the Teubner edition of the *Vita Sanctae Genovefae*, edited by C. Künstle in 1910.   Although Text C has in its favour the authority of the oldest manuscripts (eighth century), the priority of that recension is by no means generally admitted.   But the more important controversy is that regarding the authenticity of the life itself.   Bruno Krusch declares it to be a forgery, and that the author, instead of being a contemporary as he pretends, did not compile the life until more than 250 years later, towards the close of the eighth century.   It is impossible here to do more than mention the acrimonious discussion to which Krusch's pronouncement has given rise.   It must be sufficient to say that his views have by no means carried with them the support of the majority of competent critics.   Such scholars as Mgr Duchesne, Prof. G. Kurth, C. Künstle and A. Poncelet strenuously maintain that the life was really written by a contemporary, and that, so far as regards the substance of its contents, it is trustworthy.   Readers will find an excellent summary of all that is really known about St Genevieve in H. Lesêtre, *Ste Geneviève* (in the series " Les Saints "), and in the essay of E. Vacandard, *Études de critique*, vol. iv, pp. 67–124, and 255–266.   For a charming popular account of the saint, see M. Reynès-Monlaur, *Ste Geneviève* (1924).   A story in the life tells how the devil, when St Genevieve went to pray in the church at night, blew out her candle to frighten her.   She is, therefore, often represented in art with a candle.   Sometimes the devil and a pair of bellows are also depicted beside her.

ST BERTILIA OF MAREUIL, Widow   (Eighth Century)

THE life of St Bertilia was an uneventful one.   Born of noble parents, she spent her youth in exercises of charity.   In due time she married a noble youth, and they spent their lives helping the poor and sick.   On the death of her husband she lived the life of a solitary at Mareuil in the diocese of Arras, where she built a church which her cell adjoined.   She died early in the eighth century, and must be distinguished from her contemporary St Bertila of Chelles.

See *Acta Sanctorum*, January 3 ; Parenty, *Histoire de Ste Bertilie* (1847) ; Destombes, *Vies des saints des diocèses de Cambrai et d'Arras*, vol. i, pp. 37 seq. ; and P. Bertin, *Ste Bertille de Marœuil* (1943).   W. Levison has produced a critical edition of the text of the life, with a valuable introduction, in MGH., *Scriptores Merov.*, vol. vi, pp. 95–109.

4 : ST GREGORY, Bishop of Langres   (A.D. 539)

THIS saint is well known to us from the writings of St Gregory of Tours, who was his great-grandson.   Of very distinguished birth, he for forty years governed the district of Autun as count (*comes*), administering justice equitably but sternly.   It was only late in life, after the death of his wife Armentaria, that he turned from the world and gave himself unreservedly to God.   The clergy and people then elected him bishop of Langres, and for the rest of his days he showed an admirable example of devotion to his pastoral duties.   His abstemiousness in food and drink, which he was ingenious in concealing from the knowledge of others, was remarkable, and he often gave the hours of the night to prayer, frequenting especially the baptistery of Dijon, in which town he commonly lived. There the saints came to visit him and join him in chanting the praises of God ; in particular St Benignus, the apostle of Burgundy, whose *cultus* he had at first neglected, after some words of fatherly rebuke directed him to restore his dilapidated shrine, which has ever since been so famous in Dijon.   It was here that Gregory himself, who died at Langres in 539, was brought to be buried in accordance with his own desire.   His epitaph, composed by Venantius Fortunatus, suggests that any severity he had displayed as a secular ruler was expiated by the tender charity he showed to all in his last years.   Even in the miracles recorded after death he seemed to give the preference to captives who had been arrested by the officers of human justice.

See Gregory of Tours, *Vitae patrum*, bk vii ; *Historia Francorum*, bks iii, iv and v ; and *De gloria martyrum*, li.   L. Duchesne, *Fastes Épiscopaux*, vol. ii, pp. 185–186 ; DCB., vol. ii, p. 770.

ST PHARAÏLDIS, Virgin   (*c.* A.D. 740)

THERE is a great deal which is extremely confused and improbable in the accounts preserved to us of this Belgian saint, and it is difficult to know how much of her legend can be regarded as based on historical fact.   The main feature of her story is that, though she had secretly consecrated her virginity to God, she was given in marriage by her parents to a wealthy suitor, without any adequate consent on her part.   Resolutely determined to keep her vow, she refused to live with him *maritalement*, and he on his part treated her brutally.   God protected her, until at last the husband died.   Little else is recorded of her except miracles and the numerous translations of her remains.   There cannot, however, be any doubt that she became a very popular saint in Flanders, and that her *cultus* supplies abundant matter of interest to the student of folklore.   Among her own countryfolk she is called most commonly St Varelde, Verylde or Veerle.   She is represented sometimes with a goose, sometimes with loaves of bread, and more rarely with a cat. The goose may have reference to a story told of her, as also of St Werburga, that when a goose had been plucked and cooked the saint restored it to life and full plumage.   But it may also be connected with the city of Ghent or Gand, where her relics repose, for in Flemish, as in German, *gans* (*cf.* English " gander ") means a goose.   The bread without doubt must have been suggested by a miracle said to have been worked beside her tomb, when an uncharitable woman who had been asked to give a loaf to a beggar declared that she had none, and then discovered that the loaves she had been hiding were turned into stones.   St Pharaïldis is also supposed to have caused a fountain of water to spring out of the ground at Bruay, near Valenciennes, to relieve the thirst of the harvesters who were reaping for her. The water of this spring is believed to be of efficacy in children's disorders, and she is constantly invoked by mothers who are anxious about the health of their little ones.

See Hautecœur, *Actes de Ste Pharaïldis* (1882) ; Destombes, *Vies des saints de Cambrai et Arras*, vol. i, pp. 30–36 ; L. van der Essen, *Étude critique sur les Vitae des saints mérovingiens* (1907), pp. 303 *seq.* ; H. Detzel, *Christliche Ikonographie* (1896), vol. ii, p. 583.

ST RIGOBERT, Archbishop of Rheims　　(*c.* A.D. 745)

RIGOBERT seems to have been first of all abbot of Orbais, and afterwards to have been elected to the see of Rheims, but it is not easy to adjust the chronology, and his life, written much later, at the close of the ninth century, cannot be depended upon.　St Rigobert, it would appear, offended Charles Martel because he would not takes sides against Raganfred, the mayor of Neustria.　Charles accordingly banished Rigobert to Gascony and gave his bishopric to Milon, who already held the temporalities of the see of Trier.　In the end some compromise was effected, and the saint was allowed again to officiate in Rheims.　His patient acceptance of all trials, his love of retirement and prayer, and the miraculous cures attributed to him, gained him the repute of high sanctity.　He must have died between 740 and 750.

See *Acta Sanctorum*, January 4 ; Levison in MGH., *Scriptores Merov.*, vol. vii, pp. 54–80 ; and Duchesne, *Fastes Épiscopaux*, vol. iii, pp. 85-86.　There is a very important general paper on Charles Martel and his bishops : " Milo et eiusmodi similes ", by Eugen Ewig, in *St Bonifatius. Gedenkgabe zum zwölfhundertjährigen Todestag* (Fulda, 1954), pp. 412–440.

BD ROGER OF ELLANT　　(A.D. 1160)

BD ROGER OF ELLANT takes his name from the monastery of Ellant in the diocese of Rheims, founded by him in the twelfth century.　By birth an Englishman, he had crossed over to France and entered the Cistercian monastery of Lorroy in Berry.　Noted for his poverty and his exactness in carrying out the rule, he was chosen to found and build a new monastery at Ellant.　The sick and the suffering were the object of his particular care.　A chapel was dedicated in his honour in the abbey church where his body was buried.　He died January 4, 1160.

See *Acta Sanctorum*, January 4 ; and *Gallia Christiana*, vol. ix, p. 310.

BD ORINGA, Virgin　　(A.D. 1310)

ALTHOUGH there is no reason to doubt her historical existence, the story of Bd Oringa's life, told by biographers of late date, is little more than legend.　She seems to have been born and also to have spent her last years at Castello di Santa Croce in the valley of the Arno.　It is also probably true that she gathered round her a band of devout women and lived with them under the Rule of St Augustine. But the rest is a patchwork of vague traditions worked up with fictitious embellishments.　As a child, when she tended the cattle, we are told that she went aside to pray, bidding the dumb beasts not to touch the crops, and that they always obeyed her.　Her brothers beat her because she refused to marry, but she took refuge in the river, or crossed it, without ever getting wet.　At length Oringa ran away from home.　Night came upon her before she could reach Lucca, her destination, but a hare came to her, played with her, and finally went to sleep in her arms.　In the morning it ran before her and guided her safely to the town for which she was bound.　After many pilgrimages and adventures, during which she was always protected from harm, leading a life of extreme poverty and continual prayer, she returned to her native place and founded a convent there.

See *Acta Sanctorum*, under January 10 (The Augustinians keep her feast on January 4) ; and a popular sketch by M. Baciocchi de Peon, *La vergine Oringa* (1926).

5 : ST TELESPHORUS, Pope and Martyr   (*c.* A.D. 136)

S T TELESPHORUS, who figures in the list of popes as the seventh bishop of Rome, is said to have been a Greek by birth.   Towards the year 126 he succeeded St Sixtus I, and saw the havoc which the persecution of Hadrian made in the Church.   " He ended his life by a glorious martyrdom ", says Eusebius, and he is the first one of the successors of St Peter whom St Irenaeus and other early writers refer to as a martyr.   The ordinances attributed to him in the *Liber Pontificalis, e.g.* that the Mass of Christmas—a feast that did not then exist   should be celebrated at midnight, cannot with any probability be ascribed to his pontificate.   St Telesphorus is commemorated to-day in the Mass and Office of the vigil of the Epiphany.

See the *Acta Sanctorum*, January 5 ; and the *Liber Pontificalis* (ed. Duchesne), vol. i, p. 129.   In the calendar of the Carmelites this pope is claimed as a member of their order, but it is difficult to understand what historical basis can be pleaded for such a claim.

ST APOLLINARIS, Virgin   (No Date)

ALTHOUGH the Roman Martyrology on January 5 has an entry, " In Egypt, St Apollinaris, Virgin ", the pretended biography which is found in the Metaphrast and the Greek *menaia*, under the name of Apollinaris Syncletica, belongs to the category of religious romances.   It turns on the familiar theme of a girl putting on male attire and living for many years undiscovered.   In this case Apollinaris, who is the daughter of the " Emperor " Anthemius, runs away from home, disguises herself as a man, calls herself Dorotheus, and leads a hermitical life in the desert under the direction of the renowned ascetic, Macarius.   Meanwhile her sister at home is possessed by the devil, and being brought to the desert to be exorcised, is eventually consigned to the care of " Dorotheus ".   The sister is restored to her right mind, but owing to the machinations of the Evil One, " Dorotheus " is suspected of improper conduct.   She is brought before her own father to answer the charge and then reveals herself to him.   However, after obtaining her sister's complete cure by her prayers, she insists on returning to the desert, where her sex is only discovered by her fellow hermits after her death.   The entry has probably been attracted to this day by the identity of the name Syncletica with that of the saint who is commemorated on the previous day in the Greek synaxaries and today in the Roman Martyrology (see below).

See *Acta Sanctorum*, January 5 ; and *cf.* herein St Pelagia, under October 8.

ST SYNCLETICA Virgin   (*c.* A.D. 400)

SHE was born at Alexandria in Egypt, of wealthy Macedonian parents.   Her great fortune and beauty induced many young men to become her suitors, but she had already bestowed her heart on her heavenly Spouse.   Flight was her refuge against exterior assaults, and, regarding herself as her own most dangerous enemy, she began early to subdue her flesh by fasts and other mortifications.   She never seemed to suffer more than when obliged to eat oftener than she desired.   Her parents at their death left her sole heiress to their estate, for her two brothers had died before them and her sister, being blind, was committed entirely to her guardianship.   Syncletica, having distributed her fortune among the poor, retired with her sister to a disused sepulchral chamber on the estate of a relative, where, having sent for a priest, she cut off her hair in his presence as a sign whereby she renounced the world and renewed the consecration of herself to God.   Prayer and good works were from that time her principal employment ; but her strict retirement, by concealing her from the eyes of the world, has deprived us in a great measure of the knowledge of them.

Many women resorted to her to ask counsel, and her humility made her unwilling to take upon herself the task of instructing ; but charity gave her courage to speak.   Her discourses were inspired with so much zeal and accompanied by such an unfeigned humility that no words can express the deep impression they made on her hearers.   " Oh ", exclaimed Syncletica, " how happy should we be, did we but take as much pains to gain Heaven and please God as worldlings do to heap up riches and perishable goods !   By land they venture among thieves and robbers ; at sea they expose themselves to winds and waves ; they suffer shipwrecks and perils ; they attempt all, dare all, hazard all : but we, in serving so great a Master, for so immense a good, are afraid of every contradiction."   She frequently inculcated the virtue of humility   " A treasure is secure so long as it remains concealed ; but when once disclosed, and laid open to every bold invader, it is presently rifled ; so virtue is safe as long as it is secret, but if rashly exposed, it but too often evaporates in smoke."   By these and the like discourses did this devout woman excite others to charity, vigilance and every other virtue.

In the eightieth year of her age St Syncletica was seized with an inward burning fever ; at the same time her lungs were attacked, and a gangrenous affection ate away her jaws and mouth.   She bore all with incredible patience and resignation, and during the last three months of her life she found no repose.   Though the cancer had robbed her of speech, her patience served to preach to others more movingly than words could have done.   Three days before her death she foresaw that on the third day she would be released from the prison of her body ; and when the hour came, surrounded by a heavenly light and ravished by consoling visions, she surrendered her soul into the hands of her Creator, in the eighty-fourth year of her age.

The ancient beautiful life of St Syncletica is quoted in the Lives of the Fathers published by Rosweyde, bk i, and in the writings of St John Climacus.   It appears from the work itself that the author was personally acquainted with the saint.   It has been ascribed to St Athanasius, but without sufficient grounds.   See *Acta Sanctorum* for January 5.

ST SIMEON THE STYLITE   (A.D. 459)

St SIMEON was, in his life and conduct, a subject of astonishment not only to the whole Roman empire, but also to many barbarous and infidel peoples who had the highest veneration for him.   The Roman emperors solicited his prayers, and consulted him on matters of importance.   It must, nevertheless, be acknowledged that his most remarkable actions are a subject of admiration, not of imitation. They may serve, notwithstanding, for our spiritual edification, as we cannot well reflect on his fervour without being confounded at our own indolence in the service of God.

St Simeon was the son of a shepherd in Cilicia, on the borders of Syria, and at first kept his father's sheep.   Being only thirteen years of age, about the year 402, he was much moved by hearing the beatitudes one day read in church, particularly the words, " Blessed are they that mourn ; blessed are the clean of heart ".   The youth addressed himself to a certain old man to learn their meaning, and begged to know how the happiness they promised was to be obtained. He was told that continual prayer, watching, fasting, weeping, humiliation and the patient suffering of persecution were pointed out by these texts as the road to true happiness ; and that a solitary life afforded the best opportunity for the practice of virtue. Simeon upon this withdrew to a little distance where, falling upon the ground, he besought Him who desires all to be saved to conduct him in the paths which lead to happiness and perfection. At length, falling asleep, he had a vision, which he often related afterwards. He seemed to himself to be digging for the foundation of a house, and that as often as he stopped to take a little breath, which was four times, he was commanded each time to dig deeper, till at length he was told he might desist, the pit being deep enough to receive the intended foundation, on which he would be able to raise a superstructure of what kind and to what height he pleased. " The event ", says Theodoret, " verified the prediction ; the actions of this wonderful man were so much above nature, that they might well require deep foundations to build such a structure securely."

Rising from the ground, he went to a monastery near at hand ruled by an abbot called Timothy. There he remained at the gate for several days, without either eating or drinking, begging to be admitted on the footing of the lowest servant in the house. His petition was granted, and he complied with the terms of it for four months. During this time he learned the psalter by heart, and his familiarity with the sacred words greatly helped to nourish his soul. Though still no more than a boy, he practised all the austerities of the house, and by his humility and charity gained the good-will of all the monks. Having here spent two years, he removed to the monastery of Heliodorus, who had spent sixty-two years in that community so abstracted from the world as to be utterly ignorant of it, as Theodoret relates, who knew him well. Here Simeon much increased his mortifications. Judging the tough rope of the well, made of twisted palm leaves, a proper instrument of penance, he tied it close about his naked body, where it remained, unknown both to the community and his superior, till it ate into his flesh. Three days successively his clothes, which clung to it, had to be softened with liquids to disengage them ; and the incisions made to cut the cord out of his body were attended with such pain that he lay for some time as dead. On his recovery the abbot, as a warning to the rest to avoid such dangerous singularities, dismissed him.

After this he repaired to a hermitage at the foot of Mount Telanissae, where he resolved to pass the whole forty days of Lent in total abstinence, after the example of Christ, without either eating or drinking. Bassus, a priest to whom he communicated his design, gave him ten loaves and some water, that he might eat if he found it necessary. At the expiration of the forty days Bassus came to visit him, and found the loaves and water untouched, but Simeon lay stretched on the ground almost without any signs of life. Taking a sponge, he moistened his lips with water, then gave him the blessed Eucharist. Simeon having recovered a little, rose up, and by degrees found himself able to swallow a few lettuce-leaves. This was his method of keeping Lent during the remainder of his life ; and he had passed twenty-six Lents after this manner when Theodoret wrote his account of him ; in which he adds other particulars—that Simeon spent the first part of Lent in praising God standing ; growing weaker, he continued his prayer sitting ; while towards the end, being unable to support himself in any other posture, he lay on the ground. However, it is probable that in his advanced years he admitted some mitigation of this incredible austerity. When on his pillar, he kept himself during this fast tied to a pole; but in the end was able to fast the whole term without any support.   Some attribute this to the strength of his constitution, which was naturally very robust, and had been gradually habituated to an extreme privation of food.   It is well known that the hot climate affords surprising instances of long abstinence among the Indians.   A native of France has, within our memory, fasted the forty days of Lent almost in the same manner.*   But few examples occur of persons abstaining entirely from food for many days unless prepared and inured by habit.

After three years spent in this hermitage the saint removed to the top of the same mountain, where he made an inclosure, but without any roof or shelter to protect him from the weather; and to confirm his resolution of pursuing this manner of life, he fastened his right leg to a rock with a chain.   Meletius, vicar to the patriarch of Antioch, told him that a firm will, supported by God's good grace, would enable him to abide in his solitary inclosure without having recourse to any bodily restraint; whereupon the obedient servant of God sent for a smith and had his chains knocked off.   But visitors began to throng to the mountain, and the solitude his soul sighed after came to be interrupted by the multitudes that flocked to receive his benediction, by which many sick recovered their health.   Some were not satisfied unless they also touched him.

So Simeon, to remove these causes of distraction, projected for himself a new and unprecedented manner of life.   In 423 he erected a pillar six cubits† high, and on it he dwelt four years; on a second, twelve cubits high, he lived three years; on a third, twenty-two cubits high, ten years; and on a fourth, forty cubits high, built for him by the people, he spent the last twenty years of his life.   Thus he lived thirty-seven years on pillars, and was called Stylites, from the Greek word *stylos*, which signifies a pillar.   This singularity was at first censured by all as a piece of extravagance.   To make trial of his humility an order was sent him in the name of the neighbouring bishops and abbots to quit his pillar and give up his new manner of life.   The saint at once made ready to come down; but the messenger said that, as he had shown a willingness to obey, it was their desire that he should follow his vocation in God.

His pillar did not exceed six feet in diameter at the top, which made it difficult for him to lie extended on it; neither would he allow a seat.   He only stooped, or leaned, to take a little rest, and often in the day bowed his body in prayer.   A visitor once reckoned 1,244 such profound reverences made by him at one time.   He made exhortations to the people twice a day.   His garments were the skins of beasts, and he never suffered any woman to come within the inclosure where his pillar stood.   His disciple Antony mentions that he prayed most fervently for the soul of his mother after her decease.

God is sometimes pleased to conduct certain souls through extraordinary paths, in which others would find only danger of illusion and self-will.   We should, notwithstanding, consider that the holiness of these persons does not consist in such wonderful actions or in their miracles, but in the perfection of their charity,

---

* Dom Claude Léauté, a Benedictine monk of the congregation of Saint-Maur.   This fact is attested by his brethren and superiors in a relation printed at Sens in 1731; and recorded by Dom L'Isle in his *History of Fasting*.   (Some other remarkable examples may be found cited by Father Thurston in two articles in *The Month*, February and March, 1921, on "The Mystic as a Hunger Striker".)

† A cubit was a measure of from 18 to 22 inches.

patience and humility ; and it was these solid virtues which shone so conspicuously in the life of St Simeon.   He exhorted people vehemently against the horrible custom of swearing ; as also to observe strict justice, to take no usury, to be earnest in their piety, and to pray for the salvation of souls.   The great deference paid to his instructions, even by barbarians, cannot be described.   Many Persians, Armenians and Iberians were converted by his miracles or by his discourses, which they crowded to hear.   The Emperors Theodosius and Leo I often consulted him and desired his prayers.   The Emperor Marcian visited him in disguise.   By an invincible patience he bore all afflictions and rebukes without a word of complaint ; he sincerely looked upon himself as the outcast of the world ; and he spoke to all with the most engaging sweetness and charity.   Domnus, Patriarch of Antioch, and others brought him holy communion on his pillar.   In 459, on a Wednesday, September 2 (or as some say, on the previous July 24, a Friday), this incomparable penitent, bowing on his pillar as if intent on prayer, gave up the ghost, in the sixty-ninth year of his age.   Two days later his body was conveyed to Antioch, attended by the bishops and the whole country.   Many miracles, related by Evagrius, Antony and Cosmas, were wrought on this occasion.

Incredible as some of the feats of endurance may seem which are attributed to St Simeon the Elder and to the other Stylites, or " Pillar-Saints ", his imitators, there can be no doubt that the facts are vouched for by the best historical evidence.   The church historian Theodoret, for example, who is one of our principal authorities, knew Simeon well, possessed his confidence, and wrote his account while the saint was still living.   The whole question of this extraordinary phase of asceticism is discussed with great thoroughness by Hippolyte Delehaye, in his monograph *Les Saints Stylites* (1923).   This supersedes all previous works on the subject.   A popular summary by Fr Thurston of the outstanding features of this mode of life, based upon Delehaye's researches, may be found in the Irish quarterly *Studies*, December, 1923, pp. 584–596.   Besides the account of Theodoret, we have two other primary authorities for the life of St Simeon   one the Greek biography by his disciple and contemporary Antony, the other the Syriac, which also must certainly have been written within fifty years of the saint's death.   Both these texts have been critically edited by Lietzmann in his *Das Leben des heiligen Symeon Stylites* (1908) ; see also P. Peeters on Simeon's earliest biographers, in *Analecta Bollandiana*, vol. lxi (1943), pp. 71 *seq*.   Between the Syriac and the Greek accounts there are a good many points of divergence in matters of detail which cannot be gone into here.   In the Roman Martyrology St Simeon is commemorated on January 5, and the Bollandists and Butler have followed this example.   On a tree-dweller (*dendrite*) see A. Vasiliev, " Life of David of Thessalonika ", in *Traditio*, vol. iv (1946), pp. 115–147.

ST CONVOYON, ABBOT   (A.D. 868)

IN 1866 Pope Pius IX approved the *cultus* which from time immemorial had been paid in the neighbourhood of Redon in Brittany to the Benedictine monk who was the founder and abbot of the monastery of Saint Saviour.   He was himself a Breton by birth, and it was in 831 that he, with six companions, obtained a grant of land on which to build an abbey.   In the disturbed political conditions of the time, the early years of the new foundation seem to have been full of privation and hardship.   Owing in part to a charge of simony brought against certain bishops of the province, Convoyon in 848 found himself a member of a deputation sent to Rome to appeal to Pope Leo IV.   He is said to have brought back with him to his monastery a chasuble which Leo gave him, and also the relics of Pope St Marcellinus.   Later Convoyon was driven from his monastery by the incursions of the Norsemen, and was absent from it at the time of his death in 868.   In 1866 the abbey of Saint Saviour at Redon had passed into the hands of a community of the Eudist fathers, who were very active in procuring the confirmation of *cultus* for this local saint.

> Mabillon (vol. iv, 2, pp. 188 *seq.*) prints two lives of St Convoyon, one of which purports to be written by a contemporary. An interesting summary of the case presented to obtain confirmation of the cult may be found in the *Analecta Juris Pontificii* (1866), vol. viii, pp. 2177 *seq.* See also Lobineau, *Saints de la Bretagne*, vol. ii, pp. 261 *seq.*

ST DOROTHEUS THE YOUNGER, Abbot   (Eleventh Century)

TREBIZOND, on the Black Sea, was the birthplace of St Dorotheus the Younger, who is also known as St Dorotheus of Khiliokomos. He came of a patrician family, but ran away from home at the age of twelve to escape from a marriage which his parents were forcing upon him. After wandering for some time he reached the monastery of Genna at Amisos (the present Samsun), in Pontus, where he received the habit from the Abbot John. He became a pattern of monastic virtue and was raised to the priesthood. Besides being endowed with the gift of prophecy he was frequently rapt in ecstasy. One day when he was on an errand outside the monastery, a mysterious stranger told him to found a community on a mountain near Amisos, at a spot which he indicated, and to dedicate it to the Holy Trinity. Dorotheus was loth to leave his brethren, besides being uncertain as to the nature of the call, but his abbot bade him obey. The saint accordingly began to build, having at first only one companion to assist him. Other disciples soon gathered round him and he became the abbot of a great monastery to which he gave the name of Khiliokomos. Among many miracles with which he is credited he is said to have multiplied corn, to have saved from shipwreck a vessel far away out at sea and on another occasion by invoking the Holy Trinity to have caused a huge stone which crashed down during the building operations to rise unassisted and resume its proper place.

> The text of the Greek life writen by his disciple John Mauropus is printed in the *Acta Sanctorum*, June, vol. i.

ST GERLAC   (*c.* A.D. 1170)

IN the neighbourhood of Valkenburg (Holland) there is still a holy well called after St Gerlac. According to an almost contemporary biography, the hermit used this water while for seven years he lived his solitary life in the hollow of a tree. In early manhood he was devoted to feats of arms, and gave himself up to all the vices of the camp, but the news of the sudden death of his wife opened his eyes to the danger of his position. He said good-bye to the world and set out for Rome. There he did seven years' penance, tending the sick in the hospitals and practising great austerities. Afterwards he obtained the pope's sanction to become a hermit without entering a religious order. For the place of his solitary life he chose a hollow tree, situated on his own estate, although, on his coming back to his native city, he had given his possessions to the poor. The nearest church was at a considerable distance, yet for seven years he made his way thither over difficult ground at all seasons of the year, to be present at the divine offices. The monks considered his vocation an anomaly, and tried to force the bishop to make him enter their monastery. The quarrel was embittered by calumny, and the feeling against Gerlac became so incredibly violent that the monks refused him the sacraments as he lay dying. According to his biographer, Gerlac received the last rites from a venerable old man who entered his cell, gave him viaticum, anointed him, and then was never seen again.

Acta Sanctorum, January 5 ; F. Wesselmann, *Der hl. Gerlach von Houthem* (1897). Although Gerlac was never canonized, fragments are extant of a liturgical office which was recited in his honour.

6 : THE EPIPHANY OF OUR LORD JESUS CHRIST

EPIPHANY, which in Greek signifies appearance or manifestation, is a festival principally solemnized in honour of the revelation Jesus Christ made of Himself to the Magi, or wise men ; who, soon after His birth, by a particular inspiration of Almighty God, came to worship Him and bring Him presents. Two other manifestations of our Lord are jointly commemorated on this day in the office of the Church that at His baptism, when the Holy Ghost descended on Him in the visible form of a dove, and a voice from Heaven was heard at the same time " This is my beloved Son, in whom I am well pleased ; " and that of His divine power at the doing of His first miracle, the changing of water into wine at the marriage of Cana, by which He manifested His glory, and His disciples believed in Him. Upon all these accounts this festival lays claim to a more than ordinary regard and veneration ; but from none more than us Gentiles, who in the person of the wise men, our first-fruits and forerunners, were on this day called to the faith and worship of the true God.

The summons of the Gentiles to Bethlehem to pay homage to the world's Redeemer was obeyed by several whom the Bible mentions under the name and title of *Magi*, or wise men ; but is silent as to their number. The general opinion, supported by the authority of St Leo, Caesarius, Bede and others, declares for three. However, the number was small in comparison with those many others who saw that star no less than the wise men, but paid no regard to it ; admiring, no doubt, its unusual brightness, but indifferent to its divine message, or hardening their hearts against any salutary impression, enslaved by their passions and self-love. Steadfast in the resolution of following the divine call and fearless of danger, the Magi inquire in Jerusalem with confidence and pursue their inquiry in the very court of Herod himself ; " Where is He that is born King of the Jews ? " The whole nation of the Jews on account of Jacob's and Daniel's prophecies was in expectation of the Messiah's appearance among them, and the circumstances having been also foretold, the wise men, by the interposition of Herod's authority, quickly learned from the Sanhedrin, or great council of the Jews, that Bethlehem was the place which was to be honoured with His birth, as had been pointed out by the prophet Micheas many centuries before.

The wise men readily comply with the voice of the Sanhedrin, notwithstanding the little encouragement these Jewish leaders afford them by their own example to persist in their search for not one single priest or scribe is disposed to bear them company in seeking after and paying homage to their own king. No sooner had they left Jerusalem but, to encourage their faith, God was pleased again to show them the star which they had seen in the East, and it continued to go before them till it conducted them to the very place where they were to see and worship their

Saviour.   The star, by ceasing to advance, tells them in its mute language, " Here shall you find the new-born King."   The holy men entered the poor place, rendered more glorious by this birth than the most stately palace in the universe ; and finding the Child with His mother, they prostrate themselves, they worship Him, they pour forth their souls in His presence.   St Leo thus extols their faith and devotion : " When a star had conducted them to worship Jesus, they did not find Him commanding devils or raising the dead or restoring sight to the blind or speech to the dumb, or employed in any divine action ; but a silent babe, dependent upon a mother's care, giving no sign of power but exhibiting a miracle of humility." The Magi offer to Jesus as a token of homage the richest produce their countries afforded—gold, frankincense and myrrh.   Gold, as an acknowledgement of His regal power ; incense, as a confession of His Godhead ; and myrrh, as a testimony that He was become man for the redemption of the world.   But their far more acceptable presents were the dispositions they cherished in their souls : their fervent charity, signified by gold ; their devotion, figured by frankincense ; and the unreserved sacrifice of themselves, represented by myrrh.

The earliest mention of a Christian festival celebrated on January 6 seems to occur in the *Stromata* (i, 21) of Clement of Alexandria, who died before 216.   He states that the gnostic sect of the Basilidians kept the commemoration of our Saviour's baptism with great solemnity on dates held to correspond with the 10th and 6th of January respectively.   The notice might seem of little importance were it not for the fact that in the course of the next two centuries there is abundant evidence that January 6 had come to be observed throughout the East as a festival of high importance, and was always closely associated with the baptism of our Lord.   In a document known as the " Canons of Athanasius ", whose text may in substance belong to the time of St Athanasius, say A.D. 370, the writer recognizes only three great feasts in the year—Easter, Pentecost and the Epiphany.   He directs that a bishop ought to gather the poor together on solemn occasions, notably upon " the great festival of the Lord " (Easter) ; Pentecost, " when the Holy Ghost came down upon the Church " ; and " the feast of the Lord's Epiphany, which was in the month Tubi, that is the feast of Baptism " (canon 16) ; and he specifies again in canon 66, " the feast of the Pasch, and the feast of the Pentecost and the feast of the Epiphany, which is the 11th day of the month Tubi."

According to oriental ideas it was through the divine pronouncement " this is my beloved Son in whom I am well pleased " that the Saviour was first manifested to the great world of unbelievers.   In the opinion of the Greek fathers, the Epiphany (ἐπιφάνεια, showing forth), which is also called θεοφάνεια (manifestation of the deity) and τὰ φῶτα (illumination), was identified primarily with the scene beside the Jordan.   St John Chrysostom, preaching at Antioch in 386, asks, " How does it happen that not the day on which our Lord was born, but that on which He was baptized, is called the Epiphany ? "   And then, after dwelling upon certain details of liturgical observance, particularly the blessing of water which the faithful took home with them and preserved for a twelvemonth—he seems to suggest that the fact of the water remaining sweet must be due to some miracle— the saint comes back to his own question : " We give ", he says, " the name Epiphany to the day of our Lord's baptism because He was not made manifest to all when he was born, but only when he was baptized ; for until that time He was unknown to the people at large."   Similarly St Jerome, living near Jerusalem, testifies that in his time only one feast was kept there, that of January 6, to commemorate both the birth and the baptism of Jesus ; nevertheless he declares that the idea of " showing forth " belonged not to His birth in the flesh, " for then He was hidden and not revealed ", but rather to the baptism in the Jordan, " when the heavens were opened upon Christ ".

With the exception, however, of Jerusalem, where the pilgrim lady, Etheria (c. 395), bears witness, like St Jerome, to the celebration of the birth of our Lord together with the Epiphany on one and the same day (January 6), the Western custom of honouring our Saviour's birth separately on December 25 came into vogue in the course of the fourth century, and spread rapidly from Rome over all the Christian East.* We learn from St Chrysostom that at Antioch December 25 was observed for the first time as a feast somewhere about 376.   Two or three years later the festival was adopted at Constantinople, and, as appears from the funeral discourse pronounced by St Gregory of Nyssa over his brother St Basil, Cappadocia followed suit at about the same period.   On the other hand, the celebration of January 6, which undoubtedly had its origin in the East, and which from a reference in the *passio* of St Philip of Heraclea may perhaps already be recognized in Thrace at the beginning of the fourth century, seems by a sort of exchange to have been adopted in most Western lands before the death of St Augustine.   It meets us first at Vienne in Gaul, where the pagan historian Ammianus Marcellinus, describing the Emperor Julian's visit to one of the churches, refers to " the feast-day in January which Christians call the Epiphany ".   St Augustine in his time makes it a matter of reproach against the Donatists that they had not adopted this newer feast of the Epiphany as the Catholics had done.   We find the Epiphany in honour at Saragossa c. 380, and in 400 it is one of the days on which the circus games were prohibited.

Still, although the day fixed for the celebration was the same, the character of the Epiphany feast in East and West was different.   In the East the baptism of our Lord, even down to the present time, is the *motif* almost exclusively emphasized, and the μέγας ἁγιασμός, or great blessing of the waters, on the morning of the Epiphany still continues to be one of the most striking features of the oriental ritual.   In the West, on the other hand, ever since the time of St Augustine and St Leo the Great, many of whose sermons for this day are still preserved to us, the principal stress has been laid upon the journey and the gift-offerings of the Magi. The baptism of our Lord and the miracle of Cana in Galilee have also, no doubt from an early period, been included in the conception of the feast, but although we find clear references to these introduced by St Paulinus of Nola at the beginning of the fifth century, and by St Maximus of Turin a little later, into their interpretation of the solemnities of this day, no great prominence has ever been given in the Western church to any other feature but the revelation of our Lord to the Gentiles as represented by the coming of the Magi.

See H. Leclercq in DAC., vol. v, pp. 197–201 ; Vacandard, *Études de critique et d'histoire religieuse*, vol. iii, pp. 1–56 ; Hugo Kehrer, *Die heiligen Drei Könige* (1908), vol. i, pp. 46–52 and 22–31 ; Duchesne, *Christian Worship*, pp. 257–265 ; Usener-Lietzmann, *Religionsgeschichtliche Untersuchungen*, Part I ; Kellner, *Heortology*, pp. 166–173 ; G. Morin in *Revue Bénédictine*, vol. v (1888), pp. 257–264 ; F. C. Conybeare in *Rituale Armenorum*, pp.

* But to this day the non-Catholic Armenians celebrate Christmas with the Epiphany on January 6.   And it is to be remarked that even in the Western church the liturgical rank of the Epiphany feast, with Easter and Pentecost, is above that of Christmas.

165–190 ; and especially Dom de Puniet in *Rassegna Gregoriana*, vol. v (1906), pp. 497–514. See also Riedel and Crum, *The Canons of Athanasius*, pp. 27, 131 ; *Anecdota Maredsolana*, t. iii, pp. 396–397 ; *Rassegna Gregoriana*, vol. x (1911), pp. 51–58 ; and Migne, PG., vol. xlix, p. 366 (Chrysostom), and PL., vol. xxv, cc. 18–19 (Jerome), vol. xxxviii, c. 1033 (Augustine).

ST WILTRUDIS, Widow   (*c*. A.D. 986)

RADERUS in his *Bavaria Sancta* describes Wiltrudis as a maiden who obtained the consent of her brother, Count Ortulf, to refuse the proposals of marriage which had been made for her.   The truth, however, appears to be that she was the wife of Berthold, Duke of Bavaria, who, after her husband's death, about the year 947, became a nun.   Even in the world she had been renowned for her piety and for her skill in handicrafts.   After she gave herself to God her fervour redoubled and she eventually founded, about 976, an abbey of Benedictine nuns which became famous as that of Bergen, or Baring, bei Neuburg.   She became the first abbess, and died about 986.

See Rietzler, *Geschichte Bayerns*, vol. i, pp. 338 and 381 ; and Raderus, *Bavaria Sancta*, vol. iii, p. 137.

ST ERMINOLD, Abbot   (A.D. 1121)

THE medieval Life of St Erminold represents a rather unsatisfactory type of spiritual biography.   The writer seems to have been intent only on glorifying his hero, and we cannot be quite satisfied as to his facts.   Erminold, brought to the monastery of Hirschau as a child, spent all his life in the cloister.   Being conspicuous for his strict observance of rule, he was chosen abbot of Lorsch, but a dispute about his election caused him to resign within a year.   In 1114, at the instance of St Otto of Bamberg, he was sent to the newly founded monastery of Prüfening, and there he exercised authority, first as prior, and from 1117 onwards as abbot.   He is described in local calendars and martyrologies as a martyr, but his death, which took place on January 6, 1121, resulted from the conspiracy of an unruly faction of his own subjects who resented the strictness of his government.   One of them struck him on the head with a heavy piece of timber, and Erminold, lingering for a few days, died on the Epiphany at the hour he had foretold.   He was famed both for his spirit of prayer and for his charity to the poor.   A large number of miracles are recorded at his tomb after death.

See *Acta Sanctorum*, January 6 ; and also the MGH., *Scriptores*, vol. xii, pp. 481–500.

ST GUARINUS, or GUÉRIN, Bishop of Sion   (A.D. 1150)

No formal biography of St Guarinus seems to have been left us by any of his contemporaries, but a considerable local cult has been paid to him ever since his death.   He was originally a monk of Molesmes, but having been appointed abbot of St John of Aulps (*de Alpibus*), in the diocese of Geneva, he some years later wrote to St Bernard, then at the height of his fame, to ask that he and his community might be affiliated to Clairvaux.   One of St Bernard's letters in reply is still preserved, and from this and another letter of his it is evident how highly he esteemed Guarinus.   This second letter was written to console the community of Aulps when their abbot was taken from them to be made bishop of Sion in the Valais.

See *Acta Sanctorum*, January 6 ; and J. F. Gonthier, *Vie de St Guérin* (1896).

BD GERTRUDE OF DELFT, VIRGIN   (A.D. 1358)

MUCH interest attaches to the life of this mystic, who was first a servant-maid and afterwards a *béguine* at Delft in Holland.   Béguines are not, strictly speaking, members of a religious order, though they dwell in a settlement apart, perform their religious exercises in common, and make profession of chastity and obedience. But they are not vowed to poverty, and they live in little separate houses, each with one or two companions, occupied for the most part in active good works.   In her early days Gertrude had been engaged to be married to a man who left her for another girl, causing great anguish of mind to the betrothed he had forsaken. Seeing the providence of God in this disappointment, she turned her thoughts to other things, and afterwards generously befriended the rival who had somewhat treacherously stolen her lover.

As the crown of a life now spent in contemplation and austerity, our Lord was pleased to honour her, on Good Friday 1340, with the marks of His sacred wounds. We read that this privileged state had already been foretold to her by a holy friend named Lielta, and also that she had experienced a very curious bodily manifestation in the Christmas season of the previous year.   When the stigmata were thus given her, apparently as a permanent mark of God's favour, they used to bleed seven times every day.   She confided to her fellow béguine Diewerdis the news of this strange wonder.   Naturally the tidings spread, and very soon crowds came, not only from Delft, but from all the country round to behold the marvel.   This destroyed all privacy and recollection, and so Gertrude implored our Lord to come to her aid.   The stigmata consequently ceased to bleed, but the marks persisted. For the eighteen years she remained on earth she led a very suffering life, but she seems, like other mystics who have been similarly favoured with these outward manifestations, to have possessed a strange knowledge of people's thoughts and of distant and future events, of which her biographer gives instances.   The name " van Oosten ", by which she is known in the place of a surname, is stated to have come to her from her fond repetition of an old Dutch hymn beginning, *Het daghet in den Oosten* (" The day is breaking in the east ").   There seems a curious appropriateness in the fact that she died (1358) on the feast of the Epiphany when the wise men came from the east to greet their infant Saviour.   " I am longing ", she said a few minutes before her death, " I am longing to go home."

See the life in the *Acta Sanctorum*, January 6.   A short Dutch text was published at Amsterdam in 1879 by Alberdingk Thijm in *Verspreide Verhalen in Prosa*, vol. i, pp. 54–60. The hymn, *Het daghet in den Oosten*, has been printed by Hoffmann von Fallersleben in his *Horae Belgicae*.

ST JOHN DE RIBERA, ARCHBISHOP OF VALENCIA   (A.D. 1611)

PETER DE RIBERA, the father of Don John, was one of the highest grandees in Spain ; he was created duke of Alcalá, but already held many other titles and important charges.   Among the rest, he for fourteen years governed Naples as viceroy.   But above all, he was a most upright and devout Christian.   His son, therefore, was admirably brought up, and during a distinguished university career at Salamanca and elsewhere, divine Providence seems perceptibly to have intervened to shield his virtue from danger. Realizing the perils to which he was exposed, he gave himself up to penance and prayer in preparation for holy orders. In 1557, at the age of twenty-five, Don John was ordained priest; and after teaching theology at Salamanca for a while, he was preconized bishop of Badajoz, much to his dismay, by St Pius V in 1562. His duties as bishop were discharged with scrupulous fidelity and zeal, and six years later, by the desire both of Philip II and the same holy pontiff, he was reluctantly constrained to accept the dignity of archbishop of Valencia. A few months later, filled with consternation at the languid faith and relaxed morals of this province, which was the great stronghold of the Moriscos, he wrote begging to be allowed to resign, but the pope would not consent; and for forty-two years, down to his death in 1611, St John struggled to support cheerfully a load of responsibility which almost crushed him. In his old age the burden was increased by the office of viceroy of the province of Valencia, which was imposed upon him by Philip III.

The archbishop viewed with intense alarm what he regarded as the dangerous activities of the Moriscos and Jews, whose financial prosperity was the envy of all. Owing to the universal ignorance of the principles of political economy which then prevailed, the Moriscos seemed to Ribera to be " the sponges which sucked up all the wealth of the Christians ". At the same time, it is only fair to note that this was the view of nearly all his Christian countrymen, and that it was shared even by so enlightened a contemporary as Cervantes. In any case, it is beyond dispute that St John de Ribera was one of the advisers who were mainly responsible for the edict of 1609 which enforced the deportation of the Moriscos from Valencia. We can only bear in mind that a decree of beatification pronounces only upon the personal virtues and miracles of the servant of God so honoured, and that it does not constitute an approbation of all his public acts or of his political views. The archbishop did not long survive the tragedy of the deportation. He died, after a long illness most patiently borne, at the College of Corpus Christi, which he himself had founded and endowed, on January 6, 1611. Many miracles were attributed to his intercession. He was beatified in 1796 and canonized in 1960.

See V. Castillo, *Vita del B. Giovanni de Ribera* (1796); M. Belda, *Vida del B. Juan de Ribera* (1802); and P. Boronat y Barrachina, *Los Moriscos españoles y su Expulsion* (1901).

BD RAPHAELA MARY, Virgin, Foundress of the Handmaids of the Sacred Heart   (A.D. 1925)

RAPHAELA PORRAS was born in the small Spanish town of Pedro Abad, some way from Cordova, in 1850. When she was four she lost her father, the mayor of the place, who died of cholera caught when looking after the sick during an epidemic; at nineteen her mother followed, and Raphaela was left with her elder sister, Dolores, in charge of the household, which included several brothers and sisters. In 1873 both announced that they wished to become nuns. Their retiring way of life had already provoked opposition from the family; but it was eventually arranged for them to be received as novices by the nuns of Marie Réparatrice who had been invited to Cordova at the suggestion of a priest named Joseph Antony Ortiz Urruela (he had at one time studied in England under Bishop Grant of Southwark). Difficulties, however, at once arose— partly because the nuns were " foreign ", partly because of the high-handed behaviour of Don Ortiz Urruela—and the bishop asked the nuns to leave. Sixteen novices, including the two Porras girls, were given permission to remain in Cordova, and carry on as best they could under the headship of Sister Raphaela Mary-of-the-Sacred-Heart.

Early in 1877, just before Sister Raphaela and five others were to take their vows, Bishop Ceferino Gonzalez informed them that he had drawn up an entirely new rule for the community. This put the novices in an awkward position. The new rule was quite different from that in which they had been trained; on the other hand, if they refused it they all would be sent back to their homes. The course they decided on was a surprising one—no less than flight. And they carried it out. Leaving Cordova by night, they went to Andujar, where Don Ortiz Urruela had arranged for them to be sheltered by the nuns at the hospital. Naturally, there was great excitement. The civil authorities took a hand, and the bishop declared Don Ortiz Urruela " suspended "; but that enterprising priest was already in Madrid, seeing what he could do for his *protégées* there, and the bishop could really do little, as the fugitives were not a canonically-erected community. Then Don Ortiz Urruela suddenly died; but the sisters were sent a new friend in Father Cotanilla, a Jesuit, and they were allowed by the ecclesiastical authorities to settle in Madrid. In the summer of 1877 the first two, Raphaela and her sister Dolores, made their profession.

That was the startling beginning of the congregation of the Handmaids of the Sacred Heart, whose work was to be the education of children and helping with retreats. It soon began to develop and spread, and houses were opened at Jerez, Saragossa, Bilbao and Cordova—this last with the full approval of Bishop Ceferino. To-day its sisters are found in a dozen other countries besides Spain, including England and the United States. But troubles did not end with the difficulty of its birth, nor even with the granting of approval by the Holy See in 1877, when Bd Raphaela was elected mother general. Unhappily her sister Dolores, now Mother Mary-del-Pilar, did not see eye-to-eye with Raphaela in matters of administration, and there were others who supported Mother Mary : in 1893 the foundress resigned from her office as mother general, and Mary-del-Pilar was elected in her place. For the remaining thirty-two years of her life Bd Raphaela filled no office whatever in her congregation, but lived in obscurity in the Roman house, doing the housework.

It cannot be doubted that it was in these years that she earned her halo of holiness. The woman that inaugurated a religious congregation in the circumstances that she did cannot have found such self-abnegation easy. Attention has several times been drawn in these pages to people who were popularly canonized because they accepted, not formal martyrdom, but simply an unjust death : Mother Raphaela is a *beata* who lived nearly half her life cheerfully carrying a weight of unjust treatment. Courage and sweetness shone out from her face in old age. The surgeon who operated on her in her last days said it all in a sentence : " Mother, you are a brave woman "; but she had said long before, " I see clearly that God wants me to submit to all that happens to me as if I saw Him there commanding it." Bd Raphaela Mary died on the Epiphany in 1925, and she was beatified in 1952.

In English there is a good summary in pamphlet form, *In Search of the Will of God* (1950), by Fr William Lawson.

7 : ST LUCIAN OF ANTIOCH, Martyr   (A.D. 312)

S**T LUCIAN** was born at Samosata, in Syria. He became a great proficient in rhetoric and philosophy, and applied himself to the study of the Holy Scriptures under one Macarius at Edessa. Convinced that his duty as a priest required him to devote himself entirely to the service of God and the good of his neighbour, he was not content to inculcate the practice of virtue by word and example, but he also undertook to purge the Old and New Testament from the faults that had crept into them through the inaccuracy of transcribers and in other ways. Whether he only revised the text of the Old Testament by comparing different editions of the Septuagint, or corrected it upon the Hebrew text, being well versed in that language, it is certain in any case that St Lucian's edition of the Bible was much esteemed, and was of great use to St Jerome.

St Alexander, Bishop of Alexandria, says that Lucian remained some years separated from Catholic communion at Antioch, under three successive bishops. He may perhaps have favoured overmuch the heretic Paul of Samosata, condemned at Antioch in the year 269, but it is certain, at least, that Lucian died in the communion of the Church. This appears from a fragment of a letter written by him to the church of Antioch, still extant in the Alexandrian Chronicle. Though a priest of Antioch, we find him at Nicomedia in the year 303, when Diocletian first published his edicts against the Christians. He there suffered a long imprisonment for the faith, for he wrote from out of his dungeon, " All the martyrs salute you. I inform you that the Pope Anthimus [Bishop of Nicomedia] has finished his course by martyrdom." This happened in 303. Yet Eusebius informs us that St Lucian did not arrive himself at the crown of martyrdom till after the death of St Peter of Alexandria in 311, so that he seems to have continued nine years in prison.

At length he was brought before the governor, or the emperor himself, for the word which Eusebius uses may imply either. At his trial he presented to the judge an excellent apology for the Christian faith. Being remanded to prison, an order was given that no food should be allowed him ; but after fourteen days, when almost dead with hunger, meats that had been offered to idols were set before him, which he would not touch. It was not in itself unlawful to eat of such meats, as St Paul teaches, except where it would give scandal to the weak, or when it was exacted as an action of idolatrous superstition, as was the case here. Being brought a second time before the tribunal, he would to all the questions put to him give no other answer but this, " I am a Christian ". He repeated the same whilst on the rack, and he finished his glorious course in prison, either by starvation, or, according to St Chrysostom, by the sword. His acts relate many of his miracles, with other particulars ; as that, when bound and chained on his back in prison, he consecrated the divine mysteries upon his own breast, and communicated the faithful that were present : this we also read in Philostorgius, the Arian historian. St Lucian suffered at Nicomedia in Bithynia on January 7, 312, and was buried at Drepanum (Helenopolis).

We have plenty of information concerning St Lucian in Eusebius (*Hist. Eccles.*, ix, 6) in a panegyric by St John Chrysostom (Migne, PG., vol. l, p. 519), and in a rather fantastic legend preserved by the Metaphrast (Migne, PG., vol. cxiv, p. 397). See also Pio Franchi in *Studi e Documenti* (1897), vol. xviii, pp. 24-45. Father Delehaye says of St Lucian :

" Nothing could be better authenticated than the fact of his martyrdom, nothing more firmly established than his *cultus*, witnessed to by the basilica of Helenopolis, as well as by literary documents " (*Legends of the Saints*, p. 192).   Nevertheless the story of St Lucian has been chosen by H. Usener (*Die Sintfluthsagen*, 1899, pp. 168–180) as a typical example of the evolution of Christian legend out of pagan myth.   Consult the reply of Father Delehaye (*l.c.* pp. 193–197), and see also Batiffol in *Compte-rendu du Congrès catholique* (1894), vol. ii, pp. 181–186.   There is a sensitive and erudite study by G. Bardy, *Recherches sur St Lucien d'Antioche* (1936).

ST VALENTINE, Bishop   (A.D. 440 ?)

VERY little is known concerning this St Valentine, though a fairly long medieval biography of him is printed in the *Acta Sanctorum ;* but this, as all are agreed, is historically worthless.   From Eugippius in his Life of St Severinus we learn that Valentine was first of all an abbot, and then a missionary bishop in Rhaetia, and also that a disciple of Valentine who attached himself to St Severinus used every year on January 7 to offer Mass in honour of his earlier father in Christ.   Venantius Fortunatus lets us know that in a journey he made through the Tirol he came across more than one church which was dedicated in honour of the same St Valentine. From Arbeo of Freising we get the further information that Valentine was first buried at Mais in the Tirol, but that his remains were translated to Trent about the year 750, and thence in 768 to Passau.   These are all early testimonies, but there is no more evidence which can be relied on.   At a much later date a story was invented that at a subsequent removal of the relics of Valentine to a place of greater honour in Passau a leaden tablet had been found which had engraved upon it a summary of the saint's whole history.   The biographer professes to incorporate a copy of the text of this inscription, but a critical study of the document leaves no doubt that it is a clumsy forgery.

See the essay of A. Leider, " Die Bleitafel im Sarge des Hl. Valentin " in *Festgabe Alois Knöpfler* (1907), pp. 254–274 ; and the *Acta Sanctorum*, January 7.

ST TILLO   (*c.* A.D. 702)

He was by birth a Saxon, and being made captive, was carried into the Low Countries, where he was ransomed and baptized by St Eligius.   That fervent apostle sent him to his abbey of Solignac, in the Limousin.   Tillo was called thence by Eligius, ordained priest, and employed by him for some time at Tournai and in other parts of the Low Countries.   The inhabitants of the country of Iseghem, near Courtrai, regard him as their apostle.   Some years after the death of St Eligius, St Tillo returned to Solignac, and lived as a recluse near that abbey, imitating in simplicity, devotion and austerity the Antonys and Macariuses of old. He died in his solitude, about the year 702, a nonagenarian, and was honoured with miracles.   Tillo is sometimes called Theau in France, Tilloine or Tilman in Flanders, Hillonius in Germany.

His name is famous in the French and Belgian calendars, though it does not occur in the Roman Martyrology.   The Life of St Eligius names Tillo first among the seven disciples of that saint, who worked with him at his trade of goldsmith, and imitated him in all his religious exercises, before that holy man was engaged in the ministry of the Church.   Many churches in Flanders, Auvergne, the Limousin and other places are dedicated to God under his invocation.   The anonymous Life of St Tillo, in the Acta SS, is not altogether authentic ; the history which Mabillon gives of him from the Breviary of Solignac is of more authority see his *AA. SS. Benedict.*, vol. ii, p. 996.

ST ALDRIC, Bishop of Le Mans　　(A.D. 856)

THIS saint was born of a noble family, partly of Saxon and partly Bavarian extraction, about the year 800.　At twelve years of age he was sent by his father to the court of Charlemagne where, in the household of Louis the Pious, he gained the esteem of the whole court.　About the year 821 he retired from Aix-la-Chapelle to Metz, where he entered the bishop's school and received clerical tonsure.　After his ordination the Emperor Louis called him again to court, and made him his chaplain and confessor.　In 832 St Aldric was chosen bishop of Le Mans.　He employed his patrimony and his whole interest in relieving the poor, providing public services, establishing churches and monasteries, and promoting religion. In the civil wars which divided the empire his fidelity to Louis and to his successor, Charles the Bald, was inviolable.　For almost a year he was expelled by a faction from his see, Aldric having antagonized the monks of Saint-Calais by claiming that they were under his jurisdiction.　The claim was not upheld, though supported by forged documents, for which the bishop himself is not known to have been personally responsible.

Some fragments have reached us of the regulations which Aldric made for his cathedral, in which he orders ten wax candles and ninety lamps to be lighted on all great festivals.　We have three testaments of this holy prelate extant.　The last is an edifying monument of his piety : in the first two, he bequeaths lands and possessions to many churches of his diocese, adding prudent advice and regulations for maintaining good order and a spirit of charity.　The last two years of St Aldric's life he was paralysed and confined to bed, during which time he redoubled his fervour and assiduity in prayer.　He died January 7, 856, and was buried in the church of St Vincent, of which, and of the monastery to which it belonged, he had been a great benefactor.

The medieval Latin life of St Aldric has been re-edited by Charles and Froger, *Gesta domini Aldrici* (1890).　No scholar now regards it as fully reliable, but the first forty-four chapters seem to be older and more trustworthy than the rest.　Some attempts have been made to connect St Aldric with the compilation of the Forged Decretals, but this idea has not found much favour, though Paul Fournier has shown good reason for believing that they first took shape in the neighbourhood of Le Mans during his episcopate.　On the other hand, Julien Havet has argued that the first forty-four chapters of the *Gesta* were written as a piece of autobiography by Aldric himself.　In any case Havet seems to have proved that in contrast to the chapters in the later portion of the *Gesta* and those in the *Actus pontificum Cenomannis* . ., the nineteen documents incorporated in the first forty-four chapters are all authentic.　See J. Havet, *Œuvres*, vol. i, pp. 287–292, 317 *seq.*, and *Analecta Bollandiana* (1895), vol. xiv, p. 446 ; *cf.* also Duchesne, *Fastes Épiscopaux*, vol. ii, pp. 313–317, 327–328, 342–343 ; M. Besson in DHG., vol. ii, cc. 68–69.

ST REINOLD　　(A.D. 960 ?)

VERY little is known of St Reinold, monk and martyr, identified with the youngest of the " four sons of Aymon ".　Tradition connects him with the family of Charlemagne.　Apparently he made his way to Cologne and entered the monastery of St Pantaleon.　He was put in charge of certain building operations, and owing to his over-strenuous diligence, incurred the hostility of the stonemasons.　The result was that they attacked him, killed him with blows of their hammers, and flung his body into a pool near the Rhine.　For a long time his brothers in religion searched in vain for any trace of him.　His body was at last discovered through a revelation made to a poor sick woman, and it was brought back to the monastery with honour. Later on, in the eleventh century, it was translated by St Anno, Archbishop of Cologne, to Dortmund in Westphalia. St Reinold was in some places honoured as the patron of stonemasons.

The *Acta Sanctorum* for January 7 prints a short life, but it is impossible to say how much of this is purely mythical, and how much may be based on some kernel of fact. A local chronicle of Cologne states that St Reinold died in 697, and a rhythmical life of the same, printed by Floss, assigns his " martyrdom " to the episcopate of St Agilulf, Bishop of Cologne, who is supposed to have died in 750. In either case Reinold could have had nothing to do with Charlemagne. See Jordan in *Romanische Forschungen* (1907), vol. xx, pp. 1–198, and Caxton's *Romance of the Foure Sonnes of Aymon*, re-edited for the Early English Text Society.

ST CANUTE LAVARD, Martyr   (A.D. 1131)

KNUD LAVARD, " the Lord ", as he is called by his countrymen, was the second son of Eric the Good, King of Denmark. When he had come to man's estate, his uncle, King Niels, made him duke over southern Jutland with the task of defending it against the Wends ; and, from his centre at Schleswig, Canute set himself to make justice and peace reign in his territory. Unfortunately the plundering Vikings could not be induced to co-operate in this worthy object. One day, when he had condemned several of them to be hanged for their piracies, one cried out that he was of blood royal and related to Canute. The duke answered that if such was the case he should in recognition of his noble birth be hanged from the masthead of his ship, which was done.

Canute had spent part of his youth at the Saxon court, and in 1129 the Emperor Lothair III recognized his rule over the western Wends, with the title of king. This excited the anger of King Niels of Denmark, and on January 7, 1131, Canute was treacherously slain in the forest of Haraldsted, near Ringsted, by his cousins Magnus Nielssen and Henry Skadelaar. Canute, who had supported the missionary activities of St Vicelin, was canonized by Pope Alexander III in 1169 at the request of his son, Valdemar I of Denmark, and of Eskil, Archbishop of Lund. The Roman Martyrology, following the *cultus* which Canute received in Denmark, calls him a martyr, but he seems to have been a dynastic hero rather than a martyr.

See the *Acta Sanctorum*, January 7 ; C. Gertz, *Vitae sanctorum Danorum* (1908–1912) ; Schubert, *Kirchengeschichte von Schleswig-Holstein* (1907), vol. i ; and DHG., vol. xi, cc. 815–817. For the canonization, see E. W. Kemp, *Canonization and Authority* (1948), pp. 79, 86.

BD EDWARD WATERSON, Martyr   (A.D. 1593)

EDWARD WATERSON is unique among the English martyrs in having had the opportunity to turn Mohammedan and marry a Turkish girl. He was a Protestant Londoner by birth, and when a young man made a voyage to Turkey. While there he attracted the favourable notice of a wealthy Turk, who offered him his daughter in marriage on condition that he should embrace Islam. Waterson rejected the suggestion ; but on his way homewards, tarrying at Rome, he had the opportunity for conversion of another sort, and he was reconciled with the Catholic Church by Dr Richard Smith at the English College. This was in 1588. He then went on to the college at Rheims, where he was ordained priest four years later.

In June following he was sent back to England, declaring he would rather go there than own all France for a twelvemonth ; but he ministered for only a few months before being arrested and condemned for his priesthood at Newcastle-upon-Tyne. Archdeacon Trollope, from whose letters to Douay Challoner got several items of information, declared that, when Mr Waterson was tied to the hurdle to be drawn to the place of execution, the horses refused to budge ; so he had to be taken to the scaffold on foot, the bystanders saying, " It would be a vote to the papists which had happened that day " ; or, in modern idiom, " That's one up to the R.C.'s ". Again, when he came to mount the scaffold the ladder is said to have jerked about without human agency, and to have stayed still only when he made the sign of the cross over it. Then he was turned off, disembowelled and quartered.

See MMP., pp. 187–188 ; Morris, *Troubles of our Catholic Forefathers* (series III) Catholic Record Society publications, vol. v ; and Burton and Pollen, LEM.

8 : ST APOLLINARIS, BISHOP OF HIERAPOLIS   (*c.* A.D. 179)

CLAUDIUS APOLLINARIS, Bishop of Hierapolis in Phrygia, called " the Apologist ", was a famous Christian teacher in the second century. Notwithstanding the encomiums bestowed on him by Eusebius, St Jerome, Theodoret and others, we know but little of his life, and his writings, which then were held in great esteem, seem now to be all lost. Photius, who had read them and who was a very good judge, commends them both for their style and matter. He wrote against the Encratites and other heretics, and pointed out, as St Jerome testifies, from what philosophical sect each heresy derived its errors. His last work was directed against the Montanists and their pretended prophets, who began to appear in Phrygia about the year 171. But nothing rendered his name so illustrious as his apology for the Christian religion, which he addressed to the Emperor Marcus Aurelius soon after the victory that prince had obtained over the Quadi by the prayers, it is alleged, of the Christians, of which the saint made mention.

Marcus Aurelius having long attempted without success to subdue the Germans by his generals, resolved in A.D. 174 to take the field against them himself. He was beyond the Danube when the Quadi, a people inhabiting that territory later called Moravia, surrounded him in a very disadvantageous situation : so that there was no possibility that either he or his army could escape out of their hands or maintain themselves long where they were for want of water. The twelfth legion was chiefly composed of Christians. When the army was drawn up, exhausted with thirst, the Christians fell upon their knees, " as we are accustomed to do at prayer ", says Eusebius, and earnestly besought God's aid. Then on a sudden the sky was darkened with clouds, and a heavy rain poured down just as the barbarians began their attack. The Romans fought and drank at the same time, catching the rain as it fell in their helmets, and often swallowing it mingled with blood. Their assailants would still have been too strong for them, but that the storm being driven by a violent wind into their faces, and accompanied with flashes of lightning and loud thunder, the Germans, unable to see, were terrified to such a degree that they took to flight. Both heathen and Christian writers give this account of the victory.

The heathens ascribed it, some to the power of magic, others to their gods, but the Christians accounted it a miracle obtained by the prayers of this legion. St Apollinaris apparently referred to it in his apology to this very emperor, and added that as an acknowledgement the emperor gave it the name of the " Thundering Legion ". From him it is so called by Eusebius, Tertullian, St Jerome and St Gregory of Nyssa.

The Quadi surrendered the prisoners whom they had taken, and begged for peace on whatever conditions it should please the emperor to grant it them. Marcus Aurelius hereupon, out of gratitude to his Christian soldiers, published an edict, in which he confessed himself indebted for his delivery " to the shower obtained, *perhaps*, by the prayers of the Christians ". In it he forbade, under pain of death, anyone to accuse a Christian on account of his religion ; yet by a strange inconsistency, being overawed by the opposition of the senate, he had not the courage to abolish the laws already in force against Christians. Hence, even after this, in the same reign, many suffered martyrdom, though their accusers, it is asserted, were also put to death.

The deliverance of the emperor is represented on the *Columna Antoniniana* in Rome by the figure of a Jupiter Pluvius, being that of an old man flying in the air with his arms extended, and a long beard which seems to waste away in rain. The soldiers are there represented as relieved by this sudden tempest, and in a posture partly drinking of the rain water and partly fighting against the enemy, who, on the contrary, are represented as stretched out on the ground with their horses, and the dreadful part of the storm descending upon them only. The credibility of the story, which Eusebius apparently derived from the *Apology* of St Apollinaris, still remains a matter of discussion. On the one hand, it is certain that the " Thundering Legion " (*legio fulminata*) did not obtain this title from Marcus Aurelius, for it belonged to them from the time of Augustus ; on the other, there is nothing violently incredible in the facts themselves. Contemporary Christians might easily attribute such a surprising victory to the prayers of their fellow believers. There is no confirmation among pagan authorities for the text of the supposed edict of toleration. Those scholars who defend the general accuracy of the facts believe it to be at least interpolated.

St Apollinaris may have penned his apology to the emperor about the year 175 to remind him of the benefit he had received from God by the prayers of the Christians, and to implore his protection. We have no account of the time of this holy man's death, which probably happened before that of Marcus Aurelius.

For the " Thundering Legion " see Tertullian, *Apologeticum*, cap. 5, and *Ad Scapulam*, cap. 4 ; Eusebius, *Hist. eccl.*, bk v, cap. 5 ; J. B. Lightfoot, *St Ignatius*, vol. i (1889), pp. 469 *seq.* ; Mommsen in *Hermes*, 1895, pp. 90–106 ; Allard, *Histoire des persécutions*, vol. i (1903), pp. 394–396. For St Apollinaris, see *Acta Sanctorum*, February, vol. ii, pp. 4–8. His name was added to the Roman Martyrology by Baronius, but there is no evidence of any early *cultus* in either the East or West.

ST LUCIAN OF BEAUVAIS, Martyr   (A.D. 290 ?)

It is said that this Lucian preached the gospel in Gaul in the third century and came from Rome ; he was possibly one of the companions of St Dionysius of Paris, or at least of St Quentin. He sealed his mission with his blood at Beauvais, under

Julian, vicar or successor to the persecutor Rictiovarus in the government of Gaul, about the year 290.   Maximian, called by the common people Messien, and Julian, the companions of his labours, were crowned with martyrdom at the same place a little before him.   His relics, with those of his two colleagues, were discovered in the seventh century, as St Ouen informs us in his life of St Eligius.   They were shown in three gilt shrines in an abbey which bore his name, founded in the eighth century.   Rabanus Maurus says that these relics were famous for miracles when he wrote, a hundred years later.

St Lucian is styled only martyr in most calendars down to the sixteenth century, and in the Roman Martyrology ; but a calendar compiled in the reign of Louis the Pious calls him bishop, and he is honoured in that quality at Beauvais.

See the *Acta Sanctorum* for January 8, p. 640, though the two lives of this saint there printed are of little or no authority.   Duchesne in his *Fastes Épiscopaux*, vol. iii, pp. 119 and 141–152, discusses the case of St Lucian at some length, and shows good reason for believing that the whole story is mythical.   He strongly inclines to the belief that Rictiovarus never existed.   See H. Moretus, *Les Passions de S. Lucien et leurs dérivés céphalophoriques* (1953).

ST SEVERINUS OF NORICUM   (*c.* A.D. 480)

WE know nothing of the birth or country of this saint.   From the purity of his Latin he was generally supposed to be a Roman, and his care to conceal what rank he had held in the world was taken for a proof of his humility and a presumption that he was a person of birth.   He spent the first part of his life in the deserts of the East, but left his retreat to preach the gospel in Noricum (Austria).   At first he came to Astura, now Stockerau ; but finding the people hardened in vice, he foretold the punishment God had prepared for them, and repaired to Comagene (Hainburg, on the Danube).   It was not long ere his prophecy was verified, for Astura was laid waste, and the inhabitants destroyed by the Huns.   By the fulfilment of this prophecy, and by several miracles which he wrought, the name of the saint became famous.   Faviana, a city on the Danube, distressed by a terrible famine, implored his assistance.   St Severinus preached penance among them with great fruit, and he so effectually threatened a certain rich woman who had hoarded up a great quantity of provisions, that she distributed all her stores amongst the poor.   Soon after his arrival, the ice of the Danube and the Inn breaking, the country was abundantly supplied by barges up the rivers.   Another time by his prayers he chased away the swarms of locusts which were then threatening the whole produce of the year.   He wrought many miracles, yet never healed the sore eyes of Bonosus, the dearest to him of his disciples, who spent forty years without any abatement of his religious fervour.   Severinus himself never ceased to exhort all to repentance and piety ; he redeemed captives, relieved the oppressed, was a father to the poor, cured the sick, mitigated or averted public calamities, and brought a blessing wherever he came.   Many cities desired him for their bishop, but he withstood their importunities by urging that it was sufficient he had relinquished his dear solitude for their instruction and comfort.

He established several monasteries, of which the most considerable was one on the banks of the Danube near Vienna ; but he made none of them the place of his constant abode, often shutting himself up in a hermitage where he wholly devoted himself to contemplation.   He never ate till after sunset, unless on great festivals, and he always walked barefoot, even when the Danube was frozen.   Kings and princes of the barbarians came to visit him, and among them Odoacer on his march for Italy.   The saint's cell was so low that Odoacer could not stand upright in it. St Severinus told him that the kingdom he was going to conquer would shortly be his, and Odoacer finding himself soon after master of the country, wrote to the saint, promising him all he was pleased to ask ; but Severinus only desired of him the restoration of a certain banished man.   Having foretold his death long before it happened, he fell ill on January 5, and on the fourth day of his illness, repeating that verse of the psalmist, " Let every spirit praise the Lord ", he closed his eyes in death.   This happened between 476 and 482.   Some years later his disciples, driven out by the inroads of barbarians, retired with his relics into Italy, and deposited them at Luculanum, near Naples, where a monastery was built, of which Eugippius, his disciple and biographer, was soon after made abbot.   In the year 910 they were translated to Naples, where they were honoured in a Benedictine abbey which bore his name.

The one supreme authority for the life of St Severinus is the biography by his disciple Eugippius, the best text of which is to be found in the edition of T. Mommsen (1898), or in that of the Vienna *Corpus scriptorum ecclesiasticorum latinorum*, edited by Pius Knoell (1886).   See also A. Baudrillart, *St Séverin* (1908) ; and T. Sommerlad, *Wirtschaftsgeschichtliche Untersuchungen*, part ii (1903).   Sommerlad shows some reason for thinking that St Severinus belonged to a distinguished family in Africa, and that in his own country he had been consecrated bishop before he sought refuge in the East and led the life of a hermit or monk.

ST SEVERINUS, Bishop of Septempeda   (A.D. 550 ?)

THE ancient town of Septempeda in the Marches of Ancona is now called San Severino, deriving its name from a St Severinus who is believed to have been bishop there in the middle of the sixth century.   He was the brother of St Victorinus, whom Ado in his martyrology identifies with a martyr of that name.   The confusion seems to have arisen from the fact that the relics of St Severinus of Noricum were transferred to Naples, whence Ado was led to identify him with the Italian St Severinus.   The confusion is perpetuated in the present Roman Martyrology, for there is no reason to believe that Severinus of Septempeda ever had anything to do with Naples.

See the legend of SS. Severinus and Victorinus in the *Acta Sanctorum*, January 8 ; and *cf. Analecta Bollandiana*, vol. xxvii (1908), p. 466.

ST ERHARD, Bishop   (A.D. 686 ?)

THERE is better evidence for the existence of St Erhard, described as bishop of Ratisbon (he was, however, possibly only a *chorepiscopus*, a sort of bishop auxiliary), than there is for his supposed brother Albert.   A strong local tradition evidenced by place names—*e.g.* " Erhardsbrunnen ", " Erhardicrypta ", etc.—as well as by entries in calendars and other early documents, seems to imply a considerable *cultus* dating back to the eighth century and possibly earlier.   What purports to be his episcopal staff of black buffalo-horn is still preserved, as well as part of his skull.   He may be identical with an abbot of Ebersheimmünster whose name appears in a Merovingian charter of the year 684.   He is stated to have baptized

St Odilia, who, though born blind, recovered her sight on receiving the sacrament. Two or three lives of him have been printed by the Bollandists, but they are all overlaid by fabulous or legendary matter. He is in some accounts described as an Irishman, or at least of Irish descent but no great reliance can be placed upon this statement.

The most trustworthy information which is available concerning St Erhard has been collected by W. Levison in his preface to the Latin texts printed in MGH., *Scriptores Meroc.*, vol. vi, pp. 1–23.

ST GUDULA, Virgin   (A.D. 712 ?)

St Amalberga, mother of this saint, was niece to Bd Pepin of Landen. Gudula was educated at Nivelles, under the care of St Gertrude, her cousin and godmother, after whose death in 664 she returned to the house of Count Witger, her father ; having by vow consecrated herself to God, she led a most austere life in watching, fasting and prayer. By her profuse alms she was truly the mother of all the distressed. Though her father's castle was two miles from the church at Morzelle, she went thither early every morning, with a maid to carry a lantern before her ; and the wax taper being once put out, is said to have miraculously lighted again at her prayers, whence she is usually represented in pictures with a lantern. She died on January 8, perhaps in 712, and was buried at Hamme, near Brussels. In the reign of Charlemagne, her body was removed to the church of Saint-Sauveur at Morzelle, and placed behind the high altar. This emperor, out of veneration for her memory, often resorted thither to pray, and founded a nunnery, which soon after changed its name of St Saviour for that of St Goule. This house was destroyed in the irruptions of the Normans. The relics of St Gudula, by the care of Charles, Duke of Lorraine (in which Brabant was then comprised), were translated to Brussels in 978, where they were first deposited in the church of St Géry, but in 1047 removed into the great collegiate church of St Michael, since called from her St Gudule's. This saint was called colloquially Goule or Ergoule in Brabant, and Goelen in Flanders.

See her life written by Hubert of Brabant in the eleventh century, soon after this translation of her relics to St Michael's, who assures us that he took the whole relation from an ancient life of the saint, having only changed the order and style. But even if we could trust this statement, some of the miracles found in this and one or two other slightly differing accounts are very extravagant—*e.g.* that a pair of gloves given her by a friend, which she refused to use, remained suspended in the air for an hour ; or that a tall poplar-tree grew up beside her grave in a night. See for the texts the *Acta Sanctorum*, January 8, and *cf.* Destombes, *Saints de Cambrai*, vol. i, pp. 51–56. Visitors to Brussels often take the great church of Sainte-Gudule for a cathedral, but Brussels has never been an episcopal see.

ST PEGA, Virgin   (c. A.D. 719)

Pega was sister to St Guthlac and she lived a retired life not far from her brother's hermitage at Croyland, just across the border of what is now Northamptonshire, on the western edge of the great Peterborough Fen. The place is now called Peakirk, *i.e.* Pega's church. She attended her brother's funeral, making the journey by water down the Welland, and is reputed on that occasion to have cured a blind man from Wisbech. She is said to have then gone on pilgrimage to Rome, where she slept in the Lord about the year 719. Ordericus Vitalis says her relics were honoured with miracles, and kept in a church which bore her name at Rome, but this church is not now known.

The Bollandists have brought together scattered allusions from the Life of St Guthlac and elsewhere (*Acta Sanctorum*, January 8). See also DCB., vol. iv, pp. 280–281, and the forthcoming Life of Guthlac by Bertram Colgrave.

ST WULSIN, BISHOP OF SHERBORNE   (A.D. 1005)

IN a charter which purports to emanate from King Ethelred in the year 998, Wulsin is described as a loyal and trusty monk whom St Dunstan " loved like a son with pure affection ". It is a little difficult to be sure of the dates, but it would seem that when Dunstan was bishop of London he obtained a grant of land from King Edgar and restored the abbey of Westminster, making Wulsin superior of the dozen monks he placed there. In 980 Wulsin was consecrated abbot, and thirteen years afterwards he was appointed to the see of Sherborne. He seems to have died on January 8, 1005. He was evidently much beloved, and is called Saint by Malmesbury, Capgrave, Flete and others, but his name apparently is not found in the medieval English calendars.

See John Flete, *History of Westminster Abbey* (ed. Armitage Robinson, 1909), pp. 79–80 ; Stubbs, *Memorials of St Dunstan*, pp. 304, 406–408 ; Stanton, *Menology*, p. 10.

ST THORFINN, BISHOP OF HAMAR   (A.D. 1285)

IN the year 1285 there died in the Cistercian monastery at Ter Doest, near Bruges, a Norwegian bishop named Thorfinn. He had never attracted particular attention and was soon forgotten. But over fifty years later, in the course of some building operations, his tomb in the church was opened and it was reported that the remains gave out a strong and pleasing smell. The abbot made enquiries and found that one of his monks, an aged man named Walter de Muda, remembered Bishop Thorfinn staying in the monastery and the impression he had made of gentle goodness combined with strength. Father Walter had in fact written a poem about him after his death and hung it up over his tomb. It was then found that the parchment was still there, none the worse for the passage of time. This was taken as a direction from on high that the bishop's memory was to be perpetuated, and Father Walter was instructed to write down his recollections of him.

For all that, there is little enough known about St Thorfinn. He was a Trondhjem man and perhaps was a canon of the cathedral of Nidaros, since there was such a one named Thorfinn among those who witnessed the Agreement of Tönsberg in 1277. This was an agreement between King Magnus VI and the Archbishop of Nidaros confirming certain privileges of the clergy, the freedom of episcopal elections and similar matters. Some years later King Eric* repudiated this agreement, and a fierce dispute between church and state ensued. Eventually the king outlawed the archbishop, John, and his two chief supporters, Bishop Andrew of Oslo and Bishop Thorfinn of Hamar.

The last-named, after many hardships, including shipwreck, made his way to the abbey of Ter Doest in Flanders, which had a number of contacts with the Norwegian church. It is possible that he had been there before, and there is some reason to suppose he was himself a Cistercian of the abbey of Tautra, near Nidaros.

* He married Margaret, daughter of King Alexander III of Scotland. Their daughter was " The Maid of Norway ", who has a paragraph in English and Scottish history.

After a visit to Rome he went back to Ter Doest, in bad health. Indeed, though probably still a youngish man, he saw death approaching and so made his will ; he had little to leave, but what there was he divided between his mother, his brothers and sisters, and certain monasteries, churches and charities in his diocese. He died shortly after, on January 8, 1285.

After his recall to the memory of man as mentioned in the opening paragraph of this notice, miracles were reported at his tomb, and St Thorfinn was venerated by the Cistercians and around Bruges. In our own day his memory has been revived among the few Catholics of Norway, and his feast is observed in his episcopal city of Hamar. The tradition of Thorfinn's holiness ultimately rests on the poem of Walter de Muda, wherein he appears as a kind, patient, generous man, whose mild exterior covered a firm will against whatever he esteemed to be evil and ungodly.

The text of Walter de Muda's poem and other pieces were printed in the *Acta Sanctorum*, January 8. St Thorfinn is shown in his historical setting by Mrs Undset in *Saga of Saints* (1934). See also De Visch's *Bibliotheca scriptorum ordinis Cisterciensis.*

9 : ST MARCIANA, Virgin and Martyr　　(c. A.D. 303)

SHE was a native of Rusuccur, a place in Mauritania, and, courageously despising all worldly advantages to secure the possession of heavenly grace, she bid defiance to the pagan idolaters in the persecution of Diocletian. Marciana was beaten with clubs, and her chastity exposed to the rude attempts of gladiators, in which danger God miraculously preserved her, and she became the happy instrument of the conversion of one of them to the faith. At length she was torn in pieces by a wild bull and a leopard in the amphitheatre at Caesarea in Mauritania, about 100 miles west of the modern city of Algiers.

She is probably also commemorated on July 12 in the ancient breviary of Toledo, and in the Roman and some other martyrologies both on July 12 and January 9. See a beautiful ancient hymn in her praise in the Mozarabic breviary, and her acts in the *Acta Sanctorum*, though their authority is more than questionable. She was especially honoured in Spain, where she is patron of Tortosa, unless, indeed, there is really another martyr, likewise called Marciana, who, according to the Roman Martyrology, suffered at Toledo on July 12 (BHL., n. 780).

SS. JULIAN AND BASILISSA, and Companions, Martyrs (A.D. 304 ?)

ACCORDING to their "acts" and the ancient martyrologies, Julian and Basilissa, though engaged in the married state, lived by mutual consent in perpetual chastity, sanctified themselves by the exercises of an ascetic life, and employed their revenues in relieving the poor and the sick. For this purpose they converted their house into a kind of hospital, in which, if we may credit their acts, they sometimes entertained a thousand indigent persons : Basilissa attended those of her sex ; Julian, on his part, ministered to the men with such charity that he was later on confused with St Julian the Hospitaller. Egypt, where they lived, had then begun to abound with examples of persons who, either in the cities or in the deserts, devoted themselves to charity, penance and contemplation. Basilissa, after having endured severe persecution, died in peace ; Julian survived her many years, and received the crown of a glorious martyrdom, together with Celsus a youth, Antony a priest, Anastasius and Marcianilla, the mother of Celsus.

What purport to be the acts of these saints are mere romances abounding in contradictions. See the *Acta Sanctorum* for January 9. The historical existence of any such couple is more than doubtful. One of the versions of the legend of St Alexis (July 17) seems to be simply a transcription of the first paragraphs of their long *passio*.

ST PETER, Bishop of Sebastea   (A.D. 391)

THE family to which St Peter belonged was ancient and illustrious, but the names of his ancestors are long since buried in oblivion, whilst those of the saints whom his parents gave to the Church are immortal in the records of our Christian faith. In this family three brothers were at the same time eminently holy bishops, St Basil, St Gregory of Nyssa and St Peter of Sebastea ; their eldest sister, St Macrina, was the spiritual mother of many saints and excellent doctors ; and their father and mother, St Basil the Elder and St Emmelia, were banished for their faith in the reign of the Emperor Galerius Maximian, and fled into the deserts of Pontus. Finally, the grandmother was the celebrated St Macrina the Elder, who was instructed in the science of salvation by St Gregory Thaumaturgus.   Peter of Sebastea was the youngest of ten children and lost his father in his cradle, so that his eldest sister, Macrina, took charge of his education.   In this duty her only aim was to instruct him in religion : profane studies she thought of little use to one whose thoughts were set upon the world to come.   Neither did he resent these restrictions, confining his aspirations to the monastic state.   His mother had founded two monasteries, one for men, the other for women ; the former she put under the direction of her son Basil, the latter under that of Macrina.   Peter joined the house governed by his brother, situated on the bank of the River Iris.   When St Basil was obliged to surrender that charge in 362 he appointed St Peter his successor, who discharged this office for many years with great prudence and virtue.

When the provinces of Pontus and Cappadocia were visited by severe famine, he gave proof of his charity.   Human prudence would have advised him to be frugal in the relief of others till his own community were secured against that calamity ; but Peter had studied the principles of Christian charity in another school, and liberally disposed of all that belonged to the monastery to supply with necessaries the destitute people who daily resorted to him in that time of distress.   When St Basil was made bishop of Caesarea in Cappadocia in 370 he promoted Peter to the priesthood.   Basil died on January 1 in 379, and Macrina in the November of the same year.   Eustathius, Bishop of Sebastea in Armenia, an Arian and a persecutor of St Basil, seems to have died shortly after them ; for Peter was consecrated bishop of Sebastea in 380 to root out the Arian heresy in that diocese.   The evil had taken such deep root that the zeal of a saint was necessary to deal with it.   A letter which St Peter wrote, and which is prefixed to St Gregory of Nyssa's books against Eunomius, has entitled him to a place among the ecclesiastical writers ; and it is a standing proof that though he had confined himself to sacred studies, yet by good conversation and reading, and by his own natural gifts, he was inferior to none but his incomparable brother Basil and his colleague Gregory Nazianzen in solid eloquence.   In 381 St Peter attended the general council held at Constantinople. Not only his brother St Gregory of Nyssa but also Theodoret, and all antiquity, bear testimony to his sanctity, prudence and zeal.   His death occurred in summer about the year 391, and his brother of Nyssa mentions that his memory was honoured at Sebastea (probably the very year after his death) by a solemn celebration, together with that of some other martyrs of the same city. His name occurs in the Roman Martyrology on January 9.

It is a wonderful thing to meet with a whole family of saints. This prodigy of grace, under God, was owing to the example, prayers and exhortations of the elder St Macrina. From her they learned to imbibe the true spirit of self-denial and humility which all Christians confess to be the fundamental maxim of the gospel. Unfortunately it generally happens that the principle is accepted as a matter of speculation only, whereas it is in the heart that this foundation is to be laid.

We have little information about St Peter of Sebastea beyond the casual allusions contained in St Gregory of Nyssa's Life of Macrina (in Migne, PG., vol. xlvi, pp. 960 *seq.*). His letter addressed to his brother Gregory of Nyssa, entreating him to complete his treatise against Eunomius, is printed in PG., vol. xlv, pp. 241 *seq.* See also *Acta Sanctorum*, January 9 ; DCB., vol. iv, pp. 345–346 ; and Bardenhewer, *Patrology* (Eng. trans.), pp. 295–297.

ST WANINGUS, or VANENG   (*c.* A.D. 683)

FROM various Merovingian sources it appears that Vaneng was made by Clotaire III governor of that part of Neustria, or Normandy, which is called Pays de Caux, at which time he took great pleasure in hunting. Nevertheless, he was particularly devout to St Eulalia of Barcelona, called in Guienne St Aulaire. One night he seemed in a dream to hear that holy virgin and martyr repeat to him those words of our Redeemer in the Gospel, that " it is easier for a camel to pass through the eye of a needle than for a rich man to be saved ". This was the turning point in his life. He was entirely converted to God. He assisted St Wandrille in founding the abbey at Fontenelle, and founded in the valley of Fécamp a church in honour of the Holy Trinity, with a great nunnery adjoining, under the direction of St Ouen and St Wandrille. Hildemarca, a very virtuous nun, was called from Bordeaux and appointed the first abbess. Under her three hundred and sixty nuns served God in this house, and were divided into as many choirs as were sufficient, in relays, to continue the divine office night and day without interruption.

See the *Acta Sanctorum*, January 9 ; and also Vacandard, *Vie de Saint Ouen.* The *Vie de Saint Vaneng*, by C. Labbé, was re-edited by Michael Hardy in 1873 (*cf.* BHL., n. 1272).

ST ADRIAN, ABBOT OF CANTERBURY   (A.D. 710)

ADRIAN was an African by birth, and was abbot of Nerida, not far from Naples, when Pope St Vitalian, upon the death of St Deusdedit, the archbishop of Canterbury, judged him for his learning and virtue to be the most suitable person to be the teacher of a nation still young in the faith. The humble servant of God found means to decline that dignity by recommending St Theodore in his place, but was willing to share in the more laborious part of the ministry. The pope therefore enjoined him to be the assistant and adviser of the archbishop, to which Adrian readily agreed.

St Theodore made him abbot of the monastery of SS. Peter and Paul, afterwards called St Augustine's, at Canterbury, where he taught Greek and Latin, the learning of the fathers, and, above all, virtue. Under Adrian and Theodore this monastic school at Canterbury had a far-reaching influence—St Aldhelm came there from Wessex, Oftfor from Whitby, and even students from Ireland. Roman law could be studied as well as the ecclesiastical sciences ; and Bede says that there were pupils of St Adrian who had a good knowledge of Greek and spoke Latin as well as they did English. St Adrian had illuminated this island by his doctrine and the example of his holy life, for the space of thirty-nine years, when he departed to our Lord on January 9 in the year 710.

Goscelin of Canterbury has left an extremely interesting account of the discovery of St Adrian's body, incorrupt and fragrant, in 1091 (see Migne, PL., vol. clv, cc. 36–38). The account is at least indirectly confirmed by later excavations ; see *Archaeologia Cantiana* (1917), vol. xxxii, p. 18. His tomb was famed for miracles, as we are assured by Goscelin, quoted by William of Malmesbury and Capgrave ; and his name was inserted in English calendars. See the *Acta Sanctorum* for January 9, where passages from Bede and Capgrave are reproduced ; and BHL., n. 558.

ST BERHTWALD, Archbishop of Canterbury   (A.D. 731)

The claim of Berhtwald (whose name is variously spelt Berctuald, Brithwald, etc.) to be counted as a saint is somewhat questionable, and there is next to no evidence of *cultus*. He was certainly abbot of Reculver in Kent, and was elected archbishop in 692, but only consecrated a year later, in Gaul by the archbishop of Lyons ; he probably then went on to Rome for the *pallium*. Berhtwald was tactful and energetic during the course of his long episcopate—thirty-seven years—and we find him in friendly relations with St Aldhelm, St Boniface and other prominent and holy ecclesiastics ; but his attitude towards St Wilfrid was not sympathetic. He died in January 731. A letter written to Berhtwald by Waldhere, Bishop of London, is the first extant letter from one Englishman to another.

See *Acta Sanctorum*, January 9 ; DNB., vol. vi, p. 343 ; and Plummer's *Bede*, vol. ii, p. 283.

BD ALIX LE CLERCQ, Virgin, Co-Foundress of the Augustinian Canonesses Regular of the Congregation of Our Lady   (A.D. 1622)

One of the outstanding achievements of the Counter-Reformation—like some of its others, long overdue—was the beginning of proper provision for the schooling and education of girls. In 1535 St Angela Merici had founded the Ursulines for this work ; the teaching Religious of Notre Dame were begun by St Joan de Lestonnac in 1606 ; in 1609 Mary Ward opened her first school for poor children ; and to these must be added the establishment by St Peter Fourier of the Augustinian Canonesses of the Congregation of Our Lady, an undertaking in which Alix Le Clercq came to be associated as co-foundress.

She was born at Remiremont in the duchy of Lorraine in 1576. Her family was a solid one, of good position, but little is known about her life until she was nearly seventeen. By that time she was a tall, good-looking girl, fair in colouring, of a somewhat delicate constitution, attractive and intelligent : in a word Alix was, as Mgr Francis Gonne remarks, what the French call *spirituelle*. Another account, written by herself, tells us that she revelled in such pleasures as music and dancing, and being very popular was subjected to a good deal of flattery. The implication is that she " revelled " too much : perhaps she did ; but it should be remembered that, when once people have become convinced that they have any faults at all, they are apt to exaggerate them. And there is good evidence, her own, that even at this time Alix Le Clercq was not devoid of " seriousness " : " amid all the gaiety her heart was sad ", and gradually her harmless pleasures seemed to her to be no more than frivolity.

Then, when she was nineteen, she had the first of the striking dreams that became so marked a feature in her life. In this dream she was in church and approaching the altar, when beside it she saw our Lady, dressed in a strange religious habit, who beckoned her, saying, " Come, daughter, and I will welcome you ". Soon after, the Le Clercq family moved to Hymont, and Alix first met St Peter Fourier, who was parish priest of Mattaincourt, near by. It was in the church of this village, at Mass on three Sundays running, that she seemed to hear the seductive music of a dance-drum, and then seemed to see its player, an evil spirit, followed by a crowd of young people, " full of sprightly merriment ". There and then her conversion to a different sort of life was complete : " I resolved on the spot that I would not belong to such a company ".

Alix straightway cast aside her fine clothes and wore a simple peasant dress ; she hardly left her home ; and, under the careful direction of Father Fourier, she set herself to discover—not without much spiritual suffering—what it was that God required of her. Both her father and the priest proposed that she should go into a convent : but she said " No " to this, for from another dream she had learned that it was in no existing order that her vocation lay. She told St Peter Fourier that she was obsessed by the idea of a new, " active ", foundation. He was very properly sceptical about this, but at length told her to see if she could find other girls of like mind—unlikely enough in a remote village of the Vosges. But sure enough Alix found them.

And so at the midnight Mass of Christmas 1597 Alix Le Clercq, Ganthe André, and Isabel and Joan de Louvroir were allowed publicly to dedicate themselves wholly to God. Four weeks later it was made clear to St Peter Fourier that these neophytes were to found a community under his direction. But meanwhile they were the subject of adverse criticism. " The unassuming behaviour of these girls was called singularity ; their zeal, religiosity ; their simple dress, hypocritical affectation ; and their humble bearing, silliness." This gossip naturally upset Mr Le Clercq ; but he lacked imagination, and could think of nothing better than to order his daughter to go as a boarder to a convent of Tertiaries of St Elizabeth at Ormes. She obeyed ; and found this relaxed convent to be something like what we should call a women's residential club. But her father would not let her come home.

A way out of the *impasse* was opened from an unexpected quarter. Three miles from Mattaincourt, at the village of Poussay, there was an abbey of secular canon-esses, aristocratic and wealthy ladies who led a form of the conventual life mercifully no longer existing in the Church. One of these good ladies, Madame Judith d'Apremont, made up her mind to sponsor Alix Le Clercq and her three com-panions and to lodge them in a small house on her estate. Accordingly they took up their quarters there on the eve of Corpus Christi 1598 ; and after a retreat they unanimously and independently declared to Father Fourier that they believed themselves called to begin a new congregation, that for them this was what would be most pleasing to God. It was decided that their work should be education, " to teach children to read and write and sew, and especially to love and serve God " that they should never give up this work ; and that it should be done, whether for rich or poor, without charge, " as that is more pleasing to God ".

The life of the embryonic congregation was notable in these early days for a measure of physical austerity that was later to be found incompatible with the hard discipline of teaching the young.   But the spectacle of such devotion at their very door inspired some of the younger canonesses of the abbey to ask to be transferred to the new foundation—they wanted to stop having " all the privileges of the conventual life with none of its hardships "   Their lady abbess, Madame d'Amon-court, was alarmed—many monasteries in France had learned nothing from the impact of the Reformation on monasticism in other lands—fearing that her own community might be broken up ; and for some weeks there was a rather critical situation.   But again Madame d'Apremont solved the difficulty, by providing another house, this time at Mattaincourt.   It was to be the first proper convent of the new congregation.

But as yet the sisters were not formally religious, and their anomalous position upset Mr Le Clercq, who again interfered with his daughter, telling her that she was to withdraw to the Poor Clare house at Verdun.   St Peter Fourier told Alix she must obey, and in great anguish of spirit she got ready.   But her father, moved as he said by some power beyond his understanding, withdrew his order and ceased to interfere.   There then occurred a determined attempt on the part of a Franciscan Recollect friar, Father Fleurant Boulengier, to " capture " the community for the Poor Clares.   Peter Fourier's belief in the divine acceptance of his foundation wavered : he recommended, with a force only short of a direct command, that they should regularize their position by joining the Clares—Alix and her companions refused.   " We have banded together ", they said, " to look after neglected children: why should we be dragged away from this and sent to a convent that God does not want us to go to ? "

Father Fourier, in equal good faith, interpreted the will of God in the opposite sense.   It is an old dilemma.   Or was he just trying them ?   In any case, after months of uncertainty, he accepted the sisters' decision, and so did Father Fleurant.

In 1601 St Peter Fourier and Bd Alix made their second foundation, at Saint-Mihiel ; Nancy, Pont-à-Mousson, Saint-Nicolas de Port, Verdun and Châlons followed, the last, in 1613, being the first outside Lorraine.   All this time there was no sign from Rome of official approval for the new congregation.   The novel request that day-pupils should be taken, and therefore admitted into the enclosure, roused hostility (" The Church is going to the dogs, sir ! ") ; and the delay in approbation lent an edge to wagging tongues and endangered the existence of the convents.   Fourier sent Bd Alix and another sister to the Ursulines in Paris to learn more about monastic life and teaching methods and again they were invited to give up a separate existence.   This time Alix seriously considered if it were not the best thing to do.   Father (afterwards cardinal) de Bérulle settled it.   " I don't believe ", he declared to her bluntly, " that God is asking for this fusion.   Dismiss it from your mind."

It was not till 1616 that in two bulls the Holy See signified its first approval of the Augustinian Canonesses of the Congregation of Our Lady.*   Subsequently the Bishop of Toul approved their constitutions ; and St Peter Fourier then proceeded to clothe thirteen of them with the habit, designed in accordance with what Bd Alix had seen our Lady wearing in the dream recorded above ; and then they all had to begin a twelve months' novitiate, in spite of the fact that some of

---

* Their style as " canonesses " was confirmed in 1628 ; it carried with it of course the obligation and privilege of reciting the Divine Office in choir.

them had been leading a conventual life for twenty years.   But all was not well.
The papal bulls of approbation had not mentioned the congregation as a whole,
but only its convent at Nancy.   Now there was already a certain " feeling "
between this house and the others, for Nancy was under the protection of Cardinal
Charles of Lorraine, and the primate of Lorraine, Antony de Lénoncourt, had
practically taken its direction out of Father Fourier's hands into his own.   The
apparent partiality of the bulls aggravated this spirit of dissension, and a very
unhappy state of affairs resulted.   In the upshot Bd Alix had to yield her rightful
place as superioress in the congregation to Mother Ganthe André, " without
whom ", in the words of Father Fourier, " our order would never have been
established ", though she and Alix were far from being in agreement about its
organization.

   That sort of trial heroic sanctity seems to take in its stride.   But that was not
all.   Bd Alix was subjected to personal attack and the venom of slanderous rumour.
At the same time she had to face spiritual dryness, temptations and a " dark night "
of great severity.   And as, in the words of one of her nuns, " she entered into the
sufferings of others so feelingly that she made them her own ", her burden was
indeed heavy : she had plenty of opportunity to put into practice her own axiom—
common to all saints and mystics—" I value one act of humility more than a
hundred ecstasies ".   Further opportunities were provided by St Peter Fourier
himself.   Bd Alix is now recognized as the co-foundress of the Augustinian
Canonesses of Our Lady ; but it was not so while she lived, and Father Fourier
did not allow it to appear so.   He consistently and openly " kept her in her place ".
It is possible that he was, in a sense, a little afraid of her, for in contrast with his
own solid, cautious temperament, Alix Le Clercq must often have seemed to him
alarmingly " imaginative ".

   In December 1621 she was allowed to resign the office of local superioress at
Nancy, and she entered upon a few weeks of radiant peace, which was in fact a
prelude to death a month later.   She had been seriously ill for a long time, and now
when it was known the doctors had given up hope all Nancy was grieved, from the
duke and duchess of Lorraine to the school-girls and the beggar-women.   St Peter
Fourier hurried to Nancy, but he would not enter the conventual enclosure till the
bishop ordered him to do so.   Then he heard Alix's confession and prepared her
for the passage " from death to life ".   On the Epiphany she took a solemn farewell
of her community, exhorting them to love and unity, and on January 9, after a
searching agony, the end came.   Bd Alix was not quite forty-six.

   High and low acclaimed her as a saint, and steps were taken to collect evidence
for the prosecution of her cause.   But nothing was done more definitely, war
pushed it out of sight, and it was not till 1947 that Alix Le Clercq was beatified.
Her body was buried in the crypt under the convent chapel at Nancy.   During
the Revolution this convent was sacked ; it is said that Bd Alix's body was hastily
buried in the garden for safety, but all efforts to find it have failed.   That would
have pleased her humility, she whose deeds of love and spiritual insights and visions
were so far as possible concealed.   She was completely at ease only when she could
be humble and obedient, teaching the ABC and simple addition to half-a-dozen
little children at Poussay or Mattaincourt, for instance.   But in the long disagree-
ments and uncertainties about the organization of the congregation, in such matters
she was mistress of herself and of the policies she believed right ; and she was
always an excellent superior.   But a Protestant historian, Professor Pfister, has

acutely remarked that, "When she was appointed to direct the Nancy house, she had only one ambition ; and that was again to be a simple sister, teaching their letters to the four and five-year-olds in the bottom class ". The last word about Bd Alix Le Clercq is with Mother Angélique Milly—" she was the child of deep silence ".

In 1666 the Nancy convent published what purported to be a life of Alix le Clercq but was in fact an extremely valuable collection of documents bearing on that life. It was due to a copy of this book coming into the hands of the young Count Gandelet that the cause of her beatification was begun by the Bishop of Saint-Dié in 1885. The first biography proper to be published appeared at Nancy in 1773 (one of 1766 remains in manuscript), and then not another till 1858, after which there were several. *La Mère Alix Le Clercq* (1935), by Canon Edmond Renard, is the standard modern work, full, critical and well written. In English there is a short but very good biography by Margaret St L. West (1947). Reference can also be made to the standard lives of St Peter Fourier by Father Bedel (1645), Dom Vuillemin (1897), and Father Rogie, of which the last is the best. The writer of the preface to the English life of Bd Alix speaks of the excellent methods used in the schools conducted by her congregation. Fourier himself used to instruct his canonesses in pedagogy, and brief reference to some of his enlightened educational ideas is made in the notice accorded to him herein on December 9. The feast of Bd Alix is now kept on October 22.

10 : ST MARCIAN (A.D. 471)

MARCIAN was born, and spent his life, in Constantinople, of a Roman family related to the imperial house of Theodosius. From his childhood he served God, and he secretly gave away great sums to the poor. About the year 455 the Patriarch Anatolius, disregarding the saint's protests of unworthiness, ordained him priest. In this new state Marcian saw himself under a stricter obligation than before of labouring to reach the summit of Christian perfection ; and whilst he made the instruction of the poor his favourite employment, he redoubled his earnestness in providing for their bodily needs, and was careful to relax no part of his own austerities. The severity of his morals was made a handle, by those who resented the tacit censure of such an example, to fasten upon him a suspicion of Novatianism, but his meekness at length triumphed over the slander. This persecution served more and more to purify his soul. His virtue only shone forth with greater lustre than ever when the cloud was dispersed, and the Patriarch Gennadius, with the great applause of the whole body of the clergy and people, conferred on him the dignity of *Oikonomos*, which was the second in that church. St Marcian built or restored a number of churches in Constantinople, notably that known as the Anastasis, and was famous for miracles both before and after his death, which probably occurred in 471. He has been regarded by some as a writer of liturgical hymns.

He is honoured both in the Greek Menaion and Roman Martyrology. See his ancient anonymous life in Surius and in the *Acta Sanctorum*, January 10. *Cf*. also DCB., vol. iii, p. 185 ; and K. Krumbacher, *Geschichte der Byzantinischen Literatur*, p. 663.

ST JOHN THE GOOD, BISHOP OF MILAN (A.D. 660)

THE see of the leading bishopric of Liguria had been transferred in the earlier part of the seventh century from Milan to Genoa. In the pontificate of St John Camillus Bonus it was again restored to Milan. We are told that he was a strenuous defender of orthodoxy against the monothelites, and that he took part in the Council of the Lateran in 649. Beyond this we know very little of the saint who is commemorated in the Roman Martyrology on this day. There is not much indication of *cultus* until after Archbishop Aribert in the eleventh century discovered the body of St John. A second translation was carried out by St Charles Borromeo in 1582. St John is said to have died on January 3, 660.

See *Acta Sanctorum*, January 10; and *Analecta Bollandiana*, vol. xv (1896), p. 357. *Cf.* P. Olcese, *Biografia di S. Giovanni Bono* (1894).

ST AGATHO, POPE   (A.D. 681)

AGATHO, a Sicilian Greek by birth, was remarkable for his benevolence and an engaging sweetness of temper. He had been married and engaged in secular pursuits for twenty years before he became a monk at Palermo ; and was treasurer of the Church at Rome when he succeeded Donus in the pontificate in 678. He presided by his three legates at the sixth general council (the third of Constantinople) in 680 against the monothelite heresy, which he confuted in a learned letter by the tradition of the apostolic church of Rome : " acknowledged ", says he, " by the whole Catholic Church to be the mother and mistress of all churches, and to derive her superior authority from St Peter, the prince of the apostles, to whom Christ committed His whole flock, with a promise that his faith should never fail ". This epistle was approved as a rule of faith by the same council, which declared that " Peter spoke by Agatho ". This pope restored St Wilfrid to the see of York, and granted privileges to several English monasteries. A terrible plague which devastated Rome at this period may have been at least the indirect cause of his own death, which occurred in 681.

St Agatho lived in troubled times. The reason he alleges in excusing the bad Greek of the legates whom he sent to Constantinople was that the graces of speech could not be cultivated amidst the incursions of barbarians, whilst with much difficulty they earned their daily subsistence by manual labour ; " but we preserve", said he with simplicity of heart, " the faith which our fathers have handed down to us ". The bishops, his legates, say the same thing : " Our countries are harassed by the fury of barbarous nations. We live in the midst of battles, raids and devastations : our lives pass in continual alarms, and we subsist by the labour of our hands." Pope Agatho himself had died before the council concluded its sessions.

See the *Acta Sanctorum* for January 10, and especially Duchesne, *Liber Pontificalis*, vol. i, pp. 350-358 ; *cf.* Mann, *Lives of the Popes*, vol. ii, pp. 23-48.

ST PETER ORSEOLO   (A.D. 987)

THE vocation of St Peter Orseolo (Urseolus) must count among the strangest of those recorded in ecclesiastical history. Born in 928 of a distinguished Venetian family, he seems already at the age of twenty to have been appointed to the command of the fleet of the city of the lagoons, in which office he conducted a successful campaign against the Dalmatian pirates who infested the Adriatic. How far he was personally involved in the popular outbreak of 976, which ended in the violent death of the Doge Peter Candiani IV, and in the destruction by fire of a large part of the city, cannot be clearly determined. The testimony of St Peter Damian which attributes the responsibility to Orseolo can only be accepted with reserve.

It was, however, Orseolo who was chosen doge in place of the murdered Candiani, and the best modern authorities pay a high tribute to his energy and tact during his brief administration. " He was ", we are told, " a man of saintly character, but like all his race possessing higher qualities of statesmanship than were to be found in his predecessors in the ducal chair. His first care was to repair the damage wrought by the fire. He began the building of a new palace and church. He renewed the treaty with Istria. But his great service to the state lay in this, that he met and settled, to the nominal satisfaction of Otto II, the claims of the widowed dogaressa Gualdrada. . On these terms Gualdrada signed a quittance of all claims against the State of Venice." The grievances of Gualdrada had created a great political crisis, but this was now safely tided over.

Then an astounding thing happened. On the night of September 1, 978, Peter Orseolo secretly left Venice and took refuge in the Benedictine abbey of Cuxa, in Roussillon on the borders of France and Spain. His wife, to whom he had been married for thirty-two years, and his only son, who was himself destined to become one of the greatest of the Venetian doges, were apparently for a long time in entire ignorance of the place of his retreat. Still, Peter's apparently sudden resolution may not have been so entirely unpremeditated as it seems. There is early evidence for the belief that he and his wife had lived as brother and sister ever since the birth of their only child, and it has also been suggested that a letter of Ratherius, addressed to him possibly as early as 968, shows that Peter had already entertained the idea of becoming a monk. There is in any case no doubt that at Cuxa Orseolo led for a while a life of the strictest asceticism and self-effacement under the holy Abbot Guarinus ; and then, desirous of still greater solitude, he built a hermitage for himself, probably at the urging of St Romuald, whom he met at Cuxa, and who was the great propagator of this particular development of the Benedictine vocation. St Peter died in 987, and many miracles were said to have taken place at his tomb.

See Mabillon, vol. v, pp. 851 *seq.* ; Tolra, *Saint Pierre Orseolo* (1897) ; *Analecta Bollandiana*, vol. xvii (1898), p. 252 ; BHL., n. 986. And *cf.* H. F. Brown in the *Cambridge Mediaeval History*, vol. iv, p. 403 (quoted above).

ST WILLIAM, ARCHBISHOP OF BOURGES   (A.D. 1209)

WILLIAM DE DONJEON, belonging to an illustrious family of Nevers, was educated by his uncle, Peter, Archdeacon of Soissons, and he was early made canon, first of Soissons and afterwards of Paris ; but he soon took the resolution of abandoning the world altogether, and retired into the solitude of Grandmont Abbey, where he lived with great regularity in that austere order, till, seeing its peace disturbed by a contest which arose between the choir monks and lay-brothers, he passed into the Cistercians, then in wonderful repute for sanctity. He took the habit in the abbey of Pontigny, and was after some time chosen abbot, first of Fontaine-Jean, in the diocese of Sens, and secondly in 1187 of Châlis, near Senlis, a much more numerous monastery, also a filiation of Pontigny, built by Louis the Fat in 1136, a little before his death. St William always reputed himself the last among his brethren ; and the sweetness of his expression testified to the joy and peace that overflowed his soul, and made virtue appear engaging even in the midst of formidable austerities.

On the death of Henry de Sully, Archbishop of Bourges, the clergy of that church requested his brother Eudo, Bishop of Paris, to assist them in the election of a pastor. Desirous to choose some abbot of the Cistercian Order, they put on the altar the names of three, written on as many slips of parchment. This manner of election by lot would have been superstitious had it been done relying on a miracle without the warrant of divine inspiration. But it did not deserve this censure, when all the persons proposed seemed equally worthy and fit, as the choice was only recommended to God, and left to this issue by following the rules of His ordinary providence and imploring His light. Eudo accordingly, having made his prayer, drew first the name of the abbot William, to whom also the majority of the votes of the clergy had been already given. It was on November 23, 1200. This news overwhelmed William. He never would have acquiesced had he not received a double command in virtue of obedience, one from Pope Innocent III, the other from his superior, the Abbot of Cîteaux. He left his solitude with tears, and soon after was consecrated.

In this new dignity St William's first care was to bring both his exterior and interior life up to the highest possible standard, being very sensible that a man's first task is to honour God in his own soul. He redoubled his austerities, saying it was now incumbent on him to do penance for others as well as for himself. He always wore a hair-shirt under his religious habit, and never added or diminished anything in his clothing whatever the season of the year; and he never ate any flesh-meat, though he had it at his table for guests. The attention he paid to his flock was no less remarkable, especially in assisting the poor both spiritually and corporally, saying that he was chiefly sent for them. He was most gentle in dealing with penitent sinners, but inflexible towards the impenitent, though he refused to have recourse to the civil power against them, the usual remedy of that age. Many such he at last reclaimed by his sweetness and charity. Certain great men abusing his leniency, usurped the rights of his church; but William strenuously defended them even against the king himself, notwithstanding his threats to confiscate his lands. By humility and patience he overcame, on more than one occasion, the opposition of his chapter and other clergy. He converted many Albigensian heretics, and was preparing for a mission among them at the time he was seized with his last illness. He persisted, nevertheless, in preaching a farewell sermon to his people, which increased his fever to such a degree that he was obliged to postpone his journey and take to his bed. The night following, perceiving his last hour was at hand, he desired to anticipate the Nocturns, which are said at midnight; but having made the sign of the cross on his lips and breast, he was unable to pronounce more than the first two words. Then, at a sign which he made, he was laid on ashes, and thus St William died, a little past midnight, on the morning of January 10, 1209. His body was interred in his cathedral, and being honoured by many miracles it was enshrined in 1217, and in the year following he was canonized by Pope Honorius III.

See the *Acta Sanctorum* for January 10, and the *Analecta Bollandiana*, vol. iii (1884), pp. 271-361   BHL., nn. 1283-1284.

BD GREGORY X, POPE   (A.D. 1276)

THEOBALD VISCONTI belonged to an illustrious Italian family and was born at Piacenza in 1210. In his youth he was distinguished for his virtue and his success as a student. He devoted himself especially to canon law, which he began in Italy and pursued at Paris and Liège. He was acting as archdeacon of this last church when he received an order from Pope Clement IV to preach the crusade for the recovery of the Holy Land. A tender compassion for the distressed situation of the servants of Christ in those parts moved the holy archdeacon to undertake a dangerous pilgrimage to Palestine, where Prince Edward of England then was. At this time the see of Rome had been vacant almost three years, from the death of Clement IV in November 1268, since the cardinals who were assembled at Viterbo could not come to an agreement in the choice of a pope. At last, by common consent, they referred the election to a committee of six amongst them, who on September 1, 1271 nominated Theobald Visconti.

Arriving in Rome in March, he was first ordained priest, then consecrated bishop, and crowned on the 27th of the same month, in 1272. He took the name of Gregory X, and to procure the most effectual succour for the Holy Land he called a general council to meet at Lyons. This fourteenth general council, the second of Lyons, was opened in May 1274. Among those assembled were St Albert the Great and St Philip Benizi ; St Thomas Aquinas died on his way thither, and St Bonaventure died at the council. In the fourth session the Greek legates on behalf of the Eastern emperor and patriarch restored communion between the Byzantine church and the Holy See. Pope Gregory, we are told, shed tears whilst the *Te Deum* was sung. Unhappily the reconciliation was short-lived.

After the council, Bd Gregory devoted all his energies to concerting measures for carrying its decrees into execution, particularly those relating to the crusade in the East, which, however, never set out. This unwearied application to business, and the fatigues of his journey across the Alps on his return to Rome brought on a serious illness, of which he died at Arezzo on January 10, 1276. The name of Gregory X was added to the Roman Martyrology by Pope Benedict XIV ; his holiness was always recognized, and had he lived longer he would doubtless have left a deeper mark on the Church.

The account of his life and miracles in the archives of the tribunal of the Rota may be found in Benedict XIV, *De canoniz.*, bk ii, appendix 8. See likewise his life, copied from the MS. history of several popes by Bernard Guidonis, published by Muratori, *Scriptor. Ital.*, vol. iii, p. 597, and another life, written before 1297, in which mention is made of miraculous cures performed by him (*ibid.*, pp. 599, 604). There is also, of course, a copious modern literature regarding Bd Gregory X, dealing more especially with his relation to politics and his share in the election of the Emperor Rudolf of Hapsburg. It may be sufficient to mention the works of Zisterer, Otto and Redlich. The *Regesta* of Gregory X have been edited by Jean Guiraud.

11 : ST HYGINUS, POPE   (*c.* A.D. 142)

IN the Roman Martyrology St Hyginus is described as a martyr, but there is no early evidence of this. We are told in the *Liber Pontificalis* that he was a Greek by birth, but the further statement that he had been a philosopher is probably due to some confusion with another Hyginus. Eusebius lets us know that his predecessor died during the first year of the Emperor Antoninus Pius, so that it is likely that the pontificate of Hyginus lasted from 138 to 142. From St Irenaeus we learn that at this time two Gnostic heresiarchs, Valentinus and Cerdo, were present in Rome and caused trouble in the Church, but how far the trouble had progressed before Hyginus himself was summoned to his reward is not certain.

See Duchesne, *Liber Pontificalis*, vol. i, p. 131 ; *Acta Sanctorum*, January 11.

ST THEODOSIUS THE CENOBIARCH　　(A.D. 529)

ST THEODOSIUS was born at Garissus, incorrectly, it seems, called Mogarissus, in Cappadocia in 423. He was ordained reader, but being moved by Abraham's example in quitting his country and friends, he resolved to do likewise. He accordingly started for Jerusalem, but went out of his road to visit the famous St Simeon Stylites on his pillar, who foretold many circumstances of his future life, and gave him advice regarding them. Having satisfied his devotion in visiting the holy places in Jerusalem, he began to consider in what manner he should dedicate himself to God. The dangers of living without a guide made him prefer a monastery to a hermitage ; and he therefore put himself under the direction of a holy man named Longinus, who soon conceived a warm affection for his disciple. A lady having built a church on the high road to Bethlehem, Longinus could not well refuse her request that his pupil should undertake the charge of it ; but Theodosius could not easily be induced to consent : absolute commands were necessary before he would undertake the charge. Nor did he govern long ; instead he retired to a cave at the top of a neighbouring mountain.

When many sought to serve God under his direction Theodosius at first determined only to admit six or seven, but was soon obliged to receive a greater number, and at length came to a resolution never to reject any that presented themselves with dispositions that seemed sincere. The first lesson which he taught his monks was by means of a great grave he had dug, which might serve for the common burial-place of the community, that by the presence of this reminder they might more perfectly learn to die daily. The burial-place being made, the abbot one day said, " The grave is made ; who will first occupy it ? " Basil, a priest, falling on his knees, said to St Theodosius, " Let me be the first, if only you will give me your blessing." The abbot ordered the prayers of the Church for the dead to be offered up for him, and on the fortieth day Basil departed to the Lord in peace, without any apparent sickness.

When the holy company of disciples was twelve in number, it happened that at Easter they had nothing to eat- they had not even bread for the sacrifice. Some murmured, but the saint bade them trust in God and He would provide : which was soon remarkably verified by the arrival of a train of mules loaded with provisions. The sanctity and miracles of St Theodosius attracting numbers who desired to serve God under his direction, the available space proved too small for their reception. Accordingly he built a spacious monastery at a place called Cathismus, not far from Bethlehem, and it was soon filled with monks. To this monastery were annexed three infirmaries : one for the sick ; another for the aged and feeble ; the third for such as had lost their reason, a condition then commonly ascribed to diabolical possession, but due, it would seem, in many cases, to rash and extravagant practices of asceticism. All succours, spiritual and temporal, were afforded in these infirmaries, with admirable order and benevolence. There were other buildings for the reception of strangers, in which Theodosius exercised an unbounded hospitality. We are told, indeed, that there were one day above a hundred tables served ; and that food, when insufficient for the number of guests, was more than once miraculously multiplied by his prayers.

The monastery itself was like a city of saints in the midst of a desert, and in it reigned regularity, silence, charity and peace. There were four churches belonging to it, one for each of the three several nations of which his community was chiefly composed, each speaking a different language ; the fourth was for the use of such as were in a state of penance, including those recovering from their lunatic or possessed condition before-mentioned. The nations into which his community was divided were the Greeks, who were by far the most numerous, and consisted of all those that came from any province of the empire ; the Armenians, with whom were joined the Arabians and Persians ; and, thirdly, the Bessi, who comprehended all the northern nations below Thrace, or all who used the Slavonic tongue. Each nation sang the first part of the Eucharistic Liturgy to the end of the gospel in their own church, but after the gospel all met in the church of the Greeks, where they celebrated the essential part of the liturgy in Greek, and communicated all together. The monks passed a considerable part of the day and night in the church, and at the times not set apart for public prayer and necessary rest everyone was obliged to apply himself to some trade or manual labour not incompatible with recollection, in order that the house might be supplied with conveniences. Sallust, Patriarch of Jerusalem, appointed St Sabas head of all the hermits, and our saint of the cenobites, or men living in community, throughout Palestine, whence he was styled " the Cenobiarch " These two great servants of God lived in close friendship, and it was not long before they were also united in their sufferings for the Church.

The Emperor Anastasius patronized the Eutychian heresy, and used all possible means to win our saint over to his own views. In 513 he deposed Elias, Patriarch of Jerusalem, just as he had previously banished Flavian II of Antioch, and intruded Severus into that see. Theodosius and Sabas maintained boldly the rights of Elias, and of John his successor ; whereupon the imperial officers thought it advisable to connive at their proceedings, considering the great authority they had acquired by their sanctity. Soon after, the emperor sent Theodosius a considerable sum of money, for charitable uses in appearance, but in reality to engage him in his interest. The saint accepted it, and distributed it all among the poor. Anastasius, now persuading himself that Theodosius was as good as gained over to his cause, sent him a heretical profession of faith, in which the divine and human natures in Christ were confounded into one, and desired him to sign it. The saint wrote him an answer full of apostolic spirit, and for a time the emperor was more peaceable. But he soon renewed his persecuting edicts against the orthodox, despatching troops everywhere to have them put into execution. On intelligence of this, Theodosius travelled through Palestine, exhorting all to stand firm in the faith of the four general councils. At Jerusalem he cried out from the pulpit, " If anyone receives not the four general councils as the four gospels, let him be anathema." So bold an action put courage into those whom the edicts had terrified. His discourses had a wonderful effect on the people, and God gave a sanction to his zeal by some striking miracles. One of these was, that on his going out of the church at Jerusalem, a woman was healed of a cancer by touching his garments. The emperor sent an order for his banishment, which was executed ; but dying soon after, Theodosius was recalled by his successor, Justin.

During the last year of his life St Theodosius was afflicted with a painful infirmity, in which he gave proof of heroic patience and submission to the will of God ; for being advised by a witness of his sufferings to pray that God would grant him some ease, he would give no ear to the suggestion, alleging that such ideas implied a lack of patience. Perceiving that his end was close at hand, he addressed a last exhortation to his disciples, and foretold many things which came to pass after his death.   He went to his reward in 529, in the one hundred and fifth year of his age.   Peter, Patriarch of Jerusalem, and the whole country were present at his funeral, which was honoured by miracles.   He was buried in his first cell, called the cave of the Magi, because the wise men who came to find Christ soon after his birth were said to have lodged in it.   A military commander, on his march against the Persians, begged to have the hair-shirt which the saint used to wear, and believed that he owed the victory which he obtained over them to the prayers of St Theodosius.

There are two main sources for the history of St Theodosius, one the biography written by his disciple Theodore, Bishop of Petra, the other a shorter abstract by Cyril of Skythopolis. The Greek text of both of these was printed for the first time by H. Usener — see his book *Der heilige Theodosios* (1890).   To the critical material thus provided, K. Krumbacher has made important additions in the *Sitzungsberichte* of the Munich Academy for 1892, pp. 220-379.   *Cf.* also the *Byzantinische Zeitschrift* (1897), vol. vi, pp. 357 *seq.*   *Acta Sanctorum*, January 11 ; and E. Schwartz, *Kyrillos von Skythopolis* (1939), for text of the shorter life.

ST SALVIUS, OR SAUVE, BISHOP OF AMIE   (*c.* A.D. 625)

FAMOUS for miracles, Salvius succeeded Ado in the see of Amiens and flourished in the reign of Theodoric II.   His relics formerly were venerated at Montreuil in Picardy, in the Benedictine abbey which bore his name, whither they were translated from the cathedral of Amiens several years after his death, as is related in his anonymous life, a worthless compilation, largely borrowed, as Duchesne points out, from the account given of another St Salvius, of Albi, by Gregory of Tours.   A relic of Salvius was formerly kept in the cathedral of Canterbury.   This saint must not be confounded with St Salvius of Albi, nor with the martyr of this name in Africa, on whose festival St Augustine delivered a sermon.   St Salvius is styled martyr in the Roman Martyrology, but for this, as Father Bollandus himself noted nearly three centuries ago, there is no foundation.

See the *Acta Sanctorum* for January 11 ; Duchesne, *Fastes Épiscopaux ;* Corblet, *Hagiographie d'Amiens*, vol. iii, pp. 463 *seq.*

12 : ST ARCADIUS, MARTYR   (A.D. 304 ?)

THE time of this saint's martyrdom is not mentioned in his acts ; some place it under Valerian, others under Diocletian ; he seems to have suffered in some city of Mauritania, probably the capital, Caesarea.   The fury of the persecutors was at its height.   Upon the least suspicion they broke into houses, and if they found a Christian they treated him upon the spot with the greatest cruelty, their impatience not suffering them to wait for his formal indictment. Every day new sacrileges were committed ; the faithful were compelled to assist at superstitious sacrifices, to lead victims crowned with flowers through the streets, to burn incense before idols.   Arcadius, seeing the terrible conditions prevailing, withdrew to a solitary place in the country, but his flight could not be long a secret ; for his non-appearance at the public sacrifices made the governor send soldiers to his house, who, finding one of his relations there, seized him, and the governor ordered him to be kept in custody till Arcadius should be taken.

The martyr, informed of his friend's danger, went into the city, and presenting himself to the judge, said, " If on my account you detain my innocent kinsman in chains, release him ; I, Arcadius, am come in person to give an account of myself, and to declare to you that he knew not where I was." " I am willing ", answered the judge, " to pardon not only him, but you also, on condition that you will sacrifice to the gods." Arcadius refused firmly ; whereupon the judge said to the executioners, " Take him, and let him desire death without being able to obtain it. Cut off his limbs joint by joint, but do this so slowly that the wretch may know what it is to abandon the gods of his ancestors for an unknown deity ". The executioners dragged Arcadius to the place where many other victims of Christ had already suffered ; and he stretched out his neck, expecting to be decapitated ; but the executioner bid him hold out his hand, and, joint after joint, chopped off his fingers, arms and shoulders. In the same barbarous manner were cut off his toes, feet, legs and thighs. The martyr held out his limbs one after another with invincible courage, repeating, " Lord, teach me thy wisdom " for the tormentors had forgotten to cut out his tongue. After so many martyrdoms, his body lay a mere trunk. But Arcadius surveying his scattered limbs all around him, and offering them to God, said, " Happy members, you at last truly belong to God, being all made a sacrifice to Him ! " Then to the people he said, " You who have been present at this bloody tragedy, learn that all torments seem as nothing to one who has an everlasting crown before his eyes. Your gods are not gods ; renounce their worship. He alone for whom I suffer and die is the true God. To die for Him is to live." Discoursing in this manner to those about him, he died, the pagans being struck with astonishment at such a miracle of patience. The Christians gathered together his scattered limbs and laid them in one tomb.

See the *Acta Sanctorum* for January 12, where the *passio* is printed, as well as a panegyric preached by St Zeno of Verona. In spite of the fact that the *passio* is included by Ruinart in his *Acta sincera*, the document belongs rather to the category of historical romances. *Cf.* Delehaye, *Origines du culte des martyrs* (1933), p. 391.

SS. TIGRIUS AND EUTROPIUS, MARTYRS   (A.D. 404)

LENGTHY eulogium may be found on this day in the latest edition of the Roman Martyrology in the following terms : " At Constantinople, of SS. Tigrius a priest and Eutropius a reader, who, in the time of the Emperor Arcadius, having been falsely accused of causing the conflagration by which the cathedral church and the senate-hall were burnt down, as an act of reprisal, it was said, for the banishment of St John Chrysostom, suffered under the city-prefect Optatus, who was addicted to the superstitious worship of the false gods and was a bitter enemy to the Christian religion." This seems to imply that both Tigrius and Eutropius were put to death, but though Eutropius, who is described as a youth of great personal beauty and irreproachable life, undoubtedly perished under the severity of the torture to which they were both subjected, the priest Tigrius appears to have survived. We read in the *Dialogue* usually attributed to Palladius that he was afterwards banished to Mesopotamia. Tigrius was a eunuch and an enfranchised slave, and was very dear to St John Chrysostom for his gentleness and charity. The object of the torture, during which not only scourging and racking were employed, but burning torches were applied to the most sensitive parts of the bodies of the victims, was to elicit information which might lead to the discovery of the perpetrators of the outrage, but no compromising word was spoken by either of the sufferers.

See the *Acta Sanctorum* for January 12, where the accounts of Sozomen and Nicephorus Callistus are quoted at length ; *cf.* also DCB., vol. ii, pp. 11, 402, and iv, 1027. The eulogium in earlier editions of the Roman Martyrology, including the *editio typica* published in 1913, is much shorter.

ST CAESARIA, Virgin   (*c.* A.D. 529)

St Caesarius, Bishop of Arles, founded about the year 512 a great nunnery for virgins and widows, and appointed his sister, Caesaria, as its first abbess.   She soon had under her rule a community of 200 members, who seem to have devoted themselves to every kind of good work, more especially the protection and instruction of the young, the relieving of the poor and the care of the sick.   The nuns made their own clothes, and were generally employed in weaving and needlework ; they were allowed to embroider and to wash and mend clothes for persons that lived out of the convent.   The ornaments of their church were only of woollen or linen cloth, and plain.   Some of them worked at transcribing books.   They all studied two hours every day, and one of them read to the rest during part of the time they were at work.   Flesh-meat was forbidden, except to the sick, and the rule enjoined the use of baths, but pointing out that they were for health, not for enjoyment : nor were they to be indulged in during Lent.   Only the abbess and her assistant were exempt from helping in the housework ; and enclosure was permanent and complete.   St Gregory of Tours describes the abbess herself as " blessed and holy ", and Venantius Fortunatus more than once refers to her in his verse in glowing terms.   St Caesaria must have died about the year 529, probably on January 12.

See the *Acta Sanctorum* for January 12, where the rule is printed which St Caesarius drew up for the nuns ; critical edition by G. Morin in *Florilegium patristicum* (1933).   *Cf.* his article in *Revue bénédictine*, vol. xliv (1932), pp. 5–20.   Caesarius himself by his will left nearly all his property to this nunnery.

ST VICTORIAN, Abbot   (A.D. 558)

If anyone had been disposed to doubt the historic existence of St Victorian, the matter was set at rest by an inscription published by Hübner in 1900.   It is certain that Victorian, who was apparently born in Italy and then lived for some time in France, became abbot of Asan in Aragon, where he ruled for many years a vigorous and devout community.   Venantius Fortunatus, within thirty or forty years of his death, wrote a very laudatory epitaph eulogizing his virtues, his miracles and his great reputation as a teacher of monastic observance.   A Latin life of him is extant, which probably dates from the eighth century or a little later.   It is also now established that he died in 558.

See *Acta Sanctorum*, January 12 ; Venantius Fortunatus, *Carmina* (iv, 11), and especially Fita in *Boletin de la real Academia de la Historia* (1900), vol. xxxvii, pp. 491 *seq.*

ST BENEDICT, or BENET, BISCOP, Abbot of Wearmouth and Jarrow   (A.D. 690)

Benedict Biscop, a man of noble birth at the court of Oswy, king of the Northumbrians, at the age of twenty-five bade adieu to the world, made a journey of devotion to Rome, and at his return devoted himself wholly to the study of the Bible and other holy exercises.   Some time after he travelled thither a second time, burning with the desire of fuller knowledge of divine things.   From Rome he went to the great monastery of Lérins, renowned for its regular discipline ; there he took the monastic habit, and spent two years in exact observance of the rule.   After this he returned to Rome, where he received an order from Pope St Vitalian to accompany St Theodore, the new archbishop of Canterbury, and St Adrian, to England. When he arrived at Canterbury, St Theodore committed to Benedict the care of the monastery of SS. Peter and Paul at that city.   He stayed two years in Kent, giving himself up to study and prayer under the discipline of those two excellent masters.   Then he took a fourth journey to Rome, with the view of perfecting himself in the rules and practice of a monastic life.   For this purpose he made a considerable stay in Rome and other places, and he brought home with him a choice library, with relics and sacred pictures.   When he returned to Northumberland, King Egfrid bestowed on him seventy hides of land for building a monastery   this the saint founded in 674 at the mouth of the river Wear, whence it was called Wearmouth.   St Benedict went over to France, and brought back with him skilful masons, who built the church for this monastery of stone, and after the Roman fashion ; till that time stone buildings were rare in north England : even the church of Lindisfarne was of wood, covered with a thatch of straw and reeds, till Bishop Edbert had both the roof and the walls covered with sheets of lead, as Bede mentions.   St Benedict also brought over glaziers from France, for the art of making glass was then unknown here.

His first monastery of Wearmouth was dedicated in honour of St Peter ; and such was the edification which it gave that the king added a second donation of land, on which Biscop built another monastery in 685, at Jarrow on the Tyne, six miles distant from the former, this latter being called St Paul's.   These two monasteries were almost looked upon as one, and St Benedict governed them both, though he placed in each a superior, who continued subject to him, his long journeys to Rome and other absences making this substitution necessary.   In the church of St Peter at Wearmouth he set up pictures of the Blessed Virgin, the Twelve Apostles, the history of the Gospel and the visions in the Revelation of St John.   That of St Paul's at Jarrow he adorned with other pictures, disposed in such a manner as to represent the harmony between the Old and the New Testament, and the conformity of the types in the one to the reality in the other.   Thus Isaac carrying the wood which was to be employed in the sacrifice of himself, was explained by Jesus Christ carrying His cross, on which He was to finish His sacrifice ; and the brazen serpent was illustrated by our Saviour's crucifixion.   Not content with these pictures, books and relics, St Benedict on his last voyage brought back with him from Rome the abbot of St Martin's, who was the precentor of St Peter's. This abbot, John by name, was expert in music, and our saint persuaded Pope St Agatho to send him in order that he might instruct the English monks in the Gregorian chant and in the Roman ceremonial for singing the divine office.   These two monasteries thus became the best-equipped in England, and St Benedict's purchase of books was of special significance, for it made possible the work of the Venerable Bede.

About the year 686 St Benedict was stricken with paralysis in his lower limbs. He lay three years crippled and suffering, and for a considerable time was entirely confined to his bed.   During this long illness, not being able to raise his voice or make much effort, at every canonical hour some of his monks came to him, and whilst they sang the psalms appointed, he endeavoured as well as he could to join not only his heart but also his voice with theirs.   In his realization of the presence of God he seemed never to relax, and he frequently and earnestly exhorted his monks to observe faithfully the rule he had given them.   " You must not think ", he said, " that the constitutions which you have received from me were of my own devising ; for having in my frequent journeys visited seventeen well-ordered monasteries, I acquainted myself with their rules, and chose the best to leave you as my legacy."   He died on January 12, 690.   According to William of Malmesbury his relics were translated to Thorney Abbey in 970, but the monks of Glastonbury thought themselves possessed of at least part of them.   St Benet Biscop's feast is kept by the Benedictines of the English congregation and in the dioceses of Liverpool and Hexham (February 13), with a commemoration in Southwark.

The true name of this saint was Biscop Baducing, as we learn from Eddius in his life of St Wilfrid.   He is mentioned in the Roman Martyrology on this day.   Practically all our information about him is derived from Bede, who was entrusted to his care at the age of seven.   Bede wrote of his venerated abbot in his *Historia Abbatum*, as well as in his *Ecclesiastical History*, and there is also a sermon *in natale S. Benedicti (Biscop)* which is attributed to Bede and which Dr Plummer believes to be authentically his.   It is to be noted, however, that Bede's *Historia Abbatum* is founded upon an earlier *Historia Abbatum Gyrvensium*, the author of which is not known.   See Plummer's edition of the *Ecclesiastical History*, with its preface and notes ; and T. Allison in *Church Quarterly Review*, vol. cvii (1928), pp. 57–79.

13 : THIS DAY IS NOW KEPT IN HONOUR OF THE BAPTISM OF OUR LORD JESUS CHRIST IN THE RIVER JORDAN

ST AGRECIUS, BISHOP OF TRIER   (A.D. 329 ?)

THE story of St Agrecius (Agritius) has of late years acquired a certain adventitious interest owing to the discussions regarding the authenticity of the " Holy Coat of Trier ".   According to the life of the saint, a document which is certainly not older than the eleventh century, and which modern scholars pronounce to be entirely fabulous, Agrecius was first of all patriarch of Antioch, and was then, at the instance of the Empress St Helen, the mother of Constantine, appointed bishop of Trier by Pope St Silvester.   He found that that part of Germany, though evangelized more than two centuries before, had almost fallen back into paganism, and he set to work to build churches and to establish closer relations with the centre of Christendom.   In this task he was encouraged by his patroness St Helen, who in particular obtained for him a share of the precious relics which she had been instrumental in recovering from the Holy Land.   Those sent to Trier included one of the nails of the cross, the knife used at the Last Supper, the bodies of SS. Lazarus and Martha, etc., and also apparently our Lord's seamless robe.   The historically worthless character of the life discredits this story, and the ivory plaque of Byzantine origin which is appealed to as a representation of SS. Silvester and Agrecius in a chariot bringing the casket of relics to Trier is more probably to be explained as referring to another quite different translation of relics to Constantinople under the Emperor Leo I (457–474).   St Silvester is also stated to have conceded to Trier in the person of Agrecius a primacy over all the bishops of Gaul and Germany.   Setting aside these fictions, the only facts known to us regarding St Agrecius are that he assisted as bishop of Trier at the Council of Arles in 314, and that he was succeeded in the same see by St Maximinus.

See *Acta Sanctorum*, January 13 ; V Sauerland, *Trierer Geschichtsquellen des xi Jahr-hunderts* (1889), pp. 55-212   S. Beissel, *Geschichte der Trierer Kirchen* (1887), vol. i, pp. 71 *seq.* ; E. Winheller, *Die Lebensbeschreibungen der vorkarol. Bischöfe von Trier* (1935), pp. 121-145   and DHG., vol. i, c. 1014.   For the plaque, see Kraus, *Geschichte der christ-lichen Kunst*, vol. i, p. 502, and the references there given in note 4.   Kraus claims G. B. de Rossi as supporting his interpretation of the plaque.   By Kraus this ivory carving is said to be a work of the fifth century ; A. Maskell, *Ivories*, p. 419, dates it seventh to ninth century. Both are agreed that the work is Byzantine.

ST BERNO, Abbot of Cluny   (A.D. 927)

CONSIDERING the immense influence exercised by Cluny in the development of the monasticism, and indeed of the whole religious life, of western Europe from the tenth to the twelfth centuries, we know strangely little of the personality of its first abbot.   Berno seems to have been a man of good family and some wealth.   He was himself the founder of the abbey of Gigny, in which he became abbot, having already been the reforming superior of Baume-les-Messieurs, and finally he was pitched upon by Duke William of Aquitaine to rule the monastery which he planned.   The site chosen by St Berno was at Cluny, not far from Mâcon in the centre of France.   The abbey of Cluny was immediately subject to the Holy See, and in the foundations subsequently made the principle of centralization became dominant ; but in Berno's day there was no machinery for the central control of the houses with whose reform he was entrusted.   Berno ruled from 910 to 927, and perhaps the highest tribute to his personal worth was the devotion always paid to him by St Odo, who had joined him as a novice at Baume and who, after Berno's death in 927, was to succeed him at Cluny as abbot, perhaps the most famous and energetic of all its rulers.

See *Acta Sanctorum*, January 13 ; E. Sackur, *Die Cluniacenser*, vol. i, pp. 36 *seq* ; Berlière in *Revue Bénédictine*, vol. ix, p. 498 ; and P. Schmitz, *Histoire de l'ordre de St Benoît*, vol. i (1942), pp. 130-132.

BD GODFREY OF KAPPENBERG   (A.D. 1127)

GODFREY, who died at the age of thirty, belongs to the category of those youthful saints who spent the few years of their life on earth in making preparation for Heaven.   He was count of Kappenberg and lord of a great Westphalian estate in the diocese of Münster.   He was married to a young wife of a family as distin-guished as his own.   Coming, however, under the influence of St Norbert, the founder of the Premonstratensian canons, he determined to surrender his castle of Kappenberg to be converted into a monastery of that order ; and he followed this up by persuading his wife and brother to renounce the world like himself and to become religious under St Norbert's direction.   His purpose encountered the most violent opposition from his father-in-law, who even threatened to take his life.   Godfrey, however, persisted in making over all his possessions to the Premonstratensians.   He built a convent near Kappenberg, where his wife and two of his own sisters took the veil ; he also founded hospitals and other charitable institutions, and himself became a canonical novice, performing the most menial duties and washing the feet of the patients and the pilgrims to whom his hospital gave shelter.   Though he had received minor orders, he did not live long enough to reach the priesthood.   On January 13, 1127 he died in great joy of spirit, declaring that not for all the world would he wish his life to be prolonged. His feast is kept in the Premonstratensian Order on January 16.

See the *Acta Sanctorum* for January 13, where two Latin lives are printed ; also Kirkfleet' *History of St Norbert* (1916), pp. 140-151 ; Spilbeeck, *Le B. Godefroid* (1892) ; BHL.' n. 533.

BD JUTTA OF HUY, Widow   (A.D. 1228)

JUTTA (Juetta) was one of the mystics who seem to have been influenced by that remarkable ascetic revival in the Low Countries which preceded by a few years the preaching of St Dominic and St Francis in southern Europe. She was born of a well-to-do family at Huy, near Liège, in 1158. While still only a child she was forced by her father, very much against her inclination, to marry. After five years of wedded life, and after bearing her husband three children, she was left a widow at the age of eighteen. Then, after an interval, during which her good looks, to her great distress, attracted a number of suitors who pestered her with their attentions, she devoted herself for ten years to nursing in the lazar-house ; but even this life did not seem to her sufficiently austere, and she wished to exchange the role of Martha for that of Mary. She accordingly had herself walled up in a room close beside her lepers, and lived there as an anchoress from 1182 until her death, January 13, 1228. Her mystical experiences, which are set down in some detail in a contemporary Latin biography, are of great interest. By her prayers she converted her father and one of her two surviving sons, who had taken to evil courses ; the other had joined the Cistercians and became abbot of Orval. She had, as we find in the case of so many saintly mystics, an extraordinary power of reading the thoughts of others, and apparently a knowledge of distant events ; she also displayed the greatest charity in directing and helping the many souls who came to consult her in her anchorage.

See the life by Hugh of Floreffe, a Premonstratensian, printed in the *Acta Sanctorum* for January 13.

BD VERONICA OF BINASCO, Virgin   (A.D. 1497)

ALL states of life furnish abundant means for attaining holiness, and it is only owing to our sloth and tepidity that we neglect to make use of them. Bd Veronica could boast of no worldly advantages either of birth or fortune. Her parents maintained their family by hard work in a village near Milan, and her father never sold a horse, or anything else that he dealt in, without being more careful to acquaint the purchaser with all that was faulty in it than to recommend its good qualities. His consequent poverty prevented his giving his daughter any schooling, so that she never even learned to read ; but his own and his wife's example and simple instructions filled her heart with love of God, and the holy mysteries of religion engrossed her entirely. She was, notwithstanding, a good worker, and so obedient, humble and submissive that she seemed to have no will of her own. When she was weeding, reaping or at any other labour in the fields she strove to work at a distance from her companions, to entertain herself the more freely with her heavenly thoughts. The rest admired her love of solitude, and on coming to her, often found her countenance bathed in tears, which they sometimes perceived to flow in great abundance, though they did not know the source to be devotion, so carefully did Veronica conceal what passed between her and God.

Veronica conceived a great desire to become a nun in the poor and austere convent of St Martha, of the Order of St Augustine, in Milan. To qualify herself for this she sat up at night to learn to read and write. One day, being in great trouble about her little progress, the Mother of God bade her banish that anxiety, for it was enough if she knew three letters The first, purity of the affections, by setting her whole heart on God ; the second, never to murmur or grow impatient at the sins or misbehaviour of others, but to bear them with patience, and humbly to pray for them ; the third, to set apart some time every day to meditate on the passion of Christ. After three years preparation, Veronica was admitted to the religious habit in St Martha's, where her life was no other than a living copy of her rule, which consisted in the practice of evangelical perfection reduced to certain holy exercises. Every moment of her life she studied to accomplish it in the minutest detail, and was no less exact in obeying any indication of the will of a superior.

She for three years suffered from a lingering illness, but she would never be exempted from any part of her work, or make use of the least indulgence. Though she had leave, her answer always was, " I must work whilst I can, whilst I have time ". It was her delight to help and serve everyone ; and her silence was a sign of her recollection and continual prayer, of which her extraordinary gift of tears was the outward manifestation. Her biographer declares that after she had been praying long in any place the floor looked as if a jug of water had been upset there. When she was in ecstasy they sometimes held a dish beneath her face and the tears that flowed into it, so it is stated, amounted to nearly a quart (! !). She always spoke of her own sinful life, as she called it, though, indeed, it was most innocent, with feelings of intense compunction. Veronica was favoured by God with many extraordinary visions and consolations. A detailed account is preserved of the principal incidents of our Lord's life as they were revealed to her in her ecstasies. By her moving exhortations she softened and converted several obdurate sinners. She died at the hour which she had foretold, in the year 1497, at the age of fifty-two, and her sanctity was confirmed by miracles. Pope Leo X in 1517 permitted her to be honoured in her monastery in the same manner as if she had been beatified according to the usual forms, and the name of Bd Veronica of Binasco is inserted on this day in the Roman Martyrology, an unusual distinction in the case of a servant of God who has not been formally canonized.

See the life by Father Isidore de Isolanis, printed in the *Acta Sanctorum* for January 13. This contains a relatively full account of Bd Veronica's revelations, revelations which, as Father Bollandus warns his readers, must be read with caution, as they include many extravagant statements. Leo X's bull may be read in the same place. *Cf.* also P. Moiraghi, *La B. Veronica da Binasco* (1897).

14 : ST HILARY, Bishop of Poitiers, Doctor of the Church (*c.* A.D. 368)

ST AUGUSTINE, who often urges the authority of St Hilary against the Pelagians, styles him " the illustrious doctor of the churches " St Jerome says that he was a " most eloquent man, and the trumpet of the Latins against the Arians " ; and in another place, that " in St Cyprian and St Hilary, God had transplanted two fair cedars out of the world into His Church ".

St Hilary was born at Poitiers, and his family was illustrious in Gaul. He himself testifies that he was brought up in idolatry, and gives us a detailed account of the steps by which God conducted him to a knowledge of the faith. He considered, by the light of reason, that man, a moral and free agent, is placed in this world for the exercise of patience, temperance, and other virtues, which he saw must receive a recompense after this life. He ardently set about learning what God is, and quickly discovered the absurdity of polytheism, or a plurality of gods : he was convinced that there can be only one God, and that He must be eternal, unchangeable, all-powerful, the first cause and author of all things. Full of these reflections, he met with the Christian scriptures, and was deeply impressed by that sublime description Moses gives of God in those words, so expressive of His self-existence, I AM WHO AM : and was no less struck with the idea of His supreme dominion, illustrated by the inspired language of the prophets. The reading of the New Testament completed his inquiries ; and he learned from the first chapter of St John that the Divine Word, God the Son, is coeternal and consubstantial with the Father. Being thus brought to the knowledge of the faith, he received baptism when somewhat advanced in years.

Hilary had been married before his conversion, and his wife, by whom he had a daughter named Apra, was yet living when he was chosen bishop of Poitiers, about the year 350. He did all in his power to escape this promotion ; but his humility only made the people more earnest in their choice ; and, indeed, their expectations were not disappointed, for his eminent qualities shone forth so brilliantly as to attract the attention not only of Gaul, but of the whole Church. Soon after he was raised to the episcopal dignity he composed, before his exile, a commentary on the Gospel of St Matthew, which is still extant. That on the psalms he compiled after his banishment. From that time the Arian controversy chiefly employed his pen. He was an orator and poet. His style is lofty and noble, with much rhetorical ornament, somewhat studied ; and the length of his periods renders him sometimes obscure : St Jerome complains of his long and involved sentences and tragic manner—the old rhetorical tradition was not yet dead. St Hilary solemnly appeals to God that he accounted it the great work of his life to employ all his faculties to announce Him to the world, and to excite all men to the love of Him. He earnestly recommends beginning every action and discourse by prayer. He breathes a sincere and ardent desire of martyrdom, and discovers a soul fearless of death. He had the greatest veneration for truth, sparing no pains in its pursuit and dreading no dangers in its defence.

The Emperor Constantius and a synod at Milan in 355 required all bishops to sign the condemnation of St Athanasius. Such as refused to comply were banished, among whom were St Eusebius of Vercelli, Lucifer of Cagliari and St Dionysius of Milan. St Hilary wrote on that occasion his " First Book to Constantius ", in which he entreated him to restore peace to the Church. He separated himself from the three Arian bishops in the West, Ursacius, Valens and Saturninus, and the emperor sent an order to Julian, surnamed afterwards the Apostate, who at that time commanded in Gaul, to enforce St Hilary's immediate banishment into Phrygia. St Hilary went into exile about the middle of the year 356, as cheerfully as another would take a pleasure trip, and recked nothing of hardships, dangers or enemies, having a soul above the smiles and frowns of the world and his thoughts fixed only on God. He remained in exile for some three years, which time he employed in composing several learned works. The principal and most esteemed of these is that *On the Trinity*.   The earliest Latin hymn-writing is associated with the name of Hilary of Poitiers.

The emperor, again interfering in the affairs of the Church, assembled a council of Arians, at Seleucia in Isauria, to neutralize the decrees of the Council of Nicaea. St Hilary, who had then passed three years in Phrygia, was invited thither by the semi-Arians, who hoped that he would be useful to their party in crushing those who adhered strictly to the doctrine of Arius.   But no human considerations could daunt his courage.   He boldly defended the decrees of Nicaea, till at last, tired out with controversy, he withdrew to Constantinople and presented to the emperor a request, called his " Second Book to Constantius ", begging permission to hold a public disputation about religion with Saturninus, the author of his banishment. The issue of this challenge was that the Arians, dreading such a trial, persuaded the emperor to rid the East of a man who never ceased to disturb its peace.   Constantius accordingly sent him back into Gaul in 360.

St Hilary returned through Illyricum and Italy to confirm the weak.   He was received at Poitiers with great demonstrations of joy, and there his old disciple, St Martin, ere long rejoined him.   A synod in Gaul, convoked at the instance of Hilary, condemned that of Rimini in 359 ; and Saturninus, proving obstinate, was excommunicated and desposed.   Scandals were removed, discipline, peace and purity of faith were restored.   The death of Constantius in 361 put an end to the Arian persecution.   St Hilary was by nature the gentlest of men, full of courtesy and friendliness to all : yet seeing this behaviour ineffectual, he composed an invective against Constantius in which he employed the severest language, probably for good reasons not now known to us.   This piece was not circulated till after the death of the emperor.   Hilary undertook a journey to Milan in 364 to confute Auxentius, the Arian usurper of that see, and in a public disputation obliged him to confess Christ to be the true God, of the same substance and divinity with the Father.   St Hilary, indeed, saw through his hypocrisy ; but Auxentius so far imposed on the Emperor Valentinian as to pass for orthodox.   Hilary died at Poitiers, probably in the year 368, but neither the year nor the day of the month can be determined with certainty.   The Roman Martyrology names his feast on January 14.   St Hilary was proclaimed a doctor of the Church by Pope Pius IX in 1851.

A great deal has been written about St Hilary in recent years, but nothing has come to light which would gainsay the substantial accuracy of Alban Butler's account, given above in a shortened form.   The most important discovery, now generally accepted, is that of A. Wilmart (*Revue Bénédictine*, vol. xxiv (1908), pp. 159 *seq.* and 293 *seq.*).   He shows that the text printed in " The First Book to Constantius " is miscalled and incomplete.   It consists in reality, partly of a section of the letter addressed to the emperors by the Council of Sardica, partly of extracts from Hilary's work written in 356, just before his exile, under the title of " A First Book against Valens and Ursacius " (the Arian bishops).   It also seems clear that a work of Hilary's, *Liber* or *Tractatus Mysteriorum*, supposed to be lost, has not completely perished.   A large part of it was found, along with some poems or hymns of the saint, in a manuscript at Arezzo in 1887.   This *Tractatus* has nothing to do with the liturgy, as was previously conjectured, but is identical with a supposed *Liber Officiorum* otherwise attributed to him (see Wilmart in *Revue Bénédictine*, vol. xxvii (1910), pp. 12 *seq.*).   A full statement and bibliography of these new developments will be found in Fr Le Bachelet's article on St Hilary in D'I'C., vol. vi, cc. 2388 *seq.*   Other valuable contributions to the subject have been made by A. Feder in the *Sitzungsberichte* of the Vienna Academy, Phil.-Histor. Kl., clxii, no. 4, and in the texts he edited for the *Corpus Scrip. Eccles. Lat.*   So far as regards the life of St Hilary we have a biography and collection of miracles by Venantius Fortunatus printed in the *Acta Sanctorum* for January 13 (cf. BHL., nn. 580–582) ; see also

E. Watson, *The Life and Writings of St Hilary of Poitiers* (1899). As regards the hymns the reader may be conveniently referred to the supplement to Julian's *Dictionary of Hymnology*, to Walpole, *Early Latin Hymns* (1922), and especially to Feder in the fourth volume which he contributed to the Vienna *Corpus*. In England a judicial sitting and a university term are named from Hilary's feast-day, which also figures in the calendar of the Book of Common Prayer.

ST FELIX OF NOLA   (*c.* A.D. 260)

IT must be remembered that St Paulinus of Nola, who is our ultimate authority for the life of St Felix, lived more than a century after his time, and that it is probable that legendary accretions had already attached themselves to the tradition handed down. The story told by St Paulinus runs as follows :

St Felix was a native of Nola, a Roman colony in Campania, fourteen miles from Naples, where his father Hermias, who was by birth a Syrian and had served in the army, had purchased an estate and settled down. He had two sons, Felix and Hermias, to whom at his death he left his patrimony. The younger sought preferment in the world by following the profession of arms. Felix, to become in effect what his name in Latin imported, that is " happy ", resolved to follow no other standard than that of the King of kings, Jesus Christ. For this purpose he distributed most of his possessions among the poor, and was ordained priest by St Maximus, Bishop of Nola, who, charmed with his virtue and prudence, made him his right hand in those times of trouble, and looked upon him as his destined successor.

In the year 250 the Emperor Decius began a cruel persecution against the Church. Maximus, seeing himself marked out as a victim, retired into the desert, not through the fear of death but rather to preserve himself for the service of his flock. The persecutors, not finding him, seized on Felix, who in his absence was very zealous in the discharge of pastoral duties. The governor caused him to be scourged, then loaded with chains and cast into a dungeon, in which, as Prudentius informs us, the floor was spread all over with potsherds and pieces of broken glass, so that there was no place free from them on which the saint could either stand or lie. One night an angel appearing filled the prison with a bright light, and bade St Felix go to the aid of his bishop, who was in great distress. The confessor, seeing his chains fall off and the doors open, followed his guide, and was conducted to the place where Maximus lay in hunger and cold, speechless and unconscious : for, through anxiety for his flock and the hardships of his solitary retreat, he had suffered more than a martyrdom. Felix, not being able to bring him to himself, had recourse to prayer ; and discovering thereupon a bunch of grapes within reach, he squeezed some of the juice into his mouth, which had the desired effect. The good bishop, as soon as he beheld his friend Felix, begged to be conveyed back to his church. The saint, taking him on his shoulders, carried him to his home in the city before day appeared, where a devoted old woman took care of him.

Felix kept himself concealed, praying for the Church without ceasing, till the death of Decius in the year 251. He no sooner appeared again in public than his zeal so exasperated the pagans that they came to apprehend him ; but though they met him, they did not recognize him. They even asked him where Felix was, a question to which he returned an evasive answer. The persecutors, going a little further, perceived their mistake, and returned ; but Felix in the meantime had stepped a little out of the way, and crept through a hole in a ruinous wall, which was instantly closed up by spiders' webs.   His enemies, never imagining anything could have lately passed where they saw so dense a web, after a fruitless search elsewhere returned without their prey.   Felix, finding among the ruins, between two houses, an old well half dry, hid himself there for six months, and obtained during that time wherewithal to subsist by means of a devout Christian woman. Peace being restored to the Church, he quitted his retreat, and was received in the city with joy.

St Maximus died soon after, and all were unanimous in electing Felix bishop ; but he persuaded the people to make choice of Quintus, his senior in the priesthood. The remainder of the saint's estate having been confiscated in the persecution, he was advised to press his legal claim, as others had done, who thereby recovered what had been taken from them.   His answer was that in poverty he should be the more secure of possessing Christ.   He could not even be prevailed upon to accept what the rich offered him.   He rented a little spot of land, not exceeding three acres, which he tilled with his own hands to supply his own needs and to have something left for alms.   Whatever was bestowed on him he gave immediately to the poor.   If he had two coats he was sure to give them the better, and often exchanged his only one for the rags of some beggar.   He died in a good old age, on January 14, on which day he is commemorated in the martyrologies.

More than a century had elapsed after the death of Felix when Paulinus, a distinguished Roman senator, settled in Nola and was elected bishop there.   He testifies that crowds of pilgrims came from Rome and more distant places to visit the shrine of the saint on his festival.   He adds that all brought some present or other to his church, such as candles to burn at his tomb and the like ; but that for his own part he offered him the homage of his tongue and himself, though an unworthy gift.   He expresses his devotion in the warmest terms, and believes that all the graces he received from Heaven were conferred on him through the intercession of St Felix.   He describes at large the pictures of the whole history of the Old Testament in the church of St Felix, which were as so many books that instructed the ignorant.   The holy bishop's enthusiasm is reflected in his verses. He relates a number of miracles which were wrought at the tomb, as of persons cured of diseases and delivered from dangers by the saint's intercession, in several of which cases he was an eye-witness.   He testifies that he himself by having recourse to Felix had been speedily succoured.   St Augustine also has given an account of miracles performed at the shrine.   It was not formerly allowed to bury any corpse within the walls of cities, and as the church of St Felix stood outside the walls of Nola many Christians sought to be buried in it, that their faith and devotion might recommend them after death to the patronage of this holy confessor. On this matter St Paulinus consulted St Augustine, who answered him by his book *On the Care for the Dead*, in which he shows that the faith and devotion of such persons would serve them well after death, as the suffrages and good works of the living in behalf of the faithful departed are profitable to the latter.

As already stated, the poems of St Paulinus constitute our main authority for the life of St Felix.   Of these poems Bede wrote a summary in prose, which is printed, with other documents, in the *Acta Sanctorum* for January 14.   In the *Analecta Bollandiana*, vol. xvi (1897), pp. 22 *seq.*, may be found a curious illustration of the confusion introduced by the martyrologist Ado, and other hagiographers, through their invention of a " St Felix in Pincis "   This confusion was probably due to the existence of a church on the Pincio at Rome dedicated to St Felix of Nola.   Pope St Damasus pays a tribute in verse to Felix for a cure he himself had received.   *Cf.* Quentin, *Les Martyrologes historiques*, pp. 518–522.

ST MACRINA THE ELDER, Widow   (c. A.D. 340)

In more than one of his letters St Basil the Great refers to his father's mother, Macrina, by whom he was apparently brought up, and to whose care in giving him sound religious instruction he attributes the fact that he never imbibed any heterodox opinions which he had afterwards to modify. During the persecution of Galerius and Maximinus, Macrina and her husband had much to suffer. They were forced to quit their home and to hide themselves from the persecutors among the hill forests of Pontus for seven years. They often suffered hunger, and St Gregory Nazianzen declares that at times they had to depend for their food upon the wild creatures which, as he believed, by some miraculous interposition of Providence suffered themselves to be caught and killed. Even after this danger had passed, another persecution broke out in which their goods were confiscated, and it would seem that they were honoured by a formal recognition of their title to be reckoned among the confessors of the faith. Macrina survived her husband, but the exact date of her death is not recorded. In the Roman Martyrology St Macrina is described as a disciple of St Gregory Thaumaturgus, but this can hardly mean more than that she was an earnest student of his writings.

See *Acta Sanctorum* for January 14 and DCB., vol. iii, p. 779.

SS. BARBASYMAS and his Companions, Martyrs   (A.D. 346)

St Barbasymas (Barbashemin) succeeded his brother St Sadoth in the metropolitical see of Seleucia and Ctesiphon in 342. Being accused as an enemy to the Persian religion, he was apprehended with sixteen of his clergy by order of King Sapor II. The king, seeing that his threats made no impression, confined him in a loathsome dungeon, in which he was often tortured with scourgings and other atrocities, besides the continual discomfort of stench, filth, hunger and thirst. After eleven months the prisoners were again brought before the king. Their bodies were disfigured and their faces hardly recognizable. Sapor held out to the bishop a golden cup in which were a thousand gold coins, and besides this he promised him a governorship if he would suffer himself to be initiated in the rites of the sun. The saint replied that he could not answer the reproaches of Christ at the last day if he should prefer gold, or a whole empire, to His holy law ; and that he was ready to die. He received his crown by the sword, with his companions, on January 14, 346 at Ledan in Huzistan.

St Maruthas, Bishop of Maiferkat, supposed to be the author of his acts, adds that Sapor, resolving to extinguish the Christian name in his empire, published a new edict, whereby he commanded everyone to be tortured and put to death who should refuse to worship the sun, fire and water, and to feed on the blood of living creatures. The see of Seleucia remained vacant twenty years, and innumerable martyrs watered Persia with their blood. St Maruthas was not able to recover their names, but has left us a lengthy panegyric of their heroic deeds, very devotional in tone, in which he prays to be speedily united with them in glory.

See Assemani, *Acta martyrum orientalium*, vol. i, pp. 111–116 ; but the Syriac text has been more correctly edited by Bedjan, *Acta martyrum et sanctorum*, vol. ii, pp. 296–303 ; Sozomen, *Hist. Eccles.*, bk ii, c. 13 ; BHO., n. 33.

THE MARTYRS OF MOUNT SINAI (FOURTH CENTURY)

THIRTY-EIGHT solitaries on Mount Sinai were put to death by a troop of Arabians, and many other hermits in the desert of Raithu, two days' journey from Sinai, near the Red Sea, were similarly massacred by the Blemmyes. Also many anchorets on Mount Sinai were martyred by a band of desert marauders at the close of the fourth century. A boy of fourteen years of age led among them an ascetic life of great perfection. The raiders threatened to kill him if he did not discover where the older monks had concealed themselves. He answered that death did not terrify him, and that he could not ransom his life by a sin in betraying his fathers. The barbarians, enraged at this answer, fell on him with all their weapons at once, and the youth died by as many martyrdoms as he had executioners. St Nilus (*cf.* November 12) left an account of this massacre : at that time he led an eremitical life in that wilderness.

These holy solitaries are commemorated together on this day in the Eastern church, and are mentioned in the Roman Martyrology. See Martynov, *Annus ecclesiasticus graeco-slavicus*, pp. 41 *seq.* ; Nilles, *Kalendarium Manuale* (1896-1897), vol. i. The narratives of St Nilus are in Migne, PG., vol. lxxix, pp. 590-694. On the authorship of these narratives see *Analecta Bollandiana*, vol. xxxviii (1920), pp. 420 *seq.* ; and *cf.* Delehaye, *Synax. Const.*, pp. 389-391.

ST DATIUS, BISHOP OF MILAN (A.D. 552)

THE life of St Datius was spent in stormy times. During the greater part of his episcopate—which lasted at least from 530 to 552—he was engaged in strife, sometimes in defence of temporal, more often in championing spiritual, interests. To save his city of Milan from the Goths he had allied himself with Belisarius. Unfortunately he was disappointed in his hopes. Before help could come from Belisarius, Milan was invested and eventually sacked. It is possible that Datius himself was taken prisoner, and afterwards liberated through the influence of his friend Cassiodorus. Driven from Milan the bishop betook himself to Constantinople, where, in 545, he boldly supported Pope Vigilius against Justinian in the controversy concerning the "Three Chapters". He seems to have died in 552, while still at Constantinople, whence his remains were at a later date translated to his episcopal city of Milan. St Gregory the Great in his *Dialogues* recounts a curious story of a haunted house from which the devil used to frighten all intending occupants, by producing the most alarming and discordant howlings of beasts. St Datius, however, showed no fear, but put the aggressor to shame and restored perfect quiet.

See the *Acta Sanctorum* for January 14 ; DCB., vol. i, p. 789 ; and L. Duchesne, *L'Église au VIe siècle*, pp. 197-199.

ST KENTIGERN, OR MUNGO, BISHOP IN STRATHCLYDE (A.D. 603)

IF we may trust our sources, St Kentigern's mother, Thaney (Thenew, Tenoi ; *cf.* " St Enoch's " station at Glasgow) was of royal birth and, being discovered to be with child, of which the father was unknown, was sentenced to be hurled from the top of a precipitous hill (Traprain Law in Haddingtonshire). She escaped, however, without injury, and was then put into a coracle and cast adrift at the mouth of the Firth of Forth. The tide eventually carried her to Culross, on the opposite shore of the estuary, where she brought forth her child, and where St Serf took both mother and babe under his protection. The boy became very dear to him, and was given the pet name Mungo (= darling). When he had grown up, Kentigern felt himself drawn to a life of solitude and self-denial, and he accordingly retired to a place called " Glasghu ", now Glasgow. There after a while a community gathered round him, and the fame of his virtues spread, so that in the end the clergy and people of that district would have no other for their bishop ; and he was consecrated by a bishop from Ireland. St Kentigern travelled everywhere on foot, preaching the gospel to his people ; he practised the severest austerities, and recited the whole psalter every day, often standing immersed the while in the water of some ice-cold stream. During Lent he always withdrew from the company of his fellow-men, and in some desert spot gave himself up entirely to penance and prayer. This apostolic way of life was blessed, we are told, by many miracles.

The political conditions of this great tract of country, which was later known as Strathclyde and stretched southwards as far as the Ribble, were terribly unstable. The chieftains were constantly engaged in feuds among themselves, and although they recognized some sort of " king ", or supreme authority, plots and cabals were constantly being formed against him. The sequence of events, with such slender and contradictory data as we possess, is impossible to determine, but it is said that Kentigern was eventually driven into exile or flight. He made his way into Wales, where he is said to have stayed for a time with St David at Menevia, till Cadwallon, a chieftain in Denbighshire, bestowed on him the land near the meeting of the rivers Elwy and Clwyd, on which he built a monastery, called from the former of the two rivers Llanelwy, where a number of disciples and scholars put themselves under his direction, among them St Asaph. It is to be noted, however, that some Welsh historians deny that Kentigern founded this abbey, now represented by the cathedral church of Saint Asaph, or even that he was ever there ; and, indeed, while Asaph's name is common in the toponymy of the district, that of Kentigern is unknown.

Later he returned to the north, and when he again reached Strathclyde Kentigern for a while settled at Hoddam in Dumfriesshire, but before long took up his abode at Glasgow as before. His austerity of life and zeal for the spread of the Gospel continued unabated, and his biographer tells us that on one occasion a meeting took place between him and that other great apostle of Scotland, St Columba, with whom he exchanged croziers. Many extravagant miracles are recounted of Kentigern, one of which is especially famous, as the memory of it is perpetuated by the ring and the fish seen in the arms of the city of Glasgow. King Rydderch found a ring, which he had given to his queen as a love-token, upon the finger of a sleeping knight whom she favoured. He removed it without awakening the sleeper, threw it into the sea, and then asked his wife to produce the ring he had given her. In her distress she applied to St Kentigern, and he sent a monk out to fish, who caught a salmon which had swallowed the ring. A curious description of the death of the saint in the act of taking a hot bath on the octave of the Epiphany, " on which day he had been accustomed to baptize a multitude of people ", seems certainly to point to some more primitive source which the biographer had before him. The date of his death seems to have been 603, when Kentigern will have been eighty-five—not, as his biographer states, 185—years old.

His feast is kept throughout Scotland as the first bishop of Glasgow, and also in the dioceses of Liverpool, Salford, Lancaster and Menevia.

See A. P. Forbes, *Lives of St Ninian and St Kentigern* (1874), who prints the text of Joscelyn of Furness and of the incomplete anonymous life ; also his *Kalendars of Scottish Saints* (1872), pp. 362 seq. ; Skene, *Celtic Scotland*, vol. ii, pp. 179 seq. Cf. also the *Acta Sanctorum*, January 13 ; and A. W Wade-Evans, *Life of Saint David* (1923), pp. 109 seq. Forbes's KSS. is the most useful reference for the little that is known of the lesser Scottish saints in whose honour Catholic churches are still dedicated, *e.g.* Cumin (at Morar), Quivox (Prestwick), Triduana (Edinburgh), Machan (Lennoxtown). But see also M. Barrett, *A Calendar of Scottish Saints* (1904). D. D. C. Pochin Mould's *Scotland of the Saints* (1952) is useful for Scottish saints in general.

BD ODO OF NOVARA (A.D. 1200)

BD ODO, a Carthusian monk of the twelfth century, stands out from among some of his saintly contemporaries by the fact that we have good first-hand evidence concerning his manner of life. Pope Gregory IX ordered an inquiry to be made with a view to his canonization, and the depositions of the witnesses are still preserved. One or two extracts will serve to sketch his portrait better than a narrative. " Master Richard, Bishop of Trivento, having been adjured in the name of the Holy Ghost, the holy Gospels lying open before him, affirmed that he had seen the blessed Odo and knew him to be a God-fearing man, modest and chaste, given up night and day to watching and prayer, clad only in rough garments of wool, living in a tiny cell, which he hardly ever quitted except to pray in the church, obeying always the sound of the bell when it called him to office. Without ceasing, he poured forth his soul in sighs and tears ; there was no one he came across to whom he did not give new courage in the service of God ; he constantly read the divine Scriptures, and in spite of his advanced age, as long as he stayed in his cell, he laboured with his hands as best he could that he might not fall a prey to idleness." The bishop then goes on to give a brief sketch of Odo's life, noting that after he became a Carthusian he had been appointed prior in the recently founded monastery of Geyrach in Slavonia, but had there been so cruelly persecuted by the bishop of the diocese, Dietrich, that, being forced to leave his community, he had travelled to Rome to obtain the pope's permission to resign his office. He had then been given hospitality by the aged abbess of a nunnery at Tagliacozzo, who, struck by his holiness, got leave to retain him as chaplain to the community. Numerous other witnesses, who had been the spectators of Odo's edifying life, spoke of his austerities, his charity and his humble self-effacement.

One of these, the Archpriest Oderisius, deposes that he was present when Odo breathed his last, and that " as he lay upon the ground in his hair-shirt in the aforesaid little cell, he began to say, when at the point of death, ' Wait for me, Lord, wait for me, I am coming to thee ' ; and when they asked him to whom he was speaking, he answered, ' It is my King, whom now I see, I am standing in His presence.' And when the blessed Odo spoke these words, just as if someone were offering him his hand, he stood straight up from the ground, and so, with his hands stretched out heavenwards, he passed away to our Lord." This happened on January 14 in the year 1200, when Odo was believed to be nearly a hundred years old. He worked many miracles both during life and after death, but it horrified him to think that people should attribute to him any supernatural power. " Brother ", he said to one who asked his aid, " why dost thou make game of me,

a wretched sinner, a bag of putrid flesh ?   Leave me in peace ; it is for Christ, the
Son of the living God, to heal thee " ; and as he said this he burst into tears.   But
the man went away permanently cured of an infirmity which, as the witness who
recounts this attests from personal knowledge, had tortured him for many years.
The *cultus* of Bd Odo was confirmed in 1859.

See Le Couteulx, *Annales Ordinis Cartusiensis* (1888), vol. iii, pp. 263-271.   In vol. iv,
pp 59-72, the editor prints a selection of the depositions of the witnesses to the miracles
which were wrought at the tomb of Bd Odo.   As the evidence was all given within a year
of the occurrences related, it forms one of the best collections of medieval miracles preserved
to us.   The documents have been edited entire in the *Analecta Bollandiana*, vol. i (1882),
pp. 323-354.   *Cf.* also Le Vasseur, *Ephemerides*, vol. i, pp. 60-68.

ST SAVA, ARCHBISHOP OF THE SERBS   (A.D. 1237)

THE public ecclesiastical life and politics of St Sava (*i.e.* Sabas) were to a great
extent conditioned by political considerations, a circumstance common to many
churchmen in history, and nowhere more acute than in the Balkans, at the junction
of great civil and ecclesiastical powers and the meeting-place of diverse cultures.

Sava, born in 1174, was the youngest of the three sons of Stephen I, founder
of the dynasty of the Nemanydes and of the independent Serbian state.   At the
age of seventeen he became a monk on the Greek peninsula of Mount Athos, where
he was joined by his father when that prince abdicated in 1196.   Together they
established a monastery for Serbian monks, with the name of Khilandari, which
is still in existence as one of the seventeen " ruling monasteries " of the Holy
Mountain.   As abbot, Sava was noted for his light and effective touch in training
young monks ; it was remarked, too, that his influence was always on the side of
gentleness and leniency.   He began the work of translating books into the Serbian
language, and there are still treasured at Khilandari a psalter and ritual written out
by himself, and signed, " I, the unworthy lazy monk Sava ".

In the meanwhile his brothers, Stephen II and Vulkan, had fallen out over
their inheritance, and in 1207 St Sava returned home.   Religiously as well as
civilly he found his country in a bad way.   The Serbs had been Christians for
some time, but much of it was a nominal Christianity, quite uninstructed and mixed
up with heathenism.   The clergy were few and mostly uneducated, for the church
had been ruled from Constantinople or Okhrida in Bulgaria, whose hierarchs had
shown little care or sympathy for those whom they regarded as barbarians.   So
St Sava, following the example of the Benedictines in the West and the earlier
Russian monks, utilized the monks who had accompanied him from Khilandari
for pastoral and missionary work.   He established himself at the monastery of
Studenitsa, from whence he founded a number of small monasteries in places
convenient for travelling around and getting to the people.   But this did not mean
that the former Athonite had changed his mind about the necessity of solitude and
contemplation : there may still be seen in the Studenitsa valley, high and away
above the monastery, the rocky hermitage to which St Sava himself used to retire.

What happened, and the order of what happened, subsequently is more difficult
to assess, but the following represents a recent reading of the rather contradictory
evidence.   It remained desirable (and politically advantageous also) that the Serbs
should have their own bishops.   So Stephen II sent his brother to Nicaea, where
the Eastern emperor and patriarch had taken refuge from the Frankish intruders
at Constantinople.   Sava won over the emperor, Theodore II Laskaris (who was

related to the Nemanya family), and he designated Sava as the first metropolitan of the new hierarchy. The patriarch, Manuel I, was unwilling, but in the circumstances dared not oppose obstinately, and himself ordained Sava bishop, in 1219. Sava returned by way of Mount Athos, bringing with him more monks and many books that had been translated at Khilandari, and straightway set about the organization of his church. It seems that already Stephen II, "the First-Crowned", had asked to be recognized as king by Pope Honorius III and had been duly crowned by a papal legate in 1217. But in 1222 he was again crowned, by his brother as archbishop, and one source asserts that it was on this occasion that Honorius sent a crown, in response to a request from Sava, who had informed the Holy See of his own episcopal ordination.

Thus the retiring young prince, who had left home as a youth to be a monk, succeeded before he was fifty years of age in consolidating the state founded by his father by reforming the religious life of the people, giving them bishops of their own race, and sealing the sovereign dignity of his brother. St Sava is regarded as the patron-saint of Serbia and, with him as with others, the people's gratitude attributes benefits for which he was very doubtfully responsible : in this case, how to turn a plow across the head-land instead of dragging it back to the starting point, and how to make windows instead of admitting air and light by the door (*cf.* the men of the Sussex coast who said that St Wilfrid taught them how to catch fish).

The later years of St Sava's life were marked externally by two voyages to Palestine and the Near East ; the first seems to have been a pilgrimage of devotion, the second an ecclesiastical mission. On his way back from this last he was taken ill at Tirnovo in Bulgaria and there he died, with a smile on his face, on January 14, 1237. In the following year his body was translated to the monastery of Milochevo in Serbia, where it rested until 1594 when, during civil disturbances, the relics were deliberately burned by a Turkish pasha who was an Italian renegade.

The Orthodox of Serbia look on St Sava not only as the founder of their national church but also as the conscious father of their separation from Rome. And indeed it would seem this might be so—if events are looked at from the position in later times. But the position in those days was quite different. Behind the ecclesiastical authorities of Rome and Nicaea-Byzantium and Okhrida were corresponding civil powers, all of them a threat to the nascent Serbian state. Among these King Stephen II and his archbishop had to move warily ; and in any case schism between Rome and the Byzantine East was hardly definitive ; Southern Slavs, and for that matter many "Franks", did not yet know any hard-and-fast division into Catholic and Orthodox. In fact, St Sava Prosvtitely, "the Enlightener", figures in several Latin calendars and his feast is also kept in the Catholic Byzantine diocese of Krizevtsy in Croatia.

A life of St Sava was written by his disciple Domitian about 1250, but it has not survived in its original form : it was edited during the fourteenth century, with "an obvious tendenciousness in a certain ecclesiastical direction" (*i.e.* in favour of the Orthodox) says Shafarik, who cannot be suspected of partiality for the Catholic Church. Other sources are the letters of Stephen II and the history of Salona by the contemporary Latin archdeacon of Spalato, Thomas. See *Acta Sanctorum*, January 14 ; J. Martynov, *Trifolium Serbicum* ; J. Matl, "Der hl. Sava als Begründer der serbischen Nationalkirche", in *Kyrios*, vol. ii (1937), pp. 23–37 ; V. Yanich and C. P. Hankey in *Lives of the Serbian Saints* ; and a useful conference on Sava given in Belgrade by P. Bélard, printed in *L'Unité de l'Église*, no. 78 (1936). A seventeenth-century Latin bishop in Bosnia, I. T. Mrnavich, wrote a biography of St Sava, and the Franciscan poet Andrew Kachich devoted one of his best poems to him.

BD ROGER OF TODI   (A.D. 1237)

NOT much is recorded concerning Bd Roger (Ruggiero) da Todi, and in the little which is told us there seems to be a certain amount of confusion.   What can be affirmed with confidence is that he received the habit of the Friars Minor from the hands of the Seraphic Father himself in 1216, that he was appointed by St Francis to act as spiritual director to the community founded and governed by Bd Philippa Mareri at Rieti in Umbria under the rule of St Clare, that he assisted Philippa on her deathbed in 1236, and that he died himself at Todi shortly afterwards on January 5, 1237.   Pope Gregory IX, who had known him personally, permitted the town of Todi, where his remains were enshrined, to keep a feast in his honour, and Benedict XIV confirmed the *cultus* for the whole Franciscan Order.

See Mazzara, *Leggendario Francescano* (1676), vol. i, pp. 29–31 ; Léon, *Auréole Séraphique* (English trans.), vol. i, pp. 442–443.

BD ODORIC OF PORDENONE   (A.D. 1331)

IT would not be easy to find in secular literature a more adventurous career than that of the Franciscan Friar Odoric of Pordenone.   He was a native of Friuli, and his family name is said to have been Mattiussi.   About the year 1300, when he was fifteen, he received the habit of St Francis at Udine, and his later biographers expatiate upon the extreme fervour with which he gave himself to prayer, poverty and penance.   After a while he felt called to serve God in solitude, and he obtained the permission to lead the life of a hermit in a remote cell.   We are not told how long he spent in this close communion with God, but he seems to have been guided to return to Udine and to take up apostolic work in the surrounding districts. Great success followed his preaching, and crowds gathered from afar to hear him. But about 1317, when he was a little over thirty, there came to him an inspiration of a somewhat different kind, and it is difficult from the documents before us to decide how far he was influenced in his subsequent career by a simple spirit of adventure and how far by the burning desire of the missionary to extend God's kingdom and to save souls.   We shall probably not be wrong in assuming that there was a mixture of both.

It is not easy to give precise dates, but according to Yule and Cordier he was in western India soon after 1321, he must have spent three of the years between 1322 and 1328 in northern China, and he certainly died at home among his brethren at Udine in January 1331.   With regard to the route he followed in his wanderings we are better informed.   His first objective was Constantinople, and from thence he passed on to Trebizond, Erzerum, Tabriz and Soltania.   There were houses of the order in most of these cities, and he probably made a considerable stay in each, so that this part of his journey may well have occupied three years.   From Soltania he seems to have wandered about very irregularly, but eventually he came south through Baghdad to Hormuz at the entrance of the Persian Gulf, where he took ship and sailed to Salsette.   At Tana, or possibly Surat, he gathered up the bones of his four brethren who had been martyred there shortly before, in 1321, and carried them with him on his voyage eastward.   He went on to Malabar and Ceylon, and then probably rested for a while at the shrine of St Thomas at Mailapur, by the modern Madras.   Here he again took ship for Sumatra and Java, possibly also visiting southern and eastern Borneo.   China was his next goal.   Starting from Canton, he travelled to the great ports of Fo-kien, and from Fu-chau he proceeded across the mountains to Hang-chau, then famous under the name of Quinsai as the greatest city of the world, and Nan-king. Taking to the water again upon the great canal at Yang-chau, he made his way to Khanbaliq, or Peking, and there remained for three years, attached apparently to one of the churches founded by Archbishop John of Montecorvino, another heroic Franciscan missionary, now in extreme old age. There Odoric turned his face homewards, passing through Shen-si to Tibet and its capital, Lhasa, but we have no further record of the course by which he ultimately reached his native province in safety. It is interesting to note that during the latter part at least of these long journeys Odoric had for his companion an Irish friar of the same order, one Brother James. The fact is known to us from a record preserved in the archives of Udine, which tells us that after Odoric's death a present of two marks was made " for the love of God and the blessed Brother Odoric " to Brother James, the Irishman, who had been his companion on his journey.

The account which has been left us of Odoric's travels, which unfortunately was not written down by himself at the time but dictated to one of his brethren after his return, says practically nothing of any missionary labours on his part. It is, therefore, not certain how far we may credit the wonderful stories which were current in later times regarding the success which attended his preaching. Luke Wadding, the annalist, declares that he converted and baptized 20,000 Saracens, but he gives us no idea of the source of his information. It is also stated that Odoric's purpose in leaving China and returning to Europe was to obtain fresh supplies of missionaries and to conduct them himself to the Far East. At Pisa, however, St Francis appeared to him and bade him return to Udine, declaring that he himself would look after those distant missions about which Odoric was anxious. On his deathbed the worn-out apostle said that God had made known to him that his sins were pardoned, but that he wished, like a humble child, to submit himself to the keys of the Church and to receive the last sacraments. He died on January 14, 1331. Many miracles are said to have been wrought after his death, and in one of these we hear again of Brother James the Irishman, for a certain Franciscan who was a preacher and doctor of theology at Venice, and had suffered cruelly from a painful malady of the throat, asked Brother James to recommend him to his late fellow traveller, and was immediately cured. The *cultus* long paid to him was approved in 1755.

The narrative of his journeys, as dictated in Latin by Bd Odoric, will be found printed in the *Acta Sanctorum* for January 14, but the fullest account, with translation and notes, will be found in Yule-Cordier, *Cathay and the Way Thither* (1913), vol. ii. See also Wadding, *Annales, s.a.* 1331 ; M. Komroff, *Contemporaries of Marco Polo* (1928) ; and H. Matrod, *L'itinéraire . . . du b. Odoric de Pordenone* (1936). There is a fifteenth-century Welsh version of the voyages, ed. S. J. Williams, *Ffordd y Brawd Odrig* (1929). Fuller bibliographies in Yule and in U. Chevalier, *Bio-Bibliographie.*

BD GILES OF LORENZANA (A.D. 1518)

THE published lives of this Giles tell us that he was born about 1443 at Lorenzana in what was once the kingdom of Naples. His parents were a devout couple of the working class, and the boy was not hindered in the religious practices which he adopted from early youth, more especially after he came under the influence of the Franciscan friars, who made a foundation in his native town. In time he decided to serve God in solitude, settling near a little shrine of our Lady.   Here he spent most of his time absorbed in prayer, the birds and beasts becoming his familiar companions.   But the news of the miracles he was believed to work gradually attracted visitors, and being forced to seek refuge elsewhere, he next took service with a farmer near Lorenzana.   Of this stage of his life it is said that, though he spent most of his time in church, his work, God so disposing, did not suffer from his absence.   Eventually he was received into the Franciscan community as a lay-brother, and being given the care of the garden, he was allowed to build himself a little hut there, where he lived as in a kind of hermitage.   He was still the friend of the birds and all living creatures, and his miraculous cures, his ecstatic prayer and gift of prophecy were renowned far and wide.   In particular he is said to have been frequently seen raised from the ground and to have been physically assaulted by the Evil One.   He died on January 10, 1518.   The statement made that six years after his death his incorrupt body, though it had been laid in the tomb in the ordinary way, was found kneeling, rosary in hand, and the face turned towards the Blessed Sacrament, can hardly be considered to rest upon evidence sufficient to establish so strange a marvel.   The cult of Bd Giles was confirmed in 1880.

See Léon, *Auréole Séraphique* (English trans.), January 10 ; Antony da Vicenza, *Vita e miracoli del B. Egidio* (1880).

ST ANTONY PUCCI   (A.D. 1892)

THIS saint , though a member of a religious order, the Servants of Mary, spent most of his life and achieved holiness as a parish priest.   He was born of peasant stock at Poggiole, near Pistoia, in 1819 ; he was the second of seven children and was christened Eustace.   As a boy his kind and gentle disposition was noticeable, as was his industry and willingness to help, especially in his parish church, of which his father was sacristan.   Nevertheless, when Eustace's inclination to become a Servite had been finally confirmed during a pilgrimage to the shrine of our Lady at Bocca, Pucci senior and his wife opposed their son's resolution (he was their eldest boy), and it was not till he was eighteen, in 1837, that he entered the Servite priory of the Annunciation at Florence.   He took the names of Antony Mary.

During his early years as a religious Brother Antony showed those qualities of frankness and of steadiness in face of difficulties that were to distinguish him all his life.   Prayer and obedience were his first concern, and after them study.   He was ordained in 1843, and less than a year later was appointed curate of St Andrew's church in Viareggio.   In 1847, when still only 28, he became parish priest there.   Viareggio is a seaside town—a fishing-port with a ship-building yard, but chiefly a holiday resort—and here Father Antony remained for the rest of his days.

Father Antony's flock called him " Il curatino ", which can't be translated into English ; but it means that he was " a grand little man ", who was equally loved and respected.   It has been said of him that he was before his time in recognizing the need for organization, and organizations, in a parish.   But he never forgot that these things are but means to an end, and that end the life of divine charity ; and that the living example of love must come from the father of the flock.   He was the father and therefore the servant of all : the sick, the aged, the poor, all in trouble or distress, came to him, and he served them without stint.   This selflessness was never more apparent than when Viareggio was visited by two bad epidemics, in 1854 and in 1866 ; and one of the fruits of Father Antony's love for the young was his inauguration of a seaside nursing-home for children—something quite new in those days.   To the religious instruction of children he devoted much thought and work, emphasizing that what is done in church and school must be begun and finished in the home.   Nor were his concerns bounded by the limits of his parish   in his enthusiasm for the conversion of the heathen Father Antony was one of the pioneers in Italy of the work of the A.P.F. and of the Holy Childhood Society.

St Antony Pucci died on January 14, 1892 at the age of 73; his passing was greeted with an outburst of grief in Viareggio, and miracles of healing took place at his grave. He was beatified in 1952, and canonized in 1962 during the Second Vatican Council.

See the decree of beatification in the *Acta Apostolicae Sedis*, vol. xliv (1952) ; and *Un apostolo della carità* (1920), by a Servite.

15 : ST PAUL THE HERMIT   (A.D. 342)

ELIAS and St John the Baptist sanctified the desert, and Jesus Christ Himself was a model of the eremitical state during His forty days' fast in the wilderness.   But while we cannot doubt that the saint of this day was guided by the Holy Ghost to live in solitude far from the haunts of men, we must recognize that this was a special vocation, and not an example to be rashly imitated.   Speaking generally, this manner of life is beset with many dangers, and ought only to be embraced by those already well-grounded in virtue and familiar with the practice of contemplative prayer.

St Paul was a native of the lower Thebaid in Egypt, and lost both his parents when he was but fifteen years of age.   Nevertheless, he was proficient in Greek and Egyptian learning, was gentle and modest, and feared God from his earliest youth.   The cruel persecution of Decius disturbed the peace of the Church in 250 ; and Satan by his ministers sought not so much to kill the bodies, as by subtle artifices to destroy the souls of men.   During these times of danger Paul kept himself concealed in the house of a friend ; but finding that a brother-in-law coveting his estate was inclined to betray him, he fled into the desert.   There he found certain caverns which were said to have been the retreat of money-coiners in the days of Cleopatra, Queen of Egypt.   He chose for his dwelling a cave in this place, near which were a palm tree and a clear spring ; the former by its leaves furnished him with raiment, and by its fruit with food ; and the latter supplied him with water to drink.   Paul was twenty-two years old when he entered the desert.   His first intention was to enjoy liberty in serving God till the persecution should cease ; but relishing the sweets of solitude and heavenly contemplation, he resolved to return no more and never to concern himself with the things of the world ; it was enough for him to know that there was a world, and to pray that it might grow better.   He lived on the fruit of his tree till he was forty-three years of age, and from that time till his death, like Elias, he was miraculously fed with bread brought him every day by a raven.   His method of life, and what he did in this place during ninety years, is hidden from us ; but God was pleased to make His servant known a little before his death.

The great St Antony, who was then ninety years of age, was tempted to vanity, thinking that no one had served God so long in the wilderness as he had done, since he believed himself to be the first to adopt this unusual way of life ; but the contrary was made known to him in a dream, and the saint was at the same time commanded by Almighty God to set out forthwith in quest of a solitary more perfect than himself.   The old man started the next morning.   St Jerome relates that he met a centaur, or creature with something of the mixed shape of man and horse, and that this monster or phantom of the devil (St Jerome does not profess to determine which it was), upon his making the sign of the cross, fled away, after having pointed out the road.   Our author adds that St Antony soon after met also a satyr, who gave him to understand that he dwelt here in the desert, and was one of those beings whom the deluded gentiles worshipped.*   St Antony, after two days and a night spent in the search, discovered the saint's abode by a light which shone from it and guided his steps.   Having begged admittance at the door of the cell, St Paul at last opened it with a smile ; they embraced, and called each other by their names, which they knew by revelation.   St Paul then inquired whether idolatry still reigned in the world.   While they were discoursing together, a raven flew towards them, and dropped a loaf of bread before them.   Upon which St Paul said, " Our good God has sent us a dinner.   In this manner have I received half a loaf every day these sixty years past ; now you have come to see me, Christ has doubled His provision for His servants."   Having given thanks to God, they both sat down by the spring.   But a little contest arose between them as to who should break the bread ; St Antony alleged St Paul's greater age, and St Paul pleaded that Antony was the stranger : both agreed at last to take up their parts together.   Having refreshed themselves at the spring, they spent the night in prayer.

The next morning St Paul told his guest that the time of his death approached, and that he had been sent to bury him, adding, " Go and fetch the cloak given you by Athanasius, Bishop of Alexandria, in which I desire you to wrap my body." This he probably said that he might be left alone in prayer, while expecting to be called out of this world ; as also that he might testify his veneration for St Athanasius, and his high regard for the faith and communion of the Catholic Church, on account of which that holy bishop was then a great sufferer.   St Antony was surprised to hear him mention the cloak, of which he could only have known by revelation.   Whatever was his motive for desiring to be buried in it, St Antony acquiesced in what was asked of him, and he hastened to his monastery to comply with St Paul's request.   He told his monks that he, a sinner, falsely bore the name of a servant of God ; but that he had seen Elias and John the Baptist in the wilderness, even Paul in Paradise.   Having taken the cloak, he returned with it in all haste, fearing lest the hermit might be dead ; as, in fact, it happened.   Whilst on the road he saw his soul carried up to Heaven, attended by choirs of angels, prophets and apostles.   St Antony, though he rejoiced on St Paul's account, could not help lamenting on his own, for having lost a treasure so lately discovered.   He arose, pursued his journey, and came to the cave.   Going in he found the body kneeling, and the hands stretched out.   Full of joy, and supposing him yet alive, he knelt

* Educated pagans were no less credulous than their Christian contemporaries.   Plutarch, in his life of Sylla, says that a satyr was brought to that general at Athens ; and St Jerome tells us that one was shown alive at Alexandria, and after its death was embalmed, and sent to Antioch that Constantine the Great might see it.   Pliny and others assure us that centaurs have been seen.

down to pray with him, but by his silence soon perceived Paul was dead. Whilst he stood perplexed how to dig a grave, two lions came up quietly, and as it were mourning ; and, tearing up the ground, made a hole large enough. St Antony then buried the body, singing psalms according to the rite then usual in the Church. After this he returned home praising God, and related to his monks what he had seen and done. He always kept as a great treasure, and wore himself on great festivals, the garment of St Paul, of palm-tree leaves patched together. St Paul died in the year 342, the hundred and thirteenth of his age, and the ninetieth of his solitude, and is usually called the " First Hermit ", to distinguish him from others of that name. He is commemorated in the canon of the Mass according to the Coptic and Armenian rites.

The summary which Alban Butler has here given of the life of the First Hermit is taken from the short biography edited in Latin by St Jerome, and afterwards widely circulated in the West. It seems possible, though this has been much disputed, that St Jerome himself did little more than translate a Greek text of which we have versions in Syriac, Arabic and Coptic, and which contained a good deal of fabulous matter. Jerome, however, undoubtedly regarded the life as in substance historical. The Greek original seems to have been written as a supplement, and in some measure a correction, to the Life of St Antony by St Athanasius. See on the whole question F. Nau in *Analecta Bollandiana*, vol. xx (1901), pp. 121-157. The two principal Greek texts have been edited by J. Bidez (1900), the Syriac and Coptic by Pereira (1904). *Cf.* also J. de Decker, *Contribution à l'étude des vies de Paul de Thèbes* (1905) ; Plenkers in *Der Katholik* (1905), vol. ii, pp. 294-300 ; Schiwietz, *Das morgenländische Mönchtum* (1904), pp. 49-51 ; Cheneau d'Orléans, *Les Saints d'Égypte* (1923), vol. i, pp. 76-86. For a French translation of Jerome's Life of Paul, see R. Draguet, *Les Pères du désert* (1949) ; and *cf.* H. Waddell, *The Desert Fathers* (1936), pp. 35-53.

ST MACARIUS THE ELDER   (A.D. 390)

THIS Macarius was born in Upper Egypt, about the year 300, and spent his youth in tending cattle. By a powerful call of divine grace he retired from the world at an early age and, dwelling in a little cell, made mats, in continual prayer and the practice of great austerities. A woman falsely accused him of having offered her violence, for which supposed crime he was dragged through the streets, beaten and insulted, as a base hypocrite under the garb of a monk. He suffered all with patience, and sent the woman what he earned by his work, saying to himself, " Well, Macarius ! having now another to provide for, thou must work the harder ". But God made his innocence known ; for the woman falling in labour, lay in extreme anguish, and could not be delivered till she had named the true father of her child. The fury of the people turned into admiration for the saint's humility and patience. To escape the esteem of men he fled to the vast and melancholy desert of Skete, being then about thirty years of age. In this solitude he lived sixty years, and became the spiritual parent of innumerable holy persons who put themselves under his direction and were governed by the rules he laid down for them ; but all occupied separate hermitages. St Macarius admitted only one disciple to dwell with him, whose duty it was to receive strangers. He was compelled by an Egyptian bishop to receive the priesthood that he might celebrate the divine mysteries for the convenience of this colony. When the desert became better peopled, there were four churches built in it, which were served by so many priests.

The austerities of St Macarius were excessive ; he usually ate but once a week. Evagrius, his disciple, once asked him leave, when tortured with thirst, to drink a little water ; but Macarius bade him content himself with reposing awhile in the shade, saying, " For these twenty years I have never once eaten, drunk or slept as much as nature required ". His face was very pale, and his body feeble and shrivelled. To go against his own inclinations he did not refuse to drink a little wine when others desired him ; but then he would punish himself for this indulgence by abstaining two or three days from all manner of drink ; and it was for this reason that his disciple besought strangers never to offer him wine. He delivered his instructions in few words, and recommended silence, retirement and continual prayer, especially the last, to all sorts of people. He used to say, " In prayer you need not use many or lofty words. You can often repeat with a sincere heart, ' Lord, show me mercy as thou knowest best.' Or, ' O God, come to my assistance.' " His mildness and patience were invincible, and wrought the conversion of a heathen priest and many others.

A young man applying to St Macarius for spiritual advice, he directed him to go to a burying-place and upbraid the dead ; and after that to go and flatter them. When he returned the saint asked him what answer the dead had made. " None at all ", said the other, " either to reproaches or praises." " Then ", replied Macarius, " go and learn neither to be moved by abuse nor by flattery. If you die to the world and to yourself, you will begin to live to Christ." He said to another, " Receive from the hand of God poverty as cheerfully as riches, hunger and want as readily as plenty ; then you will conquer the Devil, and subdue your passions." A certain monk complained to him that in solitude he was always tempted to break his fast, whereas in the monastery he could fast the whole week cheerfully. " Vainglory is the reason ", replied the saint ; " Fasting pleases when men see you ; but seems intolerable when the craving for esteem is not gratified." One came to consult him who was molested with temptations to impurity ; the saint examining into the source, convinced himself that the trouble was due to indolence. Accordingly, he advised him never to eat before sunset, to meditate fervently at his work, and to labour vigorously without slackening the whole day. The other faithfully complied, and was freed from his torment. God revealed to St Macarius that he had not attained to the perfection of two married women, who lived in a certain town. The saint thereupon paid them a visit, and learned the means by which they sanctified themselves. They were careful never to speak idle or rash words ; they lived in humility, patience, charity and conformity to the humours of their husbands ; and they sanctified all their actions by prayer, consecrating to the divine glory all the powers of their soul and body.

A heretic of the sect of the Hieracites, called so from Hierax, who denied the resurrection of the dead, had caused some to be unsettled in their faith. St Macarius, to confirm them in the truth, raised a dead man to life, as Socrates, Sozomen, Palladius and Rufinus relate. Cassian says that he only made a dead body to speak for that purpose ; then bade it rest till the resurrection. Lucius, the Arian usurper of the see of Alexandria, sent troops into the desert to disperse the zealous monks, several of whom sealed their faith with their blood. The leading ascetics, namely the two Macariuses, Isidore, Pambo and some others were banished to a little island in the Nile delta, surrounded with marshes. The inhabitants, who were pagans, were all converted by the example and preaching of these holy men. In the end Lucius suffered them to return to their cells. Macarius, knowing that his end drew near, paid a visit to the monks of Nitria, and exhorted them in such moving terms that they all fell weeping at his feet. " Let us weep, brethren ", said he, " and let our eyes pour forth floods of tears before we go hence, lest we fall into that place where tears will only feed the flames in which we shall burn." He went to receive the reward of his labours at the age of ninety, after having spent sixty years in Skete. Macarius seems to have been, as Cassian asserts, the first anchoret who inhabited this vast wilderness. Some style him a disciple of St Antony ; but it appears that he could not have lived under the direction of Antony before he retired to Skete. It seems, however, that later on he paid a visit, if not several, to that holy patriarch of monks, whose dwelling was fifteen days' journey distant. Macarius is commemorated in the canon of the Mass according to the Coptic and Armenian rites.

See Palladius, *Historia Lausiaca*, c. 19 *seq.* ; *Acta Sanctorum*, January 15 ; Schiwietz, *Morgenländ. Mönchtum*, vol. i, pp. 97 *seq.* Bardenhewer, *Patrology* (Eng. ed.), pp. 266–267 ; Gore in *Journ. of Theol. Stud.*, vol. viii, pp. 85–90 ; Cheneau d'Orléans, *Les saints d'Égypte* (1923), vol. i, pp. 117–138.

ST ISIDORE OF ALEXANDRIA (A.D. 404)

IN early life Isidore, after distributing his large fortune to the poor, became an ascetic in the Nitrian desert. Afterwards he fell under the influence of St Athanasius, who ordained him and took him to Rome in 341. The greater part of his life, however, seems to have been passed as governor of the great hospital at Alexandria. When Palladius, the author of the *Lausiac History*, came to Egypt to adopt an ascetic life, he addressed himself first to Isidore, who advised him simply to practise austerity and self-denial, and then to return for further instruction. During his last days the saint, when over eighty years of age, was overwhelmed with persecutions, misrepresentations and troubles of every description. St Jerome denounced him in violent terms for his supposed Origenist sympathies, and his own bishop, Theophilus, who had once been his friend, excommunicated him, so that Isidore was driven to take refuge in the Nitrian desert, where he had spent his youth. In the end he fled to Constantinople to seek the protection of St John Chrysostom, and there shortly afterwards he died at the age of eighty-five.

See Palladius, *Historia Lausiaca*, and *Dialogus de vita Chrysostomi* ; and *Acta Sanctorum*, January 15.

ST JOHN CALYBITES (*c.* A.D. 450)

IT was at Gomon on the Bosphorus, among the " sleepless " monks founded by St Alexander Akimetes, that St John sought seclusion, leaving his father and a large fortune. After six years he returned disguised in the rags of a beggar, and lived unrecognized upon the charity afforded him by his parents, close to their door in a little hut (καλύβη) ; whence he is known as " Calybites ". He sanctified his soul by wonderful patience, meekness and prayer. When at the point of death he is said to have revealed his identity to his mother, producing in proof the book of the gospels, bound in gold, which he had used as a boy. He asked to be buried under the hut he had occupied, and this was granted, but a church was built over it, and his relics were at a later date translated to Rome. The legend of Calybites has either originated from, or been confused with, those of St Alexis, St Onesimus, and one or two others in which the same idea recurs of a disguise long persisted in.

See the *Acta Sanctorum* for January 15, and *Analecta Bollandiana*, vol. xv (1896), pp. 256–267. *Cf.* also *Synaxarium Cp.* (ed. Delehaye), p. 393.

ST ITA, VIRGIN   (*c.* A.D. 570)

AMONG the women saints of Ireland, St Ita (also called Ida and Mida, with other variant spellings) holds the foremost place after St Brigid. Although her life has been overlaid with a multitude of mythical and extravagant miracles, there is no reason to doubt her historical existence. She is said to have been of royal descent, to have been born in one of the baronies of Decies, near Drum, Co. Waterford, and to have been originally called Deirdre. A noble suitor presented himself, but by fasting and praying for three days Ita, with angelic help, won her father's consent to her leading a life of virginity. She accordingly migrated to Hy Conaill, in the western part of the present county of Limerick. There at Killeedy she gathered round her a community of maidens and there, after long years given to the service of God and her neighbour, she eventually died, probably in the year 570. We are told that at first she often went without food for three or four days at a time. An angel appeared and counselled her to have more regard for her health, and when she demurred, he told her that in future God would provide for her needs. From that time forth she lived entirely on food sent her from Heaven. A religious maiden, a pilgrim from afar, asked her one day, " Why is it that God loves thee so much ? Thou art fed by Him miraculously, thou healest all manner of diseases, thou prophesiest regarding the past and the future, the angels converse with thee daily, and thou never ceasest to keep thy thoughts fixed upon the divine mysteries." Then Ita gave her to understand that it was this very practice of continual meditation, in which she had trained herself from childhood, which was the source of all the rest. Ita is said to have been sought out and consulted by the most saintly of her countrymen.

It appears that St Ita conducted a school for small boys, and we are told that the bishop St Erc committed to her care one who was afterwards destined to be famous as abbot and missionary, the child Brendan, who for five years was trained by her. One day the boy asked her to tell him three things which God specially loved. She answered : " True faith in God with a pure heart, a simple life with a religious spirit, openhandedness inspired by charity—these three things God specially loves." " And what ", continued the boy, " are the three things which God most abhors ? " " A face ", she said, " which scowls upon all mankind, obstinacy in wrong-doing, and an overweening confidence in the power of money ; these are three things which are hateful in God's sight."

Not a few of the miracles attributed to St Ita are very preposterous, as, for example, the story that a skilful craftsman whose services she had retained, and to whom she gave her sister as wife, promising that he should become the father of a famous and holy son, went out to battle against a party of raiders and had his head cut off. On making a search for him, they found the trunk, but the head had been carried away by the victors. Then Ita, because her promise was still unfulfilled, set to work to pray ; whereupon the head, by the power of God, flew back through the air to unite itself to the body, and an hour later the man, standing up alive, returned with them to the convent. Afterwards he had a son who was known as St Mochoemog (hypocoristic for Coemgen), the future abbot of Liath-mor or Leagh, in Tipperary. It was St Ita who had care of him, and gave him his name, which means " my beautiful little one ", sometimes latinized as Pulcherius. St Ita's feast is celebrated throughout Ireland.

The life of St. Ita has been critically edited by C. Plummer in VSH., vol. ii, pp. 116-130. See also the *Acta Sanctorum*, January 15; J. Colgan, *Acta Sanctorum Hiberniae*; LIS., vol. i, p. 200; J. Ryan, *Irish Monasticism* (1931), pp. 138 140; and J. Begley, *Diocese of Limerick, Ancient and Modern* (1906), ch. iv.

ST MAURUS, Abbot   (Sixth Century)

AMONG other noblemen who placed their sons under the care of St Benedict to be brought up in piety and learning a certain Equitius left his son Maurus, then but twelve years old; and when he was grown up St Benedict made him his assistant in the government of Subiaco. The boy Placid, going one day to fetch water, fell into the lake and was carried the distance of a bow-shot from the bank. St Benedict saw this in spirit in his cell, and bade Maurus run and draw him out. Maurus obeyed, walked unknowingly upon the water, and dragged out Placid by the hair. He attributed the miracle to the prayers of St Benedict; but the abbot declared that God had rewarded the obedience of the disciple. Not long after, the holy patriarch retired to Monte Cassino, and St Maurus may have become superior at Subiaco.

This, which we learn from St Gregory the Great, is all that can be told with any probability regarding the life of St Maurus. It is, however, stated upon the authority of a pretended biography by pseudo-Faustus—*i.e.* Abbot Odo of Glanfeuil—that St Maurus, coming to France, founded by the liberality of King Theodebert the great abbey of Glanfeuil, afterwards called Saint-Maur-sur-Loire, which he governed until his seventieth year. Maurus then resigned the abbacy, and passed the remainder of his life in solitude to prepare himself for his passage to eternity. After two years he fell sick, and died on January 15 in the year 584. He was buried on the right side of the altar in the church of St Martin, and on a roll of parchment laid in his tomb was inscribed this epitaph " Maurus, a monk and deacon, who came into France in the days of King Theodebert, and died the eighteenth day before the month of February." That this parchment was really found in the middle of the ninth century is probable enough; but there is no reliable evidence to establish the fact that the Maurus so described is identical with the Maurus who was the disciple of St Benedict.

From the time of Bollandus and of Mabillon (who in his *Acta Sanctorum, O.S.B.*, vol. i, pp. 275-298 printed the Life of St Maurus by pseudo-Faustus as an authentic document) down to the present day a lively controversy has raged over the question of St Maurus's connection with Glanfeuil. Bruno Krusch (*Neues Archiv*, vol. xxxi, pp. 245 247) considers that we have no reason to affirm the existence of any such monk as Maurus, or any abbey at Glanfeuil in Merovingian times. Without going quite so far as this, Fr Poncelet, in many notes in the *Analecta Bollandiana* (*e.g.* vol. xv, pp. 355-356), and U. Berlière in the *Revue Bénédictine* (vol. xxii, pp. 541-542) are agreed that the life by " Faustus " is quite untrustworthy. An admirable review of the whole discussion, summing it up in the same sense, has been published by H. Leclercq in DAC., *s.v.* " Glanfeuil " (vol. vi, cc, 1283-1319). See also J. McCann, *St Benedict* (1938), pp. 274-281.

ST BONITUS, OR BONET, Bishop of Clermont   (A.D. 706)

ST BONITUS was referendary or chancellor to St Sigebert III, king of Austrasia; and by his zeal, religion and justice flourished in that kingdom under four kings. In 677 Thierry III made him governor of Marseilles, an office he carried out with distinction and liberality. His elder brother, St Avitus II, Bishop of Clermont in Auvergne, having recommended him for his successor, died in 689, and Bonet was consecrated. But after having governed that see some years with exemplary piety, he had a scruple whether his election had been perfectly canonical ; and having consulted St Tillo, then leading an eremitical life at Solignac, resigned his dignity, led a most penitential life in the abbey of Manglieu, and after having made a pilgrimage to Rome died at Lyons in 706. The colloquial form of this saint's name is Bont.

See his life, written by a monk of Sommon in Auvergne, published in the *Acta Sanctorum,* January 15 ; MGH., *Scriptores Merov.,* vol. vi ; and CMH., pp. 37-38.

ST CEOLWULF   (A.D. 760 ?)

IT is difficult to find any trace of late medieval *cultus* of this Northumbrian king, but he was held in high honour after his death, his body in 830 being translated to Norham, and the head to Durham. Bede speaks enthusiastically of his virtues and his zeal, and dedicated to him his *Ecclesiastical History*, which he submitted to the king's criticism. Ceolwulf ended his days as a monk at Lindisfarne, and it is recorded that through his influence the community, who previously had drunk nothing but water or milk, were allowed to take beer, and even wine. His relics were said to work many miracles. Simeon of Durham assigns his death to 764, but in the *Anglo-Saxon Chronicle* the date given is 760.

Practically all available information will be found collected in Plummer's edition of Bede, especially vol. ii, p. 340.

BD PETER OF CASTELNAU, Martyr   (A.D. 1208)

THIS Cistercian monk was born near Montpellier, and in 1199 we hear of him as archdeacon of Maguelone, but he entered the Cistercian Order a year or two later. To him, aided by another of his religious brethren, Pope Innocent III in 1203 confided the mission of taking action as apostolic delegate and inquisitor against the Albigensian heretics, a duty which Peter discharged with much zeal, but little success. The opposition against him, which was fanned by Raymund VI, Count of Toulouse, ended in his assassination on January 15, 1209, not far from the abbey of Saint-Gilles. Pierced through the body by a lance, Bd Peter cried to his murderer, "May God forgive thee as fully as I forgive thee". His relics were enshrined and venerated in the abbey church of Saint-Gilles.

See *Acta Sanctorum*, March 5 ; Hurter in *Kirchenlexikon*, vol. ii, cc. 2031-2033 ; H. Nickerson, *The Inquisition*, pp. 77-95.

BD FRANCIS DE CAPILLAS, Martyr   (A.D. 1648)

THE Dominicans followed the Jesuits to China early in the seventeenth century, and to the Order of Preachers belongs the honour of having produced the first native Chinese priest and bishop, Gregory Lo (1616-1691), and the first beatified martyr in China, Francis Ferdinand de Capillas. He was born of humble stock in the province of Valladolid, and joined the Preachers when he was seventeen. He volunteered for the mission in the Philippines, and received the priesthood at Manila in 1631. For ten years he laboured under a tropical sun in the Cagayan district of Luzon, regarding this apostolic field as a sort of training-ground for the still more arduous mission to which he felt himself destined. Here it was, accordingly, that he already practised great austerities, lying, for example, upon a wooden cross during the short hours he gave to sleep, and deliberately exposing his body to the bites of the insects which infest these regions. At last, in 1642, he was chosen to accompany the pioneer missionary, Father Francis Diaz, O.P., who was returning by way of Formosa to take up again the apostolate he had already begun in the Chinese province of Fokien. After learning the language an immense success is said to have attended the labours of Father de Capillas, and in Fogan, Moyan, Tingteu and other towns, he made many converts.

Unfortunately it was just at this epoch that great revolutionary disturbances shook the whole Chinese empire. The Ming dynasty came to an end, and the Manchu Tatars were called in to help to quell one party of the rebels, with the result that they themselves eventually became masters of the country. In Fokien a stout resistance was offered to the Tatars, and although they occupied Fogan they were besieged there by the armies of the Chinese viceroy. It would seem that while the town was thus invested Father de Capillas entered it by stealth to render spiritual assistance to some of his converts. The mandarins of the old administration had been tolerant and often friendly to the Christians. The new masters were bitterly hostile to the religion of the foreigner. Father de Capillas was caught, cruelly tortured, tried as a spy who was believed to be conveying information to the besiegers, and in the end put to death by having his head cut off, on January 15, 1648. In view of the question raised in the case of some of our English martyrs as to whether they really died for the faith, or were only put to death as political offenders, it is interesting to note that although Fathers Ferrando and Fonseca in their Spanish *History of the Dominicans in the Philippines* admit that sedition (*rebeldia*) was the formal charge upon which Father de Capillas was sentenced to death, the Holy See has pronounced him to be a true martyr.

In reference to this same holy Dominican, a quotation may not be out of place from Sir Robert K. Douglas :

" Why do you so much trouble yourselves ", the emperor [K'anghsi] asked on one occasion of a missionary, " about a world which you have never yet entered ? " and adopting the, to him, canonical view, he expressed his opinion that it would be much wiser if they thought less of the world to come and more of the present life. It is possible that when he said this he may have had in his mind the dying word of Ferdinand de Capillas, who suffered martyrdom in 1648 : " I have had no home but the world ", said this priest, as he faced his last earthly judge, " no bed but the ground, no food but what Providence sent me from day to day, and no other object but to do and suffer for the glory of Jesus Christ and for the eternal happiness of those who believe in His name."

See Touron, *Histoire des hommes illustres O.P.*, vol. vi, pp. 732–735 ; but especially Juan Ferrando and Joaquin Fonseca, *Historia de los PP. Dominicos en las Islas Filipinas*, vol. ii, pp. 569–587. *Cf.* R. K. Douglas, *China*, in the Story of the Nations series, pp. 61–62. For other martyrs in China see herein under February 17, May 26, July 9 and September 11. Bd Francis de Capillas was beatified in 1909.

16 : ST MARCELLUS I, POPE AND MARTYR　　(A.D. 309)

ST MARCELLUS had been a priest under Pope St Marcellinus, and succeeded him in 308, after the see of Peter had been vacant for three years and a half. An epitaph written of him by Pope St Damasus says that by enforcing the canons of penance he drew upon himself the hostility of many tepid and refractory Christians, and that for his severity against a certain apostate, he was banished by Maxentius. He died in 309 at his unknown place of exile. The *Liber Pontificalis* states that Lucina, the widow of one Pinian, who lodged St Marcellus when he lived in Rome, after his death converted her house into a church, which she called by his name. His false acts relate that, among other sufferings, he was condemned by the tyrant to keep cattle. He is styled a martyr in the early sacramentaries and martyrologies, but the fifth-century account of his martyrdom conflicts with the earlier epitaph. His body lies in Rome under the high altar in the ancient church which bears his name and gives its title to a cardinal.

The difficult question of the chronology of the brief pontificate of Pope St Marcellus has been discussed at length by Mgr Duchesne (*Liber Pontificalis*, vol. i, pp. xcix and 164) and Father Grisar (*Kirchenlexikon*, vol. viii, cc. 656–658) ; *cf.* also Duchesne in *Mélanges d'arch.* ., 1898, pp. 382–392, and CMH., pp. 42–43.

ST PRISCILLA, MATRON　　(*c.* A.D. 98)

IT is tantalizing to know so little of St Priscilla, who is commemorated in the Roman Martyrology on this day and who has given her name as foundress to what is probably the most ancient and interesting of the catacombs. She seems to have been the wife of Manius Acilius Glabrio, who, as we learn from the pagan historians Suetonius and Dion Cassius, was put to death by Domitian on the pretext of some crime of sedition or blasphemous impiety, under which charge we may perhaps recognize a conversion to Christianity. It is likely that St Priscilla was the mother of the senator St Pudens, and through him, the ancestress of SS. Praxedis and Pudentiana. St Peter, the apostle, is believed to have used a villa belonging to St Priscilla on the Via Salaria, beneath which the catacomb was afterwards excavated, as the seat of his activities in Rome. There can be no doubt that the Acilii Glabriones were intimately connected with this spot, and that many of the family in the second and third centuries were Christians and were buried in the catacombs.

See De Rossi in *Bullettino di archeologia cristiana*, 1888–1889, pp. 15 and 103 ; Marucchi in *Nuovo bullettino* . ., vol. viii (1902), pp. 217–232 ; H. Leclercq in DAC., *s.v.* " Glabrion", vol. vi, cc. 1259–1274.

ST HONORATUS, BISHOP OF ARLES　　(A.D. 429)

HONORATUS was of a consular Roman family settled in Gaul, and was well versed in the liberal arts. In his youth he renounced the worship of idols and gained to Christ his elder brother Venantius, whom he also inspired with a contempt for the world. They desired to forsake it entirely, but their father put continual obstacles in their way. At length they took with them St Caprasius, a holy hermit, to act as their instructor, and sailed from Marseilles to Greece, intending to live there unknown in some desert. Venantius soon died at Modon ; and Honoratus, having also fallen ill, was obliged to return with his conductor. He first led an eremitical life in the mountains near Fréjus.   Two small islands lie in the sea near that coast one larger and nearer the continent, called Lero, now St Margaret's ;   the other smaller and more remote, two leagues from Antibes, named Lérins, at present Saint-Honorat, from our saint.   There he settled ;   and being followed by others he founded the famous monastery of Lérins about the year 400.   Some he appointed to live in community ;   others in separate cells as anchorets.   His rule was chiefly borrowed from that of St Pachomius.   Nothing can be more attractive than the description St Hilary of Arles has given of the virtues of this company of saints, especially of the charity and devotion which reigned amongst them.

A charming legend, unfortunately of much later date, recounts how Margaret, the sister of Honoratus, converted at last from paganism by his prayers, came to settle on the other island, Lero, in order to be near her brother.   With some reluctance he was induced to promise that he would visit her once a year, when the mimosa was in bloom.   But on one occasion Margaret in great distress of soul longed for his guidance.   It was still two months from the time appointed, but she fell upon her knees and prayed.   Suddenly all the air was filled with an unmistakable perfume ;   she looked up, and there, close beside her, was a mimosa tree covered with its fragrant blossom.   She tore off a bough and sent it to her brother, who understood her appeal and tenderly acceded to the summons.   It was their last meeting, for she passed away soon afterwards.   Honoratus was by compulsion consecrated archbishop of Arles in 426, and died exhausted with austerities and apostolic labours in 429.   The style of his letters, so St Hilary, his successor, assures us, was clear and affecting, penned with an admirable delicacy, elegance and sweetness.   The loss of all these is much to be regretted.   His tomb is shown empty under the high altar of the church which bears his name at Arles, his body having been translated to Lérins in 1391.

Cf. Gallia Christiana novissima, vol. iii (1901), p. 26 ; *Revue Bénédictine*, vol. iv, pp. 180–184 ; Duchesne, *Fastes Épiscopaux*, vol. i, p. 256.   See also his panegyric by his disciple, kinsman and successor, St Hilary of Arles, and especially A. C. Cooper-Marsden, *The History of the Islands of the Lérins* (1913), illustrated with excellent photographs.   B. Munke and others have edited a medieval Latin life of St Honoratus (1911), but like the Provençal *Vida de Sant Honorat* it contains nothing of historical value.   Hilary's discourse is translated in F. R. Hoare, *The Western Fathers* (1954).

ST FURSEY, ABBOT   (*c.* A.D. 648)

THERE are few of the early Irish saints whose lives are better known to us than that of St Fursey (Fursa).   He seems to have been born near Lough Corrib—possibly upon the island of Inisquin itself.   Though conflicting accounts are given of his parentage, he was certainly of noble birth, but, as we are told, he was more noble by virtue than by blood.   His gifts of person and mind are dilated on by his biographer, but in order to equip himself better in sacred learning he left his home and his own people, and eventually erected a monastery at Rathmat (? Killursa), which was thronged by recruits from all parts of Ireland.

After a time, returning home to his family, he experienced the first of some wonderful ecstasies, which being detailed by his biographer and recounted afterwards by such writers as Bede and Aelfric, became famous throughout the Christian world.   During these trances his body seems to have remained motionless in a cataleptic seizure, and his brethren, believing him to be dead, made preparations for his burial.   The principal subject of these visions was the effort of the powers

of evil to claim the soul of the Christian as it quits the body on its passage to another
life. A fierce struggle is depicted, in which the angels engage in conflict with the
demons, refuting their arguments, and rescuing the soul from the flames with
which it is threatened. In one particular vision we are told that St Fursey was
lifted up on high and was ordered by the angels who conducted him to look back
upon the world. Whereupon, casting his eyes downward, he saw as it were a dark
and gloomy valley far beneath. Around this were four great fires kindled in the
air, separate one from the other, and the angel told him that these four fires would
consume all the world, and burn the souls of those men who through their misdeeds
had made void the confession and promise of their baptism. The first fire, it was
explained, will burn the souls of those who are forsworn and untruthful ; the
second, those who give themselves up to greed ; the third, those who stir up strife
and discord ; the fourth, those who think it no crime to deceive and defraud the
helpless. Then the fires seemed all to coalesce and to threaten him with destruction, so that he cried out in alarm. But the angel answered, " That which you did
not kindle shall not burn within you, for though this appears to be a terrible and
great fire, yet it tries every man according to the merits of his works ". Bede, after
giving a long summary of these visions, writes : " An elderly brother of our
monastery is still living who is wont to narrate how a very truthful and religious
man told him that he had seen Fursey himself in the province of the East Angles,
and heard these visions from his own lips ; adding, that though it was most sharp
winter weather and a hard frost, and this man was sitting in a thin garment when
he related it, yet he sweated as if it had been the greatest heat of summer, either
through the panic of fear which the memory called up, or through excess of spiritual
consolation ". This is certainly a very remarkable tribute to the vividness of St
Fursey's descriptions. One other curious detail in connection with the visions
is the statement that the saint, having jostled against a condemned soul, carried
the brand-mark of that contact upon his shoulder and cheek until the day of his
death.

After twelve years of preaching in Ireland, St Fursey came with his brothers,
St Foillan and St Ultan, to England, and settled for a while in East Anglia, where
he was cordially welcomed by King Sigebert, who gave him land to build a monastery, probably at Burgh Castle, near Yarmouth. This migration must have taken
place after the year 630 ; but somewhere between 640 and 644 the Irish monk
determined to cross over to Gaul. Establishing himself in Neustria, he was
honourably received by Clovis II. He built a monastery at Lagny, but died, when
on a journey, shortly afterwards, probably in 648. His remains were transferred
to Péronne. The feast of St Fursey is celebrated throughout Ireland and also in
the diocese of Northampton.

See the *Acta Sanctorum* for January 16 ; Plummer's edition of Bede's *Ecclesiastical
History*, vol. ii, pp. 169–174 ; M. Stokes, *Three Months in the Forests of France*, pp. 134–177 ;
Moran, *Irish Saints in Great Britain*, p. 315 ; Healy, *Ireland's Ancient Schools*, p. 266 ;
Gougaud, *Gaelic Pioneers of Christianity*, and *Christianity in Celtic Lands ;* Grützmacher
in *Zeitschrift f. Kirchengesch.*, vol xix (1898), pp. 190–196.

BD FERREOLUS, Bishop of Grenoble, Martyr   (c. A.D. 670)

ALTHOUGH the cult of Bd Ferreolus was confirmed by Pope Pius X in 1907,
practically nothing is known of the facts of his life. He is said to have been the

thirteenth bishop of Grenoble, but, as Mgr Duchesne points out, nothing connects him with the see but a feeble liturgical tradition.   Later accounts describe him as resisting the demands of the tyrannical mayor of the palace, Ebroin, and as having been, in consequence, driven from his see, and eventually put to death.

See Duchesne, *Fastes Épiscopaux*, vol. i, p. 232, and the *Acta Sanctorum* for January 12.

ST HENRY OF COCKET   (A.D. 1220)

THE Danes were indebted in part for the light of faith, under God, to the example and labours of English missionaries.   Henry was born in that country, and from his youth gave himself to the divine service with his whole heart.   When he came to man's estate he sailed to the north of England.   The little island of Cocket, which lies on the coast of Northumberland, near the mouth of the river of the same name, had been the home of anchorets even in St Bede's time, as appears from his life of St Cuthbert.   This island belonged to the monastery of Tynemouth, and St Henry undertook to lead in it an eremitical life.   His only daily meal, which he took after sunset, was bread and water ; and this bread he earned by tilling a little garden.   He died in his hermitage on January 16, 1127, and was buried by the monks at Tynemouth in their church.

His life by Capgrave is printed in the *Acta Sanctorum* for January 16.   *Cf.* also Stanton, *Menology*, pp. 22–23.   There seems to be no evidence of public *cultus*.

SS. BERARD AND HIS COMPANIONS, MARTYRS   (A.D. 1220)

THESE five friars were sent by St Francis to the Mohammedans of the West whilst he went in person to those of the East.   They preached first to the Moors of Seville, where they suffered much for their zeal, and were banished.   Passing thence into Morocco, they began there to preach Christ, and tried to act as chaplains to the sultan's Christian mercenaries.   The friars were looked on as lunatics and treated accordingly.   When they refused either to return whence they had come or to keep silent, the sultan, taking his scimitar, clove their heads asunder, on January 16, 1220.   These formed the vanguard of that glorious army of martyrs which the Seraphic order has since given to the Church.   When St Francis heard the news of their heroic endurance and triumph, he cried out, " Now I can truly say I have five brothers ".   They were SS. Berard, Peter, Odo, Accursio and Adjutus.

They were canonized in 1481. See the *Acta Sanctorum*, January 16 ; Wadding, *Annales Minorum*, s.a. 1220 ; and in *Analecta Franciscana*, vol. iii, pp. 579–596.   *Cf.* also Karl Müller, *Die Anfänge des Minoritenordens*, pp. 207–210 ; Léon, *Auréole Séraphique* (Eng. trans.), vol. i, pp. 99–111 ; and H. Koehler, *L'Église du Maroc*   (1934), pp. 3–20.

BD GONSALO OF AMARANTE   (A.D. 1259 ?)

IT must be confessed that many of the incidents recorded in the life of Bd Gonsalo (Gundisalvus), a Portuguese of high family, are not of a nature to inspire confidence in the sobriety of his biographer's judgement.   At the very outset we are told that when carried to the font the infant fixed his eyes on the crucifix with a look of extraordinary love.   Then, when he had grown up and been ordained priest, he is said to have resigned his rich benefice to his nephew, and to have spent fourteen years upon a pilgrimage to the Holy Land.   On his return, being repulsed by his nephew, who set the dogs on him as a vagrant, he was supernaturally directed to enter that order in which the office began and ended with the *Ave Maria*.   He accordingly became a Dominican, but was allowed by his superiors to live as a hermit, during which time he built, largely with his own hands, a bridge over the river Tamega.   When the labourers whom he persuaded to help him had no wine to drink, and he was afraid that they would go on strike, he betook himself to prayer ; and then, on his hitting the rock with his stick, an abundant supply of excellent wine spouted forth from a fissure.   Again, when provisions failed he went to the riverside to summon the fishes, who came at his call and jumped out of the river, competing for the privilege of being eaten in so worthy a cause.   Similarly, we read that " when he was preaching to the people, desiring to make them understand the effect of the Church's censures upon the soul, he excommunicated a basket of bread, and the loaves at once became black and corrupt.   Then, to show that the Church can restore to her communion those who humbly acknowledge their fault, he removed the excommunication, and the loaves recovered their whiteness and their wholesome savour " (Procter, p. 3).   It is to be feared that legend has played a considerable part in filling in the rather obscure outlines of the biography. Bd Gonsalo died on January 10, but his feast is kept on this day by the Dominicans, his *cultus* having been approved in 1560.

See Castiglio, *Historia Generale di S. Domenico e dell' Ordine suo* (1589), vol. i, pp. 299–304 ; Procter, *Short Lives of Dominican Saints*, pp. 1–4 ; *Acta Sanctorum* for January 10. The miracle of the fishes is said to have occurred not once, but repeatedly : " molte e diverse volte ".

17 : ST ANTONY THE ABBOT   (A.D. 356)

ST ANTONY was born at a village south of Memphis in Upper Egypt in 251. His parents, who were Christians, kept him always at home, so that he grew up in ignorance of what was then regarded as polite literature, and could read no language but his own.   At their death he found himself possessed of a considerable estate and charged with the care of a younger sister, before he was twenty years of age.   Some six months afterwards he heard read in the church those words of Christ to the rich young man : " Go, sell what thou hast, and give it to the poor, and thou shalt have treasure in Heaven ".   Considering these words as addressed to himself, he went home and made over to his neighbours his best land, and the rest of his estate he sold and gave the price to the poor, except what he thought necessary for himself and his sister.   Soon after, hearing in the church those other words of Christ, " Be not solicitous for to-morrow ", he also distributed in alms the moveables which he had reserved, and placed his sister in a house of maidens, which is commonly assumed to be the first recorded mention of a nunnery.   Antony himself retired into solitude, in imitation of a certain old man who led the life of a hermit in the neighbourhood.   Manual labour, prayer and reading were his whole occupation ; and such was his fervour that if he heard of any virtuous recluse, he sought him out and endeavoured to take advantage of his example and instruction. In this way he soon became a model of humility, charity, prayerfulness and many more virtues.

The Devil assailed Antony by various temptations, representing to him first of all many good works he might have been able to carry out with his estate in the world, and the difficulties of his present condition—a common artifice of the enemy, whereby he strives to make a soul dissatisfied in the vocation God has appointed. Being repulsed by the young novice, he varied his method of attack, and harassed him night and day with gross and obscene imaginations.   Antony opposed to his assaults the strictest watchfulness over his senses, austere fasts and prayer, till Satan, appearing in a visible form, first of a woman coming to seduce him, then of a Negro to terrify him, at length confessed himself vanquished.   The saint's food was only bread, with a little salt, and he drank nothing but water ; he never ate before sunset, and sometimes only once in three or four days.   When he took his rest he lay on a rush mat or the bare floor.   In quest of a more remote solitude he withdrew to an old burial-place, to which a friend brought him bread from time to time.   Satan was here again permitted to assault him in a visible manner, and to terrify him with gruesome noises ; indeed, on one occasion he so grievously beat him that he lay almost dead, and in this condition was found by his friend.   When he began to come to himself Antony cried out to God, " Where wast thou, my Lord and Master ?   Why wast thou not here from the beginning of this conflict to render me assistance ? "   A voice answered, " Antony, I was here the whole time ; I stood by thee and beheld thy combat ; and because thou hast manfully withstood thy enemies, I will always protect thee, and will render thy name famous throughout the earth."

Hitherto Antony, ever since he turned his back on the world in 272, had lived in solitary places not very far from his village of Koman ; and St Athanasius observes that before him many fervent persons led retired lives in penance and contemplation near the towns, while others followed the same manner of life without withdrawing from their fellow creatures.   Both were called ascetics, from their being devoted to the exercise of mortification and prayer, according to the import of the Greek word ἄσκησις (practice or training).   Even in earlier times we find mention made of such ascetics ; and Origen, about the year 249, says they abstained from flesh-meat no less than the disciples of Pythagoras.   Eusebius tells us that St Peter of Alexandria practised austerities equal to those of the ascetics ; he says the same of Pamphilus, and St Jerome uses the same expression of Pierius. St Antony had led this manner of life near Koman until about the year 285 when, at the age of thirty-five, he crossed the eastern branch of the Nile and took up his abode in some ruins on the top of a mountain, in which solitude he lived almost twenty years, rarely seeing any man except one who brought him bread every six months.

To satisfy the importunities of others, about the year 305, the fifty-fourth of his age, he came down from his mountain and founded his first monastery, in the Fayum.   This originally consisted of scattered cells, but we cannot be sure that the various colonies of ascetics which he planted out in this way were all arranged upon the same plan.   He did not stay permanently with any such community, but he visited them occasionally, and St Athanasius tells us how, in order to reach this first monastery, he had, both in going and returning, to cross the Arsinoitic canal, which was infested by crocodiles.   It seems, however, that the distraction of mind caused by this intervention in the affairs of his fellow men gave him great scruples, and we hear even of a temptation to despair, which he could only overcome by prayer and hard manual labour.   In this new manner of life his daily sustenance was six ounces of bread soaked in water, to which he sometimes added a few dates. He took it generally after sunset, and in his old age he added a little oil. Sometimes he ate only once in three or four days, yet appeared vigorous and always cheerful ; strangers knew him from among his disciples by the joy on his countenance, resulting from the inward peace of his soul. St Antony exhorted his brethren to allot the least time they possibly could to the care of the body, notwithstanding which he was careful not to make perfection seem to consist in mortification but in the love of God. He instructed his monks to reflect every morning that perhaps they might not live till night, and every evening that perhaps they might never see the morning ; and to do every action as if it were the last of their lives. " The Devil ", he said, " dreads fasting, prayer, humility and good works ; he is not able even to stop my mouth who speak against him. His illusions soon vanish, especially if a man arms himself with the sign of the cross." He told them that once when the Devil appeared to him and said, " Ask what you please ; I am the power of God," he invoked the name of Jesus and the tempter vanished.

In the year 311, when the persecution was renewed under Maximinus, St Antony went to Alexandria in order to give courage to the martyrs. He publicly wore his white tunic of sheep-skin and appeared in the sight of the governor, yet took care never presumptuously to provoke the judges or impeach himself, as some rashly did. The persecution having abated, he returned to his monastery, and some time after organized another, called Pispir, near the Nile ; but he chose for the most part to shut himself up in a cell upon a mountain difficult of access with Macarius, a disciple whose duty it was to interview visitors. If he found them to be *Hiero-solymites*, *i.e.* spiritual men, St Antony himself sat with them in discourse ; if *Egyptians* (by which name they meant worldly persons), then Macarius entertained them, and Antony only appeared to give them a short exhortation. Once the saint saw in a vision the whole earth covered so thick with snares that it seemed scarce possible to set down a foot without being entrapped. At this sight he cried out trembling, " Who, Lord, can escape them all ? " A voice answered him, " Humility, Antony ! "

St Antony cultivated a little garden on his desert mountain, but this tillage was not the only manual labour in which he employed himself. St Athanasius speaks of his making mats as an ordinary occupation. We are told that he once fell into dejection, finding uninterrupted contemplation above his strength ; but was taught to apply himself at intervals to manual work by an angel in a vision, who appeared platting mats of palm-tree leaves, then rising to pray, and after some time sitting down again to work, and who at length said to him, " Do thus, and relief shall come to thee ". But St Athanasius declares that Antony continued in some degree to pray whilst he was at work. He spent a great part of the night in contemplation ; and sometimes when the rising sun called him to his daily tasks he complained that its visible light robbed him of the greater interior light which he enjoyed when left in darkness and solitude. After a short sleep he always rose at midnight, and continued in prayer on his knees with his hands lifted to Heaven till sunrise, and sometimes till three in the afternoon, so, at least, Palladius informs us in his *Lausiac History*.

St Antony in the year 339 saw in a vision, under the figure of mules kicking down the altar, the havoc which the Arian persecution was to cause two years after in Alexandria. So deep was the impression of horror that he would not speak to a heretic unless to exhort him to the true faith ; and he drove all such from his

mountain, calling them venomous serpents.   At the request of the bishops, about
the year 355, he took a journey to Alexandria to confute the Arians, preaching that
God the Son is not a creature, but of the same substance with the Father ; and that
the Arians, who called him a creature, did not differ from the heathen themselves,
" who worshipped and served the creature rather than the Creator ".   All the
people ran to see him, and rejoiced to hear him ; even the pagans, struck with the
dignity of his character, flocked around him, saying, " We want to see the man of
God ".   He converted many, and even worked miracles.   St Athanasius conducted
him back as far as the gates of the city, where he cured a girl possessed by an evil
spirit.   Being desired by the governor to make a longer stay in the city, he answered,
" As fish die if they are taken from the water, so does a monk wither away if 'he
forsake his solitude ".

St Jerome relates that at Alexandria Antony met the famous Didymus, the
blind head of the catechetical school there, and exhorted him not to regret overmuch
the loss of eyes, which were common even to insects, but to rejoice in the treasure
of that inner light which the apostles enjoyed, by which we see God and kindle the
fire of His love in our souls.   Heathen philosophers and others often went to
discuss with him, and returned astounded at his meekness and wisdom.   When
certain philosophers asked him how he could spend his time in solitude without
even the alleviation of books, he replied that nature was his great book and amply
supplied the lack of all else.   When others came to ridicule his ignorance, he asked
them with great simplicity which was best, good sense or book learning, and which
had produced the other.   The philosophers answered, " Good sense."   " This,
then ", said Antony, " is sufficient of itself."   Some others wishing to cavil and
demanding a reason for his faith in Christ, he put them to silence by showing that
they degraded the notion of godhead by ascribing to it human passions ; but that
the humiliation of the Cross is the greatest demonstration of infinite goodness, and
its ignominy is shown to be the highest glory by Christ's triumphant resurrection
and by His raising of the dead to life and curing the blind and the sick.   St
Athanasius mentions that he disputed with these Greeks through an interpreter.
Further, he assures us that no one visited St Antony under any affliction who did
not return home full of comfort ; and he relates many miraculous cures wrought
by him and several heavenly visions and revelations.

About the year 337 Constantine the Great and his two sons, Constantius and
Constans, wrote a letter to the saint, recommending themselves to his prayers.   St
Antony, seeing his monks surprised, said, " Do not wonder that the emperor writes
to us, a man even as I am ; rather be astounded that God should have written to us,
and that He has spoken to us by His Son ".   He said he knew not how to answer
it ; but at last, through the importunity of his disciples, he penned a letter to the
emperor and his sons, which St Athanasius has preserved, in which he exhorts them
to constant remembrance of the judgement to come.   St Jerome mentions seven
other letters of St Antony to divers monasteries.   A maxim which he frequently
repeats is, that the knowledge of ourselves is the necessary and only step by which
we can ascend to the knowledge and love of God.   The Bollandists give us a short
letter of St Antony to St Theodore, abbot of Tabenna, in which he says that God
had assured him that He showed mercy to all true worshippers of Jesus Christ,
even though they should have fallen, if they sincerely repented of their sin.   A
monastic rule, which bears St Antony's name, may very possibly preserve the
general features of his system of ascetic training.   In any case, his example and

instructions have served as a trustworthy rule for the monastic life to all succeeding ages.   It is related that St Antony, hearing his disciples express surprise at the multitudes who embraced the religious state, told them with tears that the time would come when monks would be fond of living in cities and stately buildings, of eating at well-laden tables, and be only distinguished from persons of the world by their dress ; but that still some amongst them would rise to the spirit of true perfection.

St Antony made a visitation of his monks a little before his death, which he foretold, but no tears could move him to die among them.   It appears from St Athanasius that the Christians had begun to imitate the pagan custom of embalming the bodies of the dead, an abuse which Antony had often condemned as proceeding from vanity and sometimes superstition.   He gave orders that he should be buried in the earth beside his mountain cell by his two disciples, Macarius and Amathas. Hastening back to his solitude on Mount Kolzim near the Red Sea, he some time after fell ill ; whereupon he repeated to these disciples his orders that they should bury his body secretly in that place, adding, " In the day of the resurrection I shall receive it incorruptible from the hand of Christ ".   He ordered them to give one of his sheep-skins, with the cloak upon which he lay, to the bishop Athanasius, as a public testimony of his being united in faith and communion with that holy prelate ; to give his other sheep-skin to the bishop Serapion ; and to keep for themselves his sackcloth.   " Farewell, my children.   Antony is departing, and will no longer be with you."   At these words they embraced him, and he, stretching out his feet, without any other sign, calmly ceased to breathe.   His death occurred in the year 356, probably on January 17, on which day the most ancient martyrologies commemorate him.   He was one hundred and five years old.   From his youth to that extreme old age he always maintained the same fervour and austerity ; yet he lived without sickness, his sight was not impaired, his teeth were only worn, not one was lost or loosened.   The two disciples interred him according to his directions.   About the year 561 his remains are supposed to have been discovered and translated to Alexandria, thence to Constantinople, and eventually to Vienne, in France.   The Bollandists print an account of many miracles wrought by his intercession, particularly of those connected with the epidemic called St Antony's Fire, which raged violently in many parts of Europe in the eleventh century about the time of the translation of his reputed relics thither.

In art St Antony is constantly represented with a *tau*-shaped crutch or cross, a little bell, a pig, and sometimes a book.   The crutch, in this peculiarly Egyptian T-shaped form of the cross, may be simply an indication of the saint's great age and abbatial authority, or it may very possibly have reference to his constant use of the sign of the cross in his conflict with evil spirits.   The pig, no doubt, in its origin, denoted the Devil, but in the course of the twelfth century it acquired a new significance owing to the popularity of the Hospital Brothers of St Antony, founded at Clermont in 1096.   Their works of charity endeared them to the people, and they obtained in many places the privilege of feeding their swine gratuitously upon the acorns and beech mast in the woods.   For this purpose a bell was attached to the neck of one or more sows in a herd of pigs, or possibly their custodians announced their coming by ringing a bell.   In any case, it seems that the bell became associated with the members of the order, and in that way developed into an attribute of their eponymous patron.   The book, no doubt, has reference to the book of nature which compensated the saint for the lack of any other reading. We also sometimes find flames indicated, which are typical of the disease, St Antony's Fire, against which the saint was specially invoked.* His popularity, largely due to the prevalence of this form of epidemic (see, *e.g.* the Life of St Hugh of Lincoln), was very great in the twelfth and thirteenth centuries. He was, in particular, appealed to, probably on account of his association with the pig, as the patron of domestic animals and farm stock, so that gilds of butchers, brushmakers, etc., placed themselves under his protection. Antony is named in the preparation of the Byzantine eucharistic liturgy and in the canon according to the Coptic and Armenian rites.

The main authority for our knowledge of St Antony is the Life by St Athanasius, the authorship of which is now practically undisputed ; there is an English trans. by Dr R. T. Meyer in the Ancient Christian Writers series, and others. A very early Latin translation of the original Greek was made by Evagrius, and a Syriac version is also known. (On a second Latin rendering, see Wilmart, in the *Revue Bénédictine*, 1914, pp. 163-173.) Interesting supplementary details are also contributed by Palladius in his *Historia Lausiaca*, Cassian, and the later church historians. The literature of the subject is considerable. It will be sufficient to refer to Abbot C. Butler, *Lausiac History*, vol. i, pp. 215-228, and in the *Catholic Encyclopedia*, vol. i, pp. 553-555 ; Hannay, *Christian Monasticism*, pp. 95 *seq.*, and pp. 274 *seq.* ; H. Leclercq, art. " Cénobitisme ", in the DAC. ; and Fr Cheneau, *Saints d'Égypte*, vol. i, pp. 153-181. On the diabolical assaults and temptations which figure so prominently in the life, *cf.* J. Stoffels in *Theologie und Glaube*, vol. ii (1910), pp. 721 *seq.*, and 809 *seq.* Some fragments of what seems to be the original Coptic of three of St Antony's letters have been published in the *Journal of Theol. Studies*, July, 1904, pp. 540-545 ; their authenticity is still a matter of dispute. We only know all seven in an imperfect Latin translation. The suggestion made by G. Ghedini (*Lettere cristiane dei papiri greci*, 1923, no. 19) that a letter in Greek on a fragment of papyrus in the British Museum is an autograph of St Antony, cannot be treated seriously ; see *Analecta Bollandiana*, vol. xlii (1924), p. 173. See also G. Bardy in the *Dictionnaire de spiritualité*, vol. i, cc. 702-708 ; L. von Hertling, *Antonius der Einsiedler* (1930) ; B. Lavaud, *Antoine le Grand* (1943) ; and L. Bouyer, *St Antoine le Grand* (1950), a valuable essay on primitive monastic spirituality. H. Quefféluc's biography (1950) is " une vie romancée ". On the saint in art, see H. Detzel, *Christliche Ikonographie*, vol. ii, pp. 85-88 ; Jameson, *Sacred and Legendary Art*, vol. ii, pp. 741 *seq.* ; Drake, *Saints and Their Emblems*, p. 11. In the East St Antony is also greatly venerated, and religious communities among the Maronites and Chaldeans, and the Orthodox monks of Sinai, still profess to follow his rule. See also Reitzenstein, *Des Athanasius Werk über das Leben des Antonius* (1914) ; and Contzen, *Die Regel des hl. Antonius* (1896). There is no justification for the spelling " Anthony " in this or any other example of the name.

SS. SPEUSIPPUS, ELEUSIPPUS AND MELEUSIPPUS, MARTYRS (A.D. 155 ?)

THESE are stated in the Roman Martyrology to have been *tergemini*, three twin brothers, who, with their grandmother, Leonilla (or Neonilla), suffered martyrdom, apparently at Langres in France, in the reign of Marcus Aurelius. The whole story seems to present a typical example of a fiction which, written originally for edification or mere diversion, has been adopted in all seriousness, and transplanted to other lands far from the place of its birth. In its origin the romance is clearly connected with Cappadocia, but no early or local cult can be cited to bear out any of its incidents. How it happened that the clergy of Langres in the fifth century

* Called also the " burning sickness ", " hell fire " or " sacred fire ". It was later identified with erysipelas (called in Welsh *y fendigaid*, " the blessed ") ; but it appears originally to have been a far more virulent and contagious disorder, caused probably by the consumption of flour made from grain damaged by ergot.

or later came to believe themselves to be in possession of the relics of these martyrs cannot now be explained. The relics are supposed to have been further translated, at least in part, to the abbey of Ellwangen in Swabia.

The Latin text of the so-called acts is printed in the *Acta Sanctorum*, January 17. An unsatisfactory Greek version has also been printed by Leparev and by Grégoire, and a Georgian paraphrase by Marr. The story has been appealed to in confirmation of the theory, first enunciated by Dr Rendel Harris, that the pagan cult of the Dioscuri (the heavenly twins, Castor and Pollux) has been transplanted bodily into Christian hagiography (see, *e.g.* H. Grégoire, *Saints jumeaux et dieux cavaliers*), a fantastic thesis to which full justice has been done by H. Delehaye in the *Analecta Bollandiana*, vols. xxiii, pp. 427 *seq.* ; xxiv, 505 *seq.* ; xxvi, 334 *seq.* Cf. also C. Weymann in the *Historisches Jahrbuch*, vol. xxix, pp. 575 *seq.*

ST GENULF, OR GENOU, BISHOP   (A.D. 250 ?)

THE early episcopal lists in many French dioceses, as Mgr Duchesne has had occasion to point out, are not at all reliable, and the very existence of the bishops who, as reputed founders or patrons, are honoured with festivals of the highest rank is in some cases a matter of doubt. It seems that the abbey of Strada, founded in 828 on the banks of the Indre, acquired in the course of the same century the relics of St Genulf, who lived with another monk, St Genitus, at a place now called Celles-sur-Nahon. About the year 1000 a document was compiled which described Genulf as sent from Rome with his father, Genitus, in the third century, to preach the gospel in Gaul. They came, it is said, to a township (*civitas Giturnicensis*), where they stayed a few months, made many converts, and built a church ; then they settled in a solitude on the banks of the Nahon, and eventually died there surrounded by disciples. There is, however, nothing to identify the Giturnicenses with the Cadurcenses (Cahors), and the improbability of anyone with a German name like Genulf becoming bishop in Gaul during the third century is extreme. From this and other difficulties Mgr Duchesne concludes that the late tradition which makes St Genulf the first bishop of Cahors is quite untrustworthy. There is no scrap of respectable evidence to justify the statement, neither does the Roman Martyrology (June 17) connect " Gundulphus " with Cahors. The feast of St Genulf is, nevertheless, kept in that diocese on January 17 as a double of the first class.

See *Acta Sanctorum* for January 17, and Duchesne, *Fastes Épiscopaux*, vol. ii, pp. 126-128.

ST JULIAN SABAS   (A.D. 377)

IN the Roman Martyrology we read on this day : " In the district of Edessa, in Mesopotamia (the commemoration) of St Julian, the hermit, called Sabas, who, when the Catholic faith at Antioch had almost died out in the time of the Emperor Valens, restored it again by the power of his miracles ". Hiding himself from the world in a cave in Osrhoëne (beside the Euphrates) he practised extraordinary asceticism, eating only once in the week. After the expulsion of St Meletius, Bishop of Antioch, it was asserted by the heretics in that city that Julian Sabas, whose reputation as an ascetic stood high, had embraced Arian doctrines. When besought by the orthodox in 372 to come and refute the slander, he complied, and his presence in Antioch was attended by the most beneficial results. When his mission was accomplished he returned to his cave, and died not long afterwards.　Many stupendous miracles are attributed to him by the Greek hagiographers.

See the *Acta Sanctorum* for October 18, where Theodoret is cited as our most reliable source of information.　A Syriac version of Theodoret's account has been printed by Bedjan ; see *Analecta Bollandiana*, vol. xvi (1897), p. 184 ; and BHG., nn. 67–68.

ST SABINUS, Bishop of Piacenza　　(A.D. 420)

THE letters of St Ambrose to Sabinus bear witness to the close friendship between the two bishops, as also to the high reputation for learning which St Sabinus enjoyed, for in one letter St Ambrose asks for his criticisms of some treatises which he sent to him.　He sat in the Council of Aquileia in 381 against the Arians, and in that of Milan nine years later against Jovinian.　He is probably identical with the Sabinus who was a deacon at Milan, and was sent by Pope St Damasus to the East in connection with the Arian troubles at Antioch.　St Gregory has preserved the legend according to which St Sabinus averted a disastrous flood by writing down an order and casting the paper into the River Po.　The river obeyed, and returned to its proper channel.　He is said to have died on December 11, 420.

See *Acta Sanctorum*, January 17.

ST SULPICIUS II, or SULPICE, Bishop of Bourges　　(A.D. 647)

THE life of St Sulpicius (Pius), the second bishop of Bourges of that name, which is one of the few biographies admitted even by Krusch to be an authentic Merovingian document, does not supply very much detail, but it must have been composed within a few years of the bishop's death, and the sincerity and enthusiasm of the writer are unmistakable.　Sulpicius was the son of wealthy parents, who renounced the idea of marriage and devoted himself even from his youth to all kinds of good works, and especially to care for the poor.　Being elected bishop, he became the father of his people, defended them against the tyranny of Lullo, the minister of King Dagobert, and, as the effect of a general fast which he imposed for three days, obtained considerate treatment for them under Clovis II, Dagobert's successor. Various miracles, notably the extinction of a great conflagration by making the sign of the cross over it, were attributed to him during his life, and many more took place beside his tomb after death.

The chronological data are scanty, but we know that St Sulpicius attended the Council of Clichy in 627, and that he exchanged letters frequently with St Didier of Cahors, whom he had consecrated bishop in 630.　His austerity of life was remarkable.　He spent much of the night in prayer, fasted continually, and recited the entire psalter each day.　By the force of his example and his exhortations the whole Jewish population of Bourges was converted to Christianity.　Towards the end of his days, finding that he could no longer give the same amount of time to the care of the poor and afflicted whom he loved, Sulpicius obtained leave from the king to appoint another bishop in his place, in order that he himself might have more leisure for his works of charity.　His death, in 647, was followed by extraordinary scenes of which his biographer was evidently an eye-witness.　He compares the outcry and lamentations heard on all sides to the rumbling of thunder, and tells us that at his obsequies the vast throng of people, throwing themselves flat on the ground in their sorrow and despair, rendered it almost impossible for the clergy to carry out the offices. " O good shepherd ", they cried, " guardian of thy people, why dost thou forsake us ? To whom this day dost thou leave us ? " Though the times are far removed from our own, the sketch which his biographer has left us gives an impression of such charity, zeal and strict observance as seems befitting in the patron of that famous Paris seminary which was afterwards to bear his name.

The most reliable text of the life has been printed by B. Krusch in MGH., *Scriptores Merov.*, vol. iv, pp. 364–380, from MS. Addit. 11880, of the ninth century, in the British Museum. See also the *Acta Sanctorum*, January 17, Duchesne, *Fastes Épiscopaux*, vol. ii, pp 28–29, and BHL., n. 1146. " Pius " is an epithet to distinguish Sulpicius from a namesake.

ST RICHIMIR, Abbot   (*c.* A.D. 715)

Much obscurity overshadows the memory of St Richimir. His name is omitted from the martyrologies. Nothing is known of the place of his burial, while the country which he sanctified has long since abandoned devotion to him. Fortunately a contemporary life has been preserved. The anonymous author relates how St Richimir, while not yet in orders, went to Gilbert, Bishop of Le Mans, and asked permission to settle in his diocese, together with a few followers, and to found a monastery under the Rule of St Benedict. The bishop gladly assented, and offered him a suitable property. But Richimir preferred wild and desolate land which had yet to be cultivated. Having been ordained, he set out for the Loire and built a cell near the river. When the bishop heard of his great poverty, he gladly sent him the necessaries of life, although Richimir accepted these only reluctantly. Apparently the position was not suitable, for he abandoned it and selected a place not far distant, called later Saint-Rigomer-des-Bois. There he built a church in honour of the Apostles, and founded a monastery over which he ruled as abbot till his death about 715.

See *Acta Sanctorum*, January 17, and Mabillon, vol. iii, part i, pp. 228–232.

BD ROSELINE, Virgin   (A.D. 1329)

This holy Carthusian nun, Roseline de Villeneuve, was of very distinguished ancestry. Her father was Baron des Arcs, and her mother was a de Sabran. She had to overcome strong family opposition before she could finally execute her purpose of consecrating herself to God. She had been educated by the nuns of St Clare, but found her own vocation in following the austere Carthusian rule. She seems to have been received in the convent of Bertrand at the age of twenty-five, and twelve years later was made prioress of Celle Roubaud, in Provence, where she died, January 17, 1329. She occasionally passed a whole week together without taking food ; she punished herself with terrible disciplines, and never gave more than three or four hours to sleep. She used to teach her nuns to have a great dread of those words, " I know you not ", in order that they might make sure of hearing the greeting, " Come, ye blessed of my Father." When Roseline was asked what was the best means of getting to Heaven, she often replied, " To know oneself ". She had frequent visions and ecstasies, and possessed an extraordinary gift of reading the hearts of all who came to her. Her body was indescribably beautiful after death, and no sign of rigidity or corruption appeared in it. Five years afterwards it was still perfectly preserved, and the ecclesiastic who presided at the exhumation thought the living appearance of the eyes so wonderful that he had them enucleated and kept in a reliquary apart.   The body was still quite entire a hundred years later, and the eyes had neither shrivelled nor decayed as late as 1644. Her *cultus* was confirmed in 1851.

See the *Acta Sanctorum* for June 11 ; Le Couteulx, *Annales Ordinis Cartusiensis*, vol. v, pp. 262–268 ; Villeneuve-Flayose, *Histoire de Ste Roseline de Villeneuve* (1866).

18 : ST PETER'S CHAIR AT ROME

ST PETER, having triumphed over Satan in the East, pursued the enemy to Rome with unabated energy.   He who had formerly trembled at the voice of a servant-maid, now feared not the stronghold of idolatry and superstition. The capital of the empire of the world, and the centre of impiety, called for the zeal of the leader of the Apostles.   The Roman empire had extended its dominion beyond that of any former monarchy, and the influence of its metropolis was of the greatest human importance for the spread of Christ's gospel.   St Peter claimed that province for himself ; and repairing to Rome, there preached the faith and established his episcopal chair, and from him the bishops of Rome in all ages have derived their succession.   That SS. Peter and Paul founded that church is expressly asserted by Caius, a priest of Rome under Pope St Zephyrinus (quoted by Eusebius, *Hist. eccl.*, bk ii, c. 25), who relates also that his body was then on the Vatican hill, and that of his fellow-labourer, St Paul, on the Ostian road.   That he and St Paul planted the faith in Rome, and were both crowned with martyrdom there, is affirmed by St Dionysius, Bishop of Corinth, in the second century.   St Irenaeus, in the same century, calls the church at Rome " The greatest and most ancient church, founded by the two glorious apostles, Peter and Paul."

Nevertheless, doubt has been cast upon the historical fact of St Peter's presence in Rome.   It is pointed out that no clear contemporary statement can be adduced in proof of his residence there, that the Acts of the Apostles suggest nothing of the kind, that the only thing we know concerning his later life is that his own first epistle was written from " Babylon ", that the so-called Roman tradition is inextricably mixed up with fabulous legends about Simon Magus which no serious scholar would now dream of defending, and that the twenty-five years' Roman episcopate, attributed to St Peter with a quite suspicious unanimity by later historians such as Eusebius, cannot be reconciled with the other data they supply and with the complete silence of St Paul concerning his fellow apostle in his Epistle to the Romans.   But these difficulties have been duly considered and answered not only by Catholic apologists, but by eminent Anglicans such as Bishop Lightfoot, Professor C. H. Turner and Dr George Edmundson, as well as by Lutherans of the standing of Harnack and Zahn.   The grounds upon which the Roman tradition is based are stated concisely and clearly by the Anglican Dr F. H. Chase, Bishop of Ely, in the following passage :

The strength of the case for St Peter's visit to and martyrdom at Rome lies not only in the absence of any rival tradition, but also in the fact that many streams of evidence converge to this result.   We have the evidence of official lists and documents of the Roman church, which prove the strength of the tradition in later times, and which, at least in some cases, must rest on earlier documents.   The notice of the transference of the apostle's body to a new resting-place in 258, and the words of Caius, show that the tradition was definite and unquestioned at Rome in the first half of the third century.   The fact that Caius is arguing with an Asiatic opponent, the evidence of the [gnostic] Acts of Peter, the passages quoted from Origen, Clement of Alexandria and Tertullian, show that at the same period the tradition was accepted in the churches of Asia, of Alexandria and Carthage.   The passage of Irenaeus carries the evidence backward well within the second century, and is of special importance, as coming from one who had visited Rome, whose list of Roman bishops suggests that he had had access to official documents, and who through Polycarp was in contact with the personal knowledge of St John and his companions.

Further, Dr Chase went on to point out that the close association of the martyrdom of St Peter with that of St Paul in the reference made to them by St Clement, pope at the end of the first century, in the unquestionably genuine letter he wrote to the church of Corinth, forms a strong presumption that he, who must have known the truth, identified both apostles equally with Rome.   Dr Chase's article was written in 1900, and since then much fresh evidence has come to light.   It will be noticed that he refers to the transference of the apostle's body to a new resting place in 258.   We cannot affirm that this translation, which was in any case only temporary, is a certain fact.

The historical weight of this tradition was affirmed in eloquent terms by another Anglican divine, Dr George Edmundson, in a Bampton lecture given before the University of Oxford in 1913, wherein he states that " a tradition accepted universally and without a single dissentient voice associates the foundation and organization of the church of Rome with the name of St Peter, and speaks of his active connection with the church as extending over a period of some twenty-five years ". " It is needless ", he goes on, " to multiply references.   In Egypt and in Africa, in the East and in the West, no other place ever disputed with Rome the honour of being the see of St Peter ; no other place ever claimed that he died there, or that it possessed his tomb.   Most significant of all is the *consensus* of the oriental, non-Greek-speaking churches.   A close examination of Armenian and Syriac manuscripts   through several centuries has failed to discover a single writer who did not accept the Roman Petrine tradition."

It was undoubtedly an ancient custom throughout the West to keep as a festival the anniversary of the consecration of the bishop.   St Augustine has a treatise *de natali episcopi*, and St Leo three sermons of which the subject is the *natalis cathedrae*, " the birthday ", or anniversary, " of the chair " (*i.e.* of his installation as bishop).   That some commemoration of St Peter's enthronement as bishop of Rome should have been observed from an early date was to be expected.   In point of fact, our calendar now contains, and has contained for more than a thousand years past, two entries which recall the memory of St Peter's connection with the episcopal office.   That of the day with which we are now concerned is expressly referred to " the chair on which he first sat in Rome " ; that of February 22 professes to commemorate his earlier ministry in Antioch.   As the result of much investigation and debate the conclusion now more generally adopted is that there was originally only one feast of St Peter's chair; further, that this was kept on February 22, and had no reference to Antioch, but only to the beginning of his episcopate at Rome.* It seems, then, that any discussion of the rather complicated problem of the duplication of the feast may most fittingly be reserved for February 22.

For the present it will be sufficient to point out that, in the view of some archaeologists, the material relic known as " St Peter's chair ", which is now preserved in a casing of bronze by Bernini over the apsidal altar of St Peter's basilica in Rome, must be regarded as an important element in the development of these feasts. Some lay stress upon the fact that St Paul (Rom. xvi 5) sends greetings to " the church which is at the house of Prisca and Aquila ", seeming to point to some primitive meeting-place of a community of Roman Christians, and they urge that such a portable chair as the relic in question might naturally have been used as an improvised bishop's stool in a private house. This might, then, have been " the chair on which St Peter *first* sat in Rome ", though after a few years some more spacious place of assembly may have been provided in which a permanent seat could be constructed. It is, in any case, curious that the house of Prisca and Aquila seems to have developed in course of time into the still existing church of St Prisca on the Aventine, and that the feast of the dedication of this church was kept on February 22. On the other hand, a St Prisca, martyr, is commemorated on this day, January 18. But obviously nothing more than vague conjectures can be based on indications of this kind. All that we definitely know is that since the end of the sixth century, when the Auxerre redaction of the so-called *Martyrologium Hieronymianum* was compiled, the feast of " St Peter's chair at Rome " has been honoured pretty generally throughout the West on this day.

In a Motu Proprio of John XXIII dated July 25, 1960, this feast was dropped from the Roman Calendar.

See F. Cabrol in DAC., vol. iii, cc. 76–90 ; CMH., pp. 45–46, 109 ; and L. Duchesne, *Christian Worship* (1919), pp. 277–280. *Cf.* herein St Peter, June 29, and his Chair at Antioch, February 22.

ST PRISCA, Virgin and Martyr   (Date Unknown)

GREAT confusion and uncertainty prevail regarding the saint who is commemorated on this day under the name of Prisca. On the one hand, it is unquestionable that the so-called " acts ", dating at earliest from the tenth century, are historically worthless, for they simply reproduce, with slight changes, the legendary Passion of St Tatiana. On the other hand, there was, beyond doubt, a genuine and early *cultus* in Rome of at least one St Prisca, or Priscilla. The itineraries nearly all mention her as a martyr, and indicate the place of her interment in the catacomb of Priscilla on the Via Salaria. Moreover, as stated above in connection with St Peter's chair, there is a church on the Aventine dedicated to St Prisca which furnishes a cardinalitial title, and which, from the fourth to the eighth century, was known as the *titulus S. Priscae*, but later (*c.* 800) as *titulus Aquilae et Priscae*. This last designation clearly refers to the Aquila and his wife, Prisca, of whom we read more than once in the New Testament in connection with St Paul. The husband and wife, however, are commemorated in the Roman Martyrology on July 8, and are there assigned to Asia Minor. Many conjectures have been made to elucidate the problem, and in particular it has been pointed out that Prisca seems to have

* In the Benedictine calendar, approved in 1915, the two " chair " feasts have been subsumed in one, St Peter' Chair, on February 22.

been a favourite name among the Acilii Glabriones, and also that the name which is written in Latin as Aquila appears in Greek as Ἀκύλας ; but no clear solution has yet been arrived at.

See the *Acta Sanctorum* for January 18 ; Marucchi in *Nuovo Bullettino di archeol. crist.*, vol. xiv (1908), pp. 5 *seq.* ; Duchesne, *Liber Pontificalis*, vols. i, pp. 501, 517 ; ii, 201 ; Pio Franchi de' Cavalieri in the *Römische Quartalschrift*, 1903, p. 223 ; and De Rossi, *Roma Sotterranea*, vol. i, p. 176.

ST VOLUSIAN, Bishop of Tours   (A.D. 496)

VOLUSIAN, who was, it is stated, of senatorial rank, occupied the see of Tours from 488 to 496. From a letter addressed to him by Ruricius, Bishop of Limoges, which is couched in not very friendly terms, it would seem that Volusian was married (it must be remembered that the discipline of sacerdotal celibacy had not at this date been enforced even in the West), and that his wife had a temper which was a terror to all their acquaintance. Volusian had apparently complained that he lived in fear of the Goths. Ruricius replied, with an obvious reference to this early Mrs Proudie, that a man who could encourage an enemy in his own household had no business to be afraid of enemies from outside (*timere hostem non debet extraneum qui consuevit sustinere domesticum*). We learn from Gregory of Tours that Volusian was in the end driven from his see by the Goths, who suspected him of wishing to come to terms with the Franks, and that going into exile in Spain he died soon afterwards. Later accounts state that he was further attacked by his persecutors and decapitated, and it is probably on the ground of this supposed martyrdom that he has been honoured as a saint.

See the *Acta Sancrum*, January 18 ; MGH., *Auctores antiquissimi*, vol. viii, p. 350 ; Duchesne, *Fastes Épiscopaux*, vol. ii, p. 301 ; and H. Thurston in *The Month*, June, 1911, pp. 642–644.

ST DEICOLUS, or DESLE, Abbot   (*c.* A.D. 625)

HE quitted Ireland, his native country, with St Columban and lived with him at Luxeuil ; but when his master left France, he founded the abbey of Lure, in the diocese of Besançon, where he ended his days as a hermit. Amidst his austerities the joy and peace of his soul appeared in his countenance. St Columban once said to him in his youth, " Deicolus, why are you always smiling ? " He answered in simplicity, " Because no one can take God from me." He died probably in the year 625.

See his life and the history of his miracles in Mabillon, vol. ii, pp. 102–116, and MGH., *Scriptores*, vol. xv; pp. 675–682, both written by a monk of Lure in the tenth century. This saint is often called Deicola, but in ancient MSS. Deicolus. In Franche-Comté the French version of his name, Desle, used frequently to be given in baptism. See also Gougaud, *Gaelic Pioneers of Christianity*, pp. 134–135 ; M. Stokes, *Forests of France*, p. 177, etc. ; LIS., vol. i, p. 301 ; and J. Giradot, *La vie de St Desle* (1947).

BD BEATRICE D'ESTE OF FERRARA, Widow   (A.D. 1262)

THIS nun was the niece of another Bd Beatrice d'Este, of Gemmola, whose feast is kept on May 10. We have no full account of the life of Beatrice the younger, and it is not even quite certain whether she had been married or not before she consecrated her life to God in the Benedictine convent of St Antony at Ferrara, a convent which appears to have been founded at her special desire by the powerful family to which she belonged. She lived and died in the repute of great holiness, and it was stated in the seventeenth century that from the marble tomb in which her remains were enshrined an oily liquid still exuded which worked many surprising miracles of healing. The *cultus* of this Beatrice, which had always been maintained at Ferrara, was confirmed in 1774.

In an appendix to the January section of the *Acta Sanctorum* the Bollandists printed such fragments of information as they were able to collect concerning Bd Beatrice. See also the *Analecta Juris Pontificii* for 1880, p. 668.

BD CHRISTINA OF AQUILA, Virgin   (A.D. 1543)

THE family name of this Christina was Ciccarelli, and when she was born in the Abruzzi she received in baptism the name of Matthia. Entering the convent of Augustinian hermitesses at Aquila at an early age, she was there called Sister Christina. In the cloister she showed herself a model of virtue, but she was especially remarkable for her humility and love of the poor. She gave long hours to prayer, was often rapt in ecstasy, and seemed to possess a knowledge of future events. She is also said to have practised severe penance, and to have worked many miracles, but our information about her is scanty. When she died on January 18, 1543, it is stated that the children of Aquila went through the town proclaiming the news of her death by "shouting and singing", with the result that an enormous concourse of people attended her obsequies. The *cultus* paid to her from time immemorial was confirmed in 1841.

See P. Seeböck, *Die Herrlichkeit der katholischen Kirche* (1900), p. 297, and biographical details in the decree of confirmation.

19 : SS. MARIUS, MARTHA, AUDIFAX AND ABACHUM, Martyrs (*c.* A.D. 260)

MARIUS (Maris), a nobleman of Persia, with his wife Martha, and two sons, Audifax and Abachum, being converted to the faith, distributed his fortune among the poor, as the primitive Christians did at Jerusalem, and came to Rome to visit the tombs of the apostles. The Emperor Claudius was then persecuting the Church, and by his order a great number of Christians were driven into the amphitheatre, shot to death with arrows, and their bodies burnt. Our saints gathered and buried their ashes with respect; for which they were apprehended, and after many torments under the governor Marcian, Marius and his two sons were beheaded; Martha was drowned, thirteen miles from Rome, at a place now called Santa Ninfa. They were buried on the Via Cornelia, and they are mentioned with distinction in all the western martyrologies on January 20; but their feast is kept to-day.

We cannot place any great confidence in the "acts" of these martyrs, but the document is not contemptible; they have been printed in the *Acta Sanctorum*, January 19. See also Allard, *Histoire des Persécutions*, vol. iii, pp. 214 *seq.*; and BHL., n. 5543.

ST GERMANICUS, Martyr   (A.D. 155 ?)

WE know nothing of St Germanicus beyond what we learn from the letter of the Christians of Smyrna who, writing of the persecution which led to the arrest of St Polycarp, tell us : " But thanks be to God ; for He verily prevailed against all. For the right noble Germanicus encouraged their timorousness through the constancy which was in him, and he fought with the wild beasts in a signal way.   For when the proconsul wished to prevail upon him, and bade him have pity on his youth, he used violence and dragged the wild beast towards him, desiring the more speedily to obtain release from their unrighteous and lawless way of living.   So, after this, all the multitude marvelling at the bravery of the God-beloved and God-fearing people of the Christians, raised a cry, ' Away with the atheists !   Look for Polycarp ! ' "   This narrative, however, may count as one of the most authentic memorials now extant of the history of the early Christian Church.   Eusebius, in his *Historia Ecclesiastica*, quotes the passage, and we possess the complete text independently.   It is also noteworthy that Germanicus actually did what St Ignatius of Antioch expresses his intention of doing (*ad Rom.* 5)—*viz.* he provoked the wild beast to attack him that he might be released the sooner from the ungodly companionship of the pagans and Jews amongst whom he lived.   It is noteworthy that the Roman Martyrology also directs our thoughts to the example of St Ignatius by saying that Germanicus, " who was ground by the teeth of the beast, merited to be one with the true bread, the Lord Jesus Christ, by dying for His sake ".

See Lightfoot, *Apostolic Fathers*, part ii, vol. iii, p. 478 ; Delehaye, *Les passions des martyrs* . . (1921), pp. 12 *seq.*, and *Acta Sanctorum*, January 19.   On the date, see note to St Polycarp herein, under January 26.

ST NATHALAN, Bishop   (A.D. 678)

THE curiously extravagant legend of St Nathalan, whose cult was confirmed by Pope Leo XIII in 1898, and whose feast is now kept at Aberdeen on January 19, cannot be better given than in the words of the Aberdeen breviary : " Nathalan is believed to have been born in the northern parts of the Scotti, in ancient times, at Tullicht in the diocese of Aberdeen ; a man of great sanctity, who, after he had come to man's estate and been imbued with the liberal arts, devoted himself and his wholly to divine contemplation.   And when he learned that amongst the works of man's hands the cultivation of the soil approached nearest to divine contemplation, though educated in a noble family with his own hands he practised the lowly art of tilling the fields, abandoning all other occupations that his mind might never be sullied by the impure solicitations of the flesh.   Meanwhile, as he warred against the Devil and the perishing world, a terrible famine broke out among his neighbours, relations and friends, so that almost the whole people were in danger of perishing by hunger.   But God's saint, Nathalan, moved by the greatest pity, distributed all his grain and whatever else he had, for the name of Christ, to the poor ; but when the time of spring came, when all green things are committed to the bowels of the earth, not having aught to sow in the land which he cultivated, by divine revelation he ordered it all to be strewn and sown with sand, from which sand thus sown a great crop of all kinds of grain grew up and was greatly multiplied.

" But in the time of harvest, when many people of both sexes were collected by him to gather in the crop, there came a tempest of rain and a whirlwind, so that these husbandmen and women were forced to abstain from labour. Therefore he, excited by anger, along with the other reapers murmured a little against God ; but on the tempest abating, feeling that he had offended Him, in a spirit of penance he bound his right hand to his leg with an iron lock and key, and forthwith threw the key into the river Dee, making a solemn vow that he would never unlock it until he had visited the thresholds of the blessed Apostles Peter and Paul ; which actually took place.

" Having entered the City, approaching in meditation the monuments of the saints which are there on every side, and bewailing his sin, he worshipped the Creator whom he had heretofore offended. As he went through the chief places of the city he met a naked boy carrying a little fish for sale, which he purchased at a low price. By the divine power he found in its belly the key, unrusted, which he had flung into the Dee, and with it he opened the lock upon his leg. But the Supreme Pontiff, informed of this mighty wonder, summoned him as a man of superior holiness into his presence, and made him, in spite of his reluctance, a bishop. Rendering himself dear to all in Rome where he practised divine contemplation for many years, Nathalan, not forgetful even to extreme old age of his native soil, by permission of the Roman pontiff returned to that part of Scotland whence he sprang. Having built the churches of Tullicht, Bothelin and Colle at his own expense, he dedicated them to Almighty God, and they still exist in these provinces, dedicated in his honour. After many remarkable miracles blessed Nathalan, full of the grace of God, on the 6th of the Ides of January (January 8) commended his soul to our Lord, and went up into Heaven on high ; and being buried with great veneration at Tullicht, he affords health to the sick who piously come to invoke his aid."

St Nathalan is commemorated in the Irish martyrologies, *e.g.* those of Oengus and Gorman. See KSS., pp. 417-419 ; and LIS., vol. i, pp. 121 *seq.*

ST ALBERT OF CASHEL, BISHOP   (SEVENTH CENTURY ?)

THE greatest obscurity shrouds the history of this saint. He is commonly called archbishop of Cashel and is honoured as patron of that diocese, but it is almost certain that no such see existed at the date assigned to him. A Latin life, written apparently in the twelfth century, describes him as *natione Anglus, conversatione angelus* (an Englishman by race, an angel in conduct). We are told that he was visited in England by St Erhard, himself an Irishman and already bishop of Ardagh. Albert accompanied him back to Ireland, and in passing through Cashel, which for two years had been without a bishop, the people by acclamation elected Albert to that dignity. He had, however, only been consecrated for a short time when, during a council at Lismore, he was induced by an eloquent sermon to renounce all his honours and possessions. Together with his friend Erhard and a band of disciples he fled away to lead a pilgrim's life on the continent. They came to Rome in the time of Pope Formosus (891-896), and were welcomed by him and encouraged in their good purposes. Then they separated, and Albert for his part travelled to Jerusalem. On his return he had a longing to see his friend Erhard again, but on coming to Ratisbon found him already dead. Albert prayed that God might take him also, and he died there not many hours afterwards. In this narrative there is no mention of any actual relationship with Erhard, but other accounts represent him as Albert's brother, and in fact mention a third brother,

Hildulf, who was archbishop of Trier.　But the whole story is fabulous.　Whatever authentic information we have about St Erhard points to his having lived in the seventh century.　He cannot, therefore, have visited Rome in the time of Pope Formosus nearly two hundred years later.　St Albert's feast is kept throughout Ireland.

The Life of St Albert has been edited by W. Levison in the MGH., *Scriptores Merov.*, vol. vi, pp. 21–23.　See also the *Acta Sanctorum*, January 8 ; and LIS., vol. i, pp. 102–113.

ST FILLAN, OR FOELAN, ABBOT　　(EIGHTH CENTURY)

ST FILLAN's name is famous in the Scottish and Irish calendars, and his feast is still kept in the diocese of.Dunkeld, now on this day.　The example and instructions of his parents, Feriach and St Kentigerna, inspired him from the cradle with an ardent love of virtue.　In his youth, despising the worldly prospects to which high birth entitled him, he received the monastic habit and passed many years in a cell at some distance from a monastery not far from Saint Andrew's.　He was constrained to leave this solitude by being elected abbot.　His sanctity in this office shone forth with a bright light.　After some years he resigned this charge, and retired to a mountainous part of Glendochart in Perthshire, where with the assistance of seven others he built a church, near which he served for several years.　God glorified him by a wonderful gift of miracles, and called him to the reward of his labours on January 9, probably early in the eighth century.　He was buried in Strathfillan, and his relics were long preserved there with honour.

This account, as Butler tells us, is based upon that given in the Aberdeen Breviary.　He does not, however, reproduce any of the very extravagant incidents which are there connected with the saint.　For example, we are told that Fillan immediately after his birth was thrown by his father into a lake, and remained there a whole year tended by angels, also that when he was building his church a wolf killed the ox that used to drag the materials to the spot, whereupon through Fillan's prayers the wolf returned and drew the cart in the ox's place.　Evidently not much trust can be placed in historical materials of this description.　On the other hand, it must be said that St Fillan's name appears on January 9 in the Martyrology of Oengus (A.D. 804), and in nearly all other Irish and Scottish martyrologies and calendars ; that the honour paid to him was very widespread, for Robert Bruce had with him a relic of the saint at the battle of Bannockburn, to which, according to Hector Boece, he attributed the victory ; and that the crosier and bell believed to have belonged to him are still in existence.　The name is spelt in several ways.

Fillan's mother, ST KENTIGERNA, is commemorated on January 7 in the Aberdeen Breviary, from which we learn that she was of royal blood, daughter of Cellach, Prince of Leinster.　After the death of her husband she left Ireland, and consecrated herself to God in a religious state.　After living in great austerity and humility, she died on January 7, in the year 734 according to the *Annals of Ulster.*

See KSS., pp. 341–346 ; LIS., vol. i, pp. 134–144 ; and the *Acta Sanctorum*, January 9. As for St Kentigerna, Adam King informs us that a famous parish church bears her name on Tuch Cailleach (in Loch Lomond), a small island to which she retired some time before her death.　See the Aberdeen Breviary ; Colgan, *Acta Sanctorum Hiberniae*, vol. i, p. 22 ; and KSS., p. 373.　The " Martyrology "—*Félire*—of Oengus referred to above is often mentioned in these notes　*cf.* St Oengus on March 11.

ST CANUTE OF DENMARK, Martyr   (A.D. 1086)

St Canute (Cnut) of Denmark was a natural son of Swein Estrithson, whose uncle Canute had reigned in England. He advanced a claim to the crown of that country, but his attempt on Northumbria in 1075 was a complete failure; in 1081 he succeeded his brother Harold as king of Denmark. The Danes had received the Christian faith some time before, but, as has been said of Canute of England, their " religious enthusiasm was quaintly tinged with barbarian *naïveté* ". Perhaps the word " tinged " is hardly strong enough. Canute II married Adela, sister of Robert, Count of Flanders, by whom he had a son, Bd Charles the Good. He enacted several laws for the administration of justice and in restraint of the *jarls*, granted privileges and immunities to the clergy, and exacted tithes for their sub-sistence; unfortunately one effect of his activities was to make some churchmen feudal lords who gave more attention to their temporal than to their spiritual profit and duties. Canute showed a royal magnificence in building and endowing churches, and gave the crown which he wore to the church of Roskilde, which became the burial-place of the Danish kings.

In 1085 Canute reasserted his claim to England, and made extensive prepara-tions for invasion, in concert with Robert of Flanders and Olaf of Norway. The enterprise was brought to nothing by disputes with his *jarls* and people. They were becoming more and more restive under his imposition of taxes, tithes and a new social order, and under his brother Olaf they broke into open rebellion. Canute fled to the island of Fünen, and took refuge in the church of St Alban at Odense (said to have its name from a relic brought from England by Canute). When the insurgents surrounded the church he confessed his sins and received communion; an attack was begun, bricks and stones being thrown through the windows, and eventually the king was killed as he knelt before the altar. His brother Benedict and seventeen others perished with him. This happened on July 10, 1086.

Aelnoth, Canute's biographer, a monk of Canterbury who had spent twenty-four years in Denmark, goes on to tell us that God attested the sanctity of the slain monarch by many miraculous healings of the sick at his tomb, for which reason his relics were taken up and honourably enshrined. Canute's second successor, Eric III, having sent to Rome evidence of the miracles wrought there, Pope Paschal II authorized the veneration of St Canute, though it is not easy to see upon what his claim to martyrdom rests. Aelnoth adds that the first preachers of Christianity in Denmark and Scandinavia were Englishmen, and that the Swedes were the most difficult to convert.

See the *Acta Sanctorum*, July, vol. iii; C. Gertz, *Vitae Sanctorum Danorum*, pp. 27–168, 531–558; and B. Schmeidler in *Neues Archiv*, 1912, pp. 67–97. *Cf.* also E. A. Freeman's *Norman Conquest*, vol. iv, pp. 249, 586, 689; and F. M. Stenton, *Anglo-Saxon England* (1943), pp. 603, 608–609.

ST WULFSTAN, Bishop of Worcester   (A.D. 1095)

Wulfstan (Wulstan) was a native of Long Itchington, in Warwickshire. From early youth he loved purity, and on one occasion, believing himself to have offended by watching a woman dancing, he withdrew into a thicket and, lying prostrate, be-wailed his fault with such sorrow that henceforth he had such constant watchfulness over his senses that he was nevermore troubled with the like temptations. He made his studies in the monastery of Evesham and afterwards at Peterborough, and put himself under the direction of Brihtheah, Bishop of Worcester, by whom he was advanced to the priesthood. Having been distracted while celebrating Mass by the smell of meat roasting in the kitchen, he bound himself never to eat of it again. Not long after he became a novice in the great monastery at Worcester, where he was remarkable for the innocence and sanctity of his life. The first charge with which he was entrusted was instructing the children. He was afterwards made precentor, and then treasurer of the church, but he continued to devote himself to prayer, and watched whole nights in the church. It was only in despite of his strenuous resistance that he was made prior of Worcester and, in 1062, bishop of that see. Though not very learned, he delivered the word of God so impressively and feelingly as often to move his audience to tears. To his energy in particular is attributed the suppression of a scandalous practice which prevailed among the citizens of Bristol of kidnapping men into slavery and shipping them over to Ireland. He always recited the psalter whilst he travelled, and never passed by any church or chapel without going in to pray before the altar.

When the Conqueror deprived the English of their ecclesiastical and secular dignities in favour of his Normans, Wulfstan retained his see, an exception which later writers explain by a supposed miraculous intervention of Providence. In a synod held at Westminster, over which Archbishop Lanfranc presided, Wulfstan was called upon to surrender his crosier and ring, upon pretext of his simplicity and unfitness for business. The saint owned himself unworthy of the charge, but said that King Edward the Confessor had compelled him to take it upon him, and that he would deliver his crosier to him alone. Thereupon, going to the king's tomb, he struck his crosier into the stone ; and then went and sat down among the monks. No one was able to draw the crosier out till the saint was ordered to take it again, when it followed his hand with ease.

Be that as it may, after an initial uncertainty King William recognized Wulfstan's worth and treated him with respect and trust. Lanfranc even commissioned him to make the visitation of the diocese of Chester as his deputy. When any English complained of the oppression of the Normans, Wulfstan used to tell them, " This is a scourge of God for our sins, which we must bear with patience " He caused young gentlemen who were brought up under his care to carry in the dishes and wait on the poor at table, to teach them the true spirit of humility, in which he himself set an example. Wulfstan rebuilt his cathedral at Worcester, *c.* 1086, but he loved the old edifice which had to be demolished. " The men of old ", he said, " if they had not stately buildings were themselves a sacrifice to God, whereas we pile up stones, and neglect souls." He died in 1095, having sat as bishop thirty-two years, and lived about eighty-seven. Dr W. Hunt, in the *Dictionary of National Biography*, writes : " Wulfstan was, so far as is known, a faultless character, and, save that he knew no more than was absolutely necessary for the discharge of his duties, a pattern of all monastic and of all episcopal virtues as they were then understood ". He was canonized in 1203, and his feast is now kept in the dioceses of Birmingham, Clifton and Northampton.

The details of St Wulfstan's life are fairly well known to us from a number of short biographies. Those by Hemming and William of Malmesbury are printed by Wharton in his *Anglia Sacra*, that of Capgrave by the Bollandists in the *Acta Sanctorum* for January 19. We also obtain a good deal of information from chroniclers like Florence of Worcester and

Simeon of Durham. See also Freeman's *Norman Conquest,* vols. iv and v *passim ;* D. Knowles, *The Monastic Order in England* (1949), pp. 159–161 and *passim ;* R. R. Darlington, *The Vita Wulfstani of William of Malmesbury* (Camden Society, 3rd series, vol. xl, 1928) ; an English version of the same by J. H. F. Peile (1934) ; and J. W. Lamb, *St Wulstan, Prelate and Patriot* (1933).

ST HENRY, Bishop of Uppsala, Martyr   (A.D. 1156 ?)

For lack of reliable contemporary records only a bare outline can be given of the history of St Henry. He was an Englishman, and it is possible that he was already resident in Rome when Cardinal Nicholas Breakspear, afterwards Pope Adrian IV, was sent in 1151 as papal legate to Scandinavia. Henry seems to have accompanied him and to have been consecrated bishop of Uppsala by the legate himself in 1152. The new bishop won the favour of St Eric, King of Sweden, and when the king sailed to undertake a sort of crusade against the pagan marauders of Finland, the new bishop went with him. The Swedish warriors gained a great victory and as a result some of the Finns accepted Christian baptism. Eric sailed back to Sweden, but the bishop remained behind to continue his work, " with apostolic zeal, though occasionally hardly with apostolic wisdom ".

A convert named Lalli having committed a murder, St Henry required him to do penance, but Lalli, resentful of the indignity, lay in wait for the bishop and slew him (but there is another and quite different story of his death). Several miracles of healing and others were recorded of Henry, and although there seems to be no evidence for the assertion that the martyred bishop was formally canonized by Pope Adrian himself, he has from an early date been recognized as the patron saint of Finland. It appears from an indulgence letter of Boniface VIII in 1296 that the cathedral of Abo was already dedicated to St Henry, and when in the sixteenth century the series of paintings depicting English saints and martyrdoms was set up in the English College at Rome, the patron of Finland duly figured therein. Of much greater interest and artistic merit is a wonderful brass, still in existence, engraved (*c.* 1440) to cover the cenotaph at Nousis where his relics first rested, with twelve subordinate plaques descriptive of his legend and miracles. In 1300 the remains of St Henry were translated to the cathedral at Abo (now called Turku) and a second festival commemorating this translation was kept in Finland on June 18. In Sweden January 19 was the day of St Henry's principal feast, but the Finnish calendars assign it to January 20.

A full account of St Henry is given in an article by Professor T. Borenius in the *Archaeological Journal,* vol. lxxxvii (1930), pp. 340–358 ; and further liturgical details are supplied by Aarno Malin, *Der Heiligenkalender Finnlands* (1925), pp. 179 and 208–223. The thirteenth-century legend of St Henry is printed in the *Acta Sanctorum,* January, vol. ii, as well as elsewhere. See also C. J. A. Oppermann, *English Missionaries in Sweden and Finland* (1937), pp. 200–205 ; but *cf.* the *Analecta Bollandiana,* vol. lvii (1939), pp. 162–164.

BD ANDREW OF PESCHIERA   (A.D. 1485)

Not very much authentic detail seems to be preserved to us concerning the life of this Andrew. His family name was Gregho (their origin was Greek), and he was born at Peschiera upon the Lago di Garda. At an early age he entered the Dominican Order at Brescia, and was sent to the famous friary of San Marco at Florence to make his studies. After ordination he was bidden by his superiors to evangelize the Valtelline, a district of Switzerland and northern Italy, where heresy was rife and the people fierce and godless. An attractive picture is painted of the missionary's untiring labours amongst these unsympathetic people, of his tender devotion to the Passion, of the austerity of his life, and of his spirit of humility and poverty. Some of the miracles attributed to him are of a rather extravagant character, as when we are told that when a book was produced by the heretics to confute him in argument, he bade his opponents open their book and " an enormous viper " came out of it, typical of the poison which the book contained. He was instrumental in founding the Dominican house at Morbegno, to serve as a sort of outpost, and it was here, on January 18, 1485, that Bd Andrew died. He had spent forty-five years of his life in the Valtelline. His *cultus* was confirmed in 1820.

See the *Acta Sanctorum*, May, vol. iv, pp. 627–631 ; Procter, *Short Lives of the Dominican Saints*, pp. 7–10.

BD BERNARD OF CORLEONE　　(A.D. 1667)

PHILIP LATINI, a young man who practised the trade of a shoemaker in the town of Corleone, about twenty miles from Palermo, seems also in his youth to have had a hankering after a career of arms, and, according to his biographer, was accounted the best swordsman in Sicily. Among many other encounters, having on one occasion come into conflict with the police and wounded an officer of the law, he, as the custom was in those days, took sanctuary in a church. There he was safe from arrest, but of course could not venture to leave his refuge until the coast was clear. Being thus virtually besieged for several days, Philip, who was by nature very devout, had time to enter into himself, and realized that in the wild and adventurous life he was leading he stood in grave danger of losing his soul. He accordingly in 1631 joined the Capuchins as a lay-brother, being then twenty-seven years old, receiving the name of Bernard. From this time forth the courage and enthusiasm which he had displayed in fighting were entirely given to the practice of austerity. His fastings, watchings and macerations of the flesh were incredibly severe, and the assaults which he sustained from the enemy of mankind, who, we are told, often appeared to him in hideous forms and offered him physical violence, make very sensational reading. On the other hand, the extraordinary graces which his biographer records are on much the same scale. We hear of ecstasies and levitations, and of prophecies and miracles innumerable.

One special gift attributed to him, which makes a more attractive appeal to the feeling of our own day, was that of healing animals. He had great compassion for the poor suffering beasts, for, as he observed, they have neither doctors nor medicine nor speech to explain what is the matter with them. They were brought to him in numbers. He said the Lord's Prayer over them, and then had them led three times round the cross which stood in front of the friary church. But he cured them all (*tutte le risanava*), and, what is even more surprising, we are told that at his death he bequeathed this same power of healing animals to another member of the community who was very attached to him. Brother Bernard of Corleone died at Palermo on January 12, 1667, and was beatified in 1768.

See B. Sanbenedetti, *Vita del . F. Bernardo da Corlione* (1725), the first edition of which biography was apparently published in 1679, twelve years after Bd Bernard's death ; Father Angélique's complete biography (1901) ; Father Dionigi, *Profilo del B. Bernardo* (1934), with bibliography ; and Léon, *Auréole Séraphique* (Eng. trans.), vol. i, pp. 97–98. For an illustration of the abuses to which the privilege of sanctuary lent itself, see J. B. Labat, *Voyage en Espagne et en Italie*, 1703 et 1707, vol. iv, p. 19.

ST CHARLES OF SEZZE   (A.D. 1670)

THERE is not much which calls for special comment in the life of Charles of Sezze, Franciscan lay-brother of the Observance.   Though he was of humble birth, his parents hoped that he might be educated for the priesthood, but at school he was found a very dull pupil, and beyond learning to read and write he seems to have had no further education.   He was, however, extremely responsive to all that spoke to him of God.   Though the days of his youth were spent in labouring in the fields, he practised austere penance and took a vow of chastity.   He had more than one serious illness, and once, when he was twenty, he promised to become a religious if he was cured.   The friars of Naziano eventually accepted him as a lay-brother, and there in the noviceship his fervour redoubled.   After his profession he begged to join some of his brethren who were going to the Indies as missionaries, but he again fell seriously ill, and after convalescence was sent to live in Rome.   Here he gave a wonderful example of virtue and charity, and, despite his extreme simplicity, his company was sought by cardinals and other eminent ecclesiastics.   He died on January 6, 1670, at the age of 57, beatified in 1882, and canonized in 1959.

See the decree of beatification in the *Analecta Juris Pontificii*, 1882 ; Léon, *Auréole Séraphique* (Eng. trans.), vol. ii, pp. 64-68 ; Imbert-Gourbeyre, *La Stigmatisation* (1894), vol. i, pp. 315-316.

BD MARGARET BOURGEOYS, VIRGIN, FOUNDRESS OF THE CONGREGATION OF NOTRE DAME OF MONTREAL   (A.D. 1700)

MARGARET BOURGEOYS was the sixth of the twelve children of Abraham Bourgeoys, wax-chandler, and his wife, Guillemette Garnier, and was born at Troyes, the chief town of Champagne, in 1620.   When she was twenty years old she offered herself as a postulant first to the Carmelites and then to the Poor Clares, and was refused—for reasons unknown—by both.   She was well known in Troyes as president of the sodality of our Lady attached to the convent of the Augustinian canonesses of St Peter Fourier and Bd Alix Le Clercq ; and the Abbé Gendret took these refusals to mean that Margaret was intended to lead an unenclosed community which he had long been considering.   Such a community was in fact begun under his direction by Margaret and two others, but it came to nothing and she returned home.   Amid these rebuffs she was saved from discouragement by a vision of the Child Jesus, which, she declared, " for ever turned my eyes from all the beauty of this world ".

In 1652 there came to visit his sister in the canonesses' convent at Troyes Paul de Maisonneuve, governor of the French settlement at Ville-Marie (Montreal). He wanted a schoolmistress for his little colony ; and Margaret, who had long been interested in Canada and recognized in Maisonneuve an intimation that this was her call, agreed to go.   She landed at Quebec on September 22, 1653, and a month later was at Ville-Marie.   It was simply a fort, wherein the couple of hundred souls all lived, with a little hospital and a chapel for the Jesuit missionary when he was there.

For over four years Margaret made a sort of " uncanonical novitiate ".   She housekept for the governor, looked after the few children, helped Joan Mance at the hospital and the wives of the garrison, got the great cross restored on Mount Royal (its predecessor had been destroyed by the Indians), and had a new chapel of our Lady almost ready for the arrival of the four " gentlemen ecclesiastics " from Saint-Sulpice in 1657. In the following year the first school of Montreal was opened, in a stone building that had been a stable, with less than a dozen girls and boys and one assistant, Margaret Picart. But Margaret Bourgeoys was looking ahead : Montreal would grow, and with it her work—and there were the children of the Indians to be kept in mind. Where could she get helpers ? There was only one answer to that question ; and in the same year she sailed with Joan Mance for France. Twelve months later she was back, with her old friend Catherine Crolo and three other young women.

During the years that followed, years full of disturbance and alarms because of the Iroquois war, the school grew and Margaret added to it a kindergarten for a few adopted Indian children, household instruction for older girls, and the organization of a Marian sodality. Montreal too was growing, and with the end of the Iroquois war in 1667 the adumbration of a town began to appear. During 1670–1672 Margaret was again in France. She was given civil authorization for her work by King Louis XIV ; she obtained another half-dozen recruits ; and it seems it was now that she definitely determined to organize a religious congregation. On her return she had to pilot her little community through a period of great poverty and difficulty ; but her trust in God's providence was amply rewarded, and in 1676 the Congregation of Notre Dame was canonically erected by the first bishop of Quebec, Mgr de Laval.

But troubled times again followed. Mgr de Laval had his own ideas about the future of the congregation, which gave Mother Bourgeoys a third and fruitless journey to France, and in 1683 the convent was destroyed by fire, two sisters (one of whom was Margaret's niece) losing their lives. Mgr de Laval thought that this was the moment for the little community to amalgamate with the Ursulines, who had been in Quebec since 1639. Mother Bourgeoys humbly represented that monastic enclosure would make their work impossible ; and the bishop did not insist. That was not the end of it, however, for Mgr de Laval's successor, Mgr de Saint-Vallier, an obstinate and quick-tempered prelate, raised many difficulties before he accepted the idea of the first unenclosed foreign-missionary community for women in the Church. It was not till 1698 that twenty-four sisters were able to make simple vows, Mother Bourgeoys by then having ceased to be superioress for the past five years.

Montreal's first boarding-school was opened in 1673, and the first mission-school for Indians began in 1676 ; by 1679 there were two Iroquois girls in the community.* Schools for French children were started outside Ville-Marie on the island of Montreal (where in 1689 the Iroquois massacred every man, woman and child not protected by the fort), then farther afield near Trois-Rivières, and in 1685 Mgr de Saint-Vallier summoned the sisters to Quebec—seven missions in all. Behind these humble beginnings, which were to develop into over 200 establishments of the congregation to-day, facing reverses from savages and from fire, all the fierce hardships of colonial pioneering, struggles with poverty and some lack of comprehension from superiors, stands the indomitable figure of Bd Margaret Bourgeoys, the First Schoolmistress of Montreal. Like not a few other foundresses, she is known best in her work, in those undertakings in which she underwent the

* There were two New Englanders in this French community before the death of the foundress : captives of the Abenakis, ransomed at Montreal, who became Catholics there. Lydia Langley, of Groton, Massachusetts, was the first New England girl to become a nun.

common double trial of doubt of her own capacity for the work and a gnawing sense of her unworthiness before God. But courage was not the least of her virtues, and devotion to the good of the children and of all her neighbours urged her on, " I want at all costs ", she said, " not only to love my neighbour, but to keep him in love for me. "

C. W. Colby wrote in his *Canadian Types of the Old Regime* (New York, 1908) :

From the moment of her arrival in New France she became a source of inspiration to all about her. Less austere than Mlle Mance, less mystical than Marie de l'Incarnation, she combined fervour with an abundance of those virtues which have their roots in human affection. It is not too much to say that for almost half a century she was by influence and attainment the first woman in Montreal. Goodness radiated from her benign personality, and her work bore the more lasting results from the wisdom of her methods. But above everything else Marguerite Bourgeoys was a teacher. And when the biographer has finished his sketch of Marie de l'Incarnation* or Marguerite Bourgeoys, he had best remain content with his plain narrative. Women like those do not ask for eulogy. Their best praise is the record of their deeds, written without comment in the impressive simplicity of truth.

From the time that she resigned her superiorship at the age of 73, Bd Margaret's health and strength gradually waned, but the end came rather unexpectedly. On the last day of 1699 the aged foundress offered her life in place of that of the novice-mistress, who was very ill ; and so it came about : the young nun got better, but Mother Bourgeoys died, on January 12, 1700. She was beatified in 1950, and her feast-day is January 19.

There is a considerable literature about this *beata*. A manuscript copy of her own memoirs, written under obedience in 1698, is preserved at Montreal, and at the Quebec seminary there is the original manuscript of the unpublished biography of Margaret written by Mgr C. de Glandelet in 1715. There have been several published lives in French, from M. F. Ransonnet's (1728) to Dom A. Jamet's two volumes (1942) and Father Y. Charron's *Mère Bourgeoys* (1950, Eng. trans.), of which Canon L. Groulx says in his preface, " Rien donc, en la manière de M. Charron, de l'hagiographie abstraite et déshumanisée ". There are popular biographies in English by E. F. Butler (1932) and Sister St I. Doyle (1940).

BD THOMAS OF CORI (A.D. 1729)

THIS holy Franciscan was of humble birth, a native of Cori in the Roman Campagna. As a child he obtained some schooling from a charitable priest, but before long his parents took him away to assist them in their work of pasturing sheep. As we read of many other youthful shepherds of both sexes who figure in the lives of the saints, he turned this time of solitude spent with the dumb beasts and with God under the open sky to good account. He acquired such a habit of prayer and contemplation that when his parents both died he applied for admission, being then aged twenty-two, among the Observant friars of Cori. He was received, and six years after was ordained priest. Though he was at first employed as master of novices, he seems always to have retained his attraction for the wilderness, and he obtained leave to bury himself in the little friary of Civitella, among the mountains in the neighbourhood of Subiaco. Here Thomas spent almost all the rest of his life, offering himself sweetly and joyously for the meanest of occupations, practising

* First superioress of the Ursulines of Quebec. See Father James Brodrick's *Procession of Saints* (1949), pp. 174-201.

severe penance, preaching to the scant and rude populace, many of them brigands, who dwelt in these mountain regions, and favoured himself with many ecstasies and extraordinary graces.   In particular it is recorded of him that once when he was giving communion in the church, he fell into a trance, and was raised up, ciborium in hand, to the very roof, and then after a short interval sank slowly to earth again and went on distributing communion as before.   When elected guardian Thomas's charity and trust in Providence were unbounded ; he gave away to the poor the loaves which remained in the house, but as the community assembled to sit down at a table bare of all food, a wholly unforeseen donation was brought to supply their needs.   Though always kindly and considerate as a superior, he was strict in those things which concerned the service of God, insisting in particular that the office should be recited slowly and reverently ; *Si cor non orat*, he used to say, *in vanum lingua laborat* (If the heart does not pray, the tongue works in vain).   He died at the age of seventy-three on January 11, 1729, and was beatified in 1785.

See Luca di Roma, *Breve compendio della vita   del B. Padre Tommaso da Cori* (1786) ; Léon, *Auréole Séraphique* (Eng. trans.), vol. i, pp. 324-332.

20 : ST FABIAN, Pope and Martyr   (A.D. 250)

POPE ST FABIAN succeeded St Antherus in the pontificate about the year 236.   Eusebius relates that in an assembly of the people and clergy held to elect the new pope, a dove flew in and settled on the head of St Fabian.   This sign, we are told, united the votes of the clergy and people in choosing Fabian, though, as he was a layman and a stranger, they had no thought of him before.   He governed the Church fourteen years, brought the body of St Pontian, pope and martyr, from Sardinia, and condemned Privatus, the author of a new heresy which had given trouble in Africa.   St Fabian died a martyr in the persecution of Decius, in 250, as St Cyprian and St Jerome bear witness.   The former, writing to his successor, St Cornelius, calls Fabian an incomparable man ; and says that the glory of his death corresponded with the purity and holiness of his life.   The slab which closed the *loculus* of St Fabian in the cemetery of St Callistus still exists.   It is broken into four fragments, but clearly bears the words, in Greek characters, " Fabian, bishop, martyr ".

See Duchesne, *Liber Pontificalis*, vol. i, pp. 148-149 ; St Cyprian, Epistle ix ; H. Leclercq in DAC., vol. v, cc. 1057 1064 ; *Nuovo Bullettino di arch. crist.* (1916), pp. 207-221 ; Wilpert, *La cripta dei Papi* (1910), p. 18.   The body was afterwards transferred to the church of St Sebastian   see Grossi-Gondi, *S. Fabiano, papa e martire* (1916) and Chéramy, *Saint-Sébastien hors les murs* (1925).

ST SEBASTIAN, Martyr   (A.D. 288 ?)

ACCORDING to the " acts ", assigned without any adequate reason to the authorship of St Ambrose, St Sebastian was born at Narbonne in Gaul, though his parents had come from Milan, and he was brought up in that city.   He was a fervent servant of Christ, and though his natural inclinations were averse from a military life, yet to be better able to assist the confessors and martyrs in their sufferings without arousing suspicion, he went to Rome and entered the army under the Emperor Carinus about the year 283.   It happened that the martyrs, Marcus and

Marcellian, under sentence of death, appeared in danger of faltering in their resolution owing to the tears of their friends ; Sebastian, seeing this, intervened, and made them a long exhortation to constancy, which he delivered with an ardour that strongly affected his hearers.   Zoë, the wife of Nicostratus, who had for six years lost the use of speech, fell at his feet, and when the saint made the sign of the cross on her mouth, she spoke again distinctly.   Thus Zoë, with her husband, Nicostratus, who was master of the rolls (*primiscrinius*), the parents of Marcus and Marcellian, the gaoler Claudius, and sixteen other prisoners were converted ; and Nicostratus, who had charge of the prisoners, took them to his own house, where Polycarp, a priest, instructed and baptized them.   Chromatius, governor of Rome, being informed of this, and that Tranquillinus, the father of Marcus and Marcellian, had been cured of the gout by receiving baptism, desired to follow their example, since he himself was grievously afflicted with the same malady.   Accordingly, having sent for Sebastian, he was cured by him, and baptized with his son Tiburtius.   He then released the converted prisoners, made his slaves free, and resigned his prefectship.

Not long after Carinus was defeated and slain in Illyricum by Diocletian, who the year following made Maximian his colleague in the empire.   The persecution was still carried on by the magistrates in the same manner as under Carinus, without any new edicts.   Diocletian, admiring the courage and character of St Sebastian, was anxious to keep him near his person ; and being ignorant of his religious beliefs he created him captain of a company of the pretorian guards, which was a considerable dignity.   When Diocletian went into the East, Maximian, who remained in the West, honoured Sebastian with the same distinction and respect. Chromatius retired into the country in Campania, taking many new converts along with him.   Then followed a contest of zeal between St Sebastian and the priest Polycarp as to which of them should accompany this troop to complete their instruction, and which should remain at the post of danger in the city to encourage and assist the martyrs.   Pope Caius, who was appealed to, judged that Sebastian should stay in Rome.   In the year 286, the persecution growing fiercer, the pope and others concealed themselves in the imperial palace, as the place of greatest safety, in the apartments of one Castulus, a Christian officer of the court.   Zoë was first apprehended, when praying at St Peter's tomb on the feast of the apostles. She was stifled with smoke, being hung by the heels over a fire.   Tranquillinus, ashamed to show less courage than a woman, went to pray at the tomb of St Paul, and there was seized and stoned to death.   Nicostratus, Claudius, Castorius and Victorinus were taken, and after being thrice tortured, were thrown into the sea. Tiburtius, betrayed by a false brother, was beheaded.   Castulus, accused by the same wretch, was twice stretched upon the rack, and afterwards buried alive. Marcus and Marcellian were nailed by the feet to a post, and having remained in that torment twenty-four hours were shot to death with arrows.

St Sebastian, having sent so many martyrs to Heaven before him, was himself impeached before Diocletian ; who, after bitterly reproaching him with his ingratitude, delivered him over to certain archers of Mauritania, to be shot to death. His body was pierced through with arrows, and he was left for dead.   Irene, the widow of St Castulus, going to bury him, found him still alive and took him to her lodgings, where he recovered from his wounds, but refused to take to flight.   On the contrary, he deliberately took up his station one day on a staircase where the emperor was to pass, and there accosting him, he denounced the abominable cruelties perpetrated against the Christians.   This freedom of language, coming from a person whom he supposed to be dead, for a moment kept the emperor speechless ; but recovering from his surprise, he gave orders for him to be seized and beaten to death with cudgels, and his body thrown into the common sewer. A lady called Lucina, admonished by the martyr in a vision, had his body secretly buried in the place called *ad catacumbas*, where now stands the basilica of St Sebastian.

The story recounted above is now generally admitted by scholars to be no more than a pious fable, written perhaps before the end of the fifth century.   All that we can safely assert regarding St Sebastian is that he was a Roman martyr, that he had some connection with Milan and was venerated there even in the time of St Ambrose, and that he was buried on the Appian Way, probably quite close to the present basilica of St Sebastian, in the cemetery *ad catacumbas*.   Although in late medieval and renaissance art St Sebastian is always represented as pierced with arrows, or at least as holding an arrow, this attribute does not appear until com- paratively late.   A mosaic dating from about 680 in San Pietro in Vincoli shows him as a bearded man carrying a martyr's crown in his hand, and in an ancient glass window in Strasbourg Cathedral he appears as a knight with sword and shield, but without arrows.   St Sebastian was specially invoked as a patron against the plague, and certain writers of distinction (*e.g.* Mâle and Perdrizet) urge that the idea of protection against contagious disease was suggested, in close accord with a well-known incident in the first book of the *Iliad*, by Sebastian's undaunted bearing in face of the clouds of arrows shot at him ; but Father Delehaye is prob- ably right in urging that some accidental cessation of the plague on an occasion when St Sebastian had been invoked would have been sufficient to start the tradi- tion.   That St Sebastian was the chosen patron of archers, and of soldiers in general, no doubt followed naturally from the legend.

For the *passio* of St Sebastian see the *Acta Sanctorum*, January 20.   See also H. Delehaye in the *Encyclopaedia Britannica* (11th edn.), and in *Analecta Bollandiana*, vol. xxviii (1909), p. 489 ; and K. Löffler in the *Catholic Encyclopedia*, vol. xiii ; *cf.* also Chéramy, *Saint- Sébastien hors les murs* (1925), and the *Civiltà Cattolica*, January and February, 1918.

ST EUTHYMIUS THE GREAT, Abbot   (A.D. 473)

THE birth of this saint was the fruit of the prayers of his parents through the intercession of the martyr Polyeuctus.   His father was a wealthy citizen of Melitene in Armenia, and Euthymius was educated in sacred learning under the care of the bishop of that city, who ordained him priest and made him his deputy in the supervision of the monasteries.   The saint often visited that of St Polyeuctus, and spent whole nights in prayer on a neighbouring mountain, as he also did continu- ously from the octave of the Epiphany till towards the end of Lent.   The love of solitude daily growing stronger, he secretly left his own country at twenty-nine years of age ; and, after offering up his prayers at the holy places in Jerusalem, chose a cell six miles from that city, near the *laura* * of Pharan.   He made baskets, and earned enough by selling them to provide a living for himself and alms for the poor.   After five years he retired with one Theoctistus ten miles farther towards Jericho, where they both lived in a cave.   In this place he began to receive disciples about the year 411.   He entrusted the care of his community to Theoctistus, and

* A laura consisted of cells at a little distance from one another.

himself retired to a remote hermitage, only meeting on Saturdays and Sundays those who desired spiritual advice. He taught his monks never to eat so much as to satisfy their hunger, but strictly forbade among them any singularity in fasts or any other uncommon observances, as savouring of vanity and self-will. Following his example, they all withdrew into the wilderness from after Epiphany till Palm Sunday, when they met again in their monastery to celebrate the offices of Holy Week. He enjoined constant silence and plenty of manual labour, so that they not only earned their own living, but also a surplus which they devoted as first-fruits to God in the relief of the poor.

By making the sign of the cross and a short prayer, St Euthymius cured a young Arab, one half of whose body had been paralysed. His father, who had vainly invoked the much-boasted arts of physic and magic among the Persians to procure some relief for his son, at the sight of this miracle asked to be baptized. So many Arabs followed his example that Juvenal, Patriarch of Jerusalem, consecrated Euthymius bishop to provide for the spiritual needs of these converts, and in that capacity he assisted at the Council of Ephesus in 431. Juvenal built St Euthymius a laura on the road from Jerusalem to Jericho in the year 420. Euthymius could never be prevailed upon to depart from his rule of strict solitude, but governed his monks by vicars, to whom he gave directions on Sundays. His humility and charity won the hearts of all who spoke to him. He seemed to surpass the great Arsenius in the gift of perpetual tears, and Cyril of Scythopolis relates many miracles which he wrought, usually by the sign of the cross. In the time of a great drought he exhorted the people to penance to avert this scourge of heaven. Great numbers came in procession to his cell, carrying crosses, singing *Kyrie eleison*, and begging him to offer up his prayers to God for them. He said to them, " I am a sinner ; how can I presume to appear before God, who is angry at our sins ? Let us prostrate ourselves all together before Him, and He will hear us." They obeyed; and the saint going into his chapel prayed lying on the ground. The sky grew dark on a sudden, rain fell in abundance, and the year proved remarkably fruitful.

When the heretical Empress Eudoxia, widow of Theodosius II, frightened by the afflictions of her family, consulted St Simeon Stylites he referred her to St Euthymius. As Euthymius would allow no woman to enter his laura she built a lodge some distance away, and asked him to come and see her there. His advice to her was to forsake the Eutychians and to receive the Council of Chalcedon. She followed his counsel as the command of God, returned to orthodox communion, and many followed her example. In 459 Eudoxia desired St Euthymius to meet her at her lodge, designing to settle on his laura sufficient revenues for its main-tenance. He sent her word to spare herself the trouble, and to prepare for death. She admired his disinterestedness, returned to Jerusalem, and died shortly after. One of the latest disciples of Euthymius was the young St Sabas, whom he tenderly loved. In the year 473, on January 13, Martyrius and Elias, to both of whom St Euthymius had foretold that they would be patriarchs of Jerusalem, came with several others to visit him and accompany him to his Lenten retreat. But he said he would stay with them all that week, and leave on the Saturday following, giving them to understand that his death was near at hand. Three days after he gave orders that a general vigil should be observed on the eve of St Antony's festival, on which occasion he delivered an address to his spiritual children, exhorting them to humility and charity. He appointed Elias his successor, and foretold to Domitian, a beloved disciple, that he would follow him out of this world on the seventh day, which happened exactly as he had prophesied.   Euthymius died on Saturday, January 20, being ninety-five years old, of which he had spent sixty-eight in the desert.   Cyril relates that he appeared several times after his death, and speaks of the miracles which were wrought by his intercession, declaring that he himself had been an eye-witness of many.   St Euthymius is named in the preparation of the Byzantine Mass.

Almost all our knowledge of Euthymius is derived from his life by Cyril of Scythopolis, a Latin version of which is printed in the *Acta Sanctorum*, January 20, and a critical Greek text in E. Schwartz, *Kyrillos von Skythopolis* (1939).   See also DCB., vol. ii, pp. 398–400 ; and R. Génier, *Vie de S. Euthyme le Grand* (1909).

ST FECHIN, Abbot   (A.D. 665)

No very authentic information seems to be available regarding St Fechin, though we possess a Latin life of him, a hymn and a number of miscellaneous notices.   He is said to have been born at Luighne (Leyney), in Connaught, and to have been trained by St Nathy.   There are a good many extravagant miracles attributed to him, but two definite facts stand out   first, that he founded and ruled a community of monks, probably at Fobhar or Fore, in Westmeath ; secondly, that he perished in the terrible plague which swept over Ireland in 665.   So far as our late and unsatisfactory materials allow us to draw any inference, St Fechin never quitted his native shores, but, as such a name as Ecclefechan (" ecclesia sancti Fechani " is the form it assumes in old charters) would alone suffice to prove, the saint was certainly honoured outside his own country.   At Arbroath we hear of an annual fair being held on January 20, which was called St Vigean's market, sometimes corrupted into St Virgin's market.

See the *Acta Sanctorum* for January 20 ; LIS., vol. i, p. 356 ; and KSS., pp. 456–458. The most correct text of his life is, however, that of Plummer, printed in his VSII., vol. ii, pp. 76–86.   See also some Irish materials in *Revue Celtique*, vol. xii, pp. 318–353.

BD BENEDICT OF COLTIBONI   (*c.* A.D. 1107)

The Benedictine congregation of Vallombrosa, which developed out of the hermit-age established before 1038 in that famous valley by St John Gualbert, numbered in the days of its prime more than fifty communities, and eventually spread into France and the Tirol.   The most characteristic feature of the new organization was an attempt to combine the life of the hermit with that of the monk.   Bd Benedict Ricasoli was the son of parents who had known St John Gualbert in person, and had made over to him and his disciples a property at Coltiboni.   Here Benedict was received at an early age by Abbot Azzo, but aspiring after greater perfection and solitude than seemed possible in community life, he took up his quarters in a hut on the mountain side at some little distance from the abbey. From time to time he returned to keep some festival of the Church with his brethren, and on one of these rare visits, remaining from Christmas until the Epiphany, he showed special earnestness in exhorting the monks to fervour and to perseverance in their arduous vocation.   Their life, he told them, ought to be nothing else but a continual preparation for death, and he insistently repeated the warning, " Be ye ready, for the Son of man cometh at the hour ye think not."   Returning to his hermitage he himself soon afterwards (apparently on January 20, 1107) was sum-moned to his reward.

Rumour in later times enlarged upon the marvellous occurrences which attended his departure from this world. It was affirmed that his death was made known by the monastery bell ringing of its own accord ; that a path was miraculously cleared through the snow and ice to enable the brethren to come and see ; that he was found by them dead, but still kneeling in the act of prayer, with hands joined and eyes raised to Heaven ; and that when he was buried within the monastic enclosure a light rested over the spot, and a white lily grew spontaneously out of the ground. The cult paid to him on account of his repute for holiness was confirmed in 1907. His remains are said still to repose in the sanctuary of Galloro, near Riccia.

See the decree of the Congregation of Rites in *Analecta Ecclesiastica*, 1907, p. 247 ; and the *Acta Sanctorum* for January 20.

BD DESIDERIUS, or DIDIER, Bishop of Thérouanne　　(A.D. 1194)

ALTHOUGH there seems to be no very satisfactory evidence of *cultus*, Didier, who is said to have been the thirty-third bishop of Thérouanne, is commonly described as Blessed in hagiographical collections like those of De Ram and Guérin, and his name appears in some Cistercian and other calendars. He has an interest for many English Catholics, because he helped to found near Saint-Omer the Cistercian monastery of Blandecques, or " Blandyke ", which name has been perpetuated in English Jesuit schools as that of their monthly holiday, for in the old Saint-Omer's days the boys went to Blandyke once a month to spend the day in country air. A statue of our Lady preserved there was believed to work miracles, and as late as the eighteenth century medals were struck of our Lady of Blandyke. Bd Didier became bishop in 1169, and is said to have been remarkable for his charity and his spirit of prayer. He resigned his see three years before his death, which seems to have taken place on January 20 (or September 2), 1194 at the Cistercian abbey of Cambron, where he had been professed a monk.

See Reussens in the *Biographie nationale (belge)*, vol. v : *Gallia christiana nova*, vol. ii ; and DHG., vol ix, c. 117, and xi, 585.

21 : ST AGNES, Virgin and Martyr　　(*c.* A.D. 304 ?)

ST AGNES has always been looked upon in the Church as a special patroness of bodily purity. She is one of the most popular of Christian saints, and her name is commemorated every day in the canon of the Mass. Rome was the scene of her triumph, and Prudentius says that her tomb was shown within sight of that city. She suffered perhaps not long after the beginning of the persecution of Diocletian, whose cruel edicts were published in March in the year 303. We learn from St Ambrose and St Augustine that she was only thirteen years of age at the time of her glorious death. Her riches and beauty excited the young noblemen of the first families in Rome to contend as rivals for her hand. Agnes answered them all that she had consecrated her virginity to a heavenly husband, who could not be beheld by mortal eyes. Her suitors, finding her resolution unshakable, accused her to the governor as a Christian, not doubting that threats and torments would prove more effective with one of her tender years on whom allurements could make no impression.   The judge at first employed the mildest expressions and most seductive promises, to which Agnes paid no regard, repeating always that she could have no other spouse but Jesus Christ.   He then made use of threats, but found her endowed with a masculine courage, and even eager to suffer torment and death.   At last terrible fires were made, and iron hooks, racks and other instruments of torture displayed before her, with threats of immediate execution.   The heroic child surveyed them undismayed, and made good cheer in the presence of the fierce and cruel executioners.   She was so far from betraying the least symptom of terror that she even expressed her joy at the sight, and offered herself to the rack.   She was then dragged before the idols and commanded to offer incense, but could, St Ambrose tells us, by no means be compelled to move her hand, except to make the sign of the cross.

The governor, seeing his measures ineffectual, said he would send her to a house of prostitution, where what she prized so highly should be exposed to the insults of the brutal and licentious youth of Rome.*   Agnes answered that Jesus Christ was too jealous of the purity of His chosen ones to suffer it to be violated in such a manner, for He was their defender and protector.   " You may ", said she, " stain your sword with my blood, but you will never be able to profane my body, consecrated to Christ."   The governor was so incensed at this that he ordered her to be immediately led to the place of shame with liberty to all to abuse her person at pleasure.   Many young profligates ran thither, full of wicked desires, but were seized with such awe at the sight of the saint that they durst not approach her ; one only excepted, who, attempting to be rude to her, was that very instant, by a flash, as it were of lightning from Heaven, struck blind, and fell trembling to the ground.   His companions, terrified, took him up and carried him to Agnes, who was singing hymns of praise to Christ, her protector.   The virgin by prayer restored his sight and his health.

The chief accuser of the saint, who had at first sought to gratify his lust and avarice, now, in a spirit of vindictiveness, incited the judge against her, his passionate fondness being changed into fury.   The governor needed no encouragement, for he was highly exasperated to see himself set at defiance by one of her tender age and sex.   Being resolved therefore upon her death, he condemned her to be beheaded.   Agnes, filled with joy on hearing this sentence, " went to the place of execution more cheerfully ", says St Ambrose, " than others go to their wedding ".   The executioner had instructions to use all means to induce her to give way, but Agnes remained constant ; and having made a short prayer, bowed down her neck to receive the death stroke.   The spectators shed tears to see this beautiful child loaded with fetters, and offering herself fearlessly to the sword of the executioner, who with trembling hand cut off her head at one stroke.   Her body was buried at a short distance from Rome, beside the Nomentan road.

It is necessary to add to the account (based mainly on Prudentius) which is given above by Alban Butler, that modern authorities incline to the view that little reliance can be placed on the details of the story.   They point out that the " acts "

---

* On such vile methods of breaking down the constancy of Christian maidenhood Tertullian in his *Apologia* comments as follows : " By condemning the Christian maid rather to the lewd youth than to the lion, you have acknowledged that a stain of purity is more dreaded by us than any torments or death.   Yet your cruel cunning avails you not, but rather serves to gain men over to our holy religion."

of St Agnes, attributed unwarrantably to St Ambrose, can hardly be older than A.D. 415, and that these seem to represent an attempt to harmonize and embroider the discordant data found in the then surviving traditions.   St Ambrose, as just quoted, in his quite genuine sermon *De virginibus* (A.D. 377), says of St Agnes's martyrdom *cervicem inflexit*,* " she bent her neck ", from which it is commonly inferred that she was decapitated.   This view is supported by Prudentius's explicit statement that her head was struck off at one blow.   On the other hand, the epitaph written by Pope St Damasus speaks of " flames ", and beyond this says nothing as to the manner of her death ; while from the beautiful hymn, *Agnes beatae virginis* (which Walpole, Dreves and others now recognize as a genuine work of St Ambrose), it clearly follows that she was not beheaded, otherwise she could not after the blow was struck (*percussa*) have drawn her cloak modestly around her and have covered her face with her hand.   It seems plain that in the writer's view she was stabbed in the throat or breast.   From these apparent contradictions many critics conclude that already in the second half of the fourth century all memory of the exact circumstances of the martyrdom had been forgotten, and that only a vague tradition survived.

In any case, however, there can be no possible doubt of the fact that St Agnes was martyred, and that she was buried beside the Via Nomentana in the cemetery afterwards called by her name.   Here a basilica was erected in her honour before 354 by Constantina, daughter of Constantine and wife of Gallus ; and the terms of the acrostic inscription set up in the apse are still preserved, but it tells us nothing about St Agnes except that she was " a virgin " and " victorious ".   Again, the name of St Agnes is entered in the *Depositio martyrum* of A.D. 354, under the date January 21, together with the place of her burial.   There is also abundant subsidiary evidence of early *cultus* in the frequent occurrence of representations of the child martyr in " gold glasses ", etc., and in the prominence given to her name in all kinds of Christian literature.   " Agnes, Thecla and Mary were with me ", said St Martin to Sulpicius Severus, where he seems to assign precedence to Agnes even above our Blessed Lady.   St Agnes is, as remarked above, one of the saints named in the canon of the Mass.

It is quite possible that Father Jubaru is right in his attempt to reconcile the data supplied by Pope Damasus and St Ambrose, but it would not follow as a necessary consequence that he is also right in his theory that in the Greek " acts " we have an amalgamation of the story of two different St Agneses.   With regard to the great St Agnes, he contends that she was a child in Rome, that she consecrated to God her virginity, that she turned away from all suitors, and when persecution came that she deliberately left her parents' house and offered herself to martyrdom, that she was threatened with death by fire in an attempt to shake her constancy, but that, as she gave no sign of yielding, she was in fact stabbed in the throat.   Father Jubaru in his elaborate monograph further claims to have discovered the reliquary, containing the greater portion of the skull of the youthful martyr, in the treasury of the *Sancta sanctorum* at the Lateran.   This treasury was opened in 1903 after it had been hidden from view for many hundred years,

* A. S. Walpole, *Early Latin Hymns* (1922), p. 69, urges that *inflexit* " may mean bent aside in order to admit the point of the sword ", and quotes parallel passages from the classics in support of this view.   This is also the view of Father Jubaru.   There can be no question that stabbing in the throat was a common way of despatching the condemned, and was regarded as the most merciful form of *coup de grâce*.   St Ambrose calls the executioner " *percussor* ".

permission to do so having been obtained from Pope Leo XIII. The relic is considered by Father Grisar, S.J., and by many other archaeologists to be in all probability authentic, since a regular custom had grown up in the ninth century of separating the head from the rest of the bones when entire bodies of saints were enshrined in the churches. It also seems certain that the body of St Agnes was at that date preserved under the altar of her basilica, and further that on opening the the case in 1605 it was found without a head. From a medical examination of the fragments of the skull in the *Sancta sanctorum*, Dr Lapponi pronounced that the teeth showed conclusively that the head was that of a child about thirteen years of age. The more extravagant miracles which occur in the so-called " acts " are now admitted by all to be a fiction of the biographer. The case of St Agnes is, therefore, typical, and affords conclusive proof that the preposterous legends so often invented by later writers who wish to glorify the memory of a favourite saint cannot in themselves be accepted as proof that the martyrdom is fabulous and that the saint never existed.

In art St Agnes is commonly represented with a lamb and a palm, the lamb, no doubt, being originally suggested by the resemblance of the word *agnus* (a lamb) to the name Agnes. In Rome on the feast of St Agnes each year, while the choir in her church on the Via Nomentana are singing the antiphon *Stans a dextris ejus agnus nive candidior* (On her right hand a lamb whiter than snow), two white lambs are offered at the sanctuary rails. They are blessed and then cared for until the time comes for shearing them. Out of their wool are woven the pallia which, on the vigil of SS. Peter and Paul, are laid upon the altar in the *Confessio* at St Peter's immediately over the body of the Apostle. These pallia are sent to archbishops throughout the Western church, " from the body of Blessed Peter ", in token of the jurisdiction which they derive ultimately from the Holy See, the centre of religious authority.

Until the feast of St Peter Nolasco, displaced by that of St John Bosco, was fixed for January 28, there was in the general Western calendar on that day a " second feast " of St Agnes (she still has a commemoration in the Mass and Office of the 28th). This observance can be traced back to the Gelasian and Gregorian Sacramentaries, and is not altogether easy to explain. The addition of the words *de nativitate* or *in genuinum*, which meets us in certain liturgical texts of the seventh or eighth centuries, would seem to suggest that January 28 was the day on which St Agnes actually died, while the feast of January 21—·*de passione*, as it is sometimes described—marks the day when the martyr was brought to trial and threatened with torture. In view, however, of the prominence which the " octave " has in later times acquired in our Christian liturgy, it is curious that the one feast should occur exactly a week after the other. We have evidence that the Circumcision was called " Octavas Domini " already in the sixth century, and it must be remembered that our present Missal, following usages still more ancient, which were in fact pre-Christian in their origin, provides a special commemoration for the departed *in die septimo, trigesimo et anniversario*—in other words, the week day, the month day and the year day. It does not, therefore, seem by any means impossible that we have here a vestige of some primitive form of octave. Dom Bäumer has called attention to the fact that the primitive octave implied no more than a commemoration of the feast at the week-end without any reference to it upon the intermediate days.

The " acts " of St Agnes are printed in the *Acta Sanctorum*, January 21. The Greek " acts " were first edited by P. Franchi de Cavalieri, *S. Agnese nella tradizione e nella legenda*

(1899), together with a valuable discussion of the whole question.   See also the monograph of F. Jubaru, *Sainte Agnès d'après de nouvelles recherches* (1907) and further *Sainte Agnès, vierge et martyre* (1909) ;   DAC., vol. i, cc. 905–965 ;   *Analecta Bollandiana*, vol. xix (1900), pp. 227–228 ;   P. Franchi in *Studi e Testi*, vol. xix, pp. 141–164 ;   *Bessarione*, vol. viii (1911), pp. 218–245 ;   the *Liber Pontificalis* (ed. Duchesne), vol. i, p. 196 ;   CMH., pp. 52–53, 66 ; S. Bäumer, *Geschichte des Breviers* (1895), p. 325 ;   and, for the relics, Grisar, *Die römische Kapelle Sancta Sanctorum und ihr Schatz* (1908), p. 103.   And *cf.* St Ambrose, *De virginibus* in Migne, PL., vol. xvi, cc. 200–202 ;   and Prudentius, *Peristephanon*, 14.

ST FRUCTUOSUS, Bishop of Tarragona, Martyr   (A.D. 259)

St Fructuosus was the zealous and truly apostolic bishop of Tarragona, then the capital city of Spain.   When the persecution of Valerian and Gallienus was raging in the year 259, he was arrested by order of Emilian the governor, along with two deacons, Augurius and Eulogius, on Sunday, January 16.   He was then lying down in his bed, and only asked time to put on his shoes ;   after which he cheerfully followed the guards, who committed him and his two companions to prison. Fructuosus gave his blessing to the faithful who visited him, and on Monday he baptized in gaol a catechumen named Rogatian.   On Wednesday he kept the usual fast of the stations* till three o'clock in the afternoon.   On Friday, the sixth day after their commitment, the governor ordered them to be brought before him, and asked Fructuosus if he knew the contents of the edict of the emperors.   The saint answered that he did not, but that whatever they were he was a Christian.   " The emperors ", said Emilian, " command all to sacrifice to the gods."   Fructuosus answered, " I worship one God, who made heaven and earth and all things therein." Emilian said, " Do you not know that there are other gods ? "   " No ", replied the saint.   The proconsul said, " I will make you know it shortly.   What is left to any man to fear or worship on earth if he despises the worship of the immortal gods and of the emperors ? "   Then, turning to Augurius, he bade him pay no regard to what Fructuosus had said, but the deacon assured him that he worshipped the same Almighty God.   Emilian addressed himself to the other deacon, Eulogius, asking him if he too worshipped Fructuosus.   The holy man answered, " I do not worship Fructuosus, but the same God whom he worships ".   Emilian asked Fructuosus if he were a bishop, and added upon his confessing it, " Say, rather, you have been one ", meaning that he was about to lose that dignity along with his life ;   and immediately he condemned them to be burnt alive.

The pagans themselves could not refrain from tears on seeing them led to the amphitheatre, for they loved Fructuosus on account of his rare virtues. The Christians accompanied them, overwhelmed by a sorrow mixed with joy. The martyrs exulted to be hold themselves on the verge of a glorious eternity.   The faithful offered St Fructuosus a cup of wine, but he would not taste it, saying it was not yet the hour for breaking the fast, which was observed on Fridays till three o'clock and it was then only ten in the morning.   The holy man hoped to end the station or fast of that day with the patriarchs and prophets in Heaven.   When they were come into the amphitheatre, Augustalis, the bishop's lector, came to him weeping, and begged he would permit him to pull off his shoes.   The martyr said he could easily put them off himself, which he did.   Felix, a Christian, stepped forward and desired he would remember him in his prayers.   Fructuosus said aloud, " I am bound to pray for the whole Catholic Church spread over the world

---

* Wednesdays and Fridays were fast-days at that time ;   but only till none, that is, three in the afternoon.   This was called the fast of the stations.

from the east to the west," as if he had said, observes St Augustine, who much applauds this utterance, " If you wish that I should pray for you, do not leave her for whom I pray ". Martial, one of his flock, desired him to speak some words of comfort to his desolate church. The bishop, turning to the Christians, said, " My brethren, the Lord will not leave you as a flock without a shepherd. He is faithful to His promises. The hour of our suffering is short." The martyrs were fastened to stakes to be burnt, but the flames seemed at first to respect their bodies, consuming only the bands with which their hands were tied and giving them liberty to stretch out their arms in prayer. It was thus, on their knees, that they gave up their souls to God before the fire had touched them. Babylas and Mygdonius, two Christian servants of the governor, saw the heavens open and the saints carried up with crowns on their heads ; but Emilian himself, summoned to see too, was not accounted worthy to behold them. The faithful came in the night, extinguished the fire with wine, and took out the half-burnt bodies. Everyone carried some part of their remains home with him, but being admonished from Heaven, brought them back and laid them in the same sepulchre. St Augustine has left us a panegyric on St Fructuosus, pronounced on the anniversary day of his martyrdom.

This account of the passion of St Fructuosus belongs to that comparatively small class of the acts of the martyrs which all critics agree in regarding as authentic. Even Harnack says (*Chronologie bis Eusebius*, vol. ii, p. 473) that the document " awakens no suspicion ". It is printed in the *Acta Sanctorum*, January 21, in Ruinart and elsewhere. See Delehaye, *Les passions des martyrs*   (1921), p. 144, and also his *Origines du culte des martyrs* (1933), pp. 66–67. What more especially establishes the authenticity of the Acts of St Fructuosus is the fact that both St Augustine and Prudentius were evidently acquainted with them.

ST PATROCLUS, Martyr   (A.D. 259 ?)

Concerning the martyr St Patroclus, St Gregory of Tours comments that the popular devotion to him was greatly increased by the discovery of a copy of his *passio*. He was buried at or near Troyes, where he suffered, and over his tomb was a little oratory, but the only cleric who served it was a lector (one of the minor orders), and we may fairly infer from Gregory's language that no great interest was taken in the shrine. One fine day, however, this lector went to the bishop and showed him a hastily written manuscript which professed to be a copy of the Acts of St Patroclus. The account he gave of it was that a stranger had asked for hospitality, who had in his possession a manuscript containing the Passion of St Patroclus. The lector said he had borrowed it, and by sitting up all night had copied the document, but had, of course, returned the original to the owner who went away next morning. It is an extremely significant fact, well worthy of the attention of every student of Merovingian hagiography, that the Bishop of Troyes only scolded and cuffed him well, declaring that the lector had invented the whole story and that there had been no traveller and no manuscript. Obviously the rulers of the Church at that period were well aware that the fabrication of fictitious acts was going on freely.

St Gregory, however, declares that in this case, when a military expedition invaded Italy a short time afterwards, some of the members brought back with them a Passion of St Patroclus identical with that which the lector had copied. The result was an immense revival of devotion to the saint. He was a prominent Christian of exceptional charity and holiness. He was arrested either when a certain governor called Aurelian (259) or when the Emperor Aurelian himself came to Troyes (275). Answering fearlessly and defiantly, he was sentenced to death. In an attempt to drown him in the Seine he escaped from the executioners, but was recaptured and then beheaded. His relics were eventually carried to Soest in Westphalia, where they still repose.

See *Acta Sanctorum* for January 21 ; Allard, *Histoire des persécutions*, vol. iii, pp. 101 *seq.* ; Giefers, *Acta S. Patrocli* (1857).

ST EPIPHANIUS, BISHOP OF PAVIA   (A.D. 496)

THE reputation of Epiphanius for holiness and miracles gave him the highest credit with the weak Roman emperors of his time, and with the Kings Odoacer and Theodoric, though all of opposite interests. By his eloquence and charity he tamed savage barbarians, won life and liberty for whole armies of captives, and secured the abolition of many oppressive laws, with the mitigation of heavy public imposts and taxes. By his profuse charities he preserved many of the famine-stricken from perishing, and by his zeal he stemmed the torrent of iniquity in times of universal disorder. Epiphanius undertook an embassy to the Emperor Anthemius, and another to King Euric at Toulouse : both in the hope of averting war. He rebuilt Pavia, which had been destroyed by Odoacer, and mitigated the fury of Theodoric in the heat of his victories. He set out on a journey into Burgundy to redeem the captives detained by Gondebald and Godegisilus, but on his return died of cold and fever at Pavia, in the fifty-eighth year of his age. His death was really that of a martyr of charity, and during his lifetime he seems to have been honoured by his flock with a profusion of endearing and complimentary names. They called him the " peacemaker ", the " glory of Italy ", the " light of bishops ", and also *Papa* —*i.e.* the Father. His body was translated to Hildesheim in Lower Saxony, in 963 ; Brower thinks it lies in a silver coffin near the high altar.

See his panegyric in verse by Ennodius, his successor, reputed to be the masterpiece of that author, edited in the *Acta Sanctorum*, as also in MGH., *Auctores antiquissimi*, vol. vii, pp. 84–110. *Cf. Analecta Bollandiana*, vol. xvii (1898), pp. 124–127.

ST MEINRAD, MARTYR   (A.D. 861)

As the patron and in some sense the founder of the famous abbey of Einsiedeln in Switzerland, one of the few which have preserved unbroken continuity since Carolingian times, St Meinrad (Meginrat) cannot here be passed over. By birth he is supposed to have been connected with the family of the Hohenzollerns. He became a priest, entered the Benedictine abbey at Reichenau, and later on was given some teaching work beside the upper Lake of Zurich. His soul, however, pined for solitude, and for the opportunity of devoting himself entirely to contemplation. He consequently sought out a spot in a forest, and there, with the permission of his superiors, he settled about the year 829. The fame of his sanctity, however, brought him many visitors, and seven years later he found it necessary to move still farther south and farther from the abodes of men. The place where he finally took up his abode is now called Einsiedeln (*i.e.* Hermitage). There he lived for twenty-five years, carrying on a constant warfare with the Devil and the flesh, but favoured by God with many consolations.

On January 21, 861, he was visited by two ruffians who had conceived the idea that he had treasure somewhere stored away. Though he knew their purpose, he courteously offered them food and hospitality. In the evening they smashed in his skull with clubs, but finding nothing, took to flight.   The legend says that two ravens pursued them with hoarse croakings all the way to Zurich.   By this means the crime was eventually discovered, and the two murderers burnt at the stake. The body of the saint was conveyed to Reichenau and there preserved with great veneration.   Some forty years later Bd Benno, a priest of noble Swabian family, went to take up his abode in St Meinrad's hermitage at Einsiedeln.   Though forced, much against his inclination, in 927 to accept the archbishopric of Metz, he returned to Einsiedeln later on, gathering round him a body of followers who eventually became the founders of the present Benedictine abbey.

See the *Acta Sanctorum* for January 21, also the Life of St Meinrad in MGH., *Scriptores*, vol. xv, pp. 445 *seq*.   There are many modern accounts of St Meinrad ; see *e.g.* O. Ringholz, *Wallfahrtsgeschichte von U. L. Frau von Einsiedeln*, pp. 1–6.   The two ravens appear in the arms of Einsiedeln and are also used as the emblems of the saint.

BD EDWARD STRANSHAM, Martyr   (A.D. 1586)

EDWARD STRANSHAM, or Transham (*alias* Edmund Barber), was born at or near Oxford about 1554, went to St John's College, and there took the degree of bachelor of arts.   He was at Douay and Rheims in 1577–1578, came home for a time on account of ill-health, and then returned to Rheims.   He was ordained priest at Soissons in 1580, and in the summer of the following year came on the English mission with another priest, Nicholas Woodfen, who was to suffer martyrdom too.

Challoner quotes high commendation for both priests from Rishton and Dr Bridgewater, and Stransham laboured with such effect that in 1583 he was able to cross over to Rheims with twelve converts from Oxford for the college there.   He was in France for two years, being delayed for months in Paris where consumption threatened to put an end to his life.   But what illness failed to do, the laws of his country did.   He had been back in England only a short time when he was arrested while celebrating Mass, at a house in Bishopsgate Street Without in London. At the next assizes he and Mr Woodfen were condemned for their priesthood, and they were hanged, drawn and quartered at Tyburn on January 21, 1586, six months after their arrest.   Bd Edward Stransham was among those beatified in 1929.   The case of Mr Woodfen (*alias* Devereux, *vere* Wheeler) is still under consideration.

Further particulars may be found in an article contributed by J. B. Wainewright to the *Downside Review*, volume of 1911, at p. 205, which cites the relevant authorities.

BB. THOMAS REYNOLDS AND ALBAN ROE, Martyrs   (A.D. 1642)

THOMAS REYNOLDS, whose name was really Green, was a native of Oxford, born there about 1560.   He was educated and made his ecclesiastical studies at Rheims, Valladolid and Seville, and although he was already over thirty when he was made priest he laboured for nearly fifty years on the English mission.   He was among the forty-seven priests who were exiled in the summer of 1606 ; but, like many others of them, he came back again in secret and continued his devoted and dangerous ministry for years, until eventually he was " laid by the heels " and sentenced to death for his priesthood   but he was kept in prison for fourteen years before the sentence was carried out.   A contemporary account of this venerable old man (he was about eighty) says he " for a long course of years had preached virtue and godliness to his countrymen, no less by his example than by his words.   He was fat and corpulent, yet very infirm through past labours and sufferings. He was remarkably mild and courteous, and   had reaped much fruit in gaining many souls to God."

For all his long experience—or perhaps because of it—Mr Reynolds was of a timorous disposition, and in dread of the awful manner of death with which he was faced.   But he was encouraged and upheld by one who suffered with him at Tyburn, namely Dom Bartholomew Roe (*alias* Rouse, Rolfe, etc.).   This Benedictine monk, whose name in religion was Alban, had been born, probably at Bury St Edmunds, fifty-nine years previously.   In consequence of meeting with a man imprisoned for his faith in the abbey gatehouse at Saint Albans, Roe, who was then at Cambridge University, became a Catholic, and in due course a monk of St Laurence's at Dieulouard in Lorraine (now St Laurence's, Ampleforth).   He was evidently a man of lively disposition, for before going to St Laurence's he had been dismissed from the English college at Douay for indiscipline, and later on in England he gave offence to some over strait-laced people.   He laboured on the mission successfully nevertheless, for the few years that he was free.   His second imprisonment began about 1627 in that very Saint Albans gatehouse (it still stands) where he had received the grace of faith ; then he was for some fourteen years in the Fleet prison (he was sometimes let out on parole), where he suffered from an agonizing disease, and he there translated St John Fisher's treatise on prayer and other works into English.   At last release came.   On January 19, 1642, he was tried and sentenced for his priesthood, and two days later he and Thomas Reynolds set out for Tyburn together.

" Well, how do you find yourself now ? " asked the monk.

" In very good heart," replied Mr Reynolds.   " Blessed be God for it, and glad I am to have for my comrade in death a man of your undaunted courage."

At the scaffold they gave one another absolution, and Roe helped the aged Reynolds on to the cart, who then addressed the people, expressing forgiveness for his enemies and much moving the sheriff by invoking for that official " grace to be a glorious saint in Heaven ".   When Roe's turn came he, who had been ministering to three felons who also were to die, turned to the people and began with a cheerful " Here's a jolly company ! "   He then spoke to them, finally pointing out that his religion was his only treason, since if he would abandon it he would be at once reprieved.   His last word to men was a joking remark to one of the turnkeys from the Fleet prison.   Then the two martyrs said the psalm " Miserere " in alternate verses, and as they dropped they cried out the name of Jesus, in which one of the felons joined.   They were allowed to hang until they were dead, before, in the words of a Frenchman present, the Sieur de Marsys, " the hangman opened those loving and burning breasts, as if to give air to that furnace of charity which consumed their hearts ".

Nine Martyr Monks (1931), by Bede Camm, contains a good account of Roe and of the martyrdom of both priests.   He relies mainly on the rare *Histoire de la persécution .   en Angleterre* of Marsys ; a manuscript used by Challoner, and now at Oscott ; and some letters of Father John (Bede) Hiccocks, a Carmelite who was present, as well as MMP. (pp. 407-411).   See also D. Timothy Horner's article in *Ampleforth and Its Origins* (1952), pp. 181-195.   For Reynolds see MMP., pp. 402-407, and Pollen's *Acts of English Martyrs.* He probably came from the families of Green of Great Milton, Oxon., and Reynolds of Old Stratford, Warwickshire.

BD JOSEPHA OF BENIGANIM, Virgin   (A.D. 1696)

BD INES, to use the name by which she is best remembered amongst her own countrymen, was born in a village near Valencia in Spain in 1625. Her parents, Luis Albinana and Vincentia Gomar, were of good family but poor in this world's goods.   From earliest childhood Ines gave herself to God, shunning even the childish pastimes of her companions, and her modesty and simplicity of heart compelled the respect even of those who had little regard for virtue.   In spite of many trials which came upon her after her father's early death, she eventually accomplished her purpose of consecrating herself to God in a convent of barefooted Augustinian hermitesses at Beniganim.   Here Sister Josepha-Maria-of-St-Agnes, as she was called in religion, made great strides in perfection, regarding herself as the meanest of all, ready at every moment to render a service to the youngest of her religious sisters.   Her bodily austerities were very severe, and she often contrived to spend much of the night before the Blessed Sacrament.   After long periods of desolation and temptation most patiently borne, she was endowed by God with a remarkable gift of prophecy and of the discernment of spirits, which led to her being consulted in spiritual matters, much to her own confusion, by some of the highest grandees of Spain.   She lived until the age of seventy-one, dying on the feast of her patron St Agnes in 1696.   She was beatified in 1888.

See the brief of beatification ; and *Kirchliches Handlexikon*, under " Josepha-Maria ".

22 : ST VINCENT OF SARAGOSSA, Martyr   (A.D. 304)

THE glorious martyr St Vincent was instructed in the sacred sciences and Christian piety by St Valerius, Bishop of Saragossa, who ordained him his deacon, and appointed him, though very young, to preach and instruct the people.   Dacian, a cruel persecutor, was then governor of Spain.   The Emperors Diocletian and Maximian published their second and third edicts against the Christian clergy in the year 303, which in the following year were put in force against the laity.   It seems to have been before these last that Dacian put to death eighteen martyrs at Saragossa, who are mentioned by Prudentius and in the Roman Martyrology for January 16, and that he apprehended Valerius and Vincent.   They were soon after transferred to Valencia, where the governor let them lie long in prison, suffering extreme famine and other miseries.   The proconsul hoped that this lingering torture would shake their constancy, but when they were at last brought before him he was surprised to see them still intrepid in mind and vigorous in body, so that he reprimanded his officers for not having treated the prisoners according to his orders.   Then he employed alternately threats and promises to induce the prisoners to sacrifice.   Valerius, who had an impediment in his speech, making no answer, Vincent said to him, " Father, if you order me, I will speak." " Son," said Valerius, " as I committed to you the dispensation of the word of God, so I now charge you to answer in vindication of the faith which we defend."   The deacon then informed the judge that they were ready to suffer everything for the true God, and that in such a cause they could pay no heed either to threats or promises.   Dacian contented himself with banishing Valerius.   As for St Vincent, he was determined to assail his resolution by every torture which his cruel temper could suggest.   St Augustine assures us that he suffered torments beyo.id what any man could have endured unless supported by a supernatural strength ; and that in the midst of them he preserved such peace and tranquillity as astonished his very persecutors.   The rage and chagrin felt by the proconsul were manifest in the twitching of his limbs, the angry glint in his eyes and the unsteadiness of his voice.

The martyr was first stretched on the rack by his hands and feet, and whilst he hung his flesh was torn with iron hooks.   Vincent, smiling, called the executioners weak and faint-hearted.   Dacian thought they spared him, and caused them to be beaten, which afforded Vincent an interval of rest ; but they soon returned to him, resolved fully to satisfy the cruelty of their master.   But the more his body was mangled, the more did the divine presence cherish and comfort his soul ; and the judge, seeing the blood which flowed from his body and the frightful condition to which it was reduced, was obliged to confess that the courage of this young cleric had vanquished him.   He ordered a cessation of the torments, telling Vincent that if he could not be prevailed upon to offer sacrifice to the gods, he could at least give up the sacred books to be burnt, according to the edicts.   The martyr answered that he feared torments less than false compassion.   Dacian, more incensed than ever, condemned him to the most cruel of tortures—that of fire upon a kind of gridiron, called by the acts *quaestio legitima*, " the legal torture ".   Vincent mounted cheerfully the iron bed, in which the bars were full of spikes made red-hot by the fire underneath.   On this dreadful gridiron the martyr was stretched at full length, and his wounds were rubbed with salt, which the activity of the fire forced the deeper into his flesh.   The flames, instead of tormenting, seemed, as St Augustine says, to give the martyr new vigour and courage, for the more he suffered, the greater seemed to be the inward joy and consolation of his soul.   The rage and confusion of the tyrant exceeded all bounds : he completely lost his self-command, and was continually inquiring what Vincent did and said, but was always answered that he seemed every moment to acquire new strength and resolution.

At last he was thrown into a dungeon, and his wounded body laid on the floor strewed with potsherds, which opened afresh his ghastly wounds.   His legs were set in wooden stocks, stretched very wide, and orders were given that he should be left without food and that no one should be admitted to see him.   But God sent His angels to comfort him.   The gaoler, observing through the chinks the prison filled with light, and Vincent walking and praising God, was converted upon the spot to the Christian faith.   At this news Dacian even wept with rage, but he ordered that the prisoner should be allowed some repose.   The faithful were then permitted to see him, and coming they dressed his wounds, and dipped cloths in his blood, which they kept for themselves and their posterity.   A bed was prepared for him, on which he was no sooner laid than his soul was taken to God.   Dacian commanded his body to be thrown out upon a marshy field, but a raven defended it from beasts and birds of prey.   The " acts " and a sermon attributed to St Leo add that it was then cast into the sea in a sack, but was carried to the shore and revealed to two Christians.

The story of the translations and diffusion of the relics of St Vincent is confused and not very trustworthy.   We hear of them not only in Valencia and Saragossa, but also in Castres (Aquitaine), Le Mans, Paris, Lisbon, Bari and other places. What is quite certain is that his *cultus* spread widely through the Christian world at a very early date, penetrating even to certain Eastern regions ; and he is named in the canon of the Milanese Mass. In early art the most characteristic emblem of St Vincent is the raven which is sometimes represented as perched upon a millstone. When we only have an image with a deacon's dalmatic and a palm-branch, it is almost impossible to decide whether it is intended for St Vincent, St Laurence or St Stephen. Vincent is honoured in Burgundy as the patron of vine-dressers, the explanation for which is probably to be found in the fact that his name suggests some connection with wine.

In the above account Alban Butler has mainly followed the narrative of the poet Pruden-ius (*Peristephanon*, 5). The so-called " acts ", though included by Ruinart among his *Acta sincera*, have unquestionably been embroidered rather freely by the imagination of the compiler, who lived, it seems, centuries after the event. At the same time St Augustine in one of his sermons on St Vincent speaks of having the acts of his martyrdom before him, and it may possibly be that a much more concise summary, printed in the *Analecta Bollandiana*, vol. i (1882), pp. 259–262, represents in substance the document to which St Augustine refers. We can at least be assured of his name and order, the place and epoch of his martyr-dom, and his place of burial. See P. Allard, *Histoire des persécutions*, vol. iv, pp. 237–250 ; Delehaye, *Les origines du culte des martyrs* (1933), pp. 367–368 ; H. Leclercq, *Les martyrs*, vol. ii, pp. 437–439 ; *Römische Quartalschrift*, vol. xxi (1907), pp. 135–138. There is a good historical summary by L. de Lacger, *St Vincent de Saragosse* (1927) ; and a study of the *passio* by the Marquise de Maillé, *Vincent d'Agen et Vincent de Saragosse* (1949), on which *cf.* various papers by Fr B. de Gaiffier in *Analecta Bollandiana*. For the bishop St Valerius, see the *Acta Sanctorum*, January 28.

ST BLESILLA, WIDOW   (A.D. 383)

BUT for the letters of St Jerome, very little would be known of the youthful widow St Blesilla, daughter of St Paula. On the death of her husband, after seven months of married life, Blesilla was attacked by fever. Yielding to the promptings of grace, she determined to devote herself to practices of devotion. After her sudden recovery she spent the rest of her short life in great austerity. St Jerome, writing to her mother, speaks in very high terms of her. She herself began to study Hebrew, and it was at her request that Jerome began his translation of the book of Ecclesiastes. St Blesilla died at Rome in 383 at the early age of twenty.

See the *Acta Sanctorum*, January 22 ; and St Jerome's letters nos. 37, 38 and 39. St Blesilla is of course referred to in the more detailed lives of St Jerome and St Paula.

ST ANASTASIUS THE PERSIAN, MARTYR   (A.D. 628)

THE wood of the cross of Christ when it was carried away into Persia by Chosroës in 614, after he had taken and plundered Jerusalem, nevertheless had its victories. Of one such victory Anastasius was the visible trophy. He was a young soldier in the Persian army. Upon hearing the news of the taking of the cross by his king, he grew inquisitive concerning the Christian religion, and its truths made such an impression on his mind that when he came back to Persia from an expedition he left the army and retired to Hierapolis. He lodged with a devout Persian Christian, a silversmith, with whom he often went to prayer. The sacred pictures which he saw made a great impression, and gave him occasion to inquire more, and to admire the courage of the martyrs whose sufferings were painted in the churches. At length he went to Jerusalem, where he received baptism from the bishop Modestus. In baptism he changed his Persian name Magundat into that of Anastasius, to remind him, according to the meaning of that Greek word, that he had risen from death to a new and spiritual life. The better to fulfil his baptismal vows and obligations, he asked to become a monk in a monastery near Jerusalem. The abbot made him first study Greek and learn the psalter by heart; then, cutting off his hair, he gave him the monastic habit in the year 621.

The future martyr's first experiences of monastic life were not untroubled. He was assailed by all kinds of temptations, and by the recollection of the practices and superstitions which his father had taught him. He met these by a frank disclosure to his confessor of all his difficulties, and by extreme earnestness in prayer and monastic duties. He was haunted, however, by an intense desire to give his life for Christ, and after a time he went to Caesarea, then under Persian rule. Having boldly denounced their religious rites and superstitions, he was arrested and brought before Marzabanes the governor, when he confessed his own Persian birth and conversion to Christianity. Marzabanes sentenced him to be chained by the foot to another criminal, and his neck and one foot to be also linked together by a heavy chain, and condemned him in this condition to carry stones. The governor sent for him a second time, but could not prevail with him to renounce his faith. The judge then threatened he would write to the king if he did not comply. "Write what you please", said the saint, "I am a Christian: I repeat it, I am a Christian." Marzabanes ordered him to be beaten. The executioners were preparing to bind him on the ground, but the saint declared that he had courage enough to lie down under the punishment without moving; he only begged leave to put off his monk's habit, lest it should be treated with contempt, which only his body deserved. Having removed his outer garment he stretched himself on the ground, and did not stir all the time the cruel torment continued. The governor again threatened to inform the king of his obstinacy. "Whom ought we rather to fear," said Anastasius, "a mortal man, or God who made all things out of nothing?" The judge pressed him to sacrifice to fire, and to the sun and moon. The saint answered he could never acknowledge as gods creatures which God had made only for our use upon which he was remanded to prison.

His old abbot, hearing of his sufferings, sent two monks to assist him, and ordered prayers for him. The confessor, after carrying stones all the day, spent the greater part of the night in prayer, to the surprise of his companions, one of whom, a Jew, saw and showed him to others at prayer in the night, shining in brightness like a blessed spirit, and angels praying with him. As Anastasius was chained to a man condemned for a public crime, he prayed always with his neck bowed downwards, keeping his chained foot near his companion not to disturb him. Marzabanes let the martyr know that the king would be satisfied on condition he would only by word of mouth abjure the Christian faith, after which he might choose whether he would be an officer in the royal service or still remain a Christian and a monk, adding that he might in his heart always adhere to Christ, provided he would but for once renounce Him in words privately, in his presence, "in which", he declared, "there could be no harm, nor any great injury to his Christ". Anastasius answered firmly that he would never dissemble or seem to deny God. Then the governor told him that he had orders to send him bound into Persia to the king. "There is no need of binding me," said the saint. "I go willingly and cheerfully to suffer for Christ." On the day appointed, the martyr left Caesarea with two other Christian prisoners, under guard, and was followed by one of the monks whom the abbot had sent.   The acts of his martyrdom were afterwards written by this monk.

Being arrived at Bethsaloe in Assyria, near the Euphrates, where the king then was, the prisoners were thrown into a dungeon till his pleasure was known.   An officer came from Chosroës to interrogate the saint, who made answer to his magnificent promises, " My poor religious habit shows that I despise from my heart the gaudy pomp of the world.   The honours and riches of a king, who must shortly die himself, are no temptation to me."   Next day the officer returned and endeavoured to intimidate him by threats and upbraidings.   But the saint said calmly, " Sir, do not give yourself so much trouble about me.   By the grace of Christ I am not to be moved, so execute your pleasure without more ado."   The officer caused him to be unmercifully beaten with staves, after the Persian manner. This punishment was inflicted on three days ; on the third the judge commanded him to be laid on his back, and a heavy beam pressed down by the weight of two men on his legs, crushing the flesh to the very bone.   The martyr's tranquillity and patience astonished the officer, who went again to make his report to Chosroës. In his absence the gaoler, being a Christian by profession, though too weak to resign his place rather than detain such a prisoner, gave everyone access to the martyr. The Christians immediately filled the prison ; everyone sought to kiss his feet or chains, and kept as relics whatever had been sanctified by contact with him.   The saint, confused and indignant, strove to hinder them, but could not.   After further torments, Chosroës ordered that Anastasius and all the Christian captives should be put to death.   Anastasius's two companions, with three score and six other Christians, were strangled one after another, on the banks of the river, before his face.   He himself with eyes lifted to Heaven, gave thanks to God for bringing his life to so happy an end, and said he looked for a more lingering death, but seeing that God granted him one so easy, he embraced with joy this ignominious punishment of slaves.   He was accordingly strangled, and after his death his head was cut off.

This happened in the year 628, on January 22.   Anastasius's body, among the other dead, was exposed to be devoured by dogs, but it was the only one they left untouched.   It was afterwards redeemed by the Christians, who laid it in the monastery of St Sergius, a mile from the place of his triumph, which from that monastery was later on called Sergiopolis (now Rasapha, in Iraq).   The monk who attended him brought back his *colobium*, a linen tunic without sleeves.   The saint's body was afterwards carried to Palestine ; later it was removed to Constantinople, and lastly to Rome, where the relics were enshrined in the church of St Vincent. It is for this reason that these two quite unconnected martyrs are celebrated together in one feast.

The seventh general council convened against the Iconoclasts proved the use of sacred pictures from the miraculous image of this martyr, then kept at Rome and venerated together with his head.   These are said to be still in the church which bears the name of SS. Vincent and Anastasius.

The Greek text of the Life of St Anastasius was published by H. Usener in 1894, and an early Latin version is in the *Acta Sanctorum* for January 22.   A brief summary of the extracts read at the fourth session of the seventh oecumenical council in 787 will be found in Hefele-Leclercq, *Conciles*, vol. iii, p. 766, and the whole in Mansi, *Concilia*, vol. xiii, pp. 21-24 ; BHG., n. 6 ; BHL., n. 68.   It is very difficult to understand upon what grounds St Anastasius is stated in the Carmelite Martyrology to have been " a monk of the Carmelite Order ".

ST DOMINIC OF SORA, Abbot (A.D. 1031)

In the archives of Foligno in Etruria, the birthplace of this saint, it is stated that St Dominic's intercession was frequently invoked as a protection against thunderstorms. There seems to be no indication of the origin of this practice. It may be due to some incident in his early life of which the record is lost, for authentic documents take up the story of his career from the time that he became a monk. The whole of St Dominic's activities were devoted to the founding of Benedictine monasteries and churches in various parts of Italy, at Scandrilia, Sora, Sangro and in other towns. Each monastery that he founded was apparently given its own abbot, so that Dominic himself might be free to begin work in another place. The intervals between the various foundations were devoted to solitary prayer, until the saint received an intimation from God as to where he was to establish his next monastery. Yet in the midst of this busy life he found time to work for souls, and not infrequently the efforts he made to convert sinners were attended by striking miracles. Several of these are related by one who was probably an eye-witness, a monk named John, the disciple and constant companion of St Dominic. He died at the age of eighty in 1031 at Sora in Campania.

See the *Acta Sanctorum*, January, vols. ii and iii ; *Analecta Bollandiana*, vol. i (1882), pp. 279–322 ; and A. M. Zimmermann, *Kalendarium benedictinum*, vol. i (1933), pp. 114–117.

ST BERHTWALD, Bishop of Ramsbury (A.D. 1045)

St Berhtwald had been a monk of Glastonbury, and in 1005 he was consecrated bishop of Ramsbury, or, as the *Anglo-Saxon Chronicle* phrases it, " he succeeded to the bishop's stool of Wiltshire ". He was, in fact, the last bishop of Ramsbury, for in the time of his successor the see was removed to Old Sarum. Berhtwald, if we may trust the brief notices left us by William of Malmesbury and Simeon of Durham, seems to have been specially remembered by his contemporaries on account of his visions and prophecies, in which the Apostle St Peter was associated with the succession to the throne of St Edward the Confessor in 1042. St Berhtwald was a great benefactor to the abbey of Malmesbury as well as to his own abbey of Glastonbury, in which last he was buried after his death in 1045.

See Stanton, *Menology*, pp. 31–32 ; DNB., vol. vi, p. 344. There seems to have been no public *cultus*.

BD WILLIAM PATENSON, Martyr (A.D. 1592)

William Patenson was a native of Durham. He studied for the priesthood at Rheims, where he was ordained in 1587 and was sent on the English mission fifteen months later. He ministered for a time in the western counties, but it was in London that he was arrested, just before the Christmas of 1591. He had celebrated Mass at a house in Clerkenwell, and was breaking his fast with another priest when the pursuivants broke in. The other priest, Mr Young, got away, but Mr Patenson was taken, and brought up and condemned at the Old Bailey for being a seminary priest. There are two accounts of his zeal for the criminals with whom he was during his short time in prison : according to one of them he spent his last night in the condemned cell with seven convicted felons, and of these he brought six to repentance and the Church, so that they died publicly professing the Catholic faith. In consequence of this Bd William Patenson's execution at Tyburn was carried out deliberately without any mitigation of its atrocious cruelties, on January 22, 1592.

See MMP., pp. 185-186; Pollen's *Acts of English Martyrs*; and Catholic Record Society's publications, vol. v.

ST VINCENT PALLOTTI, FOUNDER OF THE SOCIETY OF CATHOLIC APOSTOLATE   (A.D. 1850)

ST VINCENT PALLOTTI anticipated by a century the ideas of organized Catholic Action as set forth by Pope Pius XI, who called him its " pioneer and forerunner ". At a time when anything approaching an active apostolate was deemed to be purely the concern of clergy and religious, Don Pallotti envisaged a programme under three heads : A world-wide apostolate of *all* Catholics for the spreading of the faith among those who have it not ; a similar apostolate for the confirming and deepening of the faith of Catholics themselves ; a world-wide exercise of the works of mercy, spiritual and temporal.   His own contribution to this programme was first of all his own life ; secondly, his inspiration of others with his ideas and aspirations ; thirdly, the establishment of a society of priests and brothers living the common life without vows, helped by an institute of sisters and by affiliated clergy and lay people.   This organization he called the Society of Catholic Apostolate.*

Vincent Pallotti was born in Rome, son of a well-to-do grocer, in 1795, and his vocation to the priesthood was foreshadowed at an early age.   His beginnings at school were disappointing : " He's a little saint ", said his master, Don Ferri, " but a bit thick-headed ".   However, he soon picked up, and was ordained priest when he was only twenty-three.   He took his doctorate in theology soon after, and became an assistant professor at the Sapienza.   Pallotti's close friendship with St Caspar del Bufalo increased his apostolic zeal, and he eventually resigned his post to devote himself to active pastoral work.

Don Pallotti was in very great repute as a confessor, and filled this office at several Roman colleges, including the Scots, the Irish and the English, where he became a friend of the rector, Nicholas Wiseman.   But he was not appreciated everywhere.   When he was appointed to the Neapolitan church in Rome he endured persecution from the other clergy there of which the particulars pass belief.   Equally astonishing is it that this went on for ten years before the author-ities took official notice and brought the scandal to an end.   Bd Vincent's most implacable tormentor, the vice-rector of the church, lived to give evidence for him at the informative process of his beatification.   " Don Pallotti never gave the least ground for the ill-treatment to which he was subjected ", he declared, " He always treated me with the greatest respect ; he bared his head when he spoke to me, he even several times tried to kiss my hand."

St Vincent began his organized work for conversion and social justice with a group of clergy and lay people, from whom the Society of Catholic Apostolate developed in 1835.   He wrote to a young professor : " You are not cut out for the silence and austerities of Trappists and hermits.   Be holy in the world, in your social relationships, in your work and your leisure, in your teaching duties and your

---

* Exception was taken to this name and it was changed to " Pious Society of Missions " ; in 1947 the original name was revived.   The work of the *Pallottini* among immigrants is specially notable.   They serve the English church at Rome, San Silvestro in Capite.

contacts with publicans and sinners. Holiness is simply to do God's will, always and everywhere." Pallotti himself organized schools for shoemakers, tailors, coachmen, joiners and market-gardeners, to improve their general education and pride in their trade ; he started evening classes for young workers, and an institute to teach better methods to young agriculturalists. But he never lost sight of the wider aspects of his mission. In 1836 he inaugurated the observance of the Epiphany octave by the celebration of the Mysteries each day with a different rite, in special supplication for the reunion of Eastern dissidents   this was settled at the church of Sant' Andrea delle Valle in 1847, and has continued there annually ever since.

It was well said that in Don Pallotti Rome had a second Philip Neri. How many times he came home half naked because he had given his clothes away ; how many sinners did he reconcile, on one occasion dressing up as an old woman to get to the bedside of a man who threatened--and meant it--to shoot the first priest who came near him ; he was in demand as an exorcist, he had knowledge beyond this world's means, he healed the sick with an encouragement or a blessing. St Vincent foresaw all Catholic Action, even its name, said Pius XI ; and Cardinal Pellegrinetti added, " He did all that he could ; as for what he couldn't do—well, he did that too."

St Vincent Pallotti died when he was only fifty-five, on January 22, 1850. The chill that developed into pleurisy was perhaps brought on by giving away his cloak before a long sitting in a cold confessional. When viaticum was brought he stretched out his arms and murmured, " Jesus, bless the congregation : a blessing of goodness, a blessing of wisdom. . ." He had not the strength to finish, " a blessing of power" He was beatified one hundred years later to the day, and canonized in 1963 during the Second Vatican Council.

There are biographies in Italian by Orlandi and others, and a useful sketch in French by Maria Winowska (1950). The life by Lady Herbert was revised and reissued in America in 1942.

23 : ST RAYMUND OF PEÑAFORT   (A.D. 1275)

THE family of Peñafort claimed descent from the counts of Barcelona, and was allied to the kings of Aragon. Raymund was born in 1175, at Peñafort in Catalonia, and made such rapid progress in his studies that at the age of twenty he taught philosophy at Barcelona. This he did gratis, and with great reputation. When he was about thirty he went to Bologna to perfect himself in canon and civil law. He took the degree of doctor, and taught with the same disinterestedness and charity as he had done in his own country. In 1219 Berengarius, Bishop of Barcelona, made Raymund his archdeacon and " official ". He was a perfect model to the clergy by his zeal, devotion and boundless liberalities to the poor. In 1222 he assumed the habit of St Dominic at Barcelona, eight months after the death of the holy founder, and in the forty-seventh year of his age. No one of the young novices was more humble, obedient or fervent than he. He begged of his superiors that they would enjoin him some severe penance to expiate the complacency which he said he had sometimes taken in his teaching. They, indeed, imposed on him a penance, but not quite such as he expected. It was to write a collection of cases of conscience for the convenience of confessors and moralists.   This led to the compilation of the *Summa de casibus poenitentialibus*, the first work of its kind.

Raymund joined to the exercises of his solitude an apostolic life by labouring without intermission in preaching, instructing, hearing confessions, and converting heretics, Jews and Moors ; and he was commissioned to preach the war of the Spaniards against the last-named.   He acquitted himself of his new duties with much prudence, zeal and charity, and in this indirect manner paved the way for the ultimate overthrow of the infidel in Spain.   His labours were no less successful in the reformation of the morals of the Christians detained in servitude under the Moors, which had been corrupted by their long slavery and intercourse with these infidels.   Raymund showed them that to triumph over their political foes they must first conquer their spiritual enemies, and subdue sin in themselves.   Inculcating these and the like spiritual lessons, he journeyed through Catalonia, Aragon, Castile and other countries.   So general a change was wrought hereby in the manners of the people that it seemed incredible to all but those who were witnesses of it.

It is commonly said that St Raymund of Peñafort was associated with St Peter Nolasco in the foundation of the Order of Our Lady of Ransom, usually called the Mercedarians, who were particularly concerned with ransoming captives among the Moors.   This has given rise to keen controversy.   The representatives of the order, and notably Father Gazulla, in several works contend that the Mercedarian Order was founded in 1218, at a date earlier than that at which St Raymund became a Dominican.   They allege further that a vision of our Lady was vouchsafed to St Peter Nolasco, their founder, and also simultaneously to King James of Aragon and to St Raymund, and that the institute which came into existence in consequence of this vision was originally a military order which owed nothing to Dominican influences.   All these points have been strongly contested, more particularly in the works of Father Vacas Galindo, O.P.   This writer urges that the Mercedarians, at first simply a confraternity, were not organized as a religious congregation before 1233, that St Raymund had founded the confraternity in 1222 and had given it rules based upon the Dominican constitutions and office, that the supposed triple vision of our Lady was never heard of until two or three hundred years later, and so on.

Pope Gregory IX, having called St Raymund to Rome in 1230, nominated him to various offices and took him likewise for his confessor, in which capacity Raymund enjoined the pope, for a penance, to receive, hear and expedite immediately all petitions presented by the poor.   Gregory also ordered the saint to gather into one body all the scattered decrees of popes and councils since the collection made by Gratian in 1150.   In three years Raymund completed his task, and the five books of the " Decretals " were confirmed by the same Pope Gregory in 1234.   Down to the publication of the new *Codex Juris Canonici* in 1917 this compilation of St Raymund was looked upon as the best arranged part of the body of canon law, on which account the canonists usually chose it for the text of their commentaries.   In 1235 the pope named St Raymund to the archbishopric of Tarragona, the capital of Aragon : the humble religious was not able to avert the blow, as he called it, by tears and entreaties ; but the anxiety brought on a serious illness.   To restore him to health his Holiness was obliged to consent to excuse him, but required that he should recommend a proper person.

For the recovery of his health St Raymund returned to his native country, and was received with as much joy as if the safety of the kingdom depended on his presence. Being restored again to his dear solitude at Barcelona he continued his former contemplation, preaching and work in the confessional. The number of conversions of which he was the instrument is known only to Him who by His grace was the author of them. Raymund was employed frequently in important commissions, both by the Holy See and by the king. In 1238, however, he was thunderstruck by the arrival of deputies from the general chapter of his order at Bologna with the news that he had been chosen third master general, Bd Jordan of Saxony having lately died. He wept and entreated, but at length acquiesced in obedience. He made the visitation of his order on foot without discontinuing any of his austerities or religious exercises. He instilled into his spiritual children a love of regularity, solitude, studies and the work of the ministry, and reduced the constitutions of his order into a clearer method, with notes on the doubtful passages. The code which he drew up was approved in three general chapters. In one held at Paris in 1239 he procured the establishment of this regulation, that the voluntary resignation of a superior, founded upon just reasons, should be accepted. This he contrived in his own favour, for in the year following he resigned the generalship which he had held only two years. He grounded his action on the fact that he was now sixty-five years old.

But St Raymund still had thirty-four years to live, and he spent them in the main opposing heresy and working for the conversion of the Moors in Spain. With this end in view, he engaged St Thomas to write his work *Against the Gentiles ;* he contrived to have Arabic and Hebrew taught in several convents of his order ; and he established friaries, one at Tunis, and another at Murcia, among the Moors. In 1256 he wrote to his general that ten thousand Saracens had received baptism. He was active in getting the Inquisition established in Catalonia ; and on one occasion he was accused—it is to be feared not without some reason—of compromising a Jewish rabbi by a trick.

A famous incident in St Raymund's life is said to have taken place when he accompanied King James to the island of Majorca. The king, very loose in his relations with women, promised amendment, but failed to implement his promise ; whereupon Raymund asked leave to go back to Barcelona. The king not only refused, but threatened to punish with death any person who attempted to convey him out of the island. Full of confidence in God, Raymund said to his companion, " An earthly king withholds the means of flight, but the King of Heaven will supply them." He then walked to the sea and, we are told, spread his cloak upon the water, tied up one corner of it to a staff for a sail, and having made the sign of the cross, stepped upon it without fear whilst his companion stood trembling on the shore. On this new kind of vessel the saint was wafted with such rapidity that in six hours he reached the harbour of Barcelona, sixty leagues distant from Majorca. Those who saw him arrive in this manner met him with acclamations. But he, gathering up his cloak dry, put it on, stole through the crowd and entered his monastery. A chapel and a tower, built on the place where he is supposed to have landed, transmitted the memory of this miracle to posterity. During the saint's last illness, Alphonsus, King of Castile, and James of Aragon visited him, and received his final blessing. St Raymund gave up his soul to God on January 6 in the year 1275, the hundredth of his age. The two kings, with all the princes and princesses of their royal families, honoured his funeral with their presence ; but his tomb was rendered far more illustrious by miracles. Several (including the one related above) are recorded in the bull of his canonization, published in 1601.

The principal materials for the life of St Raymund of Peñafort have been printed by Fathers Balme and Paban under the title *Raymundiana* in the *Monumenta Historica O.P.*, vols. iv and vi, and an excellent general summary will be found in Mortier, *Histoire des maîtres généraux O.P.*, especially vol. i, pp. 225–272 and 400. The best life is said to be by F. Valls Taberner, *San Ramón de Penyafort* (1936). As for the connection of the saint with the Order of Our Lady of Ransom, whatever be the truth of the case there can be no doubt that a large number of spurious documents, mysteriously found at the right moment in an iron casket at the beginning of the seventeenth century, have been made use of in support of the Mercedarian thesis. The evidence upon many points is so unsatisfactory that it becomes extremely difficult to give unreserved credence to such incidents in St Raymund's life as his miraculous voyage from Majorca. See the *Analecta Bollandiana*, vol. xxxix (1921), pp. 209 *seq.* and vol. xl (1922), pp. 442 *seq. Cf.* St Peter Nolasco, on January 28.

ST ASCLAS, Martyr   (Third Century ?)

THE fame of St Asclas was great in Egypt and throughout the East, and he is commemorated in the Roman Martyrology. His story, as epitomized in the synaxaries, runs as follows " Asclas, a native of the Thebaid, was denounced for his faith in Christ and brought before Arrian the governor. Boldly confessing his belief, he was strung up, scourged until the flesh was torn in strips from his ribs, and then cast into prison. But the governor had to pass over the River Nile in a boat, and the saint prayed that he might never reach the opposite shore until he expressly acknowledged in writing the divinity of Christ. Arrian embarked, but the boat was held up and he could get no farther ; whereupon the saint, learning of this, sent him word that only by confessing the divinity of Christ could he reach dry land once more. Then the governor called for paper, and he wrote down that mighty was the God of the Christians and that there was no other beside Him. Straightway the boat made the passage, the governor landed, and sending for the saint caused his ribs to be burnt with torches. Then he had a great stone tied to him and cast him into the river. Thus it was that Asclas gained his crown of martyrdom." It can hardly be disputed from the very form of the story that a considerable legendary element is present.

In the above quoted Synaxary of Constantinople (ed. H. Delehaye, p. 698) the feast is commemorated on May 20, but in the West on January 23. See also the *Acta Sanctorum* for this day, and Cheneau d'Orléans, *Les saints d'Égypte*, vol. i, pp. 183 *seq.*

ST EMERENTIANA, Virgin and Martyr   (c. A.D. 304 ?)

ACCORDING to the Roman Martyrology and the Breviary lesson for this day, St Emerentiana was the foster-sister of St Agnes, and consequently was of much the same age, but as yet only a catechumen. She was stoned to death two days after St Agnes's martyrdom, when praying beside her grave, and in this way received the baptism of blood. This story, which forms a kind of supplement to the " acts " of St Agnes, cannot be accepted as it stands. but there is evidence that there *was* a St Emerentiana, martyr, who was originally buried in the *Coemeterium majus*, a little farther along the Via Nomentana than the spot where the basilica dedicated to St Agnes was erected. Emerentiana was apparently honoured on September 16 with SS. Victor, Felix and Alexander, but for some reason her remains were later transferred to the basilica just mentioned, and her story by means of legendary embellishments became entwined with that of St Agnes.

See the *Acta Sanctorum* for January 21 and 23 ; and F. Jubaru, *St Agnes* (1909), pp. 145-156.

SS. CLEMENT AND AGATHANGELUS, MARTYRS (A.D. 308 ?)

CONCERNING these two martyrs, although they are held in high honour in some oriental churches, and are commemorated on this day in the Roman Martyrology, we have no reliable knowledge of any sort. Clement is supposed to have devoted himself to the instruction of children and of the poor, to have been made bishop of Ancyra in Galatia at the age of twenty, and then, after arrest, to have been dragged from city to city, enduring incredible torments for years together, but repeatedly saved from death by a series of stupendous miracles. Agathangelus was a convert whom Clement made when he was brought to Rome. Having been ordained deacon Agathangelus shared the subsequent sufferings of his master. Both are said ultimately to have perished by the sword at Ancyra. The quite untrustworthy character of their " acts " has been recognized by all critics from Baronius and Tillemont downwards.

See the *Acta Sanctorum* for January 23, and DHG., vol. i, c. 906.

ST JOHN THE ALMSGIVER, PATRIARCH OF ALEXANDRIA (A.D. 619 ?)

ST JOHN was of noble family, rich, and a widower, at Amathus in Cyprus where, having buried all his children, he employed his income in the relief of the poor, and won the respect of all by his personal holiness. His reputation raised him to the patriarchal chair of Alexandria, about the year 608, at which time he was upwards of fifty years of age. St John came to this patriarchal chair when for generations Egypt had been torn by fierce ecclesiastical strife and Monophysism was everywhere in the ascendant. " That is the background which the reader of St John's life must keep in mind ", writes Dr Baynes, " As patriarch he chose a better way— he would recommend orthodoxy to Egypt by a sympathy and charity that knew no limits." On his arrival in Alexandria St John ordered an exact list to be taken of his " masters ". Being asked who these were, he explained that he meant the poor, because they had such power in the court of Heaven to help those who had been good to them on earth. Their number amounted to seven thousand five hundred, and all these he took under his special protection. He published severe ordinances, but in the most humble terms, commanding all to use just weights and measures, in order to protect the poor from a very cruel form of oppression. He rigorously forbade all his officers and servants to take presents, seeing that these are no better than bribes, which bias the most impartial. Every Wednesday and Friday he sat the whole day on a bench before the church, that all might have free access to lay their grievances before him, and make known their necessities.

One of his first actions at Alexandria was to distribute the eighty thousand pieces of gold which he found in the treasury of his church among the hospitals and monasteries. He consecrated to the service of the poor the great revenues of his see, then the first in all the East both in riches and dignity. Besides these, a continual stream of contributions flowed through his hands representing the alms of those who were kindled by his example. When his stewards complained that he impoverished his church, his answer was that God would provide for them. To vindicate his action, he told them the story of a vision he had had in his youth, when a beautiful woman had appeared to him, with an olive garland on her head. This maiden, he was given to understand, represented Charity, or compassion for the poor, and she said to him : " I am the oldest daughter of the King. If you will be my friend, I will lead you to Him. No one has so much influence with Him as myself, since it was for me that He came down from Heaven to become man for the redemption of mankind."

When the Persians plundered Syria, and sacked Jerusalem, St John entertained the refugees who fled terror-stricken into Egypt, and sent to Jerusalem for the poor there, besides a large sum of money, corn, pulse, iron, fish, wine, and Egyptian workmen to assist in rebuilding the churches ; adding, in his letter to Modestus the bishop, that he wished it had been in his power to come in person and contribute by the labour of his hands to the carrying on of that work. No number of necessitous objects, no losses, no straits to which he saw himself often reduced, discouraged him or made him lose his confidence in the divine providence, and resources never failed him in the end. When an unfortunate debtor, whom he had relieved with bountiful alms, expressed his gratitude over-warmly, the saint cut him short, saying, " Brother, I have not yet shed my blood for you, as Jesus Christ, my Master and my God, commands me to do." A certain merchant, who had been twice ruined by shipwrecks, had as often obtained help from the good patriarch, who the third time gave him a ship laden with corn. This vessel was driven by a storm to the British islands, and a famine raging there, the owners sold their cargo to great advantage, and brought back a handsome equivalent in exchange, one half in money, the other in tin. Silver was found in the tin, and this was attributed to the virtues of the saint.

The patriarch lived himself in the greatest austerity and poverty. A person of distinction being informed that he had but one blanket on his bed, and this a sorry one, sent him a valuable rug, asking that he would make use of it for the sake of the donor. He accepted it and put it to the intended use, but it was only for one night, and this he passed in great uneasiness, with self-reproach for reposing in luxury while so many of his " masters " were miserably lodged. The next morning he sold it and gave the price to the poor. The friend, learning what had happened, bought it and gave it him a second and a third time, for the saint always disposed of it in the same way, saying with a smile, " We shall see who will get tired first ". Nor did St John spoil his approach to the problem of the indigent poor by too much finesse. He enjoyed getting money out of the wealthy, " and used to say that if with the object of giving to the poor anybody were able, without ill-will, to strip the rich right down to their shirts, he would do no wrong, more especially if they were heartless skinflints ".

Nicetas, the governor, projected a new tax, which bore very harshly upon the poor. The patriarch modestly spoke in their defence. The governor in a passion left him abruptly. St John sent him this message towards evening, " The sun is going to set," putting him in mind of the advice of the apostle, " Let not the sun go down upon your anger ". This admonition had its intended effect. The governor came at once to the patriarch, asked his pardon, and by way of atonement promised never more to give ear to informers and tale-bearers. St John confirmed him in that resolution, adding that he never believed any man whatever against another till he himself had examined the party accused, and that he made it a rule to punish all calumniators with such severity as would serve as a warning to others. Having in vain exhorted a certain nobleman to forgive one with whom he was at variance, he invited him to his private chapel to assist at Mass, and there desired him to recite with him the Lord's Prayer. The saint stopped at that petition, " Forgive us our trespasses, as we forgive them that trespass against us ". When the nobleman had recited it alone, John conjured him to reflect on what he had been saying to God in the hour of the tremendous mysteries, begging to be pardoned in the same manner as he forgave others. The other, deeply moved, fell at his feet, and from that moment was sincerely reconciled with his adversary. The saint often exhorted men against rash judgement, saying, " Circumstances easily deceive us : magistrates are bound to examine and judge criminals ; but what have private persons to do with the delinquencies of their neighbours, unless it be to vindicate them ? " Observing that many amused themselves outside the church during part of divine service, St John followed them out and seated himself among them, saying, " My children, the shepherd must be with his flock ". They were so abashed, we are told, by this gentle rebuke that they were never afterwards guilty of the same irreverence. And as he was one day going to church he was accosted on the road by a woman who demanded justice against her son-in-law, who had injured her. The woman being ordered by some standers-by to await the patriarch's return from church, he, overhearing them, said, " How can I expect that God will hear my own prayers if I disregard the petition of this woman ! " Nor did he stir from the place till he had redressed the grievance complained of.

Nicetas persuaded the saint to accompany him to Constantinople to visit the Emperor Heraclius on the approach of the Persians in 619. At Rhodes, while on their way, St John was admonished from Heaven that his death was near at hand, and he said to Nicetas, " You invite me to the emperor of the earth ; but the King of Heaven calls me to Himself ". He therefore sailed back to his native Cyprus, and soon after died happily at Amathus, in 619 or 620. The body of St John was afterwards carried to Constantinople, where it was a long time. The Turkish sultan made a present of it to Matthias, King of Hungary, who constructed a shrine for it in his chapel at Buda. In 1530 it was translated to Tall, near Bratislava ; and, in 1632, to Bratislava itself, where it may still remain. The Greeks honour this saint on November 11, the day of his death ; but the Roman Martyrology on January 23, the anniversary of the translation of his relics.

A life of St John the Almsgiver was written by two contemporaries, John Moschus and Sophronius ; this is lost. A supplementary life by another contemporary, Bishop Leontius of Neapolis in Cyprus, survives. These two sources, however, were reduced by an early editor to a single text, which was published by Father Delehaye in 1927 (*Analecta Bollandiana*, vol. xlv, pp. 5–74). It was this version that was used by Simeon Metaphrastes for his tenth-century biography. N. H. Baynes and Elizabeth Dawes in *Three Byzantine Saints* (1948) give an English translation of the Moschus and Sophronius part of this text and of the original text of Leontius. Greek text of Leontius edited by H. Gelzer (1893) ; Latin translation by Anastasius the Librarian in *Acta Sanctorum* for January 23 ; Father P. Bedjan edited a Syriac version in vol. iv of his *Acta martyrum et sanctorum*.

ST ILDEPHONSUS, Archbishop of Toledo   (A.D. 667)

THE name Ildephonsus, or Hildephonsus, seems to be the original form from which the variants Alphonsus, Alfonso and Alonzo have subsequently developed. After St Isidore of Seville, St Ildephonsus, who in accordance with a somewhat unreliable tradition is said to have been his pupil, has always been looked upon as one of the greatest glories of the Spanish church, which honours him liturgically as a doctor of the Church. He was of distinguished birth, the nephew of St Eugenius, Archbishop of Toledo, to whose office he afterwards succeeded. At an early age he became a monk in spite of parental opposition, and, joining the community of Agli (Agalia) near Toledo, he was eventually elected abbot of that monastery. We know that he was ordained deacon about the year 630, and that, though only a simple monk, he founded and endowed a community of nuns in the neighbourhood. Whilst he held the office of abbot he attended the eighth and ninth councils of Toledo, held respectively in the years 653 and 655. His elevation to the archiepiscopal dignity seems to have taken place in 657. The enthusiastic encomiums of Julian, his contemporary and successor in the see, as well as the testimony of other eminent churchmen and the evidence afforded by the ardent devotion conspicuous in his own writings, prove abundantly that the choice was a worthy one, and that Ildephonsus possessed all the virtues which became his high office. He governed the church of Toledo for a little more than nine years, and died on January 23, 667.

One feature which stands out very prominently in the literary work of St Ildephonsus, and more particularly in his tractate *De virginitate perpetua sanctae Mariae*, is the remarkable glow of enthusiasm, almost bordering upon extravagance, in the language he uses concerning our Blessed Lady. Edmund Bishop laid stress upon this trait in his valuable papers on " Spanish Symptoms ", and we may well believe it to be characteristic of the devotion of the saint as well as typical of the atmosphere in which he lived. It is not, therefore, surprising that a century after his death two legends grew up, both implying a recognition of his privileged position in relation to the Mother of God. According to one of these the martyr St Leocadia, who is one of the patrons of Toledo, rose out of her tomb when Ildephonsus was praying before it to thank him in the name of the Queen of Heaven for having vindicated the honour of her glorious mistress. The most salient feature of the other legend is that our Lady showed her gratitude to the saint by appearing to him in person seated upon his own episcopal throne, and by presenting him with a chasuble. This last story, with many embellishments, appears in nearly all the great collections of *Marienlegenden* which had such immense vogue in the twelfth and thirteenth centuries. There seems, in any case, good reason to believe that the Marian element in certain Spanish liturgical documents was strongly coloured by the language which became prevalent at Toledo in the time of St Ildephonsus.

The brief summary of the saint's career drafted by Julian, as well as the account by Cixila, will be found in the *Acta Sanctorum* for January 23, as also in the second vol. of Mabillon. See also the *Dictionnaire de Théologie*, vol. vii, cc. 739-744 ; the article by Herwegen in the *Kirchliches Handlexikon ;* E. Bishop, *Liturgica Historica*, pp. 165-210 ; and A. Braegelmann, *Life and Writings of St Ildephonsus of Toledo* (1942), which summarizes the material.

ST BERNARD, Archbishop of Vienne   (A.D. 842)

This St Bernard (often written Barnard) was born of a distinguished family about the year 778 ; in due course he entered the service of Charlemagne and married. About 800 he founded the abbey of Ambronay and later became a monk there, succeeding to the dignity of abbot. In 810 he was made archbishop of Vienne. Though our biographical materials are slight and of late date, everything points to the conclusion that he was one of the most influential as well as one of the most saintly prelates of that age.   Although he does not seem always to have acted wisely in the political disturbances which followed in the time of Louis the Debonair, his zeal for the purity of the faith and for the maintenance of ecclesiastical discipline was never called in question.   Two very complimentary letters which are supposed to have been addressed to him by Popes Paschal I and Eugenius II are, however, of doubtful authenticity.   About the year 837 he founded the abbey of Romans, and there, after his death on January 23, 842, he was buried, a highly eulogistic epitaph, which is still preserved to us, being engraved upon his tomb.

See the *Acta Sanctorum* for January 23 ; *Analecta Bollandiana*, vol. xi (1892), pp. 402 *seq.* ; Duchesne, *Fastes Épiscopaux*, vol. i, pp. 148, 158, 201, 210 ; and DHG., vol. vi, cc. 858–859.

ST LUFTHILDIS, Virgin   (*c.* A.D. 850 ?)

St Lufthildis, whose name is written in many varying forms—Leuchteldis, Liuthild, Lufthold, etc.—is one of those saints who seem to have inspired considerable local popular devotion, which is evidenced by place-names and folk traditions, but who have found no contemporary biographer to chronicle their acts. The principal feature in the story told concerning her by writers many centuries later in date was that in her youth she had much to suffer from a very cruel stepmother, who was provoked to fury by the child's love of giving to the poor.   Eventually Lufthildis left home to lead the life of a hermit, consecrating all her time to God in contemplation and the practice of penance.   Popular devotion was excited by the miracles wrought after her death, and she is still honoured in the neighbourhood of Cologne.   Her tomb was opened to inspect the relics in 1623 and again in 1901.

See the *Acta Sanctorum* for January 23 (appendix), and A. Steffens, *Die heilige Lüfthildis* (1903).

ST MAIMBOD, Martyr   (A.D. 880 ?)

St Maimbod, or Mainbœuf, is venerated on this day in the diocese of Besançon, and a church has been dedicated in his honour at Montbéliard in comparatively recent times.   He is said to have been an Irishman by birth, and seems to have belonged to that class of *peregrini*, or wandering missionaries, of whom Dom L. Gougaud wrote in his *Gaelic Pioneers of Christianity*.   We possess very little reliable information regarding him, but he is said to have been killed by a band of pagans when preaching in the neighbourhood of Kaltenbrunn in Alsace. When miracles began to be worked by his remains, Berengarius, Archbishop of Besançon, and a certain Count of Montbéliard, translated the relics to the chapel of Montbéliard, where they were destroyed in the sixteenth century during the wars of religion.

See the *Acta Sanctorum* for January 23 ; and LIS., vol. i, p. 405.

BD MARGARET OF RAVENNA, Virgin   (A.D. 1505)

Although the *cultus* of Bd Margaret does not seem to have been formally confirmed, her biography occupies several pages in the Bollandist *Acta Sanctorum*. Margaret, a native of Russi, near Ravenna, is said to have lost her sight a few months after birth, but whether she was totally blind is not clear, for she was always able to find her way into a church, a fact upon which her biographer comments naïvely, " This induces me to believe that, although blind, she saw what she wished to see ". Her early life seems to have been full of trials and sufferings, partly due to continued ill-health, partly to the offence given by her ascetical practices and love of retirement.   She was accused of hypocrisy and in many ways persecuted, but in the end she gained the esteem of most of those who had most bitterly opposed her.   In fact, some two or three hundred came at last to place themselves under her guidance and to form a religious association of persons living in the world which included both sexes, and admitted the married as well as the single.   With the assistance of the Venerable Jerome Maluselli and others she drafted constitutions, but the organization as she conceived it did not take permanent root in Italy.   On the other hand, after Margaret's death, Father Maluselli, discarding the rules which admitted laymen and women, founded on the same basis an order of clerks regular which was known as the Priests of the Good Jesus.   Margaret herself always set an admirable example of the continual prayer, humility and cheerful patience which she wished to be characteristic of the institute which she had projected, and she was famous both for her miracles and for her prophecies.   She died at the age of sixty-three on January 23, 1505.

See the *Acta Sanctorum* for January 23 ; *Kirchenlexikon*, vol. vi, cc. 1462–1463 ; Heimbucher, *Die Orden und Kongregationen*, vol. ii, pp. 35 *seq.*

24 : ST TIMOTHY, Bishop and Martyr   (*c.* A.D. 97)

ST TIMOTHY, the beloved disciple of St Paul, was probably a native of Lystra in Lycaonia.   His father was a Gentile, but his mother Eunice a Jewess.   She, with Lois, his grandmother, embraced the Christian religion, and St Paul commends their faith.   Timothy had made the Holy Scriptures his study from early youth.   When St Paul preached in Lycaonia the brethren of Iconium and Lystra gave Timothy so good a character that the apostle, being deprived of St Barnabas, took him for his companion, but first circumcised him at Lystra.   St Paul refused to circumcise Titus, born of Gentile parents, in order to assert the liberty of the gospel, and to condemn those who affirmed circumcision to be still of precept in the New Law.   On the other hand, he circumcised Timothy, born of a Jewess, that he might make him more acceptable to the Jews, and might show that he himself was no enemy of their law.   Chrysostom here commends the prudence of Paul and, we may add, the voluntary obedience of the disciple. Then St Paul, by the imposition of hands, committed to him the ministry of preaching, and from that time regarded him not only as his disciple and most dear son, but as his brother and the companion of his labours.   He calls him a man of God, and tells the Philippians that he found no one so truly united to him in spirit as Timothy.

St Paul travelled from Lystra over the rest of Asia, sailed to Macedonia, and preached at Philippi, Thessalonica and Berea.   Being compelled to quit this last city by the fury of the Jews, he left Timothy behind him to confirm the new converts there.   On arriving at Athens, however, St Paul sent for him, but learning that the Christians of Thessalonica lay under a very heavy persecution, he soon after deputed Timothy to go in his place to encourage them, and the disciple returned to St Paul, who was then at Corinth, to give him an account of his success. Upon this the apostle wrote his first epistle to the Thessalonians. From Corinth St Paul went to Jerusalem, and thence to Ephesus, where he spent two years. In 58 he seems to have decided to return to Greece, and sent Timothy and Erastus before him through Macedonia to apprise the faithful of his intention, and to prepare the alms he wished to send to the Christians of Jerusalem.

Timothy was afterwards directed to visit Corinth. His presence was needed there to revive in the minds of the faithful the doctrine which the apostle had taught them. The warm commendation of the disciple in 1 Corinthians xvi 10 no doubt has reference to this. Paul waited in Asia for his return, and then went with him into Macedonia and Achaia. St Timothy left him at Philippi, but rejoined him at Troas. The apostle on his return to Palestine was imprisoned, and after a two years' incarceration at Caesarea was sent to Rome. Timothy seems to have been with him all or most of this time, and is named by him in the title of his epistle to Philemon and in that to the Philippians. St Timothy himself suffered imprisonment for Christ, and confessed His name in the presence of many witnesses, but was set at liberty. He was ordained bishop, it seems, as the result of a special inspiration of the Holy Ghost. St Paul having returned from Rome to the East, left St Timothy at Ephesus to govern that church, to oppose false teachers, and to ordain priests, deacons and even bishops. At any rate, Chrysostom and other fathers assume that the apostle committed to him the care of all the churches of Asia, and St Timothy is always described as the first bishop of Ephesus.

St Paul wrote his first letter to Timothy from Macedonia, and his second from Rome, while there in chains, to press him to come to Rome, that he might see him again before he died. It is an out-pouring of his heart, full of tenderness towards this his dearest son. In it he encourages him in his many trials, seeks to revive in his soul that spirit of intrepidity and that fire of the Holy Ghost with which he was filled at his ordination, gives him instructions concerning the false brethren of the time, and predicts still further disorders and troubles in the Church.

We learn that St Timothy drank only water, but his austerities having prejudiced his health, St Paul, on account of his frequent infirmities, directed him to take a little wine. Upon which Chrysostom observes, " He did not say simply ' take wine ' but ' a little wine ', and this not because Timothy stood in need of that advice but because we do " St Timothy, it seems, was still young—perhaps about forty. It is not improbable that he went to Rome to confer with his master. We must assume that Timothy was made by St Paul bishop at Ephesus before St John arrived there. There is a strong tradition that John also resided in that city as an apostle, and exercised a general inspection over all the churches of Asia. St Timothy is styled a martyr in the ancient matyrologies.

The " Acts of St Timothy ", which are in some copies ascribed to the famous Polycrates, Bishop of Ephesus, but which seem to have been written at Ephesus in the fourth or fifth century, and abridged by Photius, relate that under the Emperor Nerva in the year 97 St Timothy was slain with stones and clubs by the heathen ; he was endeavouring to oppose their idolatrous ceremonies on a festival called the Katagogia, kept on January 22, on which day they walked in troops, everyone carrying in one hand an idol and in the other a club. We have good evidence that what purported to be his relics were translated to Constantinople in the reign of Constantius. The supernatural manifestations said to have taken place at the shrine are referred to as a matter of common knowledge both by Chrysostom and St Jerome.

See the *Acta Sanctorum* for January 24. The Greek text of the so-called Acts of St Timothy has been edited by H. Usener, who, in view of the small admixture of the miraculous element, inclines to regard them as reproducing a basis, derived perhaps from some Ephesian chronicle, of historical fact. The absence of any reference to the translation of St Timothy's relics to Constantinople in 356 induces him to pronounce the composition of these " acts " to be earlier than that date. *Cf.* R. Lipsius, *Die apokryphen Apostelgeschichten*, vol. ii, pt. 2, pp. 372 *seq.* ; and BHL., n. 1200 ; BHG., n. 135.

ST BABYLAS, BISHOP OF ANTIOCH, MARTYR   (c. A.D. 250)

THE most celebrated of the ancient bishops of Antioch after St Ignatius was St Babylas, who succeeded Zebinus about the year 240, but regrettably little is known about him.   According to St John Chrysostom he was the bishop who, Eusebius reports, refused admittance to the church on Easter day in 244 to Philip the Arabian —alleged to be a Christian—till he had done penance for the murder of his predecessor the Emperor Gordian.   St Babylas died a martyr during the persecution of Decius, probably in prison as Eusebius says, but Chrysostom states he was beheaded.

St Babylas is the first martyr of whom a translation of relics is recorded.   His body was buried at Antioch ; but in 351 the *caesar* Gallus removed it to a church at Daphne a few miles away to counteract the influence there of a famous shrine of Apollo, where oracles were given and the licentiousness was notorious.   The oracles were indeed silenced, and in 362 Julian the Apostate ordered that the relics of the martyr be removed.   Accordingly they were taken back to their former resting-place, the Christians accompanying them in procession, singing the psalms that speak of the powerlessness of idols and false gods.   The following evening, we are told, the temple of Apollo was destroyed by lightning.   A little later there was a third translation, made by the bishop St Meletius, to a basilica he built across the Orontes ; Meletius himself was buried next to St Babylas.

See the *Analecta Bollandiana*, vol. xix (1901), pp. 5–8, and the *Acta Sanctorum* for January 24, where two passions of St Babylas are printed, admittedly of no authority. Neither can the two panegyrics preached by Chrysostom be regarded as trustworthy historical sources, as Delehaye has shown in chap. ii of *Les passions des martyrs*   (1921), especially pp. 209 and 232. St Babylas, however, not only figures in the earliest Syriac martyrology, but was widely celebrated even in the West, and we have an account of him both in prose and verse written by St Aldhelm of Sherborne in the seventh century. These have been edited with the rest of Aldhelm's works by R. Ehwald in MGH., *Auctores antiquissimi*, vol. xv, pp. 274, 397. *Cf.* Tillemont, *Mémoires*   ., vol. iii, pp. 400–408 ; and Delehaye, *Origines du culte*   (1933), pp. 54, 58, etc.

ST FELICIAN, BISHOP OF FOLIGNO, MARTYR   (c. A.D. 254)

THE Roman Martyrology commemorates on this day an early bishop and patron of Foligno, St Felician, who is also regarded as the original apostle of Umbria.   It is difficult to say how much foundation of fact may underlie the two Latin biographies which have been preserved of him.   He is represented as having always been given up to missionary labours, as a trusted disciple of Pope St Eleutherius, who ordained him priest, and then as the friend of Pope St Victor I, who consecrated him bishop of Foligno.   If we could trust the details given in the longer of the two lives, we should be able to claim that the earliest trace of the use of the *pallium* is met with in the account of the episcopal consecration of this saint : for the pope, we are told, granted to him as a privilege that he might wear a woollen wrap outwardly round his neck,* and with this is associated in the same context the duty of consecrating bishops outside of Rome.

Felician was bishop for more than fifty years, but in the persecution of Decius he was arrested and, refusing to sacrifice to the gods, was tortured by the rack and repeated scourgings.   While he lay in prison he was tended by a maiden, St Messalina, who in consequence of the devotion she showed to him was herself accused and required to offer sacrifice ; but remaining steadfast in the faith, was then tortured until released by death.   Orders were given that Felician should be conveyed to Rome that he might suffer martyrdom there, but he died on the way, only three miles from Foligno, as a result of the torments and imprisonment he had undergone.   He was ninety-four years of age, and had been fifty-six years a bishop.

See the *Acta Sanctorum* for January 24 ; the *Analecta Bollandiana*, vol. ix (1890), pp. 379-392 ; and *A San Feliciano, protettore di Foligno* (1933), short essays, with many pictures, ed. Mgr Faloci-Pulignani.

ST MACEDONIUS   (c. A.D. 430)

THIS Syrian ascetic is said to have lived for forty years on barley moistened in water till, finding his health impaired, he ate bread, reflecting that it was not lawful for him to shorten his life in order to shun labours and conflicts.   This also was the direction he gave to the mother of Theodoret, persuading her, when in a poor state of health, to use proper food, which he said was a form of medicine.   Theodoret relates many miraculous cures of sick persons, and of his own mother among them, wrought by water over which Macedonius had made the sign of the cross.   He adds that his own birth was the effect of the anchoret's prayers after his mother had lived childless in marriage thirteen years.   The saint died when ninety years old, and is named in the Greek menologies.

Practically all our information comes from Theodoret's *Historia religiosa* (see Migne, PG., vol. lxxxii, 1399), but Macedonius also has a paragraph in the Synaxary of Constantinople (ed. Delehaye, pp. 457-458), under date February 11.   *Cf.* also DCB., vol. iii, p. 778 ; and the *Acta Sanctorum* for January 24.

BD MARCOLINO OF FORLÌ   (A.D. 1397)

THE family name of Bd Marcolino was Amanni, and he is said to have entered the Dominican noviceship when only ten years old.   The qualities most remarked in him were his exact observance of rule, his love of poverty and obedience, but especially a spirit of great humility which led him to avoid all occasions of drawing notice upon himself and to find his supreme contentment in undertaking the lowliest and most menial offices.   We are told also that he practised rigorous bodily penance, that he was a lover of the poor and of little children, and that he was favoured with continual ecstasies.   He spent so much time in praying upon his knees that calluses had formed there, as was discovered after his death.   Bd Raymund of Capua, master general of the Dominicans, had a high opinion of

* " Concessit ut extrinsecus lineo [probably an error for *laneo*] sudario circumdaretur collo ejus " (*Analecta Bollandiana*, vol. ix, p. 383).

Father Marcolino, though he was unable to make use of him in carrying out the reform of the Order of Preachers after the ravages of the Black Death and the troubles which followed on the Great Schism, because of his retiring disposition. Father Marcolino, who is said to have foretold the time of his own death, passed away at Forlì on January 2, 1397, at the age of eighty.   To the surprise of his brethren, who had failed to appreciate his holiness, a great concourse attended his funeral, drawn thither, we are told, by an angel who in the guise of a child gave notice of it in all the surrounding district.   The *cultus* was confirmed in 1750.

Our knowledge of Bd. Marcolino is largely based on certain letters of Bd John Dominici. See Mortier, *Histoire des Maîtres Généraux O.P.*, vol. iii, pp. 564-568 ; and Procter, *Short Lives*, pp. 13-15.

25 : THE CONVERSION OF ST PAUL   (A.D. 34)

THE Apostle of the Gentiles was a Jew of the tribe of Benjamin.   At his circumcision on the eighth day after his birth he received the name of Saul, and being born at Tarsus in Cilicia he was by privilege a Roman citizen. His parents sent him when young to Jerusalem, and there he was instructed in the law of Moses by Gamaliel, a learned and noble Pharisee.   Thus Saul became a scrupulous observer of the law, and he appeals even to his enemies to bear witness how conformable to it his life had always been.   He too embraced the party of the Pharisees, which was of all others the most severe, even while it was, in some of its members, the most opposed to the humility of the gospel.   It is probable that Saul learned in his youth the trade which he practised even after his apostleship —namely, that of making tents.   Later on Saul, surpassing his fellows in zeal for the Jewish law and traditions, which he thought the cause of God, became a persecutor and enemy of Christ.   He was one of those who took part in the murder of St Stephen, and by looking after the garments of those who stoned that holy martyr he is said by St Augustine to have stoned him by the hands of all the rest. To the martyr's prayers for his enemies we may ascribe Saul's conversion.   " If Stephen ", St Augustine adds, " had not prayed, the Church would never have had St Paul."

As our Saviour had always been represented by the leading men of the Jews as an enemy to their law, it was no wonder that this rigorous Pharisee fully persuaded himself that " he ought to do many things contrary to the name of Jesus of Nazareth ", and his name became everywhere a terror to the faithful, for he breathed nothing but threats and slaughter against them.   In the fury of his zeal he applied to the high priest for a commission to arrest all Jews at Damascus who confessed Jesus Christ, and bring them bound to Jerusalem.   But God was pleased to show forth in him His patience and mercy.   Saul was almost at the end of his journey to Damascus when, about noon, he and his company were on a sudden surrounded by a great light from Heaven.   They all saw this light, and being struck with amazement fell to the ground.   Then Saul heard a voice which to him was articulate and distinct, though not understood by the rest : " Saul, Saul, why dost thou persecute me ? "   Saul answered, " Who art thou, Lord ? "   Christ said, " Jesus of Nazareth, whom thou persecutest.   It is hard for thee to kick against the goad."   In other words, by persecuting My church you only hurt yourself.

Trembling and astonished, he cried out, " Lord, what wilt thou have me to do ? "
Christ told him to arise and proceed on his journey to his destination, where he
would learn what was expected of him. When he got up from the ground Saul
found that though his eyes were open he could see nothing. He was led by the
hand like a child to Damascus, and was lodged in the house of a Jew named Judas,
and there he remained three days, blind, and without eating or drinking.

There was a Christian in Damascus much respected for his life and virtue,
whose name was Ananias. Christ appeared to this disciple and commanded him
to go to Saul, who was then in the house of Judas at prayer. Ananias trembled
at the name of Saul, being no stranger to the mischief he had done in Jerusalem,
or to the errand on which he had travelled to Damascus. But our Redeemer
overruled his fears, and charged him a second time to go, saying, " Go, for he is
a vessel of election to carry my name before Gentiles and kings and the children
of Israel : and I will show him how much he has to suffer for my name." Saul
in the meantime saw in a vision a man entering, and laying his hands upon him to
restore his sight. Ananias arose, went to Saul, and laying his hands upon him
said, " Brother Saul, the Lord Jesus, who appeared to thee on thy journey, hath
sent me that thou mayest receive thy sight, and be filled with the Holy Ghost."
Immediately something like scales fell from his eyes, and he recovered his sight.
Ananias went on, " The God of our fathers hath chosen thee that thou shouldst
know His will and see the Just One and hear the voice from His mouth : and thou
shalt be His witness to all men of what thou hast seen and heard. Why dost thou
tarry ? Arise, be baptized and washed from thy sins, invoking the name of the
Lord." Saul arose, was baptized, and ate. He stayed some days with the disciples
at Damascus, and began immediately to preach in the synagogues that Jesus was
the Son of God, to the great astonishment of all that heard him, who said, " Is not
this he who at Jerusalem persecuted those who called on the name of Jesus, and
who is come hither to carry them away prisoners ? " Thus a blasphemer and a
persecutor was made an apostle, and chosen to be one of the principal instruments
of God in the conversion of the world.

St Paul can never have recalled to mind this his conversion without the deepest
gratitude and without extolling the divine mercy. The Church, in thanksgiving
to God for such a miracle of His grace and to propose to penitents a perfect model
of true conversion, has instituted this festival, which was for some time a holiday
of obligation in most churches in the West ; and we find it particularly mentioned
as such in England in the thirteenth century, an observance possibly introduced
by Cardinal Langton.

It is difficult to assign any reason for the keeping of a feast of the conversion
of St Paul on this particular day. The earliest text of the " Hieronymianum "
mentions on January 25, not the conversion, but the " *translation* of St Paul ".
The translation in question could hardly be other than the bringing of the relics
of the apostle to his own basilica after their sojourn of nearly a century in their
resting-place *ad Catacumbas*. But this commemoration of St Paul on January 25
does not appear to be a Roman feast. There is no mention of it either in the early
Gelasian or Gregorian sacramentaries. On the other hand, we find a proper
Mass in the *Missale Gothicum*, and the festival is entered in the martyrologies of
Gellone and Rheinau. Some texts, like the Berne MS. of the Hieronymianum,
show traces of a transition from " translation " to " conversion ". The calendar
of the English St Willibrord, written before the year 717, has the entry, *Conversio*

Pauli in Damasco ; while the Martyrologies of Oengus and Tallaght (both early ninth century) refer explicitly to baptism and conversion.

See the Acts of the Apostles, chaps. ix, xxii and xxvi. For the translation of St Paul's remains from St Sebastian's to his basilica, see De Waal in the *Römische Quartalschrift*, 1901, pp. 244 *seq.*, and Styger, *Il monumento apostolico della Via Appia* (1917). For a reference to the feast, see *Christian Worship* (1919), p. 281, where Mgr Duchesne points out that the Mass for Sexagesima Sunday is really in honour of St Paul. And *cf.* CMH., pp. 61–62, and *Analecta Bollandiana*, vol. xlv (1927), pp. 306–307.

ST ARTEMAS, Martyr   (Date Unknown)

We may fairly be satisfied that St Artemas has a just claim to be honoured as a saint. He was depicted and his name was inscribed in the mosaics which adorned the cupola of the ancient basilica of San Prisco near Capua. These mosaics, now unfortunately destroyed, were believed to date from about the year 500. We know also from the " Hieronymianum " that St Artemas was venerated, and is supposed to have suffered, at Pozzuoli, which is not very far from Capua. Beyond this we have no trustworthy information. But at a late date a story seems to have been connected with his name that Artemas, though hardly more than a boy himself, was teaching other boys, that he was denounced as a Christian, and that he was stabbed to death by his pupils with their styluses (sharp-pointed instruments used for writing on wax tablets). But this story is also told of St Cassian of Imola, and still earlier of St Mark of Arethusa ; and there can be little doubt that it has been borrowed from these sources and adapted to St Artemas in default of any more authentic details concerning him.

See the *Acta Sanctorum* for January 25 ; and Pio Franchi de' Cavalieri in *Studi e Testi*, vol. ix, p. 68.

SS. JUVENTINUS and MAXIMINUS, Martyrs   (A.D. 363)

These martyrs were two officers of distinction in the foot-guards of Julian the Apostate. When he was on the march in his campaign against the Persians, they let fall at table certain free reflections on the impious laws made against the Christians, wishing rather for death than to see the profanation of holy things. The emperor being informed of this, sent for them, and finding that they could not be prevailed upon to retract what they had said or to sacrifice to idols, he confiscated their estates, ordered them to be scourged, and some days after had them beheaded in prison at Antioch, January 25, 363. Christians, at the risk of their lives, stole away the bodies, and after the death of Julian, who was slain in Persia on June 26 following, erected a magnificent tomb to do them honour. On their festival Chrysostom delivered a panegyric, in which he says of these martyrs : " They support the Church as pillars, defend it as towers and are as unyielding as rocks. Let us visit them frequently, let us touch their shrine and embrace their relics with confidence, that we may obtain from thence some benediction. For as soldiers, showing to the king the wounds which they have received in his battles, speak with confidence, so they, by a humble representation of their past sufferings for Christ, obtain whatever they ask of the King of Heaven."

The scanty details recorded concerning these martyrs are mainly furnished by St John Chrysostom's panegyric. In the above quoted passage, which Butler has translated very freely, the orator rather quaintly pictures them pleading before the throne of God by holding up before Him in their hands the heads which had been cut off.   Severus of Antioch, in a hymn composed in their honour, mentions a third martyr, Longinus, who perished in their company (*Patrologia Orientalis*, vol. vii, p. 611).   See also the *Acta Sanctorum* for January 25 ; and *cf.* Delehaye, *Les origines du culte*   (1933), p. 196, and *Les passions des martyrs* pp. 228 and 230.

ST PUBLIUS, ABBOT   (*c.* A.D. 380)

ST PUBLIUS is honoured principally by the Greeks.   He was the son of a senator in Zeugma upon the Euphrates, and sold his estate and goods for the benefit of the poor.   Though he lived at first as a hermit, he afterwards became the ruler of a numerous community.   He allowed his monks no other food than vegetables and very coarse bread ; they drank nothing but water, and he forbade cheese, grapes, vinegar and even oil, except from Easter to Whitsuntide.   To remind himself of the need of a continual advance in fervour, he added every day something to his exercises of penance and devotion.   He was also remarkably earnest in avoiding sloth, being sensible of the inestimable value of time.   Theodoret tells us that the holy abbot founded two congregations, the one of Greeks, the other of Syrians, each using their own tongue in the divine offices and Holy Mysteries. St Publius seems to have died about the year 380.

We know little or nothing of St Publius beyond what is recorded of him by Theodoret in his book *Philotheus*.   See the *Acta Sanctorum* for January 25 ; and Delehaye, *Synaxarium Ecclesiae Constantinopolitanae*, pp. 423–424.

ST APOLLO, ABBOT   (*c.* A.D. 395)

AFTER passing many years in a hermitage, Apollo, who was then close upon eighty years old, formed and governed a community of many monks near Hermopolis. They all wore the same coarse white habit, all received holy communion every day, and the venerable abbot made them also a daily exhortation for the profit of their souls.   In these he insisted often on the evils of melancholy and sadness, saying that cheerfulness of heart is necessary amidst our tears of penance as being the fruit of charity and requisite to maintain the spirit of fervour.   He himself was known to strangers by the joy of his countenance.   He made it his constant petition to God that he might know himself and be preserved from the subtle illusions of pride.   It is said that on one occasion, when the devil quitted a possessed person at his command, the evil spirit cried out that he was not able to withstand his humility.   Many astonishing miracles are recorded of him, of which perhaps the most remarkable was a continuous multiplication of bread, by which in a time of famine not only his own brethren but the whole surrounding population were sustained for four months.   The saint received a visit from St Petronius, afterwards bishop of Bologna, in 393, but this, it would seem, must have been at the very end of his life, when he was over ninety years old.

For our knowledge of St Apollo we are mainly indebted to a long section of the *Historia monachorum*, which was formerly regarded as forming part of the *Lausiac History* of Palladius, but which is now recognized as a separate work, probably written in Greek by the Archdeacon Timotheus of Alexandria.   An English translation from the ancient Syriac version has been published by Sir E. A. Wallis Budge in the work entitled *The Book of Paradise of Palladius* (1904), vol. i, pp. 520–538.   The Greek text had been edited by Preuschen in his *Palladius und Rufinus* (1897).   See also the *Acta Sanctorum* for January 25 ; and P. Cheneau, *Les Saints d'Egypte* (1923), vol. i, pp. 218–225.

ST PRAEJECTUS, or PRIX, BISHOP OF CLERMONT, MARTYR   (A.D. 676)

THE episcopal see of Auvergne in the early days was honoured with many holy bishops, of whom the Christian poet, St Sidonius Apollinaris, was one of the most famous.   Later on the title of bishops of Auvergne was changed into that of Clermont, from the city of this name.   St Praejectus (called in France variously Priest, Prest, Preils and Prix) was a native of Auvergne, trained up in the service of the Church under the care of St Genesius, Bishop of Auvergne, well skilled in plainsong, in Holy Scripture and church history.   About the year 666 he was called by the voice of the people, seconded by Childeric II, King of Austrasia, to the episcopal dignity, upon the death of Felix, Bishop of Auvergne.   Partly by his own ample patrimony, and partly through the liberality of Genesius, Count of Auvergne, he was enabled to found several monasteries, churches and hospitals ; so that distressed persons in his extensive diocese were provided for, and a spirit of religious fervour reigned.   This was the fruit of the unwearied zeal, assiduous exhortations and admirable example of the holy prelate, whose learning, eloquence and piety are greatly extolled by his contemporary biographer.   Praejectus restored to health St Amarin, the abbot of a monastery in the Vosges, who was afterwards his companion in martyrdom.

As the result of an alleged outrage by Hector, the *patricius* of Marseilles—an incident very differently recounted by writers of different sympathies—Hector, after a visit to court, was arrested and executed by Childeric's orders.   One Agritius, imputing his death to the complaints carried to the king by St Praejectus, thought to avenge him by organizing a conspiracy against him.   With twenty armed men he met the bishop as he returned from court at Volvic, two leagues from Clermont, and first slew the abbot St Amarin, whom the assassins mistook for the bishop.   St Praejectus, perceiving their design, courageously stepped forward, and was stabbed by a Saxon named Radbert.   The saint, receiving this wound, said, " Lord, lay not this sin to their charge, for they know not what they do ".   Another of the assassins clove his head with a sword, and scattered his brains.   This happened in 676, on January 25.   The veneration which the Gallican churches paid to the memory of this martyr began from the time of his death, and many miracles immediately afterwards were recorded at his tomb.

The text of the Life of St Praejectus has in modern times been edited and carefully annotated by B. Krusch in MGH., *Scriptores Merov.*, vol. v, pp. 212-248.   Krusch is of opinion that, though the author does not seem to have known the saint personally, he was a contemporary, and probably a monk of Volvic in Puy-de-Dôme.   It is one of the most trustworthy and interesting of Merovingian hagiographical documents.   The greater part of the relics of St Praejectus were afterwards translated to the abbey of Flavigny in Burgundy. See also *Acta Sanctorum* for January 25 ; and Duchesne, *Fastes Épiscopaux*, vol. ii, pp. 37-38.

ST POPPO, ABBOT   (A.D. 1048)

ST POPPO was born in Flanders in 978, and was brought up by a most virtuous mother, who died a nun at Verdun.   In his youth he served for some time in the army ; but even in the world he found meditation and prayer to be sweeter than all the delights of the senses, and he renounced his profession and the marriage which had been arranged for him.   He had previously visited the holy places at Jerusalem and brought away many relics, with which he enriched the church of our Lady at Deynze.   He also made a pilgrimage to Rome, and some time after took the monastic habit at St Thierry's, near Rheims.   Richard, Abbot of Saint-Vanne, one of the great monastic reformers of the age, met Poppo about the year 1008, and found in him a man singularly well fitted to assist him in this work.   Not without great difficulty he managed to get Poppo transferred to his own monastery, and then used him to restore observance in several abbeys, Saint-Vaast at Arras, Beaulieu, and others.   St Poppo, who gradually became independent of Richard of Saint-Vanne, seems, on being appointed abbot of Stavelot, to have acted as a sort of abbot general to a whole group of monasteries in Lotharingia.   In these he was revered and preserved admirable discipline.   He was much esteemed by the emperor, St Henry II, and he seems in many political matters to have given him prudent counsel.   He died at Marchiennes on January 25 in 1048, being seventy years of age.   St Poppo received the last anointing at the hands of Everhelm, Abbot of Hautmont, who afterwards wrote his life, or, more correctly, revised the longer biography composed by the monk Onulf.

A critical edition of the life which we owe to Onulf and Abbot Everhelm is to be found in the folio series of MGH., *Scriptores*, vol. xi, pp. 291 316.   See also the *Acta Sanctorum* for January 25 ; Cauchie in the *Biographie Nationale*, vol. xviii, pp. 43 *seq.* ; and a sketch by M. Souplet, *St Poppon de Deynse* (1948).

26 : ST POLYCARP, Bishop of Smyrna, Martyr   (A.D. 155 ?)

S T POLYCARP was one of the most famous of the little group of early bishops known as " the Apostolic Fathers ", who, being the immediate disciples of the apostles, received instruction directly from them, as it were from the fountain head.   Polycarp was a disciple of St John the Evangelist, and was respected by the faithful to the point of profound veneration.   He trained many holy disciples, among whom were St Irenaeus and Papias.   When Florinus, who had often visited St Polycarp, had broached certain heresies, St Irenaeus wrote to him : " These things were not taught you by the bishops who preceded us.   I could tell you the place where the blessed Polycarp sat to preach the word of God.   It is yet present to my mind with what gravity he everywhere came in and went out ; what was the sanctity of his deportment, the majesty of his countenance, and of his whole exterior ; and what were his holy exhortations to the people. I seem to hear him now relate how he conversed with John and many others who had seen Jesus Christ, the words he had heard from their mouths.   I can protest before God that if this holy bishop had heard of any error like yours, he would have immediately stopped his ears and cried out, according to his custom, ' Good God ! that I should be reserved to these times to hear such things ! '   That very instant he would have fled out of the place in which he had heard such doctrine."   We are told that St Polycarp met at Rome the heretic Marcion in the streets, who, resenting the fact that the bishop did not take that notice of him which he expected, said, " Do not you know me ? "   " Yes ", answered the saint, " I know you, the first-born of Satan."   He had learned this abhorrence of those who adulterate divine truth from his master St John, who fled from the baths at the sight of Cerinthus.

St Polycarp kissed the chains of St Ignatius when he passed by Smyrna on the road to his martyrdom, and Ignatius in turn recommended to him the care of his distant church of Antioch, supplementing this charge later on by a request that he would write in his name to those churches of Asia to which he had not leisure to write himself.   Polycarp addressed a letter to the Philippians shortly after, which is highly commended by St Irenaeus, St Jerome, Eusebius, Photius and others, and is still extant.   This letter, which in St Jerome's time was publicly read in the Asiatic churches, is justly admired both for the excellent instructions it contains and for the perspicuity of the style.   Polycarp undertook a journey to Rome to confer with Pope St Anicetus about certain points, especially about the time of keeping Easter, for the Asiatic churches differed from others in this matter. Anicetas could not persuade Polycarp, nor Polycarp Anicetus, and so it was agreed that both might follow their custom without breaking the bonds of charity.   St Anicetus, to testify his respect, asked him to celebrate the Eucharist in his own papal church.   We find no further particulars concerning Polycarp recorded before his martyrdom.

In the sixth year of Marcus Aurelius (according to Eusebius) a violent persecution broke out in Asia in which the faithful gave heroic proof of their courage. Germanicus, who had been brought to Smyrna with eleven or twelve other Christians, signalized himself above the rest, and animated the most timorous to suffer. The proconsul in the amphitheatre appealed to him compassionately to have some regard for his youth when life had so much to offer, but he provoked the beasts to devour him, the sooner to quit this wicked world.   One Quintus, a Phrygian, quailed at the sight of the beast let loose upon him, and consented to sacrifice. The authors of this letter justly condemn the presumption of those who offered themselves to suffer (as Quintus had done), and say that the martyrdom of Polycarp was conformable to the gospel, because he did not expose himself but waited till the persecutors laid hands on him, as Christ our Lord taught us by His own example. The splendid courage of Germanicus and his companions only whetted the spectators' appetite for blood.   A cry was raised : " Away with the atheists ! Look for Polycarp ! "   The holy man, though fearless, had been prevailed upon by his friends to conceal himself in a neighbouring village during the storm. Three days before his martyrdom he in a vision saw his pillow on fire, from which he understood, and foretold to his companions, that he should be burnt alive. When the persecutors came in search of him he changed his retreat, but was betrayed by a slave, who was threatened with the rack unless he disclosed his whereabouts.

When the chief of police, Herod, sent horsemen by night to surround his lodging, Polycarp was above stairs in bed, but refused to make his escape, saying, " God's will be done "   He went down, met them at the door, ordered them supper, and desired only some time for prayer before he went with them.   This granted, he began his prayer standing, which he continued for two hours, recommending to God his own flock and the whole Church with such intense devotion that some of those who had come to seize him repented of their errand.   They set him on an ass, and were conducting him towards the city, when he was met on the road by Herod and Herod's father, Nicetas, who took him into their chariot and endeavoured to persuade him to some show of compliance.   " What harm ", they urged, " is there in saying Lord Caesar, or even in offering incense, to escape death ? "   The word Lord, however, was not as innocent as it sounded, and implied a recognition of the divinity of the emperor.   The bishop at first was silent, but being pressed, he gave them resolute answer, " I am resolved not to do what you counsel me ". At these words they thrust him out of the chariot with such violence that his leg was bruised by the fall.

The holy man went forward cheerfully to the place where the people were assembled. Upon his entering it a voice from Heaven was heard by many, " Be strong, Polycarp, and play the man " He was led to the tribunal of the proconsul, who exhorted him to have regard for his age, to swear by the genius of Caesar, and to say, " Away with the atheists ", meaning the Christians. The saint, turning towards the crowd of ungodly people in the stadium, said, with a stern countenance, " Away with the atheists ! " The proconsul repeated, " Swear by the genius of Caesar, and I will discharge you ; revile Christ ". Polycarp replied, " Fourscore and six years have I served Him and He hath done me no wrong. How then can I blaspheme my King and my Saviour ? If you require of me to swear by the genius of Caesar, as you call it, hear my free confession : I am a Christian ; and if you desire to learn the doctrines of Christianity, appoint a time and hear me." The proconsul said, " Persuade the people " The martyr replied, " I address myself to you ; for we are taught to give due honour to princes, so far as is consistent with religion. But before these people I cannot justify myself." Indeed, rage rendered them incapable of hearing him.

The proconsul threatened " I have wild beasts ". " Call for them ", replied the saint, " for we are unalterably resolved not to change from good to evil. It is only right to pass from evil to good." The proconsul said, " If you despise the beasts, I will cause you to be consumed by fire " Polycarp answered, " You threaten me with a fire which burneth for a season, and after a little while is quenched ; but you are ignorant of the judgement to come and of the fire of everlasting punishment which is prepared for the wicked. Why do you delay ? Bring against me what you please." Whilst he said this and many other things, he appeared in a transport of joy and confidence, and his countenance shone with a certain heavenly grace, insomuch that the proconsul himself was struck with admiration. However, he ordered a crier to announce three times in the middle of the stadium, " Polycarp hath confessed himself a Christian ". At this the whole multitude gave a great shout, " This is the teacher of Asia, the father of the Christians, the destroyer of our gods, who teaches the people not to sacrifice or to worship ! " They appealed to Philip the governor to let a lion loose upon Polycarp. He told them that it was not in his power, because he had brought the sports to a close. Then they all, heathen and Jews, clamoured that he should be burnt alive.

Their demand was no sooner granted than everyone ran with all speed to fetch wood from the bath-furnaces and workshops. The pile being ready, Polycarp put off his clothes and made to remove his shoes ; he had not done this before, because the faithful already sought the privilege of touching his flesh. The executioners would have nailed him to the stake, but he said, " Suffer me to be as I am. He who gives me grace to endure the fire will enable me to remain at the pile unmoved." They therefore contented themselves with tying his hands behind his back, and looking up towards Heaven, he prayed and said, " O Almighty Lord God, Father of thy beloved and blessed Son Jesus Christ, through whom we have received the knowledge of thee, God of angels and powers and of all creation, and of the whole family of the righteous who live in thy presence ! I bless thee for having been pleased to bring me to this hour, that I may receive a portion among thy martyrs and partake of the cup of thy Christ, unto resurrection to eternal

life, both of soul and body, in the immortality of the Holy Spirit.   Amongst whom
grant me to be received this day as a pleasing sacrifice, such as thou thyself hast
prepared, O true and faithful God.   Wherefore for all things I praise, bless and
glorify thee, through the eternal high priest Jesus Christ, thy beloved Son, with
whom to thee and the Holy Ghost be glory now and for ever.   Amen."   He had
scarce said Amen when fire was set to the pile.   But behold a wonder, say the
authors of this letter, seen by us who were preserved to attest it to others.   The
flames, forming themselves like the sails of a ship swelled with the wind, gently
encircled the body of the martyr, which stood in the middle, resembling not
burning flesh but bread that is being baked or precious metal refined.   And there
was a fragrance like the smell of incense.   The order was given that Polycarp
should be pierced with a spear, which was done : and a dove came forth, and such
quantity of blood as to quench the fire.

Nicetas advised the proconsul not to give up the body to the Christians, lest,
said he, abandoning the crucified man, they should worship Polycarp.   The Jews
suggested this, " not knowing ", say the authors of the letter, " that we can never
forsake Christ, nor worship any other.   For Him we worship as the Son of God,
but we love the martyrs as His disciples and imitators, for the great love they bore
their King and Master."   The centurion, seeing the contest raised by the Jews,
placed the body in the middle and burnt it to ashes.   " We afterward took up
the bones ", say they, " more precious than the richest jewels of gold, and laid them
decently in a place at which may God grant us to assemble with joy to celebrate
the birthday of the martyr."   Thus wrote these disciples and eye-witnesses.   It
was at two o'clock in the afternoon of February 23 in 155 or 166 or some other
year that St Polycarp received his crown.

An immense literature, of which we cannot attempt to take account here, has grown up
in connection with the history of St Polycarp.   The principal points round which discussion
has centred are   (1) the authenticity of the letter written in the name of the church of
Smyrna describing his martyrdom ; (2) the authenticity of the letter addressed to him by
St Ignatius of Antioch ; (3) the authenticity of Polycarp's letter to the Philippians ; (4) the
trustworthiness of the information concerning him and his relations with the apostle St John
supplied by St Irenaeus and other early writers ; (5) the date of his martyrdom ; (6) the
value and bearing of the *Life of Polycarp* attributed to Pionius.   With regard to the first
four points, it may be said that the verdict of the best authorities upon Christian origins is
now practically unanimous in favour of the orthodox tradition.   The conclusions so patiently
worked out by Bishop Lightfoot and Funk have in the end been accepted with hardly a
dissentient voice.   The documents named may therefore be regarded as among the most
precious memorials preserved to us which shed light upon the early developments of the life
of the Church.   For English readers they are accessible in the invaluable work of Lightfoot,
The Apostolic Fathers, Ignatius and Polycarp, 3 vols. ; or in the one volume abridgement
edited by J. R. Harmer (also with full translation), *The Apostolic Fathers* (1891).   As regards
the date of the martyrdom, earlier writers, in accordance with an entry in the *Chronicle* of
Eusebius, took it for granted that Polycarp suffered in 166 ; but discussions have led almost
all recent critics to decide for 155 or 156.   See, however, J. Chapman, who in the *Revue
Bénédictine*, vol. xix, pp. 145 *seq.*, gives reasons for still adhering to 166 ; and H. Grégoire
in *Analecta Bollandiana*, vol. lxix (1951), pp. 1–38, where he argues at length for 177.   As
for point (6), the *Life* by Pionius, which describes Polycarp as in his boyhood a slave ransomed
by a compassionate lady, there is now an equally general agreement among scholars that this
narrative is a pure work of fiction, though it may possibly be as old as the last decade of the
fourth century.   An attempt has been made by P. Corssen and E. Schwartz to demonstrate
that the *Life of Polycarp* is a genuine work of the martyr St Pionius, who suffered in 180 or
250 ; but this contention has been convincingly refuted by Fr Delehaye in his *Les passions
des martyrs et les genres littéraires* (1921), pp. 11–59.   There is an excellent article on St

Polycarp by H. T. Andrews in the *Encyclopaedia Britannica*, 11th edition. A handy text and translation of the martyrdom is Kirsopp Lake's in the Loeb Classical Library, *The Apostolic Fathers*, vol. ii ; and there is a translation only in the Ancient Christian Writers series, vol. vi. On the date see further H. I. Marrou in *Analecta Bollandiana*, vol. lxxi (1953), pp. 5–20.

ST PAULA, WIDOW   (A.D. 404)

THIS illustrious pattern of widows surpassed all other Roman matrons in riches, birth and endowments of mind. She was born on May 5 in 347. The blood of the Scipios, the Gracchi and Paulus Aemilius ran in her veins through her mother Blesilla. Her father claimed to trace his pedigree back to Agamemnon, and her husband Toxotius his to Aeneas. By him she had a son, also called Toxotius, and four daughters, Blesilla, Paulina, Eustochium and Rufina. She shone as a pattern of virtue in the married state, and both she and her husband edified Rome by their good example ; but her virtue was not without its alloy, a certain degree of love of the world being almost inseparable from a position such as hers. She did not at first discern the secret attachments of her heart, but her eyes were opened by the death of her husband, when she was thirty-two years of age. Her grief was immoderate till such time as she was encouraged to devote herself totally to God by her friend St Marcella, a widow who then edified Rome by her penitential life. Paula thenceforward lived in a most austere way. Her food was simple, she drank no wine ; she slept on the floor with no bedding but sackcloth ; she renounced all social life and amusements ; and everything it was in her power to dispose of she gave away to the poor. She avoided every distraction which interrupted her good works ; but she gave hospitality to St Epiphanius of Salamis and to Paulinus of Antioch when they came to Rome ; and through them she came to know St Jerome, with whom she was closely associated in the service of God during his stay in Rome under Pope St Damasus.

Paula's eldest daughter, St Blesilla, dying suddenly, her mother felt this bereavement intensely ; and St Jerome, who had just returned to Bethlehem, wrote to comfort her, and also to reprove her for what he regarded as an excess of mourning for one who had gone to her heavenly reward. The second daughter, Paulina, was married to St Pammachius, and died seven years before her mother. St Eustochium, the third, was Paula's inseparable companion. Rufina died in youth. The more progress St Paula made in the relish of heavenly things, the more insupportable to her became the tumultuous life of the city. She sighed after the desert, longed to live in a hermitage where her heart would have no other occupation than the thought of God. She determined to leave Rome, ready to leave home, family and friends ; never did mother love her children more tenderly, yet the tears of the child Toxotius and of the older Rufina could not hold her back. She sailed from Italy with Eustochium in 385, and after visiting St Epiphanius in Cyprus, met St Jerome and others at Antioch. The party made a pilgrimage to all the holy places of Palestine and on to Egypt to visit the monks and anchorets there ; a year later they arrived in Bethlehem, and St Paula and St Eustochium settled there under the direction of St Jerome.

Here the two women lived in a cottage until they were able to build a hospice, a monastery for men and a three-fold convent for women. This last properly made but one house, for all assembled in the same chapel day and night for divine service together, and on Sundays in the church which stood hard by. Their food was coarse and scanty, their fasts frequent and severe. All the sisters worked with their hands, and made clothes for themselves and others. All wore a similar modest habit, and used no linen. No man was ever suffered to set foot within their doors. Paula governed with a charity full of discretion, encouraging them by her own example and instruction, being always among the first at every duty, taking part, like Eustochium, in all the work of the house. If anyone showed herself talkative or passionate, she was separated from the rest, ordered to walk the last in order, to pray outside the door, and for some time to eat alone. Paula extended her love of poverty to her buildings and churches, ordering them all to be built low, and without anything costly or magnificent. She said that money is better expended upon the poor, who are the living members of Christ.

According to Palladius, St Paula had the care of St Jerome and—as might be expected—found it no easy responsibility. But she was also of considerable help to him in his biblical and other work, for she had got Greek from her father and now learned enough Hebrew at any rate to be able to sing the psalms in their original tongue. She too profited sufficiently by the teaching of her master to be able to take an intelligent interest in the unhappy dispute with Bishop John of Jerusalem over Origenism; but her last years were overcast by this and other troubles such as the grave financial stringency that her generosity had brought upon her. Paula's son Toxotius married Laeta, the daughter of a pagan priest, but herself a Christian. Both were faithful imitators of the holy life of our saint. Their daughter, Paula the younger, was sent to Bethlehem, to be under the care of her grandmother, whom she afterwards succeeded in the government of her religious house. For the education of this child St Jerome sent to Laeta some excellent instructions, which parents can never read too often. God called St Paula to Himself after a life of fifty-six years. In her last illness she repeated almost without intermission certain verses of the psalms which express an ardent desire of the heavenly Jerusalem and of being with God. When she was no longer able to speak, she made the sign of the cross on her lips, and died in peace on January 26, 404.

Practically all that we know of St Paula is derived from the letters of St Jerome, more particularly from letter 108, which might be described as a biography; it is printed in Migne, P.L., vol. xxii, cc. 878–905, and in the *Acta Sanctorum* for January 26. See also the charming monograph by F. Lagrange, *Histoire de Ste Paule*, which has gone through many editions since 1868; and R. Genier, *Ste Paule* (1917).

ST CONAN, BISHOP   (SEVENTH CENTURY ?)

THERE are a good many place-names which seem to bear witness to the existence of a Celtic saint named Conan or Conon, but there is no real evidence of *cultus*, and the statements which have been made about him are by no means consistent with each other. In certain breviary lessons of late date it is said that the hermit St Fiacre, born in Scotland or Ireland, was in his boyhood committed to the care of St Conan, and learnt from him those virtues which afterwards made the name of Fiacre famous. St Conan, we are told, passed from Scotland to the Isle of Man, and completed the work, begun by St Patrick or some of his disciples, of planting Christianity in that place. He is also commonly called bishop of Sodor, but the very name is an anachronism, for there is no doubt that Sodor is a corruption of the Norse term *Suthr-eyar* (Southern Islands), which was used by the Vikings for the islands off the west coast of Great Britain in opposition to the

Shetland and Orkney groups, which were northern islands. But the Viking raids did not begin before the close of the eighth century, and the name Sodor as the designation of an episcopal see cannot have been introduced until much later than that. It is quite possible, however, that Conan may have received episcopal consecration, and may have laboured in Man and the Hebrides.

See KSS., pp. 307-308 ; LIS., vol. i, p. 447 ; Olaf Kolsrud, " The Celtic Bishops in the Isle of Man " in the *Zeitschrift f. Celtische Philologie*, vol. ix (1913), pp. 357-379.

ST ALBERIC, Abbot of Cîteaux, Co-Founder of the Cistercian Order   (A.D. 1109)

THE experiences of St Alberic in his efforts to find a religious home in accord with his aspirations after high perfection throw rather a lurid light upon the untamed temper of the recruits who formed the raw material of monastic life in the eleventh century. We know nothing of his boyhood, but we hear of him first as one of a group of seven hermits who were trying to serve God in the forest of Collan, not far from Châtillon-sur-Seine. There was a certain Abbot Robert, a man of good family, who in spite of a previous failure with a community of unruly monks was in high repute for virtue. Him the hermits with some difficulty obtained for a superior, and in 1075 they moved not far off to Molesmes, where they built a monastery, with Robert for abbot and Alberic for prior. Benefactions flowed in upon them, their numbers grew, but religious fervour decayed. In time a turbulent majority set monastic discipline at defiance. Robert lost heart and withdrew elsewhere. Alberic struggled on to maintain order, but things came to such a pass that the monks beat and imprisoned their prior, and eventually, if we may trust our rather confused authorities, Alberic and Stephen Harding, the Englishman, could stand it no longer, and also quitted Molesmes. Probably, when the news of these scandals leaked out, the alms of the faithful began to dry up and the pinch made itself felt. In any case, amendment was promised, so that Robert and Alberic and Stephen were prevailed upon to return ; but the old troubles and relaxed observance soon reappeared, and Alberic seems to have been the leading spirit in persuading a group of the more fervent to establish elsewhere a new community living under a stricter rule.

In the year 1098 twenty-one monks took up their abode in the wilderness of Cîteaux, some little distance to the south of Dijon and more than seventy miles from Molesmes. These were the first beginnings of the great Cistercian Order. Robert, Alberic and Stephen were elected respectively abbot, prior and sub-prior, but shortly afterwards St Robert returned to the community he had quitted. Thus Alberic became abbot in his place, and it is to him that some of the more distinctive features of the Cistercian reform must probably be ascribed ; this way of life aimed at a restoration of primitive Benedictine observance, but with many added austerities. One of its external features was the adoption for the choir monks of a white habit (with a black scapular and hood), a change said to have been made in consequence of a vision of our Lady which was vouchsafed to St Alberic. A more notable change was the recognition of a special class of *fratres conversi*, or lay brothers, to whom the more laborious work, and particularly the field work in the distant granges, was entrusted ; but manual work was normal for all the monks, their choir observances were much shortened and simplified, and more time was available for private prayer.

Alberic's rule as abbot was not very prolonged, and much of that which was most characteristic in the final organization at Cîteaux may not improbably be traced to his successor, St Stephen.   It is Stephen also who, in an address delivered after the death of Alberic (January 26, 1109), has left us almost the only personal note we possess concerning him.   " All of us ", he said, " have alike a share in this great loss, and I am but a poor comforter, who myself need comfort.   Ye have lost a venerable father and ruler of your souls ; I have lost, not only a father and ruler, but a friend, a fellow soldier and a chief warrior in the battles of the Lord, whom our venerable Father Robert, from the very cradle of our monastic institute, had brought up in one and the same convent, in admirable learning and piety.   We have amongst us this dear body and singular pledge of our beloved father, and he himself has carried us all away with him in his mind with an affectionate love.
The warrior has attained his reward, the runner has grasped his prize, the victor has won his crown ; he who has taken possession prays for a palm for us.   Let us not mourn for the soldier who is at rest ; let us mourn for ourselves who are placed in the front of the battle, and let us turn our sad and dejected speeches into prayers, begging our father who is in triumph not to suffer the roaring lion and savage enemy to triumph over us."

See *Acta Sanctorum*, January 26 ; J. B. Dalgairns, *Life of St Stephen Harding*, and other references given herein under St Stephen on April 17.

ST EYSTEIN, ARCHBISHOP OF NIDAROS   (A.D. 1188)

IN the year 1152 an English cardinal, Nicholas Breakspeare (afterwards to be pope as Adrian IV), visited Norway as legate of the Holy See, and gave a new organization to the Church in that country, consisting of a metropolitan see at Nidaros (Trondhjem) with ten bishoprics.*   Five years later the second archbishop of Nidaros was appointed, in the person of Eystein Erlandsson, chaplain to King Inge, an appointment which violated the regulations for canonical appointments laid down by Cardinal Breakspeare.   But it proved to be the life work of the new archbishop to maintain the Church's right of conducting its affairs without inter- ference by " the rich and great ", and finally to bring the Norwegian church into the general pattern of the west European Christendom of that day.   After his appointment Eystein made his way to Rome, but it is not known exactly when or where he was consecrated bishop by Pope Alexander III and received the *pallium*. In any case he did not get back home till late in 1161, and then he came as papal legate *a latere*.   One of his first interests was to finish the enlargement of the cathedral, Christ Church, of Nidaros, and some of his building still remains.   In the account which he wrote of St Olaf, St Eystein relates his remarkably speedy recovery from an accident sustained by him when a scaffolding on this building collapsed   he attributes it to Olaf's intercession.
After the death of King Haakon II, Jarl Erling Skakke wanted to get his own eight-year-old son Magnus recognized as king of Norway.   And in 1164, probably in return for concessions touching ecclesiastical revenue, Archbishop Eystein anointed and crowned the child at Bergen, the first royal coronation in Norwegian

* Among them was Suderöyene, *i.e.* the western isles of Scotland and Man, which remained suffragan to Trondhjem till the fourteenth century   the name survives in the " Sodor and Man " diocese of the Anglican Church to-day.   Other sees were in the northern islands, Greenland and Iceland.

history.   Relations between the archbishop and the king's father continued to be close, and St Eystein was able to get accepted a code of laws some of which were of great importance for the discipline and good order of the Church.   But one matter which he does not seem to have tackled, at any rate directly, was clerical celibacy, which was not observed in the Scandinavian churches at that time (*cf.* the contemporary St Thorlac in Iceland).   It was perhaps for this reason that St Eystein founded communities of Augustinian canons regular, to set an example to the parochial clergy.

Most of St Eystein's activities as they have come down to us are matters of the general history of his country rather than his own life, and were always directed towards the free action of the spiritual power among a unified people.   This brought him into collision with Magnus's rival for the throne, Sverre, and in 1181 the archbishop fled to England; from whence he is said to have excommunicated Sverre.   Jocelyn of Brakelond, the chronicler of the abbey of St Edmundsbury in Suffolk, writes : " While the abbacy was vacant the archbishop of Norway, Augustine [the name of which Eystein is the Scandinavian form ; *cf.* the English ' Austin '], dwelt with us in the abbot's lodgings, and by command of the king received ten shillings every day from the revenues of the abbot.   He assisted us greatly to gain freedom of election. . . ."   It was on this occasion that the famous Samson was elected abbot.   It is significant that St Eystein had a strong devotion for St Thomas Becket, which later became common in the Norwegian church, and it is reasonable to suppose that he visited his shrine at Canterbury ; and it seems that it was in England that he wrote *The Passion and Miracles of the Blessed Olaf.*

Eystein returned to Norway in 1183, and he was in his ship in Bergen harbour when Sverre attacked Magnus's ships there and forced the king to flee to Denmark. In the following year Magnus lost his life in a renewal of the struggle, and it may be assumed that the archbishop was reconciled with King Sverre.   Certainly when Eystein was on his death-bed four years later Sverre visited him, and Sverre's Saga says, " They were then altogether reconciled and each forgave the other those things which had been between them."

St Eystein died on January 26, 1188, and in 1229 a synod at Nidaros declared his sanctity.   This decree has never been confirmed at Rome, although the preliminary investigations have been begun several times but have always petered out for various reasons.   Matthew of Westminster in the thirteenth century refers to him as a man whose holiness was attested by outstanding and authentic miracles. As has been said, St Eystein's work was to break the hold of a semi-barbarous nobility over the Church in Norway and to set it more free to work peacefully for her children.   This meant that his own life was one of devoted conflict, in which he learned by experience that, in the words of his friend Theodoric, " It is one thing to control the rashness of the wicked by means of earthly force and the sword, but quite another to lead souls gently with the tenderness and care of a shepherd."

The sources for the life of St Eystein have mostly to be extracted from documents of the general history of Norway, such as Sverre's Saga.   What is known of him is fitted into a more detailed account of the historical background by Mrs Sigrid Undset in her *Saga of Saints* (1934).   The manuscript of Eystein's *Passio et miracula beati Olavi* was found in England and edited by F. Metcalfe (1881).   This manuscript once belonged to Fountains Abbey.

ST MARGARET OF HUNGARY, Virgin   (A.D. 1270)

VERY great interest attaches to the life of St Margaret of Hungary, because by rare good fortune we possess in her case a complete copy of the depositions of the witnesses who gave evidence in the process of beatification begun less than seven years after her death.   No doubt the fact that she was the daughter of Bela IV, King of Hungary, a champion of Christendom at a time when central Europe was menaced with utter destruction by the inroads of the Tatars, has emphasized the details of her extraordinary life of self-crucifixion.   The Dominican Order, too, which was much befriended by Bela and his consort Queen Mary Lascaris, was necessarily interested in the cause of one of its earliest and most eminent daughters. But no one can read the astounding record of Margaret's asceticism and charity as recounted by some fifty witnesses who were her everyday companions without realizing that even if she had been the child of a beggar, such courage as hers—one is almost tempted to call it the fanaticism of her warfare against the world and the flesh—could not but have a spiritualizing influence upon all who came in contact with her.   Bela IV has been styled " the last man of genius whom the Arpads produced ", but there were qualities in his daughter which, if determination counts for anything in human affairs, showed that the stock was not yet effete.

Margaret had been born at an hour when the fortunes of Hungary were at a low ebb, and we are told that her parents had promised to dedicate the babe entirely to God if victory should wait upon their arms.   The boon was in substance granted, and the child at age of three was committed to the charge of the community of Dominican nuns at Veszprem.   Somewhat later, Bela and his queen built a convent for their daughter on an island in the Danube near Buda, and there, when she was twelve years old, she made her profession in the hands of Bd Humbert of Romans. Horrifying as are the details of the young sister's thirst for penance and of her determination to conquer all natural repugnances, they are supported by such a mass of concurrent testimony that it is impossible to question the truth of what we read.   That she was exceptionally favoured in the matter of good looks seems to be proved by the determination of Ottokar, King of Bohemia, to seek her hand even after he had seen her in her religious dress.   No doubt a dispensation could easily have been obtained for such a marriage, and Bela for political reasons was inclined to favour it.   But Margaret declared that she would cut off her nose and lips rather than consent to leave the cloister, and no one who reads the account which her sisters gave of her resolution in other matters can doubt that she would have been as good as her word.

Although the majority of the inmates of this Danubian convent were the daughters of noble families, Princess Margaret seems to have been conscious of a tendency to treat her with special consideration.   Her protest took the form of an almost extravagant choice of all that was menial, repulsive, exhausting and insanitary. Her charity and tenderness in rendering the most nauseating services to the sick were marvellous, but many of the details are such as cannot be set out before the fastidious modern reader.   She had an intense sympathy for the squalid lives of the poor, but she carried it so far that, like another St Benedict Joseph Labre, she chose to imitate them in her personal habits, and her fellow nuns confessed that there were times when they shrank from coming into too intimate contact with the noble princess, their sister in religion.   One gets the impression that Margaret's love of God and desire of self-immolation were associated with a certain element

176

of wilfulness. She would have been better, or at least she would assuredly have lived longer, if she had had a strong-minded superior or confessor to take her resolutely in hand ; but it was perhaps inevitable that the daughter of the royal founders to whom the convent owed everything should almost always have been able to get her own way.

On the other hand, there are many delightful human touches in the account her sisters gave of her. The sacristan tells how Margaret would stroke her hand and coax her to leave the door of the choir open after Compline, that she might spend the night before the Blessed Sacrament when she ought to have been sleeping. She was confident in the power of prayer to effect what she desired, and she carried this almost to the point of a certain imperiousness in the requests she made to the Almighty. Several of the nuns recall an incident which happened at Veszprem when she was only ten years old. Two Dominican friars came there on a short visit, and Margaret begged them to prolong their stay. They replied that it was necessary that they should return at once ; to which she responded, " I shall ask God that it may rain so hard that you cannot get away ". Although they protested that no amount of rain would detain them, she went to the chapel, and such a downpour occurred that they were unable, after all, to leave Veszprem as they had intended. This recalls the well-known story of St Scholastica and St Benedict, and there is in any case no need to invoke a supernatural intervention ; but there are so many such incidents vouched for by the sisters in their evidence on oath that it is difficult to stretch coincidence so far as to explain them all. Though we hear of ecstasies and of a great number of miracles, there is a certain moderation in the depositions which inspires confidence in the good faith of the witnesses. An incident which is mentioned by nearly all is the saving, at St Margaret's prayer, of a maid-servant who had fallen down a well. Amongst the other depositions we have that of the maid, Agnes, herself. Asked in general what she knew of Margaret, she was content to say that " she was good and holy and edifying in her conduct, and showed greater humility than we serving-maids ". As to the accident, we learn from her that the evening was so dark that " if anyone had slapped her face she could not have seen who did it ", and that the orifice of the well was quite open and without a rail, and that after falling she sank to the bottom three times, but at last managed to clutch the wall of the well until they lowered a rope and pulled her out.

There can be little room for doubt that Margaret shortened her life by her austerities. At the end of every Lent she was in a pitiable state from fasting, deprivation of sleep and neglect of her person.* She put the crown on her indiscretions on Maundy Thursday by washing the feet (this probably she claimed as a sort of privilege which belonged to her as the daughter of the royal founders) not only of all the choir nuns, seventy in number, but of all the servants as well. She wiped their feet, the nuns tell us, with the veil which she wore on her head. In spite of this fatigue and of the fact that at this season she took neither food nor sleep, she complained to some of the sisters in her confidence that " Good Friday was the shortest day of the year ". She had no time for all the prayers she wanted to say

---

* This neglect of cleanliness was traditionally part of the penitential discipline, and was symbolized by the ashes received on Ash Wednesday. The old English name for Maundy Thursday was " Sheer Thursday ", when the penitents obtained absolution, trimmed their hair and beards, and washed in preparation for Easter. It was also sometimes called *capitilavium* (head-washing).

and for all the acts of penance she wanted to perform. St Margaret seems to have died on January 18, 1270, at the age of twenty-eight; the process of beatification referred to above was never finished, but the *cultus* was approved in 1789 and she was canonized in 1943.

See the *Acta Sanctorum* for January 28; but more especially G. Fraknoi, *Monumenta Romana Episcopatus Vesprimiensis*, vol. i, pp. 163-383, where the depositions of the witnesses are printed in full. *Cf.* also M. C. de Ganay, *Les Bienheureuses Dominicaines*, pp. 69-89; and *Margaret, Princess of Hungary* (1945), by " S. M. C."

27 : ST JOHN CHRYSOSTOM, Archbishop of Constantinople and Doctor of the Church   (A.D. 407)

THIS incomparable teacher, on account of the fluency and sweetness of his eloquence, obtained after his death the surname of Chrysostom, or Golden Mouth. But his piety and his undaunted courage are titles far more glorious, by which he may claim to be ranked among the greatest pastors of the Church. He was born about the year 347 at Antioch in Syria, the only son of Secundus, commander of the imperial troops. His mother, Anthusa, left a widow at twenty, divided her time between the care of her family and her exercises of devotion. Her example made such an impression on our saint's master, a celebrated pagan sophist, that he could not forbear crying out, " What wonderful women are found among the Christians ! " Anthusa provided for her son the ablest masters which the empire at that time afforded. Eloquence was esteemed the highest accomplishment, and John studied that art under Libanius, the most famous orator of the age; and such was his proficiency that even in his youth he excelled his masters. Libanius being asked on his deathbed who ought to succeed him in his school, " John ", said he, " would have been my choice, had not the Christians stolen him from us."

According to a common custom of those days young John was not baptized till he was over twenty years old, being at the time a law student. Soon after, together with his friends Basil, Theodore (afterwards bishop of Mopsuestia) and others, he attended a sort of school for monks, where they studied under Diodorus of Tarsus; and in 374 he joined one of the loosely-knit communities of hermits among the mountains south of Antioch. He afterwards wrote a vivid account of their austerities and trials. He passed four years under the direction of a veteran Syrian monk, and afterwards two years in a cave as a solitary. The dampness of this abode brought on a dangerous illness, and for the recovery of his health he was obliged to return into the city in 381. He was ordained deacon by St Meletius that very year, and received the priesthood from Bishop Flavian in 386, who at the same time constituted him his preacher, John being then about forty. He discharged the duties of the office for twelve years, supporting during that time a heavy load of responsibility as the aged bishop's deputy. The instruction and care of the poor he regarded as the first obligation of all, and he never ceased in his sermons to recommend their cause and to impress on the people the duty of almsgiving. Antioch, he supposes, contained at that time one hundred thousand Christian souls and as many pagans; these he fed with the word of God, preaching several days in the week, and frequently several times on the same day.

The Emperor Theodosius I, finding himself obliged to levy a new tax on his subjects because of his war with Magnus Maximus, the Antiochenes rioted and vented their discontent on the emperor's statue, and those of his father, sons and late consort, breaking them to pieces. The magistrates were helpless. But as soon as the fury was over and they began to reflect on the probable consequences of their outburst, the people were seized with terror and their fears were heightened by the arrival of two officers from Constantinople to carry out the emperor's orders for punishment. In spite of his age, Bishop Flavian set out in the worst weather of the year to implore the imperial clemency for his flock, and Theodosius was touched by his appeal : an amnesty was accorded to the delinquent citizens of Antioch. Meanwhile St John had been delivering perhaps the most memorable series of sermons which marked his oratorical career, the famous twenty-one homilies " On the Statutes ". They manifest in a wonderful way the sympathy between the preacher and his audience, and also his own consciousness of the power which he wielded for good. There can be no question that the Lent of 387, during which these discourses were delivered, marked a turning-point in Chrysostom's career, and that from that time forward his oratory became, even politically, one of the great forces by which the Eastern empire was swayed. After the storm he continued his labours with unabated energy, but before very long God was pleased to call him to glorify His name upon a new stage, where He prepared for his virtue other trials and other crowns.

Nectarius, Archbishop of Constantinople, dying in 397, the Emperor Arcadius, at the suggestion of Eutropius, his chamberlain, resolved to procure the election of John to the see of that city. He therefore despatched an order to the count of the East, enjoining him to send John to Constantinople, but to do so without making the news public, lest his intended removal should cause a sedition. The count repaired to Antioch, and desiring the saint to accompany him out of the city to the tombs of the martyrs, he there delivered him to an officer who, taking him into his chariot, conveyed him with all possible speed to the imperial city. Theophilus, Archbishop of Alexandria, a man of proud and turbulent spirit, had come thither to recommend a nominee of his own for the vacancy ; but he had to desist from his intrigues, and John was consecrated by him on February 26 in 398.

When regulating his domestic concerns, the saint cut down the expenses which his predecessors had considered necessary to maintain their dignity, and these sums he applied to the relief of the poor and supported many hospitals. His own household being settled in good order, the next thing he took in hand was the reformation of his clergy. This he forwarded by zealous exhortations and by disciplinary enactments, which, while very necessary, seem in their severity to have been lacking in tact. But to give these his endeavours their due force, he lived himself as an exact model of what he inculcated on others. The immodesty of women in their dress in that gay capital aroused him to indignation, and he showed how false and absurd was their excuse in saying that they meant no harm. Thus by his zeal and eloquence St John tamed many sinners, converting, moreover, many idolaters and heretics. His mildness towards sinners was censured by the Nova-tians ; for he invited them to repentance with the compassion of a most tender father, and was accustomed to cry out, " If you have fallen a second time, or even a thousand times into sin, come to me, and you shall be healed ". But he was firm and severe in maintaining discipline, and to impenitent sinners he was inflexible. One Good Friday many Christians went to the races, and on Holy Saturday crowded to the games in the stadium.   The good bishop was pierced to the quick, and on Easter Sunday he preached an impassioned sermon, " Against the Games and Shows of the Theatre and Circus ".   Indignation made him not so much as mention the paschal solemnity, and his exordium was a most moving appeal.   A large number of Chrysostom's sermons still exist, and they amply support the view of many that he was the greatest preacher who ever lived.   But it must be admitted that his language was at times, especially in his later years, excessively violent and provocative.   As has been observed, he " sometimes almost shrieks at his delinquent empresses " ;   and one has a painful feeling that his invective in face of undoubted provocation from many Jews must have been partly responsible for the frequent bloody collisions between them and Christians in Antioch.   Not all Chrysostom's opponents were blameworthy men : there were undoubtedly good and earnest Christians amongst those who disagreed with him—he who became St Cyril of Alexandria among them.

Another good work which absorbed a large share of the archbishop's activities was the founding of new and fervent communities of devout women.   Among the holy widows who placed themselves under the direction of this great master of saints, the most illustrious, perhaps, was the truly noble St Olympias.   Neither was his pastoral care confined to his own flock ; he extended it to remote countries. He sent a bishop to instruct the wandering Scythians ; another, an admirable man, to the Goths.   Palestine, Persia and many other distant provinces felt the beneficent influence of his zeal.   He was himself remarkable for an eminent spirit of prayer, and he was particularly earnest in inculcating this duty.   He even exhorted the laity to rise for the midnight office together with the clergy.   " Many artisans ", said he, " get up at night to labour, and soldiers keep vigil as sentries ; cannot you do as much to praise God ? "   Great also was the tenderness with which he discoursed on the divine love which is displayed in the holy Eucharist, and exhorted the faithful to the frequent use of that heavenly sacrament.   The public concerns of the state often claimed a share in the interest and intervention of St Chrysostom, as when the chamberlain and ex-slave Eutropius fell from power in 399, on which occasion he preached a famous sermon while the hated Eutropius cowered in sanctuary beneath the altar in full view of the congregation.   The bishop entreated the people to forgive a culprit whom the emperor, the chief person injured, was desirous to forgive ; he asked them how they could beg of God the forgiveness of their own sins if they did not forgive one who stood in need of mercy and time for repentance.

It remained for St Chrysostom to glorify God by his sufferings, as he had already done by his labours, and, if we contemplate the mystery of the Cross with the eyes of faith, we shall find him greater in the persecutions he sustained than in all the other occurrences of his life.   His principal ecclesiastical adversary was Archbishop Theophilus of Alexandria, already mentioned, who had several grievances against his brother of Constantinople.   A no less dangerous enemy was the empress Eudoxia.   John was accused of referring to her as " Jezebel ", and when he had preached a sermon against the profligacy and vanity of so many women it was represented by some as an attack levelled at the empress.   Knowing the sense of grievance entertained by Theophilus, Eudoxia, to be revenged for the supposed affront to herself, conspired with him to bring about Chrysostom's deposition.   Theophilus landed at Constantinople in June 403, with several Egyptian bishops ; he refused to see or lodge with John ; and got together a cabal of thirty-six bishops in a house at Chalcedon called The Oak. The main articles in the impeachment were : that John had deposed a deacon for beating a servant ; that he had called several of his clergy reprobates ; had deposed bishops outside his own province ; had sold things belonging to the church ; that nobody knew what became of his revenues ; that he ate alone ; and that he gave holy communion to persons who were not fasting—all which accusations were either false or frivolous. John held a legal council of forty bishops in the city at the same time, and refused to appear before that at The Oak. So the cabal proceeded to a sentence of deposition against him, which they sent to the Emperor Arcadius, accusing him at the same time of treason, apparently in having called the empress " Jezebel ". Thereupon the emperor issued an order for his banishment.

For three days Constantinople was in an uproar, and Chrysostom delivered a vigorous manifesto from his pulpit. " Violent storms encompass me on all sides : yet I am without fear, because I stand upon a rock. Though the sea roar and the waves rise high, they cannot overwhelm the ship of Jesus Christ. I fear not death, which is my gain ; nor banishment, for the whole earth is the Lord's ; nor the loss of goods, for I came naked into the world, and I can carry nothing out of it." He declared that he was ready to lay down his life for his flock, and that if he suffered now, it was only because he had neglected nothing that would help towards the salvation of their souls. Then he surrendered himself, unknown to the people, and an official conducted him to Praenetum in Bithynia. But his first exile was short. The city was slightly shaken by an earthquake. This terrified the super-stitious Eudoxia, and she implored Arcadius to recall John ; she got leave to send a letter the same day, asking him to return and protesting her own innocence of his banishment. All the city went out to meet him, and the Bosphorus blazed with torches. Theophilus and his party fled by night.

But the fair weather did not last long. A silver statue of the empress having been erected before the great church of the Holy Wisdom, the dedication of it was celebrated with public games which, besides disturbing the liturgy, were an occasion of disorder, impropriety and superstition. St Chrysostom had often preached against licentious shows, and the very place rendered these the more inexcusable. And so, fearing lest his silence should be construed as an approbation of the abuse, he with his usual freedom and courage spoke loudly against it. The vanity of the Empress Eudoxia made her take the affront to herself, and his enemies were invited back. Theophilus dared not come, but he sent three deputies. This second cabal appealed to certain canons of an Arian council of Antioch, made to exclude St Athanasius, by which it was ordained that no bishop who had been deposed by a synod should return to his see till he was restored by another synod. Arcadius sent John an order to withdraw. He refused to forsake a church committed to him by God unless forcibly compelled to leave it. The emperor sent troops to drive the people out of the churches on Holy Saturday, and they were polluted with blood and all manner of outrages. The saint wrote to Pope St Innocent I, begging him to invalidate all that had been done, for the miscarriage of justice had been notorious. He also wrote to beg the concurrence of other bishops of the West. The pope wrote to Theophilus exhorting him to appear before a council, where sentence should be given according to the canons of Nicaea. He also addressed letters to Chrysostom, to his flock and several of his friends, in the hope of redressing these evils by a new council, as did also the Western emperor, Honorius. But Arcadius and Eudoxia found means to prevent any such assembly, the mere prospect of which filled Theophilus and other ringleaders of his faction with alarm.

Chrysostom was suffered to remain at Constantinople two months after Easter. On Thursday in Whit-week the emperor sent an order for his banishment. The holy man bade adieu to the faithful bishops, and took his leave of St Olympias and the other deaconesses, who were overwhelmed with grief. He then left the church by stealth to prevent a sedition, and was conducted into Bithynia, arriving at Nicaea on June 20, 404. After his departure a fire broke out and burnt down the great church and the senate house. The cause of the conflagration was unknown, and many of the saint's supporters were put to the torture on this account, but no discovery was ever made. The Emperor Arcadius chose Cucusus, a little place in the Taurus mountains of Armenia, for St John's exile. He set out from Nicaea in July, and suffered very great hardships from the heat, fatigue and the brutality of his guards. After a seventy days' journey he arrived at Cucusus, where the good bishop of the place vied with his people in showing him every mark of kindness and respect. Some of the letters which Chrysostom addressed from exile to St Olympias and others have survived, and it was to her that he wrote his treatise on the theme " That no one can hurt him who does not hurt himself ".

Meanwhile Pope Innocent and the Emperor Honorius sent five bishops to Constantinople to arrange for a council, requiring that in the meantime Chrysostom should be restored to his see. But the deputies were cast into prison in Thrace, for the party of Theophilus (Eudoxia had died in childbed in October) saw that if a council were held they would inevitably be condemned. They also got an order from Arcadius that John should be taken farther away, to Pityus at the eastern end of the Black Sea, and two officers were sent to convey him thither. One of these was not altogether destitute of humanity, but the other was a ruffian who would not give his prisoner so much as a civil word. They often travelled in scorching heat, from which the now aged Chrysostom suffered intensely ; and in the wettest weather they forced him out of doors and on his way. When they reached Comana in Cappadocia he was very ill, yet he was hurried a further five or six miles to the chapel of St Basiliscus. During the night there this martyr seemed to appear to John and said to him, " Courage, brother ! To-morrow we shall be together." The next day, exhausted and ill, John begged that he might stay there a little longer. No attention was paid ; but when they had gone four miles, seeing that he seemed to be dying, they brought him back to the chapel. There the clergy changed his clothes, putting white garments on him, and he received the Holy Mysteries. A few hours later St John Chrysostom uttered his last words, " Glory be to God for all things ", and gave up his soul to God. It was Holy Cross day, September 14, 407.

St John's body was taken back to Constantinople in the year 438, the Emperor Theodosius II and his sister St Pulcheria accompanying the archbishop St Proclus in the procession, begging forgiveness of the sins of their parents who had so blindly persecuted the servant of God. It was laid in the church of the Apostles on January 27, on which day Chrysostom is honoured in the West, but in the East his festival is observed principally on November 13, but also on other dates. In the Byzantine church he is the third of the Three Holy Hierarchs and Universal Teachers, the other two being St Basil and St Gregory Nazianzen, to whom the Western church adds St Athanasius to make the four great Greek doctors ; and in 1909 St Pius X declared him to be the heavenly patron of preachers of the word of God.   He is commemorated in the Byzantine, Syrian, Chaldean and Maronite eucharistic liturgies, in the great intercession or elsewhere.

Our principal sources for the story of St John's life are the *Dialogue* of Palladius (whom Abbot Cuthbert Butler, with the assent of nearly all recent scholars, considers to be identical with the author of the *Lausiac History*), the autobiographical details which may be gleaned from the homilies and letters of the saint himself, the ecclesiastical histories of Socrates and Sozomen, and the panegyric attributed to a certain Martyrius.   The literature of the subject is, of course, vast.   No better general account can be recommended, especially in view of its admirable setting in a background which does justice to the circumstances of the times, than that provided by Mgr Duchesne in his *Histoire ancienne de l'Église* (English trans.), vols. ii and iii ; but the definitive biography is by Dom C. Baur, *Der hl. Johannes Chrysostomus und seine Zeit* (2 vols., 1929-1930).   An English translation of the *Dialogue* of Palladius was published in 1921, and the Greek text, ed. P. R. Coleman-Norton, in 1928.   In English at the general level mention may be made of lives by W. R. W. Stephens (1883) and D. Attwater (1939), and Dr A. Fortescue's lively sketch in *The Greek Fathers* (1908).   A good introduction to the works is (Greek) *Selections from St John Chrysostom* (1940), ed. Cardinal D'Alton.   See also Puech, *St John Chrysostom* (English trans.) in the series " Les Saints " ; the volume of essays brought out at Rome in 1908, under the title Χρυσοστομικά, in honour of the fifteenth centenary ; the article by Canon E. Venables in DCB., vol. i, pp. 518-535 ; and that by G. Bardy in DTC., vol viii, cc. 660 *seq.*, where a full bibliography will be found.

ST JULIAN, Bishop of Le Mans   (Date Unknown)

In Alban Butler's time a relic was preserved at the cathedral of Le Mans which was believed to be the head of St Julian.   He was certainly also honoured in England, for his name occurs on this day in the calendar of the Eadwine Psalter of Trinity College, Cambridge (before 1170), and his feast was kept throughout the southern dioceses of England where the Sarum use was followed.   How many of the six ancient churches in this country which were dedicated to St Julian can be referred to the bishop of Le Mans is quite uncertain, for undoubtedly some of them were built in honour of the more or less mythical saint known as Julian the Hospitaller (February 12).   We know absolutely nothing which is certain about St Julian's life.   The lessons in the Sarum breviary describe him as a noble Roman who became the first bishop of Le Mans and the apostle of that part of France, and they also attribute to him some stupendous miracles.   We can only say that there is evidence in the seventh century of a chapel called *basilica Sti Juliani episcopi,* and that in the catalogues of the bishops of Le Mans, St Julian always heads the list.   A quite extravagant later legend described him as one of the seventy-two disciples of our Lord, and as identical with Simon the Leper.   It is probable that the introduction of the *cultus* of St Julian into England was due to the fact that King Henry II, who was born at Le Mans, is said to have been baptized in the church of St Julian there and may have preserved some personal devotion to the saint.

See Duchesne, *Fastes Épiscopaux*, vol. ii, pp. 309, 323, 331 ; the *Acta Sanctorum* for January 27 ; Arnold-Forster, *Studies in Church Dedications*, vol.   pp. 435-436 ; and especially A. Ledru, *Les premiers temps de l'Église du Mans* (1913).

ST MARIUS, or MAY, Abbot   (c. A.D. 555)

We have no very certain information concerning St Marius, who in the Roman Martyrology appears as Maurus, while Bobacum is given as the name of the monastery which he governed.   Both these designations seem to be erroneous.

There was an abbey of Bodon in the ancient diocese of Sisteron (Département de la Drôme), and St Marius is named as its founder and first abbot. We are told that he was born at Orleans ; that he became a monk and made a pilgrimage to the tomb of St Denis near Paris, where he was miraculously cured of an illness ; and that every year he used to spend the forty days of Lent as a recluse in the forest. In one of these retreats he foresaw in a vision the desolation which the inroads of the barbarians would soon cause in Italy, and also the destruction of his own monastery. But the evidence for all this is quite unreliable.

See the *Acta Sanctorum* for January 27 ; *Analecta Bollandiana*, vol. xxiv, pp. 96 *seq. ;* and Isnard in *Bulletin Soc. Archéol. Drôme*, vols. i and ii (1866–68).

ST VITALIAN, POPE   (A.D. 672)

POPE VITALIAN is said to have been a native of Segni in Campania, but we hear nothing of him before he was elected to the papacy in 657, nor have we any know-ledge of his life apart from his public acts. His pontificate was somewhat troubled by the strong monothelite leanings of two successive patriarchs of Constantinople and of the Emperor Constans II and his successor. A more consoling picture is offered by the pope's relations with the Church in England, as they may be read in the pages of Bede. It was in his time that St Benedict Biscop paid his first visit to Rome and that the differences between the Anglo-Saxon and Celtic bishops regarding the keeping of Easter and other points of controversy were settled at the Council of Streaneshalch (Whitby). It was also Pope St Vitalian who sent to England St Theodore of Tarsus as archbishop of Canterbury, and the African monk St Adrian, who became abbot of St Augustine's. The influence of both was very great in training the Anglo-Saxon clergy and in drawing closer the bonds between England and the Holy See. St Vitalian died in 672, and was buried in St Peter's.

Our principal sources are the *Liber Pontificalis* (ed. Duchesne), vol. i, pp. 343 *seq. ;* Bede's *Ecclesiastical History ;* and the pope's letters, though some of those attributed to him are spurious. See also the *Acta Sanctorum* for January 27, and DCB., vol. iv, pp. 1161–1163.

BD JOHN OF WARNETON, BISHOP OF THÉROUANNE   (A.D. 1130)

WE possess a contemporary biography of this John which was written by his archdeacon, John de Collemedi. A pious and clever child, he had attracted attention in early years and had been fortunate enough to number amongst his teachers Lambert of Utrecht and St Ivo of Chartres. After completing his studies he returned to his own province, and shortly afterwards retired to the monastery of Mont-Saint-Eloi, near Arras. Here the bishop of Arras became acquainted with him and, in spite of his reluctance, persuaded him to act as archdeacon in his diocese ; this was a stepping-stone to promotion to the see of Thérouanne. It needed an exercise of papal authority to constrain John to undertake the charge. As bishop he was held in the highest esteem ; the Holy See confided to him many important missions, more particularly in the matter of the reform of monastic discipline, and he was consulted by such prelates as his old master, St Ivo. Al-though firm in maintaining ecclesiastical discipline, he was pre-eminently gentle and kindly by nature : when an attempt was made to assassinate him, Bd John refused to take any action against the perpetrators of the outrage. His death occurred on January 27, 1130.

See the *Acta Sanctorum* for January 27 ; the *Biographie nationale*, vol. x, pp. 422-423 : and Destombes, *Vies des saints des diocèses de Cambrai et d'Arras*, vol. i, pp. 113-125.

28 * : ST PETER NOLASCO, Founder of the Order of Our Lady of Ransom (A.D. 1258)

PETER, of the noble family of Nolasco in Languedoc, was born about the year 1189. At the age of fifteen he lost his father, who left him heir to a great estate ; and he remained at home under the tutelage of a mother who encouraged all his good aspirations. Being solicited to marry, he set himself first to ponder seriously the vanity of earthly things ; and rising one night full of those thoughts, he prostrated himself in prayer which continued till morning, consecrating himself to God in the state of celibacy and dedicating his whole patrimony to His service. Some authors affirm that Peter took part in the campaign of Simon de Montfort against the Albigenses. The count vanquished them, and in the battle of Muret defeated and killed Peter, King of Aragon, and took his son James prisoner, a child of six years old. The conqueror is further said to have given him Peter Nolasco, then twenty-five years old, for a tutor, and to have sent them both together into Spain. But it is now generally admitted that there is no adequate evidence for connecting St Peter with the Albigensian campaign or with the education of the future King James.

The Moors at that time were masters of a great part of Spain, and numbers of Christians who had been made slaves groaned under their tyranny both there and in Africa. Compassion for the poor had always been the distinguishing virtue of Peter. The pitiful spectacle of these unfortunates, and the consideration of the dangers to which their faith and virtue stood exposed under their Mohammedan masters, touched his heart, and he soon spent his estate in redeeming as many as he could. Whenever he saw any slaves, he used to say, " Behold eternal treasures which never fail ". By his fervent appeals he moved others to contribute large alms towards this charity, and at last formed the project of instituting a religious order to maintain a constant supply of men and means whereby to carry on so charitable an undertaking. This design encountered many difficulties ; but it is said that our Lady appeared to St Peter, to the king of Aragon and to St Raymund of Peñafort in distinct visions on the same night, and encouraged them to carry the scheme into effect under the assurance of her patronage and protection. St Raymund was the spiritual director both of St Peter and of King James, and a zealous promoter of this work. The king declared himself the protector of the order, and assigned them quarters in his own palace by way of a commencement. On August 10, 1223 the king and St Raymund conducted St Peter to the church, and presented him to Berengarius, Bishop of Barcelona, who received his three religious vows, to which the saint added a fourth, to devote his whole substance and his very liberty, if necessary, to the work of ransoming slaves. The like vow was exacted of all his followers. St Raymund preached on the occasion, and

* For the commemoration of St Agnes on this day, see under that saint on January 21.

185

declared that it had pleased Almighty God to reveal His will to King James, to Peter Nolasco and to himself, enjoining the institution of an order for the ransom of the faithful detained in bondage among the infidels.* This was received by the people with acclamation. St Peter received the new habit from St Raymund, who established him first master general of the order, and drew up for it rules and constitutions. Two other gentlemen were professed at the same time with St Peter. When Raymund went to Rome, he obtained from Pope Gregory IX in 1235 the confirmation of the foundation and its rule.

King James having conquered the kingdom of Valencia, founded in it several houses of the order, one of which was in the city of Valencia itself. The town had been taken by the aid of Peter Nolasco's prayers, when the soldiers had despaired of success, and it was in fact to the prayers of the saint that the king attributed the great victories which he obtained over the infidels, and the entire conquest of Valencia and Murcia. St Peter, touching the main work of the order, ordained that two members should always be sent together amongst the infidels, to treat about the ransom of captives, and they are hence called ransomers. One of the two employed at the outset in this way was the saint himself, and Valencia was the first place which was blessed with his labours ; the second was Granada. He not only comforted and ransomed a great number, but by his charity and example was the instrument of inducing many Mohammedans to embrace the faith of Christ. He made several other journeys to those regions of the coast of Spain which were held by the Moors, besides a voyage to Algiers, where he underwent imprisonment. But the most terrifying dangers could never make him desist from his endeavours for the conversion of the infidels, burning as he was with a desire of martyrdom.

St Peter resigned the offices of ransomer and master general some years before his death, which took place on Christmas day 1256. In his last moments he exhorted his religious to perseverance, and concluded with those words of the psalmist : " The Lord hath sent redemption to His people ; He hath commanded His covenant for ever ". He then recommended his soul to God, appealing to the charity which brought Jesus Christ from Heaven to redeem us from the captivity of the Devil, and so died, being in the sixty-seventh year of his age. His relics were honoured by many miracles, and he was canonized in 1628.

Alban Butler's account of St Peter Nolasco, summarized above without substantial change, represents the version of his story which is traditional in the Mercedarian Order. But it must be confessed that hardly any detail in this narrative has escaped trenchant criticism, and that, to say the least, the facts connected with the foundation of the order are wrapped in hopeless uncertainty. Great disagreement exists, even in Mercedarian sources, regarding the date of the ceremonial foundation in the presence of Bishop Berengarius. By some this event is assigned to 1218 ; by others, as above, to 1223 ; by others again to 1228 ; and by Father Vacas Galindo, o.p., in his *San Raimundo de Peñafort* (1919), to 1234. As pointed out above under January 23, a rather heated controversy arose between the Dominicans and the Mercedarians, the former attributing a predominant influence in the creation of this work for the redemption of captives to the great Dominican, St Raymund of Peñafort ; the latter contending that he was merely

* Members of the Order of Our Lady of Ransom are commonly called Mercedarians Spanish *merced* = ransom. They now engage in general apostolic and charitable work, though the vow to ransom captives is still taken at profession.

the confidant of St Peter and that at the time of the foundation he was not yet a Dominican but a canon of Barcelona. One extremely suspicious feature in the Mercedarian case cannot easily be explained away. At the beginning of the seventeenth century, when the cause of the canonization of St Peter Nolasco was being pressed at Rome, there was discovered most opportunely behind a brick wall in the Mercedarian house at Barcelona an iron casket full of documents, hitherto quite unknown, which purported to establish upon irrefragable evidence just the points on which the promoters of the cause were most anxious to insist. The most famous of these, known as the *documento de los sellos* (the deed with the seals) was a notarial act drafted in 1260—so at least the document itself affirmed—with the express object of being submitted to the Holy See in vindication of St Peter's claims to sanctity. Now this deed, which contains an account of the apparition of our Lady to Peter himself, to King James and to Señor Raimundo de Peñafort (and which states that a swarm of bees built a honeycomb in Peter's hand when he was an infant in the cradle), after being cited for nearly three centuries as the most authentic memorial of the saint's history is now admitted to be a forgery. It is Father Gazulla himself, the Mercedarian champion (in a paper read before the Literary Academy of Barcelona, *Al Margen de una Refutacion*, 1921) who has shown that Pedro Bages, the notary whose name appears as drafting the document of the seals in 1260, had died before February 4, 1259. When this primary instrument is thus proved to be spurious, what possible value can attach to the rest of the contents of the suspicious iron casket ? It would serve no good purpose to pursue the matter further.

See the book of Fr Vacas Galindo, o.p., referred to above ; Fr P. N. Perez Merc., *San Pedro Nolasco* (1915) ; M. Even, *Une page de l'histoire de la charité* (1918) ; *Analecta Bollandiana*, vol. xxxix (1921), pp. 209 seq., and vol. xl (1922), pp. 442 seq. ; and two articles by Fr Kneller, s.j., in *Stimmen aus Maria Laach*, vol. li (1896), at pp. 272 and 357. Fr F. D. Gazulla has produced several volumes on the Mercedarian side, notably a *Refutacion* of Fr Galindo's book in 1920, and in 1934 *La Orden de N.S. de la Merced. : Estudios histórico-criticos*, 1218–1317 ; on this last *cf. Analecta Bollandiana*, vol. lv (1937), pp. 412–415.

## ST JOHN OF REOMAY, Abbot	(*c.* A.D. 544)

ALTHOUGH we have a good early biography of Abbot John, the story it tells is a very simple one. He was a native of the diocese of Langres, and took the monastic habit at Lérins. Later on he was recalled into his own country by the bishop to found the abbey from which he received his surname, but which was afterwards called Moutier-Saint-Jean. He governed it for many years with a great reputation of sanctity, and was rendered famous by miracles. It is recorded of him that he refused to converse with his own mother when she came to the abbey to visit him. He showed himself to her, however, at a distance, sent her a message to encourage her to aim at a high standard of virtue, and warned her that she would not behold him again until they met in Heaven. He went to God about the year 544, when more than a hundred years old, and was one of the pioneers of the monastic state in France.

The biography of St John of Reomay has been edited by B. Krusch in MGH., *Scriptores Merov.*, vol. iii, pp. 502–517. As Krusch has shown in his article " Zwei Heiligenleben des Jonas von Susa ", in the *Mittheilungen* of the Austrian Historical Society, vol. xiv, pp. 385 seq., the texts previously edited have no value. The author of the *vita* was Jonas of Susa, and not a contemporary.

ST PAULINUS, PATRIARCH OF AQUILEIA   (A.D. 804)

ONE of the most illustrious and holy prelates of the eighth and ninth centuries was this Paulinus of Aquileia, who seems to have been born about the year 726 in a country farm not far from Friuli.   His family had no other revenue than what they made by their farm, and he spent part of his youth tilling the soil.   Yet he found leisure for studies, and in process of time became so famous as a grammarian and professor that Charlemagne wrote to him, addressing him as Master of Grammar and Very Venerable.   This epithet seems to imply that he was then a priest.   The same monarch, in recognition of his merit, bestowed on him an estate in his own country.   It seems to have been about the year 776 that Paulinus was promoted, against his will, to the patriarchate of Aquileia,* and from the zeal, piety and talents of St Paulinus this church derived its greatest lustre.   Charlemagne required him to attend all the great councils which were held in his time, however remote the place of assembly, and he convened a synod himself at Friuli in 791 or 796 against the errors which were then being propagated against the mystery of the Incarnation.

The more serious of these false teachings took the form of what is known as the Adoptionist heresy.   Felix, Bishop of Urgel in Catalonia, professed to prove that Christ, as man, is not the natural but only the adoptive Son of God.   St Paulinus set to work to confute him in a work which he transmitted to Charlemagne. He was not less concerned in the conversion of the heathen than in the suppression of error, and was instrumental in preaching the gospel to those idolaters in Carinthia and Styria who as yet remained in their superstitions.   At the same time the conquest of the Avars by Pepin opened a new field for the bishop's zeal, and many of them received the faith through missionaries sent by St Paulinus and the bishops of Salzburg.   Paulinus strongly opposed the baptism of barbarians before they had received proper instruction and the attempt—so common in those days—to force Christianity upon them by violence.

When the duke of Friuli was appointed governor over the Hunnish tribes which he had lately conquered, St Paulinus wrote for his use an excellent " Exhortation ", in which he urges him to aspire after Christian perfection, and lays down rules on the practice of penance, on the remedies against different vices, especially pride, on an earnest desire to please God in all our actions, on prayer and its essential dispositions, on holy communion, on shunning bad company, and on other matters.   He closes the book with a most useful prayer, and in the beginning promises to pray for the salvation of the good duke.   By his fervent supplications he never ceased to draw down the blessings of the divine mercy on the souls committed to his charge.   Alcuin earnestly besought him, whenever he offered the spotless Victim at the altar, to implore the divine mercy on his behalf. St Paulinus closed a holy life by a happy death on January 11, 804.

The works of St Paulinus have been edited by J. F. Madrisi, and will be found in Migne, *PL.*, vol. xcix, cc. 17–130 ; see also the *Acta Sanctorum* for January 11 ; C. Giannoni, *Paulinus II, Patriarch von Aquileia* (1896) ; and DCB., vol. iv, pp. 246–248.

BD CHARLEMAGNE   (A.D. 814)

THE life of Charlemagne (born in 742 ; king of the Franks, 768 ; first Holy Roman emperor, 800 ; died, 814) belongs to general history, and his is a somewhat

* For this title, see herein a footnote under St Laurence Giustiniani on September 5.

surprising name to find in any book of saints. There does not appear to
have been any noticeable *cultus* of him till 1166, when it began to develop
under the rather sinister auspices of Frederick Barbarossa ; and an antipope,
Guy of Crema (" Paschal III "), appears to have equivalently sanctioned it.
It is interesting to note that St Joan of Arc associated " St Charlemagne " with
the devotion she paid to St Louis of France, and that in 1475 the observance
of a feast in his honour was made obligatory throughout that country. Prosper
Lambertini, later Pope Benedict XIV, discusses the question at some length
in his great work on beatification and canonization, and he concludes that
the title Blessed may not improperly be allowed to so great a defender of the
Church and the papacy. To-day, however, the *cultus* of Charlemagne is confined to the keeping of a feast in his honour in Aachen and two Swiss
abbeys.

The main source of our more personal knowledge of Charlemagne is the biography
written by h s contemporary and friend Einhard, the best edition being that of G. Waitz in
MGH., *Scriptores*, vol. ii, and separately. See also the *Acta Sanctorum* for January 28, and
especially the long discussion of various controverted matters in DAC., vol. iii, with full
bibliographical references. *Cf.* also the remarks of E. Amann on Charlemagne's character
in Fliche and Martin, *Histoire de l'Église*, vol. vi, p. 200, and R. Folz, *Études sur le culte
liturgique de Charlemagne*   (1951).

ST AMADEUS, Bishop of Lausanne   (A.D. 1159)

This Amadeus was of the royal house of Franconia and born at the castle of Chatte
in Dauphiné in 1110. When he was eight years old his father, Amadeus of Clermont, Lord of Hauterive, took the religious habit at the Cistercian abbey of
Bonnevaux. Young Amadeus went to Bonnevaux to be educated there, but after
a time he and his father migrated to Cluny. Amadeus senior returned to the more
austere Cistercian house, while Amadeus junior went for a short time into the
household of the Emperor Henry V. He then received the Cistercian habit at
Clairvaux, where he lived for fourteen years. In 1139 the abbot of Hautecombe
in Savoy retired and St Bernard appointed Amadeus in his place ; the monastery
had adopted the reform only four years before and its temporal affairs were in a
bad way. St Amadeus encouraged the community to bear these extra hardships
cheerfully, and by careful administration got the monastery out of its difficulties.
In 1144 he accepted, by order of Pope Lucius II, the see of Lausanne, where he
was at once involved in struggles with the nobles of the diocese and a vain effort
to induce the Emperor Conrad to go to the help of the pope against Pierleone.
When Amadeus III, Duke of Savoy, went on the Second Crusade, St Amadeus
was appointed as a sort of co-regent with his son Humbert ; and four years before
his death he was made chancellor of Burgundy by Frederick Barbarossa. Nicholas,
the secretary of St Bernard, speaks highly of the virtues of this active bishop, and
his age-long *cultus* was approved in 1910. A number of sermons of St Amadeus
are extant.

There seems to be no early life of Amadeus, but an account of him has been compiled
from various sources in such works as the *Gallia Christiana*, vol. xv, pp. 346–348, and
Manrique, *Annales Cistercienses*, under the year 1158. A more modern survey of his
career will be found in the *Cistercienser-Chronik*, vol. xi (1891), pp. 50 *seq.* and vol. xxiii
(1911), pp. 297 *seq.* and see A. Dimier, *Amédée de Lausanne* (1949) in the series " Figures
monastiques ".

BD JAMES THE ALMSGIVER   (A.D. 1304)

THERE is, or at any rate once was, a curious contest between the Friars Minor and the Servites regarding the religious status of the servant of God who is known as James the Almsgiver.   The Servites keep his feast every year on this day in virtue of a rescript of Pope Pius IX, and he is described in their martyrology as a " confessor of the Third Order of the Servants of Blessed Mary the Virgin, whose memory remaineth for a blessing among his fellow-citizens ".   On the other hand, the Third Order of the Franciscans also claims him as a recruit, although his name does not occur in the general martyrology of the Friars Minor.   Mazzara in his *Leggendario Francescano* (1676) indignantly rejects the claim of the Servites to number Bd James among the adherents of their own religious family.

The essential features of the story as told by either party are the same.   James was the son of well-to-do parents at the small town of Città delle Pieve, not far from Chiusi in Lombardy, and studied for the law.   Hearing a sermon on the words, " He that doth not renounce all that he possesseth cannot be My disciple ", he determined to become a priest, and thereafter led a most ascetic life.   Not far from Città delle Pieve he discovered a hospital with a chapel which had been allowed to fall into ruin.   He restored the buildings, furnished it as well as he could, and then devoted himself to receiving and tending all the sick and afflicted for whom he could find room.   He also, we are told, used his legal knowledge in gratuitously helping and advising those who were oppressed, and in these ways became much beloved by the poor throughout the whole country.

It happened, however, that on inquiring into the past history of his hospice, James discovered that its revenues had been scandalously appropriated for their own emolument by former occupants of the see of Chiusi.   He respectfully represented the matter to the actual bishop, laying the documents before him, but could obtain no redress.   Then he felt it his duty to take proceedings in both the ecclesiastical and civil courts, and the case in the end was given in his favour.   The bishop dissembled his resentment, and invited James to dine with him, having previously hired a band of ruffians to waylay and assassinate him on his return. The conscientious student of Italian (and other) history has often regretfully to confess that the social and ecclesiastical life of the " ages of faith " was not always so ideal as certain apologists are inclined to represent it.   The plot was carried out successfully, and for a time no trace of the murdered man was discovered.   But some shepherds passing through the forest were astonished to come upon a pear-tree and other neighbouring shrubs in full blossom, though it was still winter.   Whilst they stood wondering and somewhat alarmed at the portent, they heard, we are told, a voice which said to them, " Have no fear ; I am James, the priest, who have been murdered for defending the rights of the Church and of the poor ". It would certainly be rash to guarantee the truth of this and other supernatural incidents which are said to have attended the discovery of the body and its interment in the chapel of the hospice.   But we are told that 174 years later the remains were found still incorrupt when a second translation took place.   The date given for the murder—Mazzara calls it the martyrdom—of Bd James is January 15, 1304.

See Mazzara, *Leggendario Francescano* (1676), vol. i, pp. 95–98 ; and Spoeri, *Lebensbilder aus dem Servitenorden* (1892), p. 605.

BD ANTONY OF AMANDOLA   (A.D. 1350)

BD ANTONY seems to have been born not far from Ascoli Piceno, about the year 1260. He joined the Augustinians in 1306, the year that St Nicholas of Tolentino went to his reward, and he is said to have tried to copy the example of that great luminary of the order during the whole of his religious life. He is especially commended for his patience and for his charity towards the poor, and a great number of miracles are reported to have been wrought at his intercession. He died in 1350, and is said to have been ninety years old. His body lies at Amandola, and his feast is kept not only by the Augustinian friars but at Ancona and throughout the neighbouring district.

See J. E. Stadler, *Heiligen Lexikon* (1861).

ST PETER THOMAS, TITULAR PATRIARCH OF CONSTANTINOPLE (A.D. 1366)

THE career of St Peter Thomas presents us with a curious combination of a religious vocation and a life spent in diplomacy. Born in 1305, of humble parentage, at the hamlet of Salles in the south-west of France, he at an early age came into contact with the Carmelites, and his abilities led them gladly to admit him into their noviceship at Condom; in 1342 he was made procurator general of the order. This appointment led to his taking up his abode in Avignon, then the residence of the popes, and also indicated that in spite of high spiritual ideals he was known to be pre-eminently a man of affairs. His remarkable eloquence became known, and he was asked to deliver the funeral oration of Clement VI. It may be said that from that time forth, although he always retained the simplicity of a friar, his life was entirely spent in difficult negotiations as the representative of the Holy See. To describe the political complications in which he was called upon to intervene would take much space. It must suffice to say that he was sent as papal legate to negotiate with Genoa, Milan and Venice; in 1354 he was consecrated bishop and represented the pope at Milan when the Emperor Charles IV was crowned king of Italy. Thence he proceeded to Serbia, and afterwards was charged with a mission to smooth the difficulties between Venice and Hungary; going on to Constantinople he was instructed to make another effort to reconcile the Byzantine church with the West.

What is most surprising in our days is that Innocent VI and Urban V seem to have placed Peter Thomas virtually in command of expeditions which were distinctly military in character. He was sent to Constantinople in 1359 with a large contingent of troops and contributions in money, himself holding the title of " Universal Legate to the Eastern Church "; and when in 1365 an expeditionary force was sent to make an attack on infidel Alexandria, again the legate had virtual direction of the enterprise. The expedition ended disastrously. In the assault the legate was more than once wounded with arrows, and when he died a holy death at Cyprus three months later (January 6, 1366) it was stated that these wounds had caused, or at least accelerated, the end, and he was hailed as a martyr.

It is probable that among the reasons which led to the many diplomatic missions of St Peter Thomas we must reckon the economy thus effected for the papal exchequer at a time when it was very much depleted, for he dispensed with all unnecessary pomp and state. So far as he was himself concerned he travelled in the poorest way, and he was willing to face the great hardships which such expeditions then entailed even upon the most illustrious.   We must also not forget that though his biographers write in a tone of rather indiscriminating panegyric, they are nevertheless agreed in proclaiming his own desire to evangelize the poor, his spirit of prayer, and the confidence which his holiness inspired in others.   There are not many human touches to be found in our principal source, the biography of Mézières, but it is a tribute to the impression which the bishop made on his contemporaries that Philip de Mézières, who was himself a devoted Christian and a statesman of eminence, should speak of his friend in terms of such unstinted praise.   A decree issued by the Holy See in 1608 authorized the celebration of St Peter's feast among the Carmelites as that of a bishop and martyr, but he has never been formally canonized.

See the *Acta Sanctorum* for January 29 : Fr Daniel, *Vita S. Petri Thomae* (1666) ; Parraud, *Vie de St Pierre Thomas* (1895) ; B. J. Smet, *Life   by P. de Mézières* (1954).

BD MARY OF PISA, Widow   (A.D. 1431)

The history of Bd Mary Mancini is a standing illustration of the principle that holiness depends very little upon external circumstances.   There is, in fact, no condition of life which the interior spirit may not sanctify.   Here we have a servant of God who was twice married and many times a mother, who then lived for several years in the world as a widow, joined a relaxed religious house, reformed it, and finally founded a community of exceptionally strict observance, in which she died at an advanced age in the fragrance of sanctity.

The Mancini were a distinguished family in Pisa at a time when terrible things were occurring owing to the political factions prevalent in the Italian cities.   We are told that Catherine (Mary was the name she afterwards took in religion) at the age of five and a half had an extraordinary experience.   In an ecstasy or vision she witnessed the torture on the rack of Peter Gambacorta, who had been accused of conspiracy and was sentenced by his enemies to be hanged.   The legend goes on to say that the child prayed so hard in her horror at what she witnessed that the rope broke with which Peter was being hanged, and that his judges then commuted the death penalty.   After this our Lady appeared to her and bade her say the Lord's Prayer and the Angelical Salutation for him seven times every day, because she would eventually be supported by his bounty.   Catherine was married at the age of twelve, and had two children.   Her first husband died when she was sixteen, and, yielding to family influence, she married again.   This union lasted eight years, and she bore her husband five children, nursing him also most devotedly for a year before his death ; her children seem to have all died young.

Great pressure was used to induce Catherine to marry a third time, but she was resolute in her refusal, and she gave herself up completely to works of piety and charity.   She converted her house into a hospital, and we are told strange stories of her drinking the wine with which she washed men's sores, on one occasion experiencing such intense sweetness and consolation in this conquest of her natural repugnance that she was convinced that the mysterious stranger whom she had been tending was no other than our Saviour Himself.   During this period she was under the direction of the Dominicans and joined their third order.   It was probably through them that she was brought into relation with St Catherine of Siena, and we still possess a letter of that great saint which was addressed to " Monna

Catarina e Monna Orsola ed altre donne di Pisa ".   She had ecstasies sometimes even in the streets, and on one occasion, when thus taken by surprise, was knocked down by a mule.   Eventually she entered the relaxed Dominican convent of Santa Croce, mainly with the object of bringing it back to stricter observance.   We are told that she effected a great reform, but Sister Mary, as she was now, aspired after a life of greater austerity.   Accordingly, with Bd Clare Gambacorta, she left Santa Croce to found a new community in a convent built for them by Clare's father, the same Peter Gambacorta for whom Mary had daily prayed.   The new foundation was greatly blessed, and became a model, the fame of which spread throughout Italy.   Here Bd Mary Mancini died on December 22, 1431.   Her *cultus* was approved in 1855.

See M. C. de Ganay, *Les Bienheureuses Dominicaines* (1913), pp. 237-250 ; and Procter, *Dominican Saints*, pp. 342-345.

BD JULIAN MAUNOIR   (A.D. 1683)

It cannot be said that the Christianity of seventeenth-century France is unknown among English-speaking Catholics, but there can be no doubt that its domestic missionary work is the aspect of which we have heard least.   Monsieur Olier in Paris, Monsieur Vincent all over the place—yes.   But St John Eudes in Normandy, St Peter Fourier in Lorraine, the Oratorian Father John Lejeune in the Limousin, Languedoc and Provence, St John Francis Regis in the Velay and Vivarais, of these we know little enough, and of the missions in Brittany perhaps nothing at all.   Yet these last, in Henri Bremond's opinion, were the most successful of any, and certainly the most " picturesque "   They are associated in the first place with the names of Dom Michael Le Nobletz and of Father Julian Maunoir who, born in the diocese of Rennes in 1606, became a Jesuit in 1625, and was beatified in 1951.

No doubt the godlessness and barbarity of the Bretons, and the negligence of their clergy, at this time have been exaggerated, just as the woeful state of the Cornish before Wesley and the Welsh before Howel Harris and Griffith Jones and Daniel Rowlands has been exaggerated.   But certainly they were a very super-stitious, rough and turbulent people, and at the same time as ready to respond to a religious call as their kinsmen across the Channel.   The country of the readily used fish-knife and of " wreckers " (a phenomenon which certainly in England and probably in Brittany needs more critical examination than it commonly gets) was also the country of Armelle Nicolas and of those baroque calvaries and statues in Basse-Bretagne.   Mystics prepared the way for missioners.   And it was Father Bernard, s.j., and Dom Le Nobletz who directed the attention of Julian Maunoir to this field and urged him to learn the Breton language, which he mastered in a surprisingly short time.

The comparison of Catholic Brittany with Protestant Wales and Cornwall is not gratuitous or far-fetched.   In writing of the Breton missions Bremond uses the English word " revival " and refers to Bunyan and the *Pilgrim's Progress ;* and what he says lends point to the title, " A John Wesley of Armorican Cornwall ", given to his pamphlet on Maunoir by the Anglican historian of the Cornish saints, the late Canon Gilbert Doble.   To read Séjourné's biography of Father Maunoir and then to turn to John Wesley's *Journal* is an instructive and thought-provoking exercise, or for that matter to compare the detailed journal that Maunoir kept too.

When Father Maunoir (" Tad Maner " in Breton) began his work in 1640 there were two missionaries on the job ; when he died forty-three years later there were a thousand. Later on, Renan complained that his ancestors had been " jesuitified " and denationalized by a lot of foreign missioners. In fact, there was a handful of Jesuits, themselves mostly Breton, and a large majority of Breton pastoral clergy, who co-operated with the fathers of the Society and submitted themselves to the very rigorous discipline proposed to them by Father Maunoir. And the technique of their work was due to a priest who was a Breton of the Bretons and who was not a Jesuit, Michael Le Nobletz, " the last of the bards "

The work was primarily one of religious teaching ; " emotional preaching that swept the hearers off their feet certainly had a part, but it was secondary " Among the " teachers' aids " used were large brightly-coloured pictures (some of them can still be seen in the episcopal library at Quimper) they were illustrative of the Passion, the Lord's Prayer, the seven deadly sins and so forth, but more often allegorical—the Knight Errant, the Six Cities of Refuge, the Three Trees—that is, appeal was made to the imagination and to the " poetical " quality in the human mind, and it was these pictures, together with the liveliness and humour of the expositions that accompanied them, that reminded Bremond of Bunyan. But painted pictures were not enough, there must also be *tableaux vivants*. Hence arose the very remarkable processions, in which, for example, the way of the cross was enacted, the " actors " illustrating Father Maunoir's address at the stations, when he was often interrupted " by the sobbing and the shouts of the congregation" This was much too much like " enthusiasm " for some people and there were complaints ; but the Breton bishops backed the missioners.

Another feature was the use of religious songs (*cantiques*), some of which no doubt were old ones brought back into use, but others Maunoir composed *ad hoc*. Apparently only one survives pretty well as he wrote it, and it loses badly in translation from Breton into French ; but it is clear that Maunoir versified with power and feeling, and hymn-singing had a very notable part in the Breton " revivals ", again as in those of Wales and England in the following centuries. With this use of the mother tongue went an emphasis on devotion to the local saints of early days. St Corentin's country, Cornouaille, the diocese of Quimper, was Maunoir's field of predilection.

And just as the lives of the Celtic saints as they have come down to us are full of miracles—sometimes touching, sometimes fantastic or even positively disedifying, sometimes convincing—so Father Maunoir's evangelization was marked by numerous signs and wonders. Already in 1697 his first biographer, Father Boschet, s.j., had studied a book of his miracles and " found them so astonishing that I suspected the writer of having touched things up to glorify the holy man " But after making inquiries on the spot Father Boschet became somewhat less sceptical after all, he asks, is it surprising that Christianity should be revived in Brittany with the same helps with which it was introduced into the world ? On the natural side, Maunoir was not a man of outstanding intellectual force and was perhaps inclined to be credulous ; but he was a leader who was loved as well as obeyed, a first-rate organizer, and a man of insight not a little of the lasting success of his work was due to his missions being directed as much to the shepherds as to their flocks. The pointer used in expounding their pictures became the distinguishing badge of his missioners, and it was a good symbol—they pointed out the way.

At communion during his retreat before ordination, young Maunoir wrote, " I felt an extraordinary ardour for the salvation of souls and an overwhelming urge to work for that end in every possible way. The voice of our Lord said within me, ' I laboured, I wept, I suffered, I died for them ' " Those words sum up Bd Julian's own life ; and after his death at Plévin in Cornouaille, on January 28, 1683, pilgrims flocked in crowds to kiss the feet which had so often traversed Brittany, carrying the good news of salvation to its remotest corners.

See Fr Boschet, *Le parfait missionaire* (1697) ; X. A. Séjourné, *Histoire de   Julien Maunoir* (1895) ; H. Bremond, *Histoire littéraire du sentiment religieux en France* ., t. v, pp. 82-117 P. Pourrat, *La spiritualité chrétienne*, t. iv, p. 122 ; and G. H. Doble in *Pax*, no. 85 (1927), pp. 318-329. See also H. de Gouvello, *Le vénérable Michel le Nobletz* (1898).

29 : ST FRANCIS DE SALES, Bishop of Geneva and Doctor of the Church, Co-Founder of the Order of the Visitation   (A.D. 1622)

S T FRANCIS DE SALES was born at the Château de Sales in Savoy on August 21, 1567, and on the following day was baptized in the parish church of Thorens under the name of Francis Bonaventure. His patron saint in after-life was the *Poverello* of Assisi, and the room in which he was born was known as " St Francis's room ", from a painting of the saint preaching to the birds and fishes. During his first years he was very frail and delicate, owing to his premature birth, but with care he gradually grew stronger, and, though never robust, he was singularly active and energetic throughout his career. His mother kept his early education in her own hands, aided by the Abbé Déage, who afterwards, as his tutor, accompanied Francis everywhere during his youth. He was remarkable in his childhood for obedience and truthfulness, and seems to have been eager to learn and to have loved books. At the age of eight Francis went to the College of Annecy. There he made his first communion in the church of St Dominic (now known as St Maurice), there he also received confirmation, and a year later he received the tonsure. Francis had a great wish to consecrate himself to God, and regarded this as the first outward step. His father (who at his marriage had taken the name of de Boisy) seems to have attached little importance to it, and destined his eldest son for a secular career. In his fourteenth year Francis was sent to the University of Paris, which at that time, with its 54 colleges, was one of the great centres of learning. He was intended for the Collège de Navarre, as it was frequented by the sons of the noble families of Savoy, but Francis, fearing for his vocation in such surroundings, implored to be allowed to go to the Collège de Clermont, which was under Jesuit direction and renowned for piety as well as for learning. Having obtained his father's consent to this, and accompanied by the Abbé Déage, he took up his abode in the Hôtel de la Rose Blanche, Rue St Jacques, which was close to the Collège de Clermont.

Francis soon made his mark, especially in rhetoric and philosophy, and he ardently devoted himself to the study of theology. To satisfy his father he took lessons in riding, dancing and fencing, but cared for none of them. His heart was more and more set upon giving himself wholly to God. He vowed perpetual chastity and placed himself under the special protection of the Blessed Virgin. He was, nevertheless, not free from trials.   About his eighteenth year he was assailed by an agonizing temptation to despair.   The love of God had always meant more than anything else to him, but he was now the prey of a terrible fear that he had lost God's grace and was doomed to hate Him with the damned for all eternity. This obsession pursued him day and night, and his health suffered visibly from the consequent mental anguish.   It was a heroic act of pure love which brought him deliverance.   " Lord ", he cried, " if I am never to see thee in Heaven, this at least grant me, that I may never curse nor blaspheme thy holy name.   If I may not love thee in the other world—for in Hell none praise thee—let me at least every instant of my brief existence here love thee as much as I can."   Directly afterwards, while kneeling before his favourite statue of our Lady, in the church of St Étienne des Grés, humbly saying the *Memorare*, all fear and despair suddenly left him and a deep peace filled his soul.   This trial taught him early to understand and deal tenderly with the spiritual difficulties and temptations of others.

He was twenty-four when he took his final degree and became a doctor of law at Padua, and he rejoined his family at the Château de Thuille on the Lake of Annecy, where for eighteen months this singularly attractive youth led, outwardly at least, the ordinary life of a young noble of his time.   That he should marry was his father's greatest desire, and the bride destined for him was a charming girl, the heiress of a neighbour of the family.   However, by his distant, though courteous manner to the young lady Francis soon showed that he could not follow his father's wishes in this matter.   For a similar motive he declined the dignity offered him of becoming a member of the senate of Savoy, an unusual compliment to so young a man.   Francis had so far only confided to his mother, to his cousin Canon Louis de Sales, and to a few intimate friends his earnest desire of devoting his life to the service of God.   An explanation with his father, however, became inevitable.   M. de Boisy had been greatly chagrined by his son's refusal of the senatorship and his determination not to marry, but neither of these disappointments appeared to have prepared him for the blow of Francis's vocation.   The death of the provost of the chapter of Geneva suggested to Canon Louis de Sales the possibility that Francis might be appointed to this post, and that in this way his father's opposition might relax.   Aided by Claud de Granier, Bishop of Geneva, but without consulting any of the family, he applied to the pope, with whom the appointment rested, and the letters instituting Francis provost of the chapter were promptly received from Rome. When the appointment was announced to Francis his surprise was extreme, and it was only with reluctance that he accepted the unsought honour, hoping thereby to obtain his father's consent to his ordination.   M. de Boisy was a man of determined character and considered that his children ought to regard his expressed wish as final, and it required all the patient persuasiveness and respect which Francis could call to his aid before M. de Boisy at length gave way.   Francis put on ecclesiastical dress the very day his father gave his consent, and six months afterwards, on December 18, 1593, he was ordained priest.   He took up his duties with an ardour which never abated.   He ministered to the poor with zealous love, and in the confessional devoted himself to the poorest and humblest with special predilection. He preached constantly, not only in Annecy, but in many other places.   His style was so simple that it charmed his hearers, and, excellent scholar though he was, he avoided filling his sermons with Greek and Latin quotations, as was the prevailing custom.   He was destined, however, soon to be called upon to undertake far more difficult and hazardous work.

At this time, owing to armed hostilities and the inroads of Protestantism, the religious condition of the people of the Chablais, on the south shore of the Lake of Geneva, was deplorable, and the Duke of Savoy applied to Bishop de Granier to send missioners who might win back his subjects to the Church. In response the bishop sent a priest to Thonon, the capital of the Chablais. The first attempt was fruitless, and the priest was soon forced to withdraw. The bishop, summoning his chapter, put the whole matter before them, disguising none of the difficulties and dangers. Perhaps of all those present, the provost was the one who best realized the gravity of the task, but nevertheless he stood up and offered himself for the work, saying very simply, " My lord, if you think I am capable of undertaking the mission, tell me to go. I am ready to obey, and should be happy to be chosen." The bishop accepted at once, to Francis's great joy. But M. de Boisy took a different view of the matter and hastened to Annecy to stop what he called " this piece of folly ". In his opinion it meant sending Francis to his death. Kneeling at the feet of the bishop he exclaimed, " My lord, I allowed my eldest son, the hope of my house, of my old age, of my life, to devote himself to the service of the Church to be a confessor, but I cannot give him up to be a martyr ! " When Mgr de Granier, impressed by the distress and insistence of his old friend, seemed on the point of yielding, it was Francis who implored him to be firm, saying, " Would you make me unworthy of the Kingdom of God ? Having put my hand to the plough, would you have me look back ? "

The bishop used every argument likely to influence M. de Boisy, but he took his leave, saying, " I have no wish to resist the will of God, but I do not mean to be my son's murderer ! I cannot be a party to his throwing away his life ! May God do according to His good pleasure, but as to this undertaking, it shall never have my sanction ! " Thus Francis had the disappointment of starting on his mission without his father's blessing. It was on September 14, 1594, Holy Cross day, that, travelling on foot and accompanied only by his cousin, Canon Louis de Sales, he set forth to win back the Chablais. The Château des Allinges, six or seven miles from Thonon, was where the governor of the province was stationed with a garrison, and here the cousins, for safety's sake, were to return each night. In Thonon, the residue of the once Catholic population amounted to about twenty scattered individuals, too afraid of violence to declare themselves openly. These Francis sought out and exhorted to courage and perseverance. The missionaries worked and preached daily in Thonon, gradually extending their efforts to the villages of the surrounding country. The walk to and from Allinges, a great additional tax on their endurance, was in the following winter on several occasions a matter of extreme danger. One evening Francis was attacked by wolves, and only escaped by spending the night in a tree. When daylight came he was found by some peasants in such an exhausted condition that had they not carried him to their hut and revived him with food and warmth he would certainly have died. These good people were Calvinists, and with his thanks Francis spoke such words of enlightenment and charity that they were afterwards converted. Twice in January 1595 he was waylaid by assassins who had sworn to take his life, but on both these occasions, as also several times later, he was preserved seemingly by miracle.

Time went by with little apparent result to reward the labours of the two missioners, and all the while M. de Boisy was sending letters to his son, alternately commanding and imploring him to give up so hopeless a task. Francis could only reply that short of a positive order from the bishop he had no right to forsake his post. He himself did not lose heart, notwithstanding the enormous difficulties. To a friend near Evian he wrote, " We are but making a beginning. I shall go on in good courage, and I hope in God against all human hope." He was constantly seeking new ways to reach the hearts and minds of the people, and he began writing leaflets setting forth the teaching of the Church as opposed to the errors of Calvinism. In every spare moment of his arduous day he wrote these little papers, which were copied many times by hand and distributed widely by all available means. These sheets, composed under such stress and difficulty, were later to form the volume of " Controversies ", and in their original form are still preserved in the archives of the Visitation Convent at Annecy. This was the beginning of his activities as a writer. To all this work Francis added the spiritual care of the soldiers, quartered in the Château des Allinges, Catholic in name but an ignorant and dissolute crew. In the summer of 1595, going up the mountain of Voiron to restore an oratory of our Lady which had been destroyed by the Bernese, he was attacked by a hostile crowd, who insulted and beat him. Soon afterwards his sermons at Thonon began to be more numerously attended. The tracts too had been silently doing their work, and his patient perseverance under every form of persecution and hardship had not been without its effect. Conversions became more and more frequent, and before very long there was a steady stream of lapsed Catholics seeking reconciliation with the Church.

After three or four years, when Bishop de Granier came to visit the mission, the fruits of Francis's self-sacrificing work and untiring zeal were unmistakable. The bishop was made welcome, and was able to administer confirmation. He even presided at the " Forty Hours ", a thing which seemed unthinkable in Thonon. Catholic faith and worship had been re-established in the province, and Francis could with justice be called the " Apostle of the Chablais " A great bishop of Geneva in our own day, Marius Besson, has summed up his predecessor's apostolic spirit in a sentence that St Francis himself wrote to St Jane de Chantal " I have always said that whoever preaches with love is preaching effectively against the heretics, even though he does not say a single controversial word against them." And Mgr Besson quotes Cardinal du Perron : " I hope that, with God's help, the learning He has given me is enough easily to convince heretics of their errors ; but if you want to *convert* them, take them to my Lord of Geneva God has given him a quality through which all those to whom he speaks come away converted."

Mgr de Granier, who had long been considering Francis in the light of a possible coadjutor and successor, felt that the moment had now come to give effect to this. When the proposal was made Francis was at first unwilling, but in the end he yielded to the persistence of the bishop, submitting to what he ultimately felt was a manifestation of the Divine Will. Soon he fell dangerously ill with a fever which kept him for a time hovering between life and death. When sufficiently recovered he proceeded to Rome, where Pope Clement VIII, having heard much in praise of the virtue and ability of the young provost, desired that he should be examined in his presence. On the appointed day there was a great assemblage of learned theologians and men of eminent intellect. The pope himself, Baronius, Bellarmine, Cardinal Frederick Borromeo (a cousin of St Charles) and others put no less than thirty-five abstruse questions of theology to Francis, all of which he answered with simplicity and modesty, but in a way which proved his learning. His appointment as coadjutor of Geneva was confirmed, and Francis returned to take up his work with fresh zeal and energy. Early in 1602 he was in Paris. During his stay he was invited to preach a course in the chapel royal, which soon proved too small to hold the crowd that came to listen to his simple and moving but uncompromising words of truth. He was in high favour with Henry IV, who used every inducement to get him to remain in France, and renewed his efforts in later years when Francis was again in Paris. But the young bishop would not forsake his " poor bride ", his mountain diocese, for the " rich wife ", the more imposing see, offered him. King Henry said that " My Lord of Geneva has every virtue and not a fault "

Francis succeeded to the see of Geneva on the death of Claud de Granier in the autumn of 1602, and took up his residence at Annecy, with a household organized on lines of the strictest economy. To the fulfilment of his episcopal duties he gave himself with unstinted generosity and devotion. He thought out every detail for the government of his diocese, and apart from all his administrative work continued to preach and minister in the confessional with unremitting devotion. He organized the teaching of the catechism throughout the diocese, and at Annecy gave the instructions himself, with such glowing interest and fervour that years after his death the " Bishop's Catechisms " were still vividly remembered. Children loved him and followed him about. His unselfishness and charity, his humility and clemency, could not have been surpassed. In dealing with souls, though always gentle, he was never weak, and he could be very firm when kindness did not prevail. In his wonderful *Treatise on the Love of God*, he wrote, " The measure of love, is to love without measure ", and this he not only taught, but lived. The immense correspondence which he carried on brought encouragement and wise guidance to innumerable persons who sought his help. A prominent place in this work of spiritual direction was held by St Jane Frances de Chantal, who first became known to him in 1604, when he was preaching Lenten sermons at Dijon. The foundation of the Order of the Visitation in 1610 was the result that evolved from this meeting of the two saints. His most famous book, the *Introduction to the Devout Life*, grew out of the casual notes of instruction and advice which he wrote to Mme de Chamoisy, a cousin by marriage, who had placed herself under his guidance. He was persuaded to publish them in a little volume which, with some additions, first appeared in 1608. The book was at once acclaimed a spiritual masterpiece, and soon translated into many languages. In 1610 came the heavy sorrow of his mother's death (his father had died nine years before). " My heart was very full and I wept over that good mother more than I have wept since I became a priest," were his words afterwards, written to Mme de Chantal. Francis survived his mother twelve laborious years.

In 1622, the Duke of Savoy, going to meet Louis XIII at Avignon, invited St Francis to join them there. Anxious to obtain from Louis certain privileges for the French part of his diocese, Francis readily consented, although he was in no state of health to risk the long winter journey. But he seems to have had a premonition that his end was not far off. Before quitting Annecy he put all his affairs in order, and took his leave as if he had no expectation of seeing people again. At Avignon he led as far as possible his usual austere life. But he was greatly sought after—crowds were eager to see him, and the different religious houses all wanted the saintly bishop to preach to them. On the return journey he stayed at Lyons, where he lodged in a gardener's cottage belonging to the convent of the Visitation. Here for a whole month, though sorely in need of rest, he spared himself no labour for souls.   Being asked one day by a nun to write down what virtue he specially wished them to cultivate, he wrote on a sheet of paper, in large letters, the one word " Humility ".   In bitterly cold weather, through Advent and over Christmas, he continued his preaching and ministrations, refusing no demand upon his strength and time.   On St John's day he was taken seriously ill with some sort of paralytic seizure.   He recovered speech and consciousness, and endured with touching patience the torturing remedies used in the hope of prolonging his life, but which only hastened the end.   After receiving the last sacraments he lay murmuring words from the Bible expressive of his humble and serene trust in God's mercy. He was heard to say, " Exspectans exspectavi Dominum et intendit mihi, et exaudivit preces meas, et eduxit me de lacu miseriae et de luto faecis."—" With expectation I have waited for the Lord and He was attentive to me, and He heard my prayers and brought me out of the pit of misery and the filthy mire."   At last clasping the hand of a loving attendant, he whispered, " Advesperascit et inclinata est jam dies."—" It is towards evening and the day is now far spent."   The last word he was heard to utter was the name of " Jesus ".   While those kneeling around his bed said the litany for the dying, and were invoking the Holy Innocents, whose feast it was, St Francis gently breathed his last, in the fifty-sixth year of his age.

The beatification of St Francis de Sales in 1662 was the first solemn beatification to take place in St Peter's at Rome, where he was canonized three years later.   His feast was fixed for January 29, the anniversary of the bringing of his body to the convent of the Visitation at Annecy.   He was declared a doctor of the Church in 1877, and Pope Pius XI named him the patron-saint of journalists.   At the time of his death there was living in Paris a priest now known as St Vincent de Paul. To him Francis had entrusted the spiritual care of the first convent of the Visitation in Paris.   St Vincent said of St Francis, " This servant of God conformed so well to the divine pattern that often I asked myself with amazement how a created being —given the frailty of human nature—could reach so high a degree of perfection. . . . Going over his words in my mind I have been filled with such admiration that I am moved to see in him the man who, of all others, has most faithfully reproduced the love of the Son of God on earth."

Some people who thought St Francis de Sales too indulgent towards sinners one day spoke freely to him on the subject.   The saint replied, " If there were anything more excellent than meekness, God would certainly have taught it us ; and yet there is nothing to which He so earnestly exhorts all, as to be ' meek and humble of heart '.   Why would you hinder me from obeying the command of my Lord ?   Can we really be better advised in these matters than God Himself ? " The tenderness of Francis was particularly displayed in his reception of apostates and other abandoned sinners.   When these prodigals returned to him he used to say, speaking with all the tenderness of a father, " God and I will help you ; all I require of you is not to despair : I shall take on myself the burden of the rest." His affectionate care of them extended even to their bodily wants, and his purse was open to them as well as his heart.   He justified this to some who, disedified at his indulgence, told him that it only encouraged the sinner and hardened him in his ways, by observing, " Are they not a part of my flock ?   Has not our blessed Lord shed His blood for them ?   These wolves will be changed into lambs ; a day will come when they will be more precious in the sight of God than we are.   If Saul had been cast off, we should never have had St Paul."

An immense amount of material is available for the fuller study of the life of St Francis de Sales. A number of biographies were printed in the seventeenth century, two of them within a couple of years of his death. His own works, particularly his letters, form an almost inexhaustible mine of information. They should be consulted in the great edition of Annecy prepared by the Visitation nuns under the direction of the English Benedictine Dom Mackey, and later of Father Navatel and others. *The Spirit of St Francis de Sales* by Bishop Camus has had an immense popularity since its first appearance in 1641, and has been translated and abridged in many languages ; see also *St Francis de Sales* (1937), by M. Mueller. The most complete modern biographies are those by the Abbé Hamon (revised and supplemented edn. in 2 vols., 1909 ; English adaptation by Fr H. Burton in 2 vols., 1926-29), and by Mgr W. G. Trochu (2 vols., 1941). There is a French study of St Francis as the " Doctor of Perfection " by Canon J. Leclercq (1948). There are several slighter works accessible to English readers, some original, like that of M. M. Maxwell Scott, *St Francis de Sales and his Friends*, others translated, like the short *Life* by de Margerie. Two Anglican writers have written well of the saint : H. L. Farrer (Mrs Lear) in her *Life* (1872), and E. K. Sanders (1928).

ST SABINIAN, Martyr   (Date Unknown)

St Sabinian is commemorated in the Roman Martyrology on this day, and he is also honoured in the diocese of Troyes as the first apostle and martyr of that city. Three sets of " acts ", none of them of any historical value, profess to record the history of his martyrdom. He is said to have been born in the island of Samos, to have been converted to Christianity by reading the Bible, to have travelled to Gaul to preach the gospel before he had even been baptized, to have received this sacrament without any human minister (a voice from heaven pronouncing the words), to have been arrested on account of the conversions he effected, to have been brought before the Emperor Aurelian whose threats he defied, and finally, after a series of miraculous incidents, in the course of which fire proved powerless to burn him or arrows to wound him, to have been decapitated by the sword of the executioner. There seems to be no ancient tradition of *cultus*, and we consequently cannot safely say more than that some martyr of that name may have suffered at Troyes in one of the early persecutions under the Romans.

See the *Acta Sanctorum* for January 29 ; E. Defer, *Vie des saints du diocèse de Troyes*, pp. 27-36 ; *Analecta Bollandiana*, vol. iv (1885), pp. 139-156.

ST GILDAS THE WISE, Abbot   (c. A.D. 570)

This famous man seems to have been born about the year 500, in the lower valley of the Clyde. He must have travelled south at a somewhat early age, and we may reasonably trust the tradition which describes him as practising asceticism at Llanilltud. He was no doubt younger than either St Samson or St Paul Aurelian, but all three, either simultaneously or successively, lived under St Illtud, we are told. How long Gildas remained in Britain cannot be determined, but the terrible indictment of the scandalous lives of his contemporaries, both ecclesiastics and laymen, which he left in his *De excidio Britanniae* was written probably on British soil somewhere about the year 540. Severely as this work has been criticized as a mere jeremiad (even Bede calls it *sermo flebilis*, a pitiful tale) and as an often incoherent patchwork of the most denunciatory texts to be found in both the Testaments, it should be remembered that there is no reason to suppose that the author's object was to write a history. On the contrary, he tells us himself that his main purpose was to make known " the miseries, the errors and the ruin of Britain ", and he certainly manifests an acquaintance with Holy Scripture which must be deemed highly creditable in any writer during this period of barbarism ; nor was he ignorant of Vergil and St Ignatius of Antioch.   Moreover, there can be no question that Gildas, in spite of his querulous tone, was animated by a real zeal for morality and religion.   As a Welsh scholar of our own day has written   " A popular reverence has throughout the centuries clung to a few of the names that stand out before us in Britain and Brittany.   We have many indications that these men, who knew the poor as well as the great, the ' people ' in the Church no less than the bishops and priests who ruled it, had grasped the great fact of sin as the supreme evil for men and had ministered to the deepest need of their souls.   Those who know the works of Gildas will best appreciate this." (Hugh Williams, *Christianity in Early Britain*, 1912, p. 366.)

Little can be affirmed with confidence regarding the life of Gildas himself.   We learn on what seems fair evidence of certain Irish ascetics, such as St Finnian of Clonard, who had sojourned in Britain for a while and become disciples of St Gildas. We are also told that he himself visited Ireland, and it appears that Gildas's reputation as a scholar was such that he was consulted by distant ecclesiastics who wrote to him from there.   He seems to have lived for a time on the island of Flatholm in the Bristol Channel, where he copied a missal for St Cadoc and perhaps wrote the *De excidio*.   The last years of his life, however, were certainly spent in Brittany, where he lived for some time as a hermit on a tiny island near Rhuys, in Morbihan bay.   Here disciples gathered around him, and in spite of his desire for solitude he does not seem to have cut himself off entirely from the world, for we hear of his travelling to other places in Brittany ; the visit to Ireland has been assigned to this period, though the fact is very doubtful.   There has been much difference of opinion regarding the date of St Gildas's death.   Some put it as early as 554, but the majority of recent critics incline to *c.* 570.

The feast of St Gildas is observed in the diocese of Vannes but nowhere in Great Britain or Ireland, in spite of the fact that he was a prophetical figure of real importance, perhaps the most prominent and respected teacher of his century in Celtic-speaking lands, and an important influence in the formation of Irish monasticism.

The text of Gildas's *De excidio Britanniae* and of the *Vita Gildae*, by a monk of Rhuys, has been critically edited by T. Mommsen in MGH., *Auctores antiquissimi*, vol. xiii. See also Hugh Williams, *op. cit.*, and his *Gildas* in the Cymmrodorion Record Series, 1901, where the *vita* is printed on pp. 317–389 ; LBS., vol. iii, pp. 81–130 ; J. Fonssagrives, *St Gildas de Ruis* (1908) ; J. Ryan, *Irish Monasticism* (1931), pp. 146–166 and *passim* ; L. Gougaud, *Christianity in Celtic Lands* (1932), *passim* ; A. W. Wade-Evans, *Welsh Christian Origins* (1934), cap. xiii and *passim* , J. E. Lloyd, *History of Wales* (1939), vol. i, pp. 134–143 ; and C. E. Stevens in the *Eng. Hist. Rev.*, vol. lvi (1941), pp. 353–373. Polydore Vergil's edition of Gildas's writings (1525) was the first attempt made in England at a critical edition of an historical source.

ST SULPICIUS " SEVERUS ", BISHOP OF BOURGES   (A.D. 591)

THERE seems no sufficient reason to believe that this prelate was really called Severus.   St Gregory of Tours who gives an account of his appointment to the see of Bourges (584) in preference to other, simoniacal, candidates speaks of him with much respect and tells us of a provincial council which he convoked in Auvergne.   He also took part in the Council of Mâcon in 585.   The name Severus may have attached itself to him to emphasize the distinction between him and a later Sulpicius of Bourges, who was surnamed "Pius". It is, however, clearly the Sulpicius who died in 591 who is commemorated in the Roman Martyrology on this day, January 29. A good deal of confusion with the writer Sulpicius Severus is perceptible in the notices of the early martyrologists.

See the *Acta Sanctorum* for January 29; and Duchesne, *Fastes Épiscopaux*, vol. i, pp. 28-29. Alban Butler honours the real Sulpicius Severus with the title Saint, but there seems no sufficient authority for this; though the Bollandists refer to the ecclesiastical writer in their account of St Sulpicius, Bishop of Bourges, they point out that the temporary inclusion of the former in the Roman Martyrology was due to a confusion.

30 : ST MARTINA, Virgin and Martyr   (Date Unknown)

IN the general calendar of the Western church this day is kept as the feast of St Martina, and accordingly her name stands first today in the Roman Martyrology; and in the fuller notice which appears there on January 1, we are told that at Rome under the Emperor Alexander (Severus, 222-235) she was subjected to many kinds of torment and at length perished by the sword. Alban Butler informs us correctly that there was a chapel in Rome consecrated to her memory which was frequented with great devotion in the seventh century. We also may learn from him that her relics were discovered in a vault in the ruins of her old church, and translated in the year 1634 under Pope Urban VIII, who built a new church in her honour and himself composed the hymns used in her office in the Roman Breviary. He adds further that the city of Rome ranks her amongst its particular patrons.

Despite these attestations, the very existence of St Martina remains doubtful. Though she is represented as suffering in the City itself, there is no early Roman tradition regarding her. The "acts" of her martyrdom are full of preposterous miracles—for example, when she is wounded, milk flows from her body in place of blood—and are extravagant to the last degree. The one thing certain about them is that they bear the closest resemblance, as was long ago pointed out, both to those attributed to St Tatiana and those of St Prisca. Pio Franchi de' Cavalieri has shown with considerable probability that of these three sets, all apocryphal, those belonging to St Tatiana have formed the model for the others.

See Pio Franchi de' Cavalieri in the *Römische Quartalschrift*, vol. xvii (1903), pp. 222-236, and *Analecta Bollandiana*, vol. xxiii (1904), pp. 344-345. The Acts of St Martina are printed by the Bollandists under January 1. *Cf.* also Marucchi, *Le Forum Romain et le Palatin* (1925), pp. 246-248.

ST BARSIMAEUS, Bishop of Edessa   (A.D. 250 ?)

IN the Roman Martyrology on this day we read : "At Edessa in Syria, the commemoration of St Barsimaeus the Bishop, who after converting many gentiles to the faith and sending them to their crowns before him, followed them with the palm of martyrdom under Trajan." Alban Butler in his short notice tells us further that Barsimaeus was the third bishop of Edessa from St Thaddaeus, one of the seventy-two disciples, and also that the martyrdom took place at Edessa under Lysias, when Trajan, having passed the Euphrates, made the conquest of Mesopotamia in 114. All this has been completely exploded by Rubens Duval in a study of the Syriac Acts of Sharbil and Barsamja, which he published in the *Journal Asiatique* for 1889. He shows that the narrative, while professing to embody the most authentic documents, is vitiated by irreconcilable anachronisms. Some data will only fit the years 106 and 112 in the reign of Trajan, who is expressly mentioned, others could only be verified in the pontificate of Pope Fabian (250), who is equally mentioned. Moreover, Barsamja, according to the acts, though sentenced, was not actually put to death, and since he was a successor of Palut who was consecrated by Serapion (*c.* 209), he certainly did not live in the second century. Duval further shows that the narrative seems to be based on the Acts of Habib (St Abibus), a fourth-century martyr, and that it is consequently possible that the whole narrative is a fiction.

The Syriac acts were first printed by Cureton in his *Ancient Syriac Documents*, pp. 41–72, and subsequently by Bedjan. But see especially Rubens Duval in *Journal Asiatique*, 8th series, vol. xiv, pp. 40–58, and *cf. ibid.*, vol. xviii (1891), pp. 384–386.

ST BATHILDIS, WIDOW   (A.D. 680)

ST BATHILDIS was an English girl, who at an early age was carried over into France and sold cheaply as a slave into the household of the mayor of the palace under King Clovis II. Here she attained a position of responsibility and attracted the notice of the king, who in 649 married her. She bore him three sons, who all successively wore the crown, Clotaire III, Childeric II and Thierry III. Clovis dying in 657, when the eldest was only five, Bathildis became regent and apparently showed herself very capable at a difficult time when Merovingian power was declining in the face of the Frankish aristocracy. She seconded the zeal of St Ouen, St Leger and other holy bishops, redeemed many captives, especially of her own people, and did all in her power to promote religion. She was a benefactress of many monasteries, including Saint-Denis, Saint-Martin at Tours and Saint-Medard at Soissons, founded the great abbey of Corbie, and endowed the truly royal nunnery of Chelles.

To this last Bathildis herself retired about 665, which she is said to have long desired to do ; the notorious Ebroin and other nobles were apparently no less anxious to have her out of the way. We are told that she had no sooner taken the veil than she seemed to forget entirely her former dignity, and was only to be distinguished from the rest by her humility, serving them in the lowest offices, and obeying the abbess St Bertila as the last among the sisters. In the life of St Eligius, attributed, though unwarrantably, to St Ouen, many instances are mentioned of the veneration which St Bathildis felt for that holy prelate. Thus we learn that Eligius after his death, in a vision by night, ordered a certain courtier to reprove the queen for wearing jewels and costly apparel in her widowhood, though in so doing she had acted, not out of pride, but because she thought it due to her position whilst she was regent of the kingdom. Upon this admonition she laid them aside, distributed a part to the poor, and with the richest jewels made a beautiful cross, which she placed at the head of the tomb of St Eligius. During a long illness which preceded her death she suffered intense bodily pain which she bore resignedly, dying on January 30, 680.

In the account of St Bathildis given by Alban Butler no mention is made of a very serious charge brought against her by Eddius, the biographer of St Wilfrid, who calls her a cruel Jezebel and attributes to her the assassination of ten French bishops, among them the bishop of Lyons, whom he calls Dalfinus.   That there is much confusion here is certain, because the name of the murdered bishop was Annemund, who was the brother of Count Dalfinus.   Consequently, although Eddius has been copied by William of Malmesbury, and in part even by Bede, it is quite improbable, for a variety of reasons, that his information was in any way accurate.   Such unprejudiced authorities as Bruno Krusch, Charles Plummer and the *Dictionary of National Biography* entirely exonerate St Bathildis in this matter, and Plummer suggests that there may have been some confusion between her and Queen Brunhilda who died long before, in 613.   Butler in a footnote reports from Le Bœuf and others that " six nuns were cured of inveterate distempers, attended with frequent fits of convulsions, by touching the relics of St Bathildis, when her shrine was opened on July 13, 1631 ".

The text of the *Life of St Bathildis,* which is a genuinely Merovingian document and was written by a contemporary, has been critically edited by B. Krusch in MGH., *Scriptores Merov.*, vol. ii, pp. 475-508.   There are also frequent references to St Bathildis in the *Vita S. Eligii*, which, though not the work of St Ouen, may preserve some authentic materials, see MGH., *Merov.*, vol. iv, pp. 634-761.   See further M. J. Couturier, *Ste Bathilde, Reine des Francs* (1909) ; E. Vacandard, *Vie de St Ouen* (1902), pp. 254-263 ; BHL., nn. 905-911 and CMH., pp. 68-69.

ST ALDEGUNDIS, Virgin   (A.D. 684)

St Aldegundis was the daughter of Walbert and Bertilia, both venerated as saints, and was born in Hainault about 635.   Refusing the marriage proposed by her parents she went to live near her sister St Waldeturdis (Waudru), foundress of a convent at Mons.   Then she retired to a hermitage, from which grew up the great double monastery of Maubeuge.   We are told that she was a disciple of St Amand and that she had a number of supernatural visions.   St Aldegundis developed cancer of the breast, and she bore this agonizing malady—and the cauteries and incisions of the surgeons—with the greatest patience and trust in God till her death on January 30, 684.

The *Life of St Aldegund*, or at least the more historical portion, has been critically edited by W. Levison in MGH., *Scriptores Merov.*, vol. vi, pp. 79-90.   He pronounces, on what seems quite satisfactory evidence, that the author is not, as the *vita* claims, a contemporary. On the other hand it cannot be later than the ninth century, for it is quoted by Rabanus Maurus.   See also Van der Essen, *Étude critique sur les saints mérovingiens*, pp. 219-231 ; and *cf.* the *Acta Sanctorum* for January 30.

ST ADELELMUS, or ALEAUME, Abbot   (c. A.D. 1100)

This holy Benedictine, a Frenchman by birth, after following a career of arms, was moved to undertake a pilgrimage to Rome.   On his way he came under the influence of St Robert, abbot of the monastery of Chaise-Dieu, and determined to become a monk himself.   He completed his pilgrimage, and then returned to Chaise-Dieu, where he took the religious habit, and may later on have been chosen abbot.   However, at the instance of Constance of Burgundy, Queen of Castile, who had heard much of his holiness and miracles, he was induced to come to Burgos, where her husband eventually built a monastery for him. Adelelmus took an active part in the war against the Moors, and was credited with many miracles, one of them in favour of Queen Edith, widow of St Edward the Confessor.

We have a Latin life of St. Adelelmus written shortly after his death by a French monk Rodulph, who went to Burgos for the purpose of compiling it. It has been printed by Florez, *España Sagrada*, vol. xxvii, pp. 841–866 (and *cf.* pp. 154 *seq.*), and there is an abridgement which will be found in Mabillon, vol. vi, pt. 2, pp. 896–902. St Adelelmus's feast is kept in the diocese of Burgos, of which he is a patron ; his name in Spain is Lesmes.

ST HYACINTHA MARISCOTTI, Virgin   (A.D. 1640)

THE story of St Hyacintha is in some respects almost unique among the records of holy lives. In the case of many saints we read at some stage of their career of a momentous change of purpose and practice, which they themselves describe as their " conversion " Sometimes, as with St Augustine, this represents a turning to God from a life of sin in the world. Sometimes, as with St Teresa, the previous state was only reprehensible in contrast to the spiritual enlightenment which came later. Very rare is the case of one who, having pledged himself to a life of religious perfection, begins by being scandalously unfaithful to rule, is converted to better thoughts, relapses again, and so far recovers, in response to a new grace, as to attain in the end to the highest ideal of virtue.

Clarice Mariscotti, born of a noble family at Vignarello, was educated in the Franciscan convent at Viterbo, where one of her sisters was already a nun. She is said in her childhood to have shown little inclination for piety, and when a marriage was arranged between her youngest sister and the Marquis Cassizucchi, she herself being passed over, her pique and morose ill-humour seem to have made her almost unendurable in the family circle. As a result they, according to the evil custom of the times, practically forced her to enter a convent. She went back to the Franciscans, a community of the third order regular, at Viterbo, where she became Sister Hyacintha (Giacinta) and was admitted in due course to profession. At the same time she let it be known that though she wore the habit of a nun she intended to claim every indulgence which she could secure for herself in virtue of her rank and the wealth of her family. For ten years she scandalized the community by leading a life in which she confined herself without disguise to conformity with certain external observances, while disregarding altogether the spirit of the religious rule. At last, when she was suffering from some slight indisposition, a worthy Franciscan priest came to hear her confession in her cell, who, seeing the comforts she had accumulated around her, spoke to her severely on the subject of her tepidity and the danger she ran. Hyacintha seems to have taken the rebuke to heart and to have set about a reform with almost exaggerated fervour. This sudden conversion however showed every sign of breaking down, and she was beginning to slip back into the bad old ways, when God sent her a much more serious illness. This grace was effectual, and from that date she gave herself to a life in which cruel disciplines, constant fasts, deprivation of sleep and long hours of prayer all played their part.

What was perhaps most remarkable in such a character as hers was the fact that, becoming in time mistress of novices, she seems to have shown the most healthy common sense in the guidance of others, restraining their devotional and penitential excesses and giving very practical advice to the many who wrote to seek her counsel. For example, when asked her opinion about someone unnamed who

had a great reputation for union with God and a notable gift of tears, she replied
" First of all I should like to know how far she is detached from creatures, humble
and free from self-will, even in good and holy things, and then I should be more
ready to believe that the delight which she experiences in her devotions comes from
God.　The sort of people who most appeal to me are those who are despised, who
are devoid of self-love and who have little sensible consolation.　The cross, to
suffer, to persevere bravely in spite of the lack of all sweetness and relish in prayer :
this is the true sign of the spirit of God."　Hyacintha's charity was also remarkable,
and it was not limited to those of her own community.　Through her influence
two confraternities were established in Viterbo which devoted themselves to the
relief of the sick, the aged, decayed gentry and the poor, Hyacintha herself helping
largely to provide the necessary funds by her own begging.　She died at the age
of fifty-five, on January 30, 1640, and was canonized in 1807.　The bull of canonization states that " her mortifications were such that the prolongation of her life
was a continued miracle ", and also that " through her apostolate of charity she
won more souls to God than many preachers of her time ".

See Flaminio da Latera, *Vita della V S. Giacinta Mariscotti* (1805) ; Léon, *L'Auréole
séraphique* (Eng. trans.), vol. i, pp. 117-126 ; *Kirchenlexikon*, vol. vi, pp. 514-516.

BD SEBASTIAN VALFRÉ　　(A.D. 1710)

SEBASTIAN VALFRÉ was born at Verduno in Piedmont in 1629.　His parents were
poor and had a large family to support.　From his childhood he determined to
become a priest, and all through his years of study he maintained himself by
copying books, costing his father nothing.　We are told that all his parents were
ever able to give him was a cart-load of wine when he first left home.　He was
accepted by the Fathers of the Oratory at Turin, and joined the congregation on
St Philip's day, 1651.　He received the priesthood a year later, and for his parents'
consolation offered his first Mass at Verduno.　He gave himself up at once and
unreservedly to his priestly duties, and it was noted that from the time of his joining
it, the Turin Oratory, which had previously had much to contend with, began to
make many friends and to prosper exceedingly.　Sebastian's first office was that
of prefect of the Little Oratory, a confraternity of laymen who meet together for
devotional exercises.　This charge he retained for many years with abundant fruit,
and his wonderful gift for inspiring enthusiasm in the young seems to have led a
little later to his being appointed master of novices.　In 1661, almost immediately
after he had reached the required age of forty years, he was elected superior in spite
of his own earnest remonstrances.　We are told that his government was a perfect
copy of that of St Philip, enforcing exact observance in every detail, but showing
great tenderness to the sick, for whom nothing was thought too good.

During all this time Bd Sebastian's fame as a director of souls was constantly
growing.　He spent long hours in the confessional, being scrupulous in the regularity of his attendance, a matter upon which he laid much stress in his exhortations
to his own community.　All classes came to him, and he was prepared to bestow
endless trouble on those whom he saw in need of help or earnest to make progress.
On the other hand, aided probably by a supernatural insight, or by some strange
telepathic faculty, he was ruthless in exposing insincerity and affectation.　Amongst
his penitents was the Duke Victor Amadeus II, afterwards king of Sardinia, who
endeavoured in 1690, with Pope Alexander VIII's ready consent, to induce Father

Sebastian to accept the archbishopric of Turin, but all to no purpose. He preached sometimes as many as three sermons in one day. He also went on long missionary expeditions in the surrounding country, penetrating occasionally into Switzerland, and wonderful were the conversions which followed. Besides this, much time was devoted to instructing the young and the ignorant. He gathered together the beggars who came to the Oratory for alms, and provided food for their souls as well as for their bodies. He was indefatigable in visiting hospitals and prisons, displaying, moreover, a special affection for soldiers, whose peculiar temptations he understood and compassionated.

Like St Philip, Bd Sebastian was always cheerful, so that men judged him to be light-hearted and free from care. This was the more wonderful because we read a terrible story of his own spiritual desolation and interior trials. He was haunted by temptations to think that he was forsaken of God, that he had lost his faith, and that nothing but Hell awaited him ; yet all the while, even when he was close upon eighty, he never relaxed his apostolic work for souls, preaching out of doors in the bitter cold of January to any company of waifs and outcasts whom he could gather round him. We find him at times fearless in visiting even haunts of vice when he felt that God called him to interfere. Strange to say, his intervention on these rare occasions seems to have been wonderfully blessed, and the most brutal ruffians felt the power of his holiness, remaining abashed and dumbfounded when he denounced them in no measured terms. His life was, in fact, the model of that which ought to be led by a zealous pastor in a city where misery and evil abound, and it is in no way wonderful that he was regarded by all his contemporaries as a saint. Instances of his supernatural insight and of the fulfilment of his predictions were many. Amongst other such cases which are on record, it seems clear that he knew, some months beforehand, the time of his own death. This occurred on January 30, 1710, when he was close upon eighty-one years of age. He was beatified in 1834.

See Lady Amabel Kerr, *Life of Bd Sebastian Valfré* (1896) ; G. Calleri, *Vita del b. Sebastiano Valfré* (Eng. trans., 1849) ; P. Capello, *Vita del b. Sebastiano Valfré* (2 vols., 1872).

31 : ST JOHN BOSCO, FOUNDER OF THE SALESIANS OF DON BOSCO (A.D. 1888)

I N his life the supernatural almost became the natural and the extraordinary ordinary." These were the words of Pope Pius XI in speaking of that great lover of children, Don Bosco. Born in 1815, the youngest son of a peasant-farmer in a Piedmontese village, John Melchior Bosco lost his father at the age of two and was brought up by his mother, a saintly and industrious woman who had a hard struggle to keep the home together. A dream which he had when he was nine showed him the vocation from which he never swerved. It was the precursor of other visions which, at various critical periods of his life, indicated the next step he was to take. In this first dream he seemed to be surrounded by a crowd of fighting and blaspheming children whom he strove in vain to pacify, at first by argument and then with his fists. Suddenly there appeared a mysterious lady who said to him : " Softly, softly   if you wish to win them ! Take your shepherd's staff and lead them to pasture." As she spoke, the children were transformed into wild beasts and then into lambs. From that moment John recognized that his duty was to help poor boys, and he began with those of his own village, teaching them the catechism and bringing them to church. As an encouragement, he would often delight them with acrobatic and conjuring tricks, at which he became very proficient. One Sunday morning, when a perambulating juggler and gymnast was detaining the youngsters with his performances, the little lad challenged him to a competition, beat him at his own job, and triumphantly bore off his audience to Mass. Whilst he was staying with an aunt who was servant to a priest, John had learnt to read and he ardently desired to become a priest, but he had many difficulties to overcome before he could enter on his studies. He was sixteen when he entered the seminary at Chieri and so poor that his maintenance money and his very clothes had to be provided by charity, the mayor contributing his hat, the parish priest his cloak, one parishioner his cassock, and another a pair of shoes. After his ordination to the diaconate he passed to the theological college of Turin and, during his residence there, he began, with the approbation of his superiors, to gather together on Sundays a number of the neglected apprentices and waifs of the city.

His attention was confirmed in this field by St Joseph Cafasso, then rector of a parish church and the annexed sacerdotal institute in Turin. It was he who persuaded Don Bosco that he was not cut out to be a missionary abroad : " Go and unpack that trunk you've got ready, and carry on with your work for the boys. That, and nothing else, is God's will for you." Don Cafasso introduced him, on the one hand, to those moneyed people of the city who were in time to come to be the generous benefactors of his work, and on the other hand to the prisons and slums whence were to come the beneficiaries of that work.

His first appointment was to the assistant chaplaincy of a refuge for girls founded by the Marchesa di Barola, the wealthy and philanthropic woman who had taken care of Silvio Pellico after his release. This post left him free on Sunday to look after his boys, ·to whom he devoted the whole day and for whom he devised a sort of combined Sunday-school and recreation centre which he called a " festive oratory ". Permission to meet on premises belonging to the marchesa was soon withdrawn because the lads were noisy and some of them picked the flowers, and for over a year they were sent from pillar to post—no landlord being willing to put up with the lively band, which had increased to several hundred. When at last Don Bosco was able to hire an old shed and all seemed promising, the marchesa, who with all her generosity was somewhat of an autocrat, delivered an ultimatum offering him the alternative of giving up the boys or resigning his post at her refuge. He chose the latter.

In the midst of his anxiety, the holy man was prostrated by a severe attack of pneumonia with complications which nearly cost him his life. He had hardly recovered when he went to live in some miserable rooms adjoining his new oratory, and with his mother installed as his housekeeper he applied himself to consolidating and extending his work. A night-school started the previous year took permanent shape, and as the oratory was overcrowded, he opened two more centres in other quarters of Turin. It was about this time that he began to take in and house a few destitute children. In a short time some thirty or forty neglected boys, most of them apprentices in the city, were living with Don Bosco and his devoted mother, " Mamma Margaret ", in the Valdocco quarter, going out daily to work. He soon realized that any good he could do them was counterbalanced by outside influences, and he eventually determined to train the apprentices at home. He opened his first two workshops, for shoemakers and tailors, in 1853.

The next step was to construct for his flock a church, which he placed under the patronage of his favourite saint, Francis de Sales, and when that was finished he set to work to build a home for his increasing family. The money came—miraculously as it often seemed. The boys were of two sorts little would-be apprentices, and those in whom Don Bosco discerned future helpers and possible vocations to the priesthood. At first they attended classes outside, but, as more help became available, technical courses and grammar classes were started in the house and all were taught at home. By 1856 there were 150 resident boys, with four workshops including a printing-press, and also four Latin classes, with ten young priests, besides the oratories with their 500 children. Owing to his intense sympathy and marvellous power of reading their thoughts, Don Bosco exercised an unbounded influence over his boys, whom he was able to rule with an apparent indulgence and absence of punishment which rather scandalized the educationists of his day. Over and above all this work, he was in constant request as a preacher, his fame for eloquence being enhanced by the numerous miracles—mostly of healing—which were wrought through his intercession. A third form of activity which he pursued for years was the writing of popular books, for he was as strongly convinced of the power of the press as any member of the Catholic Truth Society. Now it would be a work in defence of the faith, now a history or other lesson book, now one of a series of Catholic readings which would occupy him for half the night, until failing sight in later life compelled him to lay down his pen.

For years St John Bosco's great problem was that of help. Enthusiastic young priests would offer their services, but sooner or later would give up, because they could not master Don Bosco's methods or had not his patience with often vicious young ruffians or were put off by his scheme for schools and workshops when he had not a penny. Some even were disappointed because he would not turn the oratory into a political club in the interests of " Young Italy ". By 1850 he had only one assistant left, and he resolved to train young men himself for the work. (It was in consequence of this that St Dominic Savio came to the oratory in 1854.) In any case something in the nature of a religious order had long been in his mind and, after several disappointments, the time came when he felt that he had at last the nucleus he desired. " On the night of January 26, 1854, we were assembled in Don Bosco's room," writes one of those present. " Besides Don Bosco there were Cagliero, Rocchetti, Artiglia and Rua. It was suggested that with God's help we should enter upon a period of practical works of charity to help our neighbours. At the close of that period we might bind ourselves by a promise, which could subsequently be transformed into a vow. From that evening, the name of Salesian was given to all who embarked upon that form of apostolate." The name, of course, came from the great Bishop of Geneva. It seemed a most unpropitious moment for launching a new congregation, for in all its history Piedmont had never been so anti-clerical. The Jesuits and the Ladies of the Sacred Heart had been expelled, many convents had been suppressed, and law after law was passed curtailing the rights of the religious orders. Nevertheless it was the statesman Rattazzi, one of the ministers most responsible for that legislation, who, meeting Don Bosco one day, urged him to found a society to carry on his valuable work, promising him the support of the king.

In December 1859, with twenty-two companions, he finally determined to proceed with the organization of a religious congregation, whose rules had received the general approval of Pope Pius IX ; but it was not until fifteen years later that the constitutions received their final approbation, with leave to present candidates for holy orders. The new society grew apace in 1863 there were 39 Salesians, at the founder's death 768, and today they are numbered by thousands, all over the world. One of Don Bosco's dreams was realized when he sent his first missionaries to Patagonia, and others soon spread over South America. He lived to see twenty-six houses started in the New World and thirty-eight in the Old. Today Salesian establishments include schools from the primary grade to colleges and seminaries, adult schools, technical schools, agricultural schools, printing and bookbinding shops, hospitals, to say nothing of foreign missions and pastoral work.

His next great work was the foundation of an order of women to do for poor girls what the Salesians were doing for boys. This was inaugurated in 1872 with the clothing of twenty-seven young women to whom he gave the name of Daughters of Our Lady, Help of Christians. This community increased almost as fast as the other, with elementary schools in Italy, Brazil and the Argentine, and other activities. To supplement the work of these two congregations, Don Bosco organized his numerous outside helpers into a new sort of third order to which he attached the up-to-date title of Salesian Co-operators. These were men and women of all classes, pledged to assist in some way the educational labours of the Salesians.

The dream or vision previously referred to struck the note for all Don Bosco's dealings with boys. It is a platitude that to do anything with them you must have a liking for them ; but the love must also be seen. It radiated from Don Bosco, and incidentally helped to form his ideas about punishment at a time when the crudest superstitions on that subject were still almost unquestioned. Fostering of a sense of personal responsibility, removal of occasions of disobedience, appreciation of effort, friendliness : these were his methods. In 1877 he wrote, " I do not remember ever to have used formal punishment. By God's grace I have always been able to get not only observance of rules but even of my bare wishes." There went with that an acute awareness of the harm done by misdirected kindness, as he was not slow to point out to parents. One of the pleasantest pictures that St John Bosco's name conjures up is those Sunday excursions into the country with a gang of boys, when he would celebrate Mass in the village church, then breakfast and games out-of-doors, a catechism lesson, and the singing of Vespers to end up— Don Bosco was a firm believer in the civilizing and spiritualizing effects of good music.

Any account of Don Bosco's life would be incomplete without some mention of his work as a church-builder. His first little church soon proving insufficient for its increasing congregation, the founder proceeded to the construction of a much larger one which was completed in 1868. This was followed by another spacious and much-needed basilica in a poor quarter of Turin, which he placed under the patronage of St John the Evangelist. The effort to raise the necessary money had been immense, and the holy man was out of health and very weary, but his labours were not yet over. During the last years of Pius IX, the project had been formed of building in Rome a church in honour of the Sacred Heart, and Pius had given the money to buy the site. His successor was equally anxious for the work to proceed, but it seemed impossible to obtain funds to raise it above the foundations.

" What a pity it is that we can make no headway," remarked the pope after a consistory. " The glory of God, the honour of the Holy See and the spiritual good of so many are involved in the undertaking. I can see no way out of the difficulty."

" I could suggest one ", said Cardinal Alimonda.

" And what might that be ? "

" Hand it over to Don Bosco : he could do it."

" But would he accept ? "

" I know him : a wish expressed by your Holiness would be honoured as a command."

The task was accordingly proposed to him and he undertook it.

When he could obtain no more funds from Italy he betook himself to France, the land where devotion to the Sacred Heart has always flourished pre-eminently. Everywhere he was acclaimed as a saint and a wonder-worker, and the money came pouring in. The completion of the new church was assured, but, as the time for the consecration approached, Don Bosco was sometimes heard to say that if it were long delayed he would not be alive to witness it. It took place on May 14, 1887, and he offered Mass in the church once shortly after ; but as the year drew on it became evident that his days were numbered. Two years earlier the doctors had declared that he had worn himself out and that complete rest was his only chance, but rest for him was out of the question. At the end of the year his strength gave way altogether, and he became gradually weaker until at last he passed away on January 31, 1888, so early in the morning that his death has been described, not quite correctly, as occurring on the morrow of the feast of St Francis de Sales. Forty thousand persons visited his body as it lay in the church, and his funeral resembled a triumph, for the whole city of Turin turned out to do him honour when his mortal remains were borne to their last resting-place. St John Bosco was canonized in 1934.

A full biography of Don Bosco in Italian, by G. B. Lemoyne, has had an enormous sale, but the standard life is that by A. Auffray (1929). Biographies and studies are numerous in many languages. Among the more recent in French are those by D. Lathoud (1938), F. Veuillot (1943), and P. Cras's *Fidèle histoire de St Jean Bosco* (1936), and such shorter works in English as H. Ghéon's *Spirit of St John Bosco* and those of F. A. Forbes and Fr H. L. Hughes. *St John Bosco's Early Apostolate* (1934), by Fr G. Bonetti, is an exhaustive study of the first quarter-century of the saint's priesthood. A new English edition of Auffray's work is in preparation.

SS. CYRUS AND JOHN, Martyrs   (*c.* A.D. 303)

Cyrus, a physician of Alexandria, who by the opportunities which his profession gave him had converted many persons to the faith, and John, an Arabian, hearing that a lady called Athanasia and her three daughters, of whom the eldest was only fifteen, were suffering grievous torment for the name of Christ at Canopus in Egypt, went thither to encourage them. They were apprehended themselves, and cruelly beaten : their sides being burnt with torches, while salt and vinegar were poured into their wounds in the presence of Athanasia and her daughters, who were also tortured after them. At length the four women, and a few days after, Cyrus and John, were beheaded, the two latter on this day. The Syrians, Egyptians, Greeks and Latins all venerate their memory.

Concerning these saints who, like SS. Cosmas and Damian, were specially honoured among the Greeks as ἀνάργυροι (physicians who took no fees), there is

a fairly abundant literature. Of special interest are three short discourses of St
Cyril of Alexandria, and a panegyric and relation of miracles by St Sophronius,
Patriarch of Jerusalem (*fl.* 638).   In these last, strong traces are said to be found
of practices resembling the incubation familiar in the temples of Aesculapius.   A
certain authority accrues to the writings of Sophronius, who had himself been
healed at the shrine of these martyrs, by the citation of extracts from them in the
proceedings of the second Council of Nicaea in 787.   From St Cyril we learn
the interesting fact that when at Menuthi in Egypt, at the beginning of the fifth
century, superstitious rites were still observed by the populace in honour of
Isis, St Cyril could think of no better plan for counteracting the mischief
than by translating thither a great part of the relics of SS. Cyrus and John.   At
Menuthi, consequently, a great shrine grew up which became a famous place of
pilgrimage.   The spot is now known as Abukir, well remembered from Nelson's
great naval victory in 1798 and the landing of Sir Ralph Abercrombie in 1801.
Abukir is simply 'Αββά Κῦρος, Abbacyrus, from the name of the first of the two
saints.   Strangely enough, outside Rome is a little church known as Santa
Passera, which represents another transformation of the same name   Abbáciro,
Pácero, Passera.

See P. Sinthern in the *Römische Quartalschrift*, vol. xxii (1908), pp. 196–239 ; H. Delehaye
in *Analecta Bollandiana*, vol. xxx (1911), pp. 448–450, and *Legends of the Saints* (1907),
pp. 152 *seq.* ; P. Peeters in *Analecta Bollandiana*, vol. xxv (1906), pp. 233–240 ; and BHG.,
pp. 33–34   St Cyril's discourses are in Migne, PG., vol. lxxxvii, c. 1110 ; and St Sophronius's relation in the same, cc. 33–79.

ST MARCELLA, Widow   (A.D. 410)

St Marcella is styled by St Jerome the glory of the Roman ladies.   Having lost
her husband in the seventh month of her marriage, she rejected the suit of Cerealis
the consul, and resolved to imitate the lives of the ascetics of the East.   She
abstained from wine and flesh, employed her time in reading, prayer and visiting
the churches of the martyrs, and never spoke with any man alone.   Her example
was followed by other women of noble birth who put themselves under her direction, and Rome witnessed the formation of several such communities in a short
time.   We have sixteen letters of St Jerome to her in answer to her questions on
religious matters, but she was by no means content simply to " sit at his feet "
she examined his arguments closely and rebuked him for his hasty temper.   When
the Goths plundered Rome in 410 they maltreated St Marcella to make her disclose
her supposed treasures, which in fact she had long before distributed among the
poor.   She trembled only for her dear pupil Principia (not her daughter, as some
have erroneously supposed), and falling at the feet of the soldiers she begged that
they would offer her no insult.   God moved them to compassion : they conducted
them both to the church of St Paul, to which Alaric had granted the right of
sanctuary.   St Marcella survived this but a short time, and died in the arms of
Principia about the end of August in 410 ; her memory is honoured on this day in
the Roman Martyrology.

All that we know of St Marcella is practically speaking derived from the letters of St
Jerome, especially from letter 127 entitled " Ad Principiam virginem, sive Marcellae viduae
epitaphium " (Migne, PL., vol. xxii, cc. 1087 *seq.*).   See also Grützmacher, *Hieronymus ;
eine biographische Studie*, vol. i, pp. 225 *seq.* ; vol. ii, pp. 173 *seq.* ; vol. iii, pp. 195 *seq.* ;
Cavallera, *Saint Jérôme* (2 vols., 1922) ; and DCB, vol. iii, p. 803.

ST AIDAN, OR MAEDOC, OF FERNS, BISHOP (A.D. 626)

ALREADY in the twelfth century we find Giraldus Cambrensis speaking of " Aidanus qui et Hybernice *Maidaucus* (dicitur) ", *i.e.* " Aidan who in Irish is called *Maidauc*." In point of fact, surprising as it may appear, these and other forms, such as Aidus, Aiduus, Maedhog, Mogue, etc., not only denote the same individual but are all variants of the same name. To Áed (which seems originally to have meant *fire*) a suffix is added, and it appears in Latin as Aidanus ; whereas by prefixing the endearing particle *Mo*, and adding the suffix *óc* we get in full accord with Irish " hypocoristic " tendencies, Mo-áed-óc -- Maedoc.

As in the case of nearly all other Irish saints of the early period, the life of St Maedoc is overlaid with legendary accretions, and any attempt to arrive at an accurate chronology is out of the question. By his parentage he seems to have belonged to Connaught, and we have wonderful stories concerning the portents which attended his birth and the miracles of his early years, as, for example, that a stag hunted by dogs took refuge with him when Maedoc was studying, but the saint rendered the poor beast invisible and the hounds retired baffled. After that we are told how he passed through Leinster and " desirous of studying the Holy Scriptures, sailed over sea to the country of the Britons, and reading these at the monastery of St David he remained a long time and performed many miracles at that place " We are told that he took with him a carload of beer, having no doubt heard of the teetotal habits of the Mynyw monks. Being rebuked once by St David he prostrated himself upon the sea-shore waiting until the word " rise " should be spoken. David forgot, and the tide came in ; but the good youth was not drowned, for the waters were built up all around him like a wall. A curious reminiscence of the deadly strife between Saxons and Britons which marked the sixth century is preserved in several passages, as for example when we read that " as long as the holy youth Aidan dwelt in the districts of the Britons with St David, the Saxons dared not come thither " ; and again that when a raiding party of Saxons did come, Aidan by his curse blinded them all, " and without hurting anyone or killing, the Saxons returned back and were blind through the whole year."

In due course St Maedoc returned to Ireland where, receiving a grant of land from King Brandubh, he built a monastery at Ferns in County Wexford. He was eventually consecrated bishop there. The record, however, preserved in the lives, both Latin and Irish, is little more than a long concatenation of miracles, some of them very bizarre. They leave a general impression of kindliness and charity, as for example when we read that one day the cook came to the saint and said " We have only a small jug of milk and a little butter left ; ought I to give it to the strangers who ask hospitality ? " " Give to everyone generously ", he was told, " as if you had all the mountain pastures to furnish supplies." But nevertheless that evening there was abundance for all the community. St Maedoc, under the form of his name Aidan or Edan, has a feast throughout Ireland today. His bell and shrine, with its satchel, are shown in the National Museum in Dublin.

The principal Latin sources for the history of St Maedoc have been published by Dr C. Plummer in VSH., vol. ii, pp. 142–163 and 295–311 (*cf.* also preface, lxxv–lxxvii), and the Irish Lives in *Bethada Náem nÉrenn* (1922), vol. i, pp. 183–290 (and *cf.* preface, xxxiii–xxxvii). See also *Acta Sanctorum* for January 31 and LIS., vol. i.

ST ADAMNAN OF COLDINGHAM (*c.* A.D. 680)

THE monastery of Coldingham, on the coast of Berwick, was a double one, for both men and women, and among its monks was an Irishman named Adamnan (Eunan), who lived a life of great austerity. One day, returning from a walk with one of his brethren, they stopped to look at the group of monastic buildings, and Adamnan suddenly burst into tears. Turning to his companion he said " The time is approaching when a fire shall consume all the buildings that we see." The other monk reported this prediction to the abbess, St Ebba, " the mother of the congregation ", and she naturally questioned Adamnan closely about it, with the result that is related in the account of Ebba herein (August 25). There seems to have been no liturgical *cultus* of Adamnan of Coldingham.

This St Adamnan is, of course, an entirely different person from St Adamnan of Iona. All we know of him comes from Bede, *Ecclesiastical History*, bk iv, ch. 23. See Plummer's edition and notes, together with KSS., p. 264, and the Bollandists (*Acta Sanctorum*, Jan., vol. iii).

ST ULPHIA, VIRGIN (*c.* A.D. 750)

THE feast of St Ulphia, whose name is written in many forms (Wulfe, Olfe, etc.), is kept in the diocese of Amiens. The late medieval biography we possess of her is of little historical value, but it is no doubt true that she led the life of a solitary under the direction of the aged hermit St Domitius. According to the legend, they both dwelt at no great distance from the church of our Lady, on the site of the present Saint-Acheul. Domitius in passing used to awaken Ulphia by knocking with his stick so that she might follow him to the offices in the church. On one occasion the frogs had croaked so loud during the greater part of the night that Ulphia had had no sleep, and the knocking failed to wake her. She accordingly forbade them to croak again, and we are assured that in that locality they are silent even to this day. After the death of Domitius, St Ulphia was joined by a disciple named Aurea, and a community was formed at Amiens under her guidance ; but she eventually returned to her solitude, and it was only in 1279, some hundreds of years after her death, that her remains were translated to Amiens cathedral.

See the *Acta Sanctorum* for January 31 and Corblet, *Hagiographie du diocèse d'Amiens* (1869).

ST EUSEBIUS, MARTYR (A.D. 884)

IN spite of his name this St Eusebius, we are told, was an Irishman who left his country like so many other *peregrini*, and eventually took the monastic habit in the famous abbey of Saint-Gall in Switzerland. He did not, however, remain there, but was permitted to go apart to lead the life of a hermit in the solitude of Mount St Victor near Röttris, in the Vorarlberg. After some thirty years it happened that when he, one day, denounced the godless lives of some of the neighbouring peasantry, one of them struck him with a scythe and killed him. A " monasterium Scottorum " (monastery for the Irish) was erected there by Charles the Fat at about the same date.

See the *Acta Sanctorum* for January 31 ; MGH., *Scriptores*, vol. ii, p. 73 ; and L. Gougaud, *Gaelic Pioneers of Christianity* (1923), pp. 11, 82, 90.

ST NICETAS, Bishop of Novgorod   (A.D. 1107)

Nicetas (Nikita), a native of Kiev, while still a young man became a monk in the monastery of the Caves there and conceived the ambition of becoming a solitary. In spite of the contrary advice of the abbot and other experienced monks he insisted on shutting himself away.   Whereupon he was subjected to a remarkable temptation.   An evil spirit of angelic appearance suggested that he should give himself to reading instead of prayer.   The first book to which Nicetas devoted himself was the Old Testament : he learned much of it by heart and received preternatural insight, so that people came to the monastery to consult him.   The older monks warned him of what would come of studying only Jewish books : he came to dislike the New Testament, and would neither read it nor hear it read.   But the prayers of his brethren at last brought him to his senses, he lost his deceptive wisdom, and humbly began his monastic life all over again, becoming a model for the whole community.

   In 1095 Nicetas was made bishop of Novgorod, and in that charge his holiness was manifested by miracles : he was said to have put out a great fire by his prayers and to have obtained rain in time of drought.   He was bishop for twelve years before he died, and about four hundred and fifty years later his relics were translated to the cathedral of the Holy Wisdom at Kiev.   In the Russian use of the Byzantine Mass, St Nicetas of Novgorod is commemorated at the preparation of the holy things.

   See Martynov's *Annus ecclesiasticus graeco-slavicus* in *Acta Sanctorum*, October, vol. xi. For other examples of dissuasion from the solitary life and of the significance of the Old Testament in early Russian Christianity, see Fedotov, *The Russian Religious Mind* (1946).

BD PAULA GAMBARA-COSTA, Matron   (A.D. 1515)

This holy Franciscan tertiary, the example of whose married life stands out in acute contrast to the laxity of the age in which she lived, was born near Brescia in 1473.   Strange and quite incredible things were afterwards related of the piety shown by her in early childhood, when, for example, she is said as an infant at the breast to have displayed her sympathy for the law of the Church by a marked abstemiousness on Fridays.   She was married at the age of twelve to a young nobleman, Lodovicantonio Costa, after all the formalities customary at that period had been duly observed.   The famous Franciscan, Bd Angelo of Chiavasso, was called into consultation, and in spite of the little maid's reluctance he formally pronounced that " the Lord had called His servant to the married state ", and wedded she accordingly was, with a splendour suited to the high rank of both families, even the wheels of the coaches, we are told, being gilded.   One authentic document is a copy of the rule of life which the bride seems to have submitted to Bd Angelo when she first settled down in her husband's home.   She was to rise every morning at day-break and say her morning prayers and rosary.   A little later she was to visit the Franciscan church in the neighbourhood, and assist at two Masses.   In the afternoon she was to recite the office of our Lady and before she went to bed she said another rosary and her night prayers.   There were also two periods of spiritual reading.   She was to fast on all vigils of our Lady and a number of other vigils, and to go to confession once a fortnight.   But the most illuminative clause is the following : " I will always obey my husband, and take a kindly view of his failings, and I will do all I can to prevent their coming to the knowledge of anyone." Her eldest son was born in 1488, she herself being then barely fifteen.

It was not long, however, before the young wife found that sad troubles were in store for her. It seems to have been her incorrigible habit of giving lavishly to the poor which first awakened her husband's resentment. As long as food was plentiful this did not so much matter, but in seasons of scarcity—and we hear of many such about this time—beggars swarmed and the worldly-wise hoarded all that their barns contained. It is true that Paula's biographers declare that in her case grain, oil and wine were supernaturally multiplied in proportion to the generosity of her alms, so that her household was not the poorer but actually the richer for her charities. We must confess, however, that the evidence is open to some suspicion. For example, there is told of Paula a story which is the exact counterpart of a well-known incident in the life of St Elizabeth of Hungary, *viz*. that going out one day with her apron full of loaves Paula met her husband, who rudely forced her to show him what she carried, whereupon he found, in that winter season, a great heap of rose blossoms. If this miracle really happened to as many saints as it is attributed to, it must have been of rather frequent occurrence.

What was quite unpardonable was Lodovicantonio's introduction into his home of a young woman of bad character, who poisoned his mind against his wife, served him as a spy, and became the actual mistress of the household. After inflicting incredible humiliation upon his wife, this young woman fell ill and died very soon afterwards, having been devotedly nursed by Paula, who brought a priest to her and obtained for her the grace of conversion. It is a curious illustration of the social life of that period, the age of the Borgias, that Paula was accused of poisoning her rival because the body was found much swollen and the illness had terminated more quickly than was expected. In the end, however, Paula, by her unalterable patience and charity, regained her husband's affection. He himself turned sincerely to God and allowed his wife to practise her devotions and to exercise charity as she pleased. Apart from other austerities she used to rise in the night to pray, kneeling without support with hands uplifted in the middle of the room ; more than once in the cold of winter she was found unconscious upon the floor, stiff and almost frozen to death. Many stories are told of her charities, as, for example, that meeting a beggar-woman in the road who had no shoes, she gave her those she was wearing, and herself returned to the castle bare-foot. We cannot be surprised that Bd Paula died in her forty-second year, on January 24, 1515. Her cult was confirmed in 1845.

See R. Bollano, *Vita . della B. Paola Gambara-Costa* (1765) ; Léon, *Auréole Séraphique* (Eng. trans.), vol. i, pp. 534–536.

ST FRANCIS XAVIER BIANCHI   (A.D. 1815)

St Francis Bianchi was born in 1743 at Arpino, in what was then the kingdom of the Two Sicilies, and was educated as an ecclesiastical student at Naples, receiving the tonsure when he was only fourteen. His father, however, would not hear of his entering a religious order, and the boy had to pass through a period of great mental anguish in the conflict between duty to his parents and what seemed the call of God. Taking counsel at last with St Alphonsus Liguori, to whom he found access during one of the saint's missions, Francis became sure of his vocation, and overcoming all opposition he entered the Congregation of Clerks Regular of St

Paul, commonly called Barnabites. In consequence probably of the ordeal through which he had passed, he then fell seriously ill and suffered acutely for three years, but he recovered eventually, and was able to make great progress in his studies, distinguishing himself particularly in literature and science. He was ordained priest in 1767, and the trust which his superiors reposed in his virtue and practical ability was shown not only by his being deputed to hear confessions at an early age, a rare concession in Italy, but also by his appointment as superior to two different colleges simultaneously, a charge which he held for fifteen years.

Many important offices were conferred upon him in the order, but his soul seems to have felt more and more the call to detach himself from external things, and to devote all his energies to prayer and the work of the ministry. He began to lead an extremely mortified and austere life, spending also long hours in the confessional, where his advice was sought by thousands. His health suffered, and his infirmities became so great that he could hardly drag himself from place to place ; nevertheless he persisted, and his unflinching resolution in placing himself at the service of all who needed his help seems to have lent a wonderful efficacy to his words and his prayers, so that he was universally regarded as a saint. At the time when the religious orders were dispersed and driven from their houses in Naples, Father Bianchi was in a most pitiable condition. His legs were terribly swollen and covered with sores, and he had to be carried to the altar. Some advantage, however, came to him from his very afflictions, for he was allowed to retain his habit and remain in the college where, all alone, he lived a life of the strictest religious observance.

There are many stories of his miraculous and prophetic powers. Two very remarkable cases of the multiplication of inadequate sums of money put aside in a drawer to meet a debt were recounted in the process of beatification, and it was also affirmed that in 1805, when Vesuvius was in eruption, Father Bianchi, at the earnest petition of his fellow townsfolk, had himself carried to the edge of the lava stream, and blessed it, with the result that the flow was stayed. Towards the end of his days the veneration he inspired in Naples was unbounded. " There may have been a Neri (black) in Rome ", the people said, " but we have our Bianchi (white) who is just as wonderful." Many years previously, a penitent of his, now known as St Mary Frances of Naples, who went to God in 1791, had promised Father Bianchi that she would appear to him three days before his death. The good priest was convinced that she would keep her word, and we are told that this visit actually took place three days before January 31, 1815, when he breathed his last. He was canonized in 1951.

See P. Rudoni, *Virtù e meraviglie del ven. Francesco S. M. Bianchi* (1823) ; C. Kempf, *The Holiness of the Church in the Nineteenth Century* (1916), pp. 96–97 ; *Analecta Ecclesiastica*, 1893, pp. 54 *seq.*

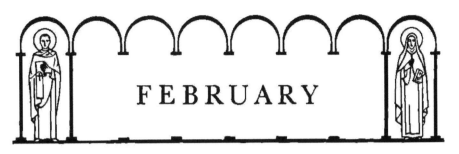

FEBRUARY

1 : ST IGNATIUS, Bishop of Antioch, Martyr   (c. A.D. 107)

ST IGNATIUS, surnamed Theophorus or God-bearer, was probably a
convert and a disciple of St John the Evangelist, but we know little that
is reliable concerning his earlier history.   According to some early writers
the apostles St Peter and St Paul directed that he should succeed St Evodius as
bishop of Antioch, an office which he retained for forty years, proving himself in
every way an exemplary pastor.   He is said by the church historian Socrates to
have introduced or popularized antiphonal singing in his diocese, but this is hardly
probable.   The peace for Christians which followed the death of Domitian only
lasted for the fifteen months of Nerva's reign and persecution was resumed under
Trajan.   In an interesting letter from the emperor to the younger Pliny, the
governor of Bithynia, the principle was laid down that Christians should be put
to death if formally delated, but that they should not be sought out otherwise.
Although Trajan was a magnanimous and humane man, yet the very gratitude which
he felt that he owed his gods for his victories over the Dacians and the Scythians
led him subsequently to persecute Christians for refusing to acknowledge these
divinities.   No reliance can unfortunately be placed in the account which legend
has bequeathed us of the arrest of Ignatius and his personal interview with the
emperor ; but from an early period it was believed that Trajan cross-questioned
the soldier of Christ in such terms as these :

" Who are you, spirit of evil, who dare to disobey my orders and who goad
others on to their destruction ? "

" No one calls Theophorus spirit of evil," the saint is said to have replied.

" Who is Theophorus ? "

" He who bears Christ within him."

" And do not *we* bear within ourselves those gods who help us against our
enemies ? " asked the emperor.

" You are mistaken when you call gods those who are no better than devils,"
retorted Ignatius.   " For there is only one God who made heaven and earth and
all that is in them   and one Jesus Christ into whose kingdom I earnestly desire to
be admitted."

Trajan inquired, " Do you mean Him who was crucified under Pontius Pilate ? "

" Yes, the same who by His death has crucified both sin and its author, and has
proclaimed that every malice of the devil should be trodden under foot by those
who bear Him in their hearts."

" Do you then carry about Christ within you ? " said the emperor.   Ignatius
answered, " Yes, for it is written, ' I will dwell in them and will walk with them.' "

When Trajan gave sentence that the bishop should be bound and taken to Rome
to be devoured by the wild beasts for the entertainment of the people, the saint

exclaimed, " I thank thee, O Lord, for putting within my reach this pledge of perfect love for thee, and for allowing me to be bound for thy sake with chains, after the example of thy apostle Paul."

Having prayed for the Church and commended it with tears to God, he joyfully submitted his limbs to the fetters and was hurried away by the soldiers to be taken to Rome.

At Seleucia, a seaport about sixteen miles from Antioch, they boarded a ship which, for some reason unknown to us, was to coast along the southern and western shores of Asia Minor, instead of proceeding at once to Italy. Some of his Christian friends from Antioch took the short route and, reaching Rome before him, awaited his arrival there. St Ignatius was accompanied for most of the way by a deacon called Philo and by Agathopus, who are supposed to have written the acts of his martyrdom. The voyage appears to have been a very cruel ordeal, for Ignatius was guarded night and day by ten soldiers who were so brutal that he says they were like " ten leopards " and he adds that he was " fighting with wild beasts on land and sea, by day and night " and " they only grow worse when they are kindly treated ".

The numerous stoppages, however, gave the saint opportunities of confirming in the faith the various churches near the coast of Asia Minor. Wherever the ship put in, the Christians sent their bishops and priests to meet him, and great crowds assembled to receive the benediction of one who was practically already a martyr. Deputies were also appointed to escort him on his way. At Smyrna, he had the joy of meeting his former fellow disciple St Polycarp, and hither came also Bishop Onesimus at the head of a deputation from Ephesus, Bishop Damas with envoys from Magnesia, and Bishop Polybius from Tralles. One of the deputies, Burrhus, was so useful that St Ignatius asked the Ephesians to allow him to stay with him as a companion. From Smyrna, the saint wrote four letters.

The letter to the Ephesians begins with high praise of that church. He exhorts them to remain in harmony with their bishop and all their clergy, to assemble often for public prayer, to be meek and humble, to suffer injuries without murmuring. He praises them for their zeal against heresy and reminds them that their most ordinary actions are spiritualized in so far as they are done in Jesus Christ. He calls them his fellow travellers on the road to God and tells them that they bear God and Christ in their breasts. He speaks in much the same terms in his letters to the churches of Magnesia and Tralles and warns them against the docetic teaching which explained away the reality of Christ's body and His human life. In the letter to Tralles Ignatius tells that community to keep from heresy, " which you will do if you remain united to God, even Jesus Christ, and the bishop and the ordinances of the apostles. He who is within the altar is clean, but he that is outside it, that is, who acts independently of the bishop, priests and deacons, is not clean." The fourth letter, addressed to the Christians in Rome, is an entreaty to them to do nothing to prevent him from winning the crown of martyrdom ; there was, he thought, some danger that the more influential would try to obtain a mitigation of his sentence. His alarm was not ill-founded. Christianity at this date had made converts in high places. Such men as Flavius Clemens, the cousin of the emperor, and the Acilii Glabriones had powerful friends in the administration. The pagan satirist Lucian (*c.* A.D. 165), who almost certainly was familiar with these letters of Ignatius, bears witness to the same effect.

" I fear your charity ", the bishop writes, " lest it prejudice me.   For it is easy for you to do what you please ; but it will be difficult for me to come to God unless you hold your hand.   I shall never have another such opportunity of attaining unto my Lord.   Therefore you cannot do me a greater favour than to suffer me to be poured out as a libation to God whilst the altar is ready ; that, forming a choir in love, you may give thanks to the Father by Jesus Christ that God has vouchsafed to bring me, a Syrian bishop, from the east to the west to pass out of this world, that I may rise again unto Him.   Only pray for me that God may give me grace within as well as without, not only to say it but to desire it, that I may not only be called but be found a Christian. .   . Suffer me to be the food of wild beasts through whom I may attain unto God.   I am God's grain and I am to be ground by the teeth of wild beasts that I may be found the pure bread of Christ. Rather entice the beasts to become my sepulchre, that they may leave nothing of my body, that when I am dead I may not be troublesome to any man.   I do not command you, as Peter and Paul did : they were apostles, whereas I am a culprit under sentence : they were free, but I am even yet a slave.   But if I suffer I shall then become the freedman of Jesus Christ and in Him I shall arise free.

I have joy of the beasts that are prepared for me and I heartily wish that they may devour me promptly : nay, I would even entice them to devour me immediately and wholly, and not to serve me as they have served some whom they have been afraid to touch.   If they are unwilling to meddle with me, I will even compel them. Excuse me in this matter.   I know what is good for me.   Now I begin to be a disciple.   May nothing visible or invisible begrudge me that I may attain unto Jesus Christ.   Come fire and cross, gashes and rendings, breaking of bones and mangling of limbs, the shattering in pieces of my whole body ; come all the wicked torments of the Devil upon me if I may but attain unto Jesus Christ. .   . The prince of this world tries to snatch me away, and to corrupt the Godward strivings of my soul.   Let none of you who are at hand lend him your aid.   Be rather on my side, that is, on God's.   Do not have the name of Jesus Christ upon your lips and worldly desires in your hearts.   Even were I myself, when I come amongst you, to implore your help, do not hearken to me but rather believe what I tell you by letter.   I write this full of life, but my longing is for death."

The guards were in a hurry to leave Smyrna in order that they might reach Rome before the games were over—for illustrious victims of venerable appearance were always a great attraction in the amphitheatre—and Ignatius himself gladly acquiesced.   They next sailed to Troas, where they learnt that peace had been restored to the church at Antioch.   At Troas he wrote three more letters.   To the Philadelphians he praises their bishop, whom he does not name, and he begs them avoid heresy.   " Use one eucharist ; for the flesh of the Lord Jesus Christ is one and the cup is one, to unite us all in His blood.   There is one altar, as there is one bishop, together with the body of the priesthood and the deacons my fellow servants, that whatever you do, you may do according to God."   In the letter to the Smyrnaeans we find another warning against the docetic heretics who denied that Christ had really assumed human flesh and that the Eucharist is actually His body.   He forbids all intercourse with such false teachers—permitting only that they should be prayed for.   The last letter is to St Polycarp, and consists mainly of advice to him, as to one greatly the writer's junior.   He exhorts him to labour for Christ, to put down false teaching, to look after widows, to hold frequent services, and reminds him that the measure of his labours will be the measure of his reward.   As St Ignatius had not time to write to other churches, he asked St Polycarp to do so in his name.

From Troas they sailed to Neapolis in Macedonia, and afterwards, we are told, they went to Philippi and, having crossed Macedonia and Epirus on foot, took ship again at Epidamnum (now Durazzo in Albania).   These details, it must be confessed, depend only upon the so-called " acts." of the martyrdom, and we can place no confidence in the description which has been left us of the closing scene.   As the saint approached Rome, the faithful are said to have come out to meet ·him, rejoicing at his presence in their midst but grieving that they were to lose him so soon.   As he had anticipated, they were desirous of taking steps to obtain his release, but he entreated them not to hinder him from going to the Lord.   Then, kneeling down with the brethren, he prayed for the Church, for the cessation of persecution, and for charity and unanimity among the faithful.   According to the same legend he arrived in Rome on December 20, the last day of the public games, and was brought before the prefect of the city, to whom the emperor's letter was delivered.   In due course the soldiers hurried him off to the Flavian amphitheatre,* and there we are told that two fierce lions were let out upon him, who devoured him immediately, leaving nothing but the larger bones.   Thus was his prayer heard.

There seems to be reasonable ground for believing that what fragments could be collected of the martyr's remains were taken back to Antioch and were venerated —no doubt at first in such a way as not to attract too much attention—" in a cemetery outside the Daphne gate ".   It is St Jerome, writing in 392, who tells us this, and we know that he had himself visited Antioch.   From the ancient Syrian Martyrology we learn that the martyr's feast was kept in those regions on October 17, and it may be assumed that the panegyric of St Ignatius preached by St John Chrysostom when he was still a priest at Antioch was delivered on that day. He lays great stress upon the point that while the soil of Rome had been drenched with the victim's blood, Antioch cherished his relics as a possession for all time. " You lent him for a season ", he told the people, " and you received him back with interest.   You sent him forth a bishop, you recovered him a martyr.   You led him out with prayers, you brought him home with the laurel wreaths of victory." But even in Chrysostom's time legend had already begun to play its part.   The orator supposes that Ignatius had been appointed by the apostle St Peter himself to succeed him in the bishopric of Antioch.   No wonder that at a later date a whole correspondence was fabricated, including letters which purported to have been exchanged between the martyr and the Blessed Virgin while she still dwelt on aarth after her Son's ascension.   Perhaps the most naïve of all these medieval fictions was the story which identified Ignatius with the little child whom our Lord (Mark ix 36) took into His arms and made the subject of a lesson in humility.

The obscurity which surrounds almost all the details of this great martyr's career is in marked contrast to the certainty with which scholarship now affirms the genuineness of the seven letters referred to above as written by him on his way to Rome.   This is not the place to enter upon a discussion of the three recensions of these letters, known as the Longer, the Curetonian and the Vossian.   The controversy, continued for centuries, has given rise to an immense literature, but the dispute is now practically settled.   It can at any rate be said that, with the

* There seems, however, to be no satisfactory reason for believing that St Ignatius suffered in the Flavian Amphitheatre or Colosseum rather than elsewhere.   See Delehaye, *Analecta Bollandiana*, vol. xvi (1897), pp. 209-252.

rarest exceptions, the present generation of patristic students are agreed in admitting the authenticity of the middle recension, which was first identified by Archbishop Ussher in 1644, and of which the Greek text was printed by Isaac Voss and by Dom Ruinart a little later in the same century.

The importance of the testimony which these letters bear to the beliefs and internal organization of the Christian Church less than a hundred years after the ascension of our Lord can hardly be exaggerated. St Ignatius of Antioch is the first writer outside the New Testament to lay stress upon the virgin-birth. To the Ephesians, for example, he writes, " And from the prince of this world were hidden Mary's virginity and her child-bearing, in like manner also the death of the Lord " The mystery of the Trinity, too, is plainly taken for granted, and we detect a definite approach to clear Christological conceptions when we read in the same letter (ch. vii), " There is one Physician, of flesh and of spirit, begotten and unbegotten, God in man, true Life in death, son of Mary and son of God, first passible and then impassible, Jesus Christ our Lord." Not less remarkable are the phrases used in connection with the Holy Eucharist. It is " the flesh of Christ ", " the gift of God ", " the medicine of immortality ", and Ignatius denounces the heretics " who confess not that the Eucharist is the flesh of our Saviour Jesus Christ, which flesh suffered for our sins and which in His loving-kindness the Father raised up ". Finally it is in the letter to the Smyrnaeans that for the first time in Christian literature we find mention of " the Catholic Church " " Wherever ", he writes, " the bishop appears, there let the people be, even as wherever Christ Jesus is, there is the Catholic Church." The saint often speaks severely of the heretical speculations—in particular, those of the docetists -which already in his day were threatening mischief to the integrity of the Christian faith. It might indeed be said that the key-note of all his instruction was insistence upon unity of belief and spirit among those who professed to be our Lord's followers. But, with all his dread of heresy, he emphasizes the need of indulgence towards the erring and urges patient forbearance and the love of the cross. The exhortation he addresses to the Ephesians provides a lesson for everyone whose religion is no empty name :

> And for the rest of men pray unceasingly—for there is in them hope of repentance—that they may attain unto God. Suffer them therefore to be instructed by the example of your works. In face of their outbursts of wrath be meek ; in face of their boastful words be humble ; meet their revilings with prayers ; where they are in error be steadfast in the faith ; in face of their fury be gentle. Be not eager to retaliate upon them. Let our forbearance prove us their brethren. Let us endeavour to be imitators of the Lord, striving who can suffer the greater wrong, who can be defrauded, who be set at naught, that no rank weed of the Devil be found in you. But in all purity and sobriety abide in Christ Jesus in flesh and in spirit.

It will be plain from what has preceded that, practically speaking, the seven letters of St Ignatius himself form the only reliable source of information concerning him. For English readers these may be conveniently consulted in the masterly work of Bishop Lightfoot, *The Apostolic Fathers* (1877–1885). A handy translation, with valuable introduction and notes, is provided in Dr J. H. Srawley's volume, *The Epistles of St Ignatius* (1935), and there is a text and translation by Kirsopp Lake in the Loeb Classical Library, *The Apostolic Fathers*, vol. i (1930). The translation and notes in the Early Christian Writers series (1946) are by Dr J. A. Kleist. Other editions, such as those of A. Lelong, F. X. Funk and T. Zahn, need not here be mentioned. The letters of Ignatius, translated into Latin and also into several oriental languages, were widely known to early Christian writers. Even the British

St Gildas, in his *De excidio Britanniae*, written about 540, quotes from that addressed to the Romans. Chrysostom's panegyric is in Migne, PG., vol. I. For further considerations on the date of the martyrdom, see H. Grégoire in *Analecta Bollandiana*, vol. lxix (1951), pp. 1 *seq.* St Ignatius is named in the canon of the Mass of the Roman, Syrian and Maronite rites.

ST PIONIUS, MARTYR   (A.D. 250 ?)

A PRIEST of Smyrna and a true heir of the spirit of St Polycarp, St Pionius was an eloquent and learned man who converted multitudes to the true faith. During the persecution of Decius (Marcus Aurelius ?) he was apprehended, together with Sabina and Asclepiades, while they were celebrating the anniversary festival of St Polycarp's martyrdom. Pionius was forewarned in a dream of his impending fate. In the morning while they were taking the " holy bread " (probably the *eulogia* blessed and distributed at Mass) with water, they were surprised and seized by Polemon, the chief priest of the temple. Throughout lengthy cross-examinations, they resisted all solicitations to offer sacrifice and, professing their readiness to suffer the worst torments and even death rather than give way, they declared that they worshipped only one God and that they belonged to the Catholic Church. When Asclepiades was asked what God he worshipped he made answer, " Jesus Christ ". Polemon said, " Is that another god ? " Asclepiades, replied, " No ; He is that same God whom they have just confessed "—a clear declaration at this early date of the consubstantiality of God the Son. When Sabina heard threats that they would all be burnt alive, she only smiled. The pagans said, " Dost thou smile ? Then thou shalt be sent to the public stews." She answered, " God will be my protector there ".

They were cast into prison, and chose to be placed in a less accessible dungeon in order that, being alone, they might be at more liberty to pray. They were dragged by force into the temple and violence was used to compel them to sacrifice. They resisted with all their might, so much so that, as the *acta* report, " it took six men to overpower Pionius ". When garlands were placed on their heads the martyrs tore them off ; and the priest whose duty it was to bring them the sacrificial food was afraid to approach them. Their constancy atoned for the scandal caused by Eudaemon, Bishop of Smyrna, who had apostatized and offered sacrifice. When the proconsul Quintilian arrived in Smyrna, he caused Pionius to be stretched on the rack and his body to be torn with hooks, and he afterwards condemned him to death. The sentence, we are told, was read out in Latin : " Pionius confesses that he is a Christian, and we order him to be burnt alive ".

In the ardour of his faith it was the martyr himself who was foremost in hastening to the stadium (the public race-course), and there he divested himself of his garments. His limbs showed no sign of the recent torture. Raising himself upon the wooden stand, he let the soldier fasten the nails. When he had thus been firmly secured the presiding officer said, " Think better of it even now and the nails shall be taken out " ; but he answered that it was his desire to die soon in order that he might rise again the sooner. Standing with his face towards the east while fuel was piled up round him, Pionius closed his eyes, so that the people thought that he had fainted. But he was praying silently, and having reached the end of his prayer, he opened his eyes and said " Amen ", his face radiant all the while the flames were rising about him. At last with the words, " Lord, receive my soul ", he gave up his spirit peacefully and painlessly to the Father who has promised to guard every soul unjustly condemned. This all seems to be the account of an eye-witness, who tells us further that when the fire was put out " we who stood by saw that his body was like the well-cared-for body of a lusty athlete ; the hair on his head and cheeks was not singed, and on his face there shone a wondrous radiance."

His acts, purporting to be written by eye-witnesses, are quoted by Eusebius and have been published by Ruinart from a Latin version, but there is also a Greek text which is probably the original. Lightfoot says of them, " These acts bear every mark of genuineness", and Delehaye, who discusses the question at some length in his *Les Passions des Martyrs* (1921), pp. 27–59, is in thorough agreement. The Greek text of the *acta* may be conveniently consulted in O. von Gebhardt, *Acta martyrum selecta*, pp. 96–114. The greater part may be found excellently translated into English in J. A. F. Gregg's *The Decian Persecution*, pp. 249–261. For the question of date, *cf.* H. Grégoire in *Analecta Bollandiana*, vol. lxix (1951), pp. 1 *seq.*

ST BRIGID, or BRIDE, ABBESS OF KILDARE, VIRGIN   (c. A.D. 525)

FOR anything in the nature of a connected story the numerous "lives" of St Brigid, written by her countrymen from one to four centuries after her death, supply no materials. Yet there cannot be any question that she must be numbered among the greatest and most highly venerated of the saints whose virtues lent glory to Ireland and helped, at least indirectly, to christianize Europe. Her memory, as it lived in the hearts of the people, was identified with an extraordinary spirit of charity. The greater part of the list of extravagant miracles which does duty for a chronicle of her work on earth is represented as being the compassionate response to some appeal which had moved her pity or roused her sense of justice. It would be a very false inference to conclude, as some have done, that because the incidents recorded of her are for the most part quite incredible, she was therefore herself no more than a myth. The people of Ireland beyond most other peoples are both imaginative and full of enthusiasm, and it follows that they are jealous of the glory of those whom they hold in honour. To record ordinary and possible things of her whom they called " the Mary of the Gael ", and regarded as the patroness of all the good women to whom Erin has given birth, would have seemed derogatory to her dignity. The very fact that strange marvels were attributed to Patrick and many lesser heroes of sanctity made it necessary that she also should not be without her crown : were not Patrick and Brigid " the columns on which all Ireland rested ? " Bare prosaic facts were not worth chronicling, or what comes to the same thing, were not judged to be worth reading in the case of one so exalted as she. It is important to have a clear perception of this curious mentality if we are not to be misled by the extravagances which swarm in such collections as Plummer's *Bethada Náem n-Érenn*, or in the *Book of Lismore*. The same caution applies in a measure to all medieval hagiography, but it is especially true of that which has been transmitted to us by Celtic pens. The example of even one extravagant Life imposed a kind of constraint upon all the biographers who came after to live up to the same standard. There must be signs and wonders, prodigies upon an heroic scale ; and if these were lacking the chronicler paid the penalty of seeing his book cast aside as stale and unprofitable. It is this unfortunate love of the sensational among simple and unsophisticated souls which explains how it has come about in all early hagiography that for one manuscript of the *acta sincera*, the really truthful record of a martyr's ordeal, we possess fifty of any story which has been so distorted and embellished with marvels that it can be regarded as little better than a romance.

What can be affirmed, then, with certainty regarding the facts of St Brigid's history is remarkably little. We are probably safe in saying that she was born about the middle of the fifty century at Faughart, near Dundalk. She undoubtedly consecrated herself to God at an early age, but the statement that she was " veiled " by St Maccaille at Mag Teloch and afterwards consecrated by St Mel at Ardagh sounds very questionable. The difficulty is increased by a gloss appended to St Broccan's hymn on St Brigid that St Mel " conferred upon her the order of a bishop ", and that from this Brigid's successor " has always a right to have bishop's orders and a bishop's honour upon her ". Father John Ryan discusses the problem in his *Irish Monasticism*, and concludes that " the story was occasioned by the exceptional honour paid, as a matter of traditional usage, to St Brigid's successor at Kildare, an honour that in some respects could be compared with the special honour shown to bishops in the hierarchy of the Church ". But, strangely enough, apart from the account of Cogitosus, St Brigid's foundation of the nunnery at Kildare is not much dwelt upon in the lives, though this seems to have been the great historic fact of her career and the achievement which made her in some sense the mother and exemplar of all the consecrated virgins of Ireland for many centuries to come.

We may perhaps most compendiously form an idea of the general tone of the early lives by translating a few paragraphs from the lessons in the *Breviarium Aberdonense*.

The holy Brigid, whom God foreknew and predestined to grow unto His own likeness, sprang from a worthy and prudent Scottish [*i.e.* Irish] stock, having for father Dubthac and for mother Brocca, from earliest years making progress in all good. For this maiden, the elect of God, full of soberness and wisdom, ever advanced towards what was more perfect. Sent by her mother to collect the butter made from the milk of the cows, as other women were sent, she gave it all to the poor. And when the others returned with their load and she sought to make restitution of the produce of the cows, turning in tender deference to our Lord, God for His virgin's sake gave back the butter with usury. In due time, when her parents wished to bestow her in marriage, she vowed chastity, and as in the presence of a most holy bishop she made her vow, it happened that she touched with her hand the wooden pillar on which the altar rested. In memory of that maiden's action long ago up to the present hour this wood remains as it were green, or, as if it had not been cut and stripped of its bark, it flourishes in its roots and heals cripples innumerable.

Saintly as she was and faithful, Brigid, seeing that the time for her espousals was drawing near, asked our Lord to send her some deformity so as to frustrate the importunity of her parents, whereupon one of her eyes split open and melted in her head. Therefore, having received the holy veil, Brigid with other consecrated virgins remained in the city of Meath, where our Lord at her prayer vouchsafed to work many miracles. She healed a stranger, by name Marcus ; she supplied beer out of one barrel to eighteen churches, which sufficed from Maundy Thursday to the end of paschal time. On a leprous woman asking for milk, there being none at hand she gave her cold water, but the water was turned into milk, and when she had drunk it the woman was healed.   Then she cured a leper and gave sight to two blind men.   Making a journey in answer to an urgent call, she chanced to slip at a ford and cut her head, but with the blood that flowed therefrom two dumb women recovered their speech.   After this a precious vessel of the king's, slipping from the hand of a yokel, was broken, and that he might not be punished it was restored uninjured by Brigid.

But among these and many similar extravagances, some legends are beautiful. One such, in particular, concerning the blind nun Dara, can hardly be told more sympathetically than in the words of Sabine Baring-Gould :

> One evening, as the sun went down, Brigid sat with Sister Dara, a holy nun who was blind, and they talked of the love of Jesus Christ and the joys of Paradise.   Now their hearts were so full that the night fled away whilst they spoke together, and neither knew that so many hours had passed.   Then the sun came up from behind the Wicklow mountains, and the pure white light made the face of earth bright and gay.   Then Brigid sighed, when she saw how lovely were earth and sky, and knew that Dara's eyes were closed to all this beauty.   So she bowed her head and prayed, and extended her hand and signed the dark orbs of the gentle sister.   Then the darkness passed away from them, and Dara saw the golden ball in the east and all the trees and flowers glittering with dew in the morning light.   She looked a little while, and then, turning to the abbess, said, " Close my eyes again, dear Mother, for when the world is so visible to the eyes, God is seen less clearly to the soul."   So Brigid prayed once more, and Dara's eyes grew dark again.

Of the saint's great religious foundation at Kill-dara (the church of the oak) and of the rule which was there followed we know little or nothing that is reliable. It is generally supposed that it was a " double monastery ", *i.e.* that it included men as well as women, for such was the common practice in Celtic lands.   It is also quite possible that St Brigid presided over both communities, for this arrangement would by no means have been without a parallel.   But the text of her rule— there is mention of a " regula Sanctae Brigidae " in the Life of St Kieran of Clonmacnois—appears not to have survived.   More than six centuries later Giraldus Cambrensis collected some curious traditions regarding this foundation.   He says, for example : " In Kildare of Leinster, which the glorious Brigid made illustrious, there are many wonders worthy of mention.   Foremost among which is the fire of Brigid which they call inextinguishable ; not that it cannot be extinguished, but because the nuns and holy women so anxiously and punctually cherish and nurse the fire with a supply of fuel that during many centuries from the virgin's own day it has ever remained alight and the ashes have never accumulated, although in so long a time so vast a pile of wood hath here been consumed.   Whereas in the time of Brigid twenty nuns here served the Lord, she herself being the twentieth, there have been only nineteen from the time of her glorious departure and they have not added to that number.   But as each nun in her turn tends the fire for one night, when the twentieth night comes the last maiden having placed the wood ready, saith, ' Brigid, tend that fire of thine, for this is thy night.'   And the fire being so left, in the morning they find it still alight and the fuel consumed in the usual way. That fire is surrounded by a circular hedge of bushes within which no male enters, and if one should presume to enter, as some rash men have attempted, he does not escape divine vengeance."

This is the story to which the poet Tom Moore alluded when he wrote of—

> The bright lamp that shone in Kildare's holy fane
> And burned through long ages of darkness and storm.

But despite the predominance of legendary material, the enthusiasm which the memory of St Brigid evoked among her countrymen is unmistakable. It would not be easy to find anything more fervent in expression than the rhapsodies of the *Book of Lismore*

> Everything that Brigid would ask of the Lord was granted her at once. For this was her desire : to satisfy the poor, to expel every hardship, to spare every miserable man. Now there never hath been anyone more bashful or more modest or more gentle or more humble or more discerning or more harmonious than Brigid. In the sight of other people she never washed her hands or her feet or her head. She never looked at the face of man. She never spoke without blushing. She was abstemious, she was innocent, she was prayerful, she was patient : she was glad in God's commandments : she was firm, she was humble, she was forgiving, she was loving : she was a consecrated casket for keeping Christ's body and His blood ; she was a temple of God. Her heart and her mind were a throne of rest for the Holy Ghost. She was single-hearted [towards God]　she was compassionate towards the wretched ; she was splendid in miracles and marvels : wherefore her name among created things is Dove among birds, Vine among trees, Sun among stars. This is the father of that holy virgin, the Heavenly Father　this is her son, Jesus Christ : this is her fosterer, the Holy Ghost : wherefore this holy virgin performs such great marvels and innumerable miracles. It is she that helpeth every one who is in straits and in danger : it is she that abateth the pestilences : it is she that quelleth the rage and storm of the sea. She is the prophetess of Christ : she is the Queen of the South　she is the Mary of the Gael.

But the language of other native writers of earlier date is at times even more far-fetched. We probably understand too little of Gaelic psychology to be quite certain of the real meaning of the phrases which we meet with in such documents as the Hymn of St Broccan, but our translators convey that Brigid was actually identified with Mary the Blessed Virgin. For example, we read :

> Brigid, mother of my high King
> Of the kingdom of Heaven, best was she born.

Or again she is called " the one mother of the Great King's Son ". It is possible that some echoes of earlier pagan mythology were mixed up with all this, for *Brig* seems to have been an abstraction, meaning " valour " or " might ", which was personified as a female goddess and particularly associated with a fire cult on February 1. This might account for some of the details in Giraldus's description of Kildare, quoted above ; but the whole subject is wrapped in the deepest obscurity. According to Charles Plummer (VSH., vol. i, p. cxxxvi), " Brigid's name is fancifully etymologized ' breosaiget ', *i.e.* fiery arrow, and certainly her legend exhibits many traits of this kind. Brigid has moreover heathen namesakes, *e.g.* ' Brigid banfile ', *i.e.* the poetess-mother of three gods of poetry. This identity of name is a great occasion of transference of myths."

In early times St Brigid was much honoured in Scotland and also in those parts of England which were more directly in contact with Celtic influences, and there are several places in Wales called Llansantffraid, St Bride's Church. In Ireland the churches dedicated to her are innumerable ; in England we know of nineteen pre-Reformation dedications. Most of these are in the West-country, but one church in London is famous, St Bride's in Fleet Street. Bridewell, originally a royal palace, seems to have acquired its name from its contiguity to St Bride's. Her feast is observed throughout Ireland, Wales, Australia and New Zealand.

The early Latin lives of St Brigid have been printed by Colgan in his *Trias Thaumaturga*, including that by Cogitosus, which approaches nearer to a formal biography than most of the others. In the *Proceedings of the R. Irish Academy*, vol. xxx (1912), pp. 307 *seq.*, Esposito has given reasons for thinking that Cogitosus was the father of Muirchu and that he flourished about 620-680. St Broccan's hymn of panegyric is printed in the *Irish Liber Hymnorum* of the Henry Bradshaw Society, vol. ii, p. 193. Canon O'Hanlon in LIS., vol. ii, devotes more than 200 pp. to St Brigid, and a full account will also be found in LBS., vol. i, pp. 264-288. See also *The Book of Lismore* (ed. Whitley Stokes) ; J. Ryan, *Irish Monasticism* (1931), pp. 134-136, 179-184 and *passim* ; Alice Curtayne, *St Brigid of Ireland* (1933) ; F. O'Briain, *St Brigid, her Legend, History and Cult* (1938) ; and M. A. O'Brien, "The Old Irish Life of St Brigid " in *Irish Historical Studies*, vol. i (1938-1939), pp. 121-134, 343-353. On this Brigid's cult in Sweden, see *Analecta Bollandiana*, vol. lxi (1943), pp. 108-116. *Cf.* L. Gougaud, *Christianity in Celtic Lands* (1932).

ST SIGEBERT III OF AUSTRASIA (A.D. 656)

DAGOBERT I, King of France, led for some time a very dissolute life, but was touched by grace at the birth of his son Sigebert, and from that hour was converted to God. Desiring to have his son baptized by the holiest prelate of his realm, he recalled St Amand, whom he had banished for the uncompromising zeal with which he had rebuked Dagobert's excesses, and he asked his pardon and promised amendment. The baptism took place with great pomp at Orleans. The young prince's education was entrusted to Bd Pepin of Landen, mayor of the palace. After the death of Dagobert in 638, Sigebert reigned in Austrasia and his brother Clovis in the rest of France. Pepin of Landen continued to be mayor of the palace, and not only proved himself a faithful minister but also formed the young prince to Christian virtue. Sigebert reigned in good understanding with his brother, and the only war in which he was involved was one occasioned by a revolt amongst the Thuringians. It ended somewhat disastrously for the Austrasian army. Sigebert was assiduous in prayer, in relieving the poor and in endowing monasteries, churches and hospitals. He founded twelve monasteries, the two principal of which were at Stavelot and Malmedy. A life filled with good works and devoted to God can never be called short. God was pleased to call this good king to the reward of his labours in the year 656, the eighteenth of his reign and the twenty-fifth of his age.

For the life of the saint, see the chronicle of Fredegarius and the *Vita Sigeberti* by Sigebert of Gembloux. A short modern biography by the Abbé Guise has been published in the series " Les Saints " (1920).

ST JOHN "OF THE GRATING ", BISHOP OF SAINT-MALO (*c.* A.D. 1170)

THIS saint is surnamed " de Craticula " from the iron grating which surrounded his tomb. He was a Breton and the son of parents in rather poor circumstances.

He received, however, an excellent education and made good progress in the arts and sciences.   He was greatly attracted by the Cistercian Order, which at that period was riveting the attention of the world, and he went himself to seek St Bernard who, after testing him, received him into his own community.   When Count Stephen de Penthièvre and his wife wished to found a monastery on their estate, St Bernard sent them John, who established a religious house at Bégard in the diocese of Tréguier.   He subsequently founded another at Buzay ; of that he became abbot, but to the great grief of his religious he was elected bishop of Aleth. As he found that the population on the isle of Aaron was increasing and that it was becoming a very important city, John transferred the seat of his diocese to that place, which he renamed Saint-Malo.

St John had great trouble over his cathedral, in which he installed canons regular of St Augustine.   It had previously been a church controlled by monks of Marmoutier at Tours, and they involved him in wearisome litigation.   When the French bishops gave their verdict against St John, he, acting on the advice of St Bernard, went himself to Rome and laid the matter before the pope, who decided in his favour.   His adversaries, however, found a pretext for raising the question afresh, and John had to travel to Rome more than once.   It was eighteen years before the affair was finally settled and his opponents silenced ; one of the letters of his correspondence with St Bernard on the subject is still extant.   His biographers dilate upon his patience under these prolonged trials and upon the conspicuous spirit of charity and forbearance which marked all his dealings with others. St John was commissioned to reform the monastery of Saint-Méen de Gaël, and, in addition to the other religious houses he had established, he founded the abbeys of Sainte-Croix de Guingamp and of Saint-Jacques de Montfort.   He lived a life of much austerity and died about 1170.

See A. Le Grand, *Vie des saints de la Bretagne Armorique* ; Lobineau, *Saints de Bretagne,* vol. ii, pp. 393–410 ; *Acta Sanctorum,* February, vol. i.

BD ANTONY THE PILGRIM   (A.D. 1267)

ANTONY MANZI, or Manzoni, was a native of Padua and belonged to a distinguished family.   His father died while he was still young and left him considerable riches, which he immediately gave away to the poor.   For this he was blamed by his fellow citizens and by his relations—especially as he had two sisters—and he was reviled in the streets and subjected to indignities of all sorts.   Resolved to live a life of poverty, he assumed the garb of a pilgrim and left Padua, wandering about until at Bazano, near Bologna, he found a sick and saintly old priest whom he served for three years for the love of God.   They lived on the alms Antony received by begging, and in turn gave away everything beyond what was required for actual sustenance.   Throughout his life he fasted, took severe disciplines, wore a rough hair shirt, and always slept on the bare ground with a stone for his pillow.   After his stay at Bazano he wandered far and wide, making pilgrimages to Rome, to Loreto, to Compostela, to Cologne and to Jerusalem.   Finally he returned to his native city where he was not more kindly regarded, even by his sisters who were nuns there, than when he took his departure many years before.   He made a home for himself in the colonnade of a church outside the walls, and there, not long after, he died.   When miracles began to be worked at his grave the Paduans who had scorned him in his lifetime sought to have him canonized ; but the pope replied that it was enough for the city of Padua to have *one* Saint Antony.   Nevertheless the *cultus* seems to have persisted and his feast is kept at Padua.

The most reliable account of Bd Antony and his miracles is that which has been published in the *Analecta Bollandiana*, vol. xiii (1894), pp. 417-425.   *Cf.* also *ib.*, vol. xiv, pp. 108 *seq.*, and the *Acta Sanctorum*, February, vol. i.

BD HENRY MORSE, Martyr   (A.D. 1645)

HENRY MORSE was born in 1595 somewhere in East Anglia, and was brought up in the Protestant faith of his parents, who were of the country gentry.   While reading law in London he decided to become a Catholic, and at the age of twenty-three went abroad and was received into the Church at Douay.   He began his studies for the priesthood there, but finished them in the Venerabile at Rome, where he was ordained.   Soon after landing at Newcastle in 1624 he was arrested and imprisoned in the castle at York.   Before leaving Rome he had obtained the agreement of the father general of the Society of Jesus that he should be admitted to the Society in England, and it so happened that a Jesuit, Father John Robinson, was a fellow prisoner at York.   Accordingly, the three years that Henry Morse spent in prison there were passed as a novitiate, and he there made his simple vows.   Eventually he was released and banished, whereupon he went to Flanders and for a time was chaplain and missioner to the English soldiers serving the king of Spain there.

At the end of 1633 Father Morse came back to England and, under the name of Cuthbert Claxton, ministered in London.   He was particularly active during the plague epidemic of 1636-37.   He had a list of four hundred infected families, Protestant as well as Catholic, which he visited regularly with physical and spiritual help.   This made so great an impression that in one year nearly a hundred families were reconciled with the Church.   He himself caught the disease three times, but each time recovered ; and he had to be warned by his superiors to moderate his zeal.   At this very time the authorities deemed it suitable to arrest Father Morse, and charge him with being a priest and with " perverting " five hundred and sixty of his Majesty's Protestant subjects " in and about the parish of St Giles in the Fields ".   On the second charge he was found not guilty, but on the first guilty ; however, Queen Henrietta Maria intervened and he was released on a bail of 10,000 florins.   When the royal proclamation was made ordering all priests to leave the country by April 7, 1641, Father Morse obeyed it in order not to involve his sureties ; and he again took up his work with the English troops abroad.

From Ghent he was in 1643 sent back to England, and laboured in the north for eighteen months, till he was apprehended on suspicion while making a sick-call on the borders of Cumberland.   He was taken off towards Durham, but on the way the Catholic wife of one of his captors, at whose house they were spending the night, enabled him to escape.   But about six weeks later he was rearrested (through his guide to a certain house losing his memory), and after some weeks in jail at Durham he was shipped from Newcastle to London.   Here he was brought to the bar of the Old Bailey and sentenced to death on the strength of his conviction nine years before.

On the day of execution Father Morse celebrated a votive Mass of the Most Holy Trinity, and was drawn on a hurdle by four horses to Tyburn, where, as well as the usual crowd of sightseers and others, the French, Spanish and Portuguese

ambassadors were present with their suites to do honour to the martyr. He told
the people that he was dying for his religion, that he had worked only for the
welfare of his countrymen, and that he knew nothing of plots against the king ; and
after he had prayed aloud for himself and for his persecutors and for the kingdom
of England, the cart was drawn away. This was on February 1, 1645. Among
the many relics of the English martyrs obtained by the Count d'Egmont, Spanish
ambassador, and carried overseas, those of Bd Henry Morse were among the most
considerable.

In the year that this martyr suffered there was published at Antwerp a volume, called
Certamen Triplex, which contained an account of his life and death (and of Bd Thomas
Holland and Bd Ralph Corby). Its author was Fr Ambrose Corby, brother of the last
named. It was reprinted in Munich in the following year, and an English translation, *The
Threefold Conflict*, appeared in London in 1858. This is the account that Challoner draws
on in MMP. See REPSJ., vol. i. The list of relics obtained by Egmont is translated and
printed in Camm's *Forgotten Shrines* (1910).

2 : THE PURIFICATION OF THE BLESSED VIRGIN MARY.
COMMONLY CALLED CANDLEMAS DAY

THE law of God given by Moses to the Jews ordained that a woman after
child-birth should continue for a certain time in a state which the law
called " unclean ", during which time she was not to appear in public or
touch anything consecrated to God. Forty days after the birth of a son, eighty days
after the birth of a daughter, the mother was to bring to the door of the tabernacle
or temple a lamb and a young pigeon or turtle-dove—the lamb for a burnt-offering
in acknowledgement of God's sovereignty and in thanksgiving for her happy
delivery, and the bird for a sin offering. These being sacrificed, the woman was
cleansed of the legal impurity. In the case of poor people, a lamb was not required,
but two pigeons or turtle-doves had to be brought.

As our Lord had been conceived by the Holy Ghost, His mother remaining a
virgin, it is evident that she was not within the intent of this law. She was, however, within its intent in the eyes of the world, and she submitted to every humbling
circumstance the law required. Devotion also and zeal to honour God by every
prescribed observance prompted Mary to this act of religion and, being poor herself,
she made the offering appointed for the poor.*

A second great mystery is honoured this day, *viz.* the presentation of our
Redeemer in the Temple. Besides the law which obliged the mother to purify
herself, there was another which ordained that the first-born son should be offered
to God and then ransomed with a sum of money. Mary complies exactly with all
these ordinances. She remains forty days at home, she denies herself all this time
the liberty of entering the Temple of God, she partakes not of sacred things,
although herself the living temple of God. On the day of her purification she walks
several miles to Jerusalem with the world's Redeemer in her arms, she makes her

* The visit of our Lady to the Temple for this purpose is also commemorated by the
Church in the Blessing of a Woman after Childbirth, commonly called " Churching ". No
idea of purification of any kind is contained in this Christian rite. for the honourable begetting
and bearing of a child incurs no sort of taint. It is perhaps not out of place to add that the
idea sometimes met that a mother should not go to church for any purpose before being
churched is unwarranted and superstitious.

offerings of thanksgiving and expiation, presents her Son by the hands of the priest to His heavenly Father, redeems him with five shekels, and receives Him back into her arms till the Father shall again demand Him. Clearly Christ was not comprehended in the law. "The King's son, to whom the inheritance of the crown belongs, is exempt from servitude—much more Christ, who was the redeemer both of our souls and bodies, was not", as St Hilary says, "subject to any law by which He was to be Himself redeemed." Nevertheless He would set an example of humility, obedience and devotion, and would publicly renew that oblation of Himself to the Father which He had made at His incarnation.

The day was marked by a third mystery, the meeting in the Temple of Simeon and Anna with the child Jesus and His parents. Holy Simeon received into his arms the object of all his longings and desires, and praised God for the happiness of beholding the longed-for Messiah. He foretold Mary's martyrdom of sorrow and announced that salvation through Christ awaited those who believed. The prophetess Anna also shared the privilege of recognizing and worshipping the world's Redeemer. He could not hide himself from those who sought Him in simplicity, humility, and ardent faith. Unless we also seek Him in these dispositions, He will not manifest Himself to us, nor will He give us His graces. When Simeon had gazed upon his Saviour, he desired no longer to see the light of this world.

It is only in comparatively recent years that we have learnt how early this celebration took its rise. A discovery made at Arezzo in 1887 revealed the existence of a hitherto unknown description of the ceremonial observed at Jerusalem, apparently in the last decade of the fourth century. It is now agreed that the author of this tractate was a certain Abbess Etheria who, leaving her convent in the northwest of Spain, undertook a long pilgrimage to the Holy Land, and wrote on her return a detailed account of her experiences. In the course of this narrative we learn how the feast of the birth of our Lord, which was then throughout the East kept with the Epiphany on January 6, was specially honoured at Jerusalem in the church of the Anastasis (Resurrection). Etheria adds details about the ceremonies, which continued during the octave, and then she goes on

> The fortieth day after the Epiphany is undoubtedly celebrated here with the very highest honour, for on that day there is a procession, in which all take part in the Anastasis, and all things are done in their order with the greatest joy, just as at Easter. All the priests, and after them the bishop, preach, always taking for their subject that part of the Gospel where Joseph and Mary brought the Lord into the Temple on the fortieth day, and Simeon and Anna the prophetess, the daughter of Phanuel, saw Him—treating of the words which they spake when they saw the Lord, and of that offering which His parents made.

There seems every probability that it was from Jerusalem that the observance of the feast spread through the Eastern world. For example, somewhere about the year 540, and possibly much earlier, we find it introduced at Ephesus under the name which it still bears among the Greeks, viz. the Hypapante (i.e. the "meeting" of Jesus with Simeon). It should be remembered that in the East, as was also at first the case in the West, this celebration is a festival of our Lord. It was the gospel incident which was commemorated, and the Blessed Virgin's part was subordinate to that of her Son. It is rather surprising to find that from an early date, at any rate from the fifth century, there seems good evidence of the existence in Palestine of a procession with candles, μετὰ κηρίων, on the feast of the Hypapante. In the Life of the Abbot Theodosius by Cyril of Scythopolis there is definite mention of the practice, and this allusion does not stand quite alone. The fact suggests at least the possibility that some Eastern influence may have introduced the custom to Rome and thence to other churches in the West, but to this question it will be necessary to return.

With regard to the origin of the ceremonial now observed on Candlemas day, *la Chandeleur*, as the French term it, in our present rite two separate elements must be carefully distinguished. The Mass and Office have no necessary connection with the blessing of candles and the subsequent procession ; the procession is unalterably attached to February 2, whereas the feast may be transferred. The same holds good in the case of the *Litaniae majores* on April 25, the feast of St Mark. Here we know that while the Christian procession of the *litaniae* dates from before the pontificate of St Gregory the Great and replaced the old pagan procession of the Robigalia, observed from time immemorial in Rome on that same day,* the feast of St Mark was of altogether later introduction. Furthermore the procession of Candlemas is a penitential procession. To this day the priest who presides wears a purple cope, and in former ages at Rome the pope, instead of riding, went barefoot, and he and his deacons wore black vestments.

The earliest writer to offer any theory as to the origin of this Candlemas procession is the Venerable Bede. In his *De temporum ratione*, written about the year 721, he represents it as a Christian version of a February lustration ordained by Numa. This is only the first in time among several hypotheses, among which attention seems to be best directed to the pagan Lupercalia. This festival was a fertility rite of high antiquity, which was also presented as a symbolical purification of the land. Goats and dogs were sacrificed and afterwards the priests, called Luperci, cutting the skins of the victims into thongs, ran naked through the city, striking everyone they met, especially women, who put themselves in their way if they desired to have children. Despite the glaring paganism of this celebration it continued for centuries. Not only are the Lupercalia marked on the 15th in every calendar which contains the month of February, but they are frequently

---

* It may be well to recall the fact that the word litanies (λιτανεῖαι, literally, supplications) in the time of St Gregory the Great and long afterwards was primarily associated with the idea of a procession, generally a penitential procession. Such religious processions were very familiar to the Roman populace in pagan days. From the earliest period in Rome and throughout Italy whenever the city, army, crops or herds seemed to be threatened by evil influences, recourse was had to a *lustratio*, a procession which went round the object to be purified or protected, leading with it the victims which were afterwards to be slaughtered, and stopping at certain stations for prayer and sacrifice. The particular lustration called the Robigalia, on April 25, had for its object, at least originally, the protection of the growing crops from *robigo* or *rubigo*, *i.e.* blight. It had begun, no doubt, in times when cultivated areas were still found in the heart of Rome, but the custom was retained, following always a traditional route, even when Rome had become a great city and the original purpose of the ceremony had been lost sight of. To eradicate such popular celebrations is next to impossible, and when the people accepted Christianity the popes and their clergy acted wisely in converting the lustration into a Christian procession, which followed the same well-known route and chanted invocations and responses closely corresponding to those now found in our Litany of the Saints.

spoken of and denounced by Christian writers. A probable view suggests that the plan of eliminating pagan abuses by providing an innocent Christian demonstration in their place was directed first against such scenes of licence and disorder as the Lupercalia. It may be, then, that this attempt took the form of deliberately borrowing from the East the ceremony of the Fortieth Day of the Epiphany with its procession and lights, precisely because it fell upon the 14th or 15th of February and thus coincided with the objectionable pagan celebration which it was desired to suppress. At a later period when the Hypapante began to be observed liturgically with Mass and Office as a feast of the Blessed Virgin, the inconsistency of keeping the birth of Christ on December 25 and the meeting with Simeon on February 15 would have forced itself insistently upon notice. Thus the candle procession, the memory of the Lupercalia having by this time grown faint, was probably transferred to the purification of our Lady on February 2, to which it properly belonged.

There are two or three considerations which point to this conclusion. In the first place the earliest mention of a procession with candles comes to us, as has already been pointed out, from the neighbourhood of Jerusalem, and that as early as about A.D. 440. Secondly, we cannot ignore the significance of the fact that the earliest references to the Roman celebration speak of it either as the Hypapante (its Greek title) or as the feast of St Simeon. It is as the " Natale Sti Simeonis " that it is entered in the calendar of St Willibrord as also in the Antiphonary of Pamelius, and we find both names in the casual reference made to it by the *Liber Pontificalis* under Pope St Sergius I. Thirdly, we know now for certain, thanks to the researches of Dom H. Peillon, that the chants which still stand in the Roman Antiphonary and are sung in the Candlemas procession are taken bodily from Greek liturgical sources. In the manuscript which Dom Peillon has identified as that principally employed by Pamelius for his edition of the antiphonary, the anthems " Ave gratia plena " and " Adorna thalamum tuum Sion " are written both in Latin and in Greek with Latin characters. There can also be little doubt that Dom Peillon is justified in regarding this manuscript as a copy of an earlier document which preserves for us with substantial fidelity the usage of the Roman church in the second half of the eighth century.

The following conclusions seem warranted :

1. The celebration of our Lord's presentation in the Temple undoubtedly began in Jerusalem about the fourth century and was marked by a procession with torches or candles on the Fortieth Day of the Epiphany, February 15.

2. The observance in the course of the fifth and sixth centuries spread throughout the Eastern church.

3. While still attached to February 15 the procession was adopted at Rome to supply a Christian substitute for the Lupercalia.

4. When the Purification of the Blessed Virgin came to be honoured in the West as an element in the Christmas cycle, the procession of the Hypapante, or feast of St Simeon, was transferred to its proper day, February 2, forty days after December 25, when the birth of our Lord was kept in Rome.

5. The Venerable Bede, though probably acquainted with what had been said by certain writers about an obscure pagan observance, the *amburbium*, deliberately refrained from making reference to it. He was satisfied that the February

procession took the place of some kind of pagan lustration.   He knew also that the Lupercalia had lasted on far into Christian times and that the *lustrum* represented a period of five years, but because exact information was not available he was intentionally vague in the statement which he made.

See McClure and Feltoe, *The Pilgrimage of Etheria*, p. 56 ; F. C. Conybeare, *Rituale Armenorum*, pp. 507 *seq.* ; I. Rahmani, *Studia Syriaca*, vol. iii, pp. 73-138 , Theodotus of Ancyra in Migne, PG., vol. lxvii, p. 1400 ; Usener, *Der hl. Theodosios*, p. 106 ; *Revue Bénédictine*, vols. xxviii (1916), pp. 301, 313, 323, and xxxiv (1922), p. 15 ; CMH., p. 75 ; and the usual reference books.   It may be noticed that there is no reason to connect the observances of February 2 with the Spanish church, as has been suggested by the author of the article on Candlemas in the *Encyclopaedia of Religion and Ethics*. The data supplied by Dom Férotin (*Liber Ordinum*, p. 454 n.) show plainly that in the Mozarabic ritual there is practically speaking no trace of such a celebration until the eleventh century.

ST ADALBALD OF OSTREVANT, Martyr   (A.D. 652)

ADALBALD was a grandson of the St Gertrude who founded the monastery of Hamage, and his father, who died early, was called Rigomer ; one of his brothers married St Bertha who, upon becoming a widow, built the monastery of Blangy in Artois and retired there : St Amand was in close touch with the whole family.   Adalbald was much at the court of Dagobert I, and would appear to have been the ideal of a young Christian noble.   He took part in several expeditions to quell the insurgent Gascons, and whilst he was in Gascony he formed a friendship with a nobleman called Ernold, the hand of whose daughter Rictrudis he obtained in marriage.   The wedding did not please some of the bride's Gascon kinsfolk, but it turned out very happily.   Both husband and wife spent much time in visiting the sick, relieving the poor and even in trying to convert criminals.   Moreover, they brought up their children, Mauront, Eusebia, Clotsindis and Adalsindis to follow in their footsteps, and all four were venerated as saints.

After some years Adalbald was recalled to Gascony, but when he had reached the vicinity of Périgueux he was attacked unawares by some of his wife's relations, who were burning to satisfy their hatred, and he succumbed.   Rictrudis was overcome with grief, but managed to get possession of her husband's body, which was buried with due honours.   Miracles were said to be worked at his tomb and his *cultus* grew both in his own country and in the Périgord.   Adalbald was accounted a martyr, because in those days the title was given to all saintly persons who died a violent death.   Possibly too the motive of religion was not altogether absent in a land where there were still many pagans.   His bones rested at first in the monastery of Elnone, and afterwards his head was taken to Douay—so at least we learn from an ancient manuscript of the church of St Amé, where there used to be a chapel dedicated in honour of St Mauront and his parents.   Their statues were long exhibited for public veneration—St Adalbald in a robe covered with lilies and holding a book, St Rictrudis in the Benedictine habit and holding the abbey of Marchiennes, and St Mauront between them, a sceptre in his right hand and towers in his left.

Our information is mainly derived from Hucbald's Life of St Rictrudis (*Acta Sanctorum*, May, vol. iii) ; and *cf. Biographie nationale (de Belgique)*, vol. i, pp. 18-21 ; and L. van der Essen, *Étude sur les Vitae des saints mérov.*   (1907), pp. 260-267.

THE MARTYRS OF EBSDORF   (A.D. 880)

THE winter of 880 was one of such extreme severity that the Rhine and the Main were frozen hard.   The young king Louis III, who had spent Christmas at Frankfurt, had great difficulties in contending with incursions of Northmen, who were forming settlements on the Scheldt and pressing south.   An army under Duke Bruno, the queen's brother, was caught on the heath of Lüneburg at Ebsdorf in Saxony and hemmed in by melting ice and snow.   The pagan Northmen descended upon them where there was no place to give battle and utterly overwhelmed them, killing Bruno, together with Theodoric, or Dietrich, the saintly old bishop of Minden, and Bishop Marquard of Hildesheim, as well as eleven nobles and fourteen of the king's bodyguard and their attendants.   The rest of the army were either driven into the swamps and drowned or taken prisoners.   Some of the accounts say that two other bishops, Erlulf of Werden and Gosbert of Osnabrück, were among those massacred, but they were actually martyred at an earlier date.   Other records give seven martyred bishops, but the whole episode has been so much mixed up with legend that it is impossible to arrive at any certainty.   The relics of the martyrs were regarded with the greatest veneration in the church of the Benedictine abbey which was subsequently erected on this spot.

See J. E. Stadler, *Heiligen-Lexikon*, vol. v, pp. 460 *seq.*

ST JOAN DE LESTONNAC, WIDOW, FOUNDRESS OF THE RELIGIOUS OF NOTRE DAME OF BORDEAUX   (A.D. 1640)

JOAN DE LESTONNAC's father belonged to a distinguished Bordelais family and, at a time when Calvinism was flourishing in Bordeaux, was a good Catholic—her mother, Joan Eyquem de Montaigne, sister of the famous Michael de Montaigne, apostatized. She tried to tamper with her child's faith, and when her endeavours failed Joan was ill-treated.   These troubles turned her heart to God and made her long for a life of prayer and mortification.   However, when she was seventeen she married Gaston de Montferrant, who was related to the royal houses of France, Aragon and Navarre.   The marriage was a very happy one, but her husband died in 1597, leaving her with four children to whom she devoted herself till they were old enough to do without her.   Two daughters eventually became nuns.   At the age of forty-seven Joan de Lestonnac entered the Cistercian monastery of Les Feuillantes at Toulouse.   This step was violently opposed by her son, and she herself was heartbroken at leaving her youngest daughter, who married only some years later.

Mme de Lestonnac, now become Sister Joan, spent six months in the Cistercian novitiate, giving great edification.   But the life was too hard for her, and at the end of that time her health completely broke down ; though she implored to be allowed to remain in the convent to die, her superiors decided that such a valuable life must be preserved for the service of God.   Before leaving she was allowed to spend a night in prayer in the chapel, and as she prayed, " Lord, if it be possible, let this chalice pass from me," the assurance was granted her that she was to found a new order for the salvation of souls, and the outline of the future Congregation of Notre Dame came before her mind.

Her health recovered almost miraculously as soon as she left Les Feuillantes. She returned to Bordeaux and visited Périgord, where she gathered round her·

several young girls who were eventually to be her first novices.   She then spent two quiet years in her country place, La Mothe, preparing for her great work.   We find her again in Bordeaux, where her directors advised her to content herself with an ordinary life devoted to works of charity.   Bordeaux being visited by the plague, Mme de Lestonnac and a band of brave women gave themselves to nursing the victims.   She now came under the influence of two Jesuits, Father de Bordes and Father Raymond, who fully realized the devastation which Calvinism was working amongst young girls of all classes who were deprived of Catholic education.   To both these priests the assurance was given simultaneously, whilst they were celebrating Mass, that it was the will of God they should assist in founding an order to counteract the evils of the surrounding heresy and that Mme de Lestonnac should be the first superior.   Thus the work began, and it grew rapidly.   The infant congregation was affiliated to the Order of St Benedict, though its rule and constitutions were founded on those of St Ignatius, and the first house was opened in the old priory of the Holy Ghost at Bordeaux.

Mme de Lestonnac and her companions received the habit from Cardinal de Sourdis, Archbishop of Bordeaux, in 1608.   After Mme de Lestonnac had been elected superior in 1610, subjects came rapidly.   They were carefully taught the religious life—their aim and object being the training and teaching of young girls of all classes.   The schools prospered beyond all expectation.   Foundations were made in many towns, Périgueux being the earliest.   The nuns lived lives of great poverty and mortification, and all seemed peaceful and happy when suddenly cruel trials fell on the foundress.   One of her nuns, Blanche Hervé, and the director of one of the houses conspired against her, and for a time their ill-considered designs succeeded.   They invented discreditable stories about her and, most surprising of all, Cardinal de Sourdis believed them.   Mother de Lestonnac was deposed and Blanche Hervé elected superior.   Blanche then treated Mother de Lestonnac most cruelly, insulting her in every possible way—even ill-treating her with physical violence.   This state of things lasted for some time, but at last Blanche's heart was touched by St Joan's unalterable patience and she repented.   As Mother de Lestonnac was now an old woman she did not wish to be reinstated as superior, and Mother de Badiffe was elected.

The last few years of the foundress were spent in retirement and preparation for death.   She passed away just after her nuns had renewed their vows, on the feast of the Purification 1640.   We are told that her body remained fresh and supple, exhaling a sweet fragrance for days after her death, and that the crowds who prayed beside her testified to the beauty of her countenance.   Many also noticed a brilliant light surrounding the bier.   In the following years a number of miracles occurred at her tomb.   For various reasons the cause of her beatification was delayed, and then came the Revolution.   The nuns were scattered and the body of their foundress lost.   In the beginning of the nineteenth century it was found again and reinterred with much solemnity at Bordeaux.   At last, greatly through the exertions of Mother Duterrail, the cause was introduced at Rome, and Joan de Lestonnac was eventually canonized in 1949.

See Duprat, *La digne Fille de Marie : la b. Jeanne de Lestonnac* (1906) ; Father Mercier, *La vén. Jeanne de Lestonnac* (1891) ; and Paula Hoësl, *Ste Jeanne de Lestonnac* (1949).   The last has been translated into English under the title *In the Service of Youth* (1951).   It must be remembered, of course, that the number of religious congregations bearing the title of " Notre Dame " is considerable and there is danger of confusion.

3 : ST BLAISE, Bishop of Sebastea, Martyr   (A.D. 316 ?)

THERE seems to be no evidence earlier than the eighth century for the *cultus* of St Blaise, but the accounts furnished at a later date agree in stating that he was bishop of Sebastea in Armenia and that he was crowned with martyrdom in the persecution of Licinius by command of Agricolaus, governor of Cappadocia and Lesser Armenia. It is mentioned in the legendary acts of St Eustratius, who is said to have perished in the reign of Diocletian, that St Blaise honourably received his relics, deposited them with those of St Orestes, and punctually executed every article of the last will and testament of St Eustratius.

This is all which can be affirmed with any faint probability concerning St Blaise, but in view of the honour in which he is held in Germany and France a few words may be said of the story contained in his legendary acts. According to these he was born of rich and noble parents, receiving a Christian education and being made a bishop while still quite young. When persecution arose, he withdrew by divine direction to a cave in the mountains which was frequented only by wild beasts. These he healed when they were sick or wounded, and they used to come round him to receive his blessing. Hunters, who had been sent to secure animals for the amphitheatre, found the saint surrounded by the beasts, and, though greatly amazed, they seized him and took him to Agricolaus. On their way they met a poor woman whose pig had been carried off by a wolf ; at the command of St Blaise, the wolf restored the pig unhurt. The incident is worth mentioning because of a ceremony which arose in connection with it. On another occasion a woman brought to him a little boy who was at the point of death owing to a fishbone in his throat, and the saint healed him. On account of this and other similar cures St Blaise has been invoked during many centuries past for all kinds of throat trouble. The governor ordered him to be scourged and deprived of food, but the woman whose pig had been restored brought provisions to him and also tapers to dispel the darkness of his gloomy prison. Then Licinius tortured him by tearing his flesh with iron combs, and afterwards had him beheaded.

In course of time many alleged relics of St Blaise were brought to the West, and his *cultus* was propagated by the rumour of miraculous cures. He is the patron saint of woolcombers, of wild animals and of all who suffer from affections of the throat. He is moreover famous in Germany as one of the fourteen *Nothhelfer* (helpers in need). In many places a blessing is given on the day of his feast or to individual sufferers at other times. Two candles (said to be in memory of the tapers brought to the saint in his dungeon) are blessed and held like a St Andrew's cross either against the throat or over the head of the applicant, with the words *Per intercessionem Sancti Blasii liberet te Deus a malo gutturis et a quovis alio malo.* We also read of " the water of St Blaise ", which is blessed in his honour, and is commonly given to cattle that are sickly.

The so-called Acts of St Blaise are indicated in BHL., nn. 1370–1380, and BHG., p. 21. *Cf.* the *Acta Sanctorum,* February, vol. i, and Detzel, *Christliche Ikonographie,* ii, 2 and 9. A. Franz, *Die Kirchlichen Benediktionen im Mittelalter,* vol. i, pp. 202–206, gives several formulas and much other information about the blessings of St Blaise. For the eighteenth-century commemoration of the saint by the Norwich woolcombers, see Parson Woodforde's *Diary,* the one-volume edition (1935), pp. 198–200.

ST LAURENCE, Bishop of Spoleto   (A.D. 576)

St Laurence was one of a party of three hundred who, being forced to leave Syria in 514 when Severus, the heretical patriarch of Antioch, was persecuting the Catholics, determined to settle in Italy.   They came to Rome, and Pope St Hormisdas ordained some of them who were not already priests, Laurence amongst the number.   He was sent to preach in Umbria, where his fervent eloquence caused many conversions and where he successfully opposed the Arian heresy then rampant in Italy.   Afterwards he retired into a monastery which he founded near Spoleto. The bishopric of that city falling vacant, the clergy chose Laurence, much against his will ; the townspeople, however, objected to having a foreigner and shut the gates of the city against him.   Thereupon the saint prayed aloud that God would indicate His will in the matter.   Immediately the gates flew open, and the people, hailing this as a miracle, received him in honour.   He laboured strenuously among them, setting an example by his devotion and charity and settling feuds and quarrels wherever he went.   For this reason the pope sent him to Bologna, which was rent by contending factions, and he succeeded in establishing peace.   He was called " the Enlightener " because he was so full of divine light that he seemed endowed with a special gift which enabled him to heal blindness—both physical and spiritual. After twenty years he obtained permission to resign his office, and he founded the monastery of Farfa, of which he became abbot and in which he died.

See the *Acta Sanctorum*, February, vol. i, pp. 361–365, and 958–959 ; *cf.* also July, vol. i, pp. 28–35, and DCB., vol. iii, p. 631.

ST IA, Virgin   (Sixth Century)

Although our knowledge of this saint rests upon nothing better than vague medieval legends, still it seems worth while to point out that the patron saint honoured at Saint Ives in Cornwall is entirely different from the supposed Persian bishop from whom Saint Ives in Huntingdonshire is believed to derive its name.

Ia was said to be an Irish maiden who intended to join a company of emigrants, SS. Gwinear, Piala and others, to west Britain.   Upon arrival at the embarking-place she found they had sailed without her, and in great grief she prayed to God for help.   As she did so she noticed a leaf floating on the water, and she touched it with her staff to see if it would sink.   Instead, it began to grow, bigger and bigger, till it became large enough to accommodate her.   She saw then that it was the answer to her prayer ; putting her trust in God, she embarked on it, and was safely floated across the sea, reaching land before the others.

These others came ashore in the Hayle estuary in Cornwall ; Ia landed a little farther to the north-west, where she built herself a hermitage and lived for the rest of her life.   The spot came to be called Porth Ia, but since the sixteenth century has been known as Saint Ives.

It is possible that this story at least represents a tradition of two different immigrations, of which St Ia belonged to the earlier.   William of Worcester in the fifteenth century and Leland in the sixteenth report local traditions connecting her with St Erth, St Uny and St Breaca, all Irish, who with St Gwinear are well known in the church-dedications and place-names of west Cornwall.   Canon Doble thinks it unlikely that these saints really came from Ireland, and Joseph Loth pointed out that Gwinear is a British name.   Wales seems more probable.

St Ia herself is well commemorated in local names, including a holy well called Venton Ia.   She is the co-titular of Saint Ives Catholic church.

The earliest reference to St Ia is in the thirteenth-century *Vita Guigneri* (Gwinear, Fingar) in the *Acta Sanctorum*, March, vol. iii, pp. 456-459.   She is discussed by Gould and Fisher in LBS., vol. iii, pp. 267-269 ; but more scientifically and no less interestingly by Canon Doble in the booklet *St Ives its Patron Saint and Church* (1939).   See also his *St Gwinear*.   Dr Henry Jenner suggested that the leaf story had its rise in the wicker and hide coracle ; *cf. Anglo-Saxon Chronicle* under the year 891.

ST LAURENCE, Archbishop of Canterbury   (A.D. 619)

LAURENCE was a priest who accompanied St Augustine to England in the year 597 and who, after acting as his envoy to obtain fuller instructions from Pope St Gregory the Great, returned to become Augustine's immediate successor in the see of Canterbury, which he occupied for eleven years.   Like Augustine he endeavoured, and failed, to induce the Britons of the West and the Irish to adopt Roman disciplinary practices.   When on King Ethelbert's death his son Edbald refused to follow his father's example in embracing Christianity, and gave himself up to idolatry and incest—taking to himself his father's widow—Laurence, who had laboured hard for his conversion, meditated retiring to France, as the bishops St Mellitus and St Justus had already done.   However, on the eve of his departure, St Peter in a dream reproached him for designing to forsake that flock for which Christ had laid down His life.   Not only did this prevent St Laurence from executing his purpose, but it had such an effect on the king (who was naturally impressed by the sight of the scars of the stripes inflicted on Laurence by the indignant apostle) that he became a Christian.   St Laurence did not long survive this happy change, dying in 619.   When his tomb was first opened in 1091, " a mighty blast of fragrance " swept through the whole monastery of St Augustine. His feast is kept in the dioceses of Westminster and Southwark.

St Laurence is mentioned in the Roman Martyrology.   We know little about him beyond what is found in Bede, *Hist. Eccles.*, bk ii, cc. 4, 6 and 7.   William of Malmesbury, *Gesta Pontificum* (Rolls Series), pp. 5, 6 etc., refers to the life by Goscelin.   Two manuscripts of this are still preserved, as Hardy records, *Catalogue of British History*, II, i, 217-218. The tomb of St Laurence has of late years been reopened, but the bodies of all the early archbishops were translated by Abbot Wido in 1091 to a place of greater honour.   A full account of the excavations was given by Sir William St John Hope in *Archaeologia*, vol. lxvi, pp. 377-400, with plans and photographs.

ST WERBURGA, Virgin   (*c.* A.D. 700)

ST WERBURGA (properly Werburh) was the daughter of Wulfhere, King of Mercia, and St Ermenilda, and so grand-daughter of St Sexburga and great-niece of St Etheldreda.   Her beauty and good qualities brought her offers of marriage, but she refused them all, saying that she had chosen the Lord Jesus for her spouse. Legend states, but the story is quite unreliable, that her greatest victory was over the attempts of Werbod, a nobleman of her father's court.   The king, it is said, was very fond of this man, and Werbod made use of his interest to try to obtain from Wulfhere the hand of Werburga in marriage.   The king agreed on condition he could gain the maiden's own consent also.   Queen Ermenilda and her sons Wulfhad and Ruffin were grieved at the news.   The two princes were in the habit of resorting to St Chad, Bishop of Lichfield, under pretext of going hunting ; for the saint lived at a hermitage in the forest, and it was by him that they were instructed and baptized. Werbod, who found them an obstacle to his plans, is said to have contrived their murder, for he showed Wulfhere the princes returning from the bishop, and so incensed him against them by slanders that the king ordered them to be put to death—partly on religious grounds, for he had been prevailed upon by Werbod to countenance and favour idolatry. Werbod, however, soon after died miserably, and Wulfhere no sooner heard that the murder had been perpetrated than he was stung with remorse, did great penance, and submitted himself to the guidance of his queen and of St Chad.

Werburga, finding him so much changed, no longer feared to tell him of her desire to be a nun, and she pleaded her cause so earnestly that her request was granted. Wulfhere conducted her in state to Ely, where they were met at the convent gate by the abbess St Etheldreda and her religious, singing hymns to God. Werburga, falling on her knees, begged to be admitted and joyfully exchanged her royal robes for a coarse habit. King Wulfhere dying in 675, his brother Ethelred succeeded him, and St Werburga, at the persuasion of her uncle, left Ely, to charge herself with the superintendence of all the houses of religious women in his kingdom, that she might establish them in the observance of the most exact monastic discipline.

Werburga seems to have spent part of her time at a royal house at Weedon in Northamptonshire, which perhaps she turned into a nunnery. Other convents in her care were at Hanbury in Staffordshire and at " Tricengeham ". This last was probably Threckingham in Kesteven, and here it was that St Werburga died on a February 3, most likely between 700 and 707. She was buried by her own wish at Hanbury, but by the end of the tenth century her relics were at Chester (perhaps removed thither, as tradition affirms, during the Danish invasions), where throughout the later middle ages her shrine in the cathedral was a place of pilgrimage. St Werburga's feast is now observed in the dioceses of Birmingham and Shrewsbury.

Much of the detail given above is of very doubtful authenticity, being based upon the biography of St Werburga written by Goscelin, who lived 400 years after her time. See the *Acta Sanctorum*, February, vol. i, pp. 391–394 ; *cf.* also the *Liber Eliensis*, i, ch. 17, 24, 36, 37, and the *Chronicon ex Chronicis* of Florence of Worcester (ed. Thorpe), vol. i, p. 32. But the most valuable discussion of her life from a historical point of view is that of Profesor James Tait in the preface to his edition of the *Chartulary or Register of the Abbey of St Werburgh, Chester* (1920), pp. vii to xiv. See also the life of Wulfhad and Ruffin printed by Fr P. Grosjean in *Analecta Bollandiana*, vol. lviii (1940).

ST ANSKAR, Archbishop of Hamburg and Bremen   (A.D. 865)

ANSKAR was born about 801 of a noble family not far from Amiens, and was sent to acquire learning at the neighbouring monastery of Old Corbie in Picardy, where a near relation of the Emperor Charlemagne loved him greatly and Paschasius Radbertus is said to have been his tutor. A vision he had of the Blessed Virgin and of the death of the Emperor Charlemagne so impressed him that he lost all youthful gaiety and thought only of preaching to the heathen as the nearest road to martyrdom. He became a monk, first at Old Corbie and afterwards at New Corbie (Corvey) in Westphalia, where he first engaged in pastoral work. Harold, King of Denmark, as a fugitive from his country, had been baptized at the court of Louis the Debonair. When he was about to return to his kingdom he took Anskar with him, as well as the monk Autbert, to convert the Danes.   They were very successful, winning many to the faith and starting a school, probably at Hedeby.   At the invitation of Björn, King of Sweden, Anskar then went with several others to spread the gospel there.   In 831 King Louis named him abbot of New Corbie and first archbishop of Hamburg, to which Pope Gregory IV added the dignity of legate of the Holy See to the northern peoples.   There he worked for thirteen years, organizing the missions in Denmark, Norway and Sweden as well as in North Germany, building churches and founding a library.

A great incursion of heathen Northmen in 845 destroyed Hamburg, whereupon Sweden and Denmark relapsed into idolatry.   Anskar still supported his desolate churches in Germany until the see of Bremen becoming vacant, Pope St Nicholas I eventually united it with Hamburg and appointed Anskar over both.   He returned to Denmark and his presence soon made the faith revive.   In Sweden the superstitious King Olaf cast lots as to whether the Christian missionaries should be admitted or not.   The saint grieved to see the cause of religion treated with such levity, and recommended the issue to the care of God.   The lot proved favourable, and the bishop established many churches, which he left under zealous pastors before his return to Bremen.

St Anskar had an extraordinary talent for preaching, and his charity to the poor knew no bounds ; he washed their feet and waited upon them at table.   When one of his disciples was loudly vaunting the miracles which the saint had wrought, Anskar rebuked him by saying, " Were I worthy of such a favour from my God, I would ask that He would grant to me this one miracle, that by His grace He would make of me a good man ".   He wore a rough hair shirt and, whilst his health permitted it, lived on bread and water.   As a stimulus to devotion he made a collection of short prayers, one or other of which he placed at the end of each psalm. Insertions of this kind may be found in many old manuscript psalters.   He died at Bremen in the sixty-seventh year of his life and the thirty-fourth of his prelacy, and the whole North bewailed him.   But although St Anskar was the first to preach the gospel in Sweden, it relapsed entirely into paganism after his death.   The conversion of the country was due to St Sigfrid and other missionaries in the eleventh century.

The materials for Anskar's life, owing no doubt to the very great veneration in which he was held, are exceptionally abundant.   There is above all the *Vita Anskarii* by his fellow missionary and successor in the episcopate, St Rembert.   It has been printed in a handy edition by G. Waitz in the series of *Scriptores rerum Germanicarum*, and an English translation with useful notes and bibliography by Dr C. H. Robinson was published in 1921.   Prof. Hauck, in his *Kirchengeschichte Deutschlands*, vol. ii, speaks enthusiastically of Anskar.   See L. Bril in the *Revue d'histoire ecclésiastique*, vol. xii (1911), pp. 17-37, 231-241 ; E. de Moreau, *St Anschaire missionnaire* . . . (1930) ; P. Oppenheim, *Der hl. Ansgar* (1931) ; and C. J. A. Opperman, *English Missionaries in Sweden* (1937), pp. 38-45.   But on this last work see *Analecta Bollandiana*, vol. lvii (1939), pp. 162-164.   And cf. Fliche and Martin, *Histoire de l'Église*, vol. vi, pp. 249-253, 447-450.

ST MARGARET "OF ENGLAND", Virgin   (A.D. 1192)

THE shrine containing the body of St Margaret, which was the glory of the church of the Cistercian nuns of Seauve Bénite, in the diocese of Puy-en-Velay, was formerly much resorted to by the whole countryside.   The old edition of *Gallia Christiana* and Dom Beaunier, the Maurist monk, confirm the local tradition that she was an Englishwoman and that her resting-place was famous for miracles.   On the other hand, she is described as being by birth a noble Hungarian in an old French biography, a manuscript copy of which was preserved by the Jesuit College of Clermont at Paris.   Her mother, who was probably at least of English extraction, took her on a pilgrimage to Jerusalem, and they both led a very penitential life, first in that city and afterwards at Bethlehem.   After St Margaret had buried her mother in the Holy Land, she made a pilgrimage to Montserrat in Spain and afterwards to our Lady's shrine at Puy.   Then she retired to the Cistercian nunnery of Seauve Bénite where she ended her days.

See *Gallia Christiana Nova*, in *Diœc, Aniciensi seu Podiensi*, vol. ii, p. 777, and *cf.* Theillière, *Notes historiques sur le monastère de la Seauve-Bénite* (1872).

BD SIMON OF CASCIA   (A.D. 1348)

THE name of Simon Fidati has attracted much attention on account of a problem of literary authorship.   Certain ascetical writings in the purest Tuscan of the *trecento*, which were traditionally attributed to Dominic Cavalca, o.p., have been claimed on the ground of internal evidence as the work of his Augustinian contemporary, this Simon.   The case is by no means clear.   No manuscript attestation supports it, and even the champions of Fidati have to suppose that if he supplied the ideas in Latin, his disciple and biographer, John of Salerno, gave them their present form by re-editing them in the speech of the people.   Still more remarkable is the contention advanced by A. V. Müller that many of the most distinctive tenets in Luther's teaching were derived from Fidati's published volume *De gestis Domini Salvatoris*.   The book had been first printed at Strassburg in 1480, and being the work of a fellow Augustinian is extremely likely to have come into Luther's hands. It certainly must be admitted that Bd Simon held some theological views which were at least incautiously expressed, and which readily lent themselves to misinterpretation.   Further, it is clear even from the short biography of his devoted disciple John of Salerno, already mentioned, that Fidati was much criticized by his contemporaries and that some did not even hesitate to call him a hypocrite.

We know little of the details of his life.   Even the summary submitted to the Congregation of Rites when a *confirmatio cultus* was petitioned for in 1833 had to confine itself for the most part to the vaguest generalities.   He must have been born about 1295, at Cascia in Umbria, and is said in early youth to have come under the influence of Angelo Clareno, whose intransigent spirit he seems to have shared. He joined the Augustinian friars, and the period of his studies must have been brief, for his career as a preacher began about 1318.   There can be no question that he possessed very remarkable gifts both of nature and grace.   His biographer recounts how when Simon was producing his great work *De gestis Domini* he had watched him write folio after folio without a pause, just as one would scribble a letter to a friend.   In the early years of his preaching his life had been extremely austere, but he found it necessary as he grew older to be more discreet in his bodily mortifications.   It is stated that he preached as a rule absolutely without preparation, leaving it to the Spirit of God to inspire him what to say.   This, however, was certainly not due to any shirking of labour, but in large measure to the fact that when he was engaged upon some great preaching mission he would have as many as thirty or even forty letters to write to penitents and others at a single sitting, and this work took him the best part of the night.   John of Salerno, who was his daily companion for seventeen years, tells us all this with an earnestness which brings conviction of its truth.

Simon was fearless in reproving offenders, and treated many even of those who sought his friendship with uncompromising harshness, but the curious effect, says his biographer, was that in many cases he only drew them to him the more.   He was like a magnet among iron filings.   He contrived to evade every post of authority within his order or outside of it, and when a certain intimate and influential friend got him nominated to an episcopal see, he treated him with such sternness that the other never dared to mention the subject again.   With all his success as a preacher, and as a man who played a part in the public life of Perugia, Florence and Siena, Bd Simon's own preference was for a life of solitude spent in prayer and among his books.   Outside of this his special interest seems to have centred in rescuing fallen women, for whom he founded a house of refuge, and in protecting young girls, for whom a similar establishment was provided as the fruit of his charitable exertions. He seems to have died in Florence, though the place is not quite certain, on February 2, 1348.

The only materials of any value for the life of Bd Simon are those contained in the volume of Fr Nicola Mattioli, *Il b. Simone Fidati da Cascia* (1898).   He prints a number of Fidati's letters, as well as the biography by John of Cremona.   The compiler of the summary printed for the Congregation of Rites in 1833 seems to have been very imperfectly acquainted with the facts of his history.   *Cf.* also A. d'Ancona and O. Bacci, *Manuale della letteratura italiana* (1904), vol. i, pp. 405-407 ; and A. V. Müller, *Una Fonte ignota del sistema di Lutero* (1921).

BD JOHN NELSON, Martyr   (A.D. 1578)

John Nelson was the son of Sir N. Nelson of Skelton in Yorkshire.   At the age of forty, hearing of the college of Douay and hoping to be able to serve his country, he went to study there and was ordained priest in 1576.   The same year he was sent upon the English mission and was apprehended in London on suspicion of being a Catholic and imprisoned.   He was tried and condemned for refusing to take the oath of Queen Elizabeth's supremacy.   He was drawn on a hurdle from Newgate to Tyburn, where he was hanged, disembowelled and quartered.   Father Nelson had been admitted into the Society of Jesus shortly before his arrest.

See MMP., pp. 7-11 ; and Camm, LEM., vol. ii, pp. 223-233.

BD STEPHEN BELLESINI   (A.D. 1840)

No very outstanding achievement marks the life of this fervent and modest religious. He was born at Trent on November 25, 1774, and in 1790 at the age of sixteen entered the Order of Hermits of St Augustine.   After being sent to make his studies at Rome and at Bologna he was constrained when the Revolution broke out to return to his native city.   Soon, however, the Augustinian community was dispersed, and Stephen then devoted himself with characteristic vigour and conscientiousness to the work of preaching and especially to the religious instruction of children.   As a result he was shortly afterwards constituted by government appointment inspector of all the schools in the Trentino, discharging his duties so much to the satisfaction of the officials that, when the Augustinian Order was restored to community life in the Papal States and Stephen insisted upon rejoining his religious brethren at Bologna, strong opposition was raised to his departure. In spite of threats of violence he carried out his purpose, and was made master of novices first at Rome and afterwards at Città della Pieve.   After some years he passed to the famous Augustinian church at Genazzano, near Palestrina, the shrine of our Lady of Good Counsel, where he became parish priest. In attending the sick during an epidemic of cholera he was himself stricken down, dying on February 2, 1840. Bd Stephen was beatified in 1904.

Two lives were published shortly after the beatification, both based upon the documents of the process—Billeri, *Vita del b. Stefano Bellesini* (1904) and Weber, *Breve vita del b. Stefano Bellesini* (1904). The former prints more extracts from Bd Stephen's letters.

4 : ST ANDREW CORSINI, BISHOP OF FIESOLE   (A.D. 1373)

THIS saint was called Andrew after the apostle of that name, upon whose festival he was born in Florence in 1302. He came of the distinguished family of the Corsini, and we are told that his parents dedicated him to God before his birth ; but in spite of all their care the first part of his youth was spent in vice and extravagance, amongst bad companions. His mother never ceased praying for his conversion, and one day in the bitterness of her grief she said, " I see you are indeed the wolf I saw in my sleep," and explained that before he was born she dreamt she had given birth to a wolf which ran into a church and was changed into a lamb. She added that she and his father had devoted him to the service of God under the protection of the Blessed Virgin, and that they expected of him a very different sort of life from that which he was leading. These rebukes made a very deep impression. Overwhelmed with shame, Andrew next day went to the church of the Carmelite friars, and after having prayed fervently before the altar of our Lady he was so touched by God's grace that he resolved to embrace the religious life in that convent. All the artifices of his former companions, and the solicitations of an uncle who tried to draw him back into the world, were powerless to change his purpose : he never fell away from the first fervour of his conversion.

In the year 1328 Andrew was ordained ; but to escape the feasting and music which his family had prepared according to custom for the day on which he should celebrate his first Mass, he withdrew to a little convent seven miles out of the town, and there, unknown and with wonderful devotion, he offered to Almighty God the firstfruits of his priesthood. After some time employed in preaching in Florence he was sent to Paris, where he attended the schools for three years. He continued his studies for a while at Avignon with his uncle, Cardinal Corsini, and in 1332, when he returned to Florence, he was chosen prior of his convent. God honoured his virtue with the gift of prophecy, and miracles of healing were also ascribed to him. Amongst miracles in the moral order and conquests of hardened souls, the conversion of his cousin John Corsini, a confirmed gambler, was especially remarkable.

When the bishop of Fiesole died in 1349 the chapter unanimously chose Andrew Corsini to fill the vacant see. As soon, however, as he was informed of what was going on, he hid himself with the Carthusians at Enna : the canons, despairing of finding him, were about to proceed to a second election when his hiding-place was revealed by a child. After his consecration as bishop he redoubled his former austerities. Daily he gave himself a severe discipline whilst he recited the litany, and his bed was of vine branches strewed on the floor. Meditation and reading the Holy Scriptures he called recreation from his labours. He avoided talking with women as much as possible, and refused to listen to flatterers or informers. His tenderness and care for the poor were extreme, and he was particularly solicitous in seeking out those who were ashamed to make known their distress : these he helped with all possible secrecy. St Andrew had, too, a talent for appeasing quarrels, and he was often successful in restoring order where popular disturbances had broken out. For this reason Bd Urban V sent him to Bologna, where the nobility and the people were miserably divided. He pacified them after suffering much humiliation, and they remained at peace during the rest of his life. Every Thursday he used to wash the feet of the poor, and never turned any beggar away without an alms.

St Andrew was taken ill whilst singing Mass on Christmas night in 1373 and died on the following Epiphany at the age of seventy-one. He was immediately proclaimed a saint by the voice of the people, and Pope Urban VIII formally canonized him in 1629. Andrew was buried in the Carmelite church at Florence ; and Pope Clement XII, who belonged to the Corsini family, built and endowed a chapel in honour of his kinsman in the Lateran basilica. The architect of this chapel, in which Clement himself was buried, was Alexander Galilei, who lived for some years in England. The same pope added St Andrew Corsini to the general calendar of the Western church, in 1737.

The two principal Latin lives of St Andrew are printed in the *Acta Sanctorum*, January, vol. ii. See also S. Mattei, *Vita di S. Andrea Corsini* (1872), and the biography by P. Caioli (1929), who makes use of certain unpublished Florentine documents.

ST THEOPHILUS THE PENITENT (No Date)

ALTHOUGH the legend of St Theophilus must almost certainly be regarded as pure romance, still it is seriously discussed in the *Acta Sanctorum*, and as an early example of a type of devil-pact story, which was firmly believed and had an enormous vogue in later ages, it claims a brief notice here.

Theophilus is described as *oeconomus*—let us say "administrator"—of the church of Adana in Cilicia, a humble, earnest man, who on being chosen bishop declined the honour, preferring to remain in his subordinate station. On his refusal of the bishopric a stranger was appointed to the see, and he, through the subtle machinations of the Devil, without any reason deposed Theophilus from his office. The injustice rankled, and the sufferer, brooding over his wrongs, was finally led on to a complete recoil from all his former good practices. Bent at all costs upon procuring his reinstatement, he consulted a Jewish sorcerer, by whom he was brought into personal communication with Satan. The Devil exacted from him a repudiation of Christ and His holy Mother, duly signed and sealed ; and on the fulfilment of this condition the bishop, by some diabolic spell, was induced to lay aside his prejudices and to restore the former administrator to his office. But when he had attained his purpose, Theophilus's remembrance of what he had done left him no peace. Eventually he did forty days' penance in the church of our Lady, humbly beseeching her intercession, and she, after administering a severe rebuke, prevailed with her Son to show mercy to the offender. After his fasts had been still further prolonged she appeared to Theophilus again in a vision during his sleep, and when he woke he found that the pact which he had signed was lying on his breast. Thereupon, prompted by gratitude and a wish to proclaim to all the world the compassion of the Mother of Mercy, he made public confession before the bishop in church of all that had happened, and the pact was burnt by the bishop's own hand in the sight of the people.

It is stated that this legend was committed to writing in Greek by one Eutychian, who professed to have been born in Theophilus's own house. See the *Acta Sanctorum*, February, vol. i. It was translated into Latin by Paul the Deacon in the ninth century, and since then the story has been told again and again with slight variations. Roswitha, the nun of Gandersheim (*c.* 980), produced a Latin metrical version (Migne, PL., vol. cxxxvii, c. 1101). It is found in all the great collections of " Marienlegenden " (see Mussafia's " Studien " in the *Sitzungsberichte* of the Vienna Academy, 1887, 1888, etc., and H. S. D. Ward, *Catalogue of Romances in the British Museum*, vol. ii, pp. 595 *seq.*) and in nearly all European languages.

ST PHILEAS, BISHOP OF THMUIS, MARTYR   (A.D. 304)

PHILEAS was of Thmuis in Egypt and a learned and eloquent man. After being converted to the faith, he was chosen bishop in his city, but was apprehended and carried prisoner to Alexandria by the persecutors. Eusebius has preserved part of a letter which he wrote in his dungeon, and sent to his flock to comfort and encourage them. Describing the sufferings of his fellow confessors at Alexandria, he says that everyone had full liberty to insult, strike and beat them. Culcian was then governor of Egypt under Maximinus. We have a long account of the trial of St Phileas before him, said to have been extracted from the court registers.

After many other questions Culcian asked, " Was Christ God ? " The saint answered, " Yes," and cited His miracles as a proof. The governor expressed great regard for Phileas, and said, " If you were a poor man you would be dispatched without more ado ; but you have sufficient not only for yourself and your family, but almost for the maintenance of a province. I pity you with all my heart, and will do my best to save you." The counsellors and lawyers, who also wished to save him, declared that he had already sacrificed in the Phrontisterium, the Academy of Literature. Phileas replied, " I have not done so by any immolation, but if you say merely that I have sacrificed, you say no more than the truth." (As he had been confined there for some time, he had probably celebrated the Holy Mysteries.) His wife, children, and other relations were present at the trial, and the governor, hoping to overcome him by his affection for them, said, " See how sorrowfully your wife stands there watching you." Phileas replied, " Jesus Christ, the Saviour of souls, calls me to His glory. He can also, if He pleases, call my wife." The counsellors out of compassion said to the judge, " Phileas asks for a delay " Culcian answered, " I grant it willingly that you may think over what to do ". Phileas said, " I *have* considered, and it is my unchangeable determination to die for Jesus Christ ".

Then the counsellors, the chief magistrate and his relations besought him to have compassion on his family and not to abandon his children while they were so young and required his care. But he stood unmoved and, raising up his heart to God, protested that he owned no other kindred than the apostles and martyrs. One of those present was a Christian called Philoromus, a tribune and the emperor's treasurer in Alexandria, so that he had his tribunal in the city where he heard causes every day. Admiring the courage of Phileas, he exclaimed, " Why do you try to overcome this brave soul and make him renounce God by impiously yielding to men ? Do you not see that he is contemplating the glory of Heaven and that he makes no account of worldly things ? " This speech drew down upon him the indignation of the court, who demanded that both men should die, and the judge assented. As they were led out to execution, the brother of Phileas said to the governor, " Phileas asks for pardon " Culcian therefore recalled him and asked if it were true. Phileas answered, " God forbid. Do not listen to this unhappy man. Far from desiring the reversal of my sentence, I am greatly obliged to the emperors, to you and to the court, for through you I become a co-heir with Christ and shall enter to-day into possession of His kingdom." After exhorting the faithful to perseverance, he was beheaded with Philoromus.

See Ruinart. *Acta martyrum sincera*, p. 494. E. Le Blant, " Notes sur les Actes de S. Phileas ", *Nuovo Bullettino di arch. crist.*, vol. ii (1896), pp. 27–33, expresses a very favourable opinion of this document, but *cf. Analecta Bollandiana*, vol. xvi (1898), p. 94, and Delehaye, *Les martyrs d'Égypte*, pp. 155–170.

ST ISIDORE OF PELUSIUM, Abbot   (*c.* A.D. 450)

St Isidore was a monk from his youth and became superior of a monastery in the neighbourhood of Pelusium in the fifth century. According to Facundus and Suidas, he was also ordained priest. During his lifetime men regarded him as a model of religious perfection, and his patriarch, St Cyril, and other prelates of his time, treated him as their father. He chose St Chrysostom for his model. We still have two thousand and twelve of his letters, full of excellent instructions in piety and showing great theological learning. They are so well expressed that according to some enthusiasts they might be used to replace the classics in the study of the Greek language. From their pages shine forth the saint's prudence, humility, undaunted zeal and ardent love of God.

There is some biographical material printed in the prefaces to Isidore's letters in Migne, PG., vol. lxxviii. See also Aigrain, *Quarante-neuf lettres d'Isidore Pélusiote* (1911), and L. Bayer, *Isidors klassische Bildung* (1915).

ST MODAN, Abbot   (*c.* A.D. 550 ?)

There is no certainty about the life of this Scottish saint. According to his legend he was a monk of great austerity of life, who against his will was made abbot of his monastery. He is said to have preached the faith at Stirling and in other places near the Forth, especially at Falkirk ; but he frequently interrupted his apostolic labours to seek solitude in the mountainous country near Dumbarton, where he would spend thirty or forty days at a time in contemplation, during which he enjoyed a foretaste of the joys of Heaven. At last, when he grew too feeble to move from place to place, he finally retired to a lonely spot near the sea surrounded by high rocks, and here he died. He is titular saint of the High Church at Stirling, and was particularly honoured at Roseneath in Dunbartonshire and at Falkirk.

See *Acta Sanctorum*, February, vol. i ; *Aberdeen Breviary*, February 4 ; and KSS. The supposed connection of St Modan with Dryburgh, which was emphasized by Butler, seems improbable, as A. P Forbes points out, since there is no reason to believe that there was any monastery at Dryburgh before a Premonstratensian abbey was founded there in the twelfth century.

BD RABANUS MAURUS, Archbishop of Mainz   (A.D. 856)

Rabanus, born about the year 784, was probably a native of Mainz, though by some writers he is said to have been a Scot or Irishman. His early education was undertaken by his parents, who afterwards took him to the neighbouring monastery of Fulda, which had been founded by St Boniface, the English apostle of Germany. The monastery school under the abbot Bangulf had a great reputation, and Rabanus responded eagerly to the instruction. He soon became a wonder to his masters and schoolfellows, so great were his abilities and so quickly did he learn. To complete his education he was sent, with his friend Hatto, to study for a year at Tours under another great Englishman, Charlemagne's learned adviser, Alcuin. In him he found an ideal master and a second father. Alcuin was much attached to him and nicknamed him Maurus, after St Benedict's favourite disciple, and he wrote him touching letters of counsel after the young man had returned to Fulda. " Be a father to the poor and needy ", he says in one of them, " be humble in rendering them service, generous in conferring benefits, and so will their blessing descend upon you "

At Fulda there was a fine library founded by Charlemagne and enriched by the zeal of the monastic scribes, and there Rabanus worked. To understand and to be able to expound the Holy Scriptures, upon which he afterwards wrote many commentaries, he learnt Greek, Hebrew and something of Syriac, and he studied the fathers and made a synopsis of their teaching. About the year 799 he received deacon's orders and was made master of the monastery school and, about the same time, he composed a metrical work in acrostic form in honour of the Holy Cross. The monks had a hard time in 805 when a famine was succeeded by a pestilence. Harder still was it for Rabanus when the abbot Ratgar ordered all the monks to set to work to build, and he had to give up his beloved books to do work for which he was quite unfitted. In 815 he was ordained priest and, under the abbot Egilius, he resumed his scholastic work as teacher. He never omitted any observance prescribed by his order, although his teaching work and his writing made very great inroads upon his time. In 822 he became abbot, and it was probably then that he wrote most of his works (though he complained ruefully that " seeing that these youngsters have enough to eat is a great hindrance ")—notably the sixty-four homilies that have come down to us which illustrate his able method of teaching. He wrote also a well-known martyrology and had great veneration for the saints. He was so obedient to the Holy See that he was called " the Pope's slave ", and such was his hatred of heresy that to him every heretic was Antichrist ; on dogmatic subjects he stood on the authority of the fathers and distrusted new departures. So widespread was his reputation that we find him constantly having to attend synods and councils at various cities. He completed the monastery buildings and built churches and oratories on all the estates belonging to his house, and he also built one or two monasteries. He resigned his office to his friend Hatto and appears to have lived some time in retirement, but in 847 he was made archbishop of Mainz, though he was seventy-one.

Henceforth Rabanus lived, if possible, more strenuously than ever, and never relaxed his old rule of life, drinking no wine and eating no meat. Three months after becoming archbishop he had to hold a synod, the result of which was a series of resolutions all tending to stricter observance of the laws of the Church. It was so evident that the new archbishop was behind these regulations that a conspiracy was formed against his life, but it was discovered, and he magnanimously forgave the plotters. A second synod took place in 852 and Rabanus was instrumental in bringing about the condemnation of the doctrines of the monk Gottschalk, who had been spreading heretical doctrines about grace and predestination, based upon an exaggeration of the teaching of St Augustine. The energies of Rabanus lasted almost to the end—he travelled about the diocese with capable priests, teaching, preaching and reconciling sinners to God. During a famine he daily fed 300 poor people at his house, and he continued his labours and his writings until his health entirely gave way; he became bedridden shortly before his death in 856. Bd Rabanus was one of the most learned men of his age.

A life of Rabanus by his disciple Rudolf has been many times printed (*e.g.* in Migne, PL., vol. cvii; in the *Acta Sanctorum*, February, vol. i; and in MGH., *Scriptores*, vol. xv, pp. 329-341). A convenient outline of his career may be found in Knöpfler's edition of his *De institutione clericorum* (1900), pp. ix-xvi; *cf.* Hauck, *Kirchengeschichte Deutschlands*, vol. ii, pp. 620 *seq.*, and Dümmler in the *Sitzungsberichte* of the Berlin Academy, 1898.

ST NICHOLAS STUDITES, ABBOT (A.D. 863)

THIS Nicholas was born at Sydonia (now Canea) in Crete, of well-to-do parents who took him in his tenth year to Constantinople to his uncle Theophanes at the monastery of Studius. The abbot was greatly struck by the little lad and allowed him to enter the monastery school, where he soon distinguished himself by his docility and eagerness to learn. At the age of eighteen he became a monk, and it was noticed that obedience to rule presented no difficulty to him, so thoroughly had he already attained to self-surrender. Nicholas was not destined to live a life of peace in those troublous times. The Saracens pillaged his home in Crete, whilst in Constantinople and Greece the Church was cruelly persecuted by the inconoclastic emperors. Before long, Nicholas, the patriarch St Nicephorus, the abbot St Theodore and others were sent into banishment, where Nicholas did all he could to assist his fellows and alleviate their sufferings. After the murder of Leo V the Armenian the persecution died down for a while and the exiles were allowed to return, but on conditions which not all of them would accept. When St Theodore died, St Nicholas, who had been a pattern disciple to others, became himself a leader and teacher. The persecution lasted on until the death of the Emperor Theophilus in 842, when his widow, Theodora, recalled the exiled servants of God and restored the venerated images to the churches. Among those who returned was the new abbot of the Studites, who was afterwards succeeded by St Nicholas.

In December 858 began the great and far-reaching dispute when St Ignatius was replaced in the patriarchal chair of Constantinople by Photius, the nominee of the Emperor Michael III. St Nicholas would have no dealings with him and went into voluntary banishment, refusing to return at the summons of Michael, who then appointed another abbot. For several years the saint wandered about, but he was eventually seized and sent back to his monastery where he was kept in strict confinement. He was consequently unable to obey the summons of Pope St Nicholas I, who wished to examine him as a witness on behalf of Ignatius. In 867 Michael was killed, and his successor, the Emperor Basil, not only restored St Ignatius, but also wished to reinstate the abbot Nicholas, who, however, excused himself on the plea of old age. He died amongst his monks, and was buried beside St Theodore, his great predecessor.

See the *Acta Sanctorum*, February, vol. i; but there is a great deal of biographical material contained in the Life of St Evaristus the Faster, printed in the *Analecta Bollandiana*, vol. xli (1923), pp. 288-325.

ST REMBERT, ARCHBISHOP OF HAMBURG AND BREMEN (A.D. 888)

ST REMBERT (or Rimbert) was born near Bruges, and became a monk in the neighbouring monastery of Torhout. St Anskar called him to his assistance in his missionary labours, and in his last illness recommended him as his successor, saying, " Rembert is more worthy to be archbishop than I am to be his deacon " After the death of Anskar in 865, Rembert was chosen archbishop of Hamburg and Bremen, with the superintendence of the churches of Sweden, Denmark and Lower Germany.   He also began the conversion of the Slavs of the North.   He sold sacred vessels to redeem captives from the Northmen, and gave the horse he was riding for the ransom of a maiden taken by the Slavs.   He was most careful never to waste a moment which could be given to serious duties or his prayers, and never in all external occupations to forget the presence of God.   He died on June 11, but is commemorated in the Roman Martyrology on February 4, the day he was chosen archbishop.   Rembert's Life of St Anskar, considering the period at which it was written, is remarkable both for its accuracy and for its style.   His letter to Walburga, first abbess of Nienheerse, is an eloquent exhortation.

See the *Acta Sanctorum*, February, vol. i, pp. 564–571 ; G. Waitz has re-edited this Latin life in the series *Scriptores rerum Germanicarum*, along with that of St Anskar, BHL., n. 7258.

ST JOAN OF FRANCE, MATRON, FOUNDRESS OF THE ANNONCIADES OF BOURGES   (A.D. 1505)

ST JOAN of France, formerly more usually known as Joan of Valois, was the daughter of King Louis XI and Charlotte of Savoy and was born in 1464.   Her small stature and misshapen body rendered her an object of aversion to her father, who married her to his cousin Louis, Duke of Orleans, in 1476.   She obtained her husband's life from her brother Charles VIII, who had determined to put him to death for rebellion.   Yet nothing could conquer his dislike of her, though she bore all things with patience, making exercises of religion her chief occupation and comfort.   When her husband came to the throne under the name of Louis XII, he desired an advantageous match with Anne, the heiress of Brittany and the late king's widow. He therefore alleged the nullity of his marriage with Joan, chiefly on the ground that she had been forced upon him by Louis XI, and he applied to Pope Alexander VI for commissaries to examine the matter.   After consideration they declared the marriage void in 1498, and Joan herself made no opposition, but rejoiced to be at liberty and in a position better to serve God.   She therefore meekly acquiesced, and the king, pleased at her submission, gave her the duchy of Berry, besides Pontoise and other townships.   She lived at Bourges, and devoted herself entirely to prayer and to works of charity.

In 1501, with the help of her confessor, the Franciscan Bd Gabriel Mary, St Joan founded an order of nuns " of the ten virtues of our Lady ", in honour of the Annunciation.   The first postulants were a group of eleven girls from a school at Bourges, some of whom were less than ten years old.   Father Gabriel Mary drew up their rule, for which after some difficulty approval was granted at Rome ; later permission was given for St Joan to be professed without doing a novitiate.   This she did at Pentecost 1504.   She died less than a year later, and was canonized in 1950.   A few houses of her order still exist, of which one is in England, at St Margaret's-at-Cliffe in Kent ; they are commonly known as the Annonciades (of Bourges) and their life is contemplative.   The order is under the direction of the Friars Minor, who keep the saint's feast on February 14.

See Maulde de la Clavière, *Jeanne de France* (1883) ; de Flavigny, *Une fille de France* (1896) ; Othon, *Le b. Gabriel Maria et l'Ordre de l'Annonciade* (1913) ; M. Cagnac, *La bse*

Jeanne de Valois (1930); J. F. Bonnefoy, *Chronique de l'Annonciade* (1937); A. Redier, *Jeanne de France* (1946); de Levis-Mirepoix, *Princess and Saint* (1950); and Anne M. C. Forster, *St Joan of France* (1950). The proceedings in the nullity suit which pronounced St Joan's marriage invalid have been published *in extenso* by M. Maulde de la Clavière in *Procédures politiques du règne de Louis XI* (1885).

BD THOMAS PLUMTREE, Martyr   (A.D. 1570)

HE appears to have been born in Lincolnshire and to have been a scholar of Corpus Christi, Oxford, taking his degree in 1546. He became rector of Stubton, but resigned his living on the change of religion under Queen Elizabeth. His next post, as master of a school in Lincoln, he also had to leave on account of his religion. He became chief chaplain to the insurgents in the Rising of the Two Earls, and in an old ballad he is described as " The Preacher of the Rebels " He celebrated Mass in Durham Cathedral on December 4, 1569. When it was found impossible to maintain the rising and the whole north was at the mercy of the queen's troops, Plumtree tried, with others, to escape, but was captured and sent back to Durham Castle. He was specially singled out for punishment and condemned to death. His gibbet was erected in the market-place, and upon his arrival there he was offered his life as the price of apostasy, but replied that he had " no desire so to continue living in this world, as meantime to die to God ". He died courageously and was buried on January 14—ten days after his death. His feast is kept today in the diocese of Hexham and Newcastle.

See Camm, LEM., vol. ii, pp. 111–186.

ST JOSEPH OF LEONESSA   (A.D. 1612)

THIS saint was born in 1556 at Leonessa in Umbria, and at the age of eighteen made his profession as a Capuchin friar in his native town, taking the name of Joseph, whereas he had previously been called Eufranio. He was humble, obedient and mortified to a heroic degree, and three days of the week he took no other sustenance but bread and water. He generally preached with a crucifix in his hand, and the fire of his words kindled a flame in the hearts of his hearers. In 1587 he was sent to Turkey as a missioner among the Christians at Pera, a suburb of Constantinople. There he encouraged and served the Christian galley-slaves with wonderful devotion, especially during a virulent pestilence in which he himself caught the infection, though he afterwards recovered. He converted many apostates, and, by preaching the faith to the Moslems rendered himself liable to the utmost severity of the Turkish law. Joseph was twice imprisoned, and the second time he was condemned to a cruel death. He was hung on a gibbet by one hand which was pierced with a sharp hook at the end of a chain, and was suspended by one foot in the same way. However, after he had been thus tortured for many hours, he was released and his sentence commuted to banishment. He landed in Venice and, after an absence of two years, arrived back at Leonessa, where he resumed his labours with extraordinary zeal. Towards the end of his life he suffered greatly from cancer, for the removal of which he underwent two operations without the least groan or complaint, holding all the while a crucifix on which he kept his eyes fixed. When it was suggested before the operation that he should be bound, he pointed to the crucifix, saying, " This is the strongest bond ; this will hold me better than any cords could do ". The operation proving unsuccessful, St Joseph died happily on February 4, 1612, at the age of fifty-eight. He was canonized in 1745.

See Giacinto da Belmonte, *Vita di S. Giuseppe di Leonessa* (1896) ; Léon, *Auréole séraphique* (Eng. trans.), vol. i ; and a useful popular work by Fr Ernest-Marie, *Le protégé des anges* (1936). Two letters of the saint have been published in the *Miscellanea francescana*, vol. ix.

ST JOHN DE BRITTO, Martyr   (A.D. 1693)

It is stated that when John de Britto as a child fell grievously ill, his mother, a lady of noble family connected with the court of Lisbon, invoked the aid of St Francis Xavier and dedicated her son to him. Be this as it may, John, though he was the favourite companion of the Infante Don Pedro, who eventually succeeded to the throne of Portugal, aspired only to wear the habit of the great missionary and to devote his life to the conversion of the infidel. Born in 1647, he made application at the age of fifteen to be received into the Society of Jesus, and in spite of much opposition he accomplished his purpose. His success in his studies was so remarkable that great efforts were made after his ordination to keep him in Portugal, but grace triumphed, and in 1673 he set sail for Goa with sixteen of his fellow Jesuits ; the rest of his life, except for a brief interval, was spent amid incredible hardships and hindrances of all kinds in evangelizing southern India. He was made superior of the Madura mission and travelled most painfully on foot through all that vast region, only ten degrees north of the equator. Those who worked with him in their letters to Europe speak in glowing terms of his courage and devotion, of the extraordinary austerity of his life, and of the rich harvest of conversions which were the fruit of his labours.

From the beginning Father de Britto realized the wisdom of the method previously adopted by the missionary Father de Nobili, *viz.* of living a life identical with that of the natives of the country, adopting their dress, abstaining from animal food, and respecting in all things lawful the ineradicable prejudices of caste. As we may learn on the unexceptionable testimony of Sir W. W. Hunter in his *Imperial Gazetteer of India* (vol. vi, pp. 245-253), " the early Jesuit missions are particularly interesting. Their priests and monks [*sic*] became perfect Indians in all secular matters, dress, food, etc., and had equal success among all castes, high and low. In the south of the peninsula they brought the old Christian settlements of the Syrian rite into temporary* communion with Rome and converted large sections of the native population throughout extensive districts." It is interesting to note also that he adds : " Schisms troubled the Church. The Portuguese king claimed, as against the pope, to appoint the archbishop of Goa ; and the Dutch adventurers for a time persecuted the Catholics along the coast." And with regard to such missionaries as John de Britto, he remarks, " All that chivalry and enthusiastic piety could effect, they accomplished ". To describe in detail the terrible odds against which de Britto had to contend would be impossible here, not the least handicap being the delicacy of his constitution which in the fevers and agues to which he was subject repeatedly brought him face to face with death. Politically also the country was in a terribly unsettled state, a condition which allowed the

* " Temporary " in the sense that in 1653 there was a very serious schism. It was to a considerable extent mended, and today the Christians of Syrian rite in Malabar are in a majority Catholics.

fanatical pagan priesthood to call into play at every turn the superstitions of the people.   Many times Father de Britto and his Indian catechists were subjected to brutal violence.   On one occasion in 1686, after preaching in the Marava country, he and a handful of devoted Indians were seized, and upon their refusal to pay honour to the god Siva, were subjected for several days in succession to excruciating tortures.   They were hung up by chains from trees, and at another time by means of a rope attached to an arm or foot and passing over a pulley, were dipped repeatedly in stagnant water, with other indescribable outrages.

Father de Britto's recovery was deemed miraculous, and not long after he was set at liberty he was summoned back to Lisbon.   Great efforts were made by King Pedro II and by the papal nuncio to induce him to remain in Europe, but he pleaded so strongly that duty called him back to Madura that he was allowed to have his way.   For three years more he returned to his mission to lead the same life of heroic self-sacrifice ; and then, through the machinations of one of the repudiated wives of the Poligar of Siruvalli, who had been baptized and therefore had given up polygamy, he was arrested and eventually put to death at Oriur, near Ramuad, by order of the Rajah Raghunatha.   Father de Britto sent two letters from his prison the day before his execution.   " I await death ", he writes to the father superior, " and I await it with impatience.   It has always been the object of my prayers.   It forms today the most precious reward of my labours and my sufferings."   The next morning, February 4, 1693, a large crowd gathered to see the end of this teacher (*guru*) who was sentenced to die because he had taught things subversive of the worship of the gods of the country.   After a long delay, for the local prince was nervous about the whole business, St John's head was struck from his body.   When the news reached Lisbon, King Pedro ordered a solemn service of thanksgiving ; and the martyr's mother was there, dressed not in mourning but in a festal gown.   St John de Britto was canonized in 1947.

The best source of information seems to be Fr J. Bertrand's *La Mission du Maduré* (1850), in the third volume of which will be found several of the saint's letters.   But the second edition of the Portuguese life by his brother F. Pereira de Britto, *Historia do Nascimento, Vida e Martyrio do Beato João de Britto* (1852), is also valuable, especially because it contains (pp. 273–287) a long letter written by his fellow labourer Fr Francis Laynes, a week after the martyrdom.   See also C. A. Moreschini, *San Giovanni de Britto* (1948). Writing in 1929 Father Thurston said, " No satisfactory life seems to exist in English.   That written by Father de Beauvais and translated in the Oratorian series is distressingly uncritical."   Since then, in 1947, Fr A. Saultière has published at Madura, under the title of *Red Sand*, a detailed biography of St John de Britto, intended primarily for young people but valuable to others as well.

5 : ST AGATHA, Virgin and Martyr   (Date Unknown)

THE cities of Palermo and Catania in Sicily dispute the honour of St Agatha's birth, but it is agreed that she received the crown of martyrdom at Catania. Her " acts ", which with many variations exist in both Latin and Greek, but which are of no historical value, state that she belonged to a rich and illustrious family and, having been consecrated to God from her earliest years, she triumphed over many assaults upon her purity.   Quintian, a man of consular dignity, thought he could carry out his evil designs upon Agatha by means of the emperor's edict against Christians. He therefore had her brought before him. Seeing herself in the hands of her persecutors, she prayed, " Jesus Christ, Lord of all, thou seest my heart, thou knowest my desires. Do thou alone possess all that I am. I am thy sheep : make me worthy to overcome the Devil." Quintian ordered her to be handed over to Aphrodisia, a most wicked woman who with her six daughters kept a house of ill-fame. In this dreadful place Agatha suffered assaults and stratagems upon her honour more terrible to her than torture or death, but she stood firm. After a month Quintian tried to frighten her with threats, but she remained un-daunted and declared that to be a servant of Jesus Christ was to be truly at liberty. The judge, offended at her resolute answers, commanded her to be beaten and taken to prison. The next day she underwent another examination, and she asserted that Jesus Christ was her light and salvation. Quintian then ordered her to be stretched on the rack—a torment generally accompanied by stripes, the tearing of the sides with iron hooks, and by burning with blazing torches. The governor, enraged at seeing her suffer all this with cheerfulness, ordered her breasts to be cruelly crushed and then cut off. Afterwards he remanded her to prison, enjoining that neither food nor medical care should be supplied to her. But God gave her comfort : she had a vision of St Peter who filled her dungeon with a heavenly light, and who consoled and healed her. Four days later Quintian caused her to be rolled naked over live coals mixed with broken potsherds. As she was carried back to prison, she prayed, " Lord, my Creator, thou hast always protected me from the cradle ; thou hast taken me from the love of the world and given me patience to suffer. Receive now my soul." After saying these words, she breathed out her life.

There is good evidence of the early *cultus* of St Agatha. Her name occurs in the Calendar of Carthage (*c.* 530), and in the " Hieronymianum ", and her praises were sung by Venantius Fortunatus (*Carmina*, viii, 4), but we can affirm nothing with confidence concerning her history. She is depicted in the procession of the saints at Sant' Apollinare Nuovo at Ravenna. As an attribute in art her breasts, which were cut off, are often shown on a dish. These in the middle ages were often mistaken for loaves, and from this a practice seems to have arisen of blessing bread on St Agatha's feast which is brought on a dish to the altar. As in Sicily she was credited with the power of arresting the eruptions of Mount Etna, so she is invoked against any outbreak of fire. Whether because warning of a fire was given by a bell, or because the molten metal in the casting of a bell resembles a stream of lava, the guilds of bell-founders took St Agatha for their patroness. Two sixth-century churches in Rome were dedicated in her honour, and she is named in the canon of the Mass.

See the *Acta Sanctorum*, February, vol. where there is, *inter alia*, a Latin version of an encomium attributed to St Methodius of Constantinople (d. 847), on which see *Analecta Bollandiana*, vol. lxviii (1950), pp. 58 *seq.* See also J. P. Kirsch in the *Catholic Encyclopedia*, vol. i, pp. 203-204 ; and, for the saint in art, Künstle, *Ikonographie der Heiligen* (1926), pp. 37-39. An Italian work on St Agatha in two vols., by B. G. Consoli, appeared in 1951.

ST AVITUS, Bishop of Vienne   (*c.* A.D. 525)

ST ALCIMUS ECDICIUS AVITUS was born in Auvergne. His father Isychius was chosen bishop of Vienne upon the death of St Mamertus and was succeeded by

Avitus in 490. Ennodius, in his Life of St Epiphanius of Pavia, says of Avitus that he was a storehouse of learning, and adds that when the Burgundians had crossed the Alps and carried home many captives out of Liguria, he ransomed a great number. Clovis, King of France, whilst yet a pagan, and Gondebald, King of Burgundy, though an Arian, held him in great respect, and after Gondebald's death in 516 his son and successor, Sigismund, was brought over to the Christian faith by St Avitus. In 517 the saint presided over a famous council at Epaon. When King Sigismund had stained his hands with the blood of his son Sigeric, on a false charge brought against him by his stepmother, St Avitus inspired him with such horror of his crime that he rebuilt the abbey of Agaunum or Saint-Maurice (*cf.* May 1). Most of the works of Avitus are lost, but we have five poems forming a series to which he himself gives the title *De spiritalis historiae gestis*, and another on virginity, dedicated to his sister Fuscina and other nuns. There are seventy-eight letters (including a well-known one to Clovis at his baptism), two complete homilies and fragments of twenty-five others. He died about 525. Ennodius and other writers of the age extol his learning, his charity to the poor and his many other virtues; but St Avitus was a man of letters rather than a theologian.

See Duchesne, *Fastes Épiscopaux*, vol. i, pp. 153-155 and 185-187; DTC., vol. i, cc. 2639-2644, and especially U. Chevalier, *Œuvres complètes de S. Avit* (1890). There is a short Latin life published in the Bollandist Catalogue of Brussels Hagiographal MSS., vol. i, pp. 57-63. *Cf.* also G. Bardy, *L'Église et les derniers Romains* (1948).

ST BERTULF, or BERTOUL   (*c.* A.D. 705 ?)

St BERTULF was born in Germany of pagan parents, but while still young he migrated to Flanders. There he found himself in a Christian atmosphere, and was so favourably impressed by what he saw and heard that he sought instruction and was baptized. He became acquainted with Count Wambert and his wife Homburga, and the count gradually made him steward over everything he possessed. Bertulf administered his office wisely and faithfully, improving his lord's property whilst not forgetting to give alms to the poor. Envious tongues accused him of wastefulness and extravagance, but Wambert gave no credence to the tales, having ample proof of his steward's fidelity, and all endeavours to entrap him failed ignominiously. When Wambert and Homburga made a pilgrimage to Rome, Bertulf accompanied them. It was told that after a tiring day on the journey, probably when they had been crossing Alpine passes, the servants pleaded that they were too exhausted to watch over the horses by night. St Bertulf undertook to take the animals to pasture and to return them all safely in the morning. This he did, although a violent storm arose, as often happens in the mountains, and Wambert was anxious about his steward; he, however, had been protected—miraculously it was averred—and was found reading peacefully, quite unaffected by the rain and the wind. Wambert treated him as a son and made him heir to his estates at Renty. When Wambert and his wife died Bertulf buried them in one of the four churches the good count had built; he himself then retired into a monastery which he founded at Renty in connection with the church of St Denis, and there he remained until his death.

See Ghesquière, *Acta Sanctorum Belgii*, vol. v, pp. 453-489; L. van der Essen, *Étude sur les Vitae des saints mérov*. (1907), pp. 422-423; and DHG., vol. viii, cc. 1112-1113.

SS. INDRACTUS AND DOMINICA, MARTYRS　　(c. A.D. 710?)

INDRACTUS was an Irishman—some say a king's son—who, we are told, came to England on his way to Rome or on his way back and was treacherously killed by Saxons, together with his sister Dominica or Drusa and seven or nine companions. Their bodies, claimed by Glastonbury Abbey, were held in great veneration. Tradition connects their names with several places in Cornwall and Somerset, but no great reliance can be placed on any of the stories told of them. One picturesque legend relates that their murderers hid their bodies, but that the place of their burial was indicated by a shaft of light which was seen by Ina, King of the West Saxons, as he wandered out of his lodging, fevered and sleepless, one dark night.

See the *Acta Sanctorum*, February, vol. i, and LBS., vol.　　pp. 318-320.

ST VODALUS, OR VOEL　　(c. A.D. 720)

THIS saint was said to be a Scot or Irishman who crossed the sea from Scotland to preach the gospel in Gaul, and who wandered about teaching until he reached Soissons. There he was cordially received by Adalgard, abbess of the great convent of St Mary, and he settled in a cottage outside the gate, living a life of poverty and holiness. The further story is mainly apocryphal. It is related that Adalgard once reproached him with not returning a silver dish which she had sent him with food. Instead of telling her that he had passed on the food to a beggar who had stolen the dish, Vodalus meekly took the blame and begged her pardon. Then, quietly withdrawing from Soissons, he determined to return to Scotland. He caught fever on the way, and by the time he took ship was nearly dead with illness and hunger. Terrible storms were encountered until the captain, surmising that they might be a judgement on him for neglecting the passenger, sent sailors to look after him and the weather improved. Vodalus was cured by an angel, who told him to return to Soissons and announced that he would be given power to heal fevers and to avert fires. He obeyed, and lived and died at Soissons where he was greatly venerated.

See *Acta Sanctorum*, February, vol. i.

ST ADELAIDE OF BELLICH, VIRGIN　　(A.D. 1015)

SHE was the daughter of Megengose, Count of Guelder, and ruled over the nunnery of Bellich on the Rhine, near Bonn, but died in 1015 as abbess of St Mary's in Cologne, both convents having been founded by her father and both being under her rule at the time of her death. Her festival is kept at Bellich, where the nunnery she instituted under the Benedictine rule was subsequently converted into a church of canonesses. She used to make it a great point that her nuns should know Latin so that they might follow the choir offices properly. She showed great prudence in other matters too, notably in the way in which she provided for the poor during a severe famine. St Heribert, Archbishop of Cologne, had the greatest respect for her and consulted her in all his difficulties.

See *Acta Sanctorum*, February, vol. i, pp. 721-727, where her life by Bertrada, a nun and her contemporary, is printed. *Cf.* DHG., vol. i, c. 517.

THE MARTYRS OF JAPAN, I   (A.D. 1597)

St Francis Xavier planted Christianity in Japan where he arrived in 1549. He himself converted and baptized a considerable number and eventually whole provinces received the faith. It is said that by 1587 there were in Japan over two hundred thousand Christians. In 1588 the haughty Emperor Cambacundono, having arrogated to himself the honours of a deity, ordered that all missionaries should leave his dominions within six months ; some obeyed, but many remained behind in disguise. In 1596 the Emperor Tagcosama,* one of the proudest and most vicious of men, was roused to fury by the boast of the captain of a Spanish ship that the object of the missionaries was to facilitate the conquest of Japan by the Portuguese or Spaniards, and three Jesuits and six Franciscans were crucified on a hill near Nagasaki in 1597.

The Franciscans were St Peter Baptist, commissary of the friars in Japan, St Martin de Aguirre, St Francis Blanco, St Francis-of-St-Michael (a lay-brother), all Spaniards ; St Philip de las Casas, born in Mexico City and not yet ordained, and St Gonsalo Garcia. The nationality of the last named, also a lay-brother, has been a subject of discussion. He was born at Bassein, near Bombay, it is generally said of Portuguese parents ; but others claim that his parents were Indian converts who took Portuguese names. If this be so, then he is the only Indian yet to have been formally canonized. Of the Jesuits, one was St Paul Miki, a high-born Japanese and an eminent preacher ; the other two, St John Goto and St James Kisai, were admitted to the order as lay-brothers shortly before they suffered. The remaining seventeen martyrs were also all Japanese ; several of them were catechists and interpreters, and all were Franciscan tertiaries. They included a soldier, St Caius Francis, a physician, St Francis of Miako, a native of Korea, St Leo Karasuma, and three boys of about thirteen who used to serve the friars at Mass, SS. Louis Ibarki, Antony Deynan and Thomas Kasaki, whose father also suffered.

Twenty-four of the martyrs, after part of their left ears had been cut off, were led through various towns, their cheeks stained with blood, as a terror to others. Upon their arrival at the place of execution near Nagasaki, they were allowed to make their confession to two Jesuits and, after being fastened to crosses by cords

---

* In Steichen's book (see bibliography below) can be found the means of rectifying the Japanese designations which have been left in the above account as they were originally printed in the pages of Alban Butler. They afford an interesting illustration of the misunderstandings into which the most conscientious chronicler is apt to be betrayed when he is dealing with matters which, owing to their remoteness in time or space, are only imperfectly comprehended. The potentate " Cambacundono ", as the name is printed above, and he who is referred to as " Tagcosama ", are in reality one and the same person, and the statement that he was " Emperor " of Japan is a pure misconception. In the histories now written by Europeans who have had the opportunity of studying the Japanese chronicles, this personage, who was beyond doubt in practice the ruler of the country from 1583 to 1598, is generally referred to as Hideyoshi. All that he did during his years of power professed to be undertaken under commission from the emperor, his relations with whom corresponded in a measure with those of the " master of the palace " towards the later Merovingian sovereigns. In 1585 Hideyoshi received from the emperor the title of *Kwampaku*, and in 1592 he abdicated this dignity and assumed that of *Taikō*. Hence we hear of him in the missionaries' letters in the former period as " Cambacundono ", and in the latter as " Tago-sama ". His real power corresponded to that of *Shōgun*—the Portuguese wrote the word Xoguno—though Hideyoshi does not seem to have been formally so designated in his lifetime.

and chains about their arms and legs and with an iron collar round their necks, they were raised into the air, the foot of each cross falling into a hole in the ground prepared for it.   The crosses were planted in a row, about four feet apart, and each martyr had an executioner near him with a spear ready to pierce his side—according to the Japanese method of crucifixion.   As soon as all the crosses had been planted, the executioners raised their lances at a given signal, and the martyrs were killed almost at the same instant.   Their blood and garments were treasured by their fellow Christians and miracles were ascribed to them.   These twenty-six witnesses to Christ were canonized in 1862.

While the heroism of the children on this occasion and in other similar tragedies at a later period must fill us with admiration, it should be remembered that it was the customary Japanese practice to involve the whole family in the condemnation of the head of the household.   As a modern historian of Japan (Captain Brinkley) has pointed out, " comprehensive punishment had long been counted one of the administrator's most effective weapons ".   An extraordinary ruthlessness, he adds, was part of the cherished traditions of the nation   " When, in consequence of falling under suspicion of treason, Hidetsugu, the Taiko's adopted son, was ordered to commit suicide, his wife, his concubine and his children were all put to death without mercy by order of the Taikō.   The Tokugawa chief, Iyeyasu, showed similar inclemency.   After he had effected the final conquest of the Osaka party, he put to death all the relatives and surviving supporters of its leader."

For other martyrs in Japan, see herein under June 1 and September 10.

See *Acta Sanctorum*, February, vol. i, pp. 729-770 ; Léon, *Auréole Séraphique* (Eng. trans.), vol. i, pp. 169-223 ; C. M. Caddell, *The Cross in Japan* (1904) ; M. Steichen, *The Christian Daimyōs* (1903) ; an account of St Gonsalo Garcia by Father P. A. Fernandez was reprinted at Bombay in 1947.   For Japanese missions in general, see bibliography for the second group of martyrs, under June 1, and an article by Father Thurston in the *Month*, March, 1905.

6 : ST TITUS, Bishop in Crete   (First Century)

S T TITUS was born a Gentile, and seems to have been converted by St Paul, who calls him his son in Christ.   His virtue and merit gained him the affection of the apostle, for we find him employed as his secretary ; and Paul styles him his brother and partner in his labours, commends his zeal for his brethren, and expresses the comfort he found in him, in so much that on one occasion he declared that he found no rest in his spirit because at Troas he had not met Titus. They went together to the council held at Jerusalem to debate the question of the Mosaic rites ; and though the apostle had consented to the circumcision of Timothy in order to render his ministry acceptable among the Jews, he would not allow the same in Titus, lest he should thereby seem to sanction the error of certain brethren, who contended that the ceremonial provisions of the Mosaic law were not abolished by the law of grace.   St Paul sent Titus from Ephesus to Corinth to remedy several occasions of scandal, as also to allay the dissensions in that church.   He was there received with great respect, and was satisfied with regard to the penance and submission of the offenders ; but he could not be prevailed upon to accept from them any present, not even so much as his own maintenance.   His love for that church was considerable, and at their request he interceded with St Paul for the pardon of the incestuous man.   He was sent by the apostle a second time to Corinth, to collect the alms for the poor Christians at Jerusalem.   All these particulars we learn from St Paul's two letters to the Corinthians.

St Paul made some stay in the island of Crete to preach the faith of Jesus Christ ; but the necessities of other churches requiring his presence elsewhere, he ordained Titus bishop for that island, and left him to finish the work he had begun.   " We may judge ", says St Chrysostom, " from the importance of the charge, how great the esteem of St Paul was for his disciple."   But at his return into Europe later the apostle ordered Titus to meet him at Nicopolis in Epirus, and to set out as soon as either Tychicus or Artemas, whom he had sent to supply his place, should arrive in Crete.   St Paul sent these instructions to Titus in the canonical epistle addressed to him.   He ordered him to establish presbyters in all the cities of the island, sums up the principal qualities necessary for a bishop, and gives him advice touching his own conduct to his flock, exhorting him to maintain strict discipline among the Cretans, of whom Paul had a poor opinion.   This letter contains the rule of episcopal life, and we may regard it as faithfully copied in the life of this disciple. After a visit to Dalmatia Titus again returned to Crete, and all that can be affirmed further of him is that he finished a laborious and holy life by a peaceful death there at an advanced old age.   St Titus has always been looked upon in Crete as the first archbishop of the see, but no special feast was at first kept in his honour in the Western church ; it was only in the time of Pope Pius IX that a feast was assigned to him on February 6.

We know practically nothing of St Titus apart from his connection with St Paul.   Such details as the statement found in the Acts of St Thecla that Titus was born at Iconium, or that of St Chrysostom that he was born at Corinth, are quite untrustworthy.   For a chronology and a fuller discussion of his character the reader must consult the books specially devoted to St Paul, such as those of Prat, Le Camus or Fouard.   See also Vigouroux, *Dictionnaire de la Bible*, vol. v, c. 2247.   Certain " Acts of Titus ", purporting to be written by " Zenas the lawyer ", mentioned in the Epistle to Titus (iii, 13), can only be regarded as a work of fiction ; still, they seem to have had a certain vogue, and the account of Titus which is given in the Synaxary of Constantinople under August 25, the date of his feast in the Byzantine church (see Delehaye's edition in the *Acta Sanctorum*, p. 921), is avowedly derived from this source.   Here Titus is represented as of royal descent and born in Crete, whence, at the age of twenty, he was called away to Judea by a voice from Heaven a year before the ascension of our Lord.   He is also stated to have lived on in Crete until he was a nonagenarian.   See R. Lipsius, *Die apokr. Apostelgesch.*, vol. ii, 2, pp. 401–406.

ST DOROTHY, Virgin and Martyr   (*c.* A.D. 303 ?)

St Aldhelm, quoting from her acts—which, however, are mostly apocryphal—says that Fabricius, the governor of Caesarea in Cappadocia, inflicted on St Dorothy the most cruel torments because she refused to marry or to worship idols and that she converted two apostate women sent to seduce her.   He also gives the well-known story from which the saint derives the apples and roses which are her attributes in art.   It relates that, as she was being led to execution, a young lawyer called Theophilus jeered at her and asked her to send him fruits from the garden to which she was going.   She promised that she would.   At the place of execution, she knelt and prayed, and suddenly there appeared an angel with a basket containing three apples and three roses which she sent to Theophilus, telling him she would await him in the garden from whence they came.   When Theophilus tasted the fruit he became a Christian and subsequently gave his life as a martyr.   St Dorothy most probably suffered under Diocletian, and her body is believed to repose in the church which bears her name in Rome. Rufinus mentions another holy virgin whom he calls Dorothy, a rich lady of Alexandria who suffered torments and voluntary banishment to preserve her faith and honour against the lust of the Emperor Maximinus, but this story is possibly due to confusion with that of the celebrated St Catherine of Alexandria.

The legendary fruits and flowers of St Dorothy may well remind us of the benefits we receive from the merits and intercession of the saints. Time after time, from the martyrdom of St Stephen onward, we find the martyrs praying for their persecutors and executioners and time after time we find that these have been converted.

See *Acta Sanctorum*, February, vol. i ; CMH., p. 79 ; and BIIL. nn. 2321-2325.

SS. MEL AND MELCHU, BISHOPS   (A.D. 488 ?)

THE records we have of these saints are conflicting, and contain so much that is obviously legendary that it is hard to arrive at actual facts. They are said to have been the sons of Conis and of Darerca, the sister of St Patrick, whom they accompanied to Ireland and helped to evangelize that country. Some of the accounts omit the name of Melchu and several commentators have thought that his name was a mistaken interpolation, especially as both he and St Mel are generally described as bishops of Ardagh. On the other hand, in the Life of St Brigid the two brothers are stated to have had no fixed sees, which might fit in with their being missionaries. St Patrick himself built the church at Ardagh and to this he appointed his nephew Mel. Acting upon the apostolic precept, he supported himself by working with his hands, and what he gained beyond bare necessaries he gave to the poor. For some time he lived with his aunt Lupait, but slanderous tongues spread serious accusations against them, and St Patrick himself came to investigate their conduct. Mel was ploughing when he arrived, but he cleared himself of the charge by miraculously picking up a live fish from the ground as if from a net, and Lupait established her innocence by carrying glowing coals without burning herself or her clothing. St Patrick was satisfied, but he told his nephew in future to do his fishing in the water and his ploughing on the land, and he moreover enjoined them to avoid scandal by separating, living and praying far apart. If Melchu was also bishop at Ardagh, he must have succeeded Mel. Two other brothers of St Mel (who is commemorated today in Ireland) are mentioned in the legends, SS Muinis and Rioch, both bishops.

See the *Acta Sanctorum*, February, vol. i ; LBS., vol. iii, pp. 461-463 ; *The Tripartite Life of St Patrick*, ed. W. Stokes, vol. i, pp. 87-89 ; LIS., vol. ii.

ST VEDAST, OR VAAST, BISHOP OF ARRAS   (A.D. 539)

ST VEDAST was very young when he left his own province, which seems to have been in the west of France. His aim was to live concealed from the world in the diocese of Toul, but there he came under the notice of the bishop who, recognizing his qualities, promoted him to the priesthood. When Clovis I, King of France, returning from his victory over the Alemanni, was hastening to Rheims to be baptized, he asked at Toul for some priest to accompany him on his journey and to prepare him. Vedast was presented to the monarch for that purpose. His biographers tell how, as they were about to cross the Aisne, a blind beggar on the bridge besought the saint to restore his sight. St Vedast prayed and made the sign of the cross on his eyes and immediately the power of vision was given back to him. This miracle confirmed the king in the faith and converted several of the courtiers. St Vedast assisted St Remigius (Rémi) in instructing the Franks until that prelate consecrated him bishop of Arras that he might re-establish the faith where it had died out.

Entering the city in 499, he restored sight to a blind man and cured one who was lame. These miracles disposed the hearts of many unbelievers to accept the Gospel, which had suffered much from the inroads of the northern marauders. Vedast could find no traces of Christianity except the ruins of a church where, within the memory of certain old people, Christians had worshipped. St Vedast found the people boorish and obstinate, but he persevered, and in the end we are told he succeeded in restoring Christianity throughout the land. He laboured nearly forty years, and left his church at his death in a flourishing condition.

There are two ancient lives of St Vedast, one seemingly by St Jonas of Bobbio, the other by Alcuin. Both will be found in the *Acta Sanctorum*, February, vol. i, and in MGH., *Scriptores Merov.*, vol. iii. See also L. Van der Essen, *Saints Mérovingiens* (1907); and W. S. Simpson, *Life and Legend of St Vedast* (1896); and E. Guilbert, *St Vaast* . (1938). Two English medieval churches were dedicated under the name of St Vedast, one of which is in London in " Foster " Lane.

ST AMAND, BISHOP   (c. A.D. 679)

THIS great missionary was born in Lower Poitou about the year 584. At the age of twenty he retired to a small monastery in the island of Yeu, near that of Ré. He had not been there more than a year when his father discovered him and tried to persuade him to return home. When he threatened to disinherit him, the saint cheerfully replied, " Christ is my only inheritance ". Amand afterwards went to Tours, where he was ordained, and then to Bourges, where he lived fifteen years under the direction of St Austregisilus the bishop, in a cell near the cathedral. After a pilgrimage to Rome, he returned to France and was consecrated bishop in 629 without any fixed see, receiving a general commission to teach the faith to the heathen. He preached the gospel in Flanders and northern France, with a brief excursion to the Slavs in Carinthia and perhaps to Gascony. He reproved King Dagobert I for his crimes and accordingly was banished. But Dagobert soon recalled him, and asked him to baptize his new-born son Sigebert, afterwards king and saint. The people about Ghent were so ferociously hostile that no preacher durst venture amongst them. This moved Amand to attempt that mission, in the course of which he was sometimes beaten and thrown into the river. He persevered, however, although for a long time he saw no fruit, and in the end people came in crowds to be baptized.

As well as being a great missionary St Amand was a father of monasticism in ancient Belgium, and a score of monasteries claimed him as founder. He did in fact found houses at Elnone (Saint-Amand-les-Eaux), near Tournai, which became his headquarters; St Peter's on Mont-Blandin at Ghent, but probably not St Bavo's there as well; Nivelles, for nuns, with Bd Ida and St Gertrude; Barisis-au-Bois, and probably three more, including Marchiennes. It is said, though the fact is not certain, that in 646 he was chosen bishop of Maestricht, but that three years later he resigned that see to St Remaclus and returned to his missions, which he always had most at heart.   He continued his labours among the heathen until a great age, when, broken with infirmities, he retired to Elnone.   There he governed as abbot for four years, spending his time in preparing for the death which came to him at last soon after 676.   That St Amand was one of the most imposing figures of the Merovingian epoch is disputed by no serious historian ; he was not unknown in England, and the pre-Reformation chapel of the Eyston family at East Hendred in Berkshire is dedicated in his honour.

Prof. Hauck in his *Kirchengeschichte Deutschlands* (vol. i, ch. 5) bears cordial testimony to the impression which the saint made upon his generation.   At the same time we have no very reliable materials for the details of his life.   B. Krusch in MGH., *Scriptores Merov.*, vol. v, pp. 395–485, has printed *inter alia* the *Vita Amandi*, which is attributed by some (*e.g.* by L. Van der Essen, *Saints mérovingiens*, pp. 336–349) to his disciple Baudemund, but Krusch rejects this attribution very positively and maintains that the *vita* cannot have been written earlier than the second half of the eighth century   however, Fr de Moreau attributes it to the beginning of that century at the latest (*cf.* the *Analecta Bollandiana*, vol. lxvii (1949), pp. 447–454).   St Amand's testament is unquestionably a genuine document ; but for the passage wherein he expresses his will that his remains should rest at Elnone and lays a curse on anyone who should move them hence, *cf.* what is said by Mgr Lesne in DHG., vol. ii, c. 944.   See the excellent book by E. de Moreau, *St Amand* (1927).

ST GUARINUS, CARDINAL-BISHOP OF PALESTRINA   (A.D. 1159)

THIS saint was born at Bologna, and even as a child he gave himself to fasting and prayer and took no pleasure in boyish pursuits and amusements.   Against the wishes of his father, who desired an heir, he decided to become a priest and was accordingly ordained.   Grieved at the lack of austerity of his associates, he withdrew more and more from their company, spending long hours in prayer and retiring into solitary places.   He was led to join the Augustinian canons of the Holy Cross at Mortaria, and there he advanced yet further in holiness.   His superiors transferred him to the church of St Frigdianus, where he was received with veneration on account of his sanctity.   Several years later he returned to Mortaria where he made some stay.   There occurred at that time a vacancy amongst the local bishops and, owing to the great reputation of Guarinus, he was elected to fill it. He was so convinced of his unworthiness that he climbed out through a window and hid until someone else had been chosen, when he quietly returned to live the life of an ordinary monk.

His fame, however, afterwards reached Pope Lucius II, himself a native of Bologna, and he sent for Guarinus who excused himself on the plea that he lacked the experience and virtues requisite, adding that after living forty years in a monastery he feared to return to the world.   The pope insisted, and he accordingly went to Rome where he was consecrated to the see of Praeneste (Palestrina), which carried with it the dignity of cardinal.   The pope gave him costly gifts and equipment to use in connection with his new office, but he sold them all and gave the proceeds to the poor, to the amazement and edification of the whole city.   Guarinus took up his abode near his titular church, spending much of his time in prayer.   At last, when he was very old, and he felt that death which he had long desired was approaching, he called his clergy round him and addressed to them his final spiritual admonitions.   All night long, as the aged saint lay on his bed rapt in contemplation, the watchers noticed that the sky outside was filled with a light so vivid that it seemed like day.   Then, in the early hours of the morning, he quietly passed to his rest.

See the *Acta Sanctorum*, February, vol. i ; BHL., nn. 8815–8816.

BD RAYMUND OF FITERO, ABBOT   (A.D. 1163)

IT was at the end of 1157, or at the beginning of 1158, when King Sancho of Castile was in residence in his capital, Toledo, that there came alarming reports of an impending attack by the Moors upon the outpost of Calatrava.   The Templars, who occupied the fortress, entreated the king to take over the castle and town, as they were too few in number to defend it, nor could they get sufficient help.   Now there happened to be staying in Toledo just then a certain Raymund, Abbot of Fitero, a Cistercian, and with him a monk called Diego Velasquez, who had formerly been a knight well trained in arms and who had been educated with King Sancho.   Velasquez urged the abbot to get the king to give him Calatrava, and Raymund, though at first unwilling, eventually petitioned Sancho to let him take over this outpost.   The ministers declared it would be folly, but the king presented the town and castle to the abbot and his abbey.   Raymund then went to the archbishop of Toledo who promised to lend him all the assistance he could ; treating the cause as a crusade he proclaimed a plenary indulgence which could be gained by all who came to the assistance of Calatrava.   The city was so greatly moved that those who could not go in person sent men or horses or money, and Raymund rode forth to Calatrava at the head of an army computed by an eyewitness to have numbered as many as 20,000.   The Moslems did not attack Calatrava after all, but out of the most promising of these recruits Raymund formed a new military order under religious rule, who took the offensive and waged war successfully against the infidels.   In this way Bd Raymund founded the military order of the Knights of Calatrava, which did great deeds in its day, and his *cultus* in Spain was approved in 1719.

See *Acta Sanctorum*, under February 1 ; *Catholic Encyclopedia*. s.v. Calatrava ; Florez, *España Sagrada*, vol. l, pp. 37–48.

ST HILDEGUND, WIDOW   (A.D. 1183)

THE parents of St Hildegund were Count Herman of Lidtberg and Countess Hedwig who, on losing her husband, retired with her third daughter, Gertrude, into the Premonstratensian convent of Dunwald.   The example of her mother was followed by Hildegund when her husband, Count Lothair, and one of her sons had died and the other, Herman, had entered a monastery.   In 1178, after a pilgrimage to Rome, she made over all her possessions to Christ, and with the consent and help of her son Herman started to convert her castle of Mehre, some way north of Cologne, into a convent.   She was somewhat delayed in executing her purpose, because her sister Elizabeth, withdrawing her consent to a first division of their inheritance, demanded a fresh settlement.   After this had been arranged, Hildegund and her daughter Hedwig (called Blessed) assumed the Premonstratensian habit and entered their new foundation, of which the saint became prioress.   The number of inmates increasing rapidly, she removed the convent to a more convenient site, where it grew and flourished, filled with holy women who maintained an unbroken stream of prayer and praise : the house, in the words of its charter, had been converted from being a fort for military exercises into a college for holy virgins. St Hildegund's son Herman was also called Blessed, and a portrait of him, standing at his mother's right hand, hung formerly in the convent church.

See the *Acta Sanctorum*, February, vol.   Dunbar, *Dictionary of Saintly Women*, vol. i.

BD ANGELO OF FURCIO   (A.D. 1327)

THIS Angelo was a native of Furcio in the Abruzzi.   His parents, for many years childless, vowed that if a boy were granted them they would dedicate him to God. They had a vision of St Michael and St Augustine, who promised them a son, who should follow the Rule of St Augustine.   At an early age his mother took him to her brother, the abbot of Cornaclano, to be educated ; here he lived the life of a little monk and despised not only the games of a child, but even such modest relaxations as were allowed to the religious.   He loved prayer and studies, and was admitted to minor orders at the age of eighteen.   His uncle dying, he returned home, where attempts were made by various people to arrange a marriage for him. His father would only say, " If it be God's will and if it please my son "   but when he was on his deathbed he related to Angelo the vision he had had before his birth. The young man was horrified to find that he had unwittingly contemplated frustrating God's purpose for him, and, as soon as he had settled the affairs of his widowed mother, he left to enter the Augustinian monastery of Vasto d'Aimone. There he made such progress that he was sent to study in Paris, and one of the most eminent teachers, Giles the Roman (Colonna) took him to live in his own house.   Angelo stayed five years in Paris, passing through the various stages of philosophical and theological learning, until he received his licentiate.   Then he returned to Italy and presented himself to the prior general of his order at Naples. Very soon the prior appointed him professor of theology in their Neapolitan college, and he gathered round him a band of eager students.   Later he was offered a bishopric, which he declined to accept.   He died in Naples, where he was greatly venerated, and his *cultus* was confirmed in 1888.

See *Acta Sanctorum*, February, vol. i ; Ossinger, *Bibliotheca Augustiniana*, pp. 375–376 ; BHL., n. 461.

7 : ST ROMUALD, ABBOT, FOUNDER OF THE CAMALDOLESE BENEDICTINES
(A.D. 1027)

ST ROMUALD, of the family of the Onesti, Dukes of Ravenna, was probably born about the year 950.   The statement of his biographer, St Peter Damian, that he lived to the age of 120 years is now universally rejected.   Though he grew up a worldly youth and a slave to his passions, yet he occasionally experienced aspirations after higher ideals.   His father, whose name was Sergius, had agreed to decide by duel a dispute he had with a relation over some property, and Romuald was an unwilling spectator of the encounter.   Sergius slew his adversary and Romuald, horrorstricken, fled to the monastery of Sant' Apollinare-in-Classe near by.   In this house he passed three years in such fervour and austerity that his observance became a standing reproach to certain lax and unfaithful monks, who were yet more exasperated when he reproved their conduct.   So, with the abbot's consent, he left the monastery and, retiring to the neighbourhood of Venice, placed himself under the direction of a hermit named Marinus. Under him Romuald made great advance in the way of perfection. Romuald and Marinus are said to have been concerned in the retirement of the doge of Venice, St Peter Orseolo, to Cuxa, and to have lived there for a time as solitaries. The example of St Romuald had such an influence on his father Sergius that to atone for his sins he entered the monastery of San Severo, near Ravenna. After a time he was tempted to return to the world, whereupon his son went thither to dissuade him from that infirmity of purpose. He succeeded in this, and Sergius stayed in the monastery for the rest of his life.

Romuald seems to have spent the next thirty years wandering about Italy, founding hermitages and monasteries. He stayed three years in a cell near that house which he had founded at Parenzo. Here he laboured for a time under great spiritual dryness, but suddenly, one day, as he was reciting the words of the Psalmist, " I will give thee understanding and will instruct thee ", he was visited by God with an extraordinary light and a spirit of compunction which from that time never left him. He wrote an exposition of the Psalms full of admirable thoughts, he often foretold things to come, and he gave counsel inspired by heavenly wisdom to all who came to consult him. He had always longed for martyrdom, and at last obtained the pope's licence to preach the gospel in Hungary ; but he was stricken with a grievous illness as soon as he set foot in the country, and as the malady returned each time he attempted to proceed, he concluded it was a plain indication of God's will in the matter and he accordingly returned to Italy, though some of his associates went on and preached the faith to the Magyars. Subsequently he made a long stay at Monte di Sitrio, but whi'st there he was accused of a scandalous crime by a young nobleman whom he had reprimanded for his dissipated life. Extraordinary as it seems, the monks believed the tale, enjoined on him a severe penance, forbade him to celebrate Mass, and excommunicated him. He bore all in silence for six months, but was then admonished by God to submit no longer to so unjust a sentence, pronounced without authority and without a shadow of foundation. He passed six years in Sitrio, observing strict silence, and, in spite of old age, increasing rather than relaxing his austerities. Romuald had some significance in missions to the Slavs and Prussians through the monastery founded for him and St Bruno of Querfurt at Pereum, near Ravenna, by Otto III in 1001. A son of Duke Boleslaus I of Poland was a monk in this monastery, and on behalf of his father presented Romuald with a fine horse. He exchanged it for a donkey, declaring that he felt closer to Jesus Christ when astride such a mount.

The most famous of all St Romuald's monasteries is that of Camaldoli, near Arezzo in Tuscany, founded by him about the year 1012. It lies beyond a mountain, the descent from which on the farther side is almost a sheer precipice looking down upon a pleasant valley, which then belonged to a lord called Maldolo, who gave it the saint, and from him it retained the name Camaldoli (Campus Maldoli). In this place St Romuald built a monastery, and by the several observances he added to St Benedict's rule he gave birth to that new congregation called the Camaldolese, in which he united the cenobitic and eremitical life. After their benefactor had seen in a vision monks climbing a ladder to heaven all dressed in white garments, Romuald changed the habit from black to white. The hermitage is two short miles distant from the monastery. It is on the mountain-side overshaded by a dark wood of fir trees. In it are seven clear springs of water. The very sight of this solitude in the midst of the forest helps to fill the mind with compunction and a love of contemplation.   On the left side of the church is the cell in which St Romuald lived when he first established these hermits.   Their cells, built of stone, have each a little garden walled round, and each cell has a chapel in which the occupant may celebrate Mass.

After some years at Camaldoli Romuald returned to his travels, and eventually died, alone in his cell, at the monastery of Val-di-Castro, on June 19, 1027.   A quarter of a century before he had prophesied that death would come to him in that place and in that manner.   His chief feast is kept today because it was on February 7, 1481 that his incorrupt body was translated to Fabriano : it was so fixed when Pope Clement VIII added his name to the general calendar in 1595.

The principal source of information for the life of St Romuald is the biography written by St Peter Damian, which has been printed in the *Acta Sanctorum*, February, vol. ii, and in many other collections.   See BHL., n. 7324.   But much subsidiary material is also available in the Life of St Peter Orseolo, the *Chronicon Venetum*, and the two Lives of St Bononius of Lucedio.   A valuable preliminary study of these sources has been made by W. Franke, *Quellen und Chronologie zur Geschichte Romualds von Camaldoli und seiner Einsiedlergenossenschaften im Zeitalter Ottos III* (1910).   See *Analecta Bollandiana*, vol. xxxi (1912), pp. 376–377 ; and also W. Franke in *Hist. Studien*, vol. cvii (1913).   Two Italian lives were published in 1927, by A. Pagnani and C. Ciampelli ; and *cf.* A. Giabbini, *L'eremo* (1945).

ST ADAUCUS, Martyr   (A.D. 303)

The Roman Martyrology for February 7 makes mention of St Adaucus in the following terms : " In Phrygia, of St Adaucus, martyr, who came of noble Italian stock and was honoured by the emperor with dignities of almost every rank, until while performing the office of *quaestor*, he was found worthy of the martyr's crown for his defence of the faith.   In the same place, of very many holy martyrs, citizens of one city, whose leader this same Adaucus was ; who, since they were all Christians and remained constant in the confession of the faith, were burnt with fire by the Emperor Galerius Maximian."   The facts rest upon the high authority of the church historian Eusebius, who was a contemporary, but while he mentions the martyrdom of St Adauc(t)us and the burning of the town in the same chapter, he does not connect the two events, though the early translation of Rufinus does.   In Eusebius the matter is presented in this form :

A small town of Phrygia, inhabited solely by Christians, was completely surrounded by soldiers while the men were in it.   Throwing fire into it they consumed them with the women and children while they were calling upon Christ.   This they did because all the inhabitants of the city and the curator himself, and the governor with all who held office, and the entire populace, confessed themselves Christians and would not in the least obey those who commanded them to worship idols.

There was another man of Roman dignity named Adaucus, of a noble Italian family, who had advanced through every honour under the emperors, so that he had blamelessly filled even the general offices of magistrate, as they call it, and of finance minister.   Besides all this he excelled in deeds of piety and in the confession of the Christ of God and was adorned with the crown of martyrdom.   He endured the conflict for religion while still holding the office of finance minister.

As against the inference that these two incidents occurred in the same place and that Adaucus set the example to his fellow-townsmen, some difficulty has been raised on the ground that a native of Italy who had had so distinguished a career would not be likely to have an official position given him in a small town in Phrygia. Rufinus, however, who lived in the same century and had travelled much, apparently saw nothing surprising in such an arrangement.

See Eusebius, *Eccles. Hist.*, bk viii, ch. 11 ; and *cf.* CMH., pp. 253–254.

ST THEODORE OF HERACLEA, Martyr　　(No Date ?)

AMONG the martyrs whom the Greeks honour with the title of Megalomartyr (*i.e.* great martyr), such as St George, St Pantaleon and others, four are distinguished above the rest : they are St Theodore of Heraclea, surnamed Stratelates (general of the army), St Theodore of Amasea, surnamed Tiro (the recruit), St Procopius and St Demetrius. St Theodore of Heraclea, with whom we are now concerned, is said to have been general of the forces of Licinius and governor of a large tract of Bithynia, Pontus and Paphlagonia. Heraclea in Pontus, originally a Greek city founded by a colony from Megara, was where the saint is supposed to have resided, and it was here that, according to one legend, he died a martyr's death, being beheaded for his faith after having been cruelly tortured by order of the Emperor Licinius.

The whole question has been very carefully studied by Father H. Delehaye in his book *Les Légendes grecques des saints militaires* (1909). In his opinion there was but one St Theodore, probably a martyr and possibly a soldier by profession. His cult seems traceable at an early date to Euchaïta, an inland town in the Heleno-pontus, and it spread widely from that centre. By degrees many fictitious and contradictory details were worked into his story by hagiographers who were in nowise concerned to adhere to historic truth in what they wrote. The divergences in the different narratives became in time so flagrant that it was necessary to have recourse to the hypothesis of two different St Theodores—the Stratelates and the Tiro, but even so their biographies overlap and cannot be kept distinct. One of the fictitious elements introduced into certain versions of the story was a conflict with a dragon, and this detail seems to have attached itself to the legend of St Theodore even earlier than to that of St George. Thus statues and pictures in which he appears mounted on horseback and piercing a dragon with a lance are not rare and are apt to be wrongly identified. The differentiation of two separate Theodores seems to have occurred somewhat earlier than Father Delehaye supposes. An Armenian homily which F. C. Conybeare believes to be of the fourth century already regards them as distinct ; and Mgr Wilpert has reproduced a mosaic which Pope Felix IV (526–530) set up in the church of St Theodore on the Palatine, in which our Saviour is represented seated, while St Peter on one side presents to Him one St Theodore and St Paul on the other side presents another.

The earliest written evidence we possess for the cult of St Theodore is a panegyric of the martyr attributed to St Gregory of Nyssa (Migne, PG., vol. xlvi, pp. 736–748). Even if it be not authentic it belongs to about the end of the fourth or the beginning of the fifth century. A selection of the most characteristic of the Greek lives of the two St Theodores is printed by Fr Delehaye in the book mentioned. An early Armenian homily on the saint has been translated into English by Prof. Conybeare in his *Monuments of Early Christianity* (pp. 217–238).   For St Theodore in art, see Künstle, *Ikonographie*, pp. 551–552, who refers in particular to an article by Hengstenberg, " Der Drachenkampf d. hl. Theodor ", in *Oriens Christianus*, 1912, pp. 18 *seq.* ; and Wilpert, *Die römischen Mosaiken*   Taf. 106–107.   *Cf.* St Theodore Tiro herein on November 9.

ST MOSES, Bishop   (*c.* A.D. 372)

St Moses, the apostle of the " Saracens ", was an Arab by birth and lived for a long time the life of a hermit at Rhinoclura, in the region between Syria and Egypt. The country was mainly inhabited by wandering bands of Saracens—worshippers of the stars—who, under their warlike queen, Mavia, waged a guerilla warfare on the Roman frontiers.   A punitive expedition sent against them appears to have been of the nature of a religious crusade, and ended in a pact whereby Mavia consented to the evangelization of her people provided they might have the holy hermit Moses as their bishop.   Lucius, the archbishop of Alexandria, would have been the right person to consecrate him, but he was an Arian and Moses refused to accept episcopal orders from him.   Eventually he succeeded in being consecrated by orthodox bishops, and thereafter spent his days in moving from place to place —he had no fixed see—teaching, preaching and converting a large proportion of his flock to the faith.   He also succeeded during the rest of his life in maintaining peace between the Romans and the Saracens.   " Saracen ", it should be noted, is a term which was applied by the later Greeks and Romans to the nomad tribes of the Syro-Arabian desert.   The exact date of the death of St Moses is not known.

See *Acta Sanctorum*, February, vol. ii.   The details are supplied by the statements of the church historians, Sozomen and Theodoret.

ST RICHARD, " King "   (A.D. 720)

In the spring of the year 720 a little party left the Hamble to go on pilgrimage to Rome and the Holy Land.   They were a Wessex family, consisting of the father, whose name is not recorded, and his sons, Willibald and Winebald.   They sailed up the Seine, landed at Rouen, visited several French shrines, and set out for Rome. But at Lucca the father died, and was buried in the church of St Frigidian (San Frediano).   Miracles were recorded at his tomb, where his relics still are and where his festival is observed with great devotion.

The son St Willibald afterwards joined St Boniface, and became first bishop of Eichstätt in Bavaria.   And we owe the above particulars to a document called the *Hodoeporicon*, in which, during his lifetime, one of his relatives, a nun of Heidenheim, set down the recollections of his early life that she had from his own mouth. It tells us all we know about the father of St Willibald and St Winebald and their sister St Walburga : but this was not enough for the faithful of Lucca and of Eichstätt, who had so great a reverence for the holy man.   So they supplied him with a name—Richard, a " life " and a background—he was a " king of the English ".   Actually there was no King Richard in England before Cœur-de-Lion, and nothing is known of the status of Willibald's father except that he could afford to go on a long pilgrimage : nevertheless he appears in the Roman Martyrology today as " sanctus Richardus rex Anglorum ".   The little we know about him is compensated by a good deal of reliable information about his children.

See the *Acta Sanctorum*, February, vol. ii and, especially, *Analecta Bollandiana*, vol. xlix (1931), pp. 353–397, where Father M. Coens uses an Eichstätt office of St Richard and an unpublished *vita* to throw some light on the evolution of his legend at Eichstätt in the tenth century and the rise of his cult at Lucca in the twelfth. In view of this article, T Meyrick's *The Family of St Richard the Saxon* (1844), the second issue of Newman's Lives of the English Saints, calls for many corrections.

ST LUKE THE YOUNGER (*c.* A.D. 946)

ST LUKE THE YOUNGER, also surnamed Thaumaturgus or the Wonderworker, was a Greek. His family came from the island of Aegina, but were obliged to leave on account of the attacks of the Saracens, and came eventually to settle in Thessaly where they were small farmers or peasant proprietors. His father, Stephen, and his mother, Euphrosyne, had seven children, of whom he was the third. He was a pious and obedient boy, and was at an early age set to mind the sheep and cultivate the fields. From a child he often went without a meal in order to feed the hungry, and sometimes he would strip himself of his clothes that he might give them to beggars. When he went forth to sow, he was wont to scatter half the seed over the land of the poor, and it was noticed that the Lord used to bless his father's crops with abundant increase. After the death of Stephen, the boy left the work of the fields and gave himself for a time to contemplation. He felt called to the religious life, and on one occasion he started off from Thessaly, meaning to seek a monastery, but was captured by soldiers who took him to be a runaway slave. They questioned him ; but when he said that he was a servant of Christ and had undertaken the journey out of devotion, they refused to believe him and shut him up in prison, treating him very cruelly. After a time they discovered his identity and released him, but upon returning home he was received with gibes and was jeered at for running away.

Although he still desired to consecrate himself to God, Luke's relations were unwilling to let him go, but two monks who, on their way from Rome to the Holy Land, were hospitably entertained by Euphrosyne, managed to persuade her to let her son travel with them as far as Athens. There he entered a monastery, but was not suffered to remain there long. One day the superior sent for him and gave the young man to understand that his (Luke's) mother had appeared to him in a vision and that, as she was needing him, he had better go home again to help her. So Luke returned once more and was received with joy and surprise ; but, after four months, Euphrosyne herself became convinced that her son had a real call to the religious life and she no longer opposed it. He built himself a hermitage on Mount Joannitsa near Corinth, and there he went to live, being at that time in his eighteenth year. He led a life of almost incredible austerity, spending his nights in prayer and depriving himself almost entirely of sleep. Nevertheless he was full of joy and charity, although at times he had to wrestle with fierce temptations. He received such graces from God that miracles were wrought through him both during his life and after his death. He is one of the early saints of whom a circumstantial story is told that he was seen raised from the ground in prayer. St Luke's cell was converted into an oratory after his death and was named Soterion or Sterion—the Place of Healing.

See the *Acta Sanctorum*, February, vol. ii. The Greek text, which was printed incomplete by Combefis and in Migne, PG., vol. cxi, cc. 441–480, has been re-edited entire in the *Analecta Bollandiana*, vol. xiii, pp. 82–121. The whole text is also found in P. Kremos, *Phocica*. BHG., p. 70.

BD RIZZERIO   (A.D. 1236)

WHEN St Francis of Assisi, seemingly on August 15, 1222, preached that unforgettable sermon at Bologna of which Thomas of Spalatro has left us a vivid picture, two well-born students of the university were so impressed that they abandoned the world and offered themselves at once for a life of poverty and toil amongst the Friars Minor.   One of these was Rizzerio, who belonged to a wealthy family at Muccia, not far from Camerino.   The incident is recorded in chapter 27 of the *Fioretti*, where, however, by some strange confusion Rizzerio is called Rinieri.   We are told that St Francis knew by revelation that both applicants were sent by God and that they would lead a holy life in the order, and accordingly, " Knowing their great fervour, he received them gladly ".   He prophesied at the same time that while Peregrine, though a learned canonist, was to remain in the path of lowliness and never become a priest, Rizzerio would " serve his brethren ".   It will be remembered that among the Franciscans the title given to the higher superiors is *minister* (*i.e.* servant), and Rizzerio accordingly received holy orders and became in the end provincial minister of the Marches.

Our early documents, notably the *Actus beati Francisci*, reproduced in the *Fioretti*, describe him as most intimate with and tenderly beloved by the saint in the last years of his life on earth, and there is a touching story of Rizzerio's temptation to despair of God's mercy.   For a long time he fought it by fasts and flagellations and prayers, but at last he determined to have recourse to his beloved father. " If ", he said, " Brother Francis shall make me welcome, and shall treat me as his familiar friend, even as he is wont to do, I believe that God will yet have pity on me ; but if not, it will be a sign that I shall be abandoned of God."   St Francis was grievously ill at the time, but he knew by revelation of Rizzerio's temptation and of his coming.   So calling Brothers Leo and Maneo he said to them, " Go quickly to meet my dearest son, Brother Rizzerio, and embrace him in my name and bid him welcome and tell him that among all the friars that are in the world I love him exceedingly."   And when at length the sorely tempted brother came to where St Francis lay, the saint rose up in spite of his illness and went to meet him. " And he made the sign of the most holy cross upon his brow and there he kissed him, and afterward said to him, ' Dearest son, God hath permitted thee to be thus tempted for thy great gain of merit ; but if thou wouldst not have this gain any more, have it not ! ' "   Then the temptation departed from him never to return. It was apparently to Brother Rizzerio also that St Francis told his original intention regarding the practice of poverty in the order, *viz.* that no friar ought to have any possessions whatever, not even books, but only his habit and breeches and the cord with which he was girded.   Brother Rizzerio seems to have died young, March 26, 1236.   His *cultus* was confirmed in 1836.

See the *Speculum Perfectionis*, ch. 2 ; the *Actus b. Francisci*, chs. 36 and 37 ; the early portions of Wadding's *Annales*, and the *Analecta Franciscana*, vol. iv, pp. 283-285.

BD ANTONY OF STRONCONE   (A.D. 1461)

LUIGI and Isabella Vici, the father and mother of Antony, were people of good position and ancient lineage.   Being fervent tertiaries they were both devoted to the Franciscan Order and seem to have raised no great opposition when their son and heir, at the early age of twelve years, sought admission among the Friars Minor as a lay-brother. His training in the religious life was superintended by his uncle, who was commissary general of the Observants in Italy. The boy, in spite of much ill-health, bravely persisted in the austerities of the life which he had chosen. So great was his progress that when he was twenty-six he was associated with Bd Thomas of Florence as deputy-master of novices at Fiesole, and thirteen years later was appointed to assist the same Thomas in a mission confided to him by the Holy See of denouncing and suppressing the Fraticelli in the Sienese territory and in Corsica. These, developing out of the party of the " Spirituals " within the Franciscan body itself, and identifying themselves with an impossible ideal of poverty and moral purity, had grown into a definitely heretical sect which rejected all constituted ecclesiastical authority.

Bd Antony, though not a priest, was employed on this mission for more than ten years, of which the last three were spent in Corsica ; but in 1431 he took up his abode in the friary of the Carceri, a place of retirement not far from Assisi, where he was more free to give rein to his intense longing for self-crucifixion. For thirty years he lived there, eating practically nothing but bread and water seasoned with wormwood, reputing himself the meanest of all and taking every opportunity which offered for humiliation and increased austerity. On one occasion, on account of his known aversion to anything which savoured of self-indulgence, he was suspected of having destroyed a number of vines which produced grapes for the community. He accepted and performed without protest the very severe penance which was enjoined him, but it was afterwards discovered that he was wholly innocent of the offence imputed to him. In 1460 Antony was transferred to the historic friary of St Damian in Assisi, and there he happily breathed his last on February 8, 1461, at the age of eighty. Many miracles followed, and popular belief maintains that Bd Antony shows to those who are devout to him the curious favour of warning them beforehand of their approaching death : a knocking is heard which seems to proceed either from his tomb or from some statue or picture representing him. A similar belief is entertained regarding two other Franciscan saints, St Paschal Baylon and Bd Matthia Nazzerei. The *cultus* of Bd Antony was confirmed in 1687.

See the *Acta Sanctorum*, February, vol. ii, where a Latin version is printed of the short life by Louis Jacobillo of Foligno. Other accounts have been written by Fathers Mariano of Florence and James of Oldis. Léon in his *Auréole Séraphique* (Eng. trans.), vol. i, has furnished an enthusiastic summary.

BD THOMAS SHERWOOD, Martyr   (A.D. 1578)

From an account written by the martyr's brother we are exceptionally well-informed regarding this heroic young man of twenty-seven, the son of most devout parents, his mother after his execution having been confined in prison for fourteen years, where eventually she died. He was not a student at the English College at Douay, as Challoner alleges, but when in London, after having made his plans to study for the priesthood, he was apprehended on suspicion of being a papist at the instigation of the son of Lady Tregonwell, a Catholic whose house he had frequented. He was sent to the Tower, where he was cruelly racked in a vain endeavour to make him disclose where he had heard Mass, and then thrust into a filthy dungeon. More's son-in-law, Roper, tried to send him money to alleviate his sufferings, but the lieutenant of the Tower would not permit of any money to be spent on him beyond six-pennyworth of clean straw for him to lie on. After six months he was tried, condemned for denying the queen's supremacy, and hanged at Tyburn.

The case is interesting because we possess the letter of the lords of the Privy Council directing that the lieutenant of the Tower and others are " to assay him [Sherwood] at the rack upon such articles as they shall think meet to minister unto him for the discovering either of the persons or of further matters ". In other words, they tortured him in order to obtain information which might convict other Catholics. In the Diary of Douay College, the death of the martyr is recorded three weeks later : " On the first of March [1578] Mr Lowe returned to us from England bringing news that a youth, by name Thomas Sherwood, had suffered, for his confession of the Catholic faith, not only imprisonment, but death itself. Amidst all his torments, his exclamation had been : ' Lord Jesus, I am not worthy to suffer this for thee, much less to receive those rewards which thou hast promised to those that confess thee.' "

See J. H. Pollen, *Acts of English Martyrs* (1891), pp. 1–20 ; and MMP., pp.

BB. JAMES SALÈS AND WILLIAM SAULTEMOUCHE, MARTYRS
(A.D. 1593)

JAMES SALÈS was born in Auvergne in 1556, son of a servant of the bishop of Clermont, who helped the lad's father to send him to the Jesuit college at Billom ; and there he entered the noviceship of the order at the age of seventeen. Saulte-mouche was a simple, honest youth employed at the same college as a servant, who became a lay-brother a few years later. James meanwhile pursued his studies and graduated at the newly founded University of Pont-à-Mousson. Apparently he was the first graduate, and late in the seventeenth century Peter Abram, when writing the history of that institution, ventured to express a hope that " he who figures first on the register of our university may one day be inscribed on the roll of the martyrs ". This anticipation was realized in 1926.

Somewhat later James pursued his studies in Paris, and it was there that the desire for martyrdom came vehemently upon the young scholastic. He accordingly applied for permission to go to the Indies. Father Aquaviva learned that his talent for preaching and teaching made him a very useful subject where he was, and he refused his request in words which now seem prophetic. " In France ", he wrote, " you will find all that the Indies have to give." In point of fact the Cévennes at that date, as well as a century later, were by no means free from peril for Catholics. It was a stronghold of the Huguenots, religious fanaticism was intense, and the whole country was in a very disturbed state. In the autumn of 1592 the mayor of Aubenas applied to the Jesuit provincial for a father to preach the Advent course with a special view to discussions with the Calvinist ministers. Father Salès was appointed and Brother Saultemouche was chosen for his companion. At the end of November they set out, the priest having about his neck a relic of Bd Edmund Campion, who had suffered at Tyburn less than a year previously. He seems to have had some presenti-ment that the crown which he had longed for was within his grasp, for he said cheerily to the porter on quitting the house, " Pray for us, dear brother, we are going to face death ".

The Advent course was completed, but the mayor begged that the preacher would remain until Easter. There seems to have been a great dearth of priests in that diocese at the time, and Aubenas was without one. Towards the beginning of February 1593 the father and brother were one night awakened by a clamour outside the walls of the town. Huguenot raiders were thundering at the gates, and knowing what had happened in other places, the two Jesuits made all haste to the church with the view of preventing a sacrilege. Father Salès gave holy communion to the brother and consumed the remainder of the sacred particles. Either by force, or, as seems more probable, by treachery, the raiders effected an entrance, and they were not long in discovering the whereabouts of the man they especially sought, for the vehemence and success of the recent controversial sermons had made a great stir. The Jesuits were seized, and when on being asked for their money the priest could produce no more than thirty sous, this seemed to infuriate their captors. They were dragged off with much brutality and brought before a kind of court of Calvinist ministers, one of whom, named Labat, seems to have borne the father a particular grudge in regard of a past encounter in which he had been put to shame. The proceedings resolved themselves into an acrimonious theological discussion. This was protracted until the next day and resulted plainly in the intense exasperation of the Protestant disputants as soon as the subject of the Holy Euchaiist was broached. The scene ended in the priest being dragged out of the hall into the open air, and there he was shot by order of the Huguenot commander. His companion, though exhorted by Father Salès to make his escape, as he might easily have done, would not quit his side. When the priest, kneeling to make a last prayer, was mortally wounded by an arquebus discharged at such close quarters that it singed his habit, the crowd fell upon the two victims with every kind of weapon, and in a few minutes had ended their bloody work amid indescribable brutalities. Brother Saultemouche had thrown his arms round Father Salès, and when his body was afterwards examined it was found to have been stabbed in eighteen places. This took place on February 7, 1593.

See J. Blanc, *Martyrs d'Aubenas* (1906), and H. Perroy, *Deux martyrs de l'Eucharistie* (1926).

BD GILES MARY (A.D. 1812)

ALTHOUGH the life of Bd Giles Mary-of-St-Joseph would have seemed singularly uneventful in the eyes of men, its very simplicity and humility made every day full of merit before the throne of God. He was born in 1729 near Taranto in Apulia. He was a rope-maker by trade, but when twenty-five years of age he was received among the Discalced Friars Minor of St Peter of Alcantara at Naples. There he spent most of his life as porter, showing intense compassion for the sick, the poor and the *lazzaroni* who formed so large a proportion of the population of that city. The distribution of alms was largely in his hands, but the more he gave away the more help seemed to flow in, and many miraculous cures are said to have been associated with his works of charity. He was also very earnest in propagating devotion to St Joseph. He died on February 7, 1812, and was beatified in 1888.

See P. P. Ausserer, *Seraphischer Martyrologium* (1889), and C. Kempf, *The Holiness of the Church in the Nineteenth Century* (1916).

8 : ST JOHN OF MATHA, Co-Founder of the Order of the Most Holy Trinity　(A.D. 1213)

S T JOHN was born at Faucon, on the borders of Provence, and when a young man was sent to Aix, where he learned grammar, the use of arms, riding and other exercises suitable for his position.　His chief interest, however, lay in the works of mercy and in prayer, and upon his return home he retired to a little hermitage not far from Faucon, with the intention of living away from the world, united to God by penance and contemplation.　However, he found his solitude so frequently broken in upon that he obtained leave from his father to study theology in Paris, where he gained his doctor's degree and was ordained priest.　During his first Mass he resolved, by a special inspiration from God, to devote himself to the task of ransoming Christian slaves from the Moslems—a work which impressed him as one of the greatest acts of charity since it benefited both their souls and their bodies.　However, before he entered upon so important an undertaking, he thought it desirable to spend some time in retirement and prayer. Accordingly, having heard of a holy hermit, St Felix of Valois, he went to him at Cerfroid and begged to be admitted to his solitude and to be instructed in the way of perfection.

One day, as they sat together on the bank of a stream, John told Felix of his plan to rescue the Christians who were held in bondage by the Mohammedans, and he spoke so eloquently that Felix offered to join him in his enterprise.　They set out for Rome in the depth of winter—it was at the close of the year 1197—to obtain the Pope's benediction.　Innocent III, convinced that these two men were led by the Holy Spirit, consented to their founding a new religious order and declared St John the first general superior.　The bishop of Paris and the abbot of St Victor were ordered to draw up the rule, which the pope approved by a bull in 1198.　He directed the religious to wear a white habit with a red and blue cross on the breast and to take the name of the Order of the Most Holy Trinity.　The two founders returned to France and presented themselves to King Philip Augustus, who authorized the establishment of their order in his kingdom, whilst Gaucher III, lord of Châtillon, gave them Cerfroid, which became the headquarters of the order.

In the years which followed the two saints founded other convents in France and sent several of their religious to accompany the counts of Flanders and Blois and other lords to the Crusades.　St John in 1201 sent to Morocco two members of the order who redeemed 186 Christian slaves.　The next year John himself went to Tunis, where he purchased the liberty of 110 more.　He returned to Provence and received gifts which he took with him to Spain, and there ransomed a number of prisoners whom the invaders held in captivity.　On a second voyage to Tunis he suffered much from the infidels, who were enraged at his zeal and at his success in exhorting the poor slaves to be constant to their faith.　As he was returning with 120 Christians whom he had ransomed, the Moslems, by damaging the rudder of his ship and tearing the sails, made certain that the vessel and its living freight would perish at sea.　But the saint, full of confidence in God, begged Him to be their pilot, and after setting his companions' cloaks in place of the useless sails, he recited his psalter, kneeling on the deck with a crucifix in his hands.　They had a prosperous voyage and landed safely at Ostia.　By this time Felix had greatly propagated the order in Italy and had obtained for it a foundation in Paris on the site of a chapel of St Mathurin, from the name of which convent these religious are called Mathurins in France. St John lived two more years in Rome, and died there ; his *cultus* was recognized in 1666.

The foregoing account, abridged from Alban Butler, reproduces what may be read in the traditional and, so to speak, official biographies of St John of Matha. In the *Petits Bollandistes* and in the lives by Gil Gonzalez de Avila and Father Calixte, still further details are supplied—for example, we are told of a mission to Dalmatia whither the saint is supposed to have been sent by Pope Innocent III in 1199 as legate. The fact is, as Paul Deslandres has pointed out in his admirable work, *L'Ordre des Trinitaires pour le rachat des captifs* (1903), the religious in question had taken no care to preserve any archives. They knew practically nothing of the history of their founder, and in the fifteenth and sixteenth centuries, feeling handicapped by this ignorance and spurred on by rivalry with the Mercedarians, Hospitallers and others, certain writers of the order deliberately compiled a fictitious record which they professed to base on documentary evidence. This procedure is the more regrettable because it did not take place in the dark ages but in comparatively modern times. It appears plain that some few individuals, under pretext of edification, did not scruple to invent a chronicle of glorious achievements, studded at every turn with supposed miracles and supernatural revelations, and to palm all this off upon their unsuspecting readers as a history of the beginnings of the order. Painful as the fact may be, it deserves to be remembered, for it forms the justification of the severely critical and sceptical attitude of the scientific hagiographers of the present day. Moreover, it is noteworthy that once the path of historical fabrication has been entered upon, all scruples soon vanish and the habit grows apace. The bogus chronicle of Gil Gonzalez de Avila was followed in course of time by the still wilder extravagances of Figueras and Domingo Lopez. A convincing illustration is ready to hand.

For the Spaniard or the Provençal of the seventeenth century Great Britain was an *Ultima Thule* about which no one was likely to know very much. It was a locality which offered every encouragement to the romancer, for fictitious detail would not be readily detected. Consequently we have a folio volume of 600 pages, *Noticias historicas de las tres Provincias del Orden de la SS. Trinidad en Inglaterra, Escocia y Hybernia* (Madrid, 1714), in which Fray Lopez professes to deal with the fate of the Trinitarian houses in England in the time of King Henry VIII. According to Lopez, there were forty-four Trinitarian houses in the British Isles when the persecution under Henry began ; they were wealthy and prosperous and they were peopled by 300 or 400 religious, *every one of whom* laid down his life for the faith. It cannot be necessary to dwell upon the fact that the Trinitarians were one of the least considerable of all the orders in the British Isles. They had only ten houses, most of them very straitened in means, and we have no reason to think that a single one of the religious was martyred. Beyond question, the statements made by Lopez, from whatever source he derived them, are a tissue of fictions. The elaborate parade of references, with names, dates, titles, etc., proves on being tested to be a mere sham, though some authentic names of persons and places connected with the Trinitarians have been worked in with the rest. Unfortunately it seems clear that the traditional biography of St John of Matha is a work of much the same character. No doubt need be felt that such a person existed, that he came from Provence, that he was an exceptionally holy and zealous man, that he founded the

Trinitarian Order for the Redemption of Captives, that he obtained an approval of his rule from Pope Innocent III, and that he died at Rome on December 17, 1213. But beyond this we know little or nothing.

The work already cited of Paul Deslandres seems to have said the last word on all these matters. For a statement from the Trinitarian standpoint the reader may be referred to Antonino-de-la-Asuncion, *Monumenta ordinis Excalceatorum SS. Trinitatis Redemptionis captivorum ad provinciam S.P.N. Joannis de Matha spectantia* (1915), and to his *Les origines de l'Ordre de la T. S. Trinité d'après les documents* (1925) ; on this last *cf.* the *Analecta Bollandiana*, vol. xlvi (1928), pp. 419–420. The book of D. Lopez referred to above was dealt with by Fr J. H. Pollen in an article in *The Month* (June 1895) entitled "Spurious Records of Tudor Martyrs ".

ST NICETIUS, or NIZIER, BISHOP OF BESANÇON   (*c.* A.D. 611 ?)

AFTER the election of St Nicetius as bishop he restored to Besançon the episcopal see which had been transferred to Nyon, on the Lake of Geneva, when Besançon had been destroyed by the Huns. A holy and learned man, he was a vigorous opponent of heresy, and is said to have been intimate with Pope St Gregory the Great, whom he visited and with whom he exchanged letters. Another of his friends was St Columban, for whom he consecrated altars at Fontaines. Luxeuil and Annegray, and whom he hospitably received at Besançon when the Irish missionary had to flee from Queen Brunehilda and her grandson Thierry II. Mgr Duchesne shows that there certainly was a Nicetius who was bishop of Besançon and also that he was at a comparatively early date venerated there as a saint. He holds, however, that it was St Nicetius who buried St Waldebert, Abbot of Luxeuil, on May 2, 670. If this were true it would certainly be impossible that Nicetius could have been a friend of St Gregory and of St Columban.

This Life, derived from Chifflet in the *Acta Sanctorum*, February, vol. ii, illustrates well the uncertainties which beset the investigator of Merovingian episcopal history. The Life of St Waldebert to which Duchesne appeals (MGH., *Scriptores*, vol. xv, p. 1173) does not seem necessarily to imply more than that St Waldebert was buried in a crypt which St Nicetius had constructed—possibly more than half a century earlier.

ST ELFLEDA, ABBESS OF WHITBY, VIRGIN   (A.D. 714)

ST ELFLEDA (Aelfflaed ; Bede spells the name Aelbfled) was the daughter of Oswy, King of Northumbria. Her father made a vow that if Heaven would give victory to his arms, he would consecrate his daughter to God and would give lands for the foundation of religious houses. As the fortune of war continued to favour him, he fulfilled his promise, and Elfleda was taken when hardly weaned to the convent of Hartlepool, and afterwards took the veil there. When the abbess, St Hilda, founded her famous monastery at Whitby, St Elfleda accompanied her thither, and after St Hilda's death was chosen abbess jointly with her mother Eanfleda. Her influence and authority extended far beyond the walls of the religious house. In the contentions which arose between St Theodore of Canterbury and St Wilfrid of York, Elfleda was always a conciliatory influence and did much to allay the animosity against Wilfrid. On one occasion she stood up before the assembled bishops and said, " Cease your discussion : I will declare to you my brother's [Aldfrid] last will, as I myself was present. He promised that if he recovered he would immediately obey the command of the Apostolic See [concerning Wilfrid] and he is known to have charged the heir to do the same in the event of his death."

Elfleda was a devoted admirer of St Cuthbert, who evidently reciprocated her affection and regarded her with great respect. On one occasion the application of his girdle had cured her, as she believed, of a severe attack of an ailment by which she had been bent almost double. In Bede's Life of St Cuthbert we have a detailed and touching account of an interview in which Cuthbert in 684 came to meet St Elfleda at Coquet island. There this " most reverend virgin and venerable hand-maid of Christ ", to use Bede's language, " who increased the lustre of her royal lineage with the higher nobility of exalted virtue ", fell at Cuthbert's feet and implored him to satisfy her anxiety regarding the future of her brother, King Egfrid. The saint in guarded terms gave her to understand that Egfrid would die within the year, that Aldfrid, his illegitimate brother, would succeed, and that he himself, Cuthbert, would be forced to accept a bishopric—all which prophecies were duly fulfilled. Elfleda seems to have died at Whitby in 714. Her fame was such that her death is recorded in the Irish annals. In William of Malmesbury's time her relics had recently been rediscovered at Whitby and honourably translated.

See the *Acta Sanctorum*, February, vol. ii ; C. Plummer's edition of Bede, *Eccles. Hist. ;* and Stanton's *Menology*, pp. 68–69. A letter of Elfleda to Adela, Abbess of Pfalzel, near Trier, is printed in Jaffé, *Monumenta Moguntina*, p. 49 ; on this see E. Ewig, *St Bonifatius Gedenkgabe zum zwölfhundertjahrigen Todestag* (1954), p. 418.

ST MEINGOLD, Martyr   (*c.* A.D. 892 ?)

The history of St Meingold, if indeed there was ever any such saint, has been overlaid with a number of unreliable and often conflicting embellishments. He appears to have been a count of Huy in what is now Belgium and, like most of the chieftains of the day, was constantly engaged in feuds with his neighbours. After a time he repented of the blood he had shed and spent seven years in deeds of penitence. In the end he was attacked and killed by some of his former adversaries at Stierke on the Moselle.

One of the tales to which we have alluded above represents him to have been the son of a certain English king, Hugh (of whom nothing else is known), and of the sister of the Emperor Arnulf. As Arnulf had no children he adopted Meingold as his heir, and as soon as he was grown to man's estate Meingold came over from England to the emperor's court, where he was received with enthusiasm. There were, however, certain lords who resented his arrival, as they thought their own standing would be shaken, and the chief of these was one Duke Albrecht, whose widowed sister, Geyla, Meingold married. Now Albrecht had compassed the death of Geyla's first husband because he had claimed property which was really part of Geyla's dowry, and he was not more disposed to yield it up to Meingold. However, with the support of the emperor, Meingold obtained possession of these estates and proceeded to stock and cultivate them, for they had been thoroughly neglected and the tenants were starving. Thereupon Duke Albrecht and his ally, Duke Baldwin, sacked the place, setting fire to houses and barns and carrying off captives. Meingold arrived to see his property in flames, and, engaging the marauders in battle, killed Baldwin. The emperor called together a council to consider the matter and urged Meingold and Albrecht to come to terms : Meingold was quite willing, and as Albrecht pretended to agree, an apparent reconciliation took place.

Soon afterwards, however, Albrecht treacherously besieged Meingold in a castle, which eventually was relieved by the imperial troops. These captured Albrecht, who was then imprisoned in the castle he had besieged. He disappeared mysteriously and his fate was unknown until the emperor, having an afternoon's fishing in the castle pond, found Albrecht's body which had been thrown there by two soldiers of the garrison. Meingold and Geyla were left in possession of their estates, but they resolved to give them up to the poor. Meingold took the garb of a penitent, and for seven years wandered about from one shrine to another. At the end of that time he came home and resolved to seek a quiet spot in which to prepare for death. Some of his ancient enemies came upon him, knowing him to be unprotected and alone, and they found him resting on the ground. When they threatened him, he stretched out his arms in the form of a cross and quietly awaited the death-stroke they dealt him. In spite of, or rather perhaps because of, this bizarre history, St Meingold is much honoured in Belgium, especially at Huy, and for some not very intelligible reason he has been adopted as the patron of bakers and millers.

Father Albert Poncelet points out that there was a historic Meingaud, Count of Wormsfeld, who was assassinated in 892. Some time afterwards a holy ascetic called Meingold died and began to be venerated in the neighbourhood of Huy, and then two or three centuries still later, this devotion led to a life being written in which some enterprising cleric fused together all that popular tradition reported concerning both the count and the hermit.

See the *Acta Sanctorum*, February, vol. ii ; and Fr Poncelet in the *Analecta Bollandiana*, vol. xxxi (1912), p. 357. *Cf.* also Dümmler, *De Arnulfo, Francorum rege*, pp. 201–204 ; and S. Balau, *Étude critique des sources de l'histoire du Pays de Liége*, p. 338.

ST CUTHMAN   (*c.* A.D. 900)

As his name shows, Cuthman was of Anglo-Saxon extraction, and was born in the south of England. He was brought up in the spirit of Christian piety by his parents, and he never disobeyed them. We are told in particular that when sent to mind his father's sheep he never failed to return at the appointed time. This employment gave him leisure to consecrate himself to God in prayer, and what gave his prayer power was his simplicity combined with detachment and obedience. Cuthman after his father's death spent all that he earned to support his decrepit mother, whom apparently he used to trundle about in a sort of barrow, for to obtain by work or from charity what was necessary for her he moved from place to place, suffering hardships and austerities cheerfully. Finding at last a home at Steyning in Sussex, he built there a little cottage as a shelter for his mother, where they might devote themselves to the service of God. No sooner was it finished than he measured out the ground near it for the foundations of a church which he proceeded to build with his own hands. The people who lived round about, fired by his zeal, contributed to assist him in completing the work. Cuthman laboured all day, conversing at the same time in his heart with God, and spent a considerable part of the night in prayer. His name was rendered famous by many miracles which were ascribed to him, both during his lifetime and after his death.

No very positive traces are left of the cult of this saint, but his name does appear in a few early calendars, notably in one of the tenth or early eleventh century (Cotton MS. Nero A ii). Two short lives are printed in the *Acta Sanctorum*, February, vol. ii. Both seem to have been derived from the abbey of Fécamp in Normandy, to which the estate of Steyning had been made over by William the Conqueror. *Cf.* Christopher Fry's play, *The Boy with a Cart* (1939) ; and the article, " A Neglected Saint ", in *Speculum*, vol. xiii (1938), pp. 448-453. The Cuthman legend also appears in Gotha MS. I, 81, from which it was printed in *Analecta Bollandiana*, vol. lviii (1940), pp. 197-199.

BD PETER IGNEUS, CARDINAL-BISHOP OF ALBANO (A.D. 1089)

IN the Roman Martyrology under February 8 mention is made of " Blessed Peter, Cardinal and Bishop of Albano, of the Order of Vallombrosa, surnamed ' Igneus ' because he passed through fire unharmed ". Of the incident here referred to a remarkable description is given in an apparently authentic letter addressed by the citizens of Florence to Pope Alexander II, which Abbot Atto has incorporated in his Life of St John Gualbert. The writers dwell upon the excitement of the populace, who were roused to fury by the simoniacal intrusion of Peter of Pavia into that see. Nothing would content them but that the lawfulness of this appointment should be left to the judgement of God by the ordeal of fire. They accordingly appealed to the monks of Vallombrosa to vindicate the cause of right.

By the command of the abbot, the monk Peter (his family name is said to have been Aldobrandini) undertakes to face the test. Two great piles of wood, ten feet long, five wide, and four and half high, are prepared with only a narrow lane, a couple of feet broad, running between them. Peter offers Mass with great devotion while the assembled crowd of nearly three thousand people pray fervently. The wood being now in full combustion, Peter removes his chasuble, retaining his alb, maniple and stole, and addresses a prayer to God, in which he beseeches the Almighty, in testimony of His abhorrence of the simony which has taken place, to preserve him unscathed in the flames, as the three youths of old were preserved in the fiery furnace of Babylon. Then, " undaunted in mind and cheerful of aspect, having made the sign of the cross and carrying a crucifix in his hand, the monk, with a certain stately solemnity, passed through the fire, sustaining no injury either to his body or to any of the things which he carried ". The writers declare that before their eyes the flames seemed to fill and expand the alb, and that Peter's feet sank up to the ankles in the red-hot ashes, but that not even the hairs on his legs were singed.* Having made the transit, the monk turned round and would have retraced his steps, but the people would not allow him. They were satisfied that God had clearly spoken, and soon after, by the formal judgement of Pope Alexander II, Peter of Pavia was deposed from the see of Florence. On the other hand the monk Peter, after being appointed abbot in another monastery, was summoned to Rome, made cardinal-bishop of Albano by St Gregory VII, and sent as legate on missions to the Italian states, to France and to Germany. It is generally stated that he died on February 8, 1089.

See the *Kirchenlexikon*, vol. ix, c. 1915 ; and Mann, *The Lives of the Popes*, vol. vi, p. 302, who points out that there is other contemporary evidence corroborating the letter of the Florentines. A short essay on the *Vita e Gesta di S. Pietro Igneo*, by I. M. Pieroni, was published at Prato in 1894. It seems highly probable that the ordeal by fire proposed by Francis di Puglia in the case of Savonarola, which, ending as it did in fiasco, brought about

* There are innumerable stories, many of which seem to rest on trustworthy evidence, of religious mystics in all parts of the world, especially in the Far East, who perform this same feat. Andrew Lang has collected some of them in his *Magic and Religion* (pp. 270-294), but there are numbers of others. See too the excellent pages by J. F. Rinn in *Sixty Years of Psychical Research* (New York, 1950), pp. 582-585.

the great reformer's downfall, must have been suggested by the historical case of Peter Igneus 400 years earlier. The letter of the citizens of Florence has been many times printed ; it may be found in Migne, PL., vol. cxlvi, cc. 693-698, and in the *Acta Sanctorum*, July, vol. ''' pp. 358-359. *Cf.* Benedict XIV (Lambertini), *De   beatificatione*, bk iv, 11, 6.

ST STEPHEN OF MURET, ABBOT   (A.D. 1124)

THIS St Stephen, sometimes called " of Grandmont ", is said to have been the son of a viscount of Thiers in the Auvergne, who accompanied his father to Italy and eventually there decided to become a monk, obtaining papal authority for the establishment in France of a community based on the example of some religious he had known in Calabria. However, the life of Stephen as it is related by the seventh prior of Grandmont is unreliable and presents a number of difficulties, chronological and other, so that the facts are far from clear. What is certain is that, probably about the year 1110, Stephen founded a monastery in the valley of Muret, near Limoges, which developed into a distinct monastic congregation that continued to exist, uneasily, till towards the end of the eighteenth century. It was known as the Order of Grandmont, from the name of the place to which his disciples migrated after St Stephen's death in 1124.

Though he did not write the rule which bears his name--" There is no rule ", he said, " except Christ's gospel "--what manner of man Stephen of Muret was can perhaps best be inferred from the life of his monks in their earlier history. It closely resembled that of the Carthusians and the Camaldolese, but was distinguished by an extreme severity that bordered on the *doctrinaire*. All property in land and fixed revenues were forbidden, no monk might go outside enclosure, and the lay-brothers were made almost completely responsible for administration. Such regulations, combined with its personal austerities, gave the order an initial appeal to enthusiastic souls and it spread rapidly, but after little more than a half-century its decline had already begun. The isolated places favoured for their houses by the earlier Grandmontines is well illustrated by the site of Craswall Priory in Herefordshire, under the north-eastern edge of the Black Mountains. King Henry II of England was a benefactor of Grandmont, and it was at his request that Pope Clement III canonized St Stephen in 1189.

The *Vita Sti Stephani* is printed in the *Acta Sanctorum*, February, vol. ii, and in Migne, PL., vol. cciv, cc. 1065-1072. See Martène, *Amplissima Collectio*, vol. vi, pp. viii *seq.* ; Heimbucher, *Die Orden und Kongregationen*, vol. i (1907), pp. 415 416 ; D. Knowles, *The Monastic Order in England* (1949), pp. 203-204, and the two articles of R. Webster there referred to, in the *Catholic Encyclopedia*, vol. vi, pp. 725-726 and vol. xiv, p. 291.

BD ISAIAH OF CRACOW   (A.D. 1471)

ISAIAH BONER was a Pole, a native of Cracow. He was sent by his parents to the academy there, where his exceptional abilities were recognized and developed, and he afterwards passed brilliantly through the higher courses of study until he acquired the degree of doctor of divinity. For a short time he was quite uncertain how he could best serve God, but he eventually chose the religious life and entered the Augustinian friary at Kazimiertz—a town which took its name from King Casimir who had built the church and the monastery. Here Isaiah set an example of singleness of heart, edifying everyone by his sanctity and learning. He was soon given the congenial task of expounding obscure and difficult passages of Holy

Scripture. This he did with much eloquence, not merely stimulating and interesting the minds of his brother friars by the subtle truths he set forth, but also attracting their souls wonderfully to the love of Christ. Sometimes, we are told, his words would descend like firebrands amongst his audience, kindling a flame of devotion which consumed all worldliness, and at another time he would expound the Bible devotionally, from the Fall onwards, in the manner of a prayer, after a special method of his own.

Whilst he was thus inspiring others, Isaiah was privately mortifying himself more and more, lest while he preached to others he should himself become a castaway. It was not so much his passions that he had to fight as the hidden powers of evil which assailed him even when his heart was uplifted in meditation and contemplation ; sometimes he was disturbed by the voices of evil spirits, sometimes he was struck with blows. His recreation was to make pilgrimages to the shrines of saints and to visit the sick, whom he cheered by directing their minds to the heavenly reward which is laid up for those who bear their sufferings on earth with resignation. To any who had a grudge against him or who showed him any antipathy, he was most humble, kneeling to ask their pardon very earnestly. As his life was drawing to a close, he had a vision of our Lady carrying the Infant Saviour. She was surrounded by angels and followed by a procession of Polish saints, and she addressed him, saying, " Isaiah, my dear servant, prepare to enter the kingdom of Heaven, prepared by God for the saints from the foundation of the world."

See the *Acta Sanctorum*, February, vol. ii, and Ossinger, *Bibliotheca Augustiniana.*

9 : ST CYRIL, Archbishop of Alexandria, Doctor of the Church   (A.D. 444)

ST CYRIL has been called the Doctor of the Incarnation, as St Augustine was styled the Doctor of Divine Grace : in the great intercession of the Syrian and Maronite Mass he is commemorated as " a tower of truth and interpreter of the Word of God made flesh "   Throughout his life he made it a rule never to advance any doctrine which he had not learnt from the ancient fathers, but his books against Julian the Apostate show that he had also read the profane writers. He often said himself that he neglected human eloquence, and it is certainly to be regretted that he did not cultivate a clearer style and write purer Greek. Upon the death of his uncle Theophilus in 412, he was raised to the see of Alexandria. He began to exert his authority by causing the churches of the Novatians to be closed and their sacred vessels to be seized-- an action condemned by the church historian Socrates, but we do not know his reasons and the grounds upon which he acted. He next drove out the Jews, who were numerous and who had enjoyed privileges in the city since the time of Alexander the Great. Their generally seditious attitude and several acts of violence committed by them decided him to take this step, which incensed Orestes the governor, although it was approved by the Emperor Theodosius. This unhappy disagreement with Orestes led to grievous results. Hypatia, a pagan woman of noble character, was the most influential teacher of philosophy at that time in Alexandria, and her reputation was so great that disciples flocked to her from all parts. Among these was the great

Bishop Synesius, who submitted his works to her criticism. She was much respected by the governor, who used to consult her even on matters of civil administration. Nowhere was the populace more unruly or more prone to lawless acts of violence than in Alexandria. Acting upon a suspicion that Hypatia had incensed the governor against their bishop, the mob in 417 attacked her in the streets, pulled her out of her chariot, and tore her body in pieces—to the great grief and scandal of all good men, and especially, it may be believed, of St Cyril. Only one other fact is known to us concerning this earlier period of his episcopate. He had imbibed certain prejudices against St John Chrysostom, having been with Theophilus at the Synod of The Oak ; Cyril had something of his uncle's obstinacy, and it was no easy matter to induce him to insert Chrysostom's name in the diptychs of the Alexandrian church.

In the year 428 Nestorius, a priest-monk of Antioch, was made archbishop of Constantinople ; and he there taught with some of his clergy that there were two distinct persons in Christ, that of God and that of man, joined only by a moral union whereby, according to them, the Godhead dwelt in the manhood merely as its temple. Consequently he denied the Incarnation, that God was made man. He also said that the Blessed Virgin ought not to be styled the mother of God, but only of the man Christ, whose humanity was but the temple of the divinity and not a nature hypostatically assumed by the divine Person. His homilies gave great offence, and protests arose from all sides against the errors they contained. St Cyril sent him a mild expostulation, but was answered with haughtiness and contempt. Both parties appealed to Pope St Celestine I who, after examining the doctrine in a council at Rome, condemned it and pronounced a sentence of excommunication and deposition against Nestorius unless, within ten days of receiving notice of the sentence, he publicly retracted his errors. St Cyril, who was appointed to see the sentence carried out, sent Nestorius, with his third and last summons, twelve propositions with anathemas to be signed by him as a proof of his orthodoxy. Nestorius, however, showed himself more obstinate than ever.*

This occasioned the summoning of the third general council which was held at Ephesus in 431, attended by two hundred bishops with St Cyril at their head as senior bishop and Pope Celestine's representative. Nestorius was present in the town, but refused to appear ; so after his sermons had been read and other evidence received against him, his doctrines were condemned, and a sentence of excommunication and deposition was pronounced. Six days later there arrived at Ephesus Archbishop John of Antioch, with forty-one bishops who had not been able to reach Ephesus in time. They were in favour of Nestorius, although they did not share his errors, of which indeed they deemed him innocent. Instead of associating themselves with the council, they assembled by themselves and presumed to depose St Cyril, accusing him in turn of heresy. Both sides appealed to the emperor, by whose order St Cyril and Nestorius were both arrested and kept in confinement. When three legates arrived from Pope Celestine, the matter took another turn. After a careful consideration of what had been done, the legates confirmed the condemnation of Nestorius, approved Cyril's conduct, and declared the sentence pronounced against him null and void. Thus he was vindicated with honour and, though the bishops of the Antiochene province continued their schism for a while, they made peace with St Cyril in 433, when they condemned Nestorius and gave

* It is debatable whether Nestorius in fact held all the opinions attributed to him ; in any case he was hardly the originator of the heresy that bears his name.

a clear and orthodox declaration of their own faith. Nestorius retired to his old monastery at Antioch, but later was exiled to the Egyptian desert.

St Cyril, who had thus triumphed over heresy by his intrepidity and courage, spent the rest of his life in maintaining the faith of the Church and in the labours of his see, until his death in 444. The Alexandrians gave him the title of Teacher of the World, whilst Pope Celestine described him as " the generous defender of the Catholic faith " and " an apostolic man ". He was a man of strong and impulsive character, brave but sometimes over-vehement, indeed violent. Abbot Chapman has suggested that more patience and diplomacy on his part might have prevented the rise of the Nestorian Church which was for so long a power in the East. But we have to thank him for the firm and uncompromising stand he took with regard to the dogma of the Incarnation—an attitude which led to the clear statements of the great council over which he presided. Although since his day Nestorianism and Pelagianism have, from time to time and under different names, tried to rear their heads in various quarters of the world, they have never again been a real menace to the Catholic Church as a whole. We ought indeed to be grateful that we, in our generation, are left in no doubt as to what we should believe with regard to that holy mystery upon which we base our faith as Christians. He was declared a doctor of the Universal Church in 1882, and at the fifteenth centenary of his death in 1944 Pope Pius XII issued an encyclical letter, " *Orientalis ecclesiae* ", on " this light of Christian wisdom and valiant hero of the apostolate ".

The great devotion of this saint to the Blessed Sacrament is manifest from the frequency with which he emphasizes the effects it produces upon those who receive it worthily. Indeed, he says that by holy communion we are made concorporeal with Christ. And it must surely be difficult for those who profess to hold the same faith as that defined in the first six general councils to shut their eyes to the vigour and conviction with which St Cyril before the year 431 affirmed his eucharistic doctrine. In a letter to Nestorius, which received the general and formal assent of the fathers at Ephesus, he had written :

> Proclaiming the death according to the flesh of the only begotten Son of God, that is, Jesus Christ, and confessing His resurrection from the dead and ascent into Heaven, we celebrate the bloodless sacrifice in our churches ; and thus approach the mystic blessings, and are sanctified by partaking of the holy flesh and the precious blood of Christ the Saviour of us all. And we receive it, not as common flesh (God forbid), nor as the flesh of a man sanctified and associated with the Word according to the unity of merit, or as having a divine indwelling, but as really the life-giving and very flesh of the Word Himself (Migne, PG., lxxvii, 113).

And he wrote to Calosyrius, Bishop of Arsinoë :

> I hear that they say that the sacramental consecration does not avail for hallowing if a portion of it be kept to another day. In saying so they are crazy. For Christ is not altered, nor will His holy body be changed ; but the power of the consecration and the life-giving grace still remain in it (Migne, PG., lxxvi, 1073).

Our knowledge of St Cyril is derived principally from his own writings and from the church historians Socrates, Sozomen and Theodoret. The view of his life and work presented by Butler is the traditional view, and we are not here directly concerned with the discussions which, owing mainly to the discovery of the work known as *The Bazaar of Heracleides,* have since been devoted to the character of Nestorius and his teaching. The literature connected with St Cyril is very copious.   A sufficient account will be found in the two articles in DTC., " Cyrille d'Alexandrie " and " Ephèse, Concile de "—as well as in Bardenhewer's *Patrology*.   See also Duchesne, *Histoire ancienne de l'Église*, vol. iii (Eng. trans.) ;   Abbot Chapman in the *Catholic Encyclopedia*, vol.   pp. 592–595 ;   and A. Fortescue, *The Greek Fathers* (1908).

ST APOLLONIA, VIRGIN AND MARTYR   (A.D. 249)

ST DIONYSIUS of Alexandria wrote to Fabius, Bishop of Antioch, an account of the persecution of the Christians by the heathen populace of Alexandria in the last year of the reign of the Emperor Philip.   The first victim of their rage was a venerable old man named Metras or Metrius, whom they tried to compel to utter blasphemies against God.   When he refused, they beat him, thrust splinters of reeds into his eyes, and stoned him to death.   The next person they seized was a Christian woman, called Quinta, whom they carried to one of their temples to force her to worship the idol.   She addressed their false god with words of scorn which so exasperated the people that they dragged her by the heels over the cobbles, scourged and then stoned her.   By this time the rioters were at the height of their fury. The Christians offered no resistance but betook themselves to flight, abandoning their goods without complaint because their hearts had no ties upon earth.   Their constancy was so general that St Dionysius knew of none who had renounced Christ.   Apollonia, an aged deaconess, was seized.   With blows in the face they knocked out all her teeth, and then, kindling a great fire outside the city, they threatened to cast her into it unless she uttered certain impious words.   She begged for a moment's delay, as if to consider the proposal ;   then, to convince her persecutors that her sacrifice was perfectly voluntary, she no sooner found herself free than she leaped into the flames of her own accord.   They next wreaked their fury on a holy man named Serapion and tortured him in his own house ; then they threw him headlong from the roof.

We meet with churches and altars dedicated in honour of St Apollonia in most parts of the Western church, but she is not venerated in any Oriental church, though she suffered in Alexandria.   To account for her action in thus anticipating her death St Augustine supposes that she acted by a particular direction of the Holy Ghost, since it would not otherwise be lawful for anyone to hasten his own end. She is invoked against toothache and all dental diseases, and her more common attributes in art are a pair of pincers holding a tooth, or else a golden tooth suspended on her necklace.

The statement of St Dionysius of Alexandria is incorporated by Eusebius in his history (vi, 41).   See also *Acta Sanctorum*, February, vol. ii ;   Künstle, *Ikonographie*, pp. 90–93, where an excellent bibliography will be found dealing mainly with the representations of St Apollonia in art ;   and *Il martirio di S. Apollonia* (1934), by G. B. Poletti, a dental surgeon. *Cf.* also an article by H. Nux in the *Revue d'odontologie*, vol. iii (1947), pp. 113 *seq.*, and Fr M. Coens in *Analecta Bollandiana*, vol. lxx (1952), pp. 138–159, where some recent bibliographical references are given.   There is a dentists' periodical in Boston, U.S.A., called *The Apollonian*.

ST NICEPHORUS, MARTYR   (NO DATE)

THERE dwelt in Antioch a priest called Sapricius and a layman named Nicephorus, who were close friends of many years, but dissension having arisen their friendship was succeeded by bitter hatred.   This continued for a time until Nicephorus, realizing the sinfulness of such animosity, resolved to seek a reconciliation.   Twice he deputed some of his friends to go to Sapricius to ask his forgiveness. The priest, however, refused to be placated. Nicephorus sent a third time—but still to no purpose, Sapricius having closed his ears even to Christ who commands us to forgive as we would be forgiven. Nicephorus now went in person to his house and, owning his fault, humbly begged for pardon; but this succeeded no better. It was the year 260, when the persecution against the Christians suddenly began to rage under Valerian and Gallienus.

Sapricius soon after was apprehended and brought before the governor, who asked him his name. "Sapricius", he answered. "Of what profession?" inquired the governor. "I am a Christian." Then he was asked if he was of the clergy. "I have the honour to be a priest", replied Sapricius, adding, "We Christians acknowledge one Lord and Master, Jesus Christ, who is God the only and true God, who created heaven and earth. The gods of the pagans are devils." The president, exasperated, gave orders for him to be tortured on the rack. This did not shake the constancy of Sapricius, who said to his tormentors, "My body is in your power, but you cannot touch my soul of which my Saviour Jesus Christ is master". The president, seeing him so resolute, pronounced sentence "Sapricius, the Christian priest, who is so ridiculously certain that he will rise again, shall be delivered over to the public executioner to be beheaded, because he has contemned the edict of the emperors".

Sapricius seemed to receive this sentence cheerfully, and was in haste to arrive at the place of execution. Nicephorus ran to meet him and, casting himself at his feet, said, "Martyr of Jesus Christ, forgive me my offence." Sapricius made no answer. Nicephorus waited for him in another street and again besought forgiveness, but the heart of Sapricius was more and more hardened and he would not even look at him. The soldiers jeered at Nicephorus for being so anxious for the pardon of a criminal about to die. At the place of execution, Nicephorus renewed his supplications, but all in vain. The executioner ordered Sapricius to kneel down that they might cut off his head. Sapricius asked, "Upon what account?"— "Because you will not sacrifice to the gods or obey the emperors." The wretched man exclaimed, "Stay, friends! Do not put me to death. I will do as you desire I am ready to sacrifice!" Nicephorus, distressed at his apostasy, exclaimed, "Brother, what are you doing? Do not renounce our master, Jesus Christ! Do not forfeit a crown you have gained by your sufferings!" But as Sapricius would pay no attention to his words, Nicephorus, weeping bitterly, said to the executioners, "I am a Christian, and believe in Jesus Christ whom this miserable man has denied: behold, I am ready to die in his stead." All were greatly astonished, and the officers despatched a lictor to the governor, asking what they should do. The governor replied that if Nicephorus persisted in refusing to sacrifice to the gods, he should perish; and he was accordingly executed. Thus Nicephorus received three immortal crowns, of faith, of humility and of charity.

Although St Nicephorus is commemorated on this day in the Roman Martyrology, and though the acts have been included by Ruinart in his collection of authentic stories of martyrdoms, there can be little doubt that Father Delehaye is absolutely right in characterizing the narrative summarized above as nothing better than a pious romance. Ruinart has not in fact been quite candid in his treatment of the text which he prints. The older Greek text contains many citations from Scripture and other comments which to the discerning eye betray the purpose of edification which the author had dominantly in view. These Ruinart, following a later recension, has omitted. The whole object of the Nicephorus narrative, as Delehaye (Les passions des martyrs et les genres littéraires, 1921, p. 220) points out, is to teach the moral lesson of the forgiveness of injuries. He holds that these acts constitute a typical specimen of " the romance of the imagination ", the hero of which never existed (see *Les légendes hagiographiques*, 1927, pp. 109 and 113). It is true that Nicephorus has been adopted as a local saint in Istria (*ib.*, p. 56), but he certainly did not belong there. See the *Acta Sanctorum*, February, vol. ii ; BHL., nn. 6085, 6086 ; BHG., nn. 1331-1334 ; *Analecta Bollandiana*, vol. xvi (1897), p. 299.

ST SABINUS, BISHOP OF CANOSA   (*c.* A.D. 566)

THE history of St Sabinus is rather difficult to disentangle, not only because it has been overlaid with legend, but also because there are two other saints of the same name inscribed in the *Acta Sanctorum* on February 9 and some points in their lives are so similar that it seems as though they had been confused. One of them was a bishop who assisted at the consecration of St Michael's sanctuary on Monte Gargano in 493 and was buried at Atripaldo, but our saint lived later and his body was interred elsewhere. He was born at Canosa* in Apulia. From his youth he only desired the things of God and cared nothing for money, except as a means of helping the poor which he did most generously. He became bishop of Canosa, and was on friendly terms with the most prominent men of his time, including St Benedict himself, who appears to have foretold to him that Rome would not be destroyed by Totila and the Goths. Pope St Agapitus I sent him to the court of the Emperor Justinian to support the newly-appointed patriarch, St Mennas, against the heretic Anthimus, and he attended the council presided over by Mennas in the year 536. On his way back through Lycia, he visited the tomb of St Nicholas at Myra and saw the saint in a vision.

In old age Sabinus lost his sight, but was endowed with great inward light and with the gift of prophecy. It is related that Totila, wishing to test it, persuaded the bishop's cupbearer to let him proffer the drinking-cup to the blind saint. No sooner had Sabinus grasped the cup than he exclaimed, " Long live that hand ; " and from thenceforth Totila and his courtiers held him to be indeed a prophet. Another occasion on which he displayed this power was when his archdeacon, Vindimus, who was eager to obtain the bishopric, wishing to hasten his death induced the cupbearer to put poison in the old man's cup. St Sabinus said to the youth, " Drink it yourself : I know what it contains ". Then, as the cupbearer started back in terror, the saint took the goblet and drained it, saying, " I will drink this, but the instigator of this crime will never be a bishop ". The poison did him no harm, but his would-be successor died that same hour, in his own house three miles away. St Sabinus died in his fifty-second year, and his body was eventually translated to Bari, where it seems to have been forgotten for a time and rediscovered in 1901. In 1562, the marble altar under which his relics lay was overlaid with silver and an inscription engraved upon it, recording the saint's chief actions.

See the *Acta Sanctorum*, February, vol. ii ; the *Dialogues* of St Gregory, bk ii, ch. 15, and bk iii, ch. 5 ; and Ughelli-Coletus, *Italia Sacra*, vol. x (1722), p. 37.

ST TEILO, BISHOP   (SIXTH CENTURY)

THERE is ample evidence from the manuscript Book of St Chad, church-dedications and the like that St Teilo was a very important man in South Wales in his time,

* Canosa in Apulia (Canusium) is quite a different place from Canossa, not far from Parma, famous in the life of Pope St Gregory VII.

but there are no extant writings about his life till some five hundred years after his death.   Around the year 1130 Geoffrey (Galfridus), a priest of Llandaff, composed a life of Teilo in the form of a sermon ; and what seems to be a longer version of this life, altered to add glory to the see of Llandaff, is contained in the *Liber Landavensis*.

Stripped of obvious accretions and borrowings from the lives of other saints, we are told that Teilo was born near Penally, hard by Tenby in Pembrokeshire, and the earlier form of his name was Eliud.   He was the pupil first of St Dubricius and then of one Paulinus (possibly St Paul Aurelian is meant), with whom he met St David.   Teilo is then made to accompany David on his mythical visit to Jerusalem.   During the yellow plague, so called " because it made everyone it attacked yellow and bloodless ", Teilo with others went abroad, the Book of Llandaff says to Brittany, where he stayed with St Samson at Dol ; and they " planted a big orchard of fruit-trees, three miles long, reaching from Dol to Cai, which is still called after their names ".

After seven years St Teilo returned to Wales, and died eventually at Llandeilo Fawr in Carmarthenshire, where (and not at Llandaff) was certainly his chief monastery and the centre of his ministry.   A dispute concerning the custody of his body arose between Llandeilo, Llandaff and Penally, " on the ground of the burial-place of his fathers being there and of his hereditary rights in the place " ; we need not believe the story that this was settled by the miraculous multiplication of his body to satisfy the three claims.   There is attributed to Teilo a reply to a question put by St Cadoc, " The greatest wisdom in a man is to refrain from injuring another when it is in his power to do so ".

In speaking of charters granted to the see of Llandaff, the *Liber Landovensis* mentions three in what is now Monmouthshire which are of interest.   The first is the grant to Teilo by Iddon ab Ynyr, " king " of Gwent, of his house, formerly belonging to St Dubricius, at Llangarth (Llanarth*), " with all its territory and sanctuary ".   The second is the not far distant Lann Maur, now Llandeilo Pertholey.   The third is also close by.   Here Iddon was faced by a force of marauding Saxons.   He asked the aid of Teilo, who was then at Llanarth.   The saint accompanied him to a hill at Cressinych by the river Trothy, where he stood and prayed to Almighty God " for His people who had been despoiled, and God gave them the victory ".   In gratitude Iddon granted the place to Teilo ; it is now called Llandeilo Crossenny.

Traces of the *cultus* of St Teilo in place-names and church-dedications are abundant all over South Wales, and are also found in Brittany, especially at Landeleau in the diocese of Quimper.   His feast is still observed in the archdiocese of Cardiff and on Caldey island.   Teilo is one of the four saints in whose honour the cathedral of Llandaff is dedicated   the others were Peter the Apostle, Dubricius and Oudoceus.   Nothing certain is known about the last named, who is reputed to have been Teilo's nephew and successor.

The text of the *Book of Llan Dâv* was reproduced and commented on in detail by J. G. Evans in 1893, and the life of St Teilo therein critically edited by J. Loth in *Annales de Bretagne*, t. ix and x (1893).   The best summary is Canon Doble's *St Teilo* (1942).   See also LBS., vol. iv, pp. 226-242, and *Analecta Bollandiana*, vol. xiv, pp. 445 *seq*.   For St Oudoceus (Euddogwy), see Doble's pamphlet.

* Llanarth is one of the few districts in Wales where the Catholic faith has never died out since the Protestant Reformation.

ST ANSBERT, Bishop of Rouen   (*c.* A.D. 695)

ANSBERT of Chaussy was chancellor to King Clotaire III, and in that position combined the recollection of a monk with the duties of a married man and of a statesman (he was at one time engaged to St Angadrisma ; *cf.* her on October 14). Later he took the monastic habit at Fontenelle under St Wandregisilus and, when that holy founder's immediate successor, St Lambert, was made bishop of Lyons, Ansbert was appointed abbot of the famous monastery.   He was confessor to King Theodoric III, with whose consent he was chosen bishop of Rouen upon the death of St Ouen in 684.   By his care, good order, learning and piety flourished in his diocese ; nevertheless Pepin, mayor of the palace, seemingly for some political motive, banished him upon a false accusation to the monastery of Hautmont, on the Sambre in Hainault, where he died.

A good deal of controversy has arisen over the Life of St Ansbert, the best text of which is that edited by W. Levison in MGH., *Scriptores Merov.*, vol. v, pp. 613-643.   Levison considers that the life is not what it claims to be, the work of Aigradus, a contemporary, but that its composition must be assigned to the end of the eighth century or the beginning of the ninth.   With this verdict, as against Vacandard (*Revue des Quest. Histor.*, vol. lxvii, 1900, pp. 600–612), the modern Bollandists agree.   See also Legris in *Analecta Bollandiana,* vol. xvii (1898), pp. 265-306 ; and Duchesne, *Fastes Épiscopaux*, vol. ii, pp. 207-208.

ST ALTO, Abbot   (*c.* A.D. 760)

THIS saint was a monk, probably an Irishman, who found his way into Germany, and about the year 743 established himself as a hermit in a wood near Augsburg. The fame of his holiness and missionary labours reached King Pepin, who made him a grant of land where he was living, and on which he founded a monastery at the place now known as Altomünster, in Bavaria.   Its church was dedicated by St Boniface about the year 750.   The abbey followed the Irish mode of life, and St Boniface wanted entirely to interdict the approach of women to its precincts and church in accordance with the strict Celtic custom.   To this St Alto would not agree, though he included the well blessed by Boniface within the monks' enclosure. After Alto's time the monastery fell on evil days, but was restored in 1000 as a Benedictine house, and still exists as an abbey of Bridgettine nuns.   Nothing further is known of St Alto ; but in the midst of a barbarous nation, at that time overrun with ignorance, vice and superstition, his humility and devotion infused into many the perfect spirit of religion, and his single life was a sensible demonstration of the power of divine grace in raising vessels of weakness and corruption to a state of sanctity.

The Life of St Alto, written by Abbot Othlonus in the middle of the eleventh century, is printed in the *Acta Sanctorum* under February 9, but the text has been re-edited in Pertz, MGH., *Scriptores*, vol. xv, pp. 843-846.   See also M. Huber in *Wissenschaft Festgabe zum Jubilaeum des hl. Korbinian* (1924), pp. 14-44 ; and Gougaud, *Gaelic Pioneers of Christianity,* p. 21.

BD MARIANUS SCOTUS   (A.D. 1088)

THE actual name of Marianus Scotus was Muiredach mac Robartaigh, and he appears to have been born in Donegal.   As a boy he was remarkable for his personal beauty and great strength, as well as for his piety and for the charming simplicity of his manners.   His parents destined him for the priesthood and he early assumed some sort of monastic habit, but without joining any community. With several companions he set out from Ireland in the year 1067, apparently with the intention of ultimately reaching Rome. At Bamberg they were kindly received by Bishop Otto of Regensburg, and under his direction they practised the strictest conventual rule, though still seculars. After a year the bishop, convinced of their vocation, advised them to enter a religious house and they were admitted to the Benedictine monastery of Michelsburg. Though they were very cordially received by the monks, they elected, as they could not speak German, to live apart from the rest, and accordingly a cell at the foot of the mountain was made over to them. There they remained for some time, but they had not forgotten their original intention of making a pilgrimage to Rome. They told the abbot, who, knowing that it was a devout practice very popular with Irishmen, gave them his blessing and a licence to continue on their way.

Upon arrival at Regensburg they were hospitably entertained at the convent of the Upper Monastery and here Marianus, who was a most skilful and industrious scribe, was able to make himself extremely useful to the Abbess Emma by transcribing books for her. His biographer, after speaking of the rapidity with which he wrote, adds : " Among all the acts which Divine Providence deigned to perform through the same person, I deem this the most worthy of praise and admiration that the holy man wrote, from beginning to end, with his own hand, the Old and New Testaments, with explanatory comments on the same books, and this he did not once or twice but repeatedly, with a view to the eternal reward—all the while clad in sorry garb, living on slender diet, attended and aided by his brethren, both in the Upper and Lower Monasteries." From the Upper Monastery he moved to the Lower, where a cell was made over to him and to his brethren, who used to prepare the vellum while he was writing. A remarkable incident was related about Marianus at this period. It was usual to prepare lights for him, as he did much of his work at night. One evening the woman whose duty it was to provide the lights forgot all about them. After she had gone to bed she suddenly remembered her omission and, calling some of her companions, she started to fulfil her duty. They came to the holy man's cell, walking on tiptoes, and then peeped through the chinks of the door. There they saw Marianus busily writing with his right hand whilst from three fingers of his uplifted left hand there proceeded three jets of light which gave an illumination more brilliant than that of many lamps. They told the abbess, and the fame of it spread far and wide. Nevertheless, as the chronicler remarks, Marianus—like Moses—was ever the meekest and humblest of men.

After remaining some time in Regensburg he proposed to resume his journey to Rome, but he first asked the Holy Spirit to make it clear to him whether it was the will of God that he should go or that he should remain where he was. His prayer was answered by a dream, in which he was told to start on his journey but to remain wherever he should first see the sun rise. He therefore got up very early and went to the church of St Peter outside the walls of the town to ask God's blessing, and, as he emerged from the building, the sun rose and he knew that he was to stay in Regensburg. Here he settled down to a life which suited his tastes and talents. He was specially remarkable for his devotion to sacred literature, and not only was he a theologian but he was also a poet. It would not be possible to give a list of all the books he transcribed or wrote probably no record was kept of the smaller books and manual psalters which, we are told, he often wrote and gave away to poor clerics and distressed widows. Early copies of at least two of his codices are still extant, and the great library in Vienna possesses a manuscript containing the Epistles of St Paul (and the apocryphal Epistle to the Laodiceans) which is quite clearly an autograph production of his.   It is written in small delicate letters and has a full marginal commentary with extracts from the fathers and other theological writers—all penned in the same handwriting   and, at the end, Marianus signs, in his mother tongue, his native Christian and family names.   Father Denis, s.j., who was librarian at the close of the eighteenth century, has given an interesting description of this document.

The abbess granted to Marianus the church of St Peter and a plot of land adjoining it, and here he built a house for himself and those of his fellow-countrymen who wished to live under his direction.   In 1078 a burgher named Bezelin built for the Irish, at his own expense, a monastery with a cloister.   The fame of Bd Marianus soon reached his native country, and relations and friends came over to join him   in fact, it was not long before his renown had spread to all parts of Ireland and disciples flocked over from every district, although the six abbots who succeeded him all hailed from the province of Ulster.   This was the origin of the Scottish or Irish monasteries of the south of Germany, some of which afterwards became so celebrated.

See the Life of Marianus in the *Acta Sanctorum*, February, vol. ii ; Rader, *Bavaria Sancta*, vol. ii, pp. 227-228 ; and *Proceedings of the Royal Irish Academy*, vol. vii, pp. 290 *seq.*

10 : ST SCHOLASTICA, Virgin   (A.D. 543)

THIS saint, who was St Benedict's sister, traditionally his twin, consecrated herself to God from her earliest years, as we learn from St Gregory.   It is not known where she lived, whether at home or in a community ; but after her brother had moved to Monte Cassino, she settled at Plombariola in that same neighbourhood, probably founding and ruling a nunnery about five miles to the south of St Benedict's monastery.   St Gregory tells us that St Benedict governed nuns as well as monks, and it seems clear that St Scholastica must have been their abbess, under his direction.   She used to visit her brother once a year and, since she was not allowed to enter his monastery, he used to go with some of his monks to meet her at a house a little way off.   They spent these visits in praising God and in conferring together on spiritual matters.

St Gregory gives a remarkable description of the last of these visits.   After they had passed the day as usual they sat down in the evening to have supper. When it was finished, Scholastica, possibly foreseeing that it would be their last interview in this world, begged her brother to delay his return till the next day that they might spend the time discoursing of the joys of Heaven.   Benedict, who was unwilling to transgress his rule, told her that he could not pass a night away from his monastery.   When Scholastica found that she could not move him, she laid her head upon her hands which were clasped together on the table and besought God to interpose on her behalf.   Her prayer was scarcely ended when there arose such a violent storm of rain with thunder and lightning that St Benedict and his companions were unable to set foot outside the door.   He exclaimed, " God forgive you, sister ; what have you done ? "   Whereupon she answered, " I asked a favour of you and you refused it.   I asked it of God, and He has granted it."   Benedict was therefore forced to comply with her request, and they spent the night talking about holy things and about the felicity of the blessed to which they both ardently aspired and which she was soon to enjoy. The next morning they parted, and three days later St Scholastica died. St Benedict was at the time alone in his cell absorbed in prayer when, lifting up his eyes, he saw his sister's soul ascending to Heaven as a dove. Filled with joy at her happiness, he thanked God and announced her death to his brethren. He then sent some of the monks to fetch her body which he placed in a tomb which he had prepared for himself. " So it happened to these two, whose minds had ever been united in the Lord, that even in the grave their bodies were not separated." But her relics are said to have been translated to France, along with those of St Benedict, in the seventh century and to have been deposited at Le Mans.

We know practically nothing of St Scholastica except from the two chapters of St Gregory's *Dialogues*, bk ii, chs. 33 and 34, summarized above.

ST SOTERIS, VIRGIN AND MARTYR   (A.D. 304)

ST AMBROSE proudly claims this saint as being the greatest honour of his family. Soteris was descended from a long line of consuls and prefects, but she derives her chief glory from the contempt which, for Christ's sake, she evinced for birth, riches, great beauty and all that the world prizes as valuable. She consecrated her maidenhood to God, and to avoid the dangers to which her beauty exposed her she took no account of it, and resolutely forswore all ornaments that might set it off. Her virtue prepared her to make a noble confession of the faith when she was brought before the magistrates after the edicts of Diocletian and Maximian against Christians. When the judge ordered that she should be struck on the face, she rejoiced to be thus treated as her Saviour had been, and though the judge ordered her to be tortured in many other ways he was unable to draw from her one groan or tear. At length, overcome by her patience and constancy, he commanded that her head should be struck off. It must be confessed that we do not clearly know whether all this happened at one time. It may be that St Soteris was arrested and tortured as a young girl in the persecution of Decius, and only suffered death fifty years later under Diocletian.

Practically speaking we are dependent upon two passages of St Ambrose for our knowledge of this martyr. He speaks of her in his *De virginibus*, iii, 7, and in his *Exhortatio virginis*, c. 12. At the same time we know from the " Hieronymianum " that she was originally buried at Rome on the Via Appia. One of the catacombs, the location of which it is difficult to determine, afterwards bore her name. Her body was later on translated by Pope Sergius II to the church of San Martino di Monti. See the *Acta Sanctorum*, February, vol. ii, and the *Römische Quartalschrift*, 1905, pp. 50–63 and 105–133.

ST TRUMWIN, BISHOP OF THE PICTS   (*c.* A.D. 690)

TRUMWIN was in 681 appointed to be bishop over the southern Picts, who were at that time subject to the English. He set up his see at the monastery of Abercorn, on the Firth of Forth. Little is known of St Trumwin's episcopate, and in 685 it came to a violent end when King Egfrid marched against the Picts and was defeated and killed in battle. Whereupon the English who were in the country of the Picts were slain or enslaved or fled south. Among the last were Trumwin and his monks. He dispersed them among various monasteries, and himself retired to the abbey of Whitby. " And there for several years ", says St Bede, " he led a life of monastic austerity with a few of his own people, to the benefit not only of himself but of many others." His relics, with those of the abbess St Elfleda and others, were found and solemnly translated during the twelfth century, but the evidence of *cultus* is slight.

Little is known of St Trumwin apart from what we learn from Bede's *Ecclesiastical History*. There is a notice in the *Acta Sanctorum* for February, vol. ii. The Anglican Bishop G. F. Browne maintained that St Trumwin erected a stone cross at Abercorn, large fragments of which are still in existence : see his book *Theodore and Wilfrith*, pp. 163–164, and *cf.* Howorth, *The Golden Days of the Early English Church*, vol. ii, p. 111 and *passim*. Consult also W. D. Simpson, *The Celtic Church in Scotland*, pp. 42–43 and 108–109.

ST AUSTREBERTA, VIRGIN   (A.D. 704)

ST AUSTREBERTA or Eustreberta was the daughter of one of King Dagobert's foremost courtiers, the Count Palatine Badefrid, and of St Framechildis. She was born near Thérouanne in Artois and was a pious and serious child, her mind set on churches and convents ; one day when she was looking at her reflection in the water she saw a veil over her head : a strange experience which made a permanent impression. When she was growing up her father began to plan a marriage for her, but the idea was so distasteful that she ran away from home, accompanied by a little brother. She found her way to St Omer, and from him she received the veil. However, knowing who she was and what anxiety would be felt concerning her, he persuaded her to let him take her back to her home. Omer explained matters to her parents, who fully recognized that she was now the bride of Christ. After remaining a short time at home, Austreberta began to be tormented by scruples, because she was still living in the world ; so her father consented to allow her to enter the nunnery of Port (afterwards Abbeville) on the Somme.

Here her piety and humility won all hearts ; the community was very observant and devout, and she was extremely happy amongst the nuns. It was told of her that one day when it was her turn to bake the bread for the house, she went to the bakery with a young girl. The oven had been heated, the fire had been taken out, the loaves were all ready, and it only remained to rake out the embers and clean the oven. Suddenly the besom blazed up and set the whole oven on fire. Austreberta, fearing that the bread would be spoilt and that no ordinary measures would be of any use, first shut the door of the bakery and then, leaning unscathed through the flames into the blazing oven, with her wide sleeves cleaned out the interior, extinguishing the flames. She charged the astonished girl, who had been standing out of the way near the door, not to mention the affair, and then quietly went on with her work, without a scorch or a mark on herself or her clothes. The only person she told was a priest. Although he was filled with admiration he said, " Daughter, do not again be so rash, lest next time you may tempt Satan to do you an injury ".

There was living at that time a man called Amalbert who had founded at Pavilly a monastery in which he had placed his daughter Aurea. He consulted St Philibert about it, and the saint advised him to appoint as superior Austreberta, who had already for a long time been abbess of Port. St Austreberta was most unwilling to leave her beloved nuns and perhaps she saw the difficulties ahead, but St Philibert insisted and she gave way. She found her new daughters undisciplined and lax, and she set to work to bring them to a better observance of rule ; but they opposed her, and at last some of them appealed to Amalbert, accusing the saint of various grave offences. He believed the charges, and after an outbreak of violent abuse worked himself into such a rage that he brandished his sword and threatened her. Austreberta remained quite calm and, drawing her veil closer to her throat, bent her neck in anticipation of the fatal blow. Her courage brought him to his senses, and henceforth she was left to rule her nuns in the way she thought fit, though perhaps not till the malcontents had been removed to another house.

The Life of St Austreberta, edited by the Bollandists (*Acta Sanctorum*, February, vol. ii), was probably compiled shortly after her death in the early years of the eighth century. Some few points are further illustrated by a life of her mother, St Framechildis, printed in the *Analecta Bollandiana*, vol. xxxviii (1920), pp. 155–166, from a manuscript in the British Museum. See also DHG., vol. v, cc. 790–792.

ST WILLIAM OF MALEVAL (A.D. 1157)

WE know nothing of the birth or parentage of this saint except that he seems to have been a Frenchman. He is thought to have been a soldier in his youth and to have led a life of dissipation. The first definite accounts we have represent him as a penitent making a pilgrimage to Rome. Here he begged Bd Eugenius III to impose a penance upon him, and the pope enjoined a pilgrimage to Jerusalem. This was in 1145, and the saint spent eight years in performing this and other pilgrimages. Upon his return to Tuscany he hid himself in some lonely spot, until he was prevailed upon to undertake the government of a monastery in the territory of Pisa. However, he found the laxity and irregularity of the monks unbearable, and as he was unable to reform them he withdrew and settled on Monte Pruno. Here he found his disciples no more amenable to discipline than the previous ones, so he determined to lead in solitude the life he had hitherto unsuccessfully proposed to others. For this purpose he fixed upon a desolate valley, the very sight of which was sufficient to daunt the most resolute. It was then called in Latin " Stabulum Rodis ", but has since been known as Maleval: it is situated in the territory of Siena. He entered this solitude in September 1155, and had no lodging but a cave until after some months he was discovered and the lord of Buriano built him a cell. During the first four months he had no company but that of wild beasts, and he ate only the herbs on which they fed. He was joined by a disciple named Albert, who lived with him till his death, which happened thirteen months later: it was Albert who recorded the last events of his life.

St William instructed his disciple in the ways of penance and perfection which he taught him even more effectually by his own example—an example, however, so transcendent that it was rather to be admired than imitated. He had the gift of prophecy and of miracles. A short time before his death a physician called Renaldo came to join them, and he and Albert buried St William's body in the garden. They continued to live according to his rule, and some time after, when others came to swell their little community, they built a chapel over the founder's grave and a hermitage to serve their own needs. This was the origin of the Gulielmites, or Hermits of St William, who afterwards spread over Italy, France, Flanders and Germany; later many of them joined the Augustinian hermit friars.

See the *Acta Sanctorum*, February, vol. ii, and the *Kirchenlexikon*, vol. xii, cc. 1609–1611; BHL., nn. 8922–8923. One of the Lives of St William of Maleval, who is also called " William the Great ", is attributed to Theobald, Archbishop of Canterbury; but the authorship seems very doubtful. *Cf.* Heimbucher, *Die Orden und Kongregationen*, vol. ii (1907), p. 180.

BD HUGH OF FOSSES   (A.D. 1164)

THE Premonstratensian Order has long venerated the memory of him who was in a true sense its second father, and who had undertaken this onerous charge in the lifetime of the founder himself.   Hugh was born at Fosses, about seven miles from Namur.   Becoming an orphan at an early age he was educated by a Benedictine community close at hand, and then passed into the service of a devout and zealous prelate, Burchard, Bishop of Cambrai.   Hugh was in attendance on his patron when the latter unexpectedly met his old friend Norbert, like himself a man of noble birth, but now going barefoot, dressed as a humble penitent, and preaching the gospel of Christ to the poor with wonderful fervour and success.   Hugh was at once captivated and besought the favour of being allowed to join Norbert as his first disciple.   In June 1119, Hugh being already a priest and about twenty-six years old, the two set out to carry on their apostolic work in Hainault and Brabant. Probably St Norbert at this time had no very definite idea of founding a new religious order, but the appeal of Bartholomew, Bishop of Laon, that he should undertake the reformation of a certain community of regular canons, and other circumstances which developed out of this frustrated effort, led to the creation of the monastery of Prémontré, which was followed by the establishment of other houses and the drafting of a religious rule.   Hugh took the initiative in the drawing up of these statutes, for on his shoulders, in the absence of Norbert who was constantly being called away for all sorts of apostolic work, much of the burden fell ; we are in particular told of a great battle with the powers of darkness, which occurred when the elder saint was at a distance.   The Devil, it seems, strove to put to flight the men of God who were converting the uncultivated wilds of Prémontré into a paradise of prayer.

In 1126 St Norbert was consecrated archbishop of Magdeburg, and two years later Hugh by a unanimous vote was elected abbot of the mother house and superior general of the order.   During the thirty-five years which his administration lasted, more than one hundred foundations of the " white canons " came into existence ; but he was now an old man, worn out by austerities and incessant labour, and on February 10, 1164 he passed to his reward.   His remains were interred in the church of Prémontré before the altar of St Andrew, and when in 1279 they were removed to a still more honourable resting-place close to the high altar we are told that the church was flooded with a celestial perfume.   These relics were happily recovered after the first world-war, despite a conflagration which consumed the church in which they were temporarily preserved.   From our fragmentary materials it is not easy to obtain a clear idea of the personal character of Bd Hugh, but he seems to have been an impetuous man who did not always realize that there might be two sides to a question in which he was keenly interested. St Bernard in a long letter addressed to him (No. 253, Migne, PL., vol. clxxxii, cc. 453–458), remonstrates strongly against the bitterness and injustice of certain complaints which Hugh had made in writing.   We do not unfortunately know the response that was returned to St Bernard's vehement but charitable appeal.

The two recensions of the *Vita Sti Norberti*, for one of which Hugh himself has been claimed as the author, constitute our most authentic source of information.   See also such modern lives of St Norbert as those of G. Madelaine (1886) in French, G. van den Elsen (1890) in Flemish, and C. Kirkfleet (1916) in English ; and H. Lamy, *Vie du b. Hugues de*

Fosses (1925). The *cultus* of Hugh was sanctioned by the Holy See in 1927, and the decree, published in the *Acta Apostolicae Sedis* for that year, pp. 316–319, contains a brief summary of his career.

BD CLARE OF RIMINI, WIDOW   (A.D. 1346)

BORN of a rich family in Rimini, Clare Agolanti married young and lived a life wholly given up to frivolity and to the gratification of her senses.   She became a widow, and, owing to party factions, was exiled for a time—returning to see her father and brother perish on the scaffold.   She still continued her careless life and married again.   When she was thirty-four, she entered a Franciscan church one day and heard a voice which said, " Clare, try to say one Pater and one Ave Maria to the glory of God, without thinking of other things".   She began to reflect seriously, and soon afterwards in the same church she had a vision of the Blessed Virgin Mary who spoke to her.   By this she was so much impressed that she resolved henceforth to live only for the world to come, and as a first step in the up-ward path she joined the third order of St Francis.   Her husband allowed her to lead almost the life of a nun, and when he died soon afterwards she gave herself up to austerities.   In place of the jewels she had formerly worn she now had rings of iron round her neck and arms and she also wore an iron cuirass which is still shown at Rimini.   To punish herself for her luxury and sensuality she slept upon rough planks, and, to mortify her fastidious taste, she forced herself at times to eat food from which even the starving would have revolted.   During Lent, she took up her quarters in a hollow in the old city wall and there she lived, exposed to all weathers.

When the Poor Clares from Regno were forced by war to take refuge in Rimini and were in great distress, Clare went begging for them from door to door.   Several women placed themselves under her direction, and with the help of friends she bought the piece of ground about that part of the old wall which contained her cell and built a convent.   She herself did not become professed or enclosed, but continued her works of charity outside.   Owing to the extreme lengths to which she carried her desire for penance she had much opposition to face.   On Good Friday she got people to tie a cord round her neck and, with her hands bound behind her back, she had herself dragged through the streets in imitation of our Lord.   These and similar practices caused even her fellow religious to regard her as unbalanced, and they locked her up to prevent her from resorting to her old haunt in the wall.   She was also accused of heresy, but upon no clear grounds. She tried to go without drinking anything at all in order to experience something of our Lord's thirst on the cross, and she nearly died in consequence.   Once she fell into an ecstasy which lasted five days, during which she was deprived of the power of speech, and for the last few months of her life she seemed to have lost consciousness and sensation : when she came to herself she was blind and could not communicate with anyone.

It is important to remember that the authority and approval of the Church are by no means involved in such extravagances as those we read of in this account of Bd Clare of Rimini.   It is extremely improbable that if such a cause were now introduced for beatification it would successfully pass the tests required by the Congregation of Rites.   She is styled Blessed because from her death onwards she seems to have been venerated locally at Rimini, and after the existence of this *cultus* had been proved by the production of sufficient evidence it was sanctioned and allowed to continue by a decree issued by Pius VI in 1784.   We must also bear in mind that just as the life of St Simeon Stylites on his pillar, and those of his many imitators, undoubtedly did enormously impress his contemporaries, from the emperor downwards, though such an existence would now be regarded even by devout Catholics as crazy ostentation or fanaticism, so the standards of taste in such matters as manifesting contempt of the world's opinion have altered very much since the fourteenth century.

For Clare's life see Mazzara, *Leggendario Francescano* (under Feb. 2), and Léon, *Auréole Séraphique* (Eng. trans.), vol. i, pp. 235-238.

11 : THE APPEARING OF OUR LADY AT LOURDES   (A.D. 1858)

ON February 11, 1858 three little girls, Bernadette Soubirous, aged fourteen, her sister Marie-Toinette, aged eleven, and their friend Jeanne Abadie, aged twelve, started out from their home in Lourdes to pick up wood. To reach a place where, as they had been told, driftwood and broken branches were likely to be found on the bank of the Gave they had to pass in front of a grotto or natural cavity in the rocky cliff of Massabielle which here skirts the course of the river on the south side, and they had first to cross a shallow millstream. The two younger girls made their way over, but exclaimed at the icy coldness of the water. Bernadette who, unlike her companions, wore stockings on account of her delicate health—she was subject to asthma—hesitated to follow their example. When, however, the other two refused to help her to cross, she began to take off her stockings. Suddenly she heard beside her a rustling sound as of a gust of wind. She looked up and saw that the trees on the other side of the river were still, but she seemed to notice some waving of boughs in front of the grotto which she had nearly reached. She paid no further attention and, removing her stockings, had already put one foot into the water when the rustling sound came again. This time she looked intently towards the grotto and saw the bushes violently agitated, and then, in the opening of a niche behind and above the branches, she perceived " a girl in white, no taller than I, who greeted me with a slight bow of the head ". The apparition, she afterwards said, was very beautiful : it was clad in white, with a blue girdle, whilst a long rosary hung over the arm. The figure seemed to the child to invite her to pray, and when Bernadette knelt down and, taking her rosary out of her pocket, began to say it, the apparition also took her rosary in her hand and passed the beads through her fingers, although the lips did not move. No words were exchanged, but at the end of the five decades, the figure smiled, withdrew into the shadow and disappeared. When the other children returned and saw Bernadette on her knees, they laughed at her. Jeanne scolded her for not helping to collect wood, and went away over the rocks on the other side of the grotto, but Toinette said, " You were frightened : did you see anything ? " Bernadette told her, making her promise to say nothing, but she told her mother that evening. Madame Soubirous questioned Bernadette. " You were mistaken . . you saw a white stone."—" No," said the child, " she had a beautiful face." Her mother thought it might be a soul from Purgatory, and forbade her to return to the grotto.

She kept away the next two days, but some children who had heard about the apparition tried to persuade her to go. Madame Soubirous, harassed, sent her to ask advice of the Abbé Pomian, but he paid no attention : the mother then told her to ask her father, who after some demur said she might go. They returned home and, taking a bottle of holy water, they went to the grotto and knelt down to say the rosary. At the third decade " the same white girl showed herself in the same place as before ". To quote Bernadette's own words. " I said, ' There she is,' and put my arm round the neck of one of them and pointed to the white girl, but she saw nothing." A girl called Marie Hillot gave her the holy water and she went forward and threw some towards the vision, which smiled and made the sign of the cross. Bernadette said, " If you come from God, come nearer ". The vision advanced a little. At that moment, Jeanne Abadie with some other children came to the top of the rock above the grotto and threw a stone down which fell near Bernadette. The apparition disappeared, but Bernadette remained kneeling and in a trance, with her eyes upraised. They could not make her move and went to fetch help. The miller Nicolau and his mother with great difficulty pulled her up the hill to his mill where she suddenly came to and cried bitterly. Here quite a crowd collected and her mother began to scold her- ·after which they all returned to Lourdes. Not one of Bernadette's relations nor the nuns who taught her the catechism would, for a moment, believe her story. Others felt sure she had seen a soul from Purgatory.

The third apparition took place on February 18, when a certain Madame Millet and a girl, an " enfant de Marie ", took Bernadette very early to the grotto. They had with them a blessed candle and pen and ink. They knelt down, and when Bernadette said, " There she is ", the young girl handed her the paper and ink. Bernadette said to the figure, " If you come from God, please tell me what you want ; otherwise go away ". As the Lady only smiled, she said, " Please have the goodness to put down in writing your name and what you want " The apparition then spoke for the first time, and said, using the Lourdes *patois*, " There is no need to write what I have to say. Will you do me the kindness to come here every day for a fortnight ? " The figure added, " I do not promise to make you happy in this life, but in the next ", and, rising towards the vault of the niche, she disappeared.

The visions of the next two days passed without any special features, except that Bernadette each day went into a trance of about a quarter of an hour's duration.

On Sunday, February 21, a large number of people accompanied her to the grotto, including Dr Dozous, then a sceptic, who felt her pulse and tested her breathing while she was in the trance. The vision said to her, " You will pray to God for sinners ". After high Mass that day, Bernadette was asked to visit the imperial procurator, J. V. Dutour, who questioned her closely and came to the conclusion that she was sincere, though deluded. After Vespers Dominic Jacomet, commissary of police, sent for her and cross-examined her rather severely, dismissing her with a caution to keep away from the grotto. These officials considered that her conduct was causing a public disturbance, and they realized also that the ground about the grotto was insecure in view of the great crowds that were now assembling there. On the 22nd, Bernadette went again to the grotto in spite of the prohibition. There was a small crowd and two policemen, but on this occasion she did not see the apparition. On the same day, the Abbé Pomian, Bernadette's confessor, decided that since it was not the chief authority, M. Dutour, who had forbidden the child to go, she need not be kept away. On the 23rd, she went to the grotto at six o'clock in the morning, and there was a crowd of two hundred people. She then saw the apparition again, and fell into a trance which lasted nearly an hour. The next day the crowd had increased to four or five hundred, and again Bernadette went into an hour's trance when the vision revealed itself. She refused, however, to divulge anything that the Lady had said to her. On Thursday the 25th, Bernadette, after repeating a decade of the rosary, dragged herself on her knees up the sloping floor of the cave, gently brushing aside the hanging sprays of foliage. At the back of the grotto she turned round and came back—still on her knees—and, after looking inquiringly at the niche, walked to the left of the grotto.* What Bernadette herself related is as follows : The Lady had said to her, " Go, drink at the spring and wash in it ". She did not know of any spring in the rock, so she turned towards the river. The Lady said she did not mean that. " She pointed with her finger, showing me the spring : I went there : I only saw a little dirty water ; I put my hand in, but could not get enough to drink. I scratched and the water came—but muddy. Three times I threw it away, but the fourth time I could drink it." The child was seen to stoop, and when she rose, her face was bedaubed with mud. She again stooped and appeared to eat a little of a bright green plant that grew there. A moment later she rose and returned to Lourdes. The crowd began by scoffing, but they were amazed later in the day when the saucerful of muddy water was seen to be running into the Gave. Within a week, it was pouring forth its 27,000 gallons of water as it does to this day. On February 26, eight hundred persons were present when Bernadette, in a trance, crawled up to the grotto, frequently kissing the ground, and by a gesture appearing to invite others to do the same. The apparition was enjoining penitence.†

The visions of the 27th and 28th followed the same course. The crowd became yet denser. Bernadette repeatedly kissed the ground and the people imitated her. In the afternoon of the latter day, she was brought before a magistrate who cautioned her again. On March 1, the onlookers had increased to 1000, and, for the first time, a priest was present. The curé of Lourdes had decided that he and his four curates must have absolutely nothing to do with the grotto, but the Abbé Dézirat, coming from a distance, was not directly under his jurisdiction. This priest was greatly impressed. A cure took place on this day, but that was not known till months later. On March 2 at 7 a.m. there were 1700 people present when Bernadette saw the apparition for the thirteenth time. She was then bidden to tell the clergy that a chapel should be built and a procession held. Bernadette went to the curé, who received her harshly, and who gave the civil officials to understand that he strongly discouraged the whole business.

March 3 was a day of great disappointment and humiliation for Bernadette. Surrounded by a vast crowd of 4000, she saw no vision and acknowledged her failure. Returning later, when the greater part of the crowd had dispersed, she

---

* There are two openings or niches in the grotto, a higher one, where our Lady's statue now stands, and a sort of tunnel leading up to it. The vision appeared in several places : on the two chief occasions, February 25 and March 25, it was at the lower opening of this " tunnel ", on the ground-floor, as Father Martindale puts it.

† In that year this day, the day on which the spring was first recognized to be a spring, was the second Friday in Lent, on which the gospel at Mass tells of the healing pool at the Sheep Gate (John v 1-15).

saw the vision and fell for a short time into a trance. On March 4, in the presence of a great gathering, there was again the apparition and trance, but no new features. This was the end of the fourteen days, but on March 25—Lady day—Bernadette started for the grotto at four or five in the morning and the Lady appeared and told her to come nearer. Bernadette then asked, " Would you kindly tell me who you are ? " At these words the apparition smiled and made no reply. Bernadette repeated her question twice more, and then the Lady, joining her hands on her breast and raising her eyes to heaven answered, " Que soy era Immaculado Conceptiou ", " I am the Immaculate Conception ".

Then she added, " I want a chapel built here ". Bernadette replied, " I have already told them what you have asked me ; but they want a miracle to prove your wish ". The Lady smiled again, and without another word passed from Bernadette's sight.

The last solemn apparition took place on April 7, when there was again a crowd of people—1200 or 1300. Bernadette remained in a trance three-quarters of an hour or more, and Dr Dozous, who was near her, stated that he saw her lift her hands and hold them arched over the flame of her burning candle which rested on the rock floor. He noticed that the flame played upon her fingers and passed between them without her taking any heed. Not only was she insensible to pain, but there was no destruction of tissue nor was there any mark. When she came out of the trance, he pushed the burning candle under her left hand which she snatched away, exclaiming : " You're burning me ". It must be admitted, however, that Father Cros in his *Histoire de Notre-Dame de Lourdes* (i, 494-499) has given reasons for discrediting this statement. No weight seems to have been attached to it by the episcopal commission which examined and reported on the facts. The eighteenth and final apparition was on July 16, the feast of our Lady of Mount Carmel. The grotto was then barricaded to exclude the public and Bernadette could only see the top of the niche above the planks from the opposite bank of the Gave, and yet the figure seemed no farther off than before. Never again, after this day, had Bernadette Soubirous any vision of our Blessed Lady during the twenty-one years she still remained on earth. To none but her had sight of any of these visions been granted.

On two points connected with the appearances of the Blessed Virgin at Lourdes it seems desirable to add a few words of comment. In the first place, certain unfriendly critics maintained * that these manifestations were organized of set purpose by the clergy at the instigation of the Roman authorities in order to confirm and popularize the dogma of the Immaculate Conception which had been defined by Pope Pius IX less than four years previously. To this it may be replied that the contemporary reports submitted by the local authorities to the prefect of the department and to the minister of the Interior absolutely exonerate the clergy from showing any belief in or sympathy with the alleged apparitions until they had taken profound hold of the people and until the strange coincidence of the discovery and persistence of the new spring had brought crowds to the grotto from all the surrounding country. Again, no one can be blind to the extreme improbability that if the church authorities had designed, as was alleged, to popularize the dogmas of the Vatican, " by appealing to the imagination and superstition of the masses ",

* See particularly the *British Medical Journal* for June 18, 1910, a number which is almost entirely devoted to the question of faith healing and the Lourdes miracles. A long article by Sir Henry Morris speaks strongly in this sense.

they would have selected as the site of the future miraculous shrine a remote spot in the Pyrenees eighty miles from any line of railway. Further, attention may be called to the fact that the subsequent career of the little visionary, Bernadette Soubirous, who upon the hypothesis of an organized imposture must have been the cunning and mendacious tool of some ecclesiastic, contradicts upon every point all the anticipations one would form in such a case. Bernadette had no more visions. She never embroidered with later and more effective enlargements the story which she told at first. She took no pleasure in the attention which was paid to her, and never put it to any sort of pecuniary profit. Shunning all excitement and still retaining the simplicity of a child, Bernadette entered a religious order of nursing sisters in 1866 at the age of twenty-two. She was sent far away from Lourdes to the noviceship of the order at Nevers, and there contentedly remained until her death twelve years later. In all the grand doings of the consecration of the basilica above the grotto and other splendid functions she had no part or share.

Secondly, attention may be drawn to a very notable confirmation of the unique character of Bernadette's visions. During those long visits to the grotto when she remained entranced, her gaze fixed upon the apparition which she beheld so clearly, presenting always an image of grace, reverence and purity which brought tears to the eyes of the rough peasants who looked on, no one ever pretended to see what she saw. There was no contagious hallucination of the crowd, no scenes of disorder, nothing of the extravagance, the cries, the physical contortions which we read of in connection with the *convulsionnaires*, or with so many of the camp-meetings of revivalists. But when the series of Bernadette's visions had quite come to an end, a veritable epidemic of false visionaries set in, which was marked by many repellent features. The reports sent to the prefect by the commissary of the police are explicit upon the point. Some of the visionaries were really pious and well-conducted girls. Marie Courrech in particular, the mayor's housemaid, bore the very highest character. She went on having visions from April to December of the same year and many people believed in her, but the difference between her trances and those of Bernadette was always very marked. Father Cros prints the testimony of an unexceptionable witness of Marie's extravagances. If these extravagances were observable in good and self-respecting young women, it is not surprising that the most preposterous antics were performed by those of indifferent character and by the children of all ages who soon began to see visions in imitation of their elders. The pious townsfolk of Lourdes and the peasants of the surrounding hamlets, now absolutely convinced of the genuineness of the first apparitions at the grotto, were prepared to treat even the youngest of their offspring as channels of divine inspiration. There seems no doubt that these children often did pass into a state of trance, and that some of them at least had real hallucinations. Of the adult " visionaries ", apart from those already mentioned, nearly all seem to have exhibited strange and repellent phenomena, hysterical convulsions, grimaces, contortions, etc. ; while, of course, in many cases, there was the gravest reason to suspect deliberate imposture.

The books on Lourdes are numberless, but, from the historical point of view, that of Fr L. J. M. Cros, *Histoire de Notre-Dame de Lourdes* (1901), 3 vols., is much the most fully documented and the most complete. A more recent work (1935) is that of Fr H. Petitot, *Histoire exacte des apparitions de N.D. de Lourdes*. *Cf.* the note to St. Bernadette on April 16 ; in B. G. Sandhurst's *We Saw Her* (*i.e.* Bernadette), published in 1953, the evidence for the visions is collected, translated and arranged with both critical acumen and deep sympathy.

SS. SATURNINUS, DATIVUS, AND OTHER MARTYRS (A.D. 304)

THE Emperor Diocletian had ordered Christians under pain of death to deliver up the Holy Scriptures to be burnt. This persecution had already raged a whole year in Africa, during which time a certain number of Christians had betrayed the cause of their Master, but many more had defended it with their blood. In Abitina, a city of proconsular Africa, Saturninus, a Christian priest, was celebrating the holy mysteries one Sunday when the magistrates with a troop of soldiers broke in upon them and seized forty-nine men and women. Among them were the priest Saturninus with his four children, namely, Saturninus the younger and Felix, who were both lectors, Mary, who had consecrated herself to God, and Hilarion, a little boy. Besides these the names are recorded of Dativus and another Felix, who were senators, Thelica, Emeritus, Ampelius, Rogatian and Victoria. Dativus and Saturninus with his children headed the procession of captives who were led before the magistrates. When questioned they confessed their faith so resolutely that the very judges applauded their courage. (It made amends for the apostasy of Fundanus, Bishop of Abitina, who had a short time previously yielded up the sacred books to be burnt ; it was recorded, however, that on that occasion a sudden violent storm had extinguished the flames.) The prisoners taken at Abitina were shackled and sent to Carthage, the residence of the proconsul, and during their journey they sang hymns and psalms to God, praising His name and rendering Him thanks.

The proconsul first examined the senator Dativus, asking him who and what he was and whether he had attended the assembly of the Christians. He replied that he was a Christian and worshipped with Christians. The proconsul asked who presided at these meetings and in whose house the assemblies took place, but, without waiting for an answer, ordered that Dativus should be racked to make him confess. Thelica when questioned as to their ringleader replied at once, " The holy priest Saturninus and all of us with him ". Emeritus boldly acknowledged that the assemblies took place in his house, and in reference to the Holy Scriptures said to be kept there replied that he kept them in his heart. In spite of torture they one and all made profession that they were Christians and that they had been present on Sundays at the " collects ", that is to say, the celebration of the liturgy. Women were as brave as men in enduring suffering and in proclaiming Christ. One young girl, named Victoria, distinguished herself particularly. She had been converted when very young and had vowed herself to the Lord, although her pagan parents had insisted upon betrothing her to a young nobleman. To escape from him she had jumped out of a window on her wedding-day and, escaping unhurt, took shelter in a church where she consecrated herself to God. The proconsul, because of her rank and for the sake of her brother who was a pagan, tried hard to induce her to renounce her faith, but she persisted in repeating, " I am a Christian". Her brother Fortunatian undertook her defence and tried to prove that she was a lunatic and that she had been enticed away by the Christians ; but Victoria, fearing lest she might lose the crown of martyrdom, made it clear by the good sense of her answers that she was in her right mind and that she had elected to be a Christian of her own free choice. Asked whether she would like to return with her brother, she said she could acknowledge no fraternal relation with those who did not keep the law of God.

St Saturninus and his children all made a noble confession of faith, including Hilarion, who was little more than a baby. " I am a Christian ", he said, " I have been at the ' collects '.   I went of my own accord ; nobody made me go."   The judge, who was sorry for him, tried to frighten him by threatening him with childish punishments, but the little boy only laughed   Then the governor said, " I will cut off your nose and ears".   Hilarion answered, " You may do it, but anyhow I am a Christian".   When the proconsul ordered them back to prison Hilarion cried out with the others, " Thanks be to God".   It appears that they all died in prison, either from the length of their confinement or from torture and the hardships they had undergone.

The " acts " of these martyrs are undoubtedly genuine, though it seems possible that some recensions of the text have been modified by transcribers in sympathy with the Donatists.   See P. Monceaux, " Les Martyrs Donatistes " in *Revue de l'histoire des religions*, vol. lxviii (1913), pp. 146–192.   The text of the acts will be found in Ruinart ; in the *Acta Sanctorum*, February, vol. ii ; and in Migne, PL., vol. viii, cc. 705–715.

ST LUCIUS, BISHOP OF ADRIANOPLE, MARTYR   (A.D. 350)

ST LUCIUS was raised to the see of Adrianople in Macedonia after the death of St Eutropius, who had been banished to Gaul for preaching against the Arians. Lucius was no less courageous than his predecessor in upholding the divinity of our Lord and he also was exiled.   He returned to his see only to encounter shameful calumnies and to be driven out once more.   He went to Rome to vindicate his innocence and there he met St Paul, Bishop of Constantinople, and the great St Athanasius—both exiles like himself.   After further difficulties and persecution St Lucius and other citizens of Adrianople were arrested because they would not enter into communion with those who had been condemned by the Council of Sardica.   The laymen were beheaded, whilst Lucius, with chains round his neck and handcuffs on his wrists, was carried away into exile, where he died in prison as the result of the treatment he had received.   The fate of his friend made a great impression upon St Athanasius, who, in more than one of his writings, treats of the constancy and courage of St Lucius and the other martyrs of Adrianople.

The story has to be pieced together from the data furnished by St Athanasius, St Hilary, the historian Socrates, etc.   See *Acta Sanctorum*, February, vol. ii ; Hefele-Leclercq, *Conciles*, vol. i, pp. 815 and 826.

ST LAZARUS, BISHOP OF MILAN   (*c.* A.D. 450)

ST LAZARUS became bishop of Milan about the year 449.   The times were troublous, for the Goths were ravaging Italy and were masters of Milan, but although St Lazarus had much to suffer at their hands he ruled his flock prudently and faithfully. St Ennodius includes him in a list of twelve holy bishops of Milan, of whom St Ambrose was the first and most eminent.   Lazarus is chiefly remembered in connection with the Rogationtide litanies which he is said to have been the first to introduce.   To invoke the protection of God at that distressful period, he ordered a three days' fast with processions, litanies and visits to various churches from the Monday to the Wednesday within the octave of the Ascension.   Afterwards, according to the same very questionable authority, St Mamertus introduced these litanies into the diocese of Vienne and changed the date to the three days before Ascension day.   The first Council of Orleans (511) ordered that this observance should be general throughout France, and it spread quickly to England and elsewhere.   Later still, Archbishop Stephen Nardini and St Charles Borromeo did much to encourage and establish this custom at Milan, which continues to the present day. St Lazarus died on March 14, probably in the year 450, after having been bishop eleven years, but his festival is kept on February 11, because saints' days are not celebrated during Lent in the diocese of Milan which, as is well known, follows its own Ambrosian rite.

See the *Acta Sanctorum*, February, vol. ii. That St Mamertus introduced the Rogation days at Vienne is beyond dispute, but there is no trustworthy evidence to establish the claim of St Lazarus to priority.

ST SEVERINUS, ABBOT   (A.D. 507)

THIS St Severinus, a Burgundian, was educated in the Catholic faith at a time when the Arian heresy was very prevalent in that land. He forsook the world in his youth and entered the monastery of Agaunum, which then consisted only of scattered cells. He became abbot and had governed his community wisely for many years when, in 504, Clovis, the first Christian king of France, who had for two years been suffering from a disease which his physicians were unable to cure, sent his chamberlain to conduct the holy man to his court, as he had heard of the wonderful recoveries obtained through his prayers. Severinus took leave of his monks, telling them that he should never see them again in this world. On his journey he healed Eulalius, Bishop of Nevers, who had been for some time deaf and dumb, and he also cured a leper at the gates of Paris. Upon his arrival he immediately restored the king to perfect health by putting on him his own cloak. As St Severinus was returning towards Agaunum, he stayed at Château-Landon in the Gâtinais with two priests who served God in a solitary chapel and who, not knowing who he was, were at once struck by his sanctity. He foresaw his death, which happened there shortly after. The beautiful church of Saint-Séverin in Paris is called after him and not after the hermit of the same name.

In editing for the MGH., *Scriptores Merov.*, vol. iii, pp. 166–183, an abstract of the Life of St Severinus, B. Krusch has shown that the long biography printed in the *Acta Sanctorum*, February, vol. ii, and elsewhere has no historical value of any sort. It was written 300 years after the death of the saint, apparently without any reliable materials. The details given above are probably all imaginary, and there is the gravest reason for thinking that Severinus could never have been either monk or abbot at Agaunum, because according to the biography he died in 507 or 508, and sound documentary evidence seems to show that Agaunum was not founded before 515. See *Analecta Bollandiana*, vol. xxxi (1912), pp. 354–355.

ST CAEDMON   (c. A.D. 680)

CAEDMON is a familiar name in the history of English literature as the herdsman who was "the father of English sacred poetry"; it is less common in lives of the saints, but his feast used to be observed in the abbey of Whitby on February 11 and it is therefore appropriate that he should be included herein. The little that is known of him is found in St Bede's *Ecclesiastical History*, and Bede's own account is too precious to be abbreviated.

"In the monastery [Whitby] of this abbess [St Hilda] there was a certain brother marked in a special way by the grace of God, for he used to make devotional and religious songs; whatever was expounded out of Scripture he soon turned into verse very expressive of fervour and penitence, and that in English, his native tongue. Many people's minds were moved to contempt of the world and desire for the heavenly life by his songs.   After his time others of the English nation attempted to compose religious poems, but none could equal him, for he did not learn the poetic art from men ; rather did he receive the free gift of song by God's grace, so that he could never make a trivial or vain poem but only such as concerned religion and befitting his religious tongue.   As he was a layman till he was well advanced in years, he had never learned anything of versifying ; and so when sometimes at a festive meal men would amuse themselves by singing in turn, he would get up from the table and go home if he saw the harp coming towards him.

" On one occasion he did this and lay down to rest in the stable where he had to take care of the cattle that night.   And as he slept one stood by him, greeted him and, calling him by name, said, ' Caedmon, sing me something '.   ' I cannot sing ', he answered, ' I left the dining-hall and came in here because I could not sing.' Then his visitor replied, ' Nevertheless you can sing to me '.   ' What shall I sing ? ' Caedmon asked.   ' Sing about the creation ', said the other.   Whereupon Caedmon straightway began to sing verses in praise of God the Creator, verses which he had not heard before, the purport whereof was as follows :

' Now must we praise the Maker of the heavenly kingdom,
' the might of God and the thought of his mind,
' the glorious Father of men,
' How he, the Lord everlasting, wrought the beginning of all wonders.
' He, the holy Creator, first fashioned
' the heavens as a roof for the children of earth ;
' then this middle-earth the Master of mankind,
' the Lord eternal, afterwards adorned,
' the earth for men, the Ruler almighty.'

" This is the sense of the words as Caedmon sang them in his sleep, but not their order, for however well composed poetry may be, it cannot be translated literally from one language into another without losing its beauty and loftiness. When he awoke he remembered all he had sung in his dream, and added more of the same kind in words that worthily showed forth God's praise.

" In the morning Caedmon told the headman who was over him about the gift he had received.   He was taken to the abbess, and told again to tell his dream and repeat the verses, so that the many learned men who were present might examine and give their judgement about the origin and nature of the gift of which he spoke. And they all agreed that heavenly grace had been given him by the Lord, and they set before him a passage of sacred history or doctrine, telling him to put it into verse were he able.   Having accepted this task, Caedmon went away, and when he came back the next morning he gave them the passage he had been told to translate, rendered into excellent verse.   Whereupon the abbess, joyfully recognizing the grace of God in the man, told him to leave the world and take the vows of religion ; and when he had been received into the monastery, she and all her people admitted him to the company of the brethren, and gave instructions that he should be taught the whole course of sacred history.*

" So he gave ear to all that he could learn, turning it over in his mind and as it were ruminating like a clean animal ;† then he made most musical verse of it and sang it sweetly to his teachers, so making them his hearers in their turn.   He sang

---

* Whitby was a double monastery.
† *Cf.* Leviticus xi 3.

of the creation of the world, the beginning of man, and all the story of Genesis, the going of the children of Israel out of Egypt, their coming into the promised land, and many other things from Holy Scripture ; the incarnation, passion and resurrection of our Lord, and His going-up into Heaven ; the coming of the Holy Ghost and the teaching of the apostles. Likewise he made many songs about the terrors of the judgement that is to come, the horrible pains of Hell, and the joys of Heaven, and others about the blessings and judgements of God, by all of which he tried to draw men away from sin to stir in them a love of well-doing and perseverance therein. For Caedmon was a very religious man, who himself submitted humbly to monastic discipline and expected others to do likewise ; and so he made a good end.

" The hour of his departure from this life was preceded by fourteen days of sickness, yet of such a kind that he could talk and go about the whole time. The house to which those who were sick and like to die were taken was close by and, on the evening of the night when he should go hence, Caedmon asked the brother attending him there to make ready a place where he might rest. The brother did as he was asked, but wonderingly, for there was as yet no sign of Caedmon's approaching death.

" When he had lain down, Caedmon talked happily and pleasantly for a time with those who were already in the infirmary, and then, it being past midnight, he asked whether the Eucharist was within. ' What need is there of the Eucharist ? ' they replied. ' The time for you to die is not yet come, seeing you talk so merrily with us as if you are in good health.' ' Bring me the Eucharist all the same,' said he. Receiving It into his hand,* he asked whether they were all in charity with him and had no complaint against him nor any quarrel or grudge. They answered that they were in perfect charity with him and without any anger ; and they in turn asked him to be of the same mind towards them. To which he answered at once, ' My children, I am in charity with all the servants of God '. Then he strengthened himself with the heavenly viaticum and prepared for entrance into another life. He asked how near it was to the time when the brethren should be awakened to sing the nightly praises of the Lord, and they answered, ' It is not far off '. ' It is well ; let us wait for that hour ', he said. Then he signed himself with the sign of the holy cross and laid his head on the pillow ; and so, falling asleep for a little while, Caedmon ended his life in quietness.

" Thus it was that he who had served the Lord with a simple and pure mind and quiet devotedness passed equally quietly from the world to behold His presence. And that tongue which had uttered so many wholesome words in praise of the Creator spake its last words also in His praise, while he signed himself with the cross and commended his spirit into His hands. And, from what has been said above, Caedmon seems to have had foreknowledge of his death."

Thus, with his usual care, delicate appreciation and living touches, wrote St Bede about fifty years later at the abbey of Wearmouth. This monastery was only some fifty miles from Whitby, so he was well placed to have informed himself as exactly as might be.

It was for long supposed, naturally enough, that the long scriptural poems, " Genesis " and the rest, in the Bodleian manuscript Junius 11, were the poems of Caedmon referred to by St Bede ; but it is now recognized that this attribution is

---

* The custom of receiving the sacred host directly into the mouth was not yet general in the Western church at this date.

impossible.   They belong to at least a generation later.   The same is true of the
" Dream of the Rood " (though it is earlier), parts of which are inscribed on the
Ruthwell cross in Annandale in Dumfriesshire.   So the only authentic fragment
of St Caedmon's verse that survives—" possibly the oldest surviving piece of
English poetry composed on English soil "—is the few lines preserved in Bede's
Latin, of which a version is given above.   The Old English translation of Bede's
Ecclesiastical History, made not by but under the direction of King Alfred, gives
a West-Saxon version of them, and an eighth-century manuscript at Cambridge
includes a Northumbrian rendering that may possibly be Caedmon's own words.

" The advent of Caedmon ", wrote the Rev. Charles Hole in the *Dictionary
of Christian Biography*, " must have been hailed by the Christian teachers much as
if a native Milton were in our days to arise in some Hindu or Chinese mission to
propagate the truth among his countrymen whom the preacher could not reach."

Bede's *Ecclesiastical History*, bk iv, c. 24.   See also the *Cambridge History of English
Literature*, vol. i, edited by F. W. Bateson (1940) ; Lingard's *Anglo-Saxon Church* (1852) ;
Hodgkin's *History of the Anglo-Saxons* (1939).   The West-Saxon " Bede " has been printed
among the publications of the Early English Text Society.   The name " Caedmon " cannot
be explained in English ; it has been conjectured that it is an adaptation of the British Celtic
name " Catumanus ".

ST GREGORY II, Pope   (A.D. 731)

THIS Gregory was born in Rome, and being conspicuous for his piety and regular
observance Pope St Sergius I ordained him subdeacon.   Under the four succeeding
popes he was treasurer of the church and afterwards library-keeper and was charged
with several important commissions.   So great was his wisdom and learning that
he was chosen to accompany Pope Constantine to Constantinople when he was
summoned there to discuss with the Emperor Justinian II certain difficulties and
differences which had arisen from the Council *in Trullo* in 692.   Upon the death
of Constantine, Gregory was chosen pope and consecrated in 715.

With unwearied zeal and watchfulness he laid himself out to extirpate heresies
on all sides and to bring about a reformation of manners.   He held synods in which
regulations were made to enforce discipline, to promote morality and to check
abuses of all kinds.   He re-erected a great part of the walls of Rome against the
Lombards, rebuilt and restored many churches, and was very solicitous for the
sick and aged.   Besides a hospital for old men, he rebuilt the great monastery near
the church of St Paul in Rome, and, after the death of his mother in 718, he converted her house into the monastery of St Agatha.   He helped to re-establish the
abbey of Monte Cassino, to which he sent the abbot St Petronax to take upon him
the government, one hundred and forty years after it had been laid in ruins by the
Lombards.   St Gregory commissioned missionaries to preach the faith of Christ
in Germany, consecrating St Corbinian and St Boniface bishops, and under
him the English pilgrims in Rome increased to the point of requiring a
church, a cemetery and a school of their own there.

Perhaps, however, it was in his dealings with the Emperor Leo III that Gregory
most fully displayed his strength and magnanimity.   Leo ordered the destruction
of holy images and enforced the execution of his edicts by a cruel persecution.   St
Germanus and other prelates in the East endeavoured to convince him, but finding
him obdurate they refused to obey, and appealed to the pope.   Gregory long
continued to use entreaties and arguments, and yet all the time strenuously en-

couraged the people of Italy to maintain their allegiance to their prince. When rebellions arose in Sicily, Ravenna and Venice he effectually opposed them; on the other hand, by his letters he encouraged the pastors of the Church to resist the heresy which the emperor endeavoured to establish by violence. St Gregory II was pope for fifteen years, dying in 731.

The sources for the life of Pope Gregory II are very fully indicated in H. K. Mann's *Lives of the Popes*, vol. i, pt. 2, pp. 141-142. The *Liber Pontificalis*, Paul the Deacon, Bede, Theophanes and Andrea Dandolo, together with John the Deacon (Sagorninus) and the letters of St Boniface, are the most important.

ST BENEDICT OF ANIANE, Abbot   (A.D. 821)

BENEDICT was the son of Aigulf of Maguelone and served King Pepin and his son, Charlemagne, as cupbearer. At the age of twenty he made a resolution to seek the kingdom of God with his whole heart. He took part in the campaign in Lombardy, but, after having been nearly drowned in the Tesino, near Pavia, in endeavouring to save his brother, he made a vow to quit the world entirely. Upon his return to Languedoc he was confirmed in his determination by the advice of a hermit called Widmar, and he went to the abbey of Saint-Seine, fifteen miles from Dijon, where he was admitted as a monk. He spent two and a half years here learning the monastic life and bringing himself under control by severe austerities. Not satisfied with observing the Rule of St Benedict, he practised those other points of perfection which he found prescribed in the Rules of St Pachomius and St Basil. When the abbot died, the brethren were disposed to elect him to fill the post, but he was unwilling to accept the charge because he knew that the monks were opposed to anything in the shape of systematic reform.

Benedict accordingly quitted Saint-Seine and, returning to Languedoc, built a small hermitage beside the brook Aniane upon his own estate. Here he lived for some years in self-imposed destitution, praying continually that God would teach him to do His will. Some solitaries, of whom the holy man Widmar was one, placed themselves under his direction, and they earned their livelihood by manual labour, living on bread and water except on Sundays and great festivals when they added a little wine or milk if it was given them in alms. The superior worked with them in the fields and sometimes spent his time in copying books. When the number of his disciples increased, Benedict left the valley and built a monastery in a more spacious place. So much did he love poverty that for a long time he used chalices of wood or glass or pewter in celebrating Mass, and if valuable silk ornaments were given him he bestowed them upon other churches. However, he afterwards changed his mind on this point, and having built a cloister and a stately church adorned with marble pillars, he furnished it with silver chalices and rich ornaments and bought a number of books. In a short time he had many religious under his direction, and at the same time exercised a general inspection over all the monasteries of Provence, Languedoc and Gascony, becoming eventually the director and overseer of all the monasteries in the empire; he reformed many with little or no opposition. One of the chief of those which came under his influence was the monastery of Gellone, founded by St William of Aquitaine in 804.

In order to have him close at hand, the Emperor Louis the Pious obliged Benedict to dwell first at the abbey of Maurmünster in Alsace and then, as he wanted him yet nearer, he built a monastery upon the Inde, later known as Cornelimünster, two leagues from Aachen, the residence of the emperor and court.　Benedict lived in the monastery yet continued to help in the restoration of monastic observance throughout France and Germany.　He was the chief instrument in drawing up the canons for the reformation of monks at the council of Aachen in 817, and presided in the same year over the assembly of abbots to enforce the restoration of discipline. His statutes, the *Capitula* of Aachen, were annexed to the Rule of St Benedict and imposed on all monks throughout the empire.　Benedict also wrote the *Codex Regularum* (Code of Rules), a collection of all the monastic regulations which he found extant ; he likewise compiled a book of homilies for the use of monks, collected from the works of the fathers ; but his most important work was the *Concordia Regularum*, the Concord of Rules, in which he gives those of St Benedict of Nursia in combination with those of other patriarchs of monastic observance to show their similarity.　This great restorer of monasticism in the West, worn out by mortifications and fatigues, suffered much from continual sickness in the latter part of his days.　He died at Inde with great tranquillity in 821, being then seventy-one years of age.

Great as was the energy and the influence of St Benedict of Aniane it must be admitted that his scheme for a peaceful revolution in the monastic life could not be carried into effect as he had planned it.　According to Edmund Bishop, the general idea of Benedict and of his patron the Emperor Louis was this : All houses were to be reduced to an absolute uniformity of discipline, observance, even of habit, according to the pattern of Inde ; visitors were to be appointed to see that the constitutions were strictly observed.　The new scheme was to be launched at the meeting of abbots at Aachen in 817.　But to plan is one thing, Mr Bishop goes on,

> to carry into effect another.　It is clear that in the general assembly of abbots, Benedict, backed as he was by the emperor, had to give up, for the sake of peace and in order to carry through substantial reforms, many details of observance by which he set great store.　His biographer and friend Ardo, too, who knew everything by personal observation and at first hand, in a roundabout way and darkly gives this to be understood.　But the decrees of this meeting of Aachen, of which Benedict was as well the author as the life and soul, were a turning-point in the history of the Benedictines, forming the basis of later legislation and practice.　After the great founder himself, Benedict of Nursia, no man has more widely affected Western monasticism than did the second Benedict, he of Aniane (*Liturgica Historica*, 1918, pp. 212–213).

Few English scholars had a better right to form an opinion on the monastic history of the ninth century than Edmund Bishop, and these words of his form a notable tribute to the work which the great monastic reformer achieved ; but, as Dom David Knowles has pointed out, his influence was quite different from that of Benedict of Nursia : " Benedict of Aniane has never been a spiritual guide for monks."

The primary authority for the life of St Benedict is the Latin biography by his disciple and friend Ardo.　The best text is that in the MGH., *Scriptores*, vol. xv.　See also the *Acta Sanctorum*, February, vol. ii ; DCB., vol. i, pp. 305–308 ; Hauck, *Kirchengeschichte Deutschlands*, vol. ii, pp. 528 *seq.* ; P. J. Nicolai, *Der Hl. Benedikt Gründer von Aniane ;* J. Narberhaus, *Benedikt von Aniane* (1930) ; W. Williams in the *Downside Review*, vol. liv (1936), pp. 357–374 ; J. Winandy in *Mélanges bénédictins* (1947), pp. 235–258 ; and D. Knowles, *The Monastic Order in England* (1949), pp. 25–30.

ST PASCHAL I, POPE   (A.D. 824)

PASCHAL, a Roman, abbot of St Stephen's on the Vatican, was elected pope on the very day of his predecessor's death. He straightway informed the Emperor Louis of his election, and the " pact of confirmation " which he received in return is the first of which the text is known. During this pontificate the iconoclast persecution was going on again in Constantinople under the Emperor Leo V, the chief defenders of orthodoxy being the patriarch, St Nicephorus, and the abbot of the monastery of Studius, St Theodore. The last-named in particular appealed to the pope, as representative of St Peter—" You have received the keys. . . . You are the rock. . ."—to come to their aid. Paschal sent legates and received a warm letter of thanks from the imprisoned Theodore ; but the legates achieved nothing. Many Greek monks fled to Rome and the pope put St Praxedis and other monasteries at their disposal.

Paschal I was very active in church building and decoration, and he translated the relics of numerous martyrs (including St Cecily) from the catacombs to the city ; in the apse of Santa Maria della Navicella may still be seen the small portrait of himself in mosaic, kneeling at the feet of our Lady, which he had put there.

In the year 823 two papal officials, who had sided against the pope in a dispute with some secular nobles, were murdered, and Pope Paschal was accused of having instigated the crime. He cleared himself by a solemn oath, but refused to hand over the criminals (members of his household), on the grounds that secular courts had no jurisdiction over them and that their crime was treason, which put them beyond the pale of the law. But when Pope Paschal died shortly afterwards, in 824, the Romans would not allow him to be buried with the usual honours in St Peter's—they apparently still believed he had been mixed up in the murder ; so he was laid to rest in the church of St Praxedis, " in the place which he had built for the purpose in his lifetime ".

The *Liber Pontificalis* contains little but a record of the pope's building operations and benefactions. For his history we have to turn to the scanty correspondence preserved to us, and to the chroniclers. There has not, of course, ever been any question of a formal canonization, and the grounds upon which Pope Paschal's name has been included in the Roman Martyrology are somewhat obscure. There is a notice devoted to him in the *Acta Sanctorum*, May, vol. iii ; but see especially H. K. Mann, *Lives of the Popes*, vol. ii, pp. 122–135.

12 : THE SEVEN FOUNDERS OF THE SERVITE ORDER
(THIRTEENTH CENTURY)

IT was between the years 1225 and 1227 that seven young Florentines joined the Confraternity of the Blessed Virgin—popularly known as the " Laudesi " or Praisers. It was at a period when the prosperous city of Florence was being rent by political factions and distracted by the heresy of the Cathari : it was also a time of general relaxation of morals even where devotional practices were retained. These young men, members of the most prominent families of the city, had from their childhood been occupied more with spiritual than with temporal affairs and had taken no part in local feuds. Whether they were all friends before they joined the Laudesi is not clear, but in that confraternity they became closely allied, and all seven grew daily more detached from the world and more devoted to the service of the Blessed Virgin. The eldest of them was Buonfiglio Monaldo, who became their leader, and the others were Alexis Falconieri, Benedict dell' Antella, Bartholomew Amidei, Ricovero Uguccione, Gerardino Sostegni, and John Buonagiunta. They had as their spiritual director James of Poggibonsi, who was chaplain of the Laudesi, a man of great holiness and spiritual insight. All of them came to realize the call to a life of renunciation, and they determined to have recourse to our Lady in their perplexity. On the feast of the Assumption, as they were absorbed in prayer, they saw her in a vision, and were inspired by her to withdraw from the world into a solitary place and to live for God alone. There were difficulties, because, though three of them were celibates, four had been married and had ties, although two had become widowers. It was necessary to make suitable provision for their dependants ; but that was arranged, and with the approval of the bishop they withdrew from the world and betook themselves to a house called La Carmarzia, outside the gates of Florence, twenty-three days after they had received their call. Their aim was to lead a life of penance and prayer, but before long they found themselves so much disturbed by constant visitors from Florence that they decided to withdraw to the wild and deserted slopes of Monte Senario, where they built a simple church and hermitage and lived a life of almost incredible austerity.

In spite of difficulties, visitors sometimes found their way to the hermits and many wished to join them, but they refused to accept recruits. So they continued to live for several years, until they were visited by their bishop, Ardingo, and Cardinal Castiglione, who had heard much about their sanctity. He was greatly edified, but he made one adverse criticism. " Your mode of life ", he said, " is too much like that of the wild creatures of the woods, so far as the care of the body is concerned. You treat yourselves in a manner bordering on barbarity : and you seem more desirous of dying to time than of living for eternity. Take heed : the enemy of souls often hides himself under the appearance of an angel of light. . . Hearken to the counsels of your superiors." The seven were deeply impressed by these words and hastened to ask their bishop for a rule of life. He replied that the matter was one that called for prayer, and he entreated them not to continue to refuse admittance to those who sought to join them. Again the solitaries gave themselves up to prayer for light, and again they had a vision of our Lady, who bore in her hand a black habit while an angel held a scroll inscribed with the title of Servants of Mary. She addressed them and said she had chosen them to be her servants, that she wished them to wear the black habit, and to follow the Rule of St Augustine. From that date, April 13, 1240, they were known as the Servants of Mary, or Servites. In accepting this rule, the Seven Founders found themselves called upon to adopt a different kind of life—much to the satisfaction of their old friend the Bishop of Florence. James of Poggibonsi, who had followed them, resolved to join them, and they were clothed by the bishop himself, Buonfiglio being elected their superior. According to custom they selected names by which they should thenceforth be known, and became Brothers Bonfilius, Alexis, Amadeus, Hugh, Sostenes, Manettus and Buonagiunta. By the wish of the bishop, all except St Alexis, who in his humility begged to be excused, prepared to receive holy orders, and in due time they were fully professed and ordained priests. The new order, which took a form more like that of the mendicant friars than that of the monastic orders, increased amazingly, and it soon became necessary to form fresh houses. Siena, Pistoia and Arezzo were the first places chosen, and afterwards the houses at Carfaggio, the convent and church of the Santissima Annunziata in Florence, and the convent at Lucca were established. Meanwhile, although the Servites had the approval of their immediate superiors, they had not been recognized by the Holy See. Again and again efforts were made to obtain recognition for them, but difficulties were raised by those who desired to see the new order abolished or absorbed in another. The Council of the Lateran had declared that no new orders should be founded, and later on the Council of Lyons had added further limitations, and therefore each time the petition of the Servites came before the pope it was set aside or ignored. It was only in 1259 that the order was practically recognized by Alexander IV, and not till 1304—over sixty years after its foundation—that it received the explicit and formal approbation of Bd Benedict XI. St Bonfilius had remained as prior general until 1256, when he begged to be relieved owing to old age. He died a beautiful death in the midst of a conference of his brethren on new year's night, 1261. St Buonagiunta, the youngest of the seven, was the second prior general, but not long after his election he breathed his last in chapel while the gospel of the Passion was being read. St Amadeus ruled over the important convent of Carfaggio, but returned to Monte Senario to end his days. St Manettus became fourth prior general and sent missionaries to Asia, but he retired to make way for St Philip Benizi, upon whose breast he died. St Hugh and St Sostenes went abroad—Sostenes to Paris and Hugh to found convents in Germany. They were recalled in 1276, and, being attacked by illness, they passed away side by side the same night. St Alexis, the humble lay-brother, outlived them all, and he was the only one who survived to see the order fully and finally recognized. He is reported to have died at the age of one hundred and ten.

There is a certain lack of precise information regarding the early history of the Seven Holy Founders. A short chronicle by Peter of Todi and the reminiscences of Father Nicholas Mati seem to constitute the nearest approach to contemporary sources. The *Annales Sacri* of Giani, continued by Garbi, are not very reliable for the beginnings of the order. The *Histoire des Sept Saints Fondateurs de l'Ordre des Servites de Marie*, by Father Ledoux (1888), has been translated into English. They were numbered among the saints by Pope Leo XIII in 1887.

ST MARINA, Virgin (No Date)

A CERTAIN man of Bithynia named Eugenius, having been left a widower, retired into a monastery and became a monk. After a time he became much oppressed by the memory of his little daughter, Marina, whom he had left in the care of a relative, and, having represented to his abbot that the child was a boy, named Marinus, he obtained his permission to bring " him " to live in the monastery. Here she was dressed as a boy, and passed as such, and lived with her father until he died, when Marinus was seventeen. She continued to live as a monk and was often employed to drive a cart down to the harbour to fetch goods. From time to time it was necessary to pass the night at an inn by the quay, and when the innkeeper's daughter was found to be pregnant, the handsome and attractive Marinus was accused of being her seducer.

When word was brought to the abbot he taxed Marinus with the charge, and " he " would not deny it; whereupon " he " was dismissed from the monastery and lived as a beggar at its gates. And when the innkeeper's daughter had weaned her boy, she brought him to Marinus and contemptuously told " him " to look after " his " child. This also Marinus suffered in silence, looking after the boy and bearing " his " shame in the face of all who passed by. After five years the abbot, at the intercession of the monks, who were impressed by this example of patience and humiliation, re-admitted Marinus and the boy to the monastery, but imposing on " him " severe penance and all the lowliest offices of the house.

But very soon after Marinus died, and when the brethren came to prepare the body for burial, its sex was discovered. The abbot was overcome with remorse at the injustice which he had unwittingly committed and with admiration for the heroism of the woman. Marina was buried with respect and lamentation, and the girl who had falsely accused her became possessed, and was released only on confessing her sin and calling upon Marina for her intercession in Heaven.

The story of this Marina, whose name appears in Greek menologies on February 12, is simply one of those popular romances of women masquerading as men of which the " lives " of SS. Apollinaris, Eugenia, Euphrosyne, Pelagia of Jerusalem and Theodora of Egypt are other examples.

For the texts of the Marina legend see L. Clugnet, *Vie et office de Ste Marine* (1905), reprinted from the *Revue de l'Orient chrétien*, Migne, PG., vol. cxv, pp. 348 *seq.*, and also the *Acta Sanctorum*, July, vol. iv. To determine the precise sequence in the tangle of plagiarisms referred to above is by no means an easy task Delehaye has discussed the matter at some length in his *Legends of the Saints*, pp. 197-206. He is of opinion that the starting-point in this group of imaginary saints was a sort of pious romance on the repentance of Pelagia ", which purported to be written by a certain James and was founded on an incident related in a sermon of St John Chrysostom. It will be noted, of course, that Marina is nothing but a Latin rendering of the Greek name Pelagia.

ST JULIAN THE HOSPITALLER　　(No Date)

ON January 27 herein reference is made under the heading, " Julian, Bishop of Le Mans ", to another St Julian known as " the Hospitaller " It is barely possible to regard the story told of him as anything but pure romance, but a strange confusion has grown up among the different St Julians, and it is very hard to disentangle the few grains of authentic fact which may possibly belong to the lives of one. or other of them. Even in the fifteenth century the difficulty was recognized, and Caxton's version of the *Golden Legend*, from which we may conveniently borrow the traditional story of " the Hospitaller ", begins by introducing us to at least three other Julians. The first was the bishop of Le Mans already mentioned, and we are told of him that some say that he was no other than Simon the leper whom our Lord healed of " meselry " (leprosy) and who " bad Jhesu Cryst to dyner ". For this reason, the writer further states, many people identify him also with the saint whom pilgrims and wayfaring men invoke for good " herborowe " (harbouring), " because our Lord was lodged in his house " ; but our medieval critic thinks this less probable. Then there was another St Julian " born in Almane (Germany) whiche was of noble lynage, and yet more noble in faythe and in vertu." This saint was a martyr and " ete never no moton ", and consequently when after his death an unprincipled cleric stole the white sheep which belonged to the church of which he was patron, he interfered in ways which the culprit found extremely disagreeable. Yet a third St Julian was " broder to one named Julie ". They were martyrs together and worked many miracles after their death, one or two of which are recounted in detail. But the Julian to whom most space is accorded is the Hospitaller " who slew his father and mother by ignorance ". His story, modernizing the spelling, is recounted thus :

"This man was noble and young and gladly went for to hunt. And on a time among all other he found a hart which returned towards him and said, 'Thou huntest me and shalt slay thy father and mother.' Hereof was he much abashed and afeared. And for dread that it should not happen to him which the hart had said to him, he went privily away so that no man knew thereof and found a prince noble and great to whom he put him in service; and he proved himself so well in battle and in services in his palace, and he was so much in the king's grace that he made him knight, and gave to him a rich widow of a castle and for her dower he received the castle. And when his father and his mother knew that he was thus gone, they put them in the way for to seek him in many places. And so long they went until they came to the castle where he dwelt, but then he was gone out and they found his wife. And when she saw them she inquired diligently who they were; and when they had said and recounted what was happened of their son, she knew verily that they were the father and mother of her husband and received them most charitably and gave to them their own bed, and made another for herself.

"And on the morrow the wife of Julian went to the church, and her husband came home whilst she was at the church. And entering into his own chamber for to awake his wife, he saw twain in his bed. And as he weened it was a man that had lain with his wife he slew them both with his sword. And after that he went out and saw his wife coming from the church. Then was he much abashed and demanded of his wife who they were tnat lay in his bed. Then she said that they were his father and his mother which had long sought him and she had them to lie in his bed. Then he swooned and was almost dead, and began to weep bitterly and to cry aloud, 'Alas! caitiff that I am, what shall I do that have slain my father and my mother? Now is that very thing happened which I supposed I had eschewed.' And he said to his wife, 'Adieu and farewell, my right dear love; I shall never rest till that I have knowledge if God will pardon and forgive me this that I have done and that I shall have worthy penance therefore.' And she answered, 'Right dear love, God forbid that ye should go without me; like as I have had joy with you, so will I have pain and heaviness.

"Then departed they and journeyed till they came to a great river over which much folk passed; where they edified an hospital for to harbour poor people, and they did their penance in bearing men over that would pass. After long time, St Julian slept about midnight, sore travailed, and it was freezing and much cold, and he heard a voice lamenting and crying, that said, 'Julian, come and help us over.' And anon he arose and went over and found one almost dead for cold. Anon he took him and bore him to the fire and did great labour to chafe and warm him. And when he saw that he could not be chafed nor warmed, he bore him into his bed and covered him in the best wise he might. And anon after, this man that was so sick and appeared as he had been meselle (a leper), he saw all shining ascending into Heaven. And he said to St Julian, his host, 'Julian, our Lord hath sent me to thee, and sendeth thee word that He hath accepted thy penance.' And a while after, St Julian and his wife rendered unto God their souls and departed out of this world."

This is the legend of St Julian, which undoubtedly was extremely popular in the middle ages. Many hospitals were, and some still are, dedicated to him, especially in the Netherlands. A number of scenes from the legend are represented in one of the stained-glass windows of Rouen Cathedral, which seems to have been put up by the guild of ferrymen in that city. Innkeepers, travellers and boatmen all placed themselves under his protection.   No very constant emblem seems to be associated with St Julian the Hospitaller, but he is often represented with a stag, or with a boat, acting as ferryman.

It would be difficult to date the origin of this romance.   It is in the *Legenda Aurea* of Bd James Voragine, and the Bollandists print the version of the story found in St Antoninus of Florence, dealing with the subject on January 29.   But the legend is certainly older than either Voragine or Antoninus ; being found, for example, in Vincent of Beauvais.   Consult the most valuable article, including an unpublished *vita*, by Fr B. de Gaiffier in *Analecta Bollandiana*, vol. lxiii (1945), pp. 144–219.   There is a considerable literature connected with this St Julian.   See, *e.g.* Gustave Flaubert, *La légende de St Julien l'Hospitalier* (1874), and A. M. Gossez, *Le St Julien de Flaubert* (1903).

ST MELETIUS, ARCHBISHOP OF ANTIOCH   (A.D. 381)

MELETIUS belonged to one of the most distinguished families of Lesser Armenia, and was born at Melitene.   His sincerity and kindly disposition gained for him the esteem of both Catholics and Arians, and he was promoted to the bishopric of Sebastea.   However, he met with such violent opposition that he left it and retired, first into the desert and afterwards to Beroea in Syria, a town of which Socrates supposes him to have been bishop.   The church of Antioch had been oppressed by the Arians ever since the banishment of Eustathius in 331, several succeeding bishops having fostered the heresy.   Eudoxus, the last of these, though an Arian, was expelled by a party of Arians in a sedition and shortly afterwards usurped the see of Constantinople.   The Arians and some Catholics then agreed to raise Meletius to the chair of Antioch, and the emperor confirmed their choice in 361, although other Catholics refused to recognize him, as they regarded his election as irregular on account of the share which the Arians had taken in it.   The Arians hoped that he would declare himself of their party, but they were undeceived when, on the arrival in Antioch of the Emperor Constantius, he was ordered with several other prelates to expound the text in the Book of Proverbs concerning the wisdom of God : " The Lord hath created me in the beginning of His ways ".   First George of Laodicea explained it in an Arian sense, then Acacius of Caesarea gave it a meaning bordering on the heretical, but Meletius expounded it in the Catholic sense and connected it with the Incarnation.   This public testimony angered the Arians, and Eudoxus at Constantinople persuaded the emperor to banish Meletius to Lesser Armenia.   The Arians gave the see to Euzoius, who had previously been expelled from the Church by St Alexander, Archbishop of Alexandria.   From this time dates the famous schism of Antioch, although it really originated with the banishment of St Eustathius about thirty years before.

The complex events of the next eighteen years, during which St Meletius was several times exiled and recalled, are a matter of general ecclesiastical history.   The fortunes of orthodox and of Arians, of Meletius and of other claimants to the Antiochene see, ebbed and flowed, largely according to the policies and views of the reigning emperors ; and some prelates and others were only too ready " to accommodate their opinions to those invested with supreme authority ", as the historian Socrates put it.   The death of the Emperor Valens in 378 put an end to the Arian persecution, and St Meletius was reinstated ; but his difficulties were not at an end, for there was another orthodox hierarch, Paulinus, recognized by many as bishop of Antioch.

In 381 the second oecumenical council assembled at Constantinople, and St

Meletius presided ; but while the council was yet sitting death took this long-suffering bishop, to the great grief of the fathers and the Emperor Theodosius who had welcomed him to the imperial city with a great demonstration of affection, " like a son greeting a long-absent father " By his evangelical meekness Meletius had endeared himself to all who knew him. Chrysostom tells us that his name was so much venerated that his people in Antioch gave it to their children ; they cut his image on their seals and on their plate, and carved it on their houses. His funeral in Constantinople was attended by all the fathers of the council and the faithful of the city. One of the most eminent of the prelates, St Gregory of Nyssa, delivered his funeral oration. He refers to the dead man's " sweet calm look and radiant smile, the kind hand seconding the kind voice " ; and closes with the words, " He now sees God face to face and prays for us and for the ignorance of the people ". Five years later St John Chrysostom, whom St Meletius had ordained deacon, pronounced his panegyric on February 12—the day of his death or of his translation to Antioch. His panegyrics by St Gregory of Nyssa and Chrysostom are still extant.

See the *Acta Sanctorum*, February, vol. ii ; BHG., p. 91 ; DCB., vol. iii, pp. 891-893 ; Hefele in the *Kirchenlexikon* ; and H. Leclercq in the *Catholic Encyclopedia*, vol. x, pp. 161–164.

ST ETHELWALD, Bishop of Lindisfarne (*c.* A.D. 740)

St Ethelwald was one of St Cuthbert's assistants, and he became first of all prior and then abbot of Old Melrose in Scotland. There he proved himself to be a man of great ability and piety, and when Eadfrith, Bishop of Lindisfarne or Holy Island, died in 721, St Ethelwald was chosen to fill his place. He was still alive when Bede wrote about him as being worthy of his high office. It is recorded of him that on Lindisfarne he erected a great cross which was afterwards removed to Durham, and that he bound the book of the gospels which his predecessor had written and which had been miraculously preserved when it had been washed overboard in a storm. He got an anchoret, St Bilfrid, to decorate the cover with metal and gems. This copy of the gospels, but not unfortunately the cover, is now preserved in the British Museum (Cotton MS., Nero D, iv). Charles Plummer described it as " the fairest manuscript that has ever come under my notice ". After ruling his diocese for many years, Ethelwald died and was buried in his cathedral. To protect them from the ravages of the Danes, the relics of St Ethelwald as well as those of St Cuthbert were removed first to Scotland, then to Chester, and finally to Durham, where they still lie in the cathedral.

Bede, Simeon of Durham and Florence of Worcester furnish all the materials we possess for any judgement of the character of this holy bishop. See especially Plummer's edition of Bede's *Ecclesiastical History*, vol. ii, pp. 297-298.

ST ANTONY KAULEAS, Patriarch of Constantinople (A.D. 901)

Antony Kauleas was a Phrygian by extraction, but was born near Constantinople at a place where his parents lived in retirement for fear of the persecution and contagious influence of the Iconoclasts. Upon his mother's death the lad entered a monastery at Constantinople, where he served God with great fervour ; in time he became abbot, and gave the religious habit to his own father. Upon the death of Stephen, brother to the Emperor Leo VI, Antony was chosen patriarch of Constantinople in 893. His predecessor had succeeded Photius when he was dismissed for the second time in 886 ; and St Antony was specially active in peace-making and conciliation in the difficult circumstances that were the legacy of the Ignatius-Photius affair. Contemporary writers speak of Antony as a man who had " the discretion of a pure mind that keeps its balance and is not deceived " " whose happy and praiseworthy life was a credit to all ". A true spirit of mortification, penance and prayer in his private and his public life characterized this great pastor, who died probably in the year 901.

See the *Acta Sanctorum*, February, vol. ii ; and Migne, PG., vol. cvi, cc. 181–200. For the representative council said to have been held in Constantinople under St Antony Kauleas, *cf.* F. Dvornik, *The Photian Schism* (1948), pt i, c. 8.

ST LUDAN (A.D. 1202 ?)

BEYOND his name and the *cultus* paid him, we know nothing for certain about St Ludan. According to tradition he was the son of a Scottish or Irish prince, and upon his father's death devoted his inheritance to charity. He built a large hospice for the care of pilgrims, strangers and the infirm of all kinds, and went on a pilgrimage to Jerusalem. As he was making his way home through Alsace he found himself one day on the road near Strasbourg and, feeling weary, he stopped to rest under an elm tree just outside the little town of Northeim and fell asleep. It was revealed to him in a dream that he was about to die, and as soon as he awoke he fell on his knees and asked God that he might receive before his death the Body of the Lord. His prayer was granted, for an angel brought him his last communion before he passed away. His death was announced by a miraculous pealing of all the bells in the countryside. A boy found in the wallet he carried a small scroll on which was written : " My name is Ludan : I am the son of the noble Scottish prince Hiltebold. For the honour of God I have become a pilgrim." He was buried in the Scheerkirche, near Hispheim, where his relics were honoured until they disappeared during the Thirty Years War.

See the *Acta Sanctorum*, February, vol. ii ; and *Archives de l'Église d'Alsace*, n.s. vol. ii (1947–48), p.p. 13–61.

BB. THOMAS HEMERFORD AND HIS COMPANIONS, MARTYRS (A.D. 1584)

IT was the name of Thomas Hemerford, with his companions, that distinguished and identified the cause of all the second group of English and Welsh martyrs (beatified in 1929) while that cause was under consideration in Rome. But actually, of the four secular priests who suffered at Tyburn on February 12, 1584, he is the one of whom least is known. He was born somewhere in Dorsetshire and was educated at St John's College and Hart Hall in the University of Oxford, where he took the degree of bachelor of law in 1575. He went abroad to Rheims, and thence to the English College at Rome, being ordained priest in 1583 by Bishop Goldwell of St Asaph, the last bishop of the old hierarchy. A few weeks later he left Rome for the English mission, but shortly after landing he was arrested, tried for his priesthood and sentenced to death. For six days before execution he lay loaded with fetters in Newgate jail, and then met the savagery of hanging, drawing and quartering with calm fortitude. Bd Thomas was a man " of moderate stature, a blackish beard, stern countenance, and yet of a playful temper, most amiable in conversation, and in every respect exemplary " There suffered with him BB. JAMES FENN, JOHN NUTTER and JOHN MUNDEN, and GEORGE HAYDOCK.

The first of these was born about 1540 at Montacute, near Yeovil, and was elected a fellow of Corpus Christi College at Oxford, but was expelled for refusing the oath of supremacy. He became a tutor and schoolmaster in his native Somerset, where he married and had two children. On the death of his wife, he, being then nearly forty years old, went to the college at Rheims, where he was ordained priest in 1580 and returned to minister in Somerset. It was not long before Mr Fenn was arrested and put in prison at Ilchester, from whence he was conveyed to London and lodged in the Marshalsea. During the two years he spent there he was most zealous in his care both for his fellow Catholics and others, giving particular attention to pirates and others condemned to death. One notably bad character he converted both to repentance and to the Church.

When he was brought to trial he was put in the dock with another priest, the Venerable George Haydock. These two had never met one another before ; yet they were charged with conspiring together at Rome (where Fenn had never been) to kill the queen, and with entering the country to do so. By direction of the judge, the jury found them guilty ; and the dishonesty of the whole business is shown by the fact that the attorney general called on Fenn while he was awaiting execution, and offered a reprieve if he would acknowledge the queen's ecclesiastical supremacy. As he was tied to the hurdle to be dragged to Tyburn his young daughter, Frances, came weeping to take leave of him and receive his last blessing ; and so Bd James Fenn went to his crown.

John Nutter was born near Burnley, at Reedley Hallows, admitted bachelor of divinity in the University of Oxford, abjured Protestantism, and in 1579 entered the English College at Rheims. Three years later he was made priest, but on his way to the mission suffered shipwreck on the coast of Suffolk and was taken ill at the same time. This combination of misfortunes led to the discovery of his priesthood, whereupon he was apprehended and treated with great lack of consideration, till the order came to send him to London. In the Marshalsea prison Nutter was distinguished for the same zeal as Mr Fenn, and his candour and forthrightness earned him the nickname of " Plain-dealing John ". After a year's confinement, whose discomforts he increased by his own penances, he was brought to trial with those mentioned above, and shared their martyrdom.

John Munden, or Mundyn, was another Dorset man, born at Coltley, near South Maperton. He was educated at Winchester and New College, Oxford, where he was deprived of his fellowship on account of his religion in 1566. Fourteen years later we hear of him at the college at Rheims (he had been schoolmastering in Dorset in the meantime) ; he left with a letter of recommendation from Dr Allen to the rector of the English College in Rome, but he does not seem to have been a student there, though he was ordained in the City in 1582. Early in the following year, while travelling from Winchester to London, he was betrayed by a lawyer named Hammond who handed him over to the magistrates at Staines. He was examined by Sir Francis Walsingham, and then lodged in the Tower, where for three weeks he lay in chains on a bare floor. When brought to trial and sentenced a year later, Bd John Munden's demeanour was so cheerful that bystanders thought he had been acquitted. The night before execution he addressed a touching letter to his " Cousin Duck " at Rheims, the text of which is still extant (Oliver's *Collections*, p. 362).

These four martyrs, together with the Venerable George Haydock, were all condemned and put to death ostensibly for high treason. What contemporaries thought is shown by the chronicler Stow, when he writes that their treason consisted " in being made priests beyond the seas and by the pope's authority ". And that was the view that the Church took when she beatified them among the other English martyrs in 1929.

See MMP., pp. 85–105 ; Burton and Pollen, LEM. ; J. H. Pollen, *Acts of English Martyrs ;* and *Publications* of the Catholic Record Society, vol. v.

13 : ST POLYEUCTUS, MARTYR   (A.D. 259)

THE city of Melitene in Armenia, which was a station of Roman troops, is illustrious for the large number of its martyrs. Of these the foremost in rank was Polyeuctus, a Roman officer of Greek parentage. While still a pagan he made friends with a zealous Christian named Nearchus who, when news of persecution reached Armenia, prepared himself to lay down his life for his faith. His only regret was that Polyeuctus was still a heathen, but he had the joy of winning him over to the truth and of inspiring him with an eager desire to die for the Christian religion. Polyeuctus openly declared himself a Christian, and was apprehended and condemned to cruel tortures. When the executioners were tired of tormenting him, they began to argue and persuade him to renounce Christ. The tears and entreaties of his wife Paulina, of his children and of his father-in-law might well have shaken a less resolute man. Polyeuctus, however, strengthened by God, only grew firmer and received the death sentence with joy. On the road to execution he exhorted the bystanders to renounce their idols, and spoke so eloquently that many were converted. He was beheaded during the persecution of Decius or Valerian.

There is good and indeed convincing evidence of the martyrdom of one St Polyeuctus at Melitene a church is known to have been dedicated to him there before 377. His name is entered on January 7, as suffering at Melitene, in the Syriac Martyrology of the fourth century, and the same entry occurs on the same day in the " Hieronymianum ". At the same time, we can by no means trust the accuracy of the history assigned to the martyr in his " acts ". The elements of romance, utilized by Corneille in his tragedy *Polyeucte*, are unmistakable. The Greek text of the acts was first published entire by B. Aubé, *Polyeucte dans l'histoire* (1882). An Armenian version has been translated by F. C. Conybeare in his book, *The Apology and Acts of Apollonius*   (1894).

ST MARTINIAN THE HERMIT   (DATE UNKNOWN)

MARTINIAN was born at Caesarea in Palestine during the reign of Constantius. At eighteen he retired to a mountain called " The Place of the Ark ", where he lived for twenty-five years as a hermit. His so-called Life contains many stories of more than doubtful authenticity. According to them, a woman of Caesarea called Zoe, hearing his sanctity much extolled, undertook the part of temptress. She pretended that she was a poor woman wandering in the desert late at night, and nearly at death's door. By this pretext she persuaded Martinian to let her remain that night in his cell. Towards morning, she threw aside her rags, showing her best clothes, and going in to Martinian told him that she was a lady of Caesarea and possessed large estates and a plentiful fortune which she offered him—together with herself. To induce him to abandon his solitary life, she quoted instances of Old Testament saints who were rich and married. He listened to her words and consented in his heart to her suggestion. However, as he was then expecting some visitors who were coming to receive his blessing, he told her that he would go to meet them on the road and dismiss them. He started out with that intention but, being touched with remorse, he speedily returned to his cell, where he made a great fire and thrust his feet into it. The pain was so intense that he could not help crying out, and the woman hearing the noise ran in and found him writhing in anguish on the ground with his feet half burnt. When he saw her, he exclaimed, " Ah, if I cannot bear this weak fire, how can I endure that of Hell ? " This example brought Zoe to repentance, and she begged him to put her in the way of securing her salvation. He sent her to Bethlehem, to the convent of St Paula, in which she lived in penitence.

For seven months Martinian was unable to rise from the ground, but as soon as his legs were healed he retired to a rock surrounded by water on every side, to be secure from danger and occasions of sin. Here he lived, exposed to all the winds of heaven, and without ever seeing any human being except a boatman who brought him twice a year biscuit, fresh water and twigs wherewith to make baskets. Six years he lived there, and then one day he saw a ship wrecked close to his island. All on board perished except one girl who, floating on a plank, cried out for help. Martinian went down and saved her life, but as he feared the danger of living on the same mountain with her, he resolved to leave her there with his provisions to await the boatman's coming in two months' time. She chose to spend the rest of her life on the rock in imitation of his penitential example ; and he, trusting himself to the waves and to God, swam to the mainland and travelled to Athens, where he made a happy end at the age of about fifty. Though not mentioned in the Roman Martyrology, St Martinian was greatly venerated in the East, particularly at Constantinople.

There is much reason to doubt the very existence of Martinian. The legend summarized above will be found in the *Acta Sanctorum*, February, vol. ii. See also Rabbow, " Die Legende des Martinian " in *Wiener Studien*, vol. xvii (1895), pp. 253–293, who prints the Greek text ; and *cf. Analecta Bollandiana*, vol. xv (1896), pp. 346–347. Rabbow has shown among other things that the Metaphrast's revision of the legend has borrowed from the Buddhistic romance of Barlaam and Joasaph. A German translation of the story has been made by H. Lietzmann in his *Byzantinische Legenden*, pp. 53–62.

ST STEPHEN OF RIETI, Abbot (*c.* A.D. 560)

STEPHEN was abbot of a monastery near Rieti in Italy, and a man of wonderful piety. Pope St Gregory the Great in his writings speaks several times of this holy man " whose speech was so rude, but his life so cultured ", and he quotes an instance of his patience. Prompted by the Devil, a wicked man burnt down his barns with the corn that constituted the whole means of subsistence of the abbot and his household. " Alas," cried the monks, " alas, for what has come upon you ! "— " Nay," replied the abbot, " say rather, ' Alas, for what has come upon him that did this deed ', for no harm has befallen me." St Gregory also relates that eye-witnesses testified that they saw angels standing beside the saint on his death-bed, and that these angels afterwards carried his soul to bliss—whereupon the watchers were so awe-stricken that they could not remain beside his dead body.

Beyond what St Gregory tells us in one of his homilies (Migne, PL., vol. lxxvi, cc. 1263-1264) and in his *Dialogues*, iv, 19 (Migne, PL., vol. lxxvii, c. 352), we know practically nothing of St Stephen of Rieti.

ST MODOMNOC   (Sixth Century)

The Irish martyrologies, and notably that of Oengus the Culdee (*c.* 804), are of great service in giving some idea of the nature of the popular appeal made by the saints they commemorate.   The eulogium of St Modomnoc (" Dominic ") takes this form   " In a little boat, from the east, over the pure-coloured sea, my Domnoc brought—vigorous cry—the gifted race of Ireland's bees."   Modomnoc is said to have belonged to the Irish royal line of the O'Neils and to have left his native land for Wales with the object of perfecting himself in learning and acquiring greater religious fervour.   Here he came under the direction of St David, who esteemed him highly.   One of his duties was to look after the bees, and a picturesque but apocryphal legend states that when Modomnoc returned to Ireland the bees insisted on following him—swarming on the ship—and that he was thus the means of introducing bees into Ireland.   In any case, with or without bees, St Modomnoc returned to his own country and settled at a place called Tipra-Fachtna, now called Tibraghny in County Kilkenny, near the river Suir.   He is said by some to have become bishop of Ossory.

No formal ancient life of St Modomnoc in Latin or Irish is now known to exist, but references to him occur in the Life of St David and elsewhere.   Plummer, *Miscellanea Hagiograph. Hibern.*, p. 217, notes that an Oxford manuscript preserves a short account in Irish of the bringing of the bees, and the notes on the *Félire* tell us that the quantity he brought was " the full of his bell "   Giraldus Cambrensis also makes reference to the story.   *Cf.* Wade-Evans, *Life of St David* (1923), p. 104.

ST LICINIUS, or LÉSIN, Bishop of Angers   (*c.* a.d. 616)

Licinius was born of a family closely allied to the French kings about the year 540. He grew up a handsome youth with charming manners and high principles, and when he was twenty his father took him to the court of his cousin, King Clotaire I. Here he signalized himself by his valour, by his chivalrous qualities and even more by his piety, for he fulfilled his Christian duties with exactitude and fervour. Fasting and prayer were constant practices with him and his heart was always upraised to God.   King Chilperic was greatly attached to him and made him count of Anjou.   Overruled by the wishes of his friends, he consented to take a wife, but his betrothed was seized with leprosy on the eve of the marriage. Licinius was so much affected by this that he resolved to carry out a design he had formerly entertained of entirely renouncing the world.   This he did in 580 ; he became a priest and entered a religious community, where he led a very austere life.

When Audouin, Bishop of Angers, died, the people, remembering the equity and the clemency with which Licinius had ruled them when he was civil governor, clamoured to have him return as their pastor.   The clergy seconded their appeal, and Licinius accepted, though unwillingly.   Thereafter his time and his substance were devoted to feeding the hungry, comforting and releasing prisoners, and curing

the souls and bodies of his people.   Although he was careful to keep discipline in
his diocese, he was more inclined to indulgence than to rigour, imitating the
tenderness which our Lord Jesus Christ showed to sinners.   By his strong and
persuasive eloquence, by the example of his severe and holy life and by miracles
which were wrought through him he succeeded in winning the hearts of the most
hardened and in making daily conquests of souls for God.   He renewed his own
spirit of devotion by frequent periods of recollection and desired to lay down his
bishopric so as to retire into solitude.   The bishops of the province refused to
listen to such a proposal, and Licinius therefore submitted to their will, spending
the rest of his life in the service of his flock, although, in his later years, he suffered
from continual infirmities.

The Life of St Licinius (BHL., n. 4917) cannot deserve confidence, for the author
pretends to be almost a contemporary, but it is certain that he did not write until more than
a hundred years afterwards.   The more favourable views expressed in a paper by J. Demar-
teau in *Mélanges Godefroid Kurth* are criticized in the *Analecta Bollandiana*, vol. xxviii
(1909), p. 106.   There is, however, no reason to doubt the existence of St Licinius or his
episcopate or the reverence in which he was held.   Duchesne, *Fastes Épiscopaux* (vol. ii,
p. 354), while treating the life as a very suspicious document, points out that a letter was
written to Licinius in 601 by Pope Gregory the Great and that he is also mentioned in the
will of St Bertram, Bishop of Le Mans, which is dated March 27, 616.

ST ERMENGILD, OR ERMENILDA, ABBESS OF ELY, WIDOW   (A.D. 703)

ST ERMENGILD, or Ermenilda, was the daughter of King Ercombert of Kent and
his wife, St Sexburga.   She married Wulfhere, King of the Mercians, and by her
zeal and piety did much to influence him to spread the Christian faith in his
dominions.   She was the mother of St Werburga and also of Coenred, who subsequently became a monk in Rome.   When King Wulfhere died in 675, Ermengild
went to join her mother, who was then building an abbey at Minster on Sheppey.
She received the veil at the monastery of Milton to which the isle belonged and
was under the rule of her mother until St Sexburga retired to Ely to be under her
sister, St Etheldreda.   Ermengild then became abbess of Minster, but after a few
years she also resigned and retired to Ely, where her daughter St Werburga was
a nun and where Sexburga had by now succeeded as abbess.   Ermengild followed
St Sexburga so that Ely had the distinction of being ruled in quick succession by
three abbesses of royal race, closely related to each other and all of them saints.
It is unlikely that St Werburga was ever abbess of Ely.

Bede, William of Malmesbury and Thomas of Ely contribute the principal materials for
this rather complicated history, but there is also an Anglo-Saxon fragment, printed in
Cockayne's *Anglo-Saxon Leechdoms*, vol. iii, p. 430, which fills in certain details.   See also
Stanton's *Menology*, pp. 67-68.

BD BEATRICE OF ORNACIEU, VIRGIN   (A.D. 1309)

SOME rather unusual mystical experiences are recorded of this Carthusian nun.
She was born at the castle of Ornacieu, in what is now the department of Isère in
the Dauphiné, and seems to have entered the Carthusian convent of Parménie at
an early age.   There she led a life of extreme austerity, favoured by constant
evidences of the special predilection of her heavenly Spouse.   For a long time in
the early years of her religious life she saw our Lord, we are told, constantly standing

beside her in a visible form, and her heart was so touched with sensible devotion that she was in danger of injuring her sight from the abundance of tears which she shed.   When it fell to her lot to act as cook and to have to tend the kitchen fire, she used to rake out the burning embers with her hands, and though the flesh was scorched she was so absorbed in God that she felt no pain.   In particular she had an intense sympathy with our Lord in His passion, and this carried her to such lengths in her desire to share His sufferings that she was wont to drive a sharp nail through the skin into the palms of her hands.   By some strange prodigy—so at least the seemingly contemporary account assures us—no flow of blood came from the wounds thus made, but only pure water, and, what is more, they healed at once, leaving no trace of any lesion.   As we are accustomed to find in mystics who have many visions and other sensible communications with the unseen, Beatrice was tormented in almost equal measure by diabolic manifestations.   Her biographer seems to insist—though it is difficult to feel quite certain on the point—that the devil assailed her physically with showers of stones and blazing darts.   She felt herself struck, he tells us, but nevertheless these missiles inflicted no pain. Such an experience would be in curious accord with the poltergeist phenomena, both ancient and modern, of which we may read in chronicles of quite another character.

Beatrice's devotion to the Holy Eucharist was also very great, and this not merely in receiving communion and in her rapt attention at Mass, but she also seems to have been one of the pioneers in realizing the treasure of graces which is opened to those who do honour to our Lord's abiding presence in the tabernacle.   Praying before the Blessed Sacrament for the release of her brother who had been taken prisoner, she had a wonderful vision of our Saviour bearing the glorious marks of the five wounds ; which appears to be an early example of the Eucharistic Christ, so well known in the representation commonly called " the Mass of St Gregory ". Our Lord, she believed, assured her that her prayer was granted, and she learnt at a later date that at that precise moment her brother in a distant land had succeeded in making his escape.   But Beatrice was afterwards sent with two other sisters to Eymeu, near Valence, to make a new foundation.   This residence was eventually found unsuitable, and the community after a while returned to Parménie ; but Bd Beatrice refused to give in to hardships and died there on November 25, 1309 (or 1303).   Her remains were later brought to Parménie, not, it was believed, without many miraculous incidents attending the translation.   In that neighbourhood she seems always to have been venerated as a saint, and her *cultus* was confirmed in 1869.

See C. Le Couteulx, *Annales Ordinis Cartusiensis*, vol. v, pp. 5-23. There are lives in French by Bellanger (1874) and Chapuis (1900) ; and see *Histoire Littéraire de France*, vol. xx, pp. 315-319.

BD CHRISTINA OF SPOLETO   (A.D. 1458)

CHRISTINA is supposed to have been a member of the Visconti family of Milan and was remarkable for her extraordinary religious precocity.   When she was little more than five, she was already leading a life of prayer and mortification.   When she was ten her parents began to speak about arranging a marriage for her : she opposed the idea because she wished to become a nun, but they persisted, as they desired heirs.   The contention had lasted two years and she was just twelve when, realizing that she was about to be forced into the marriage, she escaped with a young servant girl.   Christina assumed the habit of the Hermitesses of St Augustine, and the two girls wandered about for years, having no fixed abode and living on what they could.   When she was about twenty Christina made a pilgrimage to Assisi, and passing by way of Spoleto she went to lodge with a holy woman called Galitia. After visiting Assisi she became separated from her friend, who had left the church after paying her devotions, whereas Christina had spent the whole night there in prayer.   Next day, Christina hunted everywhere for her companion   she searched Assisi and all the neighbouring towns, but in vain.   Returning to Spoleto, she joined the staff of a hospital and spent some months nursing the sick.   All this time she never relaxed her rather sensational mortifications.   Then she again met her former hostess and friend, Galitia, who persuaded her to stay with her for a little ; while she was there Christina was taken with fever, of which she died at the age of twenty-two.   Numerous miracles of healing were reported as having taken place at her tomb and elsewhere by her intercession.

The story here epitomized is that which the Bollandists of the seventeenth century have taken over from the Augustinian historiographer, Cornelius Curtius, and have printed in the *Acta Sanctorum*, February, vol. ii.   Later investigation, however, has shown that it is almost pure romance.   There was undoubtedly a very holy penitent named Christina, who died at Spoleto on February 13, 1458, after spending three or four years in austerities the recital of which makes the modern reader shudder.   But this Christina was in no way connected with the illustrious Visconti family.   Her name was Augustina Camozzi, and she was the daughter of a worthy physician who lived near Lake Lugano.   As a girl she led a rather disorderly and very tempestuous life in the world, but died at the age of twenty-three or so after making expiation by the austerest penance.

The facts have been cleared up by M. E. Motta in the *Bolletino storico della Svizzera italiana*, vol. xv (1873), pp. 85-93.   *Cf.* also the *Analecta Bollandiana*, vol. xiii (1894), p. 411, and xxxviii (1920), pp. 434-435.

BD EUSTOCHIUM OF PADUA, Virgin   (A.D. 1469)

THERE are few stories in the records of hagiography more curious than that of Bd Eustochium.   It should be said at the outset that her *cultus* seems never to have received the formal approbation of the Holy See, though her Life has more than once been written and she is to this day liturgically honoured at Padua.   Her very birth forms a sad memorial of a period at which terrible scandals were rife in the cloister as well as in the outside world.   She was the daughter of a nun who had been seduced by a profligate, and she was actually born within the convent in which she eventually died.   The community which connived at such irregularities was afterwards dispersed by the bishop's orders and was replaced by sisters from a more observant foundation.   The little Lucrezia, to use the name by which she was christened, showed in her childhood signs of being beset by certain influences of a strongly poltergeist type, and she was believed to be possessed.   She was, however, sent to school at San Prosdocimo, the convent in which she had been born, but her conduct was in every way edifying, and when she was somewhat older she sought to be received there as a novice.   The majority of the new community were much opposed to her admission among them, for the story of her birth was well known. However, with the bishop's approval, the habit was eventually given her, and she took the name of Eustochium.   Hardly had her noviceship begun when the strangest symptoms manifested themselves.   Normally she was the most gentle, obedient and kindly of beings, full of fervour and observant of every rule, but now at not infrequent intervals her character seemed to undergo a complete transformation.   She became stubborn, rude and subject to violent outbursts of temper. Whether this was due to one of those strange dissociations of personality with which modern psychological studies have made us familiar it would be difficult to say, but it was attributed then to diabolical possession.

In any case the treatment of the afflicted girl was probably not very judicious. It terminated in a blood-curdling scene in which the novice was seized with the most horrible convulsions, shrieking, howling and eventually snatching up a knife when an attempt was made to restrain her.   She was treated as mad people were commonly treated in that age, and for several days she was kept tied up to a pillar. During these paroxysms, which recurred from time to time, she seems sometimes to have inflicted severe injuries upon herself which were said to have been caused by the devil which possessed her.   Though a period of calm succeeded, Eustochium was still regarded with hostility and suspicion, and when the abbess fell ill of a malady for which the doctors were unable to account, Eustochium was believed to have poisoned her by diabolical or magical practices in revenge for having been kept tied up.   The story of what was happening got abroad in the town, and a mob gathered round the convent who clamoured that she should be surrendered to them that they might burn her for a witch.   The bishop decided that she must be kept prisoner in one of the cells and that she should be allowed nothing but bread and water, passing the alternate days without any food at all.   This treatment seems to have continued for three months.   Fortunately the abbess recovered, but in spite of the efforts of her confessor, who declared Eustochium to be perfectly innocent, the feeling of the community against her was so strong that she was treated as an outcast.   No one would speak to her or have anything to do with her. Efforts were made to persuade her to leave the convent of her own accord, for she had as yet taken no vows.   Friendly help was promised and a marriage portion offered if she would accept a husband, but Eustochium, when quite herself, believed that God had called her to serve Him in religion and refused to consent.

For a long time the paroxysms continued to return at intervals.   Under their influence, to the horror of the sisters, Eustochium clambered or was transported to a beam high up in the roof where a false step would have meant instant destruction ; she was lifted into the air and then let fall like a stone ; she was found in her cell divested of all her garments, with marks of violence on her throat and on her limbs ; she took a knife and gashed herself with cuts from which she lost great quantities of blood ; but none the less as soon as these spasms passed, she became the same gentle, obedient unresentful creature, ready to sacrifice herself in any work of charity for those who treated her so harshly.   Eventually, at the end of four years, she was allowed to take her vows, and by degrees she gained the good will and in fact the reverence of all her fellow nuns.   She spent her last days bedridden, in much physical suffering, and died at the age of twenty-six on February 13, 1469. In preparing the body for burial the name of Jesus was found cauterized, it would seem, upon her breast.   Apparitions and many miracles are said to have followed and a celestial fragrance proceeded from the place of sepulture.   Three and a half years later, by order of the very bishop who had been instrumental in her cruel imprisonment, her body was transferred to a more honourable resting-place. Though buried without a coffin, it was found perfectly incorrupt, as if it had just been borne to the grave.

Fantastic as this story may appear, it rests upon good contemporary evidence. A short sketch was compiled and made public by Peter Barozzi, who in 1487 became bishop of Padua, where Eustochium eighteen years earlier had ended her days. Fuller biographies were later on printed by G. M. Giberti (1672) and G. Salio (1734) ; but the most reliable is undoubtedly that of the well-known Jesuit historian Giulio Cordara, which first appeared in 1765. Cordara explains that he based his whole narrative upon a manuscript relation, drawn up by the priest Jerome Salicario, who was confessor to the community during all the period of Eustochium's residence as a nun and who had himself taken a leading part in the proceedings. This relation was still preserved at San Prosdocimo and was entrusted to Fr Cordara for the purpose of his biography. A somewhat fuller account than that here printed may be found in *The Month* for February, 1926, entitled " A Cinderella of the Cloister ", by Fr Thurston.

BD ARCHANGELA GIRLANI, Virgin   (A.D. 1494)

Eleanor Girlani was born at Trino in northern Italy in the year 1460, and from earliest childhood showed herself intensely serious and devout. She went to the neighbouring Benedictine convent of Rocca delle Donne for her education, but found that her people came to see her too often and that the discipline observed by the nuns was not strict enough. Being bent on consecrating herself to God, and her father refusing his consent, she implored the intervention of the Marquess of Monferrato. In the end her father yielded, but only on condition that she took the veil in the Benedictine house already mentioned. We are told that every preparation had been made for celebrating her entry into religion there with great solemnity. The marquess himself was present in state, and the procession set out, but when the horse which Eleanor was riding had gone but a little way it stood stock still and nothing could make it advance further. In the end the company dispersed, and Eleanor returning home was met soon afterwards by a Carmelite friar who gave her a glowing account of the edifying life led by the nuns of his order at Parma. Taking Archangela as her name in religion, the girl entered there on her seventeenth birthday and took her vows a year later, in 1478.

It is strange to read that very shortly afterwards she was made prioress. How soon exactly we are not told, but since she was sent at the request of the Gonzagas to found a new Carmelite convent at Mantua, where she died, and had raised this new community to a state of great perfection before she was taken from them, the delay in advancing her to the office of superior cannot have been long. We probably must attribute a great deal of this precipitancy to her social position. As appears plainly from the records of the religious houses of women in the early middle ages, a princess or great lady who took the veil and proved herself to be reasonably observant and virtuous was almost always elected abbess as soon as a vacancy occurred. This practice seems to have lingered on through later centuries. In Archangela's case the deference paid to rank does not seem to have been misplaced. She was the model of every religious virtue, most austere in her practice of penance, charitable to all and possessed of a marvellous spirit of prayer. Many times, we are told, she was found in her cell rapt in ecstasy and raised several yards from the ground. On one occasion an ecstasy in which she was completely insensible to outward impressions lasted more than twenty-four hours. When, owing to inundations, the convent at Mantua was threatened with absolute starvation, she fell on her knees in prayer and straightway an unknown person came to the gate bringing an adequate supply of provisions.

Certain strange happenings were recorded after her death, which occurred on January 25, 1494, of which the most interesting perhaps is the pear tree tradition. Shortly after her arrival at Mantua Mother Archangela had planted a pear tree in the convent garden. Now it was believed that the tree always produced as many blossoms, and in due course as many pears, as there were sisters in the community. What is more, if a pear fell off, this was a certain indication that one of the community would die within the year. The prioress herself, as long as she was in charge, always, when a pear fell, exhorted her community to make a good preparation for death, seeing that they none of them knew for whom the warning was intended. It is also averred that the same marvel continued for many years, long after Bd Archangela's death. Her *cultus* was confirmed in 1864.

It is difficult to form any idea of the value of the evidence upon which these and similar details connected with the life of Bd Archangela are based. They may be read in a tiny booklet written by the Abbé Albarei from notes supplied by a Piedmontese Dominican. It bears the Carmelite device of cross and stars, and is entitled *Notice sur la Vie de la bse. Archangela Girlani* (Poitiers, 1865).

ST CATHERINE DEI RICCI, Virgin　　(A.D. 1590)

THIS saint was born in 1522 into a well-known Florentine family, and at her baptism was called Alexandrina. She took the name of Catherine at her religious clothing, when she was thirteen, in the Dominican convent of St Vincent at Prato, of which her uncle, Father Timothy dei Ricci, was director. Here for two years she suffered agonizing pain from a complication of diseases which remedies seemed only to aggravate ; but she sanctified her sufferings by her exemplary patience, which she derived in great part from constant meditation on the passion of Christ. Catherine while still very young was chosen novice-mistress, then sub-prioress, and in her thirtieth year was appointed prioress in perpetuity. The reputation of her holiness and wisdom brought her visits from many lay people and clergy, including three cardinals, each of whom afterwards became pope. Something similar to what is related by St Augustine about St John of Egypt happened to St Philip Neri and St Catherine dei Ricci. They had exchanged a number of letters, and although they never met in the body she appeared to him and talked with him in Rome— without ever having left her convent at Prato. This was expressly stated by St Philip Neri, who was always most cautious in giving credence to or publishing visions, and it was confirmed by the oaths of five witnesses.

Catherine is famous, even in a greater degree than other mystics who have been similarly privileged, for her extraordinary series of ecstasies in which she beheld and *enacted* in their order the scenes which preceded our Saviour's crucifixion. These ecstasies seem always to have followed the same course. They began when she was twenty years old in February 1542, and they were renewed every week for twelve years continuously. Naturally they occasioned much talk, crowds of devout or curious people sought to visit the convent. The recollection of the community was interfered with, and the inconveniences resulting were only the more acutely felt when in 1552 she was herself elected prioress. Earnest supplication was made by all the nuns at her request that these manifestations might cease, and in 1554 they came to a end. While they lasted they exhibited several features which are unusual in such cases.   Catherine uniformly lost consciousness at midday every Thursday and only came to herself twenty-eight hours afterwards, at four o'clock on the Friday afternoon.   One interruption, however, occurred in this state of rapture.   Holy communion was regularly brought to her in the morning, and she became sufficiently conscious of the outer world to receive it with intense devotion, but almost immediately afterwards she again became entranced, resuming her contemplation of the scenes of the Passion at exactly the point where she had left off.   Catherine had ecstasies at other times, and during these she usually remained quite passive, her eyes fixed on heaven.   But in her weekly Passion-ecstasy her body moved in conformity with our Lord's own gestures and movements as she witnessed them in contemplation.   For instance, when He was arrested in the garden she held out her hands as if to be bound, she stood majestically upright to represent His fastening to the pillar for the scourging, she bent her head as though to receive the crown of thorns, and so on.   What is an even more unusual feature in such experiences, she would often take occasion from the particular sufferings of Jesus Christ to address exhortations in the midst of her ecstasy to the sisters who were standing around, which she did, says one of her biographers, " with a knowledge, loftiness of thought and eloquence not to be expected from a woman, and especially from a woman neither learned nor literary ".

That Catherine was favoured with the stigmata, the wounds in hands, feet and side, as well as the crown of thorns, was also commonly asserted, and depositions to this effect submitted in the process of beatification.   Strangely enough the impression made upon those who professed to have seen the stigmata seems in each case to have been different.   Some beheld the hands pierced right through and bleeding, others saw the wound-marks shining with so brilliant a light that it dazzled them, others again perceived only " healed-up wounds, red and swollen, with a black spot in the centre, round which the blood seemed to circulate "   This remarkable diversity in the accounts of the witnesses is if possible still more pronounced in the descriptions given of that mystical phenomenon for which St Catherine is more especially famous, the ring, said to have been given her by Christ in token of His spiritual espousals with this His handmaid.   On Easter day 1542 our Saviour, we are told, appeared to her radiant with light, and then drawing from His own finger a gleaming ring He placed it upon the forefinger of her left hand, saying, " My daughter, receive this ring as pledge and proof that thou dost now, and ever shalt, belong to me."

In the *Positio super Virtutibus*, a printed summary of evidence issued, as is always now done in such cases, for the convenience of the consultors who have to pronounce upon the question of the heroic virtue of any candidate for beatification, the statements made concerning Catherine's mystic espousals occupy a great deal of space.   The promoter of the faith (popularly known as " the Devil's Advocate ") at the time when the cause was brought before the Congregation of Rites was the famous Prosper Lambertini, even better known afterwards as Pope Benedict XIV. The question of St Catherine's ring attracted his particular attention, and he made several criticisms which were replied to in detail by the postulator of the cause. St Catherine, as we have seen, was born in 1522 and died in 1590 ; unfortunately it was only in 1614 that the first juridical examination of witnesses took place in connection with the cause of beatification.   As the ring had originally become manifest in April 1542, it was practically impossible that any of the nuns who had formed part of the community when this wonder first occurred could be living to give evidence in 1614, seventy-two years afterwards.   But the phenomenon showed itself at least intermittently throughout Catherine's life and, apart from written and second-hand testimony, some few witnesses were able to give an account of what they themselves had seen.   Their evidence gives the impression of being somewhat conflicting.

Perhaps the most valuable testimonies produced in the beatification process were two written documents, one a letter of the Dominican Father Neri, dated 1549, that is seven years after the mystic espousals, the other a few notes made by Catherine's special friend and nurse in her illness, Sister Mary Magdalen Strozzi. The former recounts the apparition of our Lord on Easter Sunday and remarks particularly that the ring was placed on the index finger of her left hand.   After which he goes on :

> Within a fortnight of Easter, the true ring, that is to say the ring of gold with its diamond, was seen by three very holy sisters at different times, each of them being over forty-five years of age.   One was Sister Potentiana of Florence, the second Sister Mary Magdalen of Prato [this was Mary Magdalen Strozzi, who left the manuscript account of her beloved Mother Catherine], the third Sister Aurelia of Florence, so the superiors of our province have ascertained.
>
> A command was laid upon [Catherine] by her superior to ask a favour of Jesus Christ ; and by Him the favour was granted that all the sisters saw the ring, or at least a counterfeit presentment of it, in this sense, that for three days continuously, *i.e.* the Monday, Tuesday and Wednesday of Easter week, all the sisters beheld on the finger beside the long finger of the left hand, and in the place where she said the ring was, a red lozenge (*quadretto*) to represent the stone or diamond, and similarly they saw a red circlet around the finger in place of the ring, which lozenge and circlet Catherine averred she had never seen in the same way as the sisters, because she always beheld the ring of gold and enamel with its diamond.   Also the ring was seen in this way as a reddening of the flesh throughout the whole of Ascension day 1542, and also on the day of Corpus Christi, when it was accompanied by a most wonderful perfume which was perceived by all.*

Father Neri also goes on to remark that this reddening of the finger could not have been due to any paint or dye, for on Corpus Christi day, as he relates, Catherine was brought into the church that the governor of the city might see this red circlet. But all traces of it disappeared in his presence, though immediately afterwards it showed itself again to the nuns.

Regarding Father Neri's statement that three of the elder nuns were privileged to see the real ring of gold and red enamel, it is curious that no confirmation of this seems to be found in Sister Mary Magdalen Strozzi's own notes, though she is one of the three sisters mentioned.   What she does make perfectly clear is that for three days after Easter there was a red circle round Catherine's finger, which she describes as a ring " between skin and skin ", corresponding closely to what Dr Imbert-Gourbeyre tells of Marie-Julie Jahenny that her finger looked as if a red coral ring had been buried in the flesh.   Again, Sister Mary Magdalen's notes give a curiously touching impression of her solicitude lest Catherine had become the

---

* *Positio super Virtutibus   Summarium*, p. 352.   Cf. *Responsio ad animadversiones*, p. 79.

dupe of some wile of the Devil. She went to the confessor about it, and together they made experiments with cinnabar and other pigments, but they found they could produce nothing in the least like the reddening on Catherine's finger. Then Sister Mary Magdalen went to Catherine herself, and seems frankly to have told her doubts and scruples. These abnormal manifestations, she urged, were contrary to the spirit and traditions of the convent and were very dangerous to humility and to that desire for self-effacement which was so important in the religious life. Catherine agreed, and was delighted to let her do anything she pleased in order to get rid of the mark. She only blamed herself, and begged pardon for being the cause of so much trouble and disquiet of mind among the rest of the community. So Sister Mary Magdalen put the finger into her mouth to find if the red mark had any taste, and also left it to steep in water, and then tried to wash out the mark with soap—all, of course, without any effect. On the other hand, Catherine declared quite simply that she saw on her finger a gold ring set with a pointed diamond, and could see nothing else. " I have to take it on faith ", she said to her friend, " when you tell me that you perceive simply a red mark." The fact that St Catherine continually saw the ring and its stone with her bodily eyes, and could not see the circle of red is also definitely mentioned in the letter of Father Neri in 1549.

The facts are very puzzling. There is apparently overwhelming evidence that at certain times the marks of a red circle and lozenge showed themselves on Catherine's finger in a way that could be perceived by all. It also appears to be certain that she always with her bodily eyes saw on that finger a gold ring set with a diamond, but one cannot feel satisfied that the testimony recorded is sufficient to establish the fact that the gold ring was really seen by any others beside herself. There are so many well-attested instances of a radiance shining from the faces, hands and garments of mystics when rapt in ecstasy that we may readily agree that this is likely to have happened in the case of Catherine's finger. If so, casual witnesses may very well have persuaded themselves that in the midst of this radiance they discerned the gold ring and the diamond of which they had previously heard mention. One nun expressly said that such a bright light came from the finger that she could not see what kind of ring encircled it.

St Catherine dei Ricci died after a long illness at the age of sixty-eight on February 2, 1590. The extraordinary phenomena of which some account has just been given have tended to distract attention from other features of her life. She was distinguished by " a magnificent psychological and moral healthiness ", and like so many other contemplative saints she was a good administrator in carrying out the duties of her house and office, who was never happier than when looking after the sick, and exercised an influence well beyond the walls of her convent and her city. Not the least interesting of her characteristics was her reverence for the memory of Jerome Savonarola, to whose heavenly intercession she attributed the recovery of her health in 1540. St Catherine was canonized in 1747.

It will be sufficient to refer the English reader to the *Life of St Catherine de' Ricci*, by F. M. Capes (1905). The most authentic sources of information are, of course, the depositions of the witnesses in the process of beatification a copy of the *Summarium de Virtutibus* is in the British Museum. Several selections from the saint's lively letters have been published in Italian and French. " Tokens of espousal " are studied in Fr Thurston's collected papers, *The Physical Phenomena of Mysticism* (1952).

14 : ST VALENTINE, Martyr   (*c.* a.d. 269)

T HE commemoration of St Valentine on February 14 affords an interesting example of the peculiar difficulties which beset the student of early hagiography and of the mixture of truth and fiction which is commonly to be found in such abstracts of traditional belief as the notices in the Roman Martyrology. Alban Butler, who deserves credit for using the best sources available in his day, based his account of St Valentine upon Tillemont, an authority who was far from uncritical. From the data thus supplied, Butler, nearly 200 years ago, drew up his summary in the following terms :

> Valentine was a holy priest in Rome, who, with St Marius and his family, assisted the martyrs in the persecution under Claudius II. He was apprehended, and sent by the emperor to the prefect of Rome, who, on finding all his promises to make him renounce his faith ineffectual, commanded him to be beaten with clubs, and afterwards to be beheaded, which was executed on February 14, about the year 270. Pope Julius I is said to have built a church near Ponte Mole to his memory, which for a long time gave name to the gate now called Porta del Popolo, formerly Porta Valentini. The greatest part of his relics are now in the church of St Praxedes. His name is celebrated as that of an illustrious martyr in the sacramentary of St Gregory, the Roman Missal of Thomasius, in the calendar of F. Fronto and that of Allatius, in Bede, Usuard, Ado, Notker and all other martyrologies on this day. To abolish the heathen's lewd superstitious custom of boys drawing the names of girls, in honour of their goddess Februata Juno, on the 15th of this month, several zealous pastors substituted the names of saints in billets given on this day.

That the practice of sending valentines on February 14 is connected with any pagan observances of classical times in honour of Februata Juno seems exceedingly doubtful, and when Butler speaks of " zealous pastors substituting the names of saints in billets given on this day " he is speaking of a pious device introduced at what was relatively a very late date and of which we read, for example, in the life of St Francis de Sales. But our immediate concern here is with the martyr St Valentine, and the first objection that might be raised against the celebration of a feast in his honour is the fact that the Roman Martyrology on this day makes mention, not of one, but of two St Valentines, both martyrs put to death by decapitation and both on the Flaminian Way, though one died at Rome and the other is located some sixty miles from Rome at Interamna (Terni). Moreover, when we study the so-called " acts " of the Roman martyr, who is alone referred to by Butler, we find that the greater part of his story has been taken over bodily from a similar narrative dealing with the martyrdom of SS. Marius and Martha.

Nevertheless there seems no conclusive reason for doubting the real existence of either of these two martyrs. The evidence of early local *cultus* in both cases is strong. The Roman Valentine seems to have been a priest. He probably did suffer on February 14 in the persecution of Claudius the Goth about the year 269. He was buried on the Flaminian Way, a basilica was erected as early as 350, a catacomb was later on formed on this spot, the location of his remains was known, and they were subsequently translated. On the other hand, the connection with Interamna of a St Valentine, martyr, who is also described as bishop of that town, is attested by the martyrology known as the " Hieronymianum ", and there is some other evidence of a similar nature. It might, of course, have happened that in the persecution of the Emperor Claudius the Goth, Valentine, Bishop of Interamna, was taken to Rome after his arrest and was there put to death.

Although the story of Valentine the bishop is just as fabulous as that of Valentine the priest, it does contain an isolated fragment of what looks like genuine tradition. The acts make mention of a high official " Furiosus Placidus " who was concerned in the martyrdom, and we happen to know that a certain Furius Placidus was consul in 273. It is not, of course, necessary to suppose that if there were two martyrs named Valentine they both suffered on February 14. The mere fact that the memory of a saint was definitely associated with a particular day led in a number of cases to the inclusion of other saints of the same name among the *elogia* belonging to that day. If the Roman church honoured the memory of their St Valentine in his basilica on February 14, that would be sufficient reason for the people of Terni, if they were in any doubt as to the actual day on which their martyr suffered, to keep his festival at the same time that the Romans honoured his namesake. But clearly also it is possible that a Valentine of Interamna having actually suffered at Rome, the Romans may have venerated him with a special *cultus*, though Terni also claimed him and invented a separate legend concerning him. This is the solution which Father Delehaye seemed to favour, though Professor O. Marucchi holds fast to his belief in two separate St Valentines.

The custom, which at the present time is hardly more than a memory, for young men and maidens to choose each other for Valentines on this day, is probably based on the popular belief which we find recorded in literature as early as the time of Chaucer, that the birds began to pair on St Valentine's Day. The sending of a missive of some kind was only a natural development of this choosing. One of the earliest references to the custom of choosing a Valentine is to be found in *The Paston Letters* (no. 783). In February, 1477 Elizabeth Drews, who had a marriageable daughter and who wished to arrange a match for her with their relative John Paston, wrote to the prospective bridegroom :

> And, Cousin, upon Friday is St Valentine's Day and every bird chooseth him a mate, and if it like you to come on Thursday at night, and so purvey you that you may abide there till Monday, I trust to God that you shall speak to my husband, and I shall pray that we shall bring the matter to a conclusion. For, cousin,

> > It is but a simple oak
> > That is cut down at the first stroke.

During the same month, Margery, the marriageable daughter in question, addressed the following letter to John Paston as her Valentine :

> Unto my right well beloved Valentine John Paston, Squyer, be this bill delivered.
> Right reverend and worshipful and my right well beloved Valentine, I recommend me unto you, full heartily desiring to hear of your welfare, which I beseech Almighty God long for to preserve unto His pleasure and your heart's desire.

Her next letter is not quite so formal, and in the course of it she says :

If ye could be content with that good [her small dowry] and my poor person, I would be the merriest maiden on ground ; a good true and loving Valentine, that the matter may never more be spoken of, as I may be your true lover and bedewoman during my life.

Although on account of the custom connected with his feast the name of St Valentine was very familiar in England, no church is known to have been dedicated in his honour in this country.

The supposed " acts " of the two Valentines are in the *Acta Sanctorum*, February, vol. ii. See also O. Marucchi, *Il cimitero e la basilica di S. Valentino* (1890). *Cf. Analecta Bollandiana,* vol. xi (1892), p. 472 ; Delehaye, *Les origines du culte des martyrs* (1933), pp. 270, 315-316, his *CMH.*, pp. 92-93, and in *Bulletin d'ancienne littérature et d'archéologie chrétiennes,* vol. i (1911), pp. 161 *seq.* ; and especially Grisar, *Geschichte Roms und der Päpste*, vol. i, pp. 655-659.

ST ABRAHAM, Bishop of Carrhae   (*c.* A.D. 422)

A NATIVE of Cyrrhus in Syria, St Abraham (Abraames) became a solitary.   Fired with zeal for the spreading of the gospel, he went to a village on Mount Lebanon, the inhabitants of which were pagans.   He is said to have appeared amongst them at first as a fruit-seller, but as soon as he began to preach Christianity they rose against him and ill-treated him.   However, he gradually won his way by meekness and patience.   After he had narrowly escaped death at their hands, he borrowed money with which to satisfy the collector of taxes who was about to cast the villagers into prison on account of their failure to pay these dues.   He thus gained them all to Christ.   After instructing them for three years, he left them in the care of a priest and returned to his desert.   Some time afterwards he was ordained bishop of Carrhae in Mesopotamia, and succeeded in clearing that place of idolatry, dissensions and other evils.   St Abraham combined the recollection and penance of a monk with the vigorous execution of his episcopal duties and died in 422 at Constantinople, whither he had been summoned by the Emperor Theodosius II, who esteemed him highly and treated him with the greatest honour.   The emperor kept one of his garments of haircloth and wore it himself on certain days out of veneration for the saint.

Our main authority is the historian Theodoret, a contemporary, who speaks of St Abraham both in his *Ecclesiastical History* and in his *Philotheus*.   The passages are cited in the *Acta Sanctorum*, February, vol. ii.   *Cf.* also Tillemont and *DCB.*, vol. i, p. 8.   Carrhae is the Haran of the Bible, where Jacob served seven years for Rachel.

ST MARO, Abbot   (A.D. 433)

ST MARO chose a solitary abode not far from the city of Cyrrhus in Syria, and there, in a spirit of mortification, he lived mainly in the open air.   He had indeed a little hut covered with goatskins to shelter him in case of need, but he very seldom made use of it.   Finding the ruins of a heathen temple, he dedicated it to the true God, and made it his house of prayer.   St John Chrysostom, who had a great regard for him, wrote to him from Cucusus, the place of his banishment, and, recommending himself to his prayers, begged to hear from him as often as possible.   St Maro had had for his master St Zebinus, whose assiduity in prayer was such that he is said to have devoted to it whole days and nights without experiencing any weariness. He generally prayed standing, though in extreme old age he had to support himself on a staff. He gave advice in the fewest possible words to those who came to consult him, so desirous was he to spend all his available time in converse with God.

St Maro imitated his master in his constancy in prayer, but he treated his visitors differently. Not only did he receive them with great kindness, but he encouraged them to stay with him—although few were willing to pass the whole night in prayer standing. God rewarded his labours with most abundant graces and with the gift of healing infirmities both of mind and body ; it is consequently not surprising that his fame as a spiritual adviser spread far and wide. This drew great multitudes to consult him, and he trained many holy solitaries and founded monasteries ; we know that at least three great convents afterwards bore his name. Theodoret, Bishop of Cyrrhus, says that the great number of monks who peopled his diocese were the fruit of the saint's instructions. St Maro was called to his reward after a short illness which, says Theodoret, revealed to all the great weakness to which his body was reduced. A contest for his remains ensued amongst the neighbouring provinces. The body was finally secured by the inhabitants of a relatively populous centre who built over his tomb a spacious church with an adjoining monastery near the source of the Orontes, not far from Apamea.

It is generally said that the people called Maronites, who now mostly live in the Lebanon and have a long and honourable history among the Catholics of Eastern rite, received their name from this monastery, Bait-Marun. They venerate St Maro as their patriarch, and name him in the canon of the Mass according to their rite. They also venerate a St John Maro, who is said to have been their bishop in the late seventh century, but his very existence is problematical.

Almost all that is known about St Maro is derived from the *Philotheus* of Theodoret and from St John Chrysostom. On the origins of the Maronites see S. Vailhé in *Échos d'Orient* for 1901, 1902 and 1906 ; and P. Dib in DTC., vol. x, cc. 1 *seq.*

ST AUXENTIUS (A.D. 473)

ALTHOUGH it seems that Auxentius was the son of a Persian named Addas, he spent the greater part of his long life as a hermit in Bithynia. In his youth he was one of the equestrian guards of Theodosius the Younger, but his military duties, which he discharged with entire fidelity, did not hinder him from making the service of God his main concern. All his spare time was spent in solitude and prayer, and he often visited the holy recluses who occupied hermitages in the neighbourhood in order that he might pass the night with them in penitential exercises and in singing the praises of God. Finally, the desire of greater perfection, or the fear of vainglory, induced him to adopt the eremitical life himself. He took up his abode on the desert mountain of Oxia, only about eight miles from Constantinople but on the other side of the Hellespont in Bithynia. There he seems to have been much consulted and to have exercised considerable influence on account of his reputation for holiness.

When the fourth oecumenical council had met at Chalcedon to condemn the Eutychian heresy, Auxentius was summoned by the Emperor Marcian, not, as some of the saint's biographers would seem to suggest, as a tribute to his high character and learning, but rather under an unjust suspicion of entertaining Eutychian sympathies. Auxentius in any case cleared himself of the imputation, but when he was again left free he did not return to Oxia, but chose another cell nearer to Chalcedon on the mountain of Skopa. There he remained, leading a life of great austerity and instructing the disciples who flocked to him, until his death, which probably took place on February 14, 473. Even while St Auxentius was yet living at court the historian Sozomen wrote with enthusiasm of his steadfast faith, the purity of his life and his intimacy with fervent ascetics. Amongst those who sought his direction in his later days were a number of women. These formed a community and lived together at the foot of Mount Skopa, and they were known as the Trichinaraeae (τριχιναραῖαι), "the nuns dressed in haircloth." It was they who, after a long contest, were successful in obtaining possession of his mortal remains which were enshrined in the church of their convent.

There are several recensions of the Life of St Auxentius (for which see BHG., 2nd edn., nn. 199-203) though these all seem to be dependent on one primitive source. The whole question has been studied with very great care by J. Pargoire in the *Revue de l'Orient chrétien*, vol. viii (1903), pp. 1, 240, 426, and 550. The information there collected supersedes all such earlier notices as may be found in the *Acta Sanctorum*, February, vol. ii, or in the DCB.

ST CONRAN, Bishop   (Sixth Century ?)

THE isles of Orkney are twenty-six in number, besides the lesser, called Holmes, which are uninhabited and serve only for pasture. The faith was planted here by St Palladius and St Silvester, one of his fellow-labourers, who was appointed by him the first pastor of this church, and was honoured in it on February 5. In these islands formerly stood a great number of monasteries, the chief of which was Kirkwall. This place was the bishop's residence, and is at this day the only remarkable town in these islands. It is situated in the largest of them, which is thirty miles long, called anciently Pomonia, now Mainland. This church is much indebted to St Conran, who was bishop here in the seventh century, and whose name, for the austerity of his life, zeal and eminent sanctity, was no less famous in those parts, so long as the Catholic religion flourished there, than those of St Palladius and of St Kentigern. The cathedral of Orkney was dedicated under the invocation of St Magnus, King of Norway. On St Conran, see Bishop Lesley, *Hist. Scot.*, 1, 4.

The above notice, which is here copied unaltered from Alban Butler, has a certain interest as illustrating the process by which pure fiction becomes accepted as fact in records of this kind. Where the name of Conran ultimately came from it is hard to tell, possibly it was borrowed from Hector Boece or from Arnold Wion, but Boece, Wion and Bishop John Leslie were quite uncritical and are valueless as authorities for the remote past. The Bollandists in the *Acta Sanctorum* refer to the Conran legend on this day, but in the absence of any satisfactory material for discussion the name is only entered among the "Praetermissi et in alios dies rejecti". What is certain is that in such standard works as Skene's *Celtic Scotland* and Dietrichson's *Monumenta Orcadica* not a shadow of evidence is to be found for the statement that the name of any St Conran was famous in the Orkneys. Dietrichson mentions eight early Celtic churches in the Orkneys, but no one of these dedications makes allusion to St Conran, though several were known as St Colmskirker. It is conceivable that the Colum or Colm thus honoured was a missionary in the Orkneys, and not the famous Columba of Iona. But Colm is something quite different from Conran.

See the *Acta Sanctorum*, February, vol. ii ; Skene, *op. cit.* ; Dietrichson, *op. cit.* (Christiania, 1906) ; and J. Mooney, *Eynhallow, the Holy Island of the Orkneys* (1949) ; but *cf. Analecta Bollandiana*, vol. lxix (1951), pp. 168–169.

ST ANTONINUS OF SORRENTO, Abbot   (A.D. 830)

St Antoninus appears to have been born at Picenum, in the district of Ancona in southern Italy, and to have entered when still young a monastery under the rule of Monte Cassino—not Monte Cassino itself, as some writers have erroneously supposed. The ravages of Duke Sico of Benevento forced him to leave his convent, and he went to Castellamare near Sorrento, to the bishop St Catellus, who received him very cordially and with whom he soon formed the closest friendship. They lived and worked together, and when St Catellus felt drawn to lead for a while a solitary life on a lonely mountain-top he entrusted St Antoninus with the care of his diocese. Antoninus, however, soon followed his friend, and the two had a vision of St Michael which led them, later on, to build an oratory there, dedicated to the archangel. When St Catellus was recalled on a charge of neglecting his diocese, and then summoned to Rome and imprisoned on a false accusation, St Antoninus continued to live on his peak, which commanded an extensive view over the sea and land and which, under the name of Monte Angelo, soon became a favourite place of pilgrimage. After a time, the inhabitants of Sorrento begged him to come and live in their midst, as their bishop was in prison and they felt that Antoninus would be a help and support to them. He therefore abandoned his solitary life and entered the monastery of St Agrippinus, of which he afterwards became abbot. When he lay dying, he was understood to say that he wished to be buried neither within nor without the city wall. Accordingly his monks decided to bury him in the city wall itself.

Tradition adds that when Sicard of Benevento (the son of Sico) besieged Sorrento, he tried with battering rams to break down that portion of the city wall which contained the saint's tomb, but all in vain. During the night St Antoninus appeared to Sicard and, after upbraiding him, beat him severely with a stick. In the morning he was covered with weals and, as he was taking counsel with his advisers, word was brought him that his only daughter had become possessed with devils and was rending her garments like a madwoman. He discovered upon inquiry that this had come upon her at the very hour when he had begun his attack upon the wall. Convinced that he was withstanding the will of God, Sicard abandoned the siege and sought the intercession of St Antoninus, who obtained the girl's restoration to health. Twice more—in 1354 and in 1358—Sorrento was invested, but by the Saracens, and each time the successful repulse of the enemy was attributed to the intercession of St Antoninus, who is therefore considered the chief patron of Sorrento.

The anonymous author of the Latin life of St Antoninus lived shortly after his time, and his account is probably trustworthy in its main features. This document was first printed by A. Caracciolo in his *Antonini coenobii Agrippinensis abbatis vita* (1626). The same life with other material will be found in the *Acta Sanctorum*, February, vol. ii, and also in Mabillon.

BD CONRAD OF BAVARIA   (A.D. 1154)

Ever since the death of Conrad honour has been paid him in the diocese of Molfetta in Apulia, where he ended his days, and also by his Cistercian brethren. This *cultus* was confirmed in 1832. Conrad was the son of Henry the Black, Duke of Bavaria, and seems to have been born about the year 1105. He came to Cologne to make his studies, but desiring a more perfect way of life he became a Cistercian

at Clairvaux.   A little later, with St Bernard's permission, he journeyed to Palestine, wishing to settle as a hermit amid the scenes which the presence of our Saviour
had sanctified.   After a while, however, the disturbed conditions of the country
and broken health induced him to return to Europe.   He never reached his native
land, but being put ashore somewhere in the neighbourhood of Bari or Molfetta
—the exact locality and the length of his sojourn seem to be matters of uncertainty
—he was unable to resume his journey.   There, at any rate, worn out by his
austerities and labours of charity, he is said to have died on March 15, 1154, his
sanctity being revealed by the marvels which occurred at his tomb.   We are told
amongst other things that the lambs used to pay him reverence by coming to kneel
beside the grave.

Reliable materials for his history are scanty, but there are lives of him by Giovene and
Catacchino.   See also Rader, *Bavaria Sancta*, vol. ii, p. 252 ; and J. E. Stadler's *Heiligen-
Lexikon*.

ST ADOLF, BISHOP OF OSNABRÜCK   (A.D. 1224)

EXCEPT for the date of his episcopate chronological details are scanty in the case
of St Adolf.   He belonged to the family of the Counts of Tecklenburg (Westphalia)
and at a very early age was made a canon of Cologne.   Wishing, however, to serve
God more perfectly he entered the neighbouring Cistercian monastery of Camp.
He seems to have been still a young man when on the translation of Gerard, Bishop
of Osnabrück, to the see of Bremen in 1216, he was elected to replace him.   The
new bishop is said to have been extremely active in every work of charity and to
have made a deep impression upon the citizens by his virtues and the austerity of
his life.   At his death they paid every mark of respect to his last resting-place, and
though he has never been formally canonized, the *cultus* which began in the thirteenth century has lasted down to our own day, and is liturgically recognized in
the diocese by a feast in his honour on February 14.   The actual day of his death
was June 30, 1224.

See the *Acta Sanctorum*, February, vol. ii, but the account there given errs in attributing
to him an episcopate of twenty-one years.   This clearly appears from the documents printed
in F. Philippi's *Osnabrücker Urkundenbuch*, pp. 47-140, and *cf.* Strunck, *Westphalia Pia
Sancta*, vol. ii, pp. 188-191.

BD NICHOLAS PAGLIA   (A.D. 1255)

THERE seems to be a good deal of legendary matter in what we are told of Bd
Nicholas Paglia.   What is best attested is the fact that as a young man studying
at Bologna he heard St Dominic preach there, and was so impressed that he begged
to be received into the Order of Preachers.   He is said to have belonged to a noble
family which had estates at Giovenazzo in Apulia, and it is possible that it was the
resources which came to him by inheritance which enabled him to found a Dominican priory at Perugia in 1233 and another at Trani in 1254 or thereabouts.   We
know further that he was prior provincial of the Roman province as early as 1230
and again in 1255.   In the *Vitae Fratrum* of Gerard de Frachet, he is described as
" a holy and prudent man, well versed in sacred lore ", and two or three anecdotes
are recounted of him which suggest that he was frequently the recipient of visions
and other heavenly communications.   He died at Perugia in August 1255, and on

the ground that his remains were always held in honour there as those of a saint his *cultus* was confirmed in 1828.

See S. Razzi, *Historia degli huomini illustri* (1596), vol. i, pp. 237 *seq.* ; Procter, *Lives of the Dominican Saints* ; Taurisano, *Catalogus Hagiographicus O.P.*, p. 14.

BD ANGELO OF GUALDO   (A.D. 1325)

THE information we possess concerning this servant of God is extremely scanty. He seems to have been born about 1265 at Gualdo on the borders of Umbria. He was distinguished all his life for his extreme simplicity, innocence and gentleness. One of the greatest crimes which troubled his conscience in youth was the giving away bread to the poor, a fault for which he was scolded, but as his mother died the same day he regarded himself as in some sense guilty of hastening her end. In early life he made many pilgrimages, travelling in particular barefoot from Italy to St James of Compostela in Spain. On his return he offered himself as a lay-brother to the Camaldolese monks, but after a very short time received permission to lead a solitary life according to his desire. In this vocation he faithfully persisted for nearly forty years. When he died on January 25, 1325 it is said that the church bells in the neighbouring district rang of themselves : the people scoured the country to discover the cause, and coming to his little cell they found him dead, kneeling in the attitude of prayer. The miracles wrought at his tomb brought many to do him honour, and Pope Leo XII approved the *cultus* in 1825.

See Mittarelli, *Annales Camaldulenses*, vol. pp. 237–241, 328–329 ; J. E. Stadler, *Heiligen-Lexikon.*

BD JOHN BAPTIST OF ALMODOVAR   (A.D. 1613)

THERE seems good reason to believe that, as among the Carmelites and certain sections of the Order of Friars Minor, so among the Trinitarians towards the close of the sixteenth century there were some who realized that very great relaxations had been introduced in the discipline of religious observance, and that there was urgent need of reform. The leader of this movement in the Trinitarian Order was John Baptist-of-the-Conception. He had been born at Almodovar del Campo in 1561, had studied at Baeza and Toledo, and had taken the Trinitarian habit in the latter city. In 1594 a general chapter of the order passed a resolution that in every province two or three houses should be set aside for the purpose of observing the primitive rule in all its strictness. It appears, however, that nothing, or next to nothing, was done to carry this resolution into effect, and it was openly stated that the measure had only been drafted to please King Philip II who in his last days inclined more and more towards religious views of an extremely austere type.

The fervent piety of John Baptist took scandal at this slackness. With the aid of a generous benefactor, the Marquess of Santa Cruz, he founded in 1597 a new house of reformed Trinitarians at Valdepeñas, and two years later was able to secure at Rome approbation for his new congregation of " Barefooted Reformed ". Though a serious breach resulted in the Trinitarian Order taken as a whole—the more so because the religious supervision of the new congregation was not confided to those who wore the same habit but to Discalced Carmelites and Franciscan Observants—still the zeal, devotion and disinterestedness of the reform made a great impression upon the laity. The generous alms contributed for the ransom of captives was now largely attracted to this new and more reliable channel. As a result the hostility of the unreformed members of the order reached such a pitch that a band of them came to Valdepeñas one night with the avowed intention of ridding themselves of this inconvenient rival. They did not actually put him to death, but they bound him, threw him into a ditch, and carried off a sum of 500 reales. In spite of the opposition of their jealous brethren, the Discalced Trinitarians steadily increased in numbers, and it is stated that when Father John Baptist died thirty-four monasteries had accepted the reform. After setting a great example of good observance and patience in suffering he passed away at Cordova on February 14, 1613. He was beatified in 1819.

See P. Deslandres, *L'Ordre des Trinitaires* (1903), vol. pp. 227–228 ; Seeböck, *Die Herrlichkeit der Katholischen Kirche* (1900), p. 65.

15: SS. FAUSTINUS AND JOVITA, MARTYRS   (DATE UNKNOWN)

FAUSTINUS and Jovita were brothers, nobly born and natives of Brescia. All the incidents in their reputed " acts " are of doubtful authority, and we can only be sure of their names and martyrdom. According to the tradition of Brescia, they preached Christianity fearlessly while their bishop lay in hiding. Their zeal excited the fury of the heathen against them, and they were arrested by a heathen lord called Julian. They were tortured and dragged to Milan, Rome and Naples, and then brought back to Brescia. A single feature may be cited to illustrate the extravagance which characterizes these hagiographical romances. When taken to Rome and Naples the martyrs are represented as having baptized in the course of their journey 191,128 persons in all, 42,118 at the place called Lubras, 22,600 at the Milvian bridge, 73,200 in the city of Rome and 53,210 at Naples. As neither threats nor torments could shake their constancy, the Emperor Hadrian, who happened to be passing through Brescia, commanded them to be beheaded. The city of Brescia honours them as its chief patrons and claims to possess their relics.

On April 18 the Roman Martyrology names the martyr St Calocerus, who figures largely in the legendary history of S. Faustinus and Jovita, whose heroic confession he is said to have witnessed when, as a court official, he accompanied Hadrian to his native city Brescia and was present in the amphitheatre. The constancy of the two confessors and the refusal of the wild beasts to touch them brought about his conversion, and he was baptized by Bishop Apollonius with 12,000 other citizens. He was tortured and imprisoned in several Italian towns, notably in Asti, where he instructed St Secundus who visited him in gaol. Eventually, we are told, he was taken to Albenga in Liguria and beheaded on the seashore.

A careful study of the text of the fuller " acts " of SS. Faustinus and Jovita with all their intricate ramifications involving the story of SS. Calocerus, Calimerus, Afra, etc., has been made by Fr Fedele Savio in the *Analecta Bollandiana*, vol. xv (1896) and in subsequent publications. No good purpose could be served by attempting to summarize his conclusions here. Although it would perhaps be rash to deny the real existence of Faustinus and Jovita and that they suffered at Brescia, still the difficulties involved are serious. As F. Lanzoni in his essay, *Le origini delle diocesi antiche d'Italia* (1923), has pointed out (pp. 532–533), the two early ecclesiastical writers of Brescia, Philastrius and Gaudentius, make no reference to these local patrons, and in the case of Gaudentius, at least, who was a great preacher and a devout collector of relics, this omission is surprising. Though the " Hieronymianum " apparently contained an entry of their names, this entry in most of our best and oldest manuscripts describes them as suffering not in Brescia but in " Brittania " (!) ; CMH., p. 99. However, St Gregory in his *Dialogues* refers to a church of St Faustinus at Brescia, and in the episcopal lists of that city the sixth bishop bears the same name. This seems to show that the martyr was honoured there at an early date. St Calocerus, like the story of St Innocent of Tortona, is an excrescence upon the legend of Faustinus and Jovita. Fr Savio maintained that the supposed martyr of Albenga was identical with St Calocerus, Bishop of Ravenna, whose remains were in the eighth century translated to Albenga. As is pointed out in CMH., p. 197, this Calocerus of Brescia cannot be said to be commemorated in the " Hieronymianum ", but he figures prominently in the *acta* of St Secundus of Asti.

ST AGAPE, Virgin and Martyr   (Date Unknown)

This Agape is mentioned in many of the early martyrologies, sometimes alone, and sometimes with companions. She is specially honoured at Terni in Umbria, and is one of the patrons of that town. According to a tradition of doubtful authenticity she lived at Interamna (Terni) in the days of the martyred bishop St Valentine, under whose direction she formed a kind of community of women who lived like nuns. When persecution against the Christians broke out, it was particularly fierce at Terni and, after a bold witness for Christ, Agape received the martyr's crown, not long after the death of St Valentine. A church was built at Interturres in her honour. It is probable that she actually suffered at Antioch.

The fact that a St Agape is commemorated in the Roman Martyrology on this day and is said to have suffered at Interamna does not go far towards vindicating her historical existence. No liturgical tradition supports it. There has probably been some confusion with other martyrs of the same name. See Delehaye in *Bulletin d'ancienne littérature et d'archéologie chrétiennes*, vol. i (1911), pp. 161–168, and P. Franchi de' Cavalieri in *Studi e Testi*, no. ix, pp. 1–20.

ST WALFRID, Abbot   (c. A.D. 765)

Walfrid or Galfrido della Gherardesca was born in Pisa, of which he became a prosperous and honoured citizen. He married a wife to whom he was deeply attached, and they had five sons and at least one daughter. After a time, Walfrid and his wife Thesia felt that God was calling them to enter the religious life. Walfrid had two friends—a kinsman named Gunduald and a certain Fortis, a native of Corsica : like him they were living in the world, but were drawn to a closer service of God under monastic discipline. Together they discussed the future, and were led by a dream to choose Monte Verde, between Volterra and Piombino, as the site of their future monastery. They decided to follow the Benedictine rule of Monte Cassino and, besides their own abbey of Palazzuolo, they built at a distance of about eighteen miles a convent for women, in which their wives and Walfrid's daughter Rattruda took the veil.

The new foundation attracted many novices, and before long there were sixty monks, including Walfrid's favourite son Gimfrid and Gunduald's only son Andrew, who became the third abbot and wrote the history of St Walfrid. Gimfrid was made priest, but in an hour of temptation he fled from the monastery, taking with him men, horses and papers which belonged to the community. Walfrid, greatly distressed, sent a search party after the fugitive. On the third day, when he was praying in the midst of his monks for his son's repentance and return, he besought God also to send Gimfrid a sign which would be constantly before him as a reminder and a warning for the rest of his life. That same day Gimfrid was caught and brought back penitent, but with the middle finger of his right hand so mutilated that he could never use it again. Walfrid ruled the abbey wisely and well for ten years, and after his death was succeeded by Gimfrid, who in spite of his earlier lapse became, as Andrew records, a great and good pastor. St Walfrid's *cultus* was confirmed in 1861.

The life by Andrew is printed in the *Acta Sanctorum*, February, vol.   and also by Mabillon, vol. iii, pt 2, pp. 178–184.

ST TANCO, BISHOP OF VERDEN, MARTYR   (A.D. 808)

ST TANCO (or Tatto) was a " Scottish " monk—almost certainly a native of Ireland. Moved by missionary zeal he went over to Germany, to the abbey of Amalbarich, near Verden in Saxony. Here he gained a great reputation for learning and piety, and he was made abbot after the resignation of St Patto, who afterwards became bishop of Verden. Through an ardent desire for martyrdom Tanco also vacated his office ; and after preaching in Cleves and in Flanders succeeded Patto as bishop of Verden. His success in propagating the gospel was great, but it was a great grief to him to see so many nominal Christians enslaved to degrading passions. In order to convert or at least to confound them, he preached strenuously against the vices to which they were prone. The mob was so enraged that they attacked him fiercely, and one man stabbed him to death with a lance, thus procuring for him the martyr's crown. According to another account he overturned the statues of some false gods, and the barbarians beat out his brains with clubs and cut off his arms and legs.

There seems to be no contemporary evidence to substantiate this story, but the legend is duly recounted in the *Acta Sanctorum*, February, vol. ii ; and LIS., vol. ii, p. 567.

ST SIGFRID, BISHOP OF VÄXJÖ   (c. A.D. 1045)

THE history of St Sigfrid is somewhat obscure, owing to conflicting narratives. One account states that after King Olaf Tryggvason of Norway had been converted to Christianity (he was confirmed at Andover by St Alphege the martyr who then was bishop of Winchester), he asked the English king, Ethelred, to send him missionaries. Sigfrid, said to have been a priest of York (or possibly Glastonbury), went out from England as a missionary bishop, and with him also went two other bishops, John and Grimkel. They did not confine themselves to Norway, but passed on to Sweden which, after having been in part evangelized by St Anskar, had relapsed into idolatry. There they laboured under the protection of the archbishop of Bremen, and Sigfrid made his headquarters at Växjö. The king of Sweden, whose name also was Olaf, was himself converted by St Sigfrid, who baptized him at Husaby in a spring which afterwards bore Sigfrid's name and was the channel of many miracles. St Sigfrid continued his labours successfully for many years, and at his death was buried in the church of Växjö. Tradition has added many details to the accounts of St Sigfrid's labours. It is said that when he first arrived at Växjö he began by planting a cross and building a wooden church in which he celebrated the divine mysteries and preached. The twelve principal men of the district were converted by him, and one of them, who died almost immediately, received Christian burial and had a cross placed on his grave. So wonderfully did the truth spread, that within a short time the faith was planted in all Värend.   The fountain in which St Sigfrid baptized the catechumens long retained the names of the first twelve converts, engraved on a monument.   It is said that he ordained two bishops, for East and West Gothland.   His three nephews, Unaman a priest, Sunaman a deacon, and Vinaman a subdeacon, were his chief assistants.

After a time, St Sigfrid entrusted the care of his diocese to these three and set off to carry the light of the gospel into more distant provinces.   During his absence, a troop, partly out of hatred for Christianity and partly for booty, plundered the church of Växjö and murdered Unaman and his brothers, burying their bodies in a forest and placing their heads in a box which they sank in a pond.   The heads were duly recovered and placed in a shrine, on which occasion, we are told, the three heads spoke.   The king resolved to put the murderers to death, but St Sigfrid induced him to spare their lives.   Olaf compelled them, however, to pay a heavy fine which he wished to bestow on the saint, who refused to accept a farthing of it, notwithstanding his extreme poverty and the difficulties with which he had to contend in rebuilding his church.   He had inherited in an heroic degree the spirit of the apostles, and preached the gospel also in Denmark.   Sigfrid is said, but doubtfully, to have been canonized by Pope Adrian IV, the Englishman who had himself laboured zealously for the propagation of the faith in the North over one hundred years after St Sigfrid.   The Swedes honour St Sigfrid as their apostle.

It would be impossible here to discuss the extremely intricate and contested history of the conversion of Sweden.   It must be sufficient to refer to two valuable articles, the one by Edmund Bishop in the *Dublin Review*, January, 1885, especially pp. 182-189 ; the other by L. Bril, " Les premiers temps du Christianisme en Suède " in the *Revue d'histoire ecclésiastique*, October, 1911.   Both writers are agreed that Adam of Bremen, to whom commonly appeal is made as a primary authority, has to be used with great caution, it being his obvious purpose to glorify the share of the see of Bremen in the conversion of Scandinavia and to belittle the efforts made by English missionaries.   Secondly, they both attach importance to the data furnished by the lives of Sigfrid, though it is admitted that the earliest of these dates only from the beginning of the thirteenth century and that they embody much which is purely legendary.   The lives may best be consulted in the *Scriptores Rerum Suecicarum*, vol. ii, pt i, pp. 345-370 ; and cf. " Trois légendes de St Sigfrid " in *Analecta Bollandiana*, vol. lx (1942), pp. 82-90.   The best account is said to be in Swedish, T. Schmid, *Den hl Sigfrid* (1931).   On C. J. A. Oppermann's *English Missionaries in Sweden* (1937), see *Analecta Bollandiana*, vol. lvii (1939), pp. 162-164.   There seems to be considerable doubt whether Sigfrid was an Englishman.

BD JORDAN OF SAXONY   (A.D. 1237)

BD JORDAN was St Dominic's immediate successor, and was therefore the second master general of the Dominicans.   Nothing is actually known as to the place and date of his birth ; but his name was really Gordanus, or Giordanus, and we know that he was a Saxon and that he was a bachelor of divinity in Paris by 1219, at which date St Dominic sent to him Reginald, one of his first scholars.   Apparently it was thus that he first became known to St Dominic.   On Ash Wednesday of the following year, he and his friend Henry were clothed with the Dominican habit, and he at once came to the fore from his extraordinary eloquence.   While he was yet a novice, as he himself relates in his Life of St Dominic (one of the main sources for that saint's career), and before he had been two months in the order, he was summoned from Paris, with three other brothers, to attend the first general chapter at Bologna.   At the following chapter, at which he was not present, he was chosen prior provincial of Lombardy, and in 1222, after the death of St Dominic, he was elected master general.

Bd Jordan did great things to extend and strengthen the order, and many friaries were founded under him, notably those at Regensburg, Constance, Bâle, Freiburg and Strasbourg, and the brothers eventually extended their labours to Denmark and other distant lands.   He used to frequent places where young students foregathered, and his eloquence won them in crowds   he has been called " the first university chaplain ", and on one occasion he preached the University Sermon at Oxford ; it was perhaps here that he met and impressed Bishop Grosse-teste.   It was a sermon of Jordan's that decided Albertus Magnus to enter the order.   One learned professor, Walter the German, who had solemnly warned his pupils against the wiles and snares of the Dominican who was coming amongst them, was himself the first to fall into the net.   Not that Bd Jordan cared only for the wise and learned.   While he was still in Paris, complaints were made to him that there were some sixty novices so uninstructed or of such poor intellect that it was only with the greatest difficulty that they could be taught to read one lesson of the office.   He replied, " Let them be—despise not one of these little ones : I tell you that many amongst them will become excellent preachers," and his words proved true.   Not only could he win men, but he knew how to retain them, and he could make allowance for human weakness.   Once he had collected a number of postulants or novices in a place where there was no Dominican house.   In the evening, when he began Compline in the lodging where they were assembled, one of the young men under emotional strain began to giggle and all the others followed suit.   One of the brothers, greatly shocked, made gestures to try to stop them.   Jordan finished the office and gave the blessing ; then, addressing the brother, he asked, " Who made you novice master ? " and turning to the young men he said, " Laugh on ! You may well laugh, for you have escaped from the Devil who formerly held you in bondage.   Laugh away, dear sons ! "

Many of his sayings which have been preserved are full of religious common sense.   Someone asked him whether a paternoster on the lips of an ignorant layman could possibly have as much value as a paternoster in the mouth of a learned cleric who understood it.   He replied that a gem lost none of its value when it was in the hand of one who could not appreciate its worth.   When asked which was better—studying the Scriptures or praying—he made answer, " You might as well ask me which is better—eating or drinking."   Upon being questioned as to the best way of praying, he said, " The way in which you can pray most fervently."

Friar Jordan was on his way to the Holy Land in 1237 with two of the brothers when they encountered a great storm off the coast of Syria, and the ship was wrecked, all lives being lost.   The body of Bd Jordan was washed ashore and was interred in the Dominican church at Akka.   It is said that within a few days of his death he appeared in a vision or dream to a young Carmelite at Akka who was troubled about his vocation and had said, " This Friar Jordan was a good man—and all he got for it was to be drowned."   " Fear not, brother ", said Jordan to the doubter, " Everyone who serves Jesus Christ to the end will be saved."   It has been suggested as an hypothesis that this was the origin of the tradition of St Simon

Stock's scapular-vision of our Lady. The ancient *cultus* of Bd Jordan was confirmed in 1828.

The main original sources for a life of Jordan are his own letters and such early Dominican chronicles as the *Vitae Fratrum*, or the *Chronica* of Galvagno de la Flamma, with the *Acta Capitulorum*, both general and provincial, etc. Fr Berthier printed in 1891 a good edition of Bd Jordan's *Opera ad res O.P. spectantia* ; there is a very useful German volume, *Die Briefe Jordans von Sachsen*, with comments by B. Altaner (1925), and an edition, *B. Jordani de Saxonia epistulae* (1950), by A. Walz. The most systematic study of Bd Jordan in his public capacity has been made by Mortier in his *Histoire des Maîtres Généraux O.P.*, vol. i, pp. 137–274, and there are several special biographies by Danzas, Mothon and others, including M. Aron, *Un animateur de la jeunesse* (1931). Fr Reichert compiled a valuable *Itinerarium* of Jordan which was included in the *Festschrift zur Jubiläum des deutsches Campo-Santo*, pp. 153–160. For a fuller bibliography, see Taurisano, *Catalogus*, pp. 10–11.

BD ANGELO OF BORGO SAN SEPOLCRO (*c.* A.D. 1306)

THE decree emanating from the Congregation of Sacred Rites, which in 1921 confirmed the *cultus* of this Augustinian hermit, frankly admits that the life of Angelo said to have been written by John of St William has perished. We are consequently very ill-informed regarding his career. His family name was Scarpetti, and he was born at Borgo San Sepolcro in Umbria. He seems to have taken the Augustinian habit about the same time as his more famous contemporary St Nicholas of Tolentino. The decree referred to states that he spent part of his religious life in England and was instrumental in founding several Augustinian houses in this country. Two anecdotes are also recorded which are believed to illustrate the high favour he enjoyed with Almighty God. We are told that once when he had sternly rebuked a man of scandalous life the offender in a passion raised his arm to strike him. It was, however, instantaneously paralysed, and the miscreant only recovered the use of it by the prayer of Bd Angelo. On another occasion an innocent man who had been sentenced to death recommended himself to Angelo's prayers. He was hanged in accordance with the sentence, but when the Brothers of the Misericordia came to cut him down and bury him, they found him still alive, and the man declared that Angelo had supported him all the time so that his neck was not broken. Obviously such stories, reported at fourth or fifth hand, are not very convincing ; but there appears to be better evidence that the body of Bd Angelo remained entire down to the year 1583, exhaling, it is asserted, a sweet fragrance, and that the veneration paid to his remains at Borgo San Sepolcro as those of a saint has been continuous.

See L. Torelli, *Ristretto delle vite degli huomini etc. dell' Ordine Agostiniano*, pp. 165–166, and the decree of confirmation in the *Acta Apostolicae Sedis*, 1921, pp. 443–446.

BD JULIA OF CERTALDO, VIRGIN (A.D. 1367)

THIS is another case of confirmation of cult where very little detail seems available regarding the life of the *beata* thus honoured. Her surname is said to have been della Rena, and it has been hastily assumed that she was a kinswoman of that noble family. However, Julia was at first a domestic servant in the household of some people called Tinolfi, but in 1337 at the age of eighteen she joined the third order of the Augustinians at Florence. Finding that the distractions of a great city interfered with her recollection, she returned to Certaldo, and there, owing to her heroic and, as men believed, miraculous rescue of a child left in a burning house, she was sought out by many as a soul marvellously privileged. This decided her to avoid, as far as could be, intercourse with her fellow-men, and she had herself walled up as a recluse in a cell beside the sacristy of the church of SS. Michael and James at Certaldo. She wished in this, we are told, to follow in the footsteps of Bd Verdiana of Castelfiorentino. In this same tiny anchorage she lived for nearly thirty years, dying on January 9, 1367, at the age of forty-eight. There seems to be good evidence that after her death she was honoured as a saint, and her *cultus* was accordingly confirmed in 1819.

See I. Malenotti, *Vita della beata Giulia, vergine da Certaldo* (1819) ; and N. Risi, *Un giglio tra le spine* (1919). F Dini has shown in *Miscellanea storica della Valdelsa* (1902), pp. 56–61, that Julia did not belong to either branch of the great family della Rena.

BD CLAUD LA COLOMBIÈRE   (A.D. 1682)

A CONTEMPORARY artist has left us the portrait of Bd Claud taken when he was between thirty-five and forty-one years of age—a longish face, eyes small but bright and penetrating, a broad forehead, a well-proportioned mouth and rather a pointed chin. We are told that when he entered the Society of Jesus he was fairly strong physically, of a lively disposition, with very high ideals and in every way wise and gracious. Such gifts were to be carefully cultivated in the religious life. His intellect was trained and developed so that his outlook was broad and his judgement acute and sound. He was a lover of the fine arts ; and Olivier Patru, a member of the French Academy in 1640, corresponded with him and speaks of his writings in high praise. But these gifts would have been of little use in his work for souls if they had not been united to the interior spirit of the perfect religious animated by zeal for the glory of God. The source of his inner life was union with God in prayer, which occupied him continually. He so accustomed himself to refer everything to God that human respect and worldly motives became impossible to him. This wonderful detachment was indeed his distinguishing feature.

Bd Claud was born at Saint-Symphorien d'Ozon near Lyons in 1641. His family was well-connected, pious and in easy circumstances. There are no special records of his childhood till he was sent to the Jesuit college at Lyons for his studies. Though he acknowledged a strong aversion to the idea of a religious vocation, he conquered himself, and when he applied to be received into the Society he was at once accepted. He made his novitiate at Avignon, and after the usual two years passed into the college in that city to complete his course of philosophy. When this was ended, he was at first put to teach grammar and then the humanities, in which occupations he spent the years from 1661 to 1666. Since 1659 Avignon had been in a state of unrest ; there was continuous friction between the nobles and the people. In 1662 came the unfortunate affray in Rome between the papal guard and the suite of the French ambassador, which resulted in the occupation of Avignon, at that date still papal territory, by the troops of Louis XIV. The pupils' studies, however, were not interfered with, and the simultaneous increase of Calvinism only served to redouble the zeal of the Jesuit fathers who spent themselves in apostolic labours in the town and in the neighbouring country.

With the return of peace the townspeople of Avignon celebrated the canonization of St Francis de Sales, and the older of the two convents of the Order of the Visitation in that city was the scene of a great ecclesiastical function. This was the first occasion on which Bd Claud's gifts of oratory were displayed. He, though not yet ordained, was one of those chosen to preach the saint's panegyric in the convent church.   His text was : " Out of strength has come sweetness " (Judges xiv, 14), and the sermon was pronounced magnificent.   Meanwhile it had been decided to send the young Claud to Paris to finish his course of theology, and here he found himself in the very centre of the intellectual life of France.   Here also a great honour was conferred on him : the two sons of the famous Colbert were put under his care.   Most probably Colbert realized how gifted his sons' tutor was, and therefore, though he was no friend to the Jesuits, he had chosen Claud for such an important post.   However, his connection with the Colbert family came to an abrupt conclusion, as unfortunately a satirical phrase in an article which Claud had written was brought to the great minister's knowledge.   He was much offended, and asked that Claud might be recalled to his own province.   This, however, could not be till 1670.

The young priest was in 1673 appointed festival preacher in the college church at Avignon.   He took immense pains with his sermons, which are models of the art of preaching both for their sound doctrine and their beauty of language.   The same sermons seem to have been preached later in England, and the name of the Duchess of York (Mary of Modena, afterwards queen when James II succeeded to the throne), in whose chapel they were delivered, is traditionally attached to them in the printed editions.   During his time in Paris he had come into contact with Jansenism with its network of untruths and calumnies.   He could now from the pulpit combat these errors, animated as he was by that special love of the Sacred Heart which was to prove a most potent antidote.   At the end of 1674 Father La Chaize, Bd Claud's rector, was directed by the father general to admit him to solemn profession after he had made a month's retreat at the outset of what is called the third probation.   The retreat brought Claud many graces.   He was led to consecrate himself specially to the Sacred Heart, and in addition to the vows of profession he took a private vow to practise exact obedience to the rule of the Society of Jesus in every detail which it prescribed.   He notes that he had for some time lived as he was now pledged by this vow to live, and that he had bound himself thus formally in order to insure his perseverance.   At this date he was just thirty-three years old, the age at which our Lord died, and the inspiration came to him that he must now die still more completely to the world and to himself.   As a spiritual note of his records : " It seems right, dear Lord, that I should begin to live in thee and for thee alone, at the age at which thou didst die for all and for me in particular."

Two months after his solemn profession in February, 1675, Claud was made superior of the college at Paray-le-Monial.   It was unusual to put a young professed at the head of a house, and on the other hand gifts such as he possessed seemed hardly to have sufficient scope in a small residence of only four or five fathers such as was Paray.   We may well believe that he was sent by God for the sake of an elect soul who needed him.   That soul was St Margaret Mary Alacoque.   She was suffering and perplexed because of the extraordinary revelations of the Sacred Heart which were granted her and which became every day clearer and more intimate. In obedience to her superior, Mother de Saumaise, she had told everything to a priest, a learned man, but one who had no knowledge of these extraordinary ways. He insisted that she was suffering from delusions, and her distress was only increased.   She prayed for help and believed that our Lord answered that His faithful servant and perfect friend should be sent her.

Father La Colombière* came one day to give the community an instruction.
" As he spoke ", the saint tells us, " I heard in my soul the words ' He it is I send
you '." The first time she went to confession to him he behaved as if he knew
what was passing within her. She felt a repugnance and shrank from speaking
openly to him, though she knew it was God's will she should do so. When next
he came he told her he was glad to be the means of giving her an opportunity of
making a sacrifice to God, and thereupon " without my feeling any pain ", she says,
" he opened out my heart and showed me its depths, good and bad. He consoled
me greatly and told me not to fear God's leading as long as I was obedient, that
I must give myself entirely to Him to be treated as He willed. He taught me to
cherish the gifts of God and to receive His communications with faith and humility."
Thus he was of the greatest service to her personally, and he did much to further
the devotion to the Sacred Heart in the Church in general, realizing that this
devotion was the best antidote to Jansenism.

Father La Colombière was not long at Paray. His next mission was very
different : on the recommendation of Father La Chaize, the confessor of Louis XIV
of France, he was sent to London as preacher to Mary Beatrice d'Este, Duchess of
York. In England he preached by word and by the example of his holy life. The
love of the Sacred Heart became his favourite subject. His process tells us of his
work for souls in this country and of the many Protestants he converted. The
position of Catholics in England was extremely difficult as the hostile feeling against
them was just then intense. An agitation was set on foot to exclude the Duke of
York, who had become a Catholic, from the royal succession and to put the Prince
of Orange or some other in his place. The story of a spurious " Popish Plot ", a
tale fabricated by the infamous Titus Oates and his abettors, convulsed the country
and in this Father La Colombière amongst the rest was supposed to be implicated.
The object of the plot was said to be the murder of King Charles II and the destruction of the Established Church. Claud La Colombière was accused of having
exercised his ministry and of having converted Protestants and lapsed Catholics.
He was imprisoned in the King's Bench, but did not win the martyr's crown, as
through the intervention of Louis XIV he was simply banished from England.
His already bad health was completely broken by his imprisonment, and when he
returned to France at the beginning of 1679 it was only to lead the life of an invalid.
Although there were intervals when he rallied and active work was possible, his
lungs were seriously attacked. His superiors, hoping that the air of his native
province would be beneficial, sent him to Lyons and to Paray, and it was on a second
visit to Paray that by the direct counsel of St Margaret Mary he remained there to
die. After setting an example of great humility and perfect patience he passed
away on the evening of February 15, 1682, and it seems that the next morning St
Margaret Mary was supernaturally assured that his soul was in Heaven and needed
no prayers. Bd Claud was beatified in 1929.

See *A Jesuit at the English Court*, by Sister Mary Philip (1922), and the lives written in
French by Fr Seguin and by Fr Charrier, the former of which exists in an English translation ;
but the most up-to-date biography, fully-documented, is by Fr G. Guitton (1943). Mrs M.
Yeo's *These Three Hearts* is a reprint of a life published first in 1940. See also Frs Monier-
Vinard and Condamin, *Bx. Claude . . . Notes spirituelles* (1929), and the *Dictionnaire de
spiritualité*, vol. ii, cc. 939–941. Bd Claud's complete works, containing a good deal of
autobiographical detail, have been more than once published, and some of them translated.

* The " de " was added after his death.

In the decree of beatification Bd Claud is described as the " coadjutor " of St Margaret Mary in propagating devotion to the Sacred Heart, and as one chosen by God to direct her in the time of her trouble and vexation of spirit. For his part in spreading the devotion, *cf.* P. Pourrat, *La spiritualité chrétienne* (Paris, 1947 ; Eng. trans.), vol. iv, pp. 420–423.

16 : ST ONESIMUS, Martyr   (First Century)

ONESIMUS was a slave of Philemon, a person of note of the city of Colossae in Phrygia who had been converted to the faith by St Paul. Having robbed his master, and being obliged to fly, he met with St Paul, then a prisoner for the faith at Rome, who converted and baptized him, and entrusted him with his canonical letter of recommendation to Philemon.   By him, it seems, Onesimus was pardoned, set at liberty and sent back to his spiritual father, whom he afterwards faithfully served, for apparently St Paul made him, with Tychicus, the bearer of his epistle to the Colossians, and afterwards, as St Jerome and other fathers witness, a preacher of the gospel and a bishop.   Baronius and others confound him with St Onesimus, the bishop of Ephesus some time after St Timothy, who showed great respect and charity to St Ignatius when on his journey to Rome in 107, and is highly commended by him.

The Roman Martyrology devotes a notice to Onesimus, identifying him with this bishop of Ephesus, consecrated to that see by St Paul (!) after the episcopate of St Timothy, and stating further that he was brought in chains to Rome, was there stoned to death, and that his remains were afterwards taken back to Ephesus.   The so-called " Apostolic Constitutions ", an apocryphal document of the end of the fourth century (bk vii, c. 46), describes Onesimus as bishop of Beroea in Macedonia, and affirms at the same time that his former master Philemon became bishop of Colossae.   Nothing of this clearly is any more worthy of credit than the fantastic story which represents him as being the companion in Spain of the supposed martyrs Xanthippe and Polyxena and as being the compiler of the " acts " of their martyrdom.   The fact is that Onesimus was a very common name, especially for those of servile condition, and that anyone bearing such a name who became prominent was likely to be identified with the Onesimus of the New Testament.

Nothing is known of Onesimus except what can be gleaned from the Epistle to Philemon and the possible reference in Colossians iv 7–9.

ST JULIANA, Virgin and Martyr   (*c*. A.D. 305 ?)

The Roman Martyrology under this date commemorates at Cumae in Campania the translation of St Juliana, virgin and martyr, " who first was grievously scourged at Nicomedia by her father Africanus under the Emperor Maximian, and then tortured in divers ways by the prefect Evilasius whom she had refused to marry. Afterwards she was cast into prison where she openly fought with the Devil ; and then overcoming flames of fire and a boiling cauldron she consummated her martyrdom by having her head stricken off."   The story of St Juliana was popular in the middle ages, as is attested by the fact that a long section is devoted to her in the

Golden Legend of James of Voragine.   It is at the same time quite unhistorical, though our best manuscripts of the "Hieronymianum" point to some veneration of a St Juliana in the neighbourhood of Cumae and Naples.   We also find St Gregory the Great writing to Fortunatus, Bishop of Naples, to ask him for *sanctuaria* (substitutional relics) of this saint which might serve for the consecration of an oratory which a lady had erected on her estate in honour of St Juliana and St Severinus.   The martyrologies seem to have tried to reconcile the conflicting data which they found in their sources by the suggestion of a translation of the martyr's remains from Nicomedia to Pozzuoli or Cumae.   A prominent feature in the "acts" is a wordy contest between Juliana and the Devil, who, transforming himself into an angel of light, endeavours to persuade Juliana to comply with the wishes of her father and her suitor.   From this she is often represented in medieval art as preparing to bind a winged devil with a chain or rope.

See *Acta Sanctorum*, February, vol. ii, and BHL., nn. 4522-4524.   *Cf.* Delehaye, *Les Origines du culte des martyrs* (1933), pp. 301-302 ; Detzel, *Christliche Ikonographie*, vol. ii, p. 456.

SS. ELIAS, JEREMY AND THEIR COMPANIONS, MARTYRS   (A.D. 309)

IN the year 309, when the Emperors Galerius Maximian and Maximus were continuing the persecution begun by Diocletian, five Egyptians went to visit the confessors condemned to the mines in Cilicia, and on their return journey were stopped by the guards of the gates of Caesarea in Palestine.   They readily declared themselves to be Christians and acknowledged the motive of their journey.   Thereupon they were arrested, and on the following day, together with St Pamphilus and others, were brought before Firmilian the governor.   The judge, as was his custom, ordered the five Egyptians to be stretched on the rack before beginning his examination.   After they had suffered all manner of torture, he addressed the one who appeared to be their chief and asked him his name and his country.   The martyr, using the names which they had taken upon their conversion, said that he was called Elias and that his companions were Jeremy, Isaias, Samuel and Daniel. Firmilian asked him their country, and Elias answered that it was Jerusalem— meaning the heavenly Jerusalem, the true country of all Christians.   Elias was then tortured again, his body being scourged whilst his hands were tied behind him, and his feet squeezed into wooden stocks.   The judge then commanded that they should be beheaded, and his order was immediately carried out.

Porphyry, a youth who was a servant of St Pamphilus and who heard the sentence passed, exclaimed that they ought not to be denied burial.   Firmilian, angry at this boldness, ordered him to be apprehended, and, finding that he was a Christian and that he refused to sacrifice, ordered his sides to be so cruelly torn that his very bones and bowels were exposed.   He underwent this without a sigh or a groan. The tyrant then gave orders that a great fire should be kindled with a vacant space in the middle in which the martyr should be placed when removed from the rack. This was accordingly done, and he lay there a considerable time, surrounded by the flames, singing the praises of God and invoking the name of Jesus ; until at length he achieved a slow but glorious martyrdom.   Seleucus, an eyewitness of this victory, was heard by the soldiers applauding the martyr's constancy.   They brought him before the governor, who without more ado ordered his head to be struck off.

This story is one of overwhelming interest for all who are concerned with Christian hagiography, for it is the account given by Eusebius, the father of Church history, who was not only living in Caesarea at the time, but was the intimate friend of the St Pamphilus here named, the principal martyr who suffered on the same occasion. To mark his devotion to his friend, the historian loved to call himself " Eusebius (the disciple) of Pamphilus "   St Pamphilus, however, is commemorated separately on June 1, and will come before us again on that date. The Greek text of Eusebius, with a French translation *en face*, may conveniently be consulted in the edition of E. Grapin (vol. iii, pp. 259 283), forming part of the series of *Textes et documents pour l'étude historique du Christianisme*. It forms the eleventh chapter of the Book on the Martyrs of Palestine, of which there is an English version, with the *Ecclesiastical History*, by H. J. Lawlor and J. E. L. Oulton (1929).

ST GILBERT OF SEMPRINGHAM, FOU. GILBERTINE
ORDER   (A.D. 1189)

St GILBERT was born at Sempringham in Lincolnshire, and in due course was ordained priest. For some time he taught in a free school, but the advowson of the parsonages of Sempringham and Terrington being in the gift of his father, he was presented by him to the united livings in 1123. He gave the revenues of them to the poor, reserving only a small sum for bare necessaries. By his care, his parishioners were led to sanctity of life, and he drew up a rule for seven young women who lived in strict enclosure in a house adjoining the parish church of St Andrew at Sempringham. This foundation grew, and Gilbert found it necessary to add first lay-sisters and then lay-brothers to work the nuns' land. In 1147 he went to Cîteaux to ask the abbot to take over the foundation. This the Cistercians were unable to do, and Gilbert was encouraged by Pope Eugenius III to carry on the work himself. Finally Gilbert added a fourth element, of canons regular, as chaplains to the nuns.

Thus the Gilbertines came into being, the only medieval religious order of English origin. Except for one house in Scotland, it never spread outside this country and became extinct at the dissolution, when there were twenty-six monasteries. The nuns had the Rule of St Benedict and the canons St Augustine's. The houses were double, but it was mainly a women's order, though at its head was a canon, the master general. The discipline of the order was severe and strongly influenced by Cîteaux ; and the insistence on simplicity in church-furnishing and worship went to the extent of celebrating the choir office " in monotone in a spirit of humility, rather than to pervert the minds of the weak like the daughter of Herodias ".

Eventually St Gilbert himself assumed the office of master general of the order, but resigned the direction of it some time before his death, when the loss of his sight rendered adequate supervision impossible. So abstemious was he that others wondered how life could be supported on such slender fare. He always had at his table a dish which he called " the plate of the Lord Jesus ", into which he put all that was best of what was served up, and this was for the poor. He wore a hair-shirt, took his short rest sitting, and spent a great part of the night in prayer. During the exile of St Thomas of Canterbury, he and other superiors of his order were accused of having sent him assistance. The charge was untrue ; yet the saint chose to suffer imprisonment and to run the risk of the suppression of his order rather than deny the accusation, lest he should seem to condemn what would have been good and just. When nearly ninety he suffered from the slanders of some of the lay brothers, who were in revolt.

St Gilbert died in 1189 at the age of 106, and was canonized in 1202. His relics are said to have been taken by King Louis VIII to Toulouse, where what purports to be them are still kept in the church of St Sernin. His feast is kept in the dioceses of Northampton and Nottingham today, and by the Canons Regular of the Lateran on February 4, the day on which he is named in the Roman Martyrology.

Most of the materials for a biography of St Gilbert have been printed in the 1830 edition of Dugdale's *Monasticon*, vol. vi, pt 2. See also BHL., nn. 3524–3568. Much useful information regarding him and his order may be found in the work of Rose Graham, *St Gilbert of Sempringham and the Gilbertines* (1901). See also R. Foreville, *Le Livre de St Gilbert de Sempringham* (1943). Capgrave's Life of St Gilbert has been edited by J. J. Munro for the E.E.T.S. *Cf.* D. Knowles, *The Monastic Order in England* (1949), pp. 204–207, and references there given.

BD PHILIPPA MARERI, Virgin   (A.D. 1236)

WONDERFUL things, of which one would like to have better evidence, are reported as heralding the entrance into this world of Philippa Mareri. Wonderful things also are told of her beauty of feature, her preternatural gravity and precocious learning in childhood. She was born towards the close of the twelfth century at Cicoli in the diocese of Rieti, and the family to which she belonged were the principal landowners in that district of the Abruzzi. Her father and mother were devout Christians, and St Francis of Assisi, we are told, was more than once received in their house when he was preaching in the neighbourhood. From him Philippa imbibed a desire to aim at complete union with the suffering life of Christ our Lord. When her parents were anxious to arrange a marriage for her, she resisted the proposal with all her might, cut her hair short, wore the most unattractive clothes, and shut herself up in a corner of the house where she was hidden from the eyes of all. Her brother Thomas was furious at this conduct and did his best to break down her resolution ; but the only result of his importunity was that she finally ran away from home, and with a few companions whom she had gained over to the same way of thinking set out to lead the life of an anchoress upon Mount Marerio. There, we are told—but the evidence for all this seems far from satisfactory—they managed to get a walled enclosure built with a few huts inside and gave themselves up entirely to religious devotion and penance.

The determination thus shown had the best effect upon her brother Thomas. Touched by grace he now came to ask his sister's forgiveness. What was more, he offered her a more suitable place of retirement close to a church on an estate belonging to him. A deserted religious house was repaired and adapted to suit their needs, while a friar who had recently become a disciple of St Francis and who is now venerated as Bd Roger of Todi, was charged with the spiritual direction of the community. Other fervent souls joined them, a rule similar to that of St Clare was adopted, and Philippa was chosen abbess. The strictest poverty was maintained, and more than once the sisters seemed in danger of starving if it had not been for some supernatural intervention kindred to our Saviour's multiplication of the loaves and fishes. God's favour was also shown by other miraculous incidents ; but the nuns were not left long to enjoy the company of their foundress.

In 1236 she was seized with a painful illness, and knowing that the time of her departure was at hand, she gathered her spiritual children around her and bade them a most touching farewell, exhorting them before all else to maintain peace among themselves. She passed away on February 13, 1236. Bd Roger preached at her funeral and made no secret of his conviction that her soul was already in bliss.

See Mazzara, *Leggendario Francescano* (1676), vol. i, pp. 233 235 ; Léon, *Auréole Séraphique* (Eng. trans.), vol. and Constantini, *Vita e miracoli della b. Philippa Mareri*.

BD VERDIANA, Virgin   (*c.* A.D. 1240)

VERDIANA, whose name is variously written Viridiana and Veridiana, was born at Castelfiorentino in Tuscany of a noble family which had fallen from its high estate. When she was twelve years old, a well-to-do relation took her as a companion for his wife, who made her housekeeper. Even at that time she had a reputation for sanctity, and when she obtained permission to join a pilgrimage to St James of Compostela she had first to promise that she would come back to Castelfiorentino. Upon her return, her fellow pilgrims gave such an account of her holiness that the people begged her to stay permanently amongst them. This she consented to do if they would allow her to live the life of a recluse and would build her a hermitage. They erected one near the river Elsa, adjoining a little oratory ; it is reputed to have measured ten feet by four and to have been furnished only with a narrow stone ledge to serve as a seat. She lived for thirty-four years in her cell, and all the communication she had with the outside world was through a little window which opened into St Antony's oratory.* She ate once a day, mainly bread and water with, occasionally, a few vegetables. She slept on the bare earth except in winter when she used a plank. She had a very great love for the poor, to whom she gave nearly everything which the piety of visitors brought to her, and she only cared to receive the poor and the afflicted.

Wonderful miracles were ascribed to Bd Verdiana. It was commonly reported that two serpents had entered her cell through the tiny window and that they remained with her for years, being allowed to torment her and even eating from her plate ; but that the saint kept their presence a secret, as she did not wish her sufferings to be known. She had a visit from St Francis of Assisi himself in 1221. The two saints talked together of heavenly things and he admitted her, it was said, into his third order. She was divinely warned of her approaching death, and she closed her window and was heard reciting the penitential psalms. Tradition tells that her passing was miraculously announced by the sudden pealing of the bells of Castelfiorentino. In Florentine art Bd Verdiana appears in the habit of a Vallombrosan nun, carrying a basket with two snakes in it. It seems certain that she was associated with the Vallombrosan Order, but her connection with the Franciscan third order is by no means so clearly established. The *cultus* was approved by Clement VII in 1533.

O. Pogni, *Vita di S. Verdiana* (1936), published a Latin text written soon after her death. A later one, translated back from an Italian version, is in the *Acta Sanctorum*, February, vol. i. Canon Pogni also published Canon M. Cioni's account of the *beata* and her church and hospital at Castelfiorentino (1932–34). See also Gonnelli, *Vita di S. Verdiana* (1613). There is a notice in Léon, *Auréole Séraphique* (Eng. trans.), vol. i.

* Just such a window or hatchway can be seen at the site of an anchorhold at Lewes in Sussex, giving on to the church of St Anne.

BD EUSTOCHIUM OF MESSINA, Virgin   (A.D. 1468)

WHEN St Matthew of Girgenti was preaching in Messina, the young Countess Matilda of Calafato came under his direction and joined the Franciscan third order, giving herself up to good works.   She was for some time childless, but a daughter was vouchsafed to her in answer to her prayers.   Shortly before the child's birth a stranger told the countess that she could only be delivered in a stable, so she was taken to one, and there in 1432 she gave birth to an infant who, because of her beauty, was named Smaragda.   Deeply pious from her earliest years, the child vowed herself to a life of virginity, although her father signed a marriage contract with a suitor, who died before the nuptials could be celebrated.   After her father's death in 1446 Smaragda took the habit of St Clare in the convent of Basico, where the second rule was followed under the direction of the Franciscan Conventuals, and she then assumed the name of Eustochium.   She was distinguished for her love of poverty, her spirit of penitence and for her devotion to the passion of our Lord.   After reading an itinerary of the Holy Land, she worked out for herself a system whereby she could visit all the Holy Places in spirit and could visualize the scenes in the life of our Lord and of the Blessed Virgin Mary.   She regularly tended the sick and devoted herself especially to nursing them when the plague visited Messina.

After eleven years spent at Basico, Bd Eustochium felt that she desired a stricter rule, and Pope Callistus III allowed her to found another convent to follow the first rule of St Francis under the Observants.   In 1458-1459 her mother and sister built the convent which was called Maidens' Hill (Monte Vergine).   There she received, amongst others, her sister and her niece Paula, who was only eleven years of age.   The foundation passed through many trials during its early years.   When Eustochium became thirty—the legal age—she was elected abbess and gathered around her crowds of fervent souls.   The authority of her virtues was increased by the fame of her miracles—the sick being healed even by the kerchief which had been bathed by her tears of penitence.   She died at the age of thirty-five, her *cultus* being subsequently approved in 1782.

The most reliable account of Eustochium is to be found in a narrative written by her first disciple, Jacopa Pollicino.   It has been printed by G. Macri in the *Archivio storico Messinese*, vols. iii and iv (1903), under the title of *La leggenda della b. Eustochia da Messina*. See also Léon, *Auréole Séraphique* (Eng. trans.), vol. i.

BD BERNARD SCAMMACCA   (A.D. 1486)

IT is unfortunate that in regard to those servants of God who are publicly venerated in virtue of a confirmation of cult, reliable details are so often lacking which would give us any real insight into their lives.   Of Bernard we are told that he was born of a noble family at Catania in Sicily, that he led a wild life as a young man, that his leg was seriously injured in a brawl, and that in the course of the illness and long convalescence thus occasioned he turned to God and determined to enter the Dominican Order.   He is believed to have set a great example of obedience and humility and to have expiated the sins of his youth by severe penance.   But for the embellishments added to this account we have no guarantee.   It was said that the birds perched on his arms and sang to him, that he prophesied the future, that he was seen raised from the ground in prayer, and on another occasion that his cell was irradiated with brilliant light which came from a torch held by a child of heavenly beauty who stood beside him.   After his death on February 9, 1486 other marvels were reported.   After lying in the grave for fifteen years he appeared to the prior and bade him remove his body to a more honourable resting-place.   This was done ; his remains were found incorrupt, and during the translation the church bells rang of their own accord.   Still later a nobleman organized a raid with the object of carrying off the body to his own castle.   But Bd Bernard had no intention of allowing his relics to be kidnapped.   Before the raiders could reach the church he knocked at the door of every cell, and when the sleeping friars were rather tardy in responding to this unexpected summons he rang the great bell, which proved an effective tocsin.   The good Dominicans rushed to the church " where they found the tomb empty and the sacred body lying at the door, sur-rounded by armed men who were vainly endeavouring to raise it from the ground. It had miraculously become so heavy that the robbers were unable to move it." So the raiders took to flight, and the saint without difficulty was restored to his shrine.   The *cultus* of Bd Bernard was confirmed in 1825.

See Procter, *Short Lives of the Dominican Saints*, pp. 21–23 ; Mortier, *Maîtres Généraux O.P.*, vol. iv, p. 648 ; M. Coniglioni, *Vita del b. Bernardo Scammacca* (1926) ; Taurisano, *Catalogus Hagiographicus O.P.*, pp. 45–46.

17 : SS. THEODULUS AND JULIAN, Martyrs   (A.D. 309)

ST THEODULUS and St Julian suffered at Caesarea in Palestine im-mediately after the five Egyptians commemorated on the 16th, but they are mentioned under this date in the Roman Martyrology.   Theodulus, a wise and pious old man, occupied one of the most honourable positions in the household of Firmilian, the governor of Palestine, who held him in great esteem.   After witnessing the fortitude and patience of the five saints, he visited the prison and held the martyrs up as examples to encourage the other confessors and to prepare them for a similar ordeal.   Firmilian was so furious at this action on the part of his old servant that he sent for him, reproached him sternly for his ingratitude and, without hearing his defence, condemned him to be crucified.   Theodulus received the sentence gladly, and went joyfully to a form of death which so closely resembled that of his Saviour and by means of which he would speedily be united with Him.

Julian, who shared his triumph, was only a catechumen, held in great honour by the faithful on account of his exemplary character.   He had been absent from Caesarea and had scarcely arrived back when he was informed of the sufferings and of the execution of the martyrs which had just been taking place.   At once he ran to the spot, and finding that all was over he expressed his veneration by kissing and embracing the bodies of the saints.   The guards apprehended him and took him to the governor, who, perceiving that he was as determined as the rest, wasted no time in useless cross-examination but immediately ordered him to be burnt. Julian thanked God for the honour, and asked Him to accept his life as a voluntary sacrifice.   His cheerfulness whilst he was being tortured by slow fire amazed his executioners and the spectators.

As in the case of SS. Elias and his companions, so our knowledge of SS. Theodulus and Julian depends entirely upon Eusebius, as cited above.

ST LOMAN, BISHOP   (*c*. A.D. 450 ?)

ACCORDING to Jocelin's Life of St Patrick, Loman was the son of Patrick's sister Tigris, and was one of those disciples who accompanied him to Ireland.   The story runs that when St Patrick landed to go to Tara, he left St Loman to look after the boat and to navigate it up the Boyne.   Fortchern, the son of the chieftain of Trim, heard him singing psalms and chants in the boat, and was so attracted that he came down to the water's edge to listen.   St Loman entered into conversation with him and taught him from the little ship and they began to sing together.   Presently they were joined by Fortchern's mother, a British or Scottish princess, who, being herself a Christian, was overjoyed at the news that the gospel of Christ was being brought to Ireland.   Soon Fortchern's father, Fedelmid, came under instruction and was baptized with all his household.   He gave St Patrick land at Trim for a church, of which St Loman was consecrated bishop.   In the course of time Fortchern also became a saint and a bishop, apparently succeeding St Loman at Trim.

It has been much contested whether St Loman actually belonged to the times of St Patrick or whether, as there seems some reason to believe, he should rather be identified with a certain Bishop Loman of Trim who is known to have lived in the seventh century.

The account given above seems to be ultimately founded on the *Tripartite Life of St Patrick* (Rolls Series, vol. i, pp. 66–69), though nothing is there said of " singing psalms ", but the writer speaks only of reading the gospel.   No great reliance, of course, can be placed upon any of the Celtic legends of this period.   Colgan and the Bollandists have connected this commemoration with February 17, which is the common feast of Loman (Lommán) and the other saints of Trim ; October 11 is his proper day.   See Fr P. Grosjean's essay in the *Journal of Ecclesiastical History*, vol. i, no. 2 (1950), pp. 164–166.

ST FINTAN OF CLONEENAGH, ABBOT   (A.D. 603)

IN a tractate preserved in the Book of Leinster St Fintan is presented as an Irish counterpart of St Benedict, and there can be no question as to the high repute in which his monastery of Cloneenagh in Leix was held by his contemporaries.   An early litany speaks of " the monks of Fintan, descendant of Eochaid, who ate nothing but herbs of the earth and water ; there is not room to enumerate them by reason of their multitude ".   Quite in accord with this is a gloss in the *Félire* of Oengus   " Generous Fintan never consumed during his time aught save the bread of woody barley and muddy water of clay."   The Latin life bears out this description of extreme asceticism, which indeed St Canice of Aghaboe thought excessive and protested against.   It tells us how the saint's future holiness was foretold to his mother by an angel before his birth, how even in his boyhood he possessed the gift of prophecy and of a knowledge of distant events, how he was trained by St Columba of Tir da Glas, and how in accord with this master's direction he settled in Cloneenagh, leading an eremitical life of great austerity, but gathering round him eventually a multitude of disciples.   Apart from this we have little more than a catalogue of miracles, though the miracles are not so extravagant as those often found in Irish hagiographical documents.   The account leaves the impression that Fintan, while extraordinarily severe to himself, was gentle and compassionate in his treatment of others.   When the monks of neighbouring communities protested that his rule was too austere for human endurance, he consented to allow some mitigation for the benefit of his subjects, but would make no change in his own practice. Not a few characteristic traits of early Irish monasticism are revealed in the narrative. For example, we read of a section of the brethren at Cloneenagh who " burning with an over-great love of a pilgrim's life (the Irish *peregrini* were famous throughout Europe) and unwilling to live in their own native land departed from the monastery without the permission of their holy abbot ", and went to Bennchor and to Britain. Fintan does not seem to have taken a very stern view of their offence, and he even accorded a warm welcome to one at least of the fugitives who subsequently asked to be taken back. Again the lawlessness and violence of those rude times are brought home to us in a story which illustrates his respect for the dead. A band of marauders after making a successful raid against some neighbouring clan returned in triumph, bringing with them the gory heads of the enemies they had slain. They left the heads near the monastery, and St Fintan had them buried in the cemetery of the monks. When asked why he did this, Fintan replied," We trust in the Lord that at doomsday these men will not suffer torment, in virtue of the merits and the glory of all the saints of this holy spot who themselves will lie here interred and who will pray in their lifetime for the souls of those to be buried in their company. Since the principal part of their bodies reposes here, we hope that they will find mercy." Whatever theological misconceptions may be detected in this answer, the keen desire to be buried in close proximity to those who were thought to be sure of rising in glory was widely prevalent from the days of the catacombs to the close of the middle ages. Of the triumphant raiders just referred to, one afterwards became a monk at Cloneenagh. St Fintan, it is said, when praying in a lonely spot was surrounded by such a radiance of light that a brother who had followed him out of curiosity to observe what he did was almost blinded by the effulgence which dazzled him. We are also told that every Sunday night St Columba from his island home at Iona beheld in a vision St Fintan standing among the angels before the judgement seat of Christ. Columba told a disciple to seek out the abbot in Ireland, and described him as a man saint-like and comely, with a ruddy face and gleaming eyes, whose hair was flecked with white. The feast of St Fintan is kept throughout Ireland.

See VSH., vol. ii, pp. 96–106 (*cf.* vol. i, pp. lxx–lxxi), and Colgan, *Acta Sanctorum Hiberniae*, pp. 349–353. The Bollandist text in the *Acta Sanctorum*, February, vol. iii, pp. 17–21, presents a conflation of two different recensions of the same original. *Cf.* J. Ryan, *Irish Monasticism* (1931), pp. 127–128 and *passim*.

ST FINAN, Bishop of Lindisfarne   (A.D. 661)

St FINAN, an Irishman by birth and then a monk of Iona, succeeded St Aidan at Lindisfarne, of which he became the second bishop. His huge diocese comprised the whole of the modern counties of Northumberland, Durham and York, but he was a man of strong character as well as of most saintly life, and he appears to have exerted a firm and unquestioned sway over his half-civilized, widely-scattered and somewhat unruly flock. He was a strenuous upholder of the Celtic tradition in which he had been reared, and opposed the modern innovations introduced from the south of England by the successors of Augustine, who kept in closer touch with Rome. St Finan's ten years' rule was a peaceful one, and he lived on terms of friendship with King Oswy of Northumbria. He had the joy of baptizing Peada, prince of the Middle English, at whose request he sent St Cedd and other missionaries to preach to the Mercians. Their labours were crowned with success, and numbers of souls were converted to Christianity. After a time another royal penitent came to Finan to ask for baptism : this was Sigebert, King of the East Saxons, who had been converted through the efforts of King Oswy. Sigebert also asked for missionaries, particularly for St Cedd of whom he had heard much from Oswy. Eventually St Finan consecrated St Cedd bishop of the East Saxons and Diuma, a Scot, bishop of the Middle English. On Holy Island St Finan built a cathedral : it was of wood, after the Celtic fashion, and the roof was covered with a thatch of bent or sea-grass which is so plentiful along the Northumbrian coast. His feast is observed in the dioceses of Lancaster and Argyll.

Our principal authority is Bede, *Hist. Eccles.*, bk iii, chs. 17, 21, 22, 25.

ST SILVIN, Bishop   (*c.* A.D. 720)

NOTHING is definitely known of the parentage of St Silvin. His early manhood was spent at the court of Kings Childeric II and Thierry III. He was betrothed and was about to be married when he felt the call to abandon the world and to follow Christ in the path of poverty and celibacy, and he accordingly retired from the court. He received holy orders in Rome and afterwards became a bishop. Some accounts say that his diocese was Toulouse, others give it as Thérouanne, but as his name is not found in any register of either of these churches it seems more likely that he was ordained a regionary bishop to preach the gospel to the heathen. Silvin worked zealously in the north of France, spending most of his time in the region of Thérouanne, which was then full of pagans or of nominal Christians who were not much better than heathens. He was indefatigable in preaching to them and he gained a considerable harvest of souls by his teaching and example. Much of his private fortune was expended in ransoming slaves from the barbarians, and he devoted the rest to charity and to the building of churches. Although he was endowed with good looks and a courtly address he wore the meanest clothes and practised great austerities ; it was remarked that in his humble house he received every stranger as though he were Christ Himself. St Silvin's biographer says that for forty years he ate no bread, but lived on potherbs and fruit, and the only possession he retained for himself was a horse which he rode when he became too weak to walk. His great wish was to live the life of a hermit, but his bodily infirmities would have precluded it even had he obtained release from his episcopal duties. He appears to have died at Auchy-les-Moines near Arras, and was certainly buried in that monastery. Even in his lifetime he was held in great honour, not only on account of his charity and holiness, but also for the gift of healing with which he was credited.

There is a Latin life of St Silvin by Bishop Antenor, who must have been a contemporary, but it has undergone revision and amplification at a later date. The text will be found in the *Acta Sanctorum*, February, vol. iii, and in Mabillon. Duchesne, *Fastes Épiscopaux*, vol. iii, p. 134, thinks that Silvin was probably a " Scot ", and points out that Folcuin makes it clear that he was still living at the time of the battle of Vincy (717).

ST EVERMOD, Bishop of Ratzeburg   (A.D. 1178)

WHEN St Norbert was preaching at Cambrai in 1120 his eloquence made a deep impression upon a young man named Evermod, who thereupon forsook the world and joined the Premonstratensian canons under St Norbert's rule. He accompanied his beloved superior to Antwerp, where he laboured strenuously to repair the mischief done by the heretical teacher and firebrand, Tanchelm. In 1134 Evermod succeeded St Norbert as superior of the monastery of Gottesgnaden ; but in 1138 the urgent recommendation of Wigger, Bishop of Brandenburg, put him in charge of the abbey dedicated in honour of the Blessed Virgin at Magdeburg. Sixteen years later he was consecrated first bishop of Ratzeburg, on the confines of what is now Schleswig-Holstein, an office which he retained until his death. His apostolic energy won the admiration of all, and he is known to posterity as an apostle of the Wends.

No formal biography of St Evermod seems to have been preserved to us, but an account of his life is furnished from miscellaneous sources in the *Acta Sanctorum*, February, vol. iii. See also C. Hugo, *Sancti Ordinis Praemonstratensis Annales*, vol. i, p. 766, and vol. ii, pp. 172 and 599 *seq.*

BD REGINALD OF ORLEANS   (A.D. 1220)

Of the sons of St Dominic who have been proposed for the veneration of the faithful, Bd Reginald was the first to pass out of this world. He wore the habit for a very short time, but tradition holds that it was to him, and not to the founder himself, that our Lady appeared and made known her wish that the linen rochet which the saint's companions had hitherto worn as canons should be exchanged for the white woollen scapular of the friars. Reginald, who was born in 1183 at Saint-Gilles in Languedoc, not far from Arles, seems to have been a young man of singular promise. He had taught canon law in the University of Paris from 1206 to 1211 before he was appointed in 1212 dean of the collegiate chapter of Saint-Aignan at Orleans. In the course of a pilgrimage he came to Rome in 1218, and there met St Dominic, whom he recognized as the spiritual guide who had already been shown to him by our Lady in a time of dangerous illness. He offered himself as a disciple, and Dominic had so much confidence in him that he made him vicar of his rapidly growing religious family during the time that he himself was absent in Spain. Reginald, being bidden in that same year 1218 to betake himself to Bologna, laid the foundations of a great Dominican house in connection with the university there. Both there and at Paris, whither he was sent the next year, he had immense success both in preaching and in gaining recruits for the order. But he was already ripe for Heaven, and dying in Paris, February 1, 1220, he was buried in Notre-Dame-des-Champs. It is said that his tomb was venerated from the beginning as that of a saint, and on this ground his *cultus* was confirmed in 1875.

Our information about him is derived from the early chronicles of the Dominican Order, such, for instance, as Gerard de Frachet's *Vitae Fratrum* and Bartholomew of Trent's *Liber Epilogorum*. Memoirs have also been compiled in modern times by E. C. Bayonne, T. A. Karr and A. Gardeil. See also Mortier, *Maîtres Généraux O.P.*, vol. i, pp. 96-100 and 118-119, and Taurisano, *Catalogus Hagiographicus O.P.*, p. 8.

BD LUKE BELLUDI   (*c.* A.D. 1285)

THE devotion to St Antony of Padua is so widespread and of such early date that we cannot be surprised if those more intimately associated with him have been irradiated with his glory. Luke Belludi, born in the year 1200 of an opulent family near Padua, received the habit and cord of the Friars Minor in that city when he was twenty years old at the hands of St Francis himself. There also a little later he became the companion and intimate friend of St Antony, who, as an ancient chronicle attests, worked a great miracle at Luke's urgent request by restoring a dying child to health.   When St Antony himself in 1231 passed away at Padua in the Franciscan house known as the Aracoeli or " Arcella ", Bd Luke was one of the two friars who tended him in his last moments.   Finally it was Luke who, as provincial minister of the order, was mainly instrumental in erecting the magnificent basilica which enshrines the remains of his beloved friend and which perpetuates to this day the glory of the tender-hearted Franciscan.   We know little more of Luke beyond the fact that he was active in preaching and good works.   When he died in 1285, he was interred in the empty marble tomb which the body of St Antony had first occupied, and the slab which covered it was, it appears, used as an altar upon which Mass was celebrated.   In virtue of these and similar facts attesting the honour in which Luke has always been held in Padua, his *cultus* was confirmed in 1927.

See the decree of confirmation in the *Acta Apostolicae Sedis*, vol. xix (1927), pp. 213–216; B. Marinangeli, *Cenni sulla vita del b. Luca Belludi* (1929) ; and cf. Mazzara, *Leggendario Francescano*, vol. i, pp. 235–236.

BD ANDREW OF ANAGNI   (A.D. 1302)

IN the Franciscan supplement to the Roman Martyrology this servant of God is described as " Beatus Andreas de Comitibus " ; but it would seem that the more accurate form of his name is Andrea dei Conti di Segni (Andrew of the Counts of Segni).   In Mazzara he is called Andrea d'Anagni, from his birthplace.   As we learn from these designations he was of noble family, nephew of the Roland Conti who became Pope Alexander IV and a near kinsman of another native of Anagni, Benedict Gaetani, Pope Boniface VIII.

Laying aside all thought of worldly advancement he gave himself to the Order of Friars Minor, in which he remained a simple brother, not even aspiring to the priesthood.   His reputation for holiness was great, and it is probably true that a cardinalate was at some time offered him, and that he definitely declined to be so honoured.   Our sources of information, however, do not seem very trustworthy. One is consequently a little disposed to be sceptical about some incidents recounted in the legend of Bd Andrew.   For example : " Wadding relates that one day when he was ill and unable to take his ordinary food, a friend brought him some roasted birds.   The saint, touched with pity at the sight of the innocent creatures, would not eat, but, making the sign of the cross over them, commanded them to resume their feathers and fly away.   He was instantly obeyed, and the little birds, restored to life, took flight with chirps of joy " (Léon, i, 134).   There is no doubt that Andrew was held in great veneration both in life and after death for the miracles he was believed to work.   He breathed his last on February 1, 1302, and his *cultus* was formally approved in 1724.

See Léon, *Auréole Séraphique* (Eng. trans.), vol. i ; Mazzara, *Leggendario Francescano* (1676), vol. i, pp. 155–156.

BD PETER OF TREIA   (A.D. 1304)

THIS Peter was one of the early Franciscans and received the habit from St Francis himself.   He was born at Montecchio, near Treia, of poor parents, and he entered the order when still quite young.   He received holy orders, after which he was most devoted in carrying out the duties of the sacred ministry.   He preached boldly against licentiousness and converted many sinners.   It is related that once, when he was praying in the church of the convent of Ancona, his superiors saw him rapt in ecstasy and lifted from the ground ; our Lady, St John the Evangelist and St Francis all manifested themselves to him in visions.   He had a particular veneration for the Archangel St Michael, who appeared to him on the last day of the special Lent which he used to keep in his honour and talked with him a long time, promising him the remission of his sins.   He was united by a great bond of friendship to Bd Conrad of Offida, who lived with him for some years in the convent of Torano which St Francis had founded.   They worked and preached together and roused each other in noble emulation to higher and higher stages of sanctity, until the fame of their holiness shed a glow of distinction over their simple little community ; on the feast of the Purification one year Peter had a wonderful vision in which he saw our Lady place her Son in the arms of Bd Conrad.   After a long life of labour, adorned by miracles and the gift of prophecy, Bd Peter died at the convent of Sirolo in the Marches.   Popular devotion, which had gathered about him from the hour of his death, was sanctioned in the year 1793.

There is a pronounced atmosphere of legend in the accounts given of Bd Peter by Mazzara, *Leggendario Francescano*, vol. i, pp. 245-246, and the *Auréole Séraphique* of Fr Léon (Eng. trans.), vol. i.   They all derive from Wadding, and Wadding used, without discrimination, almost any materials that came to hand.   *Cf.* also A. Canaletti Gaudenti, *Il b. Pietro da Treja* (1937).

BD WILLIAM RICHARDSON, Martyr   (A.D. 1603)

This priest was the last martyr to suffer death for his religion during the reign of Queen Elizabeth.   He apparently belonged to a Lancashire family but was born at Wales, near Sheffield.   He went to the college at Valladolid in 1592, and from thence to Seville, where he was ordained.   It is not known how long he ministered in England (under the name of Anderson) ; but in February 1603 he was arrested in London, having been betrayed by one whom he had trusted.   His trial and condemnation for being a seminary priest were hurried through, and he was executed at Tyburn on the 17th of the same month.

Information about this martyr is very slight.   See MMP., p. 269, and Gillow's *Biog. Dict.*, vol. v, p. 414.   There are references in *Calendar of State Papers Domestic*, 1601-1603, pages 292-302.

THE MARTYRS OF CHINA, I   (Nineteenth Century)

So far as is known, Christianity was first preached in China in the seventh century, and then in its heretical Nestorian form.   The first mission from the Catholic West was established in 1294 at Khanbaliq (Peiping, Peking) by a Franciscan friar, John of Monte Corvino ; the first permanent settlement was made, by the Jesuits, during the sixteenth and seventeenth centuries ; in 1631 they were followed by the Dominicans, two years later by the Franciscans again, in 1680 by the Augustinian friars, and by priests of the Paris Foreign Missions in 1683.   This settlement has survived all persecution and other difficulties down to our own time.

In 1900 and 1909 a number of martyrs of the Chinese missions were beatified, of whom two outstanding ones suffered during this month of February.   There is something so splendidly heroic in his life, crowned by a cruel martyrdom when seventy-two years old, that BD FRANCIS-REGIS CLET claims some special notice, however brief and inadequate.   He was born at Grenoble in 1748, and joined the Congregation of the Mission (Lazarists) at the age of twenty-one.   After a brief period during which he acted as professor of theology at Annecy, he was appointed novice-master at Saint-Lazare, Paris, in 1788.   During this troubled revolutionary period it was often difficult to maintain the despatch of a regular succession of missionaries to the Far East.   An opportunity of securing a passage for two or three to China occurred in 1791, but as one of the priests appointed was accidentally detained, Father Clet offered to supply his place.   He reached Macao, and thence, after tedious delays, made his way into the interior of the empire.

It would be difficult to do justice to the arduousness of the life he led there for nearly thirty years.   Apart from the language which, beginning as he did when he was over forty, he never was able to learn well, he came into a district in which the existence of much disaffection and even open rebellion had created an atmosphere of suspicion.   The officials, at least intermittently, scrutinized all who came and went.   His life for long periods was like that described in the Epistle to the Hebrews : " they wandered about in sheepskins, in goatskins, being in want, distressed, afflicted."   The few priests who were in that vast province, then called Hukwang, died or fell into the hands of the persecutors.   For three years he carried on his work absolutely alone.   Communications were most difficult.   Many of his letters both to Europe and to his superiors at Peking went astray, and his health, tried by the climate and the hardships to which he was exposed, constantly broke down.   None the less he was beloved, and he often had the consolation of witnessing the most astounding steadfastness, in the face of indescribable torments and brutality, among the converts he had gained.   In 1818 began a period of exceptional persecution.   A strange and inexplicable darkness occurred one morning at Peking.   The emperor was frightened and, though he had hitherto been tolerant of Christian teachers, it was put into his head that the local deities were offended and that all foreign religions must be suppressed.   He issued a decree of which the effects were widespread.   Father Clet for a long time evaded capture, but owing to the malice of a pagan against a Christian convert, and afterwards to the treachery of another convert who betrayed the priest to gain the reward of 1000 taels (nearly £300) which had been offered for his apprehension, the missionary was captured and then had to endure scourgings, cruel confinement and other forms of torment which it is terrible to read of as inflicted on a man of his venerable age. The firmness of his replies only provoked his judges.   They ordered him to be repeatedly struck in the face, and in the end he was sentenced to be strangled.   This was not the simple punishment which we might suppose but, according to their barbarous custom, after the victim had been rendered unconscious by tightening the noose, the pressure was relaxed until he came to.   This was twice repeated, and it was only on the third application of the torture that Father Clet was finally despatched.   He suffered at Wuchangfu, just opposite Hankow, the capital of Hupeh.   It was February 17, 1820.

BD LOUIS GABRIEL TAURIN DUFRESSE, martyred in 1815 and among those beatified in 1900, was one of the most effective missionaries ever sent out by the Paris Society of Foreign Missions.   He went to China as a priest at the age of twenty-six, and worked for seven years in the province of Szechwan, till in 1785 he was denounced and went into hiding.   He successfully eluded capture for several months, but being afraid that the search for him would lead to the finding of some of his *confrères* he gave himself up and was imprisoned at Peking. He was released with other prisoners and deported to Manila, where he remained for four years till he accompanied the vicar apostolic, Mgr de Saint-Martin, back to Szechwan. In 1800 M. Dufresse was consecrated titular bishop of Tabraca as his auxiliary, and in the following year succeeded to the vicariate. For a time persecution was lessened and Mgr Dufresse administered his district with great vigour. Forty thousand heathen had been converted and the mission required a complete organization, which was taken in hand by a synod held in 1803. In 1811 a decree was issued ordering a search for foreign preachers. Only seven were found at Peking, three of whom were officials in charge of the observatory (European skill in astronomy and mathematics provided a lever at the imperial court of which missionaries took full advantage). But the inquisition was extended to the provinces and persecution began again in Szechwan worse than ever. On May 28, 1815, Mgr Dufresse was betrayed and taken to Chintai, the capital of the province.

It is satisfactory to be able to record that the venerable bishop, now sixty-four years old, was treated without barbarity and indeed with consideration by the local mandarins. His books were returned to him and he was allowed to speak freely in court, a permission that he availed himself of with such effect that many of his auditors were deeply moved by his passionate plea for Christianity. The several interrogations to which he was submitted were conducted without bullying and the bishop's replies were courteously listened to : his known character and works were such that his judges were somewhat prejudiced in his favour. On September 14 he was brought before the governor, who sentenced him to death by beheading. According to the law this sentence required the imperial confirmation before it could be carried out, but the governor disregarded this and ordered the execution on the spot, in order, as he hoped, to terrify and weaken the other captive Christians, who were sent for to be present. But the bearing and words of Bd Louis Gabriel had the contrary effect, and as he gave them his last blessing they affirmed aloud that they too would die for Jesus Christ, as in fact many of them did. The head of the martyr was put on a pole and with his trunk was publicly displayed for a week as a warning, guarded day and night by Christians, who when they were allowed gave them decent burial.

For those who are not experts, the map of China is a very bewildering study, and when one learns from one authority that Bd JOHN LANTRUA suffered at Shian Sa, which is said also to be in the province of Hupé, from another that the scene of his martyrdom was Tchang Cha, the capital of Hou Nan, and from the Franciscan supplement to the martyrology that he was strangled at Chansai, one is inclined to give up in despair any attempt to identify the locality. It appears, however, that the most authorized spelling is Changsha, and that this stands for a town of 500,000 inhabitants in the very centre of the country and south of the great Tungting lake —in fact Hunan, the province of which it is the capital, means nothing but " south of the lake ". Here it was that Father John ended at last by a comparatively merciful death his career of many labours and much suffering.

He was born in 1760 at Triora in Liguria, became a Franciscan at the age of seventeen, taught theology at Corneto in 1784, and was appointed guardian at Velletri in 1785, but after some years of strenuous labour he obtained leave to devote the rest of his life to the foreign missions. He left Italy in 1798, but a year's delay occurred at Lisbon before he could obtain a passage to Macao. Thence he proceeded into the interior of China, facing many dangers and hardships, for it was a period of almost unremitting persecution, but he brought encouragement to many Christians who were wavering in their faith and himself gained a rich harvest of converts.   In the provinces of Hupeh and Hunan he was at that time labouring almost alone.   In the end he was delated to the authorities, his little chapel was burnt to the ground, and all his effects seized.   To the questions put to him he made answer with all the boldness and resolution of the ancient martyrs.   Being then sent in chains a long and weary journey to a court of higher jurisdiction, he got for those who were arrested with him the privilege of being carried in a litter. Finally he was transferred to Changsha, where for six months he was kept in durance under the most intolerable conditions, his neck, feet and hands being secured with fetters.   He was dragged by force over the crucifix that it might be said that he had trampled it under foot, but he at once protested, in tones which compelled the attention of all, that this had happened against his will.   There remained no alternative for his judges but to sentence him to death.   In the last scene he prayed fervently in public and by giving a bribe to the executioners he saved himself from being stripped naked.   Then he was strangled and his body exposed to infamy. He suffered on February 7, 1816.

Among the later martyrs—he suffered on February 27, 1856— was BD AUGUSTUS CHAPDELAINE, who was born near Coutances in 1814.   His family, mainly by their own labour—he was the ninth child—farmed an estate of many hectares.   He was a generous and pious lad, and when he turned his hand to field-work it is recorded of him that he toiled like a galley-slave—*il faisait de la besogne pour quatre*.   Death, however, visited their homestead.   Two of the more vigorous sons were taken. The labour of the rest no longer sufficed, and the farm had to be broken up.   This set Augustus free to gratify the desire he had long entertained of studying for the priesthood.   In due course he was ordained, and became in 1844 curate of a parish in which his zeal worked marvels.   However, in 1851 he felt a higher call to the foreign missions, and after a short period of training at the house of the Missions Étrangères he left Paris for China.   It was only after many hardships that he eventually reached the destination assigned him.   In December 1854 he was denounced to the mandarin governor by the jealous relative of a Christian convert. He was arrested, and for some days spent a most anxious time, but the mandarin proved friendly and no harm befell him.   He laboured strenuously, and in spite of his imperfect knowledge of the language made many converts.

Later on, however, another mandarin was appointed to this district.   A new denunciation was followed by the apprehension of M. Chapdelaine with a number of his Christians.   His brave answers provoked the judge and he was ordered three hundred blows with a rattan, which left him half dead.   No cry of pain or word of complaint was heard from him, and in a day or two he seemed to be miraculously restored to health.   The mandarin believed that some spell had been employed, and a dog was accordingly killed and its warm blood thrown over him to dispel the magic.   At a second hearing of the case the missionary was sentenced to receive three hundred blows in the face with a heavy leather shoe-sole.   Many of his teeth were knocked out and his jaw fractured.   In the end he was given to understand that he might be released for a payment of 1000 taels, afterwards reduced to 300, but no such sum could be raised.   Sentence of death was therefore passed, and he was subjected to slow martyrdom by the torture of the cage.   When life was extinct his head was struck off, and we are told that three jets of blood spouted heavenwards and deeply impressed the spectators that something extraordinary had taken place.

Among the others beatified in 1900 and 1909 were the laymen PETER LIEU, strangled after encouraging his sons in prison (1834), PAUL LIEU (1818) and JOHN-BAPTIST LO (1861); the lay catechist JEROME LU (1858) and the seminarist JOSEPH SHANG (1861); JOHN PETER NÉEL, a French priest who was beheaded in 1862, together with his Chinese catechist, MARTIN; AGNES SAO KUY, a young maiden killed by torture at Kwangsi (1856); and the school-teacher AGATHA LIN, beheaded at Maoken in 1858.

For other martyrs in China see BB. Francis de Capillas (January 15), Peter Sanz and his companions (May 26), Gregory Grassi and his companions (July 9) and John Perboyre (September 11).

An excellent biography of Clet will be found in an anonymous work called *Le disciple de Jésus*, first published in 1853. There is another life in French by G. Guitton (1942), and one in English by A. S. Foley (1941). The French life of John of Triora by A. du Lys has been translated into German. See also A. Launay's works on the Chinese missions, such as *Les 52 serviteurs de Dieu* ., vol. ii, pp. 287–304, and his *Salle des martyrs du Séminaire des Missions*; H. Leclercq, *Les martyrs*, vol. x; H. Walter, *Leben, Wirken und Leiden der 77 sel. Martyrer von Annam und China* (1903); B. Wolferstan, *The Catholic Church in China* (c. 1910); and Kempf, *The Holiness of the Church in the Nineteenth Century* (1916), pp. 304–306. For the early history of the Church in China, Moule's *Christians in China before the year* 1550 (1930) is invaluable.

18 : ST SIMEON, BISHOP AND MARTYR   (*c.* A.D. 107)

IN St Matthew's Gospel, ch. xiii, we read of St Simon or Simeon who is described as one of our Lord's brethren or kinsmen. His father was Cleophas, St Joseph's brother, and his mother, according to some early writers, was our Lady's sister. He would therefore be our Lord's first cousin and is supposed to have been about eight years older than He. No doubt he was one of those brethren of Christ who are mentioned in the Acts of the Apostles as having received the Holy Spirit on the day of Pentecost. St Epiphanius says that when the Jews massacred St James the Lesser, his brother Simeon upbraided them for their cruelty. The apostles and disciples afterwards met together to appoint a successor to James as bishop of Jerusalem, and they unanimously chose Simeon, who had probably assisted his brother in the government of that church. In the year 66 civil war broke out in Palestine, as a consequence of Jewish opposition to the Romans. The Christians in Jerusalem were warned of the impending destruction of the city and appear to have been divinely ordered to leave it. Accordingly that same year, before Vespasian entered Judaea, they retired with St Simeon at their head to the other side of the Jordan, occupying a small city called Pella. After the capture and burning of Jerusalem, the Christians returned and settled among the ruins until the Emperor Hadrian afterwards entirely razed it. We are told by St Epiphanius and by Eusebius that the church here flourished greatly, and that many Jews were converted by the miracles wrought by the saints.

When Vespasian and Domitian had ordered the destruction of all who were of the race of David, St Simeon had escaped their search; but when Trajan gave a similar injunction, he was denounced as being not only one of David's descendants but also a Christian, and he was brought before Atticus, the Roman governor. He was condemned to death and, after being tortured, was crucified. Although he was extremely old—tradition reports him to have attained the age of 120—Simeon endured his sufferings with a degree of fortitude which roused the admiration of Atticus himself.

The above account of St Simeon, which follows in substance the elogium printed in the Roman Martyrology, is by no means free from difficulty. See the *Acta Sanctorum*, February, vol. iii, and Eusebius, *Hist. Eccl.*, bk iii. No final solution can be arrived at determining the identity of our Lord's " brethren ". See, *e.g.* Cornely, *Introduct. in S. Scrip.*, vol. iii, 2nd edn., pp. 595 *seq.*

SS. LEO and PAREGORIUS, Martyrs   (Date Unknown)

According to their legend these two were close friends, and when Paregorius had suffered martyrdom at Patara in Lycia, Leo was disconsolate at being deprived of the happiness of sharing his victory. But Lollian, the governor of Lycia, published an edict obliging all men to offer sacrifice on the festival of Serapis. Now the mysteries celebrated in honour of this deity were of such a licentious character that the Roman senate had at one time ordered them to be abolished. St Leo, on his way to the martyr's tomb, had to pass the temple of Serapis, and was greatly distressed to see amongst the crowds some whom he knew to be Christians, but who were led by fear to join in the worship of the false god. Soon after his return from his friend's tomb he fell asleep and had a dream in which it was revealed to him that God was calling him to a conflict similar to that which St Paregorius had endured. Filled with exultation, he determined that the next time he visited the martyr's grave he would not go through by-roads, but would make his way openly through the city. As he crossed the market-place, he saw that the Tychaeum or Temple of Fortune was illuminated with lanterns and candles. In his zeal for God he did not scruple to pull down all the lanterns he could reach and to trample the tapers under foot. When the priest cried out to the people, " If this sacrilege is not punished, the goddess Fortune will withdraw her protection from the city ", St Leo exclaimed, " Let the idol take vengeance if it can ".

The report of these proceedings soon reached the governor, who commanded that St Leo should be brought before him, and charged him with impiety to the gods and to the emperors. The martyr replied calmly, " You are mistaken in supposing that there are many gods : there is only one God, who is Lord of Heaven and earth and who does not require men to worship Him in the gross way that men worship idols."—" Answer the charges that are brought against you ", said the governor, " this is not the time to preach your Christianity. Either sacrifice to the gods or else suffer the punishment due to impiety." Leo answered, " The fear of torment shall never deter me from my duty. I am quite prepared to suffer whatever you may inflict all your tortures cannot reach beyond death. Eternal life can only be won through tribulation, for, as the Holy Scriptures teach us, narrow is the way that leadeth to life."— " Since you own that the path you tread is narrow," retorted the governor, " exchange it for ours which is broad and easy."—" I called it narrow ", said the saint, " because it is hard to enter and because at the beginning it is often beset with afflictions and persecution. But when once it has been entered, it can be kept to without great difficulty through the practice of virtue which helps to widen it and makes it easier—as many have discovered." The people cried out to the judge to silence him, but Lollian protested that he was willing to allow him liberty of speech and would even befriend him if he would only sacrifice. The confessor replied, " Would you have me acknowledge as a god that which has nothing divine about it ? " Then the governor, losing patience, ordered Leo to be scourged. Whilst the executioners were tearing his body, Lollian, who pitied his old age, continued to urge him at least to say that the gods were great. Leo retorted, " If I say they are great, it is only with reference to their power to destroy their worshippers ". The judge threatened to have him dragged over rocks and stones, but the martyr said, " You do nothing but threaten : why do you not carry out your threats ? " By this time the mob had become clamorous, and Lollian sentenced Leo to be tied by the feet, dragged to the torrent and there executed. Before he died, the martyr thanked God that he was not long separated from Paregorius, commended his soul to the care of the angels, and prayed for his enemies. After his death the executioners threw the body down a precipice but the Christians recovered it, unbruised and entire. It was noticed that his face was quite peaceful and appeared to be smiling.

This passion has been included by Ruinart in his collection of *Acta sincera*. Later criticism has not endorsed this favourable view. The story must probably be classed among the historical romances which were so widely disseminated both in East and West from the fifth century onwards (Delehaye, *Les Légendes Hagiographiques*, 1927, p. 114). Lollian was, no doubt, an historical personage, but that does not make the story true. A Latin rendering of the " acts " will be found in the *Acta Sanctorum*, February, vol. iii. The original Greek may be consulted in Migne, PG., vol. cxiv, cc. 1452–1461.

ST FLAVIAN, PATRIARCH OF CONSTANTINOPLE, MARTYR   (A.D. 449)

ST FLAVIAN, priest and treasurer of the church of Constantinople, succeeded St Proclus as patriarch or archbishop in 447. The chamberlain Chrysaphius, a special favourite with the Emperor Theodosius II, suggested to his master that he should require a present of Flavian as an expression of gratitude to the emperor for his promotion. The bishop sent him some blessed bread, according to the custom of the Church at that time, as a benediction and symbol of communion. Chrysaphius intimated that it was a very different sort of present which was expected. St Flavian answered resolutely that the revenues and treasure of the Church were designed for other uses. From that moment the favourite resolved to compass his ruin. Chrysaphius persuaded the emperor, through his wife Eudocia, to order the patriarch to make St Pulcheria, sister to Theodosius, a deaconess of his church, and so get rid of her influence over her brother. Flavian's avoidance of this was a second offence in the eyes of Chrysaphius, who was still further incensed by the saint's condemnation of the errors of Eutyches, abbot of a monastery near the city. The abbot, in his excessive zeal against Nestorius's heresy of two distinct persons in Christ, had rushed to the other extreme and, denying that our Lord had two distinct natures after the Incarnation, was the protagonist of the monophysite heresy. In a synod held by St Flavian in 448, Eutyches was accused of this error by Eusebius of Dorylaeum, and the opinion was there condemned as heretical, Eutyches being cited to appear before the council to give an account of his faith. He eventually did so, and was deposed and excommunicated. Whereupon he declared that he appealed to the bishops of Rome, Egypt and Jerusalem ; and he addressed a letter to St Leo I in which he complained of the way he had been treated and stated his case. But the pope was not misled. In a carefully-worded letter to Flavian, famous in ecclesiastical history as his " Tome " or " Dogmatic Letter ", Leo set out the orthodox faith upon the principal points in dispute.

A further council having confirmed the findings of the first one, Chrysaphius, baffled but not beaten, sought to gain his ends by other means.   He wrote to Dioscorus, St Cyril's successor in the see of Alexandria, promising him his friendship and support if he would undertake the defence of the deposed abbot against Flavian and Eusebius.   Dioscorus fell in with the proposal, and they used their interest with the Empress Eudolcia, who hoped that by striking at Flavian she would mortify her sister-in-law Pulcheria.   Theodosius was prevailed on to summon another council which should be held at Ephesus.   Dioscorus of Alexandria was invited by the emperor to preside, and with him came a number of his bishops and also of lay supporters who, it seems, were simply an organized gang of roughs. Other Eastern bishops were present, and Pope St Leo sent legates.

This assembly at Ephesus, which is commonly called by the name Leo afterwards gave it, the *Latrocinium* or Robber Synod, on account of the violence that accompanied it, opened on August 8, 449.   Eutyches was there, and two officials from the emperor with a considerable body of soldiers.   Everything was carried on by violence and open faction in favour of Eutyches, and the pope's legates were not allowed to read his letters to the council.   Amidst wild disorder the result of these proceedings was a sentence of deposition against Flavian and Eusebius.   The papal legates protested.   When Dioscorus began to read the sentence he was interrupted by several of the bishops, who besought him to proceed no further in so unwarrantable a course.   Dioscorus started up and called loudly for Elpidius and Eulogius, the imperial commissioners, who without more ado ordered the church doors to be opened, thus giving admittance to Proclus, the proconsul of Asia, who entered surrounded by soldiers and followed by a mob with clubs.   The assembly was so intimidated that, when the bishops were required to subscribe, few or none had the courage to withstand the threats of Dioscorus except the pope's legates who loudly protested and left in disgust.

St Flavian was able to appeal to Pope Leo and the other bishops in the West, and to deliver his written acts of appeal to the legates.   But during the confusion and disorder he was thrown to the ground and, egged on it is said by Dioscorus himself and the abbot Barsumas, he was kicked and beaten so severely by the soldiers and roughs that he died very shortly after—not at Ephesus as some have supposed but in his place of exile near Sardis in Lydia.   The triumph of Chrysaphius was short-lived.   The Emperor Theodosius died in the following year, and Chrysaphius was executed by order of Marcian, whose consort St Pulcheria had St Flavian's body brought to Constantinople with great honour to be buried among his predecessors in the see.   He was vindicated at the great Council of Chalcedon in 451, when Eusebius of Dorylaeum was reinstated and Dioscorus of Alexandria deprived of his see and exiled.

Despite the copious materials, supplemented in recent years by fresh Syriac documents, which we possess regarding St Flavian and the " Robber Council " of Ephesus, some of the evidence is contradictory and many points still remain obscure.   A very full discussion of these matters will be found in the text and notes of Hefele-Leclercq, *Histoire des Conciles*, vol. ii, pp. 499–880.   The Roman Martyrology does not explicitly call St Flavian a martyr, but it says that he was attacked " by the faction of the impious Dioscorus with blows and kicks and driven into exile where after three days he died ".   There is, however, some conflict of evidence as to the occasion and manner of his death.

ST HELLADIUS, Archbishop of Toledo (A.D. 633)

St Helladius in early life as a layman was attached to the court of the Visigothic kings. Not only was he a learned man but he was also an able diplomatist ; he became a royal official, and in that capacity he attended the Council of Toledo in 589 and was one of its signatories. Even at that period he had aspirations after the religious life, and St Ildephonsus, who was afterwards ordained deacon by him, describes how he loved to slip away to the monastery of Agali near the banks of the Tagus. There he would assist the brethren in their labours and help them to carry home the sheaves of corn. After some time, the call became so insistent that he abandoned the world altogether and entered the monastery. In 605 he was elected abbot and when, after the death of Archbishop Aurasius in 615, the vacant see was pressed upon him, he accepted with the greatest reluctance. He showed boundless generosity to the poor, but we have few, if any, other details of his episcopate. Some writers have conjectured that it was Helladius who instigated King Sisebut to expel the Jews from his kingdom, but there is no positive evidence to go upon. He died in 633.

See the *Acta Sanctorum*, February, vol. iii, and *cf.* Gams, *Kirchengeschichte von Spanien*, vol. ii, pt 2, pp. 82 *seq.*

ST COLMAN, Bishop of Lindisfarne (A.D. 676)

St Colman, the third bishop of Lindisfarne, equalled St Aidan and St Finan in piety and zeal ; like them, he was a native of Ireland and had been a monk of St Columba's on the island of Iona. His short episcopal rule of three years' duration is, however, chiefly remembered from the part he took in the Synod of Whitby. Differences of discipline and custom between the adherents of the Celtic tradition in the Church and those who followed the Roman use had been the cause of disputes for some years, but the question came to a head when King Oswy of Northumbria found that one year when he and his subjects were keeping Easter, his wife Eanfleda and her Kentish chaplain were observing the day as Palm Sunday. This question of the date of Easter was the burning one.

To settle the matter once for all, a synod was in 663 or 664[*] called at Whitby at the instance of King Oswy, and whilst St Wilfrid and the Frankish bishop St Agilbert defended the Roman cause St Colman upheld the Scottish use. Colman alleged the example of his predecessors and of St Columba himself, and claimed that practice to have been established in Asia by St John the Evangelist : which assertion it would have been a difficult task to prove, as Alban Butler gently observes. Agilbert, pleading himself unpractised in English, asked St Wilfrid to reply for him. He accordingly pointed out to the assembly at some length that Colman and his followers would be at fault did they refuse to follow the instructions of the Apostolic See, and claimed that the whole of the rest of the Church followed the Roman use : " Only these people [*i.e.* the Irish] with their confederates the Picts and the Britons, inhabitants of two islands in the farthest west—and not even all of them—persistently stand out against the whole world." It is so that Bede

[*] Following Bede, the date of the important synod of Whitby is generally given as 664. According to our system of reckoning it was perhaps in the autumn of 663 : see F. M. Stenton, *Anglo-Saxon England*, p. 129. But *cf.* W. Levison, *England and the Continent* (1946), pp. 265 *seq.*

reports Wilfrid's somewhat intemperate words. St Wilfrid concluded his fighting speech by quoting our Lord's commission to Peter: " Thou art Peter.   ." Oswy asked Colman if it were true that these words were spoken. " It is true," answered Colman.   Then said the king, " Can you show any such power given to your Columba ? " " None."—" Do you all ", asked Oswy, " on both sides admit that our Lord said this particularly to Peter, and that the Lord gave him the keys of the kingdom of Heaven ? " They replied : " We do." " Then ", he concluded, " I declare that I will not oppose this keeper of the gate of Heaven, and that I will obey his orders to the utmost of my power lest he shut that gate against me." This resolution of the king was approved by the assembly.*

St Colman, however, could not bring himself to accept the decision, and he preferred to resign his bishopric. With all the Irish monks of Lindisfarne and thirty of the Englishmen he withdrew, first to Iona and then to Ireland, where he founded a monastery on the Isle of Inishbofin, off the coast of Connacht. Here they could continue to carry out their traditional use, for the authorities in Rome were not disposed to press a point which involved no question of doctrine   they trusted that time would bring about the gradual adoption of the practice of the rest of the Church—and the event proved their wisdom. Even now, St Colman's troubles were not over, for his English and Irish monks could not get on together. The Englishmen complained that the Irishmen left them to do the work of harvesting and then expected to enjoy the fruit of their labours.   The saint decided to found a second house, and built a monastery at Mayo on the mainland to which he transferred the English monks. He remained abbot over the two communities until his death in 676.

St Bede could not bear the "strange practices " of the Celtic churchmen, but neither could he resist the fragrant memory of St Colman and his monks, and he wrote a long generous tribute to them. " The whole care of those teachers was to serve God, not the world, to feed the soul rather than pamper the belly   so that wherever any priest or monk went all gladly received him as God's servant . . ." St Colman's feast is observed in the diocese of Argyll and the Isles.

The story is told in Bede, *Eccl. Hist.*, bk iii, caps 25 and 26, and bk iv, cap. 4. On the paschal controversy among the Celts, see *Analecta Bollandiana*, vol. lxiv (1946), pp. 200–244 ; and *cf.* MacNaught's *Celtic Church and the See of Peter* (1927), pp. 68–93. The Colmans in the Irish martyrologies are innumerable, and it does not seem quite certain that the " chaste Colman " who left his native land and who is commemorated in the *Félire* of Oengus on February 18 is to be identified with this Colman. We are told in the Life of St Carthage that some of his monks were working beside a stream. The one in charge called out, " Colman, get into the water ". Twelve jumped in.

* The form of the tonsure was also discussed ; the Celtic monks shaved the part of the head in front of a line drawn over the crown from ear to ear. There was also supposed to be something the matter with the way they baptized. The synod of Whitby marked the end of the paschal controversy in the West, but as in other like disputes there was more than matters of discipline at stake. St Wilfrid definitely led the churches of the British Isles towards closer dependence on Rome. Had both " Celts " and " Romans " previously shown more of the Roman tolerance, the acerbities and damage of their controversy would have been considerably less.   Some of the arguments used on either side would not hold water. Italy, Gaul and Egypt all kept Easter on different dates at the end of the fourth century, to name no other variations ; even today some Eastern Catholics celebrate the feast by the discarded Julian computation.

ST ANGILBERT, Abbot   (A.D. 814)

THE early career of St Angilbert gave no indication of the sanctity to which he afterwards is said to have attained. Brought up at the court of Charlemagne and educated by Alcuin, he grew up a brilliant and able but worldly young man. Classical nicknames were in vogue amongst the aristocratic young highbrows of the time, and Angilbert was known as " Homer ". His Latin verses were greatly admired by his contemporaries, and they prove that he possessed something of the poetic genius ; but he was far removed from Homer. So greatly was he loved by Charlemagne, that it was said of him that he was the monarch's second self. Although destined eventually for an archbishopric, he is stated by his biographer Anscher to have married Bertha, a daughter of the king, and the monk Nithard distinctly claimed that he and his brother Harnid were the sons of Angilbert and Bertha. On the other hand Eginhard never even mentions Angilbert in his *Life of Charlemagne*—a strange omission if he had been Charlemagne's son-in-law, but natural enough if the union had been a mere intrigue, as it may well have been in that licentious court.

According to his biographer it was a dangerous illness that first turned Angilbert's thoughts towards the religious life. Amongst the offices he is said to have held was that of count or protector of the maritime provinces against the Northmen, who were a constant menace. We are told that on one occasion he had to cope with a most dangerous invasion when the Danes actually sailed up the Somme. On the eve of battle, St Angilbert went to implore aid at the tomb of St Riquier in the monastery of Centula, near Amiens, and he then vowed that, if successful, he would himself become one of the monks. His prayer was answered by a violent storm which utterly disorganized the enemy's fleet and made the defeat of the invaders an easy matter. Angilbert carried out his vow, and Bertha also entered a convent. It must be confessed, however, that the whole story is very doubtful. In any case the king continued to shower favours upon him : he invested him with the revenues of Centula and helped him to rebuild the abbey with great magnificence, and he made him his privy councillor as well as chief court chaplain, and entrusted him with important missions to Rome and elsewhere. Angilbert did, however, spend his last years as a monk of Centula, of which he soon became abbot. He built a fine library, and instituted amongst his monks the *laus perennis*, or continuous choir service whereby the praise of God never ceased by day or night. He lived to a great age, but managed to travel to court to append his signature to the last will and testament of his great earthly patron, who made him one of his executors. But Angilbert took to his bed immediately after his return, and died twenty-two days after the death of Charlemagne.

The two late medieval biographies of Angilbert, by Hariulf and by Anscher, are not very reliable, but they supply a certain amount of detail and they may be supplemented from contemporary letters and chronicles. The lives will be found in Mabillon, vol. iv. A good account of Angilbert is given in the *Kirchenlexikon*, vol. i, cc. 849–851 ; see also DHG., vol. iii, cc. 120–123. Modern writers are apt to set Angilbert's lapses in a very misleading light. In the *Cambridge Medieval History* (vol. ii, p. 663) Prof. G. Seeliger remarks that Charlemagne's daughter Bertha " had two sons by the pious Abbot Angilbert of St Riquier ". There is no satisfactory evidence that at that time he was either monk or priest ; it is indeed not certain that he ever was a priest.

ST THEOTONIUS (A.D. 1166)

St Theotonius is held in great honour in Portugal. A nephew of Cresconius, Bishop of Coimbra, he had been destined for the priesthood from his earliest years ; after his ordination he was appointed to Viseu, and in a short time the spiritual charge of all in that township was entrusted to him. A man of true holiness and austerity of life, he was also a great preacher whose fame spread far and wide. He resigned his office of archpriest to visit the Holy Land, but on his return continued to work at Viseu. The queen and her husband, Henry, Count of Portugal, repeatedly urged him to accept a bishopric, but he always refused. He had a great love for the poor and for the souls in Purgatory, for whom he used to sing solemn Mass every Friday. This was followed by a procession to the cemetery in which the whole population joined and in the course of which large sums of money were given in alms : these he invariably distributed amongst the poor. He was outspoken in rebuking vice, and the greatest in the land feared and respected him. When the widowed queen and Count Ferdinand (whose association with her was causing scandal) were present at one of his sermons, St Theotonius uttered from the pulpit stern words so obviously aimed at them that they were filled with confusion and beat a hasty retreat. On another occasion he was vested and about to celebrate a Mass of our Lady when he received a message from the queen, who was at the church, asking him to shorten the time he usually took. He sent back word that he was offering Mass in honour of a sovereign who was greater than any royal personage on earth, and that the queen was quite at liberty to stay or to go. Far from resenting this, she was filled with penitence and waited till after the service was over to ask pardon and to receive the saint's reprimand.

After a second pilgrimage to the Holy Land, St Theotonius found that his former preceptor, Tellus, was busied with a scheme of a new monastery at Coimbra to be composed of Canons Regular of St Augustine ; and Theotonius decided to join them, being the twelfth on the original foundation, of which he soon became prior. King Alphonsus, who greatly venerated him, heaped gifts on this monastery of the Holy Cross, as did also Queen Mafalda, although she sought in vain to be permitted to cross the threshold. In a careless age, St Theotonius was remarkable for his insistence on the exact and reverent recitation of the daily offices : he would never allow them to be gabbled or hurried. The king attributed to the holy man's prayers his victories over his enemies and recovery from illness, and in his gratitude granted the saint's request that he should liberate all his Mozarabic Christian captives. Theotonius rose to be abbot of the monastery, where he spent the last thirty years of his life, dying at the age of eighty. When Alphonsus heard of his death, he exclaimed, " His soul will have gone up to Heaven before his body is lowered into the tomb ".

The Life of St Theotonius, written by a contemporary who was one of the community of the Holy Cross which he governed so wisely, leaves the impression of an exceptionally sane and trustworthy document. There are no extravagant miracles, but there breathes in every line a true and reverent affection for the saint which it commemorates. It is printed in the *Acta Sanctorum*, February, vol. iii. *Cf.* also Florez, *España Sagrada*, vol. xxiii, pp. 105 *seq.*, and Carvalho da Silva, *Vida do admiravel Padre S. Theotonio* (1764).

BD WILLIAM HARRINGTON, Martyr (A.D. 1594)

A curious fact about this martyr is that after his death he was accused by a woman of having had a child by her before he was ordained. She was an apostate Catholic, of disorderly life, and this was only one charge among others made by her against Harrington and Catholics in general, some of them of such a kind that her testimony about anything is discredited from the start. The baselessness of the particular accusation against Harrington has been shown by Father Morris in his *Troubles of our Catholic Forefathers*. Father Pollen has noted that, at a time when Catholics were subjected to the most outrageous charges, this is the only one of its kind on record as having been made against one who died for his faith.

William Harrington was born in 1566 at Mount St John, Felixkirk, in the North Riding. When he was a youth of fifteen he met Bd Edmund Campion who was a guest in his father's house, and under the force of that example he went abroad to become a priest, first to the college at Rheims and then to the Jesuits at Tournai. But here his health gave way ; he had to give up any idea of joining that order, and for half-a-dozen or more years he returned home. Then he went back to Rheims, and was ordained in 1592. In midsummer of that year Mr Harrington came on the mission, and in the following May was apprehended in London, where he had been ministering. For nine months he was kept in prison, and bore its rigours with notable fortitude and constancy. His demeanour at his trial made a deep impression ; but he was condemned for his priesthood, and sentenced to be hanged, drawn and quartered.

The sentence was carried out on February 18, 1594, Stow in his *Chronicle* recording that, " Harrington, a seminary priest, was drawn from Newgate to Tyburn, and there hanged, cut down alive, struggled with the hangman, but was bowelled and quartered ". Of which Bishop Challoner pertinently remarks that it " cannot be drawn to an argument of his not being resigned to die, but only shows the efforts which nature will be sure to make in a man whose senses are stunned by having been half hanged, and therefore, by the motions of his hands and body, strives to resist that unnatural violence which is offered by the hands and knife of the executioner ". Bd William Harrington was only twenty-seven years old at his death.

See MMP., p. 197 ; Morris, *Troubles . .*, pp. 104–107 ; Gillow, *Biog. Dict. ;* Pollen in the *Catholic Encyclopedia*, s.v., and *The Month* for April, 1874. The source for the slander on Harrington's memory is Harsnet, *Declaration of egregious Popish Impostures* (London, 1603). The poet John Donne's brother, Henry, was imprisoned in 1593 for harbouring Harrington, and died of jail-fever.

BD JOHN PIBUSH, Martyr (A.D. 1601)

This martyr was born at Thirsk in the North Riding and was made priest at Rheims in 1587. After ministering in England for four years he was arrested at Moreton-in-the-Marsh in Gloucestershire in 1593, and taken to London, where he was confined without trial in the Gatehouse for a year. Then he was brought up at the Gloucester assizes and convicted of being a seminary priest, but was sent back to the local jail without being sentenced. In the following February he took advantage of a break-out by other prisoners to escape himself, but was careless enough to walk openly on the highway and so was retaken the next day, at Matson. He was then sent to London again, retried, and sentenced to death, on July 1, 1595.

But in fact the sentence was not carried out for another five years and more. In the meantime Mr Pibush was left to suffer in the filth and brutality of the Queen's Bench prison. Not only was his health undermined, so that his lungs rotted with tuberculosis, but he was subjected to ill-treatment from his fellow prisoners, especially when he tried to bring them to a more godly frame of mind. However, in the long run he seems to have softened both them and his jailers, for he was allowed some little privacy and was even able to celebrate Mass occasionally. His name was on the list of those imprisoned Catholics to be sent to Wisbech castle, but at the last moment it was struck off ; and after all this time in prison Mr Pibush was put to death at twenty-four hours' notice.

On February 17, 1601, he was brought before Popham, L.C.J. (who had removed his name from the Wisbech list) and asked for any reason why his sentence should not be carried out. He replied that he had never in his life done anything for which he could justly be put to death ; that he was condemned simply for being a Catholic priest ; and that he was willing to lay down his life several times over for that cause. He was then told to prepare for death, which took place the next day at St Thomas's Waterings in Southwark, a spot whose very name spoke of pilgrims to the shrine of another martyr, Thomas Becket.

See MMP., pp. 152-153 ; Gillow, *Biog. Dict.* ; Pollen, *Acts of the English Martyrs,* pp. 335-336 ; Catholic Record Society's publications, vol. v, pp. 337-340.

19 : ST MESROP, Bishop　　(A.D. 441)

IN the account of St Isaac the Great on September 9 mention is made of his work in unifying the Armenian people and laying the foundations of a literature in the national tongue, and that his chief helper therein was St Mesrop (Mashtots), who for a time had been a " civil servant ". When Armenia was partitioned between the Empire and Persia Mesrop retired to a solitary life, becoming a priest and pursuing his studies in the Greek, Syriac and Persian languages. He then became a missionary among his own people, and found himself handicapped by the fact that the Bible and the liturgy were in Syriac and that there was no adequate way of writing them in Armenian. He therefore decided in consultation with St Isaac to revive and remake an Armenian alphabet, which in due course was done with the help of other scholars, the chief basis being the small letters of the Greek alphabet.

Some years later the first Armenian translation of the Bible was completed from Syriac, St Mesrop being said to be responsible for the New Testament and the book of Proverbs. This version was soon after revised at Edessa by two of his pupils, and eventually the final revision of the Old Testament was made from the Septuagint.* The liturgy also was translated into Armenian. Mesrop preached and taught throughout Armenia and into Georgia, setting up schools and creating

* The Armenian Bible has roused the interest not only of scriptural and linguistic scholars, but of Lord Byron. He seems to have contemplated making an English version from it, but did not get further than an apocryphal letter from the church of Corinth to St Paul and the apostle's equally apocryphal reply which are found in some editions. *Cf. The Commonweal*, August 29, 1941, pp. 441-442. The Armenian Bible was first printed at Amsterdam, in 1666 ; the Psalter only at Venice a hundred years earlier.

a Georgian alphabet; he then returned to his own part of the country, where with the encouragement of St Isaac he established a school of his own. It was here, and under the direction of these two, that numerous translations from Greek and Syriac were made. St Mesrop died at the age of over eighty at Valarshapat on February 19, 441. "Mesrop the Teacher" is named in the intercession of the Mass of the Armenian rite.

There is an Armenian life of St Mesrop by his disciple Koriun or Goriun. It exists in at least two recensions (numbered in the BHO. 755 and 756). The former of these has been translated into German by Canon S. Weber in vol. i of *Ausgewählte Schriften der Armenischen Kirchenväter* (1927). With regard to the life and activities of St Mesrop, consult Tournebize, *Histoire politique et religieuse de l'Arménie* (1910), especially pp. 503–513 and 633–636 ; and also Weber, *Die Katholische Kirche in Armenien* (1903), pp. 393–421. Fr P. Peeters has expressed a high opinion of the value of Koriun's biography, so far at least as regards its broader issues of fact, and St Mesrop's claim to have created the Georgian alphabet. See the *Analecta Bollandiana*, vol. liii (1935), pp. 148–150, p. 298, with its references, and *Recherches d'histoire et de philologie orientales* (1951), vol. i, pp. 171–207. Some discussion of a divergent view will be found in the *Analecta Bollandiana*, vol. liv (1936), pp. 339–401.

ST BARBATUS, Bishop of Benevento   (A.D. 682)

WE know nothing definite about the parentage and youth of St Barbatus, although a late tradition declares him to have been a native of Benevento and to have ministered after his ordination in the church of St Basil at Morcona. He was afterwards transferred to the neighbouring Benevento, and for the remainder of his life we have a not very trustworthy biography of the ninth century. When St Barbatus began his ministry, he found even the nominal Christians steeped in pagan superstitions, including Duke Romuald, whose father Grimoald, King of the Lombards, had edified all Italy by his conversion to Christianity. They venerated a golden viper and worshipped at a tree on which they hung the skin of a wild beast. The ceremonies in honour of these terminated with public games in which the skin served for a mark at which bowmen shot arrows over their shoulders. St Barbatus preached boldly against these abuses and laboured long to no purpose, although he supplemented his exhortations with fervent prayer and rigorous fasting for the conversion of the deluded people. At length he roused them from their indifference by vividly portraying the calamities their city was bound to suffer from the army of the Emperor Constans II, who, landing soon afterwards in Italy (A.D. 663), laid siege to Benevento. In their distress and alarm they listened to the preacher and renounced their errors and pagan practices. Thereupon St Barbatus consoled them by his assurance that the siege would be raised and the emperor worsted—as actually happened. The saint with his own hand felled the tree which had been the object of their veneration and melted down the golden viper, of which he made a chalice. Hildebrand, Bishop of Benevento, had died during the siege, and St Barbatus was chosen as his successor. He was able to complete the good work he had begun and stamped out heathenism throughout the state. In the year 680 he attended the sixth general council, which was held at Constantinople against the monothelites. He did not long survive this assembly, for he died on February 29, 682, at the age of seventy years.

See the *Acta Sanctorum*, February, vol. iii. A more correct text of the life has been edited by Waitz in the MGH., *Scriptores rerum Langobardorum*, pp. 556–563. The life is not older than the beginning of the ninth century.

ST BEATUS OF LIEBANA   (*c.* A.D. 798)

IN the latter part of the eighth century there was at Toledo an aged archbishop called Elipandus, who had been infected by that subtle revival of the Nestorian heresy which asserted that Christ was only the adopted son of the Eternal Father. This false doctrine Elipandus taught openly and disseminated far and wide. Against this Goliath, God raised up another David in the form of a priest called Beatus, a monk of Liebana in the Asturian mountains. When he heard the errors of Elipandus he at once set himself to counteract his teaching, both by speech and by writing, and he was joined by Etherius, who afterwards became bishop of Osma in Catalonia. They were very successful, and won back multitudes to the true faith. This soon reached the ears of the archbishop, who was furious and wrote a scathing letter to Abbot Fidelis, apparently a dignitary of great importance in the Asturias. In it he denounced Beatus as a vagrant mountaineer (and worse things) who dared set himself against the archbishop of Toledo and the Church. As for Etherius, he was a mere youth who had been led away by the bombast of this adventurer, but Beatus must be shown his error, and if he persisted he must be delivered up for correction. This letter the abbot showed to Beatus, and the saint's reply was to publish a book with Etherius in which they set forth, none too clearly, the orthodox teaching. Beatus was influenced and praised by Alcuin, who called him " a learned man, as holy in his life as in his name ".

Ten years before the *Liber adversus Elipandum*, St Beatus had in 776 published a Commentary on the Apocalypse, of which a number of illuminated manuscripts of artistic interest exist, of ninth-century date onwards. It is likely that he was also the author of several of the hymns of the Mozarabic liturgy. Through a confusion of names, it has been mistakenly asserted that St Beatus was buried at Valcavado ; his monastery at Liebana, near Santander, was probably St Martin's, later called Santo Toribio.

See the *Acta Sanctorum*, February, vol. iii ; Florez, *España Sagrada*, vol. xxxiv, pp. 378-389 ; Gams, *Kirchengeschichte von Spanien*, vol. ii, pt 2, pp. 275-281 ; and DHG., vol. vii, cc. 89-90. And also Mateo del Alamo, " Los comentarios de Beato al Apocalipsis y Elipando " in *Miscellanea Giovanni Mercati*, vol. ii (*Studi e Testi*, vol. cxxii, 1946) ; and H. A. Sanders, *Beati in Apocalipsim libri duodecim* (American Academy in Rome, 1930).

ST BONIFACE, BISHOP OF LAUSANNE   (A.D. 1260)

ST BONIFACE was born in Brussels and was sent at the age of seventeen to study at Paris, where he in due course became one of the best-known lecturers in the university. He remained in Paris for seven more years, but disputes arose between the masters and the students, and his pupils struck and would not attend his lectures any longer. This decided him to leave Paris and he betook himself to Cologne, where a post was assigned to him in the cathedral school. He had been there only two years when he was elected bishop of Lausanne. He went to his diocese full of zeal and laboured indefatigably, but he found himself continually opposed and misunderstood throughout the eight years of his episcopate. Perhaps his long connection with the University of Paris unfitted him for dealing tactfully with his difficult people ; he appears to have publicly denounced from the pulpit the weaknesses of the clergy. Having incurred the enmity of the Emperor Frederick II, Boniface was set upon and badly wounded in 1239. Convinced that he was unfit for his office, he went to the pope and begged to be released, and his request was granted.   The saint went back to Brussels, to the Cistercian nunnery at La Cambre, where the abbess invited him to stay amongst them.   This he seems to have done, donning the Cistercian habit if he did not actually take the vows, and living the rest of his life within the precincts of the abbey.   His *cultus* was approved in 1702.

Apart from the two short Lives of Boniface which have been printed in the *Acta Sanctorum*, February, vol. iii, a great deal of information concerning him may be gleaned from contemporary chronicles, charters, etc.   All this has been turned to account by J. F. Kieckens, *Étude historique sur St Boniface* (1892) ; by Fr Rattinger in two articles in the *Stimmen aus Maria Laach*, 1896 ; and by A. Simon and R. Aubert, *Boniface de Bruxelles* (1945).   Boniface has been claimed as the first " Weihbischof ", a type of prelate without definite see, analogous to the *chorepiscopi* of the early middle ages.   We have abundant evidence that during the eighteen years or more that he resided at La Cambre, he went about consecrating churches and altars and discharging other episcopal functions.

ST CONRAD OF PIACENZA   (A.D. 1351)

This Conrad belonged to a noble family of Piacenza, where he lived with his wife, to whom he was much attached.   One day when he was out hunting he ordered his attendants to fire some brushwood to drive out the game.   This they did, but a strong wind drove the flames into the cornfields, and the conflagration spread to the neighbouring villages.   Conrad, unable to check the fire, returned home secretly with his beaters, and they said nothing about their share in the disaster. A poor man who was found picking up sticks near the fire, was accused of incendiarism and sentenced to death.   Upon hearing this, Conrad was filled with remorse and hastened to exculpate the accused and to give himself up, explaining how it had all come about.   He was ordered to make good the damage which his carelessness had caused.   The fine thus inflicted swallowed up nearly all his possessions as well as his wife's dowry.   This caused them to think very seriously, and they came to the conclusion that the finger of God was to be seen in what had happened. They agreed to give away to the poor whatever was left them, and, whilst his wife entered a convent of Poor Clares, Conrad put on the garb of a pilgrim and attached himself to some hermits who lived under the rule of the third order of St Francis, to which he was admitted.   From that time he led a life of extraordinary piety, and soon his fame began to bring him visits from his former fellow-citizens.   To avoid this publicity he decided to leave the neighbourhood ; he crossed over to Sicily and took up his abode in the valley of Noto, where he dwelt for thirty years, partly in the Hospital of St Martin and partly in a hermitage founded by William Bocherio, another nobleman who had become an anchorite.   Towards the end of his life St Conrad, to obtain more complete solitude, betook himself to the grotto of Pizzoni, three miles from Noto.

In spite of all attempts to hide himself, the fame of his sanctity spread far and wide, and when a famine occurred numbers of people came to him to implore his help.   Through his prayers relief came at once to the stricken inhabitants, and from that time his cell was besieged by sufferers of all kinds.   The Bishop of Syracuse himself visited him, and it was told afterwards that while his attendants were preparing to unpack the provisions they had brought, the bishop had asked St Conrad with a smile whether he had nothing to offer his visitors.   The holy man replied that he would go and look in his cell, from which he emerged carrying delicious newly-made cakes which the bishop accepted as miraculous and for which he gave praise to God. Some time before his death, Conrad returned the bishop's visit and made a general confession to him ; as he arrived he was surrounded by birds who fluttered round him and afterwards escorted him back to Noto. When his last hour was come, he lay on the ground in front of the crucifix and prayed for his benefactors and for the people of Noto. He was buried in the church of St Nicholas there and his tomb became a favourite shrine at which many miraculous cures took place. He is more particularly invoked for ruptures on account of the large number of people who owed their recovery from hernia to his intercession. The *cultus* of St Conrad has been approved by three popes.

See the *Acta Sanctorum*, February, vol. iii ; Mazzara, *Leggendario Francescano*, vol. i, p.' 246–254 ; and Léon, *Auréole Séraphique* (Eng. trans.), vol. i. The many marvels of which these accounts are full do not seem to be borne out by any reliable evidence.

BD ALVAREZ OF CORDOVA   (*c.* A.D. 1430)

THE birthplace of Bd Alvarez is uncertain : some authorities give it as Lisbon and others Cordova, where the greater part of his life was spent. He entered the Dominican convent of St Paul there in 1368. He became a wonderful preacher and laboured with great success first in Andalusia and afterwards in Italy. On the death of King Henry II of Castile, Alvarez became confessor and adviser of the Queen-mother Catherine (who was the daughter of John of Gaunt, Duke of Lancaster), and directed the early training of the young King John II. He completely reformed the court, but when, owing to political dissensions, the regency was divided he withdrew from court and resumed his former work as a preacher. Bd Alvarez had long formed the design, which he proceeded to carry out, of founding a Dominican house which, in accord with the reform already begun by Bd Raymund of Capua, should follow strictly the rule of St Dominic. He chose a mountainous region not far from Cordova, and there he erected the Escalaceli, Ladder of Heaven, which became a centre of piety and learning, to which men flocked from all parts of Spain. Alvarez exercised a great influence in resisting the papal claimant " Benedict XIII ", Peter de Luna, and in bringing the people and—what was much more difficult—the grandees, to acknowledge the legitimate pope.

In spite of advancing age Bd Alvarez continued his work of catechizing, teaching and preaching : he would spend his whole day in such tasks, and when he returned at night to his monastery he would devote nearly all the night to prayer. He and his brethren depended upon alms for their food, and sometimes he went to the market-place in Cordova and addressed the people, ending up by saying, " My dear brethren, the poor friars of St Dominic in the mountain recommend themselves to your charity ". His practices of penance grew ever more severe ; he crawled on his knees to a chapel dedicated to our Lady of Pity, taking the discipline as he went, and a picture still at Cordova represents him thus kneeling, his shoulders covered with blood and accompanied by angels, some of whom are clearing away little rocks from his path. He built several chapels in the monastery grounds, each one representing a " station " or scene of our Lord's passion, doubtless suggested to him by his experiences as a pilgrim in Jerusalem. It was told that one night when he had been praying in one of these, a violent storm made the brook which separated it from the monastery quite impassable. When the bell rang for Matins the holy man lifted his eyes to God, took off his black cloak, spread it on the water and walked safely across to dry land ; he resumed his cloak and returned to his place in choir as usual. The *cultus* of Bd Alvarez was confirmed in 1741.

See Touron, *Les Hommes illustres de l'Ordre de St Dominique*, vol. iii, pp. 98–110 ; Procter, *Dominican Saints*, pp. 42–44 Mortier, *Maîtres Généraux O.P.*, vol. iv, pp. 210–214. Mortier points out that the date 1420 usually assigned for the death of Alvarez cannot possibly be correct, for documentary evidence shows that he was living in 1423. The same historian seems to claim for Bd Alvarez that he was the originator in the West of the devotion of the Stations of the Cross. But the idea of a series of such shrines may be traced as far back as St Petronius of Bologna in the fifth century, and the Augustinians, Peter and John da Fabriano, erected similar stations shortly before the time of Alvarez. The idea at this period was becoming very general.

20 : SS. TYRANNIO, ZENOBIUS AND OTHER MARTYRS (A.D. 304 AND 310)

EUSEBIUS, an eyewitness of what he relates concerning these martyrs, gives the following account of them : " Several Christians of Egypt, some of whom had settled in Palestine, others at Tyre, gave astonishing proofs of their patience and constancy in the faith. After innumerable stripes and blows, which they cheerfully endured, they were exposed to wild beasts such as leopards, wild bears, boars and bulls. I myself was present when these savage beasts, accustomed to human blood, were let out upon them, and, instead of devouring them or tearing them to pieces as might naturally be expected, they stood off, refusing to touch or approach them, but turned on their keepers and any that came in their way. It was only the soldiers of Christ that they refused to attack, although these martyrs, in obedience to an order given them, tossed about their arms—which was thought to be a sure way of provoking the beasts against them. Sometimes indeed the animals were seen to rush towards them with their usual impetuosity, but they suddenly withdrew, held back by a divine power : this happened several times, to the wonder of all the onlookers. The first relay having done no execution, a second and a third was loosed upon them, but all in vain. Meanwhile the martyrs stood there unshaken, although some of them were very young. Amongst them was a youth not yet twenty who remained quite still in one position, undaunted and not trembling, with his eyes uplifted to heaven and his arms extended in the form of a cross, whilst the bears and leopards with wide-open jaws threatening immediate death seemed on the point of tearing him to pieces : but by a miracle, not being suffered to touch him, they withdrew. Others were exposed to a furious bull which had already gored and tossed into the air several infidels who had ventured too near and had left them half dead. It was only the martyrs that he could not approach : he would stop and stand scraping the dust with his hoofs, though endeavouring to rush forward, he would butt with his horns in all directions and paw the ground whilst he was being urged on by red-hot goads, but it was all in vain. After repeated trials with other wild beasts with no better success, the saints were slain by the sword and their bodies cast into the sea. Others who refused to sacrifice were beaten to death or burned or executed in some other way."

This happened in the year 304, and the Church on this day commemorates also the bishop of Tyre, St Tyrannio, who had been present at the triumph of the earlier martyrs and had encouraged them in their conflict. He had not the comfort of following them till six years later, when he was arrested, conducted from Tyre to Antioch in the company of St Zenobius, a priest and physician of Sidon, and, after suffering many torments, was thrown into the river Orontes. Zenobius died on the rack. Some time after, under Maximinus, St Silvanus, Bishop of Emesa, in Phoenicia, was devoured by wild beasts in his own city, together with two companions. Peleus and Nilus, two Egyptian priests in Palestine, were consumed by fire with several others. St Silvanus, Bishop of Gaza, was condemned to the copper mines of Phaenon near Petra in Arabia, and afterwards beheaded there with thirty-nine companions.

Whilst St Tyrannio is commemorated on this day with those who perished at Tyre in 304, St Zenobius, who suffered with him, is assigned to October 29, St Silvanus of Emesa to February 6 and St Silvanus of Gaza to May 29.

Eusebius, *Hist. Eccles.*, bk viii, cap. 13, is the principal authority, but the *Acta Sanctorum* and Le Quien, *Oriens Christianus*, supply some further discussion of geographical details, etc.

ST SADOTH, BISHOP OF SELEUCIA-CTESIPHON, MARTYR (*c.* A.D. 342)

ST SADOTH (Shadost, Sadosh, Shiadustes) appears to have acted as deacon to the bishop of Seleucia-Ctesiphon, whom he represented at the Council of Nicaea in 325. When the bishop St Simeon Barsabae suffered martyrdom during the terrible persecution by Sapor II, Sadoth was chosen to succeed him in the see, the most important in the Persian kingdom but the most exposed to the storm. This grew more violent, and for a short time Sadoth and some of his clergy took refuge in a hiding-place from which they could give assistance and encouragement to their distressed flock. During this period St Sadoth had a vision which seemed to indicate that the time had come for him to seal his faith with his blood. He described the dream to his assembled priests and deacons " I saw in my sleep a ladder surrounded with light and stretching from the earth to heaven. At the top stood the holy Simeon in great glory. He beheld me at the bottom and said with a smile, ' Climb up, Sadoth : do not be afraid. I mounted yesterday and it is your turn to-day.' This means that as he was slain last year, I am to follow him this year."

King Sapor having come to Seleucia, St Sadoth was apprehended with many clergy and others, 128 persons in all. They were cast into dungeons, where for five months they suffered incredible misery and torments. Three times they were put to the rack : their legs were bound with cords which were drawn with so much force that their breaking bones were heard to crack like sticks in a faggot. In the midst of these tortures the officers cried out to them, " Worship the sun and obey the king if you would save your lives ". Sadoth answered in the name of all that the sun was but a creature, the work of God, made for mankind, and that they would worship none but the Creator. The officers said, " Obey ! or death is certain and immediate." The martyrs cried with one voice, " We shall not die but live and reign eternally with God and His Son, Jesus Christ ". They were chained in couples and led out of the city, singing joyfully as they went, and their prayer and praise did not cease till the death of the last of the blessed company. St Sadoth himself, however, was separated from his flock and taken to Bait-Lapat, where he was beheaded after being bishop for less than a year.

See Assemani, *Bibliotheca orientalis*, vol. i, p. 188 and vol. iii, pp. 399, 613   Gregory Barhebraeus, *Chronicon*, ii, 38 ; and Le Quien, *Oriens christianus*, vol. ii, p. 1108.

ST ELEUTHERIUS, Bishop of Tournai   (A.D. 532)

A GREAT fire which destroyed Tournai Cathedral in 1092 is responsible for the loss of the relics of its first bishop, St Eleutherius, and of all the most ancient records of his life.   Very little is known about him, although many legends grew up about his life and death.   He is said to have been born at Tournai of Christian parents whose family had been converted by St Piat one hundred and fifty years before ; and to have been made bishop in 486, ten years before the baptism of King Clovis at Rheims.   He appears to have been a zealous preacher and to have converted to Christianity a great part of the Franks in his diocese.   He also vigorously opposed certain heretics who denied the mystery of the Incarnation, and was attacked by some of them as he was leaving the church one day after Mass.   He was so severely wounded in the head that he died five weeks later.   The legend of the raising to life of the governor's daughter is recounted in the ninth-century biography of the saint.   According to this extravagant fiction, the girl fell in love with the youthful bishop, and, finding him at prayer, revealed her passion.   He fled from her presence and she fell lifeless to the ground.   Eleutherius undertook to restore her life if her father would become a Christian.   He promised, but without meaning to fulfil his promises, and the saint's prayers were unavailing.   On the third day the governor was moved to contrition, and Eleutherius was then able to raise the girl from the tomb, and he then baptized her.   The governor, however, would not keep his promise, and even withdrew the girl from the hands of the Christians, until so terrible a plague broke out that he was humbled, sought instruction and was himself baptized.

See the *Acta Sanctorum*, February, vol. iii.   A long list of quasi-biographical materials is given in BHL., nn. 2455-2470, but they are none of them reliable.   The *châsse* of St Eleutherius is archaeologically interesting and has often been discussed from the point of view of medieval art.

ST EUCHERIUS, Bishop of Orleans   (A.D. 743)

ACCORDING to his biographer, apparently a contemporary, St Eucherius led a holy life from earliest childhood.   He was born at Orleans, and entered the Benedictine abbey of Jumièges about the year 714.   After he had spent six or seven years there, Soavaric, Bishop of Orleans, who was his uncle, died, and the senate and people with the clergy of the city sent a deputation to Charles Martel, mayor of the palace, to ask his permission to elect Eucherius to fill the vacant see.   Charles consented, and charged one of his officers of state to conduct the young monk from his monastery to Orleans.   The saint was filled with dismay and entreated the monks to save him from the dangers that threatened him in the world.   In spite of their reluctance they urged him to depart, setting the public good above their own desires.   He was consecrated in 721.   Unwilling as he had been to take office, he proved himself an exemplary pastor and devoted himself entirely to the care of his people, who loved and venerated him.

Eucherius did not, however, retain the favour of Charles Martel. To defray the expenses of his wars and other undertakings, and to recompense those who served him, it was the practice of that prince to seize the revenues of churches and he encouraged others to do the same. It would appear that St Eucherius strenuously opposed these confiscations, and certain persons represented this to Charles as an insult offered to his person. In the year 737, when he was returning to Paris after having defeated the Saracens in Aquitaine, Charles took Orleans on the way and ordered Eucherius to follow him to Verneuil-sur-Oise, and then exiled him to Cologne. Here the saint became so popular on account of his piety and charming character that Charles ordered him to be transferred to a fortified place near Liège, where he would be under the observation of the governor of the district. Here again the bishop won all hearts, and the governor made him distributor of alms and allowed him to retire to the monastery of Saint-Trond near Maestricht, where he spent the rest of his life in prayer and contemplation. The legend that St Eucherius saw Charles Martel burning in hell is an interpolation which does not belong to the primitive biography, but it is worth mentioning because the incident is sometimes depicted in representations of the saint in art.

The biography is printed in the *Acta Sanctorum*, February, vol. iii, and in Mabillon. See also Duchesne (*Fastes Episcopaux*, vol. ii, p. 458), who points out that whereas the author of the life makes Eucherius the immediate successor of Soavaric, the episcopal lists of Orleans mention two or three bishops as intervening. There are also other difficulties about the chronology of the life which suggest serious doubts as to its being the work of a contemporary. See " Saints de Saint-Trond " in *Analecta Bollandiana*, vol. lxxii (1954).

ST WULFRIC   (A.D. 1154)

THE burial-place of St Wulfric at Haselbury Plucknett was a popular place of pilgrimage in the middle ages. Born at Compton Martin, eight miles from Bristol, and trained for the priesthood, Wulfric lived a careless life even after his ordination, being engrossed with hawking and hunting. But while priest at Deverill, near Warminster, he was suddenly touched by divine grace, and his conversion was popularly attributed to a chance interview he had with a beggar. The man asked him if he had any of the new coins which had recently been minted and were still rare. Wulfric replied that he did not know : he would see. " You have two and a half ", said the stranger, and sure enough, when the saint opened his purse, there they lay. He gave them to him as an alms, and the beggar said, " God reward thee for thy charity ! I tell thee that soon thou shalt depart from here to go to a place where at last thou shalt find rest. If thou wilt persevere, thou shalt ere long be admitted to the fellowship of the saints." St Wulfric was casting about for a solitary spot in which he might devote himself entirely to the service of God when a knight offered him a cell adjoining the church at Haselbury in Somerset. Here he gave himself up to great austerities, and by fasting and scourging reduced himself to skin and bone. He wore chain-mail next his skin, and a curious miracle is recounted in detail of the cutting of the iron links with an ordinary pair of scissors or shears as if they were so much linen. The reason why Wulfric wanted his cuirass shortened was that it prevented him from making the innumerable prostrations which formed, perhaps as a survival of Celtic influences, so favourite a type of penitential exercise at that period. It was practised especially by St Thomas of

Canterbury and by St Gilbert of Sempringham, to take two prominent English examples.

We are told that sometimes Wulfric would at night, summer or winter, strip and get into a tub of cold water, remaining there till he had recited the whole psalter ; at other times he would spend the night in prayer in the church, where he offered Mass daily and was served by a boy named Osbern, afterwards parson of Haselbury, to whom we owe valuable information about the anchoret.   One Easter eve Wulfric was troubled in sleep by a sensual illusion ; he was so distressed thereby that the next day he made open confession of it before the whole congregation in church.   When a certain cleric from Cirencester tried to tempt him to avarice with the offer of two silver pennies, Wulfric pointed to the window-sill : " Put them there ", he said, " Somebody will come and take them."   And so it happened, to the confusion of the tempter.   Wulfric employed himself in the copying of books (he sometimes had a secretary to help him), which he bound himself, and it looks as if he also made things for the church.   The many wonders attributed to Wulfric show the veneration in which he was held, but it seems that it was for prophecy more than anything else that he was famous, even to far parts of the land : among his visitors were King Henry I and King Stephen.

St Wulfric (there is no reason to suppose that he was ever canonized) died on February 20, 1154, and was buried in the cell in which he had lived : the vestry of the present church at Haselbury stands on its site.   Later the body was moved for safety to an unmarked grave, where it probably still rests.   Wulfric had a great regard for the Cistercian Order, but the idea that he belonged to it is now rejected.

St Wulfric ought to be better known than he is, for what we read of him comes to us upon the authority of contemporaries.   There is an excellent work by Dom M. Bell, *Wulfric of Haselbury* (1933), which gives the text of the life by Abbot John of Ford, with *apparatus criticus*, introduction and notes.   Fr Bell adds the text of the first life in English, by Jerome Porter, printed at Douay in 1632 in the rare *Flowers of the Lives of the   .   Saints of the three Kingdoms*.   See also the *Acta Sanctorum*, February, vol. iii ; and R. M. Clay, *Hermits and Anchorites of England* (1914).   Wulfric's name is spelt in several ways.

BD ELIZABETH OF MANTUA, Virgin   (A.D. 1468)

VERY little incident marks the career of Bd Elizabeth Picenardi.   Her parents were people of consideration in Mantua, and she received a very religious education. Her father taught her Latin so that she was able to read daily the Little Office of our Lady, and her mother encouraged her in the practice of meditation.   She would not contemplate the idea of marriage, and after her mother's death both she and one of her sisters obtained permission to enter the third order of the Servites. We are told, but the authority for the statement does not seem very reliable, that Elizabeth made a practice of confessing and communicating daily, a thing almost unheard of in the fifteenth century.   The example of her humility and gentleness, together with the supernatural gifts with which she was credited, made a deep impression upon several young girls of her own age, and they banded themselves together to form a community of the Servite third order under Elizabeth's direction. She is said to have prophesied her own death a year before it happened.   At the age of forty, worn out by a painful internal complaint, " she rested in the Lord ", so the Servite Martyrology states, " while sweetly contemplating Jesus and his Mother amid the choirs of angels ".   Extraordinary crowds attended her funeral

and many miracles were said to have been worked at her tomb.   She was beatified
in 1804.

See Bianchi, *Memorie storiche intorno alla Vita di Elizabetta Picenardi* (1803) ; and
J. E. Stadler, *Heiligen-Lexikon.*

21 : ST SEVERIAN, Bishop of Scythopolis, Martyr   (A.D. 453)

IN the year 451 the fourth general council was called at Chalcedon to pronounce
upon the Eutychian or monophysite heresy which was spreading very rapidly
in the Eastern portion of the Church.   Dioceses were being split into factions
which, in some cases, elected rival bishops and refused communion to their
opponents.   The decision of the council, which totally condemned the heresy, was
accepted at once by a great proportion of the Palestinian monks, but there were
many exceptions.   At the head of these was Theodosius, a violent and unscrupulous
man who obtained sufficient following to enable him to expel Juvenal, Bishop of
Jerusalem, and to gain possession of the see for himself.   He then raised so cruel
a persecution in Jerusalem that he filled the city with blood, as we learn from a
letter of the Emperor Marcian.   At the head of a band of soldiers he then proceeded
to carry desolation over the country, although in certain places he met with opponents who had the courage to stand firm in their orthodoxy.   Of these no one
showed more determination than Severian, Bishop of Scythopolis, who received
as his reward the crown of martyrdom.   The soldiers seized him, dragged him
out of the city, and then put him to death.

See the *Acta Sanctorum*, February, vol. iii ; and Hefele-Leclercq, *Conciles*, vol. ii.   In
the course of a paragraph on the Holy Land, Butler refers to the dissensions and jealousies
there of those who call themselves Christians, and adds   " We have ceased to think that it
is the will of God that we should win back the Holy Land by the sword, but we may well
pray earnestly that its inhabitants may be united to the One Holy Catholic and Apostolic
Church, and that peace and goodwill may prevail amongst those to whom is committed the
custody of the Holy Places."

BD PEPIN OF LANDEN   (A.D. 646)

PEPIN OF LANDEN was never canonized, although his name appears as a saint in
some of the old martyrologies.   The wisest statesman of his time, he was mayor
of the palace to Kings Clotaire II, Dagobert I and Sigebert III, and was practically ruler of their dominions.   He was the grandfather of Pepin of Herstal,
great-grandfather of Charles Martel, and the ancestor of the Carolingian dynasty.
He has been well described as " a lover of peace, the constant defender of truth
and justice, a true friend to all the servants of God, the terror of the wicked,
the father of his country, the zealous and humble defender of religion ".   He
associated with himself as counsellors two wise and holy bishops, St Arnulf of
Metz and St Cunibert of Cologne, and though a most faithful minister to the
king, he considered himself equally the servant of the people.

First and foremost he always placed his duty to the King of kings, and when
King Dagobert, forgetful of the principles which had been instilled into him in
his youth, gave himself up to a vicious life, Pepin boldly rebuked him and never
ceased to show his disapproval until he became sincerely penitent.   Dagobert,

before his death in 638, had appointed Pepin tutor to his three-year-old son Sigebert, who under his guidance became himself a saint and one of the most blessed amongst the French kings. Pepin protected the Christian communities of the north against the invasions of the Slavs, worked hard for the spread of the Christian faith, and chose only virtuous and learned men to fill the bishoprics. His wife was Bd Itta, or Iduberga, by whom he had one son, Grimoald, and two daughters, St Gertrude and St Begga. Pepin died in 646 and was buried at Landen, but his body was translated to Nivelles, where it lies in the same tomb as that of his wife and close to the altar of St Gertrude. For many centuries their relics were carried every year in the Rogationtide processions at Nivelles.

There is a eulogistic ninth-century Life of Pepin which has been printed in large part by the Bollandists, *Acta Sanctorum*, February, vol. iii, and there are many references to him in the lives of St Gertrude of Nivelles. See also DCB., vol. iv, pp. 398–399.

ST GERMANUS OF GRANFEL, Martyr   (*c.* A.D. 677)

St Germanus was brought up almost from the cradle by Modoard, Bishop of Trier. At the age of seventeen he asked permission to retire from the world, but Modoard hesitated, telling him that, as his parents were dead, he ought to obtain the king's consent. The young man, however, decided the matter for himself, and, after giving away all his possessions to the poor, started off with three other youths to seek St Arnulf, whose example had fired them : that holy man had resigned the bishopric of Metz to live as a hermit. Arnulf received them affectionately and, after keeping them with him for some time, suggested that they should enter the monastery which he and St Romaric had founded at Romberg. Germanus first sent two of his companions to fetch his brother Numerian, who was a mere child, and together they entered the monastery which was situated in the Vosges Mountains and was afterwards known as Remiremont.

St Germanus subsequently passed on with his brother and other monks to the abbey of Luxeuil, then governed by St Walbert. When Duke Gondo was founding the monastery of Granfel in what is now the Val Moutier, Walbert, to whom he applied for an abbot, could find none worthier than Germanus, who was accordingly appointed. The Münsterthal, or Val Moutier, is a grand mountain pass through which runs the old Roman road, but at that time it was blocked by fallen rocks and could not be used. St Germanus cleared it and widened the entrance to the valley. Afterwards two other monasteries were also placed under his charge, those of St Ursitz and of St Paul Zu-Werd, but he continued to live chiefly at Granfel. Duke Cathic, or Boniface, who succeeded Gondo, inherited no share of his kindly religious spirit, and oppressed the monks and the poor inhabitants with violence and extortion. One day when he was plundering their houses at the head of a band of soldiers, Germanus went out to plead for the poor sufferers. The duke listened to him and promised to desist but, while the abbot was praying in the church of St Maurice, the soldiers began again to burn and to destroy. St Germanus, finding that remonstrance was useless, started back for the monastery with his prior Randoald, but they were overtaken by the soldiers, who stripped and killed them.

The facts are recorded in a contemporary life by the monk Bobolenus, which is printed in the *Acta Sanctorum*, February, vol. iii, and by Mabillon.

ST GEORGE, BISHOP OF AMASTRIS   (*c*. A.D. 825)

EARLY in the ninth century there lived at Cromna, near Amastris on the Black Sea, a couple, Theodosius and Megetho, who had long been childless, but upon whom in answer to prayer God bestowed a son, whom they named George. They nearly lost him when he was three years old, as he fell into the fire whilst at play and was very severely burnt. He recovered, however—miraculously as it was believed— although both hands and one foot remained permanently scarred. He grew up a youth of such singular goodness that he was the wonder of all who knew him. In due time he studied for the priesthood and his ordination was attended by crowds who had watched him grow up or who knew him by reputation. He soon decided that he must aim at complete detachment from the world and retired into the desert of Mount Sirik, where he met with an aged anchorite who undertook to train him for the hermitical life. They remained together until the old man was at the point of death, when he advised George not to remain there alone, but to go to the monastery of Bonyssa. When George presented himself he was at once accepted, although a complete stranger, and the monks received him like an old friend. They had no reason to regret it, for George soon showed himself to be remarkable even among that company of saints.

In the meantime the people of Amastris had not forgotten him, and when their bishop died they elected George to fill his place and sent to the monastery to tell him of their decision. George, however, refused to accept the office, and the deputation then carried him off by force to Constantinople to the patriarch St Tarasius, who at once recognized him. Years before, on the eve of his consecration, George had taken part in the solemn singing of the night office. It was usual at the close of such services for the choir to be given a small fee, but George had steadfastly refused to accept anything, and this had greatly impressed Tarasius, who now declared himself ready to consecrate him. The emperor, on the other hand, had a candidate of his own, but St Tarasius said that George had been properly elected and he would only yield so far as to nominate the two candidates and to tell the clergy and people of Amastris to proceed to a new election. Their choice again fell on George, who was duly consecrated and was received by his people with acclamation. He proved himself a true father to his people and as wise as he was pious. It was a time when the country was subject to attacks from the Saracens. On the eve of one of these, the farmers and countryfolk were advised to take refuge within the city walls, but they could not be convinced of their danger nor would they quit their homes. St George accordingly went round in person from farm to farm explaining the matter and urging the people to seek a safe refuge. They listened to him and obeyed. When the enemy came, they found the city strongly garrisoned, and, recognizing that their own numbers were insufficient to take it by storm, they abandoned the attack and retired.

See the *Acta Sanctorum*, February, vol. iii ; but the complete Greek text has been published in modern times by V. Vasilievsky in *Analecta byzantinorussica*, vol. iii, 1893, pp. 1–73, where he discusses the whole history of the saint in a valuable introduction.

BD ROBERT SOUTHWELL, MARTYR   (A.D. 1595)

IT is a commonly received dogma of literary criticism that a poet should be studied in relation to his times, occupation and general background. It is nevertheless usually possible, and rewarding, to consider a given writer in the light of his writings, rather than vice versa. But Robert Southwell is one of the exceptions he was not first and foremost a poet ; he was first and foremost a man, a priest, a missionary and a martyr.

He was born in or about 1561 at Horsham Saint Faith in Norfolk, being related through his mother with the Sussex Shelleys, so that there was a remote connection between the two poets, Shelley and Southwell. He was sent to school at Douay, where he was a pupil of the famous Leonard Lessius, and so made his first contact with the Society of Jesus. He then studied in Paris, under Thomas Darbyshire, who had been archdeacon of Essex in Queen Mary's time, and when he was hardly seventeen decided that he wanted to be a Jesuit himself. At first he was refused on account of his youth, and his grief at this refusal prompted the earliest of his writing that has come down to us. However, in the autumn of 1578 he was admitted to the novitiate in Rome. He eventually was made prefect of studies in the Venerable English College, and was ordained priest in 1584. Two years later, with Father Henry Garnet, he was sent on the English mission.

Father Southwell's active career as a missionary lasted for six years. In 1587 he became chaplain at the London house of Anne, Countess of Arundel, and so became acquainted with her husband, Bd Philip Howard, who was then in the Tower.* In spite of the necessary secrecy of his movements, Southwell became well-known, and was effective in his work particularly on account of his gentle, quiet disposition ; he held aloof from all political and ecclesiastical intrigue and controversy and was concerned solely with the carrying out of his priestly duties. In 1592 he was arrested by the infamous Topcliffe at Uxenden Hall, Harrow : he had been betrayed by a daughter of the house.

In a vain attempt to elicit information about his fellow Catholics, Bd Robert was examined under terrible torture at least nine times in the house of Topcliffe himself (who had boasted to the queen, " I never did take so weighty a man, if he be rightly used "), and other times elsewhere. After nearly three years in the Gatehouse and the Tower he appealed to Cecil that he should be either tried or given at least some liberty. The appeal was successful. He was brought to trial, and condemned for his priesthood. On February 21, 1595 he was hanged, drawn and quartered at Tyburn, the awed bystanders insisting that he should not be cut down until he was dead. Bd Robert Southwell was only thirty-three years old.

This is, in brief outline, what is known of Southwell's life. But we may go a little further and fill in some of the gaps, concerning both himself and his circumstances, by a short consideration of his writings. As mentioned above, the first thing that we have is a prose lament when he was refused admittance to the Society of Jesus. Foley, in his *Records of the English Province, S.J.*, says that Bd Robert wavered for a time between the Jesuits and the Carthusians—an enlightening fact when we consider the difference of life offered by these alternatives. When he had finally decided to become a Jesuit and was refused temporarily—he wrote : " Alas where am I, and where shall I be ? A wanderer in a dry and parched land. . These favours are not communicated to aliens, they are the privileges of souls admitted to the inner chamber of the King ; now feeding on the spiritual delights of Paradise, then nesting upon the couch of love they take a repose that transcendeth all delights." We possess many of his writings from the period of

* It was to console him on the death of his half-sister, Lady Margaret Sackville, that Southwell wrote his *Triumphs over Death*.

his novitiate, and they show he had a clear idea of the pains, duties and joys of a member of the Society of Jesus : " Thou also, delighting in its possession [of the Jesuit life], how inflamed should not be thy love of God ! How grateful for so high a favour ! How great a perfection is required in a religious of the Society, who should ever be ready at a moment's notice for any part of the world and for any kind of people, be they heretics, Turks, pagans or barbarians. Hence we should reflect upon the virtues necessary for a life among the Indians. . Likewise for him who may be cast by the heretics into chains, macerated by hunger and thirst, tempted by a thousand solicitations, tortured by the rack and various torments. These should always live with the enemy, keep him ever in sight, engage in continual combat, yet never yield or be overcome."

There could hardly be a better expression of the attitude of mind necessary in the Jesuit missionary. And Southwell learnt well the lesson of obedience, he took it into his mind and made it part of himself, passing it on to others by example and in his writing : he had learnt true humility. " Remembering that the rule enjoins thee to esteem *all* in thy heart as thy superior, striving to acknowledge God in each one, as in His image."

Bd Robert seems to have felt from the beginning that his part would be that of the martyr. He knew very well the conditions in which his fellow Jesuits lived and worked, in England and elsewhere ; at Rome he would hear many reports of those trials and sufferings. He heard of the execution of Bd Edmund Campion, the first English Jesuit martyr, and presumably read the eye-witness account, a sufficiently disturbing document if one is aware that oneself may soon be running the danger of a similar death. But Southwell's letter on the subject to Father Persons carries (under its disguise of a merchant's business communication) a note rather of exultation : " He [Campion] has had the start of you in loading his vessel with English wares and has successfully returned to the desired port. Day by day we are looking forward to something similar of you." His letter from Calais to the father general of his order, Father Aquaviva, written before setting out for England in 1586, expresses his desire for the martyr's crown, and gives a glimpse of the writer's sensitiveness and normal human frailty : " Nor do I so much dread the tortures as look forward to the crown. The flesh indeed is weak and profiteth nothing. Yea, while pondering these things it even recoils." He was no thick-skinned adventurer embarking on an exciting and profitable expedition, any more than he was a story-book saint saved from human suffering by angelic helpers ; rather was he a man of deep feeling, moved by his love to give up all to God, even his life : not without moments of fear and disturbance, but those powerless to move him permanently because of the strength of his will, which relied not on itself but on God's grace.

For the life of a Jesuit missionary in England in the late sixteenth century we have Father John Gerard's autobiography, telling of toil and struggle, journeyings in disguise and secret meetings, hair-breadth escapes, final capture and imprisonment, often torture and sometimes escape.* After a period of this restless life Father Southwell became chaplain to Lady Arundel, and it was then that he produced his two important prose works, *Mary Magdalen's Funeral Tears* and the

* Gerard mentions Southwell several times : once in connection with a secret conference of missionaries in Warwickshire, which was very nearly followed by capture ; another time, as learning from him [Gerard] the sporting jargon needed for easy conversation with the gentry. See Father Philip Caraman's edition of the autobiography, *John Gerard* (1951).

Epistle of Comfort, both directed to the comfort and encouragement of his fellow Catholics. We have no evidence of the date of any of his poems : he had a certain amount of spare time then, and a great deal more during the years of imprisonment, and we may assume that he was composing during either, or more probably both, of these periods.

If the poet comes a long way behind the priest and the missionary, this does not mean that Bd Robert's poetry is apart from his life : quite the contrary. His short carefully-constructed lyrics in their intensity and fervour are an expression, in a small compass and sometimes a stumbling manner, of his qualities of mind and soul ; and these qualities are best realized by an examination of that life which both conditioned and expressed them. The mixture of courage and sensitiveness ; the lyrical faith in God and love of the beauty of His works, in the midst of the worser brutalities of the age ; the strange contrast of the holy and peace-loving man evading the law by means of dark hiding-places and cunning disguises, as if he were a dangerous criminal : these are reflected vividly in the poetry. We find also the stern asceticism and devotion to a " military " discipline necessary for the work he was called to do ; the renunciation of all worldly pleasures inspired, not by a morbid desire to choke the natural feelings, but by an irresistible impulse to give up all things for the sake of one, " the pearl of great price " the eternal Christian paradox of " having nothing yet possessing all things ". The essential paradox in the fundamental truths of Christianity is the source and inspiration of Southwell's poetry. " New Prince, New Pomp ", as its name implies, reveals the contradictory values brought into the world by the new Prince whose court is a stable. In the " Lauda Sion Salvatorem " he translates—with conspicuous success in a difficult verse-form—St Thomas Aquinas's great hymn, with all its emphasis on the seeming contradiction between faith and sense, reason and revelation. The apparent simplicity of dogma, possessing on closer study this apparent contradiction, which again reveals such depths of meaning, richness of interpretation, such complementary truths, was admirably suited to Southwell's genius.

It was natural that Bd Robert should write in the popular manner of his day (whatever other reasons he might have had for doing so), and the particular " conceited " style of the late sixteenth century was well suited to the emphasis he placed on the paradoxical aspect of his faith and the feelings aroused by it within himself :

> I live, but such a life as ever dies ;
> I die, but such a death as never ends ;
> My death to end my dying life denies,
> And life my living death no whit amends.

He has been compared to Sir Philip Sidney, both for his fondness of the conceit and his general style, and we may remember that Sidney had a great influence on the young poets of his time. But the comparison has also been made for their common intensity, warmth and personal feeling. This is true so far as it goes ; yet it is the more interesting for the differences it reveals. Sidney was the perfect example of the ideal gentleman of his day—and Southwell was not that : he was a hunted and hated Jesuit, suspect of treason. Nevertheless Sidney would probably have got on well with Southwell, for they were both men of cultured intellect, lively, sweet-tempered and of great personal integrity : in Father Garnet's words, " Our dear Father Southwell . being at once prudent, pious, meek, and exceedingly winning " ; and again, " What a famous man and how much beloved was Father Southwell."

Bd Robert's poetry tends to be short, compact and intensely expressed.   Carefully designed and made indeed, but never polished   nothing so urbane as that—yet with many felicitous phrases, among many a maze of words and ideas.   These more complicated tangles are not found in the very best of his lyrics : the famous " Burning Babe " has conceits enough, but the reader is never lost in them.   The most moving of all his poems, " The Virgin Mary to Christ on the Cross ", is simple and direct, with very little conceit, and that not too startling.

Robert Southwell was the poet of the lyric   his fire, energy and passion, combined with a severe discipline imposed not only by his vocation but also by his own will, found its best expression in a few lines heavily laden with meaning and emotion, carefully controlled by the power and acuteness of his understanding.   His two long works are a less rewarding study, the " Fourfold Meditation on the Four Last Things " (a doubt has been cast on its authorship) and " St Peter's Complaint " But whatever their quality, these poems show again in what their writer was most deeply interested   in the hard facts of the four last things in the life of every man ; in the way that man's sin has wounded the love of God, the repentance He wishes to draw from the hearts of men, and in what happens if man does not repent.   In the preface to his poems we find Southwell bewailing that the great gift of poetry is being put to such an unworthy use in the profane writings of so many of his contemporaries.   He states his purpose of using the popular poetic style for his own—that is, for the divine—purpose   " to weave a new web in their own loom " We can look back to the years when, as study-master at the English College in Rome, he applied himself to the study of his own tongue ; ultimately it was for this, to be able to fight the enemy with his own weapons.   And this style was an excellent weapon, for whereas in profane poetry words would be twisted and turned to make strange meanings for the sake of wit or cleverness, in the sacred, without losing any of the intellectual dexterity, the conceit could be seen to carry with it the most profound religious teaching, partly because of the nature of the doctrine, partly because of Southwell's own skill.

The poems achieved an almost immediate popularity, for the manner, if nothing else, appealed to the general public ; to his fellow Catholics they were precious " spiritual reading " cast in a form familiar and easy to them.   He knew and expressed for them how they were feeling, for whom life was indeed—

> A wandering course to doubtful rest
> a maze of countless straying ways.

They were experiencing the frailty of present happiness and the worthlessness of worldly pleasures of which Southwell wrote ; and they needed the comfort he brought in his triumphal acclamation of the Christian's salvation, of the mercy and love of God, the words of spiritual joy uttered in the midst of suffering, and not least in translations of the songs of the Church's worship and meditations upon the life of her Lord.   The omission from these last of any meditation on the Resurrection shows how he had fixed his attention on Christ's life, suffering and death, seeing and feeling all too acutely the parallel between that Passion and the lives of himself and his fellow Catholics.

" Love is not ruled with reason, but with love.   It neither regardeth what can be nor what shall be done, but only what itself desireth to do.   No difficulty can stay it, no impossibility appal it " (*Mary Magdalen's Funeral Tears*).   It was with this outlook that Bd Robert Southwell lived and worked and died ; it is this that permeates his poetry, preventing the fierceness of his faith and the acuteness of his intellect from turning lyrical beauty into the bitterness of loveless fanaticism. He does not forbid us to seek flowers ; but he tells us to seek them in Heaven.

The fullest and standard work on Bd Robert Southwell, who shares the literary laurels of the English Jesuit province with Gerard Manley Hopkins, is Janelle's *Robert Southwell the Writer* (1935) ; a third of the book is devoted to his life and there is a full bibliography. The best edition of his works is still that of Grosart (1872). There are articles by Father Thurston in *The Month* for February and March 1895, September 1905, and others, and in the *Catholic Encyclopedia*, vol. xiv, pp. 164-165. Challoner in MMP. describes the scene on the scaffold, and gives the text of two letters from Southwell to a friend in Rome, as well as a translation of a manuscript account of his trial kept at Saint-Omer. See also Lee in DNB. ; Foley's REPSJ., vol. i ; Catholic Record Society's publications, vol. v ; Child in the *Cambridge History of English Literature*, vol. iv ; and Hood's *The Book of Robert Southwell* (1926). Trotman's edition of the *Triumphs over Death*, with the Epistle to His Father and two other letters (1914) includes a sketch of the martyr's life, and some notes and speculations of which Janelle says they " are partly inaccurate and sometimes absurd ". Bd Robert's feast is observed by the Society of Jesus. For R. C. Bald's edition of the *Humble Supplication to Her Majesty* (1953), see *Analecta Bollandiana*, vol. lxxii (1954), p. 301. A new study of Southwell by Fr Christopher Devlin is announced (1955).

BD NOEL PINOT, MARTYR (A.D. 1794)

THE fact that the cause of Bd Noel was introduced by itself and dealt with independently of the other martyrs of the French Revolution gives him a certain distinction amongst those who suffered for their faith during the Reign of Terror. He was a simple parish-priest who had been born at Angers in 1747, and had made only the ordinary studies of the secular clergy. After serving as *vicaire* in one or two churches, and distinguishing himself by his devotion to the sick when in charge of an hospital for incurables, he was in 1788 appointed *curé* in the little town of Louroux-Béconnais, where his zeal and devotion were attended by abundant fruit in the moral reformation of his parishioners.

In 1790 the Constituent Assembly forced upon King Louis XVI the measure known as the " Civil Constitution of the Clergy ", which struck at the fundamental principles of Catholic Church government and which required every priest to take an unlawful oath denounced by the Holy See. Like many other good priests, the Abbé Pinot refused to take this oath. He was arrested, and by a tribunal at Angers was sentenced to be deprived of his cure for two years. This, however, did not deter him from exercising his ministry in secret, and he was energetic in bringing back to better dispositions many priests who had not shown the same firmness as himself. When the revolt in Vendée gained some temporary success, he openly took possession of his parish again to the great joy of his flock, and even when the arms of the Republic prevailed in that region he continued his pastoral work in defiance of civil and military authority. For some time he was successful in evading the attempts persistently made to effect his capture, but at last he was betrayed by a man to whom he had shown great kindness. He was seized when actually vested for Mass and was dragged in his chasuble through the streets amid the jeers of the rabble and the soldiery. During the twelve days he was kept in prison, he was very roughly treated, and upon his reiterated refusal to take the oath he was sentenced off-hand to the guillotine. On February 21, 1794, he was led out to death still wearing the priestly vestments in which he had been arrested, and on the way to offer his final sacrifice he is said to have repeated aloud the words which the priest recites at the foot of the altar in beginning Mass : *Introibo ad altare Dei* ., " I will enter unto the altar of God, to God who giveth joy to my youth." Bd Noel Pinot was beatified in 1926.

All the essential facts will be found rehearsed in the decrees published in the *Acta Apostolicae Sedis*, vol. xi (1919), pp. 86–88, and vol. xviii (1926), pp. 425–428. See also A. Crosnier, *Le b. Noël Pinot* (1926).

22 : ST PETER'S CHAIR

WE are accustomed to use such phrases as the power of the " throne ", the heir to the " throne ", the prerogative of the " crown ", etc., substituting the concrete insignia of dignity for the office itself. The same metonomy is familiar in ecclesiastical matters. The " Holy See " is no more than the *Sancta Sedes*, the holy *chair*, for the word " see " is simply *sedes*, which has come to us through the Old French *sied*. But the Romans had another name, which they borrowed from the Greeks, for the seat occupied by a teacher or anyone who spoke with authority. This was *cathedra*, and its use in this sense can not only be traced back to the early Christian centuries, but it survives to this day, notably in the phrase " an *ex cathedra* decision ", that is to say a pronouncement in which the pope speaks as teacher of the Universal Church.

The question has been raised whether the commemoration of " St Peter's Chair " has arisen out of the honour paid to some material object venerated as a memorial and a relic, or whether the purpose of the feast was not from the first to glorify the pontifical office conferred on St Peter and his successors at their consecration. Reference has previously been made, under January 18, to the ancient *sedia gestatoria*, known as St Peter's chair, now enshrined in the apse of Rome's great basilica. De Rossi contended that this was honoured in the feast kept on February 22, but he has also given prominence to a mention by St Gregory the Great of " oil from the chair upon which Saint Peter first sat in Rome ", which seems to mean oil from the lamps which burned before a stone seat cut out of the tufa in the so-called " coemiterium Ostrianum " where St Peter used to baptize. This seat the great archaeologist associated with the feast of January 18. It may be that the two feasts originated in some such tradition, but the arguments vigorously urged by Mgr Duchesne, Marucchi, and others against the identification of the liturgical " chair of St Peter " with any material object seem to have won the day. Of the chair, ancient though it may be, now honoured at the Vatican, there is no mention, says Duchesne, before 1217. " Peter Mallius, writing of the basilica of St Peter (1159–1181) does not allude to it, and considering how constantly he enlarges on the relics therein, his silence shows that no chair of St Peter was venerated then." And when we look at the earliest collects, lessons, etc., provided for the liturgical celebration, these seem to indicate that the dominating note of the feast was the glorification of St Peter's *office*.

It has already been stated in connection with the feast of St Peter's Chair on January 18 that there was originally only one chair feast and that this was kept on February 22, having no reference to Antioch, but presumably to the beginning of St Peter's episcopate in Rome. What we know for certain is that the Philocalian calendar, which gives a list of the Roman liturgical celebrations in A.D. 354, or possibly as early as 336, contains on February 22 the entry *natale Petri de cathedra*, *i.e.* " Peter's chair feast ", for *natale* by this time, from its primitive meaning of birthday, had come to denote any kind of anniversary. We may thus be quite sure that in the middle of the fourth century, within a very few years of the death of the Emperor Constantine, the Roman church honoured St Peter by a festival which was in some way associated with his consecration to the pastoral office. That this commemoration had anything consciously to do with Antioch is highly unlikely. Not until several centuries later do we find in the calendar of St Willibrord (*c.* A.D. 704) the entry *Cathedra Petri in Antiochia*, and this is probably the earliest mention of the sort preserved to us. On the other hand it appears that in the Auxerrois " Hieronymianum " of the sixth century the entry *Cathedra Petri in Roma* must already have been attached to January 18 ; but the Gallican liturgies for the most part adhere to February 22, without any mention of Antioch.

The most important element in the case is undoubtedly the fact that on or about February 22 according to pagan usage occurred the annual commemoration of dead relatives, called the *Feralia* or *Parentalia* (when food was brought to the graves). It does not seem possible to determine a precise day, for though Ovid in his *Fasti* speaks of the Feralia under the heading February 18, still by using the phrase *parentales dies* he clearly implies that the celebration continued for more than twenty-four hours, and there are other ancient authorities who in the same connection give prominence to February 21. As Kellner points out, during the Parentalia " no marriages were celebrated, the temples remained closed, and the magistrates laid aside the external insignia of their office. Upon the commemoration of the departed followed immediately, on February 22, the festival of surviving relatives, named in consequence *Charistia* or *Cara cognatio*. This celebration had no recognized place among the functions of the official worship of the state . . nevertheless it was a very popular feast and struck its roots deeper into the life of the people than any of the official festivals ". This affords good reason for supposing that the very early institution of the feast of St Peter's Chair was simply an effort to provide a Christian substitute for the pagan rites practised at this season (*cf.* January 1 in reference to the New Year celebration, and Candlemas as regards the Robigalia and Lupercalia). Several clear testimonies point to the same conclusion. For example, in the calendar of Polemius Silvius, compiled in Gaul about the year 448, we have under February 22 the entry " the Deposition of SS. Peter and Paul ; ' the dear ties of blood ' (*cara cognatio*) so styled, because though there might be feuds among living relatives, they would be laid aside at the season of death " This plainly suggests that a Peter and Paul feast had been introduced on this day as a substitute for the pagan celebration of the Charistia. Probably the Christian festival was of much the same character liturgically whether it was called " St Peter's Chair at Rome " or " the Deposition of SS. Peter and Paul " ; it would in either case have amounted to a celebration of the special prerogatives of the Holy See.

What is perhaps most surprising as an illustration of the vitality of superstitious abuses is the fact that as late as the middle of the twelfth century, the February feast was still called " St Peter's banquet day ".[*] Beleth the liturgist, to whom we owe this information, is said to have been an Englishman, but he lived a good deal in France and it is perhaps the latter country to which he is referring. After mentioning that both the feasts of St Peter's Chair were separated by no great interval from Septuagesima, he tells us that the Antioch or February celebration was the

[*] Yet is it so surprising when we reflect what can be seen even now no farther away than the Abbots Bromley horn-dance and the so-called hobby-horse at Padstow on May 1 ?

more solemn of the two and that it was called *festum beati Petri epularum*, probably the equivalent of a homely phrase which might be rendered " St Peter's beano " " For ", he goes on, " the pagans of old were accustomed every year on a certain day in the month of February to set out a good meal beside the graves of their relatives, which the demons made away with in the night-time, though it was believed not less untruly than absurdly that the souls of the dead were refreshed therewith.   For men thought that these provisions were consumed by the souls that wandered about the graves.   However, this custom and this false persuasion could hardly be eradicated, Christians though they were.   Accordingly when certain holy men realized the difficulty and were anxious to suppress the custom altogether, they instituted the feast of St Peter's Chair, both of the Roman chair and the chair at Antioch, assigning it to the day on which these pagan abominations took place, in order that this evil practice might be utterly abolished.   Hence it is that from the spread of good food then laid out the feast acquired the name of ' St Peter's banquet day '."

It is clear that these allusions to the offerings made at the graveside must all have reference to the February feast, and this only makes it harder to understand how the feast came to be duplicated.   Various suggestions have been offered, of which the most plausible seems to be that of Mgr Duchesne, that as the original celebration on February 22 often occurred in Lent it could not be regularly kept. So " in countries observing the Gallican rite, where Lenten observance was considered incompatible with the honouring of saints, the difficulty may have been avoided by holding the festival on an earlier date."   For the selection of January 18 we may perhaps find a reason in the fact that this day is the earliest possible date on which Septuagesima can occur.   No doubt if January 17 had been chosen this would have placed the Chair feast altogether beyond the possibility of any concurrence, but there may easily have been some little miscalculation in the matter. Although Septuagesima *can* fall on January 18, this happens very rarely.   It has not occurred since 1818, and will not occur again until the year 2285.   Further, it seems highly probable that a feast of the Blessed Virgin is entered in the " Hieronymianum " on January 18 for precisely the same reason, and the conjecture suggests itself that the feast now known to us as " the Conversion of St Paul " was originally a sort of octave of the Chair feast of St Peter.   Polemius Silvius, it will be remembered, seemed to regard the latter as concerned with both apostles and called it *Depositio SS. Petri et Pauli*.

A puzzling feature in the problem is the fact that though our feast was celebrated at so early a date in Rome, it seems at a later period to have disappeared from the Roman calendar altogether.   It is not in the Gelasian or Gregorian Sacramentaries in their original form, nor in the primitive Roman Antiphonarium.   It was never adopted in Africa or in the East, and we cannot trace it at Monte Cassino or in Naples.   It may be that the pagan celebration of the Parentalia and the Charistia in Rome itself died out before the sixth century, though they lingered on in Gaul. In that case, since the feast of the Chair had effected its purpose and was now apt to interfere with the reorganized Lenten stations, it may have been suppressed at Rome in favour of this Lenten scheme.   In Gaul, however, the feast was retained. In some places it was transferred to January 18, but in many calendars it kept its old position on February 22.   To explain the duplication someone hit upon the idea that if the former celebration commemorated the beginning of St Peter's Roman episcopate, the latter must be referred to Antioch, for through the Clemen-

tine Recognitions the close connection of St Peter with Antioch was widely credited
in the fourth and fifth centuries. Eventually both feasts were adopted pretty
well everywhere in Gaul, and from thence it would seem Rome eventually readopted
them both, just as Gaul gave to Rome the Rogation days and a good many other
liturgical features.

See Abbot Cabrol in DAC., vol. iii, pp. 76-90 ; Duchesne, *Origines du culte chrétien*
(Eng. trans.), pp. 279-280 ; Kellner, *Heortology* (1908), pp. 301-308 ; De Rossi in *Bullettino
di archeologia cristiana*, 1867, p. 38. See also Belethus, *Rationale div. off.*, in Migne, PL.,
vol. ccii, cc. 9 *seq.* ; pseudo-Augustine in Migne, PL., vol. xxxix, c. 2102 ; G. Morin in
Revue bénédictine, vol. xiii, pp. 343-346 ; CMH., p. 109.

SS. THALASSIUS AND LIMNAEUS   (*c.* A.D. 450)

WE read of the holy hermits Thalassius and Limnaeus in the *Philotheus* of Theodoret, Bishop of Cyrrhus, who wrote of them from personal knowledge. He
describes Thalassius as an ascetic of wonderful simplicity and meekness, who
outshone all his contemporaries in holiness. " I often visited the man ", he says,
" and had sweet converse with him." Thalassius had taken up his abode in a cave
on a hillside south of the town of Tillima in Syria, and Limnaeus, who was much
younger than he, came to live with him as his disciple. To control too free a
tongue, Limnaeus kept complete silence for a long period, and, by similar practices,
obtained complete mastery over himself. Later on Limnaeus left Thalassius to
attach himself to another solitary the famous St Maro—under whom he completed
his training. He then went to live alone on a neighbouring mountain peak, where
he built himself a rough stone enclosure without mortar and without a roof. It
had a little window through which he could communicate with the outside world,
and a door which was usually cemented up and only opened to admit Theodoret,
his bishop. The anchoret was widely famed for his healing powers sick people
and those afflicted with evil spirits used to come to his window and he healed them
in the name of Jesus by making over them the sign of the cross. Once he trod on
a snake and it bit the sole of his foot, and when he tried to remove it, it bit his hands
also : he suffered great pain, but was healed by prayer. He had a special affection
for blind people, and used to gather them together and teach them to sing hymns.
He also built two houses for them near his cell and did all he could to help them.
Theodoret says that Limnaeus had lived thirty-eight years in this way in the open
air at the time he was writing his history.

The *Philotheus* of Theodoret is our main authority, but these saints also have a detailed
notice in the Greek synaxaries.

ST BARADATES   (*c.* A.D. 460)

ST BARADATES was another anchoret who lived in the diocese of Cyrrhus in Syria
and of whom Bishop Theodoret makes mention in his *Philotheus*. He had such a
great reputation that the Emperor Leo wrote specially to him as well as to St
Simeon Stylites and St James of Syria when he wished to ascertain the verdict of
the Eastern church upon the Council of Chalcedon. Theodoret, who calls him
" the admirable Baradates ", says that he was always devising fresh methods of
self-discipline. He lived exposed to all weathers in a tiny hut made of trellis work,
so small that he could not stand upright in it. Here he remained for a long time,
but when the patriarch of Antioch desired him to leave it, he gave proof of his

humility by immediate obedience.   He was clothed in a leather garment which covered him so completely that only his mouth and nose could be seen.   It was his practice to spend long hours in prayer with his hands upraised, and, though he was of a weakly constitution, the fervour of his spirit triumphed over the infirmity of the body.   He was also a man of learning, well versed in theology.   His answer to the Emperor's letter is still extant.

Theodoret in his *Philotheus* is again our most reliable authority.   See also the *Acta Sanctorum*, February, vol. iii.

ST MARGARET OF CORTONA   (A.D. 1297)

IN the antiphon to the " Benedictus " in the office of St Margaret of Cortona she is described as " the Magdalen of the Seraphic Order ", and, in one of our Lord's colloquies with the saint, He is recorded to have said, " Thou art the third light granted to the order of my beloved Francis.   He was the first, among the Friars Minor : Clare was the second, among the nuns : thou shalt be the third, in the Order of Penance."   She was the daughter of a small farmer of Laviano in Tuscany.   She had the misfortune to lose a good mother when she was only seven years old, and the stepmother whom her father brought home two years later was a hard and masterful woman who had little sympathy with the high-spirited, pleasure-loving child.   Attractive in appearance and thirsting for the affection which was denied her in her home, it is not wonderful that Margaret fell an easy prey to a young cavalier from Montepulciano, who induced her to elope with him one night to his castle among the hills.   Besides holding out a prospect of love and luxury he appears to have promised to marry her, but he never did so, and for nine years she lived openly as his mistress and caused much scandal, especially when she rode through the streets of Montepulciano on a superb horse and splendidly attired.   Nevertheless she does not seem to have been in any sense the abandoned woman she afterwards considered herself to have been.   She was faithful to her lover, whom she often entreated to marry her and to whom she bore one son, and, in spite of her apparent levity, there were times when she realized bitterly the sinfulness of her life.   One day the young man went out to visit one of his estates and failed to return. All one night and the next day Margaret watched with growing anxiety, until at length she saw the dog that had accompanied him running back alone.   He plucked at her dress and she followed him through a wood to the foot of an oak tree, where he began to scratch, and soon she perceived with horror the mangled body of her lover, who had been assassinated and then thrown into a pit and covered with leaves.

A sudden revulsion came as she recognized in this the judgement of God.   As soon as she possibly could she left Montepulciano, after having given up to the relations of the dead man all that was at her disposal (except a few ornaments which she sold for the benefit of the poor) ; and, clad in a robe of penitence and holding her little son by the hand, she returned to her father's house to ask forgiveness and admittance.   Urged by her stepmother, her father refused to receive her, and Margaret was almost reduced to despair, when she was suddenly inspired to go to Cortona to seek the aid of the Friars Minor, of whose gentleness with sinners she seems to have heard.   When she reached the town she did not know where to go and her evident misery attracted the attention of two ladies, Marinana and Raneria by name, who spoke to her and asked if they could help her.   She told them her story and why she had come to Cortona, and they at once took her and her boy to their own home. Afterwards they introduced her to the Franciscans, who soon became her fathers in Christ. For three years Margaret had a hard struggle against temptation, for the flesh was not yet subdued to the spirit, and she found her chief earthly support in the counsel of two friars, John da Castiglione and Giunta Bevegnati, who was her ordinary confessor and who afterwards wrote her " legend ". They guided her carefully through periods of alternate exaltation and despair, checking and encouraging her as the occasion required. In the early days of her conversion, she went one Sunday to Laviano, her birthplace, during Mass, and with a cord round her neck asked pardon for her past scandals. She had intended also to have herself led like a criminal through the streets of Montepulciano with a rope round her neck, but Fra Giunta forbade it as unseemly in a young woman and conducive to spiritual pride, though he subsequently allowed her to go to the church there one Sunday and ask pardon of the congregation. He also restrained her when she sought to mutilate her face, and from time to time he tried to moderate her excessive austerities. " Father," she replied, on one of these occasions, " do not ask me to come to terms with this body of mine, for I cannot afford it. Between me and my body there must needs be a struggle till death."

Margaret started to earn her living by nursing the ladies of the city, but she gave this up in order to devote herself to prayer and to looking after the sick poor. She left the home of the ladies who had befriended her, and took up her quarters in a small cottage in a more secluded part, where she began to subsist upon alms. Any unbroken food that was bestowed upon her she gave to the poor, and only what was left of the broken food did she use for herself and her child. Her lack of tenderness to her boy seems singular in one who showed such tenderness to other people, but it may well be that it was part of her self-mortification. At the end of three years her earlier struggles were over, and she reached a higher plane of spirituality when she began to realize by experience the love of Christ for her soul. She had long desired to become a member of the third order of St Francis, and the friars, who had waited until they were satisfied of her sincerity, at length consented to give her the habit. Soon afterwards her son was sent to school at Arezzo, where he remained until he entered the Franciscan Order. From the time she became a tertiary, St Margaret advanced rapidly in prayer and was drawn into very direct communion with her Saviour. Her intercourse with God became marked with frequent ecstasies and Christ became the dominating theme of her life. Fra Giunta has recorded a few of her colloquies with our Lord and has described some of her visions, though he acknowledges that even to him she spoke of them with reluctance and only when divinely ordered to do so or through fear of becoming the victim of delusion.

The communications she received did not all relate to herself. In one case she was told to send a message to Bishop William of Arezzo, warning him to amend his ways and to desist from fighting with the people of his diocese and Cortona in particular. Though he was a turbulent and worldly prelate he appears to have been impressed, for he made peace with Cortona soon afterwards and this was generally attributed to Margaret's mediation. In 1289 she strove to avert war when Bishop William was again at strife with the Guelfs. Margaret went to him in person but this time he would not listen, and ten days later he was slain in battle. The bishop had, however, done one good turn to Margaret and to Cortona, for in 1286 he had granted a charter which enabled her to start putting her work for the

sick poor on a permanent basis.   At first she seems to have nursed them by herself
in her own cottage, but after a time she was joined by several women, one of whom,
Diabella, gave her a house for the purpose.   She enlisted the sympathy of Uguccio
Casali, the leading citizen of Cortona, and he induced the city council to assist her
in starting a hospital called the Spedale di Santa Maria della Misericordia, the
nursing sisters of which were Franciscan tertiaries whom Margaret formed into a
congregation with special statutes ;   they were called the Poverelle.   She also
founded the Confraternity of Our Lady of Mercy, pledged to support the hospital
and to search out and assist the poor.

As Margaret advanced in life, so did she advance in the way of expiation.   Her
nights she spent, almost without sleep, in prayer and contemplation, and when she
did lie down to rest, her bed was the bare ground.   For food she took only a little
bread and raw vegetables, with water to drink ;   she wore rough hair-cloth next her
skin and disciplined her body to blood for her own sins and those of mankind.   In
spite of the wonderful graces which she received Margaret had to endure fierce
trials throughout her life.   One of them came upon her unexpectedly some eight
years before her death.   From the first there had been certain people in Cortona
who doubted her sincerity, and they continued to do so even after she had so evidently proved the reality of her conversion.   At last they began to cast aspersions
on her relations with the friars, especially with Fra Giunta, and managed to stir up
such suspicions that the veneration in which she was held was temporarily turned
to contempt and she was spurned as a madwoman and hypocrite.   Even the friars
were moved by the general indignation   restrictions were laid on Fra Giunta's
seeing her, and in 1289 he was transferred to Siena, only returning shortly before
her death.   This trial was intensified by the withdrawal of the sense of sweetness
in prayer.   There had been further misunderstandings with the friars when she
had retired the previous year by divine command to a more retired cottage at some
distance from the friars' church.   According to Fra Giunta, they realized that her
health was broken and feared lest they might lose the custody of her body after her
death.   All these trials she bore quietly and meekly and gave herself more and more
to prayer.   Thus she was led on ever higher.

Towards the latter part of her life, our Lord said to St Margaret, " Show now
that thou art converted ;   call others to repentance.   The graces I have bestowed on thee are not meant for thee alone."   Obedient to the call, she set about
attacking vice and converting sinners with the greatest eagerness and with wonderful
success.   The lapsed returned to the sacraments, wrongdoers were brought to
repentance and private feuds and quarrels ceased.   Fra Giunta says that the fame
of these conversions soon spread, and hardened sinners flocked to Cortona to listen
to the saint's exhortations, not only from all parts of Italy, but even from France and
Spain.   Great miracles of healing too were wrought at her intercession, and the
people of Cortona, who had long forgotten their temporary suspicions, turned to
her in all their troubles and difficulties.   At length it became evident that her
strength was failing, and she was divinely warned of the day and hour of her death.
She received the last rites from Fra Giunta and passed away at the age of fifty, after
having spent twenty-nine years in penance.   On the day of her death she was
publicly acclaimed as a saint, and the citizens of Cortona in the same year began to
build a church in her honour.   Though she was not formally canonized until 1728,
her festival had been by permission celebrated for two centuries in the diocese of
Cortona and by the Franciscan Order.   Of the original church built by Nicholas

and John Pisano nothing remains but a window ; the present tasteless building, however, contains St Margaret's body under the high altar and a statue of the saint and her dog by John Pisano.

The main historical source for the life of St Margaret is the " legend " of Giunta Bevegnati ; it seems probable that in MS. 61 of the convent of St Margaret at Cortona we have a copy of this corrected by the hand of the author himself. The text is in the *Acta Sanctorum*, February, vol. iii ; but it has been re-edited in more modern times by Ludovic da Pelago (1793) and E. Cirvelli (1897). See also Father Cuthbert, *A Tuscan Penitent* (1907) ; Léopold de Chérancé, *Marguerite de Cortone* (1927) ; M. Nuti, *Margherita da Cortona la sua leggenda e la storia* (1923) ; F. Mauriac, *Margaret of Cortona* (1948) ; and another life in French by R. M. Pierazzi (1947).

23 : ST PETER DAMIAN, Cardinal-Bishop of Ostia, Doctor of the Church (A D. 1072)

ST PETER DAMIAN is one of those stern figures who seem specially raised up, like St John Baptist, to recall men in a lax age from the error of their ways and to bring them back into the narrow path of virtue. He was born at Ravenna and, having lost his parents when very young, he was left in the charge of a brother in whose house he was treated more like a slave than a kinsman. As soon as he was old enough he was sent to tend swine. Another brother, who was archpriest of Ravenna, took pity on the neglected lad and undertook to have him educated. Having found a father in this brother, Peter appears to have adopted from him the surname of Damian. Damian sent the boy to school, first at Faenza and then at Parma. He proved an apt pupil and became in time a master and a professor of great ability. He had early begun to inure himself to fasting, watching and prayer, and wore a hair shirt under his clothes to arm himself against the allurements of pleasure and the wiles of the Devil. Not only did he give away much in alms, but he was seldom without some poor persons at his table, and took pleasure in serving them with his own hands.

After a time Peter resolved to leave the world entirely and embrace a monastic life away from his own country. Whilst his mind was full of these thoughts, two religious of St Benedict, belonging to Fonte Avellana of the reform of St Romuald, happened to call at the house where he lived, and he was able to learn much from them about their rule and mode of life. This decided him, and he joined their hermitage, which was then in the greatest repute. The hermits, who dwelt in pairs in separate cells, occupied themselves chiefly in prayer and reading, and lived a life of great austerity. Peter's excessive watchings brought on a severe insomnia which was cured with difficulty, but which taught him to use more discretion. Acting upon this experience, he now devoted considerable time to sacred studies, and became as well versed in the Holy Scriptures as he formerly had been in profane literature. By the unanimous consent of the hermits he was ordered to take upon himself the government of the community in the event of the superior's death. Peter's extreme reluctance obliged the abbot to make it a matter of obedience. Accordingly after the abbot's decease about the year 1043, Peter assumed the direction of that holy family, which he governed with great wisdom and piety. He also founded five other hermitages in which he placed priors under his own general direction. His chief care was to foster in his disciples the spirit of solitude, charity and humility. Many of them became great lights of the Church, including St Dominic Loricatus, and St John of Lodi, his successor in the priory of the Holy Cross, who wrote St Peter's life and at the end of his days became bishop of Gubbio. For years Peter Damian was much employed in the service of the Church by successive popes, and in 1057 Stephen IX prevailed upon him to quit his desert and made him cardinal-bishop of Ostia. Peter constantly solicited Nicholas II to grant him leave to resign his bishopric and return to his solitude, but the pope had always refused. His successor, Alexander II, out of affection for the holy man, was prevailed upon with difficulty to consent, but reserved the power to employ him in church matters of importance, as he might hereafter have need of his help. The saint from that time considered himself dispensed not only from the responsibility of governing his see, but from the supervision of the various religious settlements he had controlled, and reduced himself to the condition of a simple monk.

In this retirement he edified the Church by his humility, penance and compunction, and laboured in his writings to enforce the observance of morality and discipline. His style is vehement, and his strictness appears in all his works—especially when he treats of the duties of the clergy and of monks. He severely rebuked the bishop of Florence for playing a game of chess. That prelate acknowledged his amusement to be unworthy, and received the holy man's reproof meekly, submitting to do penance by reciting the psalter three times and by washing the feet of twelve poor men and giving them each a piece of money. Peter wrote a treatise to the bishop of Besançon in which he inveighed against the custom by which the canons of that church sang the Divine Office seated in choir, though he allowed all to sit for the lessons. He recommended the use of the discipline as a substitute for long penitential fasts. He wrote most severely on the obligations of monks and protested against their wandering abroad, seeing that the spirit of retirement is an essential condition of their state. He complained bitterly of certain evasions whereby many palliated real infractions of their vow of poverty. He justly observed, " We can never restore primitive discipline when once it is decayed ; and if we, by negligence, suffer any diminution in what remains established, future ages will never be able to repair the breach. Let us not draw upon ourselves so foul a reproach ; but let us faithfully transmit to posterity the example of virtue which we have received from our forefathers." St Peter Damian fought simony with very great vigour, and equally vigorously upheld clerical celibacy ; and as he supported a severely ascetical, semi-eremitical life for monks, so he was an encourager of common life for the secular clergy. He was a man of great vehemence in all he said and did ; it has been said of him that " his genius was to exhort and impel to the heroic, to praise striking achievements and to record edifying examples an extraordinary moral force burns in all that he wrote ".

In spite of his severity, St Peter Damian could treat penitents with mildness and indulgence where charity and prudence required it. Henry IV, the young king of Germany, had married Bertha, daughter of Otto, Marquis of the Marches of Italy, but two years later he sought a divorce under the pretence that the marriage had never been consummated. By promises and threats he won over the archbishop of Mainz, who summoned a council for the purpose of sanctioning the annulment of the marriage ; but Pope Alexander II forbade him to consent to such an injustice and chose Peter Damian as his legate to preside over the synod. The aged legate met the king and bishops at Frankfurt, laid before them the order and instructions of the Holy See, and entreated the king to pay due regard to the law of God, the canons of the Church and his own reputation, and also to reflect seriously on the public scandal which so pernicious an example would give. The nobles likewise entreated the monarch not to stain his honour by conduct so unworthy. Henry, unable to resist this strong opposition, dropped his project of a divorce, but remained the same at heart, only hating the queen more bitterly than ever.

Peter hastened back to his desert of Fonte Avellana. Whatever austerities he prescribed for others, he practised himself, remitting none of them even in his old age. He used to make wooden spoons and other little useful things that his hands might not be idle during the time he was not at work or at prayer. When Henry, Archbishop of Ravenna, had been excommunicated for grievous enormities, Peter was again sent by Alexander II as legate to settle the troubles. Upon his arrival at Ravenna he found that the prelate had just died, but he brought the accomplices of his crimes to a sense of their guilt and imposed on them suitable penance. This was Damian's last undertaking for the Church. As he was returning towards Rome he was arrested by an acute attack of fever in a monastery outside Faenza, and died on the eighth day of this illness, whilst the monks were reciting Matins round about him, on February 22, 1072.

St Peter Damian was one of the chief forerunners of the Hildebrandine reform in the Church. His preaching was most eloquent and his writing voluminous, and he was declared a doctor of the Church in 1828.

Although the biography by his disciple John (who is almost certainly John of Lodi, later bishop of Gubbio) supplies a connected account of the life of St Peter Damian, still his history is very largely written in the chronicles of the times as well as in his own letters and diatribes. John's biography is printed in the *Acta Sanctorum*, February, vol. iii, as well as in Mabillon. See also the excellent study of R. Biron, *St Pierre Damien* in the series "Les Saints", and Capecelatro, *Storia di San Pier Damiano*. For English readers Mgr Mann's *Lives of the Pope's*, vols. v and vi, provide much collateral information. *Cf.* O. J. Blum's *St Peter Damian* (1947), in which his teaching is examined ; and D. Knowles, *The Monastic Order in England* (1949), pp. 193 197, with the references there given. There is a study in German by F. Dressler (1954).

ST SERENUS THE GARDENER, MARTYR   (A.D. 302 ?)

ST SERENUS is also known as St Cerneuf at Billom in Auvergne, where some of his relics are said to be preserved. A Greek by birth, he left all that he had to serve God in the ascetic life of celibacy, penance and prayer. Coming with this intention to Sirmium in what is now Yugoslavia (its present name is Mitrovica), he bought a garden, which he cultivated, living on the fruit and vegetables it produced. When a persecution broke out against the Christians, he hid for several months, but afterwards returned to his garden. One day he found a woman walking about in it, and he asked her gravely what she was doing there within the enclosure of an ascetic. "I particularly enjoy walking in this garden", she replied. "A lady of your position ought not to be wandering about here at an unbecoming time", retorted the saint, and he would not allow her to stay. It was the hour of siesta, when it was not usual for persons of quality to be abroad, and Serenus suspected that she had come with no good intention. The lady, however, was furious at the rebuke, and immediately wrote to her husband, who belonged to the guards of the Emperor Maximian, and complained that she had been insulted by Serenus.

Her husband went to the emperor to demand justice, and said, " Whilst we are waiting on your Majesty's person, our wives in distant lands are insulted ". Whereupon the emperor gave him a letter to the governor of the province to enable him to obtain satisfaction. With this letter he set out for Sirmium, and, presenting it to the governor, charged him to avenge the affront offered. " And who is the insolent man who has dared to insult the wife of such a gentleman as yourself ? " inquired the magistrate. " A vulgar fellow—a gardener called Serenus." The governor at once sent for him and asked him his name. " Serenus ", was the reply. " Thy occupation ? "—" I am a gardener ". The governor said, " How then hast thou the insolence to affront this officer's wife in your garden ? " Serenus answered, " I have never, to my knowledge, insulted a woman in all my life. But I do remember a lady coming to my garden some time ago at an unseemly hour. She said she had come to take a walk, and I own that I told her it was improper for one of her sex and quality to be wandering abroad at such an hour." This defence caused the officer to look at the matter from another point of view it seemed that it was his wife who was in fault and he therefore withdrew, dropping the prosecution.

The governor, however, had had his suspicions aroused he thought that so scrupulous a man must of necessity be a Christian. Consequently he proceeded to cross-examine him on that point, and asked him what his religion was. " I am a Christian", was the unhesitating reply. The governor asked him where he had been lurking that he had not offered sacrifice to the gods. " It has pleased God to reserve me for this time," replied Serenus. " It seemed for a while that he had rejected me as being a stone unfit for His building, but now that He calls me to be placed in it I am ready to suffer that I may have a part in His Kingdom with His saints." The governor exclaimed, " Since thou hast sought by flight to elude the emperor's decrees and hast refused to offer sacrifice to the gods, I condemn thee to suffer death by decapitation ". The sentence was immediately carried out.

The so-called Acts of Serenus have been printed by the Bollandists (Feb., vol. iii). Although Ruinart includes them in his *Acta sincera*, the details of the story are quite unreliable ; Delehaye (*Légendes hagiographiques*, p. 115) classifies them as fictitious, but possibly based on some historic foundation.

ST ALEXANDER AKIMETES   (*c.* A.D. 430)

ALTHOUGH the name of Alexander, who was a restless and somewhat turbulent archimandrite, has never found a place in the Roman Martyrology, he is honoured in certain Eastern provinces, and his biography is given on January 15 in the *Acta Sanctorum*. Alexander was born in Asia, but in early manhood he studied in Constantinople, where he was converted through his earnest reading of the gospels, and then retired to Syria to practise asceticism. After eleven years' experience of the religious life, both as a cenobite and as an anchoret, he devoted himself to a missionary career in Mesopotamia, and is said to have converted the famous Rabulas, afterwards bishop of Edessa. After this he founded a large monastery beside the Euphrates, but before long he was on the move again, taking with him a large company of his monks. He settled for a while in Antioch, where his visit caused great disturbances, but finally established a new monastery at Constantinople. There, once more, violent animosities were aroused, and his enemies procured his banishment. After crossing the Hellespont, Alexander was mobbed and severely maltreated, but by the help of some powerful protector he managed to build another monastery at Gomon, on the Asiatic shore of the Bosphorus, where he eventually died in 430.

The fame of Alexander is mainly due to his institution of a form of choral service, the execution of which was carried on night and day without interruption, the monks being divided into relays for the purpose. They were hence called ἀκοίμητοι (sleepless ones), and it is now recognized that this type of *cursus* which Alexander created has had a considerable indirect influence upon the divine office in the Western church. So far as there was any liturgical *cultus* of St Alexander in the East, his feast seems to have been kept either on February 23 or July 3.

See the excellent article of J. Pargoire in DAC., vol. i, cc. 307–321 and also the *Revue des questions historiques*, January, 1899. A Latin version of the life is printed in the *Acta Sanctorum* for January 15; the Greek text was edited by E. De Stoop in 1911 in the *Patrologia orientalis*, vol. vi, part 5. *Cf.* also S. Vailhé in DHG., vol. i, cc. 274–282. For the *laus perennis*, *cf.* herein St Sigismund, May 1.

ST DOSITHEUS   (*c.* A.D. 530)

DOSITHEUS was brought up a pagan, entirely ignorant of the doctrines of Christianity, but he used to hear much talk about Jerusalem, and was induced, out of curiosity, to visit it. He went to see the chief sights of the city including Gethsemane, where he was impressed by a painting representing the lost being tormented in Hell. He did not understand what he saw until a stranger, an elderly lady, explained the picture and told him about the last judgement, Heaven and Hell. Greatly impressed, he asked what he should do to avoid the terrible punishment and she replied that he must fast and pray. He set about following her advice, but his friends laughed at him and told him that he had better become a monk; so making his way to the monastery at Gaza ruled by the Abbot Seridos he asked to be admitted. At first the abbot hesitated on account of his youthful appearance, but the young man's earnestness was reassuring and he accordingly accepted him with the approval of St Barsanuphius, committing him to the care of one of his monks called Dorotheus. This experienced ascetic, aware of the difficulty of passing from one extreme to another, and seeing that Dositheus was not robust, left him pretty much to his own devices at first, so far as the external practices of asceticism were concerned, but he taught him to discipline his tongue and to conquer irregular impulses. He impressed upon him the necessity of a perfect renunciation of his own will in everything, great or small, and then, as he found his strength would permit, he daily diminished his supply of food till the quantity of six pounds of bread a day, with which he had begun, became reduced to eight ounces.

After a time Dositheus was entrusted with the care of the sick—an office which he discharged to the satisfaction of all: he was so kind and cheerful that the sick loved his presence. At first, when they were unreasonable, he would sometimes lose patience and speak crossly. Then, overcome with remorse, he would run to his cell and throw himself on the ground weeping bitterly until his master came to comfort him and to assure him of God's forgiveness. After a time phthisical symptoms seem to have developed, and he suffered constant haemorrhages from the lungs, but he continued to the last to deny his own will. Unable to do anything but pray, he continually asked the direction of his master and followed it in all that he attempted. Dorotheus said, " Be instant in prayer—lose not hold of that ", and

Dositheus replied, " Master, it is well—pray for me ".   When he grew weaker he murmured, " Forgive me, master, but I cannot continue ".   " Give up the effort, then, my son, but keep God in mind as ever present beside thee." He asked Dorotheus to pray that God would soon take him, and was assured that the end was near : " Depart in peace ; thou shalt appear in joy before the Holy Trinity, and there pray for us ".

Some of the other monks murmured at Dorotheus for promising Dositheus Heaven, and for asking the intercession of one who had done nothing in the way of fasting and had moreover performed no miracles, but Dorotheus replied, " He did not fast, it is true, but he completely surrendered his own will ".   Shortly after the death of Dositheus, there came to the monastery a very holy old man who greatly desired that God would show him those departed monks of the house who had entered into glory.   His wish was granted, and he saw in a vision a number of aged saints forming a choir and amongst them there was one quite young man. Relating the vision afterwards he asked who the young man could be, and described him so exactly that none could doubt that it was Dositheus.   He has been described as a forerunner of St John Berchmans and St Stanislaus Kostka.

See the *Acta Sanctorum*, February, vol. iii.   Dositheus has never been officially recognized as a saint in either the East or the West, but there is a seemingly contemporary life which the Bollandists have translated and he is spoken of by Dorotheus the Archimandrite in the first of his " Twenty-four Discourses ".   See also P. M. Brun, " La vie de St Dosithée ", in *Orientalia Christiana*, vol. xxvi (1932), pp. 89–123, text and translation.

ST BOISIL, or BOSWELL, Abbot of Melrose   (A.D. 664)

THE famous abbey of Melrose, which at first followed the Rule of St Columba but afterwards the Cistercian, was situated on the river Tweed in a great forest which, in the seventh century, was included in the kingdom of Northumbria.   Boisil, who would appear to have been trained in his youth by St Aidan, was a priest and monk of Melrose under St Eata, whom he succeeded as abbot there.   Bede says that he was a man of sublime virtue richly endowed with the prophetic spirit, and his contemporaries were greatly impressed with his powers of prevision, as well as by his profound knowledge of the Holy Scriptures.   His fame determined St Cuthbert to go to Melrose rather than to Lindisfarne to be trained, and in later years Cuthbert often confessed how much he owed to the teaching and example of his spiritual master.   When Cuthbert first arrived at Melrose and was dismounting from his horse, Boisil said to the bystanders, " Behold a servant of God ", and Cuthbert afterwards declared that the holy abbot had foretold to him the chief events of his after life.   He loved to repeat the names of the Blessed Trinity, and had a special veneration for the holy name of Jesus, which he pronounced with such devotion as moved the hearts of all who heard him.   Boisil made frequent excursions into the villages to preach to the poor and to bring back erring souls to the paths of truth and light.

Three years beforehand he foretold the great pestilence of 664, adding that he himself would die of the Yellow Plague, but that Eata would survive it.   St Cuthbert first contracted the malady, and no sooner had he recovered than Boisil said to him, " You see, brother, that God has delivered you from this illness, and you will not get it again, nor will you die at present, but since my own death is at hand learn of me as long as I shall be able to teach you—which will not be more than seven days."—" And what will be best for me to read that may be finished in

seven days ? " asked St Cuthbert. " The Gospel of St John. I have a copy in ten
sheets which we will finish in that time "—for they were only seeking to read it
devotionally, Bede tells us, and not to treat of profound questions. It came to
pass as he foretold that at the end of seven days Boisil was taken ill and passed away
in great jubilation on account of his earnest wish to be with Christ. He had always
had a great love for the Gospel of St John, reading from it every day, for which
purpose he divided it into seven portions. St Cuthbert inherited this devotion from
him, and a Latin copy of St John's Gospel, now preserved at Stonyhurst College,
was found in his tomb. After his death St Boisil appeared to a follower of St
Egbert and told him that it was not God's will that Egbert should go as a missionary
to Germany, but that he was to labour amongst the children of Columba in Iona.
In the eleventh century the relics of St Boisil were translated to Durham.

Our chief authority is Bede, who speaks of St Boisil both in his *Ecclesiastical History*
and in his Life of St Cuthbert.   Saint Boswell's, Roxburghshire, takes its name from him
and a church at Lessuden in the same county is dedicated to him. See also the *Acta Sanctorum*, January, vol. iii. It is by no means clear why Butler notices St Boisil on this day.
The Bollandists treat of him on January 23 and March 20. From certain late Durham
calendars he would seem to have been commemorated there on July 7 or 8, as Stanton,
Menology, points out, pp. 318, 658, and September 9 is also said to have been his date.

ST MILBURGA, ABBESS OF WENLOCK, VIRGIN   (*c.* A.D. 700)

St MILBURGA was St Mildred's elder sister, and she founded the nunnery of Wenlock in Shropshire—now known as Much Wenlock. Her father Merewald and her
uncle Wulfhere, King of Mercia, assisted her greatly and endowed the house.
Archbishop St Theodore consecrated her abbess and the monastery is said to have
flourished like a paradise under her rule. She was remarkable for her humility,
but the more she humbled herself the more did God favour her with wonderful
graces. She was endowed with the gift of healing, and is said to have restored
sight to the blind. She had also great spiritual power and brought numerous
sinners to repentance by her exhortations.

Many stories are told of her   one tells how one night she remained so long in
prayer that she fell asleep and did not awake until next morning when the rays of
the sun roused her. She started up so quickly that her veil fell from her head, but
before it could touch the ground it was caught by a sunbeam which kept it poised
in the air until she could compose herself and resume it. On another occasion we
are told that a widow came to her, bringing a dead child whom she entreated the
saint to restore to life. Although Milburga reproved her, the woman refused to
go. Then Milburga threw herself down in prayer beside the child, and was
immediately surrounded by fire from Heaven. One of the sisters who entered the
room at that moment cried out to her to fly, but even as she spoke the fire disappeared, and the saint, rising from the ground, gave the child alive into its mother's
arms. After a life of holiness and good works, St Milburga was attacked by a
painful and lingering disease which she bore with complete serenity. Her last
words were, " Blessed are the pure in heart : blessed are the peacemakers ".

Her tomb was long venerated, but the Danes destroyed the abbey, and it was
almost forgotten till the Norman conquest when Cluniac monks built a monastery
on the spot. Whilst the building was going on, two boys at play there found
themselves sinking into the ground, and when the monks started excavation they

discovered the bones of St Milburga.   The beautiful ruins at Much Wenlock are those of the later house.   St Milburga was credited with having power over the birds of the air, and was invoked for the protection of the crops against their ravages.   Her feast is still observed in the diocese of Shrewsbury.   Of the third sister of this family, St Mildgytha, all that is recorded is that she was a nun, at whose tomb in Northumbria " miraculous powers were often exhibited ".

What we know of St Milburga comes to us mainly through the not very satisfactory channels of John of Tynemouth, Capgrave, William of Malmesbury and William Thorn. It is curious, however, that while many native saints of more historical importance are little noticed in our English calendars, Milburga's name appears in quite a number of them, beginning with the Bosworth Psalter, written *c.* 950.   See also the *Acta Sanctorum*, February, vol. iii ; and Stanton, *Menology,* pp. 81–82.

ST WILLIGIS, Archbishop of Mainz   (A.D. 1011)

St Willigis, a great statesman and one of the most eminent churchmen of his age, was born of humble parents in the little town of Schöningen.   Quite early he showed remarkable ability and was educated for the priesthood.   He was a canon of Hildesheim when the Emperor Otto II appointed him first of all his chaplain-in-chief and then chancellor of Germany in 971.   His outstanding qualities caused Otto to nominate him archbishop of Mainz and chancellor, as just mentioned, in spite of great opposition from those who resented his humble origin.   Willigis was indefatigable in his energy.   It was to him that Otto III, a minor, owed the crown which the archbishop placed on his head at Aachen in 983, and it was he who, after the death of the Empress Theophano, carried on the government with the Empress Adelaide.   When the promising young emperor died without issue at the age of twenty-one, it was Willigis who contrived to get his cousin Henry of Bavaria elected as his successor—a most judicious choice, for Henry is numbered among the saints.   These early emperors protected Germany from the anarchy that prevailed elsewhere in central Europe : as heads of the Holy Roman Empire they represented the unity of western Christendom, and much of their success they owed directly to St Willigis.

Absorbed as he might seem to be in politics, the saint never lost sight of his ecclesiastical duties.   He helped on the spread of Christianity in Schleswig, Holstein, Denmark and Sweden, and at all times he was careful that none but worthy men should be appointed bishops.   He consecrated the great church of Halberstadt, established the collegiate churches of St Stephen and St Victor and entirely rebuilt the cathedral in Mainz ; when it was burnt down on the very day of consecration, he patiently accepted the trial and immediately set about re-erecting it, though it was not completed until the reign of his successor.   Several great bishops were consecrated by him—notably St Adalbert of Prague, Rathgar of Paderborn, St Bernward of Hildesheim, Bd Burchard of Worms, and Eberhard, first bishop of Bamberg.   In the midst of worldly cares and successes, Willigis maintained a simple and childlike fear of God and an extraordinary humility.   A contemporary and one who knew him wrote : " His countenance remained ever unruffled, but even more remarkable was his inward peace.   He spoke little, but his few words carried more weight than many oaths from other people."   All he did was performed punctually and carefully.   He so arranged his recital of the offices that they occupied him until noon, after which he transacted business, and if any time of leisure were left over he would spend it happily in studying the Holy

Scriptures. Every day his steward had to provide food and drink for thirty poor persons and thirteen others were fed from his own table and given a present in money.

The only unedifying episode in the life of St Willigis was a dispute he had with the bishop of Hildesheim, St Bernward, over the nunnery and church of Gandersheim which stood on the boundary between their dioceses. The contention, which was caused by the mischief-making of a nun called Sophia, a sister of the emperor, caused grave scandal, and was eventually settled in favour of Hildesheim. At once the archbishop withdrew his claim, and did not hesitate to do so openly. " Brother and fellow bishop ", he said, " I resign all pretensions regarding the church and I hand over to you this staff as a token that neither I myself nor any of my successors will ever revive the claim." That he spoke and acted in good faith can be seen from the words of his opponent's biographer, who, speaking of the death of Willigis, remarks that he passed to the Lord full of years and of good works. He was honoured as a saint immediately after his death, and in the church of St Stephen a special Mass is offered on the anniversary of his death. Some of his Mass vestments are preserved, but the so-called chalice of St Willigis which was formerly used on his feast does not date from his time. The saint is chiefly known in England through the old tradition which the Rev. S. Baring-Gould popularized in his poem, " The Arms of Mayence ". It describes how the archbishop at his investment and enthronization, perceiving the empty escutcheon for his arms and having none of his own, asked that he might be allowed to choose a wheel—as a reminder of his father's trade—and it goes on to relate how the burgesses, who had sneered at him for his plebeian origin, decided after his death to adopt a wheel as the emblem of the city in thanksgiving for his peaceful and glorious reign. But the story is quite anachronistic.

No ancient biography of St Willigis is known to exist, although a brief summary of his life, corresponding to what may usually be found in the Breviary lessons, has been printed by G. Waitz in MGH., *Scriptores*, vol. xv, pp. 743–745. Abundant material concerning him may, however, be found in the chroniclers of the time, all which F. Falk has turned to good account in a series of articles in the periodical *Der Katholik* of Mainz for 1869, 1871 and 1881. There are modern biographies by H. Böhmer (1895) and J. Schmidt, the latter of which appeared as articles in *Der Katholik* for 1911 and 1912, and deals particularly with the attitude of St Willigis to the Holy See. See also H. K. Mann, *Lives of the Popes*, vols. iv and v.

24 : ST MATTHIAS, Apostle   (First Century)

CLEMENT OF ALEXANDRIA says that according to tradition St Matthias was one of the seventy-two disciples whom our Lord had sent out, two by two, during His ministry, and this is also asserted by Eusebius and by St Jerome. We know from the Acts of the Apostles that he was constantly with the Saviour from the time of His baptism until His ascension. When St Peter soon after had declared that it was necessary to elect a twelfth apostle in place of Judas, two candidates were chosen as most worthy, Joseph called Barsabas and Matthias. After prayer to God that He would direct their choice, they proceeded to cast lots, and the lot fell upon Matthias, who was accordingly numbered with the eleven and ranked among the apostles. He received the Holy Ghost with the rest soon after his election and applied himself with zeal to his mission. It is stated by Clement of Alexandria that he was remarkable for his insistence upon the necessity of mortifying the flesh to subdue the sensual appetites—a lesson he had learnt from Christ and which he faithfully practised himself.

The first part of his ministry was spent, we are told, in Judaea, but he afterwards went to other lands. According to the Greeks, he planted the faith in Cappadocia and on the coasts of the Caspian Sea ; he endured great persecution and ill-treatment from the savage people amongst whom he worked, and finally received the crown of martyrdom at Colchis. We know nothing for certain of the manner of his death, but the Greek *Menaia* and other legendary sources say that he was crucified. His body is stated to have been kept for a long time in Jerusalem and to have been translated from there to Rome by St Helen.

Apart from the short passage in the Acts of the Apostles we possess no reliable source of information concerning St Matthias, but there is a good deal of apocryphal literature connected with his name. In particular the " Acts of Andrew and Matthias in the city of the Cannibals " is a Greek fiction, dated by some as early as the second century, which had very wide currency. We have translations in Syriac, Armenian, Coptic, and even an adaptation in Anglo-Saxon. Further, Origen already knew in his time an apocryphal " Gospel of Matthias ", and there has been much discussion as to whether this is identical with a document from which Clement of Alexandria quotes a sentence or two under the name of the " Traditions " (*Παραδόσεις*) of Matthias. See, for example, Hennecke, *Handbuch zu den Neutestamentlichen Apokryphen*, pp. 90-91, 238, 544.

SS. MONTANUS, LUCIUS, AND THEIR COMPANIONS, MARTYRS (A.D. 259)

THE persecution raised by Valerian had raged for two years, during which many received the crown of martyrdom, including St Cyprian in September, 258. The proconsul Galerius Maximus, who had pronounced sentence on him, died soon after, but the procurator Solon continued the persecution ; an insurrection against him broke out in Carthage, and in it many were killed. Solon, instead of making search for the guilty, vented his fury upon the Christians and arrested eight of them, all disciples of St Cyprian and most of them clergy. The following graphic account of the proceedings is taken from the *acta* of these martyrs : " As soon as we were apprehended, we were given in custody to the officers of the quarter. When the governor's servants told us that we should be condemned to the flames, we prayed fervently to God to be delivered from that punishment, and He in whose hands are the hearts of men was pleased to grant our request. The governor modified his first intention and committed us to a very dark and incommodious prison where we found the priest Victor and some others : but we were not dismayed at the filth and darkness of the place, for our faith and joy in the Holy Ghost reconciled us to our sufferings, though these were such as cannot readily be described in words. However, the greater our trials the greater is He who overcomes them in us. In the meantime, our brother Renus had a vision in which he saw several of the prisoners going out, each preceded by a lighted lamp, whilst others, who had no such light, stayed behind. He identified us in the vision and assured us that we were of those who went forth with lamps. This gave us great joy, for we understood that the lamp represented Christ, the true light, and that we were to follow Him by martyrdom.

" The next day we were sent for by the governor to be examined. It was a triumph to us to be conducted as a spectacle through the market-place and the streets with our chains rattling. The soldiers, who did not know where the governor would hear the case, dragged us from place to place, until at length he ordered us to be brought into his closet. He put several questions to us our answers were modest but firm. At length we were remanded to prison, and here we prepared ourselves for new conflicts. The sharpest trial we endured was hunger and thirst, the governor having commanded that we should be kept without meat and drink for several days, so that even water was refused us after our work ; yet Flavian, the deacon, added great voluntary austerities to these hardships, often bestowing on others that little refreshment which was most sparingly allowed us at the public charge. God was pleased to comfort us in this our extreme misery by a vision which He vouchsafed to the priest Victor, who suffered martyrdom a few days after. ' I saw last night,' said he, ' a child whose countenance was of a wonderful brightness enter the prison. He took us to all parts to find a way of release, but there was no exit. Then said he to me, '' Thou art still concerned at being here, but be not discouraged for I am with thee carry these tidings to thy companions and let them know that they shall have a more glorious crown." I asked him where Heaven was, and he replied, '' Out of the world ".' Victor said, ' Show it to me '. The child answered, ' Where then would be thy faith ? ' Victor said, ' I cannot remember what thou commandest me tell me a sign that I may give them ' He answered, ' Give them the sign of Jacob, that is, his mystical ladder reaching to the heavens '. Soon after this, Victor was put to death. This vision filled us all with joy.

" God gave us, the night following, another assurance of His mercy by a vision to our sister Quartillosia, a fellow prisoner whose husband and son had suffered death for Christ three days before, and who followed them by martyrdom a few days after. ' I saw ', said she, ' my son who suffered he was in the prison, sitting on a vessel of water, and said to me, " God has seen your sufferings " Then entered a young man of wonderful stature, and he said, ' Be of good cheer, God hath remembered you '."

The martyrs had received no nourishment the preceding day, nor had they any on the day that followed this vision ; but at length Lucian (who was then a priest, but afterwards became bishop of Carthage), surmounting all obstacles, contrived to have food carried to them by the subdeacon Herennian and by Januarius, a catechumen. The acts say they brought the " never-failing food "—very possibly the Holy Eucharist is meant, but the matter is not clear. What is less open to question is the claim the martyrs make to have preserved fraternal charity in spite of difficulties. '' We have all one and the same spirit ", they write, " and this unites and cements us together in prayer, in mutual intercourse and in all our actions. These are those bonds of affection which put the Devil to flight, which are most pleasing to God, and which by supplication in common obtain from Him whatever is asked. These are the ties which link hearts together, and which make men the children of God. To be heirs of His kingdom we must be His children, and to be His children we must love one another. It is impossible for us to attain to the inheritance of His heavenly glory unless we keep that union and peace with our brethren which our heavenly Father has established amongst us. Nevertheless this union suffered some prejudice in our company, but the breach was soon repaired. It happened that Montanus had some words with Julian about a person who was not of our communion, but who had found his way into our company " (probably admitted by Julian). " Montanus, on this account, rebuked Julian, and

they for some time afterwards behaved with coldness, which was, as it were, a seed of discord.   But God had pity on them both and, to unite them, admonished Montanus by a dream, which he related to us as follows : ' It appeared to me that the centurions were come to us and that they led us through a long path into a spacious field, where we were met by Cyprian and Lucius.   Then we came to a very luminous place where our garments became white, and our flesh even whiter than our garments, and so wonderfully transparent that there was nothing in our hearts that was not clearly exposed to view.   Looking into myself, I discerned some dirty stain in my own bosom and, meeting Lucius, I told him what I had seen, adding that the filth I had observed within my breast denoted my coldness towards Julian.   Wherefore, brethren, let us love and cherish union with all our might. Let us be of one mind here in imitation of what shall be hereafter.   As we hope to share in the rewards promised to the just, and to avoid the punishments wherewith the wicked are threatened—as, in short, we desire to be and to reign with Christ— let us do those things which will lead us to Him and to His heavenly kingdom.' ''
Up to this point apparently we have the words the martyrs wrote in prison, but the rest of the story was compiled by certain persons present, at the recommendation of Flavian, one of the martyrs.

After suffering extreme hunger and thirst, with other hardships, during an imprisonment of many months, the prisoners were brought before the president and made a glorious confession.   Valerian's decree condemned only bishops, priests and deacons to death.   The well-meaning but mistaken friends of Flavian maintained before the judge that he was not a deacon and was therefore not included in the scope of the emperor's decree.   Consequently, although he declared himself to be one, he was not then condemned, but the others were sentenced to death. They walked cheerfully to the place of execution and each one gave exhortations to the people.   Lucius, a man of mild and retiring nature, was weak on account of ill health and the hardships of the prison : he therefore went on before the rest, accompanied by few people lest he should collapse in the pressure of the crowd and so not have the honour of shedding his blood.   Some cried out to him : '' Remember us ! ''—'' Do you also remember me '', was his reply.   Julian and Victorinus exhorted the brethren to peace, and recommended to their care the whole body of the clergy, especially those who had undergone the hardships of imprisonment. Montanus, who was endowed with great strength of body and mind, cried out many times, '' He that sacrificeth to any but the true God shall be utterly destroyed ''. He also denounced the pride and obstinacy of heretics, telling them that they might discern the true Church by the multitude of its martyrs.   A true disciple of St Cyprian and a zealous lover of discipline, he exhorted those who had fallen not to be over-hasty, but faithfully to accomplish their penance.   He exhorted the virgins to preserve their purity and to honour the bishops, whom he charged to remain in concord.   When the executioner was ready to give the stroke, Montanus prayed aloud to God that Flavian, who had been reprieved at the people's request, might follow them on the third day.   To express his assurance that his prayer was heard, he rent in pieces the handkerchief with which his eyes were to be covered and ordered one half of it to be reserved for Flavian, desiring that a place might be kept for his grave that they might not be separated even in the tomb.   Flavian, seeing his crown delayed, made it the object of his ardent desires and prayers.

To his mother, who kept close by his side and who longed to see him glorify God by martyrdom, he said, '' You know, mother, how I have longed for the privilege of dying the death of a martyr " In one of the two nights during which he survived, he was favoured with the vision of one who said to him, " Why dost thou grieve ? Thou hast twice been a confessor and thou shalt suffer martyrdom by the sword." On the third day he was brought before the governor and it was clearly to be seen what a favourite he was with the people, for they endeavoured by all means to save his life. They cried out to the judge that he was not a deacon, although he insisted that he was. A centurion presented a note which set forth that he was not. The judge accused him of lying to procure his own death. He answered, " Is it probable ? Is it not more likely that they are guilty of untruth who maintain the contrary ? " The crowd then demanded that he should be tortured, in the hope that he would recant on the rack, but the judge condemned him to be beheaded. The sentence filled him with joy, and he was led to the place of execution accompanied by a great multitude, including many priests. A shower dispersed the unbelievers, and the martyr was led to a house where he had an opportunity of taking leave of the faithful without the presence of pagan onlookers. He told them that in a vision he had asked St Cyprian whether the death stroke was painful, and that the martyr had answered, " The body feels no pain when the soul gives herself entirely to God " At the place of execution he prayed for the peace of the Church and the unity of the brethren, and appears to have foretold to Lucian that he would be bishop of Carthage—a prophecy which was fulfilled soon afterwards. When he had finished speaking, he bound his eyes with that half of the handkerchief which Montanus had left him and, kneeling in prayer, received the last stroke.

The Acts of Montanus and Lucius may be found in the *Acta Sanctorum*, February, vol. iii, and also in Ruinart, *Acta sincera ;* but the best text is that edited from a collation of several new manuscripts by Pio Franchi de' Cavalieri in a Supplementheft (No. 8) to the *Römische Quartalschrift*, 1898. Taken as a whole the document may be unhesitatingly commended as a reliable narrative of contemporary date, and this is the conclusion adhered to by such critical authorities as Pio Franchi himself (see his " Note Agiografiche " in *Studi e Testi*, vol. xxii, pp. 1–32 and 111–114) and Delehaye (*Les Passions des martyrs et les genres littéraires*, 1921, pp. 72–78). At the same time certain difficulties cannot be ignored. It has been pointed out that the whole construction of the story bears a close resemblance to the famous acts of that other group of Carthaginian martyrs, Perpetua and Felicity. Rendel Harris and Gifford in their edition of the latter text (*Acts of the Martyrdom of SS. Perpetua and Felicitas*, 1890, p. 27) have in fact gone so far as to treat the history of Montanus and Lucius as a fiction or plagiarism, based upon the Perpetua document. Without going into detail, it must be sufficient to refer to the discussion of the subject by Pio Franchi and Delehaye. It is in every way probable that the compiler of the later acts, living at Carthage, would have been familiar with the written story of Perpetua and Felicity, and that he may justifiably have regarded the manner of treatment as a model to be followed. Adhémar d'Alès (in *Recherches de Science religieuse*, vol. ix, 1918, pp. 319–378) identifies the author of the Acts of Montanus and Lucius with the deacon Pontius, who wrote an account of the martyrdom of St Cyprian, but Delehaye (in *Analecta Bollandiana*, vol. xxxix, 1921, p. 171) does not consider that a case has been satisfactorily made out.

ST PRAETEXTATUS, or PRIX, BISHOP OF ROUEN, MARTYR (A.D. 586)

ST PRAETEXTATUS became bishop of Rouen in 549 and occupied that see for thirty-five years. During this long episcopate he suffered grievous difficulties, exile and in the end martyrdom due to the rivalry between King Clotaire I's sons Chilperic and Sigebert, and the deadly feud of Chilperic's mistress, Fredegund, with Sigebert's wife, Brunhilda, sister to the poisoned second wife of Chilperic. Fredegund contrived the murder of Sigebert in 575, and Chilperic threw Brunhilda into prison at Rouen, from whence she appealed for help to Meroveus, Chilperic's son by his first wife. The young man dreaded the power of Fredegund, and was not unwilling to take up arms against his father. Furthermore, he fell in love with his step-aunt Brunhilda and married her, thus making common cause with her. Praetextatus found himself placed in a very awkward position. Meroveus had made Rouen his headquarters and expected or exacted contributions from the Church which it was difficult to refuse. The young man was the bishop's spiritual son—that is to say, he had been baptized by him, and the tie was then considered a very close one. Chilperic was ready to believe accusations against Praetextatus and summoned him to appear before a council of bishops in Paris on the charges of having broken the canons by marrying Meroveus to his aunt and also of fomenting the rebellion by giving aid to the prince. With regard to the first of these charges there is some uncertainty. It is thought by some that the bishop, in order to prevent a grievous scandal, judged the case suitable for a dispensation and actually married them and acknowledged that he had done so, but Gregory of Tours, who was present and who is the authority for all that happened, says that Praetextatus denied having married them.

At first the bishop would plead guilty to neither charge, but he was afterwards prevailed upon by false friends to acknowledge that he had favoured and helped Meroveus. He was thereupon condemned and banished to a little island off Coutances. His powerful enemies spared no trouble to blast his reputation, but St Gregory of Tours never wavered in his support. Meroveus and his brothers were put to death by order of the savage Fredegund, who was also suspected of causing the death of her husband to clear the way to the throne for her own son, Clotaire II. On the death of Chilperic, Praetextatus returned to his see by order of King Gontran of Burgundy, but sorely against the wishes of Fredegund. At the Council of Mâcon he was formally reinstated, and he took a prominent part in the deliberations of that body. He frequently remonstrated with the wicked queen, who often resided at Rouen, and her hatred for him became greater than ever. In 586 she said to him, " The time is coming when thou shalt revisit the place of thine exile."—" I was a bishop always, whether in exile or out of exile ", replied the saint, " and a bishop I shall remain ; but as for thee, thou shalt not always enjoy thy crown," and he exhorted her to abandon her evil ways. On the following Sunday, soon after midnight, as he was saying Matins in Church, an assassin sent by Fredegund stabbed him under the armpit. He was carried to his bed, where he died.

Gregory of Tours is our trustworthy authority for this story of Merovingian barbarity. See also Duchesne, *Fastes Episcopaux*, vol. ii, p. 206.

25 : SS. VICTORINUS AND HIS COMPANIONS, MARTYRS (A.D. 284)

VICTORINUS, Victor, Nicephorus, Claudian, Dioscorus, Serapion and Papias were citizens of Corinth who had made a good confession of their faith in their own country before Tertius the proconsul in 249, at the beginning of the reign of Decius. After being tortured, they passed into Egypt, but whether they were banished thither or went into voluntary banishment is not stated. They completed their martyrdom at Diospolis, the capital of the Thebaïd, under the governor Sabinus in the reign of Numerian. After the governor had tried the constancy of the martyrs with the rack and scourge, he caused Victorinus to be thrown into a great marble mortar. The executioners began by pounding his feet and legs, saying to him at every stroke, " Save thyself ! Thou canst escape this death by renouncing thy new god." But as he continued constant, the governor became impatient and ordered that his head should be battered to pieces. When Victor was threatened with the same death, his only wish was that his execution should be hastened, and pointing to the mortar he said, " Salvation and happiness await me there ! " He was immediately cast into it and pounded to death. Nicephorus, the third martyr, leaped of his own accord into this engine of destruction. The judge, angry at his boldness, commanded several executioners to beat him at the same time. Sabinus caused Claudian, the fourth martyr, to be hacked to pieces.

He expired after his feet, hands, arms, legs and thighs had been cut off. The governor, pointing to his mangled limbs and scattered bones, said to the other three, " It rests with you to avoid this punishment : I do not compel you to suffer." They answered with one voice, " We would rather ask thee to inflict on us any still more excruciating torment that thou canst devise. We will never violate the fidelity we owe to God or deny Jesus Christ our Saviour, for He is our God from whom we have our being and to whom alone we aspire." The tyrant then commanded that Dioscorus should be burnt alive and Serapion hung up by the heels and then beheaded. Papias was cast into the sea with a stone attached to his neck and drowned. This happened on February 25, the day allotted to these saints in the Western martyrologies, but the Greeks honour them on January 21, said to be the date of their confession at Corinth.

The Syriac text of the acts of these martyrs was published for the first time by Stephen E. Assemani in the eighteenth century with a Latin translation. In modern times the Syriac has been re-edited from fresh manuscript sources by Paul Bedjan. A French translation of the same acts, by F. Lagrange, was printed in 1852. The substance of the account is probably reliable, though we may suspect a certain amount of embroidery in the details.

ST CAESARIUS OF NAZIANZUS (A.D. 369)

CAESARIUS was the brother of St Gregory Nazianzen, and his father was bishop of that city. Both boys received an excellent education, but whilst Gregory went to study at Caesarea in Palestine, Caesarius repaired to Alexandria, where he distinguished himself in every branch of knowledge, specializing in oratory, philosophy and more particularly in medicine. He perfected his medical studies in Constantinople and became the foremost physician of his age, but he refused to settle there, although the city and the Emperor Constantius begged him to do so. He was afterwards recalled there and greatly honoured by Julian the Apostate, who nominated him his first physician and excepted him from several edicts which he published against the Christians. Caesarius resisted all the efforts of that prince to make him abjure his faith, and was persuaded by his father and brother to resign his post at court in spite of Julian's solicitations. Jovian restored him to his former post and Valens made him also treasurer of his private purse with control of the finances in Bithynia. A narrow escape in an earthquake at Nicea in Bithynia in 368 made such an impression upon his mind that he renounced the world, and when he died shortly after he left all he possessed to the poor.   His funeral oration was preached by his brother St Gregory.

It is from St Gregory's panegyric that most of our information is derived.   In virtue of this sermon Caesarius has been honoured as a saint and is commemorated in the Roman Martyrology.   Nevertheless it seems certain that it was only after the earthquake at Nicea and consequently only a few months before his death that Caesarius received baptism.   For the best part of the forty years he lived on earth he by his own choice was no more than a catechumen, and was consequently debarred from participating in the sacred mysteries.

ST ETHELBERT OF KENT   (A.D. 616)

ETHELBERT, King of Kent, married a Christian princess, Bertha, only child of Charibert, King of Paris. She had full liberty to practise her religion, and she brought with her a French prelate, Bishop Liudhard, who officiated in an ancient church, which he dedicated to God in honour of St Martin, at Canterbury. Tradition speaks of the piety and amiable qualities of Queen Bertha, and these no doubt made a great impression on her husband, but his conversion did not take place until the coming of St Augustine and his companions. These missionaries, sent by St Gregory the Great, first landed in Thanet, from whence they sent a message to the king announcing their arrival and explaining the reason of their coming. Ethelbert bade them remain in the island, and after some days he himself came to Thanet to hear what they had to say.   His first conference with them took place in the open air, as he was afraid they might use spells or some form of magic, which were held to be powerless out of doors.   Ethelbert, sitting under an oak, received them well and, after listening to them, told them that they might freely preach to the people and convert whom they could.   As for himself, he could not immediately abandon all that he had held sacred, but he would undertake that the missionaries should be well treated and should have the means to live.   Bede tells us that he gave them the church of St Martin in which " to sing psalms, to pray, to offer Mass, to preach and to baptize ".   Conversions took place, and it was not long before Ethelbert and many of his nobles were convinced.   They received baptism on Whitsunday, 597 ; and the king's conversion was followed by that of thousands of his subjects.

He told Augustine and his followers that they might rebuild the ancient British churches and build others but, eager as he was for the spread of God's kingdom, he would constrain no man to change his religion, for, as Bede informs us, he had learnt from his teachers that the service of Christ must be voluntary and not compulsory.   He treated all alike, although he felt a special affection for those who had become Christian.   In the government of his kingdom his thoughts were set on increasing the welfare of his people, for whom he enacted laws which were held in high esteem in England in succeeding ages.   Buildings and land at Canterbury he gave up for the use of the archbishop, who founded in the city the cathedral called Christ Church and built, outside the walls, the abbey and church of St Peter and St Paul (afterwards called St Augustine's).   In his own dominions Ethelbert established a second bishopric, that of Rochester, where he founded the church of St Andrew ; whilst in London, in the territory of the king of the East Saxons, he built the first cathedral of St Paul.   He was the means of winning over to Christianity Sabert, King of the East Saxons, and Redwald, King of the East Angles, although the latter subsequently relapsed into semi-idolatry.   Ethelbert reigned fifty-six years, dying in 616, and was buried in the church of St Peter and St

Paul where the bodies of Queen Bertha and of St Liudhard already rested. Up to the days of Henry VIII, a light was always kept lighted before his tomb. His feast is now kept in the dioceses of Westminster, Southwark and North- ampton, with a commemoration in Nottingham, and he is named in the Roman Martyrology.

We see in King Ethelbert a very noble type of convert. His reception of the missionaries and his willingness to give them a fair hearing must strike all those who read his history. After his conversion, whilst he was eager to win others, he would constrain no one, and thus aided instead of hindering the labours of the missionaries. The use of force has always been a real enemy to the progress of the faith—even when it appears for the moment to be successful—for it is opposed to the spirit of our Lord and to the essence of Christianity. The evangelization of the world will be brought about by prayer, by teaching and by example, but never by force of arms, by persecution or by compulsion of any kind.

Bede's *Ecclesiastical History* is, practically speaking, our sole authority for the life of Ethelbert (he spells the name Aedilberct). Gregory of Tours twice over alludes to the mar- riage of Bertha to a prince of Kent, but does not name him. The " Dooms " of Ethelbert should be consulted in the text of Liebermann, *Gesetze der Angelsachsen*, with its ample notes and glossary. Among general works, see F. M. Stenton's *Anglo-Saxon England* (1943). According to Dom S. Brechter's views, Ethelbert was not baptized till 601.

ST WALBURGA, Virgin   (A.D. 779)

St Walburga (Waldburg) is honoured in various parts of France under the names of Vaubourg, Gauburge and Falbourg, and in Germany and the Netherlands as Wilburga, Warpurg and Walpurgis. She was in fact an Englishwoman, the sister of St Willibald and St Winebald, and was educated at the monastery of Wimborne in Dorset, where she afterwards took the veil. When St Boniface set out on his great mission to preach Christianity to the German people, he was joined by St Walburga's brothers, and when St Tatta was asked by Boniface to send some nuns to found a convent in the newly evangelized districts, St Walburga was one of the religious who crossed to the continent under the care of St Lioba. For two years she lived at Bischofsheim, but as soon as her brother Winebald founded the double monastery of Heidenheim she was called upon to rule over the nunnery whilst he directed the monks. At his death she was appointed abbess of both houses by her other brother, Willibald, then bishop of Eichstätt, and she retained this office of superior over men and women until her death. She is said to have studied and practised medicine.

St Walburga was present in 776 at the translation of the body of St Winebald to Eichstätt, and her own body, interred at first at Heidenheim, was afterward placed beside that of her brother in the church of the Holy Cross. Although the greater part of her remains still rest there, fragments are distributed all over Europe —notably at Brussels, Antwerp, Thielt, Zutphen and Groningen. Her fame has been spread from very early times by the so-called miraculous oil—an aromatic watery fluid, perhaps possessed of natural medicinal properties, which flows through an opening in the rock on which rest her relics. Great cures have been ascribed to it even down to the present day. In art, she is represented sometimes holding three ears of corn, with which she is said to have cured a girl afflicted with a voracious appetite. On the night of one of her festivals, Walpurgisnacht, May 1, the witches were supposed to hold their revels at Blocksberg in the Hartz

Mountains : " a highly incongruous association ", as Professor Stenton remarks. Some of the *cultus* with which she was formerly honoured—including her attribute of corn—may possibly have been transferred to her from the old heathen goddess Walborg or Mother Earth. St Walburga's feast is kept in the diocese of Plymouth as well as in Germany.

The three or four medieval Latin lives are all of relatively late date, and no great trust can be placed in the details they record. But the " Hodoeporicon " of her brother St Willibald, compiled by a nun in St Walburga's own convent of Heidenheim, is a reliable document, and the Life of St Willibald, incorrectly ascribed to Bishop Reginold of Eichstätt, is also of some value. A rather uncritical narrative (*Life of St Walburge*), derived from these materials, was written by Fr T. Meyrick. A translation of the " Hodoeporicon " has been published by C. II. Talbot, *Anglo-Saxon Missionaries in Germany* (1954). The best edition of the Latin texts is that edited by Holder-Egger in MGH., *Scriptores*, vol. xv, pt 1, pp. 86-106. Fuller materials are printed in the *Acta Sanctorum*, February, vol.   See also *Analecta Bollandiana*, vol. xlix (1931), pp. 353 *seq.*

ST TARASIUS, PATRIARCH OF CONSTANTINOPLE   (A.D. 806)

ST TARASIUS, although a layman and chief secretary to the young Emperor Constantine VI and his mother Irene, was chosen patriarch of Constantinople by the court, clergy and people after having been nominated by his predecessor Paul IV, who had retired into a monastery. Tarasius came of a patrician family, had had a good upbringing, and in the midst of the court, though surrounded by all that could flatter pride or gratify the senses, he had led a life of almost monastic severity. He was most loath to accept the dignity which had been conferred upon him, partly because he felt that a priest should have been chosen, but also on account of the position created by the succession of emperors, beginning with Leo III in 726, whose policy it was for various reasons to abolish the veneration of sacred images and banish *eikons* from the churches.[*] Tarasius was called to be patriarch at a time when the Empress Irene had the imperial power in her hands as regent for her son, Constantine VI, then only ten years old. She was an ambitious, artful and heartlessly cruel woman, but she was opposed to Iconoclasm. When therefore Tarasius had been consecrated on Christmas day 784, on the understanding that a council should be held to restore the unity of the churches disrupted by the campaign against images, the way was clear for such a gathering. This, the seventh oecumenical council, eventually assembled at Nicaea in 787, under the presidency of the legates of Pope Adrian I. After due discussion it was declared to be the sense of the Church to allow to holy pictures and other images a relative honour, but not of course that worship which is due to God alone. He who reveres the image, it was emphasized, reveres the person it represents.

Tarasius, in obedience to the decision of the synod, restored holy images throughout his patriarchate. He also laboured zealously to abolish simony, and his life was a model of disinterestedness to his clergy and people. At his table and in his residence he allowed himself nothing of the magnificence of some of his predecessors. Intent on serving others, he would scarcely allow his servants to

[*] The use of sacred images had become general throughout the Church and had been encouraged by the authorities when, all danger of idolatry being over, it became necessary to impress on men's minds that God had actually become man and had been born of a human mother. For this purpose, and as a means of reviving the memory of the saints and of lifting up the soul to God, pictures and other images were introduced into the churches.

do anything for him. He permitted himself but little sleep, and all his leisure was devoted to prayer and reading. He banished the use of fine clothes from amongst his clergy, and was particularly severe against theatrical entertainments. He often took dishes from his table to distribute with his own hands to the poor, and that none might be overlooked, he visited all the charitable institutions and hospitals in Constantinople.

Some years later the emperor became enamoured of Theodota, a maid of honour to his wife, the Empress Mary, whom he had been forced to marry by his mother and whom he now resolved to divorce. To further his purpose he tried to gain over the patriarch, and sent an officer to inform him that the empress was plotting to poison him. Tarasius answered the messenger sternly, " Tell him I will suffer death rather than consent to his design ". The emperor, hoping to win him by flattery, sent for the patriarch and said to him, " I can conceal nothing from you whom I regard as my father. No one can deny that I may divorce one who has attempted my life. The Empress Mary deserves death or perpetual penance." He then produced a vessel full of poison which he pretended she had prepared for him. The patriarch, perceiving this to be an attempt to hoodwink him, replied that he was only too sure that Constantine's passion for Theodota was at the bottom of all his complaints against the empress ; he also warned him that even if she were really guilty of the crime, a second marriage during her lifetime would be adulterous. The monk John who was present also spoke so resolutely to the emperor that in his fury he drove them both from his presence. Then he turned Mary out of the palace and forced her to take the veil. As Tarasius persisted in his refusal to marry him to Theodota, it was done by Abbot Joseph, an official of the church of Constantinople. Tarasius had to face the resentment of Constantine, who persecuted him during the remainder of his reign.* We are told that spies were set to watch the patriarch's comings and goings, that none was suffered to associate with him without leave, and many of his relations and servants were banished. In the meantime, however, the Dowager Empress Irene, dissatisfied at being no longer at the head of the government, gained over the principal officers of the court and army, and having made her son prisoner caused his eyes to be put out. Irene reigned for five years, but was deposed by Nicephorus, who usurped the empire and banished her to the isle of Lesbos.

Under the reign of Nicephorus, Tarasius persevered peaceably in the functions of his pastoral office. In his last sickness, as long as he was able to move, he continued to offer the Holy Sacrifice. Shortly before his death he fell into a trance, as his biographer, who was present, relates, and he seemed to be disputing with a number of accusers who were busily scrutinizing all the actions of his life and making accusations. He appeared to be in great agitation as he defended himself against their charges. This filled all present with fear—knowing how worthy his life had been. But a wonderful serenity succeeded, and the holy man gave up his soul to God in great peace after he had ruled his patriarchal see for twenty-one years.

For the ascetical side of St Tarasius's activities our chief authority is the biography by Ignatius the deacon. The Greek text has been edited by A. Heikel in the Proceedings of

---

* On the other hand, there were those who judged that Tarasius had been too complaisant about the imperial divorce. They were led by the abbot St Plato (April 4) and by St Theodore, afterwards the Studite (November 11), who were imprisoned by Constantine.

the Helsingfors Academy. The *Acta Sanctorum,* February, vol. iii, only supplies a Latin translation. An excellent account of the Iconoclast controversy is provided in Hefele-Leclercq, *Histoire des Conciles,* vol. iii, pt 2 (1910), pp. 741 *seq. ;* and there is a summary in N. H. Baynes and H. L. B. Moss, *Byzantium* (1948), pp. 15-17, 105-108. See also Krumbacher, *Geschichte der Byzantinischen Literatur,* 2nd ed., p. 73 ; Hergenröther, *Photius,* vol. i, pp. 264-361 and *Byzantinische Zeitschrift,* 1909, pp. 57 *seq.*

ST GERLAND, BISHOP OF GIRGENTI   (A.D. 1100)

GERLAND was bishop of Girgenti in Sicily, the cathedral of which city was placed under his patronage, but beyond this fact nothing definite can be stated about him except that he was born at Besançon. From various sources and traditions his life has been reconstructed conjecturally. It is supposed that he was closely related to the two Norman counts, Robert Guiscard and Roger, who in the eleventh century set out to conquer Sicily from the Arabs ; they succeeded in their efforts, and their kinsman Gerland was entrusted with various ecclesiastical offices. He was, however, so scandalized at the dissolute conduct of those with whom he was brought in contact that he returned to his native Burgundy with the intention of leading a solitary life. Count Roger recalled him to Sicily to appoint him bishop of Girgenti, and he was consecrated by Bd Urban II. He found much to do in a land where the Moslems had ruled for so long. He re-established the cathedral, which had been reduced to ruins, built an episcopal residence, and obtained a charter of his jurisdiction. He sought out Jews and Saracens, had private interviews with them besides public conferences, and converted many, baptizing them himself. His success has been described as marvellous. Gerland died soon after returning from a visit to Rome, having apparently foreseen his approaching end.

See the *Acta Sanctorum,* February, vol. iii ; Lauricella, *S. Gerlando   di Girgenti* (1893) ; and *Analecta Bollandiana,* vol. lvii (1939), pp. 105-108.

BD ROBERT OF ARBRISSEL, ABBOT   (A.D. 1117)

ROBERT OF ARBRISSEL is commonly called Blessed, but the title is a courtesy one : attempts to bring about his beatification in the seventeenth century and again in the nineteenth came to nothing. He was a doctor of the University of Paris, and as vicar of the bishop of Rennes the vigour of his reforming zeal was ill-received, and in 1093 he had to leave his native Brittany. After a short association with St Bernard of Tiron, Bd Vitalis of Savigny and other ascetics, he in 1099 made a monastic settlement on the borders of Poitou and Anjou that developed into the famous congregation of Fontevrault.

A characteristic of this congregation was that men and women religious lived in adjacent establishments, under the authority of an abbess. Such double monasteries were not entirely new and there were to be more of them ; but the arrangement was the occasion of difficulties which aggravated the adverse criticism to which Robert of Arbrissel was subjected. He was a man of much ability and enthusiasm, but clearly lacked discretion, though the extreme eccentricities attributed to him were probably only gossip. He brought about many notable conversions, the best known being that of Bertrada, daughter of Simon de Montfort, who had left her husband, Fulk of Anjou, for King Philip I of France. She eventually became a nun of Fontevrault, which remained one of the most famous monasteries of France until the Revolution. Robert of Arbrissel died at the priory of Orsan, probably in 1117.

The most valuable study of Robert of Arbrissel is that of J. von Walter, *Die ersten Wanderprediger Frankreichs* (1903), vol. i. The principal sources are printed in *Acta Sanctorum*, February, vol. iii, but it can no longer be maintained that the letters of Bishop Marbod of Rennes and Abbot Geoffrey of Verdun, which severely criticize Robert, are not authentic it is very probable that Geoffrey was misled by vague popular rumour. See also Poncelet in *Analecta Bollandiana*, vol. xxiii (1904), pp. 375–377, and G. Niderst, *Robert d'Arbrissel et les origines de   Fontevrault* (1952).

BB. AVERTANUS AND ROMAEUS   (A.D. 1380)

LIMOGES was the birthplace of Avertanus, a holy lay-brother of the Carmelite Order. As soon as he could speak he would prattle about God and talk to Him. He was never naughty, nor did he want to play like other children, but he would pray and often appeared rapt in contemplation. Very early he began to long to join a religious order, and one night he had a vision of an angel, who enjoined him to enter the Carmelite Order. Overjoyed, he laid the matter before his parents. Although they were pious people, they were greatly distressed at the idea of losing the hope and prop of their old age ; but Avertanus persuaded them that it was the will of God and that in his cell he would not be so far away, so that in the end they yielded and dismissed him with their blessing. The prior of the Carmelite monastery of Limoges admitted him, and the brethren seem soon to have realized that the newcomer was a youth of singular holiness. They recorded that, when he received the habit, angelic voices mingled with their own chants and that the Blessed Virgin herself was seen with her hand extended in blessing above the head of the humble lay-brother. When not at prayer, it was his delight to perform the most menial tasks in the convent ; he was often found in his cell entirely rapt in ecstasy, and it was with the greatest difficulty that he could be recalled to ordinary life. At night he was wont to get up from his bed and creep on hands and knees to the top of one of the rocky hills near the monastery, where with his arms outstretched, he would pray till daybreak. He had such a horror of money that he would not touch it or speak of it or even see a coin if he could help it.

At length Avertanus was inspired with a great wish to visit the Holy Places and, with the prior's consent, he started off for Rome with a companion called Romaeus. As his biographer remarks, theirs was not the sort of pilgrimage which combines pleasure and comfort with religion. They made their way painfully over the Alps in winter, and when they reached Italy they found that the plague was raging and that the gates of the cities were closed against all strangers and tramps who might spread the disease. It was in the cities that pilgrims were usually accommodated, but the two men made their way as best they could till they reached, in the suburbs of Lucca, the hospital of St Peter, where they were taken in. The next morning Avertanus attempted to enter the city, but the gatekeepers refused to admit the gaunt and ragged pair. No doubt they were justified, for by the time Avertanus had returned to the hospital he was in a high fever, having apparently contracted the dread disease. He grew rapidly worse and, warned that his last hour was approaching, he uttered three prophecies, *viz.* that a great schism would be healed through the intercession of the Blessed Virgin, that the city of Lucca which had rejected him in life would honour him after his death, and that the hospital of St Peter would pass into the care of the Carmelites. He received the last sacraments and died happily in the midst of a vision of Christ and the angels. Romaeus did not long survive him. Stricken with the complaint and sad at the loss of his friend, he hourly grew weaker until the eighth day, when he passed away to rejoin Avertanus whom his dying eyes had beheld in glory. The *cultus* of Bd Romaeus was confirmed by Pope Gregory XVI.

See *Acta Sanctorum*, February, vol. iii. The biography given in Grossi, *Viridarium Carmelitanum*, from which the above account is mainly derived, cannot be considered a very reliable source. Avertanus is called Saint in his order. The very jejune second-nocturn lessons in the Carmelite Breviary supplement on March 4 are an indication of the slender information we possess regarding the life of Bd Romaeus.

BD CONSTANTIUS OF FABRIANO   (A.D. 1481)

EARLY in the fifteenth century, there lived at Fabriano a boy of such extraordinary goodness that even his parents would sometimes wonder whether he were not rather an angel than a human child. Once, when his little sister was suffering from a disease which the doctors pronounced incurable, Constantius Bernocchi asked his father and mother to join him in prayer by her bedside that she might recover. They did so, and she was immediately cured. At the age of fifteen he was admitted to the Dominican convent of Santa Lucia and he seems to have received the habit from the hands of Bd Laurence of Ripafratta, at that time prior of this house of strict observance. Constantius was one of those concerned with the reform of San Marco in Florence, and it was whilst he was teaching in that city that it was discovered that he had the gift of prophecy or second sight. Among other examples, the death of St Antoninus was made known to him at the moment that it took place, and this is mentioned by Pope Clement VII in his bull for the canonization of that saint. He was also credited with the power of working miracles, and besides the cares of his office he acted as peacemaker outside the convent and quelled popular tumults.

The joyous spirit conspicuous in many saints of his order was denied him. Constantius was usually sad, and when some one asked him why he so seldom laughed, he answered, " Because I do not know if my actions are pleasing to God ". He used to say the office of the dead every day and often the whole psalter, which he knew by heart. He urged this devotion on others, and said that when he desired any favour and recited the psalter for that intention, he never failed to obtain his petition. With the assistance of the municipal council, he rebuilt the friary of Ascoli and lived and died there, in spite of the entreaties of the people of Fabriano that he should spend his last years amongst them. He was esteemed so holy that it was reckoned a great favour to speak to him or even to touch his habit. Upon the news of his decease, the senate and council assembled, " considering his death a public calamity ", and resolved to defray the cost of a public funeral. The *cultus* of Bd Constantius was confirmed in 1821.

The most reliable source of information concerning Constantius is Mortier's *Maîtres Généraux O.P.*, in which he lays much stress upon the holy friar's theological attainments and the influence he exercised, after the example of Bd Raymund of Capua, in promoting the reform of the order. See also Procter, *Lives of the Dominican Saints*.

BD SEBASTIAN APARICIO   (A.D. 1600)

THE son of poor parents, Sebastian Aparicio was sent out into the fields as a child to mind the sheep. At the age of fifteen he went as servant to a widow at Salamanca, but as he found he was exposed to temptation he left her suddenly and became valet to a wealthy man. After a year he returned to more congenial work as servant to two farmers at San Lucar. He could combine his work in the fields with prayer and contemplation, and he remained there for eight years, during which period he earned enough to give marriage portions to his sisters. At the close of that time, being once more assailed by temptation, he saved himself by running away, and was moved to cut himself off completely from his native land and to go to America.

He settled in Mexico at Puebla de los Angeles, and began by doing agricultural work. Soon he found a better opening and started a carrying business—conveying merchandise from Zacatecas to Mexico City and running a sort of post. He then undertook the construction of roads, and through his enterprise and industry became a rich man. The money he made he gave away freely in charity, providing dowries, feeding the poor, and lending to farmers without asking for repayment. Sebastian's authority and prestige amongst Spaniards and Indians became immense: his judgement was accepted in the settlement of any dispute. In the midst of his wealth, he practised great austerity, sleeping only on a mat and eating the poorest food. In 1552 he retired from his business and bought a property near Mexico City, where he could live a quieter life, and for twenty years he developed the soil and bred cattle. He was often urged to marry, and, at the age of sixty, he married a poor girl at the entreaty of her relations. Upon her death he married again, but in both cases the marriage, by mutual consent, was never consummated. After the death of his second wife, when he was seventy years of age, he contracted so dangerous an illness that his life was despaired of. However, he recovered, and regarding it as a warning and call from Heaven, he made over everything he possessed to the Poor Clares and received the habit of the third order of St Francis.

At first he gave his services to the Poor Clares, but he soon felt drawn to the monastic life and entered the convent of the Friars Minor of the Observance in Mexico City. Old as he was, Sebastian was full of fervour and proved an exemplary novice, deeply humble and perfectly obedient. He was transferred first to Tecali and then to Puebla to join a community of over a hundred friars, where he spent the last twenty-six years of his life in the wearisome and humble rôle of begging brother. It was said that angels were seen to accompany the aged man on his long and arduous journeys and to guide him when he did not know the way. He had a wonderful power over beasts, and could instantly tame mules and even wild animals. To obtain food for the large community he used to have to take carts, drawn by oxen, across great tracts of country to carry the corn and other food given by charitable people, but he never had the least trouble with the animals, which obeyed the slightest movement of his lips. Bd Sebastian lived to the great age of ninety-eight, and his one sorrow at the last was that, because he was not able to retain what he swallowed, he could not receive the Blessed Sacrament. But it was carried into his cell that he might adore it, and he was so overcome with joy that he caused himself to be placed on the bare ground and poured out his soul in an ecstasy of thanksgiving to God. He was beatified in 1787.

See M. Cuevas, *Historia de la Iglesia en Mexico*, vol. i ; Léon, *Auréole Séraphique* (Eng. trans.), vol. i, pp. 313–319.

26 : ST NESTOR, Bishop of Magydus, Martyr (A.D. 251)

POLLIO, governor of Pamphylia and Phrygia during the reign of Decius, sought to curry favour with the emperor by the cruelty with which he enforced his edict against the Christians. At that time the bishop of Magydus was Nestor, who was held in great respect by Christians and pagans alike. He realized that he was a marked man, but his only care was for his flock whom he sent to places of safety whilst he remained quietly at home to pray for his people and await his fate. He was actually at prayer when he was told that the officers of justice had come for him. They greeted him respectfully, and he said, " My sons, what brings you here ? " They replied, " The irenarch [magistrate] and the curia summon thee ". Thereupon he signed himself with the sign of the cross and, with his head covered by his scarf, he followed them to the forum. As he entered, the whole court rose to its feet as a mark of respect, and he was led to a place apart and seated in a chair whilst the magistrates sat on stools. The irenarch said, " Sir, dost thou not know the order of the emperor ? "—" I know the order of the Almighty—not that of the emperor," was the reply. " Nestor, give way quietly that you may not be condemned," said the magistrate, but the bishop was inflexible and, when the irenarch warned him of tortures, replied, " The only torments that I fear are those of my God. Be assured that in torture and out of torture Him only will I confess."

Regretfully the court recognized that he must be sent to the governor, and the irenarch took him to Perga. Here he was no longer amongst friends, but his reputation had preceded him, and he was at first urged kindly and courteously to abjure his religion. He firmly refused ; whereupon Pollio caused him to be extended on an instrument of torture called the little horse, and as the executioner laid bare his sides and tore them with iron hooks, Nestor sang, " I will give thanks unto the Lord at all times : His praise shall be ever in my mouth ". The judge asked if he was not ashamed to put his trust in a man who had died such a death. " Let that be my confusion and that of all who call upon the name of the Lord ", was Nestor's answer. The crowd began to clamour that he should be put out of his sufferings, and Pollio said, " Wilt thou sacrifice or no ? Wilt thou be with us or with thy Christ ? " The martyr replied, " With my Christ I have ever been, with Him am I now, and with Him shall I be for evermore." Pollio then ordered that he should be crucified, and the sentence was carried out. As he hung on the cross, he exhorted and encouraged the Christians who stood round. His passing was like a triumph for, as he cried out, " My children, let us kneel and pray to God through the same Lord Jesus Christ," the whole of the crowd— Christians and pagans alike—knelt down and prayed, whilst he breathed forth his last breath.

The least unsatisfactory account of the martyrdom of St Nestor is that presented in a Latin text printed in the *Acta Sanctorum*, February, vol. iii. We do not possess the original Greek. Pio Franchi de' Cavalieri, " Note Agiografiche " in *Studi e Testi*, vol. xxii, p. 97, agrees with Allard in attributing to the document " a flavour of high antiquity ", even if we cannot with confidence pronounce it to be an authentic relation by a contemporary. In the notes referred to, Franchi has published another Greek recension of the story. *Cf.* also BHG., 2nd ed., n. 1328.

ST ALEXANDER, Bishop of Alexandria   (A.D. 328)

St Alexander, the successor of St Achillas in the see of Alexandria, is chiefly celebrated for the determined resistance he offered to the heresy which Arius, an Alexandrian priest, first began openly to propagate during his episcopate.   Alexander was a man of apostolic doctrine and life, charitable to the poor, and full of faith, zeal and fervour.   He admitted to the ministry by preference those who had sanctified themselves in solitude, and was happy in his choice of bishops throughout Egypt.   It seemed as though the Devil, enraged at the disrepute into which idolatry was falling, had endeavoured to repair his losses by fomenting this new and impious heresy of Arius, who taught not only that Christ was not truly God, but also that the Son was a creature, that there was a time when He did not exist, and that He was capable of sinning.   Some of the orthodox were disposed to be scandalized by the forbearance of St Alexander who, being one of the mildest of men, at first made use of gentle methods and by kindly expostulations and sound argument sought to bring Arius back to the true faith.   As his efforts proved ineffectual and the Arian faction grew in strength, the bishop summoned Arius to appear in an assembly of the clergy, where being found to be obstinate and incorrigible he was excommunicated.   At a council held in Alexandria, Arius was again tried, his sentence of excommunication being confirmed by the bishops who were present.   St Alexander wrote a letter to Bishop Alexander of Constantinople and a circular epistle to the other bishops of the Church, giving them an account of the heresy and of the condemnation of the heretic, the only two communications that have survived from his large correspondence on the subject.

In due course, in the year 325, the first oecumenical council assembled at Nicaea to deal with the matter, Pope St Silvester being represented by legates.   Arius was himself present, and both Marcellus of Ancyra and the deacon St Athanasius, whom St Alexander had brought with him, exposed the falsity of the new doctrines and completely confuted the Arians.   The heresy was emphatically and finally condemned, and Arius and a few others banished by the Emperor Constantine to Illyricum.   St Alexander, after this triumph of the faith, returned to Alexandria, where he died two years later, having named St Athanasius as his successor.

We have no proper biography of St Alexander, but Socrates, Sozomen and Theodoret supply a good deal of information.   See the *Acta Sanctorum*, February, vol. iii ; and also DCB., vol. i, pp. 79–82, and Hefele-Leclercq, *Conciles*, i, pp. 357 *seq.* and 636, note.

ST PORPHYRY, Bishop of Gaza   (A.D. 420)

Porphyry came of a family of Thessalonica (the modern Salonika) in Macedonia. Turning his back upon the world, he left friends and country at the age of twenty-five and went to Egypt, where he consecrated himself to God in a monastery in the desert of Skete.   After five years he made his way to Palestine, and took up his abode in a cave near the Jordan, where he passed five more years, until a complication of diseases obliged him to return to Jerusalem.   There he never failed daily to visit all the holy places, leaning on a stick, for he was too weak to stand upright. It happened about that time that Mark, an Asiatic who afterwards wrote his life, also came to Jerusalem as a pilgrim.   He was greatly edified by the devout assiduity with which Porphyry continually visited the scene of our Lord's resurrection and other stations, and seeing him one day struggling with difficulty to climb the steps in the church he ran to offer his assistance. Porphyry, however, refused, saying, " It is not right that I, who have come here to implore pardon for my sins, should be helped to make my task easier : rather let me undergo some trouble and inconvenience that God, seeing it, may have compassion on me." Feeble as he was, he never omitted his usual visits to the holy places and he daily partook of the Blessed Sacrament. The only thing which troubled him was that his paternal estate had not as yet been disposed of and the proceeds given to the poor. This commission he entrusted to Mark, who set out for Thessalonica and in three months' time returned to Jerusalem with money and effects of considerable value.

Mark scarcely recognized Porphyry, so completely had he recovered his health. His face had lost its pallor and was fresh and ruddy. Seeing his friend's amazement, he said with a smile, " Do not be surprised, Mark, to see me in perfect health, but only marvel at the unspeakable goodness of Christ who can easily cure what men despair of ". Mark asked him by what means he had been cured. He replied, " Forty days ago, being in great pain, I tried to reach Mount Calvary, and there I fainted away and fell into a kind of trance or ecstasy in which I seemed to see our Saviour on the cross and the good thief hanging near Him. I said to Christ, ' Lord, remember me when thou comest into thy kingdom ', and he replied by bidding the thief come to my assistance. This he did, and raising me from the ground he bade me go to Christ. I ran to Him and He came down from His cross, saying to me, ' Take this wood ' (meaning the cross) ' into thy custody '. In obedience to Him, methought I laid it on my shoulders and carried it some way. I awoke soon after and have been free from pain ever since, nor is there any sign left of the ailments from which I formerly suffered."

Mark was so much impressed by the holy man's words and example that he determined to take up his abode with him altogether. All the money he had brought was distributed amongst the poor, and consequently Porphyry found himself compelled to work for his living. He learned to make shoes and to dress leather, while Mark, who was well skilled in writing, gained a competence by copying books. He wished the saint to share his earnings, but Porphyry replied in the words of St Paul, " He that doth not work, let him not eat ". The saint led this laborious and penitential life until he was forty, when the bishop of Jerusalem ordained him priest, and committed to his charge the great relic of the holy cross. This was in 393. The saint changed nothing in his austere life, subsisting only on roots and the coarsest bread, and generally not taking food until after sunset. He continued this mode of life until his death. In 396 he was elected bishop of Gaza without his knowledge, and John, the bishop of Caesarea, wrote to the bishop of Jerusalem desiring him to send Porphyry, alleging that he wished to consult him on various difficult passages of Holy Scripture. He was therefore bidden to go, but to return in seven days.

Upon receiving this order Porphyry seemed at first disturbed, but he said, " God's will be done ". That evening he called Mark, and said to him, " Brother Mark, let us go and venerate the holy places and the sacred cross, for it will be long before we shall do so again." Mark asked him why he spoke in such a tone, and he replied that our Saviour had appeared to him the night before, and had said, " Give up the treasure of the cross which you have in custody, for I will marry you to a wife, poor indeed and lowly, but of great piety and virtue. Take care to adorn her well for, however she may appear, she is my sister."—" This," he added, " Christ signified to me last night, and therefore I fear that I may be charged with the sins of others while I seek to expiate my own—but the will of God must be obeyed." When they had done as he had said he started off with Mark and the following day, which was a Saturday, they reached Caesarea. Next morning Bishop John bade certain townsmen of Gaza lay hold of Porphyry, and while they held him he ordained him bishop. The holy man was much distressed at being promoted to a dignity for which he judged himself unfit. The Gazaeans did their best to console him, and they started for Gaza, where they arrived on Wednesday night, harassed and weary, for the heathen in the villages near Gaza, having had notice of their coming, had so broken up the roads and obstructed them with thorns and logs that they were scarcely passable.

That year there was a great drought, which the pagans ascribed to the coming of the new Christian bishop, for they said their god Marnas had foretold that Porphyry would bring calamities on the city. In Gaza there stood a famous temple dedicated to that deity, which the Emperor Theodosius I had ordered to be closed but not destroyed because of the beauty of its structure. The governor had allowed it to be reopened and when, for two months after the arrival of Porphyry, no rain had fallen, the pagans assembled in this temple to make supplication to Marnas. Then the Christians after a day of fasting and a night of prayer, went in procession to the church of St Timothy outside the walls, singing hymns. Upon their return they found the city gates shut against them. Then Porphyry and his flock besought God with redoubled fervour to bestow the boon so greatly needed, and in a short time clouds gathered and rain fell in such plenty that the heathen opened the gates and, joining them, cried out, " Christ alone is God ! He alone has overcome ! " This and the miraculous healing of a woman led to a great number of conversions, so that the pagans, perceiving their numbers decrease, became very troublesome to the Christians, whom they excluded from commerce and public offices and harassed in various ways. Porphyry, to protect himself and his flock, had recourse to the emperor, to whom he sent Mark his disciple, and afterwards followed him to Constantinople himself in company with John, his metropolitan.

Through the advocacy of St John Chrysostom and the Empress Eudoxia, Arcadius eventually was induced to grant all that was asked, including permission for the destruction of the temples of Gaza. An imperial edict to that effect was delivered to a patrician named Cynegius, who was charged to see the order carried out. When they landed again in Palestine near Gaza, the Christians came out to meet them singing hymns ; and as the two bishops and the procession passed through a square called Tetramphodos in which stood a marble statue of Venus, which was supposed to give oracles to young women about the choice of husbands, the idol fell, apparently of itself, and was broken to pieces. Ten days later arrived Cynegius with a strong guard of soldiers and the emperor's edict. In accordance with it, eight public temples were destroyed by fire, including the Marneion. After this, private houses and courts were searched and the idols were destroyed or cast into the sewers, and all books of magic were consigned to the flames. Many of the pagans desired baptism ; but many others were only angered by these proceedings, and in a riot they raised Porphyry barely escaped with his life (cf. St Marcellus on August 14). On the site of the temple of Marnas was built a church in the form of a cross, and the Empress Eudoxia sent pillars and rich marbles from

Constantinople to adorn the building, which was called after her the Eudoxiana.
At its beginning St Porphyry, with his clergy and all the Christians of the city,
went in procession from the church called Eirene singing the " *Venite, exultemus
Domino* " and other psalms, each verse being answered with an " Alleluia ".   They
all set to work carrying stones and other materials and digging the foundations
under the direction of Rufinus, a famous architect.   The church was begun in
403, took five years to build, and the bishop consecrated it on Easter day, 408.
His alms to the poor on that occasion seemed boundless, though at all times they
were very great.   St Porphyry spent the rest of his life in the zealous discharge
of his pastoral duties, and lived to see the city for the most part free from open
idolatry.

   The Life of St Porphyry by Mark the deacon is an historical document of qui te exceptional
interest.   Apart from the insight which it affords into the character of the saint, it provides
much valuable information regarding the last efforts of paganism in the Christian East.   In
1913 an English translation by G. F. Hill was published, and an annotated German version
by Dr George Rohde appeared in 1927.   The *Acta Sanctorum*, February, vol. iii, only prints
a Latin version of the Life.   The Greek text was edited for the first time by M. Haupt
in the *Abhandlungen* of the Berlin Academy in 1874, and, in 1895, more accurately by
the Philological Society of Bonn.   In 1930 H. Grégoire and M. A. Kugener published the
Greek text, with a French translation and commentary   according to them, it is not an
authentic contemporary work of Mark, but was written at least twenty-five years after
Porphyry's death.   In *Analecta Bollandiana*, vol. lix (1941), pp. 63–216, there is printed
a Latin version of a Georgian life of St Porphyry (probably of Syrian origin) : an interesting feature is that the writer seems to emphasize that paganism was brought to an end
at Gaza without the violence associated with the name of St Cyril at Alexandria.   See
also the excellent essay by F. M. Abel in the *Conférences de Saint-Etienne* (ed. Lagrange,
1910).

ST VICTOR THE HERMIT   (*c.* A.D. 610)

St BERNARD in his sermons has left us two panegyrics of the priest and hermit St
Victor, or Vittré, of Arcis-sur-Aube in Champagne.   He says : " Now in Heaven,
he beholds God clearly revealed, but not forgetting us though swallowed up in joy.
It is not a land of oblivion in which Victor dwells.   Heaven does not harden or
narrow hearts, but it makes them more tender and compassionate ; it does not
distract minds or alienate them from us ; it does not diminish but increases
affection and charity ; it augments capacity for pity.   The angels, although they
behold the face of their Father, visit us and come continually to our assistance : and
shall those now forget us who were once amongst us and who formerly suffered
what they see us to be undergoing now ?   No : I know the just await me until
Thou render to me my reward.   Victor is not like Pharaoh's cupbearer who could
forget his fellow captive.   He has not so put on the stole of glory himself as to lay
aside his pity or the remembrance of our misery."
   St Victor, born in the diocese of Troyes, was a saint from his cradle, and in his
youth prayer, fasting and almsgiving were his delight.   He received holy orders,
but the love of heavenly contemplation being always the chief inclination of his soul,
he preferred solitude to the life entailed by the care of souls.   In this the Holy
Ghost was his director, and he lived in such continual union with God through
prayer and contemplation that he seemed raised above the ordinary conditions of
this mortal life.   God glorified him by graces and miracles, but the greatest wonder
of all seems to have been the powerful example of his life, which brought about the

conversion of many sinners.   He lived a solitary life at Arcis, near Plancy-sur-Aube. His remains were translated to the Benedictine monastery of Montiéramey, and at the request of the monks St Bernard drew up an office of St Victor with a hymn of his own composition.

See the *Acta Sanctorum*, February, vol. iii.   We know practically nothing of St Victor from any authentic source.   St Bernard seems simply to have made himself the mouthpiece of vague local tradition.

BD LEO OF SAINT-BERTIN, ABBOT   (A.D. 1163)

LEO, fortieth abbot of Saint-Bertin, was a native of Furnes in Flanders.   He is described as having received an unusually good education, so that he became well versed in all branches of sacred and secular learning.   As a very young man he was attached to the court of the Count of Flanders where he held important offices, including that of almoner—although he was only twenty.   He soon retired from the world and entered the monastery of Anchin, where he distinguished himself amongst his brother monks, and ere long was called to rule the abbey of Lobbes. During the protracted wars that had desolated the country the affairs of the monastery had fallen into a bad state, but Leo succeeded in setting them in order and in restoring discipline.   In 1138 he was recalled to become abbot of Saint-Bertin —an abbey of such importance that it was known as the Monastery of Monasteries. His name appears on several contemporary charters.   That same year he went to Rome, where the main purpose of his visit was to free his abbey from the interference of Cluny, which claimed certain rights over it.   Amongst the works of St Bernard are two letters addressed " to the dear and venerable Leo and to all his community ".

When in 1146 Thierry of Alsace, Count of Flanders, took part in the Second Crusade, he was accompanied by Bd Leo, but, beyond the fact that he reached Jerusalem, nothing is known about the abbot's stay in the Holy Land.   On his return he brought with him to the chapel of St Blaise in Bruges the relic of the Precious Blood which the count had obtained and which is still treasured and venerated in that ancient city.   When the abbot was quite an old man, his monastery was entirely destroyed by fire in the year 1152.   Undismayed he started at once to rebuild it, and was fortunate in enlisting the help of a nobleman known as William of Ypres : in two years the monks were able to return, and Bd Leo lived to see the whole monastery entirely reconstructed.   In 1161 he lost his sight, and two years later he died.

See Destombes, *Vies des saints du diocèse de Cambrai*, vol. i, pp. 284–287 : *Biographie nationale (de Belgique)*, vol. xi, pp. 822–824.   It does not seem clear whether the chapel in which the alleged relic of the Precious Blood was first deposited was dedicated to St Blaise or to St Basil.   The relic purported to be drops of the actual blood of Christ our Lord collected by St Joseph of Arimathea when he washed our Saviour's body before laying it in the tomb.   The question of the nature of the veneration to be paid to such relics, apart from the question of their authenticity, was keenly debated among theologians in the fifteenth century.   See Jox, *Die Reliquien des kostbares Blut*.

BD ISABEL OF FRANCE, VIRGIN   (A.D. 1270)

A DAUGHTER of Louis VIII and Blanche of Castile and the sister of St Louis, Princess Isabel was possessed not only of rank and fortune, but also of personal beauty and exceptional qualities of mind.   Pomp and luxury attracted her so little that she confided to a nun that although she sometimes allowed herself to be richly attired to please her mother, fine clothes never gave her any pleasure.   In her girlhood she used to pray with such fervour that she was sometimes rapt in ecstasy, and she fasted three times a week besides observing the ordinary fasts, and though her mother tried to coax her to eat by promising her gifts for the poor, she entreated that other conditions might be imposed.   She was clever and eager to learn, and added Latin to her other studies that she might read the offices of the Church and the writings of the fathers.   Her fasts and the nervous strain of the life she led brought on so severe an illness that she was publicly prayed for, and her mother sent to consult a holy woman at Nanterre who was reputed to have the gift of prophecy.   The reply was that the princess would recover, but that she must never be counted among the living because for the rest of her life she would be dead to the world.   The truth of this was soon perceived when various suitors presented themselves.   She refused first Count Hugo of Austria and then Conrad, King of Jerusalem, although Pope Innocent IV sent her a letter urging her to accept him for the benefit of Christendom.   She answered him so humbly and wisely that he applauded her resolution to serve God in perpetual virginity.

Every day before her dinner Isabel would admit a number of poor people upon whom she waited herself, and after dinner she went out to visit the sick and the poor ; and she used to pay the expenses of ten knights in the Holy Land as her share in the crusade.   She was tried by several long and painful illnesses, but the ill-success of the crusade and her brother's capture were far harder trials to her. After the death of her mother she resolved to establish a house for daughters of the Order of St Francis, and obtained the approval of St Louis, who promised material aid.   The next thing was to have a rule drafted in accordance with the Rule of St Clare, and some of the greatest Franciscans of the day, including St Bonaventure himself, set to work to draw up a set of constitutions.   Thus began the famous Franciscan convent of Longchamps, whose site was within what is now the Bois de Boulogne in Paris.   It was called the Monastery of the Humility of the Blessed Virgin Mary.

Bd Isabel herself was never actually enclosed, but lived in a part of the building separate from the nuns' cells, and she wore secular clothing.   One reason for this was that her bodily sufferings would not permit her always to keep the full rule, and she was also influenced by her determination not to be elected abbess.   Moreover, by keeping part of her property, she could help to support the house and continue her gifts to the poor.   She still maintained her fasts and disciplines, and observed almost constant silence.   Before she went to communion she used always, on her knees, to beg the pardon of the few servants she retained.   In this manner of life she spent ten years.   Towards the end she passed several nights in contemplation without taking rest, and was seen rapt in ecstasy by her chaplain, her confessor and Sister Agnes who afterwards wrote her life.   Her *cultus* was approved in 1521.

Bd Isabel is dealt with in the *Acta Sanctorum* on August 31 (Aug., vol. vi), but she is commemorated by the Friars Minor now on June 8, with BB. Agnes of Bohemia and Baptista Varani.   The principal source of our information is her life by Agnes de Harcourt, Abbess of Longchamps, under whose care her last days were spent.   See also Léon, *Auréole Séraphique* (Eng. trans.), vol. iii, pp. 91–96 ; and the sketch by A. Garreau, *Bse Isabelle de France* (1943).

27 : ST GABRIEL POSSENTI   (A.D. 1862)

THIS young saint was the son of a distinguished advocate who held a succession of official appointments under the government of the States of the Church.   There were thirteen children in the family of Sante Possenti, of whom the future saint, born in 1838 and christened Francis, was the eleventh. Several died in infancy and their delicate mother was herself taken from them in 1842, when Francis was only four years old.   Mr Possenti had just then become " grand assessor ", let us say registrar, of Spoleto, and it was in the Jesuit college of that city that Francis received most of his education.   After a surfeit of the dubious marvels which meet us in the legendary story of so many aspirants for canonization, it is a distinct relief to find that the childhood of Francis Possenti, like that of Teresa Martin, was perfectly normal.   It is not recorded that he had visions at the age of four, or that he had devised extraordinary forms of self-torture before he was eight.   On the contrary he seems by nature to have possessed a warm temper which was not always under perfect control, and to have been fastidious about his dress and personal appearance.   As a youth he read novels, he was fond of gaiety and of the theatre, though seemingly the plays he frequented were innocent enough, and on account of his cheerfulness and good looks he was a universal favourite.   Though there is not the least reason to believe that he ever lost his innocence or seriously broke the law of God, he, from the shelter of the cloister, looked back upon these years with evident alarm.

> Dear Philip, [he afterwards wrote to a friend] If you truly love your soul, shun bad companions ; shun the theatre.   I know by experience how very difficult it is when entering such places in the state of grace to come away without having lost it, or at least exposed it to great danger.   Avoid pleasure-parties and avoid evil books.   I assure you that if I had remained in the world, it seems certain to me that I should not have saved my soul.   Tell me, could any one have indulged in more amusements than I ?   Well, and what is the result ?— nothing but bitterness and fear.   Dear Philip, do not despise me, for I speak from my heart.   I ask your pardon for all the scandal that I may have given you ; and I protest that whatever evil I may have spoken about anyone, I now retract it and beg of you to forget it all, and to pray for me that God may forgive me likewise.

Probably much of this self-accusatory tone was due to the sensitiveness of conscience which developed in the noviceship, but there must have been a certain relative frivolity in the years which preceded, and his friends, we are told, used in playful exaggeration to call him *il damerino*, " the ladies' man ".   As a consequence the call of God does not seem to have been at once attended to even when it was clearly heard.   Before his very promising career as a student was completed he fell dangerously ill, and he promised if he recovered to enter religion ; but when he was restored to health he took no immediate step to carry his purpose into effect. After the lapse of a year or two he was again brought to death's door by an attack of laryngitis, or possibly quinsy, and he renewed his promise, having recourse in this extremity to a relic of the Jesuit martyr St Andrew Bobola, just then beatified. Once more he was cured, miraculously as he believed, and he made application to enter the Society of Jesus. But though he was accepted, he still delayed—after all, he was not yet seventeen—possibly because he doubted whether God was not calling him to a more penitential life than that of the Society. Then his favourite sister died during an outbreak of cholera, and so, stricken with a sense of the precarious nature of all earthly ties, he at last, with the full approval of his Jesuit confessor, made choice of the Passionists. Thus in September 1856 he entered their noviceship at Morrovalle, where he was given the name in religion of Brother Gabriel-of-our-Lady-of-Sorrows.

The rest of Gabriel's career is simply a record of an extraordinary effort to attain perfection in small things. His brightness, his spirit of prayer, his charity to the poor, his consideration for others, his exact observance of every rule, his desire (constantly checked by wise superiors) to adopt forms of bodily mortification which were beyond his strength, his absolute submission in all matters in which he could practise obedience evidently made an ineffaceable impression upon all who lived with him. Their testimony in the process of his beatification is most convincing. It was a life of continual self-surrender, but the most charming feature of the whole was the cheerfulness with which the offering was made. Naturally there is not much to chronicle in such an existence. But as an illustration of the simple means—simple except for the weariness of the endless renewal of such acts of self-repression—by which heroic sanctity may be reached, the following may be quoted from one of his biographies :

> He was always eager to do more bodily penance, and for a long time, to take a single example, he asked permission to wear a chain set with sharp points. Leave was refused, but he still begged for it with modest persistence. His director replied, " You want to wear the little chain ! I tell you what you really ought to have is a chain on your will—yes, that is what you need. Go away, don't speak to me about it." And he retired deeply mortified. Another time when he was asking leave for the same thing, " Well, yes," I said, " wear it by all means ; but you must wear it outside your habit and in public, too, that all may see what a man of great mortification you are." Though stung to the quick, he wore it as I directed ; besides, to satisfy his thirst for penances, I made fun of him before his companions ; but he accepted all in silence, and did not even ask to be dispensed from thus becoming a laughing stock.

After only four years spent in religion, in the course of which Brother Gabriel had given rise to the expectation of great and fruitful work for souls once the priesthood had been attained, symptoms of tuberculous disease manifested themselves so unmistakably that from henceforth he had to be exempted, very much against his will, from all the more arduous duties of community observance. Patience under weakness and bodily suffering, and a ready submission to the restrictions imposed by superiors upon his ardent nature, became the keynote of his effort after perfection. Young and old were indescribably impressed by the example which he gave, but he himself shrank from any sort of favourable notice, and not long before his death he succeeded in securing the destruction of all his private notes of the spiritual favours which God had bestowed upon him. He passed away in great peace in the early morning of February 27, 1862, at Isola di Gran Sasso in the Abruzzi. St Gabriel-of-our-Lady-of-Sorrows was canonized in 1920.

See N. Ward, *Life of Gabriel of our Lady of Sorrows* (1904); Anselm de la Dolorosa, *Vida de San Gabriel de la Virgen Dolorosa* (1920); *Lettere di San Gabriele dell' Addolorata* (1920); and C. Hollobough, *St Gabriel, Passionist* (1923).

SS. JULIAN, CRONION AND BESAS, MARTYRS   (A.D. 250)

DURING the persecution of Christians under Decius many of the citizens of Alexandria, especially amongst the rich and those who held public office, apostatized and sacrificed to idols under stress of fear. St Dionysius, Bishop of Alexandria, who records and deplores this in a letter to Fabian, adds : " Others, firm and blessed pillars of the Lord, confirmed by the Lord Himself and receiving of Him strength suited to the measure of their faith, proved themselves noble witnesses of His kingdom. Foremost of these was a man afflicted with gout and unable to walk or to stand, Julian by name, who was apprehended together with his two bearers. One of these immediately denied his faith, but the other, Cronion, surnamed Eunus, and the aged Julian himself, after having confessed the Lord, were carried on camels through the whole city, a very large one, as you know, and were scourged and at length consumed in an immense fire in the midst of a crowd of spectators. A soldier named Besas, who was standing by and who opposed the insolence of the multitude while these martyrs were on their way to execution, was assailed by them with loud shouts, and this brave soldier of God, after he had shown his heroism in the great conflict of piety, was beheaded."

The Roman Martyrology mentions on December 7 a certain soldier, martyred at Alexandria under Decius, whom it calls Agatho. He was set to guard the dead bodies of some martyrs, and resolutely refused to allow the crowd to come near in order to insult and mutilate them. The angry mob therefore denounced him to the magistrate, and upon his confessing Christ he was sentenced to death and beheaded. Dom Quentin has shown that this martyr is really the same as St Besas, just mentioned. Rufinus in translating the *Ecclesiastical History* of Eusebius omitted the name of the soldier, and it was supplied as Agatho by the martyrologist Ado out of his own head.

The letter of St Dionysius here referred to is quoted in Eusebius, *Eccles. Hist.*, bk vi, ch. 41. See Feltoe's edition of Dionysius of Alexandria, pp. 11–12. Dom Quentin explains the confusion about Besas in his *Martyrologes historiques*, pp. 449, 462, 611, 658.

ST THALELAEUS THE HERMIT   (*c.* A.D. 450)

FOR our knowledge of the holy recluse Thalelaeus we are chiefly indebted to Theodoret, who says that he was personally acquainted with him. He was a native of Cilicia, and for some time he lived in a hut beside a heathen shrine near Gabala, to which people used to go to sacrifice. The evil spirits or the pagan priests tried to scare him away by fearful apparitions and hideous noises, but the holy man stood his ground and converted many of those who had come to worship in the temple. Theodoret says that he himself conversed with some of these converts. Afterwards St Thalelaeus contrived for himself a sort of penitential cage. He made two wheels and joined them by bars into a kind of barrel, but open between the bars. He shut himself up in this, and it was so small and cramped that his chin rested on his knees. He had been in it ten years when Theodoret saw him and asked him why he had chosen so strange an abode. The penitent answered, " I punish my criminal body that God, seeing my affliction for my sins, may be moved to forgive them and to deliver me from the torments of the world to come, or at least to mitigate their severity ". John Moschus, in the *Spiritual Meadow*, relates that Thalelaeus the Cilician spent sixty years in the ascetic life, weeping almost without intermission ; and that he used to say to those that came to him, " Time is allowed us by the divine mercy for repentance and satisfaction, and woe be to us if we neglect it ". He was surnamed Epiklautos, " weeping much ".

See the *Acta Sanctorum*, February, vol. iii, where the passage from Theodoret's *Philotheus* is quoted, and *cf.* DCB., vol. iv, p. 882.

ST LEANDER, Bishop of Seville　　(A.D. 596)

It was mainly through St Leander's efforts that the Western Goths or Visigoths, who had ruled in Spain for a hundred years, were converted from the errors of Arianism. His father was Severian, Duke of Cartagena, at which place the saint was born, and his mother was the daughter of the Ostrogothic King Theodoric. His brothers were St Fulgentius, Bishop of Ecija, and St Isidore, who succeeded him in the see of Seville. He had a sister, St Florentina, and according to tradition a second sister who married King Leovigild. This, however, is not certain ; if true it must have added enormously to his difficulties, for Leovigild was a determined Arian. Even as a boy, Leander was remarkable for his eloquence and fascinating personality ; while still quite young he took the monastic habit at Seville, where he gave himself for three years to devotion and study. Upon the death of the bishop of Seville he was unanimously chosen to succeed him, but his change of condition made little or no alteration in his mode of living. He immediately set to work to fight against the prevalent heresy of Arianism, and through his prayers and his eloquence caused many conversions, including that of Hermenegild, the eldest son of King Leovigild. In 583 St Leander went to Constantinople on an embassy to the emperor, and there he became acquainted with St Gregory the Great, who had been sent there as legate by Pope Pelagius II. The two men formed a close and lasting friendship, and it was at the suggestion of Leander that Gregory wrote his *Morals on the Book of Job.*

Upon his return, he continued his fight for the true faith, but in 586 Leovigild caused his son St Hermenegild to be put to death for refusing to receive communion from the hands of an Arian bishop, and he banished several Catholic prelates, including St Leander and his brother St Fulgentius. Even in exile the bishop continued his fight, writing two works against Arianism and a third to meet the objections that had been raised against his arguments. Before long, however, Leovigild recalled the exiles, and when he found that he was on his death-bed he sent for St Leander and entrusted to him his son and successor Reccared to be instructed in the Catholic faith. Nevertheless, through fear of his people, St Gregory tells us, Leovigild himself died unreconciled to the Church. Reccared, under the guidance of St Leander, became an ardent and well-instructed Catholic. Leander spoke with so much wisdom on the controverted points to the Arian bishops that, by force of his reasoning rather than by his authority, he brought them over to the truth and thus converted the whole nation of the Visigoths. He was equally successful with the Suevi, a people of Spain whom Leovigild had perverted. No one rejoiced more than did St Gregory the Great at the wonderful blessings bestowed by Almighty God on the labours of the holy bishop, and he wrote him an affectionate letter in which he congratulated him warmly and also sent him the pallium.

In 589 St Leander presided over the third Council of Toledo, at which a solemn declaration of the consubstantiality of the Three Persons of the Trinity was drawn up, and twenty-three canons were passed relating to discipline, for the holy prelate was no less zealous in the reformation of manners and morals than in restoring the purity of the faith.   The following year another synod was held at Seville to complete, establish and seal the conversion of the nation to the true faith.   St Leander was deeply sensible of the importance of prayer, and he laboured to encourage true devotion in all, but especially in those who were consecrated to God under a religious rule.   His letter to his sister Florentina, usually called his Rule of a Monastic Life, turns chiefly on the contempt of this world and on prayer. A very important work of his was his reform of the Spanish liturgy.   In this liturgy and in the third Council of Toledo, in conformity with the practice of the Eastern churches, the Nicene Creed was appointed to be said at Mass in repudiation of the Arian heresy.   Other Western churches, and eventually Rome itself, adopted this practice later.

St Leander was tried by frequent illness, particularly by the gout, and St Gregory, who was afflicted with the same complaint, alludes to it in one of his letters.   According to an old Spanish tradition, the famous picture of our Lady of Guadalupe was a present from the pope to his friend Leander.   Of the bishop's many writings none have come down to us except his Rule of a Monastic Life, and a homily in thanksgiving for the conversion of the Goths.   He died in 596, and his relics are now in a chapel of Seville Cathedral.   In Spain St Leander is honoured liturgically as a doctor of the Church.

See the *Acta Sanctorum*, March, vol. ii ; Gams, *Kirchengeschichte von Spanien*, vol. ii, pt 2, pp. 37 *seq.* and 66 *seq.* ; DTC., vol. ix, p. 95.   There is also an excellent article on St Leander by Mrs Humphry Ward in DCB., vol. iii, pp. 637–640 ; and *cf.* F. H. B. Daniell's article on Reccared, vol. iv, pp. 536–538.

ST BALDOMERUS, or GALMIER   (*c.* A.D. 660)

St Galmier was a locksmith in Lyons who lived in great poverty and austerity, spending all his leisure moments in holy reading and prayer.   He gave his earnings —and sometimes even his tools—to the poor, and to everyone he met he used to say, " In the name of the Lord, let us always give thanks to God ".   Viventius, abbot of Saint Justus, came upon him when he was at prayer, and was greatly struck by the fervour of his devotion, but he was still more impressed when he entered into conversation with him.   The abbot offered him a cell in his monastery, and here he devoted himself almost entirely to contemplation.   His biographer says that as a mark of God's special favour the wild birds of the air whom no man had ever caught or tamed used to come at the hour of his meal and eat out of his hands, whilst he would say to them, " Take your refreshment and always bless the Lord of Heaven ".   Bishop Gundry ordained him subdeacon, in spite of his reluctance. He was sometimes venerated as the patron of locksmiths, and is represented in art with pincers and other implements of his trade.

St Baldomerus is commemorated under this name in the Roman Martyrology, but we have no reliable materials for his history.   See the *Acta Sanctorum*, February, vol. iii ; Detzel, *Christliche Ikonographie*, vol. ii, p. 179.

ST ALNOTH   (*c.* A.D. 700)

AT Weedon in Northamptonshire there stood a house which was presented by Wulfhere, King of Mercia, to his daughter St Werburga and was converted by her into a monastery.   On the estate lived a cowherd called Alnoth, a man of singular simplicity and holiness.   It is told in Goscelin's Life of St Werburga that she one day saw her steward cruelly belabouring the poor serf for some fancied fault. Although she might well have used her authority to command the bailiff to stop, the saint in her humility cast herself at his feet and besought him to spare the good cowherd, who, she felt sure, was more acceptable to God than any of themselves. Later on, Alnoth became a hermit, and lived in the woods at Stowe near Bugbrooke. He was murdered by robbers—for what reason is not clear, as he possessed nothing that they could plunder.   He was buried at Stowe and his memory was long venerated in the neighbourhood, a festival being kept in his honour.

See the *Acta Sanctorum*, February, vol. iii.   There seems to be no mention of St Alnoth in any of the early English calendars.

ST JOHN OF GORZE, ABBOT   (A.D. 974)

THE father of John of Gorze was well on in years when his son was born at Vandières near Pont-à-Mousson, and, though he lived long enough to have him well educated at Metz and at Saint-Mihiel, he died before John attained to manhood.   The youth was called upon to look after the family property, and was thus brought into touch with leading men in church and state.   The benefices of Vandières and of Saint-Laurent in the village of Fontenoy were vested in him, and he did much to adorn and beautify these churches, especially Saint-Laurent, where he would sometimes spend several days in prayer when he was free from secular business.   Although the world still had attractions for him, he was greatly influenced by an old priest who had a special devotion to the Divine Office and by a holy deacon named Bernier. The church and monastery on his estate were dependent on the nunnery of St Peter at Metz, and he used often to go there to serve at Mass.   The accidental discovery of the austerity practised by the nuns and those who were under their care brought home to him the ease and luxury in which he was living.   From that moment he turned his mind entirely to spiritual matters.   He is credited with having learnt the Bible by heart, and is said to have acquired an extraordinary knowledge of the *Comes*, the Penitentials, the canons of ecclesiastical law, the homilies of the fathers, and the lives of the saints, so that he could recite them as though he were reading from a book.

A pilgrimage to Rome brought John into touch with various holy persons who helped him to advance in the spiritual life, and he visited Monte Gargano, Monte Cassino—and Vesuvius.   Upon his return to Lorraine, he formed a great friendship with Archdeacon Einhold of Toul, whom he persuaded to give away his possessions and to join him on another pilgrimage to Rome.   However, Adelborn, Bishop of Metz, interposed, and the two then betook themselves to the almost deserted abbey of Gorze in 933.   They soon instilled new life into the monastery, and Einhold became abbot, with John as his prior ; so severe were the austerities which he undertook that his superior felt obliged to moderate them.   The Emperor Otto I having asked for two monks to go as his ambassadors to the court of the Caliph Abdur-Rahman of Cordova, John was chosen as the chief spokesman, and he fulfilled his mission with so much courage and wisdom that he won the admiration

of the Mussulman chief.   On his return in 960 he was elected abbot of Gorze, and
he proceeded to introduce reforms which spread to other Benedictine monasteries
in Upper Lorraine ; the reform, like that of the contemporary St Gerard of Brogne,
was marked by its physical severity.   It seems rather uncertain whether John
should be styled "Saint", or "Blessed" :   the Bollandists give the latter
description, but he is popularly spoken of as St John of Gorze.

A full and historically important biography of John of Gorze was written in 980 by his
friend John, abbot of St Arnulf at Metz, but the only manuscript we possess is unfortunately
incomplete.   The text has been edited by the Bollandists (*Acta Sanctorum*, February,
vol. iii), by Mabillon, and in the MGH., *Scriptores*, vol. iv, whence it has been reprinted in
Migne, PL., vol. 137, cc. 241–310.   See also Mathieu, *De Joannis Abbatis Gorziensis Vita*
(1879), and Sackur, *Die Cluniacenser*, vol. i.

BD MARK BARKWORTH, Martyr   (A.D. 1601)

MARK BARKWORTH (*alias* Lambert) was born in Lincolnshire in 1572, and brought
up a Protestant.   He was a graduate of the University of Oxford, and while
travelling on the continent visited the seminary at Douay, where he was shortly
afterwards received into the Church.   He began studying for the priesthood there,
and concluded his course at Valladolid, where he was ordained in 1599.   At this
time there was a movement towards the Order of St Benedict among the students
in the English college at Valladolid, and of this movement Mr Barkworth seems to
have been the leader ; it was viewed with strong disfavour by the Jesuit fathers
who conducted the college, and when Barkworth left Spain for the English mission
in the year of his ordination, and in company with Bd Thomas Garnet, he was still
a secular priest.   So on his way through Navarre he visited the abbey of Hirache
and was there accepted as a Benedictine novice, with the privilege of making his
profession at the hour of death, if there were no opportunity for him to do so before.
     Within a few months of his arrival in England Father Mark was arrested, and
it was while in prison that he told a Genoese soldier, Hortensio Spinola, of a vision
of St Benedict from whom he had learned that he would die a martyr and a monk.
It is said that for this reason he would not make use of opportunities for escape ;
and in February 1601 he was brought to trial at the Old Bailey, together with the
Venerable Roger Filcock.   The jury included three men who were not only apostates but probably former fellow students of Father Mark, and so with antecedent
knowledge that he was a priest.   His answers to questions caused several demonstrations in court, and he was sentenced without any witnesses having been called.
     The day of his execution was very cold and it was snowing heavily.   By some
means Father Mark got hold of a Benedictine habit, which he put on, and had his
head shaved in the monastic form of tonsure.   When he and Father Roger Filcock
arrived at Tyburn the dead body of Bd Anne Line (see below) was hanging from
the gallows : he kissed the edge of her dress and her hand, saying, "Thou hast got
the start of us, sister, but we will follow thee as quickly as we may ".   He addressed
the people, reminding them that Pope St Gregory had sent monks of St Benedict to
preach the gospel to their heathen ancestors, "And I come here to die ", he said,
"as a Catholic, a priest and a religious of the same order ".   He had made his
profession in two senses.   Then as he was about to be turned off the cart he sang
"in manner and form following : *Haec est dies Domini, gaudeamus, gaudeamus,
gaudeamus in ea* "—" This is the day of the Lord ; let us rejoice, rejoice, rejoice
in it."   The contemporary account of the subsequent butchery is one of the most

horrible in the records of the English martyrs ; but Father Filcock was allowed to hang till he was dead. While the martyrs were being quartered it was noticed that Father Mark's knees were calloused by constant kneeling. A young man picked up one of his legs and showed it to the attendant Protestant ministers, asking " Which of you gospellers can show such a knee ? " Bd Mark Barkworth died on February 27, 1601, the first English Benedictine martyr.

There is a complete account of this *beatus* in Camm's *Nine Martyr Monks* (1932). The principal sources are MMP., pp. 253–256, wherein is used a manuscript provided by the English monks of Douay ; Raissius in his *Catalogus Christi Sacerdotum* ; Blackfan, *Annales Collegii Sti Albani in oppido Valesoleti*, and the usual Benedictine authorities.

BD ANNE LINE, MARTYR   (A.D. 1601)

THIS Anne was daughter to William Heigham, a gentleman of Dunmow in Essex and a strong Protestant, who disinherited his son and daughter when they became Catholics. Anne married Roger Line, of Ringwood, in the New Forest of Hampshire. Shortly afterwards Mr Line was imprisoned for recusancy and then allowed to go abroad, to Flanders, where he died in 1594. His widow, who suffered from extreme ill-health, then devoted the rest of her life to the service of her hunted co-religionists. When the Jesuit, Father John Gerard, organized a house of refuge for clergy in London, Mrs Line was put in charge of it ; but after Father Gerard's escape from the Tower in 1597 she began to come under suspicion of the authorities, and had to find a new residence. But this also was tracked down, and on Candlemas day 1601 the pursuivants broke in just as Father Francis Page, S.J., had vested for Mass. He managed to remove his vestments and escape detection, but Mrs Line, Mrs Gage and others were taken.

A friend at court brought about the release of Mrs Gage, but Anne Line was brought before Lord Chief Justice Popham at the Old Bailey, charged with having harboured a priest from overseas. She was so ill at the time that she had to be carried into court in a chair. When asked if she were guilty of the charge, she replied in a loud voice for all to hear, " My lords, nothing grieves me more but that I could not receive a thousand more." The prosecution, which had only one witness, signally failed to prove its case ; the jury nevertheless, at the judge's direction, found a verdict of guilty, and Anne was sentenced to death. She spent her last days and hours with composure and spiritual comfort, and when brought to Tyburn to be hanged she kissed the gallows and knelt in prayer up to the last moment. There suffered with her Roger Filcock, a Jesuit, who had long been Mrs Line's friend and confessor, and Bd Mark Barkworth. Father Filcock's cause is among those still under consideration.

See MMP., pp. 257–259 ; John Gerard's autobiography (tr. P. Caraman, 1951), pp. 82–86 ; and Gillow, *Biog. Dict.*

28 : MARTYRS IN THE PLAGUE OF ALEXANDRIA   (A.D. 261)

PESTILENCE raged throughout the greater part of the Roman empire during the years from 249 to 263. In Rome, five thousand persons are said to have died in one day and Alexandria in particular suffered severely : St Dionysius of Alexandria tells us that his city had already been afflicted with famine, and this was followed by tumults and violence so uncontrolled that it was safer to travel from one extremity of the known world to the other than to go from one street of Alexandria to the next.   To these scourges succeeded the plague, which raged until there was not one house in that great city that escaped or which had not some death to mourn.   Corpses lay unburied, and the air was laden with infection, mingled with pestilential vapours from the Nile.   The living appeared wild with terror, and the fear of death rendered the pagan citizens cruel to their nearest relations ; as soon as anyone was known to have caught the infection, his friends fled from him : the bodies of those not yet dead were thrown into the streets and abandoned.

At this juncture, the Christians of Alexandria came forward and displayed a great example of charity.   During the persecutions of Decius, Gallus and Valerian they had been obliged to remain hidden, and had held their assemblies in secret or in ships that put out to sea or in pestilential prisons.   Now, however, they came forth, regardless of danger, and set to work to tend the sick and to comfort the dying. They closed the eyes of the plague-stricken and carried them when dead upon their shoulders, washing their bodies and decently burying them, although they knew they were likely to share the same fate.   In the words of the bishop : " Many who had healed others fell victims themselves.   The best of our brethren have been taken from us in this manner : some were priests, others deacons and some laity of great worth.   This death, with the faith which accompanied it, appears to be little inferior to martyrdom itself."   The Roman Martyrology, recognizing the force of these words of St Dionysius, in fact honours those loving Christians as martyrs.   Their charity in thus relieving their persecutors when attacked by sickness may well make us ask ourselves what our attitude is to the sick poor, who are not our enemies but who are, in most cases, our fellow Christians.

Our knowledge of the charity of the Christians of Alexandria is derived from Eusebius, who in bk vii, ch. 22, of his *Ecclesiastical History* inserts a long quotation from the letter of St Dionysius referred to above.   The Greek text may be conveniently consulted in Feltoe's edition of *The Letters and other Remains of Dionysius of Alexandria*, pp. 79–84.

ST PROTERIUS, Patriarch of Alexandria, Martyr   (A.D. 457)

St Cyril's successor as patriarch of Alexandria was an unprincipled man named Dioscorus, who patronized the heretic Eutyches and upheld his errors.   The leader of the orthodox party was Proterius, who had been ordained by Cyril.   Dioscorus, knowing his great reputation and hoping to win him over to his views, had appointed him archpriest and entrusted him with the care of his church, but when the patriarch began to show himself to be clearly heretical, Proterius openly opposed him.   The Council of Chalcedon condemned and deposed Dioscorus in 451, and Proterius was elected in his place.   The city of Alexandria, always notorious for its riots and tumults, divided into two parties, the one demanding the return of Dioscorus and the other supporting Proterius.   The schismatic party was headed by two priests, Timothy Elurus and Peter Mongus (Elurus, $a\ddot{\imath}\lambda ov\rho os$, means " cat ", and Mongus, $\mu o\gamma\gamma \acute os$, means " croaker ").   So great and so frequent were the tumults they raised against Proterius that during the whole of his pontificate he was never out of danger of falling a victim to violence, in spite of the decision of the Council of Chalcedon and of the imperial orders.   Dioscorus being dead, Elurus, who had contrived to get himself consecrated, was proclaimed by his party the sole lawful bishop in Alexandria.   The imperial commander drove Elurus out, and this so enraged the

Eutychian party that their menaces obliged St Proterius to take sanctuary in the baptistery adjoining the church of St Quirinus. The rabble had no respect for sanctuary, and, breaking into the church, they stabbed him to death during Holy Week in the year 457. Not satisfied with this, they dragged his dead body through the streets, cut it in pieces, burnt it and scattered the ashes in the air. The bishops of Thrace, in a letter they wrote to the Emperor Leo soon after, declared that they reckoned Proterius among the martyrs and hoped to find mercy through his intercession.

There is no special biography of Proterius, but in the *Acta Sanctorum*, February, vol. iii, the principal texts, letters, etc., which make reference to him have been collected. See also Hefele-Leclercq, *Conciles*, vol. ii, p. 858.

SS. ROMANUS AND LUPICINUS, ABBOTS (*c.* A.D. 460 AND 480)

St ROMANUS had reached the age of thirty-five when he withdrew into the forests of the Jura Mountains between Switzerland and France to live there as a hermit. He took with him Cassian's *Lives of the Fathers of the Desert*, a few tools and some seeds, and found his way to an uninhabited spot at the confluence of the Bienne and the Alière, enclosed between steep heights and difficult of access. Here under the shelter of an enormous fir tree he spent his time praying, reading and cultivating the soil. At first his solitude was disturbed only by the beasts and an occasional huntsman, but before long he was joined by his brother Lupicinus and by one or two more. Other recruits soon flocked to them, including their sister and a number of women.

The two brothers soon built the monastery of Condat and then that of Leuconne, two miles to the north, whilst for the women they established the nunnery of La Beaume (the site of the present village of Saint-Romain-de-la-Roche). The brothers ruled as joint abbots in perfect harmony, although Lupicinus was inclined to be the stricter; he generally lived at Leuconne, and when at one time the brethren at Condat were making their food more palatable, he came over and forbade the innovation. Although they strove to imitate the anchorites of the East, they were obliged to modify some of their austerities owing to climatic and other differences. The Gauls were naturally great eaters, and these monks spent much of their time in very hard manual labour, but they never touched flesh-meat and were only allowed milk and eggs when they were ill. They wore wooden sabots and the skins of animals sewn together, which protected them from the rain, but not from the bitter cold in winter or from the summer rays of the sun reflected from the perpendicular rocks.

St Romanus made a pilgrimage to what is now Saint-Maurice in the Valais, to visit the place of martyrdom of the Theban Legion. He cured two lepers on the way, and, the fame of this miracle reaching Geneva, the bishop, the clergy and the whole town turned out to greet him as he was passing through. He died about the year 460, and was buried, as he had desired, in the church of the nunnery where his sister ruled. Lupicinus survived his elder brother by some twenty years, and he is commemorated separately on March 21. In the longer Latin biography the austerity of Lupicinus is much dilated on, but there are also wonderful things told of his compassion for his monks and of his spirit of faith. When starvation seemed to threaten he obtained from God by his prayers a multiplication of the corn which remained to them ; and when his subjects, yielding to temptation, planned to leave or actually quitted the monastery, he did not deal harshly with them, but was only intent on animating them with courage to persevere in their vocation.

The historical value of the Lives of Romanus, Lupicinus and Eugendus (January 1), which had gravely been called in question not only by Bruno Krusch, but also by Quesnel and Papebroch, was vindicated by Mgr Duchesne in a remarkable paper called " La Vie des Pères du Jura " in *Mélanges d'archéologie et d'histoire*, vol. xviii (1898), pp. 3–16. M. Poupardin in *Le Moyen Age*, vol. xi (1898), pp. 31–48, pronounced in a similar sense. *Cf.* M. Besson, *Nos origines chrétiennes*. The text of the Life of Romanus and Lupicinus may be found in the *Acta Sanctorum*, February, vol. iii, but it has been more recently edited by Krusch in MGH., *Scriptores Merov.*, vol. iii, pp. 131–153. In the former it has been divided into two sections, so far as it treated separately of Romanus and Lupicinus ; the latter prints the whole continuously.

ST HILARUS, POPE   (A.D. 468)

UNDER St Flavian of Constantinople on February 18 mention has been made of the ominously-named " Robber Council " held at Ephesus in 449, when the heresiarch Eutyches was upheld by rebel bishops and those who maintained orthodoxy were abused and physically maltreated, St Flavian so that he died. The legates of Pope St Leo I were powerless : they made their protest and withdrew, barely escaping with their lives. One of these legates was Hilarus, a Sardinian by birth. His letter to the Empress St Pulcheria is extant, in which he apologizes for not personally delivering to her the pope's letter after the synod, explaining that owing to the violence and intrigues of Dioscorus he could not get to Constantinople and was only just able to escape to Rome. As a votive offering for his preservation at this time he afterwards built the chapel of St John the Apostle in the baptistery of St John Lateran. Over the door may still be seen the inscription he put up there : *Liberatori suo beato Iohanni evangelistae Hilarus episcopus famulus Christi :* " Hilarus, bishop and servant of Christ, to his liberator, the blessed John the Evangelist."

On the death of Leo the Great in 461 the deacon Hilarus was elected to the pontifical chair, and he was a worthy successor to Leo. Little or nothing is known of his personal life ; but his chief work as pope seems to have been the strengthening of ecclesiastical discipline and administration in Gaul and Spain, both by curbing the excesses of individual bishops and by maintaining their rights. On one occasion he publicly rebuked the Emperor Anthemius in St Peter's for favouring teachers of unsound doctrine. Pope St Hilarus died on February 28, 468 and was buried in the church of St Laurence outside the walls of Rome, where also he had provided a library and two public baths.

Beside the notice in the *Liber Pontificalis* (Duchesne, vol. i, pp. 242–248) and the letters, which may be consulted in Thiel and in Jaffé, the Bollandists reproduce most of the relevant materials in the *Acta Sanctorum*, September, vol. iii. See also Hefele-Leclercq, *Conciles*, vol. ii ; Grisar, *Geschichte Roms und der Päpste*, pp. 323 and *passim ;* and DCB., vol. iii, pp. 72–74.

ST OSWALD OF WORCESTER, ARCHBISHOP OF YORK   (A.D. 992)

ST OSWALD, of Danish extraction, was the nephew of St Odo, Archbishop of Canterbury. He was educated by Odo and became a priest of Winchester, but he crossed over to France and took the monastic habit at Fleury.   In spite of invitations from his uncle to return to England he could not be prevailed upon to do so until he heard that the archbishop was dying, but he arrived too late to see him alive.   Oswald then joined his other uncle, Oskitell, Archbishop of York, remaining with him for some years.   Oswald's piety and great qualities attracted the attention of St Dunstan who, upon being appointed to Canterbury, recommended him to King Edgar, by whose order he was made bishop of Worcester. He at once founded a monastery of twelve monks at Westbury-on-Trym, and he subsequently built the great abbey of Ramsey on an island formed by marshes and the River Ouse in Huntingdonshire, *c.* 970.   Oswald was a great supporter of St Dunstan's plans for the revival of religion and for the spread of the monastic order. He and St Ethelwold, Bishop of Winchester, were the prelates specially charged to enforce the decree that the clergy must either live single lives or resign their cures. In his own diocesan city Oswald showed great forbearance and tact in dealing with the lax clergy of St Peter's.   Instead of removing them, he founded another church near by which was served by Benedictine monks and to which all the people soon flocked.   Seeing their church empty the clergy of St Peter decided that they also would embrace the monastic rule, and they carried out their resolution.

The saint spent much of his time in visiting his diocese, preaching without intermission and reforming abuses ; he also fostered the study of letters and encouraged learned men to come from abroad.   In the year 972, he was promoted to the see of York, but by the wish of the king and with the pope's sanction he retained Worcester, and although he divided his time between the two dioceses, Worcester remained the place of his predilection, and he loved to worship with the monks in the monastery church of St Mary which he had founded and which became the cathedral of Worcester.   Every day St Oswald used to wash the feet of twelve poor persons whom he afterwards fed at his own table.   On February 29, 992 he had just wiped and kissed the feet of the last poor man and was yet on his knees, saying, " Glory be to the Father and to the Son and to the Holy Ghost ", when he gently passed away.   As his body was being borne to burial at Worcester it was noticed that a white dove was hovering over it.   St Oswald's feast is observed in the archdiocese of Birmingham.

There are several early lives of St Oswald, the more valuable of which have been edited by James Raine for the Rolls Series in the first and second volumes of his *Historians of the Church of York*.   The earliest biography there printed must have been written by a monk of Ramsey between 995 and 1005, shortly after the saint's death.   See also Stanton, *Menology*, pp. 89–91, from which we may learn that St Oswald's name is entered under this day in a considerable number of medieval English calendars, and D. Knowles, *The Monastic Order in England* (1949), pp. 40–56 and *passim*.

BD ANGELA OF FOLIGNO, Widow   (A.D. 1309)

ANGELA of Foligno must always take her place among the great mystics and contemplatives of the middle ages, side by side with Catherine of Siena and Catherine of Genoa.   She has a very marked and distinct individuality of her own, and presents an unusual type of the great Franciscan revival which influenced central Italy so strongly.   She seems in many ways the opposite to her great spiritual father, St Francis.   His life was *action*, Angela's was *thought, vision* ;   Francis saw God in all His creatures—Angela saw all creatures in God ;   but the underlying principle is the same, namely, joyful love.

Very little is known of Bd Angela's history—not even her surname.* The date of her birth must have been about 1248, and she belonged to a good family of Foligno, where she was born and lived She was married to a rich man and was the mother of several sons.   In her early life she was careless and worldly ; indeed, according to her own account, her life was not only pleasure-seeking and self-indulgent, but actually sinful.   Then suddenly about 1285 there came to her the vision of the True Light, the call to a love full of fruitful suffering, to the peace of greater and more living joys than any on earth.   It was a sudden, vivid conversion, a conversion of her whole point of view, impetuous, painful, joyous.   The life she had thought harmless, even if without any higher aim, she now saw in its true perspective, as sinful, and from this conviction of sin was born in her a craving for penance, suffering, renunciation—renunciation complete and joyful, that has lost all to find all, the victorious faith of her great model, St Francis, whose third order she eventually joined.

For some time after her conversion she continued outwardly her life in the world.   Then gradually all ties were broken.   Her mother, to whom she was much attached, though, perhaps naturally, she hindered her in her new life, died ; then before long her husband ; and finally her sons, and though her biographer exults over the providence displayed in thus removing all hindrances to her spiritual ascent, she was herself not inhuman, and Brother Arnold tells us how cruelly she suffered as blow after blow fell upon her.   Still, her conversion had been so complete, so violent, that all things, joy or sorrow, as with St Francis, were but one, a living unity.   For these early Franciscans nothing existed but the love of God.

What little we know of Angela's life is told us mostly by Brother Arnold, a Friar Minor, who was her confessor and who prevailed upon her to dictate the account of her visions to him.†   He tells us that after a time she gave up all her possessions, selling last of all a " castle " which she loved very much.   That this sacrifice was asked of her had been revealed in a vision, in which she was told that if she would be perfect she must follow St Francis in his absolute poverty.   Arnold tells us pathetically how, time after time, when he read over to her what he had written, she exclaimed that he had misunderstood her and given quite a wrong meaning to her words.   At other times she would cry out that when her visions were put into words they were blasphemous, and Arnold warns us not to be scandalized at the heights of ecstasy to which Angela rises, and adds that the greater her ecstasy the deeper was her humility.   For instance, when she says she has been raised " for ever " to a new state of light and joy, she does not speak in any spirit of over-confidence or spiritual pride.   She simply tells us that her state is one of continual progress, that she is entering into a new light, a new sense of God, a solitude which she has not yet inhabited.

She gathered round her a family of tertiaries, both men and women.   We hear from Brother Arnold that she had one special companion, " una vergine Cristiana ", who lived with her and who was evidently not exempt from human respect, for

---

* Father Ferré is able to tell us from his examination of the Assisi manuscript that she was known among her family and intimates as " Lella ", but this was probably only a pet name derived from Angela.

† Later research has shown that the third of the three sections into which the manuscript is divided cannot, as was previously supposed, have been written or edited by Brother Arnold.

when she and Angela were walking from Foligno, perhaps climbing the heights to Spello or Assisi, or going along that wonderful plain of Umbria to Rivotorto or Santa Maria degli Angeli, Angela would fall into ecstasy, her face shining and her eyes burning. The companion became much embarrassed and, thinking to set a good example, covered her own head, imploring Angela to do the same, telling her that her eyes were like lamps. " Hide yourself—what will people say of you ? Hide yourself from the eyes of men." " Never mind," said Angela, " if we meet anyone God will take care of us." Arnold adds that the companion had to accustom herself to such episodes as Angela's states of ecstasy occurred at any moment.

One Holy Thursday she said to the companion, " Let us go and look for Christ our Lord. We will go to the hospital and perhaps amongst the sick and suffering we shall find Him." She could not go empty-handed, and the only things they possessed were their veils for covering their heads on which the companion set such store. These Angela hastily sold to buy food to take to the hospital, " and so we offered food to these poor sick people, and then we washed the feet of the women, and the men's hands, as they lay lonely and forsaken on their wretched pallets— more especially was a poor leper much consoled ", and great was the joy and sweetness they experienced on their way home, and so they found the Lord Christ on this Maundy Thursday. And so this strange life of great simplicity and of such overwhelming spiritual experience ran its course, and at the end of 1308 she knew that death was near. She had all her spiritual children assembled and laid her hand in blessing on the head of each, leaving them as her last will and testament words of wonderful confidence and assurance. Bd Angela died happily and in great peace on January 4, 1309.

We have one other detail of her outer life. Ubertino di Casale entered the Order of Friars Minor in 1273. For fourteen years his life was zealous and exemplary. He was a man of great learning, and these years were spent in various universities. He then fell away grievously into carelessness and sin. He tells us he made Angela's acquaintance in a wonderful manner which he does not relate, and that she revealed to him his most secret thoughts, " God speaking through her ", as he says, and that she brought him back to a holy life. He adds that he was only one of a large family of spiritual children who owed the life of their souls to her.

Though so little is known of her outer life, she has revealed her inner life very fully. " I, called Angela of Foligno, walking in the path of penance, made eighteen spiritual steps before I knew all the imperfection of my life." These eighteen steps begin with the consciousness of sin, then, through the shame of confession, to the mercy of God, to self-knowledge, to the cross of Christ. At the ninth step, " the way to the cross ", she discards her rich clothing, her delicate food, but this is all still done very much against the grain, for she is not yet really controlled by divine love. At the tenth step comes the vision of Jesus Christ, which is granted to her in answer to her prayer : " What can I do to please thee ? " The vision of Christ and His passion reveals to her the smallness of all her sufferings, and she tells us that she wept so continuously and so bitterly that she had to bathe her eyes for a long time with cold water. After the vision of the Cross she knows true penitence, and she decides on a life of absolute poverty. So one by one she climbs her steps. She learns more and more of the Passion. God Himself through the Lord's Prayer teaches her to pray. She finds what graces come from our Blessed Lady, and at the eighteenth step she says that she realizes God most vividly, and so delights in prayer that she forgets to eat. At this stage she sells her much-loved castle.

Angela tells us that she has dwelt in two abysses, of height and of depth. Now, after the eighteenth step, she is hurled from the abyss of height and we have a terrible chapter telling of her temptations. She seems to herself to be stripped of every good wish or thought. She is tried by the most horrible sensual temptations, haunted by longings for sins of which she had never heard. At last the light broke through and she had a short reprieve. What she calls the next abyss was the temptation to false humility, great self-consciousness and scrupulosity. She wanted to tear off her clothes and run about the town naked, with fish and meat hung round her neck, crying out, " This is a most vile woman who stinks of evil and falsehood, who spreads vice and sin wherever she goes. Yes, that is what I am—a humbug. I pretend I eat no fish or meat, and really I am a glutton and a drunkard. I pretend I wear common rough clothing, but at night I sleep under the softest coverings, which I hide in the morning." She implored the Friars Minor and her tertiaries to believe these self-accusations. At last she was delivered from this curse of false humility only to fall into the other extreme of great spiritual pride. She was filled with anger, bitterness, ill-nature. This state of torment began in 1294 and lasted more than two years. At last her poor tortured soul was lifted out of this abyss of darkness and she was comforted with a vision of God as the highest good, and more and more, as her life proceeded, she was filled with great joy and happiness —that joy which was the keynote of the early Franciscan life. Over and over again in her visions she is shown the love and goodness and kindness of God ; more and more she grasps the underlying principle that St Francis taught, which binds all things together and " makes of all things one "—namely, love. When she is in the state of love everything that could be said about God or the life of Christ in Holy Scripture would only be a hindrance—she is " in God " and reads much greater and incomparable words. When she comes to herself after this experience she is so peaceful and happy that she says she is full of love " even for the devils ". She is so lost in love that not even the passion of our Lord can sadden her—all is joy. Sometimes the soul contemplates the human flesh of God which died for us, at other times joyful love wipes out all the sorrow of the Passion. " Therefore ", she concludes, " the Passion is to me only a shining path of life."

A large part of the book of visions is taken up with these wonderful, vivid, but always restrained descriptions of every detail of Christ's passion and crucifixion. More and more she rises above the pain and suffering in the spirit of her Lord Himself, " who for the joy set before Him endured the cross and despised the shame ". She tells us that assisting at a representation of the Passion (apparently a kind of mystery play) in the open air she was so overcome with this spirit of joy that she seemed to herself to be taken up and hidden in the shining wound of the side of Christ. Wonderful favours and visions were granted her at Mass and holy communion. One of the last recorded visions is *Peace*. Something had disturbed her and she had lost her joy and peace. At last God spoke to her and told her she was favoured above anyone in the valley of Spoleto. Her soul cried out, Why, then, did God desert her ? The answer was that she must trust more and more, and gradually peace returned to her, greater than she had ever known.

The book concludes with a vision she calls the path of salvation, in which she speaks of the blessedness of those who know God, not by what He gives, but by

what He is in Himself.   " ' Lord ', she cried, ' tell me what thou dost want of me ;
I am all thine.'   But there was no answer, and I prayed from Matins till Terce—
then I saw and heard."   There was an abyss of light—an abyss in which the truth
of God was spread out like a road on which those passed who went to Him and those
also who turned away from Him, and the voice of God said to me, " In truth the
only way of salvation is to follow my footsteps from the cross on earth to this light ".
Here the divine Word became clearer and more distinct, and the path was bathed
in light and splendour as far as the eye could reach.

We know very little about Bd Angela of Foligno apart from her own disclosures regarding
herself.   These are printed in the *Acta Sanctorum* for January 4, and they were re-edited
by Boccolini in the eighteenth century, and by Faloci-Pulignani from 1899.   An Italian
arrangement of the same materials had appeared in 1536, of which there is an English rendering by Mary G. Steegman, which was published under the title *The Book of the Divine
Consolation of Bd Angela of Foligno* (1909).   But a re-editing of the sources was highly
desirable (*cf.* the article " Les œuvres authentiques d'Angèle de Foligno " in the *Revue
d'histoire franciscaine*, July, 1924) ; this was done from MS. 342 in the municipal library at
Assisi by Fr P. Doncœur, text (1925) and French translation (1926), and by Fr M. J. Ferré
(text and translation, 1927).   See also L. Lecléve, *Ste Angèle de Foligno* (1936) ; and Fr
Doncœur's bibliography in the *Revue d'ascétique et de mystique*, July, 1925.   The *cultus* of
Bd Angela has been approved by Pope Innocent XII and other pontiffs (she is sometimes
called Saint).

BD VILLANA OF FLORENCE, MATRON   (A.D. 1360)

BD VILLANA was the daughter of Andrew de' Botti, a Florentine merchant, and was
born in 1332.   When she was thirteen she ran away from home to enter a convent,
but her attempts were unsuccessful and she was forced to return.   To prevent any
repetition of her flight, her father shortly afterwards gave her in marriage to Rosso
di Piero.   After her marriage she appeared completely changed : she gave herself
up to pleasure and dissipation and lived a wholly idle and worldly life.   One day,
as she was about to start for an entertainment clad in a gorgeous dress adorned with
pearls and precious stones, she looked at herself in a mirror.   To her dismay the
reflection that met her eyes was that of a hideous demon.   A second and a third
mirror showed the same ugly form.   Thoroughly alarmed and recognizing in the
reflection the image of her sin-stained soul, she tore off her fine attire and, clad in
the simplest clothes she could find, she betook herself weeping to the Dominican
fathers at Santa Maria Novella to make a full confession and to ask absolution
and help.   This proved the turning point of her life, and she never again fell
away.
      Ere long Villana was admitted to the third order of St Dominic, and after this
she advanced rapidly in the spiritual life.   Fulfilling all her duties as a married
woman, she spent all her available time in prayer and reading.   She particularly
loved to study St Paul's epistles and the lives of the saints.   At one time, in her
self-abasement and in her love for the poor, she would have gone begging for them
from door to door had not her husband and parents interposed.   So completely
did she give herself up to God that she was often rapt in ecstasy, particularly during
Mass or at spiritual conferences ; but she had to pass through a period of persecution when she was cruelly calumniated and her honour was assailed.   Her soul
was also purified by strange pains and by great bodily weakness.   However, she
passed unscathed through all these trials and was rewarded by wonderful visions
and colloquies with our Lady and other saints.   Occasionally the room in which

she dwelt was filled with supernatural light, and she was also endowed with the gift of prophecy. As she lay on her deathbed she asked that the Passion should be read to her, and at the words " He bowed His head and gave up the ghost ", she crossed her hands on her breast and passed away. Her body was taken to Santa Maria Novella, where it became such an object of veneration that for over a month it was impossible to proceed with the funeral. People struggled to obtain shreds of her clothing, and she was honoured as a saint from the day of her death. Her bereaved husband used to say that, when he felt discouraged and depressed, he found strength by visiting the room in which his beloved wife had died. Bd Villana's *cultus* was confirmed in 1824.

See the *Acta Sanctorum* for August 26 (Aug. vol. v) ; Procter, *Lives of Dominican Saints*, pp. 50–52 ; M. C. Ganay, *Les Bienheureuses Dominicaines*, pp. 153–175.

BD HEDWIG OF POLAND, MATRON   (A.D. 1399)

THERE are two Hedwigs (Jadwiga) of royal blood, both of whom Butler commemorates on the same day (October 17). The younger of these, whose claim to liturgical celebration is not clearly made out, seems to be honoured in her own country on the last day of February with a popular *cultus*. The cause of her beatification was indeed introduced, but it has never been prosecuted to a successful issue. She was born in 1371, and was the youngest daughter of Louis, nephew and successor to Casimir III, King of Poland. After his death in 1382 it was pressed upon Hedwig as a religious duty to accept for a husband the still pagan Jagiello, Duke of Lithuania. Diplomatically such an alliance seemed most advantageous for Poland and the Church, as the duke was not only willing in view of the marriage to accept Christianity himself, but promised that all his people should become Christians also. Hedwig, child as she still was in years (she was then thirteen), had to make a decision according to her conscience. A sympathetic pen in modern times has given this account of her surrender :

> Covering herself with a thick black veil she proceeded on foot to the cathedral of Cracow, and repairing to one of the side chapels, threw herself on her knees, where for three hours with clasped hands and streaming eyes she wrestled with the repugnance that surged within her. At length she rose with a detached heart, having laid at the foot of the cross her affections, her will, her hopes of earthly happiness ; offering herself, and all that belonged to her, as a perpetual holocaust to her crucified Redeemer, and esteeming herself happy, if so by this sacrifice she might purchase the salvation of those precious souls for whom He had shed His blood. Before leaving the chapel she cast her veil over the crucifix, hoping under that pall to bury all human infirmity that might still linger round her heart, and then hastened to establish a foundation for the perpetual renewal of this type of her soul's sorrow. This foundation yet exists ; within the same chapel the crucifix still stands, covered by its sable drapery, being commonly known as the " crucifix of Hedwig ".

Jagiello seems to have been sincere. He received baptism, together with the new name of Ladislaus, and we read strange stories of the " conversion " of the Lithuanian people—how the temples of the false gods were destroyed wholesale, and how men, women and children drawn up in platoons, " were sprinkled [for their baptism] by the bishops and priests, every division receiving the same name."

All through the troubled years which followed, Hedwig was the most stable as well as the most judicious element in the government of the kingdom.   She exercised a moderating influence upon the policy of her husband, she came to the rescue of the poor suffering people, who too often had to pay the penalty for the mistakes or the selfishness of their rulers, she won the love of her subjects by her gentleness and boundless charity, and yet she showed that she could defend herself with dignity against Ladislaus's irrational outbursts of jealousy.   It was only in her asceticism that she seemed to forget the need of a measure of prudence.   But she was conscientious in all wifely duties, and her husband beyond doubt regarded her with deep affection as well as with a certain feeling of awe.   When at last there was promise of an heir to the throne he was extravagant in the preparations he wished made.   From the frontier where he was conducting a campaign he wrote about providing jewels and rich draperies.   Hedwig replied   " Seeing that I have so long renounced the pomps of this world, it is not on that treacherous couch—to so many the bed of death—that I would willingly be surrounded by their glitter.   It is not by the help of gold or gems that I hope to render myself acceptable to that Almighty Father who has mercifully removed from me the reproach of barrenness, but rather by resignation to His will and a sense of my own nothingness."   Humanly speaking, she was not altogether wise in her use of penance and prayer.   On the anniversary of her great renunciation she went out unattended to make a vigil in the cathedral before the veiled crucifix.   Her ladies-in-waiting found her there, hours later, rapt in ecstasy or possibly in a swoon.   Not long afterwards the birth of a daughter, who lived only a few days, cost the mother her life.   It was believed that many miracles were wrought at her tomb.

See the *Dublin Review*, October, 1864, pp. 311–343 ; A. B. C. Dunbar, *Dictionary of Saintly Women*, vol. i, pp. 366–369 ; H. Sienkiewicz, *Knights of the Cross*, ch. 4 ; and the *Cambridge History of Poland*, vol. i (1950), for the historical background of the marriage that united Poland and Lithuania for 400 years.

BD ANTONIA OF FLORENCE, WIDOW (A.D. 1472)

THE town of Aquila in the Abruzzi contains the relics of three distinguished Franciscans—St Bernardino of Siena, Bd Vincent of Aquila and Bd Antonia of Florence.   Antonia married whilst still quite young, lost her husband after a few years and, desiring after her widowhood to consecrate herself to God, she resisted the efforts of her relations who wished her to marry again.   When in 1429 Bd Angelina of Marsciano sent two of her religious to found in Florence the fifth of her convents of regular tertiaries of St Francis, Antonia was one of the first to enter the new house.   The following year the superioress of the Observance, who recognized her exceptional merits and powers, transferred her to Foligno and placed her in charge of the convent of St Anne, which was the original house founded by Bd Angelina.   Here Antonia had the privilege of being under the immediate direction of the foundress.   Three years later she was sent to rule a recently established community at Aquila, and once again she set the example of a holy life poured forth in acts of charity.   Bd Angelina died the second year after Antonia had gone to Aquila, and she lost another of her chief supports in the person of St Bernardino of Siena, who died in 1444 at Aquila.

When St John Capistran visited the town, Antonia told him that she desired a stricter rule, and he so fully sympathized with her wishes that he obtained for her the monastery of Corpus Christi, which had just been built for another order, and thither she retired in 1447 with eleven of her nuns to practise the original rule of St Clare in all its rigour.   Girls gave up brilliant prospects to join her and the convent soon had to be enlarged to contain the hundred or more nuns who sang the divine praises day and night.   Humility and patience were the outstanding qualities of Bd Antonia, who for fifteen years bore uncomplainingly a most painful disease, and in her spiritual life had to undergo severe trials.   Her son was nothing but a trouble to her : he dissipated his whole fortune, and he and her other relations used to come and worry her with their quarrels and affairs.   It was also a great blow to her when the Franciscans of Aquila, to whom St John Capistran had entrusted the care of the convent, gave up the direction of the nuns ; but they subsequently resumed the spiritual guidance of the community.   She was a true daughter of St Francis in her love for poverty, which she called the Queen of the House.   She was full of tenderness to her spiritual daughters, and when after seven years she resigned her office, she retained the affection and veneration of the whole community.   Bd Antonia at times was seen to be in ecstasy and upraised from the ground, and once a fiery globe appeared to rest upon her head and to light up the place in which she prayed.   When she died in 1472 the bishop, magistrates and people of Aquila insisted on conducting her funeral with great solemnity at the public charge.   Her cult was confirmed in 1847.

See Léon, *Auréole Séraphique* (Eng. trans.), vol.   pp. 36–40 ; Mazzara, *Leggendario Francescano*, vol. i, pp. 287–289.

BD LOUISA ALBERTONI, Widow   (A.D. 1533)

Louisa's (Lodovica) father, Stephen Albertoni, and her mother, Lucrezia Tebaldi, belonged to distinguished Roman families.   She was born in 1473, and lost her father while yet an infant.   Her mother married again, and Louisa was brought up first by her grandmother, and then by two of her aunts ; and she was induced by family influence to marry James de Cithara, a young man of noble family and great wealth.   She bore him three daughters and lived with him on terms of deep affection, but he died in 1506.   Becoming in this way her own mistress, Louisa gave herself up almost entirely to prayer, assuming finally the habit of the third order of St Francis.   Her contemplation of the Passion was so uninterrupted, and the devotion with which she called to mind the sufferings of our Lord so intense, that she is said to have nearly lost her sight by the tears in which these hours of prayer were spent.   What remained of her time was given to the service of the sick and the poor, and to visiting the seven great basilicas of Rome.   She lived in the deepest poverty, her whole fortune expended in alleviating the distress of those around her.

The methods of relief which her humility adopted were often somewhat original, as when, for example, she baked a great batch of bread to be distributed at random to the poor, putting into the loaves gold and silver coins of different values, and praying at the same time that the largest alms might providentially find their way to those who most needed help.   Louisa in fact stripped herself so generously of all she possessed that the time came when she had nothing left to give : her relatives supplied her with her daily food, but she kept little even of this for herself.   In these last years of her life she enjoyed profound peace of soul and was constantly rapt in ecstasy, during which times, as we are told by her biographers, she was not seldom raised physically from the ground.   She fell asleep in the Lord on January 31, 1533, as she repeated, like her Divine Master, the words " Father, into thy hands I commend my spirit ".   Many miracles are said to have taken place when her body lay in the church awaiting burial, and afterwards at her tomb.   Her *cultus* was confirmed in 1671.

See G. Paolo, *Vita della B. Lodovica Albertoni* (1672) ; Léon, *Auréole Séraphique* (Eng. trans.), vol. i, pp. 127-132 ; B. Mazzara, *Leggendario Francescano* (1676), vol. i, pp. 145-155.

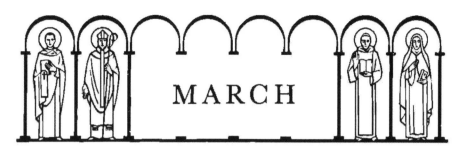

MARCH

1 : ST DAVID, OR DEWI, BISHOP IN MYNYW, PATRON OF WALES (A.D. 589 ?)

IT is certainly unfortunate that we have no early history of St David (as we anglicize his name Dewi), the patron of Wales and perhaps the most celebrated of British saints. All the accounts preserved to us are based on the biography written about 1090 by Rhygyfarch (Ricemarch), son of Bishop Sulien of Saint Davids. Rhygyfarch was a learned man and his claim to have drawn on old written sources is probably justified ; but he was concerned to uphold the fabulous primacy of the see of Saint Davids and he appears incapable of distinguishing historical facts from the wildest fables.

According to the legend David was the son of Sant, of princely family in Ceredigion, and of St Non (March 3), grand-daughter of Brychan of Brecknock ; and he was born perhaps about the year 520. " The place where holy David was educated ", says Rhygyfarch, " was called Vetus Rubus [Henfynyw in Cardigan] and he grew up full of grace and lovely to behold. And there it was that holy David learnt the alphabet, the psalms, the lessons for the whole year and the divine office ; and there his fellow disciples saw a dove with a golden beak playing at his lips and teaching him to sing the praise of God." Ordained priest in due course, he afterwards retired to study for several years under the Welsh St Paulinus, who lived on an island which has not been identified. He is said to have restored sight to his master, who had become blind through much weeping. Upon emerging from the monastery, David seems to have embarked upon a period of great activity, the details of which, however, are at least for the most part pure invention. To quote again from his biographer : " He founded twelve monasteries to the glory of God : first, upon arriving at Glastonbury, he built a church there ; then he came to Bath, and there, causing deadly water to become healing by a blessing, he endowed it with perpetual heat, rendering it fit for people to bathe in ; afterwards he came to Croyland and to Repton ; then to Colfan and Glascwm, and he had with him a two-headed altar ; after that he founded the monastery of Leominster. Afterwards, in the region of Gwent, in a place that is called Raglan, he built a church ; then he founded a monastery in a place which is called Llangyfelach in the region of Gower." Finally, and here we are on surer ground, he settled in the extreme south-west corner of Wales, at Mynyw (Menevia), with a number of disciples and founded the principal of his many abbeys.

The community lived a life of extreme austerity. Hard manual labour was obligatory for all, and they were allowed no cattle to relieve them in tilling the ground. They might never speak without necessity, and they never ceased praying mentally, even when at work. Their food was bread, with vegetables and salt, and they drank only water, sometimes mingled with a little milk. For this reason

St David was surnamed " The Waterman ", as being the head of those strictly teetotal ascetic Welsh monks whom St Gildas criticized as being sometimes more abstemious than Christian, and whose aim was to reproduce the lives of the hermits of the Thebaïd. When any outsider wished to join them, he had to wait at the gate for ten days and be subjected to harsh words ere he could be admitted. Always from Friday evening until dawn on Sunday a strict vigil was kept and prayer was maintained uninterruptedly, with only one hour's repose, on the Saturday after Matins.

We are told that a synod was held at Brefi in Cardigan to suppress the Pelagian heresy, which was springing up in Britain for the second time. There is, however, no trace of any preoccupation about Pelagianism in the decrees which were said to have been passed by the assembly. St David was invited to attend, but was unwilling to go until St Deiniol and St Dubricius came in person to fetch him. At the synod David is said to have spoken with such grace and eloquence as to silence his opponents completely, and he was thereupon unanimously elected primate of the Cambrian church, Dubricius having resigned in his favour. St David was obliged to accept, but he did so on condition that the episcopal seat should be transferred from Caerleon to Mynyw—now Saint Davids—a quiet and solitary place.

An extraordinary story, fabricated presumably to demonstrate the imaginary metropolitan status of Saint Davids, represents David as having made a pilgrimage to the Holy Land, where he was consecrated archbishop by the patriarch of Jerusalem. He is alleged to have called at Caerleon another council, known as the Synod of Victory, because it was said to mark the extirpation of Pelagianism in Britain. It ratified the decrees of Brefi and also a code of rules which had been drawn up for the regulation of the British church. Giraldus, in his paraphrase of Rhygyfarch, adds " The decrees of these two synods which Bishop David had promulgated by word of mouth, he also committed to writing with his own sacred hand, and commanded them to be kept for his own church and several others throughout Wales. But, like many other excellent treasures of his noble library, they have disappeared owing to age and negligence, and also in the frequent attacks of pirates who, arriving in summer-time in ships of war from the Orkney Islands, had been wont to lay waste the maritime provinces of Wales." Of St David himself Giraldus tells us that he was the great ornament and example of his age and that he continued to rule his diocese until he was a very old man. At his death, which, according to Geoffrey of Monmouth, took place in his monastery at Mynyw, St Kentigern at Llanelwy saw his soul borne to Heaven by angels. His last words to his monks and neighbours are recorded as, " Be joyful, brothers and sisters. Keep your faith, and do the little things that you have seen and heard with me." His body was subsequently translated from the monastery church to Saint Davids cathedral, where the empty tomb is still shown. It is said that the relics werere moved to Glastonbury, but they were apparently at Saint Davids in 1346.

In art St David is represented standing on a mound with a dove on his shoulder in allusion to the legend that when he was speaking at Brefi, a snow-white dove descended upon his shoulder, whilst at the same time the earth on which he stood rose up to form a hill, from the summit of which his voice could be heard like a trumpet by the whole assembly. In Shakespeare's *Henry V* allusion is made to the practice of Welshmen wearing leeks on St David's day, and it is called " an ancient tradition begun upon an honourable respect ", but no adequate explanation of the usage is forthcoming. There is no mention of leeks in St David's life. Pope Callistus II is said to have approved the cult of St David about the year 1120 and to have granted an indulgence to those who should visit his shrine—" two visits to Menevia being reckoned equal to one visit to Rome "—but this is doubtful. There can, however, be no question that he was a highly popular saint in his own country. More than fifty pre-Reformation churches in South Wales are known to have been dedicated in his honour. Moreover, even in England, Archbishop Arundel in 1398 ordered his feast to be kept in every church throughout the province of Canterbury. His feast is now observed in Wales and in the dioceses of Westminster and Portsmouth.

The earliest surviving mention of St David's name occurs in the *Catalogue of Saints of Ireland* (*c.* 730?) and in the *Martyrology of Oengus* (*c.* 800), but no details are added. The text of Rhygyfarch's Life has been accurately edited by A. W. Wade-Evans in *Y Cymmrodor*, vol. xxiv, and the same scholar has published a translation in English, abundantly annotated, together with some other relevant documents, in the *Life of St David* (1923) ; the Latin text is printed also in his *Vitae Sanctorum Britanniae* (1944). The adaptation of Rhygyfarch by Giraldus Cambrensis may be found in vol. iii of his works in the Rolls Series. See also LBS., vol. ii, pp. 285–322 ; J. E. Lloyd, *History of Wales* (1939), vol. i, pp. 152–159 ; S. M. Harris, *St David in the Liturgy* (1940) ; J. Barrett Davies in *Blackfriars*, vol. xxix (1948), pp. 121–126. For David's influence on the Irish church, see J. Ryan, *Irish Monasticism* (1931), pp. 113–114, 160–164 and *passim* ; and on the alleged canonization, *Analecta Bollandiana*, vol. xlix (1931), pp. 211–213. An extremely full bibliography of all materials relating to St David has been published by Wyndham Morgan in connection with the Cardiff Public Library. See also the very beautiful volume printed at the Gregynog Press in 1927, Ernest Rhys, *The Life of St David ;* and Diana Latham, *The Story of St David* (1952).

ST FELIX II (III), POPE   (A.D. 492)

ACCORDING to the Roman Martyrology this Pope Felix was an ancestor (great-great-grandfather) of Pope St Gregory the Great ; it recalls Gregory's statement that when his aunt, St Tharsilla, lay dying, Felix appeared in vision and summoned her to Heaven. The martyrology calls him Felix III, through the long-standing but erroneous numeration of the antipope Felix as Pope St Felix II (see July 29).

Little certain is known about him personally, but he was a straightforward, courageous Roman of the type of Leo I, and he has his place in general church history in connection with the monophysite troubles. In 482 the Emperor Zeno published a document called the *Henotikon*, which had been devised by the patriarch of Constantinople, Acacius, to placate the dissenting monophysites by ignoring the decisions of the Council of Chalcedon. Two years later St Felix held a synod at the Lateran and excommunicated Acacius and his supporters for a betrayal of the Catholic faith. St Felix thus appears in the common role of the Roman pontiffs as an upholder of an oecumenical council against the secular power, while much of the East meekly accepted the emperor's " line ". But the resulting " Acacian schism " unhappily lasted for thirty-five years, and helped to pave the way for the eventual separation of the Byzantine church.

In the west, Felix helped in the restoration of the African church after its long persecution by the Arian Vandals. He died in 492 after a pontificate of nearly nine years, and his feast is kept in Rome.

See Duchesne's edition of the *Liber pontificalis*, vol. i, pp. 252–253 ; DCB., vol. ii, pp. 482–485, s.v. Felix III ; and works of general ecclesiastical history.

ST ALBINUS, or AUBIN, Bishop of Angers   (*c.* A.D. 550)

THE great popularity of St Aubin appears to be due, not so much to his career, which presents no remarkable features, as to the many miracles attributed to him not only during his life but more particularly after his death.   His *cultus* spread over France, Italy, Spain, Germany and even to distant Poland, and he became the titular patron of an immense number of French parishes.   Born in the diocese of Vannes in Brittany, the saint belonged to a family said to have originally come from England or Ireland.   While still young he entered the monastery of Tincillac, about which little is known, and there he led a life of great devotion.   At the age of about thirty-five he was elected abbot, and, under his rule, the house flourished exceedingly and became a garden of virtues.   Consequently, when the see of Angers fell vacant in 529 the clergy and citizens of Angers turned their eyes to Aubin.   Greatly against his will, but much to the joy of the bishop of Rennes, St Melanius, he was appointed bishop of Angers and proved himself a capable and enlightened pastor.

St Aubin preached daily, and whilst always generous to the sick and needy he was specially concerned with helping poor widows who were struggling to bring up large families.   The ransoming of slaves was another good work very dear to his heart, and he spent large sums of money in buying back prisoners who had been carried off in the numerous raids of the barbarians.   Tradition says that one of these captives was ransomed, not from the pirates, but from King Childebert himself.   This was a lovely girl called Etheria upon whom the monarch had cast eyes.   He caused her to be carried off from her home and imprisoned in a fortress. As soon as this came to the ears of the bishop, he went to the castle to demand her release, and such was the respect he inspired that the guards delivered her up at once.   The legend adds that one soldier tried to detain the maiden and used threats and violence, but St Aubin breathed upon him and he fell down dead.   The king made no further attempt to recapture the girl, but was undignified enough to demand a ransom which, we are told, was paid by the saint.   Whether or not there is any truth in the story, it is certain that King Childebert had a great veneration for the bishop, but in other quarters he was very unpopular because of the energy with which he enforced the decrees of the Councils of Orleans in 538 and 541 against incestuous marriages.

St Aubin was credited with very many miracles.   Besides numerous cases of the healing of the sick and the restoration of sight to the blind, we read of a youth called Alabald who was raised from the dead by his intercession.   Once, after he had pleaded in vain with a judge to release some criminals, a great stone fell during the night from the prison wall and thus enabled the prisoners to regain their liberty. They immediately came to seek the saint and assured him that they would in future lead reformed lives.

The principal source for the life of St Albinus is a short biography by Venantius Fortunatus, the most critical text of which is to be found in MGH., *Auctores antiquissimi*, vol. iv, " opera pedestria ", pp. 27–33.   His name is entered in the " Hieronymianum ", and St Gregory of Tours refers to the *cultus* paid to him.   See Duchesne, *Fastes Épiscopaux*, vol. ii, pp. 347–349, 353–354 ; DHG., vol. v. cc. 254–255 ; and the *Acta Sanctorum*, March, vol. i.

ST SWITHBERT, Bishop   (A.D. 713)

ST SWITHBERT (Suidbert) was one of a band of twelve missionaries who, headed by St Willibrord, started in 690 to evangelize the pagans of Friesland.   A

Northumbrian by birth, and brought up as a monk near the Scottish border, Swithbert, like so many other Englishmen of his period, had crossed over to Ireland in search of higher perfection. Here he had come under the direction and influence of St Egbert, who, though long consumed with zeal for the conversion of Lower Germany, had been restrained by divine command when he prepared a ship and was on the point of embarking in person. His place had then been taken by his disciple and devoted friend St Wigbert, but the mission was a complete failure, and after labouring for two years Wigbert returned home. Egbert, however, refused to be discouraged and never slackened in his appeal for volunteers, until he succeeded in collecting and training this second mission which he despatched. By this time the conditions had become much more favourable. The missionaries landed at the mouth of the Rhine and, according to Alcuin, made their way as far as Utrecht, where they set to work to preach and to teach.

Swithbert laboured mainly in Hither Friesland, which comprised the southern part of Holland, the northern portion of Brabant and the provinces of Guelderland and Cleves. His efforts were successful and multitudes were converted to the faith by his eloquence and zeal. His fellow labourers pressed him to obtain consecration that he might the better preside over his converts, and he returned to England for that purpose and also probably to collect more workers. There in 693 he was consecrated regionary bishop by St Wilfrid who, banished from his own see of York, was preaching the faith in Mercia. Bede tells us that this took place at the time when the see of Canterbury was still vacant after the death of St Theodore, and doubtless St Swithbert was well known to St Wilfrid, who hailed from his own country of Northumbria. The newly appointed bishop then returned to his flock, but did not long remain with them—possibly because Pepin of Herstal was not satisfied at his election, but more likely simply to extend the missionary field. After settling the churches he had founded, he left them in the care of St Willibrord and his companions and penetrated further into the country, up the right bank of the Rhine, where he converted to the faith a considerable number of the Boructuari, who inhabited the district between the Ems and the Lippe. A few years later, however, the Saxons invaded the country, which they devastated and occupied, and the saint, finding his work undone, withdrew into Frankish territory where he resolved to retire from the world and prepare his soul for death. Pepin, at the request of his wife Plectrudis, bestowed upon him a small island in the Rhine where he built a monastery which flourished for many years. Round this monastery grew up the town of Kaiserswerth, six miles north of Düsseldorf, but it is now united to the mainland, a channel of the Rhine having changed its course.

St Swithbert died in his abbey about the year 713, and has ever since been held in great veneration in Holland and the other places where he laboured. He is joint patron of St Peter's, Kaiserswerth, where his relics, which were found in 1626 in a silver shrine, are still preserved and honoured. Many miracles were ascribed to him and he is appealed to as a patron against angina. He is sometimes spoken of as St Swithbert the Elder, to distinguish him from St Swithbert the Younger, Bishop of Werden, with whom he was formerly often confused. One very interesting memorial of St Swithbert which still survives is a manuscript of Livy now preserved in Vienna. This codex of fifth-century date seems to have belonged to him, for it bears his name and he is described in it as bishop of Dorostat, now Wijk-bij-Duurstede on the Rhine.

The principal source for the life of St Swithbert is Bede's *Ecclesiastical History* (bk v, chs. 9–11) with Plummer's notes, but see also Alcuin, *De Sanctis Ebor.* (v, 1073, in Jaffé's edition). The life by Marcellinus, printed in Surius, is a shameless fabrication. A panegyric and hymn by Radbod, Bishop of Utrecht, may be consulted in Migne, PL., vol. cxxxii, cc. 547–559. *Cf.* also the *Acta Sanctorum*, March, vol. i, and Bouterwek, *Der Apostel des Bergischen Landes*; BHL., 7939–7942; Van der Essen, *Étude sur les saints mérovingiens*, pp. 428 *seq.*; and W. Levison, *England and the Continent*   (1946), pp. 57–58.

ST RUDESIND, OR ROSENDO, BISHOP OF DUMIUM   (A.D. 977)

ST RUDESIND, or San Rosendo as he is called by his Spanish fellow countrymen, came of a noble Galician family. According to his biographer, Brother Stephen of Celanova, his mother was praying in St Saviour's church on Mount Cordoba when the birth of this son was divinely foretold to her. Rudesind grew up a serious and saintly youth, and when the see of Dumium (now Mondoñedo) fell vacant, the people demanded that he should be appointed. In vain did he plead that he was only eighteen and quite unsuitable   they insisted, and eventually he had to accept consecration. As a bishop he was a great contrast to his cousin Sisnand, Bishop of Compostela, who neglected his duties and spent all his time in sports and dissipation. This caused such scandal that King Sancho put him in prison, and requested Rudesind to take over the diocese, which he did very reluctantly. On one occasion, when King Sancho was away, the Northmen descended upon Galicia, whilst at the same time the Moors invaded Portugal. Bishop Rudesind gathered together an army and, with the battle-cry, " Some put their trust in chariots and some in horses, but we will call on the name of the Lord ", he led his men first against the Northmen whom he drove back to their ships, and then against the Moors whom he forced to retire into their own territories.

But at the death of King Sancho in 967 Sisnand broke out of prison and on Christmas night attacked Rudesind, whom he threatened with death unless he vacated the see. The holy man made no resistance and retired into the monastery of St John of Caveiro which he had founded, and here he remained until he was instructed in a vision to build another abbey in a place that would be shown him. To his joy he found the place of his dream at Villar—a valley owned by his forefathers—" full of springs and streams and suitable for flowers, grain and herbs, as well as for fruit trees ". Here he began to build and in eight years he completed the monastery, which he called Celanova. Over it he placed a saintly monk named Franquila, under whose obedience he chose to serve. With the help of this abbot he continued to build more monasteries as well as to enforce in those already founded a stricter observance of the Rule of St Benedict. After the death of Franquila, he was elected abbot, and so great was his influence that bishops and abbots came to him for advice and instruction and other religious houses placed themselves under his jurisdiction.

Many miracles are related by his biographer Stephen as having been wrought through St Rudesind—demoniacs and epileptics were healed, the blind cured, stolen property restored and captives liberated ; and he prefaces his catalogue with a simple little personal experience of his own. " When I was at a tender age ", he says, " my parents delivered me over to study letters. In order to escape from the toil of study and also from canings (which are the common lot of boys) I used to hide in the woods. As I could not be made amenable, even when I was securely tied up, my master, moved by a divine inspiration, went to the tomb of St Rudesind, lit a candle and prayed that if I were destined by the Just Judge for the order of the clergy, He would constrain me by the bonds of His virtue and would open my heart to learn. After this I became more docile, as I have often heard him say, and not so very long afterwards I received the religious habit in that very monastery." St Rudesind was canonized in 1195.

It is not certain whether the life attributed to the monk Stephen was really written by him, and in any case he lived nearly two centuries after the saint he commemorates. By far the greater part of the documents printed in the Bollandist *Acta Sanctorum* are taken up with the miracles after Rudesind's death. Much obscurity envelops his connection with the two sees, Dumium and Compostela, and whether he did not retire to Celanova before he was called away to take his cousin's place. See A. Lopez y Carballeira, *San Rosendo* (1909) ; and Gams, *Kirchengeschichte Spaniens*, vol. ii, pt 2, pp. 405-406. In Antony de Yepes, *Coronica General de la Orden de San Benito*, vol. v, pp. 14-16, is printed a Spanish translation of the bulls of beatification and canonization of San Rosendo. *Año Cristiano*, by Justo Pérez de Urbel (5 vols., 1933-1935) is useful for this and other Spanish saints, but it makes no claim to be a critical work.

BD ROGER LE FORT, Archbishop of Bourges (A.D. 1367)

Roger le Fort finds recognition in the Bollandist *Acta Sanctorum* on this day, though his cult has never been formally approved. He is said to have owed his elevation to the bishopric of Orleans to a jest. On the day of the election he had been criticizing the unseemly eagerness of the canons in pushing their claims without any thought of the responsibilities and difficulties involved in such a dignity. In mock earnest he said to one of those who were entering the chapter-house, " I hope the electors will think of me on the present occasion, for I too should like to be a bishop ! " The canon, taking the words seriously, informed the rest, and the whole gathering acclaimed the name of the new candidate. The presiding prelate then rose and said, " Brethren, Heaven and earth are witnesses that you have made choice of Messire Roger for your bishop. Concurring as I do with your judgement, I declare that he upon whom your votes have fallen is the preordained pontiff of this city, for he is a man of eminent sanctity and wisdom. Assuredly this is the decision of the Holy Spirit, whom we cannot resist without guilt." Thereupon Roger was unanimously elected. It was in vain that he protested that he had only spoken in jest and that he had neither the desire nor the ability to undertake such a charge : the voice of the people came to ratify the choice of the clergy, and he was compelled to submit. On his entry into Orleans at his consecration an ancient custom was revived and all the prisoners in the city prison were released.

Roger was afterwards translated to Limoges, and in 1343 he became archbishop of Bourges. He is perhaps best remembered in connection with the feast of the Conception of our Lady, which he established in his diocese and which he did much to popularize. When he died, at the age of ninety, it was found that he had left all his possessions to enable poor boys to receive a good education. The archbishop's unsullied reputation and piety had caused him to be greatly venerated during his life, and immediately after his death his tomb became a place of pilgrimage where many miracles were said to be worked.

See the *Acta Sanctorum*, March, vol. i, and Cochard, *Saints de l'Église d'Orléans*, pp. 487-495.

BD BONAVITA   (A.D. 1375)

A BLACKSMITH by trade and a Franciscan tertiary, Bd Bonavita lived and died in the little town of Lugo, fourteen miles west of Ravenna. It is recorded of him that whether walking or sitting, at work or at leisure, indoors or out of doors, he was liable to become so rapt in contemplation as to be oblivious to all that was round about him. He had the true Franciscan spirit, and when one bitter winter's day he found a poor wretch half frozen outside the church he stripped and gave the man his own clothes. The little urchins of the town pursued the nearly naked black-smith with abuse and stones, but he reached home unhurt and unperturbed. Upon another beggar he bestowed his newly-mended shoes, and he made it his regular practice not only to feed the hungry, but to visit the prison and to help bury the dead.

A disastrous fire broke out which destroyed many of the houses in Lugo, but although nearly the whole population turned out in the hope of arresting its progress, Bonavita appears not even to have noticed it. When his attention was at last aroused he proceeded to the spot where the conflagration was raging, and as soon as he made the sign of the cross the fire was totally extinguished. We are told that through the same holy sign he also wrought many other wonders, but it must be admitted that the evidence for these marvels is not very satisfactory. The cult of this good tertiary seems never to have been formally approved.

See the *Acta Sanctorum*, March, vol. i, where the details given are derived mainly from Wadding, *Annales*, s.a. 1375.

BD CHRISTOPHER OF MILAN   (A.D. 1484)

BD CHRISTOPHER, who is called the apostle of Liguria because of his great success in evangelizing that part of Italy, received the Dominican habit at Milan, early in the fifteenth century. Soon after his ordination he began to be known as a great preacher, and his fame afterwards spread far and wide. His biographers record that his sermons, which brought about conversions and improvement of morals wherever he went, were always based on the Bible, the theology of St Thomas and the writings of the fathers, and that he denounced those preachers who, in their attempts to be popular and up-to-date, aired new-fangled notions and scorned to preach on the gospel for the day. Like a true missionary he wandered fearlessly and untiringly over dangerous passes and difficult country in his labours for souls. At Taggia, where he was particularly successful, the grateful inhabitants built Father Christopher a church and a monastery of which he became prior. He was endowed with the gift of prophecy. One day, as he was watching the people of Castellano dancing in the square, he exclaimed, "' You are now dancing merrily, but your ruin is nigh and your joy will be changed into sorrow "—a forecast which was fulfilled a few years later when the plague carried off most of the inhabitants. He also foresaw the destruction of Trioria by the French, and he warned the population of Taggia that they would flee from their city though not pursued, and that their river would leave its banks and destroy their gardens—prophecies which came true in every particular. When his last illness came upon him, he was preaching the Lent at Pigna. He had himself carried to his beloved Taggia and there breathed his last. His cult was confirmed in 1875.

See Mortier, *Histoire des Maîtres Généraux O.P.*, vol. iv, pp. 371-372 and 648 ; Procter, *Lives of Dominican Saints*, p. 56 ; Taurisano, *Catologus Hayiographicus O.P.*, pp. 44-45.

BD PETER RENÉ ROQUE, Martyr   (A.D. 1796)

This devoted Breton priest was born at Vannes in 1758. After his studies in the seminary of that city he was ordained in 1782, and for a while became chaplain to the Dames de la Retraite ; but four years later he made his way to Paris to join the Lazarists, or Congregation of the Mission of St Vincent de Paul. Even before his noviceship was completed he was sent to act as professor of theology in his native town, and there when the Revolution broke out he showed the utmost heroism in devoting himself to every form of apostolic work. He refused to take the Constitutional Oath which was tendered him and for some time lived disguised and in hiding. In the end, having been betrayed by some miscreant, he was arrested by the revolutionaries ; but even confinement in gaol did not put an end to his activities, for he found means to write in defence of religion and to render numberless services, both bodily and spiritual, to his fellow-prisoners. On being sentenced to death, Father Roque fell on his knees and gave fervent thanks to God. He was guillotined on March 1, 1796, and as soon as peace was restored to the Church an episcopal process was begun with a view to his beatification. This came about in 1934, and in the same year his remains were enshrined in Vannes cathedral.

See L. Brétaudeau, *Un Martyr de la Révolution à Vannes* (1908) ; M. Misermont, *Le bx P. R. Rogue* (1937), and the decrees in the *Acta Apostolicae Sedis*, vol. xxi (1929), pp. 564-567, and vol. xxvi (1934), pp. 304-308 and 292-296, which include a biographical summary.

2 : THE MARTYRS UNDER THE LOMBARDS   (c. A.D. 579)

ST GREGORY THE GREAT in one of his Dialogues has preserved for us the record of those martyrs under the Lombards whom we commemorate on this day, who were in fact contemporaries of his own. It was about the middle of the sixth century that the Lombards from Scandinavia and Pomerania, who had already descended upon Austria and Bavaria, penetrated yet further south into Italy, bringing ruin and desolation in their train. Not content with material destruction, they attempted in many cases to pervert the Christian population, forcing their pagan rites upon them. In one place they endeavoured to induce forty peasants to eat meat offered to idols : when they refused to a man, the invaders killed them all with the sword. In the case of another party of prisoners, their captors sought to make them join in the worship of their favourite deity, a goat's head, which they carried in procession and to which they bowed the knee, singing obscene songs in its honour. The greater part of the Christians—about 400 in number—chose rather to die than to flout God thus.

See St Gregory's *Dialogues*, bk iii, chs. 26-27.

ST CHAD, or CEADDA, Bishop of Lichfield   (A.D. 672)

St Chad was one of four holy brothers of whom all became priests and two—St Chad himself and his elder brother St Cedd—were raised to the episcopate. Angles by race and born in the kingdom of Northumbria, Cedd and Chad were trained at Lindisfarne under St Aidan. Chad went to Ireland after the death of Aidan and appears to have spent some years with St Egbert at Rathmelsigi.   He was recalled to England, however, by St Cedd to take charge of the abbey of Lastingham which he had founded in a wild and solitary spot on the Yorkshire moors south-west of Whitby.   The new abbot was not left long in his retirement.   Within a year he was summoned by King Oswy to become bishop of York, although St Wilfrid had already been designated by Oswy's son Alcfrid (to whom he had given over part of the kingdom) and had actually gone to France to be consecrated by St Agilbert because he objected to being consecrated by those who held the Scottish view about the keeping of Easter.   It has been conjectured by some that Oswy feared that Wilfrid, like Agilbert, would accept a French see, and by others that he was influenced by the Scottish party, but all we actually know is what we learn from the words of the Venerable Bede.

" King Alcfrid ", he writes, " sent the priest Wilfrid to the king of the Gauls to have him consecrated for himself and his subjects.   Now he sent him for ordination to Agilbert, who, as we stated above, had left Britain and had been made bishop of Paris.   By him Wilfrid was consecrated with great pomp, several bishops having assembled for that purpose in a town called Compiègne belonging to the king. While he was still abroad, King Oswy, following his son's example, sent to Kent a holy man of modest character, well versed in the Scriptures and practising with diligence what he had learnt from them, to be ordained bishop of the church of York.   This was a priest named Ceadda (or Chad).   But when they reached Kent, they found that Archbishop Deusdedit had departed this life and that as yet no other had been appointed in his place.   Thereupon they turned aside to the province of the West Saxons, where Wine was bishop, and by him the above-mentioned Chad was consecrated bishop, two bishops of the British nation, who kept Easter in contravention of canonical custom from the 14th to the 20th of the moon, being associated with him, for at that time there was no other bishop in all Britain canonically ordained besides Wine.   As soon as Chad had been consecrated bishop, he began most strenuously to devote himself to ecclesiastical truth and purity of doctrine and to give attention to the practice of humility, self-denial and study   to travel about, not on horseback, but on foot, after the manner of the apostles, preaching the gospel in the towns and the open country, in cottages, villages and castles, for he was one of Aidan's disciples and tried to instruct his hearers by acting and behaving after the example of his master and of his brother Cedd."

When St Theodore, the new archbishop of Canterbury, arrived in England in 669 and came on his first visitation to Northumbria, he adjudged the see of York to Wilfrid and charged Chad with being improperly ordained.   The saint humbly replied, " If you consider that I have not been properly consecrated, I willingly resign this charge of which I never thought myself worthy.   I undertook it, though unworthy, under obedience."   St Theodore was so deeply impressed by the respondent's humility and holiness that, before allowing him to retire to Lastingham, he supplied whatever was defective in his episcopal consecration, and soon after, at the death of Jaruman, Bishop of Mercia, he asked King Oswy to let St Chad have that see.   In consideration of his age the archbishop forbade him to continue to make his visitations on foot, and to enforce his command lifted him on a horse with his own hands.   St Chad moved the seat of the diocese from Repton to Lichfield. King Wulfhere gave him land on which to build a monastery at " Ad Barvae " in the province of Lindsey, and the abbey of Bardney in the same district is believed to have owed its foundation to him. Hard by the church in Lichfield he built a house of retreat, and thither in his leisure time he was wont to betake himself, to pray and read with the seven or eight monks he had settled there, including his friend Owen. This monk, Bede tells us, declared that one day he heard sweet singing—which melody descended from heaven into the bishop's oratory, filling the same for about half an hour and then mounting up again to heaven. After this the bishop opened his window and, seeing him at his work, bade him call the other brethren. When the monks entered the oratory, he exhorted them to keep peace among themselves and to practise with fervour the rules of regular discipline. Then he added that the day of his death was at hand, " for ", said he, " that gracious guest who was wont to visit our brethren has vouchsafed to come to me also to-day and to call me out of this world. Return therefore to the church and speak to the brethren that they in their prayers recommend my passage to the Lord." Chad then fell into what is described as " a languishing distemper " which increased until the seventh day when, " after receiving the body and blood of our Lord, he departed this life, escorted by the soul of his brother Cedd and by a joyful company of angels "

Though St Chad only ruled over the Mercians for two and a half years, his virtues left a deep impression upon all that country. Thirty-one churches were dedicated in his honour in the Midlands and several wells bear his name. Bede, to whom we owe most of the details of St Chad's life, says that he received some of his information from those who studied under the saint.

According to legend sometimes reproduced in art, St Chad was once praying by a stream in a wood, when a hart escaped from its pursuers and leapt into the water. The saint moved with compassion sent it to graze in the wood, and when the huntsmen, the two sons of King Wulfhere, pressed on to secure their prey, he first read them a little homily on kindness to animals and in the end converted them to the faith. Their father was a renegade Christian who had never allowed them to be baptized, and when he discovered that the young men had renounced paganism he murdered them both. Afterwards, seized with remorse, he sought out St Chad (to whose sylvan retreat he was conducted by the hart), and after having made confession to him and done penance, he built several abbeys by way of atonement and completed Peterborough minster, which had been begun by his father. Though the story is extravagant, an entry in Codex E of the Anglo-Saxon Chronicle does bring the name of Wulfhere into connection with Peterborough as contributing to its endowment. Part of St Chad's relics are in the cathedral at Birmingham which bears his name, and a seventh-century manuscript, known as St Chad's Gospel, is preserved in Lichfield cathedral library. The saint's feast is kept in several English dioceses, and Birmingham has a second feast, of the translation of his relics.

Nearly everything that can be regarded as historically trustworthy concerning St Chad's life will be found in the text and notes of C. Plummer's edition of Bede's *Ecclesiastical History*. The data furnished by such sources as Eddius, William of Malmesbury, Capgrave, etc., are unimportant and for the most part legendary. There is an attractive volume by an Anglican clergyman, the Rev. R. H. Warner, *The Life and Legends of St Chad* (1871), in which many out-of-the-way materials have been laid under contribution, such as a Middle English metrical life attributed to Robert of Gloucester, and sundry references in Bradshaw's *Life of St Werburg*. There is also an interesting paper dealing with St Chad's relics in the *Journal of the Archaeological Institute*, vol. xxxiii, pp. 72 seq., and further information will be found in *The History of St Chad's Cathedral, Birmingham* (1904). There is a Life of St Chad, apparently unpublished, in the Codex Gothanus — see *Analecta Bollandiana*, vol. lviii (1940), p. 96.

BD CHARLES THE GOOD, MARTYR   (A.D. 1127)

BECAUSE of his wise and beneficent rule as well as for his personal holiness, Charles, Count of Flanders and Amiens, fully deserved the title of " the Good " which his subjects bestowed upon him.   His father was St Canute, King of Denmark, who had been slain in St Alban's church, Odense, in 1086.   Charles, who was but five years old at the time, was taken by his mother to the court of her father, Robert, Count of Flanders, and in due time was knighted with his father's sword which, if we may believe an old legend, had come into his possession in a singular way.   As a small boy, we are told, Charles had been taken to the prison of Bruges to visit those who were confined there, and amongst others Ivend Trenson, who had long been detained as a hostage and who happened to have been entrusted with the sword of King Canute at the time of his murder.   The prisoner was lying on his pallet with the sword under his pillow, and the child, perceiving it, asked permission to gird it on.   " It is only right that you should keep it altogether," said Ivend, " for it was your father's sword."   Charles carried it home in triumph and obtained from his grandfather the liberation of the hostage and his companion.   When Robert II joined the crusade in Palestine, his nephew accompanied him and covered himself with glory and scars ; moreover, upon their return home, Charles helped his uncle to fight against the English.   Robert was succeeded by his son Baldwin who, having no children, designated his cousin Charles as his heir.   He also brought about his marriage with Margaret, daughter of Renault, Count of Clermont.   Finally he associated Charles with himself in the government of Flanders, so that when he died, the populace, who had become accustomed to Charles's wise and benevolent rule, received him with acclamation.

There were, however, other claimants, and for several years Charles had to face a great deal of turbulent resistance to his authority.   As soon as he was free from external aggression he devoted himself to the task of inaugurating an era of peace and justice amongst his subjects.   He enacted excellent laws, enforced them strictly, and by his example even more than by legislation sought to civilize the people.   When he was reproached with unfairly espousing the cause of the poor against the rich, he said, " It is because I know so well the needs of the poor and the pride of the rich."   He had such a horror of blasphemy that any member of his household who swore by God's name was punished by a fast of forty days on bread and water.   One of his humane regulations forbade the taking away of a child without the consent of its parents, and he was so stern with those who oppressed the helpless that the poor lived in peace and security.   This security was troubled first by an eclipse of the sun in August 1124, which was held by the superstitious to portend awful calamities, and then by a terrible famine which occurred a year later, after an exceptionally long and hard winter.

Daily at Bruges and at each of his castles Bd Charles fed a hundred poor men, and at Ypres he distributed 7800 two-pound loaves in one day.   He reprimanded the inhabitants of Ghent for allowing men to die at their gates, and in order that the grain might be used for bread he forbade the brewing of beer.   All the dogs were killed by his command, and a fixed price was set for the sale of wine.   He ordered the land to be sown everywhere in a proportion of two-thirds in grain and one-third in peas or beans which grow fast.

Discovering that certain nobles had bought up grain and were hoarding it that they might retail it at exorbitant prices, Charles and his almoner Tancmar obliged them to sell at once and at a reasonable charge. This aroused their fury, and the chief of these profiteers, Lambert, with his brother Bertulf, the dean of St Donatian's at Bruges, formed a plot to murder the count. In this they were joined by Erembald, magistrate of Bruges, together with his sons, who owed Charles a grudge for having repressed their violence. The count, who used to go every morning barefoot to pray before Mass in the church of St Donatian, was warned one day, as he was starting, that there was a conspiracy on foot against him. He replied quietly, " We are always in the midst of dangers, but we belong to God. If it be His will, can we die in a better cause than that of justice and truth ? " As he was saying the psalm " *Miserere* " before the altar of our Lady in the church he was set upon by the conspirators : his arm was cut off by one of them and his head was cloven by Bertulf's nephew, Borchard. The relics of the martyr are preserved in the cathedral of Bruges and his festival is observed with great solemnity. His *cultus* was confirmed in 1883. The chronicler Galbert notes as a marvel that the news of the murder, which took place on Wednesday morning, reached the inhabitants of London on Friday at the first hour, " and yet no one could have crossed the sea in that time ".

The sources for the history of Charles the Good are abundant and reliable. Walter, Archdeacon of Thérouanne, a contemporary, wrote one account, and Galbert, a notary at Bruges, also a contemporary, provided another describing still more fully the events which followed the martyrdom. Both these documents will be found in the *Acta Sanctorum*, March, vol. i, as also in Migne, PL. and in MGH., *Scriptores*, vol. xii, pp. 537–623. See BHL., nn. 1573–1576. Further materials are contributed by other chroniclers, *e.g.* by Abbot Suger. *Cf.* Le Glay, *Histoire du bx Charles le Bon*, and *Analecta Bollandiana*, vol. xi (1892), pp. 188–197. This article contains some few criticisms upon what is undoubtedly the best available text of Galbert, that edited by H. Pirenne for the " Collection de Textes pour servir à l'étude et l'enseignement de l'Histoire ". The edition is provided with a preface, a map and many useful notes.

BD FULCO OF NEUILLY (A.D. 1201)

THE early life of this great preacher, whose activities seem to have centred in the north of France, is said to have been by no means free from reproach, but after a serious conversion he set about his priestly duties at Neuilly-sur-Marne with fervour and success. His sermons, delivered with intense enthusiasm in a simple, popular style, attracted hearers from far and near, and soon he began to undertake missionary journeys through Normandy, Picardy and Burgundy, fearlessly denouncing the evils of the time and bringing numberless sinners to repentance. The general licence of manners and the extortions of usurers formed the theme of his discourses, and he had often to pay the penalty of the freedom with which he spoke. He was more than once thrown into prison, but escaped miraculously (?) from custody, and was reputed to have a strange knowledge of men's thoughts and to have worked innumerable cures upon those who had recourse to him in their infirmities. A remarkable feature in his apostolic career, considering the ideas of the age in which he lived, was his repudiation of any conspicuous practice of asceticism. Ralph Coggeshall, the English chronicler, records that he took his night's rest like other people, attempted no unusual fasts and accepted gratefully any food that was set before him. It may have been this which at a later date started rumours unfavourable to his disinterestedness. In certain comments of the worthy Cardinal James de Vitry we seem to find the echo of some such gossip.

All the chroniclers, however, are agreed that Fulco never flattered and was no respecter of persons. According to Roger Hoveden it was he who told King Richard Cœur-de-Lion that unless he married off his three disreputable daughters, he would certainly come to a bad end. When Richard exclaimed in a fury that the words proved his censor to be a hypocrite and an impostor, for he had no daughters, the holy man answered, " Yes, but indeed you have three daughters, and I will tell you their names. The first is called Pride, the second Avarice and the third Lust."

The fame of the French priest's missionary labours attracted the notice of Pope Innocent III, and in the year 1198 he commissioned Fulco to preach the new Crusade, accounted the Fourth, throughout the northern part of France. His eloquence had already produced marvellous effects, and if we may credit his own statement, as reported by Coggeshall, 200,000 people in the course of three years had taken the cross at his hands. Fulco was himself to have joined in the expedition, but before starting he fell ill and died on March 2, 1201. His tomb was still venerated at Neuilly-sur-Marne in the eighteenth century. The *cultus* formerly paid to him seems never to have been authoritatively confirmed.

Contemporary chroniclers, such *e.g.* as Roger Hoveden, Rigord and Ralph Coggeshall, as well as the later Jordan, provide a good deal of information about Fulco. See also Raynald's continuation of Baronius's *Annales Ecclesiastici, s.a.* 1198, nn. 38-42. A letter addressed by Innocent III to " Brother Fulco " is printed in his *Regesta* (Migne, PL., ccxiv, 375), but there seems no evidence that the preacher belonged to any religious order.

BD AGNES OF BOHEMIA, Virgin   (A.D. 1282)

BD AGNES of Bohemia, or " of Prague ", whom St Clare called her " half self " and who founded the first establishment of Poor Clares north of the Alps, was a descendant of St Wenceslaus (" Good King Wenceslaus ") ; her father was Ottokar I, who succeeded to the throne of Bohemia in 1197, and her mother was sister of Andreas II, King of Hungary   St Elizabeth of Hungary was her first cousin and two years her junior. Agnes was only three years old when, in 1208, she was betrothed to Boleslaus, the son of Henry, Duke of Silesia, and of St Hedwig, and she was immediately sent away from home, under the care of her nurse and a suitable retinue, to the monastery of Trebnitz in Silesia, which her fiancé's mother had founded. Here, according to a fourteenth-century Latin document in the Bamberg library, " she was taught the rudiments of faith and morals by a daughter of St Hedwig "—who must have been Gertrude the abbess. Boleslaus died when the little girl was only six, and she returned to Bohemia, where she was placed in the Premonstratensian convent of Doxan. Two years later she was recalled to her father's court, and when, at the age of nine, she was betrothed to the Emperor Frederick II's son Henry, she was sent away again—this time to the Austrian court to learn the German language and customs. The life had no attraction for Agnes, and more and more she turned her mind to God, practising in private strict fasts and austerities. She was seized with a great desire to consecrate herself to a life of virginity, and prayed fervently that she might be enabled to follow the call. Her life at the time can hardly have been a happy one, for Duke Leopold of Austria, to whose care she had been committed, was plotting to break off her engagement and to marry his own daughter to the prince. In this he was eventually successful, and Agnes was once more sent back to her home—joyfully enough, we may be sure, and feeling that her prayers had been answered.

But she was not long left in peace.   Proposals for her hand came from Henry III of England as well as from Frederick II, who had become a widower, and in spite of her vehement objections her brother, King Wenceslaus, affianced her to the emperor.   From this time Bd Agnes increased her penances and prayers, and under her jewelled robes wore a hair-shirt and a girdle studded with iron points.   Often she would rise before dawn and barefoot and meanly clad sallied forth, escorted by the most devout of her ladies, to visit the churches.   Upon her return she would bathe her bleeding feet, resume the attire fitted to her rank, and attend to her duties as a princess and visit the sick.   She was twenty-eight years old and a beautiful woman when, in 1235, the emperor sent an ambassador to Prague to escort her to Germany that the marriage might take place.   Wenceslaus would listen to no remonstrances ; but Agnes found means to delay her departure and wrote to Pope Gregory IX, entreating him to prevent the marriage because she had never consented to it and had long desired to be the spouse of Christ.   Gregory, although for the moment he had made peace with Frederick, knew him well enough to be able to sympathize with the unwilling victim.   He sent his legate to Prague to undertake her defence and to Agnes herself he wrote letters which she showed to her brother.   Wenceslaus was greatly alarmed.   On the one hand he feared to anger the emperor, but on the other he did not wish to alienate the pope or to force his sister to marry against her will.   Eventually he decided to tell Frederick and to let him deal with the matter.   The emperor on this occasion showed one of those flashes of magnanimity which have made his complex character so fascinating a study to historians.   As soon as he had satisfied himself that the objection came, not from the King of Bohemia, but from Agnes herself, he released her, saying, " If she had left me for a mortal man, I should have made my vengeance felt ; but I cannot take offence if she prefers the King of Heaven to myself."

Now that she was free, Agnes set about consecrating herself and her possessions wholly to God.   Her father had brought the Friars Minor to Prague, probably at her suggestion, and she built or completed a convent for them.   With the help of her brother she endowed a great hospital for the poor and brought to it the Knights Hospitallers of the Cross and Star, whose church and monastery still remain in the same place, and the two also built a convent for Poor Clares.   The citizens would fain have shared in the work, but the king and his sister preferred to complete it alone.   Nevertheless it is said that the workmen, determined to do their part, would often slip away unperceived in the evening in order to avoid being paid.   As soon as the convent was ready, St Clare sent five of her religious to start it, and on Whitsunday 1236 Bd Agnes herself received the veil.   Her profession made a great impression : she was joined by a hundred girls of good family, and throughout Europe princesses and noble women followed her example and founded or entered convents of Poor Clares.   Agnes showed the true spirit of St Francis, ever seeking the lowliest place and the most menial work, and it was with difficulty that she was induced, when nominated by Pope Gregory IX, to accept the dignity of abbess—at least for a time.   After much entreaty she obtained for the Poor Ladies of Prague the concession obtained in 1238 by St Clare at San Damiano, namely, permission to resign all revenues and property held in common.   The four letters from St Clare to Bd Agnes which have come down to us express her tender affection for her devoted disciple, to whom she also sent, in response to her request for a souvenir, a wooden cross, a flaxen veil and the earthen bowl out of which she drank.   Agnes lived to the age of seventy-seven and died on March 2, 1282.   Her *cultus* was confirmed by Pope Pius X; the Friars Minor now keep her feast on June 8, with BB. Isabel of France and Baptista Varani.

The questions relating to the sources of Bd Agnes's life are very fully treated by Dr W. W. Seton in his volume *Some New Sources for the Life of Bd Agnes of Bohemia.* The better-known documents have been printed in the *Acta Sanctorum,* March, vol. i, but Dr Seton has found and edited an earlier Latin text (fourteenth century), together with a fifteenth-century German version which presents sundry expansions of the original. He also vindicates the authenticity of the four letters addressed to Agnes by St Clare. A popular account may be found in Léon, *Auréole Séraphique* (Eng. trans.), vol. i, pp. 339-348, and in Mazzara, *Leggendario Francescano,* March, nn. 19-21.

BD HENRY SUSO   (A.D. 1365)

THE fourteenth century was a period of remarkable spiritual activity in Germany, where the religious revival took the form of a pronounced mysticism. Most of its chief exponents came, either directly or indirectly, under the influence of the Dominican, Meister Eckhart, and were to be found, sometimes in convents, some-times as itinerant prophets, and sometimes as the heads of small societies of people calling themselves friends of God, who lived more or less in the world without being of it and who devoted much time to religion and to good works. The teaching of these leaders was propagated through their writings, through their preaching, and also through table-talks which seem rather to have corresponded to modern retreat-addresses. Of all Eckhart's pupils perhaps the most famous was Henry Suso.

His real name was Von Berg, but he preferred to be known by the surname, Seuse, of his mother, a very holy woman who suffered much at the hands of her dissolute husband. The date of his birth is uncertain and all we know of his early years is derived from a paragraph in his autobiography (but *cf.* below) where, writing of himself as he always does in the third person, he says : " In his childhood it had been his custom when the beautiful summer came and the tender flowrets first began to spring up, never to pluck or touch a flower until he had greeted, with the gift of his first flowers, his spiritual love, the sweet blooming rosy maid, God's mother." At the age of thirteen he entered the Dominican priory at Constance, which town, as Bihlmeyer has shown, was also his birthplace. The building, which was beautifully situated on a small island at the point where the Rhine flows out of the lake, is still in existence, but now serves as a factory. Here he remained until he had been professed, when he was transferred to Cologne that he might study at the *studium generale* in that city. For several years he appears to have lived a somewhat careless life, satisfied with the avoidance of any gross or serious sin, but in his eighteenth year he received what he describes as " a secret illumination and drawing sent by God " which " speedily wrought in him a turning away from creatures ". " Forsake all " were the words that rang in his ears, and he deter-mined to obey at once, making no reservations. In vain did the Devil seek to deter him by maxims of worldly wisdom, suggesting that his conversion was too rapid, that he could not count upon corresponding to grace, that perseverance was im-possible, and that moderation was the secret of success. Heavenly wisdom taught him how to meet these suggestions and how to overcome them.

Bd Henry was wonderfully moved to make himself " the servant of the Eternal Wisdom ", whom he beheld afar off in vision (one thinks of Solovyev half a mil-lennium later); his veneration for the Holy Name caused him to cut its letters in his flesh; his deep love for the Mother of God, his whole highly-charged religious outlook, expressed themselves in ways that are loosely called " mystical ", sometimes touching, sometimes perhaps rather extravagant. In the same spirit he inflicted on himself bodily penances of the greatest severity, exercising upon them an ingenuity that in later times would seem somewhat morbid. Besides these physical mortifications, Henry Suso was tormented by inner sufferings in the shape of imaginations against faith, intense sadness or nervous depression and a haunting fear that he was doomed to lose his soul whatever he might do. He says of himself : " After the terrible suffering had lasted about ten years, during which period he never looked upon himself in any other light than as one damned, he went to the holy Master Eckhart and made known to him his suffering. The holy man delivered him from it and thus set him free from the hell in which he had so long dwelt." The time also came—when Bd Henry was about forty years old—when he gave up his outward mortifications, for God showed him that these practices were but a beginning and that he must now press on in quite another direction if he wished to reach perfection. Instead of remaining at home and cultivating his own soul only, he must now go forth to save his neighbour. It was also revealed to him that, though he was freed from the crosses he had borne in the past, there were others in store for him. Whereas he had afflicted himself at will, he would be afflicted and persecuted by others, meeting with ingratitude and losing his good name and his friends.

Suso had distinguished himself when a student at Cologne, and now that he began to go forth preaching his learning and eloquence brought him many disciples of both sexes. He is said to have preached for thirty-seven years, converting many sinners and working miracles. On one occasion, when he was speaking at Cologne, the congregation were amazed to see his face shining like the sun. Nevertheless trouble followed him wherever he went. Upon the flimsy accusation of a child he was charged with theft and sacrilege, at another time he was suspected of poisoning, and elsewhere he was accused of faking a miracle and was obliged to fly for his life. In the Netherlands he was reprimanded for writing heretical books, and although he was afterwards exculpated his distress at the charge brought on a serious illness. His sister, a nun, fell into grievous sin and ran away from her convent ; he never rested until he had found her, and after bringing her to repentance placed her in another community where she died a holy death. Another of his efforts to reclaim an erring woman did not turn out so well. A sinner who had placed herself under his direction had professed to be leading a better life, but when he discovered that she was continuing her evil ways he refused to continue to assist her with alms. In revenge she accused him of being the father of her child, and the charge seems to have been believed. Perhaps his own charitable action may have seemed to substantiate it, for when someone took to him the baby whom its mother had abandoned he received it lovingly and adopted it until he could find it a suitable home. In view of the scandal, the master general of the order caused an inquiry to be made into the matter, and the truth being established his character was vindicated.

At a time when his monastery was burdened with debt, Suso was elected prior. Instead of seeking to raise money by begging or borrowing, he ordered a special Mass to be said in honour of St Dominic, trusting to the saint's dying promise never to abandon his children. The other friars murmured : " The prior must be crazy. Does he think God will send food and drink from heaven ? " As Bd Henry was still standing in choir, deep in thought, he was called out to receive a gift of twenty pounds of Constance money from a canon who had been admonished by God to come to his assistance. Not only did the monastery wipe off its debt, but it never lacked provisions during his term of office.

Bd Henry died at Ulm, on January 25, 1365, and was buried in the Dominican convent. It has been maintained that two hundred and forty years later his body was accidentally disinterred by workmen and was found incorrupt, wearing the Dominican habit. There is, however, no serious evidence for this identification. The burgomaster ordered the body to be covered up again, and all traces of it have been lost. The *cultus* of Bd Henry was confirmed in 1831.

Suso left several devotional books of great beauty, one of which, *The Book of Eternal Wisdom*, was extraordinarily popular during the latter part of the middle ages. His so-called " autobiography " is said to have been preserved to us by his spiritual daughter, Elizabeth Stagel, of the Dominican convent of Töss, near Winterthur. Consisting mainly of materials supplied by him, it shows evident marks of having been edited by someone other than himself—so much so that of late years the authenticity of the whole has been called in question. His books record some of the many occasions when the veil between this world and the next was lifted for him. Not only had he visions of our Lord, the Blessed Virgin and the saints, but many of those whom he had known appeared to him after death—notably his parents, Elizabeth Stagel and his beloved teacher Eckhart, whom he beheld in glory. In reply to his question asking how he might attain to eternal happiness, the master replied in words which might serve as an epitome of the life of Suso himself : " To die to self in perfect detachment, to receive everything as from God, and to maintain unruffled patience with all men, however brutal or churlish they may be."

Both the life and the writings of Bd Henry Suso have of late years given rise to much discussion. Those interested may be referred for fuller information to the third part of Xavier de Hornstein's very painstaking volume *Les grands mystiques allemands du XIVᵉ siècle* (1922). It contains a clear statement of conflicting views with a good bibliography. See also Wilms, *Der s. Heinrich Seuse* ; R. Zeller, *Le bx Henri Suso* (1922) ; and J. Ancelet-Hustache, *Le bx Henri Suso* (1943). Several editions of Suso's works have appeared since Father Denifle in 1880 brought out the first critical text of *Die deutschen Schriften*. That of K. Bihlmeyer (1907) may be specially recommended both for the writings themselves and for the introduction thereto. There is an excellent French translation of the *Œuvres mystiques* by Father Thiriot. and see B. Lavaud, *L'œuvre mystique de Henri Suso* (3 vols., 1946). In English, the translation of the " Autobiography " made many years ago by Father T. F. Knox, after falling out of copyright, was reprinted by other publishers with an introduction by Dean Inge ; " S.M.C." in *Henry Suso Mystic, Saint and Poet*, brings out his relevance to our times. There is an English translation by R. Raby of the *Horologium Sapientiae* (1868), and of its shorter original form, *The Little Book of Eternal Wisdom*, with *The Little Book of Truth* (1952), by J. M. Clark, who has also translated *The Life of the Servant* (1952), that is, Suso's autobiography. See also J. A. Bizet, *Henri Suso et le déclin de la scolastique* (1947).

3 : SS. MARINUS AND ASTYRIUS, MARTYRS   (*c.* A.D. 262)

EUSEBIUS, in his *Ecclesiastical History*, describes the martyrdom of St Marinus. As a man who belonged to a noble family of Caesarea in Palestine, and had served with distinction in the army, he was about to be honoured with the decoration of the vine switch (κλῆμα), emblematic of the dignity of " centurion ", when a rival, who was in the running for the same distinction, raised the objection that since Marinus was a Christian and would not sacrifice to the emperor, he was therefore disqualified. Achaeus, the governor, accordingly questioned him, and eliciting a confession of his faith, gave him three hours in which to reconsider his position. As he left the judgement hall he was met by Theotecnus, bishop of the city, who leading him into the church made him stand close to the altar. Pointing to the sword which hung at his side and then to the book of the gospels, he told him to choose between the two. Marinus without hesitation stretched out his hand and took the book. "Hold fast then to God", said the bishop, " that, strengthened by Him, thou mayest obtain what thou hast chosen. Go in peace." Upon returning before the judge he declared his faith with as great determination as before, and was immediately led away to execution.

St Astyrius, a Roman senator in high favour with the emperor, was present at the martyrdom. Wrapping the body in the cloak he was wearing he carried it away on his own shoulders and gave it honourable burial. Eusebius does not say that Astyrius himself was put to death, but Rufinus in his Latin version of the history assumes this, and both the Roman Martyrology and the Greek Menaion (under August 7) commemorate the senator as a martyr.

All the information we possess regarding these saints is derived from Eusebius, *Eccl. Hist.*, bk vii, chs. 15 and 16.

SS. EMETERIUS AND CHELIDONIUS, MARTYRS   (A.D. 304)

BEYOND their names and the fact of their martyrdom, scarcely anything is actually known about St Emeterius and St Chelidonius, the patrons of Santander. Prudentius, who composed a long poem in their honour, says that the persecutors burned the acts of their martyrdom, " grudging us the history of so glorious a triumph " Tradition says that they were the sons of St Marcellus, both of them soldiers like their father, and that they perished by the sword, under Diocletian, at Calahorra in Spain. According to a story related by St Gregory of Tours, the ring of St Emeterius and the *orarium* (handkerchief ?) of St Chelidonius were caught up into heaven at the moment of their execution.

This seems to be one of the cases in which an early local *cultus* and tradition fully guarantee the fact of the martyrdom, though we lack knowledge of anything more than the names of the martyrs and the date and place where they suffered. Prudentius mentions them in more than one of his poems, and they are noticed in the " Hieronymianum " (CMH., p. 124). The chapter devoted to them by Gregory of Tours is no. 92 of his *In gloria martyrum*.

ST ARTHELAIS, VIRGIN   (*c.* A.D. 560 ?)

DURING the reign of the Emperor Justinian, there lived in Constantinople a charming and virtuous girl, the daughter of the proconsul Lucius and his wife Anthusa. Many were the suitors for the hand of Arthelais, but the emperor, hearing of her beauty, sent messengers to her father asking that she should be handed over to him. Her parents and she were dismayed, and concluded that the only way to avoid dishonour was by flight. It was arranged that she should go to her uncle Narses Patricius at Benevento, and her father escorted her as far as Buda in Dalmatia, where he left her to prosecute her journey under the charge of three attendants. Hardly had he departed when they were set upon by robbers, who seized Arthelais whilst her servants took to flight. After three days' imprisonment she was miraculously delivered and rejoined her escort, but the wrath of God fell upon her captors. The travellers crossed the sea in safety and arrived at Sipontum, from whence they sent messengers to Narses, who, however, had already started to meet them, having been apprised of their arrival in a dream.   From Sipontum they passed on to Lucera and thence to Benevento, where the whole population came out to greet her.   From the Golden gate of the city she walked barefoot to the church of our Lady, where she offered gifts, the bells in the meantime pealing forth in her honour.   She then gave herself to unceasing prayer and fasted every day except Sunday—thereby, no doubt, undermining her health, for she died of fever at the age of sixteen amid general lamentation.

These historical details cannot be regarded as trustworthy.   Besides the two very short biographies printed in the *Acta Sanctorum*, March, vol. i, a longer account is furnished in the text translated from a Greek original by a certain Peter.   See S. Borgia, *Memorie istoriche di Benevento*, vol. i, pp. 143-176.

ST NON, or NONNITA   (Sixth Century)

SINCE the revised March volume of Butler's *Lives* was published a church has been opened on the cliffs near Saint Davids by the Passionist fathers dedicated in honour of our Lady and St Non.   It therefore seems desirable to say a word about this obscure saint, if only to show how little is known about her.

If St Non is obscure, she is also famous in the Celtic lands as the mother of St David, and the few references to her are mostly to be found in Rhygyfarch's (Rice-march) life of St David and its derivatives.   According to his story there was in the sixth century a religious house of women at Ty Gwyn, north-west of the village-city that we now call Saint Davids and close to the Whitesand bay (Porth Mawr) from which tradition says St Patrick set out to convert the Irish.   In this nunnery was a young woman of noble birth and great beauty named Non ; she came under the notice of a local chieftain, called Sant, who violated her ; and the fruit of this association was St David.   He is supposed to have been born during a storm, at the spot on the coast, south of modern Saint Davids and overlooking St Bride's Bay, where the ruins of the medieval St Non's chapel still stand.   Two hundred yards away is the Catholic church referred to above, built in part of stones from old ecclesiastical buildings of the district.   David was baptized in the spring at Porth Clais, it is said, by or at the instance of St Ailbhe, who is stated to have been Non's nephew and who was responsible, according to some writers, for her leaving the nunnery after her violation.

What truth there is in all this no one can say.   It at least seems likely that she was not a nun ; the Latin form of her name, Nonna, means " nun ", and so could easily be misunderstood.   According to some Irish writers she subsequently had other children.   And it may well be that, whether before or after David's birth, she was Sant's wife.   Later in life she is said to have gone into Cornwall and then settled in Brittany, where place-names and church dedications give some support to the statement.   In the west of England in the middle ages she was esteemed to be buried at Altarnun in Cornwall, but Dirinon, in the department of Finistère in Brittany, seems to have a better claim.   Her grave is shown in the church there, covered by a striking medieval table-tomb on which is a recumbent effigy of the saint.   In both Brittany and Wales there was considerable devotion to St Non in the past ; she was often called Non the Blessed, and the bards refer to her beauty. Lewis Glyn Cothi (fifteenth century) in a poem swears " by the hand of Non ", perhaps a reference to the legend that while in labour with David she left the impression of her hand on a stone which was by her side.

See bibliographical note to St David (March 1).   A mystery play in Breton, *Buhez Santes Nonn*, formerly performed at Dirinon, was translated from a manuscript of about 1400 into French in the *Revue Celtique* (vol. viii, 1887).   See also LBS., *s.v.* Non and David, with numerous references.   There are holy wells of St Non at Saint Davids, at Dirinon and at several places in Cornwall, though the best-known one here, at Altarnun, is now dried up ; the Saint Davids well is now in the grounds of the Passionist retreat there.   For an interesting reference to St David's birth, see *Blackfriars*, vol. xxix (1948), pp. 123–125 ; and *cf.* G. H. Doble in the *Cornish Times* for August 17, 1928 (reprinted separately, *St Nonna*, same year) : he suggests that the Cornish St Non was a man.

ST WINWALOE, or GUÉNOLÉ, Abbot   (Sixth Century)

THE accounts of the early life of St Winwaloe are so conflicting that it has been suggested that there were two holy men of that name, one of whom was born in Britain and became the disciple of St Samson, whereas the abbot who is commemorated on this day was born in Brittany, whither his parents, Fracan and Gwen, had migrated from Britain and settled at Ploufragan.   On account of his beauty, the boy was named Winwaloe, or " He that is fair ", and, because he was their third son, his parents consecrated him to God from his birth.   They were tenderly attached to him, and in spite of their vow they kept him with them until he was fifteen, although he had given early evidence of a vocation for the religious life.   A violent thunderstorm which they took to be a sign from Heaven finally decided them to part from him, and his father took him to a monastery on the little island of Lauré, under an Abbot Budoc.   Here St Winwaloe and his two brothers appear to have spent several years.   It is told of him that while he was still at home he was one day walking with his father when he perceived a number of sails on the horizon, and with boyish exaggeration exclaimed, " I see a thousand ships ".   They turned out to be pirates who landed on the coast, but Fracan and his followers completely defeated them.   Winwaloe, who had been praying earnestly during the fight, persuaded his father to build a monastery with the spoil, and a cross which marks the spot where the invaders landed is called to this day, " The Cross of the Thousand Sails ".

St Winwaloe made such progress as a monk that the thought occurred to him of sailing to Ireland to carry on the labours of St Patrick, but that saint, appearing in a vision, dissuaded him.   Thereupon Budoc sent him with eleven monks to found another monastery.   After wandering through the northern part of Brittany they found, as they thought, a suitable island at the mouth of the river Aulne, and there they built themselves a settlement of huts which afterwards gave to the island its name of Tibidy or " The House of Prayer ".   The place proved, however, to be exposed to such violent storms that, after three years, the monks were obliged to abandon it and to settle on the mainland.   With the assistance of the rough Prince Grallo, who had a great veneration for St Winwaloe, they founded the monastery of Landévennec in a sheltered valley on the opposite side of Brest harbour, and there the holy abbot ruled over a large number of monks for many years, until at last in extreme old age he died when standing at the altar after giving the kiss of peace.

The popularity of the saint is attested by the number of dedications made to him and by the many variations of his name.   He appears as Winwalocus, Guinvaloeus, Wingalotus, Galnutius, Guingalois, Guignolé, Guénolé and in several other spellings.   St Winwaloe's name is entered in two or three late medieval English calendars, but there seems to have been little *cultus* outside the area of Celtic influences ; there are dedications to him in Cornwall, at Gunwalloe, Landewednack and elsewhere.

The legendary character of the sources upon which this history is based is made evident by the extravagant miracles with which it is freely embroidered. The longest form seems to have been the composition of Wrdisten, Abbot of Landévennec, who lived more than 300 years after the time of St Winwaloe. The text of Wrdisten's very tedious and discursive biography may be found in the *Analecta Bollandiana*, vol. vii (1888), pp. 167-264. In LBS., vol. iv, pp. 353-362, there is a discussion of the various texts and abridgements of the life. See also G. H. Doble, *St Winwaloe* (1940) ; and Fr J. Le Jollec, *Guénolé, le saint de Landévennec* (1952), who gives an account of the abbey of Landévennec, whose restoration has been undertaken by the Benedictines of Kerbénéat, and of the saint's *cultus*.

ST ANSELM OF NONANTOLA, ABBOT   (A.D. 803)

WHEN the Langobard King Aistulf was reigning in Italy, he was greatly assisted in his military campaigns by his brother-in-law, Anselm, Duke of Friuli. The duke was not only a valiant soldier but also an ardent Christian, and founded first a monastery with a hospital at Fanano in the province of Modena and then a larger abbey twenty miles further south at Nonantola. Desirous of consecrating himself entirely to God, he then went to Rome, where he was clothed with the habit of St Benedict and appointed abbot over the new community. He also received from Pope Stephen III permission to remove to Nonantola the body of Pope St Silvester ; and as Aistulf enriched the abbey with gifts and granted it many privileges it became very celebrated throughout all Italy. Abbot Anselm came to rule over more than one thousand monks, besides having charge of a great hospital and hospice for the sick and for pilgrims. This he had built near the monastery and dedicated it in honour of St Ambrose. After the death of Aistulf, his successor Desiderius banished the holy abbot to Monte Cassino, where he remained for seven years, but Charlemagne restored him to Nonantola, where he died in a good old age, after having spent fifty years in religion.

The short Latin life of St Anselm, which has been several times printed (*e.g.* by Mabillon, by Muratori, and in MGH.), was edited with much illustrative matter by P Bartolotti in 1892, *Antica vita di S. Anselmo di Nonantola*.

ST CUNEGUND, WIDOW   (A.D. 1033)

ST CUNEGUND was piously trained from her earliest years by her parents, Siegfried of Luxemburg and his saintly wife Hedwig. She married St Henry, Duke of Bavaria, who gave her as a wedding present a crucifix of eastern workmanship which is said to be identical with one now existing in Munich. Later writers have asserted that they both took a vow of virginity on their wedding-day, and the story is accepted in the Roman Martyrology ; but historians now seem to agree that there is no reliable evidence to corroborate the statement. In the middle of the eleventh century Cardinal Humbert knew nothing of the alleged celibate marriage he attributed their childlessness to divine punishment for what he regarded as Henry's exploitation of the Church. Upon the death of the Emperor Otto III, Henry was elected king of the Romans, and his coronation by St Willigis at Mainz was followed, two months later, by that of his wife at Paderborn. In 1013 they went together to Rome to receive the imperial crown from Pope Benedict VIII.

In spite of her exemplary life, Cunegund is said by the hagiographers of a later age to have become the victim of slanderous tongues, so that even her husband's confidence in her was momentarily shaken. Feeling that her position required her vindication, the empress asked to be allowed the ordeal by fire, and walked unscathed over red-hot ploughshares. Henry was eager to make amends for his unworthy suspicions, and they lived thenceforth in the closest union of hearts, striving in every way to promote the glory of God and the advancement of religion. But this story too is insufficiently supported.

It was partly at the instigation of St Cunegund that the emperor founded the monastery and cathedral of Bamberg, to the consecration of which Pope Benedict came in person, and she obtained for the city such privileges that by common report her silken threads were a better defence than walls. During a dangerous illness she had made a vow that if she recovered she would found a convent at Kaufungen, near Cassel, in Hesse. This she proceeded to do, and had nearly finished building a house for nuns of the Benedictine Order when St Henry died. Her later biographers relate a quaint story about the first abbess. It appears that the empress had a young niece, called Judith or Jutta, to whom she was much attached, and whom she had educated with great care. When a superior had to be found for the new convent, St Cunegund appointed Judith and gave her many admonitions and much good advice. No sooner, however, did the young abbess find herself free, than she began to show symptoms of frivolity and lax observance. It was soon noticed that she was ever the first in the refectory and the last to come to chapel, and that she was a gossip and listened to tales. In vain did her aunt remonstrate with her. The climax came when she failed to appear in the Sunday procession and was found feasting with some of the younger sisters. Filled with indignation St Cunegund sternly upbraided the culprit, and even struck her. The marks of her fingers remained impressed upon the abbess's cheek until her dying day, and the marvel not only converted her, but had a salutary effect upon the whole community.

On the anniversary of her husband's death in 1024 Cunegund invited a number of prelates to the dedication of her church at Kaufungen. There, when the gospel had been sung at Mass, she offered at the altar a piece of the true cross, and then, putting off her imperial robes, she was clothed in a nun's habit, and the bishop gave her the veil. Once she had been consecrated to God in religion, she seemed entirely to forget that she had ever been an empress and behaved as the lowest in the house, being convinced that she was so before God. She feared nothing more than anything that could recall her former dignity. She prayed and read much and especially made it her business to visit and comfort the sick. Thus she passed the last years of her life, dying on March 3, 1033 (or 1039). Her body was taken to Bamberg to be buried with her husband's.

It is to the contemporary chroniclers, rather than to the relatively late biography of St Cunegund, that we must look for a trustworthy statement of the facts of her life. The latter is under suspicion of having been written with a view to her future canonization, which eventually came about in the year 1200. J. B. Sägmüller, in particular (*Theologische Quartalschrift*, 1903, 1907, 1911), has shown good reason for doubting that the childlessness of the emperor and empress was due to any compact between the parties to live together as Mary and Joseph ; *cf.* A. Michel in the same, vol. xcviii (1916), pp. 463–467. The biography, in varying forms, has been edited in the *Acta Sanctorum* (March, vol. i) and by G. Waitz in MGH., *Scriptores*, vol. vii. There are popular but rather uncritical modern lives of St Cunegund written by Toussaint and by H. Müller, the latter including an account of both St Henry and St Cunegund in one narrative. *Cf.* Hauck, *Kirchengeschichte Deutschlands*, vol. iii, p. 539.

ST GERVINUS, Abbot (A.D. 1075)

St Gervinus came of a family which is said to have been related to Bruno, Bishop of Toul, who afterwards was raised to the papacy as Leo IX. He was born in the district of Rheims and received his education at the episcopal school. A clever and eager student, he was greatly attracted by the Latin classics, and was at one time in danger of being led astray by the sensuous charm of the poetry he read, but by the grace of God he triumphed over temptation. After his ordination to the priesthood he became one of the canons of Rheims, and was thus comfortably provided for. Finding, however, that the life of a secular priest did not satisfy him, he entered the abbey of Saint-Vanne at Verdun, where he soon was noted for his wide knowledge, his eloquence and his modesty. In 1045 Henry I, King of France, appointed Gervinus abbot of Saint-Riquier, but he would not accept until he had received the suffrages of all the monks. His term of office was marked by the building of several chapels and sanctuaries, by his prudence in the management of the affairs of the abbey and by the zeal he displayed in collecting Greek and Latin manuscripts for the library. Pilgrims used to throng the church, and the abbot sometimes spent nearly the whole day in hearing confessions. Nor was his zeal confined to his abbey, for he made excursions through Picardy, Normandy, Aquitaine and as far as Thuringia, preaching and hearing confessions. When Pope St Leo IX in 1050 came in person to Rheims to consecrate the church of St Remigius and to preside over a council, the abbot of Saint-Riquier accompanied him on his journey back to Rome.

More than once St Gervinus visited England, where his abbey owned estates, and each time he preached the word and visited English shrines. St Edward the Confessor esteemed him highly, and a curious story is told that Queen Edith, sharing her husband's admiration, on their first meeting came forward according to the English custom to welcome the abbot with a kiss. Gervinus, thinking this unseemly, drew back and declined the proffered salute. Queen Edith was so furious that her husband had some difficulty in placating her, but the scene ended in her making the abbot a present of a very handsome cloak.

So great was the veneration in which he was held that he was called " the holy abbot " even during his lifetime. Although, for the last four years of his life, he suffered from a terrible form of leprosy, he continued to carry on all his customary duties as before, and he would often bless God for sending him the trial. On March 3, 1075, when he offered his last Mass in the little underground church of Notre-Dame de la Voûte which he had built, he was so ill that he could scarcely finish, and had to be carried back to his cell as soon as it was over. To his monks who stood round him in consternation he said, " Children, to-day our Blessed Lady has given me my discharge from this life ", and he insisted upon making a public confession of his sins. He then had himself taken back to the church and laid before the altar of St John Baptist, where he died. When his body was then washed, it was noticed that no trace of the leprosy remained.

The main source of our knowledge of the life of St Gervinus is the Chronicle of Saint-Riquier compiled by Hariulf. It is printed in Migne, PL., vol. clxxiv, and extracts also in MGH.

BD SERLO, Abbot of Gloucester   (A.D. 1104)

The claims of Serlo to be included in the calendar are perhaps doubtful, but he is described as " Blessed " in the Benedictine martyrologies of Ménard and Bucelin, while as abbot of a famous English monastery he has an interest for English readers. By birth he seems to have been a Norman, and he entered the Benedictine Order at Mont-Saint-Michel.   In 1071 he was recommended to William the Conqueror by St Osmund (then chancellor of Salisbury) as a good religious to whose rule the abbey of Gloucester might suitably be confided, and he was consecrated abbot at the hands of St Wulfstan, Bishop of Worcester.   When he came to Gloucester there were only two adult monks and about eight young boys : he left when he died a community of more than a hundred professed.

In July 1100 the abbot thought it his duty to write boldly to King William II telling him of the vision which had been vouchsafed to one of the Gloucester monks —it may have been himself—which announced that the cup of the king's iniquities was full to overflowing, and that the vengeance of Heaven was about to strike him down.   Ordericus, the chronicler, tells us that the letter was brought to Rufus on the very morning that he was setting out on the hunting excursion from which he was never to return.   After reading the letter the king laughed, gave his orders for the hunt to William Tirel, and said aloud in the presence of all : " I wonder why my lord Serlo has been minded to write thus to me, for he is, I believe, a good abbot, and a judicious old man.   In his extreme simplicity he passes on to me, busied with so many affairs, the nightmares of his snoring monks, and from a long distance has even sent them to me in writing.   Does he suppose that I follow the example of the English, who will defer their journey or their business for the dreams of wheezing old women ? "   Thereupon the king mounted his horse and rode off, only to be pierced an hour or two later by Tirel's sharp arrow glancing from a tree (?).

Serlo himself died in 1104 after ruling the abbey for more than thirty years. William of Malmesbury, a younger contemporary, writes of him : " How much the grace of God, conspiring with his industry, elevated the place [Gloucester Abbey], what eloquence can sufficiently explain ?   The management of the abbey in spirituals is what the weak may look up to and the strong not despise.   This was effected by the discipline of Serlo, a man humble to the good, but menacing and terrible to the proud of heart."   Serlo seems to have been a writer of ability both in prose and verse, but it is difficult to disentangle his compositions from what has been written by others who bore the name of Serlo and from those of Godfrey of Winchester.

See the *Historia et Cartularium Monasterii Sancti Petri Gloucestriae*, vol. i (Rolls Series), pp. xvii–xxii, as also the *Gesta Regum* of William of Malmesbury (Rolls Series), vol. ii, p. 512, and Symeon of Durham (Rolls Series), vol. ii, p. 236.   There is also a notice of Serlo in the DNB. and in T. D. Hardy, *Catalogue of British History*, vol. ii, p. 27.

ST AELRED, Abbot of Rievaulx   (A.D. 1167)

Aelred (Ailred) was of good family, son of the " hereditary " priest of Hexham, and was born there in 1110.   After a good education he was invited by St David, King of Scotland, to his court, and made master of his household, where he gained the esteem of all.   His virtue shone with bright lustre in the world, particularly his meekness, which Christ declared to be the distinguishing mark of His true disciples.   The following is a memorable instance of his gentle bearing.   A certain person of quality having insulted and reproached him in the presence of the king, Aelred heard him out with patience, and thanked him for his charity in telling him his faults.   This behaviour made such an impression on his adversary that he asked his pardon on the spot.   Another time, whilst he was speaking on a matter of importance, someone interrupted him very harshly and rudely   the servant of God heard him with tranquillity, and afterwards resumed his discourse with the same calm and presence of mind as before.   He wished to devote himself entirely to God by forsaking the world ; but the claims of friendship detained him some time in it. Reflecting, however, that he must sooner or later be separated by death from those he loved most, he condemned his own cowardice, and broke these ties of friendship at no little cost to himself.   He describes his feelings during this crisis, and says, " Those who saw me, judging by the courtly atmosphere in which I lived, and not knowing what passed within my soul, said, speaking of me   ' Oh, how well is it with him ! how happy he is ! '   But they knew not the anguish of my mind   for the deep wound in my heart caused me a thousand torments, and I was not able to bear the intolerable stench of my sins."   But after he had taken his resolution, he says, " I began then to know, by a little experience, what immense comfort is found in Thy service, and how sweet that peace is which is its inseparable companion."

To cut himself off from the world, Aelred left Scotland, and embraced the austere Cistercian life at Rievaulx in Yorkshire, where a noble lord called Walter Espec had founded a monastery in 1132.   At the age of twenty-four he became a monk under the first abbot, William, a disciple of St Bernard.   Fervour lending strength to his delicate body, he practised severe austerities and employed much of his time in prayer and reading.   He surrendered his heart with great ardour to the love of God, and by this means finding all his mortifications sweet and light, he cried out, " This is a yoke which does not crush but liberates the soul ; this burden has wings, not weight."   He speaks of the love of God always with rapture, and from his frequent outbursts these thoughts seem entirely to have absorbed him. " May thy voice (says he) so sound in my ears, good Jesus, that my heart may learn how to love thee, that my mind may love thee, that the interior powers of my soul and the very marrow of my heart may love thee, and that my affections may embrace thee, my only true good, my sweet and delightful joy !   What is love, O my God ? If I mistake not, it is the wonderful delight of the soul, so much the more sweet as more pure, so much the more overflowing and enlivening as more ardent.   He who loves thee, possesses thee ; and he possesses thee in proportion as he loves, because thou art love.   This is that abundance with which thy beloved are inebriated, melting away from themselves, that they may pass into thee by loving thee."   He had taken much delight in his youth in reading Cicero's *De amicitia* : but after his conversion found that author and all other reading tedious which was not sweetened with the honey of the holy name of Jesus and seasoned with the word of God.   This he tells us himself in his book, *On Spiritual Friendship*.   He was much edified with the very looks of a monk called Simon, who had despised high birth, an ample fortune and all the advantages of mind and body to serve God in that penitential state.   This monk went and came as one deaf and dumb, always recollected in God ; and was such a lover of silence that he would scarce speak a few words on necessary occasions.   His very silence however, was sweet and full of edification.   Aelred says of him, " The very sight of his humility stifled my pride, and made me blush at the immortification of my looks.   The silence practised among us prevented my ever addressing him of set purpose ; but one day, on my speaking a word to him inadvertently, his displeasure at my infraction of the rule appeared in his looks, and he suffered me to lie some time prostrate before him to expiate my fault ; for which I grieved bitterly, and for which I could never forgive myself."

St Aelred, much against his inclination, was made abbot of a new monastery of his order, founded at Revesby in Lincolnshire, in 1142, and soon after, in 1147, abbot of Rievaulx, where he presided over three hundred monks. Describing their life, he says that they drank nothing but water ; ate sparingly and of the coarsest food ; laboured hard, slept little, with boards for their bed ; never spoke except to their superiors on necessary occasions ; carried the burdens which were laid on them without refusing any ; went wherever they were led ; gave not a moment to sloth or amusements of any kind, and never had any lawsuit or dispute. St Aelred also speaks of their mutual charity and of the peace in which they lived, and he is not able to find words to express the joy which the sight of every one of them inspired in him. His humility and love of solitude made him steadfastly refuse the bishoprics which were pressed upon his acceptance. Reading and prayer were his delight. Even in times of spiritual dryness, if he opened the divine books, he found his soul flooded with the light of the Holy Ghost. In the *Revue Bénédictine* for April, 1925, Dom A. Wilmart printed for the first time a very beautiful prayer of St Aelred, which is called his " Oratio Pastoralis ". It is a sort of examination of conscience upon the duties and responsibilities incumbent upon him as superior of a large community. The document throws much light upon the saint's interior spirit and upon the deep and tender affection with which he regarded the monks committed to his charge. He adapted Osbert of Clare's life of St Edward the Confessor for the translation of his relics in 1163, and preached at Westminster on that occasion.

It appears clearly from Aelred's biographers, notably from the life by Walter Daniel, that in spite of all the saint's stern asceticism there was something singularly gentle and lovable about him in his relations with others. " For seventeen years I lived under his rule ", writes Walter, " and during all that time he dismissed no one from the monastery." Towards the close of his life he was a great sufferer, apparently from gout and stone ; in 1157 we find the general chapter of the Cistercians granting him exemptions which the state of his health demanded. Nevertheless he is heard of in Scotland in 1159 and again in 1165, and other visits of his can be traced to different parts of England, and on one occasion to Cîteaux itself. For one afflicted as he was, such journeys must have been a torment. But by 1166 he could leave his monastery no more, and after a lingering illness he died, on January 12, 1167, in the shed alongside the infirmary which for ten years had been his living and sleeping quarters. Of those last days, Aelred's patience and trust in God, the love and grief of his monks, Walter Daniel has left us a most moving account. It must be admitted that Alban Butler is not at his best in his treatment of St Aelred, who is one of the most attractive of English saints, a great teacher of friendship, divine and human, and a man who, quite apart from his writings, must have exercised a great influence through the monasteries he founded from Rievaulx. He was himself, " One whom I might fitly call friendship's child for his whole occupation is to love and to be loved " (*De spirituali amicitia*).

It seems that St Aelred was canonized in 1191 ; his feast is kept on March 3 in the dioceses of Liverpool, Hexham and Middlesbrough, and by the Cistercians.

Besides the admirable study of St Aelred by Father Dalgairns (in Newman's series of *Lives of the English Saints*), which may be truly described as one of the classics of hagiography, a very complete and up-to-date account of the saint is provided by F. M. Powicke's *Ailred of Rievaulx and his Biographer Walter Daniel* (1922). This writer shows that the life by Walter Daniel, a contemporary monk of Rievaulx, is the source from which both the two biographies previously known have been condensed. In 1950 Professor Powicke published Daniel's biography in Latin and English, with notes and a long introduction. We also obtain a good many sidelights upon Aelred's character from his own treatises and sermons. All these, with the exception of his book on the Hexham miracles, will be found printed in Migne, PL., vol. cxcv. There is a great devotional glow in many of his ascetical writings, notably in his *Speculum charitatis*. He was the author also of several short biographies— *e.g.* that of St Ninian—and of historical and theological tractates. There is a translation of *De spirituali amicitia* by Fr Hugh Talbot, called *Christian Friendship*. T. E. Harvey's *St Aelred of Rievaulx* (1932) is an excellent short book by a Quaker. See also D. Knowles, *The Monastic Order in England* (1949), pp. 240-245, 257-266 and *passim*. Aelred's name is variously spelt. In the DNB., for example, he appears as " Ethelred ", in Powicke and others as " Ailred " See, further, the *Acta Sanctorum* for January 12 ; and the *Dictionnaire de Spiritualité*, vol. i, cc. 225-234.

BD JACOPINO OF CANEPACI   (A.D. 1508)

THE life of this good Carmelite lay-brother seems to have been one of those in which perfection is found by prayer, austerity and charity, and in which there is little to relate of striking achievements or of intercourse with the outer world. He was born of humble parents in the township of Piasca in the diocese of Vercelli, and being animated with an intense devotion to the Blessed Virgin he sought admission at Vercelli among the Carmelites of the old observance. The example of his fervour was a stimulus to all. His special work was to collect alms, begging from door to door throughout the town, and in the discharge of this humble duty he seems to have found many opportunities for consoling those in trouble or saying a word of good advice to the tempted or the fallen. Worn out with toil, austerities and infirm health, he died on his seventieth birthday in 1508. A *cultus* is said to have begun at his tomb shortly after his death on account of the miracles worked there, and this was approved in 1845.

The outlines of Bd Jacopino's life are sketched in the office sanctioned for his feast, and there is a short biography, *Vita del b. Giacobino di Ayloche* (1846).

BD TERESA VERZERI, VIRGIN, FOUNDRESS OF THE DAUGHTERS OF THE SACRED HEART   (A.D. 1852)

TERESA VERZERI, born at Bergamo in Lombardy on July 31, 1801, was one of the several children of Antony Verzeri and his wife Helen, of the family of the counts of Pedrocca-Grumelli. The Verzeris had a devotion to St Jerome ; a son (who became bishop of Brescia) was named after him, and Teresa was given as a second name Eustochium, after the daughter of St Paula, the dear friends of Jerome who were in turn the heads of the community of women near his monastery at Bethlehem. This choice of name proved to be prophetic.

Teresa Verzeri is said to have first thought of becoming a nun when she made her first communion at the age of ten. Such aspirations are not uncommon at such a time ; but by the time of her confirmation Teresa's inclination had hardened into a resolution. In this she received the help and encouragement of Canon Joseph Benaglio, of the cathedral chapter of Bergamo ; but it is not easy to say whether at this time the good canon could not make up his own mind about Teresa or whether he was trying her. For three separate times she entered the Benedictine convent of St Grata on his instructions, and each time on his instructions she left it again. This unquestioning obedience brought upon her a certain amount of contempt and mockery, which she bore bravely and cheerfully. It was certainly a hard apprenticeship.

After her third withdrawal from the convent Teresa gave herself entirely to the religious instruction of girls, at a small house in the country called Gromo, and this proved to be the seed of the new congregation which she was to establish. She was joined by one of her sisters, Antonia, and by two other young women, Virginia Simoni and Catherine Manghenoni ; and these four made simple vows before Canon Benaglio, who designated them as teachers of the young. They imposed a stern way of life on themselves, with long periods of silence and fasting ; and Teresa herself had many spiritual difficulties, doubts and temptations to contend with. But recruits began to come in, some of them of good education, and they eventually included three more of her own sisters, Mary, Judith and Catherine, and even her mother, who was now a widow. The community lived under the general direction of Canon Benaglio, and with his help a rule and constitutions were drawn up. The rule envisaged charitable works of several kinds : schools for poor children, visiting sick women, recreational and religious centres for girls in moral danger, and, above all, retreats for lay women, to be conducted according to the Spiritual Exercises of St Ignatius.

At first the bishop of Bergamo, Mgr Charles Gritti-Morlacchi, viewed the new institute with favour, but afterwards he put obstacles and discouragements in its way. A further and worse trial for Teresa Verzeri arose from her own undecidedness and humility. Was God really calling her to this work as a foundress, seeing that there were other similar congregations already in existence, notably the Society of the Sacred Heart of St Madeleine Sophie Barat? Sister Teresa visited Turin, where in 1832 Mother Barat began her work of retreats for women, and she there felt strongly drawn towards a fusion of her budding institute with that of Madeleine Sophie. But it became clear to her that God's will was otherwise ; there was room and need for two separate congregations, though so alike. There were then these and other difficulties to be overcome and much patience to be exercised and disappointments to be borne before the new congregation could be said to be solidly established. At length in 1841 Mother Teresa Verzeri and her companions were allowed to make their solemn vows, which were received for the Church by the prefect himself of the Congregation of Bishops and Regulars, Cardinal Constantine Patrizi. A few days later the Holy See's approbation of the congregation was issued, and this approbation was confirmed in 1847 ; on this second occasion permission was given to the mother foundress to open a house of her institute in Rome itself.

Among those who helped Bd Teresa Verzeri in her difficulties was Bd Ludovic Pavoni, of Brescia. He printed the constitutions of her congregation at his institute, at a time when to do so was to risk serious displeasure ; he simply refused to be intimidated by gossip and intrigue. Furthermore, he asked Mgr Speranza to do what he could to forward the cause of the Daughters of the Sacred Heart, and when Bd Teresa acquired an old monastery at Brescia, Canon Pavoni was the architect and contractor for the alterations and personally supervised their carrying out. On her behalf he went several times to Bergamo and Trento, and made himself responsible that Mass should be celebrated daily in their mother house. In fact nothing was too much for Bd Ludovic to do for these sisters ; he and Bd Teresa had a very high regard for one another, and this mutual esteem has continued in their respective congregations for the century that has passed since the death of their founders.

For four more years, after opening the Rome house, Bd Teresa grew in grace and holiness, and her foundation with her. Then, in a cholera epidemic that swept northern Italy, she was struck down and died, at Brescia, on March 3, 1852. The crowds at her funeral bore witness to the reputation of holiness that was already hers ; as time passed it continued to increase, and she was beatified in 1946.

See the brief of beatification, printed in the *Acta Apostolicae Sedis*, vol. xxxix, no. 1 (1947). There seem to be no biographies of Teresa Verzeri in other languages than Italian ; apparently several volumes of her letters have been published : *cf. Un apostolo della gioventù derelitta* (Bd Ludovic Pavoni), pages 209–211 and footnotes (1928).

4 : ST CASIMIR OF POLAND   (A.D. 1484)

ST CASIMIR, to whom the Poles gave the title of " The Peace-maker ", was the third of the thirteen children of Casimir IV, King of Poland, and of Elizabeth of Austria, daughter of the Emperor Albert II. Casimir was the second son ; he and his two brothers, Ladislaus and John, had as their tutor John Dlugosz, the historian, a canon of Cracow and a man of extraordinary learning and piety. All the princes were warmly attached to the holy man, but Casimir profited the most by his teaching and example. Devout from his infancy, the boy gave himself up to devotion and penance, and had a horror of anything approaching softness or self-indulgence. His bed was often the ground, and he was wont to spend a great part of the night in prayer and meditation, chiefly on the passion of our Saviour. His clothes were plain, and under them he wore a hair-shirt. Living always in the presence of God he was invariably serene and cheerful, and pleasant to all. The saint's love of God showed itself in his love of the poor who are Christ's members, and for the relief of these the young prince gave all he possessed, using in their behalf the influence he had with his father and with his brother Ladislaus when he became king of Bohemia. In honour of the Blessed Virgin Mary Casimir frequently recited the long Latin hymn " *Omni die dic Mariae* ", a copy of which was by his desire buried with him. This hymn, part of which is familiar to us through Bittleston's version, " Daily, daily sing to Mary ", is not uncommonly called the Hymn of St Casimir, but it was certainly not composed by him ; it is three centuries older than his time.

The nobles of Hungary, dissatisfied with their king, Matthias Corvinus, in 1471 begged the King of Poland to allow them to place his son Casimir on the throne. The saint, at that time not fifteen years old, was very unwilling to consent, but in obedience to his father he went to the frontier at the head of an army. There, hearing that Matthias had himself assembled a large body of troops, and withal finding that his own soldiers were deserting in large numbers because they could not get their pay, he decided upon the advice of his officers to return home. The knowledge that Pope Sixtus IV had sent an embassy to his father to deter him from the expedition made the young prince carry out his resolution with the firmer conviction that he was acting rightly. King Casimir, however, was greatly incensed at the failure of his ambitious projects and would not permit his son to return to Cracow, but relegated him to the castle of Dobzki. The young man obeyed and remained in confinement there for three months. Convinced of the injustice of the war upon which he had so nearly embarked, and determined to have no further part in these internecine conflicts which only facilitated the further progress into Europe of the Turks, St Casimir could never again be persuaded to take up arms, though urged to do so by his father and invited once more by the disaffected Hungarian magnates. He returned to his studies and his prayers, though for a time he was viceroy in Poland during an absence of his father. An attempt was made to induce him to marry a daughter of the Emperor Frederick III, but he refused to relax the celibacy he had imposed on himself.

St Casimir's austerities did nothing to help the lung trouble from which he suffered, and he died at the age of twenty-three in 1484 and was buried at Vilna, where his relics still rest in the church of St Stanislaus. Miracles were reported at his tomb, and he was canonized in 1521.

A Latin life of St Casimir by Zachary Ferreri was printed at Cracow in 1521 and has been reproduced in the *Acta Sanctorum*, March, vol. i, and there is also a biography by Prileszky in the *Acta Sanctorum Hungariae* (1743), vol. i, pp. 121–132. A popular account in German is that of Felix Iózefowicz, *Der heilige Kasimir*, commending the saint as a patron for young students. In the article devoted to St Casimir in the *Catholic Encyclopedia*, Prof. L. Abraham gives references to several works in Polish of more modern date. Casimir is sometimes referred to as king of Poland and Hungary, though he never occupied the throne of either country. The fact that he is accorded apparently only one line in the *Cambridge History of Poland*, vol. i (1950) shows perhaps how little impression he made in secular affairs. The so-called Hymn of St Casimir forms one division of the great *Mariale*, a remarkable rhyming Latin lyric of the twelfth century, which has been attributed both to St Anselm and to St Bernard of Clairvaux. The true author is probably Bernard of Morlaix, or Cluny. Casimir's love of these verses is a testimony at once to his good literary taste and to his devotion to the Mother of God. At a time when certain enthusiastic sympathizers with Polish aspirations were eager to claim the *Omni die dic Mariae* as a sort of national anthem, a book was brought out which printed the text of the hymn along with translations in various modern languages in the metre of the original. When a second edition was in contemplation, Cardinal Wiseman was invited to contribute an English version of this hymn. His rendering was afterwards published separately, with a musical setting, but it is now little known.

ST LUCIUS I, POPE   (A.D. 254)

ALMOST immediately after his accession the persecution which had been initiated by Decius was renewed under Gallus, and Pope Lucius I was banished to a place the name of which has not been recorded. But he had been but a short time in exile when he and his companions were recalled, to the great joy of his people who flocked in crowds to meet him. On this occasion St Cyprian wrote him a letter of congratulation. In it he assures the pope that he had not lost the palm of martyrdom, although, like the three children in the fiery furnace, he had been preserved by God from death. The letter adds : " We do not cease in our sacrifices and prayers to God the Father and to Christ His Son, giving thanks and offering supplication that He who perfects all may consummate in you the glorious crown of your confession. He perhaps has only recalled you that your glory may not be hidden, for it is fitting that the victim who owes to his brethren an example of virtue and faith should be sacrificed in their presence." In another letter, which St Cyprian afterwards wrote to Pope St Stephen, he quotes St Lucius as having condemned the Novatian heretics for their refusal of absolution and communion to those who had fallen but were penitent.

According to Eusebius, St Lucius did not occupy the pontifical chair for more than eight months.   Although in the Roman Martyrology on this day Lucius is described as " Martyr in the persecution of Valerian ", it is practically certain that he was no longer living when the persecution of Valerian began, and it is improbable that he suffered death as a martyr.   The chronographer of 354 does not insert his name in the "depositio martyrum ", but in the "depositio episcoporum ", and the remnants of the catacomb inscription discovered by De Rossi supply no indication of martyrdom.   No credence can be given to the statement of the *Liber Pontificalis* that St Lucius, as he was being led to death, virtually nominated Stephen as his successor.

Certain relics of St Lucius are said to be treasured in Bologna, whilst a head, reputed to be that of this pope, was long venerated in the cathedral of Roeskilde, near Copenhagen—the burial-place of the Danish kings—and Pope Lucius is honoured as chief patron of that city ; but most probably the relics in Sweden and in Bologna are the remains of one of the two other saints of the name of Lucius who are commemorated on this same day.   The pope's body was buried in the catacomb of St Callistus, but the remains after an early translation were transferred to the church of St Cecilia, where they now lie, by order of Clement VIII.

See Duchesne, *Liber Pontificalis*, vol. i, pp. xcvii and 153 ; St Cyprian (Hartel), pt ii, pp. 695 and 748 ; De Rossi, *Roma Sotterranea*, vol. ii, 62-70 ; and *cf.* the *Acta Sanctorum*, March, vol. i, and Allard, *Histoire des persécutions*, vol. iii, pp. 27 *seq.*

SS. ADRIAN AND HIS COMPANIONS, MARTYRS   (A.D. 875 ?)

IN the ninth century, during one of their numerous descents upon the coast of Scotland, the Dànes massacred St Adrian and a number of his companions who, after having helped to evangelize Fifeshire, had retired into a monastery on the Isle of May in the Firth of Forth.   The early history of these saints is uncertain. According to the Aberdeen Breviary, St Adrian was of royal descent and a native of Pannonia in Hungary, where he became a bishop.   Fired by missionary zeal, he came to Scotland with Clodion, Gaius, Stolbrand, Monan and 6602 other companions—all of whom perished with him.   As a missionary bishop he appears to have had no fixed see, but he has been credited with the bishopric and even the archbishopric of Saint Andrews.   Some modern historians identify St Adrian with the Irish St Odhran, and are disposed to follow Boece, who states that all the martyrs were Angles and Scots.   The Angles may well have been the followers of St Acca who, when driven from Northumberland, founded a bishopric among the Picts, whilst the Scots or Irish will have been Adrian and his friends, who were probably obliged by Danish invasions to leave Ireland and so came to the Firth of Forth.   Fordun gives the number of martyrs as 100 ; there certainly was a battle in 875 between the Scots and the Danes, in the course of which many of the Scots were killed.   In the Aberdeen Breviary, printed in 1509, the martyrs had an office with nine lessons, and Wyntoun celebrates their death in a metrical chronicle :

> And upon Haly Thurysday
> Saint Adrian thai sloe in May
> With mony of his cumpany
> In that haly Ile thai ly.

St David I built a priory on the island and placed it under the Benedictines of Reading, but it afterwards passed to the canons regular of Saint Andrews.   The Isle of May became a favourite place of pilgrimage, and as such it was visited several times by the Scottish King James IV.

See the Aberdeen Breviary, and KSS., pp. 266–268.

ST PETER OF CAVA, Bishop of Policastro   (A.D. 1123)

PETER PAPPACARBONE was a native of Salerno in Italy, a nephew of St Alferius, founder of the monastery of Cava, and entered upon the religious life at a very early age under St Leo, the second abbot.   He distinguished himself at once by his piety, abstemiousness and love of solitude.   At this time the fame of the abbey of Cluny had spread far and wide, and the young monk was so attracted by what he had heard that about 1062 he obtained permission to leave Cava and go to France. When the older monks at Cluny would have sent him to the school to be trained, their abbot, St Hugh, disagreed, saying that Peter might be young in years but that he was a full-grown man in devotion.   The abbot's opinion was abundantly justified, for Peter proved himself well among that household of holy men and he remained there for some six years.   He was then recalled to Italy, having been released by St Hugh apparently at the request of the archdeacon of Rome, Hildebrand (who was afterwards Pope St Gregory VII).

St Peter was appointed the first bishop of Policastro, but he found himself unfitted for the turmoil of the world and for the secular cares which devolved upon him.   He obtained permission to resign and retired to Cava, where Abbot Leo, realizing that he himself was becoming too old to govern, nominated him as his successor and withdrew.   The monks by their votes had confirmed the election of their new superior, but soon found the strict rule he had brought from Cluny extremely irksome : they began to murmur and rebel, and some of them carried their complaints to the aged Leo in his retirement.   St Peter, far from resisting and equally far from relaxing the rule, quietly left and betook himself to another monastery.   It was not long before the monks of Cava, urged by Abbot Leo, came to entreat St Peter to return, which he consented to do.   Thereafter it was remarked that those who had the most vehemently opposed him were now foremost in welcoming the rule they had previously spurned.

Under the government of Abbot Peter the monastery flourished amazingly. Not only did numbers of aspirants to the religious life flock to him from all sides, but men and women in the world showered money and lands upon the community, which was enabled to minister far and wide to the sick and the poor.   The abbey itself had to be enlarged to admit the new members, and a new church was built, to the dedication of which came Pope Urban II, who had been with St Peter at Cluny and had remained his close friend.   The description of this occasion was preserved in the chronicles of Cava, where it is stated that Bd Urban talked freely with the abbot and monks, as though " forgetting that he was pope ".   St Peter lived to a great age and died in 1123.

The abbey of Cava still exists, and in 1912 the monks gave proof of their devotion to the founders of their observance by reprinting from the unique ancient manuscript in their possession the Lives of Alferius, Peter and two other early abbots, purporting to be written by Hugh of Venosa, a younger contemporary of St Peter.   It is to this biography, which may be found in the *Acta Sanctorum* (March, vol. i) as well as in Ughelli and Muratori, that we owe all our knowledge of St Peter of Cava.

BD HUMBERT III OF SAVOY   (A.D. 1188)

HUMBERT III, Count of Savoy, was born in 1136 at Avigliana, and his parents, Amadeus III of Savoy and Matilda of Vienne, were at pains to give him a good and religious education.. They entrusted his training to Bd Amadeus, Bishop of Lausanne, under whom the youth made great progress, especially in the life of prayer. Called to rule at his father's death, he sacrificed a desire for solitude to the task imposed upon him, and though a mere boy when he took up the reins of government he showed himself fully equal to his position, finding it quite possible to reconcile the duty of a secular ruler with that of self-sanctification. When his wife died childless, the count sought in the monastery of Aulps the consolation he needed, and would fain have remained there, but his vassals came to entreat him not to abandon them and to take steps to ensure the succession in his family. Yielding to these representations he again took up the burden and contracted two, if not three, more marriages. By his second wife, Germana of Zähringen, he had a child, Agnes, who was betrothed to John Lackland, afterwards king of England, but both mother and daughter died before the marriage could take place. During this period Humbert had occasion to repel aggression by force of arms, and he then proved himself as capable in warfare as in peace. " Brave in contest, undaunted in reverse, just and moderate in victory, he was ever unflinching in his adherence to what he held to be just." His reputation for wisdom and probity reached far beyond the limits of his own country, and won for him the confidence of his contemporaries. We read, however, that on one occasion he came into violent conflict with St Anthelmus, Bishop of Belley. Happily the two holy men, though they had lost their tempers badly, arrived at a very edifying reconciliation.

The time came at last when Count Humbert felt that he was justified in retiring from the world to prepare himself for death. He accordingly withdrew to the Cistercian abbey of Hautecombe, where he gave himself up to the humblest and most austere practices of the religious life. According to some authorities, however, he was not suffered to remain long in retirement : the call of his people, who were again threatened with invasion from Germany, summoned him from the cloister to take command of the army. Though forewarned of his approaching death he marched with them as far as Chambéry, where he died in 1188. This account of the close of his troubled career is, it must be confessed, very doubtful. There is good reason to believe that Bd Humbert died peacefully in his Cistercian retreat, where also was buried nearly a century later Bd Boniface of Savoy, who had been archbishop of Canterbury. The *cultus* of Bd Humbert was approved in 1838.

There seems to be no early biography of Bd Humbert. The facts have to be gathered from the imperfect and often conflicting accounts of the chroniclers. Most of the story can be gleaned from the important work of Samuel Guichenon, *Histoire généalogique de la royale Maison de Savoye*, of which the first edition appeared in 1660. See also the convenient little volume of F. G. Allaria *Il b. Umberto III storia e leggende* (1879). It is noteworthy that Guichenon strongly maintains that Humbert was married, not three, but four times, and that his fourth wife, when he retired to his Cistercian abbey, herself became a nun at Messines in Flanders.

BD CHRISTOPHER BALES, MARTYR   (A.D. 1590)

CONISCLIFFE in the diocese of Durham was the birthplace of Christopher Bayles, or Bales (who also took the name of Rivers). He received his education abroad at the

English College in Rome and at the Douai College at Rheims, and was then ordained and sent on the English mission in 1588. After labouring for nearly two years, he was arrested and imprisoned. The misery of his confinement was aggravated by his bodily weakness, for he was consumptive, but nothing could overcome his courage and patience. He was cruelly racked in prison to force him to admit where he had said Mass and by whom he had been harboured, and on one occasion he was left hanging by the wrists for twenty-four hours.

Eventually he was brought to trial and found guilty of treason, for having been ordained priest beyond the seas and for coming to England to exercise his priestly office. When the judge asked him in the usual form whether he had anything to say in his defence, Bales answered that he wished to put one question " Was St Augustine, the monk sent by the Pope of Rome to preach the Catholic faith in England, guilty of treason in complying with that commission ? " The court replied in the negative. " Why, then ", asked the martyr, " do you arraign and condemn me for a traitor who do the same thing as he did, and to whom nothing can be objected but what might equally be objected against him ? " They replied that the difference lay in the fact that, by English law, such action had now been made treason. Having been accordingly sentenced to death, he was hanged, disembowelled and quartered in Fleet Street on March 4, 1590.

See MMP., p. 160, and J. H. Pollen, *Acts of English Martyrs.* The Penkevel Papers in the Westminster Archives and Fr Grene's *Collectanea* at Stonyhurst furnish contemporary evidence, and *cf.* John Gerard's autobiography (ed. Caraman, 1951), pp. 8–9.

BD PLACIDA VIEL, VIRGIN   (A.D. 1877)

VICTORIA EULALIA JACQUELINE VIEL, who was to become second superior general of the Sisters of the Christian Schools, was born in the Norman village of Val-Vacher in 1815, the eighth child of a farmer. The only schooling she had herself was seven years at a sort of dame's school in the near-by town of Quettehou. She was serious and shy by disposition, leading the quiet ordered life of a farmer's daughter and housekeeping for her brother until she was seventeen, when she went on a visit to her aunt, who was a member of St Mary Magdalen Postel's community at Saint-Sauveur-le-Vicomte. Victoria was so impressed by what she saw there that she offered herself to the community and was accepted, receiving the name of Placida at her clothing.

Mother Mary Postel was then nearly eighty, and by the end of Sister Placida's noviciate had decided that this young sister was the one most likely to succeed herself at the head of the community. Placida was therefore sent for a short period of intensive training to the normal-school in Argentan ; on her return she was set to teach in the boarding-school, and the foundress quietly initiated her into the duties and responsibilities of administration, even to the extent of sending her to open new houses. In five years' time Placida was made novice-mistress ; but this was soon interrupted by her being sent to Paris to beg funds for the restoration of the abbey church at Saint-Sauveur and to do other important convent business.

On July 16, 1846 St Mary Magdalen Postel died, and at the ensuing general chapter of the Sisters of the Christian Schools Sister Placida was chosen in her place. Her aunt, Sister Mary, had expected to be the choice ; and although the new superioress gave her a maximum of authority and responsibility, Sister Mary, who had already shown hostility to her niece, was the source of much worry and unpleasantness to Mother Placida for the next ten years. Indeed, she stayed at the mother-house as little as possible so long as her aunt lived, directing her society " from the rough winding highways and byways of central and western France " which she traversed so often collecting funds and on other business of the rapidly-growing convents : notably the getting of official civil recognition, a long and wearisome business, which once took her on a mysterious secret visit to the Count de Chambord in Vienna.

Mother Placida directed the institute for thirty years, and it was a period of great expansion : orphanages, nursery-schools, workrooms and free elementary schools were opened, one of the largest and best-loved foundations being the orphanage of the Holy Heart of Mary in Paris, where by 1877 there were 500 children being looked after ; and the foundress's undertaking of the rebuilding of the great church at the mother-house was carried to a triumphant conclusion. Cardinal Guibert, Archbishop of Bordeaux, speaking of the state of France in the 1870s echoed what had been said of Bd Anne Javouhey, and remarked, " I know only one man capable of restoring order in France. He is at Saint-Sauveur-le-Vicomte, and his name is Mother Placida." In reading of her life and achievements one gets an impression of great charm and good-humour, and of quietness and confidence in her determination that what St John Baptist de la Salle had done for boys should be spread wider yet among girls ; thirty-six poor-schools were opened in Normandy—and *Les ordonnances de Louis XIV* was abolished as a reading-book for beginners, or for anyone else.

Bd Placida's life was of the simplest from every point of view. We read of no great spiritual trials or mystical graces ; but occurrences to all seeming miraculous were not wanting. These and other things she consistently attributed to the intercession in Heaven of Mother Postel, the preliminary steps towards whose beatification she took. Bd Placida herself died on March 4, 1877, being only 62 years old ; and she was beatified in 1951. During the time she was at the head of the Sisters of the Christian Schools their convents in France had risen from 37 to 105, and their religious from 150 to over 1000.

See, in French, D. Meunier, *Une gerbe de merveilles* (1931) ; L. Canuet, *Bonne Mère Placide* (1925) and the biography by P. de Crisenoy (1943) ; in English, *Bd Placide Viel* (1951), by S[ister] C[allista]. *Cf.* also lives of St Mary M. Postel (July 16).

5 : SS. ADRIAN AND EUBULUS, MARTYRS (A.D. 309)

THE seventh year of Diocletian's persecution, when Firmilian was governor of Palestine, Adrian and Eubulus came from Batanea to Caesarea to visit the holy confessors. At the gates of the city they were asked their business and their destination, and frankly acknowledged that they had come to minister to the followers of Jesus Christ. They were immediately brought before the president, by whose orders they were scourged, their sides were torn with iron hooks, and they were condemned to be thrown to the wild beasts. Two days later, at the local festival of the goddess Fortune, Adrian was first exposed to a lion which mangled but did not kill him, and then slain with the sword ; Eubulus suffered a similar fate a day or two after. The judge had offered him his liberty if he would sacrifice to idols, but the saint preferred to die, and was the last to suffer at Caesarea in this persecution, which had lasted for twelve years, under three successive governors, Flavian, Urban and Firmilian.   Retribution soon overtook the cruel Firmilian, for that same year he fell into disgrace and was beheaded by the emperor's order—as his predecessor Urban had been two years previously.

The historian Eusebius, who was a contemporary, is our reliable source of information concerning these martyrs.   See his *Martyrs of Palestine*, xi, 29–31.

ST PHOCAS OF ANTIOCH, Martyr   (Date Unknown)

Phocas, in the words of the Roman Martyrology (derived ultimately from St Gregory of Tours), " after suffering many outrages in the name of the Redeemer, triumphed over the Old Serpent and has his victory made manifest to-day by this marvel ; to wit, that whenever a man, bitten by a venomous snake and full of faith, touches the door of the martyr's basilica, the poison loses its power and he is cured ". The Bollandists have identified him with St Phocas of Sinope (" the Gardener "), of whom relics were deposited in the church of St Michael at Antioch.

St Gregory of Tours, *De gloria martyrum*, bk i, ch. 98 ; his words have been adopted by Florus and the other later martyrologists.   See Delehaye, *Origines du culte des martyrs* (1933), pp. 169, 205, and CMH., pp. 128, 374–375.

ST EUSEBIUS OF CREMONA   (*c.* A.D. 423)

St Eusebius of Cremona paid a visit as a young man to Rome and during his stay made the acquaintance of St Jerome.   There sprang up between the two an intimacy which proved lifelong, and when Jerome proposed to journey to the Holy Land Eusebius determined to accompany him.   Arrived at Antioch, they were joined by the widow St Paula and her daughter St Eustochium, who accompanied them in their pilgrimages to the Holy Places and Egypt, before they all settled at Bethlehem.   In view of the large number of poor pilgrims who flocked to Bethlehem, St Jerome proposed to build a hostel for them ; and it was apparently to collect funds for that purpose that he sent Eusebius and Paulinian first to Dalmatia and then to Italy, where they seem to have sold the property St Eusebius owned at Cremona as well as that of St Paula in Rome.

In Rome Eusebius found himself involved in an acrimonious dispute with Rufinus, a priest of Aquileia, who was charged with making a garbled translation of Origen and disseminating false doctrine.   St Jerome had opposed his teaching, and Eusebius identified himself with his master.   Rufinus attacked Eusebius violently, and complained that through his agency his translation of Origen had been stolen and tampered with.   Later on, we find St Jerome accusing Rufinus of hiring a monk to get possession of a letter from St Epiphanius to John of Jerusalem —the monk having undertaken to make a Latin translation of it for Eusebius who, though an excellent Latin scholar, knew no Greek.   The details of these protracted controversies are obscure and not very edifying.   It seems that Eusebius was largely responsible for having eventually induced Pope St Anastasius to condemn the writings of Origen.

In 400 he again visited his native town, and is said to have remained in Italy. The account attributed to him of Jerome's last illness is certainly a forgery.   Several of St Jerome's commentaries are dedicated to his friend, whose body is said to have been buried beside that of his master at Bethlehem ; but the fact is very doubtful.

An altar in the crypt of the church of the Nativity is dedicated in honour of St Eusebius. A tradition states that St Eusebius was the founder of the monastery of Guadalupe in Spain, and that he introduced into the Peninsula the Order of Hieronymites, but the legend is baseless.

Nearly all the reliable information we possess concerning St Eusebius of Cremona comes from the works and letters of St Jerome. The long life printed in the *Acta Sanctorum* (March, vol. i) was compiled by Francis Ferrari from this source, but very uncritically. See also DCB., vol. ii, pp. 376–377, and Cavallera, *St Jérôme, sa vie et son œuvre* (1922).

ST GERASIMUS, ABBOT   (A.D. 475)

ST GERASIMUS was a native of Lycia in Asia Minor, where he embraced the life of a hermit. Passing thence to Palestine, he fell for a time into the errors of Eutyches, then very prevalent, but St Euthymius brought him back to the true faith. He appears afterwards to have stayed at several settlements in the Thebaïd and then to have returned to the Holy Land, where he became intimate with St John the Silent, St Sabas, St Theoctistus and St Anastasius of Jerusalem. So great a number of disciples gathered round him that he established for them by the Jordan, near Jericho, a *laura* of 70 cells, with a *cenobium* for the training of aspirants. His monks observed almost complete silence ; their only bed was a reed mat and no fire was ever lighted in their cells, the doors of which might never be closed. Bread, dates and water were their usual food, and their time was divided between prayer and manual work : to each one was set an appointed task which he was expected to finish by Saturday. Severe as was the rule, St Gerasimus made it severer still for himself, and never ceased doing penance for his temporary lapse into heresy. He was wont, it is said, to spend the whole of Lent without taking any food but the Holy Eucharist. So highly did St Euthymius esteem his convert that he used to send to him for training those of his followers whom he regarded as called to the highest perfection. The fame of St Gerasimus was second only to that of St Sabas, and at the time of the Council of Chalcedon in 451 his name was honoured throughout the East. His great laura long survived its founder and was still flourishing a hundred years after his death.

John Moschus in his *Spiritual Meadow* furnishes us with a charming anecdote. One day when the abbot was beside the Jordan, a lion came up to him evidently in great pain, walking on three feet with the fourth paw in the air. Gerasimus examined the paw and, seeing that a sharp thorn had entered, extracted it, bathed the foot and bound it up. After this, the lion would not leave him, but became tamer than any domestic animal. Now the monastery had a donkey that was used for fetching water, and after a time the lion was sent to take care of it when it went to pasture. One day, Arab traders stole the donkey, and the lion returned home to the monastery alone and very dejected. Questioned, it could only be silent and look over its shoulder. " Thou hast eaten him ", said the abbot. " Blessed be God. But henceforth thou must do what the donkey did." Accordingly the lion had to carry the water-bottles for the community. Shortly afterwards the Arab thief passed again with the ass and with three camels, and the lion, recognizing them, chased the man off, seized the donkey's bridle in his mouth, and brought it and the camels back in triumph to the monastery. St Gerasimus saw his mistake and gave his favourite the name of Jordan. When the old abbot died the poor beast was disconsolate. The new abbot said to him, " Jordan, our friend has left us orphans and has gone to join the Master whom he served, but do thou take thy food and eat." But he only moaned and roared the more. At last Sabbatius, the abbot, led him to the grave of Gerasimus, and weeping knelt down beside it saying, " See where he is buried." Then the lion stretched himself over the grave and beat his head upon the ground and could not be prevailed upon to leave, but was found dead there a few days later. It has been suggested that the lion which has become the attribute of St Jerome was really the lion of St Gerasimus, confusion having arisen when, as sometimes happened, St Jerome's name was spelt Geronimus.

The *Acta Sanctorum*, March, vol. i, prints more extracts from the Life of St Euthymius, by Cyril of Scythopolis, which mention Gerasimus, as well as quotations from John Moschus. But besides these sources a Life of Gerasimus has also been edited in Greek by Papadopoulos Kerameus in the fourth volume of his *Analecta*. He ascribes it to Cyril of Scythopolis, but H. Grégoire in the *Byzantinische Zeitschrift* (vol. xiii, pp. 114–135) has given substantial reasons for setting aside this attribution.

ST KIERAN, or CIARAN, OF SAIGHIR, Bishop in Ossory
(c. A.D. 530 ?)

Of the sons of Erin senior to or associated with St Patrick, one of the most celebrated is St Kieran, whom the Irish designate as the first-born of their saints. Very conflicting accounts of him appear in the legendary lives, where he seems to have been confused with other holy men of his name and where, in order to reconcile discrepancies of date, he is sometimes credited with having lived to the age of 300. According to some he was a native of Ossory, according to others Cork was his birthplace. Having received some elementary knowledge of Christianity, he is said to have made a journey to Rome, at the age of about thirty, in order to be more fully instructed in the faith, and after a stay of some years to have returned to Ireland accompanied by four learned men, all of whom were afterwards raised to the episcopate. Some writers maintain that he was ordained bishop in Rome, and that it was in Italy, on his homeward journey, that he first met St Patrick, who was not yet a bishop ; but others, with more show of probability, assert that St Kieran was one of the twelve whom St Patrick upon his arrival in Ireland consecrated bishops to assist him in evangelizing the country. We read that he made himself a cell in a lovely spot surrounded by woods near a famous spring, and for some time lived the life of a hermit. Ere long, however, disciples gathered about him and he constructed a monastery or collection of huts, round which subsequently sprang up a town called after him Sier-Ciaran and Saighir, or Saigher. He is venerated as the first bishop of Ossory, a diocese now including Kilkenny and parts of Leix and Offaly, and his feast is observed throughout Ireland.

Many legends, some fantastic and some poetical, have grown up round St Kieran, but only two or three of them can be set down here. The holy man had had for his nurse St Cuach, who afterwards became abbess of Ros-Bennchuir, a place situated in a part of Ireland very remote from Saighir. Nevertheless, every Christmas night, when St Kieran had offered Mass and had given communion to his monks, he celebrated again at Ros-Bennchuir and gave communion to Cuach. How he got there and back in the same night was never known, for he told no one, but, as the chronicler truly remarks, God could if He willed convey this faithful servant, as He had in the past conveyed the prophet Habakkuk from Palestine to Chaldaea.

St Kieran lent some oxen to Cuach to help her to cultivate her fields. He sent no word that they were arriving and the animals found their own way to the abbess, who, divining from whence they came, set them to work at the plough. They remained for several years at Ros-Bennchuir, but when they judged that the land was in a good state of cultivation the wise beasts of their own accord returned to their master.

One day a boy called Crichidh came to St Kieran, who took him in and employed him in the monastery. But the mischievous lad, " at the instigation of the Devil ", extinguished the paschal fire which was lighted at Easter and was kept burning for the rest of the year, the only source from which all lights in the monastery were kindled. Then said the aged St Kieran, " Brothers, our sacred fire has been put out on purpose by that rascally boy Crichidh, for he is always doing things to annoy us. Now we shall have no fire until next Easter unless the Lord sends us some ", and he went on to foretell that the miscreant would meet with an untimely death. The very next day when the boy went out into the woods, he was eaten up by a wolf.

Tidings of this reached St Kieran the Younger at Clonmacnois to whom the lad belonged, and he came to Saighir. It was bitterly cold and the monks had no means of warming their guests or of cooking a meal. Then St Kieran the Elder upraised his hands to God in prayer, and immediately there fell into his lap a glowing fire-ball which he carried in his skirt to his guests, who were able to warm themselves by its heat. As soon as supper was announced and they had all sat down to table, Kieran of Clonmacnois said, " I will not eat here until my boy who has been killed in this place has been restored to me safe and sound." The other Kieran replied, " We knew why you had come. The Lord will bring him to life for us. Therefore eat freely, for the boy is just coming." Even as he spoke the lad entered and sat down to supper with the brethren, who all gave thanks to God.

Aengus, King of Munster, had seven minstrels who were wont to sing him sweet lays of the deeds of heroes to the accompaniment of their harps. As they wandered through the land they were murdered by the king's enemies, who threw their bodies into a bog and hung their harps upon a tree which overshadowed the swamp. Aengus was very sad, for he did not know what had become of them, and, being a Christian, he would not consult magicians. St Kieran, however, was divinely enlightened as to their fate and came and told Aengus where they were. At the king's request, the saint went to the spot, and when he had fasted for a day the water from the bog evaporated and he could plainly discern the bodies of the bards lying side by side in the mud. St Kieran recalled them to life in the name of the Holy Trinity, and although they had lain in the bog for a month they arose as out of sleep, and taking down their harps they sang their sweetest songs to the king and to the bishop. Then, amid a shower of blessings from Aengus and his people, St Kieran returned to Saighir and the bog has remained dry ever since.

Both the Latin and the Irish lives of St Kieran have been edited and annotated by C. Plummer. See his VSH., vol. i, pp. 217-233, and *Bethada Náem n-Érenn* (Eng. trans.), vol. ii, pp. 99-120. The newly-found Latin life in MS. Gotha I. 81, is printed in *Analecta Bollandiana*. vol. lix (1941), pp. 217-271. There is, of course, only a very slender kernel of history to be looked for in these legends, and the stories themselves are differently narrated in different texts. For example, in the first Irish life the boy Crichidh becomes " Trichem, a rich man, cunning in many kinds of evil ". The Latin life, BHL., 4658, is to be found both in Colgan and the *Acta Sanctorum*, March, vol. i ; and there is an analysis of it in G. H. Doble's *St Perran* (1931). See also LBS., vol. ii, pp. 119-138 ; and J. Ryan's *Irish Monasticism* (1931) ; and *cf.* next notice.

ST PIRAN, ABBOT (SIXTH CENTURY ?)

THE identification of the Cornish St Piran (or Perran) with St Kieran (Ciaran) of Saighir goes back to the middle ages ; but the most recent investigation, that of Canon Doble, follows the early Bollandists, and Dr Plummer and Joseph Loth, in rejecting it. He conjectures that, the identification having been made on the strength of the resemblance of name (initial C in Irish is P in Cornish), and there being a connection between Ossory and Bodmin priory, a west-country cleric appropriated the life of Kieran for Piran. The life has suffered in the process, and nothing of Cornish interest has been added.

It is specially disappointing if we know nothing of St Piran because there is more information about his medieval *cultus* than that of any other Cornish saint, and the remains of his chapel at the centre of this *cultus* are a " relic " of great interest. They were discovered by chance, buried in the sand at Perranzabuloe (Piran-in-the-Sand), on the coast north of Perranporth, at the end of the eighteenth century and properly excavated in 1910. It is not likely that the ruin goes back to the saint's time, but it, with the adjacent cross, was probably the centre of the Celtic monastic settlement that revered Piran as its founder.

Other places bearing the saint's name are Perranarworthal and Perran Uthnoe (the present Catholic church at Truro is dedicated in his honour), there are traces of his *cultus* in Wales, and it is widespread in Brittany. So late as the middle of the eighteenth century the tin-miners of Breage and Germoe kept the feast of St Piran as their patron on March 5 ; this date, like his life, was borrowed from St Kieran : but Wilson's Martyrology (1608) gives his date at Padstow as May 11.

Canon Doble's monograph, *St Perran, St Keverne and St Kerrian* (1931), with C. Henderson's section on the *cultus*, is most valuable. The medieval Latin life, " a recension of a recension " derived from the life of Kieran of Saighir, is in John of Tynemouth's *Nova Legenda Angliae*. The newly-found *Vita Sancti Pirani* in the Gotha MS. I. 81 is printed in *Analecta Bollandiana*, vol. lix (1941), pp. 217-271. And see Doble in *Old Cornwall*, Winter, 1942.

ST VIRGIL, ARCHBISHOP OF ARLES (*c.* A.D. 610)

ST VIRGIL was born in Gascony, but was educated at the monastery on Saint-Honorat--one of the Lérins islands two miles south of Cannes which are so familiar a sight to the dwellers in the French Riviera. He became a monk there and afterwards abbot—if we are to believe the anonymous biographer who is our chief authority for his life, but who, living some centuries later, romances freely to glorify his hero. According to him, the saint was walking one night by the shore when he noticed a strange ship drawn up on the beach. He could plainly discern the sailors working on the deck and it was evident that they must also have perceived him, for two of them disembarked and came to meet him. Accosting him by name, they assured him that his reputation had spread to foreign lands, and that if he would accompany them to Jerusalem he would give great joy to the faithful and would attain to great sanctity. Virgil was not to be deceived, and, making the sign of the cross, he replied, " The wicked wiles of the deceiver cannot beguile the soldiers of Christ, nor can you entrap those whom God forewarns. For prayer has so fortified the island of St Honoratus that the dragon is cast forth, nor has the Devil any power to do harm." Immediately the ship and its sailors vanished. The name of Virgil does not appear in the list of abbots of Lérins, and in other chronicles he is spoken of as a monk of Lérins who afterwards became abbot of Saint-Symphorien at Autun.

It is certain that he was called from monastic life to become archbishop of Arles, receiving the pallium from Pope St Gregory I, by whom he was appointed apostolic vicar for the kingdom of Childebert II. The Venerable Bede mentions him in connection with the mission to England of St Augustine it would appear that it was St Virgil who was the consecrator of Augustine, at the special request of Gregory. The archbishop was an able and vigorous administrator whose zeal, in one instance, outran his discretion, for we find St Gregory remonstrating with his friend for his attempts to convert the Jews of his diocese by force, and recommending him to confine his efforts to prayer and preaching.

St Virgil built several churches in Arles, and the story goes that when the basilica of St Honoratus was under construction and the stone pillars were being brought there, it was suddenly found impossible to move them. No reason could be found until the archbishop repaired to the spot. His enlightened eyes at once perceived what was hidden from others, *viz.* that the Devil in the form of a little Negro of enormous strength was hanging on to the stone column and frustrating all efforts to drag it along. St Virgil spoke sternly to the fiend and he vanished in a dreadful stench, leaving the pillars free to be drawn to their destination. His biographer gives many instances of the saint's powers as a wonder-worker ; according to him, Virgil wrought many miracles of healing, raised to life several dead persons and destroyed a terrible serpent which had been causing great damage. The people of Arles undoubtedly had great confidence in his protection, for they were convinced that so long as they retained his body alive or dead in their midst, the great archbishop would deliver them from all their foes. He was buried in the church of St Saviour which he had built.

The legendary biography of St Virgil has been printed in the *Acta Sanctorum,* March, vol. i. See also Duchesne, *Fastes Épiscopaux*, vol. i, pp. 259-260.

ST JOHN JOSEPH OF THE CROSS (A.D. 1734)

ON the feast of the Assumption 1654, in the island of Ischia, off Naples, a boy was born, who, being baptized the same day, received the names of Carlo Gaetano. His parents, Joseph Calosirto and Laura Garguilo, were a well-to-do and most exemplary couple, who strove to bring up their numerous family in the right way. Their house was ever open to the poor—especially to the shamefaced poor who were loath to beg—and Madonna Laura used to prepare food and medicaments for those in need, to whom she dispensed them with her own hands. Of their seven sons, five entered religion, but little Carlo was pre-eminent amongst them for his precocious piety and for his sweet disposition. Generally the boy's sanctity was recognized and approved by his relations, who left him free to follow his own devices even when—to the modern mind at least—they might seem extravagant and imprudent. To be freer to pray, Carlo chose as his bedroom a remote attic, and as he could not afford to buy any instrument of penance, he managed to make himself one with nails, and he undertook many severe fasts while still a mere child. After such a childhood it was but natural that the boy should feel a strong vocation for the religious life, and, with the hope of obtaining divine guidance to choose aright, he made a fervent novena.

Two Spanish Franciscan friars of the " Alcantarine " reform in the course of a begging tour came to the hospitable house of Madonna Laura. Carlo, whose novena had just come to an end, was greatly impressed by the poverty and conversation of these sons of St Francis and went to their convent in Naples, Santa Lucia del Monte, to consult with the superiors. Here he met Father Carlo-of-the-Wounds-of-Jesus, and this experienced director discerned in the youth the germs of a great vocation. For nine months he put him through a strenuous course of self-abnegation and trained him in the method of mental prayer bequeathed by St Peter of Alcantara. Then the aspirant, only sixteen years old, was clothed with the religious habit, and that habit, we are told, he never laid aside night or day in all the sixty-four years that he lived as a friar. It was at his clothing that he took the name of John Joseph-of-the-Cross. The new novice did not disappoint the expectation of his superiors : his fervour, humility and obedience were such that he seemed like another Peter of Alcantara. It is a proof of the high esteem in which he was held that when the Neapolitan Alcantarines were about to build a monastery at Piedimonte di Alife, they chose John Joseph to start a tradition of regular observance, although he was not yet twenty-one and was not a priest. To labour with his hands in such a cause was a congenial task to the young friar, who strove to make the new house an exact replica of St Peter's little monastery at Pedrosa. Day after day through the bitterest cold he might be seen toiling up the mountain with bare and bleeding feet, carrying stone for the builders.

It had been the wish of St John Joseph to remain a deacon in imitation of the Seraphic Father St Francis, but his superiors decided that he should be raised to the priesthood, and on Michaelmas day 1677 he celebrated his first Mass. A month later, when at an unusually early age he was entrusted to hear confessions, it was found that the young priest, who from his purity of heart had grown up ignorant of evil, was endowed with an extraordinary insight and wisdom in the tribunal of penance. About this time he formed the plan of building in the wood near the convent some little hermitages, like those of the early Franciscans, where he and his brethren could spend periods of retirement in even stricter austerity than was possible in the house. He easily obtained the permission of his superiors, and these hermitages became the means of great spiritual advancement.

From this congenial life the saint was recalled to the mother-house to be charged with the delicate and difficult task of novice-master. Here again he acquitted himself successfully, inculcating upon his novices strict observance of the rule, but not exacting from them the austerities he practised himself. Indeed, he was most particular that they should have regular times of recreation. He was again transferred to Piedimonte to be superior, and though he obtained leave to lay down the office for a short period, which he devoted to the direction of souls, he was soon recalled to take up the charge of governing his brethren a second time. He was then passing through a season of great aridity and desolation, but he was consoled by a vision of a departed lay-brother who reassured him as to his condition. It was after this vision that St John Joseph began to show powers as a wonder-worker, not only by miracles of healing, but also by supplying and multiplying food for the house ; his fame spread so rapidly that when he went back to Ischia, to visit his mother in her last illness, he had the unusual experience of being acclaimed as a saint in his native town. A second period as novice-master was succeeded by a third term as superior at Piedimonte, at the close of which an illness brought him

to death's door—the malady had been brought on by hardships and austerities—
and hardly had he recovered when he was called upon to take the lead in a crisis
which threatened the very existence of the Italian Alcantarines.

It had been laid down by a papal brief that the office of minister provincial and
other important charges among the Italian branch of Alcantarines should always
be confided to Spaniards. This led to great friction, partly no doubt on account of
racial differences, but also because of the fact that, as the Spanish friars in Italy were
comparatively few, suitable superiors were often not forthcoming. The troubles
increased until the Spaniards obtained entire separation from the Italians, with
possession of the two Neapolitan houses, one of which was Santa Lucia del Monte.
Disorganized and threatened with total suppression, the Italian friars turned to St
John Joseph to help and direct them, and it was mainly through his wisdom,
personality and reputation that they held together, lived down slander and opposition, and gained permission to turn themselves into a province. At one period in
Naples it was as much as they could do to keep a roof over their heads, and they
were without many of the ordinary necessaries of life—but Father John Joseph took
all these hardships cheerfully, as being in keeping with the teaching of the founder.
As soon as the branch was well started the saint, who had been made the first
minister provincial, was bent on taking measures to lay down his office and to retire
into obscurity. Obscurity for him, however, was out of the question, for his
holiness, his miracles and the conversions he wrought made him more and more
famous. By this time he was growing old and was partially paralysed, but when he
appeared in the streets, hobbling along with the help of a stick, he was followed by
crowds who wanted his advice or his blessing, or sought surreptitiously to cut—or
even to bite—pieces from his habit. In 1722 the two Neapolitan houses were
restored to them, and St John Joseph returned to Santa Lucia where, as he had
prophesied when he had left it, he was ultimately to lay his bones.

One of the many miracles reported by his biographer is worthy of record
because of the sensation it created at the time and because of the large number of
persons who appear to have witnessed it. It was in the octave of the feast of St
Januarius and John Joseph had gone into the cathedral to honour the saint's relic,
when, in the seething crowd, there slipped from his hand the stick without which
he could not move a step. Undismayed he appealed to the saint whose festival
was being kept, and immediately he was transported first to beneath the pulpit and
then to the door of the cathedral. He was sitting on the steps without a stick when
there drove up in a coach the Duke of Lauriano who, surprised to see him there,
asked if there was anything the matter. " I have lost my steed ", replied the friar
cheerfully, and when the duke offered to carry him to his coach, John Joseph refused
his offer with thanks and motioned him to enter the cathedral, saying, " You will
see the walking-stick there." The duke obeyed, but before he had reached the
high altar he heard a cry of " A miracle ! A miracle ! " from the congregation and,
looking round, he saw the stick flying through the air at a distance of about two
hand's-breadths above the heads of the congregation. Those who were outside
beheld the stick pass through the door, strike St John Joseph lightly on the chest
with its handle, and then return to his hand. The old man grasped it joyfully and
hobbled away home as fast as he could, for the crowd were following him with
acclamations and were tearing pieces from his ragged old habit. Besides miracles
and the gift of prophecy John Joseph was endowed with other supernatural gifts,
such as ecstasies, levitation and heavenly visions : moreover, during a great part

of his life he could read the thoughts of those who came to consult him as clearly as though they had been writtten words.

As the day of his death approached, St John Joseph was divinely warned and spoke of it freely to those around him, but he continued to carry on his usual avocations.   At two o'clock in the morning of March 1, 1734, he had a violent apoplectic seizure from which he never recovered, although he lingered on for five days, passing away at the age of eighty.   He was buried at Santa Lucia del Monte in the habit he had worn so long, and his tomb almost immediately became a very popular place of pilgrimage.   He was canonized in 1839.

See Diodato dell' Assunta, *Saggio istorico* (1789), and *Compendium vitae, virtutum et miraculorum B. Joannis Josephi a Cruce* (1839).

6 : SS. PERPETUA, FELICITY AND THEIR COMPANIONS, MARTYRS (A.D. 203)

THE record of the passion of St Perpetua, St Felicity and their companions is one of the greatest hagiological treasures that have come down to us. In the fourth century these acts were publicly read in the churches of Africa, and were in fact so highly esteemed that St Augustine found it necessary to issue a protest against their being placed on a level with the Holy Scriptures.   In them we have a human document of singularly vivid interest preserved for us in the actual words of two of the martyrs themselves.

It was in Carthage in the year 203 that, during the persecution initiated by the Emperor Severus, five catechumens were arrested.   They were Revocatus, his fellow-slave Felicity (who was shortly expecting her confinement), Saturninus, Secundulus and Vivia (Vibia) Perpetua, at that time twenty-two years of age, the wife of a man of good position, and the mother of a young child.   She had parents and two brothers living—a third, names Dinocrates, having died at the age of seven. These five prisoners were joined by Saturus, who seems to have been their instructor in the faith and who underwent a voluntary imprisonment with them because he would not leave them.   Perpetua's father, of whom she was the favourite child, was an old man and a pagan, whereas her mother was probably a Christian— as was also one of her brothers, the other being a catechumen.   The martyrs, after their apprehension, were kept under guard in a private house, and Perpetua's account of their sufferings is as follows : " When I was still with my companions, and my father, in his affection for me, was trying to turn me from my purpose by arguments and thus weaken my faith, ' Father ', said I, ' do you see this vessel— waterpot or whatever it may be ? . .   Can it be called by any other name than what it is ? '   ' No ', he replied.   ' So also I cannot call myself by any other name than what I am—a Christian.'   Then my father, provoked at the word ' Christian ', threw himself upon me as if he would pluck out my eyes, but he only shook me and in fact he was vanquished. .   Then I thanked God for the relief of being, for a few days, parted from my father   and during those few days we were baptized, the Spirit bidding me make no other petition after the rite than for bodily endurance. A few days later we were lodged in prison, and I was greatly frightened because I had never known such darkness.   What a day of horror !   Terrible heat, owing to the crowds !   Rough treatment by the soldiers !   To crown all I was tormented with anxiety for my baby.   Then Tertius and Pomponius, those blessed deacons who ministered to us, paid for us to be removed for a few hours to a better part of the prison and obtain some relief.   Then all of them went out of the prison, and I suckled my baby, who was faint for want of food.   I spoke anxiously to my mother on his behalf and encouraged my brother and commended my son to their care. I was concerned because I saw their concern for me.   Such anxieties I suffered for many days, but I obtained leave for my baby to remain in the prison with me, and, being relieved of my trouble and anxiety for him, I at once recovered my health, and my prison suddenly became a palace to me and I would rather have been there than anywhere else.

" Then my brother said to me : ' Lady sister, you are now in great honour -so great that you may well pray for a vision in which you may be shown whether suffering or release be in store for you.'   And I, knowing myself to have speech of the Lord for whose sake I was suffering, confidently promised, ' To-morrow I will bring you word.'   And I made petition and this was shown me.   I saw a golden ladder of wonderful length reaching up to heaven, but so narrow that only one at a time could go up ; and on the sides of the ladder were fastened all kinds of iron weapons.   There were swords, lances, hooks, daggers —so that if anyone went up carelessly, or without looking upwards, he was mangled and his flesh caught on the weapons.   And at the foot of the ladder was a huge dragon [or ' serpent '] which lay in wait for those going up and sought to frighten them from making the ascent. Now the first to go up was Saturus, who had given himself up of his own accord for our sakes, because our faith was of his own building and he had not been present when we were arrested.   He reached the top of the ladder, and, turning, said to me, ' Perpetua, I wait for you, but take care lest the dragon bite you,' and I said, ' In the name of Jesus Christ, he will not hurt me.'   And the dragon put out his head gently, as if afraid of me, just at the foot of the ladder ; and as though I were treading on the first step, I trod on his head.   And I went up and saw a large garden, and sitting in the midst a tall man with white hair in the dress of a shepherd, milking sheep ; and round about were many thousands clad in white.   And he raised his head and looked upon me and said, ' Welcome, child.'   And he called me and gave me some curds of the milk he was milking, and I received it in my joined hands and ate ; and all that were round about said Amen.   At the sound of the word I awoke, still eating something sweet.   And at once I told my brother, and we understood that we must suffer and henceforth began to have no hope in this world.

" After a few days there was a report that we were to be examined.   Moreover, my father arrived from the city, worn with anxiety, and he came up that he might overthrow my resolution, saying, ' Daughter, pity my white hairs !   Pity your father if I am worthy to be called father by you, if I have brought you up to this your prime of life, if I have preferred you to your brothers.   Make me not a reproach to men !   Look on your mother and your mother's sister, look upon your son who cannot live after you are gone.   Lay aside your pride, do not ruin us all, for none of us will ever speak freely again if anything happens to you.'   So spoke my father in his love for me, kissing my hands and casting himself at my feet ; and with tears called me by the name, not of ' daughter ', but of ' lady '.   And I grieved for my father's sake, because he alone of all my kindred would not have joy at my martyr-dom.   And I comforted him, saying, ' It shall happen as God shall choose, for assuredly we lie not in our own power but in the power of God.'   And he departed full of grief. Another day, whilst we were taking our meal, we were suddenly summoned to be examined and we arrived at the market-place. The news of this soon spread and brought a vast crowd together. We were placed on a platform before the judge, who was Hilarian, procurator of the province, the proconsul being lately dead. The rest, who were questioned before me, confessed their faith. When it came to my turn, my father appeared with my baby, and drawing me down from the step besought me, ' Have pity on your child.' The president Hilarian joined with my father and said, ' Spare your father's white hairs : spare the tender years of your child. Offer a sacrifice for the prosperity of the emperors.' I replied, ' No.'—' Are you a Christian ? ' asked Hilarian, and I answered, ' Yes, I am.' As my father attempted to draw me from my resolution, Hilarian commanded that he should be beaten off and he was struck with a rod. This I felt as much as if I myself had been struck, so greatly did I grieve to see my father thus treated in his old age. Then the judge passed sentence on us all and condemned us to the wild beasts ; and joyfully we returned to our prison. Then, as my baby was accustomed to the breast, I sent Pomponius the deacon to ask him of my father, who, however, refused to send him. And God so ordered it that the child no longer required to suckle, nor did the milk in my breasts distress me." Secundulus seems to have died in prison before his examination. Before Hilarian pronounced sentence, he had caused Saturus, Saturninus and Revocatus to be scourged and Perpetua and Felicity to be hit on the face. They were reserved for the shows which were to be exhibited for the soldiers in the camp on the festival of Geta, whom his father Severus had made *caesar* when his brother Caracalla was created *augustus* four years previously.

St Perpetua relates another of her visions in the following words : " A few days later, while we were all praying, I happened to name Dinocrates—at which I was astonished, because I had not had him in my thoughts. And I knew that same moment that I ought to pray for him, and this I began to do with much fervour and lamentation before God. The same night this was shown me. I saw Dinocrates coming out of a dark place where there were many others, hot and thirsty ; his face was pale with the wound which he had on it when he died. Dinocrates had been my brother according to the flesh, and had died pitiably at the age of seven years of a horrible gangrene in the face. It was for him that I had prayed and there was a great gulf between us, so that neither of us could approach the other. Near him stood a font full of water, the rim of which was above the head of the child, and Dinocrates stood on tiptoe to drink. I was grieved that though the font had water he could not drink because of the height of the rim, and I awoke realizing that my brother was in travail. But I trusted that I could relieve his trouble and I prayed for him every day until we were removed to the garrison prison—for we were to fight with the wild beasts at the garrison games on Geta Caesar's festival. And I prayed for him night and day with lamentation and tears that he might be given me. The day we were in the stocks, this was shown me. I saw the place I had seen before, but now luminous, and Dinocrates clean, well-clad and refreshed ; and where there had been a wound, there was now only a scar ; and the font I had perceived before had its rim lowered to the child's waist ; and there poured water from it constantly and on the rim was a golden bowl full of water. And Dinocrates came forward and began to drink from it, and the bowl failed not. And when he had drunk enough he came away—pleased to play, as children will. And so I awoke and I knew he suffered no longer.

" Some days later, Pudens, the officer who had charge of the prison, began to show us consideration, perceiving that there was some great power within us, and he began to admit many to see us for our mutual refreshment.   When the day of the games drew near, my father came, overwhelmed with grief, and he began to pluck out his beard and throw himself upon the ground and to curse his years and to say such words as none could listen to unmoved.   I sorrowed for the unhappiness of his old age.

" On the eve of the day we were to suffer I saw in a vision Pomponius the deacon come hither and knock loudly at the prison door, which I opened to him.   He was dressed in a white robe without a girdle, wearing shoes curiously wrought, and he said to me, ' Perpetua, we are waiting for you : come.'   Aud he took me by the hand and we began painfully and panting to pass through rough and broken country till we reached an amphitheatre, and he led me into the middle, saying, ' Fear not ; I am here with you and I labour with you.'   Then he departed.   And I saw a huge crowd watching, and because I knew that I was condemned to the beasts, I wondered that there were none let loose on me.   Then there came out an ill-favoured Egyptian with his attendants to fight against me.   And another troop of goodly young men came to be my supporters.   And I was stripped and changed into a man and my attendants rubbed me down with oil for the combat ; and I saw the Egyptian, opposite, rolling in the dust.   And there came forward a man so wonderfully tall that he rose above the top of the amphitheatre, clad in a purple robe without a girdle, with two stripes, one on each side, running down the middle of the breast, and wearing shoes curiously made of gold and silver ; and he was carrying a rod like a trainer, and a green bough on which were golden apples.   Having called for silence, he said, ' This Egyptian, if he overcome her, shall kill her with a sword, and if she overcome him, she shall receive this bough.'   And he withdrew.   And we approached each other and began to use our fists.   My opponent tried to catch hold of my feet, but I kept on striking his face with my heels ; and I was lifted up into the air and began to strike him as would one who no longer trod the earth. But when I saw that the fight lagged, I joined my hands, linking my fingers.   And I caught hold of his head and he fell on his face ; and I trod on his head.   And the people shouted, and my supporters sang psalms.   And I came forward to the trainer and received the bough ; and kissing me, he said, ' Peace be with thee, daughter.'   And I began in triumph to go towards the Gate of Life ;[*] and so I awoke.   And I saw that I should not fight with beasts but with the Devil : but I knew the victory to be mine.   I have written this up to the day before the games. Of what was done in the games themselves, let him write who will."

St Saturus also had a vision which he described in writing.   He and his companions were conducted by angels into a beautiful garden, where they met martyrs named Jocundus, Saturninus and Artaxius, who had lately been burnt alive, and Quintus, who had died in prison.   Then they were led to a place which seemed as though it were built of light, and sitting in it was One white-haired with the face of a youth—" whose feet we saw not "—and on His right and on His left and behind Him were many elders, and all sang with one voice, " Holy, holy, holy."   They stood before the throne, and " we kissed Him, and He passed His hand over our faces.[†]   And the other elders said to us, ' Stand up '.   And we stood up and gave

---

[*] *Porta sanativaria.*   See below, penultimate paragraph.
[†] *Cf.* Apocalypse vii, 17   " And God shall wipe away all tears from their eyes.'

the kiss of peace. And the elders said to us, ' Go and play '." Then Saturus said to Perpetua, " You have all you desired "; and she replied, " Thanks be to God that as I was merry in the flesh, so am I still merrier here." He adds that as they went out they found before the gate their bishop Optatus, and Aspasius, a priest, alone and sorrowful. They fell at the martyrs' feet and begged them to reconcile them, for they had quarrelled. As Perpetua was talking to them in Greek, " beneath a rose-tree," the angels told the two clerics to compose their differences, and charged Optatus to heal the factions in his church. Saturus adds : " We began to recognize many brethren and martyrs there, and we all drew strength from an inexpressible fragrance which delighted us ; and in joy I awoke."

The rest of the acts were added by another hand—apparently that of an eyewitness. Felicity feared that she might not suffer with them, because women with child were not allowed to be exposed for punishment. All joined in prayer on her behalf, and she was delivered in the prison, giving birth to a daughter, whom one of their fellow-Christians adopted. The apprehension that the captives might use magic to obtain their deliverance caused the tribune who had charge of the martyrs to treat them harshly and to refuse to allow them to see visitors ; but Perpetua remonstrated with him and he relented somewhat, ar.d admitted certain of their friends, whilst Pudens their gaoler, " who now believed," did all he could for them. The day before the games, they were given the usual last meal, which was eaten in public, and was called " the free feast ", but the martyrs strove to make of it an *agape*, a love-feast, and to those who crowded round them they spoke of the judgements of God and of the joy of their own sufferings. Their courage astonished the pagans and caused the conversion of many.

The day of their triumph having arrived, the martyrs set forth from the prison as though they were on their way to Heaven. After the men walked Perpetua, " abashing with the high spirit in her eyes the gaze of all ", and Felicity beside her " rejoicing to come from the midwife to the gladiator, to wash after her travail in a second baptism ". At the gates of the amphitheatre the guards wished to force the men to wear the robes of the priests of Saturn and the women the dress consecrated to Ceres, but Perpetua resisted so strenuously that the officer allowed them to enter the arena clad as they were. Perpetua was singing a psalm of triumph, whilst Revocatus, Saturninus and Saturus threatened the bystanders and even Hilarian, as they passed his balcony, with the judgement of God. The crowd, enraged at their boldness, yelled that they should be scourged, and accordingly, as they passed in front of the gladiators, each received a lash. Saturninus had expressed a hope that he might be exposed to various sorts of beasts to gain a more glorious crown, and he and Revocatus, after being attacked by a leopard, were also set upon by a bear. Saturus, on the other hand, had a great horror of bears and hoped that a leopard would despatch him at once. He was exposed to a wild boar which turned upon its keeper, who received such wounds that he died soon afterwards, whereas Saturus was only dragged along by the beast. Then the martyr was tied up before the bear, but the bear refused to come out of his den, and Saturus was reserved for a second encounter. This gave him an opportunity of speaking to the gaoler Pudens, who had been converted. He encouraged him, saying, " You see that what I desired and foretold has come to pass : not a beast has touched me. Believe steadfastly. See, I go forth yonder, and with one bite from the leopard, all will be over." It happened as he had foretold ; a leopard sprang upon him and in a moment he was covered with blood. The mob jeered and cried out, " He is well washed [baptized] ! " whilst the martyr said to Pudens, " Farewell : keep the faith and me in mind, and let these things not confound but confirm you." Then he took a ring from the gaoler's finger, and having dipped it in his blood, he returned it to Pudens as a keepsake, and so died, going to await Perpetua, according to her vision.

In the meantime Perpetua and Felicity were exposed to a savage cow. Perpetua was tossed first and fell on her back, but sat up and gathered her torn tunic round her, pinning up her dishevelled hair lest she should seem to be mourning. Then she went to the help of Felicity, who had also been tossed, and side by side they stood expecting another attack ; but as the mob cried out that it was enough, they were led to the gate Sanavivaria, through which victorious gladiators left the arena. Here Perpetua seemed to return as from an ecstasy and asked when she was to fight the cow. Upon being told what had happened, she could not believe it until she saw on herself and on her clothing the marks of what she had suffered. Then, calling her brother she said to him and to the catechumen Rusticus, " Stand fast in the faith and love one another ; and do not let our sufferings be a stumbling-block to you." By this time the fickle people were clamouring for them to come out into the open, which they did willingly, and after giving each other the kiss of peace, they were killed by the gladiators, Perpetua guiding to her own throat the sword of her nervous executioner, who had failed to kill her at the first stroke, so that she shrieked out with pain. " Perhaps so great a woman   could not else have been slain except she willed it."

In 1907 Father Delattre discovered and pieced together an ancient inscription found in the Basilica Majorum at Carthage, where the bodies of these martyrs were buried—as we know from Victor Vitensis, a fifth-century African bishop, who had seen the place where they were interred. It reads : " Here are the martyrs Saturus, Saturninus, Revocatus, Secundulus, Felicity and Perpetua, who suffered on the nones of March." It cannot, however, be confidently maintained as a matter of certainty that the inscription discovered is that of the *tombstone* of the martyrs. The proper day for their commemoration, that on which they suffered, is *nonis Martii* (March 7), but the feast, owing to its concurrence with that of St Thomas Aquinas, has now been transferred to March 6. No saints are more uniformly honoured in all the early calendars and martyrologies. Their names appear not only in the Philocalian calendar at Rome of the year 354, but also in the Syriac calendar compiled probably in the neighbourhood of Antioch at the end of the same century.

The Acts of SS. Perpetua and Felicity have naturally produced a very considerable literature. Both Latin and Greek texts' may be conveniently consulted in the edition of Dean Armitage Robinson in *Texts and Studies*, vol. i, pt 2. There are English translations by R. W. Muncey, *The Passion of St Perpetua* (1927) and E. C. E. Owen, *Some Acts of the Early Martyrs* (1927). But the best is by W. H. Shewring, *The Passion of Perpetua and Felicity* (1931), with a Latin text and an excellent introduction. The theory that the Greek text was the original and the Latin a translation has now been generally abandoned, and no one seems to have followed Hilgenfeld in his curious contention that the document was first drafted in the Punic language. A considerable number of scholars, notably among Catholics Fr Adhémar d'Alès, have inclined to the view that the editor of the acts was no other than Tertullian himself. One reason which weighs in favour of this theory is to be found in the traces which appear of Montanist teaching and phraseology ; but these, as Delehaye has shown, are but slight, and there is no reason for identifying the acts with heretical teaching of any sort. See Delehaye, *Les Passions des martyrs et les genres littéraires* (1921), pp. 63–72. *Cf.* Monceaux, *Histoire littéraire de l'Afrique chrétienne*, i, pp. 70–96, and A. J. Mason, *Historic Martyrs* (1905), pp. 77–106.

ST FRIDOLIN, Abbot   (Sixth Century ?)

The history of St Fridolin, " the Traveller ", presents many difficulties to the historian, for the accounts which have come down to us are so conflicting that even the very century of his birth is uncertain. The " acts " of his life, long preserved at Säckingen, were unfortunately lost, and our chief authority, a somewhat unreliable one, is a biography written by one Balther, who had read a copy of the acts and who professed to have reproduced them from memory, the prior of the monastery which owned it having refused him permission to keep the book.

Fridolin was reported to be an Irishman of good family who became a priest. He exercised his ministry by wandering from city to city preaching the word of God ; but soon he felt the call to a missionary career and left his native land, in spite of the entreaties of his disciples, his relations and even the Irish prelates. His first landing-place was some distant shore which cannot with certainty be identified. Passing on to France, he travelled as an itinerant preacher until he reached Poitiers, where he was hospitably received by the monks of the monastery of St Hilary, which he eventually joined. The church had been left in ruins by the ravages of the Vandals and the bones of the founder had been lost, and Fridolin was most anxious to find them. His wish was gratified by a vision in which St Hilary told him where his body lay buried. It was agreed to rebuild the church and to place the relics in a suitable shrine, and St Fridolin was chosen abbot to carry out the work.

News of the discovery having reached King Clovis III, that monarch summoned the bishop and the abbot to appear before him. According to the legend, a magnificent banquet was given, at which many nobles, pagan and Christian, were entertained, and the king filled a costly goblet and he offered it to St Fridolin. By some misadventure the cup fell off the table and was broken into four pieces. Clovis, half in jest, suggested that the saint should work a miracle over them and thus exalt God's name before his pagan guests. St Fridolin took the fragments, bent over them in prayer, and then restored the cup entire and without a flaw. Immediately upon his return to Poitiers, Fridolin set to work to restore the monastery, which had fallen into disrepair, as well as to rebuild the church, in which he caused part of the relics to be deposited with great ceremony. Two of the saint's nephews, who had come over from Northumbria to join him, assisted him in his work, and not long after their arrival St Fridolin had another vision of St Hilary, who said to him : " Brother Fridolin, why do you delay in doing what you promised to God and to me when you were separating a certain portion of my remains to carry with you ? Do not tarry any longer in this place, which your nephews will take care to have dedicated to the service of Almighty God after your departure." In answer to Fridolin's inquiry as to where he should go, he was directed to a certain island in the Rhine.

On his way he is said to have founded the monastery of Hilera on the Moselle and to have built a church in honour of St Hilary in the Vosges mountains. Passing through the town now called Strasbourg, he erected another church under the same patronage. At Coire, in the present canton of Grisons in Switzerland, he stayed for some time with the bishop, and is credited with the foundation of yet another church of St Hilary. Whilst at Coire he ascertained that there was an uncultivated island in the Rhine which corresponded to the island of his dream ; being unable to obtain any particulars beyond the fact that it was called Säckingen, he started out to examine it for himself with a view to making a settlement there.　His motives were misunderstood, and he was so severely belaboured that he was forced to beat a retreat and to seek a charter granting him possession of the island.　Authorities differ as to the ruler from whom he obtained this charter : some say Thierry I of Austrasia, and others Sigismund of Burgundy ; but eventually he was able to build a church and monastery.　He is also stated to have founded a convent for nuns and to have obtained lands for its endowment from the lord of Glarus.　In later times the canton of Glarus was subject to the abbess of Säckingen.　The last years of St Fridolin's life were spent at the head of his monastery, but he appears also to have founded a sort of school for very young boys in which he encouraged sports and at times joined in them.　His many travels to spread the gospel earned him the name of " Viator ", and it is recorded that in later centuries Scottish or Irish pilgrims who went to Rome used to track his progress along the Rhine.

For the biography by Balther, see MGH., *Scriptores Merov.*, vol. iii, pp. 354–369, and the *Acta Sanctorum*, March, vol. i.　Extravagant as the legend is, it was very well known in the later middle ages, more particularly in Switzerland and the adjacent provinces.　Hence a considerable literature has gathered round it.　See more particularly the monograph of C. Benziger, *Die Fridolins-legende nach einem Ulmer Druck des Johann Zainer* (1913).

SS. CYNEBURGA, CYNESWIDE and TIBBA　(Seventh Century)

Bede tells us that Cyneburga, a daughter of King Penda of Mercia, was married to Alcfrid, a son of King Oswy of Northumbria.　It is not known what happened to Alcfrid after he rebelled against his father, but after a time Cyneburga found herself free to leave the north and to return to her own land.　On a piece of fenland on the borders of Northampton and Huntingdon, her brothers or she founded a convent which she entered.　The place was afterwards called Cyneburgecester, and it is now known as Castor.　Round her gathered a band of women who served God in much holiness, whilst she as their abbess outshone them all and was remarkable for the wisdom and care with which she watched over her nuns.　Here she was joined by her sister St Cyneswide, who from her earliest years had devoted herself to God alone.　Her brother, King Wulfhere, had betrothed her to Offa, son of the king of the East Saxons, but she so wrought upon her affianced husband that he released her.　She eventually succeeded her sister as abbess.

A third holy woman, who is associated with the other two and was venerated on this day, is their kinswoman St Tibba, of whom it is recorded that she spent many years in solitude and devotion, but whether she lived in the abbey or in some cell in the neighbourhood history does not record.　They were all laid to rest eventually in the abbey of Medeshamstede (Peterborough), which the two sisters must have helped to establish, for their names appear in the list of those who took part in the assembly which sanctioned its foundation, and they were reckoned among its patrons.　In the reign of Henry I the bones of these three saints were restored to Peterborough from Thorney, whither they had been taken when Peterborough was for a second time ravaged by the Danes, and a festival was instituted to honour the translation.　According to Camden, St Tibba was specially honoured at Ryhall in Rutlandshire, so she may possibly have at one time occupied a cell in that neighbourhood, where, indeed, the Anglo-Saxon Chronicle (*s.a.* 963) says she was at first buried.

We know little of St Cyneburga beyond what may be found in the text and notes of Plummer's edition of Bede's *Historia Ecclesiastica.* What is stated in William of Malmesbury and the *Peterborough Chronicle* is not very trustworthy. The references to Cyneburga in the *Cartularium Gloucestriae* are due to confusion with another saint of that name *cf.* J. B. L. Tolhurst, " St Kyneburga of Gloucester ", in *Pax,* Summer 1943, pp. 85–87. The names Alcfrith and Cyneburh may clearly be read in the runes of the Bewcastle Cross in Cumberland.

ST CHRODEGANG, Bishop of Metz (a.d. 766)

St Chrodegang was born near Liège, and was probably educated at the abbey of S.-Trond. We are told that he spoke his own tongue and Latin with equal fluency ; in appearance he was singularly prepossessing, and his kindness and gracious manners endeared him to all. Charles Martel recognized his exceptional qualities, and chose him as his secretary and referendary. After the death of Charles, Chrodegang, though still a layman, was in 742 invested with the bishopric of Metz ; he combined in such an eminent degree sanctity with sagacity that nothing but good could result from such an appointment, and everywhere the holy man used his influence for the furtherance of justice and for the public weal. His biographers extol his almost boundless charity and his special solicitude for widows and orphans. As ambassador from Pepin, mayor of the palace, to Pope Stephen III, Chrodegang was concerned closely with Pepin's coronation as king in 754, his defeat of the Lombards in Italy, and the handing over of the exarchate of Ravenna and other territory to the Holy See.

St Chrodegang, having thus contributed to set the papacy on a firmer basis and to establish the Frankish supremacy in Italy, turned his attention to the spiritual affairs of his diocese. The laxity and lawlessness of the times had not been without influence on the clergy : many of them had become overmuch entangled in worldly affairs, and the younger ones were not being adequately trained in knowledge and discipline. He started with those of his own city and cathedral, for whom he drew up a series of regulations, founded to a considerable degree on the Rule of St Benedict. He brought together in clergy-houses all the ecclesiastics—higher and lower—and obliged them to assist at the choir offices and to live a common life according to rule. The code which has come down to us consisted originally of thirty-four chapters. At the daily meetings, one of these sections had to be read, and from this reading the meeting came to be called " the chapter ". Soon the name " chapter " became attached to those present, whilst those who were bound by these canons (rules) were called *canonici* or canons, the conventuals who had their own regulations becoming known as " regulars ". The reputation of St Chrodegang caused his reform to spread beyond his own diocese and later it attracted the attention of Charlemagne ; the emperor caused it to be enacted that all bodies of clerics should live either the collegiate life—according to canon—or else as regulars or monks. Thus was the saint a notable influence in the " canon regular " movement that reached beyond France and Germany to Italy and the British Isles.

Another of the activities of St Chrodegang was the building and restoration of churches, monasteries, and charitable institutions. The abbey of Gorze, which he loved above all others, was one of his foundations. For these monasteries the pope sent him the bodies of three saints whose shrines attracted crowds of pilgrims, and as a further mark of favour the Holy See accorded him precedence of all the other Frankish bishops—even, according to some authorities, sending him the pallium.

It is generally agreed that the church of Metz under Chrodegang was the first in the north to adopt the pure Roman liturgy and the Gregorian chant. The choir school which he established became famous, and in 805 Charlemagne ordered that all choirmasters should be drawn from the school at Metz. Its reputation lasted for several centuries, and when the fathers of Cîteaux wished to perpetuate the very best traditions in the matter of choral service they turned to the church of Metz and adopted its antiphonary. St Chrodegang died on March 6, 766, and his body was laid to rest at Gorze.

As a source of reliable history the biography of St Chrodegang attributed to John of Gorze and printed in MGH., *Scriptores*, vol. x, cannot claim confidence, but from Paul Warnefrid, *De Episcopis Mettensibus* (in *Scriptores*, vol. ii, of the same series), and from other chroniclers we are fairly well informed concerning the saint's activities. The primitive text of Chrodegang's rule for his canons is best studied in the edition of Wilhelm Schmitz, *S. Chrodegangi Regula canonicorum mit Umschrift der Tironischen Noten* (1889). See also the paper of Dr H. Reumont in the *Festschrift für Georg von Hertling* (1913), pp. 202–215 ; the *Acta Sanctorum* (March, vol. i) ; A. Hauck, *Kirchengeschichte Deutschlands*, vol. ii, pp. 62–68 ; DCB., vol. i, pp. 498–503 ; and J. C. Dickinson, *The Origin of the Austin Canons* (1950), pp. 16–20.

SS. BALRED AND BILFRID   (EIGHTH CENTURY)

ST BALRED or Balther was a priest who led the solitary life in the kingdom of Northumbria, which comprised the south of Scotland. He appears to have lived at one time at Tyningham, at another period inhabiting a cell on the Bass Rock. A legend recounts that there was then a dangerous shoal in the Firth of Forth, which was visible only at low tide and was the cause of many shipwrecks ; it stood between the Bass Rock and the mainland. According to the lesson in the Aberdeen Breviary, St Balred, out of pity for sailors, decided to move it. Going out to the rock, he stood upon it and it floated away under him " like a little boat wafted by a fair wind ", and was steered by him to the neighbouring shore, where it remained and became known as St Baldred's Rock. After a life of great austerities and trials, the holy hermit died at Aldham, and a dispute arose with the neighbouring parishes of Tyningham and Preston for the possession of his body. Tradition relates that in the morning it was found that there were three precisely similar bodies and so each parish was able to have its own.

The relics were lost during a Danish attack, but two centuries later a priest called Elfrid discovered through a dream the body of St Balred, which was removed to Durham together with the remains of another hermit, St Bilfrid the goldsmith, who was honoured with him on March 6. Bilfrid, as the inscription on it states, adorned with gold, silver and gems St Cuthbert's famous Book of the Gospels, which, after being miraculously rescued uninjured from the sea, was long preserved in Durham, but now forms one of the treasures of the Cottonian Library in the British Museum.

Here again, as pointed out in Stanton's *Menology* (pp. 105 and 633), some confusion seems to have arisen between two different holy men, the Baldredus of the Aberdeen Breviary, who was a bishop, and the Baltherus of Symeon of Durham, who was a priest. Moreover, if Baldredus, as stated in the Breviary, was a bishop under St Kentigern, he cannot have died more than 150 years later, as Baltherus is said to have done. See KSS., pp. 273–274.

ST CADROE, OR CADROEL, ABBOT   (A.D. 976)

ST CADROE was the son of a Scottish prince or thane, who was sent over to Ireland for his education, and so greatly distinguished himself at Armagh that he was credited with having read " all that ever poet has sung, orator spoken and philosopher thought ".   Upon his return to Scotland he set to work to foster vocations and to train priests because—to quote the old chronicler—" the Scots had many thousands of schoolmasters and but few fathers ".   After some years he was divinely moved to relinquish his country and his father's house, and amid general lamentations he left Scotland with his pilgrim's staff in hand.

After visiting shrines in England and Wales he came south to London, where he was kindly received by an aged man named Hegfrid.   In the middle of the night Cadroe was aroused by his host, who told him that the town was on fire.   Cadroe made his way to the scene of the conflagration and, earnestly invoking God's help, lifted his hands towards heaven.   The flames immediately died down and London was saved.   The news of the miracle spread far and wide and reached King Edmund, who invited the saint to visit him in his royal city of Winchester.   Then St Odo, bishop of that see and afterwards archbishop of Canterbury, escorted him to the coast, from whence he sailed to France with a dozen companions.   At Péronne they were befriended by a lady who enabled them to settle in the forest of Thiérache, in a monastery which they dedicated to St Michael.   St Cadroe refused to become abbot and went on to Fleury, where he received the Benedictine habit, but he returned to St Michael's after he had passed through the novitiate.   He became abbot of Waulsort, on the Meuse, which he ruled for several years, until the bishop of Metz begged him to take charge of the abbey of St Clement at Metz which had fallen upon evil days.   He completely reformed it and succeeded in raising it to even more than its former glory.

No doubt can be entertained that St Cadroe ruled the abbey of Waulsort, for, as Mabillon points out, a charter of the Emperor Otto III in the year 991 refers to him as " Cadroel of blessed memory ".   But it is not easy to pronounce upon the historical value of the Latin life written, probably in the eleventh century, by one Reimann or Ousmann—the name is uncertain.   It is not a mere romance, in spite of its occasionally extravagant tone.   The text is published most fully by Colgan, *Acta Sanctorum Hiberniae*, under March 6, but it has also been edited by the Bollandists and by Mabillon.   See also Skene, *Chronicles of the Picts and Scots*, pp. 106-116 ; KSS., pp. 293-294 ; and *cf.* Gougaud, *Gaelic Pioneers of Christianity*.

ST OLLEGARIUS, OR OLDEGAR, ARCHBISHOP OF TARRAGONA   (A.D. 1137)

THE father of Ollegarius (Olaguer in Spanish) and his mother both came of noble Visigothic families.   Catalonia was suffering severely from the ravages of the Saracens, and it was apparently as a votive offering for protection from their incursions that Ollegarius was dedicated by his parents to God and to St Eulalia in the church of which that saint was patroness in Barcelona.   At the age of fifteen the boy was made over to the canons attached to the church, and with him was given an endowment of vineyards, buildings and other property.   In those days it was not essential that a canon should be a priest, or even a celibate, and therefore it did not seem extraordinary that the youth should be appointed provost when he had scarcely reached manhood—the importance of his family and his personal piety would sufficiently justify such a choice.   When he had been raised to the priesthood he was sent to France to the monastery of St Adrian, in which canons regular had lately been installed, and was made prior, the first of several such offices that he held.   The story goes that, the bishopric of Barcelona falling vacant in 1115, Count

Raymond was desirous of appointing Ollegarius, but the holy man shrank from taking the office and withdrew into hiding.   The count, not to be beaten, went to Rome to obtain confirmation of his choice, and, fortified with a papal bull and accompanied by a legate, he tracked Ollegarius to his retreat amongst the canons of Maguelonnes and overcame his resistance.   The new bishop proved himself both a zealous overseer and an able administrator, and was soon translated to the archiepiscopal see of Tarragona.

In 1123 Ollegarius went to Rome to attend the first Council of the Lateran, where he asked Pope Callistus II and the assembly to enact that the privileges which were being offered to those who would take part in the crusades in Palestine should be extended to those who would fight the Moslems in Spain.   His petition was granted, and he returned home as apostolic delegate charged to preach a crusade against Moors.   Success crowned his efforts, and Count Raymond succeeded in obtaining sufficient reinforcements to inflict severe losses on the Moors and to drive them from some of their strongholds.   Ollegarius also did much to encourage and extend in his diocese the newly formed Order of Knights Templars.   His metropolitan city of Tarragona had been almost entirely destroyed by the Moors, and he set to work to rebuild and restore it.   Ollegarius also made the care of the sick poor, and in particular the mentally afflicted, the object of his special solicitude.   Although he was closely bound to the ruling family, he did not hesitate to denounce Count Raymond III when the count sought to reimpose an unjust tribute which his father, Raymond Berengarius, had remitted.   At a synod in 1137 the archbishop, who was old and in failing health, was suddenly taken ill.   He was carried from the council-chamber to his bed, from which he never rose again.

There is a Latin life, or rather two separate lives, of Ollegarius which have been printed by Florez in his *España Sagrada*, vol. xxix, pp. 472–499, together with a collection of the saint's miracles.   In Spain, and especially in Catalonia, his memory was at one time cherished very devoutly, and he was the subject of many popular biographies, such as that of Jaime Rebullosa, *Vida y milagros del d. Olaguer* (1609).   See also the *Acta Sanctorum*, March, vol. i.

ST CYRIL OF CONSTANTINOPLE   (*c.* A.D. 1235 ?)

In the Carmelite supplement to the Roman Martyrology we may read on this day the following entry : " In the Holy Land, of St Cyril, Confessor, of the Carmelite Order, who by his learning and holiness brought many to the faith of Christ and ruled his order with great praise for twenty-seven years.   At length, in the reign of the Emperors Philip and Otto, he had rest in a blessed end."   The unsatisfactory character of this notice is revealed at once by the fact that while the Emperors Philip of Swabia and Otto IV must unquestionably be here referred to, Otto was not the colleague but the opponent and successor of Philip.   Moreover Otto IV died in 1218, while Brocard, the predecessor of Cyril in the office of prior general of the Carmelites, was still living at that date.   It would serve no good purpose to enter into any detail regarding the fanciful biography which at a later period was invented for St Cyril and which still holds its place in the lessons of the Carmelite Breviary. According to this, Cyril was a gifted priest of Constantinople who had rendered marvellous services to the Church in controversy with the Greek Orthodox over the question of the *Filioque*, and who had been sent by the Emperor Manuel Comnenus on an embassy to Pope Alexander III.   In point of fact we know no more about St Cyril than the circumstance that about the year 1232 he succeeded to the office of prior general in Palestine, retaining it for not more than three years, and secondly that, owing in part to a most extravagant confusion of his name with that of St Cyril of Alexandria and St Cyril of Jerusalem, there were attributed to him long after his death a supposed treatise on the procession of the Holy Ghost, a dissertation upon the development cf the Carmelite Order, and a much-controverted Oracle or Prognostic, " solemnly transmitted from Heaven by angelic hands to St Cyril of Constantinople, the Carmelite ". The first of these alleged writings probably never existed in any shape or form, while the second and third were forgeries. Owing, however, to the enormous vogue which attached in the thirteenth century to the mystic and prophetical utterances which passed under the name of Joachim of Flora, the supposed *Oraculum* of St Cyril, the first mention of which occurs about the year 1295, came to play a part in the controversy over Joachim's " Eternal Gospel ". As a result Cyril's name became widely known, and by the aid of much confusion with the other Cyrils who had lived 800 or 900 years earlier he was venerated by his brethren as a saint and doctor of the Church. It should be mentioned, however, that no commemoration of this " St Cyril of Constantinople " finds a place in the Roman Martyrology.

The case of St Cyril has been very frankly and thoroughly investigated by Fr Benedict Zimmerman. The outcome of his researches is presented summarily in the *Catholic Encyclopedia* (vol. iv, p. 595), but a fuller discussion will be found in his *Monumenta Historica Carmelitana*, pp. 295-311, and in his contribution to U. Chevalier's *Bibliothèque liturgique*, vol. xiii, pp. 289-291 and 329-332. The fictitious history of the saint may be read in some detail in the *Acta Sanctorum*, March, vol. i. The literature which centres round Cyril's *Oraculum* and Joachim of Flora, notably certain contributions by Cardinal Ehrle to the *Archiv für Litteratur und Kirchengeschichte*, is duly indicated in Fr Zimmerman's notes.

BD JORDAN OF PISA   (A.D. 1311)

JORDAN OF PISA is perhaps best known at the present day as one of the creators of the modern Italian language. A contemporary of Dante and a preacher of great eloquence and learning, he was among the first to use the Tuscan dialect instead of Latin in his addresses and sermons—thus fixing and enriching the spoken language, as Dante and Petrarch gave a stable form to the written word. Nothing is known of his parentage or early youth, but from a passage in one of his sermons it is thought that he was studying in Paris in 1276. " Consider ", he says, " a man who has obtained the friendship of the king of France : what honour may he not receive ? I have seen such a man with my own eyes—a man of mean and low extraction who managed to win the friendship of the king. The entire court and all the barons bowed down before him and paid him incredible honour simply because he was the king's friend." The allusion was certainly to Peter de la Brosse, who, after acting as barber-surgeon to St Louis IX, became the intimate friend of his son, King Philip the Bold. The first thing we know about Jordan is that he received the Dominican habit at Pisa in 1280, and that he was afterwards sent to complete his studies at the University of Paris.

At the Dominican provincial chapter at Rieti in 1305 he was appointed lector in Florence, and during the three years that he occupied that post he made the house of Santa Maria Novella famous throughout Italy for the high standard of excellence of its studies. Whilst teaching in the schools, Bd Jordan never forgot that he belonged to the Order of Preachers, and he was one of the greatest orators of his age. In Florence he sometimes preached five times a day, in the churches and in

the open air.   Often he would begin to treat of a subject in the morning in one
church, continue it at noon in another, and finish it in the evening in a third, the
Florentines following him from church to church.   Many of his hearers took notes,
some of which have come down to us and are treasures of the language of the time.
His teaching was simple but powerful   he preached Christ crucified and the doctrine of the faith illustrated by examples from Holy Scripture and by anecdotes from
the lives of the saints.   He often refers to the necessity and importance of preaching,
and to the work of St Dominic, before whose time, Jordan said, " there were
scarcely any schools of theology : now they fill the whole of Christendom, and every
great community has its own school—a most useful thing.   Before him, only
bishops announced the word of God : it was their distinctive office.   Priests,
monks and hermits did no more than preach by example."

The effect of his own preaching—especially in Florence—was quite wonderful,
and the tone of public morality in the city was entirely changed.   He was also
careful to ensure the perseverance of his penitents by constantly pointing out to
them the means of perseverance, daily attendance at Mass, frequent use of the
sacraments, morning and evening prayer, recalling the presence of God, reading,
meditating on the vanity of this world and on the eternity that awaits us.   Often
after he had spoken for a couple of hours, he would be completely exhausted, and
sometimes his disciple Ventura—afterwards Bd Silvester of Valdiseve—would wait
at the foot of the pulpit stairs to refresh him with wine.   The two men were close
friends, and Ventura afterwards entered the Camaldolese monastery in Florence as
a lay-brother.   Many of Jordan's other penitents likewise became famous for their
sanctity.   In the chronicle of the Dominican convent at Pisa it is noted that the
holy man had learnt by heart " the Breviary, the Missal, the greater part of the
Bible with its marginal notes, the second part of the *Summa* of St Thomas and many
other things ".   Of the confraternities which Jordan founded in Pisa, one, the
Confraternity of the Holy Redeemer, still retains its primitive constitution.   In
1311 Bd Jordan was appointed professor of theology in the friary of St James in
Paris, but he was taken ill on the way and died at Piacenza.   His *cultus* was confirmed in 1833.

See S. Razzi, *Historia degli Uomini illustri O.P.*, vol. i, pp. 66 *seq.* ; A. Galletti, " Fra
Giordano da Pisa, predicatore del secolo xiv " in *Archivio storico italiano*, vol. xxxiii (1899) ;
Procter, *Lives of Dominican Saints*, pp. 01-64 ; Taurisano, *Catalogus Hagiographicus O.P.*
(1918), p. 25.

ST COLETTE, Virgin   (A.D. 1447)

ALL human institutions, however excellent, are apt to degenerate after the death of
their founders or the immediate successors of those founders.   If they are to continue they need to be reanimated with their original ideals or else remodelled to
bring them up to date.   We find this with the great religious orders, which all have
their ups and downs, their periods of activity and eclipse, and it is as the reformer
of one of the most austere of these families, the Poor Clares, that St Colette did her
chief work in the world.   The impression she made upon her order was very great,
and one branch still bears after her the name of Colettines.   The circumstances
of her birth were humble, her father being a carpenter at the abbey of Corbie in
Picardy ; her parents were devout people who gave to their little girl the name of
Nicolette, in honour of St Nicholas of Myra.   Colette, as she was called, was a

singularly attractive child, very lovely to behold, but so tiny that her father was quite concerned about it. The child prayed that she might grow taller, and her prayer was answered. As she grew older she lived at home almost as a solitary, busying herself with prayer and manual work, and her parents, recognizing that she was led by the spirit of God, allowed her full liberty. Nevertheless, even in her retirement, her beauty attracted so much attention that Colette, finding it a hindrance, prayed that her complexion might be changed, and we read that her face became so thin and pale that she was scarcely recognizable, but that her sweet and modest demeanour continued to make her singularly attractive to all who saw her.

Both her parents died when Colette was seventeen, leaving her under the care of the abbot of Corbie; after a time in a convent, she distributed to the poor the little she had inherited and entered the third order of St Francis. The abbot gave her a small hermitage beside the church of Corbie, where she lived a life of such austerity that her fame spread far and wide and many sought her prayers and advice. After a while, however, she received no more visitors, and for three years maintained complete silence and seclusion. Doubtless during that period she had pondered much over the condition of the order to which she was affiliated and had spoken of it to her confessor, Friar Henry de Baume, for we read that he dreamt he saw Colette tending a vine covered with leaves but fruitless, and that after she had pruned it it began to bear an abundance of grapes. Colette herself also had visions, in one of which the Seraphic Father St Francis appeared and charged her to restore the first rule of St Clare in all its original severity. Not unnaturally, she hesitated, but she received what she recognized as a sign from Heaven when she was struck blind for three days and dumb for three days more. Encouraged by her director, she left her cell in 1406, and straightway made an attempt to explain her mission in one or two convents, but soon discovered that, if she was to succeed, she must be invested with the proper authority. Barefoot, dressed in a habit made up of patches, Colette set out for Nice to seek Peter de Luna, who at that epoch of the great schism was acknowledged by the French as pope, under the name of Benedict XIII. He received her with great consideration, and not only professed her under the rule of St Clare, but was so much impressed that he constituted her superioress of all convents of Minoresses that she might reform or found, with a mission to the friars and tertiaries of St Francis as well. At the same time he appointed Father Henry de Baume to act as her assistant.

Armed with these powers, St Colette went from convent to convent, travelling through France, Savoy and Flanders, and at first she met with violent opposition, being treated as a fanatic and even accused of sorcery. But rebuffs, ill-will, and calumnies were all alike received with joy, and after a while she began to meet with a more favourable reception, especially in Savoy, where her reform gained both sympathizers and recruits, and from thence it passed to Burgundy, France, Flanders and Spain. Besançon was the first house of Poor Clares to receive her revised rule, in 1410. Her fame spread far and wide and was enhanced by the many miracles she wrought. " I am dying to see that wonderful Colette who raises people from the dead ", wrote the Duchess of Bourbon. She saw her, and no family was more deeply influenced by the saint. This peasant woman exercised a singular spell over people of high rank in the world, like Blanche of Geneva, the Duchess of Nevers, Amadeus II of Savoy, the Princess of Orange, and Philip the Good, Duke of Burgundy.

It is said that, as Colette made a stay at Moulins in 1429, she met St Joan of Arc on her way with an army to besiege La Charité-sur-Loire, and one would be pleased to imagine an interview between these two remarkable women, so unlike in their missions but so similar in their spirit.   Unfortunately no evidence exists of any personal intercourse between them.   One place closely connected with St Colette is Le Puy-en-Velay, where her convent has had an unbroken life to this day.   Altogether she founded seventeen new convents, besides reforming numerous old ones, and several houses of Franciscan friars accepted her reform.

Underlying all her external activity was St Colette's life of prayer which sustained her throughout her whole career.   She beheld our Lord in a vision suffering and dying on the cross, and always on Fridays, from six in the morning until six in the evening, she meditated unceasingly on the Passion, neither eating nor drinking nor doing anything else.   In Holy Week particularly, but also at other seasons, she would be rapt in ecstasy when assisting at Mass or when praying in her cell, which was sometimes irradiated with a supernatural light, whilst her own countenance shone with celestial brightness.   Almost always after holy communion she was rapt in an ecstasy which lasted for many hours.   Once she had a vision of men and women falling from grace in appalling numbers, like the flakes in a snowstorm, and ever afterwards she would daily pour forth fervent prayer for the conversion of sinners and for the souls in Purgatory : indeed we read that she actually died in a transport of intercession for sinners and for the Church.   Like her spiritual father St Francis, Colette was a lover of animals, especially of those that are weak and gentle : lambs and doves she would gather round her and the shyest of birds would eat out of her hand.   For children too she had a great affection, and she liked to play with them and to bless them—as her Saviour had done.

It was in Flanders, where she had established several houses, that St Colette was seized with her last illness.   She foretold her own death, received the last sacraments and died in her convent at Ghent in her sixty-seventh year.   Her body was removed from Ghent by the Poor Clares when the Emperor Joseph II was suppressing a number of religious houses in Flanders, and borne to her convent at Poligny, thirty-two miles from Besançon.   She was canonized in 1807.

Although much manuscript material for the history of St Colette which is known to have existed in the sixteenth century has now disappeared, we are not destitute of contemporary and first-hand sources.   The text of the narrative of Father Henry de Baume, her confessor for thirty-three years, seems to have been lost, as also the memoirs of Fr Francis Claret, another of her spiritual guides, but the record compiled by her devoted friend and daughter in religion, Sister Perrine, still survives.   Moreover, we have a good number of the saint's own letters and the copious but disjointed recollections of Fr Peter de Vaux, her confessor in her last years.   It is interesting to note that a copy of this life by Peter de Vaux was made and richly illuminated by command of Margaret, Duchess of Burgundy, who was the sister of Edward IV, King of England.   She presented it to a convent of Colettines and wrote at the end in her own hand, " Votre Loyal fylle Margarete d'Angleterre ; priez pour elle et pour son salut ".   This manuscript is now in the convent of the Poor Clares at Ghent. The lives by Sister Perrine and Peter de Vaux, formerly printed in a Latin translation by the Bollandists, together with some extracts from the processes, have been edited by Fr Ubald d'Alençon in the language in which they were written (1911).   In modern times we have biographies by Bizouart, Germain, Pidoux, Imle and Poirot.   See also some valuable notes by Ubald d'Alençon in the *Archivum Franciscanum Historicum*, vols. ii and iii (1909-1910). The admirable biography of the saint by Mme Sainte-Marie Perrin has been translated into English with some useful additions (1923), as has the life by Fr Sellier (1864).

7 : ST THOMAS AQUINAS, Doctor of the Church   (A.D. 1274)

THE family of the counts of Aquino was of noble lineage, tracing its descent back for several centuries to the Lombards. St Thomas's father was a knight, Landulf, and his mother Theodora was of Norman descent. There seems something more northern than southern about Thomas's physique, his imposing stature, massive build and fresh complexion. The precise year of his birth is uncertain, but it was about 1225 and took place in the castle of Rocca Secca, the ruins of which are still to be seen on a mountain crag dominating the fertile plain of Campagna Felice and the little town of Aquino. Thomas was the youngest of four sons, and there were also several daughters, but the youngest little girl was killed by lightning one night, whilst Thomas, who was sleeping in the same room, escaped unscathed. Throughout life he is said to have been very nervous of storms, often retiring into a church when lightning was about. Hence the popular devotion to St Thomas as patron against thunderstorms and sudden death.

A few miles to the south of Rocca Secca, on a high plateau, stands the abbey of Monte Cassino, the cradle of Western monasticism and one of the holiest spots in Europe, whose abbot at this time was a kinsman of the Aquino family, Landulf Sinibaldo. As a child of five Thomas was taken here as an oblate (*cf.* cap. lix of St Benedict's Rule), and he remained till he was about thirteen, living in the monastery and getting his schooling there. He was taken away probably because of the disturbed state of the times, and about 1239 was sent to the University of Naples, where for five years he studied the arts and sciences, and even began to " coach " others. It was in Naples that he became attracted by the Order of Preachers, whose church he loved to frequent and with some of whose members he soon became intimate. The friars, who saw him often absorbed in prayer in their midst, noticed on several occasions rays of light shining about his head, and one of them, Father John of San Giuliano, exclaimed, " Our Lord has given you to our order ". St Thomas confided to the prior that he ardently desired to become a Dominican, but in view of the probable opposition of his family, he was advised to foster his vocation and to wait for three years. Time only confirmed his determination, and, at the age of about nineteen, he was received and clothed in the habit of the order.

News of this was soon carried to Rocca Secca, where it aroused great indignation —not because he had joined a religious community, for his mother was quite content that he should become a Benedictine, and indeed probably saw in him the destined abbot of Monte Cassino, but because he had entered a mendicant order. Theodora herself set out for Naples to persuade her son to return home. The friars, however, hurried him off to their convent of Santa Sabina in Rome, and when the angry lady followed in pursuit, the young man was no longer to be found there. The master general of the Dominicans, who was on his way to Bologna, had decided to take Thomas with him, and the little party of friars had already set out on foot together. Theodora, not to be baulked, sent word to the saint's elder brothers, who were serving with the emperor's army in Tuscany, desiring them to waylay and capture the fugitive. As Thomas was resting by the roadside at Aquapendente near Siena, he was overtaken by his brothers at the head of a troop of soldiers, and after a vain attempt to take his habit from him by force, was brought back, first to Rocca Secca and then to the castle of Monte San Giovanni, two miles distant, where he was kept in close confinement, only his worldly-minded sister Marotta being allowed to visit him. They sought to undermine his determination in every way, but after a time began to mitigate the severity of his imprisonment. During his captivity Thomas studied the *Sentences* of Peter Lombard, learned by heart a great part of the Bible, and is said to have written a treatise on the fallacies of Aristotle.

Other devices for subduing him having failed, his brothers conceived the infamous plan of seducing him by introducing into his room a woman of bad character. St Thomas immediately seized a burning brand from the hearth and chased her out of the place. We are told that he immediately fell into a deep sleep in which he was visited by two angels, who seemed to gird him round the waist with a cord emblematic of chastity.*

This captivity lasted two years before Thomas's family gave up and in 1245 permitted him to return to his order. It was now determined to send him to complete his studies under St Albert the Great, and he set out in company with the master general, John the Teutonic, who was on his way to Paris ; from thence Thomas went on to Cologne. The schools there were full of young clerics from various parts of Europe eager to learn and equally eager to discuss, and the humble, reserved new-comer was not immediately appreciated either by his fellow students or by his professors. His silence at disputations as well as his bulky figure led to his receiving the nickname of " the dumb Sicilian ox ". A good-natured companion, pitying his apparent dullness, offered to explain the daily lessons, and St Thomas humbly and gratefully accepted the offer ; but when they came to a difficult passage which baffled the would-be teacher, his pupil explained it to him so clearly and correctly that his fellow student was amazed. Shortly afterwards a student picked up a sheet of Thomas's notes, and passed it on to the master, who marvelled at the scholarly elucidation. The next day St Albert gave him a public test, at the close of which he exclaimed, " We call Brother Thomas ' the dumb ox ' ; but I tell you that he will yet make his lowing heard to the uttermost parts of the earth ". But Thomas's learning was exceeded by his piety, and after he had been ordained priest his union with God seemed closer than ever. His disciple and biographer William da Tocco writes that from that time he used to spend hours in prayer, both during the day and at night, and, he adds, " when consecrating at Mass, he would be overcome by such intensity of devotion as to be dissolved in tears, utterly absorbed in its mysteries and nourished with its fruits ".

There are chronological difficulties about these years of St Thomas's life, but certainly in 1252, at the instance of St Albert and Cardinal Hugh of Saint-Cher, he was ordered to Paris to teach as a bachelor in the university. Academical degrees were then very different from what they are now, and were conferred only in view of the actual work of teaching. In Paris Thomas expounded the Holy Scriptures and the *Liber sententiarum* of Peter Lombard ; he also wrote a commentary on these same Sentences, and others on Isaias and St Matthew's Gospel. Four years later he delivered his inaugural lecture as master and received his doctor's chair, his duties being to lecture, to discuss and to preach ; and towards the end of the time he began the *Summa contra Gentiles*. From 1259 to 1268 Paris saw nothing of her most popular professor, for he was in Italy. Here he was made a preacher general, and was called upon to teach in the school of selected scholars attached to the papal

* It has been suggested that the first part of this story is simply an exaggerated version of the visit to Thomas of his sister Marotta. He certainly converted her to better ways, and she became a Benedictine nun and abbess at Capua. After her death she appeared to St Thomas, asking him to offer Masses for her in Purgatory.

court, and, as it followed the pope in his movements, St Thomas lectured and preached in many of the Italian towns.   About 1266 he began the most famous of all his written works, the *Summa theologiae*.

In 1269 he was back again in Paris.   St Louis IX held him in such esteem that he constantly consulted him on important matters of state, but perhaps a greater testimony to his reputation was the resolution of the university to refer to his decision a question upon which they were divided, *viz.* whether in the Blessed Sacrament of the altar the accidents remained really or only in appearance.   St Thomas, after fervent prayer, wrote his answer in the form of a treatise which is still extant, and laid it on the altar before making it public.   His decision was accepted by the university first and afterwards by the whole Church.   It was on this occasion that we first hear of the saint receiving from our Lord's own lips a formal approval of what he had set down.   Appearing in a vision, the Saviour said to him, " Thou hast written well of the sacrament of my Body " ; and almost immediately afterwards Thomas passed into an ecstasy and remained so long raised from the ground that there was time to summon many of the brethren to behold the spectacle.   Later on, towards the end of his life, when the Angelic Doctor was at Salerno and was busied with the third part of his *Summa* which deals with Christ's passion and resurrection, a sacristan saw him at night kneeling before the altar in ecstasy.   Then a voice, which seemed to come from the crucifix, said aloud, " Thou hast written well of me, Thomas ; what reward wouldst thou have ? "   To which he answered, " Nothing but thyself, Lord ".   A story of a different kind is told of an occasion when Thomas had been invited to lunch with King St Louis.   During the meal he suddenly had an idea about a matter on which he had been writing, and banging his fist on the table he exclaimed, " That's finished the Manichean (?) heresy ! " The prior tugged at Thomas's *cappa* and reminded him that he was at table with the king, and Thomas pulled himself together and apologized for his absent-mindedness.

During his second, as during his first, period in Paris the university was torn by dissensions of different kinds, and in 1272 there was a sort of " general strike " among the faculties, in the midst of which St Thomas was recalled to Italy and appointed regent of the study-house at Naples.   It was to prove the last scene of his labours.   On the feast of St Nicholas the following year he was celebrating Mass when he received a revelation which so affected him that he wrote and dictated no more, leaving his great work, the *Summa theologiae*, unfinished.   To Brother Reginald's expostulations he replied, " The end of my labours is come.   All that I have written appears to be as so much straw after the things that have been revealed to me."

He was ill when he was bidden by Pope Gregory X to attend the general council at Lyons for the reunion of the Greek and Latin churches and to bring with him his treatise " Against the Errors of the Greeks ".   He became so much worse on the journey that he was taken to the Cistercian abbey of Fossa Nuova near Terracina, where he was lodged in the abbot's room and waited on by the monks.   In compliance with their entreaties he began to expound to them the Canticle of Canticles, but he did not live to finish his exposition.   It soon became evident to all that he was dying.   After he had made his last confession to Father Reginald of Priverno and received viaticum from the abbot he gave utterance to the famous words, " I am receiving thee, Price of my soul's redemption : all my studies, my vigils and my labours have been for love of thee.   I have taught much and written much of the most sacred body of Jesus Christ ; I have taught and written in the faith of Jesus Christ and of the holy Roman Church, to whose judgement I offer and submit everything." Two days later his soul passed to God, in the early hours of March 7, 1274, being only about fifty years of age. That same day St Albert, who was then in Cologne, burst into tears in the presence of the community, and exclaimed, " Brother Thomas Aquinas, my son in Christ, the light of the Church, is dead. God has revealed it to me."

St Thomas was canonized in 1323, but it was not until 1368 that the Dominicans succeeded in obtaining possession of his body, which was translated with great pomp to Toulouse, where it still lies in the cathedral of Saint-Sernin. St Pius V conferred upon him the title of doctor of the Church, and in 1880 Leo XIII declared him the patron of all universities, colleges and schools. Of the holy man's writings, which fill twenty thick volumes, this is not the place to give any detailed account : they were mainly philosophical and theological. He commented much on Aristotle, whose teaching he was in some sense the first to utilize in order to build up a complete system of Christian philosophy. With regard to his method it has been said that he applied geometry to theology, first stating his problem or theorem, and then propounding difficulties. This he follows up with a train of relevant passages drawn from the Bible, the Church's tradition and various theological works, and concludes with a categorical answer to all the objections made at the beginning.

St Thomas also wrote dissertations on the Lord's Prayer, the Angelical Salutation and the Apostles' Creed, besides composing commentaries on many parts of the Holy Scriptures and treatises in answer to questions propounded to him. Of all his works the most important was the *Summa theologiae*, which is the fullest exposition of theological teaching ever given to the world. He worked at it for five years, but, as already stated, he never finished it. It was the greatest monument of the age, and was one of the three works of reference laid on the table of the assembly at the Council of Trent, the other two being the Bible and the Pontifical Decrees. It is almost impossible for us, at this distance of time, to realize the enormous influence St Thomas exerted over the minds and theology of his contemporaries and their immediate successors. Neither were his achievements confined to matters of dogma, Christian apologetic and philosophy. When Pope Urban IV, influenced by the visions of Bd Juliana of Liège, decided to institute the feast of Corpus Christi, he appealed to St Thomas to compose the liturgical office and the Mass for the day. These give proof of an extraordinary mastery of apt expression, and are as remarkable for their doctrinal accuracy as for their tenderness of thought. Two of the hymns, the " Verbum supernum " and " Pange lingua ", are familiar to all Catholics, because their final verses, " O salutaris " and " Tantum ergo ", are regularly sung at Benediction ; but others of the saint's hymns, notably the " Lauda Sion " and the " Adoro te devote ", are hardly less popular.

Of the many noble characteristics of St Thomas Aquinas perhaps the two which may be considered with the greatest profit are his prayerfulness and his humility. He was ever wont to declare that he learnt more at the foot of the crucifix than from books. " His marvellous science ", says Brother Reginald, " was far less due to his genius than to the efficacy of his prayers. He prayed with tears to obtain from God the understanding of His mysteries, and abundant enlightenment was vouchsafed to his mind." St Thomas was singularly modest about his great gifts.

Asked if he were never tempted to pride or vainglory, he replied, " No ", adding that if any such thoughts occurred to him, his common sense immediately dispelled them by showing him their utter unreasonableness. Moreover he was always apt to think others better than himself, and he was extremely modest in stating his opinion he was never known to lose his temper in argument, however great the provocation might be, nor was he ever heard to make a cutting remark or to say things which would wound other people.

We are not as well informed about the life of St Thomas as we should like to be—especially about his early years—but there is a considerable amount of more or less contemporary evidence. William da Tocco, the author of the biography printed in the *Acta Sanctorum*, was a pupil of his, and so also was Ptolemy of Lucca, who devotes a good deal of space to him in his *Ecclesiastical History*. A great part of the testimony presented when evidence was taken with a view to canonization has been preserved and is printed by the Bollandists. Besides this, the letters and chronicles of the period, and Denifle's great work, the *Chartularium Universitatis Parisiensis*, supply an abundance of collateral information. But for fuller details the reader must be referred to the *Bibliographie thomiste* (1921) compiled with great care by Frs Mandonnet and Destrez. For the English public we have the very copious *Life and Labours of St Thomas of Aquin* (1871), by Abp. R. B. Vaughan, and smaller biographies by Frs Conway and Kavanagh, and two works dealing with the more philosophic aspect of the work of the Angelic Doctor, M. Grabmann, *Thomas Aquinas, his Personality and Thought* (1928), trans. from the German ; and Fr M. C. d'Arcy, *Thomas Aquinas* (1930). Those who desire to obtain an insight into the spirituality of St Thomas, to learn, in other words, what made him a saint, may be recommended to make acquaintance with the admirable sketch of L. H. Petitot, *Saint Thomas d'Aquin : la vocation, l'œuvre, la vie spirituelle* (1923). This is largely based upon the very thorough researches of Fr Mandonnet, notably his *Siger de Brabant*. On the other hand the contributions to the subject made by modern German scholars, notably by Endres and Grabmann, should not be neglected. Among more recent publications in English may be mentioned J. Maritain, *The Angelic Doctor* (1931) ; G. K. Chesterton, *St Thomas Aquinas* (1933) ; A. Sertillanges, *St Thomas Aquinas and His Work* (1933) ; G. Vann, *St Thomas Aquinas* (1940) ; R. Coffey, *The Man from Rocca Sicca* (1944). But the standard biography, in which critical science and " unction " are neatly combined, is *St Thomas Aquinas* (1945), by Fr Angelo Walz, tr. into English by Fr Sebastian Bullough (1951) ; this has extensive bibliographies. There are anthologies of the saint's writing by Fr d'Arcy (1939) and Fr Thomas Gilby (1951 and 1955).

ST PAUL THE SIMPLE (*c.* A.D. 339)

PAUL, surnamed " the Simple " on account of his childlikeness, is not to be confused with St Paul, the first hermit, of whom an account has been given under January 15. This second Paul, also an anchorite, became one of the most eminent of the early followers of St Antony in the Egyptian Thebaïd. Up to the age of sixty he had lived the life of a labourer, but the misconduct of his wife, whose infidelity he had surprised, contributed to wean him from all earthly ties. Leaving her without a word, the old man went an eight days' journey into the desert to seek St Antony and to beseech him to accept him as a disciple and to teach him the way of salvation. The great patriarch, judging him to be too old to enter upon a hermit's life, repulsed him, bidding him return to the world to serve God by hard work, or at any rate to enter some monastery where they would put up with his stupidity. He then shut the door. Paul, instead of obeying, remained outside, fasting and praying continuously until the fourth day, when Antony opened the door and discovered him still there. " Go away, old man ", he exclaimed. " Why are you so persistent ? You cannot remain here."—" I cannot die anywhere but here ", replied his would-be disciple. Realizing that Paul had had no food, and fearing lest he should actually have the old man's death on his conscience, Antony admitted him rather reluctantly, saying, " You can be saved if you are obedient and do what I enjoin." The reply was, " I will do whatever you command."

The neophyte was thereupon subjected to a course of training which was calculated to discourage anyone less determined. First he was bidden to stand outside and pray until he was told to stop—and he obeyed, undisturbed by the heat of a scorching sun and without having broken his fast. Next he was invited to enter the cave and to weave mats and hurdles as he saw St Antony do. This also he performed, praying all the while. When he had made fifteen mats he was told that they were badly made and that he must take them to pieces and start over again. He complied without a murmur, although he was still fasting. This done, St Antony bethought him of another test, telling him to moisten with water four six-ounce loaves of bread—the bread being exceedingly hard and dry. When the food was ready, instead of eating, he instructed Paul to sing psalms with him and then to sit down beside the loaves until the evening, when it would be time to eat. At night they would pray together and then take a short rest, rising at midnight for further prayers which continued until daybreak. After sunset each one would eat a loaf and Antony would ask his disciple if he would like another, receiving the reply, " Yes, if you do." To Antony's rejoinder, " It is enough for me ; I am a monk ", the old man would meekly reply, " Then it is enough for me ; I also wish to be a monk." The same routine was repeated day after day, but sometimes the training would take another form. Paul would have to spend the time drawing water and pouring it away, or weaving rushes into baskets and undoing them, or sewing and unsewing his garments ; but whatever he was told to do he did it cheerfully and promptly. Once St Antony overturned a pot of honey and told him to collect it all from the ground without picking up any dust.

On another occasion, when there were guests at the hermitage and a general conversation was going on, Paul asked if the prophets were before Jesus Christ or Jesus Christ before the prophets. St Antony, mortified at his disciple's display of ignorance, told him sharply to hold his tongue and go away. Paul at once did so, and continued to keep silence until the matter was reported to Antony, who had forgotten all about it. When he had elicited the fact that Paul's silence was simply a question of obedience, he exclaimed, " How this monk puts us all to shame ! He immediately obeys man's simplest order, while we often fail to listen to the word which comes to us from Heaven." When the training was deemed complete, Antony established Paul in a cell at a distance of three miles from his own, and there he was wont to visit him. He recognized in the old man singular spiritual gifts and certain powers of healing and exorcising greater than his own. Often when he could not effect a cure, he would send the sufferer on to St Paul, who would restore him at once. Another divine gift he possessed was the power to read men's thoughts. As each one came into church he could tell by glancing at his face what was in his mind and whether his thoughts were good or bad. By such signs of God's predilection St Antony came to esteem his aged follower above all his other disciples, and frequently held him up to them as a model.

The substance of all that precedes is to be found in the 22nd chapter of Palladius's *Lausiac History*, with a few additions from the *Historia Monachorum* as translated by Rufinus. Seeing that Palladius wrote sixty or seventy years after the death of Paul the Simple it is likely that his account is embellished by some legendary accretions. A detailed account of Paul may also be found in J. Bremond, *Les Pères du désert*, vol. i, pp. xli–xliii and 94–96.

ST DRAUSIUS, or DRAUSIN, Bishop of Soissons   (*c.* A.D. 674)

ONE of the treasures now preserved in the museum of the Louvre in Paris is an interesting and beautiful Romano-Gallic sarcophagus which is actually the tomb of St Drausius, though the relics it contained were scattered at the time of the Revolution.   Up to that period it had stood in the cathedral of Soissons, where the saint's shrine was held in the utmost veneration.   Five foot six in length, the tomb is made of hard stone, dug out for the body and adorned with sculptures outside.

Drausius was educated by St Anseric, Bishop of Soissons, and was appointed archdeacon by Anseric's successor.   So highly did Bishop Bettolin esteem his young subordinate that when he himself was about to retire, on the plea that his election had not been valid, he urged that Drausius should be chosen in his place. The new bishop soon proved himself a most zealous administrator, whilst by his sermons and instructions he gained many to Christ.   His abstinence was such that his life was one constant fast, and although he suffered nearly all his life from most painful maladies, he added to his sufferings by voluntary mortifications.   He founded two religious houses, one for men and the other for women, to serve as havens of rest in those troublous times, and also that through the prayers of the communities the blessing of God might descend upon the city.   From Bettolin he bought land beside the Aisne, and there he built his monastery for men at Rethondes.   The nunnery was at Soissons itself, and in establishing it St Drausius was greatly assisted by Leutrude, the wife of Ebroin, mayor of the palace.   In 664 the church of Notre-Dame de Soissons was completed and dedicated.   Already at this date a single church was not considered sufficient for the needs of a great community, and St Drausius therefore built two other chapels, one for the abbess and obedientiaries, and another for sick nuns, guests and the poor whom they received.   The holy bishop only lived long enough to complete his work, and died on March 5 about the year 674.

St Drausius's fame extended to other countries, and it is recorded that St Thomas of Canterbury had recourse to him before returning to England, where he foresaw martyrdom awaiting him.   As it was supposed that those who spent a night in intercession at the tomb of the saint became invulnerable against all hostile machinations, Italians and Burgundians, when they had war in their own country, were wont to make pilgrimages to the shrine of St Drausius to enable them to bid defiance to their enemies.   All this comes to us on the authority of John of Salisbury who, writing in 1166, remarks that Robert de Montfort had passed a night at the shrine in prayer before his encounter with Henry, Earl of Essex.

There is a short Latin life of St Drausius which has been printed in the *Acta Sanctorum* (March, vol. i).   See also Duchesne, *Fastes Épiscopaux*, vol. iii. p. 90, from whom we may learn that in signing his name the saint wrote variously Drusio, Draucio, and Drauscio.

ST ESTERWINE, Abbot   (A.D. 686)

ST ESTERWINE spent his early years at the court of Northumbria where his noble birth, handsome looks and gracious speech seemed to offer him every chance of advancement.   Feeling called, however, to the religious life, he betook himself to the abbey of Wearmouth, lately founded by his kinsman, St Benedict Biscop.   The high qualities which had endeared him to the court were no less conspicuous in the monastery, and his exceptional abilities, coupled with his piety and humility, made him eminently fitted for a post of authority.   When St Benedict, finding that duty often called him away, decided that it would be to the interest of the monastery that another abbot should be appointed to rule in his absence, his choice fell upon St Esterwine, who held office wisely and successfully for four years—until his death, which took place whilst Benedict was still absent in Rome.　Though aware that his sickness was mortal, St Esterwine lay in the common dormitory of the monks until four days before the end, when he caused himself to be carried to a quiet spot where he could prepare himself for death.　He passed away while his monks were singing the night office.

Nearly all that is to be known concerning St Esterwine will be found in the text and notes of Plummer's Bede.　The older *Historia Abbatum* should be consulted, as well as Bede's own narrative.　*Cf.* also Stanton's *Menology*, p. 106.

ST ARDO　(A.D. 843)

ARDO is remembered chiefly through the life he wrote of his superior, St Benedict of Aniane, " the reviver of monastic discipline, the second father of monasticism in the West ".　A Frank by race, he was a native of Languedoc, but not much is known of his history, which appears to have been uneventful.　He changed his name of Smaragdus to Ardo, and became one of the earliest followers of Benedict of Aniane, from whom he received the habit.　He was raised to the priesthood and was made director of the schools attached to the monastery.　He won the special regard of his abbot, who generally chose him as his travelling companion.　It seems to have been on one of these journeys that he became known to Charlemagne, who presented him with a curiosity in the shape of a stone which resounded like brass. When, in 814, St Benedict was about to leave Aniane to settle at Aachen he chose Ardo as provisional superior of Aniane.　History furnishes us with no further details as to his life or death.　The only one of his writings that has survived is the biography of Benedict, which he compiled at the request of his brethren.

In the ninth century all knowledge and science was kept alive by the monks, who alone saved it from extinction.　Among the schools of the day that of Aniane, of which Ardo was director, was perhaps the most prominent.　St Benedict, its founder, had collected a considerable library and had selected some excellent masters.　We know there was a singing master, a reading master, and teachers of literature and arts, as well as experienced theologians.　Several of the boys trained under Ardo became bishops, and many of the others helped to spread the method of Aniane in the schools attached to the great religious houses of France and Germany.

Although the Bollandists reject the claims of Ardo to be included in the register of saints, Mabillon seeks to prove that he must have been the subject of a definite *cultus*, because he has his own office in the Aniane Breviary and his relics were publicly venerated.　See his *Acta Sanctorum O.S.B.*, vol. iv, pt 1, p. 558, where we learn also that Ardo's head was preserved in a casket of silver-gilt, and his body in a wooden chest " wonderfully carved ".

ST THEOPHYLACT, BISHOP OF NICOMEDIA　(A.D. 845)

ST THEOPHYLACT came as a boy from Asia to Constantinople and became known to St Tarasius, who took a liking to him and gave him a good education.　Finding that he had a vocation to the religious life, the patriarch sent him and another of his disciples, St Michael the Confessor, to a monastery which he had recently founded beside the Bosphorus.　After they had lived there some years and had been thoroughly tested, St Tarasius raised them both to the episcopate, Theophylact becoming bishop of Nicomedia and Michael bishop of Synnada.

When Leo V revived Iconoclasm, St Nicephorus, the successor of St Tarasius in the see of Constantinople, summoned a council to maintain the Catholic doctrine in the presence of the emperor.   The case was ably and eloquently argued by St Theophylact and other learned men, but Leo remained obdurate.   When all had spoken and there was a slight pause, Theophylact stood up and prophesied, saying, " I know that you are scornful of the patience and long-suffering of God.   But, like a hurricane, calamity and a terrible death will overtake you, and there shall be none to deliver you."   Leo was infuriated and ordered them all into banishment   St Theophylact was imprisoned in a fortress in Caria, where he died thirty years later. As for the words of his prophecy, they were fulfilled to the letter.   When he was in his chapel on Christmas day 820, Leo was attacked by conspirators, and although he seized the cross from the altar and fought desperately with it against his foes, he was cut down and killed before assistance could arrive.

We read of the liberality of St Theophylact, his generosity to the poor, his care of widows, orphans and the insane, and of his tenderness to the blind, the lame and the sick, for whom and for travellers he established hospices.

In the *Acta Sanctorum* under March 8 will be found a summary of such information as it is possible to collect concerning St Theophylact, who must not, of course, be confused either with the historian Theophylact who lived in the seventh century, or with the arch-bishop and scripture commentator who wrote at the close of the eleventh.   St Theophylact was duly honoured in the Greek *Menaion* and in the synaxaries.   See Delehaye, *Synaxarium Constantinopolitanum*, pp. 519–522 ; and *Analecta Bollandiana*, vol. l (1932), pp. 67 *seq.*

8 : ST JOHN OF GOD, Founder of the Brothers Hospitallers   (A.D. 1550)

THIS St John was born in Portugal and spent part of his youth in the service of the bailiff of the count of Oroprusa in Castile.   In 1522 he enlisted in a company of soldiers raised by the count, and served in the wars between the French and the Spaniards and afterwards in Hungary against the Turks.   From contact with licentious companions in the army, he gradually lost the practice of religion and fell into grievous excesses.   The troop having been disbanded, he went to Andalusia, where he entered the service of a woman near Seville as a shepherd. At the age of about forty, stung with remorse for his past misconduct, he resolved to amend his life, and began to consider how he could best dedicate the rest of his life to God's service.   Compassion for the distressed led him to leave his situation in the hope that by crossing to Africa he might succour the Christian slaves there and perhaps win the crown of martyrdom.   At Gibraltar he met a Portuguese gentleman who had been condemned to banishment.   This exile and his wife and children were bound for Ceuta in Barbary, and John was so full of pity for them that he attached himself to the family and served them without wages. At Ceuta the man fell ill, and John hired himself out as a day labourer to earn a little money for their benefit.   However, he sustained a great shock owing to the apostasy of one of his companions, and as his confessor assured him that his going in quest of martyrdom was an illusion, he resolved to return to Spain.

Upon reaching Gibraltar the idea suggested itself that by turning pedlar and selling sacred pictures and books he might find opportunities of doing good to his customers. He succeeded well in this business, and in 1538, when he was forty-three, he was able to open a shop in Granada. Now on St Sebastian's day, which is kept as a great festival in that city, it happened that they had invited as special preacher the famous John of Avila. Amongst those who flocked to hear him was this other John, who was so affected by his sermon that he filled the church with his cries, beating his breast and imploring mercy. Then, as though demented, he ran about the streets, tearing his hair and behaving so wildly that he was pelted with sticks and stones and returned home a pitiable object. There he gave away his stock and began roaming the streets distractedly as before, until some kindly persons took him to Bd John of Avila. The holy man spoke to him in private, gave him advice and promised him help. John was quieted for a time, but soon returned to his extravagances and was carried off to a lunatic asylum, where, according to the practice of the times, the most brutal methods were employed to bring him to his senses. When John of Avila was informed of what had befallen, he came to visit his penitent and told him that he had practised his singular method of penance long enough, and advised him to occupy himself for the future in something more conducive to his own spiritual profit and that of his neighbour. This exhortation had the effect of instantly calming John—much to the astonishment of his keepers—but he remained in the hospital, waiting upon the sick, until St Ursula's day 1539, when he finally left it.

His mind was now set upon doing something to relieve the poor, and he began selling wood in the market-place to earn money for feeding the destitute. Soon afterwards he hired a house in which to harbour the sick poor, whom he served and catered for with such wisdom, zeal and economy as to astonish the whole city. This was the foundation of the order of Brothers of St John of God, which has since spread all over Christendom. John was busy all day long tending his patients, and at night he used to go out and find new objects of charity he soon ceased to go daily in quest of provisions, for people of their own accord brought him all that was necessary for his little hospital. The archbishop of Granada favoured the undertaking and gave considerable sums to extend it. This encouraged others to contribute in various ways, and the modesty and patience of St John did quite as much as his wonderful efficiency to make the hospital popular. The bishop of Tuy invited the holy man to dinner and put questions to him which he answered in such a manner as to impress the prelate most favourably with his prudence and common sense. It was this bishop who gave him the name of " John of God " and who prescribed for him a kind of habit, although John never thought of founding a religious order : the rules which bear his name were only drawn up six years after his death, and religious vows were not introduced among his brethren before the year 1570, twenty years after he had disappeared from the scene.

To make trial of the saint's disinterestedness, the marquis of Tarifa came to him in disguise to beg an alms, and received from his hands twenty-five ducats--which was all John had. The marquis, in addition to returning the loan, bestowed on him 150 gold crowns, and sent to his hospital daily during his stay in Granada good supplies of bread, mutton and poultry. St John was always generous, but he was willing to give more than money to help those in distress. When a fire broke out in his hospital he carried out most of the sick on his own back, and, although he passed and repassed through the flames and stayed in the midst of them several times, he received no hurt. Moreover, his sympathies were universal. Unlike many beneficent persons, he did not confine his charity to his own hospital he considered himself bound to try to succour every distressed person of whom he had tidings. He therefore organized inquiries into the wants of the poor throughout the province, relieved some in their homes, provided work for others, and with singular tact and wisdom laid himself out in every way to comfort and assist the afflicted members of Christ. He was particularly careful to provide for young girls in distress to protect them from the temptations to which they are often exposed. Nor did his solicitude stop there. Crucifix in hand, St John would seek out hardened sinners and with tears exhort them to repentance. Although his life seemed to be one of continual action, he accompanied it with perpetual prayer and corporal austerities. Frequent ecstasies and an exalted spirit of contemplation shed lustre upon the other qualities, but pre-eminent amongst his virtues was the extraordinary humility which appeared in his actions, not least of all amidst the honours he received at the court of Valladolid, whither business sometimes called him.

Worn out at last by ten years' hard service, St John fell ill. The immediate cause was over-fatigue through his efforts to save his wood and other things for the poor in a flood, and to rescue a drowning man. At first he concealed his symptoms that he might not be compelled to diminish his work, but he carefully went over the inventories of the hospital and inspected the accounts. He also revised the rules of administration, the time-tables, and the devotional exercises to be observed. His archbishop sent for him in consequence of a complaint that he harboured tramps and women of bad character. When told of the charges John dropped to his knees at the prelate's feet and said, " The Son of man came for sinners, and we are bound to seek their conversion. I am unfaithful to my vocation because I neglect this, but I confess that I know of no bad person in my hospital except myself alone, who am indeed unworthy to eat the bread of the poor." He spoke with such evident sincerity that the archbishop dismissed him with respect, leaving all things to his discretion.

As his disease gained greater hold it became impossible to conceal it, and the news quickly spread. Lady Anne Ossorio came in her coach to visit him, and found him lying in his habit in his little cell, with an old coat spread over him instead of a blanket, whilst under his head was a basket. The good lady, who seems to have been as practical as she was kind, despatched a messenger to the archbishop, who immediately sent an order to John to obey her during his illness as he would obey himself. In virtue of this authority Lady Anne prevailed with him to leave his hospital. He named Antony Martin superior over his helpers, and before leaving he visited the Blessed Sacrament, remaining there so long that the masterful Lady Anne caused him to be lifted forcibly into her coach, in which she conveyed him to her own home where he was looked after with delicate attention. He complained that whilst our Saviour in His agony drank gall, he, a miserable sinner, was served with good food. The magistrates begged him to give his benediction to his fellow townsfolk. This he was loath to do, saying that his sins made him the scandal and reproach of the place, but that he recommended to them his brethren, the poor and those who had served him. At last, at the wish of the archbishop, he gave the city his dying blessing. St John passed away, on his knees before the altar, on March 8, 1550, being exactly fifty-five years old. He was buried by the archbishop, and the whole of Granada followed in procession.

St John of God was canonized in 1690, and in 1886 Pope Leo XIII, as the Roman Martyrology records, " declared him the heavenly patron of all hospitals and sick folk ", with St Camillus of Lellis, to whom Pope Pius XI in 1930 added nurses of both sexes. Because of his early venture in hawking books and pictures he is also sometimes specially honoured by book and print sellers.

The facts set out in the life, compiled, it would seem, about twenty years after the founder's death by Francis de Castro, who was rector of St John's own hospital at Granada, may be taken as substantially reliable : De Castro's biography, written in Spanish, has been reproduced in Latin in the *Acta Sanctorum* (March, vol. i). Modern resettings of the same story are fairly numerous. The best known are those of A. de Govea (1624) and L. del Pozo (1908) in Spanish ; and those of Sagnier (1877) and R. Meyer (1897) in French. In English a translation of the life by G. de Villethierri was included in the Oratorian Series in 1847, and there are lives by E. Baillon (1884), by M. and F. Leonard, and by N. McMahon (1952). *Cf.* also Heimbucher, *Die Orden und Kongregationen*, vol. ii, pp. 245-251, who gives details of the developments of the institute founded by St John. In art the saint is commonly represented with a pomegranate surmounted by a little cross. The *granada*, which is the Spanish for pomegranate, stands for the city of Granada, and the reference is to a vision in which the Child Jesus told him, " Thou wilt find thy cross in Granada ".

ST PONTIUS (*c.* A.D. 260)

WHEN St Cyprian, the great bishop of Carthage, was banished to Curubis, his deacon Pontius volunteered to accompany him, and remained with him until his death. In those days the tie between a bishop and his deacon was a close one, and in this case circumstances no doubt drew the two men together into a somewhat intimate relationship. Pontius must have had ample opportunities for obtaining information about the bishop's earlier life and activities. But he seems to have been preoccupied with the idea of producing a tractate which would eclipse in popularity the " acts " of Perpetua and Felicity, and in his biography of St Cyprian, from the date of his baptism to his martyrdom, it is the last scenes which rouse his enthusiasm almost to the exclusion of other matter. This *Vita et passio Cypriani*, as it is called, won high praise for its style and matter from St Jerome and other great churchmen. Certain modern writers, on the other hand, have depreciated the tractate as being uncritical and over-laudatory, not realizing that it was written professedly as a panegyric—to glorify the martyr—and that a critical biography in the modern sense would have been neither comprehensible nor acceptable to the circle for whom it was intended. Quite incidentally the author exhibits his own piety and zeal for the Christian faith. When St Cyprian was condemned, Pontius was spared—probably because he was not considered to be of much importance. As he had longed for martyrdom, this was a great disappointment to him, and he ends his account of St Cyprian with the words : " Greatly, very greatly do I exult in his glory, but even more greatly do I grieve that I have remained behind." How and where he died we do not know, but there is no reason to suppose that he suffered martyrdom.

It is only through St Jerome that we know the name of the author of the Life of St Cyprian, which is referred to again under Cyprian on September 16. Here it is sufficient to give a reference to Delehaye, *Les passions des martyrs et les genres littéraires* (1921), pp. 82-110, and to point out that Harnack has re-edited and annotated the text of Pontius, *Das Leben Cyprians von Pontius*, in the series *Texte und Untersuchungen*, vol. xxxix. This Pontius must not be identified with the martyred Pontius whose feast is observed on May 14.

SS. PHILEMON AND APOLLONIUS, Martyrs   (*c.* A.D. 305)

St Apollonius was a Christian deacon of Antinoë in the Thebaïd, and Philemon was a popular musician and entertainer who was converted through his instrumentality. They were apprehended during the persecution of Diocletian and brought before a judge of the name of Arrian, who had already put to death SS. Asclas, Timothy, Paphnutius and several other martyrs. After being questioned and tortured they were removed to Alexandria, where they were condemned to death and cast into the sea. The so-called acts of these martyrs as circulated in Greek by the Metaphrast are very extravagant. They end, as these romances usually do, with the conversion and martyrdom of the judges, but the earlier part may conceivably be founded on fact—especially in view of the circumstance that timorous Christians in time of persecution did occasionally hire pagans to offer sacrifice in their stead and to bring back to them a certificate to the effect that they had complied with the law. The Church compelled such *libellaticii*, as they were called, to do penance, but did not everywhere regard them as apostates.

According to these " acts ", Apollonius, alarmed at the prospect of torture, went to a well-known piper and dancer called Philemon and offered him four gold pieces if he would go and sacrifice in his place. Philemon agreed, but asked him for some of his clothes and for his hooded cloak with which he might conceal his face. Thus disguised he went before the judge, who began to question him and required him to carry out the rite imposed. Then the Holy Spirit came upon Philemon, and he avowed himself a Christian and refused to offer sacrifice. The judge argued with him, and then said, " Send for the piper Philemon : perhaps his sweet tunes will drive away the fancies of this fool ". Being unable to find Philemon, the officers brought his brother Theonas, who promptly revealed the identity of Philemon. The judge treated the incident as a joke, quite in keeping with the jester's powers of impersonation, but made it clear that he must now in earnest comply with the emperor's edicts. This Philemon stoutly refused to do. Arrian told him that it was folly for him to pretend to be a Christian, seeing that he was not baptized. Upon hearing these words the piper was greatly distressed, but when he prayed to God there descended upon him a cloud from heaven, and in that cloud he was baptized. Then Arrian appealed to his professional pride, reminding him how greatly he would be missed at the forthcoming games, and asking how he could bear to think of his beloved pipes being played by unskilled hands. Again Philemon prayed, and this time there came down from heaven fire which consumed the pipes.

In the meantime the officers had arrested Apollonius, who now appeared before the tribunal very penitent for his cowardice and eager to proclaim himself a Christian. As both men persisted in their refusal to sacrifice, they were sentenced to have their heads struck off. Before the execution, Philemon asked that a great pot should be brought into court and a living baby placed inside. Then, the lid having been replaced, he directed the officers to shoot at it with their bows. They did so, and the pot was transfixed with their arrows, but the child within was found to be unscathed. Thereupon Philemon said, " The Christian's body like the pot may be riddled with wounds, whilst the soul within, like the baby, remains unhurt ". At these words the judge ordered the archers to direct their arrows upon the prisoner, but the musician raised his hand and all the arrows remained poised in mid-air, with the exception of one which turned back and blinded Arrian himself. The judge's sight was, however, miraculously restored by clay from the martyr's tomb.

This led to his conversion as well as to that of four officials sent to hold an inquiry, and eventually all five were put to death by being sewn up in sacks and cast into the sea.

The story of the death of these martyrs, divested of its later accretions, is told in the *Historia Monachorum*, which was transluted by Rufinus (see Preuschen, *Palladius und Rufinus*, pp. 80-82). Rufinus declares that he had visited the shrine and seen the relics. There was evidently a *cultus* in his time. But there is no mention of the burning of the pipes or of the shooting with arrows ; there is indeed a cloud-burst, but this only puts out the fire in which the martyrs were at first sentenced to be burned alive. Another version of the tale appears in the synaxaries see Delehaye, *Synax. Constant.*, pp. 307-308. Here the commemoration of the martyrs is attached to December 14 ; but the Roman Martyrology registers their names on March 8.

ST SENAN, BISHOP   (A.D. 560)

ST SENAN of Scattery Island (Inis Cathaigh) was the most celebrated of the twenty-two saints who, according to Colgan, bore the name of Senan, and some of the episodes recorded in his life and certain of the miracles with which he is credited may well have belonged originally to one or other of his less well known namesakes. Senan came of Christian parents in Munster, and the legends, as is often the case, lay stress upon his youthful precocity ; we are told that when he was out with his mother and she began to pluck and to eat some berries, the child gently reproved her for eating between meals. On another occasion, when the family was moving home elsewhere, Senan was told to get the house ready by arranging the furniture and cooking utensils in their place. Absorbed in prayer he neglected to do so, and was scolded by his mother. The boy told her to trust in God who would repair his negligence, and immediately the pots and pans shot up to their places on the shelves and the furniture began to move automatically into position—to the great edification of all present.

After some time as a fighting-man Senan determined to enter upon the religious life. He therefore betook himself to a holy abbot called Cassidus, who trained him in monastic discipline. After a time the abbot was told in a vision to send his young disciple to St Natalis, abbot of Kilmanagh in Ossory. In his new home St Senan was soon distinguished for his piety and docility as well as for many remarkable miracles. One day he was sent to mind a herd of cows, and, in order that the abbey might have enough milk, he sought to prevent the calves from having access to the cows. At first he was unsuccessful ; but when he laid his staff on the ground between them and retired to pray, the animals were unable to cross the barrier. On another occasion he was working at the mill, and, as it was growing dark, he asked the cook for some candles. He replied that he had none for the moment, but expected soon to have some ready. As Senan did not return to him for a week, the cook was curious to know how he had managed without candles or whether he was neglecting his work. He therefore peeped through the mill-door and was amazed to see the millstones working automatically, whilst the saint was reading in a corner by the light of a candle which the cook recognized as being the last one which he himself had supplied. These and similar wonders spread Senan's fame, and multitudes flocked to him to be healed, to ask his prayers and to be instructed. Natalis decided that he was now fit to be placed over others, but when Senan asked where he was to go, Natalis replied that such direction must be sought from God. St Senan started out towards East Leinster, and was directed by an angel to a place called Inis Conerthe, which is probably identical with the present Enniscorthy. After some time spent there, the saint journeyed to Rome, from which he returned through France, England and Wales. He appears to have stayed with St David, and we are told that when they parted David presented his friend with his staff, which St Senan brought back to Ireland.

Landing on a small island off the coast of Leinster, he was warned by an angel that this was not the place where he could rest and be buried, but that he must go on and build many cells and churches to God's glory and must do much to promote the increase of monastic discipline in Ireland before he could settle down. Accordingly he made a foundation at Inishcarra, near Cork (where he was joined by some Italian monks), and others elsewhere. At length he was told that the time had come for him to choose his final retreat. From the summit of Mount Tese an angel pointed out Arnanaingel, the Hill of the Angels, rising up in the distance, in the estuary of the Shannon, and promised not only that he and his monks should possess the island on which it stood, but also that other holy men should succeed them there. This piece of land, which is now called Scattery Island, lies south of Kilrush Quay, and contains a round tower which local tradition attributes to St Senan, and also a small church of St Senan, part of which is of great antiquity. Accompanied by the angel, the saint afterwards made a circuit of the island, and when he saw the waves dashing against the cliffs, he criticized the place as being too exposed, but the angel gave him the assurance that none of his monks would be drowned when crossing the water in obedience to their superior.

The monastery soon became famous and many men came there, but it was St Senan's rule that no woman should be allowed to land on the island. Legend, however, relates that St Cannera, knowing she was about to die, greatly desired to receive viaticum and to be buried there. An angel brought her across the water, but on the shore she was met by Senan, who refused to allow her to proceed. If Christ will receive my soul, why should you reject my body ?" she asked. " That is true," replied St Senan, " but for all that, I will not allow you to come here go back and do not plague us. You may be pure in soul but you are a woman." —" I will die before I go back ", retorted St Cannera ; and she gained her point, for she died on the shore and was buried in the island.

At some period of his life, St Senan appears to have been consecrated a bishop but the chroniclers do not say when or where. As his last hour was approaching, the holy man was moved to revisit the monastery of St Cassidus and the nunnery of St Scotia, his aunt. On his return journey, in a field at Killeochailli, he heard a voice saying, " Senan, servant of God, thou art called to Heaven ", and that very day he passed away. His monks brought his body back to Iniscattery. According to another legend, he was restored to life for a short time and sat up in his coffin to nominate his successor and to deliver a long discourse to the assembled monks, who were not unnaturally much impressed by what they had seen and heard.

The documents printed by Colgan in his *Acta Sanctorum Hiberniae* and thence re-edited by the Bollandists (March, vol. i) seem substantially to exhaust the available material for the life of St Senan. There is an Irish life preserved in the Book of Lismore and one or two other manuscripts ; it has been edited by Whitley Stokes in the *Anecdota Oxoniensia* (1890) and Colgan gives an abbreviated Latin translation of it. For his *cultus* in Cornwall see G. H. Doble, *Saint Senan, Patron of Sennen* (1928) ; but this may be another man. See also Gleeson in the *North Munster Antiquarian Journal*, 1940, pp. 14-30 ; and *Analecta Bollandiana*, vol. lxvi (1948), pp. 199-230. St Senan has a commemoration today throughout Ireland.

ST FELIX OF DUNWICH, Bishop of the East Angles   (A.D. 648)

Sigebert, ruler of the East Angles, had previously been an exile in Gaul, where he had accepted the Christian faith and received baptism. On becoming king he in 631 obtained a bishop, Felix, from the archbishop of Canterbury, St Honorius, to direct the evangelization of the East Anglian people. This Felix was a Burgundian and was, it seems, already a bishop before coming on the English mission.

Sigebert, whom Bede describes as " a most Christian and learned man ", appointed Dunwich in Suffolk to be the episcopal see of Felix, who for seventeen years preached the gospel in what are now the counties of Norfolk, Suffolk and Cambridge ; he was very successful in bringing the people " to the faith and works of righteousness and the gift of everlasting happiness ". A school was set up, for which Felix secured teachers who could conduct it on the Kentish model. From this slender foundation later writers have argued that this institution was the germ of Cambridge University, and would have us honour King Sigebert and St Felix as its founders. But neither Bede nor even William of Malmesbury makes any mention of Cambridge. The young East Anglian church was further strengthened at this time from another quarter, when St Fursey came from Ireland and established a monastery, probably at Burghcastle.

Dunwich, where St Felix died and was buried in 648, has been entirely swallowed up by the gradual inroads of the sea, although it was once a considerable town. The relics of the saint were translated first to Soham, near Ely, and then to Ramsey abbey, where they still were in the twelfth century. St Felix (whose name is found in Felixstowe) is mentioned in the Roman Martyrology as the apostle of the East Angles ; his name appears in a number of English medieval calendars, and his feast is observed today in the diocese of Northampton.

All our reliable information is derived from Bede's *Ecclesiastical History*, bks ii and iii.

ST JULIAN, Archbishop of Toledo   (A.D. 690)

At the time of his death in 690 St Julian, Archbishop of Toledo, was the most important person in Spain. He is said to have been of Jewish extraction, but his parents were Christian and he was baptized in the chief church of Toledo, as we learn from his successor in the episcopal chair, who gives a short account of his life. The youth was trained by another prelate of Toledo, St Eugenius II, and he had as companion a lad who was afterwards known as Gudila Levita. Bound by community of tastes as well as by affection, the friends at first gave themselves to prayer, study and retirement, but apostolic zeal drew them into the world to labour for the conversion of sinners. St Julian, who was an able theologian and a learned man, rose promptly to a position of importance, and when Wamba, the last of the Visigothic kings, was given over by the physicians, it was Julian who gave him the monastic habit and shaved his head that he might " die in religion ". The Life of King Wamba written by Julian has survived, and is much valued by historians as it enables them to know more of the reign of that monarch than they can learn of his predecessors or successors.

Julian was chosen to occupy the see of Toledo in 680, and he seems to have ruled his diocese with the same wisdom which characterized him in secular affairs. His biographer assures us that he was endowed with all graces of soul and body, and was so kind that everyone who appealed to him for assistance went away comforted and

content.   He presided over several synods and succeeded in obtaining for his see
the supremacy over all Spain.   He is consequently recognized as archbishop of
Toledo, though the term was not in general use in Spain at that period.   Later
writers have censured Julian for encouraging the kings to revive persecution against
the Jews ; but it should be noted that the really scandalous and cruel law which
enacted that all adult Jews should be sold as slaves, while their children were to be
taken from them at the age of seven and reared in Christian families, was not passed
until the sixteenth council of Toledo, five years after his death.

The bishop was a voluminous writer.   Amongst his literary works was a revision
of the Mozarabic liturgy in use in Spain at that period, a book against the Jews, and
the three books of the " Prognostics ", which treat of death and the state of the soul
after death.   In this work he states that love and the wish to be united to God are
sufficient to extinguish in us the natural fear of death ; and that the blessed in
Heaven pray for us, earnestly desire our happiness and know our actions—either in
God whom they behold and in whom they discern all the truth they are concerned
to know, or else through the angels, God's messengers upon earth.

The very brief memoir written by Felix, Julian's successor in the see of Toledo, is the
principal source of information concerning him.   See the *Acta Sanctorum*, March, vol. i ;
but something also may be learnt from the chroniclers and the acts of the councils over which
he presided.

ST HUMPHREY, or HUNFRID, BISHOP OF THÉROUANNE   (A.D. 871)

THE Benedictine abbey of Prüm in the Eifel was celebrated in the ninth century,
and it attracted amongst others a young man named Humphrey, who came thither
from France and received the habit.   It was when St Egilon was abbot and Humphrey and St Ansbald (the future rebuilder of the abbey) were fellow monks at
Prüm that there arrived in the monastery a very sick old man, the Emperor Lothair
I, to end his life amongst the brethren.   He only survived six days, and doubtless
Humphrey was one of those of whom it is recorded in an ancient chronicle that
" the brothers reverently buried the emperor in the church of the Holy Saviour ".
Within a year died another important personage—St Folkwin, Bishop of Thérouanne ; and Humphrey was elected in his stead.   The position in which the new
bishop found himself was one of great difficulty, and it is little to be wondered at if
the simple monk was appalled at the prospect before him.   In the report of the
Council of Toulouse at which St Humphrey was present we read something of the
condition of the country—devastated by the Normans, insufficiently defended, and
with everything in disorder.

The diocese of Thérouanne suffered even more than others.   The invading
Northmen had penetrated as far as they could in their ships and had then descended
upon the country, laying waste the fields and burning the towns and villages.   At
Whitsuntide they seized the great monastery of Saint-Bertin at Saint-Omer and set
it on fire, after having looted it and put to death with cruel tortures four monks who
had been left in charge.   The town of Thérouanne was also attacked, and the
bishop was obliged to seek safety in flight.   Dismayed and discouraged, Humphrey
appealed to Pope St Nicholas I for permission to lay down his charge and to retire
into a monastery.   The pope answered kindly and sympathetically, but would not
grant the petition.   " Do you not know, dearest brother ", he wrote, " that if it is
dangerous for the pilot to desert the ship when the sea is calm, it is far worse if he

abandons his post in troubled waters ?" Whilst making it quite clear that Humphrey was justified in escaping from his persecutors, the pope urged him to hold himself in readiness to return as soon as the storm blew over, again to gather together and encourage his scattered flock. The barbarians did actually withdraw shortly afterwards, and St Humphrey went back to his devastated see and played a noble part in encouraging the people to return to their homes and restore their sanctuaries. He assisted Abbot Adelard to rebuild Saint-Bertin and after Adelard's death, Humphrey was chosen to succeed him, and ruled the abbey wisely and well whilst continuing to be bishop of Thérouanne. But in 868 he was ousted from Saint-Bertin by King Charles the Bald, who wished to replace him by a creature of his own, a secular canon named Hildwin. St Humphrey continued to rule his diocese and died three years later. By his order the feast of the Assumption became generally observed throughout his province : up till then it had only been fitfully kept in certain churches.

No proper biography of St Humphrey seems to be known, but a good deal of information concerning him has been collected by the Bollandists in the *Acta Sanctorum*, March, vol. i. See also Destouches, *Vies des saints de Cambrai et Arras*, vol. i, pp. 310-314 ; Duchesne, *Fastes Épiscopaux*, vol. iii, p. 136.

ST DUTHAC, BISHOP OF ROSS (c. A.D. 1065)

St Duthac was greatly venerated in Scotland before the Reformation, and his memory is still preserved in place-names—notably Kilduthie, Arduthie near Stonehaven and Kilduich on the Loch of Duich. Tayne, where he was buried and where a church was built in his honour, is called in Gaelic Dhuich Baile, or Duthac's Town, and near it still stands St Duthac's Cairn, although the biennial fairs called by his name are no longer held in the town. Educated in Ireland, like so many of his countrymen, he returned to labour in Scotland as a priest and became bishop of Ross. His reputation for sanctity was enhanced by his miracles and predictions he is said to have foretold the invasion of the Danes which took place ten years after his death. The victory of the Scots under Alexander Stewart, great-grandfather of King Robert II, was ascribed to the intercession of St Andrew and of St Duthac, whose shrine became a favourite place of pilgrimage.

Legendary history relates that St Duthac, as a child, was once sent by his master to fetch embers from the forge to kindle a fire, and that he carried home the live coals in his kilt without being singed. In later life, when a kite stole a ring and some meat from one of the saint's disciples, St Duthac summoned the bird, which relinquished the ring but was allowed to retain the flesh. On another occasion a canon slew an ox at Dornoch, and after distributing portions to the poor, determined to carry a piece to the saint who lived some way off. The canon travelled on a dark and stormy night, but the spit on which he bore the meat shone like a lamp and led him safely on his way until he had delivered up his gift, in its first freshness, to the holy bishop. His feast is kept in the diocese of Aberdeen.

See the *Acta Sanctorum*, March, vol. i ; KSS., pp. 328-329 ; and the lessons of the Aberdeen Breviary.

ST VEREMUND, ABBOT (A.D. 1092)

Of the religious houses in the kingdom of Navarre in the eleventh century the chief in importance was the Benedictine abbey of Hyrache, which under the direction of

St Veremund became second to none in all Spain.   He had entered the monastery as a mere boy under his uncle, Abbot Munius, from whom he afterwards received the habit.   He grew up an exemplary monk, distinguished especially for his boundless love of the poor.   In illustration of this, a story appears amongst the chronicles of the abbey.   When serving as doorkeeper Veremund was sometimes carried away by his zeal to distribute to the poor more than the prescribed allowance of food, and the abbot, meeting him one day as he was going to the door with a great number of pieces of bread gathered up in his tunic, asked him what he was carrying.   "Chips", replied the young man—" pieces of bread being, as it were, like chips for warming the poor within ", explains the chronicler.   When, at the abbot's command, Veremund opened out his tunic the bread had been changed into chips—" God thus showing through this miracle ", to quote the words of the narrative, " that the liberality of Veremund to the poor was pleasing in His eyes and that his ambiguity was not a lie but a mystery."

Upon the death of Munius, St Veremund succeeded him as abbot and led his brethren on by precept and example to ever higher degrees of perfection.   He appears to have possessed the gift of healing the sick, and is said to have arrested in a marvellous way a fire which was about to destroy the crops of the abbey.   His care for the reverent and accurate recitation of the Divine Office won for him high approval and praise from Rome, and he was an upholder of the particular Spanish usages, called Mozarabic.   The kings of Navarre made grants to his abbey, and the rise of the town of Estella was due to one of these donations.   One night shepherds watching their flocks were amazed to see a shower of stars fall on a hill which was afterwards known in the local dialect as Yricarra, " Starry ".   A search at the spot where the meteorites had fallen was rewarded by the find of a remarkable statue of our Lady with the Holy Child, and King Sancho Ramirez was so much impressed that he started to build a city to be called Estella upon the same spot.   He presented the site to Veremund, with the request that he would dedicate the new town to the Mother of God.   Thus it came to pass that practically every building in Estella paid rent or tribute to the abbey.

At one time there arose a great famine in Navarre, and the poor flocked to their good friend the abbot, and the numbers were increased by pilgrims on their way to or from Compostela.   The monks' granaries and store-houses were bare, but three thousand persons had collected and their wailing rent the air.   Veremund had gone up to the altar to celebrate Mass, and when he reached that part where the priest prays for the people, he made intercession with tears for the starving crowd. Suddenly there appeared a white dove, which flew down low over the heads of the people, seeming to touch them in its passage, and then disappeared as suddenly as it had come.   Meanwhile the people experienced a wonderful feeling of contentment   not only was their hunger appeased, but their mouths were filled with a delicious taste, as though they had been regaled with some heavenly and invigorating food.   In their joy and relief they cried aloud and gave thanks and glory to God for His goodness.

See the *Acta Sanctorum*, March, vol. i, and Mabillon.

ST STEPHEN OF OBAZINE, Abbot   (A.D. 1154)

The parents of this Stephen lived in the Limousin district of France, and the youth from his childhood was addicted to religious exercises and to works of charity.

After his ordination he felt called to a stricter life, and renouncing all pleasures he began to practise mortifications.   Having made friends with another priest of similar views, he determined to embrace with him the solitary life and to retire into the forest of Obazine, a wild district about two leagues from Tulle.   On the day they were to start they gave a feast to their friends and distributed all their possessions to the poor.   After a time others desired to join them, and the holy men felt called to accept these disciples.   Stephen's friend Peter accordingly went to Limoges to ask the sanction of Bishop Eustace, and they were allowed to build a monastery and to celebrate the Holy Mysteries on condition that they maintained the rules handed down by ancient custom.   These eremitical monasteries were not, of course, single buildings, but collections of huts, in each one of which lived one or two solitaries.

The austerities practised by the little community were extreme, and Stephen, though he had a gentle and kindly nature, was rigid in enforcing them.   All their time was occupied with prayer, reading and manual labour, and they never ate until evening.   St Stephen did not look upon himself as in any way above the others, and he cooked and carried water like the rest : but they had no written rule, because Stephen was their living rule.   His brethren nominated him superior, but he left the direction of the community to Peter.   Stephen also founded a convent for women which soon contained 150 nuns, with a rule almost as severe as that of the men.   It was said of them that they lived so much separated from the world and in such simplicity that they appeared to be only tied to earth by bonds which they were not allowed to break.

After some years St Stephen, fearing lest the discipline of his communities should grow relaxed after his death because they had no written constitutions, applied to the monastery of Dalon, belonging to the Order of Cîteaux, to ask that some monks might be sent to instruct his own in the rule of that order.   In 1142 he himself received the Cistercian habit and the bishop of Limoges gave him his blessing as abbot.   He died twelve years later.

There is a Latin life of St Stephen of Obazine of considerable bulk which has been printed by Baluzius and of which a summary will be found in the *Acta Sanctorum*, March, vol. i.

BD VINCENT, BISHOP OF CRACOW   (A.D. 1223)

VINCENT KADLUBEK was born at Karnow in Poland about the year 1150.   He studied in Italy and France, took his master's degree, and held several ecclesiastical offices, of which provost of the cathedral chapter of Sandomir was one.   In 1208 he was elected to the bishopric of Cracow.   At this time the archbishop of Gniezno, Henry Kietlicz, was energetically implementing the reforms of Pope Innocent III in Poland, and he received notable support from Bishop Vincent, his fellow student. The country was in a state of political disorder and religious demoralization, and Bd Vincent looked particularly to the religious orders to help him in his task : with the object of strengthening their influence he became a benefactor of several monasteries, and at the same time seconded their efforts by his own preaching and frequent visitations.   He took an active part in politics, and was solicitous for the temporal welfare of the common people.

In 1218 Vincent resigned his see and retired to the monastery of Jedrzejow, where he was professed a monk of the Cistercian reform.   It was perhaps, but not certainly, in these last years of his life that he was engaged in that historical work for which he is best remembered, for he was the first Polish chronicler. His " Chronicle of the Kings and Princes of Poland ", in four books, is valuable in so far as part of it was written from his own experience, and it has been reprinted in modern times. But his uncritical acceptance of popular legends has caused him to be likened to Geoffrey of Monmouth ; and "the Latin which he employs is detestable. " Vincent Kadlubek died at his monastery on March 8, 1223, leaving a great reputation for holiness, and in 1764 his ancient *cultus* was confirmed by the Holy See.

See Manrique, *Annales Cistercienses,* vol. iv ; Henriquez, *Menologium Cisterciense ;* and the *Cambridge History of Poland,* vol. i (1950), pp. 154-155. In some calendars Bd Vincent appears as Saint.

9 : ST FRANCES OF ROME, WIDOW   (A.D. 1440)

THE gentle saint who was known first to her fellow-citizens and then to the Church at large as Santa Francesca Romana, St Frances the Roman, possessed to an extraordinary degree the power of attracting the love and admiration of those who came in contact with her. Nor has her charm ended with her death, for she is still honoured by countless souls who seek her intercession and pray before her tomb in Santa Maria Nuova. On her feast day and within its octave, crowds flock to visit Tor de' Specchi and the Casa degli Esercizi Pii (the successor of the old Palazzo Ponziano), the rooms of which are annually thrown open to the public and every memorial and relic of the saint exhibited.

She was born in the Trastevere district of Rome in 1384, at the beginning of the Great Schism of the West, which was to cause her much grief as well as adversely to affect the fortunes of her family. She did not live to see harmony completely restored. Her parents, Paul Busso and Jacobella dei Roffredeschi, were of noble birth and ample means, and the child was brought up in the midst of luxury but in a pious household. Frances was a precocious little girl, and when she was eleven she asked her parents to allow her to become a nun, only to be met by a point-blank refusal. Her parents, who were excellent people and much attached to her, had quite different plans for their attractive little daughter. Within a year they announced to her that they had arranged to betroth her to young Lorenzo Ponziano, whose position, character and wealth made him a suitable match. After a time Frances withdrew her objections, and the marriage was solemnized when she was barely thirteen. At first she found the new life very trying, although she did her best to please her husband as well as her parents-in-law, and Vannozza, the young wife of Lorenzo's brother Paluzzo, discovered her one day weeping bitterly. Frances told her of her frustrated hopes, and learnt to her surprise that this new sister of hers would also have preferred a life of retirement and prayer. This was the beginning of a close friendship which lasted till death, and the two young wives strove together henceforth to live a perfect life under a common rule. Plainly dressed they sallied out to visit the poor of Rome, ministering to their wants and relieving their distress, and their husbands, who were devoted to them, raised no objection to their charities and austerities. This life was for a time interrupted by a severe and somewhat mysterious illness to which Frances fell a victim, and which her relatives sought to remedy by the aid of magic. We are told that after a year St Alexis appeared to her in a vision. He inquired if she was prepared to die or if she wished to recover. She replied that she had no will but the will of God. The saint then informed her that it was God's will that she should recover and work for His greater glory, and, after throwing his cloak over her, he disappeared. Her infirmity had disappeared also.

After this the lives of the sisterly pair became even stricter than before, and daily they went to the hospital of Santo Spirito in Sassia to nurse the patients, singling out more particularly those suffering from the most repellent diseases. Their mother-in-law, Donna Cecilia, not unnaturally, was afraid lest they might injure their health, and thought that their avoidance of banquets and entertainments might be misconstrued in society and bring discredit on the family, but her sons, to whom she appealed, refused to interfere in any way. In 1400 a son was born to Frances, and for a time she modified her way of life to devote herself to the care of little John Baptist (Battista). The following year Donna Cecilia died, and Frances was bidden by her father-in-law take her place at the head of the household. In vain she pleaded that Vannozza was the wife of the elder brother : Don Andrew and Vannozza insisted that she was the more suitable, and she was obliged to consent. She proved herself worthy of this position, discharging her duties efficiently whilst treating her household not as servants but as younger brothers and sisters, and trying to induce them to labour for their own salvation. In all the forty years that she lived with her husband there was never the slightest dispute or misunderstanding between them. When she was at her prayers, if summoned by Lorenzo or asked to give orders about the house, she laid all aside to respond to the call of that duty. " It is most laudable in a married woman to be devout ", she was wont to say, " but she must never forget that she is a housewife. And sometimes she must leave God at the altar to find Him in her housekeeping." Her biographers relate that once when she was reading our Lady's office a page was sent to fetch her. " Madonna, my master begs you to come to him ", said the lad. She immediately closed the book and went. Three more times this interruption happened ; but when at last she opened the book for the fifth time she found the words of the antiphon were written in letters of gold. In addition to the eldest, two other children of Frances are known, a younger boy, Evangelist, and a girl, Agnes ; and she allowed no one but herself to look after them during childhood.

Although, like so many other interior souls, Frances was sorely tried all her life by violent temptations, which in her case sometimes took the form of hideous or enticing visions, and sometimes resembled bodily assaults, still for several years outward prosperity seemed to smile upon her and her family. The first indication of the clouds that were gathering came in the form of a famine and pestilence, mainly the result of the civil wars which were then convulsing Italy. Plague-stricken people were dying in the streets, and disease and starvation decimated Rome. Frances was unremitting in her efforts to relieve the sufferers and, with the help of Vannozza, tried to succour all she came across. Even the plentiful stock of provisions at the Palazzo Ponziano was exhausted at last, and the two women went from door to door begging for food for the poor in spite of rebuffs and insults. It was then that she received her father-in-law's consent to sell her jewels, and she never from that time forth wore any but the plainest dresses.

In 1408 the troops of Ladislaus of Naples, the ally of the antipope, had entered Rome and a soldier of fortune, Count Troja, had been appointed governor. The

Ponziani had always supported the legitimate pope, and in one of the frequent conflicts Lorenzo was stabbed and carried home to Frances, to whose devoted nursing he owed his restoration to health.   Troja resolved to leave the city after having wreaked his vengeance on the principal papal supporters.   Amongst these were the Ponziani, and he not only arrested Vannozza's husband Paluzzo, but also demanded as a hostage little Battista ; but whilst his mother Frances was praying in the church of Ara Coeli the boy was released in circumstances that seemed to be miraculous.   Then, in 1410 when the cardinals were assembled at Bologna for the election of a new pope, Ladislaus again seized Rome.   Lorenzo Ponziano, who as one of the heads of the papal party went in danger of his life, managed to escape, but it was impossible for his wife and family to follow him.   His palace was plundered and Battista was taken captive by the soldiers of Ladislaus, though he afterwards got away and was able to join his father.   The family possessions in the Campagna were destroyed, farms being burnt or pillaged and flocks slaughtered, whilst many of the peasants were murdered.   Frances lived in a corner of her ruined home with Evangelist, Agnes and Vannozza, whose husband was still a prisoner, and the two women devoted themselves to the care of the children and to relieving as far as their means would allow the sufferings of their still poorer neighbours.   During another pestilence three years later, Evangelist died.   Frances then turned part of the house into a hospital, and God rewarded her labours and prayers by bestowing on her the gift of healing.

Twelve months after the death of Evangelist, as his mother was praying one day, a bright light suddenly shone into the room and Evangelist appeared accompanied by an archangel.   After telling her of his happiness in Heaven he said that he had come to warn her of the impending death of Agnes.   A consolation was, however, to be vouchsafed to the bereaved mother.   The archangel who accompanied Evangelist was henceforth to be her guide for twenty-three years.   He was to be succeeded in the last epoch of her life by an angel of still higher dignity.   Very soon Agnes began to fail, and a year later she passed away at the age of sixteen. From that moment, as Evangelist had promised, the angel was always visible to St Frances, though unseen by others.   Only when she committed a fault did he fade away for a time, to return as soon as she felt compunction and made confession. The form he took was that of a child of about eight years old.   But, weakened by what she had gone through, Frances herself fell a victim to the plague.   So ill was she that every hope of recovery was abandoned, but the disease suddenly left her, and she began to regain her health.   It was at this time that she had a vision of Hell so terrible that she could never allude to it without tears.

After many delays Pope John XXIII summoned the Council of Constance which was to prepare the healing of the Great Schism, and in that same year 1414 the Ponziani regained their property after being recalled from banishment.   Lorenzo was now a broken man and lived in retirement, being tended with the utmost devotion by his faithful wife.   It was his great wish to see his son Battista married and settled before his death, and he chose for him a beautiful girl called Mobilia, who proved to have a violent and overbearing temper.   She conceived a great contempt for Frances, of whom she complained to her husband and his father, and whom she ridiculed in public.   In the midst of a bitter speech she was struck down by a sudden illness, through which she was nursed by the saint.   Won by her kindness Mobilia found her contempt turned to love, and thenceforward she sought to imitate her saintly mother-in-law.   By this time the fame of the virtues and miracles of St

Frances had spread over Rome, and she was appealed to from all quarters, not only to cure the sick but also to settle disputes and heal feuds. Lorenzo, whose love and reverence for her only increased with age, offered to release her from all the obligations of married life provided only that she would continue to live under his roof.

She was now able to carry out a project which had been taking shape in her mind of forming a society of women living in the world and bound by no vows, but pledged to make a simple offering of themselves to God and to serve the poor. The plan was approved by her confessor Dom Antonio, who obtained the affiliation of the congregation to the Benedictines of Monte Oliveto, to which he himself belonged. Known at first as the Oblates of Mary, they were afterwards called the Oblates of Tor de' Specchi. The society had lasted seven years when it was thought desirable to take a house adapted for a community, and the old building known as Tor de' Specchi was acquired. Whatever time she could spare from her home duties St Frances spent with the oblates, sharing in their daily life and duties. She never allowed them to refer to her as the foundress, but insisted that all should be subject to Agnes de Lellis who was chosen superioress. Three years later Lorenzo died and was laid beside Evangelist and Agnes ; and St Frances announced her intention of retiring to Tor de' Specchi. On the feast of St Benedict she entered her foundation as a humble suppliant and was eagerly welcomed. Agnes de Lellis immediately insisted upon resigning office and Frances had to take her place in spite of her protestations.

Her life was now lived closer than ever to God. Her austerities indeed she could not well increase, for she had long subsisted on dry bread with occasionally some vegetables ; she had scourged herself and made use of horsehair girdles and chains with sharp points. But now visions and ecstasies became more frequent, and she sometimes spent whole nights in prayer. One evening in the spring of 1440, though feeling very ill she tried to get back home after visiting Battista and Mobilia. On the way she met her director, Dom John Matteotti, who, shocked at her appearance, ordered her to return at once to her son's house. It was soon evident that she was dying, but she lingered on for seven days. On the evening of March 9 her face was seen to shine with a strange light : " The angel has finished his task : he beckons me to follow him ", were her last words. As soon as it was known that she was dead, the Ponziani Palace was thronged by mourners and by those who brought their sick to be healed. Her body was removed to Santa Maria Nuova, where the crowds became even greater as the report of miracles wrought there was spread abroad. She was buried in the chapel of the church reserved for her oblates. Her congregation still survives at Tor de' Specchi, where the oblates carry on educational work ; their dress remains that of the Roman noble ladies of the period. St Frances was canonized in 1608, and Santa Maria Nuova is now known as the church of Santa Francesca Romana.

By far the most important source for the Life of St Frances of Rome is the collection of visions, miracles and biographical details compiled first of all in Italian by John Matteotti and afterwards, with omissions and additions, translated by him into Latin. Matteotti had been the saint's confessor during the last ten years of her life, but there is no evidence that he had been acquainted with her at an earlier date. The seventeenth-century biography which has been printed under the name of Mary Magdalen Anguillaria, superioress of Tor de' Specchi, adds little to the materials provided by Matteotti, though it may have incorporated some new facts from the processes which preceded the canonization. All these sources in a Latin version will be found in the *Acta Sanctorum*, March, vol. ii. There is a short but very sympathetic life of St Frances in English by Lady Georgiana Fullerton published in 1855 ; and lives in French by Rabory (1884), Rambuteau (1900) and Mrs Berthem-Bontoux (1931), the last a solid but rather prolix work.   The Italian text of Matteotti has been edited by Armellini, but *cf.* M. Pelaez in the *Archivio Soc. Romana di Storia patria*, vols. xiv and xv (1891–1892).

ST PACIAN, BISHOP OF BARCELONA   (*c.* A.D. 390)

ST PACIAN is chiefly remembered through his writings, for very little is known of his history.   At some time in his life he married—probably before he became a priest—and his son, Flavius Dexter, was chamberlain to the Emperor Theodosius and captain of the royal bodyguard under Honorius.   St Jerome, who was intimate with Dexter, had the greatest regard for the father, whose eloquence, learning and sanctity he extolled while dedicating to the son his *Catalogue of Illustrious Men.*

St Pacian lived to old age and was a voluminous writer ; but of his many works the only ones which have come down to us are an exhortation to penance, a sermon on baptism and three epistles addressed to a nobleman called Sympronian, who had embraced the Novatian heresy and had sent Pacian a letter in which he censured the Church for allowing repentance and absolution for all sins and also for taking the title of Catholic.   In his reply St Pacian makes the now famous retort : " Christianus mihi nomen   Catholicus vero cognomen.   Illud me nuncupat : istud ostendit.   Hoc probor : inde significor."—" My name is Christian, my surname Catholic.   The one puts me in a class, the other gives me a character.   The second is a testimonial, the first is a label."   Elsewhere he insists that those alone are embraced in the unity of the Church who are united to the chair of St Peter.   " To Peter alone did the Lord speak " (Thou art Peter, etc.) " that from him, the one, He might establish unity."—" Ut ex uno fundaret unum."

Amongst St Pacian's lost writings was one entitled *Cervulus*, directed against an obscene heathen pageant which took place annually at the new year and in which, apparently, Christians sometimes participated.   The performance, which centred round a little stag and which is alluded to by St Ambrose and other writers, consisted of masquerades in which those who took part were dressed up as wild animals. Like many a modern censor the bishop found that his strictures acted rather as an advertisement, and at the beginning of his treatise on penance he deplores that the chief effect of his censure was to make more people curious to witness the objectionable revels.

A brief account of St Pacian will be found in the *Acta Sanctorum*, March, vol. ii.   See also Bardenhewer's *Patrologie.*

ST GREGORY, BISHOP OF NYSSA   (*c.* A.D. 395)

ST GREGORY of Nyssa, upon whom the seventh general council, the second at Nicaea, bestowed the title of " Father of the Fathers ", was the brother of St Basil the Great, St Peter of Sebastea and St Macrina, and the son of St Basil and St Emmelia, herself the daughter of a martyr.   He was born at Caesarea in Cappadocia, and must have been left an orphan at an early age for he was brought up by his elder brother Basil and by his sister Macrina.   In a letter to his younger brother Peter, Gregory speaks of Basil as " our father and master ", and throughout his life he looked up to him with the greatest affection and veneration.   After an excellent education in secular and religious knowledge he became a rhetorician and married a wife called Theosebeia.   He had become a reader in the Church, but was led to accept a wholly secular post as professor of rhetoric, a branch in which he excelled. The post was not very congenial   he complained that his scholars were more intent upon military than upon academic distinction, and when St Gregory Nazianzen wrote him a sharp letter of reprimand in which he urged him to renounce " that ignoble glory ", as he expressed it, the epistle had the desired effect of bringing the young man back to the sacred ministry.   He was promoted to the priesthood, and it has been suggested that he ceased to live with Theosebeia as his wife, but there is no evidence to show this.   Celibacy at that date was not a matter of precept for the clergy even in the West, and in any case we do not know whether she still remained under his roof or whether, as some have thought, she joined St Macrina in her convent.   St Gregory Nazianzen, who had a great regard for Theosebeia, was wont to refer to her as his friend's " holy and blessed sister ", and in the eloquent oration which he preached at her funeral he calls her " the boast of the Church and the blessing of our generation."

St Gregory is thought to have spent the first few years of his priesthood in some sort of retirement—perhaps on the Iris in Pontus.   In the meantime, his brother Basil, the bishop of Caesarea, was having a hard struggle against heresy and opposition on all sides, and amongst his opponents was his own uncle, the Pontic bishop Gregory.   This division in a family otherwise so united seemed a terrible scandal to the younger Gregory, and in hopes of bringing about a reconciliation he devised the extraordinary expedient of forging letters purporting to come from his uncle to Basil tendering the olive branch.   Of course the fraud was promptly exposed, and brought upon the real author his brother's wrathful reprimand, not unmingled, however, with a little amusement.

It was apparently at Basil's suggestion that Gregory was chosen bishop of Nyssa in 372.   It was part of his policy to place orthodox prelates on the outposts of his diocese to try to stem the inroads of heresy, and he accordingly consecrated his brother, sorely against Gregory's desires, to this remote see on the confines of Lower Armenia.   As soon as he arrived in Nyssa he was faced with difficulties. The city was a hotbed of Arianism, and one of the emperor's courtiers had wanted the bishop's chair for himself or for a friend.   Gregory, with the best will in the world, was wanting in tact, and he had not much notion of ruling a province.   In the hopes of helping Basil he called a synod of provincial bishops at Ancyra, but as he could not handle the delegates the meeting did more harm than good to Basil's cause.   No wonder then that, when Gregory was suggested to his brother as one of his envoys to Pope St Damasus in Rome, Basil should have negatived the proposal, saying that his brother was entirely inexperienced in ecclesiastical affairs and was no diplomatist.

Supported by the Arians, the governor of Pontus, Demosthenes, called a meeting at which a certain Philocares accused Gregory of embezzling church property as well as of irregularity in his election, and soldiers were sent to arrest him.   The bishop suffered himself to be led away, but discouraged by the brutality of his gaolers he contrived to escape and reached a place of safety.   His enemies pretended that his flight was an evidence of guilt, and St Basil wrote them a strong letter in which he pointed out that the treasurer of the church had entirely acquitted Gregory of any irregularity.   However, a synod of Galatian and Pontic bishops deposed him, and he wandered about whilst a usurper took possession of his see until the year 378, when the Emperor Gratian restored him after his lengthy banishment.

His people received him with open arms, but his joy at returning was clouded by the death of St Basil and by that of St Macrina which occurred soon afterwards. Of his sister's approaching end he had a premonition, and he was able on the afternoon before her death to have a long conversation with her which he afterwards recorded.

From the time of St Basil's death, Gregory became a man of influence, and a period of great activity opened out for him. He was present at the Council of Antioch which was called to deal with the errors of the Meletians, and the orthodox bishops of the East there assembled sent him on a mission to Palestine and Arabia to remedy the disorders which heresy had caused in the Arabian church. To assist him in his work, the Emperor Theodosius gave him the use of government post-horses and carriages. At the General Council of Constantinople in 381 Gregory occupied an important place. He had come to be regarded as " the common mainstay of the Church ", and to be on Gregory's side was considered in his day as a proof of orthodoxy. The council, which had been called by the Emperor Theodosius, asserted the faith of Nicaea and strove to put an end to Arianism. At that assembly he seems to have been charged with a kind of inquisitorship over Pontus. Towards the end of his life he paid another visit to Palestine, and was so much shocked by the abuses he found among the pilgrims as well as by the heretical atmosphere to which they were exposed, that he came to the conclusion that pilgrimages under the conditions then prevailing were not a form of devotion to be recommended. In a letter or treatise on those who go to Jerusalem he remarks that pilgrimages form no part of the gospel precept, and adds that he himself derived no benefit from visiting the Holy Places.

Three episcopal sees having been fixed by the Emperor Theodosius as centres of communion in the East, Gregory of Nyssa, Helladius of Caesarea and Otreius of Melitene were the bishops selected. This honour, however, seems to have gained for Gregory the jealousy and ill-will of Helladius, who considered himself his metropolitan and resented being placed on an equality with him. In one of Gregory's letters he gives a graphic description of the discourtesy with which Helladius had treated him. At Constantinople, on the other hand, he was highly honoured and much consulted. He preached there the funeral orations on St Meletius of Antioch and on the Princess Pulcheria and the Empress Flaccilla. He also delivered a discourse at the enthronization of St Gregory Nazianzen, and, at a much later period, the oration at the dedication of the great church which the prefect Rufinus erected near Chalcedon. Although it is known that he lived to a great age, the exact date of his death is uncertain.

The veneration in which Gregory was held during his life and the even greater esteem with which he was regarded for some time after his death, is not altogether endorsed by modern ecclesiastical writers, who are indisposed to regard him as the main destroyer of Arianism and as the originator of those clauses which the Council of Constantinople inserted into the Nicene Creed. Nevertheless it is certain that he exercised a predominant influence in this the second great oecumenical council, and that his orthodoxy was quite unquestioned, although it may be admitted that he inclined to Universalism and to the theory that all things would be restored in Christ at the last day. The writings of St Gregory show him to be well versed in the pagan philosophers, and he used the teaching of Plato in much the same way that the schoolmen used that of Aristotle. Of Christian teachers he was most influenced by Origen, whose allegorical interpretations of Holy Scripture he largely adopted. His literary works, which were greatly admired for their diction, are valuable for their accurate exposition of the Christian faith and interesting for their intermixture of everyday ideas with elaborate mystical and poetical speculations. Of his voluminous writings the chief are his great Catechetical Discourse, which was an instruction on the Christian faith, two works against Eunomius and Apollinaris which are the main source from which knowledge of these heresies has been derived, and numerous commentaries on Holy Scripture. On the ascetic side may be mentioned his book on Virginity, a number of sermons on Christian life and conduct, and sundry panegyrics on the saints. His letters, of which about twenty are extant, are natural and charming. Amongst them may be mentioned one which narrates the life and death of St Macrina, one to three ladies in Jerusalem, and one which describes in a truly modern manner the beauties of a house and villa in Galatia where he stayed on a visit. Both he and his brother Basil had an appreciation of the beauties of nature seldom found in the writers of the early centuries.

Our knowledge of the life of St Gregory of Nyssa is derived from many various sources, and more especially from the correspondence of his friends. See the *Acta Sanctorum*, March, vol. ii ; Bardenhewer, *Patrology* (Eng. trans.), pp. 195-206 ; Bardenhewer's larger work on the Fathers which is accessible in French as well as in German ; and DTC., vol. vi, cc. 1847-1852, etc. There is also an excellent account of Gregory in DCB., vol. ii, pp. 761-768. Recent works on the saint's thought are H. Urs von Balthasar, *Présence et Pensée* (1942), and J. Daniélou, *Platonisme et théologie mystique* (1944).

ST BOSA, BISHOP OF YORK (A.D. 705)

WHEN St Wilfrid of York had been driven out in consequence of his dissensions with King Egfrid and his diocese was divided into two sees, it was a monk of Whitby, Bosa by name, who was chosen to become bishop of Deira, the southern portion, whilst Eata of Lindisfarne was appointed to Bernicia. They were both consecrated by St Theodore, Archbishop of Canterbury, in 678. Bosa, who is described by the Venerable Bede as " beloved by God . a man of singular merit and holiness ", made his seat at York, and governed his province wisely and well until his death, being succeeded by St John of Beverley. Bede says that St Acca, for whom he had the greatest regard, had been brought up and trained from boyhood by St Bosa at his school in York, and that he owed much to the example and teaching of this holy master.

All the facts will be found in the text and notes of Plummer's edition of Bede.

ST CATHERINE OF BOLOGNA, VIRGIN (A.D. 1463)

JOHN DE' VIGRI, the father of St Catherine of Bologna, was a lawyer and diplomatic agent to Nicholas d'Este, Marquis of Ferrara. At the request of his patron, he sent Catherine at the age of eleven as maid of honour to young Margaret d'Este, whose studies she shared and whose most intimate companion she became. Amongst other lessons, the two girls worked at Latin, in which language Catherine afterwards wrote several small works. When a marriage was arranged between Margaret and Robert Malatesta she desired to retain her friend in her service, but Catherine had already felt the call to the religious life. Soon after returning home she lost her father, and almost immediately she joined a company of Franciscan tertiaries at Ferrara, who lived a semi-monastic life under the guidance of a woman called Lucy Mascaroni.

Although only fourteen at the time of her admission, Catherine at once aimed at a perfection so exalted as to win the admiration of her sisters.   From this early age she was subject to visions, some of which indeed came from God, whilst others were of Satanic origin, as she was afterwards forced to conclude.   In order to help others to distinguish between divine visions and the artifices of Satan, Catherine subsequently declared that she had learnt to recognize when it was our Lord who was really deigning to visit her, by the holy light of humility which, at such times, always preceded the rising sun, for, as she went on to explain, " she used to experience at the approach of the Divine Guest a sentiment of respect which would inwardly bow her spirit, or make her outwardly bow her head ; or else she would be aware that the origin of her faults, past, present or future, was in herself   she used to consider herself too as the cause of all the faults of her neighbours, for whom she felt a burning charity.   And Jesus would enter into her soul like a radiant sunshine. to establish there the profoundest peace."   The Devil then sought to instil into her mind blasphemous thoughts and doubts, the most grievous of which concerned the real presence of Jesus Christ in the Blessed Sacrament.   This caused her intense misery, until at last God revealed the whole doctrine to her, and so completely answered her difficulties that her doubts left her for ever.   He also assured her that if the conscience is pure the effects of the sacrament are independent of sensible fervour, nor do doubts hinder its efficacy, provided no consent is given to them ; and, moreover, that those who are patient under such trials gain more by their communions than if they were favoured with spiritual consolation.   Probably as the result of all she had gone through, St Catherine became oppressed by a constant and overpowering inclination to sleep, which she regarded as a diabolic temptation, but which may well have been a merciful dispensation to relieve the bodily and mental strain which had preceded.   This too passed away and peace settled upon her soul.

She now began to write down an account of her trials and the favours she had received, thinking that it might help others after her death.   Not wishing the sisters to see this diary, she used to sew it up in the cushion of a chair, but the others, suspecting that she was doing something of the sort, searched for and found the manuscript.   Their indiscretion was soon discovered by Catherine, and taking the leaves she threw them into the oven furnace.   This oven was under her special charge, for she was the baker, and at one time, indeed, finding that the glare was injuring her eyes and fearing lest she might become a burden to the community, she mentioned her apprehensions to the superior, who, however, told her to remain at her post and leave her health to God.   When she had been baker for a considerable period, St Catherine became novice-mistress, and it was about this time that she had a remarkable vision which is often represented in art and which may best be described in her own words.   Writing of herself in the third person she says : " She asked permission of her mistress to pass the night of Christmas in the church of the monastery and she obtained it.   She went there as soon as she could, with the intention of reciting a thousand Ave Marias in honour of our most Blessed Lady : and this she really did with all the attention and fervour of which she was capable, and she was occupied in this way till midnight, the hour when it is believed our Saviour was born.   At this very hour she saw our Blessed Lady appear. holding in her arms the Infant Jesus, swathed in linen bands as new-born infants commonly are.   This kind mother came to her and gave her Son to her.   I leave you to picture the joy of this poor creature when she found herself holding the Son of the eternal Father in her arms. Trembling with respect, but still more overcome with joy, she took the liberty of caressing Him, of pressing Him against her heart and of bringing His face to her lips.   When the poor creature we speak of dared to move her lips towards the Divine Infant's mouth, He disappeared, leaving her, however, filled with joy." Two works she wrote about this time consisted of a series of non-metrical verses on the mysteries of the life of our Lord and of His Mother, which she called a " Rosary ", and which was treasured after her death in her monastery at Bologna, and a treatise on the Seven Spiritual Weapons which was published posthumously and had a great circulation throughout Italy.

Already some years earlier the little community governed by Lucy Mascaroni had embraced the strict Rule of St Clare and had removed to a more suitable building, but it was felt by St Catherine and the more austere sisters that the full regularity of the convent could not be obtained until it should become enclosed. The inhabitants of Ferrara, however, long resisted this innovation, and it was mainly through the prayers and efforts of St Catherine that enclosure was conceded, and finally sanctioned by Pope Nicholas V.   Catherine was then appointed superioress of a new convent of strict observance at Bologna, and although she shrank from the office and would have preferred to remain in Ferrara, she received a divine intimation that she was to go and made no further protest.   She and the religious who accompanied her were received at Bologna by two cardinals, by the senate and magistrates, and by the entire population, and there they established the convent of Corpus Christi.   Despite the strictness of the enclosure, the fame of the sanctity and healing powers of St Catherine, as well as her gifts of prophecy, attracted so many would-be postulants that room could not be found for them all.

After working hard all the week, she would devote the free time she had on Sundays and festivals to copying her breviary, illuminating it with colours.   The whole of this breviary, with the figures of our Lord, our Lady and the saints was her work and is still preserved.   She also composed a number of hymns and painted several pictures.   Three precepts which Catherine practised all her life she was wont to impress upon her daughters.   The first was always to speak well of others, the second was to practise constant humility, and the third was never to meddle in matters which were no business of hers.   Strict beyond measure with herself, she was most tender to the weaknesses of other people, and when the triennial election of the abbess was pending the only objection that could be urged against her re-election was that the rules lost their force through her kindness.   When she was novice-mistress and thought some of the younger sisters were insufficiently fed, she used to beg for eggs (hard-boiled, presumably), which she slipped into their bags after having peeled them and left the shells on her own plate.   This caused her to be censured for sensuality at the annual visitation, but she received the reproofs humbly as though they had been deserved.

The saint's health, which had been failing since before her return to Bologna, ere long broke down altogether.   On the first Sunday in Lent of 1463 she was attacked by violent pains, and was obliged to take to her bed, from which she never rose again.   On March 9 she rendered up her soul to God, and her passing was so peaceful that the watching sisters did not realize that she was dead until they perceived a sweet fragrance and noticed that her face had become so fresh and beautiful that she looked like a young girl of fifteen who was sleeping.   Her body was buried without a coffin and remained in the ground for eighteen days, when it was disinterred, owing to the cures which were reported and to the sweet scent

which proceeded from the grave.   It was found to be incorrupt, and has ever since
been preserved in the chapel of the convent church in Bologna.   There the entire
body may be seen through glass and behind bars   it is in a sitting posture and
richly habited, but the face and hands, which are uncovered, are now black with
damp and age.   St Catherine is honoured as a patron of artists.   The miniatures
executed by her, which are still preserved in her convent of Corpo di Cristo at
Bologna, are said to have been painted with remarkable delicacy.   Two pictures of
hers are also still in existence.   One is in the Pinacoteca at Bologna, the other in
the Academy of Fine Arts at Venice.   She was canonized in 1712.

The outlines of St Catherine's history may be learnt from a short memoir published
nearly fifty years after her death by a Franciscan friar, Denis Paleotti, but more completely
from the biography of Father J. Grassetti who, though he only wrote in 1610, had access
at Bologna to such records as existed concerning her.   Both these lives, originally composed
in Italian, were printed by the Bollandists (*Acta Sanctorum*, March, vol. ii) in a Latin translation.   It seems regrettable that the most valuable source of first-hand information concerning Catherine Vigri has apparently never yet been printed.   This is the *Specchio d'illumin-
azione*, a memorial of the saint penned by her fellow religious and subject, Sister Illumínata
Bembi, whose manuscript is still preserved in the convent.   Most modern biographies
depend almost entirely on Grassetti.   The most imposing of these is that of J. E. Duver,
Vie de sainte Catherine de Bologne (1905) ; there is another in French by J. Stiénon du Pré
(1949).   A very useful collection of essays bearing on the subject of Catherine appeared
at Bologna in 1912 under the title *La Santa nella storia, nelle lettere e nell' arte*.   See also
Léon, *Auréole Séraphique* (Eng. trans., vol. i, pp. 394–437) and Dunbar, *Dictionary of Saintly
Women*, vol. i, pp. 160–161.   An English translation of Grassetti was included in the
Oratorian Series.

ST DOMINIC SAVIO   (A.D. 1857)

THE year 1950 saw the canonization of a twelve-year-old girl, Mary Goretti, as a
martyr and the beatification of a fifteen-year-old boy, Dominic Savio, as a confessor.
The Church has raised several child martyrs to her altars, but the case of Dominic
Savio seems to be unique.   He was canonized in 1954.

He was born at Riva in Piedmont in 1842, the son of a peasant, and grew up
with the desire to be a priest.   When St John Bosco began to make provision for
training youths as clergy to help him in his work for neglected boys at Turin,
Dominic's parish-priest recommended him.   An interview took place, at which
Don Bosco was most deeply impressed by the evidence of grace in the boy's soul,
and in October 1854, when he was twelve, Dominic became a student at the Oratory
of St Francis de Sales in Turin.

His own personality apart, Dominic was best remembered at the oratory for
the group he organized there.   It was called the Company of the Immaculate
Conception, and besides its devotional objects it helped Don Bosco in his work by
undertaking various necessary jobs, from sweeping the floors to taking special care
of boys who for one reason or another were misfits.   When the time came, in 1859,
for St John Bosco to form the kernel of his now world-wide Salesian congregation,
among the twenty-two present were all the original members of the Company of
the Immaculate Conception ; all, that is, except Dominic Savio   he had been
called to the congregation of Heaven two years before.

Early on at the oratory Dominic prevented a brutal fight with stones between
two boys by characteristically direct action.   Holding up a little crucifix between
them, " Before you fight ", he said, " look at this, both of you, and say, ' Jesus

Christ was sinless, and He died forgiving His executioners ; I am a sinner, and I am going to outrage Him by being deliberately revengeful '. Then you can start—and throw your first stone at me." The rascals slunk away. He was scrupulous in observing the discipline of the house, and some of the wilder spirits did not like it when he expected them to be equally scrupulous. They called him a sneak, and told him to " run and tell Don Bosco "—thereby showing how little they knew about Don Bosco, who would not tolerate tale-bearing. Likely enough Dominic laughed it off ; for he was a ready laugher, and sometimes it got him into trouble with the masters. But if he was no tale-bearer he was a good story-teller, and that endeared him to his companions, especially the younger ones.

It was a specially happy dispensation of Providence that brought Dominic Savio under the care of so moderate and wise a man as St John Bosco : otherwise he might have developed into a young fanatic and spoiled himself by excess. Don Bosco insisted on cheerfulness, on careful attention to daily duties, on joining in the games, so that Dominic would say, " I can't do big things. But I want all I do, even the smallest thing, to be for the greater glory of God." " Religion must be about us like the air we breathe ; but we must not weary the boys with too many devotions and observances and so forth ," Don Bosco used to say. And, true to that spirit, he forbade Dominic to inflict the least bodily mortification upon himself without express permission. " For ", he said, " the penance God wants is obedience. There is plenty to put up with cheerfully—heat, cold, sickness, the tiresome ways of other people. There is quite enough mortification for boys in school life itself." Nevertheless he found Dominic shivering in bed one cold night, with all the bed-clothes save one thin sheet thrown off. " Don't be so crazy," he said, " You'll get pneumonia ." " Why should I ? " replied Dominic. " Our Lord didn't get pneumonia in the stable at Bethlehem."

The most important source for the details of Dominic Savio's short life is the account written by St John Bosco himself. In writing it he was careful not to set down anything that he could not vouch for, and he was most particularly careful when dealing with the spiritual experiences that were accorded to this boy : such things as supernatural knowledge—of people in need, of their spiritual state, of the future. Or the occasion when Dominic was missing all the morning till after dinner. Don Bosco found him eventually in the choir of the church, standing in a cramped position by the lectern, rapt in prayer. He had been there for about six hours, yet thought that early Mass was not yet over. Dominic called these times of intense prayer " my distractions " They would sometimes overtake him at play : " It seems as though Heaven is opening just above me. I am afraid I may say or do something that will make the other boys laugh."

St John Bosco tells us that the needs of England had an important part in this boy's prayers ; and he records " a strong distraction " in which Dominic saw a wide mist-shrouded plain, with a multitude of people groping about in it ; to them came a pontifically-vested figure carrying a torch that lighted up the whole scene, and a voice seemed to say, " This torch is the Catholic faith which shall bring light to the English people ". At Dominic's request Don Bosco told this to Pope Pius IX, who declared that it confirmed his resolution to give great care and attention to England.

Dominic's delicate health got worse and worse, and in February 1857 he was sent home to Mondonio for a change of air. His complaint was diagnosed as inflammation of the lungs, and according to the practice of the day he was bled,

bled to excess.   The treatment seems certainly to have hastened his end.   He received the last sacraments, and on the evening of March 9 he asked his father to read the prayers for the dying.   Towards the end of them he tried to sit up. " Good-bye, father ", he murmured, " the priest told me something.   But I can't remember what.   ."   Suddenly his face lit up with a smile of intense joy, and he exclaimed, " I am seeing most wonderful things ! "   He did not speak again.

The cause of the beatification of Dominic Savio was begun in Rome in 1914. It met with some opposition, on the ground of his extreme youth.   Pope Pius X on the other hand regarded his age as a point in favour of beatification.   This view eventually prevailed ; but Dominic Savio was not beatified till 1950, sixteen years after the canonization of Don Bosco.

The definitive text of the biography written by St John Bosco is that published at Turin in 1950, edited by Fr E. Ceria.   An English translation, by Mary Russell, was published in 1934.   Other Italian lives are by Cardinal Salotti (1921) and Don Cojazzi (1950), and among the French ones is A. Auffray's *Un Saint de quinze ans* (1950).   There is an excellent short account by Fr John Sexton, issued by the Salesian Press in London in 1950.

10 : THE FORTY MARTYRS OF SEBASTEA   (A.D. 320)

THE Emperor Licinius who at one time had extended a measure of toleration to Christians, reversed his policy after his breach with his brother-in-law Constantine and a fresh persecution was begun.   In Cappadocia he published a decree ordering every Christian, on pain of death, to abandon his religion. When Agricolaus, the governor of Cappadocia and Lesser Armenia, communicated this decree to the army, forty young soldiers of various nationalities stationed at Sebastea refused to sacrifice to idols.   The forty, who are said to have all belonged to the famous " Thundering Legion ", appeared before the tribunal at Sebastea (now Sivas in Turkey) saying that they were Christians and that no torments would induce them to forsake their religion.   The governor at first tried persuasion, representing to them the disgrace which would follow upon their refusal to obey and promising promotion if they would conform.   Finding them inexorable, he commanded that they should be tortured and cast into prison.   Here they sang together Psalm xc, " He that dwelleth in the aid of the most High shall abide under the protection of the God of Heaven ", and they were comforted by a vision of our Lord who encouraged them to persevere.

Then the governor, incensed at their obstinacy, subjected them to a strange ordeal which he had devised.   The cold in Armenia is very severe, especially in March when the north wind rages.   Under the walls of the city stood a pond or lake which was frozen hard, and on it the prisoners were condemned to be exposed quite naked and to be left there night and day.   Agricolaus also ordered that a fire and a warm bath should be prepared on the edge of the lake to tempt them to apostasy.   The martyrs, without waiting to be stripped, undressed themselves, encouraging each other and saying that one bad night would purchase for them a happy eternity.   Together they prayed, " Lord, we are forty who are engaged in this conflict : grant that forty may be crowned and that we may not fall short of that sacred number ".   Their guards were continually urging them to offer up sacrifice and so to pass on to the fire and the warm bath, but all in vain.   St Gregory of Nyssa asserts that they endured for three days and three nights this lingering death. Out of the whole number, only one failed and allowed himself to be led to the shore. As it turned out, the reaction of the heat after the intense cold was too great and he died in the bath, thus losing the life he had striven to save as well as the palm of victory. This defection greatly grieved the others, but they were consoled by seeing his place filled and their number miraculously completed.

One of the soldiers who had been set to guard the prisoners, being off duty, sat down by the fire, and he fell asleep and had a strange dream. He seemed to be standing by the lake when suddenly the sky was filled with beautiful angelic forms. One by one they descended upon the ice bearing robes and crowns with which they invested the martyrs. The soldier counted : there were thirty-nine crowns. This vision and the desertion and fate of the apostate wrought his instantaneous conversion. By a special inspiration of the Holy Ghost, he flung off his clothes, stepped on to the ice, and took his place among the survivors, proclaiming himself a Christian. By his martyrdom he obtained the grace of what is known as the " baptism of blood " as well as the fortieth crown which had been forfeited by the deserter. God had indeed heard the petition of His servants and had answered it in this wholly unexpected way.

By the following morning most of the victims were dead, but a few still lingered on, notably Melito, the youngest. Agricolaus ordered that the arms and legs of the survivors should be broken and the bodies cast into a furnace where they would be consumed. With their dying lips they sang faintly, " Our soul hath escaped from the snare of the fowler : the snare is broken and we are set free ". The officials left Melito to the last : they pitied his youth and hoped that he would give way when he found himself alone, but his mother, a poor widow, reproached the executioners for their mistaken kindness. As she drew near to her son he looked up at her with his dimmed eyes, and being unable to smile he made a little sign of recognition with his feeble hand. Fortified by the Holy Ghost, she urged him to persevere to the end, and lifted him up and placed him herself upon the waggon with the rest of the victims. The bodies of the martyrs were burned and their ashes thrown into the river, but the Christians managed secretly to rescue some of the charred remains or bought them with money. A portion of the precious relics were kept at Caesarea, and St Basil says of them, " Like bulwarks they are our protection against the inroads of enemies ". He adds that everyone implored the succour of the martyrs, who raised up those who had fallen, strengthened the weak and increased the fervour of the saints.

St Basil the Elder and St Emmelia, the parents of the four saints, Basil the Great, Gregory of Nyssa, Peter of Sebastea and Macrina, procured a share of these relics some of which Emmelia gave to the church she built near Annesis. The enthusiasm with which they were received was extraordinary, and according to St Gregory of Nyssa they were honoured by miracles. He adds, " I buried the bodies of my parents by the relics of these holy martyrs, that in the resurrection they may rise with the encouragers of their faith ; for I know they have great power with God, of which I have seen clear proofs and undoubted testimonies ". St Gaudentius, Bishop of Brescia, writes in his sermons on these martyrs, " God gave me a share of these venerable relics and granted me to found this church in their honour ". He says that as he passed through Caesarea on his way to Jerusalem they were presented to him by the two nieces of St Basil, who had received them from their uncle. Portions of their relics were also taken to Constantinople, as we learn from Sozomen and Procopius.

Perhaps the most interesting feature connected with the memory of these champions of the faith is the preservation of a document known as " The Testament of the Forty Holy Martyrs of Christ " The Greek text has been in print for more than a couple of centuries, but it is only of recent years that its authenticity has come to be recognized. It is a unique but perfectly genuine relic of the age of persecution. Though it cannot well be here inserted entire, the summary account written by Father H. Delehaye, the Bollandist, will not be out of place.

" Meletios, Aetios and Eutykhios, prisoners of Christ, salute the bishops, presbyters, deacons, confessors and other ' ecclesiastics ' of the whole Christian world, and make known their wishes regarding the disposal of their mortal remains after the consummation of their martyrdom. They desire that all their relics be placed in the care of the priest Proidos and certain other persons, in order that they may repose together in Sareim near Zela. Meletios writes this exordium in the name of all.

" At this point Aetios and Eutykhios, speaking for their companions, conjure the families of the martyrs not to give way to excessive grief, and carefully to fulfil their last wishes as to the disposal of their remains. When their ashes shall be gathered together, let no one retain any particle for himself, but deliver everything to the persons designated. Should anyone disobey this injunction, they hope he may fail of obtaining the favours which he looks for from the possession of the relics.

" The martyrs then express their solicitude for one of their number, a young man named Eunoikos, whose tender age might probably move the persecutors to clemency. If, say they, he shall win the palm of martyrdom with us, let him repose with us. In case he should be spared, let him remain faithful to the law of Christ, in order that, on the day of the resurrection, he may enjoy the blessed lot of those whose sufferings he has shared.

" Here, it seems, Meletios again takes the pen. He addresses himself to his brothers, Krispinos and Gordios, exhorting them to be on their guard against the deceitful pleasures of this world, and to hold themselves in constant readiness by a strict adherence to the precepts of our Lord. He wishes these exhortations to be taken to heart by all the followers of Christ.

" Then begins a list of salutations : ' We salute the lord priest Philip, and Proklianos and Diogenes and at the same time the holy church. We salute the lord Proklianos of Phydela with the holy church and all who are his. We salute Maximos with the church, Magnos with the church. We salute Domnos with his, and Iles our father, Valens with the church.' Again Meletios intervenes : ' And I, Meletios, salute my relations Lutanios, Krispos and Gordios, etc.' There follow other salutations, general and particular ; and finally ' We salute you, we the forty brethren united in captivity,' with the forty names. ' We, the forty prisoners of Christ, have signed by the hand of Meletios, one of us ; we have confirmed all that has been written, for we were all in full agreement with it.' "

It is extremely improbable that all, or even many, of the forty would have been able to write for themselves. Therefore Meletios set down the names in their place. But the names preserved in the *acta* are those of the " Testament ", and we may fairly draw the inference that there was sound historical evidence for part of the story, though not necessarily for such extravagant excrescences as that the stones hurled at them recoiled upon the throwers or that their ashes were recovered after being cast into the water.

The Greek *passio*, which seems to be the source from which all the other versions of the "acts" are derived, was first edited by R. Abicht in the *Archiv für Slavische Philologie* (vol. xviii, pp. 144 *seq.*). The text may now most conveniently be consulted in O. von Gebhardt, *Acta Martyrum Selecta*, pp. 166–181, where the "Testament" is also printed. The Latin, Armenian and Old Slavonic versions have no particular importance. On the other hand, the panegyrics of St Basil, St Gregory of Nyssa, St Ephraem, St John Chrysostom and St Gaudentius of Brescia bear valuable witness to the veneration in which the martyrs were held already at the close of the fourth century. See on these homilies Delehaye, *Les Passions des Martyrs* ., pp. 184–235. There are certain inconsistencies between the details furnished by the *passio* and those of the panegyrics, notably as to the question whether the martyrs were exposed to their ordeal in the middle of the town or upon a frozen lake outside it. On this see Pio Franchi de' Cavalieri in *Studi e Testi*, no. 22, fasc. 3, pp. 64–70, and Delehaye in *American Catholic Quarterly Review*, 1899, pp. 161–171. *Cf.* also Bonwetsch, *Studien zur Geschichte d. Theologie*, vol. pt 1, pp. 71–95; and BHG., nn. 1201–1208.

SS. CODRATUS AND HIS COMPANIONS, MARTYRS   (A.D. 258 ?)

THE parents of St Codratus were Greek Christians belonging to the city of Corinth. They both died early and, according to one tradition, he was actually born in the wilderness whither his mother had retired to escape persecution under Decius and where she died. It was commonly reported that he grew up in the desert and was divinely nourished with food from the skies—the clothes with which his mother had covered him adapting themselves miraculously to his growth. In any case, he emerged from his retirement to study medicine and surrounded himself with a band of disciples, most of whom seem to have led ascetical lives.

Under the Emperors Decius and Valerian, Jason was the prefect of Greece entrusted with the enforcement of the cruel laws against the Christians. St Codratus was one of those summoned to appear before him, and the judge strove at first to persuade him to offer sacrifice to the gods and so escape punishment. The holy man, who was attended by five of his faithful disciples, protested that eternal salvation was dearer to them than life, and instead of defending himself, he is said to have given a summary of God's dealings with men from the creation of the world to the death and resurrection of our Lord. Jason scornfully rejected the doctrine that God had become man and had suffered for us, and finding that argument and persuasion had no effect upon the martyr, he ordered him to be scourged.

Then the prefect addressed himself to Cyprian, a mere boy, thinking that he would be more readily won, but Codratus exhorted his companions to be steadfast. They were all of them subjected to tortures and then cast to the wild beasts, which, however, refused to touch them. Finally they were led out of the city to the place of execution, where they were beheaded. The names of the other four were Dionysius, Anectus, Paul and Crescens.

No confidence can be placed in the Greek acts and the synaxaries in which this history is recounted. See the *Acta Sanctorum*, March, vol. ii.

ST MACARIUS, BISHOP OF JERUSALEM   (c. A.D. 335)

PRESERVED in the pages of the historian Eusebius is the letter which Constantine wrote to Macarius, Bishop of Jerusalem, entrusting him with the construction of a church on the spot where the Empress Helen had discovered the site of Christ's sepulchre, and giving him practically a free hand in its design and in the choice of workmen and materials. He lived to complete the basilica he had undertaken. We know from the testimony of St Athanasius that Macarius was a sincere and upright man, filled with the true apostolic spirit. He succeeded Bishop Hermon in 314 at the time when the Arian heresy was beginning seriously to menace the Church, and we know from the testimony of St Athanasius that he proved himself a valiant champion of the true faith. At the Council of Nicaea his name appears first of the Palestinian bishops in the list of the signatories.

According to the popular legend, Macarius was not only present at the finding of Christ's cross, but was also actually the means of identifying it. When the necessary excavations had been made three crosses were discovered, and it was at first doubtful which of the three was that on which our Lord had suffered. If we may trust the account which Rufinus gives in his Ecclesiastical History " It happened that in the city there was a woman lying ill, nigh unto death. Macarius was bishop of that church at the time. When he saw the queen and the rest standing by, he said, ' Bring hither all the crosses that have been found, and God will show us which it was that bore the Lord '. Then having entered with the queen and the others into the house of the woman who was ill, he knelt down and prayed thus : ' O God, who through thine only-begotten Son hast inspired the heart of thine handmaid to seek the holy wood upon which our salvation depends, show plainly which cross was identified with the glory of the Lord and which served for the punishment of slaves. Grant that as soon as the health-giving wood touches this woman who is lying half-dead, she may be recalled to life from the gates of death.' When he had spoken these words, he touched her with one of the crosses—and nothing happened. Then he applied the second— equally without effect. As soon, however, as he touched her with the third cross, she started up open-eyed and, with her strength fully restored, began to glorify God and to run about the house with greater agility than before her illness. The queen; having obtained her desire through such a clear indication, erected with royal pomp a marvellous temple on the spot where she had found the cross."

Constantine's great basilica was consecrated on September 13, 335, the year which is generally considered to have been that of the death of its supervisor and builder Macarius.

It must be confessed that there is some discrepancy between the accounts given by St Ambrose and the church historians concerning the miracle by which the cross was identified, but this is dealt with more fully on May 3. See the *Acta Sanctorum*, March, vol. ii ; DCB., vol. iii, p. 765 ; and F. J. Bacchus in the *Catholic Encyclopedia*, vol. ix, pp. 482-483.

ST SIMPLICIUS, POPE   (A.D. 483)

ST SIMPLICIUS, who succeeded St Hilarus in 468, occupied the papal throne at a most difficult and troublous period. Already all the provinces of the West outside Italy had fallen into the hands of the barbarians. who were mostly pagans or Arians, and during his tenure of the chair of St Peter Rome itself was permanently occupied by Odoacer, the ruler of the Heruli, and the empire of the West ceased to exist. The people, ground down under the taxes of the Roman governors and impoverished by devastating raids, offered but little resistance to the conquerors who exacted no imposts from them. St Simplicius was greatly concerned to alleviate their miseries and to sow the seeds of the faith among the barbarian invaders. In the East he was engaged in a protracted struggle with monophysite influences. He

vindicated the binding force of the Council of Chalcedon against those who sought
to set it aside, and laboured zealously to maintain the faith which he saw betrayed
on every hand. Simplicius died in 483 and was buried in St Peter's.

It would be possible to compile a long biography of St Simplicius, for his activities made
themselves felt in secular as well as ecclesiastical history, but regarding his virtues as a servant
of God we know little beyond generalities ; neither is there any great evidence of *cultus*.
See the *Liber Pontificalis* (Duchesne), vol. i, pp. 249–251 ; Hefele-Leclercq, *Conciles*, vol. ii,
pp. 912–930 ; and the excellent notice by J. P. Kirsch in the *Catholic Encyclopedia.*

ST KESSOG, BISHOP AND MARTYR   (SIXTH CENTURY)

ST KESSOG (Mackessog) is believed to have come of the royal race of Munster, his
father being king at Cashel. The story is told that on one occasion, when several
of the neighbouring princes and their sons were being entertained, Kessog, with
two of the visitors, boys like himself, fell into a lake and only Kessog escaped with
his life. For some reason he was blamed by the victims' parents, who threatened
to burn Cashel and devastate the province. Kessog had recourse to prayer and
the life of the two boys was restored. The saint passed over to Scotland, where,
after having been attached to the Culdees, he was elected itinerant bishop and
laboured in the provinces of Leven and Boyne ; he made his headquarters on
Monks' Island in Loch Lomond, and from there he evangelized the whole of the
surrounding country.

There is considerable uncertainty about his fate. According to one tradition
he suffered death for the truth at Bandry   according to another he was martyred
in foreign parts and his body, embalmed with sweet herbs, was brought back to
Scotland and buried at Luss. From these herbs, which germinated and were
called in Gaelic *luss*, the parish afterwards derived its name. The Scots used to
invoke him as a battle-cry until they adopted St Andrew as the national patron, and
they long held him in honour. They represented him in their art as an archer with
a quiver at his back and a bent bow in his hands. In Lennox, of which he is the
patron, St Kessog's bell was venerated in the seventeenth century, and the church
of Auchterarder is dedicated in his honour. At Inverness there is a Kessog Ferry,
and in Cumbrae a Kessog's Fair is held on the third Wednesday in March, whilst
the fair of Fel-ma-Chessaig is held on March 21, which, according to the old style,
would be March 10. Malcolm, Earl of Lennox, gave a charter to John of Luss
" for the reverence and honour of our patron, the most holy man, the blessed
Kessog ", and at Buchanan is, or was, another charter wherein Robert Bruce
granted a sanctuary-girth of three miles " to God and St Kessog " at Luss.

See KSS., pp. 373–374, and the Aberdeen Breviary. There is also a short notice of
him in the *Acta Sanctorum*, March, vol. ii.

ST ANASTASIA PATRICIA, VIRGIN   (NO DATE)

THE history of this Anastasia rests on very slender authority. She is stated to have
been the daughter of a patrician of Egyptian race and to have been a lady-in-waiting
in the court of Constantinople. Her beauty won the heart of the Emperor Justinian
and the jealousy of the Empress Theodora. She was as good as she was fair, and
when she found herself the object of the emperor's attentions she escaped by night
and made her way to Alexandria, where she entered a convent. The emperor
did not forget her, and after the death of Theodora he caused a search to be made,

intending to raise her to the throne as his wife. News of this reached Anastasia and she fled into the desert, where she wandered about until she came to the community ruled over by Abbot Daniel, whom she told her history and her plight. Without delay he gave her the habit of a monk and the necessary instructions for becoming a hermit. Then he enclosed her in a cave at a considerable distance from his own cell and left her—charging her on no account ever to emerge or to allow anyone to enter her hermitage. After that, she saw no more of him. His disciples used to bring water and food which they placed before her door, but they never knew her sex.

Thus did " Anastasius the Eunuch " live for twenty-eight years, and in all that time she never beheld the face of man, but gave herself up to prayer and mortification. Only when she felt the hand of death upon her did she send a message to the aged abbot, requesting him to come to her. Full of foreboding, Daniel hastened to the cell, accompanied by one of his disciples, and there he found her at the point of death. After a few parting words, he gave her communion and stood by while her soul left her body. Then the abbot and his disciple buried her in her habit according to the wish she had expressed just before her death. It is supposed that her relics were afterwards removed to Constantinople.

The story in all probability is pure romance. The theme is one very familiar to the Greek hagiographers ; see, for example, the legend of St Apollinaris Syncletica (January 5) and that of St Pelagia (October 8), and *cf.* Delehaye, *Les Légendes Hagiographiques* (1927), pp. 188–189. The tale of Anastasia Patricia may be found in certain copies of the synaxaries, and it is printed by Delehaye, *Synax. Constant.*, cc. 524–528, as well as in the *Acta Sanctorum*, March, vol. ii.

ST DROCTOVEUS, OR DROTTÉ, ABBOT (*c.* A.D. 580)

AUXERRE was the birthplace of St Droctoveus. He was educated under St Germanus in the abbey of Saint-Symphorien at Autun, and afterwards became a monk in that community. The rule followed was a very strict one, and we are told that Droctoveus was foremost amongst his brethren for his spirit of mortification and prayer. When Germanus was appointed bishop of Paris, he still wished to lead the religious life, and a monastery was accordingly attached to the church which King Childebert built, dedicated in honour of the Holy Cross and St Vincent. Probably St Droctoveus was placed by St Germanus over the new abbey and he continued to govern it until his death. He is lauded by the chroniclers as the embodiment of all Christian and monastic virtues, and Venantius Fortunatus has left us some verses in his honour, but any detailed record of his life was destroyed by Northmen when they burnt the monastery. The monks of his house subsequently adopted the Benedictine rule, and when the body of St Germanus had been laid there both church and abbey took the name of Saint-Germain. The site is that of the present well-known church of Saint-Germain-des-Prés.

See Mabillon, vol. i, pp. 239-243 ; and the *Acta Sanctorum*, March, vol. ii.

ST ATTALAS, ABBOT (A.D. 627)

ST ATTALAS, a Burgundian, spent his youth with Aregius, Bishop of Gap, to whom his parents had confided him. There he received excellent instruction in letters, but found that he was not making sufficient spiritual progress. He therefore made his way to the monastery of Lérins, where he entered, but later resolved to seek a stricter community. At the celebrated monastery of Luxeuil, which St Columban had founded on the site of the old Roman town of Luxovium, he found all the austerity he desired, and of all the pious band Attalas was perhaps the one most after Columban's heart : he recognized in him a kindred spirit and took special pains to lead him on to perfection. When the holy abbot and his Irish companions were exiled from France by Theodoric, King of Austrasia, whom he had boldly rebuked for his vices, Columban took Attalas with him on his travels, which ended in Lombardy, when Agilulf, King of the Lombards, gave him land for the foundation of a monastery at Bobbio, a lonely spot in the Apennines. St Columban was seventy years of age at the time, and as he only lived one year after the foundation of Bobbio much of the credit for the establishment and prestige of the great monastery is certainly due to Attalas, who succeeded him as abbot in 615. The new superior had many difficulties with which to contend, the chief of which was disloyalty amongst his brethren. Once the authority of St Columban was removed, they murmured against the severity of the rule and broke out into rebellion.

Like St Columban, Attalas contended strenuously against Arianism, which was rife in the districts about Milan. He was endowed with the power of healing, and Jonas the Scot, who wrote his life, was eye-witness of some of the cures which he effected. Fifty days before his death, St Attalas was divinely warned to get ready for a long journey. Doubtful whether this meant an expedition to foreign parts or the passage to eternity, the abbot put everything in order in the monastery and prepared himself for a voyage. Falling ill with fever he realized that the warning referred to death, and when the disease increased, he asked to be laid outside the door of his cell, beside which stood a cross which he always touched on leaving or returning to it. As he wished to be alone for a while, all withdrew except St Blimond (afterwards abbot of Saint-Valéry), who remained near at hand in case St Attalas might require assistance. The dying man besought mercy of God with many tears, and then he saw Heaven unveiled, and contemplated it for several hours. Afterwards he recalled his monks and bade them carry him back to his cell. The following day he rendered up his soul to his Creator, and was buried at Bobbio beside his master Columban. The body of St Bertulf was afterwards placed in the same tomb and the three holy men were venerated together.

See Mabillon, vol. ii, pp. 115–118. The short contemporary biography of St Attalas by his disciple Jonas is also printed by the Bollandists (March, vol. ii) and by Migne, PL., vol. lxxxvii, cc. 1055–1062. But the best edition is by B. Krusch in MGH., *Script. merov.*, vol. iv, pp. 113–119.

ST HIMELIN   (*c.* A.D. 750)

THE holy priest Himelin was by birth said to be an Irishman, closely related to St Rumold of Malines, and he is remembered by the following legend. Returning from a pilgrimage to Rome, in the days of King Pepin of France, he was taken very ill one evening at Vissenaeken, near Tirlemont in Brabant. As he rested by the roadside, weary and thirsty, he asked for a drink of water from the maid-servant of the parish priest, as she passed with a pitcher of water which she had drawn from the well. She had been strictly forbidden to let anyone touch the vessel for fear of infection, as plague was raging in the district, so " I cannot let you drink out of the pitcher, for my master has forbidden it ", she replied. Then, pitying his evident misery, she added, " But if you will come to the house, you shall have both food and drink." The pilgrim, however, insisted, and assured her that if she would only let him take a draught of the water, her master would be well satisfied. She complied with his request and returned home. No sooner had the parish priest tasted the water than he perceived that it had been changed into delicious wine, and on questioning the girl he elicited from her what had previously happened to the pitcher. Deeply impressed by the miracle the good man ran out and brought back the sick pilgrim to his house, where he nursed him tenderly until his death, although he could not induce him to lie on a better bed than a heap of straw. St Himelin was buried at Vissenaeken, the church bells of which pealed forth at his passing, although no human hands had set them in motion. His shrine is still a resort for pilgrims, especially on his feast-day, March 10.

See the *Acta Sanctorum*, March, vol. ii.

BD ANDREW OF STRUMI, Abbot   (A.D. 1097)

About the middle of the eleventh century the city of Milan was torn between the rival factions of Archbishop Guido and the " Pataria ", a nickname which has never been quite satisfactorily explained they were the reform party who, under the leadership of the deacon Arialdo and a knight called Herlembald, strove against simony and concubinage amongst the clergy. Of all Arialdo's disciples perhaps the most prominent was Andrew, then known as " the Ligurian ", a native of Parma, who became his closest friend and associate.

The archbishop excommunicated Arialdo, who was, however, exculpated at Rome, Guido himself coming under ecclesiastical censure for simony. He continued, nevertheless, to harass the Pataria, and having seized Arialdo he is said to have wreaked his vengeance upon the unfortunate deacon, whose eyes were blinded and body mutilated in the most barbarous manner. At the risk of his life, Andrew penetrated several times into the enemy's territories, first to learn the fate of his master and then to try to recover his body. Shepherds led him to a lonely spot where they had seen the body deposited, but it was no longer there, having been disinterred and cast into the water. It was washed up again—miraculously as it seemed—at the very spot from which it had been cast, and Andrew was enabled with the assistance of Herlembald to remove it, still incorrupt after ten months.

After seeing Arialdo's body duly honoured at Milan, where he is venerated as a martyr, Andrew retired into the Vallombrosan Order, to which he appears to have been admitted by Abbot Rudolf, who was also in close sympathy with the Pataria. Rudolf's successor promoted Andrew to be abbot of San Fedele at Strumi on the Arno, and he was then able to devote part of his time to literary work. From his close association with Arialdo, he was eminently competent to amplify and supplement the Life of Arialdo, which had been begun by Abbot Rudolf. He also wrote the Life of St John Gualbert. Busily occupied as he was, Bd Andrew still retained the public spirit which had made him a leader of the Pataria. Italy was in a very disturbed condition owing to the struggle between the Emperor Henry IV and Pope Urban II, and Florence and Arezzo were paralysed by mutual antagonism. The abbot of Strumi came forward as a peacemaker between them ; and so well did he manage the situation that he earned the confidence of both parties, and the peace which he negotiated continued unimpaired during the rest of his life. The prestige he obtained had a totally unforeseen result : a number of churches, priories and hospitals in the dioceses of Florence and Arezzo and throughout the Casentino placed themselves under his supervision and became affiliated to the Vallombrosan Order.

Bd Andrew died in 1097. Most of his writings appear to have perished about the year 1530 when, at the time of the siege of Florence, the mother-house of the Vallombrosans was almost entirely destroyed by fire, the library being burnt with nearly all its books and manuscripts, which included the records and documents of the beatified members of the community.

See the *Acta Sanctorum*, March, vol. ii.

BD JOHN OF VALLOMBROSA   (*c.*   1380)

JOHN OF VALLOMBROSA was a Florentine who entered the monastery of the Holy Trinity in his native city. He was a clever man and spent hours of the day and night poring over books. In the course of his studies he became interested in necromancy and began to practise the black arts in secret. He had become thoroughly vicious and depraved when reports of his proceedings reached the ears of the abbot of Vallombrosa, who summoned him before a commission of monks and formally accused him. At first John lied and denied that he had had any dealings with magic, but when incontrovertible evidence was brought against him he acknowledged his guilt. His punishment was a lengthy imprisonment in a pestilential prison where he lost his health and was reduced to a skeleton.

When at last he was liberated John could scarcely walk, but he was sincerely penitent. Although the abbot and the monks would fain have restored him to their fellowship he asked to be allowed to continue voluntarily the life he had been compelled to lead. " I have learnt ", he said, " in this dark and long imprisonment, that there is nothing better. nothing more holy, than solitude : in solitude I intend to go on learning divine things and to try to rise higher. Now that I am free from temporal fetters I am resolved, with the help of Christ, to waste no more time." With the consent of the abbot he embraced the life of a hermit and soon became known as the foremost amongst the solitaries of the countryside for his sanctity and great learning. His letters and treatises, some written in Latin and some in the vernacular, were handed about from one to another and were prized for their subject-matter as well as for the elegance of their diction. He seemed as though divinely inspired to touch the hardest hearts and to expound the most abstruse points of Holy Scripture.

The " hermit of the cells ", as he came to be called, lived to extreme old age and enjoyed the friendship and esteem of St Catherine of Siena. Writing to Barduccio of Florence after her death, John says that whilst he was mourning over her loss she came to him in a vision, and gave him the consolation of witnessing her celestial glory.

There is a short life printed in the *Acta Sanctorum* under Andrew of Strumi, March, vol. ii, 3rd ed., pp. 49-50. *Cf.* Zambrini, *Opere volgari a stampa dei sec. 13 e 14,* pp. 238, 263-264, etc.

BD PETER GEREMIA   (A.D. 1452)

THE life of this holy man was written by one of his brethren who knew him well and had lived with him in the same friary. Born in Palermo, Peter was the son of a jurist and fiscal agent to King Alfonso I and at the age of eighteen was sent to the

University of Bologna to study law with a view to succeeding to his father's office. There he made such progress that he was often called upon to take the chair of the professor when the latter was prevented from delivering his lectures. Peter was on the eve of taking his degree when he had a strange experience which he ever afterwards looked upon as a supernatural interposition. He was sitting one evening in his room, buried in study, when he was disturbed by loud and persistent rapping on his window—which was on the third storey. Startled, he inquired who the unseen visitor could be and what he wanted. " I am your cousin ", replied a voice. " After I had taken my degree, I also was called to the bar where, as you know, I gained honour and distinction. Blind and miserable wretch that I was, I spent my whole time in defence of others, and I even, against my conscience, undertook unjust cases in order to obtain money and fame. I found no one to plead my own case before the judgement-seat of God, and I am now condemned to everlasting torment. But before I am cast into Hell I am sent to warn you to flee from the courts of men if you wish to be acquitted before the judgement-seat of God."

Peter lost no time in acting upon the warning. Then and there he took a vow of perpetual chastity, and the next morning he bought an iron chain which he wound three times round his body and riveted there. This was found embedded in his flesh fifty-one years later when his body was being prepared for burial. He then obtained admission into the Dominican convent at Bologna. When news of this reached the ears of his father he was greatly incensed and travelled to Bologna, intending to remove the novice by force and compel him to complete his legal studies. Peter refused to see his parent, but sent a message saying that he was well and needed nothing that his relations could give him except their prayers. Whilst the father raged and threatened, the young man was asking as a special grace that he might neither be unfaithful to his vocation nor forfeit the love of his parents, to whom he was greatly attached. When an interview was at last arranged, the father was completely softened and gave Peter his blessing.

After he was raised to the priesthood he became a celebrated preacher and brought many to repentance and newness of life. St Vincent Ferrer when he visited Bologna sought him out to congratulate him on the work he was doing and to urge him to continue labours which God had so wonderfully blessed. Summoned as a theologian to the Council of Florence, Bd Peter found his learning and eloquence greatly extolled by Pope Eugenius IV, who wished to raise him to high ecclesiastical honours. He declined all preferment, but was obliged to accept the post of apostolic visitor in Sicily, though he stipulated that his powers should be limited to the restoration of regular observance in religious houses where irregularities had crept in during the Great Schism. In this delicate task he was entirely successful, and his preaching to the people was no less popular than in Italy. He died at Palermo in 1452, and his *cultus* was confirmed in 1784.

A picturesque story is told of Bd Peter when he was prior of Palermo. One day the procurator told him that there was no food in the house. It was a Friday, and the prior, knowing that a fisherman in the neighbourhood had had a good haul of tunny, took boat and went to beg a few of the fish for his brethren. The man refused roughly. Peter said nothing and started back in his boat, when lo ! all the fish broke through the nets and were escaping out to sea. The fisherman, aghast, followed in pursuit of Peter and besought pardon. He made the sign of the cross over the sea, and thereupon the fish again became entangled in the nets, and the man eagerly bestowed on the prior as much fish as he needed.

See the *Acta Sanctorum*, March, vol. i ; Taurisano, *Catalogus Hagiographicus O.P.*, p. 38 ; Mortier, *Maîtres Généraux O.P.*, vol. iv, pp. 152-212 ; and M. A. Coniglione, *Pietro Geremia* (1952).

BD JOHN OGILVIE, MARTYR   (A.D. 1615)

THE father of John Ogilvie was baron of Drum-na-Keith, lord of large territories in Banffshire and head of the younger branch of Ogilvies, whilst his mother, through whom he was connected with the Stewarts and the Douglases, was the daughter of Lady Douglas of Lochleven, Queen Mary's gaoler.   The family, like many Scottish families at that time, was partly Catholic and partly Presbyterian, but John's father, though not unfriendly to the old faith, brought his eldest son up as a Calvinist, and as such sent him at the age of thirteen to be educated on the continent.   There the lad became interested in the religious controversies which then and until a much later date were popular in France and in lands under French influence.   The best Catholic and Calvinistic protagonists took part in these disputations, which profoundly influenced the intellectual world.   Ere long the boy felt himself called to reconsider his position, and according to a speech ascribed to him in a Scottish version of his trial, he went to consult Italian, French and German scholars, who contrasted the unbroken faith of the Church with the novelty of the reformed doctrines and laid stress upon the unity which is characteristic of the Catholic organization alone.   Confused, John withdrew himself from controversy and fastened upon two texts of Holy Scripture : " God wills all men to be saved and to come to the knowledge of the truth ", and " Come to me, all who suffer and are laden, and I will refresh you ".   He began to see that the Catholic Church could embrace all kinds of people and that in her could be found men and women of every class who could and did despise the world.   These reflections and the testimony of the martyrs decided him, and it was in order to belong to the Church of these martyrs that he decided to become a Catholic and was received into the Church at the Scots College in Louvain in 1596, at the age of seventeen.

His next three years were spent in various continental educational centres. Lack of funds caused Father Crichton, the head of the Scots College, to dismiss many of his pupils, including John Ogilvie, who betook himself to the Scottish Benedictines at Ratisbon, with whom he remained six months, studying the arts and perhaps acquiring something of the Benedictine outlook, which is independent of national traditions.   He next passed on to the Jesuit College at Olmütz, which he entered as a lay student, and henceforth we find him intimately connected with the Jesuits.   The Society, though not much more than fifty years old, was at the height of its fame, and had attracted some of the finest minds of the age.   Within a year of joining the college, John asked to be admitted to the Society, but at that very moment an outbreak of plague compelled the authorities to close the college. Not to be deterred, the young man followed the superior to Vienna, obtained his consent, and after probation was admitted a novice at Brünn.   For the next ten years he worked and trained in Olmütz, Gratz and Vienna.   To quote the words of the Rev. W. E. Brown in his Life of John Ogilvie : " During these ten years in the Austrian province of the Society of Jesus, Ogilvie was undergoing a rigorous discipline.   Renaissance learning and scholastic method were combined into an intellectual training, consistent and, as far as knowledge went, complete. His spiritual life was being formed by a discipline no less severe. And all this time he was learning pre-eminently that discipline of the will which was the hall-mark of the Jesuit, which guaranteed the readiness of his obedience and his detachment from all earthly ties."

By the express command of Aquaviva, father general of the Society, John Ogilvie came to the French province, and it was in Paris that he received priest's orders in 1610. In France the young man was brought into contact with two Jesuits who had undertaken missionary work in Scotland, and had made expeditions thither still hoping, through the nobles, to win over King James. Both Crichton and Gordon had suffered arrest, and Gordon had spent three years in the Tower of London. It seemed to them that conditions were more unpromising than ever, and they were utterly dispirited. Therefore, when in 1611 the father general charged them to " consider the affairs of Scotland ", all they could do was to draw up a record of past failure and a declaration of the futility of any further efforts in that kingdom, in view of the tightening of the penal laws. It was at this time that Ogilvie formed the project of devoting his life to the work, and he wrote to the father general offering himself for the mission. In reply he received a stern reminder that it was for his superiors to recommend whom they would, and neither Crichton nor Gordon wished him to go. Undeterred, the young man returned to the charge, and after two and a half years of worrying and importunity received orders to proceed to Scotland.

In consequence of the strict regulations against the entry of priests into Great Britain, he travelled under the name of John Watson, and figured henceforth sometimes as a horse-dealer and sometimes as a soldier returning from the European wars. The Jesuit Moffat and a secular priest named Campbell crossed with him, but they parted at Leith and Ogilvie went north. He soon found out that the Catholic nobles on whom he had relied were only anxious to be left alone. Most of them had conformed, at least outwardly, to the established religion, and none but a very few middle-class uninfluential families were prepared to receive a proscribed priest. We know little of his movements during the next six months. According to his own depositions, he spent six weeks in the north of Scotland and apparently wintered in Edinburgh, but he does not seem to have gained any converts or to have made much headway. Realizing this, he reverted to the methods attempted by the earlier Jesuits and went to London, where he got into touch with King James, or one of his ministers, to whom he proposed some semi-political project the details of which are lost. On the strength of this, he made a journey to Paris to consult his superior, Father Gordon, who rebuked him sharply for leaving his mission and sent him back to Scotland.

Upon his return to Edinburgh, John Ogilvie made his headquarters at the house of William Sinclair, a parliamentary advocate and a sincere Catholic. Here he met a Franciscan namesake, and the two ministered to the little congregations which met at the houses of Sinclair, John Philipps and Robert Wilkie. Ogilvie soon increased his flock and became famous for his insistence on greater devotion among Catholics. He also appears to have acted as tutor to Sinclair's elder boy Robert, who afterwards became a Jesuit. Warming to his work, he now began to extend it in other directions, and set about visiting Catholics in prison—a risky proceeding in a place where all visitors were watched—and he even climbed to the castle and obtained leave to see old Sir James MacDonald, who recalled his ministrations in after years.   During the summer months of 1614 he made some converts, and Sinclair afterwards maintained that the number was great, considering the shortness of the time.   Towards the end of August he went to Glasgow, where he was harboured by a widow called Marion Walker, who ended her days in prison for the faith.   She had made of her house a centre where wandering priests could celebrate Mass and hear confessions.   In Glasgow he succeeded in entering into relations with Sir John Cleland and Lady Maxwell, who were both secret Catholics, and also in reconciling to the faith several members of the Renfrewshire gentry.   At the same time he was building up a congregation among the bourgeoisie.   Shortly after his return to Edinburgh, news came that five other persons in Glasgow wished to be reconciled and he hurried back to Glasgow.   On May 4 he celebrated Mass, one of the five would-be converts, Adam Boyd by name, being present.   After the service the man said he desired instruction, and requested the priest to come at four o'clock in the afternoon to the market-cross, where a messenger would meet him and conduct him to a safe place.   Ogilvie agreed, and Boyd immediately went to Archbishop Spottiswoode, a former Presbyterian minister who was now one of the king's most capable lieutenants, and who from his residence in Glasgow kept watch upon Catholics and Presbyterians alike.   It was agreed between them that one of the archbishop's most muscular servants, Andrew Hay, should meet Adam Boyd and Ogilvie in the market-place.   At the same time Boyd denounced all those whom he suspected of having dealings with Ogilvie.

The appointment was kept, and the Jesuit arrived in the square accompanied by James Stewart, the son of the former provost, who, recognizing Hay, tried to induce Ogilvie to return home.   Stewart and Hay fell into a dispute which ended in a free fight in which outsiders took part, but finally Ogilvie was borne along to the provost's house.   Thither came also Spottiswoode and his guards, and the prisoner was called upon to come forward, only to be received by a blow from the archbishop.   " You are overbold, sir, to say your Masses in a reformed city ! " the prelate exclaimed.   " You act as a hangman, sir, and not as a bishop in striking me ", was the spirited if impolitic answer he received.   Immediately he was assailed by the servants and citizens, dragged by the beard, torn by men's nails, and only saved by the personal intervention of Lord Fleming, who happened to be present. A search was made in which he was stripped naked, but all that could be found on him was a purse of gold, another of silver, a few medicaments, a breviary and a compendium of religious controversy.

The following morning he was brought before the archbishop and the burghal court of Glasgow, and was asked, " Have you said Mass in the king's dominions ? " Knowing that this came under the criminal law the prisoner replied, " If this is a crime, it should be proved, not by my word, but by witnesses ".   Questioned as to why he had come to Scotland, he replied boldly, " I came to unteach heresy and to save souls ".   In response to the query, " Do you recognize King James ? " he said, " King James is *de facto* king of Scotland " ;   and when interrogated in respect to the Gunpowder Plot, he answered, " I detest parricide and praise it not "— " parricide " being the recognized term for the assassination of a sovereign.   All questions which would incriminate himself or endanger the life of others he refused to answer, and the trial dragged on until he had been without food for twenty-six hours and was trembling with fever.   Then at last the judge allowed him to warm himself by the fire, but even there he was insulted by one of the archbishop's retainers, who then proceeded to express his desire to throw the prisoner into the fire. " Your action would never be more welcome than it is now, when I am shivering with cold," replied the priest. At last he was sent back to his cell, where he was bound by the feet to an enormous iron bar which kept him lying on his back, for he was too weak to carry it about. Spottiswoode obtained permission to use the torture of the boot, but though it was fitted to his leg, the complete process does not appear to have been carried out upon him. His misery was increased by a report, spread by his captors, to the effect that he had betrayed the names of his friends.

When it was found that neither the threat of " the boot " nor yet promises of the king's favour if he would give way could obtain from the prisoner the betrayal of the unknown Catholics of Scotland, it was determined to deprive him of sleep and thus weaken his power of resistance. For eight days and nights he was kept from sleep by being prodded with sharp-pointed stakes, by being dragged from his couch, by shouts in his ears, by having his hair torn and by being flung upon the floor. Only because the doctors declared that another three hours would prove fatal was he allowed a day and a night's rest before being brought up for his second examination, which took place in Edinburgh before the lords commissioners appointed by the king's missives for his examination and trial. The charge against him was now completely changed. Ogilvie, the authorities declared, had been guilty of high treason in refusing to acknowledge the king's jurisdiction in spiritual matters ; but actually the whole object of the privy council was, not to convict him of saying Mass, or even to condemn him for asserting the papal jurisdiction in Scotland, but to discover, through him, what Scotsmen would be prepared to welcome a return to the Catholic faith. While he lay in prison, the authorities had encouraged people to visit him and had spread rumours that he had betrayed his friends, for they hoped that these, when arrested, would betray themselves and others. All the tortures he underwent were directed to the same end, and only when foiled in all their efforts to obtain from him the desired information did they press the question of the power of the pope to depose a monarch. To this—which was a moot point among the theologians of the day—the prisoner consistently replied that he would answer that question to the pope alone.

After the second trial, Ogilvie was taken back to Glasgow, where he seems to have been, at first, kindly treated. The report of his heroism in prison had gone through the length and breadth of Scotland, and even his keepers, including the archbishop, desired nothing so much as that he should recant and accept the royal supremacy. Soon, however, there came for the prisoner a questionnaire drawn up by no less a person that King James himself. To these five questions, which dealt entirely with the relations between church and state, he could only return answers which practically sealed his fate. His treatment in prison grew more rigorous. Nevertheless he still continued to write, in Latin, an account of his arrest and subsequent treatment and managed to transmit the pages through the crack between the door and the floor to persons who were passing outside—ostensibly on their way to visit other prisoners.

Though the gallows had been erected in readiness, there was still the show of a trial to be gone through. For the last time Father Ogilvie appeared before his judges. He was told that he was being tried, not for saying Mass, but for the answers he had given to the king's questions. In the face of the archbishop's offers of his patronage if he would retract his replies to the questionnaire he boldly declared, " In all that concerns the king, I will be slavishly obedient ; if any attack his temporal power, I will shed my last drop of blood for him. But in the things of spiritual jurisdiction which a king unjustly seizes I cannot and must not obey."

He was accordingly condemned for high treason and sentenced to a traitor's death. His friend John Browne, who attended him to the end and heard his last words, asserted that even on the scaffold he was offered his freedom and a fat living if he would abjure his religion—a sure proof, if further proof were needed, that his offence was his faith and not his politics. As the ladder was removed and his body swung in the air, the crowd groaned and anathematized the cruelty and injustice of those who had done the martyr to death. The cause of John Ogilvie was not included in that of the English martyrs, but he was beatified separately, December 22, 1929 ; his feast is kept in Scotland and by the Society of Jesus.

See W. E. Brown, *John Ogilvie* (1925), which includes a translation of documents from the process of beatification ; James Forbes, *Jean Ogilvie, Écossais, Jésuite ;* G. Antonelli, *Il b. Giovanni Ogilvie* (1929), with some attractive illustrations.

11 : ST CONSTANTINE, Martyr (Sixth Century)

ACCORDING to the lessons in the Aberdeen Breviary the early career of King Constantine of Cornwall gave no promise of the holiness to which he afterwards attained ; but after the death of his wife, daughter of the king of Brittany, he was so grief-stricken that he resolved to mend his ways and gave up his kingdom to his son. Concealing his rank and identity, he found his way to Ireland, where he entered the monastery of St Mochuda at Rahan. There he served for seven years, performing the most menial offices and carrying sacks of corn to and from the mill. According to the legend, he was finally identified by a monk who happened to be in the granary one day and overheard him laughing over his work and saying to himself : " Is this indeed King Constantine of Cornwall who formerly wore a helmet and breastplate and who now drudges at a handmill ? " He learnt letters, was raised to the priesthood, and was sent to Scotland, where he was associated first with St Columba and then with St Kentigern. He is said to have preached the faith in Galloway and then to have become abbot of a monastery at Govan. As an old man Constantine went on a mission into Kintyre, but was attacked by pirates, who cut off his right arm. Calling his followers he gave them his blessing, and slowly bled to death. Scotland regarded him as her first martyr, and his feast is still observed in the diocese of Argyll and the Isles.

Cornwall, Wales and Ireland also had traditions of a Cornish king named Constantine who became a monk, but no confidence can be placed in their often contradictory details ; nor is there any good reason to suppose that Constantine of Cornwall was identical with Gildas's " tyrannical Whelp of the unclean Lioness of Domnonia ".

The principal source is the Aberdeen Breviary and Martyrology. The Bollandists (*Acta Sanctorum*, March, vol. ii) seem to have adopted in the main the conclusions of Colgan in his *Acta Sanctorum Hiberniae*. See KSS., pp. 311–314, and especially Canon Doble's excellent summary, *St Constantine* (1930), no. 26 in his Cornish Saints series. The annals of Tigernach (so-called) enter under the date 588 " Conversio Constantini ad Dominum " ; the Annals of Ulster, however, record it in 587, and the *Annales Cambriae* give it under 589.

ST SOPHRONIUS, Patriarch of Jerusalem   (*c.* A.D. 638)

St Sophronius was born in Damascus.   Although threatened at one time with blindness through over-study, he eventually became so great an adept in Greek philosophy that he was surnamed "the Sophist".   Falling under the influence of the celebrated hermit John Moschus, he joined forces with him, and they travelled widely in Syria, in Asia Minor and in Egypt, where he appears to have taken a monk's habit about the year 580.   The two friends lived together for some years in the laura of St Sabas and at the monastery of St Theodosius near Jerusalem. Ever eager to advance in the practice of asceticism they visited the monasteries and many famous solitaries in Egypt and then went on to Alexandria, where St John the Almsgiver, the patriarch, detained them for two years to assist him in reforming his diocese and opposing heresy.   It was in that city that John Moschus wrote his *Spiritual Meadow*, which he dedicated to Sophronius.   About 620 Moschus died in Rome, where they had gone on pilgrimage, and Sophronius eventually returned to Palestine, where his piety, learning and orthodoxy led to his being elected patriarch of Jerusalem.

No sooner was he established in his see than he assembled all the bishops of his patriarchate to condemn monothelite teaching, and composed a synodal letter to explain and state the Catholic doctrine on the subject contested.   This letter, which was afterwards confirmed in the sixth general council, was sent by St Sophronius to Pope Honorius and to Sergius, Patriarch of Constantinople, who had persuaded Honorius to write evasively on this question as to one or two wills in Christ.   It seems evident that Honorius never professed to pronounce upon the matter in dispute, but his silence was ill-timed, as it gave the appearance of conniving at heresy.   Sophronius, seeing that the emperor and many Eastern prelates were fighting against the truth, felt that it was his duty to defend it with greater zeal than ever.   He took his suffragan Stephen, Bishop of Dor, to Mount Calvary, and there adjured him by Christ who was crucified on that spot, and by the account he would have to render at the last day, "to go to the Apostolic See, where are the foundations of holy doctrine, and not to cease to pray till those in authority there should examine and condemn the novelty".   Stephen obeyed and remained in Rome for ten years, until he saw the heresy condemned by Pope St Martin I at the Council of the Lateran in 649.

Sophronius soon had other troubles to contend with.   The Saracens had invaded Syria and Palestine, taking Damascus in 636 and Jerusalem in 638.   During that time he had done all he could to help and strengthen his flock, sometimes at the peril of his life.   He preached to them a most pathetic Christmas sermon when the Mohammedans were beleaguering the city and the faithful could not go out to keep the festival at Bethlehem according to custom.   After the town fell, St Sophronius fled, and is thought to have died of grief soon afterwards, perhaps in Alexandria. Besides the synodal letter, St Sophronius wrote biographies and homilies, as well as hymns and anacreontic odes of considerable merit.   The Life of John the Almsgiver, which he compiled in collaboration with John Moschus, has not come down to us, and another large work, in which he cited 600 passages from the fathers in support of the doctrine of Christ's twofold will, has likewise perished.

The identity of Sophronius "the Sophist" with Sophronius the patriarch of Jerusalem has been called in question   see S. Vailhé in the *Revue de l'orient chrétien*, vols. vii and viii

(1902–1903). We have no direct evidence that the patriarch was associated with John Moschus. It has, however, been generally assumed that " the Sophist " who travelled with Moschus is the man who was afterwards patriarch ; so *e.g.* by the Bollandists (*Acta Sanctorum.* March, vol. ii). *Cf.* Bardenhewer, *Patrology* (Eng. trans.), pp. 559–561 and 564–565 ; and DCB., vol. iv, pp. 719–721.

ST VINDICIAN, Bishop of Cambrai   (A.D. 712)

BULLECOURT near Bapaume was the birthplace of St Vindician who, upon the death of St Aubert about 669, was elected to succeed him as bishop of Cambrai. We are told that he visited all the parishes in his diocese and converted many sinners. He translated the body of St Maxellendis, who had been murdered by Harduin, a nobleman whom she had refused to marry. A great sensation was caused on that occasion by the sudden cure of blindness and conversion of the murderer. At Caudry, where the relics were deposited, Vindician settled an establishment of pious women to serve God and to watch over them. Monasteries sprang up plentifully under his fostering care, and we find him soon afterwards consecrating the chapels of two more new convents and assisting, when invited by St Amand, at the consecration of the church of the monastery of Elnone.

Upon his return to his own diocese, St Vindician found that it had become the scene of a terrible tragedy. St Leger (Leodegar), Bishop of Autun, had incurred the displeasure of the savage Ebroin, mayor of the palace, who had blinded him, mutilated his face and had him beheaded in the forest of Sarcy in Artois. The horror-stricken bishops held a consultation as to what should be done. Tradition says that they decided to send Vindician as their spokesman to King Thierry to make a solemn protest. It was an embassy fraught with danger, but he accepted it and succeeded in gaining access to the king. Vindician came straight to the point. It was the duty of a bishop, he said, to reprove those who have fallen from grace lest they perish in their sin and the bishop with them. He went on to call upon the king to listen to a solemn expostulation in regard of the murder of St Leger which had been perpetrated with his connivance. It was a crime so great that the assembled bishops hardly knew what atonement could be made for such an outrage. The king must humbly seek reconciliation with God, acknowledging his fault and saying with the patriarch Job, " I have not concealed my fault, but have confessed it in the presence of all the people "

King Thierry declared that he recognized his offence and would try to make amends. The monastery of Arras—since called Saint-Vaast—became the special recipient of his bounty as being near the place where St Leger had died. That monastery, which had been begun by St Aubert on the spot where St Vaast used to retire for prayer and contemplation, had become for St Vindician the object of his particular solicitude. Carrying out the intentions of his predecessor, he was anxious to establish at Arras a community of men eager for the sanctification of souls. With that end in view he spared neither pains nor expense, and has consequently always been considered the primary benefactor of the abbey. He attempted to obtain for Arras the body of St Leger, but after some contention it was given to Poitiers. We find the holy bishop concerned in one more consecration, when he dedicated the church of the abbey of Hamage. No special events mark the rest of his life. He continued to rule over his diocese, and in his old age would often retire to Mont-Saint-Eloi or to Saint-Vaast to renew his fervour. He had reached his eightieth year when he was seized with the fever which proved fatal. He was on a visit to Brussels, but his body at his own request was buried on Mont-Saint-Eloi.

There is no early biography of St Vindician, and it is to be feared that some of the details incorporated in the account of him furnished by the Bollandists (*Acta Sanctorum*, March, vol. ii) and by the Abbé Destombes (*Vies des Saints des diocèses de Cambrai et Arras*, vol. i, pp. 320–335) are based upon a forgery. See the article of A. Poncelet, *Analecta Bollandiana*, vol. xxvii, pp. 384–390. But there can be no question as to the important part played by this saint in the ecclesiastical history of the Low Countries in the seventh century: Van der Essen, *Saints Mérovingiens*, pp. 276–277.

ST BENEDICT, ARCHBISHOP OF MILAN   (A.D. 725)

VERY little is known about St Benedict Crispus. After he became archbishop of Milan he had a great lawsuit at Rome, being what Ughelli describes as " a very earnest defender " of his episcopal rights : but he lost his case. He has an interest for English people as he composed the epitaph for the tomb in St Peter's of the young Anglo-Saxon prince Caedwalla (April 20). Benedict is named in the Roman Martyrology.

See the *Acta Sanctorum*, March, vol. ii.

ST OENGUS, ABBOT-BISHOP   (*c.* A.D. 824)

ST OENGUS (or Aengus) sometimes called " the Hagiographer ", is better known as " the Culdee " or " God's Vassal "—a Celtic title which came to be applied to those who practised a particularly rigid observance, especially in the order of divine service, but which was attached specially to him as to one who made an important contribution to the devotional literature of the Church and who lived according to the strictest rule of religion. He came of royal race in Ulster, and was born about the middle of the eighth century. In early youth he entered the famous monastery of Clonenagh in Leix, which, under its saintly abbot Maelaithgen, then enjoyed a great reputation for learning, for sanctity and for its numbers. Here he made rapid advance until he had reached a point at which it could be said of him that no one in his time could be found in Ireland to equal him in virtue and in sacred knowledge. To shun the world more entirely he retired to a cell at Dysartenos some seven miles from the monastery, where he hoped to continue unnoticed the austerities he practised. Besides making three hundred genuflexions, it was his custom to recite the whole Psalter daily, dividing it into three parts, one of which he recited in his cell, another under a spreading tree, and the third whilst he stood tied by the neck to a stake, with his body partially immersed in a tub of cold water. His fame soon attracted too many visitors, and he departed secretly from his hermitage.

At the church of Coolbanagher, Oengus had a vision of angels who seemed to surround a particular tomb, singing hymns of celestial sweetness. Inquiry from the local priest elicited the fact that the tomb was that of a poor old man who formerly lived at the place. " What good did he do ? " asked Oengus. " I saw no particular good done by him ", replied the priest, " but that his customary practice was to recount and invoke the saints of the world, as far as he could remember them, both at his going to bed and his getting up, in accordance with the custom of the old devotees."—" Indeed ", said Oengus, " he who would make a poetical composition in praise of the saints should doubtless have a high

reward, when so much has been vouchsafed to the efforts of this holy devotee."
From this moment his metrical hymn in honour of the saints began to shape itself
in Oengus's mind, although he did not immediately put it into words, fearing
that he was unworthy and that his verses might not be dignified enough for so
lofty a subject.

Continuing his journey, he finally reached the great monastery of Tallaght near
Dublin, and asked to be received as a serving-man—concealing his name and
scholarship. He was accepted by the abbot, St Maelruain, and for seven years he
was given the meanest and most laborious offices, but he was well satisfied because
he found plenty of time to raise his heart and thoughts to Heaven. His identity,
however, was discovered in a singular way. One day as he was working in the
monastery barn a scholar, who did not know his lesson and was therefore playing
truant, took shelter in the granary and asked to be allowed to stay. Oengus took
the little fellow in his arms and lulled him to sleep. When he awoke he had
learnt his lesson perfectly. That, at least, was what he told the abbot, who cross-
questioned him after hearing him repeat his lesson with unprecedented fluency and
intelligence. Whether Maelruain thought that a miracle had been performed, or
whether he realized that the humble serving-man was a teacher of exceptional
ability, he ran out to the barn and embraced St Oengus with tender affection,
divining or eliciting that he was the missing Oengus of Dysartenos. Blamed for
the misplaced humility which had deprived the community of the benefit of his
learning and experience, he fell on his knees and begged the abbot's pardon. From
that moment the two saints became the closest of friends, and St Oengus, freed
from menial work, set about composing the metrical hymn known in the Irish
language as the *Félire* and in Latin as the *Festilogium*, although it does not appear
to have been circulated until after the death of St Maelruain in 787, for the name
of that abbot is included and he is called the " Bright Sun of Ireland ". As he
meant to imitate the practice of the old man who was buried at Coolbanagher,
Oengus could hardly be expected, consistently with the recital of the whole Psalter
and his other devotions, to do more than invoke the principal saints in this metrical
hymn, the repetition of which he is said to have added to his daily exercises. He
remained on for some years at Tallaght, but after the death of St Maelruain
he turned his steps back to Clonenagh, where he had spent his youth. Here
he appears to have been made abbot in succession to Maelaithgen, and to have
been raised to episcopal dignity in accordance with the practice prevalent in
Ireland at the time of making the superiors of religious houses bishops without a
definite see.

As he felt his end approaching, he withdrew to Dysartbeagh and there finished
his Félire and perhaps composed some of his other works now lost, but whether
he built a monastery in that place or whether he had a hermitage whilst continuing
to guide a religious community elsewhere is uncertain. The exact date of his death
is contested, but it is not thought that he lived to a great age. As he is said to have
died on a Friday we may choose between 819, 824, and 830, in each of which years
March 11, which is certainly his day, fell on a Friday.

The Life of St Oengus printed by the Bollandists in the *Acta Sanctorum* (March, vol. ii)
is taken from Colgan. There seems to be no early biography in either Latin or Irish, and
the saint is not commemorated liturgically in any Irish diocese. Some useful illustrative
material has been collected by Whitley Stokes in the edition of the *Félire* which he edited
for the Henry Bradshaw Society. See also Abp J. Healy, *Ireland's Ancient Schools and*

Scholars, pp. 404–413 ; J. O'Hanlon in the *Irish Ecclesiastical Record* for 1869, as also in his LIS. ; and L. Gougaud, *Christianity in Celtic Lands* (1932).

ST EULOGIUS OF CORDOVA, Martyr   (A.D. 859)

St Eulogius has been described as the principal glory of the Spanish church in the ninth century.   The descendant of a stock which had owned land in Cordova since the Roman occupation, he was one of a family of four brothers and two sisters. Cordova was then in the hands of the Moors, who had made it their capital, and Christianity, although to a certain extent tolerated, was hampered by vexatious restrictions : public worship was allowed on payment of a monthly tax, but Christians were forbidden under pain of death to make converts.   At the same time many of them held high office under their conquerors, and the saint's youngest brother Joseph was an important official in the court of Abdur Rahman II.

Eulogius received his early education from the priests of Saint Zoïlus, and when he had learnt all they could teach him he placed himself under the illustrious writer and abbot Sperandeo.   Here he had as fellow pupil Paul Alvarez, and they contracted a lifelong friendship, Alvarez afterwards becoming his biographer.   Their studies completed, Eulogius was raised to the priesthood, whilst his friend married and took up a literary career.   The two carried on a voluminous correspondence, but agreed to destroy their letters as being too effusive and lacking in polish.   In his Life of St Eulogius, Alvarez gives a delightful description of his friend, whom he represents as pious, mortified, learned in all branches of knowledge, but especially in the Holy Scriptures, of an open countenance, so humble that he often deferred to the opinions of those whose judgement was greatly inferior to his own, and so kindly that he won the love of all who had dealings with him.   Visiting hospitals and monasteries was his recreation, and he was in such high esteem that he was asked by the monks to draw up new rules for them.   To do this he not only went to stay in Spanish houses, but also visited monasteries in Navarre and Pamplona, comparing their regulations and selecting what was best in each code.

In 850 the Moors started a sudden persecution of Christians in Cordova, either because certain Christians were indiscreet in inveighing openly against Mohammed, or else because they had attempted the conversion of some of the Moors.   Matters were made worse for the faithful when an Andalusian bishop called Reccared, instead of defending the flock of Christ, opened the door of the fold to the fury of the wolves.   Why he should have turned against his own clergy is not clear : probably he was a " moderate " man and preferred peace and toleration to missionary zeal and persecution.   Whatever the reason, it was he who was responsible for the arrest of the priests of Cordova and of their bishop.   They were shut up in prison and Eulogius, who was of their number, occupied himself in reading the Bible to the rest and in encouraging them to remain faithful to God.   From his dungeon he wrote his Exhortation to Martyrdom, addressed to two maidens, Flora and Mary.   " They threaten to sell you as slaves and dishonour you ", he said, " but be assured that they cannot injure the purity of your souls, whatever infamy they may inflict upon you.   Cowardly Christians will tell you in order to shake your constancy that the churches are silent, deserted and deprived of the sacrifice on account of your obstinacy : that if you will but yield temporarily you will regain the free exercise of your religion.   But be persuaded that, for you, the sacrifice most pleasing to God is contrition of heart, and that you can no longer draw back or renounce the truth you have confessed." The girls were spared the threatened humiliation and were executed with the sword, declaring with their dying breath that as soon as they should find themselves in the presence of Jesus Christ they would ask for the release of their brethren. Six days after their death the prisoners were set free, and Eulogius immediately composed a metrical account of the passion of the martyrs in order to induce others to follow in their footsteps. His brother Joseph was deprived of his office at court and he himself was compelled to live from thenceforth with the traitor Reccared, but he continued to instruct and confirm the faithful both by his voice and by his pen.

In 852 several others suffered martyrdom, and that same year the Council of Cordova forbade anyone to provoke arrest of set purpose. As the persecution waxed hotter under Abdur Rahman's son and successor the zeal of Eulogius only increased, and he kept numerous weak Christians from falling away, besides encouraging others to martyrdom. In the three volumes which he entitled *The Memorial of the Saints* he described the sufferings and death of all who perished in that persecution. He also wrote an *Apologia*, directed against those who denied to these victims the character of true martyrs on the grounds that they had wrought no miracles, that they had sought death instead of awaiting it, that they had perished at one blow without previous torture, and that they had been killed, not by idolaters, but by men who acknowledged the one true God. In defending these he was also defending himself, because he had approved and encouraged their action.

After the death of the archbishop of Toledo, the clergy and people cast their eyes upon St Eulogius as the most prominent leader of the Church, but although he was canonically elected he did not live to be consecrated. For his activities he was a marked man and could not long escape the fate to which he had urged others. There was a young woman in Cordova called Leocritia who had been converted to Christianity by a relative and baptized, although her parents were Moslems. For a follower of Islam to become a Christian was punishable by death, and the girl's parents discovering her change of faith beat her and treated her cruelly in order to induce her to apostatize. She made her sufferings known to St Eulogius, who with the help of his sister Anulona assisted her to escape and concealed her amongst faithful friends. Her place of hiding, however, was discovered, and she and all those concerned in her escape were brought before the kadi. Eulogius, undaunted, offered to show the judge the true road to heaven, and declared that the prophet Mohammed was an impostor. The kadi threatened to have him scourged to death. The martyr replied that it would be to no purpose as he would never change his religion. The kadi then gave orders that he should be taken before the king's council. There one of the council led him aside and said, " Although ignorant people rush headlong to their death, a man of your learning and standing ought not to imitate their folly. Be guided by me. Say but one word—since necessity requires it : afterwards you may resume your own religion and we will promise that no inquiry shall be made." Eulogius replied with a smile, " If you could but conceive the reward which awaits those who persevere in the faith until the end, you would resign your dignities in exchange for it ! " He then began boldly to proclaim the gospel to them, but the council, to avoid listening, promptly sentenced him to death. As he was being led away, one of the servants struck him on the face for having spoken against Mohammed : he at once turned the other cheek and meekly received a second blow. He was led out of the city to the place of execution,

and with great composure allowed himself to be decapitated.   St Leocritia suffered
four days later.

As stated above, for our knowledge of the history of St Eulogius we are almost entirely
dependent upon the short Latin biography of his friend Alvarez or Alvarus.   This has
been printed in the *Acta Sanctorum*, March, vol. ii, and also in Migne, PL., vol. cxv, cc.
705–720, and other collections.   See further Gams, *Kirchengeschichte von Spanien*, vol. ii,
pp. 299–338, and the article "Eulogius" in the *Kirchenlexikon*.   *Cf.* Dozy, *Histoire
des Musulmans d'Espagne*, vol. ii, pp. 1–174, and W. von Baudissin, *Eulogius und Alvar*
(1872).   There is a popular account tr. into English, J. Perez de Urbel, *A Saint under
Moslem Rule* (1937).

ST AUREA, Virgin   (*c.* A.D. 1100)

When Spain lay under the Moorish yoke it became the custom for those Christians
who desired to live the religious life to build their monasteries in desolate mountain
fastnesses where their conquerors seldom troubled to molest them.   One of these
was San Millán de la Cogolla above the Upper Ebro in the diocese of Calahorra.
It was primarily a Benedictine abbey for men but, as was not unusual at the time,
there was a settlement for women a short distance away, and these women were
under the direction of the abbot of La Cogolla.   Down below, in the village of
Villavelayo, lived a couple, Garcia Nunno, or Nunnio, and Amunia his wife, with
their daughter Aurea.   Constant study of the Holy Scriptures and meditation on
the lives of St Agatha, St Eulalia and St Cecilia determined her to devote herself
to God in the religious life, and she sought admittance to the convent of San Millán.
Receiving the habit she lived a life of complete abnegation as a solitary.   Aurea
was rewarded by a vision of her three patron saints who assured her of God's
approval and promised her a crown of glory ; the fame of her penances and miracles
spread, and her assistance and intercession were eagerly sought.   She became the
victim of a painful disease, dying in her mother's arms, in the presence of the monk
who wrote her life.   Her mother, who did not long survive her, was buried by her
side.

The evidence is not very satisfactory.   Mabillon in the *Annales* says nothing of St Aurea ;
but a summary account is in the Bollandist *Acta Sanctorum*, March, vol. ii.

BD CHRISTOPHER MACASSOLI   (A.D. 1485)

This Bd Christopher of Milan must not be confused with a Dominican of the same
name and place who is commemorated on March 1.   Christopher Macassoli
entered the Franciscan Order at an early age.   Love of poverty, great purity of
heart and complete trust in God were his distinguishing characteristics.   As
a priest he converted many by his preaching and example.   At Vigevano he
helped to enlarge the friary in which he lived, and thousands of people flocked
to receive his counsel and to ask his intercession with God.   He died in 1485
and Pope Leo XIII in 1890 confirmed the local *cultus* which had been unbroken
since his death.   We are told that the little chapel of St Bernardino at Vigevano,
where his remains repose in a tomb built into the wall, is covered with votive
offerings made by the faithful in acknowledgment of miraculous answers to
prayer.

See Mark of Lisbon, *Croniche dei Minori* (Italian adaptation by B. Barezzi), vol. iv,
251–252.

BD JOHN BAPTIST OF FABRIANO (A.D. 1539)

THE life led by John Baptist Righi of Fabriano is much extolled in the chronicles of the Order of Friars Minor. He was a priest, but though said to be a man of great natural ability he would never, out of humility, acquire more learning than was needful for ordination. The rigour of his fasts recalled the asceticism of the fathers of the desert. He often passed the entire week from Sunday to Sunday without taking food, and during the long Lent which he kept from the Epiphany until Easter day he never ate except on Sundays and Thursdays. After the termination of the night office, instead of retiring to his cell to rest, he used to remain praying in the church, and on one occasion was discovered there by the sacristan rapt in ecstasy, while diffusing around him a heavenly perfume which had attracted the intruder to the corner in which John Baptist had hidden himself. He was a little man and very frail, but he would not consent to protect himself from the cold by using any more clothing than his single patched habit. He wore himself out rendering services to others, for though he was most earnest in insisting that the rule should be observed with strict fidelity, he spared no pains to secure for his brethren, and especially for the sick, such alleviations as they really needed. After his death at the friary of Massaccio in 1539 miracles were reported to have been worked at his tomb, and a considerable *cultus* followed, which was confirmed in 1903.

See Ciro da Pesaro, *Vita e culto del B. Giovanni Righi* (1904) ; the author has made use of a short biography written about sixty years after Father John's death. *Cf.* also Mark of Lisbon, *Croniche dei Minori*, vol. iii, pp. 602-603.

BB. JOHN LARKE, JERMYN GARDINER AND JOHN IRELAND, MARTYRS (A.D. 1544)

JOHN LARKE is sometimes erroneously described as having been Sir Thomas More's chaplain, whereas he was actually rector of Chelsea, the church which Sir Thomas habitually attended when in London, his town house being situated in that parish. We have no details concerning Larke's parentage, birth or upbringing, but it is conjectured that he must have been an old man when he suffered martyrdom. In 1504 he had been appointed rector of St Ethelburga, Bishopsgate, the incumbency of which he continued to hold until shortly before his death.* In 1526 he became rector of Woodford in Essex, but he resigned the living four years later when he was nominated to Chelsea by Sir Thomas More, who as lord chancellor held the right of appointment from the abbey of Westminster. He seems to have had the greatest veneration for his patron, and Cresacre More in his life of Sir Thomas says that " his death so wrought on the mind of Dr Larke, his own parish priest, that he, following the example of his own sheep, afterwards suffered a most famous martyrdom in the same cause of supremacy ". The title of " doctor " appears to have been one of courtesy only. Though he never took the oath or sacrificed his principles to preserve his life and benefices, Larke does not appear to have been molested until 1544, when he was arrested and charged with treason, together with a secular priest named John Ireland, of whom little is known, and a young man called German or Jermyn Gardiner, a secretary and probably a relation of Stephen

* A remarkable painting of Larke may be seen in this interesting church, one of the few in the City to be spared by the great fire of 1666.

Gardiner, Bishop of Winchester. German was a zealous Catholic who, though sometimes spoken of as a priest, was almost certainly a layman.

The trial of Larke, Ireland and Gardiner took place at Westminster on February 15, 1544, and the record in the state papers contains the following statement :

> The Jury say upon their oath that John Heywood, late of London, gentleman, John Ireland, late of Eltham in the county of Kent, clerk, John Larke, late of Chelsea in the county of Middlesex, clerk, and German Gardiner, late of Southwark in the county of Surrey, gentleman, not weighing the duties of their allegiance nor keeping God Almighty before their eyes, but seduced by the instigation of the devil, falsely, maliciously and traitorously [have acted] like false and wicked traitors against the most serene and Christian prince, our Lord Henry VIII, by the grace of God King of England, France and Ireland, Defender of the Faith, and upon earth Supreme Head of the English and Irish Church—choosing, wishing and desiring and cunningly machinating, inventing, practising and attempting—together with many other false traitors unknown, in confederacy with them to deprive our said King Henry VIII of his royal dignity, title and name of " Supreme Head of the English and Irish Church " which has been united and annexed to his imperial crown by the laws and proclamations of this his realm of England.

The prisoners were all condemned and sentenced to death, but John Heywood, whose name figures first in the report of the trial, recanted after he had been placed on the hurdle, and received the king's pardon. The rest remained steadfast and perished at Tyburn on March 7, 1544. The feast of John Larke in the diocese of Brentwood is assigned to this day.

See Camm, LEM., vol. i, pp. 541-547.

ST TERESA MARGARET REDI, Virgin   (A.D. 1770)

To the list of youthful saints who of late years have been honoured by the Church is now to be added the name of the Carmelite nun, Teresa-Margaret-of-the-Sacred Heart, canonized in 1934. Anne Mary Redi, as she was called in the world, belonged to Arezzo, but the greater part of her life was spent at Florence and within convent walls. Born in 1747, she was sent to Florence at the age of ten to be educated by the nuns of the community of St Apollonia. She remained with them for seven years, giving a most admirable example of obedience, modesty, prayerfulness, diligence and all the virtues appropriate to a child at school. Reclaimed by her parents when her education was completed, she remained for a few months at home, but received what seemed to her a supernatural admonition from St Teresa of Avila that she was called to the Carmelites. She accordingly entered the convent of St Teresa at Florence in 1765. She would have wished to enter as a lay-sister, but this was not allowed, and after a most edifying noviceship she took her vows as a choir-nun.

There is not much to chronicle in the retired life Teresa Margaret led in a cloistered order, but those who had known her during the five years she was spared to them spoke in glowing terms of her extraordinary fidelity to her Christian vocation. We have the actual words used by her fellow Carmelites when summoned to give evidence in the episcopal process instituted not long after her death in view of her beatification. She was especially devout to the Sacred Heart and marvellously charitable, putting to profit every opportunity which a cloistered life could afford of sacrificing herself for the benefit of others. Her prayers, penances and a practice of poverty far more rigid than the rule required probably shortened her life. Moreover, she was much employed in tending the sick of the community, maintaining an unclouded brightness and equanimity even when she herself was far more fit to be a patient than a nurse. After her death at the age of twenty-three her body lay exposed for fifteen days without a sign of decomposition, and it has remained incorrupt until the present time. The devotion paid to her, especially in the city of Florence, has been attended with many miracles.

The *summarium de virtutibus* printed for the process of beatification may be found in the library of the British Museum. See also Fr Lorenzo, *La b. Teresa Margherita* (1930); and Fr Stanislas, *Un angelo del Carmelo* (1930), of which there is an adapted English version by Mgr J. F. Newcomb, *St Theresa Margaret* . (1934). She is honoured liturgically among the Carmelites on March 11, though March 7 was the day of her death.

12 : ST GREGORY THE GREAT, Pope, Doctor of the Church
(A.D. 604)

POPE GREGORY I, most justly called "the Great", and the first pope who had been a monk, was elected to the apostolic chair when Italy was in a terrible condition after the struggle between the Ostrogoths and the Emperor Justinian, which ended with the defeat and death of Totila in 562. The state of Rome itself was deplorable : it had been sacked four times within a century and a half, and conquered four times in twenty years, but no one restored the damage done by pillage, fire and earthquake. St Gregory, writing about 593, says : " We see what has become of her who once appeared the mistress of the world. She is broken by all she has suffered from immense and manifold misfortunes. Ruins upon ruins everywhere ! Where is the senate ? Where are the people ? . We, the few who are left, are menaced every day by the sword and innumerable trials. . Deserted Rome is in flames : her buildings also."

The saint's family, one of the few patrician families left in the city, was distinguished also for its piety, having given to the Church two popes, Agapitus I and Felix III, Gregory's great-great-grandfather. Little is known of Gordian, Gregory's father, except that he was a *regionarius*—whatever that might be—and that he owned large estates in Sicily as well as a house on the Coelian Hill ; his wife Silvia is named as a saint in the Roman Martyrology. Gregory appears to have received the best education obtainable at that time in Rome, and to have taken up the career of a public official. In 568 a fresh calamity fell upon Italy in the form of the first Lombard invasion, and three years later the barbarian horde came alarmingly near Rome. At that time of panic Gregory probably showed something of the wisdom and energy which distinguished him later, for at the age of about thirty we find him exercising the highest civil office in Rome—that of prefect of the city. In that capacity he gained the respect and esteem of the Romans and developed an appreciation of order in the administration of affairs which he retained throughout his life. Faithfully and honourably though Gregory fulfilled his duties, he had long been feeling the call to a higher vocation, and at length he resolved to retire from the world and to devote himself to the service of God alone. He was one of the richest men in Rome, but he gave up all, retiring into his own house on the Clivus Scauri, which he turned into a monastery and which he placed under the patronage of St Andrew and in the charge of a monk called Valentius, of whom Gregory writes that he was " the superior of my monastery and of myself ". The few years the saint spent in this seclusion were the happiest of his life—although his excessive fasting brought on gastric troubles and sowed the seeds of the painful infirmity which tormented him for the rest of his life.

It was not likely that a man of St Gregory's talents and prestige would be left long in obscurity at such a time, and we find him ordained seventh deacon of the Roman church, and then sent as papal *apocrisiarius* or ambassador at the Byzantine court. The contrast between the magnificence of Constantinople and the miserable condition of Rome could not fail to impress the saint, but he found the etiquette of the court wearisome and the intrigues revolting. He had the great disadvantage of knowing no Greek, and more and more he lived a monastic life with several of the monks of St Andrew's who had accompanied him. In Constantinople he met St Leander, Bishop of Seville, with whom he formed a lifelong friendship, and at whose request he began a commentary on the Book of Job which he afterwards finished at Rome and which is generally known as his *Moralia*. Most of the dates in St Gregory's life are uncertain, but it was probably about the beginning of the year 586 that he was recalled to Rome by Pelagius II. He immediately settled down again, deacon of Rome though he was, in his monastery of St Andrew, of which he soon became abbot ; and it seems that it is to this period we must refer the celebrated story told by the Venerable Bede on the strength of an old English tradition.

St Gregory, it appears, was one day walking through the market when he noticed three golden-haired, fair-complexioned boys exposed for sale and inquired their nationality. " They are Angles or Angli ", was the reply. " They are well named," said the saint, " for they have angelic faces and it becomes such to be companions with the angels in heaven." Learning that they were pagans, he asked what province they came from. " Deira."—" De ira ! " exclaimed St Gregory. " Yes, verily they shall be saved from God's ire and called to the mercy of Christ. What is the name of the king of that country ? "—" Aella."—" Then must Alleluia be sung in Aella's land." So greatly was he impressed by their beauty and by pity for their ignorance of Christ that he resolved to preach the gospel himself in Britain, and started off with several of his monks. However, when the people of Rome heard of their departure they raised such an outcry that Pope Pelagius sent envoys to recall them to Rome.

The whole episode has been declared apocryphal by modern historians on the ground of the flimsiness of the evidence. They also point out that Gregory never alludes to the incident, and moreover that even in his most informal writings he never indulges in puns. On the other hand, the first part of the story—the scene in the market-place—may easily be true : men sometimes pun in familiar conversation who would abstain from the practice when writing. Also it might plausibly be urged that St Gregory's admiration for the fair complexion and hair of the English lads, while natural enough in an Italian, is not the sort of trait which it would have occurred to a northern scribe to invent ; while finally there can be no dispute that Gregory later on was deeply interested in St Augustine's mission, however it came about.

The trental of Masses or Gregorian Masses for the Dead are also connected in origin with this period. Justus, one of his monks, being ill, acknowledged to having three golden crowns hidden away, and the abbot sternly forbade the brethren to have any communication with him or to visit him on his death-bed.   Upon his death he was excluded from the monks' burial ground and was interred under a dunghill, the pieces of gold being buried with him.   Nevertheless, as he died penitent, the abbot ordered that Mass should be offered for thirty days for the repose of his soul, and we have St Gregory's own testimony that at the close of that time the dead man's soul appeared to Copiosus, his natural brother, assuring him that he had been in torments but was now released.

A terrible inundation of the Tiber was followed by another and an exceptionally severe outbreak of the plague : Rome was again decimated, and in January 590 Pelagius died of the dread disease.   The people unanimously chose Gregory as the new pope, and to obtain by penitence the cessation of the plague he ordered a great processional litany through the streets of Rome.   From seven churches in the city proceeded seven columns of people, who met at St Mary Major.   St Gregory of Tours, after the report of one who was present, describes it : " The procession ordered for Wednesday took place on three successive days : the columns proceeded through the streets chanting ' Kyrie eleison ' while the plague was still raging ; and as they walked people were seen falling and dying about them.   Gregory inspired these poor people with courage, for he did not cease preaching and wished that prayer should be made continually."   The faith of the people was rewarded by the speedy diminution and cessation of the plague, as we learn from contemporary writers, but no early historian mentions the appearance of the Archangel Michael sheathing his sword on the summit of Hadrian's mausoleum during the passing of the procession.   This legend, which subsequently gained great credence, accounts for the figure of the angel which now surmounts the ancient pile and for the name of Sant' Angelo which the castle has borne since the tenth century. Although St Gregory had thus been publicly devoting himself to the help of his fellow-citizens, his inclinations still lay in the direction of the contemplative life, and he had no intention of becoming pope if he could avoid it : he had written to the Emperor Maurice, begging him not to confirm the election ; but, as we are told by Gregory of Tours, " while he was preparing to run away and hide himself, he was seized and carried off to the basilica of St Peter, and there, having been conse- crated to the pontifical office, was given as pope to the city ".   This took place on September 3, 590.

A correspondence with John, Archbishop of Ravenna, who had modestly censured him for trying to avoid office, led to Gregory's writing the *Regula Pastor- alis*, a book on the office of a bishop.   In it he regards the bishop as first and foremost a physician of souls whose chief duties are preaching and the enforcement of discipline.   The work met with immediate success, and the Emperor Maurice had it translated into Greek by Anastasius, Patriarch of Antioch.   Later St Augus- tine took it to England, where 300 years later it was translated by King Alfred, and at the councils summoned by Charlemagne the study of the book was enjoined on all bishops, who were to have a copy delivered to them at their consecration.   For hundreds of years Gregory's ideals were those of the clergy of the West and "formed the bishops who have made modern nations ".   To the twofold duty of enforcing discipline and of preaching the pope set himself vigorously from the moment of his assuming office.   He promptly and publicly deposed the Archdeacon Laurence, the most important ecclesiastic in Rome, " on account of his pride and misde- meanours, about which we think it our duty to keep silence ", says an old chronicle ;

he appointed a *vice-dominus* to look after the secular affairs of the papal household, he enacted that only clerics should be attached to the service of the pope, he forbade the exaction of fees for burial in churches, for ordinations, or for the conferring of the pallium, and he prohibited deacons from conducting the sung part of the Mass lest they should be chosen for their voices rather than for their character.   In the matter of preaching, St Gregory was no less zealous   it was the great work he did for the churches of Rome.   He liked to preach during Mass and preferred to choose as his subject the gospel for the day.   We still possess a number of these homilies, which are popular and eloquent : they always end with a moral lesson which each one is to apply to himself.

In his instructions to his vicar in Sicily and to the overseers of his patrimony generally, Gregory constantly urged liberal treatment of his vassals and farmers and ordered that money should be advanced to those in difficulties.   He was indeed an ideal papal landlord ; his tenants were flourishing and content, and yet money flowed into the treasury.   After his death he was blamed for the empty coffers left to his successors, but his huge charities—which took almost the form of state relief —must have saved multitudes from starvation in that distressful period.   Large sums were spent in ransoming captives from the Lombards, and we find him commending the bishop of Fano for breaking up and selling church plate for that object and advising another prelate to do the same.   In view of a threatened corn shortage he filled the granaries of Rome, and a regular list was kept of the poor to whom grants were periodically made.   Cases of " decayed gentlewomen " seem to have received special consideration.   St Gregory's sense of justice showed itself also in his enlightened treatment of the Jews, whom he would not allow to be oppressed or deprived of their synagogues.   He declared that they must not be coerced but must be won by meekness and charity, and when the Jews of Cagliari in Sardinia complained that their synagogue had been seized by a converted Jew who had turned it into a church, he ordered the building to be restored to its former owners.

From the very outset of his pontificate the saint was called upon to face the aggressions of the Lombards, who from Pavia, Spoleto and Benevento made incursions into other parts of Italy.   No help was obtainable from Constantinople or from the exarch at Ravenna, and it fell upon Gregory, the one strong man, not only to organize the defences of Rome, but also to lend assistance to other cities. When in 593 Agilulf with a Lombard army appeared before the walls of Rome and general panic ensued, it was not the military or the civil prefect but the Vicar of Christ who went out to interview the Lombard king.   Quite as much by his personality and prestige as by the promise of an annual tribute Gregory induced him to withdraw his army and leave the city in peace.   For nine years he strove in vain to bring about a settlement between the Byzantine emperor and the Lombards ; Gregory then proceeded on his own account to negotiate a treaty with King Agilulf, obtaining a special truce for Rome and the surrounding districts.   Anticipating a few years we may add that Gregory's last days were cheered by news of the re-establishment of peace.

It must have been a relief to the saint to turn his thoughts sometimes from the busy world to his writings.   Towards the end of 593 he published his celebrated *Dialogues*—one of the most popular books of the middle ages.   It is a collection of tales of visions, prophecies and miracles gathered from oral tradition and designed to form a sort of picture of Italian efforts after holiness.   His stories were obtained from people still living who, in many cases, claimed to be eye-witnesses of the events recorded. St Gregory's methods were not critical, and the reader today must often feel misgivings as to the trustworthiness of his informants. Modern writers have wondered whether the *Dialogues* could have been the work of anyone so well balanced as St Gregory, but the evidence in favour of his authorship seems conclusive ; and we must remember that it was a credulous age and that anything unusual was at once put down to supernatural agency.

Of all his religious work in the West that which lay closest to Gregory's heart was the conversion of England, and the success which crowned his efforts in that direction was to him—as it necessarily is to Englishmen—the greatest triumph of his life. Whatever may be the truth of the Angles and Angels story, it seems most probable that the first move in regard to the sending of a mission came from England itself. This is the inference to be drawn from two letters of St Gregory still preserved. Writing to the French Kings Thierry and Theodebert he says : " News has reached us that the nation of the Angli greatly desires to be converted to the faith, but that the bishops in their vicinity pay no heed (to their pious wish) and refuse to second it by sending preachers." He writes to Brunhilda in almost exactly the same terms. The bishops alluded to are most probably the bishops of northern France—not the British (" Welsh ") or Scottish bishops. In this difficulty the pope's first action was to order the purchase of some English slaves, boys of about seventeen or eighteen, in order to educate them in a monastery for the service of God. Still, it was not to them that he intended primarily to entrust the work of conversion. From his own monastery of St Andrew he selected a band of forty missionaries whom he sent forth under the leadership of Augustine. It is not necessary to retell here the further history of that mission, already dealt with on May 26. Well may we say with the Venerable Bede : " If Gregory be not an apostle to others, he is one to us, for we are the seal of his apostleship in the Lord."

During nearly the whole of his pontificate St Gregory was engaged in conflicts with Constantinople—sometimes with the emperor, sometimes with the patriarch, occasionally with both. He protested constantly against the exactions of Byzantine officials whose pitiless extortions reduced the Italian country people to despair, and remonstrated with the emperor against an imperial edict which prohibited soldiers from becoming monks. With John the Faster, Patriarch of Constantinople, he had an acrimonious correspondence over the title of Oecumenical or Universal which that hierarch had assumed. It only meant the general or superior authority of one archbishop over many, but the use of the title Oecumenical Patriarch seemed to savour of arrogance, and Gregory resented it. For his own part, though one of the most strenuous upholders of the papal dignity, he preferred to call himself by the proudly humble title of *Servus servorum Dei*—Servant of the servants of God— a title still retained by his successors. In 602 the Emperor Maurice was dethroned by a military revolt under Phocas, who murdered the old emperor and his whole family in the most brutal fashion. The writing of a tardy but rather painfully diplomatic letter to this cruel usurper is the only act which has exposed the pope to hostile criticism. The letter consists mainly of hopes that peace is now assured ; in the interest of his defenceless people Gregory could not afford to launch denunciations.

Into the thirteen years of his pontificate Gregory had crowded the work of a lifetime. His deacon Peter declared that he never rested, and he certainly did not spare himself, though he suffered from chronic gastritis and was a martyr to gout. He became reduced almost to a skeleton, and the sands of life were running low, yet he dictated letters and looked after the affairs of the Church to the very end.

Almost his last action was to send a warm winter cloak to a poor bishop who suffered from the cold. Gregory was buried in St Peter's, and as the epitaph on his tomb expresses it, " after having conformed all his actions to his doctrines, the great consul of God went to enjoy eternal triumphs."

St Gregory has been credited with the compilation of the Antiphonary, the revision and rearrangement of the system of church music, the foundation of the famous Roman *schola cantorum*, and the composition of several well-known hymns. These claims have been contested, though he certainly had considerable effect on the Roman liturgy. But his true work lies in other directions. He is venerated as the fourth doctor of the Latin church, in which capacity he may be said to have popularized St Augustine and to have given clear expression to certain religious doctrines which had not previously been perfectly defined. For several centuries his was the last word on theology, though he was a popular preacher, catechist and moralist rather than a theologian. Perhaps his chief work was in strengthening the position of the Roman see. As the Anglican Milman writes in his *History of Latin Christianity* : " It is impossible to conceive what would have been the confusion, the lawlessness, the chaotic state of the middle ages without the medieval papacy ; and of the medieval papacy, the real father is Gregory the Great." Not without reason did the Church bestow upon him that seldom granted title of Magnus, " the Great ".

As stated above, King Alfred the Great had a translation made of St Gregory's *Regula Pastoralis*, and presented a copy to each of his bishops. This he equipped with both a preface and an epilogue written by himself, and he also prefixed some Anglo-Saxon verses, of which the following prose translation may give an idea :

> This message Augustine brought over the salt sea from the south to the islanders, as the pope of Rome, the Lord's champion, had formerly decreed it. The wise Gregory was versed in many true doctrines through the wisdom of his mind, his hoard of studious thoughts. For he gained over most of mankind to the guardian of Heaven [St Peter], he the best of Romans, wisest of men, most gloriously famous. Afterwards King Alfred translated every word of me into English and sent me to his scribes south and north ; ordered more such to be brought to him after the exemplar, that he might send them to his bishops, for some of them needed it who knew little Latin.

St Gregory's own letters and writings are the most reliable source of information for the history of his life, but in addition to these we have a short Latin biography by a monk of Whitby which probably dates from the early years of the eighth century, another by Paul the Deacon late in the same century, and a third by John the Deacon, between 872 and 882. We have also valuable notices in Gregory of Tours, Bede and other historians, and especially in the *Liber Pontificalis*. For the letters of St Gregory the edition of P. Ewald and L. M. Hartmann in MGH. should of course be consulted. A valuable modern life in brief compass is that of Mgr Batiffol in the series " Les Saints " (Eng. trans., 1929). See also the *Acta Sanctorum*, March, vol. ii ; Mann, *Lives of the Popes*, vol. i ; Snow, *Life of St Gregory the Great* ; Fliche and Martin, *Histoire de l'Eglise*, vol. v (1938) ; and amongst Anglican writers the very careful work of Dr J. H. Dudden, *St Gregory the Great* (1905) ; but the literature of the subject is, of course, vast. See the bibliographies in DAC. and DTC.

ST MAXIMILIAN, MARTYR   (A.D. 295)

THE *passio* of St Maximilian is one of that small collection of precious documents that is an authentic, contemporary and practically unembroidered account of the trial and death of an early martyr. It runs as follows :

In the consulate of Tuscus and Anulinus, on March 12, at Theveste in Numidia,* Fabius Victor was brought before the court, together with Maximilian. The public prosecutor, Pompeian, opened the case, and said, " Fabius Victor is here with Caesar's commissary, Valerian Quintian. I demand that Maximilian, son of Victor, a conscript suitable for service, be measured." The proconsul Dion asked the young man his name, and he answered, " What is the good of replying ? I cannot enlist, for I am a Christian " ; and added when the proconsul told the usher to take his height, " I cannot serve, I cannot do evil. I am a Christian." The proconsul repeated his order, and the usher reported that Maximilian measured five feet ten inches. Then the proconsul said he was to be given the military badge, but Maximilian persisted, " Never !—I cannot be a soldier."

DION : You must serve or die.

MAXIMILIAN : I will never serve. You can cut off my head, but I will not be a soldier of this world, for I am a soldier of Christ.†

DION : What has put these ideas into your head ?

MAXIMILIAN : My conscience and He who has called me.

DION (to Fabius Victor) : Put your son right.

VICTOR : He knows what he believes, and he will not change.

DION (to Maximilian) : Be a soldier and accept the emperor's badge.‡

MAXIMILIAN : Not at all. I carry the mark of Christ my God already.

DION : I shall send you to your Christ at once.

MAXIMILIAN : I ask nothing better. Do it quickly, for there is my glory.

DION (to the recruiting-officer) : Give him his badge.

MAXIMILIAN : I will not take the badge. If you insist, I will deface it. I am a Christian, and I am not allowed to wear that leaden seal round my neck. For I already carry the sacred sign of the Christ, the Son of the living God, whom you know not, the Christ who suffered for our salvation, whom God gave to die for our sins. It is He whom all we Christians serve, it is He whom we follow, for He is the Lord of life, the Author of our salvation.

DION : Join the service and accept the seal, or else you will perish miserably.

MAXIMILIAN : I shall not perish : my name is even now before God. I refuse to serve.

DION : You are a young man and the profession of arms befits your years. Be a soldier.

MAXIMILIAN : My army is the army of God, and I cannot fight for this world. I tell you, I am a Christian.

DION : There are Christian soldiers serving our rulers Diocletian and Maximian, Constantius and Galerius.

MAXIMILIAN : That is their business. I also am a Christian, and I cannot serve.

DION : But what harm do soldiers do ?

MAXIMILIAN : You know well enough.

DION : If you will not do your service I shall condemn you to death for contempt of the army.

---

* Now Tebessa in Algeria. It is suggested that this is a copyist's mistake, and that the martyrdom was really somewhere near Carthage. *Cf.* the penultimate paragraph.

† It was this insistence of the early Christians on being soldiers of Christ that gave us our word " pagan " : *paganus* = a civilian. *Cf. Shorter Oxford Dictionary*, edition of 1936.

‡ A leaden seal (*bulla*), worn round the neck. *Cf.* the modern identity disc.

MAXIMILIAN : I shall not die.   If I go from this earth my soul will live with Christ my Lord.

DION : Write his name down.   Your impiety makes you refuse military service, and you shall be punished accordingly as a warning to others.

He then read the sentence : " Maximilian has refused the military oath through impiety.   He is to be beheaded."

MAXIMILIAN : God liveth !

Maximilian's age was twenty-one years, three months and eighteen days.   On his way to death he said to the assembled Christians, " Beloved brethren, make haste to attain the vision of God and to deserve a crown like mine with all your strength and with the deepest longing."   He was radiant ; and, turning to his father, he said, " That cloak you got ready for when I was a soldier, give it to the lictor.   The fruits of this good work will be multiplied an hundredfold.   May I welcome you in Heaven and glorify God with you ! "

Almost at once his head was cut off.

A matron named Pompeiana obtained Maximilian's body and had it carried in her litter to Carthage, where she buried it close to the holy Cyprian, not far from the palace.

Victor went home joyfully, thanking God for having allowed him to send such a gift to Heaven, whither he was not long in following his son.   Amen.

The text of the *passio* is in *Acta Sanctorum*, March, vol. ii, and Ruinart, *Acta sincera*. See Allard, *Histoire des Persécutions*, vol. iv ; Delehaye, *Les Passions des martyrs*   ., pp. 104–110.   In the third century the Roman army was recruited chiefly from volunteers, but the sons of veterans were under obligation to serve.   St Maximilian's rejection of this obligation has been the occasion of needless embarrassment to some writers (*e.g.* Paul Allard) ; the conflicting views on soldiering current in the early Church can be conveniently examined (without necessarily accepting all his conclusions) in the work of a Protestant scholar, Dr C. J. Cadoux, *The Early Christian Attitude to War.   Cf.* St Victricius (August 7) and St Martin of Tours (November 11).   In the Roman Martyrology, St Maximilian is called Mamilianus, and the place of his martyrdom is erroneously given as Rome.

SS. PETER, GORGONIUS AND DOROTHEUS, MARTYRS
(A.D. 303)

WHEN the Emperor Diocletian was in residence at Nicomedia in Asia Minor it was reported to him that there were Christians in his own household.   He accordingly caused images of the gods to be set up and ordered that all suspected persons should offer sacrifice to them.   The Christians boldly refused, and the first to incur his vengeance was Peter, his major-domo.   We read in Eusebius and elsewhere of the terrible tortures he had to endure.   Stripped naked, he was suspended in the air while he was scourged until his bones were laid bare ; vinegar mixed with salt was poured over the quivering flesh.   Upon seeing this, Dorotheus, who was set over the imperial bedchamber, and Gorgonius, another high official, exclaimed, " Sire, why do you punish Peter for sentiments in which we all share ?   His faith, his opinions and his religion are ours also.   Hitherto we have fought for you : from henceforth we will serve God whose creatures we are."   They and another official named Migdonius were thereupon tortured and then put to death.   Peter, whose spirit was undaunted, was cut down and trampled underfoot and finally slowly roasted like meat on a spit, pieces of flesh being cut off from time to time.   In the midst of his agony he uttered no cry of pain, but exclaimed exultingly, " The gods of the heathen are but devils : it is the Lord who made the heavens ".

We know practically nothing of these martyrs except what is found in the *Ecclesiastical History* of Eusebius, bk viii, ch. 6. But it is noteworthy that the Syriac Calendar or *Breviarium* of the end of the fourth century mentions on this day the names of martyrs who suffered at Nicomedia, and amongst these we find those of Peter and Dorotheus, to whom Eusebius gives prominence. It is probable that the " Egdunus and seven others at Nicomedia " commemorated in the Roman Martyrology all belong to the same group. The " Migdonius " mentioned above and the " Egdunus " of the martyrology are probably mere miswritings of the same name. *Cf.* note to St Gorgonius on September 9.

ST PAUL AURELIAN, Bishop of Léon   (*c.* A.D. 573)

THE Bretons are fortunate in having a life of one of the fathers of Christianity in their country written before the wholesale destructions by the Northmen, with some authentic particulars of its author. He was a monk of Landévennec, named Wrmonoc, who knew the Léon country well ; he based his work, he tells us, on an earlier life, and finished it in the year 884. The following is a summary of this document.

Paul Aurelian (afterwards known as St Pol de Léon), was the son of Perphius, a British chief, and was born in Penychen (or elsewhere) in South Wales. At the monastic school to which he had asked to be sent he had as his fellows St David, St Samson and St Gildas : this was at Ynys Byr under St Illtyd, and Paul was present at the well-known miracle of the enlargement of that island. When he was sixteen his master allowed him to withdraw to a lonely spot elsewhere (Llanddeusant in Carmarthenshire ?), where he built some cells and a chapel. There he lived for years a life of prayer, praise and study, and there after he had been raised to the priesthood he gathered round him twelve companions who lived in cells near his own. From this retreat he was recalled to a troubled world by a king called Mark, who besought him to come to " Villa Bannheddos " and evangelize his people. This he did so successfully that they wished to make him their bishop. He was reluctant to consent, and while casting about in his mind what to do an angel appeared to him, who told him that his vocation lay beyond the sea. King Mark was loath to let him go, and churlishly refused his request for a parting present in the shape of a little bell—one of seven which were rung before meals.

The holy man with his twelve companions took ship and arrived at the coast of Armorica or Brittany. But before setting sail from British soil he touched at a bay (in Cornwall ?) where his sister lived a solitary life with a few other nuns.* She prevailed upon him to stay some days, and on the eve of his departure besought him with tears to obtain for her a favour from God. The place, though convenient for their purpose, was too confined and close to " tiresome relatives ". " It is easy for you to obtain what I want if you will but pray to God for it : ask that the sea may be forced into a stationary bed and that the land may be a little extended." Then St Paul and his sister knelt down on the shore in prayer, having first put two rows of stones along low-water mark ; and immediately the sea receded and left dry ground behind. And the stones grew up into mighty pillars which acted as a dyke and kept out the sea.

* Her name is given as Sitofolla, and attempts have been made to identify her with that mysterious person St Sativola--Sidwell--who was venerated at Exeter. *Cf.* Fr P. Grosjean in *Analecta Bollandians*, vol. liii (1935), pp. 359-365.

St Paul and his disciples came to the island of Ushant, where they landed at the place which is now called Porz-Pol. There they built cells and lived happily for some time, until the angel St Paul had seen before appeared again and told him to move further.

Coming to the mainland they went inland and made a settlement at Ploudal-mézeau. Then Paul, again urged on by the angel, made his way to the lord of the district, a good Christian named Withur, who befriended them and gave them the island of Batz, where St Paul settled down and built a monastery. Wonderful tales are told about the benefits the saint conferred. He killed a dragon that had done untold mischief, he taught the people how to get honey by gathering a swarm of wild bees and setting them in a hive, and he tamed a wild sow whose descendants remained at Léon for many generations.

When Paul was talking one day to Withur, a fisherman came to show them a fish he had caught. In its head was embedded a bell which—curiously enough—turned out to be the very bell which King Mark had refused to give St Paul. (In proof of the authenticity of this incident the peasants of Léon point to an ancient hand-bell which is preserved in their cathedral, made of red copper mingled with silver. Miraculous properties were attributed to it.)

The people who had profited so much from the teaching and miracles of St Paul now began to clamour to have him as their bishop. Withur was equally anxious, but he knew how unwilling the holy man would be to accept such a dignity and therefore he had recourse to a stratagem. He gave him a letter which he asked him to deliver personally to King Childebert in Paris, as it contained matter of great importance. It actually contained a request that St Paul should be appointed bishop. He protested with tears, but the king had him consecrated and then sent him back to Léon, where he was received with acclamation. The name of the *oppidum* where his seat was fixed was changed to St-Pol-de-Léon in memory of him. He continued to live the same austere life as before, his only food being bread and water except on great festivals, when he took a little fish. It seems that Withur had given him his own house on the island of Batz as a monastery for his monks, and thither the holy bishop loved to retire at intervals for prayer and contemplation.

He lived to extreme old age, but had resigned office for some years before his death. After having outlived two of his followers whom he had ordained to succeed him in his episcopacy, he died in his monastery at Batz. St Paul was endowed with the gift of prophecy and foretold the incursions of the Marcomanni (North-men), says Wrmonoc, and he recounts the saint's last moments very simply and movingly.

For discussion of this narrative—which must by no means be taken at its face value—the reader may be referred to the works mentioned below. It may be added that there are considerable traces of St Paul Aurelian in Wales, and in Cornwall at Paul, close to the western shore of Mount's Bay. If his sister's little monastery was in fact close by, on Gwavas Lake (as Charles Henderson thought), it is an interesting coincidence that, when driven out by the French Revolution, the last bishop of Léon, John Francis de la Marche, landed in Mount's Bay in 1791, nine days before St Paul's feast. That feast is now observed in the diocese of Quimper and at the monastery on Caldey.

The earliest manuscript (tenth century) of Wrmonoc's Life of St Paul Aurelian was printed by C. Cuissard in the *Revue Celtique*, vol. v (1883), pp. 417-458 ; a later manuscript (eleventh-twelfth century) is printed in *Analecta Bollandiana*, vol. i (1882), pp. 209-258 ;

see also vol. ii, pp. 191–194. The fullest and best discussion of the subject is by Canon G. H. Doble, *St Paul of Léon* (1941), where the more important parts of the Wrmonoc *vita* are translated ; *cf.* the same writer's article, " St Paulinus of Wales ", in *Laudate*, July 1941. See also LBS., vol. iv, pp. 75–86 ; and F. Duine, *Sources hagiographiques   de Bretagne*, pp. 58–61.

ST THEOPHANES THE CHRONICLER, Abbot   (A.D. 817)

It was at the court of the Emperor Constantine V that St Theophanes grew up. His father had died early, leaving him heir to a large estate and entrusting him to the guardianship of the emperor.   He was induced to marry, but by mutual agreement his wife became a nun ; Theophanes also retired from the world and seemingly built two monasteries, the first of which was situated on Mount Sigriana, near Cyzicus.   When he established the second, on the island of Kalonymos, which was part of his heritage, he made this his home, and there spent six years.   Eventually he returned to Mount Sigriana and remained on as abbot.   In 787 Theophanes was invited to take part in the Second Council of Nicaea, which sanctioned the use and veneration of sacred images.   But Leo the Armenian in 814 reversed the policy of his predecessors, and strove to suppress the *cultus* of images.   Recognizing how widespread was the authority and reputation of St Theophanes, he attempted to win him over to his side by civilities and crafty letters.   But the holy man was well armed against all the devices which could be used to ensnare him. At the age of fifty he had begun to be grievously afflicted with the stone and with another painful internal disease ; but, called to Constantinople by the emperor, he obeyed the call, although he was at the time tortured by these agonizing infirmities.

Leo sent him a message that flattered and then threatened.   To this Theophanes replied   " Being now far advanced in years and much broken with pain and the weakness of my body, I have neither relish nor inclination for any of those things which I despised, for Christ's sake, in my youth.   As to my monastery and my friends, I commend them to God.   If you think to frighten me into compliance by your threats, as a child is awed by the rod, you are only losing your pains."   The emperor sent several emissaries to argue with him, but he remained inflexible. He was condemned to be scourged and imprisoned, and, after receiving 300 stripes, was confined for two years in a close and stinking dungeon, where he was left almost without the necessaries of life, although his malady was ever increasing.   At last he was removed from prison and banished to the island of Samothrace, where he died March 12, 817, seventeen days after his arrival, as the result of the treatment he had endured.   He left a Chronography or short history of the world to the year 813, starting from A.D. 284, the date which terminated an earlier history written by his friend George Syncellus, secretary of the patriarch St Tarasius.

The importance of the work of St Theophanes as a chronicler of Byzantine history has led to much attention being paid to his life.   The complete biography of the saint by Methodius was edited completely for the first time by D. Spyridon in the periodical 'Ἐκκλησιαστικὸς Φάρος, vol. xii (1913). The lives previously known seem all to be dependent on this.   Moreover, we have a panegyric delivered by his fellow monk and disciple, St Theodore Studites, which is to be found in the *Analecta Bollandiana*, vol. xxxi (1912), pp. 11 25, as well as certain letters of the same Theodore printed in Migne, PG., vol. xcix. cc. 1197 *seq.* *Cf.* BHG., nn. 1788–1792.   The *Chronographia* of Theophanes has been edited by De Boor (1885), with a valuable introduction.   See also Pargoire in *Βυζαντινὰ Χρονικά*, vol. ix (1902), pp. 31–102 ; Krumbacher, *Gesch. der Byz. Literatur*, pp. 342–347 ; and *Analecta Bollandiana*, vol. xxxi (1912), pp. 11–25, 148–156.

ST ALPHEGE, Bishop of Winchester   (A.D. 951)

St Alphege the Elder, or the Bald, as he is called to distinguish him from one of his successors, St Alphege the Martyr, is now chiefly remembered for his indirect part in the restoration of monasticism in England by encouraging his kinsman St Dunstan to become a monk.   No doubt the bishop's arguments sank into his mind, but it required a dangerous illness to decide him.   St Alphege, on hearing of his purpose, was greatly rejoiced and lost no time in investing him with the habit, and later had the joy of raising him to the priesthood.   Two others were ordained on that occasion, St Ethelwold and another monk named Ethelstan.   The spirit of prophecy came upon St Alphege, and addressing the new priests he is reported to have said, " To-day, before God, I have laid my hands upon three men, of whom two will attain to the grace of the episcopal order—one in the city of Winchester and then at Canterbury, and the other will also occupy my seat in legitimate succession later on.   The third, after doing much evil and wallowing in sensual pleasures, will come to a miserable end."   His words were fulfilled in every particular.   The good bishop's life was one of great holiness and he was famous for his prophetical gifts.

The Life of Dunstan by " B ", together with the histories of William of Malmesbury and Simeon of Durham, are the principal sources for the little we know of St Alphege, whose name figures in two or three medieval calendars.

ST BERNARD OF CAPUA, Bishop of Caleno   (A.D. 1109)

St Bernard of Capua, of whose antecedents and early life no records are available, became chaplain and adviser to Duke Richard II, son of Prince Jordan of Capua. He gained the confidence of his patron so entirely that it was said that Richard would undertake nothing without first consulting his confessor.   When the see of Foro-Claudio was vacant he was appointed by Pope Victor III, and he soon began to consider removing his episcopal seat.   Foro-Claudio was in an exposed place— not easily defended—on the high-road between Rome and Naples, whereas at a short distance off, in a far better position, stood Caleno.   The change was accordingly made.   On Monte Massico hard by lay the body of the hermit St Marcius (Martin), mention of whom is made in the *Dialogues* of St Gregory ; and Arachis, Duke of Benevento, came with a great retinue intending to remove the body and to take it to Benevento.   Mass was celebrated for them in the presence of the relics, but suddenly there came an earthquake, and the duke, interpreting this as a warning that it was not God's will that the body should leave the neighbourhood, returned home.   Then St Bernard and his priests went up to the mountain, and having brought the precious treasure to their new cathedral enclosed it in the altar.

The account of this saint in the *Acta Sanctorum*, March, vol. ii, is based upon certain breviary lessons cited by Ughelli and by Michael Monachus in his *Sanctuarium Capuanum*. The authority is not very satisfactory, but there can be no doubt of St Bernard's historical existence.

ST FINA, or SERAPHINA, Virgin   (A.D. 1253)

The old town of San Geminiano in Tuscany treasures with special veneration the memory of Santa Fina, a young girl whose claim to be recognized as a saint lay in the perfect resignation with which she accepted bodily suffering.   She was born of parents who had seen better days but had fallen into poverty.   The child was she and several other sisters lived in great self-abnegation and from midnight to midday served God in unbroken prayer. Diseases and sufferings of many kinds were cured through the prayers of Bd Justina, and still more wonderful miracles of healing were wrought after her death. She died in 1319 and her *cultus* was approved in 1890.

All that we know of Bd Justina is contained in the short life printed in the *Acta Sanctorum*, March, vol. ii.

BD NICHOLAS OWEN, Martyr   (A.D. 1606)

Perhaps no single person contributed more to the preservation of the Catholic religion in England during the penal times than a humble artisan called Nicholas Owen, who in the reign of James I saved the lives of many priests by his extra-ordinary skill in devising hiding-places for them. Nothing is known of his antecedents or early life, but it is thought that he may have been a builder by trade. Familiarly known as " Little John " and " Little Michael ", he also passed under the names of Andrewes and Draper. Summarizing contemporary records Father Tanner says of him : " A great servant of God in a diminutive body, Nicholas Odoenus, otherwise Owen, spent eighteen years with Fathers Henry Garnet and John Gerard in the capacity of a faithful and most useful servant. Born in England in an age of licence, he lived a singularly innocent life, untainted by the allurements of the world ; his confessor, who had known his conscience from his earliest childhood, solemnly asserts that he preserved his baptismal innocence unsullied until death. With incomparable skill he knew how to devise a place of safety for priests in subterranean passages, to hide them between walls, and to bury them in impenetrable recesses. But what was much more difficult of accomplishment, he so disguised the entrances to these as to make them most unlike what they really were. Moreover he kept these places so close a secret with himself, that he would never disclose their existence to anyone else. He alone was both their architect and their builder, working at them with inexhaustible industry and labour, for generally the thickest walls had to be broken into and large stones excavated, requiring stronger arms than were attached to a body so diminutive as to give him the nickname of ' Little John '. And by his skill many priests were preserved from the fury of the persecutors, nor is it easy to find anyone who had not often been indebted for his life to Owen's hiding-places—a benefit redounding to all Catholics, whose progress in virtue and whose access to the sacraments were thus due to him. His unwonted success in constructing these hiding-places would seem to have been a reward from Heaven for his remarkable piety ; for when he was about to design one, he commenced the work by receiving the most holy Eucharist, sought to aid its progress by continual prayer, and offered the completion of it to God alone, accepting of no other reward for his toil than the merit of charity and the consolation of labouring for the good of Catholics."

When he had worked for some years in this way, Father Garnet admitted him to the Society of Jesus, before 1580, and he was amongst the first English lay-brothers—although, for good reasons, his connection with the order was kept secret. He was with Father John Gerard when they were betrayed by an unsuspected traitor and apprehended together on St George's day, 1594. He was imprisoned in the Counter and was subjected to terrible tortures to force him to disclose the names of other Catholics. He and Brother Richard Fulwood were hung up for three hours together, with their arms fixed into iron rings, and their bodies hanging in the air, and Owen's suffering was increased by heavy weights which were attached to his feet. This was the notorious " Topcliffe " rack, which was also applied to Father Southwell. No information could be obtained from either of the prisoners, and Nicholas was released for a sum of money which a Catholic gentleman paid, because, as Father Gerard testified, his services in contriving priests' hiding-places were indispensable to them and many others.

He soon proved that he could do more than conceal them : he could deliver them from prison. The wonderful escape of Father Gerard from the Tower was almost certainly planned by Owen, although it was carried out by Brothers Fulwood and Lilly, who were less well-known to the prison authorities. Owen himself was waiting at a fixed spot with horses. Father Gerard in his narrative says : " After we landed . I with Richard Fulwood went to a house which Father Garnet had in the suburbs, and there I and Little John shortly before daylight mounted our horses which he had ready there for the purpose, and rode straight off to Father Garnet who was then living a short distance in the country." Father Gerard also mentions a narrow escape which Owen had when he had been lent by Garnet to construct hiding-places in a new house which Gerard had taken and was about to occupy. Suspicion had been aroused and the house was surrounded, " but the house was so large that although they had a numerous body of followers, they were not able to surround it entirely, nor to watch all the outlets so narrowly but what Little John managed to make off safely ".

At length, after a faithful service of twenty years, Owen fell once more into the hands of his enemies together with Father Garnet and Father Oldcorne. He came voluntarily out of the hiding-place in which he had carefully concealed them, in order that he might be captured and, by passing for a priest, save the lives of the fathers as more useful to the Church. He was apprehended with Brother Ralph Ashley, the servant of Father Oldcorne. At first a " free custody " was allowed in order that those who visited him might be watched, but Owen's prudence baulked the intentions of his captors. He was then removed from the Marshalsea to the Tower of London, the keeper of which, Wade, was possessed by a fanatical hatred of the Catholic faith. He kept his victim suspended day after day, sometimes for six hours together, although he was ill and suffering from a hernia, which was girt with an iron band. Owen consistently refused to answer Wade's questions and would speak to God alone, invoking the aid of Jesus and Mary. In the end the prolonged strain so extended the martyr's body that his bowels broke in a terrible way, the iron band assisting to tear and enlarge the wound, and in the midst of terrible anguish Brother Nicholas passed to his eternal reward.

Attempts were made to vilify his memory and to attribute his death to suicide, but his courage was too well known and the lie obtained little credence. A piece of evidence which has only been made available of recent years is contained in a despatch of the Venetian ambassador, Giustiniani, who on March 13, 1606, wrote to his government as follows (the portion in square brackets is in cypher) :

> I ought to add that while the king (James) was talking to me he let fall that last night one of the Jesuits, conscience-stricken for his sins, stabbed himself deeply in the body twice with a knife. When the warders ran up at the noise they found him still alive. He confessed to having taken a share in the plot at the suggestion of his provincial (Garnet), and now, recognizing his crime,

he had resolved to kill himself, and so escape the terrible death that overhung him, as he deserved. [Public opinion, however, holds that he died of the tortures inflicted on him, which were so severe that they deprived him not only of his strength, but of the power to move any part of his body, and so they think it unlikely that he should have been able to stab himself in the body, especially with a blunt knife, as they allege. It is thought that as he confessed nothing and is dead, they have hoodwinked the king himself by publishing this account] in order to rouse him and everybody to greater animosity against the Catholics and to make the case blacker against his companion the provincial.

King James's statement that Brother Owen in his dying agony " confessed to having taken a share in the plot at the suggestion of his provincial ", is not only supremely improbable in itself, but is refuted by the fact that not the least use was made of this alleged confession at Garnet's trial.

Father Gerard wrote of Brother Owen : " I verily think no man can be said to have done more good of all those who laboured in the English vineyard. For, first, he was the immediate occasion of saving the lives of many hundreds of persons, both ecclesiastical and secular, and of the estates also of these seculars, which had been lost and forfeited many times over if the priests had been taken in their houses ; of which some have escaped, not once but many times, in several searches that have come to the same house, and sometimes five or six priests together at the same time. Myself have been one of the seven that have escaped that danger at one time in a secret place of his making. How many priests then may we think this man did save by his endeavours in the space of seventeen years in all shires and in the chiefest Catholic houses of England ! "

The most reliable information we possess concerning Bd Nicholas Owen is to be found in the writings of his companion and contemporary, Father John Gerard, which are printed in *The Condition of Catholics under James I*, by Fr John Morris ; and see the translation of his autobiography by Fr P. Caraman (1951). See also REPSJ., vol. iv, pp. 245-267. Giustiniani's despatch, which alone enables us to fix the exact date of the death of Bd Nicholas, is printed in the *Calendar of State Papers, Venetian*, vol. x, pp. 327-328.

13 : ST EUPHRASIA, or EUPRAXIA, Virgin   (c. A.D. 420)

THE Emperor Theodosius I had a kinsman Antigonus, who died within a year of the birth of his daughter Euphrasia, and the emperor took the widow and her child under his protection. When the little girl was five years old he arranged to betroth her to the son of a wealthy senator—in accordance with the custom of the time—the marriage being deferred until the maiden should have reached a suitable age. The widow herself began to be sought in marriage, and she withdrew from court and went with Euphrasia to Egypt, where she settled down near a convent of nuns. Euphrasia, then seven years of age, was greatly drawn to the nuns and begged to be allowed to stay with them. To humour her and thinking it was only a childish fancy, her mother left her there for a little, expecting her soon to weary of the life, but the child was persistent, although she was told that she would have to fast and to sleep on the ground and to learn the whole Psalter if she remained. The abbess then said to the mother, " Leave the little girl with us, for the grace of God is working in her heart. Your piety and that of Antigonus have opened to her the most perfect way   The good woman wept for joy, and leading her child before the image of our Lord she said, " Lord Jesus Christ, receive this child.   Thee alone doth she love and seek, and to thy service alone doth she commend herself."   Then turning to Euphrasia she exclaimed, " May God who laid the foundations of the mountains, keep you always steadfast in His holy fear ". A few days later the child was clothed in the nun's habit, and her mother asked if she were satisfied.   " Oh, mother ! " cried the little novice, " it is my bridal robe, given me to do honour to Jesus my beloved."   Soon afterwards the mother went to rejoin her husband in a better world, and as the years went by Euphrasia grew up a beautiful girl in the seclusion of the convent.

In due time the emperor, presumably Arcadius, sent for her to come to Constantinople to marry the senator to whom he had betrothed her.   She was now twelve years old and an heiress, but she wrote him a letter begging him to allow her to follow her vocation and requesting him to distribute her parents' property to the poor as well as to enfranchise all her slaves.   The emperor carried out her requests ; but Euphrasia was sorely tried by vain imaginations and temptations to know more of the world she had forsaken.   The abbess, to whom she opened her heart, set her some hard and humbling tasks to divert her attention and to drive away the evil spirits from which she suffered in body as well as in soul.   Once the abbess ordered her to remove a pile of stones from one place to another, and when the task was completed she continued to make her carry them backwards and forwards thirty times.   In this and in whatever else she was bidden to do, Euphrasia complied cheerfully and promptly : she cleaned out the cells of the other nuns, carried water for the kitchen, chopped the wood, baked the bread and cooked the food.   The nun who performed these arduous duties was generally excused the night offices, but Euphrasia was never missing from her place in the choir, and yet at the age of twenty she was taller, better developed and more beautiful than any of the others.

Her meekness and humility were extraordinary.   A maid in the kitchen once asked her why she sometimes went without food for the entire week, a thing no one but the abbess ever attempted.   When the saint said she did it out of obedience, the woman called her a hypocrite, who sought to make herself conspicuous in the hope of being chosen superior.   Far from resenting this unjust accusation, Euphrasia fell at her feet and besought her to pray for her.   As the saint lay on her death-bed, Julia, a beloved sister who shared her cell, besought Euphrasia to obtain for her the grace of being with her in Heaven as she had been her companion on earth, and three days after her friend's demise, Julia was taken also.   The aged abbess who had originally received Euphrasia remained for a month together very sad at the loss of her dear ones.   She prayed earnestly that she might not have to linger on now that the others had gone to their reward.   The following morning when the nuns entered her cell they found only her lifeless body, for her soul had fled in the night to join the other two.   According to Russian usage St Euphrasia is named in the preparation of the Byzantine Mass.

The remarkable Greek life, which is the source of all we know concerning St Euphrasia, has been printed in the *Acta Sanctorum*, March, vol. ii.   There seems good reason to regard it as a more or less contemporary and, in its main features, a trustworthy narrative.   Certainly the asceticism it reflects is the asceticism of that age.   Within a few years of the date at which Euphrasia died, St Simeon Stylites set up his first pillar.   Of Euphrasia, as of her abbess, it is stated that she stood upright in one spot for thirty days until she lost consciousness and fell down in a swoon. Etheria in her pilgrimage (*c.* 390) tells us much of the *ebdomadarii* who made it a point of honour and endurance to pass an entire week without food from Sunday to Saturday evening. Moreover, the whole atmosphere of the document recalls vividly the ascetic ideals set before us in the Life of St Melania the Younger, who was a contemporary. See also A. B. C. Dunbar, *Dictionary of Saintly Women*, vol. i, pp. 292–293.

ST MOCHOEMOC, ABBOT   (SEVENTH CENTURY)

THE accounts we have of St Mochoemoc are overladen with fantastic legends. Perhaps all that we should be justified in asserting is that he was the nephew of St Ita, who had charge of him in his youth, that he entered the monastery of Bennchor (Bangor) in County Down, that he was afterwards commissioned by St Comgall to found a settlement at Arderin, that he eventually established a flourishing community at Liath-mor, where he became the teacher of St Dagan and St Cuanghas, and that he died at a very advanced age.

Tradition, however, declares him to have been the son of St Ita's sister Nessa and of Beoan, whom Ita had so marvellously raised to life. The boy was so handsome that he was named Coemgen (Pulcherius), but his aunt called him by the pet-form Mochoemog, and by that name he was always known. His father and mother came to St Ita and said, " Lady, the grace of God shines wonderfully in your little favourite, our son   we are earthly, and he is so spiritual that he cannot live with us." She at once replied, " Bring him hither and I will rear him myself." So she watched over him until he was twenty and superintended his studies. Then she blessed him and sent him to St Comgall at Bangor, where he was ordained. Recognizing his sanctity the abbot said one day to him, " My son, it is necessary that you should become the spiritual father of others, and that you should erect a house for God's service wherever He may decree."

So Mochoemoc set out with other monks and settled first at Arderin on Slieve Bloom, but later he departed to the country of Eile. There the chieftain offered to give him a lonely wooded place, and this the saint willingly accepted. Now when Ita had parted from her nephew she had given him a little bell, saying, " Here is this silent bell for you : it will not sound till you have reached the place of your resurrection." As soon as Mochoemoc had reached the land granted him, the bell tinkled, and the saint gave thanks to God because he knew it was to be the place of his resurrection. There also he found a great wild hog, which greeted the monks, and Mochoemoc exclaimed, " As the colour of that hog is *liath*—grey—so shall it be the name of this place for ever." Here then at Liath he founded his principal church which was called Liath-mor or Liath-Mochoemoc, but the place is now known as Leamokevoge in County Tipperary. Round the holy man gathered a number of disciples, and St Mochoemoc built for them a great monastery in which they lived in peace. At last, when he had founded many monasteries, the saint was warned that his time was come, and having blessed his monks and Liath he went to his reward a very old man.

There was formerly venerated in Scotland, particularly in the district about Glasgow, a maiden St Kennoch whose history is wrapped in great obscurity. We are met first with the difficulty that while in the text of the Aberdeen Breviary the name is printed Kenoca, the form in the calendar of the same book, as well as in the Aberdeen Martyrology and in the Arbuthnott calendar, is Keuoca or Kevoca. On the other hand, " Kennocha " appears among the virgins and widows in the ancient Litany of Dunkeld. Forbes, in his *Kalendars of Scottish Saints*, suggests that an ancient Irish monk—no other than Mochoemoc of Leamokevoge—has here through some confusion been transformed into a woman. The Kevoge, in fact, which we find in Leamokevoge is simply the saint's name, and it may obviously be identified with Kevoca. No certain conclusion is possible. The statement that St Kennoch lived in the time of King Malcolm II (1005-1034) rests apparently only on the authority of Adam King (1588), which is quite worthless in such a matter.

There is a Latin Life of St Mochoemoc and an Irish text which is the translation of it. The Latin was printed by Colgan, and also in the *Acta Sanctorum*, March, vol. ii. It has been re-edited in VSH., vol. ii, pp. 164-183 ; see also LIS., vol. iii. For St Kennoch, see the *Acta Sanctorum*, March, vol. ii, and KSS.

ST GERALD OF MAYO, ABBOT   (A.D. 732)

ST GERALD was an Englishman, a native of Northumbria, who became a monk at Lindisfarne. After the Council of Whitby which prohibited the Celtic observance of Easter in Northumbria, St Colman left England accompanied by all the Irish monks and thirty of the English novices. At Inishbofin, an island off the coast of Mayo, he founded a monastery for his community, but as he found that the Englishmen and the Irish could not agree, he built a second house on the mainland for the English monks. It is not certain whether Gerald was one of the original thirty or whether he followed later, for we know that English and other students long continued to frequent Colman's school at Mayo of the Saxons, as it came to be called. At first St Colman acted as abbot over the two monasteries, but Gerald afterwards succeeded him in the English house, which flourished exceedingly. He is sometimes spoken of as a bishop, notably in the litany of Irish saints from the Book of Leinster, but this is very doubtful, as even his so-called acts which attribute to him many marvellous miracles only allude to him as an abbot. It has been suggested that the title *pontifex* or president of the English which was bestowed upon him gave rise to the idea that he was a bishop, whereas it probably only meant that the abbot of Mayo had certain privileges as protector of his countrymen who were strangers in Ireland. St Gerald, who lived to old age, must have witnessed the introduction into his abbey of the Roman observance of Easter. He is also credited, though on doubtful authority, with the foundation of the abbeys of Elytheria or Tempul-Gerald in Connaught and of Teagh-na-Saxon, as well as of a nunnery which he is said to have placed under the care of his sister St Segretia.

The extravagant Latin Life of St Gerald printed by Colgan has been re-edited by Plummer, VSH., vol. ii, pp. 107-115. See also the *Acta Sanctorum*, March, vol. ii, and LIS. vol. iii.

ST NICEPHORUS, PATRIARCH OF CONSTANTINOPLE   (A.D. 828)

THE father of St Nicephorus was secretary and commissioner to the Emperor Constantine Copronymus, but when that tyrant declared himself a persecutor of the orthodox faith, his minister maintained the honour due to holy images with so much zeal that he was stripped of his dignities, scourged, tortured and banished. Young Nicephorus grew up with his father's example before him to encourage him in boldly confessing his faith, while an excellent education developed his exceptional abilities. After Constantine VI and Irene had restored the use of sacred pictures and images, Nicephorus was introduced to their notice and by his sterling qualities that an ancient Irish monk—no other than Mochoemoc of Leamokevoge—has here through some confusion been transformed into a woman. The Kevoge, in fact, which we find in Leamokevoge is simply the saint's name, and it may obviously be identified with Kevoca. No certain conclusion is possible. The statement that St Kennoch lived in the time of King Malcolm II (1005-1034) rests apparently only on the authority of Adam King (1588), which is quite worthless in such a matter.

There is a Latin Life of St Mochoemoc and an Irish text which is the translation of it. The Latin was printed by Colgan, and also in the *Acta Sanctorum*, March, vol. ii. It has been re-edited in VSH., vol. ii, pp. 164-183 ; see also LIS., vol. iii. For St Kennoch, see the *Acta Sanctorum*, March, vol. ii, and KSS.

ST GERALD OF MAYO, ABBOT   (A.D. 732)

St GERALD was an Englishman, a native of Northumbria, who became a monk at Lindisfarne. After the Council of Whitby which prohibited the Celtic observance of Easter in Northumbria, St Colman left England accompanied by all the Irish monks and thirty of the English novices. At Inishbofin, an island off the coast of Mayo, he founded a monastery for his community, but as he found that the Englishmen and the Irish could not agree, he built a second house on the mainland for the English monks. It is not certain whether Gerald was one of the original thirty or whether he followed later, for we know that English and other students long continued to frequent Colman's school at Mayo of the Saxons, as it came to be called. At first St Colman acted as abbot over the two monasteries, but Gerald afterwards succeeded him in the English house, which flourished exceedingly. He is sometimes spoken of as a bishop, notably in the litany of Irish saints from the Book of Leinster, but this is very doubtful, as even his so-called acts which attribute to him many marvellous miracles only allude to him as an abbot. It has been suggested that the title *pontifex* or president of the English which was bestowed upon him gave rise to the idea that he was a bishop, whereas it probably only meant that the abbot of Mayo had certain privileges as protector of his countrymen who were strangers in Ireland. St Gerald, who lived to old age, must have witnessed the introduction into his abbey of the Roman observance of Easter. He is also credited, though on doubtful authority, with the foundation of the abbeys of Elytheria or Tempul-Gerald in Connaught and of Teagh-na-Saxon, as well as of a nunnery which he is said to have placed under the care of his sister St Segretia.

The extravagant Latin Life of St Gerald printed by Colgan has been re-edited by Plummer, VSH., vol. ii, pp. 107-115. See also the *Acta Sanctorum*, March, vol. ii, and LIS. vol. iii.

ST NICEPHORUS, PATRIARCH OF CONSTANTINOPLE   (A.D. 828)

THE father of St Nicephorus was secretary and commissioner to the Emperor Constantine Copronymus, but when that tyrant declared himself a persecutor of the orthodox faith, his minister maintained the honour due to holy images with so much zeal that he was stripped of his dignities, scourged, tortured and banished. Young Nicephorus grew up with his father's example before him to encourage him in boldly confessing his faith, while an excellent education developed his exceptional abilities. After Constantine VI and Irene had restored the use of sacred pictures and images, Nicephorus was introduced to their notice and by his sterling qualities

obtained their favour. He distinguished himself by his opposition to the Iconoclasts and was secretary to the Second Council of Nicaea, as well as imperial
commissioner. Although a brilliant speaker, a philosopher, a musician and in
every respect fitted for statesmanship, he always had a great inclination for the
religious life, and while still occupied with public affairs had built a monastery in a
solitary spot near the Black Sea. After the death of St Tarasius, Patriarch of
Constantinople, no one could be found more worthy to succeed him than Nicephorus. As he was a layman at the time, his election was opposed by some as
uncanonical, and it was only at the express request of the emperor that he could be
induced to accept office. During the consecration, as a public testimony of his
faith, he held in his hand a treatise he had written in defence of images, and at the
conclusion he laid it up behind the altar as a pledge that he would ever defend the
tradition of the Church.

The new patriarch ere long still further antagonized the hostile rigorists. At
the request of the emperor, Nicephorus, with the consent of a small synod of
bishops, pardoned and reinstated in office a priest called Joseph, who had been
deposed and exiled for celebrating a marriage between the Emperor Constantine VI
and Theodota during the lifetime of the lawful Empress Mary. No doubt he acted
in this way to avoid worse evils, but the party which was headed by St Theodore
Studites refused to have any dealings or even to be in communion with the patriarch
and with those who supported what they called the " Adulterine Heresy " they
went so far as to appeal to the pope. St Leo III sent them an encouraging reply
but, being imperfectly informed about the whole matter and having received no
communications from Archbishop Nicephorus, he took no further action. After
a time, however, a reconciliation was brought about between the patriarch and St
Theodore (who meanwhile had been imprisoned and his monks dispersed). It was
not until then that Nicephorus sent to the pope a letter announcing his apppoint-
ment to the see of Constantinople, with an apology and a rather lame excuse for
his delay in making the customary notification. At the same time, in view of
attacks that had been made upon his orthodoxy, he added a lengthy confession of
faith and promised that in future he would give due notice at Rome of any important
questions that might arise.

St Nicephorus was a zealous administrator and applied himself with patient
determination to improving morals and restoring discipline in the various monasteries under his control as well as amongst the clergy generally, with the support of
St Theodore. But Leo the Armenian became emperor in 813. He was an Iconoclast, although he did not at first express his opinions and evaded the confession of
faith which Nicephorus tried to elicit before consecrating him. It was only when
he felt his position assured that he allowed his views to become known. He
attempted by crafty suggestions to win over Nicephorus to favour his design of
destroying the images which had been replaced in the churches after their use had
been vindicated and sanctioned by the Second Council of Nicaea. The patriarch
replied, " We cannot change the ancient traditions we respect the holy images,
as we do the cross and the book of the gospels." Leo, however, persisted in his
antagonism, which he proceeded to propagate without at first showing his hand too
clearly. He privately encouraged some soldiers to insult an image of Christ which
was fixed to a great cross at the Bronze Gate of Constantinople, and then ordered
the figure to be removed on the plea of preventing a second profanation. Shortly
afterwards the emperor, having assembled in his palace certain Iconoclastic bishops,

sent for the patriarch and his fellow dignitaries. They entreated Leo to leave the
government of the Church to her pastors, one of them saying, " If this is an
ecclesiastical affair, let it be discussed in the church, not in the palace." The
emperor in a rage drove them all from his presence.

Some little time later the heterodox bishops held a meeting and cited the
patriarch to appear before them. To their summons he replied, " Who gave you
this authority ? If it was he who pilots the vessel of Old Rome, I am ready. If
it was the Alexandrine successor of the Evangelist Mark, I am ready. If it was the
patriarch of Antioch or he of Jerusalem, I make no opposition. But who are you ?
In my diocese you have no jurisdiction." He then read the canon which declared
those men excommunicated who presume to exercise any act of jurisdiction in the
diocese of another bishop. On their side they proceeded to pronounce against him
a sentence of deposition. After several attempts had been made against his life
he was sent by the emperor into exile, and spent his fifteen remaining years at the
monastery which he had built on the Bosphorus. Although Leo's successor
Michael the Stammerer would not bring back the sacred images which Leo had
banished from the churches, he was no persecutor and would have restored the
patriarch had he been willing to keep silence on the disputed question ; but
Nicephorus would not purchase his liberty at the expense of his conscience, and he
felt that silence would be tantamount to consent. In exile he could and did continue
to defend his tenets in writings which have lasted to this day.

His chief works were an Apology for orthodox teaching regarding sacred images
and another larger treatise in two parts, the first of which consisted of a defence of
the Church against the charge of idolatry, and the second, known as the Antirrhetica,
was a confutation of the writings on images of Constantine V. Besides several
other treatises, mostly dealing with Iconoclasm, he left two historical works known
as the *Breviarium* and the *Chronographia*, the one a short history from the reign
of Maurice to that of Constantine and Irene, and the other a chronicle of events
from the beginning of the world. In the collection of the councils may still be
found the seventeen canons of Nicephorus, in the second of which he declares it
to be unlawful to travel on Sunday without necessity.

In 846, by order of the Empress Theodora and in the patriarchate of St
Methodius, the body of St Nicephorus was translated from the island of Prokenesis
to Constantinople, where it was deposited in the church of the Apostles on March
13—the day appointed for the commemoration of the saint in the Roman Martyrology.

The principal source for the life of St Nicephorus is a biography of the deacon Ignatius.
It has been edited by De Boor in modern times, but is also found in the *Acta Sanctorum*,
March, vol. ii. There is a good account of this disturbed period in Hergenröther, *Kirchengeschichte*, vol. i, and in the article " Nicephorus " in the *Kirchenlexikon ;* and summaries
of the Iconoclast controversy in Baynes and Moss, *Byzantium* (1948), pp. 15–17, 105–108,
by H. L. B. Moss and H. Grégoire. *Cf.* Hefele-Leclercq, *Histoire des Conciles*, vol. iii,
pt 2 (1910), pp. 741 *seq.*

ST ANSOVINUS, BISHOP OF CAMERINO   (A.D. 840)

ST ANSOVINUS was born at Camerino in Umbria, but no details of his early life
have been preserved. After his ordination to the priesthood he retired into a
solitary spot at Castel-Raimondo, near Torcello, where he soon acquired a reputation for sanctity and miracles. It was even believed that when he came to church

he crossed the river on his cloak which he cast into the water, and that, when the rays of the sun dazzled him as he was offering the holy sacrifice, he hung the linen purificator in the air and it shaded his eyes. The Emperor Louis the Pious when in Italy chose him as his confessor, and ratified his election to the see of Camerino. The saint, however, had no wish to accept the dignity, and when he did consent it was with the proviso that he should not be expected to provide soldiers for the imperial army. Although such military service was usual in feudal and semi-feudal states, he considered it unsuitable and contrary to the law of the Church.

Ansovinus proved himself a wise and prudent pastor. Not only was he liberal to the poor, but in seasons of dearth he husbanded all the resources at his command with such sagacity that he was able to relieve the sufferings of the needy. Indeed, it was said that when he had entirely emptied a granary, it was supernaturally refilled. The saint had the gift of healing and was instrumental in curing many sick persons. He was in Rome when he was seized with a form of fever which he and those about him recognized as likely to prove fatal. In spite of the protests of his friends he insisted upon returning home to die amongst his own people. They carried the sick man out to his horse, and when the animal saw him that strange instinct which dumb creatures often possess impelled him to kneel down to enable his master to mount. Ansovinus reached Camerino and was able to give a last blessing and to receive the viaticum before he quietly expired.

A singular miracle with which he is credited is worth relating, if only to account for the attribute commonly connected with St Ansovinus. He was on his way to Rome to be consecrated when he and his friends arrived at Narni, where they stayed for refreshment. They called for wine, and the innkeeper brought some. Ansovinus, detecting that it had been watered, remonstrated with the man, who answered rudely that they could take it or leave it—it was all they would get. The saint then asked for cups, but the innkeeper said that he only provided wine and that visitors were expected to bring their own drinking-cups. So St Ansovinus took off his cape and told the host to pour the wine into the hood. He did so, under protest, and the hood retained the wine, whilst the water with which it had been mixed ran away.

The life printed in the *Acta Sanctorum*, March, vol. ii, which purports to have been written by a certain Eginus not less than a century after the death of the saint, is a wordy and unconvincing document consisting mainly of miracles. But the *cultus* of St Ansovinus is recognized, and his name is entered in the Roman Martyrology. See also M. Santoni, *Culto di Sant' Ansovino* (1883).

ST HELDRAD, ABBOT   (*c.* A.D. 842)

THE father of St Heldrad was a feudal lord in Provence, whose castle was near Aix at a town called Lambesc, the exact situation of which appears to be uncertain. Heldrad, while still quite young, succeeded to a large fortune, a considerable proportion of which he expended in good works. Not far from the town, at a spot where several important roads met, a market was held which was a veritable Vanity Fair, with much fraud and blasphemy. Beside the market St Heldrad built a church and a hospice, where all guests, rich or poor, were received without payment. He also laid out a garden where vegetables could be grown by the people. In spite of all he had done, he was not satisfied and resolved to give up everything for Christ's sake and to seek the way of perfection. Part of his possessions he gave to the bishop for the upkeep of the works he had established, and the rest was devoted to the poor. Meanly clad in the guise of a pilgrim, he started forth, visiting first the holy places of western France and of Spain, but not finding anywhere the kind of life to which he felt called.

Then he began tramping through Italy. Quite casually he heard from other pilgrims of the Benedictine monks of Novalese who, in their monastery at the foot of the Alps, not only exercised hospitality day and night, but also, it is said, took charge of a hospice on the top of the pass of Mont Cenis. Léon Lallemand, in his *Histoire de la Charité* (vol. ii, p. 183), speaks of a refuge on Mont Cenis constructed by Charlemagne on the site of an ancient temple of Jupiter, and it is possible that this was in charge of the monks of Novalese. One would like to think that in the winter season the brethren used to set out to seek travellers who were lost in the snow, bringing them back to the hospice to tend them and aid them on their journey. But positive evidence of this is lacking. The short summer season only gave the monks time to gather wood for fuel and to lay in provisions for the winter. It was in the autumn that Heldrad presented himself at the door of the abbey. The abbot Amblulf had had a premonition with regard to his coming and therefore received him with special cordiality.

Here at last Heldrad found the life of devotion and active charity which satisfied his aspirations. For a time the abbot tested him by entrusting him with the care of the monastery vineyards, but before long he gave him the habit. Raised to the priesthood, Heldrad no doubt took part in perilous mountain expeditions, perhaps even anticipating the work subsequently taken up by the canons of the Great St Bernard. What is more certain is that he was charged with the training of the young religious; he does not, however, seem to have been tied to the spot, for at one time we find him at Cluny whither he had been summoned by Louis the Pious. After the death of Amblulf, Charlemagne's son Hugh was appointed abbot, but he was so often absent that the abbey would greatly have suffered but for Heldrad, who acted as administrator with so much success that he was elected abbot upon the death of Hugh. In this capacity he did much for the monastery. Within the fortified enclosure he erected a tower, the upper part of which served as a signalling-station, whilst the lower part contained the treasures of the house and the famous library which was his special care. Not satisfied with succouring travellers on the Mont Cenis he established another hospice on the Lautaret Pass, now called the Monestier de Briançon. St Heldrad's death took place about 842. He was held in such veneration that his relics were long carried in procession in the valley of Novalese at Rogationtide, and his *cultus* was approved in 1903.

Nearly all that can be learnt about St Heldrad will be found collected in the volume published by C. Cipolla, *Monumenta Novaliciensia Vetustiora* (1898), including a fragmentary rhythmical life which may possibly be assigned to the ninth century and which is certainly not later than the tenth, and also a prose life which had previously been printed in the *Acta Sanctorum* (March, vol. ii) and elsewhere. This latter, according to Bethmann (MGH., *Scriptores*, vol. vii, p. 73 n.), may be assigned to the early eleventh century. A short poem addressed to Heldrad is printed among the *Poetae Latini Aevi Carolini*, ii, p. 549.

## SS. RODERIC AND SOLOMON, MARTYRS	(A.D. 857)

THE history of the two martyrs Roderic and Solomon has been preserved for us by their contemporary St Eulogius, who wrote, either from his own knowledge or from the testimony of eye-witnesses, the acts of all those who perished before him in the persecution in which, as narrated above (March 11), he himself laid down his life. It must be acknowledged that these acts give an unfavourable impression of the mentality of the general run of Christians in Moorish Spain at that epoch. Families were divided, apostasy was common, and the Moors themselves were scandalized at the unfaithfulness of Christians and cast their laxity in their teeth. No wonder then that Eulogius begins his book with the words, " In those days, by a just judgement of God, Spain was oppressed by the Moors ". The story of St Roderic may serve as an illustration.

The martyr was a priest of Cabra who had two brothers, one of whom had become a Mohammedan whilst the other was a bad Christian who had practically abandoned his faith. One night the two brothers fell into an altercation which became so heated that they came to blows, and Roderic rushed in to separate them. Thereupon they both turned on him and beat him until he fell senseless to the ground. The Mohammedan then had him placed upon a litter and carried through the streets, whilst he himself walked beside the stretcher proclaiming that Roderic had apostatized and wished to be publicly recognized as a Mohammedan before he died. The victim was too ill to speak, but he suffered great anguish of mind, and as soon as he had recovered the use of his limbs he made his escape.

Not long afterwards, the Mohammedan brother met him in the streets of Cordova and immediately haled him before the kadi on the charge of having returned to the Christian faith after having declared himself a Mohammedan. Roderic indignantly denied ever having forsaken the Christian religion, but the kadi refused to believe him and cast him into one of the vilest dungeons in the city. There he found another prisoner, named Solomon, who had been confined there on the same charge. The two encouraged each other during the long and weary imprisonment by which the kadi had expected to wear out their constancy. As they remained inflexible, they were separated, but when that also proved ineffectual they were condemned and decapitated. St Eulogius, who saw their dead bodies exposed beside the river, noticed that the guards threw into the stream the pebbles stained with the martyrs' blood lest the people should pick them up to preserve them as relics.

Our primary authority is the *Apologeticus* of St Eulogius, from which the Bollandists in the *Acta Sanctorum* (March, vol. ii) have extracted the relevant passages. See also Florez, *España Sagrada*, vol. xii, pp. 36 *seq*.

BD AGNELLO OF PISA   (A.D. 1236)

THE founder of the English Franciscan province, Bd. Agnello, was admitted into the order by St Francis himself on the occasion of his sojourn in Pisa. He was sent to the friary in Paris, of which he became the *custos* or guardian, and in 1224 St Francis appointed him to found an English province, although he was as yet only a deacon. Of the eight brothers selected to accompany him three were Englishmen, but only one was in priest's orders, namely, Richard of Ingworth. True to the precepts of St Francis, they had no money, and the monks of Fécamp paid their passage over to Dover. They made Canterbury their first stopping-place, whence Richard of Ingworth, Richard of Devon and two of the Italians went on to London to see where they could settle. The rest were lodged at the Poor Priests' House, sleeping in a building which was used as a school by day. While the scholars were there, the friars were penned up in a small room at the back, and only after the boys had gone home could they come out and make a fire.

It was the winter of 1224, and they must have suffered great discomfort, especially as their ordinary fare was bread and a little beer, which was so thick that it had to be diluted before they could swallow it. Nothing, however, damped their spirits, and their simple piety, cheerfulness and enthusiasm soon won them many friends. They were able to produce a commendatory letter from Pope Honorius III, so that the archbishop of Canterbury, Stephen Langton, in announcing their arrival, said, " Some religious have come to me calling themselves Penitents of the Order of Assisi, but *I* call them of the Order of the Apostles " By this name they were at first known in England, and when some of them were to be ordained acolytes at Canterbury four months after landing, the archdeacon, in bidding the candidates come forward, said, " Draw near, ye brothers of the Order of the Apostles ".

In the meantime Richard of Ingworth and his party had been well received in London and had hired a dwelling on Cornhill. They were now ready to push on to Oxford, and Agnello came from Canterbury to take charge of the London settlement. Everywhere the friars were received with enthusiasm, and Matthew Paris himself attests that Bd Agnello was on familiar terms with King Henry III. Although the minister provincial was not himself a learned man, yet he established a teaching centre which afterwards greatly influenced the university. To that school, in which Grosseteste, afterwards bishop of Lincoln, was a lecturer, flocked numbers of eager youths who were trained as friars and who, before many years were over, helped to raise Oxford to a position hardly inferior to Paris as a centre of learning.

Agnello seems to have died at the age of forty-one, only eleven years after he landed at Dover, but his reputation for sanctity and prudence stood high amongst his fellows. It is stated that his zeal for poverty was so great that " he would never permit any ground to be enlarged or any house to be built except as inevitable necessity required ". In particular the story runs that he built the infirmary at Oxford " in such humble fashion that the height of the walls did not much exceed the height of a man ". During Mass and when saying the Divine Office he shed tears continually, " yet so that neither by any noise nor by groans nor by any contortion of the face could it be known that he wept " He was stern in resisting relaxations in the rule, but his gentleness and tact led him to be chosen in 1233 to negotiate with the rebellious Earl Marshal. His health is said to have been undermined by his efforts in this cause and by a last painful journey to Italy. On his return he was seized with dysentery at Oxford and died there, after crying out for three days, " Come, sweetest Jesus ". The cult of Bd Agnello was confirmed in 1892 ; his feast is observed in the archdiocese of Birmingham today and by the Friars Minor on the 11th.

The narrative of Thomas of Eccleston, *De adventu Fratrum Minorum*, together with the Chronicle of Lanercost, and the *De conformitate* of Bartholomew of Pisa are the most reliable sources of information. See especially the translation of Thomas of Eccleston with its appendixes, by Father Cuthbert, and the text edited by A. G. Little. See also the last-named's *The Grey Friars in Oxford* (1892) ; E. Hutton, *The Franciscans in England* (1933) ; and Father Gilbert, *Bd Agnellus and the English Grey Friars* (1937).

14 : ST LEOBINUS, OR LUBIN, BISHOP OF CHARTRES   (*c.* A.D. 558)

THE parents of St Lubin were peasants in the country near Poitiers, and from childhood he was set to work in the fields. As a boy he was keen to learn, and his thirst for knowledge increasing with years he went to a monastery—probably Noailles—where he was employed in menial tasks. His work occupied him all day, and he was obliged to do most of his studying at night, screening his lamp as best he could, because the monks complained that the light disturbed their slumbers. By humility and perseverance he advanced in religious knowledge until he had reached an honourable place in the house. In some way, however, he came into contact with St Carilef, and it was probably at his suggestion that Lubin sought out the hermit St Avitus, who recommended him to spend some time longer in a monastery and then to return to him in Le Perche.

After sundry misadventures Lubin settled down for five years in an abbey near Lyons, until in a war between the Franks and the Burgundians the monastery was raided and the monks took to flight, only Lubin and an old man remaining behind. The raiders, who were intent on plunder, tried to discover from the old man where the treasures were concealed, and he referred them to St Lubin. As they could obtain no information from him they had recourse to torture—fastening a cord round his head and tightening it. After this they tied his feet and dipped him, head first, into the river, but failing to make him divulge anything they eventually left him for dead. He recovered, however, and with two companions returned to Le Perche where St Avitus received him into his monastery. After the death of St Avitus, Lubin again lived the life of a hermit. Bishop Aetherius of Chartres nominated him abbot of Brou and raised him to the priesthood. He seems to have found his responsibilities too onerous and longed to lay down office and become a simple monk at Lérins, but St Caesarius, to whom his own bishop sent him for advice, told him to go back to Brou and not to leave his people like sheep without a shepherd. He obeyed, but soon after his return was promoted to succeed Aetherius as bishop of Chartres. He brought about various reforms and continued to be very famous for his miracles. He took part in the Fifth Council of Orleans and in the Second Council of Paris, dying on March 14, about 558, after a long illness.

The ancient Life of St Leobinus has been edited by B. Krusch in MGH., *Auct. Antiquiss.*, vol. iv, part 2, pp. 73–82, as an appendix to the works of Venantius Fortunatus, who was at one time believed to have been the author. Fr A. Poncelet considers that the biography in its present form cannot be older than the middle of the ninth century. See the *Analecta Bollandiana*, vol. xxiv (1905), pp. 25–31, and p. 82. *Cf.* Duchesne, *Fastes Épiscopaux*, vol. ii, p. 422, and the *Acta Sanctorum*, March, vol. ii.

ST EUTYCHIUS, OR EUSTATHIUS, MARTYR   (A.D. 741)

DURING the reign of the Emperor Leo the Isaurian, when the empire was being attacked and seriously threatened by the invading forces of Islam, persecution came almost equally from both sides. On the one hand the emperor was so determined an opponent of the *cultus* of sacred images that the orthodox faithful were continually subjected to imprisonment and exile, whilst, on the other hand, the fanatical hatred of the Arabs was directed against all Christians alike, and their victories over Romans were apt to be celebrated by a fresh holocaust of victims. Eutychius or Eustathius, the son of a patrician, was taken prisoner with many others by the Arabs. He was carried off and kept for many months in captivity, until the khalif, when another expedition of his against the Christians had suffered reverses, growing infuriated, wreaked his vengeance on the prisoners. For refusing to abjure the Christian faith Eutychius was put to death at Carrhae in Mesopotamia with several companions—perhaps at the stake—after enduring horrible tortures. His relics are said to have worked many miracles.

See the *Acta Sanctorum*, March, vol. ii, where the brief account given is based entirely upon the *Chronography* of Theophanes.

ST MATILDA, WIDOW   (A.D. 968)

A DESCENDANT of the celebrated Widukind who led the Saxons in their long struggle against Charlemagne, St Matilda was the daughter of Dietrich, a Westphalian count, and of Reinhild, a scion of the royal Danish house. The little girl, who was born about the year 895, was confided to the care of her paternal grandmother, the abbess of the convent of Erfurt. Here, not far from her home, Matilda was educated and grew up to womanhood, excelling all her companions, we are told, in beauty, piety and learning. In due course she married the son of Duke Otto of Saxony, Henry, called " the Fowler " because of his fondness for hawking : the union was an exceptionally happy one, and Matilda ever exerted a wholesome and restraining influence over her husband. Just after the birth of their eldest son Otto, three years after their marriage, Henry succeeded to his father's dukedom, and when, about the beginning of the year 919, King Conrad died childless, he was raised to the German throne. It was well indeed for him that he was a capable soldier, for his life was one of warfare—in which he was singularly successful.

By Henry himself and his subjects his successes were attributed as much to the prayers of the queen as to his own prowess. Throughout her life she retained the humility which had distinguished her as a girl, and in the royal palace she lived almost like a religious. To her court and to her servants she seemed less a queen and mistress than a loving mother, and no one in distress ever applied to her in vain. Her husband rarely checked her liberal almsgiving or showed irritation at her pious practices, having entire confidence in her goodness and trusting her in all things. After twenty-three years of marriage King Henry died of an apoplectic fit in 936. Matilda had gone to the church to pour forth her soul in prayer for him at the foot of the altar when it was announced to her that he had passed away. At once she asked for a priest to offer the holy sacrifice for his soul, and cutting off the jewels that she was wearing gave them to the priest as a pledge that she renounced, from that moment, the pomps of the world.

Five children had been born to Henry and Matilda—Otto, afterwards emperor, Henry the Quarrelsome, St Bruno, subsequently archbishop of Cologne, Gerberga, who married Louis IV, King of France, and Hedwig, the mother of Hugh Capet. Although it had been Henry's wish that his eldest son Otto should succeed him, Matilda favoured her younger son Henry and persuaded a few nobles to vote for him ; but Otto was chosen and crowned. Unwilling to give up his claims, Henry raised a rebellion against his brother, but finding himself worsted, sued for peace, was pardoned by Otto, and at Matilda's intercession was made duke of Bavaria. The queen was now living a life of almost complete self-abnegation ; her jewellery had gone to help the poor, whilst her bounties were so lavish as to arouse criticism. Her son Otto accused her of having treasure in hiding and of wasting the crown revenues : he called upon her to give an account of all she had spent and set spies to watch her movements and her donations. The bitterest part of her suffering was the discovery that her favourite Henry was aiding and abetting his brother. She bore all with invincible patience, remarking, with a touch of pathetic humour, that it was a consolation to know that her sons were united—even though it was only in their persecution of herself. " I would willingly endure all they could do against me if it would keep them together—provided that they could do it without sin ", she is reported to have said.

To satisfy them, Matilda resigned her inheritance to her sons and retired to the country residence where she had been born. But no sooner was she gone than Duke Henry fell ill and disaster began to descend upon the state. It was generally felt that these misfortunes were due to the treatment meted out to their mother, and Otto's wife Edith persuaded him to ask her forgiveness and to restore all he had taken from her. Matilda freely forgave both her sons and returned to court, where she resumed her works of mercy. But though Henry had ceased to persecute her, his conduct continued to cause her great sorrow. He again revolted against Otto and afterwards punished an insurrection of his own Bavarian subjects with almost incredible cruelty ; even the bishops were not spared. In 955 when Matilda saw him for the last time, she prophesied his approaching death and entreated him to repent before it was too late. The news that he had died, which reached her shortly afterwards, almost prostrated her and cut away one of the last ties that bound her to earth. She set about building a convent at Nordhausen, and made other foundations at Quedlinburg, at Engern and also at Poehlen, where she established a monastery for men. That Otto no longer resented her spending her own revenue in religious works is evident from the fact that when he went to Rome to be crowned emperor he left the kingdom in her charge.

The last time Matilda took part in a family gathering was at Cologne at the Easter of 965. Thither came also the Emperor Otto, " the Great ", and her other surviving children and grandchildren. After this appearance she practically retired from the world, spending her time in one or other of her foundations, chiefly at Nordhausen. Urgent affairs had called her to Quedlinburg when a fever from which she had been suffering for some time grew gradually worse and she realized she was dying. She sent for Richburga, who as lady-in-waiting had assisted her in her charities and was now abbess of Nordhausen. According to tradition, the queen proceeded to make a deed of gift of everything in her room until she was told that there was nothing left but the linen which was to serve as a winding-sheet. " Give that to Bishop William of Mainz ", she said designating her grandson. " He will need it first." He actually died, very suddenly, twelve days before his grandmother's decease on March 14, 968. Matilda's body was buried beside that of her husband at Quedlinburg, and she was locally venerated as a saint from the moment of her death.

The MGH. contain the best text of the two ancient lives of St Matilda—the older in *Scriptores*, vol. x, pp. 575–582, the more recent in *Scriptores*, vol. iv, pp. 283–302. Further information may be gleaned from the contemporary chroniclers and charters. See also the *Acta Sanctorum*, March, vol. ii ; L. Clarus, *Die hl. Mathilde ;* L. Zöpf, *Die Heiligenleben im 10 Jahrhundert ;* and L. E. Hallberg, *Ste Mathilde.*

BD JAMES, Archbishop of Naples   (A.D. 1308)

Viterbo was the birthplace of James Capocci, who entered the Augustinian Order at an early age.   Giving great promise of eminence both in piety and learning he was sent to make his higher studies at the University of Paris, where he attended the lectures of his illustrious fellow Augustinian, Aegidius Romanus, who had been the pupil of St Thomas Aquinas and was an enthusiastic upholder of the teaching of the Angelic Doctor.   After returning for a while to Italy and acting as theological instructor to his own brethren, Capocci was sent to make a second stay in Paris, where he took his doctor's degree, and thereupon lectured in that city and subsequently at Naples.   It is recorded of him that he solemnly expressed his conviction that God had sent into the world three teachers to enlighten the Universal Church —first Paul the Apostle, then later on Augustine, and now in these last days Brother Thomas.   In 1302 Bd James was appointed archbishop of Benevento by Pope Boniface VIII, but only a few months later the same pontiff translated him to the archiepiscopal see of Naples, in which office he won the veneration of all by his virtue and his learning.   His death in 1308 was followed by many spontaneous manifestations of the ardour with which his memory was cherished by his flock, and the *cultus* then begun was confirmed in 1911.

See the rescript for the *confirmatio cultus*, which is printed in the *Acta Apostolicae Sedis*, vol. iii (1911), p. 319.   Some idea of the mental attitude of Bd James towards questions much discussed in his day may be obtained from his work *De regimine christiano*, which was printed and edited by H. X. Arquillière in 1926, and also from the article of M. Grabmann in the *Festgabe Josef Geyser* (1930), vol. i, pp. 209–232.

15 : ST LONGINUS, Martyr   (First Century)

THE story of St Longinus, who is commemorated on this day in the Roman Martyrology and is there associated with the city of Caesarea in Cappadocia, may conveniently be given in the terms of Bd James of Voragine's *Golden Legend*.   St Longinus, according to this account, was the centurion who, standing by Pilate's direction with other soldiers beside the cross of our Lord, pierced His side with a lance, and seeing the portents which followed, the darkening of the sun and the earthquake, believed in Christ.   But what influenced him most, as some relate, was that though his sight was failing him, either through age or infirmity, the blood of our Saviour running down the lance touched his eyes, and straightway he saw clearly.   For this reason he gave up his soldiering, and, after being instructed by the apostles, he led a monastic life in Caesarea of Cappadocia, by his words and example winning many souls to Christ.   Having been brought to trial and refusing to offer sacrifice, the governor ordered all his teeth to be knocked out and his tongue cut off.   Nevertheless Longinus did not in consequence lose his power of speech. Catching up an axe, he broke the idols into fragments, and cried aloud, " Now we shall see whether they are gods ".   But a pack of demons issuing forth from the idols entered into the governor and his attendants.   Then gibbering and howling they fell down at Longinus's feet.   Thereupon Longinus said to them, " Why take ye up your abode in idols ? "   Who answered, " Where the name of Christ is not heard and the sign of His cross is not imposed, there is our dwelling-place ". Meanwhile the governor continued to rave and he was now blind.   So Longinus said to him, " Know that thou canst only be cured when thou hast put me to death. But as soon as I shall have surrendered my life by thy act, I will pray for thee, and I will obtain for thee health both of body and of soul." Straightway then the governor ordered his head to be cut off ; and immediately this was done he threw himself down beside the corpse and with tears manifested his repentance. But in that same moment he recovered his sanity along with his sight, and he ended his life in the doing of all good works.

The untrustworthy character of this account, which is supported by no documentary evidence of the early centuries, is patent upon the face of it. The " centurion " of Mark (xv 29) is unwarrantably identified with the " soldier " (John xix 34) who pierced the side of Jesus. To this latter, in the apocryphal " Gospel of Nicodemus ", otherwise known as the " Acts of Pilate ", the name Longinus is given in its later recensions ; but there seems every probability that it was suggested by the Greek word λόγχη (a lance), the weapon he is recorded to have used. There is a Syriac manuscript of the gospels in the Laurentian Library at Florence written by a certain monk Rabulus in 586, which contains a miniature of the crucifixion. In this the soldier piercing our Lord's side has the name Loginus written over his head in Greek characters. This may, however, have been a later addition. What we know for certain is that there were several different stories in circulation regarding Longinus which have given rise to different feasts at different dates. The most notable legend is that of Mantua, which claims that Longinus came to that city shortly after the death of our Lord, and that there, after preaching the gospel for some years, he suffered martyrdom. He is said, moreover, to have brought with him a portion of the precious blood shed upon the cross, which relic is alleged to be still preserved at Mantua, as well as the body of the saint.

There is a considerable literature connected with these fables. Some account of it will be found in C. Kröner, *Die Longinuslegende* (1899), but a still fuller treatment in R. J. Peebles, *The Legend of Longinus in Ecclesiastical Tradition and English Literature* (1911). See also the *Acta Sanctorum*, March, vol. ii ; and F. I. Dölger, *Antike und Christentum*, bk iv (1933), pp. 81–94.

ST MATRONA, Virgin and Martyr   (Date Unknown)

THERE are three saints of this name who are commemorated in the *Acta Sanctorum* on March 15. One only of the three appears in the Roman Martyrology, where she is honoured with the following eulogium : " At Thessalonica, of St Matrona, the servant maid of a certain Jewess, who worshipped Christ by stealth and went daily to the church for secret prayer. She was discovered by her mistress and in many ways tormented until at last she was beaten to death with stout rods and in the confession of Christ rendered up her pure soul to God." The same account, slightly developed, is found in the Greek synaxaries, and we meet it in the West in the early part of the ninth century with certain additional details describing how the martyr, on two occasions being left overnight bound with thongs to a bench, was found in the morning miraculously released. Of this St Matrona no *cultus* seems to survive. In Barcelona, however, there is, or was, what purport to be the remains of a virgin of the same name who, though born in that region, was taken to Rome, and there, on account of the services she rendered to the Christians in prison, was arrested and put to death, her body being brought back to her own country. A third St Matrona, who is not a martyr, is honoured on this day in the neighbourhood of Capua. She is said, however, to have been of royal birth and to have come from Portugal. She suffered grievously from dysentery, and was supernaturally directed to go to Italy to find a cure, for the relief of which disease she is now invoked.

See the *Acta Sanctorum*, March, vol. ii ; A. B. C. Dunbar, *Dictionary of Saintly Women*, vol. ii, p. 77 ; Quentin, *Les Martyrologes Historiques*, p. 181.

ST ZACHARY, POPE   (A.D. 752)

DETAILS of the early life of St Zachary are lacking, but he is known to have been born at San Severino of a Greek family settled in Calabria, and he is believed to have been one of the deacons of the Roman church. Upon the death of St Gregory III, he was unanimously elected pope. No better selection could have been made : a man of learning and of great personal holiness, he joined a conciliatory spirit to far-sighted wisdom, and was able to cope with the grave problems which confronted him upon his accession. The position of Rome was one of much peril. The Lombards were again preparing to invade Roman territory, when the new pope decided to treat directly with their ruler, and went himself to Terni to visit him. He was received with respect, and his personality produced such an impression that Liutprand returned all the territory that had been taken from the Romans in the preceding thirty years. Moreover he made a twenty years' treaty and released all his prisoners. Peace having been made with Rome, Liutprand prepared to attack Ravenna. The exarch immediately turned to St Zachary and implored his assistance. The pope, after sundry unsuccessful efforts, went in person to Pavia, where his intervention induced the king to abandon his offensive. Liutprand died soon afterwards, and his second successor, Rachis, was encouraged by Zachary eventually to become a monk at Monte Cassino. But his brother Aistulf was a different sort of man : in the last years of St Zachary's pontificate he captured Ravenna, bringing the Byzantine imperial exarchate finally to an end, and Rome was again threatened.

Pope Zachary's relations with Constantinople, where the Emperor Constantine V maintained Iconoclasm, were rendered unimportant by political upheavals there, but in the further West progress was continuous. This was in the first place due to St Boniface, with whom the pope kept in close touch and to whom he gave every encouragement. By this time the power of the Merovingian kings in France had passed completely to the mayors of the palace, and in 751 Pepin the Short sent an embassy to the pope asking if he did not think that one who exercised sovereign rule ought to be king. Zachary, with equal diplomacy, replied that he did think so, and Pepin was accordingly elected king at Soissons and anointed by the papal legate St Boniface—a happening full of significance for both papacy and secular sovereignty.

Amid all his activities Pope Zachary found time to translate St Gregory's *Dialogues* into Greek, and he was always full of care for the poor and oppressed. He provided a home for nuns driven out of Constantinople by the icono-clasts, he ransomed slaves in the Roman market who otherwise would have been sold by the Venetians to the Saracens, and early in his pontificate he threatened with excommunication those who should sell Christian slaves to Jews. Zachary was venerated as a saint immediately after his death, which happened in March 752.

There is a fairly satisfactory account of St Zachary in the *Liber Pontificalis*, but for fuller detail we have to turn to his letters and to the chronicles, such as the Annals of Lorsch. See H. K. Mann, *Lives of the Popes*, vol. ii, pp. 225–288, and Cardinal Bartolini, *Di S. Zaccaria Papa* (1879). Hodgkin, Gregorovius and other secular historians speak appreciatively of his work.

ST LEOCRITIA, or LUCRETIA, Virgin and Martyr   (A.D. 859)

St Leocritia lived in Cordova when it was a Moorish city and when the conversion of a follower of Islam was punishable by death. Her parents were wealthy and influential Moslems, but she herself had been converted to Christianity by a relation called Litiosa, and had been baptized. At first she kept her religion secret, but as time went on she practised it more openly and admitted her faith to her parents. Angry and alarmed, they sought to make her apostatize by entreaties, by threats and finally by blows and confinement. She managed to send word to St Eulogius, asking if he could find her a refuge with his sister Anulona, and the messenger brought back a favourable answer. She now awaited an opportunity to escape. Her apparently passive attitude had led her parents to think she was about to comply with their wishes, and they accordingly gave her permission to attend a wedding ; she contrived to slip away from the gathering and to rejoin her Christian friends. Her absence was soon discovered and a great hue and cry was raised, followed by the arrest and examination of any Christians suspected of having had communication with her. Leocritia was handed on from one Christian family to another, St Eulogius visiting her from time to time to instruct her more fully and to strengthen her for the fate that awaited her. At length she was discovered, and both she and St Eulogius were brought before the judge. When St Eulogius was asked why he had concealed her, " I have been entrusted with the office of a preacher ", he replied, " and it is my holy duty to enlighten all who seek the light of the faith. To no seeker may I refuse to show the way of life. What I have done for her I would also have done for you, if you had asked me." They were both flogged and condemned to death. After St Leocritia had been decapitated, her body was thrown into the Guadalquivir. It was afterwards deposited at Oviedo, beside that of St Eulogius.

A short account of St Leocritia is given in the *Acta Sanctorum*, March, vol. ii.

BD WILLIAM HART, Martyr   (A.D. 1583)

This martyr, born at Wells in Somerset, went to Lincoln College, Oxford, and there came under the influence of Dr Bridgewater, who, on account of his Catholic principles, soon after resigned the rectorship and took refuge in Douai. Hart followed his example, and though a delicate man, suffering at times paroxysms of pain from the stone, he faced with marvellous cheerfulness the many hardships entailed by his life as a refugee. After teaching at Rheims he passed on to Rome, and being there ordained priest, returned to the English mission and laboured in Yorkshire. He was particularly remarkable for his joyous spirit and for his courage and charity in visiting those Catholics who were imprisoned in York Castle. On one occasion, when suspicion was aroused, he only escaped capture by letting himself down over the wall into the moat, where he was up to the chin in mud and water. Not long afterwards he was betrayed by an apostate and seems to have been arrested on Christmas night in the house of Bd Margaret Clitherow, who was one of his penitents. He suffered much in the dungeon into which he was cast, not only from physical hardships, but also from the persistent attempts of Protestant ministers to argue with him even at the very foot of the gallows. He was hanged, but the crowd would not allow him to be cut down and disembowelled alive.

See Challoner (MMP., pp. 72–79), who prints a very touching letter written by the martyr to his Protestant mother a few days before his death ; and Camm, LEM., vol. pp. 300 *seq.*

ST LOUISA DE MARILLAC, WIDOW, CO-FOUNDRESS OF THE VINCENTIAN SISTERS OF CHARITY (A.D. 1660)

To the modern reader it must seem strange that this valiant woman, who had been a wife and a mother before she consecrated her widowhood to the service of God, was best known to her contemporaries as Mademoiselle Le Gras, Le Gras not being even her maiden name but the name of her husband. The title Madame, however, in seventeenth-century France, was given only to great ladies of the high nobility, and Louisa de Marillac, though well-born and married to an important official in the service of the queen, was not of the rank to whom that compliment was paid. Her father, Louis de Marillac, was a country gentleman of ancient lineage, and her father's brothers after rising to fame became even more celebrated in history as the tragic victims of the resentment of Cardinal Richelieu. Louisa, born in 1591, lost her mother when still a child, but had a good up-bringing and education, thanks partly to the nuns of Poissy to whose care she was confided for a while, and partly to the personal instruction of her own father, who, however, died when she was little more than fifteen. She had wished at one time to become a Capuchin sister but her then confessor, himself a Capuchin, dissuaded her because her health was too frail. In the end a suitable husband was found for her and she consented to marry Antony Le Gras, a man who seemed destined for a distinguished career. A son was born to them, and her twelve years of married life were happy enough except that before very long her husband fell ill of a lingering sickness in which she nursed him most devotedly. Unfortunately she was tempted to regard this visitation as a punishment for her own infidelity to grace, and these anxieties of conscience became the occasion of long spells of aridity and doubt. It was, however, her good fortune to make the acquaintance of St Francis de Sales, who spent some months in Paris during the year 1619. From him she received the wisest and most sympathetic of guidance. But Paris was not his home, and though he confided her to the spiritual care of his favourite disciple, Mgr Le Camus, Bishop of Belley, the latter's visits to the capital were rare and apt to be somewhat uncertain.

Not long before the death of her husband, Louisa made a vow not to marry again but to devote herself wholly to the service of God, and this was followed a little later by a strange spiritual illumination in which she felt her misgivings dispelled and was given to understand that there was a great work which she was called to do in the future under the guidance of a director to whom she had never yet spoken. Her husband's state of health had long been hopeless. He died in 1625, but before this she had already made the acquaintance of " M. Vincent ", as the holy priest known to us now as St Vincent de Paul was then called, and he, though showing reluctance at first, consented eventually to act as her confessor. St Vincent was at this time organizing his " Confraternities of Charity ", with the object of remedying the appalling misery and ignorance which he had found existing among the peasantry in country districts.   With his wonderful tact and zeal he was soon able to count upon the assistance of a number of ladies (whom he styled *Dames de Charité*), and associations were formed in many centres which undoubtedly effected a great deal of good.   None the less experience showed that if this work was to be carried on systematically and was to be developed in Paris itself, good order was needed and a copious supply of helpers.   The aristocratic ladies of charity, however zealous, could not spare enough time from their other duties, and in many cases had not the physical strength, to meet the demands made upon them.   For the purpose of nursing and tending the poor, looking after neglected children and dealing with rough-spoken male folk, the most useful recruits were as a rule those in humble station, who were accustomed to hardships. But they needed supervision and guidance from one whom they thoroughly respected and who had the tact to win their hearts and to show them the way by example.

Coming by degrees to be better acquainted with Mlle Le Gras, St Vincent found that he had here at hand the very instrument he needed.   She had a clear intelligence, unflinching courage, a marvellous endurance in spite of feeble health and, perhaps most important of all, the readiness to efface herself completely, realizing that the work was wholly for God and not for her glory.   Never perhaps was a greater or more enduring religious enterprise set on foot with less of sensationalism than the founding of that society which was at first known by the name of the " Daughters of Charity " (*Filles de la Charité*) and which has now earned the respect of men of the most divergent beliefs in every part of the world.   It was only after some five years personal association with Mlle Le Gras that M. Vincent, who was ever patient to abide God's own good time, sent this devoted soul in May 1629 to make what we might call a visitation of the " Charity " of Montmirail. This was the precursor of many similar missions, and in spite of much bad health, of which St Vincent himself was by no means inconsiderate, his deputy, with all her reckless self-sacrifice did not succumb.   Quietly, however, and very gradually, as activities multiplied, in the by-ways of Paris as well as in the country, the need of robust helpers made itself felt.   There were many girls and widows of the peasant class who were ready to give their lives to such work, but they were often rough and quite illiterate.   To obtain the best results instruction was necessary and tactful guidance.   Vincent's own energies were already taxed to the uttermost, most of his time being necessarily given to his company of mission priests.   Moreover, much of the work of the " Charities " had necessarily to be done by women, and to organize and superintend that work a woman was needed who was well acquainted with the instruments upon whom she had to depend.

Hence it came about that in 1633 a sort of training centre or noviceship was established in what was then known as the Rue des Fossés-Saint-Victor.   This was the unfashionable dwelling which Mlle Le Gras had rented for herself after her husband's death, and she now gave hospitality to the first candidates who were accepted for the service of the sick and poor, four simple people whose very names are unrecorded.   These with Louisa as their directress formed the grain of mustard seed which has grown into the world-wide organization known as the Sisters of Charity of St Vincent de Paul.   But expansion was rapid.   Soon it became evident that some rule of life and some guarantee of stability was desirable.   Louisa had long wanted to bind herself to this service by vow, but St Vincent, always prudent and content to wait for a clear manifestation of the will of God, had restrained her ardour. But in 1634 her desire was gratified ; and this naturally paved the way for a scrutiny of the whole position and the possibilities of the future. St Vincent had now complete confidence in his spiritual daughter, and it was she who drafted something in the nature of a rule of life which was to be followed by the members of their association. The substance of this document forms the kernel of the religious observance of the Sisters of Charity down to the present day. But although this was a great step forward, the recognition of the Sisters of Charity as an institute of nuns was still far distant. St Vincent himself insisted that he had never dreamed of founding a religious order. It was God who had done it all. These poor souls, as he often reminded them, must look upon themselves as nothing but Christian women devoting their energies to the service of the sick and the poor. " Your convent ", he said, " will be the house of the sick ; your cell, a hired room ; your chapel, the parish church ; your cloister, the streets of the city or the wards of the hospital ; your enclosure, obedience ; your grating, the fear of God ; your veil, holy modesty." If at the present day the white cornette and the grey stuff gown to which his daughters have remained faithful during nearly three centuries at once attract the eye in any crowd, that is only due to the modern abandonment of the peasant costume of past ages. In the towns of Normandy and Brittany not so long ago the white linen headdresses of the country-women were such that a Sister of Charity who had strayed amongst them would not easily have been distinguishable in the throng. St Vincent, the foe of all pretension, was reluctant that his daughters should claim even that distinction and respect which attach to the religious habit of those who are consecrated to God. It was not until 1642 that he allowed four of the company to take annual vows of poverty, chastity and obedience, and it was not until 1655—though this delay was mainly due to political and accidental causes—that Cardinal de Retz, Archbishop of Paris, despatched from Rome the formal approbation of the company and placed them definitely under the direction of St Vincent's own congregation of priests.

Meanwhile the good works of the Daughters of Charity had multiplied apace. The patients of the great Paris hospital of the Hôtel-Dieu had passed in large measure under their care, the brutal treatment of an abandoned child had led St Vincent to organize a home for foundlings, and despite the illiteracy of many of their own recruits the associates had found themselves compelled to undertake the teaching of children. In all these developments Mlle Le Gras had borne the heaviest part of the burden. She had set a wonderful example at Angers in taking over the care of a terribly neglected hospital. The strain had been so great that in spite of the devotion of her Daughters of Charity she had suffered a severe breakdown, which at first was reported, but incorrectly, to be a case of plague infection. In Paris she had nursed the plague-stricken herself during an outbreak of the epidemic and in spite of her delicate constitution had survived the ordeal. Her frequent journeys, necessitated by the duties of her office, would have tried the endurance of the most robust, but she was always at hand when her presence was needed, full of hope and creating around her an atmosphere of joy and peace. As we may learn from her letters to St Vincent and others, two things only troubled her ; the one was the respect and veneration with which she found her visits welcomed, the other was her anxiety for the spiritual welfare of her son Michael. With all her occupations she never forgot him. St Vincent himself kept an eye on Michael, and was satisfied that the young man was a thoroughly good fellow, but with not much stability of character. He had no vocation for the priesthood, as his mother had hoped, but he married and seems to have led a good and edifying life to the end. He came with his wife and child to visit his mother on her deathbed and she blessed them tenderly. It was the year 1660, and St Vincent was himself eighty years old and very infirm. She would have given much to see this beloved father once more, but that consolation was denied her. Nevertheless her soul was at peace, her life's work had been marvellously blessed, and she uncomplainingly made the sacrifice, telling those around her that she was happy to have still this one deprivation left which she could offer to God. The burden of what, in those last days, she said to her grieving sisters was always this : " Be diligent in serving the poor . . . love the poor, honour them, my children, as you would honour Christ Himself." St Louisa de Marillac died on March 15, 1660, and St Vincent followed her only six months later. She was canonized in 1934.

No more valuable source exists for the biographer of St Louisa than the *Vie de Saint Vincent de Paul*, by Father P Coste, together with the saint's correspondence and discourses which had previously been collected and published by the diligence of the same painstaking editor. Some value also attaches to the *Vie de Mlle le Gras*, which was brought out by M. Gobillon in 1676, and to three others of more modern date, that by the Countess de Richemont in 1882, that of Mgr Baunard in 1898, and that of E. de Broglie in the series " Les Saints " (Eng. trans., 1933). A slight but attractive, if not always accurate, sketch was written by Kathleen O'Meara under the title of *A Heroine of Charity*, and there are other popular accounts by M. V. Woodgate (1942) and Sister M. Cullen. All the lives of St Vincent de Paul mentioned herein under July 19 necessarily include much information concerning St Louisa.

ST CLEMENT HOFBAUER   (A.D. 1820)

ST CLEMENT MARY HOFBAUER is sometimes called the second founder of the Redemptorists, because it was he who first planted the congregation of St Alphonsus Liguori north of the Alps. To him is due the further credit of having done more than any other individual to bring about the collapse of " Josephinism ", that Austrian counterpart of Erastianism which treated ecclesiastics as functionaries of the state and subject to secular control. Born in 1751 in Moravia, St Clement, whose baptismal name was John, was the ninth of the twelve children of a grazier and butcher who had changed his Slavonic surname Dvorak to the German equivalent Hofbauer. Even as a child the boy longed to become a priest, but poverty stood in the way, and, at the age of fifteen, he was apprenticed to a baker. Later he was employed in the bakery of the Premonstratensian monastery at Bruck, where his self-sacrifice during a time of famine won him the favour of the abbot, who allowed him to follow the classes of the Latin school attached to the abbey. After the abbot's death, the young man lived as a solitary, until the Emperor Joseph's edict against hermitages obliged him to take up his old trade again, this time in Vienna. From that city he twice made pilgrimages to Rome, in company with his friend Peter Kunzmann, and on the second occasion they obtained permission from Bishop Chiaramonti of Tivoli (afterwards Pope Pius VII) to settle as hermits in his diocese. Within a few months, however, it was borne in upon him that his work was to be that of a missioner, not a solitary, and he accordingly returned to Vienna. One day, after he had been serving Mass at the cathedral of St Stephen, he offered to fetch a carriage for two ladies who were detained in the porch by a downpour of rain, and this chance meeting led to the accomplishment of his heart's desire, for the two ladies, discovering that he had not the means to prosecute the necessary studies for the priesthood, paid not only for him but also for his friend Thaddeus Hübl. As the University of Vienna was tainted with rationalistic teaching, they returned to Rome, and there, being greatly attracted by the Redemptorists, they both sought admission into the novitiate. St Alphonsus himself, who was still alive at the time, rejoiced greatly when he heard of the new-comers from the north, foreseeing the establishment of his congregation in Austria.

The two friends were professed and ordained in 1785, Clement being then already 34 years old. They then were sent back to Vienna, but since the Emperor Joseph II, not content with the overthrow of the Jesuits, had already suppressed several hundred monasteries belonging to other orders, it was useless to think of making a new foundation there. He was then charged by his superiors to begin a mission in Courland, and started northwards with Thaddeus Hübl. On the way St Clement met his old friend Emmanuel Kunzmann, who had continued to live in the hermitage at Tivoli, but was then on a pilgrimage. Their encounter seemed providential. Kunzmann soon determined to join the other two as a lay-brother, and became the first Redemptorist novice to be received north of the Alps. At Warsaw the papal nuncio placed at their disposal the church of St Benno. There were several thousand German Catholics in the city who, since the suppression of the Jesuits, had had no priest who knew their language. In his anxiety to retain the Redemptorists, the nuncio wrote to Rome and obtained the postponement of the mission to Courland in view of the work to be done in Warsaw. They began their labours in the utmost poverty   they had no beds, and the priests slept upon the table while Brother Emmanuel rested in a chair. They borrowed their cooking utensils, and as the lay-brother knew nothing of cooking, Clement was obliged to help him. In the early days they preached in the streets, but when the government prohibited outdoor sermons, they remained in St Benno's, which became the centre of a continuous mission. Between the years 1789 and 1808 the work done by St Clement and his brethren was extraordinary : five sermons were preached every day, three in Polish and two in German, for although St Clement's work lay primarily with the Germans, he wished to help all, and the work amongst the Poles received a great impetus after the reception of the first Polish novice, John Podgorski. The church of Holy-Cross-in-the-Fields was handed over to Clement and served from St Benno's. Numbers of Protestants were brought to the church, and St Clement was particularly successful in the conversion of Jews. In addition to this apostolic ministry the holy man also accomplished a great social work. The constant wars had left the lower classes in great misery, and the condition of many of the children was pitiful. To provide for them, he opened an orphanage near St Benno's and collected alms for their support. On one of his begging expeditions, a man who was playing cards in a tavern replied to his appeal by spitting in his face. St Clement, undeterred, said, " That was a gift to me personally ; now please let me have something for my poor children "   the man who had insulted him afterwards became one of his regular penitents. A school for boys was also founded, while confraternities and other associations helped to ensure the permanence of the good work thus begun. As his community increased, he began to send out missionaries and to establish houses in Courland as well as in Poland, Germany and Switzerland —but they all had eventually to be abandoned, owing to the difficulties of the times.

After twenty years of strenuous labours, St Clement had to give up his work in Warsaw also, in consequence of Napoleon's decree suppressing the religious orders. The previous year the saint had lost his beloved friend Father Hübl, who had died of typhus contracted when he was giving the last sacraments to some Italian soldiers. A police-agent risked his life to warn the Redemptorists of their impending expulsion. They were therefore prepared for the official visitation when it came on June 20, 1808, and surrendered themselves without delay. They were taken to the fortress of Cüstrin on the banks of the Oder and there imprisoned ; but such was their influence on their fellow prisoners and on the people outside who used to crowd round the prison to listen to the Redemptorists' hymns, that the authorities decided not to keep them there lest their presence should cause too many conversions. It was decided that the community should be broken up and that each member should return to his native country. St Clement, however, determined to settle in Vienna, in the hope of founding a religious house there in the event of the repeal of the laws of Joseph II, and after great difficulties, including another imprisonment on the Austrian frontier, he succeeded in reaching the city where he was to live and work for the last twelve years of his life.

At first he laboured quietly, helping in the Italian quarter, but before long the archbishop appointed him chaplain to the Ursuline nuns and rector of the public church attached to their convent. There he was free to preach, to hear confessions and perform all priestly duties, and soon from this centre fresh vigour was infused into the religious life of Vienna. His confessional was besieged not only by the poor and simple, but by ministers of state and university professors. As one of his biographers remarks : " By the sheer unaided force of his holiness, he, a man to whom the opportunity of acquiring anything like wide intellectual culture had been denied, gained such an ascendency over the minds of his contemporaries that he came to be regarded as an oracle of wisdom by leaders of thought both in the world of politics and letters." It was actually St Clement Mary Hofbauer and his friends and penitents, one of whom was Prince Ludwig of Bavaria, who were mainly responsible for defeating at the Congress of Vienna the attempt to create a national German church independent of the pope. The saint interested himself specially in the diffusion of good literature, but perhaps his crowning work was the establishment of a Catholic college, which proved an inestimable boon to Vienna, supplying many priests and monks as well as well-instructed laymen who afterwards occupied important positions in every civic career. All through his life St Clement had a great devotion to the sick, whom he loved to visit, and he is said to have been present at two thousand death-beds. He was summoned to rich and poor alike, and never refused a call. He was a particularly good friend to the Catholic Armenian Mekhitarist monks who had come to Vienna not long before ; and in his dealings with Protestants he was much helped by his realization that, as he wrote in a letter to Father Perthes in 1816, " If the Reform in Germany grew and maintained itself it was not through heretics and philosophers, but through men who truly aspired after interior religion ".

In spite of all his good works and public spirit St Clement was the object of frequent persecution by the supporters of " Josephinism ", and the police kept an unwearying eye on him. They reported in 1818 that, " Pietism and bigotry are increasingly becoming the fashion of the day. The confessional, however, is the decisive factor in keeping this fashion alive " and it indeed seems that his work as a confessor and director was a principal source of the influence that made of St Clement Hofbauer " the apostle of Vienna ". Once he was forbidden to preach, and his opponents, after the failure of their attempts at the Congress of Vienna, accused him of being a spy who reported to Rome all that was done in the Empire. The Austrian chancellor asked that he should be expelled, but Francis I heard such a good report of Clement from the archbishop and from Pope Pius VII, that he not only forbade any further annoyance of the Redemptorists, but in an interview with the saint spoke encouragingly of the prospect of a legal recognition of his congregation.　　The saint's two great objects were now practically attained : the Catholic faith was once more in the ascendant, and his beloved congregation was about to be firmly planted on German soil.　　He did not live to see the actual realization of his hopes, but he was perfectly satisfied.　　" The affairs of the congregation will not be settled until after my death ", he said.　　" Only have patience and trust in God.　　Scarcely shall I have breathed my last when we shall have houses in abundance."　　The prophecy was soon to be fulfilled.　　Towards the end, in 1819, St Clement was suffering from a complication of diseases, but he worked as hard as ever.　　On March 9 he insisted upon walking through a storm of snow and wind to sing a requiem Mass for the soul of Princess Jablonowska, who had helped him greatly when he was living at Warsaw.　　He nearly fainted at the altar, and on his return home took to his bed, from which he was not again to rise.　　There, six days later, he breathed his last in the presence of many of his friends.　　All Vienna crowded the streets to do him honour when his body was borne by twelve of his dearest disciples into the cathedral through the great doors, which were only opened on solemn occasions ; and in 1909 he was canonized.

There are excellent biographies in German by A. Innerkofler, M. Meschler and M. Haringer (this last was translated into English by Lady Herbert of Lea), but the best is that of J. Hofer, *Der heilige Klemens Maria Hofbauer : Ein Lebensbild* (1921).　　Much information may be gleaned from Fr H. Castle's *Life of St Alphonsus Liguori*, and there are English accounts by Fr O. R. Vassall-Phillips and Fr J. Carr.　　See also an article by W. C. Breitenfeld in *The Tablet*, January 5, 1952, pp. 7–9, and E. Hosp, *Der hl. K. M. Hofbauer* (1951).

16 : ST JULIAN OF ANTIOCH, Martyr　　(Date Unknown)

AMONGST the many St Julians who are registered as martyrs in the Roman Martyrology, perhaps the most important is the Cilician saint from Anazarbus who is honoured on this day.　　From the fact that his body— one knows not how or wherefore—was afterwards conveyed to Antioch, he is often referred to as St Julian of Antioch.　　In the church dedicated to him just outside that city St John Chrysostom preached a panegyric which is still preserved, and the great orator appeals to the marvellous effects which, as all men might witness, were produced by his relics in the exorcising of evil spirits, as evidence of the glory of the martyr and his power with God.　　What we learn from the panegyric and from the synaxaries about St Julian's history is not very much or probably very reliable. He is said to have been subjected to almost every form of torment which malignity could devise, and to have been paraded for a whole year as a kind of show through the various cities of Cilicia.　　In the end he was sewn up with scorpions and vipers in a sack and thrown into the sea.　　We are not told, however, at what period this happened or how the body was recovered.　　But the *cultus* of the martyr at Antioch in Chrysostom's time was clearly very real and vigorous, and portions of his relics seem to have been conveyed to distant parts of the world.

Our main authority is the panegyric of St Chrysostom mentioned above (Migne, PG., vol. 1, cc. 665–676). The Greek synaxaries give an account of St Julian under March 16 ; the " Hieronymianum " mentions him both under December 26 and February 14. See also Delehaye, *Les origines du culte des martyrs* (1933), pp. 166, 200; *Synax. Const.*, p. 541 ; CMH., p. 148.

ST ABRAHAM KIDUNAIA   (Sixth Century)

The birthplace of St Abraham was near Edessa in Mesopotamia, where his parents occupied an important position, being possessed of great riches. They chose for him a bride, and although he felt called to a celibate life he did not dare to oppose their wishes. In accordance with the custom of the time and country, a seven-days' festivity preceded the actual marriage, and on the last day Abraham ran away to conceal himself in the desert. A search was made for the fugitive, who at length was discovered absorbed in prayer. All appeals and entreaties having failed to shake his resolution, his friends finally withdrew, and he walled up the door of his cell, leaving only a little window through which food could be passed. When his parents died, he inherited their riches, but he commissioned a friend to distribute all his goods to the poor. His only remaining possessions were a cloak, a goatskin garment, a bowl for food and drink, and a rush mat on which he slept. " He was never seen to smile ", says his biographer, " and he regarded each day as his last. And yet he preserved a fresh complexion and as healthy and vigorous a body (although he was naturally delicate) as though he were not leading a penitential life.
.   And, what is even more surprising, never once, in fifty years, did he change his coat of goatskin, which was actually worn by others after his death."

Not far from Abraham's cell there was a colony of idolaters who had hitherto resisted with violence all attempts to evangelize them, and who were a source of constant grief to the bishop of Edessa. The bishop accordingly appealed to him to leave his hermitage and preach to the people. Reluctantly St Abraham allowed himself to be ordained priest and did as he was bidden. Coming to the town which was called Beth-Kiduna he found the citizens determined not to listen, and on all sides were signs of idolatry and appalling abominations. He asked the bishop to build a Christian church in the midst of the pagan settlement, and when it was completed, the saint felt that his time had come. After praying earnestly, he went forth and cast down the altars and destroyed every idol he could see. The infuriated villagers rushed upon him, beat him and drove him from the village. During the night he returned, and was found in the morning praying in the church. Going out into the streets he began to harangue the people and to urge them to give up their superstitions, but they again turned on him, and seizing him dragged him away, stoned him and left him for dead. Upon recovering consciousness he again returned, and though constantly insulted, ill-treated and sometimes attacked with sticks and stones, he continued for three years to preach, without any apparent result. Suddenly the tide turned : the saint's meekness and patience convinced the people that he was indeed a holy man, and they began to listen. " Seeing them at last so well disposed, he baptized them all in the name of the Father and of the Son and of the Holy Ghost, to the number of a thousand persons, and thenceforth he read the Holy Scriptures assiduously to them every day while instructing them in the principles of faith, of Christian justice and of charity." Thus for a year he continued to build up his converts, and then, fearing that he himself was becoming too much absorbed in the things of this world, he determined to leave his flock to the care of others and stole away at night to hide himself once more in the desert. St Abraham lived to the age of seventy. At the news of his last illness, the whole countryside flocked to receive his benediction, and after his death each one sought to procure some fragment of his clothing.

To the story of Abraham, which is in substance perhaps authentic, is attached the unhistorical legend of his niece Mary, to which in all probability the narrative owes the wide popularity it enjoyed both in the East and in the West. Mary is said to have been only seven years old when she became an orphan and was sent to her uncle, her sole surviving relation. For her he built a little cell near his own, and trained her in learning and piety until she had reached the age of twenty. She was then seduced by a false monk who came under pretence of receiving instruction from St Abraham, and having left her cell secretly she made her way to Troas, where she led the life of a common prostitute. Her uncle did not know what had become of her, and for two long years he ceased not to weep and to pray for her. Learning the truth at last, he resolved to seek out the lost sheep and to reclaim her if possible. He borrowed a horse and disguised himself in a soldier's uniform. He found where Mary was living, and sent word inviting her to sup with him, but not disclosing his identity. She made her appearance in a garb and with a lightness which plainly indicated her degradation, but she did not recognize her uncle, although she felt embarrassed in his presence. When the meal was over, laying aside his disguise, he grasped her hand and made a moving appeal until she was overcome with sorrow. Then, filled with hope and joy, he began to comfort her, undertaking to take all her sins upon himself if only she would return with him and resume her former holy life. Mary promised that henceforward she would obey him in all things, and Abraham led her back into their solitude. After three years God showed her that she was pardoned by granting her the gift of healing and of working miracles, the legend relates.

In accord with the Roman Martyrology, Alban Butler and one or two modern writers, notably Mgr Lamy, St Ephraem has been spoken of as the author of the narrative just summarized this attribution seems now to be definitely rejected and the saint assigned to the sixth century. See the *Acta Sanctorum*, March, vol. ii ; the *Analecta Bollandiana*, vol. x (1891), pp. 5–49, where a Syriac text is printed, and vol. xxvi (1907), pp. 468–469 ; Delehaye's *Synax. Const.*, under October 29 ; DHG., vol. i, cc. 175-177 ; A. Wilmart on the Latin versions of the story in the *Revue bénédictine*, vol. l (1938), pp. 222-245 ; and especially E. de Stoop in *Musée belge*, vol. xv, pp. 297-312.

ST FINNIAN LOBHAR, ABBOT   (*c.* A.D. 560 ?)

THE records we have of this St Finnian are conflicting and untrustworthy, and even the century of his birth is uncertain. On his father's side he was descended from the kings of Munster, but his mother's family came from Leinster, and it was in Bregia on the east coast of Leinster that he appears to have been born. He was called Lobhar, " the Leper ", from a painful scrofulous affection from which he suffered for many years—the name of leprosy being attached by the Irish (and others) to various forms of skin trouble. He is said to have been a disciple of St Columba, but it is possible that he lived much later and was only educated at one of the houses of the Columban observance. On reaching manhood he set out for the south of Ireland, where Bishop Fathlad conferred holy orders upon him and perhaps raised him to episcopal rank. In any case his virtues and miracles began to make him famous, and people flocked to him to be cured of their diseases. It is related that a woman brought her small boy, who was blind, mute and a leper from birth, and that the saint prayed earnestly that the child might recover. It was revealed to him that if he wished his prayer answered he must bear the leprosy himself. He cheerfully agreed, and was covered with ulcers from the crown of his head to the sole of his foot. One day, as he sat reading by a lake, his book fell in and sank. The water was too deep for anyone to recover it, but presently it rose to the top and was restored to the saint undamaged. In that place he built a church and made a cemetery. Some writers identify the spot with the famous Innisfallen, and regard Finnian as the founder of the abbey.

If we may believe the " acts ", the saint afterwards went to a place later called Clonmore, where he suffered greatly from his infirmity, and then, wishing to revisit his own country, he came to Swords, where he found St Columba, who gave over Swords abbey to Finnian and took his departure. The new abbot ruled for many years, exercising hospitality, healing the sick and living a life of great austerity. For one quarter of each night he sat in cold water to sing the psalms, the rest of the night he lay on the bare ground. Elsewhere, however, we read that St Finnian spent the last thirty years of his life presiding over Clonmore monastery, which had been founded by St Maidoc.

See the Bollandists in the *Acta Sanctorum*, March, vol. ii, whose account is largely based upon Colgan's *Acta Sanctorum Hiberniae*, pp. 627-629, and upon a late Latin life which they consider to be of English origin. If we may trust the verses attributed to St Meling (seventh century) by the glossator of the *Félire*, St Finnian Lobhar rested at Clonmore in the same grave with St Onchu.

ST EUSEBIA, ABBESS   (*c.* A.D. 680)

St Eusebia was the eldest daughter of St Adalbald of Ostrevant and of St Rictrudis. After the murder of her husband, Rictrudis retired to the convent of Marchiennes with her two younger daughters, and sent Eusebia to the abbey of Hamage, of which her great-grandmother St Gertrude was abbess. Eusebia was only twelve years old when St Gertrude died, but she was elected her successor, in compliance with her dying wishes and in accordance with the custom of the times, which required that the head of a religious house should, when possible, be of noble birth, so that the community should have the protection of a powerful family in times of disturbance. St Rictrudis, who was now abbess of Marchiennes, not unnaturally considered Eusebia far too young to have charge of a community, and bade her come to Marchiennes with all her nuns. The little abbess was loath to comply, but she obeyed, and arrived with her community and with the body of St Gertrude, when the two communities were merged into one and all settled down happily, except Eusebia. The memory of Hamage haunted her, until one night she and some of her nuns stole out and made their way to the abandoned buildings, where they said office and lamented over the non-fulfilment of St Gertrude's last injunctions.

Though this escapade did not go unpunished, St Rictrudis, finding that her daughter was still longing for Hamage, consulted the bishop and other devout men, who advised her to yield to Eusebia's wishes. She therefore consented to her return and despatched her back with all her nuns. She had no reason to regret her action, for the young abbess proved herself wise and capable, re-establishing discipline as in the days of St Gertrude, whom she strove to imitate in all things. No special incidents appear to have marked Eusebia's after life. She was only in her fortieth year when she had a premonition of her impending end, and gathering her nuns round her, gave them her parting instructions and blessing. As she finished speaking a great light spread throughout her room and almost immediately her soul ascended to Heaven.

See the *Acta Sanctorum*, March, vol. ii ; Destombes, *Vies des Saints de Cambrai*, i, pp. 349-353 ; and *Analecta Bollandiana*, vol. xx (1901), pp. 461-463.

ST GREGORY MAKAR, Bishop of Nicopolis   (*c.* A.D. 1010)

St Gregory Makar, it is said, was born in Armenia and, desiring to serve God in solitude in a land where he was not known, he found his way to a monastery near Nicopolis in Little Armenia and joined the community. The bishop of Nicopolis after some time attached him to his own person, ordaining him priest and encouraging him to preach against prevailing heresies. Thus when this bishop died the clergy and people chose Gregory to be their shepherd. In that capacity he shone not only by his virtue and eloquence, but also as a wonder-worker, especially in healing the sick. Nevertheless he was not satisfied he still longed for a solitary life and he feared that the adulation of his people would lead him to vainglory. He therefore left the city secretly, and in the company of two Greek monks made his way westwards, first to Italy and then to France.

At Pithiviers in the diocese of Orleans Gregory felt inspired to settle, and he built himself a hermitage and set about leading the life of a recluse after the Eastern manner, hitherto little practised in France. He abstained from all food on Mondays, Wednesdays, Fridays and Saturdays, and even on Tuesdays and Thursdays never ate till after sundown. His ordinary food was a handful of lentils, steeped in water and exposed to the sun, supplemented by a little barley bread and sometimes by a few roots eaten raw. Much as St Gregory wished to live in solitude, it soon became known that a holy hermit had settled at Pithiviers, and visitors began to throng to his cell. He worked many miracles of healing and gave wise spiritual counsel. The faithful brought him offerings, but these for the most part he distributed to the poor. For seven years St Gregory lived in his hermitage, combining the severe life of a solitary with the missionary zeal of a great preacher, and when he died the whole countryside was filled with lamentations.

The Latin Life of St Gregory has been printed in the *Acta Sanctorum*, March, vol. ii. See also Cochard, *Saints de l'Église d'Orléans*, pp. 384-393.

ST HERIBERT, Archbishop of Cologne   (A.D. 1021)

St Heribert, one of the most distinguished of the prelates who have ruled over the diocese of Cologne, was born in the town of Worms in the Palatinate of the Rhine, and as he showed himself eager to learn he was sent to the celebrated abbey of Gorze in Lorraine. There he would fain have entered the Benedictine Order, but his father had other ambitions for him and recalled him peremptorily to Worms, where the young man was given a canonry and was raised to the priesthood. Heribert gained the confidence of the Emperor Otto III, whose chancellor he became, and in 998 he was raised to the see of Cologne amid general approval.

The one dissentient was Heribert himself, who declared and honestly believed that he was quite unfitted for the high dignity. From Benevento, whither he was summoned by Otto, he passed on to Rome, and there received the *pallium* from Pope Silvester II. He then returned to Cologne, which he entered humbly with bare feet on a cold December day, having sent the *pallium* on before him. It was on Christmas eve that he was consecrated archbishop in the cathedral of St Peter, and from that moment he devoted himself indefatigably to the duties of his high calling. State affairs were never allowed to hinder him from preaching, from relieving the sick and needy, and from acting as peacemaker throughout his diocese. He did not despise the outward splendour which his position required, but under his gold-embroidered vesture he always wore a hair-shirt. The more the business of the world pressed upon him, the more strenuously did he strive to nourish the spiritual life within.

Soon after taking possession of his see, Heribert accompanied the emperor on another visit to Italy, which was to prove Otto's last, for he died there, probably of smallpox, not, as alleged, by poison. In accordance with his master's last wishes St Heribert brought his body back to Aachen, where it was buried. He also bore with him the imperial insignia for he foresaw that there would be a contest for the imperial crown, and he felt in duty bound to retain possession of the insignia with which he had been entrusted until he could hand them over to the properly constituted sovereign. Unfortunately the nearest claimant, Duke Henry of Bavaria, misinterpreted his attitude and concluded that the archbishop would have preferred to see some other sovereign chosen. The consequence was that St Heribert was in disfavour with the duke, and continued to be so long after St Henry II had been duly elected king and emperor, and in spite of the fact that the prelate had immediately yielded up the insignia, proving himself on every occasion one of the emperor's most loyal supporters. Henry does not appear to have taken from him the chancellorship, for his name appears appended to edicts of the years 1007 and 1008, but it was only towards the close of Henry's reign that the emperor learned to appreciate the virtue and good faith of the great archbishop, and there was a public and moving reconciliation between the two saintly men who had been so long estranged.

St Heribert would gladly have freed himself from secular business to be at liberty to devote the rest of his life to the spiritual needs of his diocese and people. On the opposite side of the Rhine, at Deutz, he and Otto III had begun a monastery and church which he afterwards completed with the help of money which that emperor had bequeathed to him. His own income he habitually divided between the Church and the poor, reserving for his personal use only what was absolutely necessary. He would often steal away and seek out the sick and poor in their homes and in hospitals ; he relieved them, washed their feet, and by his example inspired others to do likewise. Not did he confine his charity to Cologne, but sent money to priests he could trust in other towns to be spent on assisting the destitute. At a time of great drought the archbishop instituted a penitential procession from the church of St Severinus to that of St Pantaleon, and exhorted the multitude to do penance and to trust in God. Some of those present declared that they saw a white dove flying close to the saint's head as he walked with the procession. Entering the church of St Severinus Heribert went up to the high altar and, bowing his head in his hands, gave himself to earnest prayer for his people. Scarcely had he risen from his knees when a torrential rain poured down upon the city and the countryside, and the harvest was saved. Another procession which he instituted to avert plague and famine took place round the walls of the city in Easter week and was kept up each year until the end of the eighteenth century. He is still invoked for rain.

Zealous for the maintenance of discipline amongst the clergy, Heribert was assiduous in his visitations, and it was when visiting Neuss for one of these pastoral visits that he contracted a fever which he soon recognized as destined to be fatal. With great fervour the saint received viaticum and then suffered himself to be borne back to Cologne. After being laid at the foot of the crucifix in the cathedral of St Peter and commending himself and his flock to the mercy of God, he was carried to his own house, and shortly afterwards he breathed his last. His body was laid at Deutz, where in after years many miracles were attributed to his intercession.

The archbishop had been the founder of the abbey and minster of Deutz, and the monks were naturally solicitous that his memory should be held in veneration. A short biography of him was accordingly written by Lanthert, one of the monks, and it has been printed both by the Bollandists and in vol. iv of MGH (*Scriptores*). This life, rewritten and somewhat expanded by the more famous Rupert of Deutz, will also be found in the *Acta Sanctorum*, March, vol. ii, and in Migne, PL., vol. clxx, cc. 389–428. The text of what purported to be a bull of canonization, issued seemingly by Pope Gregory VII, was at one time accepted without suspicion, but of late years it has been shown to be almost certainly a forgery of the seventeenth century. See the *Analecta Bollandiana*, vol. xxvii (1908), p. 232 ; and vol. xxxii (1913), p. 96. There is a long account of St Heribert in Kleinermanns, *Die Heiligen auf den erzb. Stuhl von Köln*, vol.

BD JOHN, BISHOP OF VICENZA, MARTYR   (A.D. 1183)

JOHN was a native of Cremona and a member of the family of Sordi or Surdi ; the name of Cacciafronte, by which he was generally known, was that of his stepfather, who wished the boy to adopt it. At the age of fifteen John was made a canon of Cremona, but the following year he entered the Benedictine abbey of St Laurence. Eight years later he became prior of St Victor and in 1155 he was recalled to be abbot of St Laurence. It was said by the monks that obedience was no hardship under his rule, for he was the first to practise what he enforced, and he made the spiritual and temporal welfare of the community his constant care. Bd John espoused the cause of Pope Alexander III against Octavian, Cardinal of St Cecilia, who, under the title of Victor IV, claimed to occupy the chair of St Peter. For his zeal in organizing penitential processions and urging the people of Cremona to remain loyal to Alexander, the good abbot was banished by the Emperor Frederic Barbarossa, who favoured the antipope. He lived for several years the life of a solitary in Mantuan territory and was then called upon to fill the bishopric of Mantua. He continued to practise great austerity, his food, clothing and furniture being of the plainest, and he daily fed the poor at his own table. He did much to remedy abuses and kept a strict watch over church property, although he was so indifferent to his own possessions and position that he wrote to urge the pope to reinstate Bishop Graziodorus, his predecessor, who had abandoned Mantua to follow the antipope, but who had afterwards repented. The Holy See acceded to his request and John resigned Mantua, but was soon given the see of Vicenza, where he became as popular as he had been in Mantua.

His death was due to an act of revenge. It was usual to farm out ecclesiastical property to tenants, whose rent formed part of the episcopal revenues. Amongst the farmers on the estates of the bishopric of Vicenza was a man called Peter, who not only would not pay his dues but also treated the property as his own. The bishop expostulated with him gently at first, and then more severely. Remonstrance proving ineffectual, excommunication followed. Peter thereupon waylaid Bd John and killed him with a dagger, the holy man exclaiming with his last breath, " Do thou forgive him, Lord " The people of Vicenza were filled with grief and anger. Determined to punish the murderer, they set fire to his house : he managed to escape, but was never heard of again.

Two interesting documents containing a brief report of the official inquiry made at Cremona in 1223 and at Vicenza in 1224 into the life of Bd John are printed by the Bollandists in an appendix to the *Acta Sanctorum*, March, vol. ii ; see also A. Schiavo, *Della vita e dei tempi del B. Giovanni Cacciafronte* (1866).

BD TORELLO (A.D. 1282)

THE town of Poppi in the Casentino was the birth place of Bd Torello, who under parental care passed an almost blameless youth. After his father's death, however, he was led away into evil courses, until one day, when he was playing at bowls with some of his dissolute companions, a cock flew out from a hen-roost and, perching upon his arm, crowed three times-- as though to wake him from the sleep of sin. Torello stood stock-still in amazement, convinced that this was a divine warning. Thereupon he sought out the abbot of San Fedele, at whose feet he poured forth his confession and from whom he received absolution and good advice. Torello then left Poppi, and striking out into the woods wandered about for eight days. At length he reached a great rock, under the shelter of which he remained for another eight days, subsisting on herbs and three little loaves which he had taken with him. Upon that rock he resolved to build himself a hermitage in which to serve God for the rest of his life, and he therefore returned to Poppi to distribute to the poor all his property except the little he required to carry out his plan.

He bought a small parcel of land about the rock for a garden and had a hut built just large enough to contain him, and there he lived a most penitential life. He wore next his skin a half-shaven pigskin garment with bristles so prickly that they cut into his flesh. He allowed himself barely three hours for sleep, and often he would go for two days without food, whilst his ordinary fare consisted of four ounces of bread and a little water. His manner of life was hidden from all but one chosen friend. Against temptations he would lacerate his body until the blood flowed and stand in cold water till he trembled with shivering fits. Increasing age and illness compelled him to eat more and to mix a little wine with the water he drank. Death overtook him at the age of eighty as he knelt in prayer ; he had spent over fifty years in his hermitage. Many miracles were attributed to Torello—notably the rescue of a boy from a wolf and the taming of the wolf, who used afterwards to sleep at the entrance of the hermitage. Bd Torello is sometimes claimed as a Vallombrosan and sometimes as a Franciscan, but though he took the habit of a penitent from the abbot of Poppi he belonged to no order. His *cultus* was approved by Pope Benedict XIV.

The text of a short Latin Life of Torello is printed in the *Acta Sanctorum*, March, vol. ii. Also, in the eighteenth century, when his *cultus* was confirmed, several biographical sketches were published in Italian or Latin by Maccioni, Soldani, Cinatti, Bellogrado and others.

BB. JOHN AMIAS AND ROBERT DALBY, MARTYRS   (A.D. 1589)

JOHN AMIAS (or Anne) and Robert Dalby were two Yorkshire men who, after being educated in the Douai College at Rheims, were ordained priests, were sent on the English mission, and suffered death together in 1589. Amias, a widower and formerly a clothmonger at Wakefield, had ministered for seven or eight years in England before he was captured, whereas Dalby, who had been a Protestant minister, had only come back to England the year before he was apprehended. Not much detail as to their labours seems to be extant, but we have a graphic description of their death in Dr Champney's manuscript history as quoted by Challoner. He says: "This year on March 16, John Amias and Robert Dalby, priests of the College of Doway, suffered in York as in cases of high treason, for no other cause but that they were priests ordained by the authority of the See of Rome, and had returned into England and exercised there their priestly functions for the benefit of the souls of their neighbours. I was myself an eye-witness of the glorious combat of these holy men, being at that time a young man in the twentieth year of my age; and I returned home confirmed by the sight of their constancy and meekness in the Catholic faith, which by God's grace I then followed. For there visibly appeared in those holy servants of God so much meekness, joined with a singular constancy, that you would easily say that they were lambs led to the slaughter."

After describing the execution Dr Champney adds "The sheriff's men were very watchful to prevent the standers by from gathering any of their blood or carrying off anything that had belonged to them. Yet one, who appeared to me to be a gentlewoman, going up to the place where their bodies were in quartering, and not without difficulty making her way through the crowd, fell down upon her knees before the multitude, and with her hands joined and eyes lifted up to heaven, declared an extraordinary motion and affection of soul. She spoke also some words, which I could not hear for the tumult and noise. Immediately a clamour was raised against her as an idolatress, and she was drove away; but whether or no she was carried to prison, I could not certainly understand."

See MMP., pp. 152-153, and J. H. Pollen, *Acts of English Martyrs*, pp. 329-331.

17 : ST PATRICK, ARCHBISHOP OF ARMAGH, APOSTLE OF IRELAND   (A.D. 461)

IF", says Alban Butler, "the virtue of children reflects an honour on their parents, much more justly is the name of St Patrick rendered illustrious by the lights of sanctity with which the Church of Ireland shone during many ages, and by the colonies of saints with which it peopled many foreign countries." The field of his labours, he adds, was the remote corner of the then known world, and he himself was born upon its confines. Whether his birthplace, the village of "Bannavem Taberniae", was near Dumbarton on the Clyde, or in Cumberland to the south of Hadrian's Wall, or at the mouth of the Severn or elsewhere is of no great moment. We may infer from what he says of himself that he was of Romano-British origin. His father Calpurnius was a deacon and a municipal official, his grandfather a priest, for in those days no strict law of celibacy had yet been imposed on the Western clergy. The saint's full name in the Roman style was not improbably Patricius Magonus Sucatus. He tells us that when he was sixteen he " knew not the true God ", meaning probably no more than that he lived thoughtlessly, like those around him, not heeding much the warnings of the clergy " who used to admonish us for our salvation " We cannot be far wrong in supposing that he was born about 389, and that about 403 he with many others was carried off by raiders to become a slave among the still pagan inhabitants of Ireland. There for six years he served his master, and amid the bodily hardships of this bondage his soul grew marvellously in holiness. It is the generally accepted tradition that these years were spent near Ballymena in Antrim upon the slopes of the mountain now called Slemish, but according to another view the place of his captivity, near the forest of Fochlad (or Foclut), was on the coast of Mayo. If this be true, then Crochan Aigli (Croagh Patrick), which was the scene at a later date of his prolonged fast, was also the mountain upon which in his youth he had lived alone with God tending his master's herds. Wherever it may have been, he tells us himself how " constantly I used to pray in the daytime. Love of God and His fear increased more and more, and my faith grew and my spirit was stirred up, so that in a single day I said as many as a hundred prayers and at night nearly as many, so that I used to stay even in the woods and on the mountain [to this end]. And before the dawn I used to be aroused to prayer, in snow and frost and rain, nor was there any tepidity in me such as now I feel, because then the spirit was fervent within."

After six years he heard a voice in his sleep warning him to be ready for a brave effort which would bring him back to freedom in the land of his birth. Accordingly he ran away from his master and travelled 200 miles to the ship of whose approaching departure he had had some strange intimation. His request for free passage was refused at first, but, in answer to his silent prayer to God, the sailors called him back, and with them he made an adventurous journey. They were three days at sea, and when they reached land it was only to travel in company for a month through some uninhabited tract of country until all their provisions gave out. It is St Patrick himself who narrates how hunger overcame them. " And one day the shipmaster began to say to me, ' How is this, O Christian, thou sayest that thy God is great and almighty ; wherefore then canst thou not pray for us, for we are in danger of starvation ? Hardly shall we ever see a human being again.' Then said I plainly to them, ' Turn in good faith and with all your heart to the Lord my God, to whom nothing is impossible, that this day He may send you food in your journey, until ye be satisfied, for he has abundance everywhere ! And, by the help of God, so it came to pass. Lo, a herd of swine appeared in the way before our eyes, and they killed many of them, and in that place they remained two nights ; and they were well refreshed and their dogs were sated, for many of them had fainted and were left half dead by the way. And after this they rendered hearty thanks to God, and I became honourable in their eyes ; and from that day they had food in abundance. Moreover, they found wild honey, and gave me a piece of it. But one of them said, ' This is an idol-offering '. Thanks be to God, I tasted none of it."

At length they reached human habitations—probably in Gaul—but the fugitive was safe, and thus eventually Patrick, at the age of twenty-two or twenty-three, was restored to his kinsfolk. They welcomed him warmly and besought him not to depart from them again, but after a while, in the watches of the night, fresh visions came to him, and he heard " the voices of those who dwelt beside the wood of Foclut which is nigh to the western sea, and thus they cried, as if with one mouth, ' We beseech thee, holy youth, to come and walk among us once more '." " Thanks be to God ", he adds " that after many years the Lord granted to them according to their cry."

With regard to the order of events which followed there is no certainty. St Patrick could hardly have set out upon such an undertaking as the conversion of Ireland without study and preparation, without priestly orders, without some sort of commission from ecclesiastical authority. It seems therefore beyond dispute, and it is quite in agreement with the statements of the saint's earliest biographers, that he spent several years in France before he made any attempt to take up his work in Ireland. The evidence for a considerable sojourn on the island of Lérins (off Cannes) is strong, and so also is that which represents him as being in personal contact with Bishop St Germanus, at Auxerre. Some have maintained that he journeyed to Rome at this period and was despatched on his special mission to the Irish by Pope St Celestine I. Since the publication of Professor Bury's *Life of St Patrick* the view has gained favour that he was three years at Lérins, from 412 to 415, that he then spent some fifteen years at Auxerre, during which time he received holy orders, that meanwhile Pope Celestine had sent Palladius to Ireland, who after less than a twelvemonth died among the Picts in North Britain, and that then, in 432, St Germanus consecrated Patrick bishop to replace Palladius and carry on his work of evangelization, which as yet was hardly begun.

To trace in detail the course of the saint's heroic labours in the land of his former captivity is impossible, left as we are to the confused, legendary and sometimes contradictory data supplied by his later biographers. Tradition declares that his first effort was made in the north beside that Slemish where, according to Muirchu, he had pastured the cattle and prayed to God as a slave. We may or may not accept the story that, apprised of the coming of his former bondsman, the master who had owned him elected to set fire to his own house and perish in the flames. But it seems probable that there is an historical basis for a preliminary stay of St Patrick in Ulster, whence after the foundation of Saul he embarked with characteristic energy on his attempt to gain the favour of the High-King Laoghaire, who held his court at Tara in Meath. There is doubtless much that is purely mythical in the legend of the encounter of Patrick with the magicians or Druids, but it is clear that something momentous was decided on that occasion, and that the saint, either by force of character or by the miracles he wrought, gained a victory over his pagan opponents which secured a certain amount of toleration for the preaching of Christianity. The text of the *Senchus Mor* (the old Irish code of laws), though in its existing form much later than St Patrick's time, makes definite reference to some under-standing arrived at at Tara, and associates the saint and his disciple St Benen (Benignus) with the work of its composition. We are there told how " Patrick requested the men of Erin to come to one place to hold a conference with him. When they came to the conference the gospel of Christ was preached to them all ; and when the men of Erin heard of the killing of the living and the resuscitation of the dead, and all the power of Patrick since his arrival in Erin ; and when they saw Laoghaire with his druids overcome by the great signs and miracles wrought in the presence of the men of Erin, they bowed down in obedience to the will of God and Patrick."

Although King Laoghaire seems not to have become a Christian himself, certain members of his family did, and from that time the work of the great apostle, though carried on amid manifold hardships and often at the risk of his life owing to the lawless violence of those whom he thwarted or rebuked, was openly favoured by many powerful chieftains. The druids, as the most interested representatives of paganism, were his bitter opponents. A strange prognostic is preserved to us by Muirchu which was alleged to have been current amongst them even before the preaching of the gospel began. " Adze-head [this was a reference to the form of the tonsure] will come, with his crook-headed staff, and his house [chasuble, *casula* — a little house] holed for his head. He will chant impiety from his table in the east of his house. All his household shall answer, Amen, Amen." And they added, " When, therefore, all these things come to pass, our kingdom, which is a heathen one, will not stand." How full of peril the mission was we learn from the incident of Odhran, St Patrick's charioteer, who by some presentiment asked to take the chief seat while Patrick himself drove. Odhran was killed by a spear-thrust intended for his master, while the saint himself escaped. But the work of the evangelization of Ireland went steadily on, despite opposition. Proceeding northwards from Tara, Patrick overthrew the idol of Crom Cruach in Leitrim, and built a Christian church in the place where it had stood. Thence he passed to Connaught, and amongst his other doings there Tirechan has preserved the story of the conversion of Ethne and Fedelm, the two daughters of King Laoghaire, though the incident of the shamrock, used as an illustration of the Trinity in their instruction, is an accretion of much later date. But the whole history of his preaching in Ulster again, as well as in Leinster and Munster, cannot be told here.

When Patrick had gathered many disciples round him, such, for example, as Benignus, who was destined to be his successor, the work of evangelization was well under way. He maintained his contacts abroad, and it has been suggested that the " approval " of which we read was a formal communication from Pope St Leo the Great. In 444, according to the Annals of Ulster, the cathedral church of Armagh, the primatial see of Ireland, was founded, and no long time probably elapsed before it became a centre of education as well as administration. There is good reason to believe that St Patrick held a synod—no doubt at Armagh, though this is not expressly mentioned— and although, again, there may be interpolations, many of the decrees then enacted are still preserved to us as they were originally framed. The names of Auxilius and Iserninus, the southern bishops, which are attached to his *Collectio Canonum Hibernensis*, support the presumption of authenticity. It is likely that the synod was held towards the close of Patrick's days, and he must have been by that time a man in broken health, for the physical strain of his austerities and endless journeys cannot, apart from some miraculous intervention of Providence, have failed to produce its effect. Nevertheless the story of his forty days' fast upon Croagh Patrick and of the privileges he then extorted from the divine clemency by his importunity in prayer must be connected with the end of his life. As Tírechán briefly tells us : " Patrick went forth to the summit of Mount Aigli, and he remained there for 40 days and 40 nights, and the birds were a trouble to him, and he could not see the face of the heavens, the earth or the sea on account of them ; for God told all the saints of Erin, past, present and future, to come to the mountain summit—that mountain which overlooks all others, and is higher than all the mountains of the West—to bless the tribes of Erin, so that

Patrick might see [by anticipation] the fruit of his labours, for all the choir of the saints of Erin came to visit him there, who was the father of them all."

The British chronicler Nennius gives a similar account, but adds that " from this hill Patrick blessed the people of Ireland, and his object in climbing to its summit was that he might pray for them and see the fruit of all his labours. Afterwards he went to his reward in a good old age, where now he rejoices for ever and ever. Amen." It seems certain that Patrick died and was buried, in or about the year 461, at Saul on Strangford Lough, where he had built his first church. That he spent his last days as abbot of Glastonbury is quite untrue.

It need hardly be said that in all the ancient lives of St Patrick the marvellous is continuously present and often in a very extravagant form. If we were dependent for our knowledge of him upon such material as is supplied in the *Vita Tripartita* we should understand little of his true character. Too many of the wonder-workers who are portrayed for us by Celtic hagiographers remain featureless, simply from the profusion of incredible marvels which reduces all to a dead level of unreality. Fortunately in the case of the apostle of Ireland we have a slender collection of his own writings, and these show us the man himself as he was and felt and acted. It is only by a study of the " Confession ", the *Lorica* and the Coroticus letter, that we come to understand the deep human feeling and the still more intense love of God which were the secret of the extraordinary impression he produced upon those with whom he came into contact. If he had not possessed a strongly affectionate nature which clung to his own kith and kin, he would not have referred so many times to the pang it had cost him to leave them, turning a deaf ear to their efforts to detain him. He was deeply sensitive. If he had not been that, he could never have laid so much stress upon his disinterestedness. The suggestion that he was seeking profit for himself in the mission he had undertaken stung him almost beyond endurance. All that was most human, and at the same time most divine, in Patrick comes out in such a passage as the following, from his " Confession ".

> And many gifts were proffered me, with weeping and with tears. And I displeased them, and also, against my wish, not a few of my elders ; but, God being my guide, in no way did I consent or yield to them. It was not any grace to me, but God who conquereth in me, and He resisted them all, so that I came to the heathens of Ireland to preach the gospel and to bear insults from unbelievers so as to hear the reproach of my going abroad and to endure many persecutions even unto bonds, the while that I was surrendering my liberty as a man of free condition for the profit of others. And if I should be found worthy, I am ready to give even my life for His name's sake unfalteringly and very gladly, and there I desire to spend it until I die, if only our Lord should grant it to me.

On the other hand, the marvel of the wondrous harvest which God had allowed him to reap was always before his eyes and filled him with gratitude. It is unquestionably true that, in his apostolate of less than thirty years, Patrick had converted Ireland as a whole to Christianity. This is not a mere surmise based upon the unmeasured encomiums of his enthusiastic biographers. It is the saint himself who alludes more than once to the " multitudes " (*innumeros*), the " so many thousands ", whom he had baptized and confirmed. And again he says " Wherefore then in Ireland they who never had the knowledge of God, but until now only worshipped idols and abominations —how has there been lately prepared a people of the Lord, and they are called children of God ?   Sons and daughters of Scottic chieftains are seen to become monks and virgins of Christ."   Paganism and rapine and vice had not entirely loosed their hold.   The saint in this same " Confession ", which was written in his later days, still declares   " Daily I expect either a violent death or to be robbed and reduced to slavery or the occurrence of some such calamity."   But he adds   " I have cast myself into the hands of Almighty God, for He rules everything ; as the Prophet saith, ' Cast thy care upon the Lord, and He Himself will sustain thee '."   This was apparently the secret of the inexhaustible courage and determination manifested by St Patrick throughout his whole career.

The literature of the subject is naturally vast.   The primary source of any accurate knowledge must always be St Patrick's own writings, referred to above.   The most valuable text of the " Confession " (though incomplete) is that contained in the " Book of Armagh " This manuscript, written in the first years of the ninth century, contains also the memoirs of St Patrick compiled by Muirchu and Tirechan, as well as other documents.   The whole was very carefully edited by Dr John Gwynn for the Royal Irish Academy in 1913.   The documents bearing on St Patrick had previously been published by Fr Edmund Hogan in the *Analecta Bollandiana*, vols. i and ii (1882–1883), and elsewhere.   The *Vita Tripartita* is most readily accessible in the edition prepared for the Rolls Series by Whitley Stokes (1887). It is there supplemented by the Muirchu and Tirechan collections and other documents, notably by the hymns of Secundinus (Sechnall) and Fiacc, which last are also critically edited in the *Irish Liber Hymnorum* published by the Henry Bradshaw Society.   Other later lives of St Patrick were printed for the first time by Colgan in his *Trias Thaumaturga* (1647).   A very convenient little book containing in English the most material documents connected with St Patrick's life is that of Dr N. White, *St Patrick, his Writings and Life* (1920).   Modern biographies of the saint are very numerous, the most noteworthy being those of J. B. Bury (1905) and the still more comprehensive volume of Abp J. Healy (1905), which last includes a text and translation of the documents of which St Patrick himself is the author.   Prof. Bury's work is particularly valuable as exploding from an agnostic standpoint the theory of Prof. Zimmer that Palladius and Patrick were one and the same person and that the story of Patrick's life is a myth.   But the identification of Palladius and Patrick has been revived in a modified form by T. F. O'Rahilly, *The Two Patricks* (1942).   See also biographies by H. Concannon (1931), K. Müller (*Der hl. Patrick*, 1931), E. MacNeill (1934) ; J. Ryan, *Irish Monasticism* (1931). pp. 59-96 and *passim* ; *Codices Patriciani Latini* (1942), a descriptive catalogue ed. by L. Bieler, with notes thereon by the editor in *Analecta Bollandiana*, vol. lxiii (1945), pp. 242-256 ; Dr Bieler's *Life and Legend of St Patrick* (1949), with Fr P. Grosjean's notes on the same in *Analecta Bollandiana*, vol. lxii (1944), pp. 42-73 ; and for Patrick's birthplace, his stay in Gaul and other matters, *Analecta Bollandiana*, vol. lxiii (1945), pp. 65-119.   Dr. Bieler has edited the texts, and see his *Works of St. Patrick* (1953) in English.

ST JOSEPH OF ARIMATHEA   (First Century)

WE know nothing authentically of St Joseph of Arimathea beyond what is recorded in the Gospels.   He is mentioned by all four evangelists and we learn from them that he was a disciple of our Lord, but " secretly, for fear of the Jews ".   He was " a counsellor, a good and a just man ".   He had not taken any part in the vote of the Sanhedrin against Jesus and " was himself looking for the kingdom of God ". The scenes beside the cross would seem to have given him courage, so " he went in boldly to Pilate and begged for the body of Jesus ".   Having obtained his request, he bought fine linen, and wrapping the body therein he laid Him in a sepulchre which was hewed out of the rock and in which " never yet any man had been laid ".   History has no more to tell us about Joseph, but the apocryphal gospels, and in particular that fuller redaction of the " Gospel of Nicodemus ", which was originally known as the "Acts of Pilate", contain further references, but of a legendary kind.

But the most astonishing of the legends associated with the name of Joseph of Arimathea is of much later date. It was at one time supposed that William of Malmesbury in his *De Antiquitate Glastoniensis Ecclesiae* (*c.* 1130) was already familiar with the story of the coming of this Joseph to Glastonbury. This, however, has been shown to be an error. It was not until more than a century later that a chapter by another hand, embodying this fiction, was prefixed to William's book. Here at last we are told how when St Philip the Apostle was preaching the gospel in Gaul, he was accompanied by Joseph of Arimathea, who was his devoted disciple. St Philip sent over to England twelve of the clerics in his company and placed them all under Joseph's direction. The king in Britain to whom they addressed themselves would not accept their Christian teaching, but he gave them an island, Yniswitrin, afterwards known as Glastonbury, in the midst of the swamps, and there at the bidding of the archangel Gabriel they built a church of wattles in honour of our Blessed Lady, thirty-one years after the passion of Jesus Christ and fifteen after the assumption of the Blessed Virgin. This tale, before the end of the fourteenth century, is found very much developed in John of Glastonbury's history of the abbey. John informs us that besides St Philip's twelve disciples, no less than one hundred and fifty other persons, men and women, came from France to Britain to spread the gospel, and that at our Lord's command all of them crossed the sea borne upon the shirt of Josephes, the son of Joseph of Arimathea, on the night of our Saviour's resurrection, and reached land in the morning. They were afterwards imprisoned by the "king of North Wales", but, on being released, St Joseph, Josephes and ten others were permitted to occupy the isle of Yniswitrin, which is here identified not only with Glastonbury but also with Avalon. Here, as previously stated, the chapel of wattles was built, and in due course St Joseph of Arimathea was buried there.

Neither in Bede, Gildas, Nennius, Geoffrey of Monmouth, the authentic William of Malmesbury nor any other chronicler for eleven hundred years do we find any trace of the supposed coming of Joseph of Arimathea to Glastonbury. Not even in the legend as presented by John of Glastonbury about the year 1400 is mention made of the Holy Grail, though this is so conspicuously associated with Joseph and his son Josephes in the Grail romances. On the other hand, much is made by the later Glastonbury writers of two silver cruets which Joseph is supposed to have brought with him, one containing the blood and the other the sweat of our Saviour. But when this legend did obtain currency towards the close of the fourteenth century, it was enthusiastically adopted as a sort of national credential, and at the Councils of Constance (1417) and of Basle (1434) the English representatives claimed precedence on the ground that Britain had accepted the teaching of Christianity before any other country of the West. It might at any rate be said that the claim was not less well-founded than that made by France in virtue of the coming of SS. Mary Magdalen, Martha and Lazarus to Provence, or by the Spaniards on the ground of the preaching of the gospel in Spain by the apostle St James.

An admirable account of this example of medieval myth-making was published by Dean J. Armitage Robinson in *Two Glastonbury Legends* (1926), in which full bibliographical references are provided. The learned writer's sober exposition of the facts of history is particularly valuable in view of the mass of extravagant fictions obtained by automatic script—not the less pernicious because the writers who produced them printed them, no doubt, in good faith—with which the country was flooded after the publication of Bligh Bond's *Gate of Remembrance* in 1918. See also the *Acta Sanctorum*, March, vol. ii articles by Henry Jenner in *Pax*, no. 48 (1916), pp. 125 *seq.*, and by Fr Thurston in *The Month*, July 1931, pp. 43 *seq.* ; and T. D. Kenrick, *British Antiquity* (1950).

THE MARTYRS OF THE SERAPEUM (A.D. 390)

THEOPHILUS, Archbishop of Alexandria (the same who later compassed the downfall of St John Chrysostom) obtained a rescript from the Emperor Theodosius authorizing him to convert a temple of Dionysius into a Christian church. This proceeding led to riots, in the course of which many were killed in the streets. The insurgents made their headquarters in the great temple of Serapis, from which they made sallies and seized a number of Christians, whom they tried to induce to offer sacrifice to Serapis, and upon their refusal put them to a cruel death. The emperor expressed his admiration of those who had received the crown of martyrdom, and in order not to dishonour their triumph he pardoned their murderers ; but he ordered the destruction of all the heathen temples in Egypt. When his letter was read in Alexandria, the pagans abandoned the temple of Serapis, and the idol having been cast down, it was thrown into a fire. The populace had been told that if it were touched the heavens would fall and the earth revert to chaos, but as soon as they realized that no terrible judgement followed upon its destruction, many heathens embraced Christianity. Two churches were built on the site of the temple of Serapis. one of the most famous buildings of the ancient world.

The accounts furnished by Theodoret, Rufinus, and other early church historians have been extracted and annotated in the *Acta Sanctorum*, March, vol. ii. For a vivid account of the scene in the Serapeum, see DCB., vol. iv, p. 1000. There seems to have been no ecclesiastical *cultus*, but an entry was added to the Roman Martyrology by Baronius.

ST AGRICOLA, BISHOP OF CHALON-SUR-SAÔNE (A.D. 580)

ST AGRICOLA, or Arègle, as he is popularly called in France, was a contemporary of St Gregory of Tours, who knew him well and was greatly impressed with the simplicity of his life. The saint came of a Gallo-Roman family of senatorial rank, but it seems to have been the father of another Agricola who adopted Venantius Fortunatus and educated him with his own son. In the year 532, during the reign of the sons of Clovis, Agricola was raised to the bishopric of Chalon-sur-Saône. His new position, which obliged him to keep up an appearance of state and to exercise hospitality, made no change in the simplicity and penitential abstinence of his daily life. St Gregory says that he never dined, and that he never broke his fast until the evening, when he partook of a light meal standing. Whole-heartedly devoted to the spiritual welfare of his people, St Agricola spent much time and money upon the enlargement and adornment of the churches of his diocese. His interests, however, were not entirely restricted to his own see, and he was present at many councils. After governing his diocese for forty-eight years and translating to his own cathedral city the remains of the recluse St Didier, St Agricola died at the age of eighty-three, and was buried in the church of St Marcellus, where his body was found three hundred years later. His relics are still preserved above the high altar.

St Gregory of Tours is the main authority (see Migne, PL., vol. lxxi, cc. 362 and 895), and *cf.* Duchesne, *Fastes Episcopaux*, vol. ii, p. 193 ; P. Besnard, *Les origines*   *de l'église chalonnaise* (1922), pp. 62–65.

ST GERTRUDE OF NIVELLES, Virgin　　(A.D. 659)

St Gertrude, the younger daughter of Bd Pepin of Landen and of Bd Itta, Ida or Iduberga, was born at Landen in 626. She had a brother, Grimoald, who succeeded his father, and a sister, St Begga, who married the son of St Arnulf of Metz. Gertrude was brought up carefully by her parents, who fostered her naturally religious disposition. When she was about ten years old, her father gave a feast at which he entertained King Dagobert and the chief nobles of Austrasia. One of these lords asked the monarch to bestow the hand of Gertrude on his son, who was present. Dagobert, no doubt thinking to please the little girl, sent for her and, pointing to the handsome young man in his brave attire, asked the child if she would like him for a husband. To his surprise Gertrude answered that she would never take him or any earthly bridegroom, as she wished to have Jesus Christ as her only lord and master. No one seems to have thought of overruling the girl's determination, which was indeed applauded by the king and the assembly. Upon being left a widow, Bd Itta consulted St Amand, Bishop of Maestricht, as to how she and her daughter could best serve God, and by his advice began to build a double monastery at Nivelles. Lest any attempt should be made to interfere with Gertrude's vocation, her mother herself cut off her hair, shaving her head to the shape of a monk's tonsure. As soon as the new foundation was ready both mother and daughter entered it, but Itta insisted upon making Gertrude superior, while she herself served under her daughter, though assisting her from time to time with her advice. The young abbess proved herself fully equal to the position. She won the respect not only of her nuns but of the many pilgrims of distinction who visited the house. Amongst the latter were St Foillan and St Ultan on their way from Rome to Péronne, where their brother St Fursey was buried. St Gertrude gave them land at Fosses on which to build a monastery and a hospice. Foillan became its abbot, but Ultan and some others were retained at Nivelles (according to Irish writers) in order to instruct the community in psalmody.

Bd Itta died in 652, and St Gertrude, feeling the charge of so large an establishment, committed much of the external administration to others. This gave her more time for the study of the Holy Scriptures and enabled her to add to her mortifications. So severely did she treat her body that by the time she was thirty she was worn out by fasting and want of sleep, and felt compelled to resign in favour of her niece Wulfetrudis, whom she had trained, but who was only twenty years old. The saint now began to prepare for death by increasing her devotions and disciplines. Her biographer relates that once, when she was praying in church, a globe as of fire appeared above her head and lit up the building for half an hour. Holy though she was, when the time of her departure approached she was afraid because of her unworthiness, and sent to ask St Ultan at Fosses whether he had had any revelation with regard to her. The holy man sent back word that she would die the following day while Mass was being celebrated, but that she need have no fear, for St Patrick with many angels and saints was waiting to receive her soul. St Gertrude rejoiced at the message, and on March 17, while the priest was saying the prayers before the preface, she rendered up her soul to God. In compliance with her wish she was buried in her hair-shirt without shroud or winding-sheet, and her head was wrapped in a worn-out veil which had been discarded by a passing nun.

St Gertrude has always been regarded as a patroness of travellers, probably owing to her care for pilgrims and to a miraculous rescue at sea of some of her monks who invoked her name in great peril. Before starting on a journey it was once the custom to drink a stirrup-cup to her honour, and a special goblet, of old used for the purpose, is preserved at Nivelles with her relics. She came to be regarded also as a patroness of souls who, on a three days' journey to the next world before the particular judgement, were popularly supposed to lodge the first night with St Gertrude and the second night with St Michael. The most constant emblem with which St Gertrude (who was widely invoked and a very popular saint in Belgium and the Netherlands for many centuries) is associated is a mouse. One or more mice are usually depicted climbing up her crozier or playing about her distaff. No really satisfactory explanation of this symbolism has ever been given, though many suggestions have been made—for example, that while Gertrude was spinning, the Devil in the form of a mouse used to gnaw her thread in order to provoke her to lose her temper. In any case she was specially invoked against mice and rats, and as late as 1822, when there was a plague of field-mice in the country districts of the Lower Rhine, a band of peasants brought an offering to a shrine of the saint at Cologne in the form of gold and silver mice. There may also have been some underlying transference to her of traits derived from the Freya or other pagan myths. St Gertrude is further invoked for good quarters on a journey and for gardens. Fine weather on her feast day is regarded as a favourable omen, and this day is treated in some districts as marking the beginning of the season of out-door garden work.

There is an early Latin Life of St Gertrude (which has been critically edited by B. Krusch in MGH., *Scriptores Merov.*, vol. ii, pp. 447–474), as well as a number of other documents of which details will be found in the BHL., nn. 3490–3504. See also Mabillon and the Bollandist *Acta Sanctorum*. A full account of the folk-lore connected with St Gertrude of Nivelles is provided in Bächtold-Stäubli, *Handwörterbuch des deutschen Aberglaubens* (1927), vol. iii, cc. 699–786, with a comprehensive bibliography ; and *cf.* Künstle, *Ikonographie der Heiligen*, pp. 280–281. See also A. F. Stocq, *Vie critique de ste Gertrude* (1931).

ST PAUL OF CYPRUS (*c.* A.D. 760)

AMONG the victims of the persecution initiated by the Emperor Constantine Copronymus against those who venerated the sacred images, one of the most outstanding was a Cypriot called Paul, who was hailed before the governor of Cyprus, and given the alternative of trampling upon the crucifix or of suffering the torture of the rack which was standing beside him. Without a moment's hesitation Paul cried out, " Far be it from me, Lord Jesus Christ, only begotten Son of God, to trample on thy divine image ", and stooping down he kissed the figure on the cross. The irate governor gave orders that he should be stripped and pressed between two boards. His body was then torn with iron combs and finally hung, head downwards, over a fire until it was consumed. The author of the Acts of St Stephen the Younger says that his example helped greatly to encourage the Constantinopolitan martyrs, and consequently some writers have thought that St Paul suffered in Constantinople, but the not very copious evidence shows that he almost certainly was martyred in the island of Cyprus.

See the *Acta Sanctorum*, March, vol. ii ; the account is based on the Greek *Menaia*. The entry in the Roman Martyrology, assigning this martyr to Constantinople, seems to have been due to a mistake of Baronius.

BD JOHN SARKANDER, MARTYR   (A.D. 1620)

JOHN SARKANDER, who was to end his life as a martyr for the seal of confession, was born on the borders of Austrian Silesia, of well-connected parents who were more pious than affluent. His father died when he was thirteen, and his mother took special pains to find a suitable teacher for her fourth son, John, whose great abilities she recognized. He was eventually sent to the Jesuit college at Prague, and in due course raised to the priesthood. Returning to the diocese of Olmütz (Olomuc), he attracted the attention of the bishop, Cardinal von Dietrichstein, who appointed him parish priest of Holleschau (Holeshov). Since the fifteenth century that district had been a hotbed of the Hussite heresy and the Bohemian Brothers, but supported by the local landowner, Baron von Lobkovitz, and with the help of members of the Society of Jesus, Sarkander rekindled the faith amongst the inhabitants and reconciled about 250 heretics to the Church. By so doing he incurred the enmity of a powerful neighbouring landowner, Bitowsky von Bystritz, who was violently anti-Catholic and regarded Lobkovitz as a dangerous rival.

In 1618, at the beginning of the Thirty Years War, a revolt broke out in Moravia: the Protestants seized the reins of government and set about destroying Catholic institutions. On the advice of his friends, Sarkander left Holleschau and betook himself eventually to Cracow, where he remained for several months. As soon, however, as he could prudently do so, he returned to his parish and strove to reorganize his scattered flock. The country was still in a very disturbed state, and in February 1620 Polish troops, sent to the assistance of the emperor, came pouring across Moravia, pillaging on their way. When they drew near to Holleschau, Sarkander, at the head of his parishioners, went out to meet them carrying the Blessed Sacrament. As pious Catholics the Poles dismounted, fell on their knees and asked for the priest's blessing. Not only did they leave Holleschau intact, but they left a warning to the troops who followed that they should spare the village. Sarkander had indeed saved Holleschau, but he had signed his own death-warrant. His enemy Bitowsky immediately accused him of having treasonably brought the Poles into the country. His visit to Poland was misconstrued, and it was declared that he had planned the incursion as the agent of Baron von Lobkovitz, so he was carried off to Olmütz, where he was loaded with chains and confined in a subterranean dungeon. The commission which tried him was composed almost entirely of Hussites, and they called upon him to disclose who had brought the Polish troops into the country and what Baron von Lobkovitz, who was known to be his penitent, had told him in the confessional. Sarkander denied that he had anything to do with the coming of the Poles, but refused absolutely to divulge the secrets of the confessional. Thereupon he was subjected to the rack in its severest form, and four days later was again racked, and branded for two hours with torches. Moreover, the next morning, after being racked for three hours, he was plastered with feathers which had been dipped in a mixture of pitch, sulphur and oil and was then set on fire. He survived this atrocious treatment and lingered on for a month, reduced to almost complete helplessness, but praying continually, until on March 17, after receiving the last sacraments, he passed peacefully and joyfully to his reward.

The words Sarkander had used to those who sought to make him reveal the secrets of the confessional are worthy of record : " I know nothing, and nothing has been entrusted to me in the holy sacrament of penance. Anything that may ever have been confided to me in that way is not retained in my memory. I have buried it in oblivion out of veneration for the inviolable seal of confession, and I would choose, with God's help, rather to be torn in pieces than sacrilegiously to violate the seal of confession." Bd John Sarkander was venerated as a martyr from the time of his death, and was beatified in 1859.

We are indebted to John Scintilla, a Catholic magistrate of Olmütz, for an account of the proceedings of the commission which tried the martyr. He was constrained by his official position to be present at the first session and he afterwards drafted a report for Cardinal von Dietrichstein. See Liverani, *Della vita e passione del Ven. Giovanni Sarcander* (1835), and the articles in the *Catholic Encyclopedia* (under " John "), and the *Kirchenlexikon* (under " Sarkander "). There is a fuller biography in Polish, P. Matuszynski, *Zywot bl. Jana Sarkandra meczennika* (1875).

18 : ST CYRIL, ARCHBISHOP OF JERUSALEM, DOCTOR OF THE CHURCH (A.D. 386)

IT was the lot of St Cyril of Jerusalem, a man of gentle and conciliatory disposition, to live at a time of bitter religious controversy. The Duc de Broglie characterizes him as " forming the extreme right wing of Semi-Arianism, touching on orthodoxy, or the extreme left wing of orthodoxy, bordering on Semi-Arianism, but there is nothing heretical in his teaching ", and Newman describes him more accurately when he says : " He seems to have been afraid of the word ' Homoousios ' (consubstantial), to have been disinclined to the friends of Athanasius and to the Arians, to have allowed the tyranny of the latter, to have shared in the general reconciliation, and at length, both in life and death, to have received honours from the Church which, in spite of whatever objections may be made to them, appear, on a closer examination of his history, not to be undeserved " (Preface to the translation of Cyril's *Catecheses*, p. ii). If he was not born in Jerusalem (about 315), he was certainly brought up there, and his parents, who were probably Christians, gave him an excellent education. He acquired a wide knowledge of the text of Holy Scripture, of which he made great use, some of his instructions consisting almost entirely of biblical passages connected and interwoven with each other. He seems to have been ordained priest by the bishop of Jerusalem, St Maximus, who thought so highly of his abilities that he charged him with the important duty of instructing the catechumens. His catechetical lectures were delivered for several years— those to the *illuminandi*, or candidates for baptism, taking place in Constantine's basilica of the Holy Cross, usually called the Martyrion, and those to the newly-baptized being given during Easter week in the circular Anastasis or church of the Resurrection. They were delivered without book, and the nineteen catechetical discourses which have come down to us are perhaps the only ones ever committed to writing. They are most valuable as containing an exposition of the teaching and ritual of the Church in the middle of the fourth century, and are said to be " the earliest example extant of anything in the shape of a formal system of theology ". We find in them also interesting allusions to the discovery of the cross, to the proximity of the rock which closed the Holy Sepulchre, to the weariness his hearers must be experiencing after their long fast, and so on.

The circumstances under which Cyril succeeded St Maximus in the see of Jerusalem are obscure. We have two stories recorded by his opponents, but they are quite inconsistent with each other, and St Jerome, who is responsible for one of them, seems to have been prejudiced against him. In any case it is certain that St Cyril was properly consecrated by the bishops of his province, and if the Arian Acacius, who was one of them, expected to find in him a pliable tool he was doomed to disappointment. The first year of his episcopate was marked by a physical phenomenon which made a great impression on the city, and of which he sent an account to the Emperor Constantius in a letter which has been preserved. Its genuineness has been questioned, but the style is undoubtedly his, and, though possibly interpolated, it has resisted adverse criticism. The letter says "On the nones of May, about the third hour, a great luminous cross appeared in the heavens, just over Golgotha, reaching as far as the holy mount of Olivet, seen, not by one or two persons, but clearly and evidently by the whole city. This was not, as might be thought, a fancy-bred and transient appearance : but it continued several hours together, visible to our eyes and brighter than the sun. The whole city, penetrated alike with awe and with joy at this portent, ran immediately to the church, all with one voice giving praise to our Lord Jesus Christ, the only Son of God."

Not very long after Cyril's accession, misunderstandings began to arise between him and Acacius, primarily about the precedence and jurisdiction of their respective sees, but also over matters of faith, for Acacius had now become imbued with the full Arian heresy. Cyril maintained the priority of his see as possessing an "apostolic throne", whilst Acacius, as metropolitan of Caesarea, claimed control over it and pointed to a canon of the Council of Nicaea which ran, "Since a custom and old tradition has obtained that the bishop of Aelia [Jerusalem] should receive honour, let him hold the second place, the metropolitan [of Caesarea] being secured in his own dignity". Disagreement increased to open strife, and finally Acacius called a small council of bishops of his own party, to which Cyril was summoned, but before which he refused to appear. To the charge of contumacy was added that of having sold church property during a famine to relieve the poor. This he had certainly done, as it was also done by St Ambrose, St Augustine and many other great prelates, who have been held fully justified. However, the packed meeting condemned him and he was driven out of Jerusalem. He made his way to Tarsus, where he was hospitably received by Silvanus, the semi-Arian bishop, and where he remained pending the hearing of an appeal which he had sent to a higher court. Two years after his deposition, the appeal came before the Council of Seleucia, which consisted of semi-Arians, Arians and a very few members of the strictly orthodox party—all from Egypt. Cyril himself sat among the semi-Arians, the best of whom had befriended and supported him during his exile. Acacius took violent exception to his presence and departed in anger, though he soon returned and took a prominent part in the subsequent debates. His party, however, was in the minority, and he himself was deposed, whilst Cyril was vindicated and reinstated.

Acacius thereupon, making his way to Constantinople, persuaded the Emperor Constantius to summon another council. Fresh accusations were made in addition to the old ones, and what particularly incensed the emperor was the information that a gold-brocaded vestment presented by his father Constantine to Macarius for administering baptism had been sold, and had been seen and recognized on a comedian performing on the boards of a theatre. Acacius triumphed and obtained a second decree of exile against Cyril within a year of his vindication. But upon the death of Constantius in 361, his successor Julian recalled all the bishops whom his predecessor had expelled, and Cyril returned to his see with the rest. Comparatively few martyrdoms marked the reign of the Apostate, who recognized that the blood of the martyrs is the seed of the Church, and who sought by other and more insidious means to discredit the religion he had abandoned. One of the schemes he evolved was the rebuilding of the Temple at Jerusalem in order to falsify the prophecy of our Lord, who had foretold its permanent and utter ruin. The church historians Socrates, Theodoret and others expatiate in great detail upon the attempt made by Julian to rebuild the Temple and to appeal to the national sentiment of the Jews to further this scheme. Gibbon and other more modern agnostics scoff at the record of preternatural occurrences, the earthquakes, the visible balls of fire, the collapsing walls, etc., which led to the abandonment of the enterprise, but even Gibbon is constrained to admit that the story of these prodigies is confirmed not only by such Christian writers as St John Chrysostom and St Ambrose, but, "strange as it may seem, by the unexceptionable testimony of Ammianus Marcellinus, the philosophic soldier", and a heathen. St Cyril, we are informed, looked on calmly at the vast preparations made for the rebuilding of the Temple and prophesied that it would fail.

In 367 St Cyril was banished for the third time, Valens having decreed the expulsion of all prelates recalled by Julian, but about the date of the accession of Theodosius he was finally reinstated and enjoyed undisturbed possession of his see for the last eight years of his life. He was distressed on his return to find Jerusalem torn with schisms and party strife, overrun with heresy and stained by appalling crimes. The Council of Antioch to which he appealed for help sent him St Gregory of Nyssa, who, however, found himself unable to do much and soon departed, leaving to posterity in his "Warning against Pilgrimages" a highly-coloured description of the morals of the holy city at this period.

In 381 both Cyril and Gregory were present at the great Council of Constantinople—the second oecumenical council—and the bishop of Jerusalem on this occasion took his place as a metropolitan with the patriarchs of Alexandria and Antioch. At this gathering the Nicene Creed was promulgated in its amended form, and Cyril, who subscribed to it with the rest, accepted the term "Homoousios", which had come to be regarded as the test word of orthodoxy. Socrates and Sozomen have described this as an act of repentance. On the other hand, in the letter written by the bishops who had been at Constantinople to Pope St Damasus, Cyril is extolled as one who had at various times been a champion of orthodox truth against the Arians; and the whole Catholic Church, by including him among her doctors (in 1882) confirms the theory that he had been, all along, one of those whom Athanasius calls "brothers, who mean what we mean and only differ about the word". He is thought to have died in 386 at the age of nearly seventy, after an episcopate of thirty-five years, sixteen of which were spent in exile. Of St Cyril's writings, the only ones which have survived are the Catechetical Lectures, a sermon on the Pool of Bethesda, the letter to the Emperor Constantius, and three small fragments.

Our knowledge of St Cyril's life and work is mainly derived from the church historians and from the writings of his contemporaries. The *Acta Sanctorum*, March, vol. ii, and especially Dom Touttée in his preface to the Benedictine edition of this father, have brought together the most notable references. See also the articles devoted to St Cyril in

Bardenhewer's *Patrology*, the DCB. and the DTC.   J. H. Newman's preface to the translation
of the *Catechetical Discourses* is still of value ; see also the text and translation published by
Dr F. L. Cross in 1952.   There is an excellent sketch of St Cyril in A. Fortescue's *Greek
Fathers* (1908), pp. 150–168.

ST ALEXANDER, BISHOP OF JERUSALEM, MARTYR   (A.D. 251)

St ALEXANDER was a student with Origen in the great Christian school of Alexandria,
at first under St Pantaenus and then under his successor Clement.   He was chosen
bishop of his native city in Cappadocia, and during the persecution of Severus he
made a good confession of his faith.   Although not put to death, he was imprisoned
for several years, until the beginning of the reign of Caracalla.   His former master,
Clement, who had been forced to leave Alexandria, undertook to convey a letter to
the church of Antioch, in which St Alexander sent his congratulations upon the
election of St Asclepiades—the news of which, he said, had lightened the chains
with which he was loaded.   When released from prison, he made a pilgrimage to
Jerusalem, and there we read that moved by some celestial portent the people
appointed him coadjutor bishop of that see.   This event, which took place in 212,
is the earliest recorded instance of an episcopal translation and coadjutorship, and
it had to be ratified by the hierarchy of Palestine assembled in council.   The two
bishops were still governing the church of Jerusalem when St Alexander wrote to
another see : " I salute you in the name of Narcissus who here, in his 116th year,
implores you with me to live in inviolable peace and union."   St Alexander came
into conflict with Bishop Demetrius of Alexandria, who censured him for having
taken part in the ordination of Origen and for having encouraged him while still a
layman to teach in the churches.   We have Origen's testimony that Alexander of
Jerusalem excelled all other prelates in mildness and in the sweetness of his discourses.   Amongst the benefits which he conferred on the city was the formation
of a great theological library which still existed when Eusebius wrote and of which
he made considerable use.   In the persecution of Decius, St Alexander was seized
and made a second public confession.   He was condemned to the beasts, but they
could not, we are told, be induced to attack him, and he was taken back to prison
in Caesarea where he died in chains.   The Church reckons him as a martyr.

Eusebius in his *Ecclesiastical History* (bk vi) is the primary source of information concerning St Alexander, from whose letters he quotes a few extracts.   See also the *Acta
Sanctorum*, March, vol. ii ; and Bardenhewer, *Geschichte der altkirchlichen Literatur*, vol. ii,
pp. 271–273.

ST FRIGIDIAN, OR FREDIANO, BISHOP OF LUCCA   (A.D. 588 ?)

St FRIGIDIAN, or Frediano as he is called in Italy, was an Irishman by birth or by
extraction.   He is said to have been the son of a king of Ulster and to have been
educated in Ireland, where he was raised to the priesthood.   Irish writers have
tried to identify him with St Finnian of Moville, but St Frediano lived for over
twenty-eight years in Lucca and died there, whereas Finnian ended his days in
Ireland, where he had spent the greater part of his life.   On a pilgrimage to Italy
Frediano visited Lucca, and was so greatly attracted by the hermitages on Monte
Pisano that he decided to settle there himself as an anchorite.   His repute for
sanctity caused him to be chosen for the bishopric of Lucca ; it required, however,
the intervention of Pope John II to induce Frediano to give up his life of solitude.
After seven years of peaceful rule he was temporarily driven out of the city by the

Lombard invaders, who sacked and burnt the cathedral; but the holy bishop returned, and when the ferocity of the invaders had begun to abate he set to work to repair the damage. He rebuilt his cathedral on a new site outside the north wall of the city. This church, which now bears his own name, was by him dedicated to the Three Deacons (Stephen, Vincent and Laurence). We are told that he showed goodwill and charity to all, relieved the necessitous, clothed the naked, comforted the sorrowful and visited the sick. His influence extended to the conquerors, many of whom were converted. He never ceased to aspire to the solitary life, and would retire from time to time to some lonely hermitage. It is stated that he formed a community of clergy, with whom he lived, sharing their austere discipline. This association continued after his death, and we read that when relaxation had crept in among the canons of the Lateran, Pope Alexander II (*d.* 1073), who had been bishop of Lucca, " sent for some regular canons from San Frediano, as from a house of strict observance ". It was not till 1507 that the congregation of San Frediano was merged into that of St John Lateran.

One of the many miracles said to have been worked by St Frediano has become specially famous, because it is recorded in the *Dialogues* of St Gregory, who writes : " Nor shall I be silent on this also which was related to me by the venerable Venantius, Bishop of Luni. I learned from him two days ago that at Lucca there had lived a bishop of marvellous power, by name Frediano, of whom the inhabitants relate this great miracle : that the river Auxer [Serchio] running close under the walls of the city and often bursting from its bed with great force, caused grievous damage to its inhabitants, so that they . . strove to divert its course . but failed in the attempt. Then the man of God Frediano made them give him a little rake, and advancing to where the stream flowed, he knelt in prayer. He then got up and ordered the river to follow him. As he dragged the rake behind him, the waters left their usual course and ran after it, making a new bed wherever the saint marked the way. Whence thus ever following on, it ceased to do injury to the fields and crops."

When St Frediano felt his death approaching he gathered his brethren round him, and while they were singing hymns of praise and thanksgiving, he fell into a placid sleep and passed to his rest. His relics were, it is said, miraculously rediscovered during the reign of Charlemagne ; in 1652 the bones were put together and the skeleton now lies in a glass coffin under the high altar of the cathedral at Lucca. As well as at Lucca the feast of St Frediano is kept throughout Ireland (as St Frigidian) and by the Canons Regular of the Lateran.

See Colgan, *Acta Sanctorum Hiberniae*, pp. 634–641, and especially Guerra and Guidi, *Compendio di storia ecclesiastica Lucchese dalle origini . . * (1924). On St Finnian or Winnin, with whom St Frediano has been wrongly identified, see KSS., pp. 465–466. See also A. M. Tommasini, *Irish Saints in Italy* (1937), pp. 360–377 ; A. Pedemonte, *S. Frediano* (1937), who denies that the saint was Irish, and, with less reason, dates him in the third century ; and M. Giusti in *Bollettino storico lucchese*, vol. xi, pp. 1–27.

ST EDWARD THE MARTYR (A.D. 979)

ST EDWARD was the son of King Edgar, sovereign of all the English, by his first wife, Ethelfleda, who did not long survive the birth of her son ; he was baptized by St Dunstan, then archbishop of Canterbury. After Edgar's death a party sought to set aside Edward in favour of Ethelred, a boy hardly ten years old, who was Edgar's son by his second queen, Elfrida. Edward himself was but a youth when he came to the throne, and his reign lasted a brief three years. The guidance of St Dunstan was unable to commend him to the disaffected thegns, for which the young king's violent temper was perhaps partly responsible. The chroniclers, who are all agreed that he was murdered, are not in accord as to the actual perpetrator of the deed, but William of Malmesbury claims to describe the crime in detail. He tells us that, from the moment of Edward's accession, his stepmother had sought an opportunity to slay him. One day, after hunting in Dorsetshire, the king, who was weary and wished to see his little stepbrother, of whom he was fond, determined to visit Corfe Castle, the residence of Elfrida, which was close at hand. Apprised of his arrival, the queen went out to meet him and noticed that he was alone, having outstripped his companions and attendants. She feigned pleasure at seeing him and ordered a cup to be brought to allay his thirst. As he drank, Elfrida made a sign to one of her servants, who stabbed the young king with a dagger. Although Edward immediately set spurs to his horse and tried to regain his escort, he slipped from the saddle, his foot caught in the stirrup, and he was dragged along till he died. "This year", says the Anglo-Saxon Chronicle under 979, "was King Edward slain at eventide at Corfe-gate, and was buried at Wareham without any kind of kingly honours." William of Malmesbury says that Elfrida had his body thrown into a marsh, thinking thus to dispose of it, but a pillar of light caused it to be discovered, and it was taken up and buried in the church at Wareham. His relics were afterwards removed to Shaftesbury. Elfrida herself was in the end seized with remorse for her crime and, retiring from the world, she built the monasteries of Amesbury and Wherwell, in the latter of which she died.

The earliest account of the murder attributes it to Ethelred's retainers; there is no good evidence for Queen Elfrida's alleged part in it, which is not mentioned till over a hundred years after the event. Edward was a martyr only in the broad sense of one who suffers an unjust death, but his *cultus* was considerable, encouraged by the miracles reported from his tomb at Shaftesbury; and his feast is still observed in the diocese of Plymouth.

Our principal authorities are William of Malmesbury, Florence of Worcester, the Anglo-Saxon Chronicle, Osbern the hagiographer and, earliest of all, the author of the Life of St Oswald in the *Historians of the Church of York* (Rolls Series), vol. i, pp. 448-452. See also F. M. Stenton, *Anglo-Saxon England* (1943), pp. 366-369; and particularly R. M. Wilson, *Lost Literature of Medieval England* (1952), pp. 111-112.

ST ANSELM, Bishop of Lucca   (A.D. 1086)

IT was in 1036 that St Anselm was born in Mantua, and in 1073 his uncle, Pope Alexander II, nominated him to the bishopric of Lucca, left vacant by his own elevation to the chair of St Peter, and sent him to Germany to receive from the Emperor Henry IV the crozier and the ring— in accordance with the regrettable custom of the time. Anselm, however, was so strongly convinced that the secular power had no authority to confer ecclesiastical dignities that he could not bring himself to accept investiture from the emperor and returned to Italy without it. Only after he had been consecrated by Alexander's successor, Pope St Gregory VII, did he consent to accept from Henry the crozier and the ring, and even then he felt scruples of conscience on the subject. These doubts led him to leave his diocese and to withdraw to a congregation of Cluniac monks at Polirone. A dignitary of such high-minded views could ill be spared, and Pope Gregory recalled him from his retirement and sent him back to Lucca to resume the government of his diocese. Zealous with regard to discipline, he strove to enforce among his canons the common life enjoined by the decree of Pope St Leo IX. In acute discordance with the edifying example accredited to them above in our notice of St Frediano, the canons refused to obey, although they were placed under an interdict by the pope and afterwards excommunicated. Countess Matilda of Tuscany undertook to expel them, but they raised a revolt and, being supported by the Emperor Henry, drove the bishop out of the city in 1079. St Anselm retired to Canossa, to the Countess Matilda, whose director he became, and in all the territories under her jurisdiction he established strict order among the monks and the canons. He was wont to say that he would prefer that the Church should have neither, rather than that they should live undisciplined lives. He himself was most austere, and always spent several hours daily in prayer : he never drank wine, and found some pretext for avoiding delicate food at well-served tables. Although he used to celebrate every day, he was moved to tears in saying Mass, and he lived so continually in the presence of God that no secular affairs could banish the remembrance of it.

As one of Pope Gregory's most faithful supporters, he drew upon himself much persecution. His chief services to the pontiff were rendered in connection with investitures, the suppression of which was at that period a matter of life or death to the orderly government of the Church. This abuse had been gradually increasing until it had become a grievous scandal, especially in Germany. It had its roots in the feudal system, under which bishops and abbots had become owners of lands and even of cities, for which they naturally paid allegiance to the sovereign, receiving in exchange temporal authority over the territories they governed. But the consequence was that in course of time all sacred offices were shamelessly sold to the highest bidder or bestowed on profligate courtiers. Gregory had no more vigorous supporter than Anselm of Lucca, who had himself protested against receiving investiture at secular hands. After the death of Gregory, the next pope nominated St Anselm to be his legate in Lombardy—a post which entailed the administration of several dioceses left vacant in consequence of the investitures quarrel. Thus Anselm was apostolic visitor, but he was never actually made bishop of Mantua, as some of his biographers have claimed. We read that he was a man of great learning, and had made a special study of the Bible and of its commentators : if questioned on the meaning of any passage of Holy Scripture—a great part of which he knew by heart—he could cite at once the explanations given by all the great fathers of the Church. Amongst his writings may be mentioned an important collection of canons and a commentary on the Psalms which he began at the request of the Countess Matilda, but which he did not live to complete. The holy bishop died in his native town of Mantua, and the city has since adopted him as its principal patron saint.

The main source of information is the life of the saint, formerly attributed to Bardo, *primicerius* of the cathedral of Lucca, though Mgr Guidi has shown that the true author must have been a priest belonging to the suite of the Countess Matilda (see *Analecta Bollandiana*, vol. xlviii, p. 203). This " Bardo " life has been many times printed, *e.g.* by Mabillon, the Bollandists, and in MGH., *Scriptores*, vol. xii. But there is also a long poem by Ranierius (7300 lines), first printed by La Fuente (1870), on which *cf.* Overmann in the *Neues Archiv*, vol. xxi (1897). See also the *Acta Sanctorum*, March, vol. ii, and P. Schmeidler in the *Neues Archiv.*, vol. xliii. Anselm's *Collectio Canonum* has been critically edited in recent times by Thaner.

BD CHRISTIAN, Abbot of Mellifont (A.D. 1186)

BEYOND the fact that he was abbot of the first Cistercian monastery ever established in Ireland, practically nothing at all can be stated with certainty about Bd Christian, otherwise called Christian O'Conarchy or Giolla Criost Ua Condoirche. The various traditions and legends are confused and conflicting. According to some accounts, he was born at Bangor in Ulster, and Colgan says that he was the disciple and afterwards the archdeacon of St Malachy of Armagh, and that he probably accompanied that prelate on a visit to Rome, staying at Clairvaux on his way there. He would appear to have been one of the four disciples who remained behind at Clairvaux on the homeward journey and who received the habit from St Bernard himself. Upon his return to Ireland, St Malachy was anxious to introduce the Cistercian Order into his country, and at his prompting Donough O'Carroll set about building Mellifont. Malachy applied to the founder for a superior and some monks to start the new foundation, and St Bernard sent Christian and several French brothers in 1142.

Abbot Christian is said by some writers to have become bishop of Lismore and papal legate for Ireland. An ancient anonymous Irish annalist notes the year 1186 as the date of the death of Christian, the illustrious prelate of Lismore, " formerly legate of Ireland, emulator of the virtues which he saw and heard from his holy father St Bernard and from the Supreme Pontiff, the venerable man Eugenius, with whom he was in the novitiate at Clairvaux ".

See Colgan, *Acta Sanctorum Hiberniae*, and LIS., vol. iii, p. 839.

ST SALVATOR OF HORTA (A.D. 1567)

ST SALVATOR is usually described as " of Horta " because he spent many years in the Franciscan friary of that place, although he was born at Santa Columba in the diocese of Gerona in Spain. He came of a poor family, and lost both his parents while still a child. Migrating to the town, he worked as a shoemaker in Barcelona, but at the age of twenty, as his heart was set on the religious life, he became a Franciscan of the Observance. Employed in the kitchen, his virtue quickly matured in these humble surroundings, but he thirsted for greater austerity, and passed on, first to the convent of St Mary of Jesus at Tortosa, and then to the solitude of St Mary of the Angels at Horta in the same diocese. In that house of very strict observance he made a protracted stay, but eventually he returned to Barcelona, where his supernatural gifts attracted much notice, and where the blind, lame and deaf came to him to be healed. He always walked barefoot, scourged himself daily, and kept long and rigorous fasts. He was specially devoted to our Lady and to St Paul, who appeared to him on several occasions, notably on his death-bed. St Salvator had gone to Sardinia in compliance with the orders of his superiors when he was seized with an illness which proved fatal. He died at Cagliari, being forty-seven years of age, in 1567. He was venerated as a saint during his lifetime, and was eventually canonized in 1938.

A full biography by Father Serpi, who was the promoter of the cause of St Salvator in the process of beatification, is printed in the *Acta Sanctorum*, March, vol. ii. See also Léon, *Auréole Séraphique* (Eng. trans.), vol. i, pp. 470–483.

19: ST JOSEPH, HUSBAND OF OUR LADY ST MARY   (FIRST CENTURY)

ACCORDING to the Roman Martyrology March 19 is " the [heavenly] birthday of St Joseph, husband of the most Blessed Virgin Mary and confessor, whom the Supreme Pontiff Pius IX, assenting to the desires and prayers of the whole Catholic world, has proclaimed patron of the Universal Church ". The history of his life, says Butler, has not been written by men, but his principal actions, through the inspired evangelists, are recorded by the Holy Ghost Himself. What is told in the gospels concerning him is so familiar that it needs no commentary. He was of royal descent and his genealogy has been set out for us both by St Matthew and by St Luke. He was the protector of our Lady's good name, and in that character of necessity the confidant of Heaven's secrets, and he was the foster-father of Jesus, charged with the guidance and support of the holy family, and responsible in some sense for the education of Him who, though divine, loved to call Himself " the son of man ". It was Joseph's trade that Jesus learnt, it was his manner of speech that the boy will have imitated, it was he whom our Lady herself seemed to invest with full parental rights when she said without qualification, " Thy father and I have sought thee sorrowing ". No wonder that the evangelist adopted her phrase and tells us, in connection with the incidents which attended the Child's presentation in the Temple, that " His father and mother were wondering at those things which were spoken concerning Him."

None the less our positive knowledge concerning St Joseph's life is very restricted, and the " tradition " enshrined in the apocryphal gospels must be pronounced to be quite worthless. We may assume that he was betrothed to Mary his bride with the formalities prescribed by Jewish ritual, but the nature of this ceremonial is not clearly known, especially in the case of the poor ; and that Joseph and Mary were poor is proved by the offering of only a pair of turtle-doves at Mary's purification in the Temple. By this same poverty the story of the competition of twelve suitors for Mary's hand, of the rods deposited by them in the care of the High Priest and of the portents which distinguished the rod of Joseph from the rest, is shown to be quite improbable. The details furnished in the so-called " Protevangelium ", in the " Gospel of Pseudo-Matthew ", in the " History of Joseph the Carpenter ", etc., are in many respects extravagant and inconsistent with each other. We must be content to know the simple facts that when Mary's pregnancy had saddened her husband his fears were set at rest by an angelic vision, that he was again warned by angels—first to seek refuge in Egypt, and afterwards to return to Palestine—that he was present at Bethlehem when our Lord was laid in the manger and the shepherds came to worship Him, that he was present also when the Infant was placed in the arms of Holy Simeon, and finally that he shared his wife's sorrow at the loss of her Son and her joy when they found Him debating with the doctors in the Temple. St Joseph's merit is summed up in the phrase that " he was a just man ", that is to say, a godly man. This was the eulogy of Holy Writ itself.

Although St Joseph is now specially venerated in connection with prayers offered for the grace of a happy death, this aspect of popular devotion to the saint was late in obtaining recognition. The *Rituale Romanum*, issued by authority in

1614, while making ample provision of ancient formularies for the help of the sick and dying, nowhere—the litany not excepted—introduces any mention of the name of St Joseph.   Many Old Testament examples are cited, our Lady of course is appealed to, and there are references to St Michael, SS. Peter and Paul, and even to St Thecla, but St Joseph is passed over, and it is only in recent times that the omission has been repaired.   What makes this silence the more remarkable is the fact that the account given of the death of St Joseph in the apocryphal " History of Joseph the Carpenter " seems to have been very popular in the Eastern church, and to have been the real starting-point of the interest aroused by the saint.   More-over, it is here that we find the first suggestion of anything in the nature of a litur-gical celebration.   The recognition now universally accorded to St Joseph in the West is commonly said to have been derived from Eastern sources, but the matter is very obscure.   In any case it is worthy of note that the " History of Joseph the Carpenter " was almost certainly first written in Greek, though it is now known to us only through Coptic and Arabic translations.   In this document a very full account is given of St Joseph's last illness, of his fear of God's judgements, of his self-reproach, and of the efforts made by our Lord and His mother to comfort him and to ease his passage to the next world, and of the promises of protection in life and death made by Jesus to such as should do good in Joseph's name.   It is easy to understand that such alleged promises will have made a deep impression upon simple folk, many of whom no doubt believed that they carried with them a divine warrant of fulfilment.   At all periods of the world's history we find such extrava-gances developing hand in hand with great popular movements of devotion.   The wonder would seem to be that for nearly a thousand years we find no recognizable traces either in East or West of any great response to such an appeal.   Dr L. Stern, a high authority, who interested himself much in this document, believed that the Greek original of the " History of Joseph the Carpenter " might be as old as the fourth century, but this estimate of its antiquity, as Father Paul Peeters thinks, is probably excessive.

As regards the West and certain Irish references, Father Paul Grosjean con-cludes (see bibliography below) that the oldest explicit mention of St Joseph about March 19 that we have is in a manuscript preserved at Zurich (Rh. 30, 3) ; this martyrology, from Rheinau, is of the eighth century, and originated in northern France or Belgium.   The references in the Martyrology of Tallaght and the *Félire* of Oengus, writes Father Grosjean, are concordant witnesses (depending on one another) to a continental tradition, that of the copy or abridgement of the " Martyrology of Jerome " that the writers used ; and that tradition is further attested, a little later, by two abridgements of the *Hieronymianum* from Reichenau and one from Rheims.   The idea that the Irish Culdees celebrated a feast of St Joseph on March 19 is a mistaken one.   The *Félire* is indeed the work of a Culdee, but it is not a calendar : it is a devotional poem commemorating certain saints whose names are taken arbitrarily, day by day, from an abridged martyrology of continental origin, with supplements for Ireland.   The evidence of Oengus is very valuable, because it testifies to the presence of the names of the saints he mentions in the document that he used ; but a martyrology is not a liturgical calendar, and it does not enable us to conclude that such and such a saint was celebrated on such and such a day at Tallaght or in some other Irish monastery.

These early references were a starting-point for future developments, but they only came slowly.   In the first printed Roman Missal (1474) no com-

memoration of St Joseph occurs, nor does his name appear even in the calendar.
We find a Mass in his honour at Rome for the first time in 1505, though a Roman
Breviary of 1482 assigns him a feast with nine lessons.   But in certain localities and
under the influence of individual teachers a notable *cultus* had begun long before
this.   Probably the mystery plays in which a prominent rôle was often assigned to
St Joseph contributed something to this result.   Bd Herman, a Premonstratensian
who lived in the second half of the twelfth century, took the name of Joseph, and
believed that he had received assurance of his special protection.   St Margaret of
Cortona, Bd Margaret of Città di Castello, St Bridget of Sweden and St Vincent
Ferrer seem to have paid particular honour to St Joseph in their private devotions.
Early in the fifteenth century influential writers like Cardinal Peter d'Ailly, John
Gerson and St Bernardino of Siena warmly espoused his cause, and it was no doubt
mainly due to the influence they exercised that before the end of the same century
his feast began to be liturgically celebrated in many parts of western Europe.   The
claim which has been made that the Carmelites introduced the devotion from the
East is quite devoid of foundation ; St Joseph's name is nowhere mentioned in
the " Ordinarium " of Sibert de Beka, and though the first printed Carmelite
Breviary (1480) recognized his feast, this seems to have been adopted from the
usage already accepted in Belgium, where this breviary was set up in type.   The
Carmelite chapter of 1498 held at Nîmes was the first to give formal authorization
to this addition to the calendar of the order.   But from that time forward the
devotion spread rapidly, and there can be no question that the zeal and enthusiasm
displayed by the great St Teresa in St Joseph's cause produced a profound impression upon the Church at large.   In 1621 Pope Gregory XV made St Joseph's
feast a holiday of obligation, and though this has been subsequently abrogated in
England and elsewhere there has been no diminution down to our own time in the
earnestness and the confidence of his innumerable clients.   The number of
churches now dedicated in his honour and the many religious congregations both
of men and women which bear his name are a striking evidence of the fact.

The vast devotional literature which centres round the *cultus* of St Joseph does not call
for attention here.   From the historical point of view we must be content to refer to the
Acta Sanctorum, March, vol. iii, and to a small selection of modern essays of which the best
seems to be that of J. Seitz, *Die Verehrung des hl. Joseph in ihrer geschichtlichen Entwicklung
bis zum Konzil von Trent dargestellt* (1908).   See also three articles in the *Revue Bénédictine*
for 1897   Canon Lucot, *St Joseph   Étude historique sur son culte* (1875) ; Pfülf in the
Stimmen aus Maria Laach, 1890, pp. 137 161, 282-302   Leclercq in DAC., vol. vii ; and
Cardinal L. E. Dubois, *St Joseph* (1927), in the series   Les Saints "   On the festivals
celebrated in honour of the saint see especially F. G. Holweck, *Calendarium Festorum Dei
et Dei Matris* (1925), p. 448.   *The Man Nearest to Christ* (1944). by Fr. F. L. Filas is an
excellent popular work, well documented.   U. Holzmeister's *De sancto Ioseph quaestiones
biblicae* (1945) is a very useful summary of history and tradition.   The last word to date
on the subject of the earliest liturgical references is from Fr P. Grosjean, in *Analecta
Bollandiana*, vol. lxxii (1954), fasc. 4, " Notes d'hagiographie celtique ", no. 26.   My
grateful thanks are due to Fr Grosjean for an advance copy of this article.

ST JOHN OF PANACA, Abbot   (Sixth Century)

During the monophysite disturbances in the East, a Syrian called John left his
native land and, coming to the West, settled not far from Spoleto.   There he built
an abbey of which he became superior, and he also founded another religious house
near Pesaro.   An untrustworthy legend informs us that when the holy man was
leaving Syria, he prayed   " Lord God of Heaven and earth, God of Abraham,

Isaac and Jacob, I beseech thee, the true light, to enlighten me who hope in thee and to prosper my way before me, and to let it be to me for a sign of my resting-place when the person to whom I shall give my psalter shall not return it to me that same day ." He landed in Italy and had travelled as far as the neighbourhood of Spoleto when he met a handmaid of the Lord, to whom he lent his psalter. When he asked her to return it, she said, " Where are you going, servant of God ? Remain here and resume your journey to-morrow." John agreed to tarry the night, and remembering his prayer he said to himself, " This is indeed what I asked of the Lord : here will I stay." The next morning he received back his psalter and had walked the distance of four bow-shots when there appeared an angel, who led him to a tree under which he told him to sit, adding that it was the Lord's will that he should remain in that place and that there he would have a great congregation and would find rest.

It was the month of December and the ground was hard with frost, but the tree under which John was seated was blossoming like a lily. Some passing huntsmen asked him whence he came and what he was doing there. The holy man told them his whole history and they were filled with astonishment—especially at his clothes, the like of which they had never seen. " Please do not hurt me, my sons ", said John, " for I have come here in the service of God." But the request was un-necessary, as they had already noticed the tree which was blossoming and recognized that the Lord was with him. Far from wishing to do him harm they were eager to announce his arrival to the bishop of Spoleto, who hurried out to greet him and found him praying under the tree. They wept for joy when they met, and all who were present gave glory to God. In that place John built his monastery, and there he lived until forty-four years later, when he fell asleep in peace and was buried with hymns and songs.

St John, who in the Roman Martyrology is said to have built his abbey " apud Pinnensem civitatem ", appears in the Martyrology of Ado. His festival is still kept at Spoleto. See the *Acta Sanctorum*, March, vol. iii.

SS. LANDOALD AND HIS COMPANIONS (*c.* A.D. 668)

FOR the life of St Landoald and his companions we have only a very untrustworthy biography written in 981, three hundred years after their death, to replace their original acts said to have been lost in 954. When St Amand decided to resign the see of Maestricht, in order to resume work as a missionary bishop in the provinces which are now Holland and Belgium, he went to Rome to obtain the pope's sanc-tion. St Martin I not only signified his warm approval, but selected several companions to assist him in his labours. Of these the principal was Landoald, a priest of the Roman church who came of a Lombard family and was filled with missionary zeal. A deacon, St Amantius, and nine other persons completed the party, which included St Adeltrudis, St Bavo's daughter, and St Vindiciana, Landoald's sister. They reached the territory between the Meuse and the Scheldt, and here Landoald remained, at the request of St Remaclus. He found a wide scope for his energies in the huge diocese of Maestricht, the country having been only partly evangelized and the people still addicted to gross superstitions and vices.

At Wintershoven, on the river Herck, Landoald made his headquarters, and there he built a church which St Remaclus dedicated about the year 659. Childeric II, King of Austrasia, made Maestricht one of his residences, and there he became interested in the little community at Wintershoven, to whose support he contributed. It was necessary to send a messenger from time to time to receive the royal gifts, and one of St Landoald's disciples, Adrian by name, was deputed for that purpose. Returning from one of these expeditions, he was attacked and murdered by thieves, and was honoured as a martyr. St Landoald did not long survive his disciple, and is thought to have died before St Lambert succeeded to the see of Maestricht after the murder of St Theodard. He was buried in the church of Wintershoven, but his body was several times moved, eventually to Ghent in 980. There is said to have been another translation of part of the relics back to Wintershoven in 1624, which seems to have been the occasion for the fabrication of other spurious documents.

See the *Acta Sanctorum*, March, vol. iii ; *Analecta Bollandiana*, vol. iv (1885), pp. 196–198, and vol. xxvii (1908), p. 475. See also Pirenne in *Biographie nationale* (*de Belgique*), vol. xi, pp. 256–257 ; Balau, *Sources de l'histoire de Liége*, pp. 135–139, but especially Holder-Egger in the *Aufsätze an Georg Waitz gewidmet*, pp. 622–665, and L. Van der Essen, *Saints Mérovingiens*, pp. 357–368.

ST ALCMUND, Martyr   (*c.* A.D. 800)

There were two Alcmunds to whom honour was paid in the north of England. One was a bishop of Hexham who died in 781, and is commemorated on September 17. The other is styled martyr and is said to have been put to death on March 19. This Alcmund was the son or nephew of Alhred, King of Northumbria, who according to the Anglo-Saxon Chronicle was driven from York in 774. It would seem that somewhere about 792, Osred, stated to have been the brother of Alcmund, made an attempt to regain possession of the Northumbrian kingdom, which he had previously ruled for a while, but was " seized and slain ". It is possible that Alcmund took part in, or repeated, this attempt and shared his brother's fate. Eardwulf, who was " hallowed for king " in 795, is said to have been responsible for the crime. The slender items of information preserved by different writers are hopelessly inconsistent. If veneration was paid to Alcmund's remains shortly afterwards, this would seem to be due to the fact that many miracles were alleged to have been worked at his tomb at Lilleshall ; these relics were afterwards trans- lated to Derby. Several churches were dedicated in his honour in Shropshire and Derbyshire.

See Stanton, *Menology*, pp. 124, 636 ; Dugdale, *Monasticon*, vol. vi, p. 262 ; and *Analecta Bollandiana*, vol. lviii (1940), pp. 178–183.

BD ANDREW OF SIENA   (A.D. 1251)

Bd Andrew de' Gallerani was a distinguished soldier, who led the Sienese to victory against the Orvietans. Having killed a man for openly blaspheming God, he was obliged to escape from justice or from the vengeance of his victim's friends, and retired to a family estate near the sea-coast. When he returned to Siena, it was to devote himself entirely to good works. He founded in that city the Society of Mercy to assist the sick, and established a hospital. The rest of his life was divided between charitable activities and prayer. His society, the members of which wore a special kind of cloak bearing a cross and the letter M, continued until the year 1308, when it was merged in the Dominican Order. Many miracles were attributed to Bd Andrew. Once he healed a foot which had already begun to mortify; once he walked dry-shod and untouched by the rain through the streets of Siena whilst a violent downpour was raging; on another occasion, when he returned to his home late at night from a distant errand of mercy, the gates and doors of his house opened to him of their own accord.

There is an early and seemingly trustworthy Latin life which has been printed in the *Acta Sanctorum*, March, vol. iii.

20 : SS. PHOTINA AND HER COMPANIONS, MARTYRS   (NO DATE)

ACCORDING to the Roman Martyrology, "Photina the Samaritan woman, Joseph and Victor her sons, the army officer Sebastian, Anatolius, Photius, the sisters Photis, Parasceve and Cyriaca, all confessed Christ and attained martyrdom". The story which is preserved by the Greeks is purely egendary. It asserts that Photina was the Samaritan woman whom our Lord talked with at the well. After preaching the gospel in various places she went to Carthage, where she died after suffering three years' imprisonment for the faith. St Victor, an officer in the imperial army, was made governor in Gaul and converted St Sebastian. The martyrs were brought to Rome, where some of them were burned over a slow fire and then flayed, whilst the rest were beheaded after being horribly tortured. A Spanish legend states that St Photina converted and baptized Domnina (who was Nero's daughter) with one hundred of her servants.

See the *Acta Sanctorum*, March, vol. iii, and Delehaye, *Synox. Constant.*, cc. 549-552. It is difficult to understand how Baronius could have included this entry in the Roman Martyrology. He seems in his notes to suggest that this commemoration had come to Rome by way of the monks of Monte Cassino. The story, however, in its divergent forms had wide currency in the East, and there was a Syrian convent of St Photina on Mount Sion at Jerusalem. *Cf.* the *Analecta Bollandiana*, vol. xxxviii, pp. 197 and 406.

ST MARTIN, ARCHBISHOP OF BRAGA   (A.D. 579)

ST MARTIN OF BRAGA is said by St Gregory of Tours to have surpassed in learning all the scholars of his age, and the Christian poet Fortunatus described him as having inherited the merits as well as the name of St Martin of Tours. His early history is uncertain. The story that he was a native of Pannonia is possibly the mistake of some scribe who confused him with St Martin of Tours. He is said to have made a pilgrimage to Palestine, and it was perhaps with returning pilgrims that he made his way to Galicia in Spain. There the Suevi held the mastery and had propagated Arian doctrines. St Martin, however, by his earnest preaching brought Galicia back to the Catholic Church. He began by converting and instructing King Theodomir, and subsequently reconciled many other Arians and lapsed Catholics. He built several monasteries, the principal among which, Dumium, served him as a centre for his missionary efforts.

The Suevian monarchs out of regard for him made Dumium the seat of a bishopric (now Mondoñedo), of which he became the first occupant, and so closely did they attach Martin to their court that he was called "the Bishop of the Royal Family". Nevertheless he never relaxed his own severe monastic rule of life, and maintained strict discipline in the government of his monks. He was afterwards promoted to the see of Braga, which made him metropolitan of the whole of

Galicia, and he held that dignity until his death.   Besides his main work as a missionary, St Martin rendered great service to the Church by his writings.   The chief of these are a collection of eighty-four canons, a *Formula vitae honestae*, written as a guide to a good life at the request of King Miro, a description of superstitious peasant customs entitled *De correctione rusticorum*, a symposium of moral maxims, and a selection of the sayings of the Egyptian solitaries.   St Martin died in 579 at his monastery at Dumium, and his body was translated to Braga in 1606.

Our principal authorities are here Gregory of Tours and Venantius Fortunatus.   See the *Acta Sanctorum*, March, vol. iii ; Florez, *España Sagrada*, vol. iv, pp. 151–158 ; Gams, *Kirchengeschichte Spaniens*, vol. ii, pt 1, pp. 472–475.   A cordial appreciation of the work and scholarship of St Martin of Braga may be found in the *Cambridge Medieval History*, vol. iii, pp. 489–490.   Prominence is also given to him in Ebert's *Geschichte der Literatur des Mittelalters*, vol. i, 2nd ed., pp. 579–584.   There is an account of his life in *Martini Episcopi Bracarensis Opera Omnia* (1950), ed. C. W. Barlow.

ST CUTHBERT, Bishop of Lindisfarne   (A.D. 687)

Nothing authentic is known about the parentage and birthplace of St Cuthbert. Irish hagiographers claim him as an Irishman, whereas all the Saxon chroniclers maintain that he was born in the Lowlands of Scotland.   According to Bede's metrical biography he was a Briton, and Bede in the preface to his prose History of St Cuthbert distinctly states that he has written nothing which is not well attested.   The name Cuthbert is undoubtedly Saxon and not Celtic.   We first make his acquaintance when he was about eight and was under the charge of a widow named Kenswith, whom he regarded as a mother and who treated him as her son.   He was then a healthy, lively little lad, full of fun, and the ringleader of the boys of the countryside, all of whom he could beat in running, jumping and wrestling.   One day, in the midst of their play, one child burst into tears, and exclaimed, " Oh, Cuthbert, how can you waste your time in idle sport—you whom God has set apart to be a priest and a bishop ? "   These words made so deep an impression on his mind that, from that moment, he developed a gravity beyond his years.   The occupation to which he was bred—that of a shepherd—gave him ample opportunities of quiet communing with God on the great pasturages or folklands of Northumbria.   It was at the end of August 651 that Cuthbert, then about fifteen years of age, had a vision which decided him to consecrate his life to God.   The summer day was followed by a dark night without moon or stars, and Cuthbert was alone and in prayer.   Suddenly a beam of dazzling light shone across the black sky, and in it appeared a host of angels carrying, as though in a globe of fire, a soul to heaven.   Later he learnt that the holy bishop St Aidan had died that night at Bamborough.   Although this was actually the turning-point in his life, he does not appear at once to have given up the world.   It has been suggested that he may have been called upon to fight against the Mercians, for it was on horseback and armed with a spear that he eventually appeared at the gate of Melrose Abbey and asked to be admitted amongst the brethren.   We are not told whether St Boisil the prior had any previous knowledge of him, or whether he instantaneously read the thoughts of his heart, but, as Cuthbert dismounted, he turned to one of the monks and said, " Behold a servant of the Lord ! "

In the year 660 the abbot of Melrose received land for another monastery, and upon an elevation at the confluence of the rivers Ure and Skell was built the abbey of Ripon, to which St Eata came in 661, bringing with him Cuthbert as guest-master. We read that on one cold winter's morning, as he entered the guest-chamber, he found a stranger already installed there. Fetching water he washed the visitor's hands and feet and offered refreshment. The guest courteously declined, saying that he could not wait because the home to which he was hastening lay at some distance. Cuthbert nevertheless insisted and went off to fetch some food. At his return he found the cell untenanted, but upon the table lay three loaves of singular whiteness and excellence. There was no footprint on the snow which surrounded the abbey, and St Cuthbert felt sure that he had indeed entertained an angel. The stay of Eata and Cuthbert at Ripon was of short duration. A year later King Alcfrid transferred the abbey to St Wilfrid, and, in the words of Bede, "Eata with Cuthbert and the rest of the brethren whom he had brought with him was driven home and the site of the monastery he had founded was given for a habitation to other monks".

Cuthbert returned to Melrose. The whole country was being ravaged by a disease known as "the yellow plague", and it prostrated Cuthbert. When, however, he was told that the monks had spent the whole night in prayer for his recovery, he cried, "What am I doing in bed ? It is impossible that God should close His ears to such men ! Give me my staff and my shoes." Getting up he immediately began to walk ; his will at the time seemed to triumph over his disease, but he never really regained his health. Under the infliction men and women were again, as Bede tells us, putting faith in charms and amulets. To assist the stricken people and to revive Christianity St Cuthbert now entered upon a strenuous missionary effort which extended over the years that he was prior, first at Melrose, and afterwards at Lindisfarne. Over hill and dale he travelled, sometimes on horseback, sometimes on foot, ever preferring the remoter hamlets because they had less chance of being visited. Like Aidan he taught from house to house, but whereas Aidan, who did not know the dialect, was always accompanied by an interpreter, Cuthbert could talk to the peasants in their own tongue and with their own Northumbrian accent. He knew the topography, having wandered over the lowlands with his flocks, and he could enter into the lives of his hearers and was content with their simple fare. Of pleasing appearance moreover and of cheery, winning address, he made his way at once to the hearts of his hosts, so that his teaching was extraordinarily successful. From the coast of Berwick to the Solway Firth he carried the gospel message, and everywhere he was a welcome and honoured guest.

At Coldingham, where he visited the monastery, a monk who watched him reported that he used to rise quietly at night from amongst the sleeping brethren, and making his way to the beach would enter the sea, and with the water up to his armpits would chant praises to God. A legend still current amongst the border peasantry tells of two otters—more probably seals— which followed the holy man back over the rocks and licked his half-numbed feet and wiped them with their coats until warmth was restored. If we may believe the tradition of St Cuthbert's visit to the Picts of Galloway, it was from Coldingham that he sailed with two companions, landing at the estuary of the Nith on the day after Christmas. Snowdrifts prevented them from penetrating inland, whilst a succession of storms made re-embarkation impracticable, and they seemed in danger of dying from hunger. The two companions were discouraged and depressed, but Cuthbert's faith never wavered. He assured them that all would be well, and presently they discovered, at the foot of a cliff, slices of dolphin's flesh which sustained them until the storm abated and they were able to take once more to the sea. It is said that a church was afterwards built to mark the spot, and the name of the town, Kirkcudbright, which grew up near it, has preserved the memory of St Cuthbert's visit.

Meanwhile great changes were taking place at Lindisfarne, and it seemed at one moment as though Holy Island might lose altogether the famous community which had made it the most venerable sanctuary in the north. The disputes over the date of Easter had culminated in the celebrated Council of Whitby, at which King Oswy decided for the Roman use. St Colman returned to Lindisfarne, but soon decided that he could not conform and preferred to resign. Followed by all the Irish monks and thirty of the English, and bearing the body of St Aidan, he left England and made new homes in Ireland. To fill his place St Eata was recalled from Melrose and given the rank of bishop, and Cuthbert accompanied him again to act as his prior. Their task was no easy one, for many of the remaining monks were set against the innovations, whilst Eata and Cuthbert, whatever their private feelings may have been, were determined to enforce the decisions of the Council of Whitby. They had to face opposition and even insult, but Cuthbert's conduct was beyond praise : never once did he lose patience or self-control, but, when the malcontents became too offensive, he would quietly rise and close the discussion, only to resume it when passion had subsided. The life St Cuthbert led at Lindisfarne was similar to that at Melrose. He carried on his apostolic labours amongst the people, preaching and teaching and ministering not only to their souls but also to their bodies, by virtue of the gift of healing which was bestowed upon him. Wherever he went crowds flocked to hear him, to open their hearts to him, and to beg him to heal their sick. The days were not long enough, and he would sometimes forgo sleep on three nights out of four that he might spend the time in prayer by the sea-shore, or in the recitation of psalms as he paced up and down the church, or in meditation and manual work in his cell.

After some years at Lindisfarne, the longing to lead a life of still closer union with God led him with his abbot's consent to seek solitude. His first hermitage was at no great distance from the abbey—probably in the islet off Holy Island which local tradition associates with him and calls St Cuthbert's Isle. The place, wherever it may have been, appears not to have been sufficiently secluded, for in 676 he moved to a bleak and desolate island of the Farne group, two miles from Bamborough. The spot was then uninhabited, and afforded him at first neither water nor corn, but he found a spring and though the first crop which he planted failed entirely the second crop—which was barley—yielded sufficient to sustain him. In spite of the storms which then, as at all times, were wont to rage round the islands, visitors persisted in coming, and St Cuthbert build a guest-house near the landing-stage to lodge them. Only once did he leave his retreat, and that was at the request of the abbess St Elfleda, King Oswy's daughter. This meeting took place on Coquet Island, and Elfleda urged him on that occasion to accept a bishopric which King Egfrid was anxious to bestow upon him. Shortly afterwards he was elected bishop of Hexham. He refused to leave his island cell, and was only induced to consent when King Egfrid came in person to Farne, accompanied by Bishop Trumwin. Very reluctantly Cuthbert gave way, but stipulated to be allowed to remain in his hermitage for the six months that would elapse before his consecration. During that period he visited St Eata and arranged for an exchange of dioceses, whereby Eata would take Hexham and Cuthbert would have the see of Lindisfarne with charge of the monastery.

On Easter day 685 he was consecrated in York Minster by St Theodore, Archbishop of Canterbury. As a bishop the saint " continued to be the same man that he was before "—to quote his anonymous biographer. The two years of his episcopate were mainly spent in visiting his diocese, which extended far to the west and included Cumberland. He preached, taught, distributed alms, and wrought so many miracles of healing that he won during his lifetime the name of " the Wonderworker of Britain ", which the remarkable cures effected at his tomb caused him to retain after his death. He was making his first visitation of Carlisle, a few weeks after his consecration, when, by some strange telepathic gift or by divine revelation, he was apprised of the overthrow of the Northumbrian army and of the death in battle of King Egfrid. Defeat in war was followed by a recurrence of the plague, which was so severe that many villages were entirely deserted. The good bishop went fearlessly amongst his people ministering to the sick and dying, his very presence inspiring hope and often restoring health. On one occasion he revived with a kiss a widow's son in whom life appeared to be extinct.

But labours and austerities had sapped St Cuthbert's constitution, and he realized that he had not long to live. Upon his second visit to Carlisle he told his former disciple St Herbert, the hermit of Derwentwater, that they would meet on earth no more, consoling his afflicted friend by obtaining from Heaven the promise that they would die on the same day. After a farewell visitation through the diocese, he laid down the pastoral staff, and after celebrating the Christmas of 686 with the monks in Holy Island, he withdrew to his beloved Farne to prepare for his end. " Tell us, my lord bishop ", said one of the monks who assembled to bid him farewell, " when we may hope for your return."—" When you shall bring back my body ", was the reply. His brethren often visited him during the last three months, although he would not allow anyone to stay and minister to him in his growing weakness. Fever set in and he endured terrible trials from the spirits of evil during a stormy period of five days, when no one could approach the island. He wanted to be buried in his retreat, but yielded to the entreaties of his monks who wished that his bones should rest amongst them at the abbey. " You will bury me ", he said, " wrapped in the linen which I have kept for my shroud, out of love for the Abbess Werca, the friend of God, who gave it to me." His last instructions were given to Abbot Herefrid who sat beside him and asked for a message to the brethren. " Be of one mind in your councils, live in concord with the other servants of God : despise none of the faithful who seek your hospitality : treat them with kindly charity, not esteeming yourselves better than others who have the same faith and often live the same life. But hold no communion with those who err from the unity of the Catholic faith. Study diligently, carefully observe the canons of the fathers, and practise with zeal that monastic rule which God has deigned to give you by my hands. I know that many have despised me, but after my death it will be found that my teaching has not deserved contempt."

These were St Cuthbert's last words as Bede learnt them from the lips of Herefrid. He then received the last sacraments and died peacefully, seated, with his hands uplifted and his eyes gazing heavenwards. A monk immediately climbed the rock on which now stands the lighthouse and waved two lighted torches—for it was night—to announce to the brethren at Lindisfarne that the great saint had passed to his rest. His body, which at first was laid in the abbey and remained at Lindisfarne for 188 years, was removed when the Northmen began to descend upon the coast, and after many translations was deposited in a magnificent shrine in

Durham Cathedral, which continued to be a favourite place of pilgrimage for the north of England until the Reformation.   In the reign of Henry VIII the shrine was desecrated and plundered, but the monks secretly buried the relics.   In 1827 St Cuthbert's body was again discovered, and the various articles through which it was identified were removed to the cathedral library.   Although the genuineness of the relics is generally admitted, yet there is another tradition, according to which St Cuthbert's remains still lie interred in another part of the cathedral, known only to three members of the English Benedictine Congregation, who hand on the secret before they die.

St Cuthbert is usually represented as carrying in his hands the head of King Oswald.   This was buried with him for safety, and was found when the bishop's coffin was opened and examined at Durham in 1104.   Sometimes the compassionate otters appear at his feet, but more often he is accompanied by a bird—probably representing one of the wild fowl, known as St Cuthbert's birds, which once swarmed in the Farne Islands.   Several beautiful legends are told about the saint's friendship with these creatures whom he tamed and to whom he promised that they should never be disturbed.   Two ancient copies of the gospels are specially connected with the saint.   One is the famous eighth-century Lindisfarne Gospels, which the scribe who wrote it laid on St Cuthbert's tomb and which was beautifully adorned by St Bilfrid.   It was accidentally dropped overboard by monks who were taking it to Ireland, but was washed up on the shore practically undamaged, and is now at the British Museum.   The other is the seventh-century Gospel of St John which was buried with St Cuthbert and is one of the most cherished possessions of Stonyhurst College.   His ring is treasured at Ushaw.

St Cuthbert's life was one of almost continuous prayer.   All that he saw spoke to him of God, and his conversation was habitually about heavenly things.   Bede says, " He was aflame with the fire of divine charity ; and to give counsel and help to the weak he considered equal to an act of prayer—knowing that He who said ' Thou shalt love the Lord thy God ', also said ' Thou shalt love thy neighbour as thyself '."   As well as in several northerr English dioceses, the feast of this great saint is kept in Saint Andrews and in Meath.   Hexham has a second, translation, feast on September 4.

Our sources of information concerning St Cuthbert are in an exceptional degree authentic and reliable.   No medieval historian commands more respect than Bede, and supplementary details of later date—notably in the account of the translations, etc., by Simeon of Durham (his complete works have been edited in the Rolls Series) and in the discoveries made when the tomb was opened in 1827 (for which see Raine, who did not like monks, *Saint Cuthbert*, 1828)—also confirm the earlier narratives.   Much incidental information will be found in the notes to Plummer's edition of Bede's *Ecclesiastical History*.   The archaeological aspects of the question may be best studied in the catalogue of Haverfield and Canon Greenwell, *Inscribed Stones*, etc., and in the Durham vol. i of the *Victoria County History*.   The Irish account of St Cuthbert was printed in the eighth volume of the publications of the Surtees Society.   The early anonymous life of the saint was edited with that written by Bede by Fr Stevenson, who also has printed a convenient English translation (1887) of the Bede life. There is a very full biography by Abp C. Eyre (1849) which is specially useful for its plans and maps ; another by Provost Consitt (1887) ; and an excellent popular sketch by Mrs H. Colgrave (1947).   A new edition of the anon. and Bede lives is by B. Colgrave, *Two Lives of St Cuthbert* (1940) ; and for some miracles at Farne see *Analecta Bollandiana*, vol. lxx (1952), pp. 5-19.   See also Craster in the *English Historical Review*, April 1954 (important for the translations of the relics).

ST HERBERT (A.D. 687)

St Herbert's Island on Lake Derwentwater derives its name from the holy anchoret and priest who lived and died there in the seventh century. He was the disciple and close friend of St Cuthbert, and it was his custom every year to visit his master at Lindisfarne and thus to renew his fervour. St Cuthbert in the year before he died had occasion to come to Carlisle, and St Herbert repaired to him there instead of going all the way to Lindisfarne. They talked together for some time, and then St Cuthbert told his friend that if he had anything to ask he must ask it at once, because the time of his own departure was at hand and they would meet no more in this world. St Herbert wept bitterly, beseeching his spiritual father not to abandon him, but to pray that, as they had served God together in this life, they might be allowed at the same moment to behold His glory in heaven. St Cuthbert paused for a moment in prayer, and then replied, " Weep no more, but rather rejoice, dear brother, for God in His mercy has heard our prayer and has granted our petition ". Almost immediately afterwards St Herbert was seized with a painful illness which lasted until March 20 of the following year, when both saints were called from this world to enter Heaven together. In the fourteenth century an indulgence was granted to pilgrims who should visit St Herbert's Island, and the present Catholic church at Windermere is dedicated in his honour. St Herbert is best remembered in these days through Wordsworth's lines, beginning " If thou in the dear love of some one friend .".

See the Lives of St Cuthbert, prose and metrical, by Bede, and the *Acta Sanctorum*, March, vol. iii. There is a brief account of St Herbert in the " Lives of the English Saints ", edited by J. H. Newman. This was written by John Barrow, of Kendal, principal of St Edmund's Hall, who, when he became a Jesuit in 1867, changed his name to William Bernard.

ST WULFRAM, Archbishop of Sens (A.D. 703 ?)

The father of St Wulfram was an officer of King Dagobert, and the saint himself, though early raised to the priesthood, was summoned to the court. When Lambert, the occupant of the archiepiscopal seat of Sens, died, Wulfram was elected to succeed him, and discharged his episcopal duties very devotedly for two and a half years. He then made a solemn abdication, moved by a desire to labour among the heathen Frisians, coupled probably with doubts as to the canonicity of his appointment, for St Amatus (Amé), the rightful archbishop, was still alive. He had been unjustly banished by Thierry III and had survived both Méry and Lambert who had been installed in his place. In preparation for his missionary labours Wulfram retired to the abbey of Fontenelle and there obtained monks to assist him in his mission.

They travelled by sea and, upon landing in Friesland, they were successful in converting a number of people, including one of King Radbod's sons, and strove to wean the natives from the practice of offering human sacrifices. In reply to St Wulfram's remonstrances King Radbod declared that it was the custom of the country, and that he could not and would not interfere. It had become the practice to cast lots for the victim, who was usually a child of noble birth. A boy called Ovon was chosen in this way, and St Wulfram begged that he might be spared. The king replied that Wulfram was at liberty to rescue the child by the power of his God if he could. The saint betook himself to prayer, and after the boy had been left hanging for two hours, the rope broke and the lad fell to the ground. He

was still alive and was given to Wulfram, who sent him to Fontenelle, where he
became a monk and a priest and in later life supplied the details of the saint's
mission to Friesland.   St Wulfram also, in a wonderful way, rescued two children
who were being drowned as victims to the sea-goddess.   According to a story,
which, however, is not to be found in the earliest manuscripts of his life, King
Radbod was so impressed by the saint's miracles that he consented, half unwillingly,
to be baptized.   But at the last moment he suddenly asked where his ancestors
were, and was informed by St Wulfram that Hell was the portion of all idolaters.
Upon hearing these words Radbod drew back, declaring that he chose Hell with
his ancestors rather than Heaven without them.   After working for many years
among the Frisians St Wulfram went back to Fontenelle, where he died.   His relics
were translated first to Blandigny and then to Abbeville, where they are still
venerated.

   The Latin Life of St Wulfram (printed by Mabillon, vol. iii, pt 1, and critically edited
by W. Levison in MGH., *Scriptores Merov.*, vol. v) professes to be written by Jonas, monk
of Fontenelle, and a contemporary of the saint.   Despite the attempted vindication by Abbé
Legris (*Analecta Bollandiana*, vol. xvii, pp. 265–306) it seems certain that it must have been
compiled nearly a hundred years later (see *Analecta Bollandiana*, vol. xix, p. 234 ; vol. xxix,
p. 450) and that it is not historically trustworthy.   There is a short account of St Wulfram
by W. Glaister in English, and in French by Sauvage and La Vieille (1876).   *Cf.* Duchesne,
Fastes Épiscopaux, vol.   p. 413.

THE MARTYRS OF MAR SABA   (A.D. 796)

THE story of the sufferings of the monks of Mar Saba, between Jerusalem and the
Dead Sea, has been graphically told by one of themselves, Stephen the Wonder-
worker, known also as " the Poet ", from the hymns which he composed.   The
Arabs had been devastating Palestine for some time, burning monasteries as well
as despoiling churches, and the monks of the laura of St Sabas doubted whether to
remain or to fly.   Coming to the conclusion that their home would assuredly be
destroyed if they left, they decided to remain, hoping that through their poverty
they might be spared.   Soon afterwards a party of Arabs rode down from the hills
and, when some of the monks went forth to beg to be left in peace, demanded
money.   In vain did the brethren assure them that they were pledged to poverty
and owned nothing.   The new-comers drove them back into the settlement, and
followed them there to ransack their cells and church.   They could find nothing of
value, and after desecrating the church and burning some of the hermitages, they
withdrew.   About thirty of the monks had been wounded, but Thomas, the leech,
bound up their wounds.   The monks repaired the other damage as best they could
and resumed their customary life.   A week later, as they were keeping their
Saturday vigil in church, an aged white-haired brother from the monastery of St
Euthymius brought a letter advising them that the marauders were about to return.
In their terror the hermits tried to find hiding-places, and Sergius, the sacristan,
concealed the sacred vessels—the only treasure which the laura possessed.

   The marauders did not fail to reappear, and at once searched for the monks,
many of whom they drove from their hiding-places.   The first to suffer death was
the sacristan, who had escaped, fearing lest under torture he might reveal the place
where he had secreted the sacred vessels.   When ordered to return he refused, and
bared his neck to the executioner's sword.   John, the hospitaller, they found at the
top of the hill, near the guest-house of which he had charge.   He was stoned,

hamstrung and then dragged by the feet over the rocks down into the church, where the Arabs hoped to force him to disclose hidden valuables. They failed, but he was suffocated with smoke as he lay there. Patricius tried to save those who were concealed with him by giving himself up when the enemy discovered the entrance to their hiding-place. He and others were then driven into a winding cavern and the Arabs blocked up the entrance with thorns and brushwood, which they set on fire. The dense smoke entered the cave, choking and blinding the poor victims. At intervals their tormentors would summon them to come out through the smouldering embers, question them, and drive them back. They would then pile on more fuel. Finally, after having pillaged and burnt the settlement and its church, they departed, taking with them everything that was portable. Of the monks who had been driven into the cavern, eighteen had died of suffocation and most of the others were at their last gasp.

The Greek narrative is printed in full in the *Acta Sanctorum*, March, vol. iii. See also Delehaye, *Synax. Constant.*, p. 548, in which text the marauders are called " Ethiopians ".

BB. EVANGELIST AND PEREGRINE   (*c.* A.D. 1250)

DURING their school days in Verona, two boys, afterwards known as Evangelist and Peregrine, struck up a friendship which was to last throughout their lives and to extend beyond the grave. Both wished to give themselves to God in religion, and whilst uncertain what order to enter, they were favoured with a vision which led them to join a community of the Hermits of St Augustine outside Verona. Their conduct was exemplary, but the prior asked them one day why they usually prayed out of doors, with their eyes fixed on the sky. They replied that it was because they always saw our Lady there with her divine Son and with St Anne, as they had appeared in the vision which had brought them to join the hermits. The supernatural favours which they received, far from elating the two friends, only rendered them the more humble, and they were always eager to perform the most menial duties, as well as to do any good service to their brethren. They were both of them endowed with the gift of healing, and cured the sick people who came to them from all sides. Evangelist was warned by an angel of his approaching death, and passed peacefully away while upon his knees. Peregrine besought God that He would allow him to join his friend and, as he prayed, Evangelist appeared to him in glory and assured him that he was about to follow him. A few hours later he breathed his last, and the two were buried in the same grave. Their *cultus* was confirmed in 1837.

See the *Acta Sanctorum*, July, vol. vi.

BD AMBROSE OF SIENA   (A.D. 1286)

SIENA venerates on this day the memory of one of the noblest of her sons, Ambrose Sansedoni. His parents belonged to two of the most distinguished Sienese families, and his father, nicknamed for his valour " Buonattaco ", was foremost in all schemes for the defence of Christendom against the Moors. The boy was born with an abnormally large head and apparently without having the use of his arms and legs. One day, when his nurse had taken him to the Dominican church of St Mary Magdalen, he was seen to struggle, and upon being extricated from the swathing bands in which he was wrapped like a Della Robbia *bambino*, it was found that his limbs were as vigorous as those of any other child. Many instances of his precocious piety are given by his biographers, and as he grew older he developed a great devotion for the sick and poor, visiting the hospital every Sunday and the prison every Friday. At seventeen Ambrose decided to join the Order of Preachers. His superiors were not slow in recognizing his ability, and they sent him to Cologne, where he had St Albert the Great as his master and St Thomas Aquinas as a fellow student. So intelligent a pupil could not fail to make progress under such a teacher, and before long he was besieged in his cell by applicants asking for help in their difficulties. This popularity was distasteful to him, and he besought his superiors to allow him to retire into solitude. Having won their consent he withdrew from public life—but not for long. Influential people urged the Dominicans to recall him and to set him to preach. For three years he taught theology in Paris, where the students crowded to his lectures. He was sent to preach in Germany, France and Italy, and we are told that his sermons seemed inspired. Sinners were converted and enemies settled their differences amicably; some of his hearers declared that while he stood in the pulpit they had seen the Holy Spirit descend upon his head in the form of a dove.

Like many other Italian saints, men and women, the eloquent friar did not confine his energies to spiritual exhortations, but was called upon to take part in important public affairs. By his persuasive words he managed to reconcile the prince electors, who in their private quarrels were on the eve of kindling civil war. He arrested a new heresy in Bohemia which was causing strange disorder, and when charged by Bd Gregory X to preach the crusade he obtained a generous response to his appeals. Twice did he reconcile with the Holy See the people of Siena, who, having taken the part of Manfred, the bastard son of Frederic II, had been placed under an interdict. Several writers assert that when Ambrose entered the consistory to plead for his fellow-townsmen, his face was illuminated with so supernatural a light that the pope exclaimed, " Father Ambrose, you need not explain your mission ; I grant whatever you wish ".

In spite of all the important missions with which he was entrusted, and of the success which attended his efforts, Ambrose ever remained singularly humble. The pope wished to make him a bishop, but he never could be induced to consent, although he filled the office of master of the sacred palace. After the death of Gregory he sought retirement in one of the houses of his order. Here he often swept out the church, the dormitories and the cloisters, and never gave more than four hours to sleep. After Matins he prayed for two hours in choir and studied the rest of the night until Prime. During the forty-five years that he was a religious Ambrose ate meat once—out of obedience—and on Fridays he took nothing but bread and water. Even to old age he continued to preach, and his sermons lost none of their fire and eloquence. At the beginning of Lent 1286, when preaching one day against usury, he spoke with such vehemence that he broke a blood-vessel. The following morning, as the haemorrhage had stopped, he tried to continue his sermon, but the trouble began again, and it was evident that his days were numbered. He died in his sixty-sixth year, and the *cultus* which had been paid to him in Siena from the time of his death was confirmed in 1622.

Ample materials for the biography of Bd Ambrose will be found in *Acta Sanctorum*, March, vol. iii, and they include a very interesting collection of contemporary testimonies to the numerous miracles worked at his tomb. Departing from the usual practice, Pope Clement VIII seems to have ordered his name to be inserted in the Roman Martyrology before any formal canonization or *confirmatio cultus* had taken place ; but Baronius in his note upon this eulogium supplies a number of references to Dominican and other writers who bore testimony to the sanctity of Ambrose and the miracles he had worked. For a fuller bibliography see Taurisano, *Catalogus Hagiographicus O.P.*, p. 22.

BD JOHN OF PARMA (A.D. 1289)

JOHN BURALLI, the seventh minister general of the Franciscans, was born at Parma in 1209, and he was already teaching logic there when at the age of twenty-five he joined the Franciscans. He was sent to Paris to prosecute his studies and, after he had been ordained, to teach and to preach in Bologna, Naples and Rome. His eloquence drew crowds to his sermons, and great personages flocked to listen to him. It has been stated that in 1245, when Pope Innocent IV convoked the first general council of Lyons, John was deputed to represent Crescentius, the minister general, who owing to his infirmities was unable to attend, but this is incorrect ; the friar who went to the council was Bonaventure of Isco. John, however, that same year journeyed to Paris to lecture on the " Sentences " in the university, and in 1247 he was chosen minister general of the order. The work that lay before him was exceedingly difficult, for many abuses and a spirit of strife had crept in owing to the lax observance of Brother Elias. We are fortunate in having a first-hand description of Bd John's activities, written by his fellow townsman Brother Salimbene, who was closely associated with him for a long time. We learn that he was strong and robust, so that he could bear great fatigue, of a sweet and smiling countenance, with polished manners, and full of charity. He was the first among the ministers general to visit the whole order, and he travelled always on foot. Outside the friaries he would never allow his dignity to be known, and he was so humble and unassuming that on coming to a house he often helped the brothers to wash vegetables in the kitchen. A lover of silence and recollection, he was never heard to utter an idle word, and when dying he admitted that he would have more to answer for in respect of his silence than of his speech.

He began his general visitation with England, and when King Henry III heard that he was at hand to pay his respects, he rose from table and came out of doors to embrace the humble friar. In France John was at Sens visited by St Louis IX who, on the eve of his departure for the crusades, came to ask his prayers and blessing on the enterprise. The king, who arrived in pilgrim guise, staff in hand, struck Brother Salimbene as looking delicate and frail. He took food with the brothers in the refectory, but could not persuade John of Parma to sit beside him. Burgundy and Provence were next visited. At Arles, a friar from Parma, John of Ollis, came to ask a favour. Would the minister deign to give to him and to Salimbene a commission to preach ? John, however, was not going to make favourites of his compatriots. " Of a truth, if you were my blood-brothers ", he replied, " you would not obtain that office from me without an examination." John of Ollis was not easily snubbed. " Then if we *must* be examined, will you call on Brother Hugh to examine us ? " Hugh of Digne, the former provincial, was actually in the house. " No ! " said the minister promptly. " Brother Hugh is your friend and he might spare you, but call hither the lecturer and tutor of the house." Brother Salimbene cannot resist telling us that he himself passed the test, but that John of Ollis was sent back to do some more studies.

Soon after John of Parma's return from a mission as papal legate to the Eastern emperor, trouble broke out in Paris, whither he had sent St Bonaventure, as one of the greatest scholars of the Friars Minor. William of Saint-Amour, a secular doctor of the university, had raised a storm against the mendicant orders and attacked them in a scurrilous libel. Bd John went to Paris, and is said to have addressed the university professors in terms so persuasive and humble that all were moved, and the doctor who was to have replied could only say, " Blessed art thou, and blessed are thy words " The storm abated, and the minister general then applied himself to the restoration of discipline. Even before he had gone to the East he had held a general chapter at Metz, where measures were taken to secure the proper observance of the rule and constitutions and to insist upon the Roman Missal and Breviary being strictly adhered to. He obtained several papal bulls which assisted him, and Pope Innocent IV bestowed on the order the convent of the Ara Coeli in Rome, which became the residence of the minister general.

In spite of all his efforts Blessed John met with bitter opposition, partly caused by his Joachimite leanings. He became convinced that he was not capable of carrying through the reforms which he felt were essential. Whether he acted spontaneously or in obedience to pressure put upon him by the papal curia is not clear, but he resigned office in Rome in 1257, and when asked to nominate a successor chose St Bonaventure. The selection was a happy one, and St Bonaventure is sometimes spoken of as the Second Founder ; but the way had been prepared for him by his predecessor's firm government. John now retired to the hermitage of Greccio, the place where St Francis had prepared the first Christmas crib. He spent the last thirty years of his life there in retirement from which he only emerged two or three times when summoned by the pope. When, as a very old man of eighty, he heard that the Greeks had relapsed into schism, he begged that he might be allowed to go again to plead with them. He obtained the pope's consent and started off, but as he entered Camerino he realized he was dying, and said to his companions, " This is the place of my rest ". He went to his reward on March 19, 1289, and many miracles were soon after reported at his tomb. His *cultus* was approved in 1777.

John of Parma played so considerable a part in the early developments of the troubles which culminated in the Fraticelli revolt that his name figures more or less prominently in a multitude of books dealing with the Franciscan movement. Salimbene's picture of him, even as transmitted through the distorted medium of Dr Coulton's *From St Francis to Dante*, is unforgettable. Salimbene's text is published in MGH., *Scriptores*, vol. xxxii. We have no ancient biography, but two or three modern ones in Italian, notably by B. Affó (1777) and by Luigi da Parma (1909). See also Léon, *Auréole Séraphique* (Eng. trans.), vol. i, pp. 493–512, and Edouard d'Alençon in DTC., vol. viii, cc. 794–796. Although the Joachimite *Introductorius evangelii aeterni* was at one time attributed to John of Parma, it certainly was not written by him but by Gerard of Borgo-San-Donnino ; and even the authorship of the *Sacrum commercium beati Francisci cum domina paupertate* commonly assigned to him is uncertain ; see the critical edition of this latter brought out by Edouard d'Alençon in 1900.

BD MAURICE OF HUNGARY (A.D. 1336)

MAURICE CSAKY belonged to the royal Hungarian dynasty, his father being count of Csak, but the exact place of his birth is not known. From childhood he was seriously disposed, and loved to hear and read the lives of the saints, and he wished to enter a monastery ; but his aspirations were overruled, and at the age of twenty he was married to the daughter of the Palatine Prince Amadeus. His bride was in every way worthy of him, and they were tenderly attached to each other ; but after some years they agreed to part and to retire into the cloister. Maurice chose the Order of Preachers, and entered the friary on the island of St Margaret. The step taken by the young couple created a great sensation, and Ladislaus, governor of Budapest, actually caused Maurice to be imprisoned for five months to test his resolution. He emerged from captivity with his intention unshaken, but his superiors in the order thought it wise to transfer him from Hungary to Bologna. Later the young friar returned to his own country as an emissary of peace. So eager was he to avert strife that he would rush in between combatants and exhort them to come to terms. When he was appointed sacristan he made this office an opportunity for almost unbroken devotion to the Blessed Sacrament. A great love for the poor was another characteristic of a singularly winning personality. Maurice died at Raab and was buried in the monastery of Javarin.

A Latin Life of Bd Maurice is printed by the Bollandists in the *Acta Sanctorum*, March, vol. iii. See also F. Kaindl in *Archiv f. österreichische Geschichte*, vol. xci (1902), pp. 53–58. Although there seems never to have been any formal beatification or *confirmatio cultus*, Bd Maurice is, or at any rate was, honoured liturgically in his native country.

BD MARK OF MONTEGALLO   (A.D. 1497)

THIS great promoter, if he was not the originator, of those charitable loan-banks known as *monti di pietà*, was born in the town of Santa Maria di Montegallo, in the diocese of Ascoli. He studied with distinction at Perugia and Bologna, and after qualifying as a doctor he married. Before long, however, both he and his wife realized vocations to the religious life and separated by mutual consent, she to become a Poor Clare at Ascoli and he to enter a Franciscan community at Fabriano. Soon he was launched upon a preaching and missionary career which was to last for forty years. Once, as he knelt in prayer, a voice had murmured in his ear : " Brother Mark, preach love ", and love had become his favourite theme as he tramped up and down the country from Sicily to the valley of the Po. He seemed absolutely indefatigable in his zeal for souls, and often combined the healing of their bodies with that of their consciences.

Out of compassion for the poor who fell into the clutches of usurers Mark established houses where the impoverished could borrow the money they needed on very small security, and sometimes on no security at all. To found one such bank in Vicenza he preached with such eloquence that the money required was collected in one day, and the office was built and launched within a year. Pitiful and kind as Bd Mark was to others, he was merciless to himself. Even on his journeys he omitted nothing of the scourgings, night-watches and mortifications he practised in the friary. Dawn often found him deep in prayer which had begun at midnight. At Camerino, where the plague was rife, he prophesied the cessation of the pestilence if the people would repent. Believing his words they crowded to the tribunal of penance, confessing their sins, and the scourge was stayed. Besides the house at Vicenza, other loan-banks and hostels were started at Bd Mark's instigation, notably one at Fabriano which a friend of his built, and another at Perugia, founded by St James of the Marches. When he lay dying at Vicenza he asked that the Passion should be read to him, and as the reader pronounced the words, " It is consummated ", he breathed his last. In some Italian cities Bd

Mark of Montegallo was called "A new star of love", and the description seemed singularly appropriate to one who was all aglow with the fire of charity.

See the *Acta Sanctorum*, March, vol. iii, where the Bollandists have printed extracts from Wadding's *Annales* together with a rhythmical Latin eulogy written by a contemporary. *Cf.* Léon, *Auréole Séraphique* (Eng. trans.), vol. i, p. 530.

BD BAPTIST OF MANTUA (A.D. 1516)

BD BAPTIST came of a Spanish family on his father's side, but his mother was a native of Brescia in northern Italy, and he himself was born at Mantua. Because of his ancestry he, like his father, was known by the nickname, or possibly the surname, of Spagnuolo—the Spaniard. As a child he displayed great ability, and while still young he received a good grounding in philosophy and rhetoric. There were irregularities in his youth which led to trouble at home ; but in the end Baptist felt himself called to the religious life, and he joined the Carmelite community at Ferrara. From the outset he sought to follow the path of perfection, but he also devoted himself to literature and sacred science with such success that in his Latin composition and verse he was accounted the equal of the most famous humanists of the age. God bestowed on him in a remarkable degree the gift of counsel, which was widely recognized, especially among the Carmelites of Mantua, by whom he was six times re-elected vicar general of the Reform. It was not only in the cloister that he gave inspiration and help, but he endeared himself to many people living in the world, and to the poor and destitute to whom he was a father. Princes and popes held him in the utmost esteem, partly for his scholarship and partly for the tact he displayed in dealing with delicate negotiations. When away from his convent and in secular surroundings never did he abate any of the rules of his order or depart from that poverty to which he had pledged himself ; on several occasions he was visited with illness when a little relaxation would have been permissible, yet he continued all his customary mortifications and practices of devotion in spite of ill-health.

Sorely against his wish Bd Baptist was elected prior general of the Carmelite Order, but the special command of the pope was required before he could be induced to accept the office. In spite of his humble opinion of his own capacities, he proved himself a most able and exemplary superior. He had a great devotion to our Lady and lost no opportunity of extolling her and extending her veneration. His incredibly vast output of Latin verse (55,000 lines) was nearly all animated by some religious purpose. He glorified the marvels of Loreto and sang of the feasts of the Church, desiring above all things to prove that good literature need not necessarily be associated with paganism. His fellow-townsmen of Mantua thought so highly of his merits as a poet that they set up a bust of him in rivalry with that of Virgil. Baptist dedicated one of his longest effusions to that great connoisseur of letters, Pope Leo X, but he did not hesitate to tell him that one of the gravest needs of the time was the reform of the Roman curia, "which was infected by a deep corruption disseminating poison throughout all countries". "Help, holy father Leo", the poet exclaimed, "for Christendom is nigh its fall."

Returning to Mantua at the end of his days, Baptist endured with exemplary patience a painful illness, to which he succumbed, passing peacefully to his eternal reward in the spring of 1516. The whole city turned out to honour him on the day of his burial, and a number of miracles, ascribed to his intercession, established his *cultus* immediately after his death. He was beatified in 1885.

See F. Ambrosio, *De rebus gestis   Baptistae Mantuani* (1784); G. Fanucci, *Della vita di Battista Spagnoli* (1887); Villiers, *Bibliotheca Carmelitana*, i, pp. 217 240; B. Zimmerman, *Monumenta historica Carmelitana* (1907), pp. 261 and 483-504, where several interesting letters of Bd Baptist are printed. *Cf.* also Pastor, *History of the Popes*, vol. viii, pp. 204 207.

BD HIPPOLYTUS GALANTINI   (A.D. 1619)

HIPPOLYTUS GALANTINI was one of those who have attained to great holiness amid the cares of a secular life. The son of a worthy Florentine silk-weaver, he learnt and followed his father's trade, by which he earned his living. He was only twelve years old when he attracted the notice of Archbishop Alexander de' Medici— afterwards Pope Leo XI—who allowed him to help the priests in instructing children. He would fain have entered a religious order, but was debarred by ill-health, and adopted in his father's house a rule of life which was a counterpart of that of the cloister. By fasts, scourgings and long night-watches he obtained complete mastery over rebellious nature, and acquired a spiritual discernment which more than compensated for his lack of secular education. Without influence, without money and without book-learning Hippolytus succeeded in founding a secular institute devoted to teaching the main principles of religion and Christian duty to ignorant children of both sexes and even to uninstructed adults. For his associates he composed a rule about the year 1602, and his example inspired others all over Italy to imitate his work. The Institute of Christian Doctrine was the name given to the congregation thus founded, but they were popularly known as the " Vanchetoni " Hippolytus had only reached the age of fifty-five when he was seized with a painful and serious illness which proved fatal. His sufferings were alleviated by celestial visions, and he passed away whilst kissing a picture of his crucified Lord. His name is still greatly venerated in Tuscany and among the Franciscans, who reckon him as one of their tertiaries. He was beatified in 1824.

See D. A. Marsella, *De B. Hippolyto Galantinio* (1826); Moroni, *Dizionario di erudizione*, vol. xx, pp. 262 *seq.*, and xxxvi, 75-77; Léon, *Auréole Séraphique* (Eng. trans.), vol. i, pp. 513 516.

21 : ST BENEDICT, ABBOT, PATRIARCH OF WESTERN MONKS   (*c.* A.D. 547)

IN view of the immense influence exerted over Europe by the followers of St Benedict, it is disappointing that we have no contemporary biography of the great legislator, the father of Western monasticism ; for St Benedict, it has been said, " is a dim figure, and the facts of his life are given us in a clothing which obscures rather than reveals his personality " The little we know about his earlier life comes from the *Dialogues* of St Gregory, who does not furnish a connected history, but merely a series of sketches to illustrate the miraculous incidents in his career.

Benedict was of good birth, and was born and brought up at the ancient Sabine town of Nursia (Norcia). Of his twin sister Scholastica, we read that from her infancy she had vowed herself to God, but we do not hear of her again until towards the close of her brother's life. He was sent to Rome for his " liberal education ", being accompanied by a " nurse ", probably to act as housekeeper. He was then in his early teens, or perhaps a little more. Overrun by pagan and Arian tribes, the civilized world seemed during the closing years of the fifth century to be rapidly lapsing into barbarism the Church was rent by schisms, town and country were desolated by war and pillage, shameful sins were rampant amongst Christians as well as heathens, and it was noted that there was not a sovereign or a ruler who was not an atheist, a pagan or a heretic. The youths in schools and colleges imitated the vices of their elders, and Benedict, revolted by the licentiousness of his companions, yet fearing lest he might become contaminated by their example, made up his mind to leave Rome. He made his escape without telling anyone of his plans excepting his nurse, who accompanied him. There has been considerable difference of opinion as to his age when he left the paternal roof, but he may have been nearly twenty. They made their way to the village of Enfide in the mountains thirty miles from Rome. What was the length of his stay we do not know, but it was sufficient to enable him to determine his next step. Absence from the temptations of Rome, he soon realized, was not enough ; God was calling him to be a solitary and to abandon the world, and the youth could no more live a hidden life in a village than in the city —especially after he had miraculously mended an earthenware sieve which his nurse had borrowed and had accidentally broken.

In search of complete solitude Benedict started forth once more, alone, and climbed further among the hills until he reached a place now known as Subiaco (Sublacum, from the artificial lake formed in the days of Claudius by the banking up of the waters of the Anio). In this wild and rocky country he came upon a monk called Romanus, to whom he opened his heart, explaining his intention of leading the life of a hermit. Romanus himself lived in a monastery at no great distance, but he eagerly assisted the young man, clothing him with a sheepskin habit and leading him to a cave in the mountain. It was roofed by a high rock over which there was no descent, and the ascent from below was rendered perilous by precipices as well as by thick woods and undergrowth. In this desolate cavern Benedict spent the next three years of his life, unknown to all except Romanus, who kept his secret and daily brought bread for the young recluse, who drew it up in a basket let down by a rope over the rock. Gregory reports that the first outsider to find his way to the cave was a priest who, when preparing a dinner for himself on Easter Sunday, heard a voice which said to him, " You are preparing yourself a savoury dish whilst my servant Benedict is afflicted with hunger ". The priest immediately set out in quest of the hermit, whom he found with great difficulty. After they had discoursed for some time on God and heavenly things the priest invited him to eat, saying that it was Easter day, on which it was not reasonable to fast. Benedict, who doubtless had lost all sense of time and certainly had no means of calculating lunar cycles, replied that he knew not that it was the day of so great a solemnity. They ate their meal together, and the priest went home. Shortly afterwards the saint was discovered by some shepherds, who took him at first for a wild animal because he was clothed in the skin of beasts and because they did not think any human being could live among the rocks. When they discovered that he was a servant of God they were greatly impressed, and derived much good from his discourses. From that time he began to be known and many people visited him, bringing such sustenance as he would accept and receiving from him instruction and advice.

Although he lived thus sequestered from the world, St Benedict, like the fathers in the desert, had to meet the temptations of the flesh and of the Devil, one of which has been described by St Gregory. "On a certain day when he was alone the tempter presented himself. For a small dark bird, commonly called a blackbird, began to fly round his face, and came so near to him that, if he had wished, he could have seized it with his hand. But on his making the sign of the cross, the bird flew away. Then such a violent temptation of the flesh followed as he had never before experienced. The evil spirit brought before his imagination a certain woman whom he had formerly seen, and inflamed his heart with such vehement desire at the memory of her that he had very great difficulty in repressing it; and being almost overcome he thought of leaving his solitude. Suddenly, however, helped by divine grace, he found the strength he needed, and seeing close by a thick growth of briars and nettles, he stripped off his garment and cast himself into the midst of them. There he rolled until his whole body was lacerated. Thus, through those bodily wounds he cured the wounds of his soul", and was never again troubled in the same way.

Between Tivoli and Subiaco, at Vicovaro, on the summit of a cliff overlooking the Anio, there resided at that time a community of monks who, having lost their abbot by death, resolved to ask St Benedict to take his place. He at first refused, assuring the community, who had come to him in a body, that their ways and his would not agree—perhaps he knew of them by reputation. Their importunity, however, induced him to consent, and he returned with them to take up the government. It soon became evident that his strict notions of monastic discipline did not suit them, for all that they lived in rock-hewn cells; and in order to get rid of him they went so far as to mingle poison in his wine. When as was his wont he made the sign of the cross over the jug, it broke in pieces as if a stone had fallen upon it. "God forgive you, brothers", the abbot said without anger. "Why have you plotted this wicked thing against me? Did I not tell you that my customs would not accord with yours? Go and find an abbot to your taste, for after this deed you can no longer keep me among you ." With these words he returned to Subiaco—no longer, however, to live a life of seclusion, but to begin the great work for which God had been preparing him during those three hidden years.

Disciples began to gather about him, attracted by his sanctity and by his miraculous powers, seculars fleeing from the world as well as solitaries who lived dispersed among the mountains; and St Benedict found himself in a position to initiate that great scheme, evolved perhaps or revealed to him in the silent cave, of "gathering together in this place as in one fold of the Lord many and different families of holy monks, dispersed in various monasteries and regions, in order to make of them one flock after His own heart, to strengthen them more, and bind them together by fraternal bonds in one house of the Lord under one regular observance, and in the permanent worship of the name of God " He therefore settled all who would obey him in twelve wood-built monasteries of twelve monks, each with its prior. He himself exercised the supreme direction over all from where he lived with certain chosen monks whom he wished to train with special care. So far they had no written rule of their own but according to a very ancient document " the monks of the twelve monasteries were taught the religious life, not by following any written rule, but only by following the example of St Benedict's deeds " Romans and barbarians, rich and poor, placed themselves at the disposal of the saint, who made no distinction of rank or nation, and after a time parents came to entrust him with their sons to be educated and trained for the monastic life. St Gregory tells us of two noble Romans, Tertullus the patrician and Equitius, who brought their sons, Placid, a child of seven, and Maurus, a lad of twelve, and devotes several pages to these young recruits (see St Maurus, January 15, and St Placid, October 5).

In contrast with these aristocratic young Romans, St Gregory tells of a rough untutored Goth who came to St Benedict and was received with joy and clothed in the monastic habit. Sent with a hedge-hook to clear the thick undergrowth from ground overlooking the lake, he worked so vigorously that the head flew off the haft and disappeared into the lake. The poor man was overwhelmed with distress, but as soon as St Benedict heard of the accident he led the culprit to the water's edge, and taking the haft from him, threw it into the lake. Immediately from the bottom rose up the iron head, which proceeded to fasten itself automatically to the haft, and the abbot returned the tool saying, " There ! Go on with your work and don't be miserable ". It was not the least of St Benedict's miracles that he broke down the deeply-rooted prejudice against manual work as being degrading and servile : he believed that labour was not only dignified but conducive to holiness, and therefore he made it compulsory for all who joined his community—nobles and plebeians alike.

We do not know how long the saint remained at Subiaco, but he stayed long enough to establish his monasteries on a firm and permanent basis. His departure was sudden and seems to have been unpremeditated. There lived in the neighbourhood an unworthy priest called Florentius, who, seeing the success which attended St Benedict and the great concourse of people who flocked to him, was moved to envy and tried to ruin him. Having failed in all attempts to take away his character by slander, and his life by sending him a poisoned loaf (which St Gregory says was removed miraculously by a raven), he tried to seduce his monks by introducing women of evil life. The abbot, who fully realized that the wicked schemes of Florentius were aimed at him personally, resolved to leave Subiaco, lest the souls of his spiritual children should continue to be assailed and endangered. Having set all things in order, he withdrew from Subiaco to the territory of Monte Cassino. It is a solitary elevation on the boundaries of Campania, commanding on three sides narrow valleys running up towards the mountains, and on the fourth, as far as the Mediterranean, an undulating plain which had once been rich and fertile, but having fallen out of cultivation owing to repeated irruptions of the barbarians, it had become marshy and malarious. The town of Casinum, once an important place, had been destroyed by the Goths, and the remnant of its inhabitants had relapsed into—or perhaps had never lost—their paganism. They were wont to offer sacrifice in a temple dedicated to Apollo, which stood on the crest of Monte Cassino, and the saint made it his first work after a forty days' fast to preach to the people and to bring them to Christ. His teaching and miracles made many converts, with whose help he proceeded to overthrow the temple, its idol and its sacred grove. Upon the site of the temple he built two chapels, and round about these sanctuaries there rose little by little the great pile which was destined to become the most famous abbey the world has ever known, the foundation of which is likely to have been laid by St Benedict in the year 530 or thereabouts. It was from here that went forth the influence that was to play so great a part in the christianization and civilization of post-Roman Europe : it was no mere ecclesiastical museum that was destroyed during the second World War.

It is probable that Benedict, who was now in middle age, again spent some time as a hermit ; but disciples soon flocked to Monte Cassino too. Profiting no doubt by the experience gained at Subiaco, he no longer placed them in separate houses but gathered them together in one establishment, ruled over by a prior and deans under his general supervision. It almost immediately became necessary to add guest-chambers, for Monte Cassino, unlike Subiaco, was easily accessible from Rome and Capua. Not only laymen but dignitaries of the Church came to confer with the holy founder, whose reputation for sanctity, wisdom and miracles became widespread. It is almost certainly at this period that he composed his Rule, of which St Gregory says that in it may be understood " all his manner of life and discipline, for the holy man could not possibly teach otherwise than he lived ". Though it was primarily intended for the monks at Monte Cassino, yet, as Abbot Chapman has pointed out, there is something in favour of the view that it was written at the desire of Pope St Hormisdas for all monks of the West. It is addressed to all those who, renouncing their own will, take upon them " the strong and bright armour of obedience to fight under the Lord Christ, our true king ", and it prescribes a life of liturgical prayer, study (" sacred reading ") and work, lived socially in a community under one common father. Then and for long afterwards a monk was but rarely in holy orders, and there is no evidence that St Benedict himself was ever a priest. He sought to provide " a school for the Lord's service ", intended for beginners, and the asceticism of the rule is notably moderate. Self-chosen and abnormal austerities were not encouraged, and when a hermit, occupying a cave near Monte Cassino, chained his foot to the rock, Benedict sent him a message, saying, " If you are truly a servant of God, chain not yourself with a chain of iron but with the chain of Christ ". The great vision, when Benedict saw as in one sunbeam the whole world in the light of God, sums up the inspiration of his life and rule.

The holy abbot, far from confining his ministrations to those who would follow his rule, extended his solicitude to the population of the surrounding country   he cured their sick, relieved the distressed, distributed alms and food to the poor, and is said to have raised the dead on more than one occasion. While Campania was suffering from a severe famine he gave away all the provisions in the abbey, with the exception of five loaves. " You have not enough to-day ", he said to his monks, marking their dismay, " but to-morrow you will have too much ". The following morning two hundred bushels of flour were laid by an unknown hand at the monastery gate. Other instances have been handed down in illustration of St Benedict's prophetic powers, to which was added ability to read men's thoughts. A nobleman he had converted once found him in tears and inquired the cause of his grief. The abbot replied, " This monastery which I have built and all that I have prepared for my brethren has been delivered up to the heathen by a sentence of the Almighty. Scarcely have I been able to obtain mercy for their lives." The prophecy was verified some forty years later, when the abbey of Monte Cassino was destroyed by the Lombards.

When Totila the Goth was making a triumphal progress through central Italy, he conceived a wish to visit St Benedict, of whom he had heard much. He therefore sent word of his coming to the abbot, who replied that he would see him. To discover whether the saint really possessed the powers attributed to him, Totila ordered Riggo, the captain of his guard, to don his own purple robes, and sent him, with the three counts who usually attended the king, to Monte Cassino. The impersonation did not deceive St Benedict, who greeted Riggo with the words, " My son, take off what you are wearing ; it is not yours " His visitor withdrew in haste to tell his master that he had been detected. Then Totila came himself to the man of God and, we are told, was so much awed that he fell prostrate. But Benedict, raising him from the ground, rebuked him for his evil deeds, and foretold in a few words all that should befall him. Thereupon the king craved his prayers and departed, but from that time he was less cruel. This interview took place in 542, and St Benedict can hardly have lived long enough to see the complete fulfilment of his own prophecy.

The great saint who had foretold so many other things was also forewarned of his own approaching death. He notified it to his disciples and six days before the end bade them dig his grave. As soon as this had been done he was stricken with fever, and on the last day he received the Body and Blood of the Lord. Then, while the loving hands of the brethren were supporting his weak limbs, he uttered a few final words of prayer and died—standing on his feet in the chapel, with his hands uplifted towards heaven. He was buried beside St Scholastica his sister, on the site of the altar of Apollo which he had cast down.

The fact that we know practically nothing of the life of St Benedict beyond what is told us by St Gregory, or what may be inferred from the text of the Rule, has not stood in the way of the multiplication of biographies of the saint. Among those in foreign languages, the lives by Abbots Tosti, Herwegen, Cabrol and Schuster have been translated into English ; perhaps the best life of English origin is that by Abbot Justin McCann (1938). See also T. F. Lindsay's *St Benedict* (1950) *High History of St Benedict and His Monks* (1945), by a monk of Douay ; and Zimmermann and Avery's *Life and Miracles of St Benedict* (1950), being bk ii of St Gregory's " Dialogues " For those who wish to learn something of the spirit of the saint, Abbot Cuthbert Butler's *Benedictine Monachism* (1924) and Abbot Chapman's *St Benedict and the Sixth Century* (1929) may be strongly recommended, especially the first. See also P. Renaudin, *St Benoît dans l'Histoire* (1928). A convenient edition of the Rule, Latin and English, has been published by Abbot Hunter-Blair (1914), a critical revision of the Latin text by Abbot Butler (1933), text and translation by Abbot McCann (1952), and a commentary by Abbot Delatte (Eng. trans., 1921). See too *The Monastic Order in England* (1940), pp. 3–15 and *passim*, by Dom David Knowles, and his *The Benedictines* (1929).

ST SERAPION, BISHOP OF THMUIS   (c. A.D. 370)

SURNAMED " the Scholastic " on account of his learning both in sacred and in secular knowledge, St Serapion for some time presided over the catechetical school of Alexandria ; he afterwards retired into the desert, where he became a monk and formed a friendship with St Antony, who at his death left him one of his tunics. Serapion was drawn from his retreat to be placed in the episcopal seat of Thmuis, a city of Lower Egypt near Diospolis. He took part in the Council of Sardica in 347, was closely associated with St Athanasius in defence of the Catholic faith, and is said by St Jerome to have been banished by the Emperor Constantius. He informed Athanasius about the new Macedonian heresy which was being propagated and the four letters which Athanasius, from the desert where he lay concealed, wrote to Serapion were the first express confutation of that error to be published. St Serapion laboured with great success against the Arians and the Macedonians, and he also compiled an excellent book against the Manicheans. He wrote several learned letters and a treatise on the titles of the Psalms, which are lost, but for us his most important work is the *Euchologion*, discovered and published at the end of last century. Socrates says that St Serapion made a short epigram or summary of Christian perfection which he often repeated : "The mind is puri-fied by spiritual knowledge (or by holy meditation and prayer), the spiritual passions of the soul by charity, and the irregular appetites by abstinence and penance." He is thought to have died in banishment, but the exact date of his death is not known.

See the *Acta Sanctorum*, March, vol. iii ; DCB., vol. iv, p. 613 ; and CMII., pp. 154–155. There has been much confusion in the martyrology entries. There is a short account of Serapion's career in the preface to Bishop John Wordsworth's booklet *Bishop Serapion's Prayerbook* (1910), being a translation of the prayers of his *Euchologion*.

ST ENDA, ABBOT, AND ST FANCHEA, VIRGIN   (c. A.D. 530)

THE little which is recorded of St Fanchea (whose day is January 1) is of a very fabulous character, and is nearly all contained in the Life of St Enda, her brother. Fanchea, who along with other Irish maidens had consecrated herself to God, knew that Enda had taken part in a raid against his enemies, one of whom had been slain in the fight. The shouts of the victors as they returned from their expedition penetrated the convent walls. Fanchea recognized her brother's voice, but at the same time received a supernatural intimation that he was called to serve God in great sanctity of life. She accordingly reproved him for the deed of blood upon which he had been engaged, and when he promised to settle peacefully at home if she would give him one of her maidens in marriage, she pretended to be ready to comply. But it pleased God that the maiden in question should die at that very time, and when she brought her brother to see the bride that had been promised him, he found only a corpse, pale and rigid in death. Enda thereupon gave himself up to a monastic life ; but even so thoughts of warlike exploits still recurred, and his sister impressed it upon him that when these temptations came he ought to put his hand to his shaven head to remind himself that he now wore, not a regal diadem, but the tonsure (*corona*) of his Master, Christ. Finally, still by her advice, Enda left Ireland and went to Rome, whither, after a long interval, Fanchea, with some of her nuns, set out to visit him, only spreading her cloak upon the sea, and being wafted over the waters. In Rome she asked Enda to return to Ireland for the good of his people. He promised to do so after a year, but she herself on reaching home surrendered her soul to God before he could follow her. It has been stated that St Fanchea built a nunnery at Ross Oirthir, or Rossory, in Fermanagh, and that her remains were deposited and long venerated at Killaine, but the evidence does not seem very satisfactory.

All that we are told of St Enda's history previous to his settlement at Aranmore is quite legendary, except perhaps for an important stay at Candida Casa, the monastery founded by St Ninian in Galloway. After his alleged visit to Rome, where he was ordained priest, Enda landed at Drogheda and built churches on both sides of the river Boyne. Afterwards he crossed Ireland and went to see Oengus, King of Munster, who was married to another of his sisters, and lived at Cashel. From his brother-in-law he asked for the isle of Aran that he might found a religious establishment there. Oengus urged him to choose a more fertile place nearer at hand, but when St Enda persisted that Aran was to be the place of his resurrection and that it was good enough for him, Oengus yielded, declaring that he willingly gave it to God and to Enda, whose blessing he craved in return.

To this island St Enda brought his disciples, and the fame of his austerity and sanctity led many others to join them. The saint built, on the eastern side of Aranmore, a great monastery at Killeany, over which he presided, and half the land was apportioned to it, whilst the rest of the island was divided between ten other smaller houses which he founded and over which he set superiors. We are told that not only did he live a most penitential life himself, but that he exacted a very strict discipline from all under his charge. A legend relates that every night he tested his brethren by putting them in turn into a curragh, or wicker-work canoe, and setting it afloat without the hide covering which rendered it watertight. If a man was free from sin, the water could not get in. All the monks—including the abbot himself—escaped a wetting, except Gigniat the cook, who when questioned admitted that he had added a little to his own portion of food from that of Kieran, son of the artificer. St Enda ordered him to leave the island, saying, " There is no room here for a thief; I will not permit this at all ".

With St Finnian of Clonard, St Enda was a father of monachism in Ireland : with him organized monasticism, properly speaking, seems to have begun. One of his best-known disciples was St Kieran of Clonmacnois, just referred to.

The Latin Life of Enda has been printed by Colgan and in the *Acta Sanctorum*, March, vol. iii, but more critically by Plummer in his VSH., vol. ii, pp. 60-75, and *cf.* J. Healy, *Ireland's Ancient Schools and Scholars*, pp. 163-187. See J. Ryan, *Irish Monasticism* (1931), pp. 106-107. Fanchea's name is variously written Faenche, Faenkea, Fainche, Fuinche, etc.

BD SANTUCCIA, Matron   (A.D. 1305)

THE picturesque town of Gubbio in Umbria was the birthplace of Santuccia Terrebotti. She married a good man and they had one daughter, called Julia, who died young. The bereaved parents thereupon decided to retire from the world and to devote the rest of their days to God in the religious life. For some time Santuccia ruled a community of Benedictine nuns in Gubbio, but upon receiving the offer of the buildings which had once been occupied by the Templars on the Julian Way, she transferred herself and her sisters to Rome. There she inaugurated a community of Benedictine nuns who called themselves Servants of Mary, but were popularly known as Santuccie. The *cultus* of Bd Santuccia has never been confirmed.

See Garampi, *Memorie ecclesiastiche ; Spicilegium Benedictinum* (1898), vol. ii ; and the *Acta Sanctorum*, March, vol. iii.

22 : ST PAUL OF NARBONNE   (*c.* A.D. 290)

WE learn from St Gregory of Tours that St Paul of Narbonne was sent from Rome with several other missionaries to plant the faith in Gaul. Two of the band, St Saturninus of Toulouse and St Dionysius of Paris, received the crown of martyrdom, but St Paul of Narbonne, St Trophimus of Arles, St Martial of Limoges and St Gatian of Tours, after passing through many dangers and founding churches in the places now connected with their names, finally died in peace. Prudentius says that the name of Paul shed lustre on the city of

Narbonne.   No attention need be paid to an extravagant legend which has identified St Paul of Narbonne with the Sergius Paulus who was proconsul at Cyprus when the apostle St Paul withstood the magician Elymas.

See the *Acta Sanctorum*, March, vol. iii, and Duchesne, *Fastes Épiscopaux*, vol. i, p. 303.

ST BASIL OF ANCYRA, Martyr   (A.D. 362)

IN the middle of the fourth century when Arians and semi-Arians were propagating their heresies, Basil was a priest of Ancyra, a holy man who had been trained by the saintly Bishop Marcellus in the full doctrine of the Catholic Church.   After Marcellus had been banished by the Emperor Constantius, and a semi-Arian, another Basil, intruded into his see, the priest Basil never ceased exhorting his people to remain staunch to the orthodox faith.   In 360 the extreme Arians obtained the upper hand, and not only deposed the semi-Arian bishop, but ordered the degradation of St Basil, whom they forbade to hold religious assemblies.   He, however, disregarding their orders, supported his own flock, won over many who had been led astray, and boldly defended the faith in the presence of Constantius himself.   When Julian the Apostate came to the throne, open persecution of Christians almost ceased for a time, as the emperor trusted to subtler means of undermining their faith.   In some cases, however, he grew impatient, and permitted—if he did not actually urge—the punishment of well-known Christian leaders.   Basil, who had continued to do his utmost to thwart the imperial policy in Ancyra, was arrested and accused of sedition, of overturning altars, of inciting the people against the gods and of speaking irreverently against the emperor and his religion.   He made a bold confession, and after being suspended by his wrists and ankles and having his flesh torn with rakes, he was cast into prison, and eventually put to death.   This martyred presbyter must not be confused with his opponent, the better-known Bishop Basil of Ancyra.

There is a fantastic account, upon which no reliance can be placed, of the torments endured by St Basil.   See his so-called acts, a short Greek romance which appears to have been written in the tenth century by John, a monk of the monastery of St Elias.   This was critically edited by M. Krascheninnikov in 1907, and it will be found also in the *Acta Sanctorum*, March, vol. iii.   But there can be no reasonable doubt that Basil did suffer martyrdom, for Sozomen speaks of him in his *Eccles. Hist.*, v, 11.

ST DEOGRATIAS, Bishop of Carthage   (A.D. 457)

WHEN Carthage was seized by the Vandals in 439, the Arian barbarians expelled Bishop Quodvultdeus and set him adrift with most of his clergy in a water-logged hulk, which, however, managed eventually to reach Naples.   After fourteen years, during which Carthage remained without a chief pastor, Genseric, at the request of Valentinian, allowed the consecration of another bishop.   He was a priest of the name of Deogratias, who by his example and teaching strengthened the faith of his people and succeeded in winning the respect of pagans and Arians alike.   Two years after the bishop's consecration, Genseric sacked Rome and returned to Africa with a multitude of captives.   These unfortunate people were distributed between the Vandals and the Moors, regardless of natural ties, husbands being separated from wives and parents from their children.   To buy them back, Deogratias sold the gold and silver vessels and ornaments of the altar, and thus redeemed a great number of families.   As there were not enough houses in Carthage available for their accommodation, the bishop gave over two of the largest churches which he filled with bedding, and organized a daily distribution of food. Some of the baser spirits among the Arians, resenting his activity, lay in wait to kill him, but the project failed. Worn out by his efforts, however, Deogratias died after an episcopate of little over three years, and was deeply mourned by his own flock and by the exiles who had found in him their great protector. The Carthaginians would have torn his body to pieces to obtain relics, but his corpse was secretly buried while the public prayers were being chanted, and was thus preserved from dismemberment.

Victor, Bishop of Vita, in his *Historia Persecutionis Vandalicae*, is the principal authority for what we know of St Deogratias. See the *Acta Sanctorum*, March, vol. iii.

BD ISNARDO OF CHIAMPO   (A.D. 1244)

CHIAMPO, where Bd Isnardo was born, is a village near Vicenza. As a youth he seems to have fallen under the spell of St Dominic's eloquence, and joining the Order of Preachers he received the habit from the holy founder himself about the year 1219, along with Bd Guala Romanoni. Isnardo, we are told, in spite of the fact that he led an extremely ascetic life, was very stout, and physical exertion of any kind was a matter of much difficulty to him. Nevertheless nothing could daunt his energy as a preacher, and his persuasiveness and learning were such that he made many conversions. On one occasion a scoffer ridiculing the speaker's corpulence shouted out, " I could no more believe in the holiness of an old porpoise like Brother Isnardo than I could believe that that barrel there would jump up of itself and break my leg ". Whereupon, we are told, the barrel did fall upon his leg and crush it. Isnardo was one of the first Dominicans to preach in Pavia, and when a house of the Order was founded there he was elected prior in 1240. In this house he passed away in 1244, being credited with many miracles both before and after his death. His *cultus* was confirmed in 1919.

See G. M. Pio, *Delle vite degli huomini illustri di S. Domenico* (1607), pp. 205-206 ; the decree confirming the *cultus* in *Acta Apostolicae Sedis*, vol. xi (1919), pp. 184-186 ; and R. Majocchi, *B. Isnardo da Vicenza* (1910). On this last *cf. Analecta Bollandiana*, vol. xxxiii (1914), pp. 100-101.

ST BENVENUTO, BISHOP OF OSIMO   (A.D. 1282)

ST BENVENUTO SCOTIVOLI was born at Ancona and intended for the law, which he studied at Bologna, but feeling that God called him to labour for souls he was ordained to the priesthood. By Pope Alexander IV he was appointed archdeacon of Ancona, besides being made administrator of the diocese of Osimo. The seat of the bishopric had been removed from that town to Recanati, because the people of Osimo had espoused the cause of the Emperor Frederick II against the Holy See, but Benvenuto succeeded in the difficult task of reconciling the city with the papacy. The episcopal chair was then restored to Osimo, of which in 1264 he was nominated bishop by Alexander's successor, Urban, and he was also appointed governor of the Marches of Ancona. Before his consecration Benvenuto was admitted into the Franciscan Order, and during the remaining eighteen years of his life he continued to wear his Minorite habit, which was long preserved at Osimo with his relics. It had ever been his earnest desire to imitate St Francis, and as he felt death approaching, he asked to be carried into the church and laid on the bare ground that he might die like the Seraphic Father. Whilst the psalms were being intoned by the clergy round him, he passed away to his eternal rest.

See the *Acta Sanctorum*, March, vol. iii, and Léon, *Auréole Séraphique* (Eng. trans.), vol. i, pp. 517-519. It is stated that Benvenuto was canonized by Pope Martin IV, and consequently less than four years after his death.

BD HUGOLINO OF CORTONA   (*c.* A.D. 1470)

VERY little seems to be known of the Augustinian hermit Hugolino Zefferini of Cortona.   When Father Papebroch the Bollandist wrote to a high authority of the Augustinian Order to obtain information, a courteous reply was returned to the effect that the archives of their house in Cortona had unfortunately perished in a conflagration, and that a manuscript life of the holy man which they had once possessed had either been lost or stolen.   All they could send was a seventeenth-century engraving which contained representations of a certain number of miracles alleged to have been wrought in connection with the relics of the *beatus*.   One of the most surprising of these had reference to a lily which, growing out of the corpse of the deceased thirty years after his burial, effected the cure of a woman who was blind.   Other traditions stated that when the first lily had been thoughtlessly plucked, two other lilies grew out of the wounds of the hermit's incorrupt body. From the conflicting accounts given it is not even clear whether Bd Hugolino belonged to Cortona or to Mantua, and whether he lived in the fourteenth century or in the fifteenth.   It seems, however, to be certain that his relics were preserved and venerated at Cortona, and the *cultus* paid to him there was approved by Pope Pius VII in 1804.

See the *Acta Sanctorum*, March, vol. iii.   Two short Italian biographies are also cited, one by F. Baldelli (1704), the other by N. Fabbrini (1891).

ST NICHOLAS VON FLÜE   (A.D. 1487)

NICHOLAS VON FLÜE (" Bruder Klaus ") occupies a unique place in the estimation of his countrymen.   Ecclesiastics, patriots, politicians, historians and poets of all creeds have sung his praises, and it may safely be asserted that no religious figure in the history of Switzerland has given rise to so varied and voluminous a body of literature.   The holy man, who was born near Sachseln in Unterwalden in 1417, belonged to a much respected family of small farmers, owners of the Kluster Alp or pasture in the Melchthal and of the estate of Flüeli on the Sachsterberg, from which they derived their surname.   His father Henry also held a civil post in the cantonal service, whilst his mother, Emma Robert, was a native of Wolfenschiessen.   She was a deeply religious woman who brought up her two sons, Nicholas and Peter, to belong as she did to the brotherhood of the Friends of God (*Gottesfreunde*).   The members of this society were scattered over Germany, Switzerland and the Netherlands, and were drawn from both sexes and all classes.   Adhering loyally to the Catholic Church, they sought by strictness of life as well as by constant meditation on the passion of our Lord and similar devotions, to enter, as their name implied, into specially close relationship with God.   Some of them lived in their own families, others formed small communities, and a few retired from the world altogether to lead an eremitic life.   Nicholas was specially responsive to the training he received, and was remarkable from childhood for his piety, his love of peace and his sound judgement.

At the age of twenty-two, and in spite of his peace-loving disposition, Nicholas fought in the ranks in the war with Zürich. Fourteen years later, on the occasion of the occupation of the Thurgau, he again took up arms, but this time he was captain of a company. The high esteem in which he was held caused him to be appointed magistrate and judge and to be sent on various occasions as deputy for Obwalden to councils and meetings, where his clear-sighted wisdom carried great weight. He was repeatedly offered the highest post of all, that of *landamman*, or governor, but he could never be induced to accept it. He had married a religious-minded girl called Dorothea Wissling, and their union had been a happy one. Of their ten children, John, the eldest son, became *landamman* during his father's lifetime, and the youngest studied at the University of Bâle, and was afterwards for many years parish-priest of Sachseln. Throughout the years of his married life, Nicholas had continued the devout practices of his youth. To quote the testimony of his eldest son : " My father always retired to rest at the same time as his children and servants ; but every night I saw him get up again, and heard him praying in his room until morning. Often too he would go in the silence of the night to the old church of St Nicholas or to other holy places." In obedience to what seemed to him a supernatural call to contemplation, for he had many visions and revelations, he used at times to withdraw into solitude in the valley of the Melch, but when he was about fifty he felt irresistibly drawn to abandon the world altogether and to spend the rest of his days far from home as a hermit. His wife did not oppose him, for the Friends of God recognized such vocations as sent from on high. Nicholas resigned his offices, took leave of his wife, his father and his children in the early autumn of 1467 and set forth barefoot and bareheaded, clad in a grey-brown habit and carrying his rosary and his staff.

His destination appears to have been Strasbourg, in the neighbourhood of which was a settlement of the brethren, Alsace having been their headquarters. Before crossing the frontier, however, he received hospitality from a peasant whom he discovered to be also a Friend of God, and in the course of conversation his host sought to deter him from leaving the country, assuring him that the Swiss were unpopular in Alsace and elsewhere abroad on account of their rough manners, and that he might fail to find the peaceful retreat he sought. That night there was a terrific thunderstorm, and as Nicholas looked at the little town of Liechstall beyond the frontier, the flashes of lightning made it appear to be in flames. He took this to be a sign which confirmed the advice he had received, and immediately retraced his steps. One evening during the homeward journey, as he lay under a tree, he was seized with such violent gastric spasms that he thought his last hour had come: the pain passed off, but from that time he lost all desire for ordinary food or drink, and became in fact incapable of taking either. Later that autumn, hunters who had been looking for game in the Melchthal brought home news that they had come across Nicholas on his pasture land of the Klüster, where he had made himself a shelter of boughs under a larch tree. His brother Peter and other friends went to beseech him not to remain there to die of exposure, and he was persuaded to move to Ranft, another part of the valley, where the people of Obwalden soon built him a little cell with a chapel attached.

In this spot, which was situated above a narrow gorge, the loneliness of which was emphasized by the roar of the mountain torrent in the valley below, St Nicholas spent nineteen peaceful years.　The hours from midnight to midday were passed in prayer and contemplation, but in the afternoon he would interview those who found their way to his hermitage to seek his advice on spiritual or even on temporal matters.　God had given him the spirit of counsel, as he once admitted to his friend Henry Imgrund, and he continued to exercise it as he had done in the past. Strangers also were attracted by the fame of this remarkable man, who was reported to live without eating and drinking.　Never very talkative, he was particularly sparing of his words to those who came out of mere curiosity.　So also, when questioned as to his abstention from food, he would only reply, " God knows ". That no one brought him provisions the cantonal magistrates proved by having all approaches to his cell watched for a month, and unprejudiced foreigners, such as Archduke Sigismund's physician and envoys from the Emperor Frederick III, satisfied themselves of the truth of the report and were profoundly impressed by the hermit's sincerity.　Once a year Nicholas took part in the great Musegger procession in Lucerne, but otherwise he only left his retreat to attend divine service and occasionally to visit Einsiedeln.　The gifts of the faithful enabled him in his later years to found a chantry for a priest in connection with his own little chapel, and he was thus able to assist at Mass daily and to communicate often.

At this epoch the Swiss Confederation had just passed through the most glorious phase in its history.　Within six years, in the three battles of Grandson, Morat and Nancy, the sturdy mountain folk had vindicated their independence and had routed the hitherto unconquered Charles the Bold, master of the two Burgundies and nearly the whole of Belgium : their reputation was so great that every prince in Europe sought their alliance.　The hour of their most signal triumph proved nevertheless to be the hour of their greatest danger, for internal dissensions threatened to undo the success which their arms had won.　Quarrels arose over the division of booty and between the country party and the towns. Another source of contention was the proposal to include Fribourg and Soleure (or Solothurn) in the confederation.　At length agreement was reached on most points and was embodied in a document known as the Edict of Stans.　On the subject of the inclusion of Fribourg and Soleure, however, no accommodation could be reached, and feeling ran so high that it seemed that the question would have to be settled by arms.　The meeting was breaking up in disorder when the parish-priest of Stans suggested seeking a final opinion from Nicholas von Flüe.　The deputies gave their consent and he set out to seek the hermit.　His suggestion was no casual or sudden inspiration.　As we know from the protocols of the Council of Lucerne, that city, which occupied an ambiguous position between the two parties, had, at an early stage of the strife, sent delegates to Brother Nicholas to obtain his advice, and it is quite possible that other districts had done the same.　It has been even suggested that the Edict of Stans, a most statesmanlike charter, may have been drafted in the hermit's cell.　In any case, it is greatly to the credit of the deputies that, in the heat of their quarrel, they should have been willing to refer the matter to him.　The chronicler Diebold Schilling, who represented his father at the council, tells us that the priest Imgrund arrived back in Stans streaming with perspiration, and that, seeking out the deputies in their lodgings, he besought them with tears to reassemble immediately to hear the message which he must impart to them alone.　Schilling does not record the words of that message, but he informs us that within an hour the council had arrived at a unanimous agreement.　Fribourg and Soleure were to be admitted into the Swiss Confederation, but upon certain conditions, which were accepted for them by Hans von Stall, the delegate of Soleure. The date was December 22, 1481.

That Christmas was a specially joyful one throughout Switzerland, and the Stans Council expressed in laudatory terms its gratitude to Nicholas for his services. Letters of thanks from Berne and Soleure to the holy man are still extant, as well as a letter written on his behalf by his son John, thanking Berne for a gift which would be expended upon the Church. (He himself could neither read nor write, but used a special seal by way of a signature.) Several of the hermit's visitors have left accounts of their interviews with him, and that written by Albert von Bonstetten, dean of the monastery of Einsiedeln, is particularly interesting. He describes the recluse as tall, brown and wrinkled, with thin grizzled locks and a short beard. His eyes were bright, his teeth white and well preserved, and his nose shapely. He adds, " He praises and recommends obedience and peace. As he exhorted the Confederates to maintain peace, so does he exhort all who come to him to do the same." The dean held him in great veneration, but with regard to the prophetical gifts ascribed to Nicholas in some quarters, he says cautiously that he had received no evidence of them from trustworthy sources. Six years after the Council of Stans, Nicholas was seized with his last illness, which lasted only eight days, but caused him intense suffering. He bore it with perfect resignation and died peacefully in his cell, on his birthday, having attained the age of seventy. Immediately his death became known he was honoured in all Switzerland both as a patriot and as a saint, though it was only in 1669 that his *cultus* was formally sanctioned : he was canonized in 1947. His skeleton lies in a shrine under a black marble canopied altar which stands close to the entrance to the choir of the present church of Sachseln, and the habit in which he died is preserved in a cupboard in the south apse. The two " Flüe houses " at Flüeli date back to the days of St Nicholas, and although they have been greatly modernized one room in his dwelling-house remains intact.

In 1917 the fifth centenary of the birth of " Bruder Klaus " was celebrated throughout Switzerland with quite remarkable enthusiasm. Perhaps the most valuable result of the interest thus awakened was the publication of a great historical monograph by Robert Durrer, a scholar with an unrivalled knowledge of the archives of his country. In these two quarto volumes, entitled *Bruder Klaus*, which together total some 1350 pages, will be found all the available material bearing on the life of Nicholas von Flüe. The collection includes two early sketches of the career of Bruder Klaus, one by Albrecht von Bonstetten, the other by Heinrich von Gundelfingen, but these are supplemented by a mass of documentary evidence derived from ancient records and other sources. A comprehensive nineteenth-century biography is that of J. Ming, *Der selige Bruder Nikolaus von Flüe*, and others have since been written by A. Baumberger, F. X. Wetzel and J. T. de Belloc, in Italian by F. Andina (1945), and in French by A. Andrey (1941) and C. Journet (1947). See also the *Acta Sanctorum*, March, vol. iii, and the *Kirchenlexikon*, vol. ix, pp. 316-319.

23 : SS. VICTORIAN AND HIS COMPANIONS, MARTYRS (A.D. 484)

HUNERIC, the Arian king of the Vandals, succeeded his father Genseric in 477. He at first showed a certain moderation in regard to his orthodox Catholic subjects in Mauretania, but in 480 a policy of relentless persecution was again resorted to. Amongst the more conspicuous victims were a group of martyrs who are honoured on this day. Victorian, in particular, a native of

Hadrumetum, who was one of the wealthiest citizens of Carthage, had been appointed proconsul by Huneric himself. When the persecuting edicts were published, the Vandal king did all in his power to induce this representative Catholic to conform to Arianism. When promises and threats alike failed to shake his adherence to the true faith, the courageous witness to Christ was subjected to horrible torments, but persevered gloriously until death released him. With Victorian the Roman Martyrology associates four others who suffered about the same time. Two of these, who were brothers, were subjected to the same torture which, more than a thousand years later, was employed by the priest-hunter, Topcliffe, to test the constancy of the Elizabethan martyrs. The two Brothers were hung up by the wrists and heavy weights were attached to their feet. We are told that when one of them gave signs that his resolution was weakening, the other exhorted him so powerfully to endure further that the faint-hearted brother cried out to the executioners not to diminish but to augment his pains. Both were afterwards seared with red-hot plates of iron, but bore all patiently to the end.

Our authority for these facts is the *Historia Persecutionis Vandalicae* by St Victor, Bishop of Vita, a contemporary.

ST BENEDICT THE HERMIT   (*c.* A.D. 550)

St GREGORY the Great, in his *Dialogues*, has preserved the memory of a hermit or solitary monk, named Benedict, who resided in some part of the Campagna and was barbarously shut up in an oven by the Goths when, under the leadership of Totila, they were devastating Italy. By a miracle, he was preserved from death, and was liberated unhurt the next day. He lived at the time of St Benedict of Nursia, who was personally acquainted with him. The holy man appears to have died a natural death in 543 or 550, and he may perhaps be identified with a St Benedict whose relics are venerated at Lavello, in the diocese of Venosa, who is also commemorated upon this day.

The *Dialogues* of St Gregory the Great (bk iii, ch. 18) are here our only authority, but the Roman Martyrology registers the name of St Benedict the Hermit on this day.

ST ETHELWALD THE HERMIT   (A.D. 699)

AFTER the death of St Cuthbert, the hermitage he had inhabited on Farne Island was occupied by St Ethelwald, or Oidilwald, a monk from Ripon. He found Cuthbert's cell in a very dilapidated condition, and asked for a calf's skin to nail over the ill-adjusted planks of the wall against which he was wont to pray, because the wind, howling in his ear through the gaps, hindered his devotions. Farne is not very far distant from Lindisfarne or Holy Island, from which its cliffs are plainly visible on a clear day, but ocean swells and currents as well as fierce gales formerly rendered the group of islands inaccessible for weeks together. Bede relates a miracle wrought by St Ethelwald over the elements, which was told him by one of those for whom it was performed. Three monks from Lindisfarne had paid a visit to the hermit on a fine day, and had been greatly edified by his discourses. After they had started on their homeward journey, a terrific storm suddenly arose and they were in danger of their lives. Looking back, they saw St Ethelwald appear at the entrance of his cell and then fall on his knees in prayer. The wind immediately dropped, and a breeze wafted them safely home. No sooner, however, had they disembarked and secured their boat, than the storm began again with redoubled fury and raged for the rest of the day. After living for twelve years on Farne, St Ethelwald died and was buried at Lindisfarne. Owing to Danish incursions, his relics were exhumed more than once, but they were eventually translated to Durham.

Bede and the books cited above in the notice of St Cuthbert tell us all that is to be known of St Ethelwald, but particular reference should be made to the account of him included in the volume of *Hermit Saints* (1844) in the series " Lives of the English Saints ", edited by J. H. Newman. A verse translation is there given of an incident concerning St Ethelwald.

BD PETER OF GUBBIO   (*c.* A.D. 1250 ?)

No particulars have been preserved about the life of Bd Peter, a member of the Ghisengi family of Gubbio, who joined the Brictinian Hermits of St Augustine and is said to have become provincial. Attention was directed to him because of the wonders which were reported to have taken place at his tomb. During the night office a voice was heard chanting the alternate verses of the *Te Deum*, and when the community traced the sound and discovered that it proceeded from the vault where he was buried, they found his body in a kneeling posture with open mouth and joined hands. It was translated to a more honourable resting-place, where it remained incorrupt. Hence pilgrims, even from distant places, flocked to Gubbio to venerate his relics. The last translation of his body took place in 1666. Pope Pius IX confirmed his *cultus*.

See the *Acta Sacntorum*, March, vol. iii.

BD SIBYLLINA OF PAVIA, Virgin   (A.D. 1367)

Sibyllina Biscossi, left an orphan in early childhood, constrained to earn her bread as a servant-maid before she was ten years old, unable to read or write, and afflicted with total blindness at the age of twelve, can have known little of comfort or joy in the sense which the world attaches to these terms. When her blindness rendered her incapable of doing any useful work, some kind Dominican tertiaries of Pavia, in which city she was born and died, took her to live with them. Intensely devout and full of faith, the child was at first convinced that if she prayed hard enough St Dominic would restore her sight. The days slipped by and nothing happened, but at last, when all hope of cure seemed to have left her, she had a dream, or perhaps a vision. She thought that St Dominic took her by the hand and led her through a long, long passage in pitchy darkness where the felt presence of evil beings would have caused her to faint with terror had it not been for the hand-clasp of her guide. But a glimmer of light showed itself beyond, which became more intense as they struggled forwards, and in the end they emerged into glorious sunshine in a home of ineffable peace.

When she awoke Sibyllina was at no loss for an interpretation. God meant her to remain blind ; and so she determined to second the divine purposes which had already made her so pointedly an exile in this world. She made arrangements to become a recluse and was enclosed in an anchorage beside the Dominican church. At first she had a companion living with her, who died after three years and no one took her place. Sibyllina as a solitary led a life of incredible austerity, but she lived until the age of eighty. People of all classes came to consult her in their troubles and conversed with her through the window of her cell, while many miracles were ascribed to her intercession. It is recorded of her that she was specially devout to the Holy Ghost and that she regarded Whitsunday as the greatest feast of the year. When she died in 1367 she had been a recluse for sixty-five years. Her body was still incorrupt in 1853 when her cult was confirmed.

See G. M. Pio, *Delle vite degli huomini illustri di S. Domenico* (1607), cc. 467–469 ; Procter, *Lives of the Dominican Saints*, pp. 72–74 ; M. C. de Ganay, *Les Bienheureuses Dominicaines*, pp. 179–191.

ST JOSEPH ORIOL (A.D. 1702)

St Joseph Oriol was born in Barcelona and spent almost all his life in that city. His father having died while he was still in the cradle, his mother contracted a second marriage with a shoemaker, who loved his little stepson as though he had been his own child. Joseph early became a choirboy at the church of St Mary-of-the-Sea, and the clergy, noticing that he spent hours in prayer before the Blessed Sacrament, taught him to read and write, foreseeing in him a vocation to the priesthood. They subsequently enabled him to follow the university courses. At the death of her second husband, Joseph's mother was left very poor, and the son went to live with his foster-mother, who was tenderly attached to him. The young man's life as a student was most exemplary. After he had taken his doctor's degree and had been raised to the priesthood, Joseph accepted some tutorial work in a family of good position to enable him to support his mother. Here also he gained all hearts and was looked upon as a saint, but he remained under no illusions about himself, for God made known to him how far he was from perfection. In consequence of that revelation, he took a vow of perpetual abstinence, and lived for the rest of his days on bread and water. He also increased his bodily penances and wore such miserable clothes that he was often insulted in the streets of Barcelona.

Relieved of the support of his mother by her death in 1686, Joseph started for Rome to venerate the tombs of the apostles, and made the whole journey on foot. Here he was presented by Pope Innocent XI to a benefice in his native Barcelona, and as a priest with the cure of souls he continued to live in the most complete self-abnegation. The one little room which he hired at the top of a house contained only a crucifix, a table, a bench and a few books—it was all he needed. The income of his cure went for the relief of the poor, being expended in alms to the living and in Masses for the dead. No bed was necessary for one who never slept for more than two or three hours at night. St Joseph had a great gift for direction, and whatever time he could spare was spent in the confessional. At one time, indeed, he was accused of over-severity and of inflicting penances which were injurious to health. His critics succeeded in gaining the ear of the bishop, who forbade him to hear confessions, but the prohibition did not last long. The prelate in question died soon afterwards and his successor reinstated Joseph in all his faculties. Throughout his ministry his zeal was all-embracing, including the most opposite extremes. He was fond of teaching little children, but he also had a great influence over soldiers, whom he won by his gentleness and sympathy. Strangely enough, in the midst of this busy life, St Joseph was suddenly seized with an ardent desire for martyrdom, and decided to go at once to Rome to place himself at the disposal of the Congregation *de Propaganda Fide*. In vain did the people of Barcelona entreat him not to leave them ; in vain did two wise priests urge him to take time for reflection.   His decision was made ; his purpose unalterable   and he started off for Italy.   At Marseilles, however, he fell ill, and the Blessed Virgin in a vision told him that his intention was accepted but that it was God's will that he should go back to Barcelona and spend the rest of his life in caring for the sick.

His return was attended with extraordinary demonstrations of joy.   The fame of his wonderful healing powers spread far and wide, and sufferers came from long distances to be cured of their infirmities.   Miracle after miracle was reported, and at one time the saint's confessor forbade him to perform such cures in church because of the disturbance which they caused.   As a matter of fact St Joseph always sought to direct attention away from himself and to associate bodily cures with the tribunal of penance, but powers such as his could not be hidden.   Like many other wonder-workers, he also possessed the gift of prophecy, and amongst other predictions he foretold the time of his own death.   After receiving the last sacraments he asked for the *Stabat Mater* to be said aloud, and died on March 23, 1702.   He was in his fifty-third year.   Immense crowds collected round the bier of the dead saint, and on the day of the funeral it became necessary to close the cathedral before his burial could be proceeded with.   His few little possessions were eagerly sought for as relics, and the tribute of popular veneration only augmented with the lapse of years.   St Joseph Oriol was canonized in 1909.

The bull of canonization (*Acta Apostolicae Sedis*, vol. i (1909), pp. 605-622), of almost unprecedented length, gives a full summary of his career.   The principal published life is that of J. Ballester de Claramunt, *Vida de San José Oriol, presbitero* (1909)   but there are others both in Spanish and Catalan by M. E. Anzizu and by Masden, and one in Italian by Salotti.

24 : ST GABRIEL THE ARCHANGEL

BY a decree of the Congregation of Sacred Rites dated October 26, 1921, issued by command of Pope Benedict XV, it was directed that the feast of St Gabriel the Archangel should be kept in future as a greater double on March 24 throughout the Western church.   As the question of the liturgical celebration of festivals in honour of the great archangels will be more naturally treated in connection with the older feast of St Michael on September 29, it will be sufficient here to point out that according to Daniel (ix 21) it was Gabriel who announced to the prophet the time of the coming of the Messiah, that it was he again who appeared to Zachary " standing on the right side of the altar of incense " (Luke i 10 and 19) to make known the future birth of the Precursor, and finally that it was he who as God's ambassador was sent to Mary at Nazareth (Luke i 26) to proclaim the mystery of the Incarnation.   It was therefore very appropriate that Gabriel should be honoured on this day which immediately precedes the feast of the Annunciation of the Blessed Virgin.   There is abundant archaeological evidence that the *cultus* of St Gabriel is in no sense a novelty.   An ancient chapel close beside the Appian Way, rescued from oblivion by Armellini, preserves the remains of a fresco in which the prominence given to the figure of the archangel, his name being written underneath, strongly suggests that he was at one time honoured in that chapel as principal patron.   There are also many representations of Gabriel in the early Christian art both of East and West which make it plain that his connection with the sublime mystery of the Incarnation was remembered by the faithful in ages long anterior to the devotional revival of the thirteenth century. This messenger is the appropriate patron-saint of postal, telegraph and telephone workers.

See the *Acta Apostolicae Sedis*, vol. xiii (1921), and the note to Michael the Archangel on September 29.

ST IRENAEUS, Bishop of Sirmium, Martyr   (A.D. 304)

An account of the sufferings and death of St Irenaeus, Bishop of Sirmium, is contained in the acts of his martyrdom which, while untrustworthy as to details, seem undoubtedly to be based on some authentic historical records. Sirmium, then the capital of Pannonia, stood on the site of the present Mitrovica, forty miles or more to the west of Belgrade, and St Irenaeus, quite apart from his position as leader of the Christians, must have been a man of considerable local importance. It was during the persecution of Diocletian that he was apprehended as a Christian and brought before Probus, governor of Pannonia. When commanded to offer sacrifice to the gods he refused, saying, " He that sacrifices to the gods will be cast into hell-fire ! " " The edicts of the most clement emperors require that all should sacrifice to the gods or suffer under the law ", replied the magistrate. " The law of my God bids me rather to suffer all torments than to sacrifice to the gods ", is said to have been the saint's retort. He was put to the rack, and whilst being tortured was again urged to sacrifice, but his resolution remained unshaken. All the bishop's relations and friends were greatly distressed. His mother, his wife and his children surrounded him. His wife, in tears, threw her arms round his neck and begged him to preserve his life for her sake and for that of his innocent children. His sons and daughters cried, " Father, dear father, have pity upon us and upon thyself ", whilst his mother sobbed aloud, and servants, neighbours and friends filled the court-house with their lamentations.

The martyr steeled himself against their appeals for fear that he might seem to offer to God a divided allegiance. He repeated those words spoken by our Lord, " If anyone renounce me before men, him will I renounce before my father who is in Heaven," and he avoided making any direct answer to their entreaties. He was again committed to prison, where he was detained a long time, suffering still more hardships and bodily torments, by which it was hoped to shake his constancy. A second public examination produced no more effect than the first, and in the end sentence was passed that for disobedience to the imperial edict he should be drowned in the river. Irenaeus is said to have protested that such a death was unworthy of the cause for which he suffered. He begged to be given an opportunity to prove that a Christian, strong in his belief in the one true God, could face without flinching the persecutor's most cruel torments. It was conceded to him that he should first be beheaded and that then his body should be cast from the bridge into the river.

The narrative of the martyr's death, drawn up originally in Greek, has been included by Ruinart in his collection of *Acta sincera*. But, as Delehaye has pointed out, the documents which Ruinart has brought together under this head vary greatly in value, and it cannot be maintained that the Passion of St Irenaeus represents the highest type of such acts : see Delehaye, *Les Légendes hagiographiques* (1927), pp. 114–116. The text may also be read in the *Acta Sanctorum*, March, vol. iii, the Greek original being printed in the appendix.

ST ALDEMAR, Abbot   (*c.* A.D. 1080)

CAPUA was the birthplace of the holy priest and monk Aldemar, surnamed the Wise. His parents sent their son to be educated and trained at the abbey of Monte Cassino, where he was raised to the diaconate. Princess Aloara of Capua asked that he might become the director of the convent which she had built in Capua. Here it soon became evident that God had bestowed upon him the gift of miracles, and these gave rise to so much talk that the abbot recalled him to Monte Cassino. The princess, however, would not consent to his removal and, the quarrel between them growing bitter, Aldemar, to bring it to an end, made his escape to Boiano, where he joined three brothers who lived like canons attached to the church. However, he did not find the peace he sought, for one of the brethren took an intense dislike to him which developed into hatred. He actually tried to kill Aldemar with a cross-bow, but either through his own clumsiness or by a miraculous interposition of Providence, the missile pierced his own arm, and he was only cured through the prayers of his intended victim. St Aldemar then withdrew from the little company and built the monastery of Bocchignano in the Abruzzi, the first of several religious houses, all of which remained under his direction. He had a very great love of animals, and when a swarm of bees made a hive of one of the cupboards in his monastery, he would not allow them to be disturbed. It was whilst he was making a visitation of the houses he had founded that he was stricken with a fever which proved fatal.

A short Latin life by Peter, a deacon of Monte Cassino, has been edited by Mabillon, and by the Bollandists in the *Acta Sanctorum ;* see also Michael Monachus, *Sanctuarium Capuanum.*

ST CATHERINE OF VADSTENA, Virgin   (A.D. 1381)

ST CATHERINE (Karin) ULFSDOTTER was the fourth of the eight children of St Bridget, who with Catherine is commonly called " of Sweden ", though they were not of the royal house. In that religious family she first learned to love God, and at an early age she was entrusted to the care of the abbess of Risaberga. Catherine was betrothed by her parents to a devout young nobleman, Eggard von Kürnen (Kyren), who was of German descent, and the wedding was solemnized in due course ; but St Catherine is celebrated with the office of a virgin, for it is said that the young couple agreed from the outset to live together in perpetual continency. In her new position the young wife led a life of austerity which Eggard countenanced if he did not actually encourage, but her brother Charles was greatly incensed when she tried to induce his own wife to follow her example. After the death of her husband Ulf, St Bridget went to live in Rome, and Catherine afterwards told her namesake of Siena that on the day her mother left Sweden she, her daughter, forgot how to smile. In 1350 she got Eggard's leave to visit her mother in Rome, where-upon brother Charles wrote a violent letter to Eggard forbidding him to allow her to go. The letter came into Catherine's hands, but she was not deterred and set out under protection provided by one of her uncles. She was then about nineteen years old.

St Bridget had long desired a companion, and when her daughter, after a few weeks' stay, proposed to return home, she besought her earnestly not to go but to work with her in Rome for the cause of Christ. What followed is not altogether clear or easy to understand, seeing that Catherine was under obligation to her husband, to whom she appears to have been deeply attached. But remain in Rome she did, though not without moments of great unhappiness " I lead a wretched life, caged up here like an animal, while the others go and nourish their souls at church. My brothers and sisters in Sweden can serve God in peace " ; for owing to the disorders of the city her mother, when she went out, made Catherine stop at home indoors. In the circumstances it may be reasonably supposed that her dream of our Lady reproaching her for her discontent was a product of nervous depression, though poor Catherine took it very seriously. Bridget, however, believed it to be revealed to her that her daughter's husband was about to die, as indeed he did before the year was out ; and Catherine then seems to have lost all desire to go back to Sweden.

When it became known that this beautiful girl was a widow, she began to be importuned for her hand, and some of her suitors, in spite of her emphatic refusals, went so far as to lay plans for kidnapping her. One day, as she was on her way to worship at the church of St Sebastian, a Roman count, Latino Orsini, was actually lying concealed with his servants in a vineyard beside the road. Suddenly a stag made its appearance, and so diverted their attention that St Catherine passed by unobserved. * On another similar occasion, the same would-be abductors were temporarily blinded—so at least the leader of the party afterwards testified in the presence of the pope. But the outward beauty of the saint was only a mirror of the inward graces of her soul. Her charity was so great, extending beyond deeds to words, that she was never heard to say an angry or impatient word or to utter an unkindly criticism. Years later she prayed that the Bridgettine Order might always be kept from the poisonous venom of detraction, and she warned her niece Ingegerda, afterwards abbess of Vadstena, against uncharitable judgements, saying that both the backbiter and the listener carried the devil in their tongues. She shunned all display and wore her clothes until they were threadbare ; yet she is stated to have cast a kind of radiance over her material surroundings, so that the very cover of her bed and the curtain behind her head seemed to be of gorgeous texture and hue.

For the next twenty-five years, Catherine's life was almost identified with that of her mother, in whose good works she took an active part. Besides the vocal prayers to which she had always been addicted, the daughter now spent four hours of every day in meditation on the Passion. She was praying in St Peter's one day when she was accosted by a woman in a white dress and a black mantle, whom she took to be a Dominican tertiary. The stranger asked her to pray for one of her fellow-countrywomen, from whom she would presently receive valuable assistance and who would set a crown of gold upon her head. Shortly afterwards came tidings of the death of a sister-in-law, who bequeathed to her the golden headdress which—like other women of her rank and country— she wore on great occasions. The tiara was broken up and on the proceeds of the sale St Bridget and her daughter lived for two years. From time to time they made pilgrimages to Assisi and elsewhere, and at last St Bridget resolved to pay a final visit to the Holy Land. She was accompanied by Catherine. Bridget herself did not long survive her return to Rome, and her body was that same year conveyed back to Sweden to be buried in her convent church at Vadstena.

The monastery had not yet been canonically erected, its religious living without vows and without habit. To St Catherine now fell the task of forming the

* *Cf.* a somewhat similar story told of the English St Osyth (October 7).

community according to the rule which her mother had laboured so long to get approved ; but a year later she returned to Rome to forward the cause of Bridget's canonization.   Not till the end of five years did she come back to Sweden, with the canonization still not accomplished—the " Great Schism " had broken out meanwhile—but with a ratification of the Bridgettine rule from Pope Urban VI.   During this time in Italy, St Catherine Ulfsdotter formed a friendship with St Catherine Benincasa of Siena, and Urban wished to send them together on a mission to Queen Joanna of Naples, who was supporting the claimant pope who called himself Clement VII.   Catherine is said to have refused to go to the court of the woman who had seduced her brother Charles, as is mentioned in the notice herein of St Bridget on October 8.   But Bd Raymund of Capua in his life of Catherine of Siena explains it otherwise   he himself, he says, dissuaded the pope from sending the two Catherines into so dangerous a *milieu*.

It seemed as though Catherine's work was now done, for immediately after her final retirement to Vadstena her health began to fail.   She continued the practice she had long observed of making a daily confession, but the gastric trouble from which she suffered made it impossible for her to receive the Blessed Sacrament. She used therefore to ask that the Body of the Lord might be brought to her sickroom that she might adore It and offer up her devotions in Its presence.   Commending her soul to God in a final prayer, she passed away peacefully on March 24, 1381.   It was remarked that a bright star appeared over the house at the moment of her death and remained until the funeral.   Her obsequies were attended by all the bishops and abbots of Scandinavia, as well as by the son of the king and by the whole neighbouring population.   St Catherine has never been formally canonized, but her name was added to the Roman Martyrology and her feast is observed in Sweden and elsewhere as well as by the Bridgettines.   She is said to have written a book entitled *The Consolation of the Soul*, consisting of extracts and maxims from Holy Scripture and various devotional works, but no copy has been preserved to us.

There is a short Latin biography of St Catherine which was written in the first quarter of the fifteenth century by one of the monks of Vadstena, Ulf Birgersson.   It may be found in the *Acta Sanctorum*, March, vol. iii, and it was one of the first books printed in Sweden. A more critical text appears in the *Scriptores rerum Sueciarum*, vol. iii.   Some of the documents and collections of miracles connected with her projected canonization have also been printed in both the works just named.   The full text of the canonization documents has been edited by I. Collijn, *Processus seu Negocium Canonizacionis b. Katerinae de Vadstenis* (1942-1946).   St Catherine's life was so intimately bound up with that of her mother, that perhaps the best account of the daughter will be found in the biographies of St Bridget, for whom see under October 8.

SS. SIMON OF TRENT   WILLIAM OF NORWICH
(A.D. 1475 and 1144)

IN accord with the Roman Martyrology, which on this day commemorates " the passion of St Simeon, a boy, most cruelly slain by Jews at Trent and afterwards glorified by many miracles ", Alban Butler devotes some little space to two alleged cases of ritual child-murder for which the Jews were held responsible.   Of the many reputed examples of this crime, the truth of which was universally credited in the middle ages, only that of St Simon, or Simeon, finds recognition in the martyrology. According to the statement drawn up at Trent shortly after the tragedy, a Jewish physician decoyed and kidnapped a little Christian child, two and a half years old, in view of the celebration of the Jewish pasch. After crucifying the boy and draining his blood, the officials of the synagogue hid the body for a short time and eventually threw it into the canal. The crime was discovered ; and those suspected, under torture, admitted their guilt. Horrible punishments were inflicted after conviction, while on the other hand a profusion of miracles followed beside the tomb of the infant. In the case of William of Norwich, which occurred more than three centuries earlier, the victim was twelve years old. Here again it is alleged that the boy was enticed away, gagged, bound and crucified. The body was carried in a sack by two Jews to Mousehold Wood for the purpose of burying it there, but being surprised apparently before their task was completed they left it hanging on a tree.

It is to the credit of Butler's sober judgement that even while he accepts without question the traditional belief that the various child victims were really put to death by Jews in hatred of the Christian faith, he adds that " it is a notorious slander of some authors, who, from these singular and extraordinary instances, infer this to have been at any time the custom or maxim of that people ". Butler's protest is certainly well-founded. No scrap of serious evidence has ever been adduced which would show that the use of Christian blood formed any part of Jewish ritual. There is little room for doubt that in each of these cases a child had been deliberately killed by somebody ; and it is possible that such child-murders may occasionally have been committed by Jewish maniacs, or as an act of private vengeance, or by necromancers who wished to use the blood for some magical rite. This is not the place for a discussion of the problem which, in some instances—notably in that of " el santo Niño de la Guardia ", the official records of which have been published in the Spanish *Boletin de la real Academia de la Historia,* vol. xi—presents many perplexing features, but even medieval and eastern Jews must, as a people, unquestionably be acquitted of any participation in, or sympathy with, such crimes. Moreover, if we confine our attention to the two martyrs here in question, there is no conclusive evidence—that of confessions under torture being worthless—that the guilt was brought home to those who were really the culprits.

For Simon of Trent the more important documents will be found in the *Acta Sanctorum,* March, vol. iii ; in Muratori, *Rerum Italicarum Scriptores,* vol. xx, pp. 945 *seq. ;* and in G. Divina, *Storia del beato Simone da Trento* (1902), but *cf.* the critical discussion of the last-named work in *Analecta Bollandiana,* vol. xxiii (1904), pp. 122–124. For William of Norwich the only real authority is Thomas of Monmouth, whose manuscript was edited for the first time by Dr A. Jessopp and M. R. James in 1896. On the general question of these alleged Jewish ritual murders, the English reader may be referred to H. L. Strack, *The Jew and Human Sacrifice* (Eng. trans.), and to Father Thurston in *The Month,* June 1898, pp. 561–574, and November 1913, pp. 502–513. A number of cases of such alleged martyrdoms are discussed also by W. H. Hart, *Cartularium of Gloucester* (Rolls Series), vol. i, pp. xxxix to li. Concerning the similar case of St Wernher, at Trier in 1275, the Bollandists have printed the greater part of the documents which were prepared for the canonical process. See the *Acta Sanctorum,* April, vol. ii, where the very unsatisfactory nature of the evidence must strike every reader. The vindication of the Jews by Cardinal Ganganelli (afterwards Pope Clement XIV) in 1759, has been translated by C. Roth, *The Ritual Murder Libel and the Jews* (1935), and *cf.* Dr Roth's *History of the Jews in England* (1941).

BD DIDACUS, OR DIEGO, OF CADIZ   (A.D. 1801)

BD DIDACUS JOSEPH OF CADIZ was popularly called " the apostle of the Holy Trinity ", because of his devotion to the mystery of the Three Divine Persons and the ingenuity with which he contrived to make the theological dogma of the Blessed

Trinity the subject of his eloquent and most fruitful sermons.   He was born on March 29, 1743 in Cadiz, and was baptized Joseph Francis.   His parents brought him up devoutly, and he preserved throughout his life his baptismal innocence.   As a child he liked to construct and decorate little altars, and the same instinct led him when he was older to wait at the church doors in the early morning that he might offer his services to any priest who wanted a server.   Constant attendance at the Capuchin church where he made his communions, and the reading of the lives of Capuchin saints, led Diego to desire to enter the Order of St Francis, but he was refused at first as he seemed to be insufficiently educated.   However, he overcame this obstacle, and on being at last accepted began his novitiate at Seville as Brother Diego or Didacus.   In due course he was raised to the priesthood and sent to preach.   From the first it became evident that he was endowed with gifts of no mean order, for his sermons wherever he went brought conviction of sin and amendment of life.   Throughout Spain, but more particularly in Andalusia, the holy man journeyed, teaching and preaching in remote villages and crowded towns, shrinking from no fatigue or hardship so long as there was work to do for souls.   He was content simply to preach the gospel, indulging in no rhetorical artifices or flowery language.   A wonderful intuition or sympathy seems to have brought him into touch with his hearers, so that he won the hearts alike of the poor and of the well-to-do, of young students in schools and of professors in universities.   His work in the tribunal of penance was complementary to his preaching, for it enabled him to direct and strengthen those whom his sermons had touched.   Any free time during the day was spent in visiting prisons and hospitals or in similar works of charity, whilst a great part of the night was given to prayer.

It is related that in preaching about the love of God, there were occasions when Father Diego was raised supernaturally into the air so that he required assistance to regain the floor of the pulpit.   Sometimes the largest churches could not contain the crowds who flocked to hear him, and he would preach in a square or in the streets, whilst the crowds stood for hours entranced.   At the close of his sermons he had to be protected from the people, who tried to tear pieces from his habit as relics.   Popularity, however, could not injure one so humble as Bd Diego   slights and insults might serve, he thought, as a very inadequate expiation for his sins. He shunned all presents, and, if obliged to accept them, he immediately distributed them to the poor : money he absolutely refused.   Immediately his death became known in 1801 he was acclaimed as a saint, and Pope Leo XIII proclaimed his beatification in 1894.

See C. Kempf, *The Holiness of the Church in the Nineteenth Century* ; *Analecta Ecclesiastica*, 1894, pp. 151 seq. ; Damase de Soisey, *Le bx Diego Joseph de Cadiz* (1902).

25 : THE ANNUNCIATION OF THE BLESSED VIRGIN MARY
COMMONLY CALLED LADY DAY

THIS great festival takes its name from the tidings announced by the angel Gabriel to the Blessed Virgin Mary concerning the incarnation of the Son of God.   It was the divine purpose to give to the world a saviour, to the sinner a victim of propitiation, to the righteous a model, to this maiden—who should remain a virgin—a son, and to the Son of God a new nature, a human nature, capable of suffering pain and death, in order that He might satisfy God's justice for our transgressions. The Holy Ghost, who was to her in place of a husband, was not content with rendering her body capable of giving life to the God-man, but enriched her soul with fullness of grace, that there might be a sort of proportion between the cause and the effect, and that she might be the better qualified to co-operate in this mystery of holiness : therefore the angel begins his address with " Hail ! full of grace ". If Mary had not been deeply rooted in humility, this manner of salutation and the purport of that great design for which her co-operation was asked might easily have elated her, but in her lowliness she knew that the glory of any graces she possessed belonged to God. Her modesty had suggested a doubt, but once that was set at rest, without further inquiry she gives her assent in that all-potent submission : " Behold the handmaid of the Lord, be it done to me according to thy word." The world was not to have a saviour until she had given her consent to the angel's proposal : she gives it, and behold the power and efficacy of her *Fiat !* In that moment the mystery of love and mercy promised to mankind thousands of years earlier, foretold by so many prophets, desired by so many saints, is accomplished upon earth. In that instant the Word of God becomes for ever united to manhood : the soul of Jesus Christ, produced from nothing, begins to enjoy God and to know all things, past, present and to come : at that moment God begins to have a worshipper who is infinite, and the world a mediator who is omnipotent : and to the working of this great mystery Mary alone is chosen to co-operate by her free assent.

There is some reason to think that of all the great mysteries of our Lady's life the Annunciation may have been the first to be honoured liturgically, and that the date of that event having once been identified, however this came about, with March 25, it became the starting-point for the whole of what may be called the Christmas cycle. If our Lord became incarnate on March 25, it would be natural to suppose Him born on December 25. His circumcision would then follow on January 1, and His presentation in the Temple and the purification of His mother on February 2, the fortieth day after that on which the shepherds were summoned to the manger at Bethlehem. Moreover as the day of the Annunciation was " the sixth month with her that is called barren ", the birth of St John Baptist would follow just a week before the end of June. What we know for certain is that already in the very early years of the third century Tertullian (*Adv. Judaeos*, ch. viii) states definitely that our Saviour died on the cross upon March 25. Moreover, this tradition, if it can so be called, is confirmed by other early writers --notably by Hippolytus in the first half of the same third century, who not only in his Commentary on Daniel indicates this same day as that of our Lord's passion, but in his Chronicle assigns to March 25 " the begetting of Christ " as well as His crucifixion. With this we find St Augustine in agreement, who in his *De Trinitate* (iv, 5) declares that Jesus was put to death upon March 25, the same day of the year as that on which He was conceived.

At the same time it must not be assumed that this recognition of a particular day in the calendar as the actual anniversary of the coming of the angel to Mary necessarily implied that any liturgical celebration had already been instituted to commemorate it. Apart from the birth and resurrection of our Lord and the feast of Pentecost, the primitive calendar of the Church seems only to have paid formal

honour to the heavenly birthdays of its martyrs.   But by degrees all the greater
episodes in the history of man's redemption came to be honoured separately by a
special offering of the Holy Sacrifice with formularies of prayer appropriate to the
occasion.   Early Christian literature unfortunately abounds in apocryphal documents, often fathered without warrant upon writers whose names are famous in
church history.   Also there are genuine discourses and treatises which have been
interpolated with foreign matter, or which, in the process of translation into other
tongues, have taken on a colouring which belongs, not to the original, but to the
country or period at which the translation was made.   All this must of necessity
impose very great caution in drawing inferences from literary allusions which
cannot be securely dated.   Though St Gregory Thaumaturgus, who lived in the
third century, is credited with not less than six sermons which have the Annunciation for their principal subject, there is no solid ground for believing any one of
them to be authentic, much less for supposing that any such festival was kept at
that date.   But before the year 400 a church in commemoration of the Annunciation was built at Nazareth, and the building of a church may be taken as good
evidence of some liturgical celebration of the occasion it expressly commemorates.
Such a solemnity would be likely to be adopted in course of time in other localities,
and may gradually have diffused itself throughout the Christian world.   There
seems to be some indication of this in a sermon of St Proclus of Constantinople,
before 446, but a more satisfactory example is provided by a discourse of St
Abramius, Bishop of Ephesus, about a century later.   As the oriental tradition was
always opposed to the celebration of the eucharistic liturgy during Lent on any day
except Sunday (or, in some countries, Saturday also), it was the practice to keep
no feasts during the great fast.   This must have stood in the way of any general
recognition of the Annunciation, and in fact we find the Council *in Trullo* in 692
making a definite rule that the liturgy was not to be celebrated on week-days during
Lent with the single exception of the feast of the Annunciation on March 25.   From
the discourse of St Abramius just referred to we learn that there had previously
been a commemoration of this mystery (which of course may be regarded as a feast
of our Lord as well as of His mother) on the Sunday before Christmas.   The
observance of the festival in March among the Greeks is clearly attested about the
year 641 by the *Chronicon Paschale*.

In the West the history seems to have been very similar.   The liability of the
commonly accepted date to coincide with the solemn observances of Holy Week,
or in any case with the " scrutinies " and fasts of Lent, was always an obstacle to
the celebration of a feast in March.   We learn from St Gregory of Tours that in
the sixth century some festival of our Lady—its special purpose is not mentioned—
was kept in Gaul " in the middle of January ".   The Auxerre *Hieronymianum*
(*c*. 595) apparently indicates more precisely January 18, but refers expressly to her
passing away (*depositio*).   The choice of this date seems to have been determined
by the wish to avoid the possibility of concurrence with the earliest possible day
on which Septuagesima could fall, and it therefore points to a liturgical celebration
which was something more than a mere entry in the martyrology.   In Milan, at
Aquileia, and at Ravenna, as well as among such memorials as remain to us of the
early Mozarabic rite in Spain, we find indications of a commemoration during
Advent, stress being laid upon our Lady's special relation to the mystery of the
Incarnation ; while among the decrees of the Council of Toledo in 656 we have
a definite pronouncement on the subject.   This enactment deplores the then

prevalent diversity of usage with regard to the date on which the feast of the Mother of God was kept, it points out the difficulty of observing it on the actual day when the angel came to her to announce the conception of her divine Son, owing to the likelihood that the festival would occur during Passiontide, and it enacts that in future it should be celebrated on December 18, exactly a week before Christmas. The statutes of Sonnatius, Bishop of Rheims (*c.* 625), let us know that the " Annunciation of Blessed Mary " was kept as a holiday, with abstention from servile work, but there is nothing to tell whether it fell on January 18 or in March. It seems, however, to have been generally recognized that the proper day was March 25, and there can be little doubt that when under Pope St Sergius, at the end of the seventh century, we find that the Annunciation, together with three other feasts of our Lady, was celebrated liturgically at Rome, it was kept, Lent notwithstanding, in March as the Greeks kept it. Henceforward the feast, obtaining recognition in the Gelasian and Gregorian sacramentaries, was gradually received throughout the West as part of the Roman tradition.

See Abbot Cabrol's article " Annonciation " in DAC., vol. i, cc. 2241–2255 ; S.Vailhé, *Echos d'Orient*, vol. ix (1906), pp. 138–145, also the same periodical, vol. xxii (1923), pp. 129–152 ; M. Jugie, in *Byzantinische Zeitschrift*, vol. xiv (1913), pp. 37–59, and in *Analecta Bollandiana*, vol. xliii (1925), pp. 86–95 ; and K. A. Kellner, *Heortology* (1908). On the date of the Crucifixion and its identification with the day of our Lord's conception *cf.* also the admirable article of C. H. Turner on the " Chronology of the New Testament " in Hastings, *Dictionary of the Bible.*

THE GOOD THIEF   (A.D. 29)

ON the supposition that our Lord was crucified upon March 25 the Roman Martyrology for this day contains the following entry : " At Jerusalem the commemoration of the holy thief who confessed Christ upon the cross and deserved to hear from Him the words : ' This day shalt thou be with me in paradise.' " We know no more of his history than is contained in the few sentences devoted to him by the evangelist St Luke, but, as in the case of most of the other personalities mentioned in the gospels, such as Pilate, Joseph of Arimathea, Lazarus, Martha, a story was soon fabricated which gave him a notable place in the apocryphal literature of the early centuries. In the Arabic " Gospel of the Infancy " we are told how, in the course of the flight into Egypt, the Holy Family was waylaid by robbers. Of the two leaders, named Titus and Dumachus, the former, stirred by compassion, besought his companion to let them pass unmolested, and when Dumachus refused, Titus bribed him with forty drachmas, so that they were left in peace. Thereupon the Blessed Virgin said to her benefactor, " The Lord God shall sustain thee with His right hand and give thee remission of sins ". And the Infant Jesus, intervening, spoke, " After thirty years, mother, the Jews will crucify me in Jerusalem, and these two robbers will be lifted on the cross with me, Titus on my right hand Dumachus on my left, and after that day Titus shall go before me into paradise ". This story, with others, subsequently found popular acceptance in western Christendom, though the names there most commonly given to the thieves were Dismas and Gestas. But we also find Zoathan and Chammatha, and yet other variants. That genuine devotional feeling was sometimes evoked by the incident of the pardon of the good thief upon the cross seems to be shown by the vision of St Porphyrius (*c.* 400), to which passing reference was made herein on his day (February 26). We find the two thieves represented in pictures of the crucifixion at a quite early date, as, for example, in the Syriac manuscript illuminated by Rabulas in 586, which is preserved in the Laurentian Library at Florence. The words of the good thief, "Lord, remember me when thou shalt come into thy kingdom", are adapted to very solemn usage in the Byzantine Mass, at the "great entrance" and again at the communion of the ministers and people.

See the *Évangiles apocryphes*, edited by P. Peeters, vol. ii ; the article " Larrons " in the *Dictionnaire de la Bible ;* Bauer, *Leben Jesu im Zeitalter der N.T. Apokryphen*, pp. 221-222 ; Rendel Harris in *The Expositor*, 1900, vol. i, pp. 304-308 ; and *Notes and Queries*, 10th series, vol. xi, pp. 321 and 394 ; vol. xii, p. 133. Echoes of the legend of the Good Thief are met with both in the medieval *Cursor Mundi*, ll. 16739 *seq.*, in Longfellow's *Golden Legend*, and elsewhere.

ST BARONTIUS   (*c.* A.D. 695 ?)

AFTER a career " in the world " Barontius about the year 675 withdrew with his young son to the abbey of Lonray in Berry ; but though he professed first to distribute all his property he secretly retained some of it for his own use. One day after Matins he was suddenly attacked with violent pains, accompanied by difficulty of breathing, and he fell into a state of coma which lasted many hours. Upon coming to himself he described a series of extraordinary visions which he had experienced. He thought that two demons had seized him by the throat and had tortured him till the hour of Terce, but that St Raphael had come to his assistance and had delivered him from their hands. He had then been brought before St Peter, and the devils had accused him of the sins of his past life, but Peter (who was also the patron of the monastery) had defended him and had declared that he had expiated his lapses, but imposed a penance for his deceit about the property. After having sent him to witness the torments of Hell (where Barontius recognized certain bishops suffering for their avarice) and a wait in Purgatory, St Peter had bidden him return to his monastery, give his remaining possessions to the poor, and be careful not to relapse into sin.

Deeply impressed by this experience, Barontius went on a pilgrimage to the tomb of the Apostle in Rome, and then retired to a hermitage near Pistoia, together with another monk, named Desiderius. In 1018 a monastery was built on the site where the two hermits had lived and died. It was dedicated under the name of St Barontius, but it is possible that this recluse Barontius and he of the vision were not the same person.

We have two documents which supply information concerning St Barontius—the Vision and the Life. The former, as W. Levison has shown in MGH., *Scriptores Merov.*, vol. v, pp. 368-394, is of early date, possibly the close of the eighth century, and is an interesting specimen of the same type of experience as those of Fursey and Drithelm recorded in the pages of Bede. The life can hardly be older than the year 1000, and little reliance can be placed upon the incidents it professes to record. Both these texts had previously been edited by the Bollandists and Mabillon.

ST HERMENLAND, ABBOT   (*c.* A.D. 720)

ST HERMENLAND was born in the diocese of Noyon, and from his earliest youth aspired to the religious life. His parents, however, had worldly ambitions for him and sent him to the court of King Clotaire III, where he was appointed cup-bearer. A marriage was arranged for him and preparations for the wedding were already in train when, convinced that he was opposing the will of God, Hermenland opened his heart to the king, who, though grieved at the prospect of losing him, consented to allow him to follow his true vocation. He went to the abbey of Fontenelle in Normandy and received the habit from St Lambert ; and when St Pascharius, Bishop of Nantes, appealed to the monastery for monks to take part in the evangelization of his diocese, Lambert chose Hermenland to be the superior of the twelve brethren whom he sent. Pascharius established them in a monastery which he had built in the estuary of the Loire, on the island called Aindre, and there they kept the Rule of St Columban as they had observed it at Fontenelle.

In this solitude St Hermenland and his brethren lived a life of great austerity, and in spite of their isolation their fame spread rapidly amongst the inhabitants of the mainland. Parents brought their children to be educated by the monks, who taught them to be good Christians as well as to love learning. The abbot sought to escape at times from the many visitors who frequented the monastery, and at certain seasons, notably in Lent, he would retire with several other monks to Aindrette, a neighbouring islet, for a period of retreat and special austerity. St Hermenland had the gift of prophecy and could read men's thoughts, besides being famous as a wonder-worker. It was said that once, when one of the monks was speaking with great relish about a lamprey which he had tasted at the table of the bishop of Nantes, Hermenland asked, " Don't you think that God is able to send us one here ? " As he spoke a wave washed up a lamprey at his feet, and that one small fish, distributed by the abbot, fed the whole community of monks. Another legend relates that when the saint had occasion to visit Coutances, he was offered hospitality by a citizen who had only a little wine left to set before his guests. Although a large number of people partook of the wine, the barrel, instead of being emptied, was found to have been miraculously filled. When the saint grew old, he resigned office and retired to Aindrette, where he spent his last years in solitude.

The Life of St Hermenland, attributed to the monk Donatus, which had previously been printed by the Bollandists and by Mabillon, has been critically edited in modern times by W. Levison. He pronounces that it is not the work of a contemporary, but was written at least fifty years after the saint's death, and that it is of little value as a historical document see MGH., *Scriptores Merov.*, vol. v, pp. 674–710, and *cf.* the *Analecta Bollandiana*, vol. xxix (1910), p. 451.

ST ALFWOLD, BISHOP OF SHERBORNE   (*c.* A.D. 1058)

ST ALFWOLD became bishop of Sherborne during the reign of St Edward the Confessor in succession to his brother Bertwin. He had been a monk at Winchester, and he brought with him a picture of St Swithun, the patron of that city, and spread devotion to him in Dorsetshire. He was an extremely abstemious man, and in a country where self-indulgence in food was general and where even bishops were expected to keep a rich table, he drank water from a rough bowl and ate off a common platter. St Alfwold had a great veneration and love for St Cuthbert, and loved to repeat an antiphon from his office in memory of him. Quite late in life he visited Durham to honour Cuthbert's relics, and when the shrine was opened he talked familiarly with the great saint—as a man talks to his friend. It is said that when a sharp dispute arose between him and Earl Godwin, that noble was seized with a sudden illness which only left him when he had begged Alfwold's forgiveness. As the saint was dying, he tried to repeat once more his favourite antiphon from St Cuthbert's office, but he lost the power of speech when he was half-way through and made a gesture to those round his bed to complete the sentence for him. After his death the see of Sherborne was united to that of Ramsbury to form the diocese of Salisbury.

Our principal authority is William of Malmesbury's *Gesta Pontificum* (Rolls Series, pp. 179-181). There seems to be little evidence of *cultus*.

BD THOMASIUS   (A.D. 1337)

BD THOMASIUS, or Thomas, was a native of the village of Colle-Stracciario— popularly called Costacciaro—about seven miles from Gubbio in Umbria. Even as a child his heart was set on practices of piety, and his father would take him about the country to visit shrines and places of pilgrimage. It was in this way that he made the acquaintance of the Camaldolese hermits of St Romuald in their settlement at Sitria, and he was so greatly attracted by their way of life that he obtained his father's consent to entering their order. He spent several years among them, but he longed for a yet more penitential and solitary life. With the abbot's consent, he took possession of an old cave on Monte Cupo or Cucco, which was supposed to have been occupied at one time by St Jerome. For years he lived in this solitude, and his manner of life, as his biographer says, was only known to God. That he must have lived on roots and wild fruit is certain, because the faithful, not knowing of his existence, could not provide him with food as they did other hermits. At last, by accident, he was discovered by some travellers who had lost their way. His mortifications and fasts had reduced him to skin and bone, and pitiful people brought food and drink, but he would not alter his mode of life, and gave away everything to the poor who also began to gather round him. Several young men wished to join him and to submit to his discipline, but he would not bind them to any promises and left them free to come or to go. They treasured up his sayings and his miracles, and one of them afterwards wrote his life. Thomasius is said to have died in 1337, worn out by austerities and privations.

See the *Acta Sanctorum*, March, vol.   and Mittarelli, *Annales Camaldulensium*, v, pp. 360 *seq.*

BD MARGARET CLITHEROW, MARTYR   (A.D. 1586)

WE are fortunate in possessing ample information about Margaret Clitherow, thanks to the biography written by her confessor, Father John Mush, supplemented by details from other contemporary documents. In York we can still see the guildhall in which she was tried, the castle in which she was imprisoned, the house in the Little Shambles which is the reputed home of her married life, and the room with the dormer window at the Black Swan inn, which tradition points out as the place which she hired as a Mass-house, when her own private chapel was considered unsafe.

Margaret was the daughter of a wealthy wax-chandler, called Thomas Middleton, who was a freeman of the city of York and had held the office of sheriff for the year 1564-65. He died shortly afterwards, and his wife within five months married a man of inferior condition of the name of May, who took up his residence with the family at the Middleton house in Davygate. It was from there that Margaret was married in 1571 to John Clitherow, a grazier and butcher, who like her own father was well-to-do and had held civic appointments. He had been bridgemaster and then chamberlain—becoming thus entitled to the address of Mr before his name.

Margaret was bred a Protestant, but two or three years after her marriage she embraced the Catholic faith, which she had been led to study, as her biographer tells us, " finding no substance, truth nor Christian comfort in the ministers of the new gospel, nor in their doctrine itself, and hearing also many priests and lay people to suffer for the defence of the ancient Catholic faith ". Her kindly, easy-going husband seems to have made no opposition then or at any time to what she chose to do. He was not of the stuff of which heroes are made, and continued to conform to the state religion, but he had one brother a priest, and a certain Thomas Clitherow who was imprisoned in York Castle for his religion in 1600 was probably another brother. Mr Clitherow was wont to say that he found but two faults in his wife : she fasted too much, and she would not accompany him to church.

Quite at first it seems that Margaret was able to practise her faith without much difficulty and could seek out backsliders and win converts, but the laws became harsher or were more strictly enforced. She was warned by cautious friends to be more circumspect : fines were imposed upon Mr Clitherow for his wife's continued absence from church and she herself was imprisoned in the castle—once for two whole years. The conditions there, as we know from contemporary records, were very bad, the cells were dark, damp and verminous, and many of the captives died during their confinement ; yet Margaret treated these periods as times of spiritual retreat, praying and fasting four days a week—a practice she continued after her liberation. It is not clear at what date she began to open her house to fugitive priests, but she continued to do so to the end, in spite of the enactment of the law which made the harbouring of priests an offence punishable by death. Father Thompson, Father Hart, Father Thirkill, Father Ingleby and many others had been hidden in the secret priest's chamber, the entrance to which " was painful to him that was not acquainted with the door, by reason of the straitness thereof, and yet large enough for a boy ". Moreover, in order that none should be deprived of Mass when it could be had, Father Mush tells us : " She had prepared two chambers, the one adjoining to her own house, whereunto she might have resort at any time, without sight and knowledge of any neighbours. The other was a little distant from her own house, secret and unknown to any but to such as she knew to be both faithful and discreet. This place she prepared for more troublesome storms, that God might yet be served there when her own house was not thought so safe, though she could not have access to it every day as she desired." She also supplied and tended all that was required for the service of the altar, both vestments and vessels.

Possessed of good looks, full of wit and very merry, Margaret's was a charming personality. " Everyone loved her ", we read, " and would run to her for help, comfort and counsel in their distresses. . Her servants also carried that reverent love to her that notwithstanding they knew when priests frequented her house, and she would reasonably sharply correct them for their faults and negligences, yet they had as great a care to conceal her secrets as if they had been her natural children." In many cases people of a different faith from hers were the first to try to shield her and to warn her of impending danger. Moreover, like a true Yorkshire woman, she was a good housewife and capable in business. In " buying and selling her wares ", we learn, " she was very wary to have the worth of them, as her neighbours sold the like, as also to satisfy her husband who committed all to her trust and discretion ", but we are not surprised to find that she often urged her husband to give up the shop with all its worries and to confine his energies to the wholesale business.

Every day was begun with an hour and a half devoted to private prayer and meditation. It there was a priest available, Mass followed, and during it she would kneel behind her children and servants in the lowliest place beside the door—perhaps to be able to give the alarm in case of surprise. Twice a week, on Wednesday and Sunday, she tried to make her confession. Although not an educated woman she had learnt much from the priests who frequented the house, and three books she knew thoroughly, the Bible, Thomas à Kempis and Perrin's Exercise. At some time—perhaps in prison—she had committed to memory the whole of the Little Office of our Lady in Latin, " not knowing what God might do with her ". The thought of the martyred priests whom she had known and who had suffered at Knavesmire was constantly in Mrs Clitherow's mind, and when her husband was away she would sometimes go on pilgrimage barefoot with other women to the place of execution outside the city walls. At all hours a dangerous proceeding owing to spies, it was particularly perilous during the day, and therefore they generally went by night, and Margaret would remain meditating and praying under the gallows " as long as her company would suffer her " These expeditions were cut short, for Margaret, during the last year and a half before her final arrest, was compelled to remain confined in her own house, " at liberty under bonds "—apparently because she had sent her eldest son to school beyond the seas.

On March 10, 1586 Mr Clitherow was summoned to appear before the York tribunal set up by the Great Council of the North, and in the absence of the master his house was searched. Nothing suspicious was found until the officials reached a remote room where the children and a few others were being taught by a schoolmaster named Stapleton, whom they took for a priest. In the confusion that ensued he eluded them and escaped through the secret room, but the children were questioned and threatened. An eleven-year-old boy from abroad, who was living with the family, was terrorized into disclosing the entrance to the priest's chamber. No one was in occupation, but in a cupboard were found vessels and books which were obviously used for Mass. These were seized and Margaret herself was apprehended and led first before the council and then to prison in the castle. Once reassured as to the safety of her family, her high spirits never forsook her, and when two days later she was joined by Mrs Ann Tesh, whom the same boy had betrayed as frequenting the sacraments, the two friends joked and laughed together until Margaret exclaimed, " Sister, we are so merry together that I fear, unless we be parted, to lose the merit of our imprisonment ". Just before the summons to appear before the judge she said, " Yet before I go, I will make all my brethren and sisters on the other side of the hall merry ; " and, " looking forth of a window toward them—they were five and thirty and might easily behold her from thence—she made a pair of gallows with her fingers and pleasantly laughed at them ". After the charge had been read, accusing her of harbouring and maintaining priests and of attending Mass, the judge asked her whether she was guilty or not guilty. She replied, " I know no offence whereof I should confess myself guilty ", and when questioned as to how she would be tried she would only say, " Having made no offence, I need no trial ".

From this position she never swerved, although she was brought up several times and urged to plead and to choose trial by jury. It would be death in any case, as she well knew, but if she accepted trial her children, servants and friends would be called up as witnesses, and either they would lie to save her, and thus commit perjury, or they would have to give evidence and so suffer the scandal and sorrow of having caused her death. Many attempts were made to persuade her to apostatize or at least submit to trial, and one Puritan divine who had argued with her in prison had the courage to stand up in court and declare that condemnation on the charge of a child was contrary to the law of God and of man. Judge Clinch, who would have wished to save her, was overruled by others of the council, and he finally pronounced the terrible sentence which the English law decreed for anyone who would not plead, *viz.* that she should be pressed to death. She heard the sentence with the utmost serenity and said, " God be thanked ; all that He shall send me is welcome. I am not worthy so good a death as this."

After this she was imprisoned in John Trew's house on the Ousebridge where even then she was not left in peace, but was visited by various people who tried in vain to shake her constancy, including her stepfather Henry May, who had been elected mayor of York. She was never allowed to see her children, and only once did she see her husband and then only in the presence of the gaoler. She was to suffer on March 25, which was the Friday in Passion week, and the evening before she sewed her shroud and then spent the greater part of the night on her knees. At eight in the morning the sheriff came to conduct her to the toll-booth a few yards from the prison, and " all marvelled to see her joyful, smiling countenance ". Arrived at the place of execution, she knelt down to pray and some of those present desired her to join them in prayer. She refused, as Bd William Hart had done almost exactly three years before. " I will not pray with you, nor shall you pray with me ", she said. " Neither will I say Amen to your prayer, nor shall you to mine." But she prayed aloud for the pope, cardinals, clergy, Christian princes and especially for Queen Elizabeth, that God would turn her to the faith and save her soul. She was then obliged to strip and to lie flat on the ground, with a sharp stone under her back and her hands were bound to posts at the side. A door was laid over her and weights placed upon it to the quantity of seven or eight hundredweights. Her last words, as they descended upon her were, " Jesu, Jesu, Jesu, have mercy upon me ! " She was about a quarter of a hour in dying, but her body was left for six hours in the press. At the time of her death she was something over thirty years old.

To her husband she had sent her hat " in sign of her loving duty to him as to her head ", and to her twelve-year-old daughter Agnes her shoes and stockings to signify that she should follow in her steps. The little girl became a nun at Louvain, whilst two of the martyr's sons were afterwards priests. One of Margaret Clitherow's hands is preserved in a reliquary at the Bar Convent, York.

Fr John Morris, in his *Troubles of our Catholic Forefathers*, vol. iii (1876), very fully investigated the materials available for the life of Margaret Clitherow and printed an accurate text of the contemporary memoir by John Mush, the martyr's confessor. Nothing substantial has since been added ; but see Burton and Pollen, LEM., vol. i, pp. 188–199 ; J. B. Milburn, *A Martyr of Old York* (1900) ; and Margaret T. Monro, *Bd Margaret Clitherow* (1948).

BD JAMES BIRD, Martyr (A.D. 1593)

James Bird was a layman and only nineteen years old when he suffered martyrdom. His father was a Protestant gentleman of Winchester, and James had been brought up by him in that religion. Becoming convinced of the truth of the Catholic faith he was received into the Church and went abroad, spending some time at the Douay College at Rheims. Upon his return to England, his zeal for religion led to his being apprehended and imprisoned. He was accused of high treason, in that he had become reconciled with the Church of Rome and had asserted that the pope was the head of the Church on earth. Bird pleaded guilty to both charges, and was sentenced to death, but he was offered life and liberty if he would once attend a Protestant service. He refused thus to compromise his conscience, and when his father entreated him to make this one concession, he replied that, as he had always obeyed him in the past so would he willingly have obeyed him now, if he could have done so without offending God. After enduring a long imprisonment he was brought to the scaffold, and endured the extreme penalty with perfect serenity. He was hanged, drawn and quartered at Winchester, and his head was set up on a pole upon one of the city gates.

See MMP., pp. 188–189 ; and J. H. Pollen, *Acts of English Martyrs*, p. 231.

ST LUCY FILIPPINI, Virgin   (A.D. 1732)

The institute of the " Maestre Pie " is not as well-known outside of Italy as it deserves to be, but at a period when compulsory education was still undreamed of it worked wonders both for the religious and the social improvement of the women of that country. Atlhough St Lucy was not the actual foundress of this remarkable organization, she was perhaps the most zealous, the most influential and the most holy of all its early promoters. Born in 1672 at Tarquinia in Tuscany, about sixty miles from Rome, she was left an orphan at an early age, and when still quite young her seriousness of purpose, her great piety and remarkable gifts brought her to the notice of the bishop of the diocese, Cardinal Marcantonio Barbarigo, who persuaded her to come to Montefiascone to take part in an educational institute for training teachers which he had established in that city under the direction of religious. Lucy threw herself heart and soul into the work and was there brought into contact with Bd Rose Venerini, whom as the successful and most devoted organizer of a similar work in Viterbo, the cardinal had summoned to Montefiascone, that she might give his own foundation the benefit of her experience.

No pupil could have shown more aptitude than St Lucy. Her modesty, her charity, her intense conviction of the value of the things of the spirit, together with her courage and her practical common sense, won all hearts. The work prospered amazingly. New schools for girls and educational centres multiplied in all directions, and in 1707, at the express desire of Pope Clement XI, she came to Rome and there founded the first school of the Maestre Pie in the Via delle Chiavi d'Oro. She was only able to remain in the city a little more than six months, her duties calling her elsewhere, but the children came in crowds which far exceeded the accommodation which could be provided for them, and Lucy before she left was known to half the district as the *Maestra santa* (the holy schoolmistress). Like Rose Venerini, she had a great gift of easy and convincing speech. Unfortunately her strength was not equal to the strain that was put on it. She became seriously ill in 1726, and in spite of medical care in Rome itself was never able to regain her normal health, dying a most holy death on March 25, 1732, the day she had herself predicted. St Lucy Filippini was canonized in 1930.

See the *Acta Apostolicae Sedis*, vol. xxii (1930), pp. 433–443 (the canonization) ; F. de Simone, *Vita della serva .   Lucia Filippini* (1732) ; and *La B. Lucia Filippini* (1926).

26 : ST CASTULUS, Martyr (A.D. 286)

DURING the reign of Diocletian, Pope St Caius was greatly concerned for the safety of the Christians in Rome. Certain legendary acts tell us that Castulus, a zealous Christian, who was the emperor's chamberlain, offered to arrange for religious services to be held actually in the palace itself, because no search was likely to be made there ; and moreover, that he sheltered Christians in his own house, which adjoined the palace, and showed them the place of rendezvous. Not satisfied with thus serving the Church, he and his friend Tiburtius went about Rome converting men and women to Christianity and bringing them to the pope to be baptized. Eventually he was betrayed by an apostate Christian called Torquatus, and brought before Fabian, prefect of the city. He was cruelly tortured and then cast into a pit and smothered with sand. A cemetery and a church on the Via Labicana were named after St Castulus.

While the Acts of St Castulus, printed in the *Acta Sanctorum* (March, vol. iii), are historically valueless and are partly plagiarized from those of St Sebastian, there is no reason to doubt the historical existence of the martyr or that his remains were interred in the catacomb which bears his name. The friable nature of the sandstone in this cemetery, which easily crumbles, may have some relation to what is said of the manner of the martyr's death. See Leclercq in DAC., vol. ii, cc. 2372-2375.

ST FELIX, Bishop of Trier (c. A.D. 400)

St FELIX was consecrated bishop of Trier in 386 and took part in a synod held in his episcopal city at which St Martin was also present. He was a most holy man and extremely liberal to the poor. He built a monastery and a church which he dedicated to our Lady and the Theban Martyrs and in which he placed the alleged relics of the advance-guard of the Theban Legion—Thyrses the General and nine others. Because he had been elected by those who were said to have compassed the death of Priscillian, St Ambrose and Pope St Siricius refused to hold ecclesiastical communion with St Felix, and it was probably for this reason that he resigned his see in 398 and retired to the monastery he had built, which was subsequently called after St Paulinus. He died an edifying death and many miracles were reported as having taken place at his tomb. Sulpicius Severus speaks of him with much respect.

See the *Acta Sanctorum*, March, vol. iii, and Duchesne, *Fastes Épiscopaux*, vol. iii, p. 36.

ST MACARTAN, Bishop (c. A.D. 505)

VERY little is known of St Aedh Mac Cairthinn, although his feast is kept throughout Ireland, in the diocese of Clogher, of which see he is said to have been the first bishop, as a double of the first class. On August 15, which was at one time reckoned as his special day, we find this cryptic utterance in the *Félire* of Oengus : " Fer da chrich, a fair champion." " Fer da chrich ", used here as a name, means " man of two districts ", and the gloss goes on to explain that this " man of two districts " was the abbot of Dairinis, or Bishop Mac Cairthinn, adding : " Aedh is truly the man's name, grandson of Aithmet, with many deeds, his name at Clochar of the churches was afterwards Bishop Mac Cairthinn ; ' man of two districts ' was his name at first ; I will tell you his history, a true brother with victory, with fame,

to Mael-ruain, to his teacher.   He was the maternal uncle of Mael-ruain, Oengus's
tutor, and from him Mael-ruain brought ' Fer da chrich's ' bell, which is in
Tallaght."   Little more is told in the fragmentary Latin life still preserved, except
the extravagant miracles with which the saint defeated the attempts of the local
chieftain to drive him from Clogher.   St Macartan is believed to have been consecrated bishop by St Patrick himself.

> A mutilated Latin life is printed by Colgan, and in the *Acta Sanctorum* (under August 15),
> from the Codex Salmanticensis.   See also LIS., vol. viii, pp. 208 *seq.*

ST BRAULIO, Bishop of Saragossa   (A.D. 651)

At the college founded in Seville by St Isidore, one of the more promising of the
alumni was a boy of noble birth called Braulio, who grew up to be so eminent a
scholar that Isidore regarded him as a friend and disciple rather than a pupil, and
used to send him his own writings to correct and revise.   Braulio prepared for the
priesthood and was ordained, and when in 631 the see of Saragossa became vacant
at the death of his brother Bishop John, the neighbouring prelates assembled to
elect a successor and their choice fell upon Braulio.   They are said to have been
assisted in their selection by the appearance of a globe of fire which rested above
Braulio's head, whilst a voice pronounced the words, " Behold my servant whom
I have chosen and upon whom my spirit rests ".   As a pastor, St Braulio laboured
zealously to teach and encourage his people, and at the same time to extirpate the
Arian heresy which continued to flourish even after the conversion of King Reccared.   He kept in close touch with St Isidore, whom he assisted in his task of
restoring church order and regularizing ecclesiastical discipline.   A small portion
of the correspondence between the two saints has survived to this day.   So great
was St Braulio's eloquence and his power of persuasion, that some of his hearers
asserted that they had seen the Holy Spirit, in the form of a dove, resting on his
shoulder and imparting in his ear the doctrine he preached to the people.   He took
part in the fourth Council of Toledo, which was presided over by his friend and
master St Isidore, and also in the fifth and sixth.   The last-named assembly charged
him to write an answer to Pope Honorius I, who had accused the Spanish bishops
of negligence in the fulfilment of their duties.   His defence was dignified and
convincing.

The good bishop's duties did not prevent his constant ministrations in his
cathedral church and in that of our Lady " del Pilar ", where he spent many hours
of the day and night in prayer.   Luxury of all kinds he abhorred : his garments
were rough and plain, his food simple and his life austere.   An eloquent preacher
and a keen controversialist, he could carry conviction by his telling arguments and
absolute sincerity.   His liberality to the poor was only matched by his tender care
of all his flock.   The close of his life was saddened by failing eyesight—a heavy
trial to anyone, but especially to a scholar.   As his end drew near, he realized that
he was dying, and the last day of his life was spent in the recitation of psalms.
According to a legend, which, however, appears to be comparatively modern,
heavenly music resounded in the chamber of death, and a voice was heard to say,
" Rise, my friend, and come away ! "   The saint, as though waking from sleep,
replied with his last breath, " I come, Lord : I am ready ! "

Of St Braulio's writings, we have a Life of St Emilian with a poem in his
honour, forty-four letters, which were discovered at Leon in the eighteenth century

and shed great light on Visigothic Spain, and an eulogy of St Isidore, as well as a catalogue of his works.   He is said to have completed some writings which St Isidore left unfinished, and he is almost certainly the author of the Acts of the Martyrs of Saragossa.   St Braulio is the patron of Aragon and one of the most famous of the Spanish saints.

See the *Acta Sanctorum*, March, vol. ii ; Florez, *España Sagrada*, vol. xxx, pp. 305 *seq.* ; Gams, *Kirchengeschichte Spaniens*, vol. ii, pt 2, pp. 145–149 ; DTC., vol. ii, cc. 1123 *seq.* ; DHG., vol. x, cc. 441 *seq.* ; and C. H. Lynch, *St Braulio* (1938).   But the indispensable work is now the critical edition of the saint's letters by J. Madoz, published in Madrid in 1941.

ST LUDGER, Bishop of Münster   (A.D. 809)

IT was in the abbey school of Utrecht, presided over by St Boniface's friend Gregory, that St Ludger (Liudger), a Frisian, received his earlier education.   In the life which the pupil afterwards wrote of his master he tells us that in that school " some were of noble Frankish families ; some were English ; some of the new seed of God planted among the Frisians and Saxons ; others of the Bructeri and the Suevi ; others of sundry nations whom God had sent thither.   Of all these, I, Ludger, am the least—yea, the weakest and most insignificant."   At his own request the boy had been sent to Utrecht at an unusually early age by his parents ; amongst the memories of his childhood, he cherished the recollection of having once seen the great St Boniface, " when the hair of his head was white and his body decrepit with age ".   Ludger was preparing for the diaconate when there arrived in Utrecht a priest from York, Alubert, who had been moved to preach the gospel in Friesland.   St Gregory welcomed him eagerly, and urged him to have himself consecrated regionary bishop.   Alubert rather unwillingly consented, but only on condition that he should be given one or two native clergy.   Sigbold and Ludger were appointed to him, and the three returned to York, where Alubert was consecrated bishop, Sigbold ordained priest and Ludger deacon.   There they met the famous Alcuin, whom the archbishop of York had set over the cathedral school. Ludger was attracted to him as steel to a magnet, and when he had to accompany his friends back to Utrecht he earnestly entreated permission to return to England to continue his studies under the most learned man and the greatest teacher of the age.   St Gregory wished to retain him, but he was allowed to go back to England. He sat at Alcuin's feet for three and a half more years, and would, no doubt, have stayed longer, but for an untoward incident.   In a quarrel, the son of an English earl had been killed by a Frisian merchant, and to avert the vengeance of the English it was thought expedient that all Frisians in England should return to their own land.   Ludger accordingly returned to Utrecht, where he received a warm greeting from Gregory, who died not long afterwards, entrusting his monastery to his nephew Alberic.

Abbot Alberic sent Ludger to rebuild the wrecked church over the reputed grave of St Lebuin at Deventer.   While he was occupied with this work, the true place of burial was revealed to him in a dream, and he was able to include the tomb in the new building.   As soon as the church had been consecrated, Ludger was sent with several companions to preach on the frontiers of Friesland, where he made a number of converts and destroyed several pagan shrines.   In these much treasure was found—the greater part of which was appropriated by Charlemagne, but one-third was returned for ecclesiastical use.   Ludger was still only a deacon, and it was felt that he ought to be raised to the priesthood. Accordingly, when Alberic went to Cologne to be consecrated bishop, he took with him Ludger, and there ordained him priest and gave him spiritual charge of the Ostergau. At Dokkum, the place of St Boniface's martyrdom, he seems to have built a church, for the porch of which Alcuin sent him from England some lines of his own composition. For seven years St Ludger worked with great success, founding churches, converting pagans and bad Christians and in general laying the foundations of a flourishing Christian community. Suddenly all his efforts were brought to a standstill, and his work to outward appearance ruined, through an invasion of Friesland by the Saxons, under Widukind ; they overran the country, destroyed the churches, drove out the priests and compelled the people to return to heathen rites. Ludger conducted his disciples to a place of safety and then started on a pilgrimage to Rome, accompanied by his brother Hildegrim and his nephew Gerfrid. They went on to Monte Cassino, and here Ludger spent three years, not taking the Benedictine vows, but studying and observing the Rule, for, as we read, " he was anxious to build a monastery on his own estate, and this was afterwards done at Werden ".

Meanwhile Alcuin, whom Charlemagne had attached to his court, brought his friend Ludger to the monarch's notice, and it seems not improbable that the emperor had met the saint on the occasion of his visit to Monte Cassino. In any case St Ludger returned to his country in 785, prepared to resume his missionary labours now that the field was again open to him. Charlemagne formed such a high opinion of him that he gave him spiritual charge over five provinces of Friesland. Aided by his knowledge of the people and of their speech, the holy man's labours were abundantly blessed, although he had but few helpers. He crossed the water to Heligoland, where he preached to the inhabitants and converted many, baptizing them in the fountain in which St Willibrord had once baptized three converts. On the return journey, he cured a blind minstrel named Bernlef, who embraced Christianity and afterwards accompanied the saint on his missionary journeys. These successes induced Charlemagne to offer Ludger the recently subjugated province of north-west Saxony or Westphalia, and the ardent missionary willingly accepted the additional charge. Although by no means a strong man, he laboured untiringly in this fresh field, travelling over the country, teaching and preaching indoors and in the open air, and baptizing his converts himself. Ludger's gentleness, persuasiveness and attractive personality did more to reconcile and settle the Saxons than all the emperor's repressive measures.

His headquarters he made at Mimigerneford, where he built a monastery, from which the town derived its later name of Münster, and in it he instituted the rule of St Chrodegang of Metz for clergy living in community. As the number of the faithful increased it became necessary to have a bishop, and Ludger was accordingly consecrated at Cologne about 804 by Archbishop Hildebald. With the help of his brother Hildegrim, the saint not only succeeded in evangelizing Westphalia, but crossed the Weser into what was formerly known as Eastphalia. His unquenchable zeal prompted him to go still further north, to preach to the Northmen of Denmark and Scandinavia, but Charlemagne refused his consent, realizing no doubt that the saint was growing old and that there were limits even to his powers. Years before, at Utrecht, St Ludger had beheld in a vision his lately deceased master Abbot Gregory, who from a height appeared to be dropping scrolls and fragments which he bade him collect. Automatically he obeyed and gathered them into three piles. The dream had been interpreted by one of the monks to mean that Ludger would become the spiritual guide of three peoples ; but the saint had then ruefully exclaimed, " Would that God would rather grant me fruit in the place over which I now have charge ! " Legend has attributed to Ludger many monastic foundations, but with some of these, notably that at Helmstädt, which was after-wards called by his name, he had certainly nothing to do. Werden, however, undoubtedly owed its existence to his exertions. It was ruled by his relations until 877, and became one of the most important abbeys in Germany.

In spite of all his external activity, the holy man allowed nothing to interfere with his devotions, public or private. He was so particular about attention at offices, even whilst he was travelling, that when one of his clergy stooped to mend the fire during Matins, to prevent the smoke from blowing into the bishop's face, he was rebuked at the close of the service. St Ludger was once accused to Charle-magne of wasting his income in indiscriminate almsgiving and neglecting the embellishment of the churches in his care. The prince, who loved to see churches magnificent, considered this a serious charge, and ordered him to appear before him to reply to it. On the morning after his arrival, a chamberlain came to summon him, but found him at prayer. The saint sent back word that he would follow when he had finished his devotions. A second messenger was despatched and yet a third before he was ready, and Charlemagne indignantly asked him why he had not immediately obeyed his summons. " Because I believed that the service of God was to be preferred to yours or to that of any man," replied the accused calmly. " Such indeed was your will when you invested me with the office of a bishop, and therefore I deemed it unseemly to interrupt the service of God, even at the command of your majesty." St Ludger suffered great pain towards the end of his life, but he continued his labours until the last day—which was Passion Sunday, 809. That morning he preached at Coesfeld and then hurried to Biller-beck, where he preached again and said Mass. In the evening he peacefully died, surrounded by his disciples and in the presence of his sister, the Abbess Gerburgis. Münster and Werden disputed for the possession of his body, but he had expressed a wish to be buried at Werden. The greater part of his relics remain there to this day.

Our sources of information regarding the life of St Ludger are abundant and, on the whole, reliable. The biography by his admirer Altfrid, who was bishop of Münster from 839 to 849, was compiled from the statements of those who had lived with the saint. The other lives are not so trustworthy. All these documents will be found critically edited by W. Diekamp in his *Geschichtsquellen des Bisthums Münster*, vol. iv ; most of them had pre-viously been printed by the Bollandists and Mabillon. There are modern biographies in German by Hüsing, by Pingsmann and by Krimphove. and for English readers there is an excellent account by Stubbs in DCB., vol. iii, pp. 729–731. See also Hauck, *Kirchengeschichte Deutschlands*, vol. ii, pp. 349, 354 and 406.

ST BASIL THE YOUNGER (A.D. 952)

THE story of the hermit St Basil the Younger, originally written by his disciple Gregory, has come down to us through Greek channels in which fable has obviously become intermingled with history. According to this tradition, he had a cell not far from Constantinople, but was arrested on suspicion of being a spy, under the rule of Leo VI and Alexander, and was conducted to Constantinople. Under cross-examination, as he refused to reply to the charges brought against him, he

was beaten with sticks and suspended by the feet.   He was afterwards exposed to
the lions, but since they did him no injury, he was then cast into the sea, but was
brought safely back to land by dolphins—a very favourite form of rescue in Greek
folk-lore, both pagan and Christian.   Early the following morning he made his way
into the city, where he cured of fever a bedridden man who received him into his
house.   His miracles and sanctity soon made him famous, but he was several times
severely mishandled on account of his stern denunciation of wickedness in high
places.   When Constantine Porphyrogenitus was attempting to obtain a share in
the empire, the holy man foretold his failure and uttered many other remarkable
prophecies ; and Basil never scrupled to admonish the princesses Anastasia and
Irene when he deemed that reproof was necessary.   He died at the age of 100, and
was buried in the church of a nunnery in Constantinople.

See the *Acta Sanctorum*, March, vol. iii, where the Greek text is printed.

27 : ST JOHN DAMASCENE, Doctor of the Church   (*c.* A.D. 749)

S T JOHN OF DAMASCUS, the last of the Greek fathers and the first of
the long line of Christian Aristotelians, was also one of the two greatest poets
of the Eastern church, the other being St Romanus the Melodist.   The whole
of the life of St John was spent under the government of a Mohammedan khalif,
and it exhibits the strange spectacle of a Christian father of the Church protected
from a Christian emperor, whose heresy he was able to attack with impunity because
he lived under Moslem rule.   He and St Theodore Studites were the principal
and the ablest defenders of the *cultus* of sacred images in the bitterest period of the
Iconoclastic controversy.   As a theological and philosophical writer he made no
attempt at originality, for his work was rather to compile and arrange what his
predecessors had written.   Still, in theological questions he remains the ultimate
court of appeal among the Greeks, and his treatise *Of the Orthodox Faith* is still to
the Eastern schools what the *Summa* of St Thomas Aquinas became to the West.

The Moslem rulers of Damascus, where St John was born, were not unjust to
their Christian subjects, although they required them to pay a poll tax and to submit
to other humiliating conditions.   They allowed both Christians and Jews to occupy
important posts, and in many cases to acquire great fortunes.   The khalif's doctor
was nearly always a Jew, whilst Christians were employed as scribes, administrators
and architects.   Amongst the officials at his court in 675 was a Christian called
John, who held the post of chief of the revenue department—an office which seems
to have become hereditary in his family.   He was the father of our saint, and the
surname of al-Mansur which the Arabs gave him was afterwards transferred to the
son.   The younger John was born about the year 690 and was baptized in infancy.
With regard to his early education, if we may credit his biographer, " His father
took care to teach him, not how to ride a horse, not how to wield a spear, not to
hunt wild beasts and change his natural kindness into brutal cruelty, as happens to
many.   John, his father, a second Chiron, did not teach him all this, but he sought a
tutor learned in all science, skilful in every form of knowledge, who would produce
good words from his heart ; and he handed over his son to him to be nourished
with this kind of food ".   Afterwards he was able to provide another teacher, a
monk called Cosmas, " beautiful in appearance and still more beautiful in soul ",

whom the Arabs had brought back from Sicily amongst other captives. John the elder had to pay a great price for him, and well he might for, if we are to believe our chronicler, " he knew grammar and logic, as much arithmetic as Pythagoras and as much geometry as Euclid ". He taught all the sciences, but especially theology, to the younger John and also to a boy whom the elder John seems to have adopted, who also was called Cosmas, and who became a poet and a singer, subsequently accompanying his adopted brother to the monastery in which they both became monks.

In spite of his theological training St John does not seem at first to have contemplated any career except that of his father, to whose office he succeeded. Even at court he was able freely to live a Christian life, and he became remarkable there for his virtues and especially for his humility. Nevertheless, after filling his responsible post for some years, St John resigned office, and went to be a monk in the laura of St Sabas (Mar Saba) near Jerusalem. It is still a moot point whether his earlier works against the iconoclasts were written while he was still at Damascus, but the best authorities since the days of the Dominican Le Quien, who edited his works in 1712, incline to the opinion that he had become a monk before the outbreak of the persecution, and that all three treatises were composed at St Sabas. In any case John and Cosmas settled down amongst the brethren and occupied their spare time in writing books and composing hymns. It might have been thought that the other monks would appreciate the presence amongst them of so doughty a champion of the faith as John, but this was far from being the case. They said the new-comers were introducing disturbing elements. It was bad enough to write books, but it was even worse to compose and sing hymns, and the brethren were scandalized. The climax came when, at the request of a monk whose brother had died, John wrote a hymn on death and sang it to a sweet tune of his own composition. His master, an old monk whose cell he shared, rounded upon him in fury and ejected him from the cell. " Is this the way you forget your vows ? " he exclaimed. " Instead of mourning and weeping, you sit in joy and delight yourself by singing." He would only permit him to return at the end of several days, on condition that he should go round the laura and clear up all the filth with his own hands. St John obeyed unquestioningly, but in the visions of the night our Lady appeared to the old monk and told him to allow his disciple to write as many books and as much poetry as he liked. From that time onwards St John was able to devote his time to study and to his literary work. The legend adds that he was sometimes sent, perhaps for the good of his soul, to sell baskets in the streets of Damascus where he had once occupied so high a post. It must, however, be confessed that these details, written by his biographer more than a century after the saint's death, are of very questionable authority.

If the monks at St Sabas did not value the two friends, there were others outside who did. The patriarch of Jerusalem, John V, knew them well by reputation and wished to have them amongst his clergy. First he took Cosmas and made him bishop of Majuma, and afterwards he ordained John priest and brought him to Jerusalem. St Cosmas, we are told, ruled his flock admirably until his death, but St John soon returned to his monastery. He revised his writings carefully, " and wherever they flourished with blossoms of rhetoric, or seemed superfluous in style, he prudently reduced them to a sterner gravity, lest they should have any display of levity or want of dignity ". His works in defence of eikons had become known and read everywhere, and had earned him the hatred of the persecuting emperors.

If his enemies never succeeded in injuring him, it was only because he never crossed the frontier into the Roman empire. The rest of his life was spent in writing theology and poetry at St Sabas, where he died at an advanced age. He was proclaimed doctor of the Church in 1890.

The gospel of the man with the withered hand, which is appointed in the Roman Missal for the Mass of St John Damascene, refers to a story once widely credited but now regarded as apocryphal. When the saint was still revenue officer at Damascus, the Emperor Leo III, who hated him but could not take him openly, sought to destroy him by guile. He therefore forged a letter purporting to have been written to him by John to inform him that Damascus was poorly defended and to offer his aid in case he should attack it. This forgery Leo sent to the khalif with a note to the effect that he hated treachery and wished his friend to know how his official was behaving. The infuriated khalif had John's right hand cut off, but sent him the severed member at his request. The saint bore it into his private chapel and prayed in hexameter verse before an image of the Mother of God. By our Lady's intercession it was joined again to his body and was immediately employed to write a thanksgiving.

The formal biography of the saint written in Greek by John of Jerusalem about a century and a half after his death is pretentious in style and untrustworthy in the data it supplies. It is possibly no more than a translation of an Arabic original (see the *Analecta Bollandiana,* vol. xxxiii, 1914, pp. 78–81). It was edited by Le Quien and is reprinted in Migne (PG., vol. xciv, cc. 429–490) with Le Quien's valuable comments. The brief notice of John Damascene in the *Synax. Constant.* (ed. Delehaye, cc. 279–280) is probably more reliable. There is an excellent account of St John by J. H. Lupton in DCB., vol. iii, pp. 409–423, and by Dr A. Fortescue in his book, *The Greek Fathers,* pp. 202–248. A still fuller and more up-to-date estimate of the work of this great doctor of the Church is that of M. Jugie in DTC., vol. viii, cc. 693–751, where his writings and theological teaching are discussed in detail. See also J. Nasrallah, *S. Jean de Damas* (1950).

ST JOHN OF EGYPT (A.D. 394)

EXCEPTING St Antony, no desert hermit acquired such widespread fame as St John of Egypt, who was consulted by emperors and whose praises were sung by St Jerome, Palladius, Cassian, St Augustine and many others. He was born in the Lower Thebaïd at Lycopolis, the site of the present city of Asyut, and was brought up to the trade of a carpenter. At the age of twenty-five, he abandoned the world and placed himself under the direction of an aged anchoret, who for ten or twelve years trained him in obedience and self-surrender. John obeyed unquestioningly, however unreasonable the task imposed : for a whole year, at the command of his spiritual father, he daily watered a dry stick as though it had been a live plant and carried out other equally ridiculous orders. He continued thus until the old man's death, and it is to his humility and ready obedience that Cassian attributes the extraordinary gifts which he afterwards received from God. Another four or five years seem to have been spent in visiting various monasteries. Finally he retired to the top of a steep hill near Lycopolis and made in the rock a succession of three little cells—one as a bedroom, another as a workroom and living-room, and the third as an oratory. He then walled himself up, leaving only a little window through which he received the necessaries of life and spoke to those who visited him. During five days of the week he conversed only with God, but on Saturdays and Sundays men—but not women—had free access to him for his instructions and

spiritual advice.   He never ate until sunset, and his fare was dried fruit and vegetables.   At first and until he became inured, he suffered severely because he would
not eat bread or anything that had been cooked by fire, but he continued this diet
from his fortieth year until he was ninety.

He founded no community, but was regarded as a father by all the ascetics of
the neighbourhood, and when his visitors became so numerous that it seemed
necessary to build a hospice for their reception, the establishment was managed by
his disciples.   St John was especially famous for his prophecies, his miracles and
his power of reading the thoughts and of discovering the secret sins of those who
visited him.   Wonderful cures were effected by the application to the sick and
blind of oil which the man of God had blessed.   Of his many prophecies the most
celebrated were those made to the Emperor Theodosius I.   John told him that he
would be victorious against Maximus, and Theodosius thereupon confidently took
the offensive and defeated him.   So again in 392, four years later, when Eugenius
seized the empire of the West, Theodosius once more had recourse to the recluse.
He sent the eunuch Eutropius into Egypt with instructions to bring back St John
if possible, but in any case to find out from him whether he should march against
Eugenius or await his attack.   The saint refused to leave his cell, but sent word
that Theodosius would be victorious, though at the price of much blood, and that
he would not long survive his triumph.   The prediction was fulfilled : Eugenius
was defeated on the plains of Aquileia and Theodosius died less than six months
later.

Shortly before St John's death he was visited by Palladius, who gives a most
interesting account of his journey and reception.   The venerable hermit told him
that he was destined one day to be consecrated bishop, and made other disclosures
of things of which he could not normally have knowledge.   Similarly, when some
monks came from Jerusalem, John recognized at once that one of them was a
deacon, though the fact had been suppressed.   The recluse was then ninety years
of age and died shortly afterwards.   Divinely warned of his approaching end, he
had shut his window and commanded that no one should come near him for three
days.   He died peacefully at the end of that period, when on his knees at prayer.
In 1901 the cell he had occupied was discovered near Asyut.

The Bollandists in the *Acta Sanctorum* (March, vol. iii) have extracted the principal
references made to St John of Egypt in Palladius's *Lausiac History*, in the *Historia Monachorum*, and elsewhere.   For the text of Palladius we have to consult C. Butler, or Lucot ;
for the *Historia Monachorum*, see Preuschen, *Palladius und Rufinus.*

BD WILLIAM TEMPIER, Bishop of Poitiers   (A.D. 1197)

BD WILLIAM TEMPIER, the forty-sixth bishop of Poitiers and the third to bear the
name of William, was born at Poitiers.   At a very early age he entered the monastery of St Hilaire-de-la-Celle in his native city and became one of the canons regular.
He was remarkable for his piety and austerity and rose to be superior.   In 1184 he
was chosen to succeed Bishop John in the episcopal chair of Poitiers.   A strenuous
opponent of simony and of any secular control of ecclesiastical affairs, he had to
endure persecution and calumny in defence of the rights of the Church.   Dying
in 1197, he was buried behind the high altar of the church of St Cyprian in Poitiers,
and his tomb became a place of pilgrimage, because of the miracles of healing
reported to have been wrought there.

See the *Acta Sanctorum*, March, vol. iii.

28 : ST JOHN OF CAPISTRANO   (A.D. 1456)

CAPISTRANO is a little town in the Abruzzi, which of old formed part of the kingdom of Naples.   Here in the fourteenth century a certain free-lance —whether he was of French or of German origin is disputed—had settled down after military service under Louis I and had married an Italian wife.   A son, named John, was born to him in 1386 who was destined to become famous as one of the great lights of the Franciscan Order.   From early youth the boy's talents made him conspicuous.   He studied law at Perugia with such success that in 1412 he was appointed governor of that city and married the daughter of one of the principal inhabitants.   During hostilities between Perugia and the Malatestas he was imprisoned, and this was the occasion of his resolution to change his way of life and become a religious.   How he got over the difficulty of his marriage is not altogether clear.   But it is said that he rode through Perugia on a donkey with his face to the tail and with a huge paper hat on his head upon which all his worst sins were plainly written.   He was pelted by the children and covered with filth, and in this guise presented himself to ask admission into the noviceship of the Friars Minor.   At that date, 1416, he was thirty years old, and his novice-master seems to have thought that for a man of such strength of will who had been accustomed to have his own way, a very severe training was necessary to test the genuineness of his vocation.   (He had not yet even made his first communion.)   The trials to which he was subjected were most humiliating and were apparently sometimes attended with supernatural manifestations.   But Brother John persevered, and in after years often expressed his gratitude to the relentless instructor who had made it clear to him that self-conquest was the only sure road to perfection.

In 1420 John was raised to the priesthood.   Meanwhile he made extraordinary progress in his theological studies, leading at the same time a life of extreme austerity, in which he tramped the roads barefoot without sandals, gave only three or four hours to sleep and wore a hair-shirt continually.   In his studies he had St James of the Marches as a fellow learner, and for a master St Bernardino of Siena, for whom he conceived the deepest veneration and affection.   Very soon John's exceptional gifts of oratory made themselves perceptible.   The whole of Italy at that period was passing through a terrible crisis of political unrest and relaxation of morals, troubles which were largely caused, and in any case accentuated, by the fact that there were three rival claimants for the papacy and that the bitter antagonisms between Guelfs and Ghibellines had not yet been healed.   Still, in preaching throughout the length and breadth of the peninsula St John met with wonderful response.   There is undoubtedly a note of exaggeration in the terms in which Fathers Christopher of Varese and Nicholas of Fara describe the effect produced by his discourses.   They speak of a hundred thousand or even a hundred and fifty thousand auditors being present at a single sermon.   That was certainly not possible in a country depopulated by wars, pestilence and famine, and in view of the limited means of locomotion then available.   But there was good evidence to justify the enthusiasm of the latter writer when he tells us : " No one was more anxious than John Capistran for the conversion of heretics, schismatics and Jews.   No one was more anxious that religion should flourish, or had more power in working wonders ; no one was so ardently desirous of martyrdom, no one was more famous for his holiness.   And so he was welcomed with honour in all the provinces of Italy. The throng of people at his sermons was so great that it might be thought that the apostolic times were revived. On his arrival in a province, the towns and villages were in commotion and flocked in crowds to hear him. The towns invited him to visit them, either by pressing letters, or by deputations, or by an appeal to the Sovereign Pontiff through the medium of influential persons."

But the work of preaching and the conversion of souls by no means absorbed all the saint's attention. There is no occasion to make reference here in any detail to the domestic embarrassments which had beset the Order of St Francis since the death of their Seraphic Founder. It is sufficient to say that the party known as the " Spirituals " held by no means the same views of religious observance as were entertained by those whom they termed the " Relaxed ". The Observant reform which had been initiated in the middle of the fourteenth century still found itself hampered in many ways by the administration of superiors general who held a different standard of perfection, and on the other hand there had also been exaggerations in the direction of much greater austerity culminating eventually in the heretical teachings of the Fraticelli. All these difficulties required adjustment, and Capistran, working in harmony with St Bernardino of Siena, was called upon to bear a large share in this burden. After the general chapter held at Assisi in 1430, St John was appointed to draft the conclusions at which the assembly arrived, and these " Martinian statutes ", as they were called, in virtue of their confirmation by Pope Martin V, are among the most important in the history of the order. So again John was on several occasions entrusted with inquisitorial powers by the Holy See, as for example to take proceedings against the Fraticelli and to inquire into the grave allegations which had been made against the Order of Gesuats founded by Bd John Colombini. Further, he was keenly interested in that reform of the Franciscan nuns which owed its chief inspiration to St Colette, and in the tertiaries of the order. In the Council of Ferrara, later removed to Florence, he was heard with attention, but between the early and the final sessions he had been compelled to visit Jerusalem as apostolic commissary, and incidentally had done much to help on the inclusion of the Armenians with the Greeks in the accommodation, unfortunately only short-lived, which was arrived at at Florence.

When the Emperor Frederick III, finding that the religious faith of the countries under his suzerainty was suffering grievously from the activities of the Hussites and other heretical sectaries, appealed to Pope Nicholas V for help, St John Capistran was sent as commissary and inquisitor general, and he set out for Vienna in 1451 with twelve of his Franciscan brethren to assist him. It is beyond doubt that his coming produced a great sensation. Aeneas Sylvius (the future Pope Pius II) tells us how, when he entered Austrian territory, " priests and people came out to meet him, carrying the sacred relics. They received him as a legate of the Apostolic See, as a preacher of truth, as some great prophet sent by God. They came down from the mountains to greet John, as though Peter or Paul or one of the other apostles were journeying there. They eagerly kissed the hem of his garment, brought their sick and afflicted to his feet, and it is reported that very many were cured. . The elders of the city met him and conducted him to Vienna. No square in the city could contain the crowds. They looked on him as an angel of God." John's work as inquisitor and his dealings with the Hussites and other Bohemian heretics have been severely criticized, but this is not the place to attempt any justification. His zeal was of the kind that sears and consumes, though he was merciful to the submissive and repentant, and he was before his time in his attitude to witchcraft and the use of torture. The miracles which attended his progress wherever he went, and which he attributed to the relics of St Bernardino of Siena, were sedulously recorded by his companions, and a certain prejudice was afterwards created against the saint by the accounts which were published of these marvels. He went from place to place, preaching in Bavaria, Saxony and Poland, and his efforts were everywhere accompanied by a great revival of faith and devotion. Cochlaeus of Nuremberg tells us how " those who saw him there describe him as a man small of body, withered, emaciated, nothing but skin and bone, but cheerful, strong and strenuous in labour. . He slept in his habit, rose before dawn, recited his office and then celebrated Mass. After that he preached, in Latin, which was afterwards explained to the people by an interpreter." He also made a round of the sick who awaited his coming, laying his hands upon each, praying, and touching them with one of the relics of St Bernardino.

It was the capture of Constantinople by the Turks which brought this spiritual campaign to an end. Capistran was called upon to rally the defenders of the West and to preach a crusade against the infidel. His earlier efforts in Bavaria, and even in Austria, met with little response, and early in 1456 the situation became desperate. The Turks were advancing to lay siege to Belgrade, and the saint, who by this time had made his way into Hungary, taking counsel with the great general Hunyady, saw clearly that they would have to depend in the main upon local effort. St John wore himself out in preaching and exhorting the Hungarian people in order to raise an army which could meet the threatened danger, and himself led to Belgrade the troops he had been able to recruit. Very soon the Turks were in position and the siege began. Animated by the prayers and the heroic example in the field of Capistran, and wisely guided by the military experience of Hunyady, the garrison in the end gained an overwhelming victory. The siege was abandoned, and western Europe for the time was saved. But the infection bred by thousands of corpses which lay unburied round the city cost the life first of all of Hunyady, and then a month or two later of Capistran himself, worn out by years of toil and of austerities and by the strain of the siege. He died most peacefully at Villach on October 23, 1456, and was canonized in 1724. His feast was in 1890 made general for all the Western church, and was then transferred to March 28.

The more important biographical materials for the history of St John of Capistrano are printed in the *Acta Sanctorum*, October, vol. x. See BHL., nn. 4360–4368. But in addition to these there is a considerable amount of new information concerning St John's writings, letters, reforms and other activities which has been printed during the present century in the *Archivum Franciscanum Historicum* edited at Quaracchi ; attention may be called in particular to the papers on St John and the Hussites in vols. xv and xvi of the same periodical. This and other material has been used by J. Hofer in his *St John Capistran, Reformer* (1943), a work of much erudition and value. English readers may also be referred to a short life by Fr V. Fitzgerald, and to Léon, *Auréole Séraphique* (Eng. trans.), vol. iii, pp. 388–420.

ST GUNTRAMNUS (A.D. 592)

Guntramnus (Gontran), king of Burgundy and part of Aquitaine from 561 to 592, is said to have been very popular among his people, who certainly honoured him as a saint after his death ; and his name has found its way into the Roman Martyrology. But his claims to holiness scarcely would obtain formal canonization for him today. Nearly all we know of him is derived from the pages of St Gregory of Tours. Though far from disciplined himself (he divorced one wife and executed the unsuccessful physicians of another), he encouraged the holding of three synods to improve the discipline of the clergy, endowed churches and monasteries, and dealt justly with his subjects.

The relevant chapters of Gregory of Tours are reprinted in the *Acta Sanctorum*, March, vol. iii.   There is an excellent summary in DCB., vol. ii, pp. 820-822.

ST TUTILO   (*c.* A.D. 915)

St Tutilo was educated by Iso and Marcellus in the celebrated Benedictine monastery of Saint-Gall, where he had as schoolfellows Bd Notker Balbulus and Ratpert.   They all three became monks in the abbey, Tutilo being appointed head of the cloister school and Notker librarian.   Handsome, eloquent and quick-witted, St Tutilo appears to have been a universal genius, for he is described as a poet, an orator, an architect, a painter, a sculptor, a metal worker and a mechanic.   Music, however, was his passion, and he could play all the various instruments taught to the monastery scholars.   Although he did not invent liturgical tropes, he certainly cultivated them, and he was probably associated with his friend Notker in writing sequences and in fitting words to the final Alleluia in the gradual.   King Charles the Fat had a great admiration for St Tutilo, and remarked that it was a pity such a genius should be hidden away in a monastery.   The saint himself shrank from publicity, and when obliged to go to large cities like Metz and Mainz, where his artistic talents were in great request, he strove to avoid notice and shrank from compliments.   He was wont to adorn his pictures and sculptures with an epigram or motto, and there are still at Constance, Metz, Saint-Gall and Mainz paintings attributed to him, but of his poetical and musical works only three little elegies and one hymn have been printed.   He died about the year 915 and was buried in the chapel of St Catherine, which was renamed St Tutilo's in his honour.

See *Histoire littéraire de la France*, vol. v, pp. 671–673 ; Wagner, *Einführung in die Gregor. Melod.*, vol. i, p. 282 ; L. Gauthier, *Hist. Poés. Liturg.*, vol. i (Tropes), pp. 35-36.

29 : SS. JONAS AND BARACHISIUS, MARTYRS   (A.D. 327)

WE are able to quote here from what purport to be the genuine acts of the martyrs SS. Jonas and Barachisius, compiled by an eye-witness called Isaias, an Armenian in the service of King Sapor II.   The Greek versions contain certain additions and interpolations, but the original Syriac text has been published by Stephen Assemani and by Bedjan.

In the eighteenth year of his reign, Sapor or Shapur, King of Persia, began a bitter persecution of Christians.   Jonas and Barachisius, two monks of Beth-Iasa, hearing that several Christians lay under sentence of death at Hubaham, went thither to encourage and serve them.   Nine of the number received the crown of martyrdom.   After their execution, Jonas and Barachisius were apprehended for having exhorted them to persevere and to die.   The president began by appealing to the two brothers, urging them to obey the King of Kings, *i.e.* the Persian monarch, and to worship the sun.   Their answer was that it was more reasonable to obey the immortal King of Heaven and earth than a mortal prince.   Barachisius was then cast into a narrow dungeon, whilst Jonas was detained and commanded to sacrifice. He was laid flat on the ground, face downwards, with a sharp stake under the middle of his body, and beaten with rods. The martyr continued all the time in prayer, so the judge ordered him to be placed in a frozen pond ; but this also was without effect. Later on the same day Barachisius was summoned and told that his brother had sacrificed. The martyr replied that he could not possibly have paid divine honours to fire, a creature, and spoke so eloquently of the power and infinity of God that the Magians in astonishment said to one another that if he were permitted to speak in public he would draw many to Christianity. They therefore decided for the future to conduct their examinations by night. In the meantime they tortured him too.

In the morning Jonas was brought from his pool and asked whether he had not spent a very uncomfortable night. " No ", he replied. " From the day I came into the world I never remember a more peaceful night, for I was wonderfully refreshed by the memory of the sufferings of Christ." The Magians said, " Your companion has renounced ! " but the martyr, interrupting them, exclaimed, " I know that he long ago renounced the Devil and his angels ". The judges warned him to beware lest he perish abandoned by God and man, but Jonas retorted, " If you possess your vaunted wisdom judge whether it is not wiser to sow corn rather than to hoard it. Our life is seed, sown to rise again in the world to come, where it will be renewed by Christ in immortal life." He continued to defy his tormentors, and after further tortures he was squeezed in a wooden press till his veins burst, and finally his body was divided piecemeal with a saw and the mangled segments thrown into a cistern. Guards were appointed to watch the relics lest the Christians should steal them away.

Jonas having been thus disposed of, Barachisius was once more advised to save his own body. His reply was : " This body I did not frame, neither will I destroy it. God who made it will restore it, and will judge you and your king." So he was again subjected to torments, and was finally killed by having hot pitch and brimstone poured into his mouth. Upon receiving news of their death, an old friend bought the martyrs' bodies for five hundred drachmas and three silk garments, promising never to divulge the sale.

The Syriac text may be found in S. E. Assemani, *Acta Sanctorum Martyrum Orientalium,* vol. i, with a Latin translation. Bedjan in the last century re-edited the text, without a translation, in his *Acta Martyrum et Sanctorum,* vol. ii. The Greek version was first printed by Delehaye in the *Analecta Bollandiana,* vol. xxii (1903), pp. 395–407, and subsequently with a Latin translation in vol. ii of the *Patrologia Orientalis,* pp. 421–439. The account given in the synaxaries is also of some value : see Delehaye's edition of the *Synax. Constant.,* cc. 567–570.

SS. MARK, Bishop of Arethusa, and CYRIL, Martyr (*c.* A.D. 365)

The Eastern churches commemorate on this day St Mark, Bishop of Arethusa on Mount Lebanon. Baronius in the Roman Martyrology substituted St Cyril of Heliopolis, excluding Mark as a teacher of doubtful orthodoxy. St Mark's Confession of Faith in itself is unexceptionable, but amongst the anathemas which follow it is a strange and ambiguous passage which might easily be understood in an heretical sense. It may well be that it has been incorrectly reported, and the Bollandists have vindicated the bishop's orthodoxy. In any case the encomiums passed upon him by St Gregory Nazianzen, Theodoret and Sozomen when they relate his sufferings would lead us to conclude that, even if tainted at one time with Semi-Arianism, he had subsequently joined the strictly orthodox party and had fully expiated any previous vacillation.

During the reign of the Emperor Constantius, Mark of Arethusa had demolished a heathen temple, and had built a church and made many converts to the Christian faith. He had by so doing incurred the resentment of the pagan population who, however, could take no revenge whilst the emperor was a Christian. Their opportunity came when Julian the Apostate succeeded to the throne and enacted that those who had destroyed heathen temples must either rebuild them or pay a heavy fine. Mark, who was both unable and unwilling to obey, fled from the fury of his enemies, but upon learning that some of his flock had been apprehended he returned and gave himself up. The old man was dragged by the hair through the streets, stripped, scourged, thrown into the city sewer, and then handed over to the tender mercies of schoolboys to be pierced and torn by their pointed iron styles or pens. They bound his legs with cords so tight as to cut his flesh to the bone and screwed off his ears with small cord. Finally they smeared him over with honey and, shutting him in a kind of cage, hung him up at midday in the heat of summer to be the prey of wasps and gnats. He was so calm in the midst of his sufferings that he derided his tormentors for having raised him nearer heaven whilst they themselves were grovelling upon earth.

At length the fury of the people was turned to admiration and they set him free, whilst the governor appealed to Julian for his pardon. The emperor eventually consented, saying that it was not his wish to give the Christians any martyrs. Even the pagan rhetorician Libanius seems to have realized that the cruelty which evoked such heroism only lent strength to the Christian cause, and he implored the persecutors to desist. Then we are told by the historian Socrates that the people of Arethusa were so much impressed by the bishop's fortitude that they asked to be instructed in a religion which was capable of inspiring such resolution, and that many of them embraced Christianity. Thus Mark was left in peace to the end of his life and died during the reign of Jovian or of Valens.

St Cyril was a deacon of Heliopolis, a city near the Lebanon. In the reign of Constantius, by destroying many idols, he too had earned the hatred of the pagan population. Upon the accession of Julian, they set upon him and killed him, ripping open his stomach and, it is stated, eating his liver.

See the *Acta Sanctorum*, March, vol. iii ; and Delehaye, *Synax. Constant.*, pp. 565–568.

SS. ARMOGASTES, ARCHINIMUS AND SATURUS, MARTYRS
(*c.* A.D. 455)

GENSERIC, King of the Vandals, after he had renounced the orthodox faith, became a fierce persecutor of his Catholic subjects, and enacted that no Catholic should hold any post in his household. Armogastes, who had been in the service of Genseric's son Theodoric, was accordingly deprived of his honours and dignities in the court and most cruelly tortured. Cords were bound tightly round his head and legs, but as he lifted up his eyes to heaven and made the sign of the cross, they broke of themselves. This happened several times, although stronger and yet stronger cords were employed. He was then suspended by one foot, with his head hanging down, but he still refused to conform. Theodoric would have beheaded him, but the Arian priests deterred him, saying that it would only cause Armogastes to be honoured by the people as a martyr.   Theodoric therefore banished him to Byzacena to work in the mines, but afterwards, in order publicly to disgrace him, ordered him to be transferred to Carthage and there set to mind cattle.   This brave man, however, regarded it as a glorious thing to be dishonoured before men in the cause of God.   Not long afterwards he was divinely warned that his end was drawing near.   He accordingly gave instructions as to his place of burial to a devout Christian called Felix and died at the time he had foretold.

Archinimus is supposed to have been a native of Mascula who, refusing to abjure the eternal Godhead of Christ, was threatened with death, but reprieved at the last moment.   Saturus, the third of the martyrs, was master of the household to Huneric, who, on the score of his faith, threatened to deprive him of his estate.   His wife besought him to purchase his pardon at the expense of his conscience but he refused, saying to her in the words of Job, " You have spoken like one of the foolish women ".   He was deprived of everything and reduced to beggary, but, says Victor of Vita, " of his baptismal robe they could not rob him ".

Victor of Vita is our only authority for these martyrdoms.   The text is quoted by the Bollandists in the *Acta Sanctorum*, March, vol. iii.   Some difficulty is caused by the word Archinimus, which in the Roman Martyrology appears as *archimimus*, so that the second martyr figures as " Mascula, the chief-actor," whereas the true reading probably is " Archinimus, a native of Mascula ", Archinimus being a proper name ; but there are other possibilities.

SS. GUNDLEUS AND GWLADYS   (SIXTH CENTURY)

GUNDLEUS, the Latin form of Gwynllyw (now corrupted to Woolo), was the name of a chieftain of south-east Wales, whose wife Gwladys was, we are told, one of the many children of Brychan of Brecknock.   According to one account Gundleus asked Brychan for his daughter's hand and was refused ; whereupon he came to Talgarth with a force of three hundred men and carried the lady off.   An embroidery of this story is that Brychan, following in pursuit, was beaten off by King Arthur, though not before his " knights " Cai and Bedwyr had persuaded him not to try to get Gwladys for himself.   Certainly such a kidnapping would have been an appropriate beginning to the marriage, for though their first-born was the great St Cadoc, much of the life of Gwladys and her husband was given over to violence and brigandage.   At length Cadoc set himself to reform his parents, and was successful.   They retired from the world and lived close to one another on what is now Stow Hill at Newport in Monmouthshire, where the ancient St Woolo's church stands.   The place was pointed out to them in a dream : " On rising ground above the river there stands a white steer : there shall be your dwelling-place."

Here they lived austerely on the fruits of their labour, " washing themselves as often in the cold winter as in the hot summer ", going down the hill at night to the river Usk for the purpose—the account can be interpreted as meaning that they went to and from their bath naked, a distance of about half a mile each way.   However, Cadoc insisted that his parents should separate altogether ; so Gwladys removed first to the bank of the river Ebbw and then to Pencarnau in Bassaleg (where the Catholic church is now dedicated in her honour).   Both passed the remainder of their days in devout retirement, and the memory of Gwynllyw and Gwladys is preserved in several place-names and church-dedications in the district.

The text and translation of a Latin life of St Gundleus, compiled about 1130, is printed in A. W. Wade-Evans, *Vitae Sanctorum Britanniae* (1944). Capgrave's abridgement of this is given in the *Acta Sanctorum*, March, vol. iii. *Cf.* the note to St Cadoc on September 25 ; T. D. Hardy, *Descriptive Catalogue of Materials* (Rolls Series), vol. i, pt 1, pp. 87–89 ; and see LBS., vol.   pp. 202–204 and 234 *seq.*, for useful summaries of the material.

ST RUPERT, BISHOP OF SALZBURG   (*c.* A.D. 710)

THE early history of St Rupert was formerly very obscure, and there has been considerable difference of opinion as to the date at which he actually flourished. According to the most reliable sources he was a Frank, though Colgan claims him as an Irishman whose Gaelic name was Robertach. It may now be affirmed with certainty that before his missionary undertakings began he was already bishop at Worms, and in that case there is no great likelihood that he paid a visit to Rome, for, as bishop, he would not require any special authorization for such an enterprise. It was probably about the year 697 that he arrived with several companions at Regensburg and presented himself before Duke Theodo, without whose permission nothing much could be done. He may have brought credentials from the French King Childebert III, who was always anxious for the conversion of recently sub-jugated provinces. The duke, it seems, was still a pagan, but his sister is said to have been a Christian, and there is no room for doubt that many in Bavaria had received the message of the gospel before this date. Theodo not only gave the new-comers a welcome, but consented to listen to their preaching and to receive instruction. His conversion and baptism were followed by that of many of the nobles, and no serious opposition was offered to the work of the missionaries. The people were well disposed, and St Rupert and his followers met with conspicuous success. One heathen temple at Regensburg and another at Altötting were almost immediately adapted for Christian worship. Other churches were built and nearly the whole population was re-established in the Christian faith. The missionaries pushed their way also along the Danube, and at Lorch St Rupert made many converts and performed several miracles of healing.

It was, however, neither Regensburg nor Lorch which the saint made his headquarters, but the old ruined town of Juvavum, which the duke gave him and which was rebuilt and called Salzburg. Theodo's generosity enabled Rupert to erect there a church and a monastery with a school which were dedicated to St Peter, besides other sacred edifices. The neighbouring valley with its salt springs formed part of the duke's donation. St Rupert had been ably seconded by his companions, three of whom, Vitalis, Chuniald and Gislar, were afterwards reckoned as saints, but before long it became imperative to obtain more help. He therefore returned to his native land to enlist recruits, and succeeded in obtaining twelve more workers. He also induced his sister or niece St Erentrudis to enter a nunnery which he built at Nonnberg and of which she became the first abbess. A considerable number of churches and places bear St Rupert's name and are traditionally connected with him, but many of them were no doubt dedicated to him in after times. Besides the great work of evangelization the saint did much to civilize his converts and promoted the development of the salt mines. It was he who gave to Juvavum its modern name of Salzburg, and it was there he died, probably about the year 710. St Rupert's feast is kept in Ireland as well as in Austria and Bavaria.

The most reliable source is a document known as the *Gesta S. Hrodberti* written in the first half of the ninth century. It has been edited by W. Levison in MGH., *Scriptores Merov.*, vol. vi. Other texts are cited in BHL., nn. 7391-7403, but they are much less reliable. See also Hauck, *Kirchengeschichte Deutschlands*, vol. i, pp. 372 seq. W. Levison in the *Neues Archiv*, vol. xxviii, pp. 283 seq. and L. Gougaud, *Les saints irlandais hors d'Irlande* (1936). The saint's name appears in many forms.

BD DIEMODA, OR DIEMUT, Virgin　　　(c. A.D. 1130)

DIEMODA, or Diemut, was a Bavarian and a friend of the celebrated recluse Bd Herluka of Epfach, who no doubt greatly influenced her. Diemut had joined the nunnery of Wessobrunn, but she could not feel content in community life and aspired to seclusion as a solitary. She opened her heart to the abbot of the neighbouring monastery and he, after testing her, sanctioned the call and walled her into a tiny cell adjoining the church. Here she gave herself to prayer and penance, and to copying books for the service of the church and of the abbey. In the monastery library of Wessobrunn before its secularization there were at least fifty volumes, patristic and liturgical, in the beautiful handwriting of Bd Diemut. At her death her body was laid in the old minster, but the relics were transferred in 1709 to the abbey church of Wessobrunn.

See Hefner in the *Oberbayerischen Archiv*, vol. i, pp. 355-373 ; Hardy, *Descriptive Catalogue* (Rolls Series), vol. iii, pp. xxx-xxxii, where a list is given of the books she copied ; *Kirchenlexikon*, vol. iii, cc. 1721-1722. There seems to have been no public *cultus*.

ST BERTHOLD　　(c. A.D. 1195)

ACCORDING to certain late and untrustworthy authorities St Berthold was born at Limoges and studied theology in Paris, where he was raised to the priesthood. With his kinsman Aymeric, who afterwards became Latin Patriarch of Antioch, he accompanied the Crusaders to the East and found himself in Antioch at the time when it was being besieged by the Saracens. We are told it was divinely revealed to him that the investment of the town was a punishment for the sins and especially for the licentiousness of the Christian soldiers. Berthold offered himself up as a sacrifice, and vowed that if the Christians were delivered from their great peril he would devote the rest of his life to the service of the Blessed Virgin. In a vision he saw our Lord, accompanied by our Lady and St Peter, and above their heads a great cross of light. The Saviour addressed Berthold and spoke of the ingratitude of the Christians in view of all the blessings He had showered upon them. In consequence of the appeals and warnings of the holy man, the soldiers and the citizens were brought to repentance. Although they were weak with fasting and privations, when the next assault took place they were completely victorious and the city and the army were delivered. All this, however, is legend.

What is more certain is that through the efforts of one Berthold, a relative of the Patriarch Aymeric, a congregation of priests was formed on Mount Carmel, Berthold appearing to have drawn into his community many of the scattered Latin hermits who had previously inhabited the district. Moreover, through his detachment and sanctity, he was an inspiration to the whole Order of Carmelites, of which he is often called the founder. It seems that he may have been its first superior, receiving some encouragement from Aymeric, who was, however, never, as has been asserted, legate of the Holy See. Berthold's life was to a great degree a hidden one, and there is little more to record, except that he undertook the erection or the re-erection of the monastic buildings, and that he dedicated the church in honour of the prophet Elias—as Peter Emilianus afterwards informed King Edward I of England in a letter dated 1282. St Berthold ruled the community for forty-five years, and seems to have remained with them down to the time of his death, which occurred about the year 1195.

Father Papebroch, the Bollandist, writing in the *Acta Sanctorum*, March, vol. iii, maintained that St Berthold was the first superior of the Carmelite Order, and that the hermits whom he gathered round him had no more connection with Elias than the fact that they lived near Mount Carmel and venerated his memory. This contention led to a deplorably acrimonious controversy, now more than two centuries old, but all scholars have long been agreed that the Bollandist view was fully justified. Historical evidence is lacking which could establish any sort of continuity between St Berthold's group of Carmelite hermits and the "Sons of the Prophets".

See B. Zimmerman, *Monumenta Historica Carmelitana*, pp. 269–276, in the *Catholic Encyclopedia*, vol. iii, pp. 354–356, and in DTC., vol. ii, cc. 1776–1792; the *Acta Sanctorum*, March, vol. iii ; *Analecta Ord. Carmel.*, vol. iii, pp. 267, 368 *seq.* ; C. Kopp, *Elias und Christentum auf dem Karmel* (1929) ; and Fr François, *Les plus vieux textes du Carmel* (1945).

ST LUDOLF, BISHOP OF RATZEBURG   (A.D. 1250)

ALTHOUGH he did not actually die for the faith, St Ludolf is often honoured as a martyr because he patiently bore persecution, disgrace and banishment for the extension and freedom of the Church. He was a canon regular of the Premonstratensian Order, but was elected bishop of Ratzeburg in 1236. He still continued to live the life of a monk, and gave the rule of St Norbert to the chapter of his cathedral ; he built and endowed the Benedictine nunnery of Rehna, which long preserved and venerated his memory. He came several times into conflict with Duke Albert of Sachsen-Lauenberg, who imprisoned, ill-treated and finally banished him. At Wismar, however, he was hospitably received and entertained by Duke John the theologian. He died in 1250 as the result of the ill-treatment he had previously received. St Ludolf was canonized in the fourteenth century and is venerated at Wismar in Mecklenburg.

See the *Acta Sanctorum*, March, vol. iii, and the *Kirchenlexikon*, *s.v.* Ratzeburg.

30 : ST REGULUS, OR RIEUL, BISHOP OF SENLIS   (c. A.D. 250 ?)

ST RIEUL is the patron of the city and diocese of Senlis, of which he is said to have been the first bishop. He probably lived in the third century, as he is spoken of as having been the contemporary of other saints who are known to have flourished at that period. The cathedral of Senlis was burnt, and with it perished all its archives, including the ancient records of the early bishops. According to his quite apocryphal acts, St Rieul was converted by St John the Evangelist and accompanied St Dionysius the Areopagite (Denis) to France, where, as bishop of Arles, he shepherded the Christian colony founded by St Trophimus. He subsequently went to Paris in search of the relics of the martyrs St Denis, St Rusticus and St Eleutherius, and then undertook the conversion of the people of Senlis. Possibly there were two bishops of the name of Rieul—one of Arles and the other of Senlis—and their history has been confused ; but in any case the connection with St John the Evangelist is certainly a fiction.

See the *Acta Sanctorum*, March, vol. iii ; BHL., nn. 7106–7109 ; Duchesne, *Fastes Épiscopaux*, vol. iii, pp. 117 and 147.

ST JOHN CLIMACUS, Abbot   (*c.* A.D. 649)

THE *Ladder* (*Klimax*) *to Paradise* was a book which was immensely popular in the middle ages and won for its author, John the Scholastic, the name " Climacus " by which he is generally known. The saint's origin is hidden in obscurity, but he was possibly a native of Palestine and is said to have been a disciple of St Gregory Nazianzen. At the age of sixteen he joined the monks settled on Mount Sinai. After four years spent in testing his virtue, the young novice was professed, and was placed under the direction of a holy man called Martyrius. Under the guidance of his spiritual father, he left the monastery and took up his residence in a hermitage nearby—apparently to enable him to check a tendency to waste time in idle conversation. He tells us himself that, under the direction of a prudent guide, he succeeded in shunning rocks which he could not have escaped if he had presumed to steer alone. So perfect was his submission that he made it a rule never to contradict anyone, or to contest any statement made by those who visited him in his solitude. After the death of Martyrius, when St John was thirty-five years of age, he embraced the completely eremitical life at Thole—a lonely spot, but sufficiently near to a church to enable him, with the other hermits and monks of the region, to assist on Saturdays and Sundays at the divine office and the celebration of the holy mysteries. In this retirement the holy man spent forty years, advancing ever more and more in the way of perfection. He read the Bible assiduously, as well as the fathers, and was one of the most learned of the desert saints, but his whole aim was to conceal his talents and to hide the extraordinary graces with which the Holy Ghost had enriched his soul. In his determination to avoid singularity he partook of all that was allowed to the monks of Egypt, but he ate so sparingly that it was a case of tasting rather than of eating. His biographer records with admiration that so intense was his compunction that his eyes seemed like two fountains which never ceased to flow, and that in the cavern to which he was wont to retire for prayer the rocks used to resound with his moans and lamentations.

As a spiritual director he was in great request. At one time indeed some of his fellow-monks, either through jealousy or perhaps justifiably, criticized him for wasting time in unprofitable discourse. John accepted the accusation as a charitable admonition and imposed upon himself a rigorous silence in which he persevered for nearly a twelvemonth. The whole community then besought him to resume advising others, and not to bury the talents which he had received ; so he resumed his instructions, and came to be regarded as another Moses in that holy place, " for he went up into the mountain of contemplation, talked to God face to face, and then came down to his fellows bearing the tables of God's law, his Ladder of Perfection " This work, which he wrote at the request of John, abbot of Raithu, consists of thirty chapters illustrating the thirty degrees for attaining to religious perfection from the first step of renunciation which rests on the three pillars of innocence, mortification and temperance, to the thirtieth and final step upon which are seated the three theological virtues of faith, hope and charity. It treats first of the vices and then of the virtues, and it is written in the form of aphorisms or sentences illustrated by many curious anecdotes of monastic life.

We are told that God bestowed upon St John an extraordinary grace of healing the spiritual disorders of souls. Amongst others to whom he ministered was a monk called Isaac who was brought almost to the brink of despair by temptations of the flesh. John recognized the struggle he was making, and after commending his faith said, " My son, let us have recourse to prayer ". They prostrated themselves in humble supplication and from that moment Isaac was released from those temptations. Another disciple, a certain Moses, who appears to have at one time lived near or with the saint, after carrying loads of earth for planting vegetables, was overcome with fatigue and fell asleep in the heat of the day under a great rock. Suddenly he was awakened by his master's voice and rushed forward, just in time to avoid being crushed by the fall of an overhanging crag. St John in his solitude had been aware of the impending danger and had been praying to God for his safety.

The good man was now seventy years old, but upon the death of the abbot of Mount Sinai he was unanimously chosen to succeed him. Soon after, the people in the time of a great drought applied to him as to another Elias, begging him to intercede with God on their behalf. The saint recommended their distress to the Father of mercies, and his prayer was answered by an abundance of rain. Such was his reputation that St Gregory the Great, who then sat in St Peter's chair, wrote to the holy abbot, asking for his prayers and sending him beds and money for the use of pilgrims to Sinai, who were numerous. For four years St John governed the monks wisely and well. It was, however, with reluctance that he had accepted the charge, and he found means to lay it down shortly before his death. He had attained the age of fourscore years when he passed away in the hermitage which had been so dear to him. His spiritual son George, who had succeeded him as abbot, entreated the dying saint that they might not be separated. John assured him that their prayers were heard, and the disciple followed his master within a few days. Besides the *Climax*, we have another work of St John's—a letter written to the abbot of Raithu, in which he describes the duties of a true shepherd of souls. In art, John is always represented with a ladder.

Although there is what professes to be an ancient Life of St John Climacus, written by Daniel, a monk of Raithu, this contains no more in the way of fact than is to be found in the *Synax. Constant*. The whole history is very obscure, and the note of F Nau in the *Byzantinische Zeitschrift*, vol. xi (1902), pp. 35-37, must be accepted with great reserve in view of the criticism of L. Petit in DTC., vol. viii, cc. 690-692. This last article makes it probable that John was married in early life and that he only became a monk after the death of his wife. The accounts given in such works as DCB., and the *Kirchenlexikon* for the most do little more than expand the jejune data furnished by Daniel. See also *Échos d'Orient*, 1923, pp. 440-450.

ST ZOSIMUS, Bishop of Syracuse   (*c.* A.D. 660)

THE parents of St Zosimus were Sicilian landowners, who dedicated their little boy to the service of St Lucy and placed him, when he was seven years old, in the monastery that bore her name near Syracuse, not far from their home. There his main occupation seems to have been to watch near the relics of the saint. The duty was not altogether congenial to the little lad, accustomed as he was to a free open-air life on a farm, and once, when the abbot Faustus had set him a particularly distasteful task, he ran away and went home. He was brought back in disgrace, and the enormity of his offence impressed upon him. That night, in his dreams, he saw St Lucy rise from her shrine and stand over him with a menacing countenance. As he lay in terror, there appeared beside her the gracious figure of our Lady interceding for him, and promising in his name that he would never do such a thing again. As time went by, Zosimus became more reconciled to the life of the cloister, his visits home became fewer and shorter, and he settled down to the regular round of prayer, praise and contemplation with the other monks.

For thirty years he lived almost forgotten. Then the abbot of Santa Lucia died, and there was great uncertainty and discussion over the choice of a successor. Finally the monks went in a body to the bishop of Syracuse and begged him to make the appointment for them. The prelate, after scrutinizing them all, asked if there was no other monk belonging to the convent. Thereupon they remembered Brother Zosimus, whom they had left to mind the shrine and to answer the door. He was sent for, and no sooner had the bishop set eyes upon him than he exclaimed, " Behold him whom the Lord hath chosen ". So Zosimus was appointed abbot, and a few days later the bishop ordained him a priest. His biographer says that he ruled the monastery of Santa Lucia with such wisdom, love and prudence that he surpassed all his predecessors and all his successors. When the see of Syracuse fell vacant in 649, the people elected Zosimus, who, however, did not wish to be raised to the dignity, whilst the clergy chose a priest called Vanerius, a vain and ambitious man. Appeal was made to Pope Theodore, who decided for Zosimus and consecrated him. In his episcopate the holy man was remarkable for his zeal in teaching the people and for his liberality to the poor ; but it is difficult to judge of the historical value of the anecdotes which purport to have been recorded by a contemporary biographer. At the age of nearly ninety St Zosimus died, about the year 660.

There is a short and fragmentary Latin life printed in the *Acta Sanctorum*, March, vol. iii. See also Cajetan, *Vitae Sanctorum Sicul.*, vol. i, pp. 226-231, and animad. 181-183. Gams describes him as a Benedictine, but he is not noticed by Mabillon ; he was perhaps a " Basilian ".

ST OSBURGA, ABBESS OF COVENTRY, VIRGIN (*c.* A.D. 1016)

NOTHING is known of the life of St Osburga, except that she is supposed to have been the first abbess of the nunnery founded by King Canute at Coventry and that her death occurred about 1016. On the other hand it is possible that she flourished at a much earlier period. We first hear of her in 1410, when her shrine was already the object of popular *cultus* and the scene of so many miracles that the clergy and people of Coventry petitioned for the observance of her festival. A synod was therefore called, which issued a decree commanding that, in the archdeaconry of Coventry, the feast of St Osburga should be kept with the solemnity due to a patron saint. It does not seem certain what day was chosen. Devotion to St Osburga lingered on at Coventry until after the Reformation, and her feast is still kept in the archdiocese of Birmingham on this day.

See Stanton, *Menology*, p. 137 ; *cf.* Leland's *Collectanea*, vol. i, p. 50, and Dugdale, *Monasticon*, vol. iii, pp. 175 and 182.

BD DODO　　(A.D. 1231)

IN spite of his evident vocation to the religious life, Bd Dodo was constrained by his parents to marry.　At his father's death, however, he was able to fulfil his aspirations, for his wife and his mother retired into a convent and he was free to join the Premonstratensians.　With the abbot's permission, he afterwards betook himself to a lonely spot where he lived in complete solitude for four years, his only visitors being the evil spirits who strove to tempt him.　He moved to another place in Friesland, called Asch or Hasch, and there he redoubled his austerities.　As he lay prostrate before the crucifix one day, the figure spoke to him and told him that he would have to remain long upon the cross.　He possessed the gift of healing, and many sick persons recovered health at his hands.　In extreme old age he was killed by a falling wall, and after his death, marks of our Lord's wounds are said to have been found upon his body.　This early case of alleged stigmatization is interesting because it may possibly be of older date than that of St Francis ; but it seems likely that the wounds were caused by the falling masonry.　The story that Dodo induced the Frisians to relinquish a number of their savage pagan customs may belong to someone else of the same name.　As a solitary he would hardly have had occasion to intervene, as the legend says he did, to stop the practice of keeping the victims of assassination unburied until vengeance had been taken on the murderers, or on some members of their family.

See the *Acta Sanctorum*, March, vol. iii.　As to the alleged stigmata, *cf.* Fr Thurston in *The Month*, July 1919, pp. 39-50.

BD AMADEUS IX OF SAVOY　　(A.D. 1472)

AMADEUS IX, who, like his ancestor Humbert III, afterwards attained to beatification, was the son of Duke Louis I of Savoy and Anne of Cyprus, and grandson of the antipope " Felix V ".　Amadeus was born at Thonon in 1435 and was betrothed in the cradle to Yolande, daughter of Charles VII of France, thereby cementing peace between the two countries.　He is described as handsome, accomplished and endowed with exceptional spiritual graces ; unfortunately he was subject all his life to severe attacks of epilepsy, which at times completely prostrated and incapacitated him.　His marriage, which took place in 1451, was a happy one, but of his four sons and two daughters, the majority died very young. In the province of Brescia, which was given to him as his portion, the young prince lived a congenial and secluded life, away from the cares and tumults of the court, but upon his father's death he was called to take up the government of Savoy and Piedmont.　He was a clement ruler, but inflexible in suppressing bribery and in preventing the oppression of the poor by the rich.　Indeed, in cases which came before him personally, he was so much disposed to espouse the cause of the weak that Duke Galeazzo of Milan once jestingly remarked that whereas in the rest of the world it was better to be rich than poor, in the duchy of Savoy it was the beggars who were favoured and the wealthy who were harshly dealt with.

Amadeus could not bring himself to refuse alms to anyone, and after he had exhausted the contents of his purse, he would give away his own clothing and anything he had about him.　He is even said on one occasion to have broken up the jewelled collar he wore and to have distributed the fragments.　When an ambassador had been loudly boasting of the numerous packs of hounds and the many different breeds of dogs kept by his master, the duke led him to a terrace outside the palace which was furnished with tables round which the poor of the city were being fed. " These are my packs and my hunting-dogs ", he remarked. " It is with the help of these poor people that I chase after virtue and hunt for the kingdom of Heaven." The ambassador objected that some amongst them were vicious and undeserving, mere idlers and hypocrites. " I would not judge them too severely ", replied Amadeus gently, " lest God should judge me likewise and withhold His blessing." He had the greatest horror of blasphemy and would not retain in his service anyone who used profane language. He was very liberal in all his benefactions, yet the finances of the state were not impoverished. On the contrary, through his wise administration, debts incurred by his predecessors were paid off, his exchequer which he had found empty was replenished, and he was able to provide marriage portions for three of his sisters without incurring any debts or imposing any fresh taxes.

In his private life he was extremely austere, and far from allowing himself any relaxations on the score of ill-health, he gave it out that he was obliged to fast on account of it. Beginning every day by private meditation and by hearing Mass, it is also stated that he frequented the sacraments more constantly than was usual at that period. Like all truly magnanimous men, he bore no malice towards those who treated him ill. He had received much provocation from the Sforzas of Milan, but when, upon the death of Duke Francis, his son Galeazzo, in his haste to reach Milan quickly from the Dauphiny, tried to pass incognito through Savoy and was arrested, Amadeus treated him with honour and provided an escort to conduct him to Milan. Afterwards Galeazzo was ungrateful enough to attack him, but Amadeus brought the war to an end and gained his friendship by giving him his sister Bona in marriage. It must be confessed that some historians judge his policy less favourably, and declare that his conciliatory attitude resulted in Savoy becoming a centre of continual strife. His brothers rebelled against him several times, but he always forgave them and made excuses for them. Because of his malady, Amadeus resigned the government into the hands of his wife, but his subjects rose in revolt and he himself was imprisoned until his brother-in-law, King Louis XI, came and set him at liberty. Though then only in his thirty-seventh year, his disease had sapped his strength, and he recognized that his end was approaching. Having exhorted his sons and nobles in words which are often inscribed on representations of the holy man, " Be just : love the poor and the Lord will give peace to your lands ", Bd Amadeus rendered up his soul to God on March 30, 1472. He was beatified in 1677.

See the *Acta Sanctorum*, March, vol. iii ; J. F. Gonthier, *Œuvres historiques*, vol. iii, pp. 95-121 ; E. Fedelini, *Les Bienheureux de la Maison de Savoie* (1925).

31 : ST BALBINA, Virgin (Date Unknown)

IN the Roman Martyrology today we read the following notice : " At Rome, of St Balbina, Virgin, daughter of blessed Quirinus, Martyr, who was baptized by Pope Alexander and chose Christ as her spouse in holy virginity ; after completing the course of this world she was buried on the Appian Way near her father." This account was unfortunately dependent upon a wholly gratuitous insertion of the martyrologist Ado, who borrowed certain details from the Acts of Pope Alexander which Bede had prudently ignored, and used the names Quirinus, Theodora and Balbina to fill three successive blank days in the month of March. The so-called Acts of Balbina are merely a late plagiarism from the Acts of Alexander. All that is known to us is that midway between the Via Appia and the Via Ardeatina there was a cemetery of Balbina, probably so called because it was constructed on the estate of a Christian lady named Balbina. On the other hand there seems to have been a Balbina, called daughter of Quirinus, but she cannot have been identical with the first-named Balbina because she lived at a much earlier date, and was buried in the catacomb of Praetextatus. Balbina was honoured in a little fourth-century church on the Aventine which bore her name, but it is difficult to decide which Balbina was intended.

The fabulous story of St Balbina is printed in the *Acta Sanctorum*, March, vol. iii, but it is all extracted from the Acts of Alexander, in one version of which Balbina is represented as a martyr. See also Dom Quentin, *Les martyrologes historiques*, especially pp. 113 and 490 ; Leclercq in DAC., vol. ii, pp. 137-157 ; and J. P. Kirsch, *Die Römischen Titelkirchen im Altertum*, pp. 94-96.

ST ACACIUS, OR ACHATIUS, BISHOP   (THIRD CENTURY)

THIS Acacius has been claimed as a bishop of Antioch in Pisidia by some and of Melitene in Armenia Minor by others ; a third view is that he was not a bishop at all. But a report of his trial has been preserved, in a document of which the Greek original is lost. According to this, Acacius was the great support of the Christians of Antioch, and as such was haled before the consular agent Martian. He declared that Christians were loyal subjects of the emperor, who prayed for him regularly, but when invited to an act of worship of the same emperor he refused.

Thereupon ensued a discussion between Martian and Acacius which ranged over the seraphim, Greco-Roman mythology, the Incarnation, Dalmatian morals, the nature of God and the religion of the Kataphrygians. When ordered to accompany the officer to sacrifice in the temple of Jupiter and Juno, Acacius replied, " I cannot sacrifice to someone who is buried in the isle of Crete. Or has he come to life again ? " Then Martian made an accusation of magic and wanted to know where were the magicians who helped him ; and to Acacius's rejoinder that all came from God and that magic was hateful to Christians he objected that they must be magicians, because they had invented a religion. " You make your own gods and are afraid of them ; we destroy them ", responded Acacius. " When there are no masons, or the masons have no stone, then you have no gods. We stand in awe of our God—but we did not make Him ; He made us ; for He is Master. And He loves us, for He is Father ; and in His goodness He has snatched us from everlasting death."

Finally Acacius was required to disclose the names of other Christians, on pain of death, and he would not. " I am on trial and you ask for names. If you cannot overcome me alone, do you suppose you would be successful with the others ? You want names—all right : I am called Acacius, and I have been surnamed Agathangelus [' good angel ']. Do what you like." Acacius was then returned to prison and the proceedings of the examination forwarded to the emperor, Decius, who, we are told, could not forbear to smile when reading them. The upshot was that Martian was promoted to the legation of Pamphylia and Acacius received the imperial pardon, an interesting and unusual circumstance.

St Acacius is called a martyr but there is no evidence that he was eventually put to death for the faith, which may account for his never having received any *cultus* in the West ; but his name figures in Eastern calendars on March 31 and other dates.

The *acta disputationis* (appropriately so called) are in *Acta Sanctorum* for March, vol. iii, and in Ruinart.   Father Delehaye assigns them to his third category of such documents, *viz.* an embroidery of an otherwise reliable document   see his *Les Passions des Martyrs.* See also Allard, *Histoire des Persécutions*, vol. ii ; and J. Weber, *De actis S. Achatii* (1913) ; but *cf.* the unfavourable judgement passed on Weber's dissertation by Delehaye in *Analecta Bollandiana*, vol. xxxiii (1914), pp. 346–347.

ST BENJAMIN, Martyr   (*c.* A.D. 421)

KING YEZDIGERD, the son of Sapor II, put an end to the cruel persecution of Christians which had raged in Persia under his father, and the Church had been in the enjoyment of peace for twelve years when a bishop named Abdas, with mis-directed zeal, burnt down the Pyraeum, or Temple of Fire, the chief object of worship of the Persians.   The king threatened to destroy all the churches of Christians unless Abdas would rebuild the temple.   This he refused to do, and Yezdigerd put him to death and initiated a general persecution which was intensified under his son Varanes and lasted for forty years.   Theodoret, who was living in the neighbourhood at the time, gives an appalling account of the cruelties practised.

One of the foremost of the martyrs was a deacon called Benjamin.   After he had been beaten and then imprisoned for a year, an ambassador from the emperor at Constantinople obtained his release, promising on his behalf that he would refrain from speaking about his religion.   Benjamin, however, declared that he could not observe such a condition, and in fact he lost no opportunity of preaching the gospel.   He was again apprehended and brought before the king. At the trial his only reply to the indictment was to ask the monarch what he would think of a subject who would renounce his allegiance and join in war against him. The tyrant ordered that reeds should be thrust in between his nails and his flesh and into all the tenderest parts of his body and then withdrawn.   After this torture had been repeated several times, a knotted stake was inserted into his bowels to rend and tear him.   The martyr expired in the most terrible agony.

Besides Theodoret (*Eccles. Hist.*, bk v, ch. 38), which source is reproduced in the *Acta Sanctorum*, March, vol. iii, an account of these martyrs has been preserved both in Syriac and Armenian.   See Peeters in the *Analecta Bollandiana*, vol. xxviii (1909), pp. 399–415, who throws great light upon certain inconsistencies in the narrative, and shows that Theodoret has probably used a Syriac original.   *Cf.* also the *Historisches Jahrbuch*, vol. xxxiv (1913), pp. 94 *seq.* ; and Labourt, *Le Christianisme dans l'Empire perse*, pp. 105–112.

ST GUY OF POMPOSA, Abbot   (A.D. 1046)

ST GUY, or Guido, who is also called Guion, Wido, Witen and Wit, was born near Ravenna, and his father and mother took great pride in him ; and, mainly to please them, he was very careful of his appearance and dress.   One day, how-ever, he was smitten with compunction for this form of vanity.   He went to Ravenna, where the patronal feast of St Apollinaris was being celebrated, and stripping off his fine clothes he gave them to the poor and donned the shabbiest garments he could find.   To his parents' mortification, he started off in that garb for Rome, and whilst he was there he received the tonsure.   A divine inspiration led him to place himself under the guidance of a hermit called Martin, who lived on a little island in the river Po.   For three years they remained together, and then the recluse sent him to the abbey of Pomposa, near Ferrara, to learn monastic life in a large community.   That monastery and that of St Severus at Ravenna were actually under the ultimate direction of the hermit, who decided the appointment of the superiors.

St Guy's outstanding merits were such that he rose to high office, becoming abbot first of St Severus and then of Pomposa upon the nomination of Martin, confirmed by the vote of the monks.   His reputation drew so many (including his father and his brother) to join the community, that the number of monks was doubled, and it became necessary for St Guy to build another monastery to accommodate all.   After a time he delegated to others the secular part of his office, and concentrated on the more purely spiritual side, especially on the direction of souls. At certain seasons of the year he was accustomed to withdraw to a cell about three miles from the abbey, where he lived in such unbroken abstinence and devotion that he seemed to be sustained by fasting and prayer.   During Lent especially, he treated his body with a severity which tortures could hardly have surpassed, and yet he was extraordinarily tender to his monks and they were devoted to him.   St Peter Damian, who at his request delivered lectures on the Sacred Scriptures in the abbey of Pomposa for two years, dedicated to St Guy his book *De perfectione monachorum*.

Holy as he was, St Guy did not escape persecution.   For some reason, Heribert, Archbishop of Ravenna, conceived a bitter hatred against him and actually determined to destroy his monastery.   Warned of the approaching attack, the abbot's only measure of defence was a three days' fast, which the whole community observed.   When the archbishop and his soldiers arrived at the gates, Guy went out to meet them, and with the utmost deference and humility led him into the church.   Heribert's heart was touched : he begged the abbot's pardon, and promised him his protection for the future.   Towards the close of his life, St Guy retired into solitude, but he was summoned to Piacenza by the Emperor Henry III, who had come to Italy and wished to consult the abbot, of whose sanctity and wisdom he had heard much.   The aged man obeyed very unwillingly, and took a tender farewell of his brethren, telling them that he should see their faces no more. He had arrived at Borgo San Donnino near Parma, when he was attacked by a sudden illness, from which he died on the third day.   A contest took place for the custody of his body between Pomposa and Parma ; the emperor settled the matter by having the relics taken to the church of St John the Evangelist at Speyer, which was afterwards renamed St Guido-Stift.

There is a short Latin life which has been printed both by the Bollandists, *Acta Sanctorum*, March, vol. iii, and by Mabillon.

BD JOAN OF TOULOUSE, Virgin   (Fourteenth Century)

As early as the year 1240 the Carmelite brothers from Palestine made a settlement at Toulouse.   Twenty-five years later, when St Simon Stock was passing through Toulouse on his way to Bordeaux, he was approached by a woman called Joan, who begged him to affiliate her to his order, although she was living in her own home. The prior general consented, clothed her with the Carmelite habit, and allowed her to take a vow of perpetual chastity.   As far as it was possible Joan followed strictly the rule of St Albert of Jerusalem, and she was venerated not only as the first Carmelite tertiary, but as the founder of the Carmelite tertiary order.   She daily frequented the fathers' church, and combined penance with love, depriving herself almost of the necessaries of life to relieve the sick and poor.   She used also to train young boys in the practices of holiness, with a view to preparing them to enter the Carmelite Order.   It was her custom to carry about with her a picture of the crucified Redeemer, which she studied as though it had been a book.   Bd Joan was buried in the Carmelite church of Toulouse and her tomb was thronged by those who sought her aid.   For 600 years she was honoured, and her body was re-enshrined several times—notably in 1805, when a little book of manuscript prayers was found beside her.

The above is a summary of the story of Bd Joan (whose *cultus* was confirmed in 1895) as it is related in the lessons for her feast in the Carmelite supplement to the Breviary, but there has apparently been considerable confusion.   It seems clear that she in fact lived at Toulouse towards the end of the fourteenth, not the thirteenth, century, and that she was not a tertiary but a recluse.

See the Breviary lessons referred to above, and Fr Bonifatius, *Die sel. Johanna von Toulouse* (1897) ; and Fr B. Zimmerman's *Monumenta historica Carmelitana*, p. 369, and *Les saints déserts des Carmes déchaussés* (1927), pp. 17–18, where the problem is examined.

BD BONAVENTURE OF FORLI   (A.D. 1491)

BD BONAVENTURE TORNIELLI was born at Forlì and was a man of good family.   He does not seem to have entered the Order of Servites until 1448, when he was thirty-seven years old, but his fervour and austerity of life rapidly enabled him to make up for lost time.   After his ordination he prepared himself for apostolic work by a year of retirement, and then began to preach with wonderful eloquence and success.   He was especially commissioned by Pope Sixtus IV to undertake this apostolic mission, and throughout the papal states, Tuscany and the Venetian province his sermons were productive of a notable reformation of life.   Towards the close of 1488 he was elected vicar general of his order, an office in which he gave proof of great administrative ability and charity.   But he still continued his missionary work, and he had just finished preaching the Lent at Udine when on Maundy Thursday 1491 God called him to Himself, worn out by age and the hardships of the life he had been leading.   His relics were ultimately conveyed to Venice, where a *cultus* grew up marked by many miraculous cures.   This *cultus* was confirmed in 1911.

See the decree of confirmation printed in the *Acta Apostolicae Sedis*, vol. iii (1911), pp. 659–660 ; and F. Cornelius, *Ecclesiae Venetae*, vol. ii, pp. 34–51.

THE spirit and example of the world imperceptibly instil the error into the minds of many that there is a kind of middle way of going to Heaven ; and so, because the world does not live up to the gospel, they bring the gospel down to the level of the world.   It is not by this example that we are to measure the Christian rule, but by the words and life of Christ.   All His followers are commanded to labour to become perfect even as our heavenly Father is perfect, and to bear His image in our hearts that we may be His children.   We are obliged by the gospel to die to ourselves by fighting self-love in our hearts, by the mastery of our passions, by taking on the spirit of our Lord.   These are the conditions under which Christ makes His promises and numbers us among His children, as is manifest from His words which the apostles have left us in their inspired writings.   Here is no distinction made or foreseen between the apostles or clergy or religious and secular persons.   The former, indeed, take upon themselves certain stricter obligations, as a means of accomplishing these ends more perfectly ; but the law of holiness and of disengagement of the heart from the world is general and binds all the followers of Christ.

THE END OF VOLUME I

Individual members of groups, e.g. of martyrs, are not entered in this index if they have only a bare mention in the text. A general date-index of names, covering the whole work, will be found at the end of Volume IV